Northern European Art *in the* Norton Simon Museum

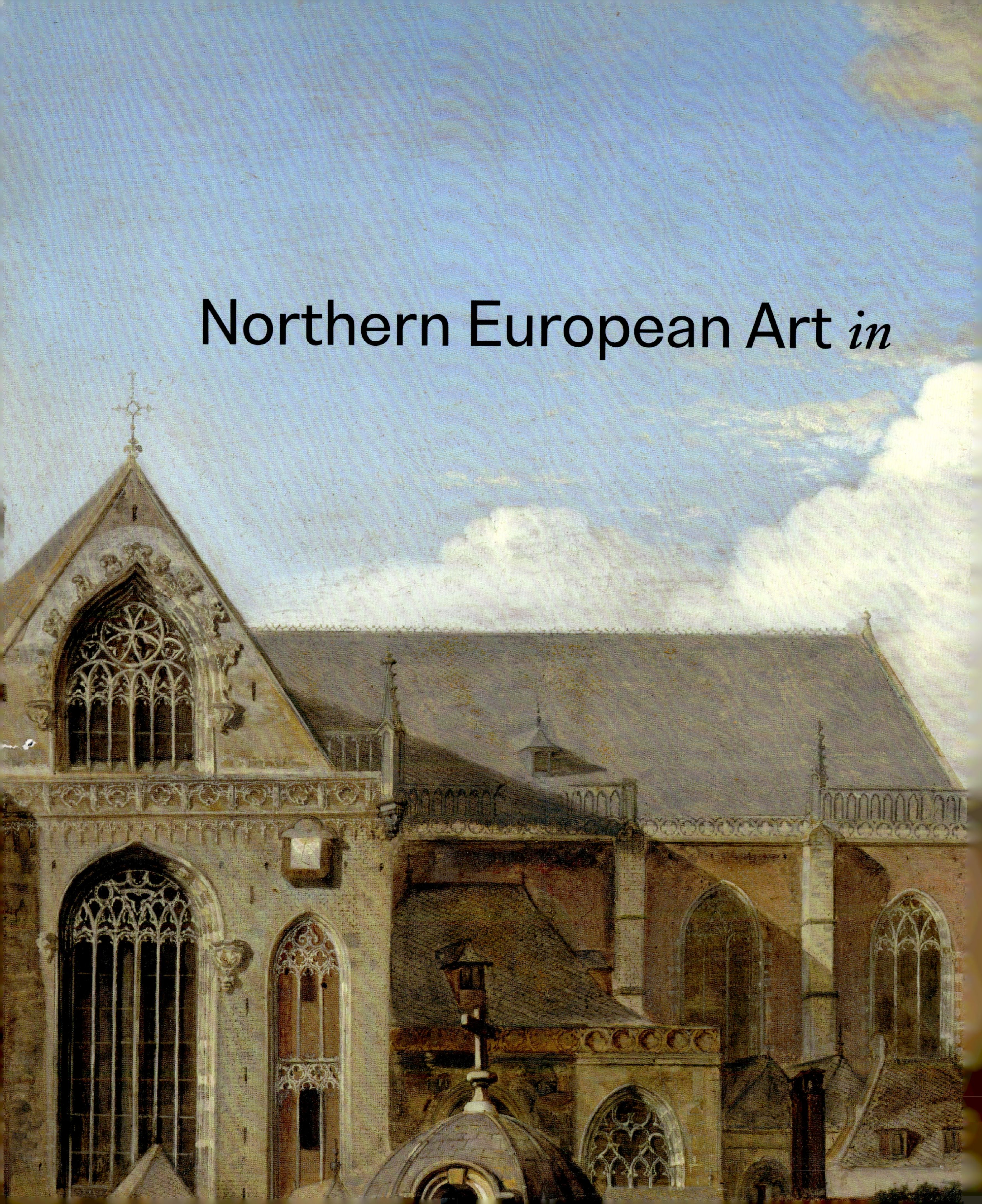
Northern European Art *in*

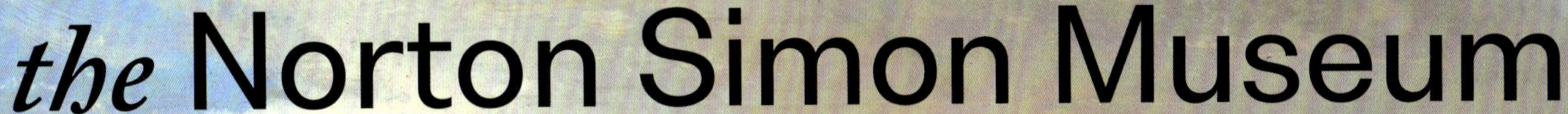

the Norton Simon Museum

Amy Walsh

Technical notes by
Rosamond Westmoreland

With contributions by
Ulrich Birkmaier
Lisa Forman
Devi Ormond
William W. Robinson
Gloria Williams Sander
Carol Togneri
Mark Watters
Nancy E. Yocco

Norton Simon Art Foundation
Pasadena, California

Distributed by
Yale University Press
New Haven and London

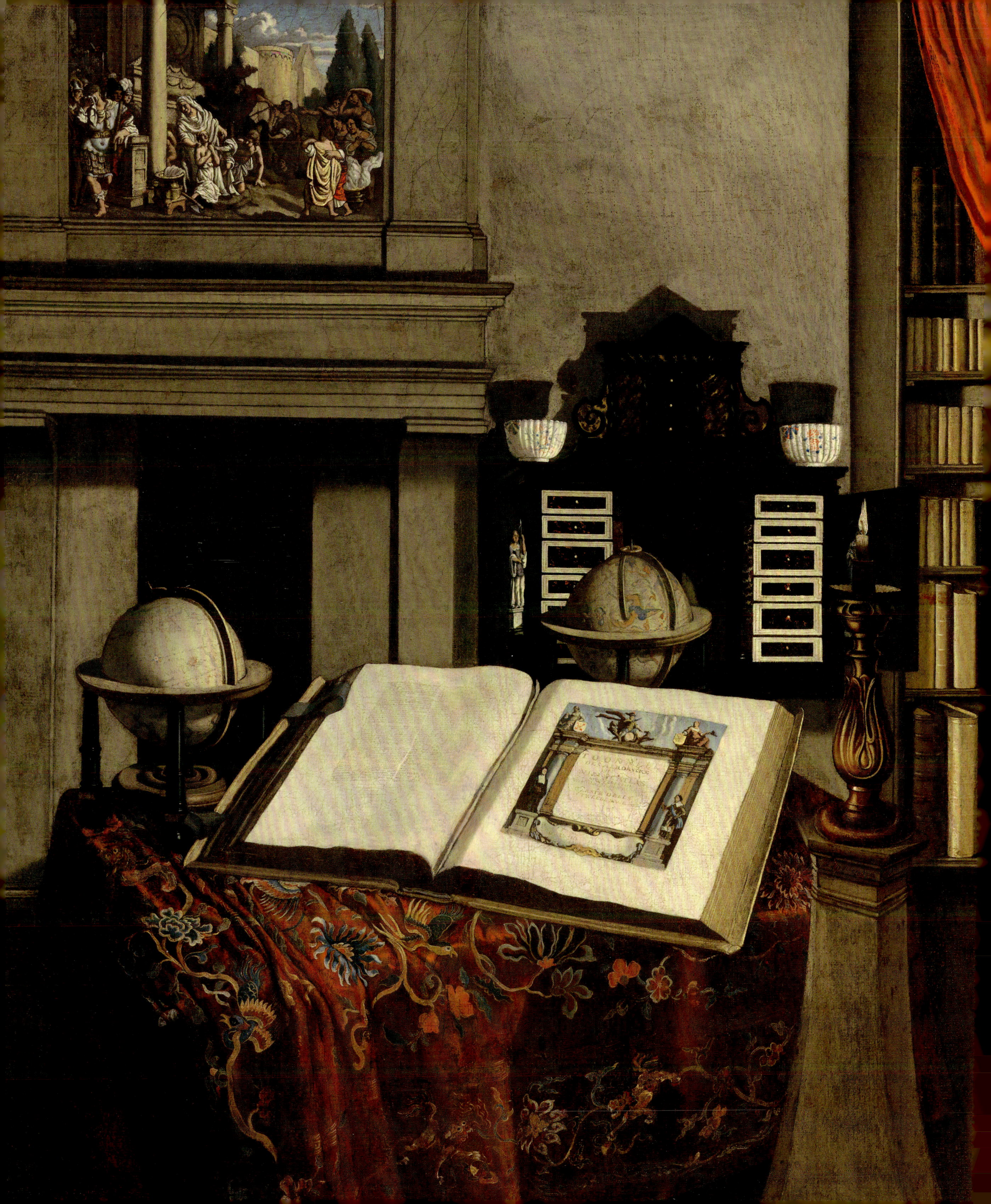

Contents

7 Foreword
9 Acknowledgments
13 Introduction

18 **Catalogue**

473 Sources and Exhibitions Cited
513 Photographic Credits
515 Index

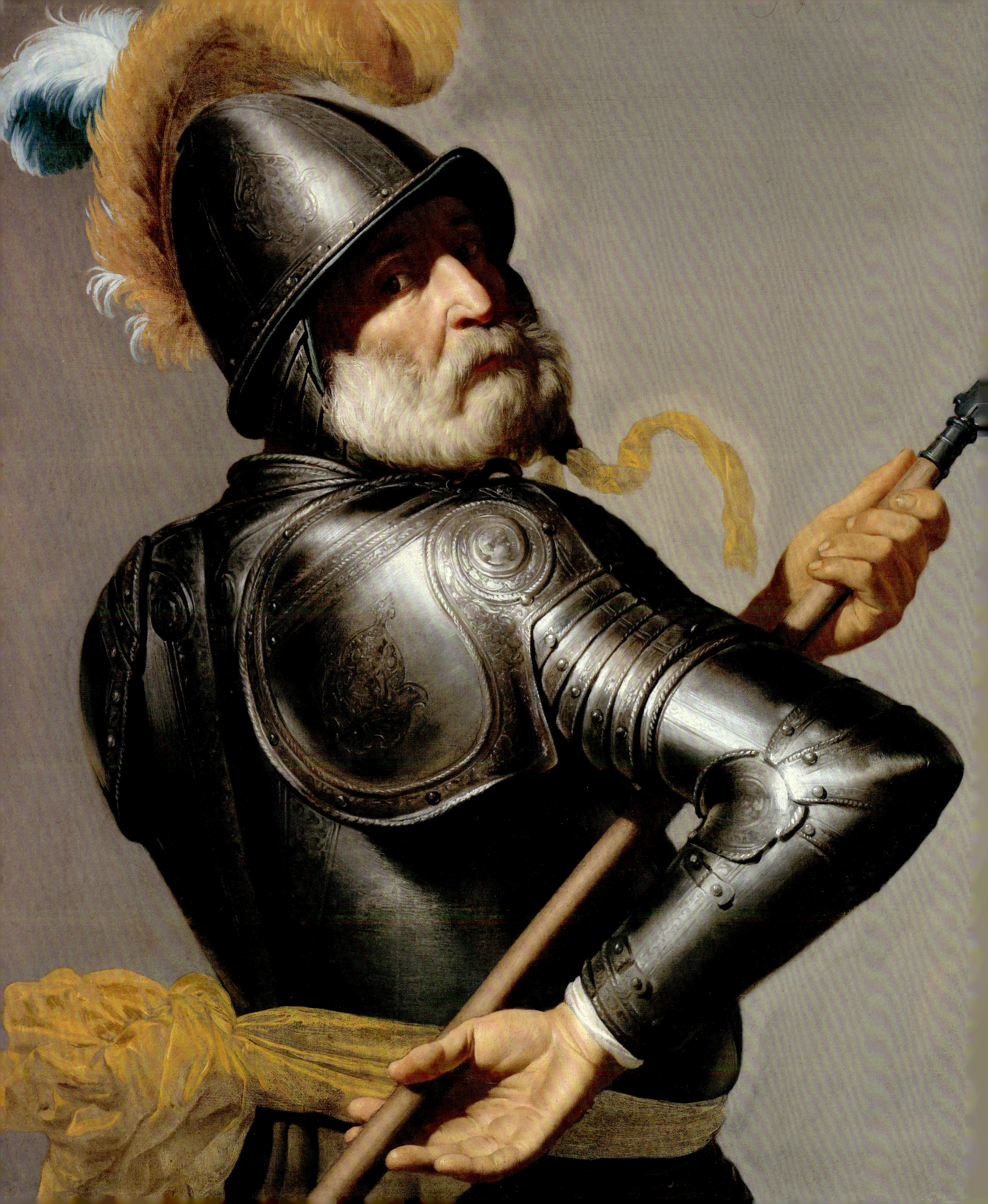

Foreword

Norton Simon began collecting art in 1954, when he was in his late forties, after building a fortune as the founder of Norton Simon Inc., an international company that included Hunt-Wesson Foods, Canada Dry Corporation, and Avis Car Rental, among many others. Over the next thirty-five years he assembled one of the finest private art collections of the twentieth century, transforming it in 1975 into the museum that bears his name.

This catalogue is the tenth in a series of volumes that celebrates the strengths of the Norton Simon Museum's holdings and features Dutch, Flemish, Early Netherlandish, and German paintings from the fifteenth through the eighteenth centuries. Acquired by Simon over a twenty-five-year period—predominantly in the 1960s and 1970s—this selection of works includes icons from the Museum's collections, such as Rembrandt's *Self-Portrait* (cat. 66), Lucas Cranach I's *Adam* and *Eve* (cats. 17–18), and Rubens's *Holy Women at the Sepulchre* (cat. 71), as well as treasures by lesser-known but no less accomplished artists like Sébastien Stoskopff (cat. 92) and Johannes Cornelisz. Verspronck (cat. 95). Simon could be an infamously protracted buyer, often stretching out the period of negotiation for a year or more, but he also led with his intuition, ultimately basing purchases on his personal response to a work of art.

Northern European Art in the Norton Simon Museum illuminates ninety-five extraordinary paintings and works on paper. An introductory essay by Carol Togneri, former Chief Curator at the Norton Simon Museum, addresses Simon's ambition and foresight as a collector and recounts some of his most public and dramatic acquisitions. The catalogue's entries—authored by curator and provenance researcher Amy Walsh, with technical reports by conservator Rosamond Westmoreland and contributions from a number of specialists in the field—offer insights into the historical context, ownership trajectories, and conservation assessment of these objects. Across a rich range of genres, from portraiture and landscape to still-life and religious themes, Simon consistently selected works of art that emphasize the humanity of their subjects. This quality—familiar to anyone who has visited the Norton Simon Museum—enables paintings made centuries ago to transcend their era, eliciting empathy and engagement from viewers that continue to inspire us today.

We are grateful to the J. Paul Getty Foundation, in its earlier iteration as the Getty Grant Program, for a publication grant that initiated this project. Over the course of the book's development, my predecessors Sara Campbell Abdo and Carol Togneri, along with staff at the Museum, worked assiduously to support the research and study of this part of the collection and to bring the catalogue to completion. I joined the Norton Simon Museum in the final stages of the book's development and benefited from the exceptional collaboration of the current staff and the expert team at Marquand Books in finalizing the manuscript for publication. I particularly wish to acknowledge the dedication and the contributions of Alexandra Kaczenski, former Curatorial Assistant, who was essential to all aspects of the final phase of the book's review and submission; Kate Austin, Rights and Reproductions Coordinator, who oversaw photography and imaging for works of art reproduced in the book; and John Griswold, Head of Conservation and Installations, who reexamined a number of the paintings in the catalogue, conducted new infrared reflectography to identify underdrawings, and added to and clarified important matters in the technical entries. Dane Reeb, Curatorial Assistant, and Rachel Weiss, Graduate Intern, provided editorial and research assistance for which I am most grateful. They, along with curators Gloria Williams Sander and Maggie Bell, served as dedicated proofreaders during the final stages of review. At Marquand Books, I thank Gina Broze, Melissa Duffes, Tom Eykemans, Leah Finger, Jeremy Linden, Adrian Lucia, and Kestrel Rundle, whose combined talents produced this handsome volume. Tom Fredrickson copyedited the manuscript, and it benefited from his thoughtful revisions.

This catalogue, like those before it, has had the commitment and support of the Museum's President, Walter W. Timoshuk, along with the Board of Trustees of the Norton Simon Art Foundation. I thank them for their unwavering dedication to scholarship of the collection.

Emily Talbot
Chief Curator

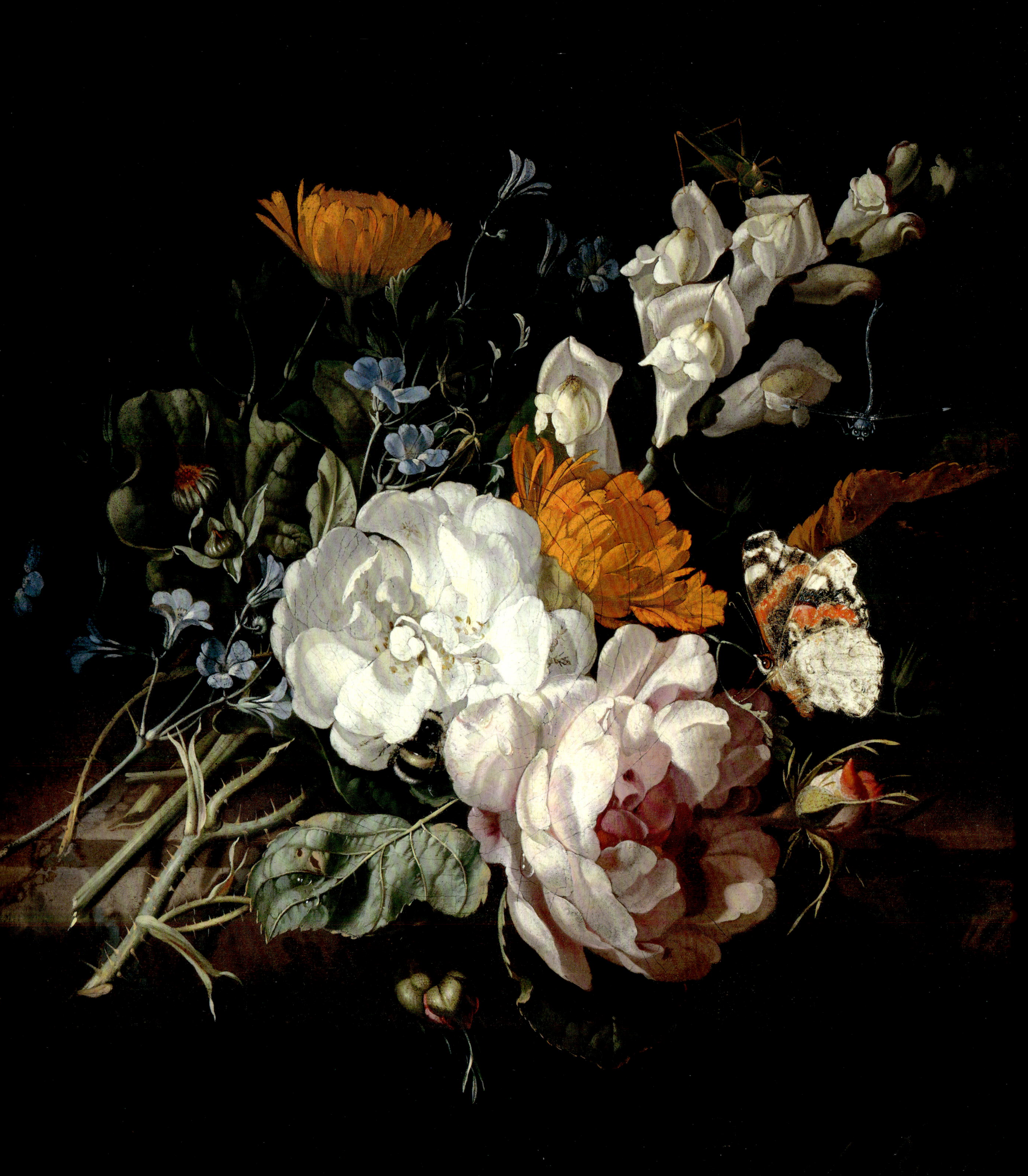

Acknowledgments

Norton Simon was a man with impeccable taste and an insatiable desire to assemble a world-class art collection. His focus was always on the objects themselves, which he constantly reevaluated and exchanged in an effort to improve the collection's overall quality. The series of recent publications to which this book belongs owes its existence to the people he entrusted with the care and maintenance of his collection—those who recognized the need to research and share knowledge of these outstanding works of art. In 1994 Norton Simon Museum curator Gloria Williams Sander proposed this project and made the initial request to the Getty Grant Program (now the J. Paul Getty Foundation). Its generous two-year grant enabled Rosamond Westmoreland and me to research each of the ninety-three paintings in the collection from the point of view of both conservation and art history. It has been both a personal and a professional honor and pleasure to research and write about the Norton Simon Museum's beautiful and important paintings.

I have benefited greatly from the knowledge and support of many people, but I am most grateful for the support of the Norton Simon Art Foundation, particularly Walter W. Timoshuk, Carol Togneri, Sara Campbell Abdo, and Gloria Williams Sander throughout the book's long gestation. It is to the organizational and editorial skills and perseverance—not to mention patience and friendship—of Carol and Sara in resolving editorial details that I owe the birth of this catalogue. And to Emily Talbot and Alexandra Kaczenski, who nurtured the final text to publication, I extend my appreciation and gratitude.

There are many people at the Norton Simon Museum who make things work on a daily basis. I am particularly grateful for the practical help and cheerful cooperation of the administration, accounting, and security departments, the curatorial staff, preparators, and registrar. Especially helpful were Jacqui Chambers, Andrea Clark, Andrea Cook, Ronald Dykhuizen, Lisa Escovedo, Kimberly Gilhooly, Sharon Goodman, Stanley Halstead, Wayne Horton, Thomas Norris, Dane Reeb, Caroline Sam, Cindy Schembri, Jenna Siman, John Sudolcan, Sally Swaney, and Jeffrey Taylor. Kate Austin, building on initial work by Brittany Traub, handled every detail of photography for this book, and she procured all rights for illustrations used throughout from a variety of museums, private collections, and dealers. John Griswold reviewed all the technical entries, made suggestions and updates, and answered lingering questions. William W. Robinson and Nancy E. Yocco, Gloria Williams Sander, and Carol Togneri contributed interesting entries on three individual works of art, and Ulrich Birkmaier and Devi Ormond contributed updated technical entries based on their close study and treatment of these objects. In addition to her contributions to the final editing of the text and her skilled management of the book's production, Emily Talbot provided immeasurable help during the COVID-19 lockdown in 2020 and 2021 in arranging access to all the files for the objects in this book as well as books from the Museum's library.

One of the most pleasant and helpful experiences has been the opportunity to discuss the paintings in the collection with the many colleagues who have visited the Norton Simon Museum. I am grateful for their interest and their generosity in sharing their knowledge and opinions. In addition to the visits of individuals, the study trip by the Curators of Dutch and Flemish Art (CODART) to Los Angeles in January 2010 provided a special opportunity for me to gather opinions and insights about the collection from a group of colleagues. My thanks to the participants of that study trip and to Gerdien Verschoor, then director of CODART, and her staff.

Thanks are due to the many curators, conservators, and academic scholars who have contributed to this catalogue through emails, letters, and conversations, as well as their own publications. Among the many people who have shared knowledge and opinions are: Ann Jensen Adams, Maryan Ainsworth, Konstantin Akinsha, Pam Ambrose, Ronni Baer, Katharine Baetjer, Jeremy Bangs, Kathryn Beebe, Kristin Lohse Belkin, Maggie Bell, Marianne Berardi, Pieter Biesboer, Ulrich Birkmaier, Cynthia von Bogendorf Rupprath, Marten Jan Bok, Jennifer Boynton, Pieter van den Brink, Christopher Brown, Edwin Buijsen, Quentin Buvelot, Alan Chong, Elizabeth DeRosa, Lloyd DeWitt, Blaise Ducos, Charles Dumas, Frits Duparc, Rudi Ekkart, Jan Piet Filedt Kok, Nancy Fox, Michiel Franken, David Freedberg, Barbara and Thomas Gaehtgens, Ivan Gaskell, Walter S. Gibson, Larry Goedde, Erik Goldner, Naomi Gorse, Michael Hall, John Hand, Egbert

Haverkamp-Begemann, Fiona Healy, Karen Hearn, S. A. C. Dudok van Heel, Valentine Henderiks, Mark Henderson, Guus van den Hout, Jeremy Howarth, Michael Jaffé, Roswitha Juffinger, Lea Eckerling Kaufman, Morgan Kavanagh, George Keyes, Jennifer Kilian, Marijke de Kinkelder, Wouter Kloek, Elly Klück, Erik Jan and Carolyn Kortenhorst, Susan Koslow, Gerbrand Kotting, Suzanne Laemers, Erik Löffler, Anne-Marie Logan, Petra Mandt, Andrew McLean, Fred Meijer, Carolyn Mensing, Norbert Middelkoop, Cynthia Morris, Ute Neidhardt, Judith Niessen, Devi Ormond, JoAnne Paradise, Ruud Priem, Joseph Rishel, William Robinson, Pieter Roelofs, Sandra Rosenbaum, Francis Russell, Simon Schama, Gary Schwartz, Christine Sellin, George Shackelford, Colin Slim, Seymour Slive, Leonore van Sloten, Eric Jan Sluijter and Nicolette Sluijter-Seijffert, Joaneath Spicer, Mary Sprinson de Jesús, Arthur Stoegmann, Ariane van Suchtelen, Dominique Suhr, Yvonne Szafran, Paul Taylor, Tijn Thörig, Ilona van Tuinen, Ilja Veldman, Michiel Verweij, Christiaan Vogelaar, Jørgen Wadum, Adriaan Waiboer, Dean Walker, Gregor Weber, Dennis Weller, Ernst van de Wetering, Arthur Wheelock, Martha Wolff, Margreet Wolters, Anne Woollett, Nancy Yeide, and Eric Zafran. For any inadvertent omissions, I beg forgiveness.

Throughout the years, Burton Fredericksen contributed provenance information on the paintings in the collection. His dedication to the history of collecting and provenance and his generosity in sharing his extensive knowledge is legendary. I am also grateful for the friendship and help of other members of the Getty Provenance Index, in particular Patricia Teter, Anna Cera Sones, Libby Spatz, Julia Armstrong-Totten, and Christian Huemer.

Without the many resources and staff of the Getty Research Institute, this project would not have been possible. I am forever grateful for the riches it holds. My sincere thanks and appreciation to the GRI administration and curators who have built the collection and to the research librarians, circulation staff, and staff of the Special Collections, who over the years have generously helped me with my research. Special thanks go to Sally McKay and the Getty research library's circulation staff who assisted in a plethora of ways while the GRI was closed during the COVID-19 lockdown. Further from home, the Rijksbureau voor Kunsthistorisches Documentatie was invaluable for the research of Dutch paintings. Over the years I have benefited from the expertise of many members of the staff. Without exception they have generously shared their knowledge and have patiently guided me to hidden treasures.

I have also profited from the resources and assistance of staff at the Frick Art Reference Library as well as the libraries of the Courtauld Institute of Art, the Metropolitan Museum of Art, the Mellon Centre for British Art, the Rubenianum, the National Gallery of Art in Washington, the Research Library at the Los Angeles County Museum of Art, and the various libraries of the University of California, Los Angeles, and Columbia University. I am also grateful to the staff of the Nationaal Archief and the Koninklijke Bibliotheek in The Hague and the National Archives at College Park, Maryland, for their assistance.

Susan Koslow and Ilja Veldman, among others, kindly let me use them as sounding boards for complicated catalogue entries. Maryan Ainsworth, Burton Fredericksen, Walter Liedtke, Ann Lowenthal, Fred Meijer, and Arthur Wheelock read various drafts of the manuscript and provided valuable insights and suggestions. I am very grateful to each of them for their careful reading of the text and considered comments, which have greatly contributed to this catalogue. For their editorial help, thanks to Fronia Simpson, Jennifer Boynton, Casie Kesterson, and Nancy Bryan. Tom Fredrickson copyedited the final manuscript, and we are grateful for his keen eye.

Over the years, many colleagues have graciously welcomed me to their galleries and storerooms, taking time from their busy schedules to accommodate my needs and interests and to share their insights into works in their museums as well as those in the Norton Simon Museum. To everyone, I am extremely grateful. For their extraordinary kindness and help in opening closed doors at the Kunsthistorisches Museum and Gemäldegalerie der Akademie der bildenden Künste during the holidays, special thanks to Wolfgang Prohaska and Renate Trnek.

It is a pleasure to acknowledge and thank the dealers who have provided information about the provenance of paintings, the location of works of art, or information about and photographs of works formerly or presently in their possession: Hans Cramer, Anthony Crichton-Stuart, Derek Johns, Jack Kilgore, Otto Naumann, Robert Simon, Anthony Speelman, and the Old Master paintings staff of Sotheby's and Christie's, especially Clarissa Post, Lucien Simmons, and Christopher Apostle.

A special thank-you for the support and inspiration of my many former colleagues at the Los Angeles County Museum of Art, including J. Patrice Marandel, Claudia Einecke, and Melissa Pope in European Paintings and Sculpture, and Joseph Fronek, Virginia Rasmussen, and Elma O'Donoghue in Paintings Conservation.

Throughout the long process of researching and writing about the northern European paintings at the Norton Simon Museum I have had the real pleasure and privilege of working with Rosamond Westmoreland, whose knowledge of and keen insight into the techniques and conservation of Old Master paintings have guided me to a greater understanding and appreciation of the works in the collection. To Roz, her late husband, Richard, and her family, I extend my sincere appreciation and respect.

Friends and family have sustained me in many ways. While far from home, I have enjoyed the warm hospitality of many friends, including Eric Jan Sluijter and Nicolette Sluijter-Seijffert, Norbert Middelkoop and Leonora van Sloten, Cynthia von Bogendorf Rupprath, Marten Jan Bok and Kitty

Kilian, Saskia and Edwin Buijsen, Wolfgang Prohaska, Gary and Loekie Schwartz, Madeline Aria, Gail Aronow, Katharine Baetjer, Elizabeth DeRosa, Milli Gervasi, Margaret Lawson, and Kathryn and Peter Scudese. I am also grateful to my family and old friends closer to home, especially my sister Jane Walsh-Brown and brother-in-law Jim Brown, my late aunt Mary Waites and cousin Barbara Pape, and old friends Margaret McNally and Jonathan Wacks, Bob and Kris Dworkoski, Barbara Hausman-Smith and Charlie Smith, Margaret McMillen, JoAnne and Arnold Paradise, Susan Pitt and Greg Ohler, the late Mary Jane Rothe, and Jeannine Wiest.

Finally, I am deeply grateful to my parents, Margaret and Arthur Walsh, for their inspiration and loving support throughout my life. My mother had looked forward to the publication of this book but unfortunately died before she could hold it in her hands. I offer this book now to my wise and wonderful daughter, Kate Scudese, who as a teenager patiently put up with my piles of books and files and preoccupation with artists long dead. Thank you for dragging me away from my desk to be with you and for continuing to delight me with the joy of sharing your life with Peter, Alexander, and Theodore.

The nature of scholarship is that it builds on the work of others. I am grateful for the preceding years of scholarship that have provided a foundation on which to stand. To family and friends, colleagues, and scholars as well as those in the future who will build on this research, I dedicate this book with great appreciation.

Amy Walsh
Former Curator of European Paintings
and Head of Provenance Research,
Los Angeles County Museum of Art

In addition to the many generous people cited above, I would also like to recognize colleagues whose specific knowledge was particularly helpful in the technical examination of the paintings. They include Joseph Fronek, John Hand, Dare Hartwell, Ella Hendriks, Ann Hoenigswald, Isabel Horovitz, Melanie Gifford, Mark Leonard, Elisabeth Mention, Cathy Metzger, Andrea Rothe, Yvonne Szafran, Jørgen Wadum, Arie Wallert, Elizabeth Walmsley, and Ernst van de Wetering. Furthermore, my thanks go to Gloria Williams Sander, Andrea Clark, Lisa Escovedo, Jeffrey Taylor, Carol Togneri, the Security Staff, and John Sudolcan and the Preparations Department at the Norton Simon Museum, all of whom made my work there studying these paintings an extremely enjoyable experience. And finally, my thanks to Amy Walsh, from whom I have learned a great deal about northern European paintings over these collaborative years. Her generosity and enthusiasm were as invigorating as our many discussions about this remarkable collection of paintings.

Rosamond Westmoreland
Paintings Conservator

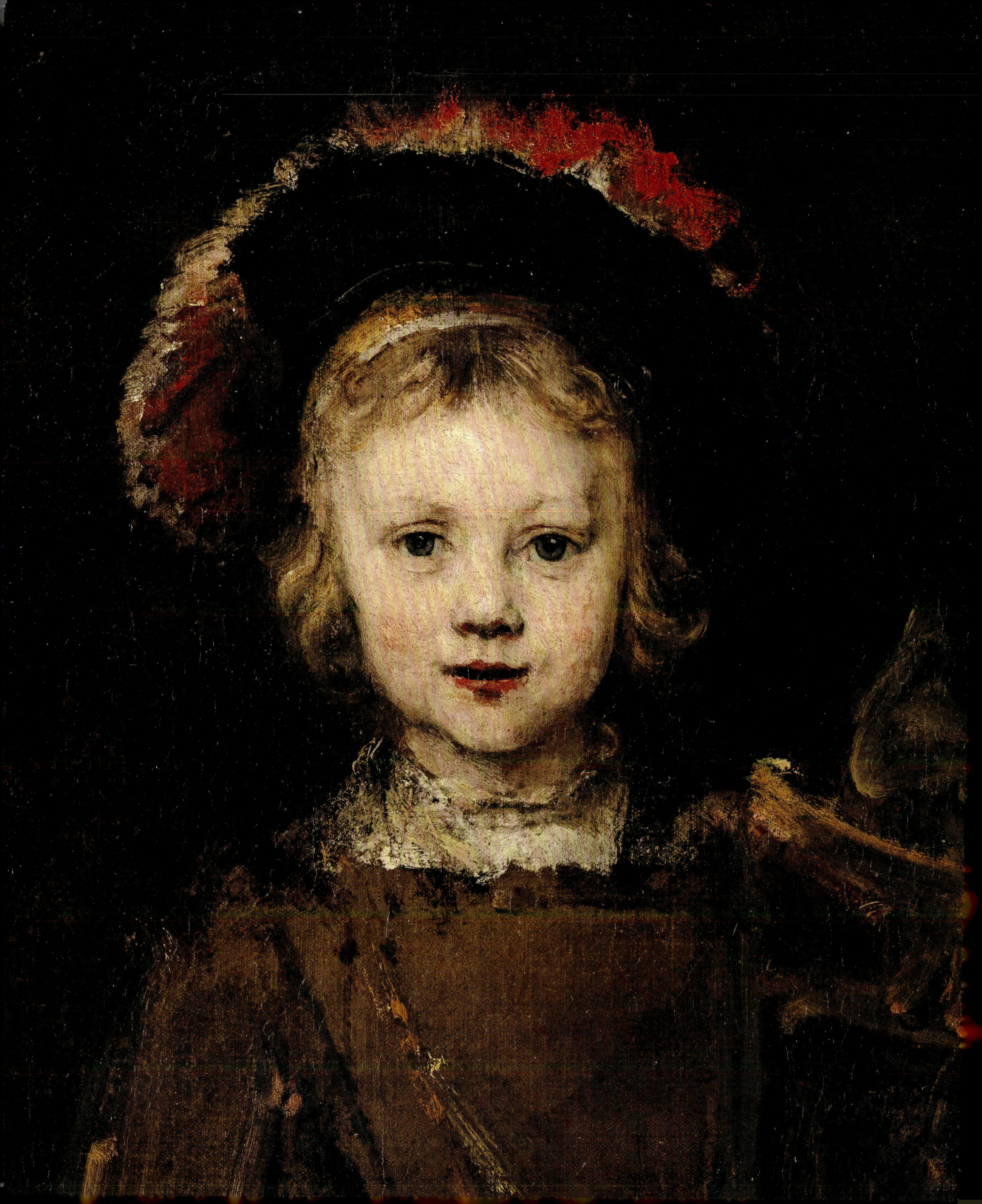

Introduction

When Mr. Simon is sitting down he is bidding. If he bids openly when sitting down, he is also bidding. When he stands up he has stopped bidding. If he then sits down again he is not bidding until he raises his finger. Having raised his finger he is continuing to bid until he stands up again.

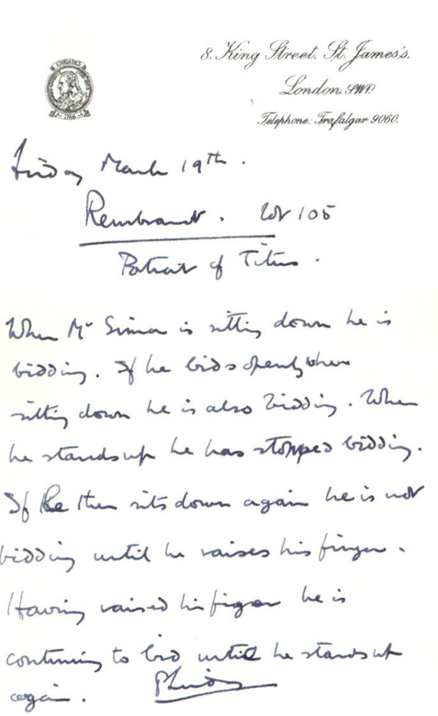

8, King Street, St. James's,
London, SW1
Telephone: Trafalgar 9060.

Friday March 19th.
Rembrandt. Lot 105
Portrait of Titus.

When Mr Simon is sitting down he is bidding. If he bids openly when sitting down he is also bidding. When he stands up he has stopped bidding. If he then sits down again he is not bidding until he raises his finger. Having raised his finger he is continuing to bid until he stands up again.

Fig. 1. Notes by Christie's Patrick Lindsay regarding Norton Simon's bidding strategy.

These were the famously abstruse directions, written in the hand of Patrick Lindsay, one of Christie's directors in London, to serve as a reminder to the auctioneer, Peter Chance, of the agreed-upon bidding arrangements with Norton Simon for the afternoon of 19 March 1965 (fig. 1). The sole object of Simon's desire that day was Rembrandt's arresting portrait of a young boy, at that point identified as the artist's son, Titus, and now one of the most celebrated and endearing images in his Pasadena museum (fig. 2; cat. 67). The oft-told story is recounted in detail in Sara Campbell Abdo's seminal 2010 book on the formation of Simon's collection, *Collector Without Walls: Norton Simon and His Hunt for the Best*. Along with Suzanne Muchnic's updated 2019 biography (*Odd Man In: Norton Simon and the Pursuit of Culture*), Campbell Abdo's book remains the ultimate source for understanding Simon's wide-ranging ambitions and his often unconventional methods for acquiring things, be they works of art or corporations. And while his success in creating a collection of such potency and fame is largely credited to his business acumen and competitiveness, his desire for the objects that remain in the collection parallels the voracity and fascination with art embodied by other private American collectors of the twentieth century whose eponymous museums continue to exist today.

Simon's successful—albeit confounding—bid on the Rembrandt portrait in 1965 deserves retelling in this catalogue, one that celebrates his discerning eye for paintings made by Dutch, Flemish, Netherlandish, and German artists. One cannot ignore the fact that, in his thirty-five-year journey as a collector of art, some of the highest prices he ever paid for such works were for the three Rembrandts that remain in the Museum today. But it was the *Portrait of a Boy in Fancy Costume* that cemented Simon's standing as a serious collector and contender in the international art market. The painting had been owned by the Earls of Spencer at Althorp for almost a century and was then in the Cook Collection for another fifty years until the family put it up for auction. Simon was keen to have objects that came from prestigious collections, and he no doubt took the painting's provenance into consideration when ruminating on its purchase. His desire to remain anonymous during the bidding for this painting prompted the obfuscated directions he supplied to Lindsay prior to the auction, but that veil was quickly lifted once the auctioneer misread Simon's silent bids and knocked

Fig. 2. Rembrandt Harmensz. van Rijn, detail of *Portrait of a Boy in Fancy Costume* (cat. 67).

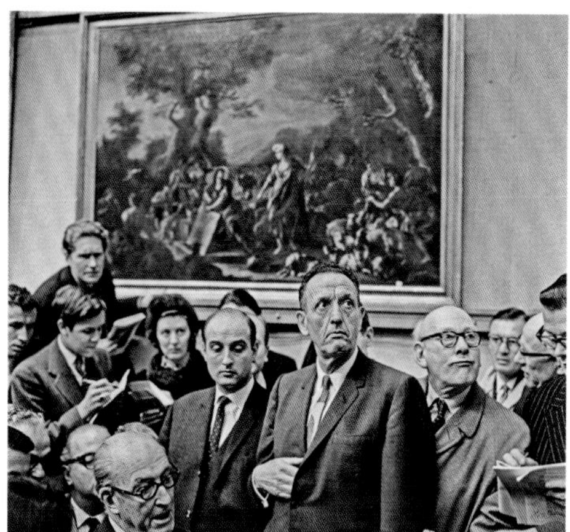

Fig. 3. Norton Simon protesting the winning bid at Christie's, 19 March 1965.

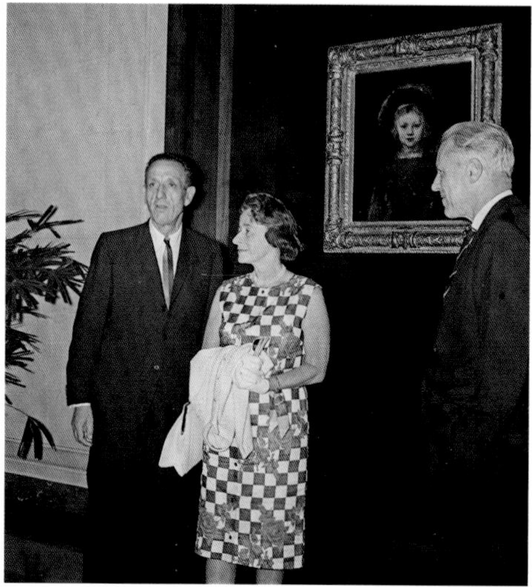

Fig. 4. Norton and Lucille Ellis Simon (left) with John Walker, director of the National Gallery of Art (right), at the opening of *Exhibition of Rembrandt's "Portrait of the Artist's Son Titus"* on 28 May 1965. National Gallery of Art, Washington, DC, Gallery Archives.

down the painting for $2.1 million to a dealer representing the Greek shipping tycoon Stavros Niarchos. Simon rose in the overcrowded saleroom, protested, and, after complaining vociferously that the auctioneer had missed his signals, succeeded in having the bidding reopened and ultimately relayed the winning bid at $2.2 million. Film footage and still photographs captured the shocked audience, many of whom had never witnessed such uproar in the staid confines of the prestigious and proper London auction rooms (fig. 3). Some suggested that the entire drama had been cunningly orchestrated by Simon to garner attention, but he would later say that news of the important painting itself should have taken precedence over the rampant press coverage about the man who purchased it. Soon after the auction, he would pose formally for press photos with his first wife, Lucille Ellis Simon, in front of the Rembrandt painting as it hung on loan at the National Gallery of Art in Washington, DC (fig. 4).

This was hardly the first time Simon had presented himself as a tough negotiator. He had been known for his shrewd business deals and takeovers starting as early as the late 1920s. The son of a small business entrepreneur, Simon's legendary talent for quick calculations and playing odds parlayed his early acquisitiveness into major corporate deals. By the early 1940s, he had achieved resounding success by investing in a steel company, and in the late 1950s he turned a small food-packing company in Fullerton, California, into a major concern, Hunt Foods Inc. His investments allowed him to delve into other businesses as varied as the Ohio Match Company, Wesson Oil, Canada Dry, and the Northern Pacific Railway. When he began to purchase art in the mid-1950s, at the suggestion of his wife, Lucille, he had a somewhat conservative start, focusing primarily on French nineteenth-century paintings and sculpture, some contemporary American objects, and a handful of Old Masters from local Los Angeles dealers.

His first purchases of Dutch art in 1956 took the form of two Rembrandt portraits—*Portrait of a Woman, probably Hendrickje Stoeffels* (fig. 5) and *The Philosopher* (fig. 6)—both of which have been downgraded in attribution since then. Like many others to follow, those paintings would later be dispersed, with *Portrait of a Woman* going to Simon's first wife as part of their divorce settlement in 1970. Two Rembrandt etchings, also purchased in 1956, would likewise be separated from the collection in 1958, when they were donated as unrestricted gifts to Pomona College in Claremont, California. Works on paper remained of interest to Simon, however, as he would eventually amass almost 400 prints by Rembrandt, holdings to be surpassed only by his acquisitions of hundreds of Goya etchings as well as more than 700 Picasso prints during his lifetime. While he would later divest himself of many extraordinary drawings and other works on paper, he retained an outstandingly accomplished book of Dutch seventeenth-century watercolors featuring 158 different varieties of achingly beautiful tulips (cat. 24), which may have appealed to Simon not only for their aesthetic qualities but also for their origins as tools of commerce.

Simon's notoriety at this point brought him in contact with high-profile dealers who offered even more significant opportunities for acquisition. By the 1960s his collection contained works by Renoir, Gauguin, Pissarro, Degas, and Manet, but he continued to refine his holdings as his eye sharpened. He added to the northern European collection with a superb Rubens (cat. 72), a Frans Hals portrait (cat. 29), a Van der Heyden interior (cat. 34), and, most importantly at this juncture, *Christ Giving His Blessing* by Hans Memling (cat. 55). This was to be one of his rare early purchases of a religious painting by a Netherlandish artist. Shortly after acquiring the panel in April 1964, he was dismayed to learn that the dealer from Knoedler and Co. who sold the painting to him had peddled a very similar composition by the same artist to another client in the late 1950s (fig. 55a). Heated correspondence between Simon and Knoedler commenced, and Simon quickly dressed down the dealership for not revealing this other version to him prior to his purchase.

On the same day he bought the Memling, Simon also purchased from Knoedler *An Unknown Genoese Noblewoman*

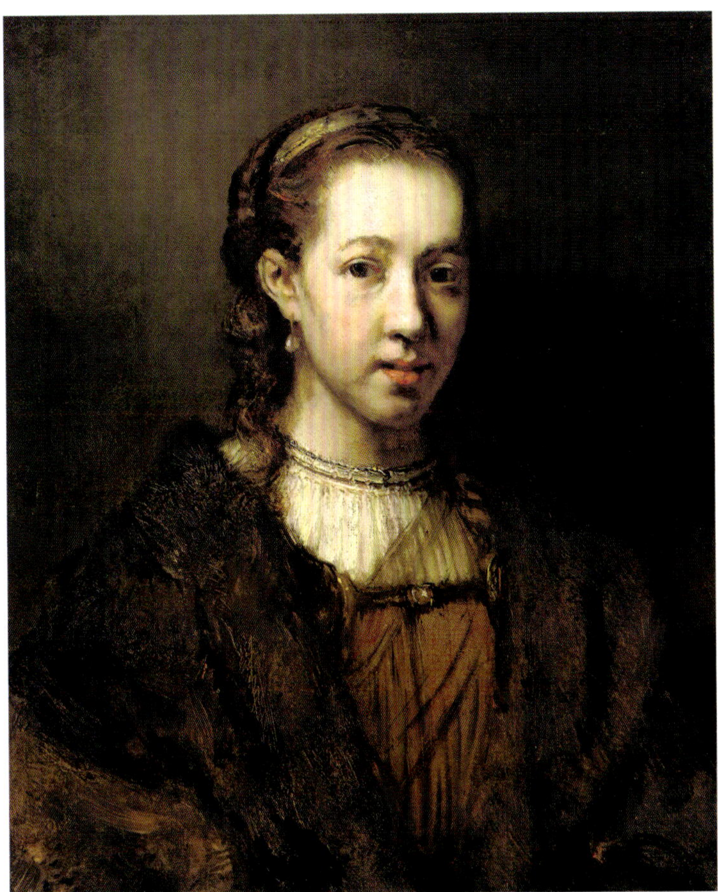

Fig. 5. Attributed to Jacobus Leveck (formerly attributed to Rembrandt van Rijn), *Portrait of a Woman, probably Hendrickje Stoeffels*, ca. 1653, oil on canvas, 25¾ × 12¼ in. (65.5 × 54 cm), Agnes Etherington Art Centre, Queen's University, Kingston. Gift of Isabel Bader, 2019 (62-017.07).

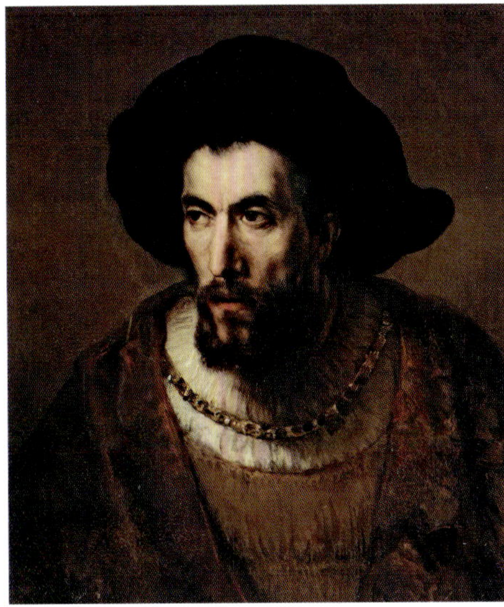

Fig. 6. Formerly attributed to Rembrandt van Rijn, *The Philosopher*, ca. 1650–55, oil on canvas, 26¼ × 23 in. (66.7 × 58.4 cm), Collection of the Haggerty Museum of Art, Marquette University, Milwaukee.

(formerly *Marchesa Lomellini Durazzo*) by Anthony van Dyck, which he would later sell in 1973 (fig. 7). This popular Flemish master ultimately evaded Simon's grasp, a gap in the Museum's current holdings that is still evident today. On the other hand, Simon managed to purchase nine paintings by Rubens, eight of which remain in the collection (cats. 69–76).

Three days prior to purchasing the Memling and Van Dyck, Simon finalized the stunning purchase of the entire stock of the venerable New York dealership Duveen Brothers, along with its extensive library and building at 18 East Seventy-Ninth Street in New York. This, too, involved complicated and drawn-out negotiations. The collection comprised more than 300 paintings, drawings, watercolors, sculptures, and tapestries as well as furniture and decorative arts, and it ended up costing $4 million, with treasures by artists such as Giorgione, Francesco di Giorgio, Luini, Ribera, and Clodion. Within this vast deal were nineteen objects from the northern European school, eight of which remain in Pasadena today, including works by Daniël Mijtens I (cat. 57), Rubens (cats. 75–76), and Gerard David (cat. 21).

The years 1968 and 1969 saw a flurry of acquisitions, and it seems clear that by this point Simon was already considering the notion of calling his growing collection a museum—specifically, however, a "museum without walls." Portions of the growing number of objects were being lent to university galleries, museums, and his own Hunt Foods corporate headquarters. His place on the board of the Los Angeles County Museum of Art ensured that there was a stopping off location for his purchases, one where they could be studied and treated by conservators. But any hopes on the part of the LACMA board that Simon's collection and funds would eventually land there were to be dashed in the following decade. By the 1970s Simon was flirting with other museums, including the Fine Arts Museums of San Francisco, the National Gallery of Art in Washington, the J. Paul Getty Museum, and others that recognized Simon's fledgling, fifteen-year-old collection as an enviable achievement.

By the end of 1969, this group of works would have an impressive footing in the northern schools, with significant paintings by Rembrandt (cat. 66), Jan Steen (cats. 88–89), and Gerrit Dou (cat. 22) counted among them. In the early 1970s, superb examples by Lucas Cranach I (cats. 17–18), Jacob van Ruisdael (cat. 78), Gabriel Metsu (cat. 56), Cornelis Cornelisz. van Haarlem (cat. 16), and Maarten van Heemskerck (cats. 31–32) would join the roster. Simon's most acquisitive years for the entire collection were from 1972 to 1975, tellingly the years that led up to his securing his own museum in Pasadena in which to exhibit these treasures (fig. 8). Jan Lievens's haunting *Panoramic Landscape* from 1640 (cat. 49) would be purchased in 1974, a real testament to Simon's growing discernment for rare and exceptional examples by various artists. His last Rubens purchase, the impressive *Saint Ignatius of Loyola*, ca. 1616 (cat. 73), had been sold, along with its pendant and other paintings, from the Jesuit Church in Brussels in 1777, soon after the suppression of the Jesuit colleges, convents, and churches. It would remain with the Earls of Warwick for 180 years before being sold from Warwick Castle to Simon in the last days of 1974.

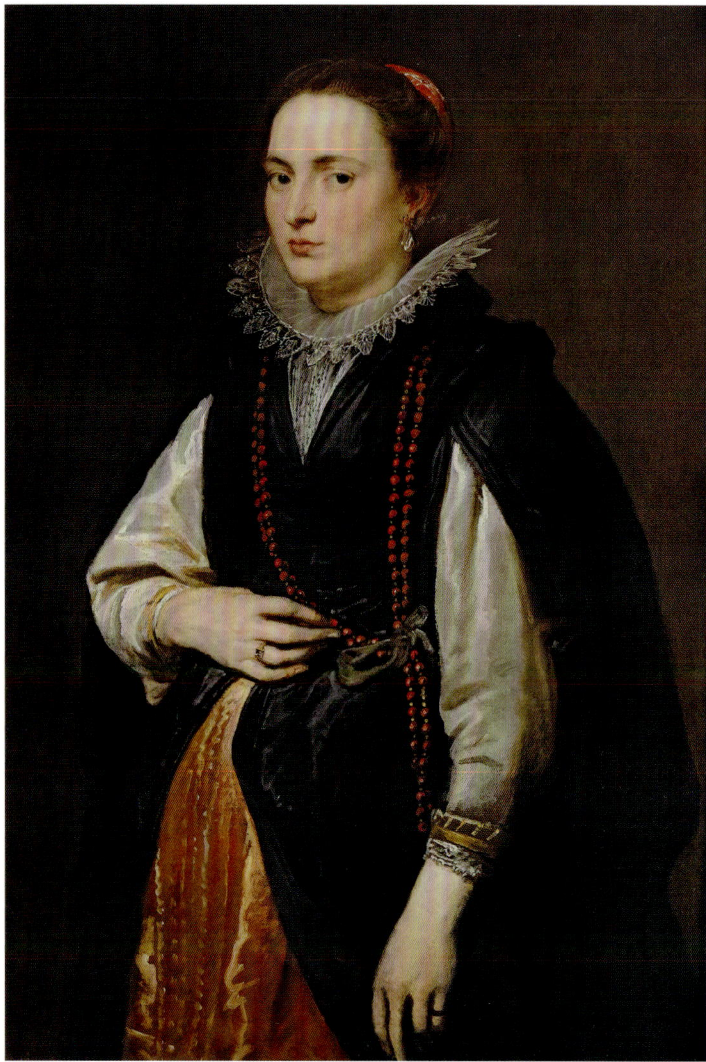

Fig. 7. Anthony van Dyck, *An Unknown Genoese Noblewoman* (formerly *Marchesa Lomellini Durazzo*), ca. 1621–27, oil on canvas, 39½ × 29½ in. (100.4 × 74.9 cm), private collection, courtesy of The Weiss Gallery, London.

The last ten years of northern European acquisitions witnessed additional Dutch, German, and Flemish works joining a now formidable collection: another Lievens (cat. 48) and paintings by Jacob Jordaens (cat. 40), Willem Reuter (cat. 68), and Quiringh Gerritsz. van Brekelenkam (cat. 13). But the most outstanding purchases were the last Rembrandt to join the collection, *Portrait of a Bearded Man in a Wide-Brimmed Hat,* dated 1633 (cat. 65), and the sublime Dieric Bouts *Resurrection* (cat. 11). As discussed by Amy Walsh in the entry for the Rembrandt, the sitter in the portrait may now have been successfully identified as Jacob Jacobsz. van Couwenhoven, a wealthy Rotterdam brewer. The painting has impressive provenance, having once been owned by Henry Clay Frick (who sold it in order to purchase a Vermeer) as well as Baron Thyssen-Bornemisza of Lugano, Switzerland, a name now associated with the great museum in Madrid. As for the Bouts, it is one of four very fragile *tüchlein* paintings executed in glue tempera on a fine linen canvas that were

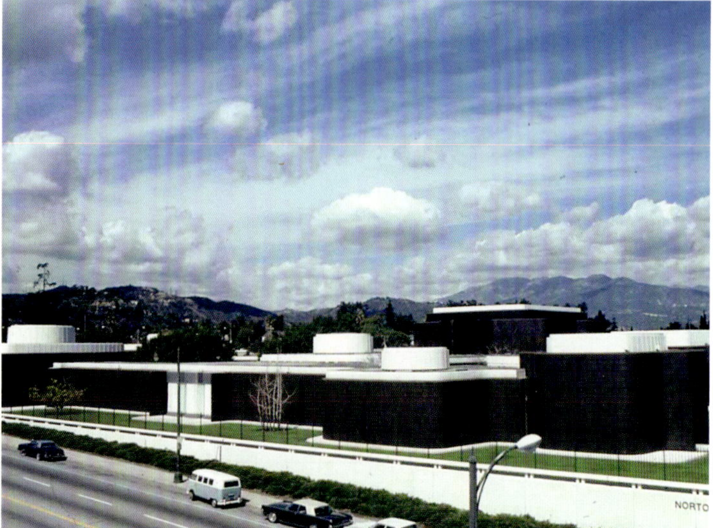

Fig. 8. Norton Simon Museum, ca. 1976.

meant to hang together as a polyptych. It was known as early as 1858 to be owned by the Milanese Guicciardi family.

When the sale of the Bouts *Resurrection* was announced by Sotheby's in London for 16 April 1980, Simon decided he would "have some fun" with a scheme that involved one of his staff members in the audience holding three empty envelopes as a bluff, while Simon, absent from the saleroom floor, remained on the phone with a Sotheby's specialist. The idea was to have all eyes on the staff member as he was instructed to open the envelopes when the bidding reached certain points. In yet another concocted scheme reminiscent of that for the purchase of the Rembrandt *Portrait of a Boy in Fancy Costume*, Simon managed to create his own version of a shell-and-pea game that infuriated the auctioneer and competitive bidders. The painting was knocked down to Simon for the highest price he had ever paid in his entire collecting career: $4,214,000. Weeks later at his museum, Simon would proudly pose in front of the Bouts with his second wife, the actress Jennifer Jones Simon (who had been present at the auction but was apparently oblivious to the devised strategy). The underbidder was the National Gallery in London, which owned one of the other panels: an *Entombment* that had been purchased directly from the Guicciardi family in 1860 for £120 (about $24,000 today). Five years after Simon's acquisition, the J. Paul Getty Museum would purchase another section of Bouts's altarpiece, an *Annunciation*, for about $5 million.

Simon would continue buying art—primarily paintings but also Southeast Asian sculpture and Picasso and Goya etchings—until the end of 1989. His late additions of works by Guercino, Cagnacci, Van Gogh, Degas, Courbet, and even a group of forty-two artists' letters (fig. 9) would amaze the art world both for their beauty and for the boldness of the unconventional museum founder who continued to supplement his collection with pieces of rarity and importance. The

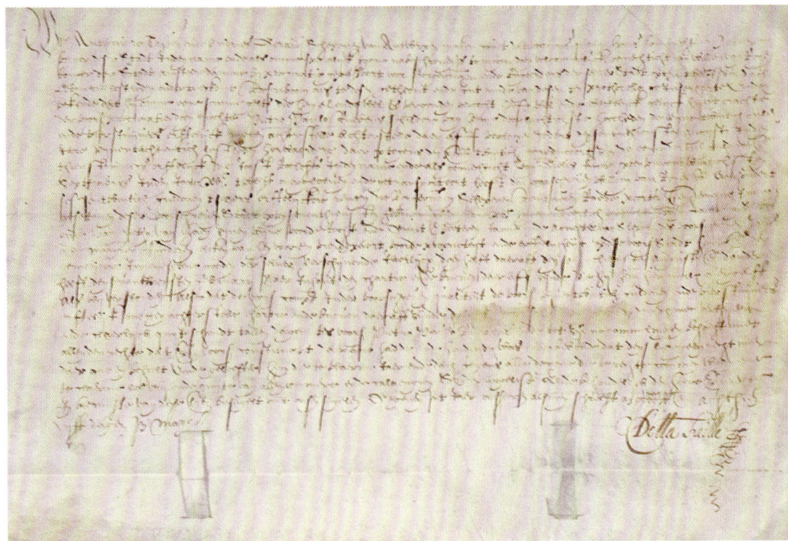

Fig. 9. Peter Paul Rubens, *Autograph Letter (Written in Secretary's Hand in Dutch, Signed by Rubens on Verso)*, 1618, ink on vellum, 8⅝ × 13⅜ in. (21.9 × 34 cm), Norton Simon Art Foundation.

ninety-five catalogue entries that follow represent a small but consequential portion of the more than 12,000 works of art that today make up the combined collections of the Norton Simon Museum. The founder's choices of still lifes, portraits, landscapes, and mythological scenes by some of the most celebrated artists from northern Europe stop Museum patrons in their tracks on entering the galleries; it is as if they have suddenly come upon an old acquaintance. Just as the inscrutable Simon structured his entities and built his art collection with cunning and curatorial precision, he also managed to make the art that hangs in his galleries of northern European art enlighten visitors about the culture and history of Holland, Belgium, and Germany from centuries past. In the pages that follow, Amy Walsh is your worthy guide to this remarkable legacy.

Carol Togneri
Former Chief Curator, Norton Simon Museum

Catalogue

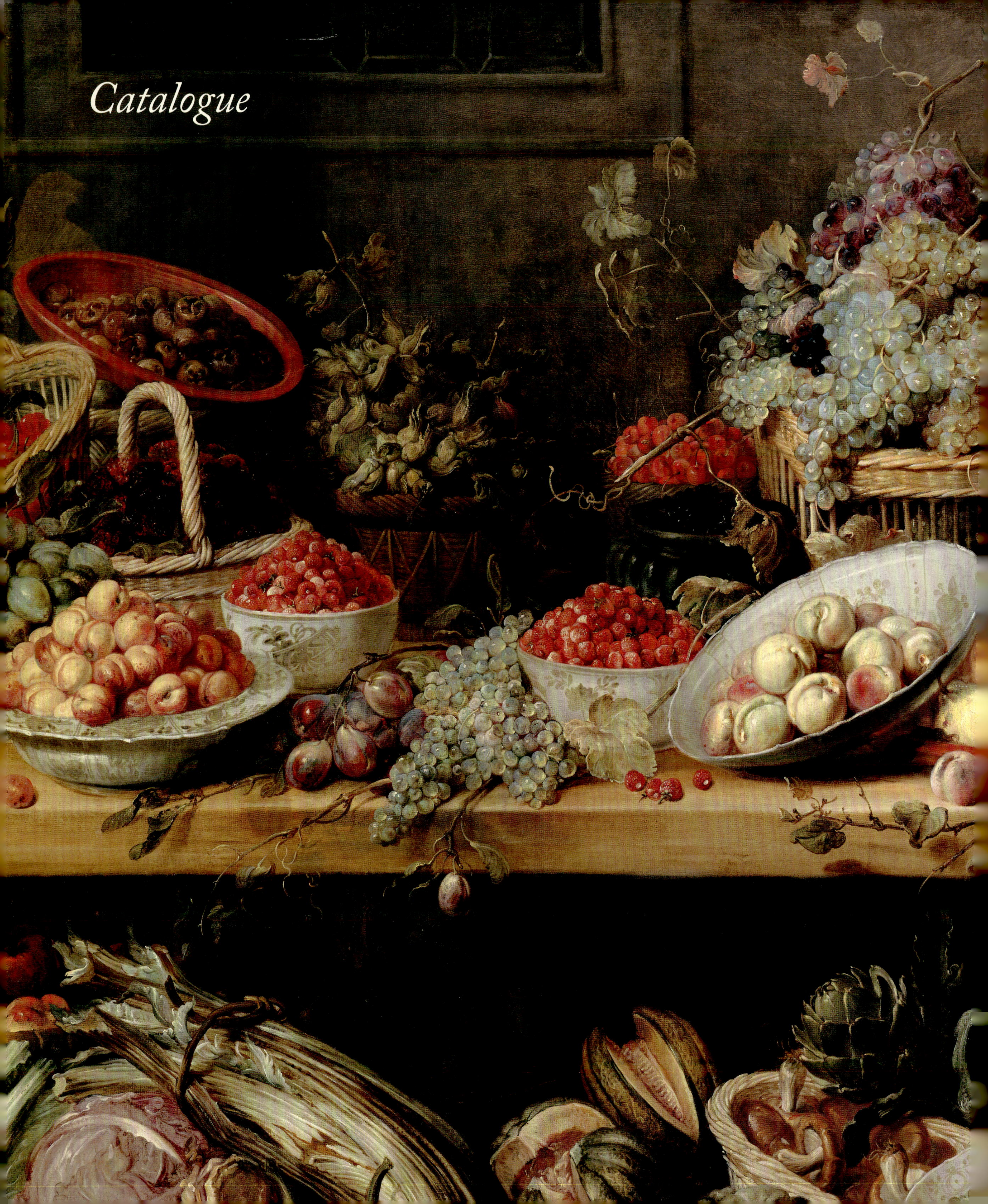

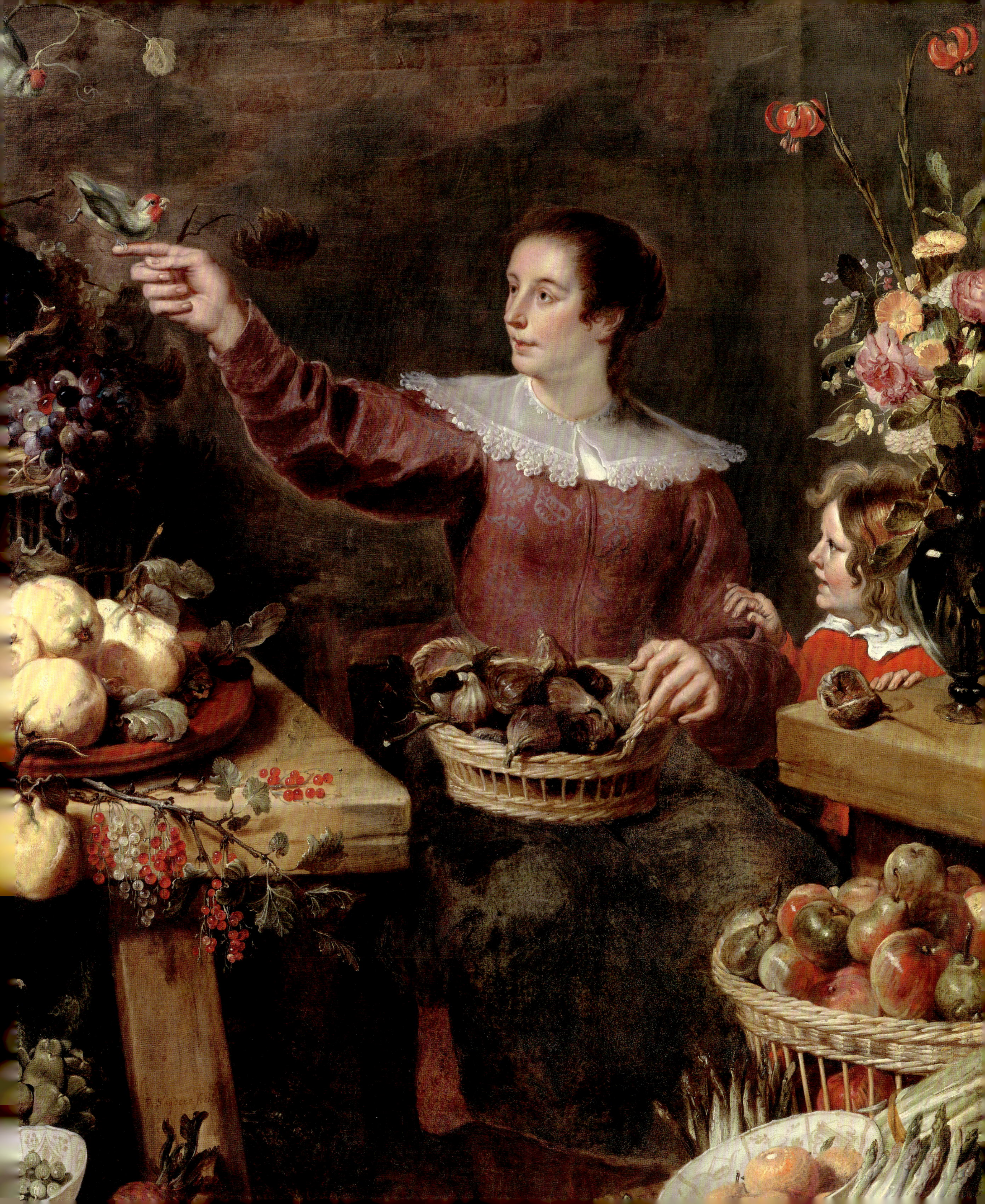

1, 2

Master of Alkmaar

Netherlandish
Alkmaar, active ca. 1490–1515

The Flagellation of Christ

ca. 1500–10

Oil on panel, 18¾ × 9¼ in. (47.6 × 23.5 cm)
Norton Simon Art Foundation, M.1969.36.1.P

Christ Carrying the Cross

ca. 1500–10

Oil on panel, 18⅝ × 9⅜ in. (47.3 × 23.9 cm)
Norton Simon Art Foundation, M.1969.36.2.P

Provenance

William, 1st Baron Bagot (1728–1798), Blithfield, Rugeley, Staffordshire, by descent to;[1] William, 2nd Baron Bagot (1773–1856), Blithfield, Rugeley, Staffordshire, as Van Eyck, by descent to;[2] Gerald, 5th Baron Bagot (1866–1946), Blithfield, Rugeley, Staffordshire; his estate (sale, Sotheby's, London, 17 October 1945, lot 73, as Early Dutch School, sold to); [Thomas Agnew & Sons, London, as Master of Alkmaar, stock nos. 9101 (*The Scourging of Christ*, purchased with Leonard F. Koetser) and 9102 (*Calvary*, purchased with R. Buttery), sold 15 March 1954 to]; [M. Knoedler and Co. Inc., Paris and New York, stock nos. A5663 and A5664 owned with Pinakos Inc. (Rudolf Heinemann), New York, sold 1969 to]; Norton Simon Art Foundation.

Exhibited

London 1946, nos. 26–27; Paris 1969, no. 13; on loan, Phoenix Art Museum, 20 February–21 June 1970; on loan, Los Angeles County Museum of Art, 22 June 1970–26 July 1972; Princeton 1972–74, pp. 28–31, nos. 3 (*Flagellation*), 4 (*Carrying the Cross*).

References

Neale 1819–23, vol. 3 (1820), n.pag.; Neale 1829–31; Neale 1847, vol. 1 (1847), n.pag.; S. Campbell 2010, p. 330, nos. 711A–B, ill.

Technical Notes

The Flagellation of Christ

The uncradled support is a vertically grained oak panel. The left and right sides of the panel have exposed wood margins that are unprimed and unpainted; the absence of similar margins at the top and bottom suggests that these edges were trimmed. Shaped hardwood strips ⅜ inch wide that conform to the curve of the slightly warped panel have been screwed into the top and bottom edges. The thick, off-white ground has a slight vertical striation, unrelated to wood grain, which suggests that the ground was applied by brush. The presence of barbes at the left and right edges indicates that the panel was installed in a framework before the ground was applied. At the top and bottom, the ground continues without interruption. Thinly painted dark lines surround numerous design elements, such as the heads of some spectators, the blue leggings of the man at the far right, and Christ's legs. Hatching on the proper left arm, back, and waist of the man in the right foreground may also be part of an underdrawing. The smoothly brushed paint appears to be an oil medium. The artist combined opaque paint with layering of semitransparent glazes. The paint has become somewhat transparent. Pentimenti are visible to the eye and have been confirmed by X-radiographs. In the gray balustrade across the upper portion of the painting, the arms of the man second from left on the balcony were previously positioned in front of the balustrade, or, more likely, the balustrade was raised from its original height. Part of the garment of the man at the far right of the balcony was changed. Other areas in which changes have become visible are on the back contour of Christ's proper right leg and foot and on the left side of his torso. Throughout the painting there is a very fine, dense network of cracks. Abrasion is fairly widespread. Thinly painted glazes are disturbed or almost removed; flesh tones are abraded, especially in the face and hair of the man at far left, the face of Christ, and the face and hat of the man in the green shirt behind Christ. The painting was cleaned in 1954. The majority of retouching is in the face and figure of Christ and the blue leggings of the man at lower right. The varnish, an aged synthetic resin as suggested by ultraviolet-light examination, is a thin layer, moderately yellowed.

Christ Carrying the Cross

The uncradled support is a vertically grained oak panel. The left and right edges are slightly beveled on the reverse. The presence of barbes at the bare left- and right-side margins indicates that the panel was primed in a framework such as an altarpiece. The absence of these at the top and bottom edges is a strong indication that they have been cut down. Shaped hardwood strips that conform to the slight warp of the panel have been screwed into the top and bottom edges. When these strips were removed, the cleanly sawn top and bottom edges were found to be lighter colored than the exposed left and right edges, which further demonstrates the alteration to the original panel. The thick ground is off-white. The shallow vertical striation could be from the ground having been applied by brush and not smoothed afterward.

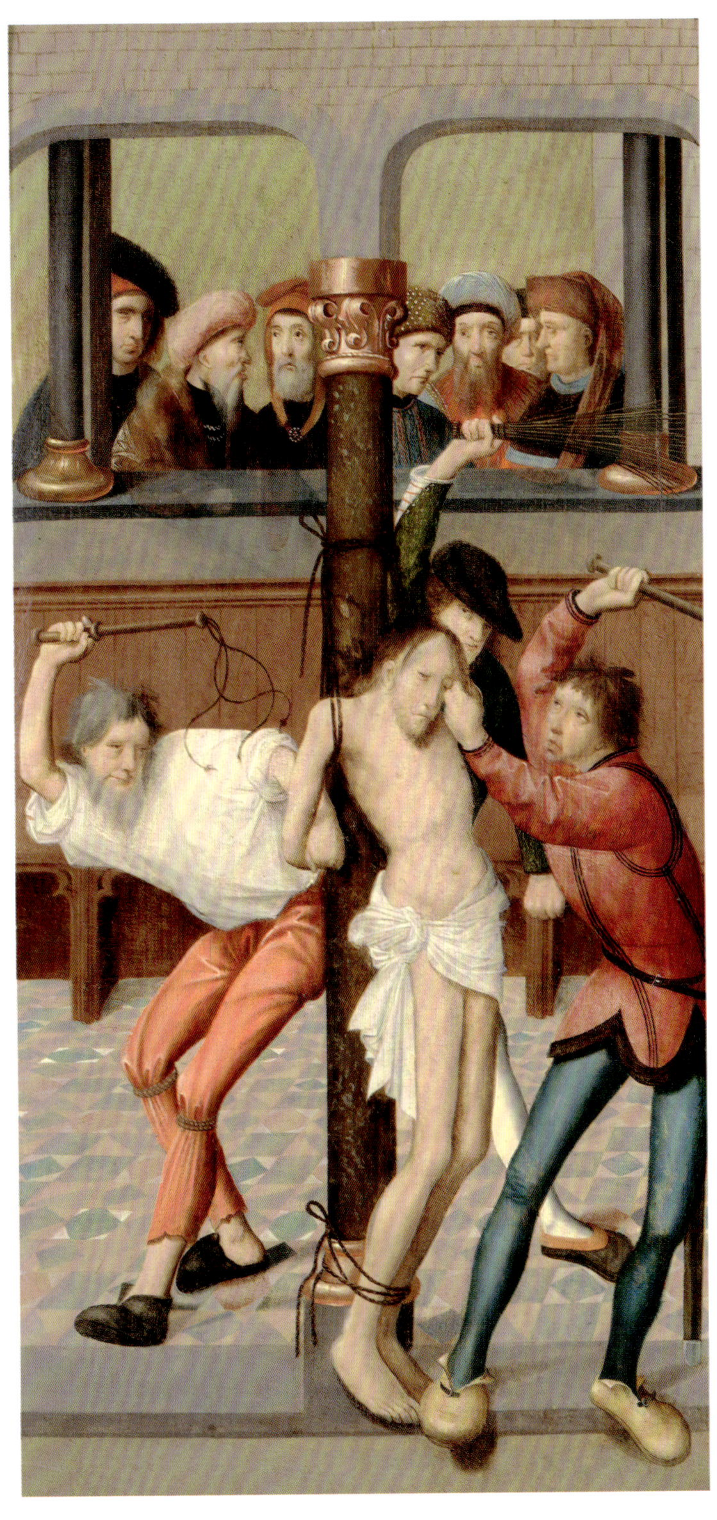

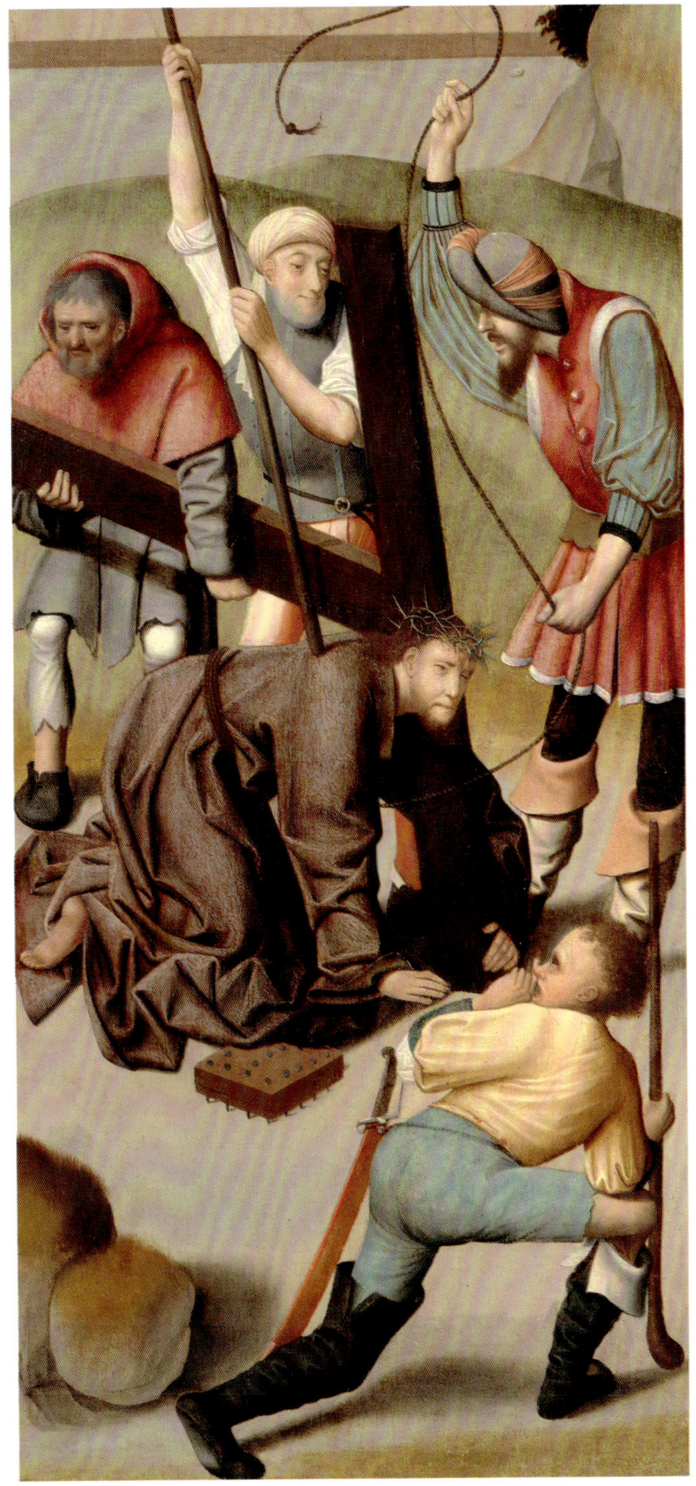

Microscopic examination of the surface revealed no drawing except for a thin red line at the far left edge of Christ's robe, beneath his foot. The artist used both rich opaque paint as well as thinned, semitransparent glazes. The robe of Christ is an extraordinarily thin glaze; magnification shows red pigment particles dispersed in the medium. The brighter red of the man's cloak at the upper left is similar. Brushmarking is slight, evident at contours of more thickly painted areas. The paint exhibits very fine, very dense cracking throughout. Although the paint is generally fairly well preserved, some abrasion has occurred, such as in the trousers of the man at the lower right foreground. A loss at bottom center has been filled and retouched; there is also a repaired loss in the boulder at the lower left and at the bottom right corner. According to notes in the files, the painting was cleaned in 1954 before entering the collection. Ultraviolet-light examination suggests the varnish is a thin layer of aged synthetic resin, moderately yellowed. There is minor scattered retouching below the varnish.

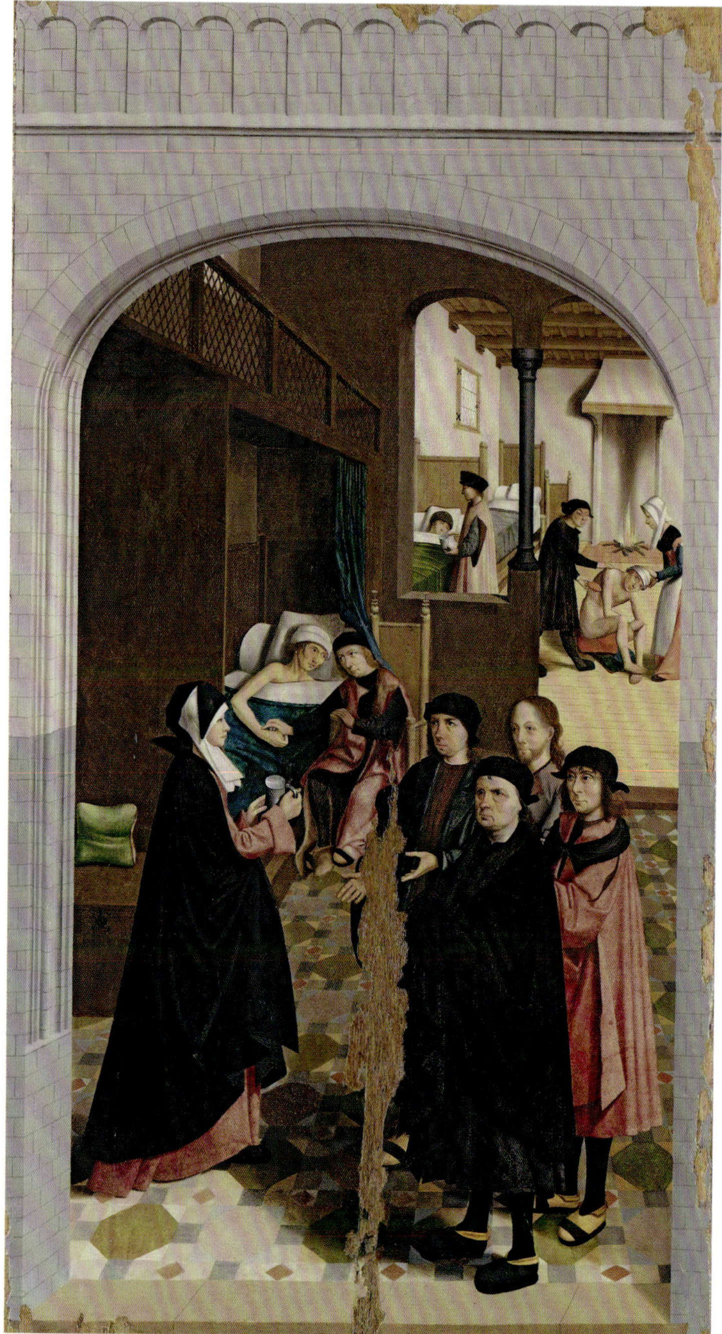

Fig. 1a. Master of Alkmaar, *Visiting the Sick*, from *The Seven Works of Mercy*, 1504, oil on panel, 40 ¾ × 22 ⅜ in. (103.5 × 56.8 cm), Rijksmuseum, Amsterdam.

The *Flagellation of Christ* and *Christ Carrying the Cross* depict two events preceding the Crucifixion, which are described only briefly in the Gospels.[3] According to Matthew and Mark, after Pilate had washed his hands he ordered that Christ be scourged, which Roman law prescribed as a prelude to crucifixion. Following the Flagellation, Christ was mocked and crowned with thorns; then, bearing his own cross, he was led to Golgotha, the site of his Crucifixion. In *Christ Carrying the Cross*, Christ has fallen under the weight of his cross, his knee on the spike block affixed to the hem of his robe; Simon of Cyrene, dressed as a sixteenth-century peasant, supports the bottom of the cross, while tormentors prod and harass Christ.

The narrative details included in the Pasadena panels were probably inspired by the popular literary narratives of the life and Passion of Christ, which embroidered details from Old Testament prophecies onto the original Gospel accounts.[4] Psalm 22, which the Church Fathers accepted as the prophetic expression of Christ's words during the Passion and which became the Good Friday Passion Psalm in the liturgy, was particularly influential. It was the principal source for the characterization of Christ's tormentors as calves, bulls, lions, unicorns, and dogs. The identification of these tormentors with dogs was especially popular in the late Middle Ages in the narrative Passion tracts and may be suggested here by the man lunging across the foreground.[5] A contemporary Dutch manuscript makes this reference explicit: "And they led him with tumult, pushing and pursuing him just like mad dogs that hunt a wolf; they raged and grimaced at him because he didn't move as quickly as they wished."[6]

The ideal of the *imitatio Christi* dominated popular piety in the early sixteenth century, when these two panels were painted. The faithful were instructed to pray before scenes of Christ's suffering and, by identifying with his human experience, to come closer to God.[7] The Flagellation marks the beginning of Christ's physical suffering, which continued as he carried the cross. The latter event also represented a metaphor for following in Christ's path. Matthew 16:24 was often cited in this context: "If anyone would come after me, let him deny himself and take up his cross and follow me."[8] Simon of Cyrene, who assisted Christ in carrying the cross (as in the Pasadena panel), was presented as the prototype

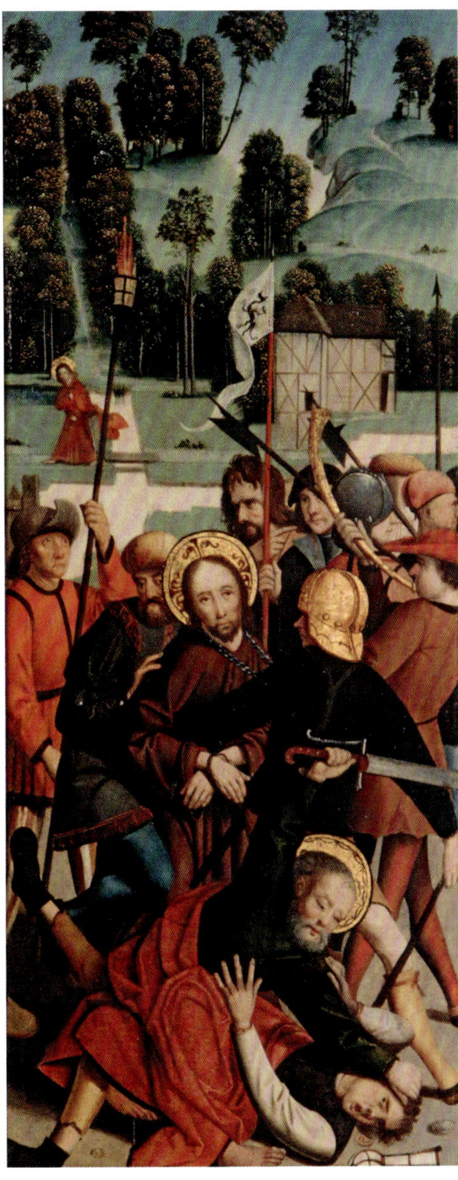

Fig. 2a. Master of Alkmaar, *The Arrest of Christ*, 1490–ca. 1510, oil on panel, 23 ¾ × 10 ¼ in. (60.3 × 26 cm), Spencer Museum of Art, Lawrence.

for Christians to follow. A short prayer included beneath an image of Christ carrying the cross published in Germany in the 1460s exemplifies the way in which contemporaries responded to these images: "Oh, dear Lord Jesus, as thou hast carried thy Cross, so grant me, dear Lord, that I [may] patiently bear all adversity and sorrows, that I therewith lay low all villainy and temptations of the body and of the battle over the evil spirit."[9]

The original context of the Pasadena panels is unknown: They may have formed part of an altarpiece of which the center panel or sculpture represented the Crucifixion or they may have been part of a polyptych of the Passion of Christ arranged horizontally. The integrity of the panels, which show evidence of having been painted within a frame, has been distorted by later alterations. Both panels were cut at the top and bottom, probably by the eighteenth century. The uniform, narrow, unpainted margins evident along both sides of the panels are missing at the top and bottom where the paint surface continues to the cut edges.[10] The greater reductions, possibly as much as six inches, probably came from the tops of the panels.[11] Contemporary images of Christ Carrying the Cross often include a reference to Pilate's house or the city gates of Jerusalem or to Calvary with Christ's crucifixion between the two thieves, as in *Christ Carrying the Cross, with the Crucifixion* (Metropolitan Museum of Art, New York), the interior left panel of the *Lamentation* Triptych by Gerard David (ca. 1460–1523).[12] The Pasadena panel may, like these, have included the suggestion of a distant town or building on a hill. The top of *The Flagellation of Christ* probably originally extended the brick facade of the building to include a cornice similar to that in the panel *Visiting the Sick* by the Master of Alkmaar in the Rijksmuseum, Amsterdam (fig. 1a).

Attributed to Jan van Eyck (ca. 1390–1441) in the eighteenth century, *The Flagellation of Christ* and *Christ Carrying the Cross* were exhibited by Thomas Agnew & Sons in 1946 as the work of the Master of Alkmaar. The artist's sobriquet derives from the polyptych *The Seven Works of Mercy*, dated 1504, which belonged to the Sint-Laurenskerk in Alkmaar before being acquired by the Rijksmuseum in 1918. The maker of the Amsterdam panels, who was previously identified with one of the Haarlem-based Van Waterlant brothers, is currently believed to be the Alkmaar painter Cornelis Buys I, who probably led a large workshop, possibly in Amsterdam, active between ca. 1495 and 1532.[13]

The Pasadena paintings share with the Amsterdam panels an interest in cast shadows and clear, elegant color, as well as robust, angular movements and individualized facial expressions.[14] The manner of framing the scene of the *Flagellation*—with arches extending into a brick facade that appears to lie on the picture plane, the tiled floor, tilted space, and columns placed between a wall and arch—is also characteristic of the interior scenes in the Amsterdam polyptych, such as the panel depicting *Visiting the Sick*. The overlapping rounded hills in *Christ Carrying the Cross* are also similar to those in *The Resurrection* by the Master of Alkmaar (Rijksmuseum, Amsterdam).

In support of the attribution of the Pasadena paintings to the Master of Alkmaar (whom he identifies as the brothers Claas and Mourijn van Waterlant), Jeremy Bangs draws particular attention to the similarity of the faces and poses in the Pasadena panels to those in works traditionally attributed to the master: the *Triptych with Adoration of the Magi, Saint Antony Abbot, and Saint Adrian* (Rijksmuseum, Amsterdam), *The High Priest Refusing Joachim's Sacrifice* and *The Meeting of Joachim and Anna under the Golden Gate* (Frans Hals Museum, Haarlem), and *Christ before Pilate* and *Pilate Washing His Hands*, the locations of which are unknown.[15] Bangs compares "the characteristic face of the figure at the left in the *Flagellation* to faces seen in Haarlem and Amsterdam," such as that of Joachim, and observes, "The odd or contorted pose of the foreground figure in the panel of *Christ*

Carrying the Cross has its cousin in the foreground figure in the triptych at Amsterdam."[16]

The expressive, almost caricature-like facial features with strong noses and the exaggerated, angular movements of the figures in the Pasadena panels distinguish them within the oeuvre of the Master of Alkmaar. Some of the differences may be attributable to the more violent subject matter and the influence of the dynamic scenes and characterizations in the popular contemporary prints by Israhel van Meckenem II (1440/45–1503) and others.[17] In the Pasadena panel of the *Flagellation*, seven men, individually characterized and dressed in a mixture of invented "biblical" and contemporary European costumes like those in *Pilate Washing His Hands*, stoically observe from behind a balustrade as three tormentors, whips raised above their heads, appear to spiral around the flaccid figure of Christ. The same exaggeration appears in the figure of the tormentor lunging across the foreground of *Christ Carrying the Cross*. The stylized energy of the animated postures and expressions in the Pasadena panels recall that of the figures in the violent scene of *The Arrest of Christ* (fig. 2a).[18] The stiff, exaggerated movement of the lunging man also resonates in the profile figure of Christ striding with bent knees in *Resurrection of Christ* (Rijksmuseum, Amsterdam) and in the figure in the foreground of *Pilate Washing His Hands*. The description of the eyes in the Pasadena panels as slits beneath strongly arched lids, with the eye socket defined by the line of the eyebrow continuing down a long, pointed nose, is also characteristic of the artist.

The numerous points of agreement between the Pasadena and Amsterdam panels strongly support the attribution of *The Flagellation of Christ* and *Christ Carrying the Cross* to the artist traditionally identified as the Master of Alkmaar. If the current attribution of the Amsterdam paintings is accepted, the author of the Pasadena paintings was, thus, also the Alkmaar painter Cornelis Buys I.

1. According to Sotheby's sale catalogue, 17 October 1945, lot 73a/b, the paintings were collected by the 1st Baron Bagot.

2. In 1820 Neale mentioned seeing the paintings now at the Norton Simon Museum together with a *Nativity*, all attributed to Van Eyck, at Blithfield, Staffordshire, the seat of Lord Bagot; see Neale 1819–23, vol. 3 (1820), n.pag. At the Blithfield, Rugeley, sale (London, Sotheby's, 17 October 1945, lot 40), however, the *Nativity* was sold separately as an early German panel, apparently no longer considered related to *The Flagellation of Christ* and *Christ Carrying the Cross*, which were called "Early Dutch School." According to an article by A. C. R. Carter, "Art Heirlooms Realise £15,026, £1,850 for Nativity," from an unidentified newspaper attached to a copy of the catalogue of the Bagot estate sale, now at the Getty Research Institute (hereafter cited as GRI), "Dr. James Hasson, who was physician to the French forces in England during the war, outbid a big company of professional collectors at Sotheby's yesterday by giving £1,850 for an early German panel depicting the Nativity. At one time this was attributed to Jan van Eyck, and was bought by the 1st Baron Bagot (1728–1798). Among other Bagot heirlooms were two early Dutch panels of the Road to Calvary, and the Scourging, for which Mr. Colin Agnew paid £1,520." For the painting of the *Nativity*, see Bagot 1824, p. 156, which gives a transcription of a letter dated 8 January 1781 from Horace Walpole to the 1st Baron Bagot discussing the subject of this painting. Lord Bagot assumed the painting represented a marriage, but Walpole thought it was "a father and mother presenting their son . . . to the Virgin."

3. Accounts of the Flagellation of Christ are found in Matthew 27:26, Mark 15:15, Luke 23:16, and John 19:1; Christ Carrying the Cross is told in Matthew 27:32, Mark 15:21, Luke 23:26–27, and John 19:17.

4. The first comprehensive interpolations of extra-Gospel narration were the *Meditationes vitae Christi* by Pseudo-Bonaventure from the late thirteenth century and *Vita Christi* by Ludolph of Saxony from the early fourteenth century, which were followed and further developed by German and Dutch devotional texts of the fifteenth and sixteenth centuries. Marrow 1977, p. 168, notes, "The brutal figures, cruel anecdotes, and entirely new events, sometimes of grotesque character, that appear in depictions of the Passion during the late Middle Ages and Early Renaissance all occurred for the first time in narrative Passion tracts."

5. Marrow 1977, p. 169, identifies the source as Psalm 21, but quotes from Psalm 22.

6. Marrow 1977, p. 179. The quotation is his translation from the Dutch manuscript in the Koninklijke Bibliotheek, The Hague, MS 133 E 4, fol. 116r–v.

7. Marrow 1977, p. 167.

8. Matthew 16:24.

9. Gibson 1972–73, p. 86, notes, "In a late 15th-century Dutch Passion narrative, the account of Christ's tortures and his taking up of the cross is followed by an exhortation to the reader to bear God's whips with patience; man is flailed by God for the cleansing of his sins and the testing of his virtues."

10. Ridges, or "barbes," of red paint along the vertical edges of the painted surfaces further suggest that the panels were prepared and painted while inserted in a grooved frame. Filedt Kok 2008, p. 152, describes similar findings on all four sides of the panels of the *Seven Works of Mercy*. Regarding the construction of altarpieces, see Verougstraete-Marcq and Van Schoute 1989.

11. This estimate is based on the dimensions of two panels of similar width by Mourijn and Claas van Waterlant: *Christ in Limbo* (61.5 × 24.5 cm) and the *Arrest of Christ* (59 × 23.5 cm; present location of both unknown). See Bangs 1999, p. 85, figs. 16–17; and M. Friedländer 1967–76, vol. 10, pl. 32, no. 51.

12. See New York 1998–99, pp. 292–95, ill.; the central panel of the altarpiece is the *Lamentation* (Philadelphia Museum of Art), the right is the *Resurrection, with Pilgrims of Emmaus* (Metropolitan Museum of Art, New York).

13. I am grateful to Jan Piet Filedt Kok for introducing me to Judith Niessen, the author of the entries on Alkmaar in Filedt Kok 2008 and Niessen 2010. In her article and in an email to the author (Norton Simon Museum curatorial files; cited hereafter as NSM) dated 14 August 2011, she dismissed any connection of the Master of Alkmaar with Haarlem and noted recent research by Sebastian Dudok van Heel, which suggests that "the Master of Alkmaar can be identified after all with the brother of Jacob Cornelisz., Cornelis Buys the Elder." See Dudok van Heel 2011, p. 59; Niessen 2010, p. 298n21, summarizes his argument. Niessen believes that the diversity within the group of paintings attributed to the Master of Alkmaar suggests a large workshop "with one leading artist and several independent co-workers."

14. Regarding *The Seven Works of Mercy*, which were severely damaged by vandals in 1582 and also suffered from prolonged exposure to damp, see Filedt Kok 2008, pp. 152–56; and

De Bruyn Kops 1976. See also Niessen 2010, especially p. 267, for discussion of stylistic characteristics. In response to the author's inquiry, Judith Niessen (email to the author, 14 August 2011) generously offered her opinion regarding the Pasadena panels: "From the web-photos (and the old b/w I have studied before), I do feel your panels are part of the same group [discussed in her 2010 article]. Indeed, similar figure types and details can be found on various paintings I discussed in my article, and there are even some good comparisons to make with the *Seven Acts* [*sic*] *of Mercy*. It seems however that the handling of paint and the colouring is slightly different from what I have seen and studied but this can well be a result of the images."

15. Jeremy Bangs, in discussion with the author, 29 May 2004, and email, 8 June 2004 (NSM). See Bangs 1999, pp. 65–152, figs. 10–11, 32–33, 40–41; and M. Friedländer 1967–76, vol. 10, pl. 28–29, no. 49, pl. 32, no. 52, pl. 34, no. 54. Niessen 2010 rejects this identification.

16. Bangs, email to the author, 8 June 2004.

17. See, for example, Van Meckenem, *The Bearing of the Cross* (Bartsch 1978–, vol. 17, p. 208, vol. 22, p. 211); and Lucas van Leyden, *The Bearing of the Cross*, dated 1509 (Bartsch 1978–, vol. 64, p. 373).

18. Bangs 1999, fig. 17. Thanks to Cynthia Morris for identifying the current location of this painting: In 1992 it was donated by her parents, Drs. Mark and Bette Morris, to the Spencer Museum of Art, University of Kansas.

3

Balthasar van der Ast

Dutch
Middelburg 1593/94–1657 Delft

Still Life with Fruits and Flowers

ca. 1630

Signed, lower left, on edge of table:
"· B · van der · Ast ·"
Oil on panel, 16 9/16 × 30 1/4 in. (42.1 × 76.8 cm)
The Norton Simon Foundation, F.1972.43.4.P

Provenance
Probably Willem J. Dreesmann (1885–1954), Amsterdam, by descent to his daughter; Pia van Spaendonck-Dreesmann (1917–1995), Tilburg, the Netherlands.[1] [Alfred Brod, London, in 1959].[2] [Kunsthandel Gebr. Douwes, Amsterdam, inv. no. 7696, by 1962 until at least 1963].[3] [G. Cramer Oude Kunst, The Hague, sold 1972 to]; The Norton Simon Foundation.

Exhibited
Probably London 1948, no. 21, as "A large plate of Delft ware heaped with grapes over a quince, an apple and a plum, stands on a table beside a low glass vase holding flowers. More fruit, a crab, shells, a snail and beetles on the table. Butterflies, a dragonfly and other insects hovering, or on the wing, 20 1/2 × 30 in. [50.8 x 76.2 cm]";[4] London 1962, no. 1; Amsterdam 1962, no. 1; [unidentified Italian exhibition, after 1962, no. 6];[5] Delft 1963, as exhibited by Kunsthandel Gebr. Douwes, Amsterdam; Delft 1972; on loan, Virginia Museum of Fine Arts, Richmond, 1 October 1972–16 December 1974.

References
Bol 1960, p. 82, no. 98, as panel, 52 × 76 cm; Graevenitz 1972, p. 1186; Olbricht 1972, p. 756, ill.; Gerson 1976, p. 164, fig. 5; Pasadena 1980, p. 49, ill.; Kahr 1982, pp. 193–94, fig. 147; P. Sutton 1986, p. 215, fig. 311; Pasadena 1989, p. 72, ill.; Cornette and Mérot 1999, p. 204; S. Campbell 2010, pp. 141, 345, no. 858, ill.

Technical Notes
The support is a horizontally grained oak panel with a reverse that retains its original wide chisel marks and hand-beveled edges. Before the panel was prepared with a ground layer, it was enlarged by the addition of a 3/8-inch-wide oak strip glued to the top edge. A crack at the lower left corner has been repaired with a small rectangle of wood glued to the reverse. The moderately thin smooth white ground, which leaves the wood grain visible, continues without interruption over the join of the strip at the top edge. Microscopic examination did not reveal underdrawing. Oil paint was smoothly applied in thin, opaque layers, as well as in translucent glazes. Textures were closely observed. For example, the snail at the bottom center was painted in a quick, sure drawing in brown paint directly over the foreground color, with a tiny pure white highlight at the center of its shell. Often the contours of objects were softened. The use of glazes, possibly applied with a blender brush, produced fuzzy contours where colors merge. The soft skin of fruit is handled differently from flowers, which are crisply painted. Brushstrokes are not evident, and very few distinct color boundaries exist. There may be a substantial amount of abrasion throughout, such as that in the background and the dark leaves at the top. Retouching, not identifiable with ultraviolet light, has been done carefully. Some of the gray background has been repainted, particularly around the dragonfly, covering small losses at the top center and the edge of the table. In other areas of compensation, thin washes of color have been floated onto the painting. The thick varnish is moderately yellowed. Ultraviolet-light examination suggests this is a natural resin, possibly with an additive.

Still Life with Fruits and Flowers is characteristic of the hybrid still lifes for which Balthasar van der Ast is best known. In this asymmetrical composition, a blue-and-white Chinese export porcelain (kraakware) plate of fruit appears off-center to the right, and a secondary area of interest, a disproportionately small floral arrangement in a thorn-prunted rummer, appears on the left.[6] Compared to the tight, symmetrical bouquets painted by Van der Ast and his contemporaries about ten years earlier, such as that portrayed in *Flowers in a Glass Beaker* (cat. 9), here the bouquet is looser and more graceful in its rhythmic play of stems, and the grape leaves that sail like kites above the plate of fruit reflect Van der Ast's personal style. A large dragonfly perches on one of the grape leaves in the shadows on the right, while a colorful moth hovers against the dark background between the flowers and fruit. The brightly lit, colorful display of insects, fruit, and shells organized in groups of two or three recalls the illuminated border of a manuscript page. A bright red crayfish marks the center of the foreground, to the left of which a small snail appears to be moving slowly to the right.[7]

Superficially, the additive display of objects on a tabletop with minimal overlap in *Still Life with Fruits and Flowers* resembles compositions painted during the first decade of the seventeenth century, such as *Still Life with Cherries and Strawberries in Porcelain Bowls*, 1608 (Staatliche Museen, Berlin) by Osias Beert (ca. 1580–1623/24). Within Van der Ast's own body of work, the somewhat awkward arrangement of

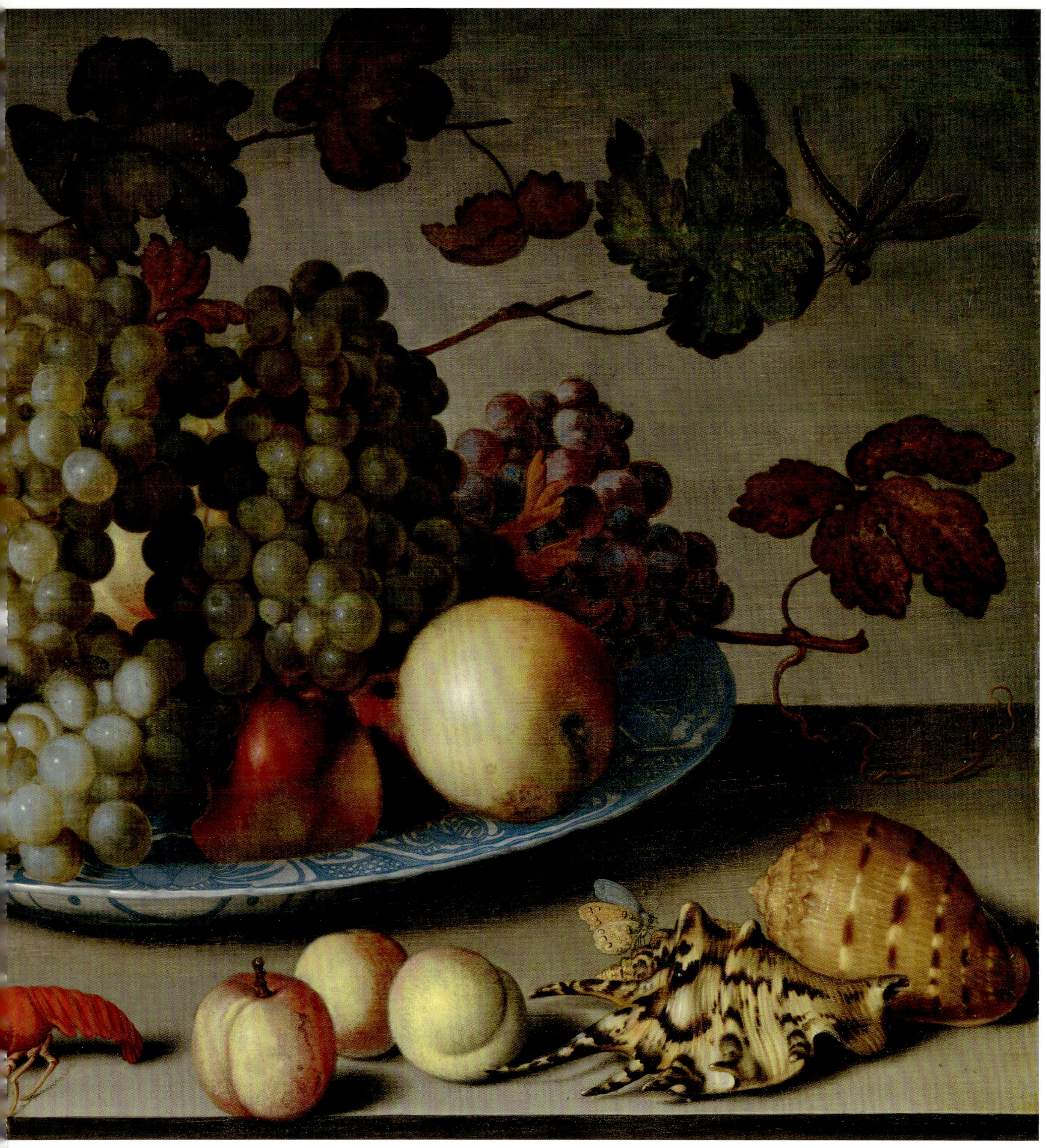

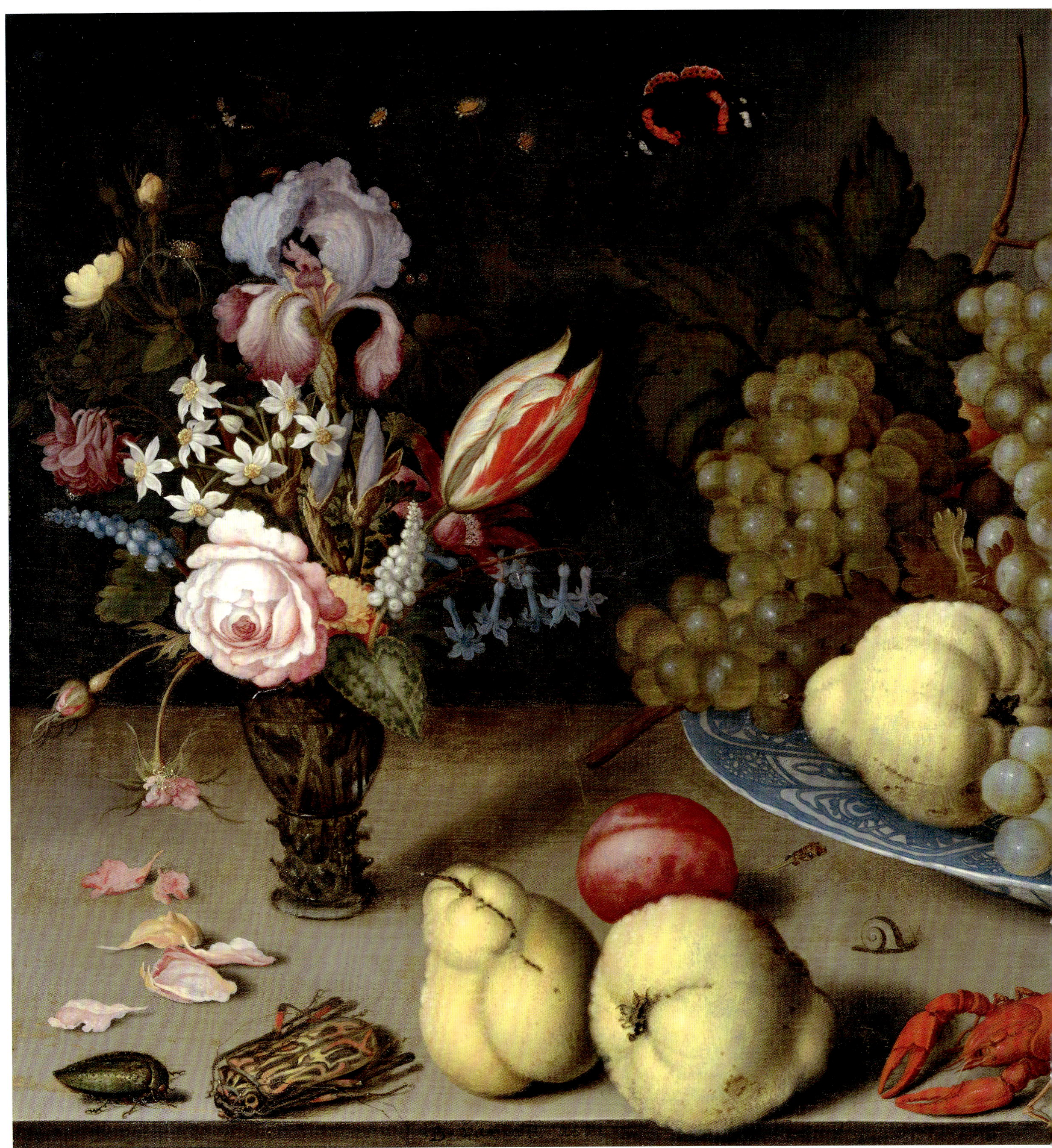

the objects in two tiers is a subtle variation on such still lifes as his 1623 *Fruit Still Life with Two Parrots* (fig. 3a), in which the objects in the picture are actually displayed on two levels of a table. Significant differences in perspective and tonality, however, suggest that the Pasadena painting dates from about 1630, during the artist's last years in Utrecht or shortly after his move to Delft. The lower vantage point in the present picture eliminates the disturbing illusion of a tilted tabletop found in the earlier paintings and increases the impression of actual space. By silhouetting the objects against the background rather than against the table, Van der Ast could represent the vase of flowers and plate of fruit in proper perspective, thereby increasing the illusion of depth. A visual wedge that recedes toward the right as the color of the background changes from dark to light greenish-gray helps to integrate the composition horizontally.

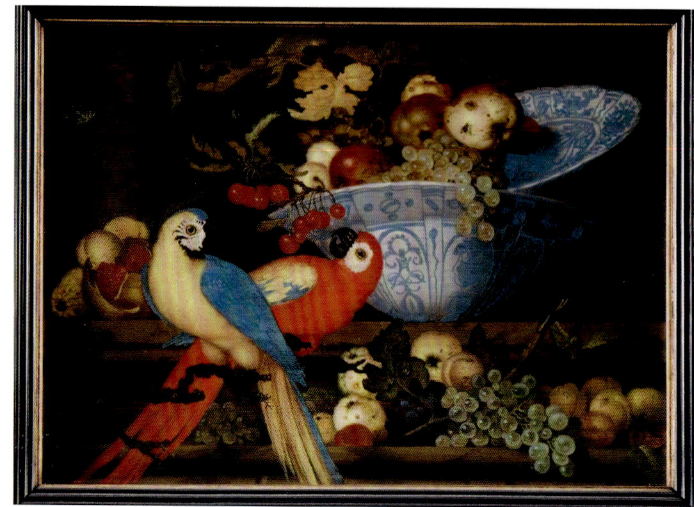

Fig. 3a. Balthasar van der Ast, *Fruit Still Life with Two Parrots*, 1623, oil on panel, 8⅝ × 12 in. (22 × 30.5 cm), Statens Museum for Kunst, Copenhagen.

Van der Ast used light to unify the disparate parts of the composition within a shared atmosphere. Light from an unseen source in the upper left dramatically highlights the colorful display of fruit, insects, and flowers against the shadowed background. The same light casts shadows across the foreground, reflects on the grapes, and penetrates the plate of fruit, illuminating apples beneath the grapes. Departing from his early, detailed manner, which relied heavily on layering of opaque paint and glazes, Van der Ast here applied thin coats of paint with relatively soft, painterly brushwork and limited glazes. Variations in the handling of paint suggest differences in texture among the soft flower petals, the firm surfaces of the grapes, and the hard, rough shells. The mottled surfaces of the pears in the left foreground, for example, are rendered with films of paint and glazes that create soft, fuzzy boundaries, while the pear and apple on the right have a smooth gloss and defined outlines, and the grapes are broadly painted. Van der Ast used glazes selectively for the flowers, freely sketching the form of the pink rose with rapid strokes of cherry red. The brushstrokes used to apply the thin, transparent paint to define the blue iris match neither the smooth glazes of his brother-in-law and teacher, Ambrosius Bosschaert I (1573–1621), that characterize Van der Ast's early paintings nor the tiny brushstrokes of Jan Brueghel II (1601–1678).

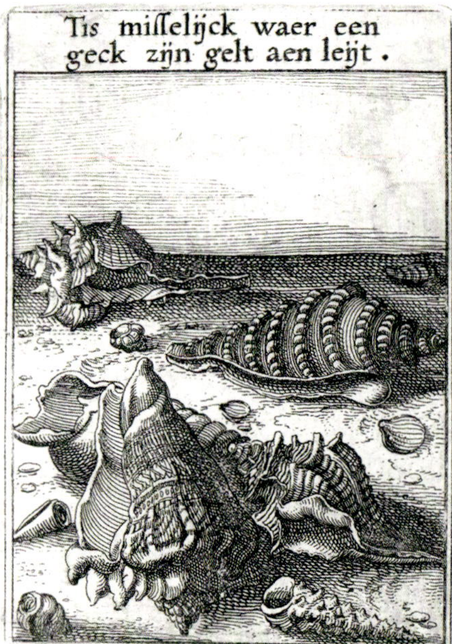

Fig. 3b. Roemer Visscher, *Tis misselijck waer een geck zijn gelt aen leijt [It's disgusting where a fool leaves his money]*, engraving, emblem IV from *Sinnepoppen* (Amsterdam, 1614). (91-B28047) Getty Research Institute, Los Angeles.

Van der Ast's sensuous still life is a celebration of his artistic skill, but it could also remind the viewer of the vanity of earthly possessions.[8] The combination of shells, crayfish, beetles, and the imported plate with flowers and fruit recalls the cabinets of curiosities housing specimens of exotic new plants, animals, shells, and artifacts traded globally and sold by local merchants to collectors. While appreciated as examples of the wonders of God's creation, the obsession with collecting these natural specimens was scorned as frivolous. Two emblems in *Sinnepoppen*, a popular emblem book published by Roemer Visscher in Amsterdam in 1614, for example, warn against the current craze of collecting shells and tulips. The motto for emblem IV (fig. 3b), illustrated by shells, is titled "It's disgusting where a fool leaves his money" (Tis misselijck waer een geck zijn gelt aen leijt), and the one for emblem V, illustrated by two tulips, bears the title "A fool and his money are soon parted" (Een dwaes en zijn gelt zijn haest gescheijden).[9] Some contemporaries viewed the import of these foreign luxury objects, including Chinese porcelain, as markers of Dutch decadence and moral decline.[10]

Flowers, which seduce by their beauty but last only a short time, were a favorite metaphor for the brevity of earthly existence and a reference to *vanitas*, a warning to prepare oneself for eternal life rather than take pride in earthly possessions and achievements. A poem on a cartouche beneath a floral still life by Jan Brueghel I (1568–1625; private collection, formerly with Richard Green, London) from the beginning of the seventeenth century has an explicit message: "Look upon this flower which appears so fair, and fades so swiftly in the strong light of the sun. Mark God's word: only it flourishes eternally. For the rest, the world is naught."[11] Van der Ast referred poignantly to inevitable death and decay with the pink rose that droops under its own weight and has already dropped petals on the table. Filled to the brim with fruit, the blue-and-white bowl also enhances this reading, as moralists and artists associated porcelain's fragile nature with *vanitas*.[12] The dark bruises on the fruit, as well as the beetles and the dragonfly, both insects that will bore into and destroy the flowers and fruit, are further reminders to viewers of their own ultimate return to dust.

1. Pia Dreesmann was married to Charles Franciscus Josephus Maria van Spaendonck (1912–2001). The introduction to the sale catalogue of her collection (Amsterdam, Sotheby Mak van Waay, 20 October 1999) notes, "This private collection was originally part of the highly important collection of the late Mr. W. J. Dreesman[n], the renowned Dutch collector." Cat. 8 in this volume, attributed to Cornelis Bisschop (1630–1674), was also formerly in Spaendonck's collection in Tilburg.

2. Noted on the mount of the photograph of the painting Brod sent to the RKD–Netherlands Institute for Art History (cited hereafter as RKD).

3. According to the mount of the photograph from Douwes now in the GRI. Douwes probably owned the painting in partnership with Terry-Engell, since he exhibited it both before and after the Terry-Engell exhibition (London 1962).

4. See London 1948, no. 21. Amsterdam 1962 states that the painting was exhibited in 1950 by the Eugene Slatter Gallery, London, as no. 21. This is presumably an error in date, as a painting by Van der Ast entitled *Fruit and Flowers*, likely cat. 3, appears as no. 21 in a 1948 exhibition of Dutch and Flemish Masters at the Eugene Slatter Gallery. This is confirmed by a label on the back of the painting from an unidentified Italian exhibition to which Douwes lent the painting, which lists among previous exhibitions: "Eug. Slatter, London, 1948, no. 21." Although the description of no. 21 agrees with the Pasadena painting, the vertical measurement is four inches larger. This may indicate that by 1962 four inches of the Pasadena painting had been cut from the top of the panel or that it was a different painting and that the connection came from Bol 1960, p. 82, no. 98, which cites the dimensions as 52 × 76 cm. A painting with similar dimensions to the Slatter painting was exhibited by Kunsthandel P. de Boer in Amsterdam, 1934, no. 229: "Stilleven; op een Delftsche schotel met vruchten. Daarnaast schelpen," panel, 58 × 75 cm.

5. A white paper label (approx. 2½ × 4½ in.) glued to the back of the painting has the following information typed on it: "6. BALTHASAR VAN DER AST, *Natura morta con frutta e fiori*, tavola: 42 × 77 cm; firmato." The label stamped "Kunsthandel Gebr. Douwes" cites the 1962 Terry-Engell exhibition and thus must postdate 1962.

6. Van der Ast's deep dish with a broad rim divided into panels is characteristic of blue-and-white porcelain, which was produced in China during the early seventeenth century for export to Europe. Often called kraakware, a reference to the Portuguese name for the ships, carracks, on which the porcelain was transported to Europe, this ceramic was admired for its thin walls and greenish-blue glaze without crackle. See D. F. Lunsingh Scheurleer 1974 and Rinaldi 1989. Van der Ast included such objects in other still-life paintings; see Amsterdam/Salem 2015–16, p. 176, cats. 45a–b. "Thorn prunts" are the large, applied-glass drops broadly melted on the wall of the vessel and drawn out to a point. For a recent study on Van der Ast's still-life paintings, see Aachen/Gotha 2016.

7. Snails appear most frequently in the paintings Van der Ast produced from 1624 to 1627. By the late 1620s, snails and other shells had become an independent genre within the artist's oeuvre. See Lokin 2016, p. 65.

8. Regarding the theoretical ideals of a painting, see Taylor 1995, pp. 78–113.

9. Visscher 1614. Regarding the tulip, see Schama 1987b, pp. 350–66; Segal 1992; and Pavord 1999.

10. Weststeijn 2022, pp. 446–49.

11. Ertz 1979, vol. 3, no. 426, pp. 900f., ill. Translation from the Dutch: "Wat kyck ghy op dees blom, die u soo schone schynt / En door des sonnen cracht seer lichtelyck verdwindt / Ledt op godts woordt alleen dwelck eeuwich bloeyen siet / Waerin verkeert de rest des werelts dan, is niet." Ter Kuile 1985, p. 38.

12. Weststeijn 2022, pp. 449–50.

4

Nicolaes Berchem

Dutch
Haarlem 1621/22–1683 Amsterdam

Pastoral Scene

1679

Signed and dated lower right on peasant's bag: "NBerchem F: 1679" (*NB* in ligature)
Oil on panel,
26 ¾ × 25 ¼ in. (67.9 × 64.1 cm); with added wood strips 27 ¼ × 25 ⅞ in. (69.2 × 65.7 cm)
The Norton Simon Foundation, F.1972.15.4.P

Provenance

Anonymous (sale, Amsterdam, Yver, 23 April 1801, lot 1, "In een Landschap ziet men eenige Herders en Herderinnen by een staande Koe, een Bok en Schaapen, dit Schildery is warm van couleur, fix en meesterlyk behandeld op Paneel, hoog 26, breed 25 duim," sold for ƒ430 to); Farret.[1] F. Kamermans (sale, Rotterdam, A. Lamme, 3 October 1825, lot 2, bought in by); [Arnoldus Lamme (1771–1856), Rotterdam].[2] Jean-François Boursault (sale, Paris, Paillet, 7 May 1832, lot 8, sold to); [Henry Artaria (d. by 1850) for];[3] Edmund Higginson, Esq. (1802–1871), Saltmarshe, Herefordshire (sale, London, Christie's, 4 June 1846, lot 122, sold to);[4] [John] Hickman.[5] Frederick C. Dickson (sale, London, Sotheby's, 30 June 1971, lot 4, sold to); [Edward Speelman Ltd., London, sold 1972 to]; The Norton Simon Foundation.

Exhibited

On loan, Allen Memorial Art Museum, Oberlin, 6 January 1972–8 May 1973; on loan, Los Angeles County Museum of Art, 9 May 1973–26 November 1974.

References

Higginson 1842, p. 4, no. 8; Hofstede de Groot 1907–28, vol. 9 (1926), no. 221; Pasadena 1980, p. 61, ill.; P. Sutton 1986, p. 219; Pasadena 1989, p. 61, ill.; Aikema 1996, pp. 168, 207n32, fig. 140; Biesboer 2006, pp. 32 and 161n76; S. Campbell 2010, p. 339, no. 788, ill.

Technical Notes

The support is an uncradled, vertically grained oak panel with beveled edges in its original state, with no cracks or planar deformations. The cream-colored ground layer is thin, which allows the texture of the panel to remain a prominent part of the surface. Microscopic examination of the surface reveals light golden-brown underpainting, visible in tiny losses at the left edge and beneath the chin of the standing woman. A grayish-beige layer is seen in a small loss in the sky at the top edge. In the proper right leg and foot of the man reclining at the lower right and the feet of the standing man at the right, it is possible to see outlines drawn in brown paint where the artist worked out the composition. The fluidly brushed oil paint is generally rich and opaque. Lively brushwork describes the figures and animals. The painting is in a very well-preserved state, with only a few other small paint losses at the right edge. The darkened, natural-resin varnish has a wax component. The inscribed date of "F: 1679" is partially obscured, perhaps by the varnish, although it is possible an early overpainting under the aged varnish may be responsible. The painting was cleaned in 2004 by Roz Westmoreland, Beverly Hills.

Dated 1679, two years after Nicolaes Berchem permanently settled in Amsterdam, *Pastoral Scene* is a dramatic departure from the panoramic landscapes animated by small-scale figures he had painted during the previous two decades. Here, large, robust shepherds and animals bathed in warm, southern light dominate a compact composition. The only relief from the press of figures is on the right, where the composition opens to the sky and a view of a distant range of mountains. The combination of lively brushwork and compressed, ambiguous spatial relationships is characteristic of Berchem's works from 1679 to 1680, notably *Shepherds and Their Flocks* and *Shepherds with a Woman Washing* (both Kunsthistorisches Museum, Vienna).[6]

In his quest for a new aesthetic, Berchem was drawn to a print by Aegidius Sadeler (ca. 1570–1629; fig. 4a) after *The Annunciation to the Shepherds* by Jacopo Bassano (ca. 1510–1592) and adopted its basic composition for this *Pastoral Scene*.[7] In Berchem's painting the posture and costume of the milkmaid as well as her relationship to the cow are virtually identical to Sadeler's print. He also incorporated the prominent figure of the shepherd with a broad-brimmed hat who sits on the ground leaning back on his left elbow. In other areas of the painting, Berchem made adjustments to Bassano's design. To accommodate the standing woman on the left, for example, he moved the milking group farther to the right than in the print. The cow, which in both works is parallel to the picture plane, raises its head in Berchem's painting and looks toward the viewer. Although the shepherd leaning over the cow's back can be read as a variation of the print's figure of the younger shepherd behind the lowered head of the cow, Berchem's figure, like the woman twisting in the left foreground and the alert cow, contributes to a more vibrant and complex space.

Berchem similarly transformed the fully clothed man in the Sadeler print into a partially nude river god. A prolific

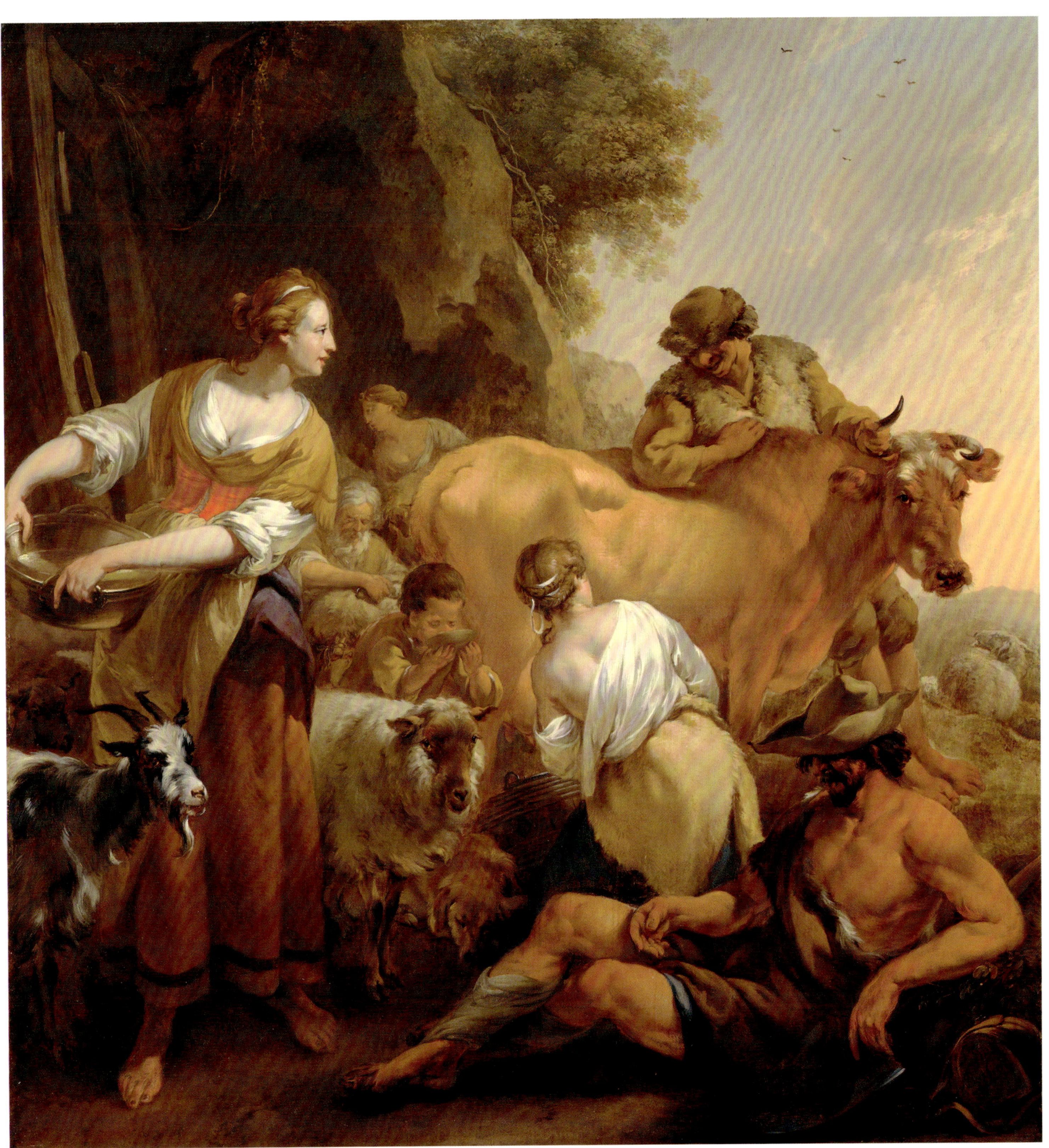

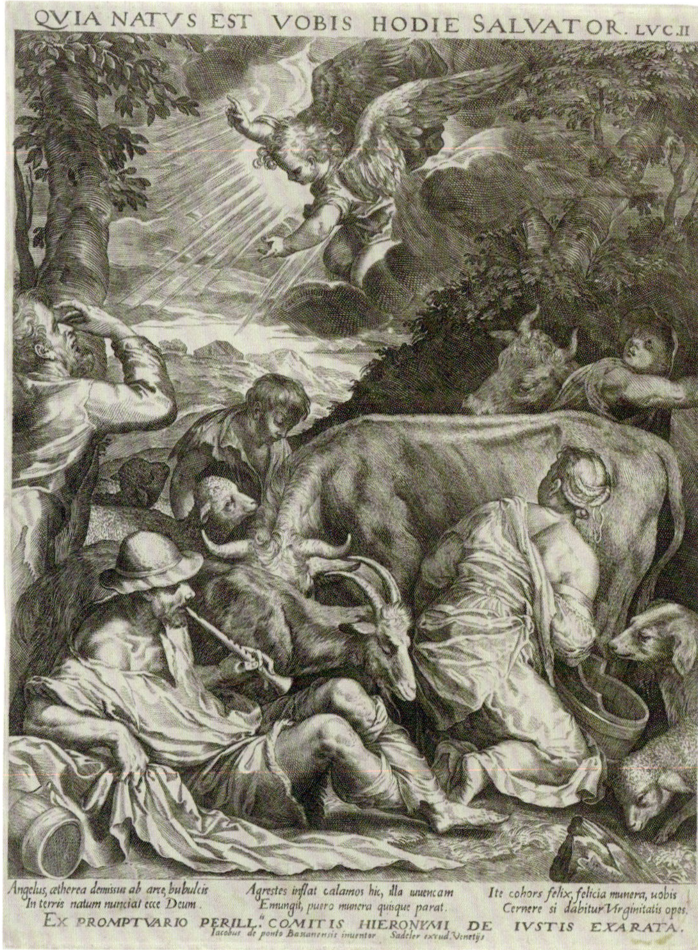

Fig. 4a. Aegidius Sadeler after Jacopo Bassano, *Proclamation to the Shepherds*, 1593, engraving, 10⅝ × 8⅛ in. (27.1 × 20.8 cm), Rijksmuseum, Amsterdam.

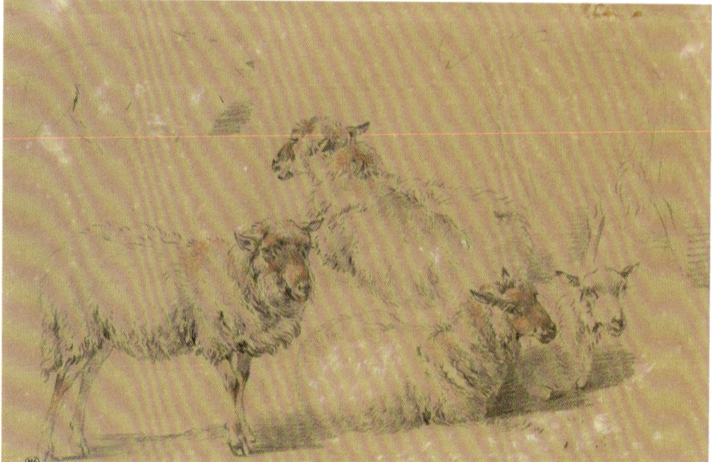

Fig. 4b. Nicolaes Berchem, *Study of Six Sheep*, 17th century, black chalk, red chalk, white highlights, beige washed paper, 6¾ × 10⅝ in. (17 × 27 cm), Musée du Louvre, Paris.

draftsman who made numerous figure and animal studies, Berchem corrected Bassano's more ascetic figure with a drawing made after an antique sculpture or a studio model (or both).[8] He also must have used drawings for other details; many of these drawings remained in his studio until his death, when his widow, Catharina de Groot, sold them at auction in 1683.[9] The head of the cow (for which there is no known drawing) is, for example, identical in shape to that in a painting in the collection of the Earl of Warwick, signed and dated 1636. For the head of the goat in the lower left corner of *Pastoral Scene*, Berchem may have relied on one of the studies of different views of the animal that he made from life. Another sheet of drawings of sheep in the Musée du Louvre is closely related to the sheep facing the viewer (in front of the boy; fig. 4b).[10] Berchem certainly also used study drawings, such as *Study of a Young Farm Woman* (Prentenkabinet, Staatlichen Museen, Berlin), for the standing woman on the left who holds a basin in the Pasadena painting.[11] In this twisting, wonderfully free figure, caught in flickering light, one finds the lively, fractured brushstrokes of Berchem's mature paintings, which break surfaces into facets of color, creating a sense of transience.

Using a palette of reds and browns, Berchem created the impression of a searing hot summer afternoon in a foreign place, far from the cool, moist atmosphere of the Dutch countryside as depicted in *Evening in the Meadows* by Aelbert Cuyp (1620–1691; cat. 20). Both artists represented classical concepts of the idyllic countryside in these paintings: Cuyp through the realism of the native Dutch scene, Berchem through the portrayal of idealized contemporary Italian and classical Arcadian figures.

Berchem's attraction to Bassano and pastoral subjects reflects the continuing appreciation for Virgil's *Eclogues*, the first-century CE Roman text that proffers the ideal classical world of Arcadia, where shepherds live in idyllic peace and harmony. The late sixteenth-century revival of the *Eclogues* spawned a new genre of pastoral literature and painting, particularly in Venice (where the Bassanos, Giorgione, and Titian were the chief practitioners) and later throughout Europe.[12] In the Netherlands, Karel van Mander's translations of Virgil's *Eclogues* (as *Ossental*) and *Georgics* (as *Landt-werck*), both of which featured an idealized rural world based on reality, initiated a new literary genre. Not surprisingly, interest in such subjects was strongest among artists who had traveled to Italy, including the Bamboccianti, the Dutch and Flemish genre and animal painters who had worked in Italy under the influence of Pieter van Laer (1599–after 1642) and returned north to paint scenes of the Italian countryside populated by Arcadian figures.[13] In *Pastoral Scene*, Berchem, a second-generation member of the Bamboccianti, returned to the model of the Venetian Bassanos for a dramatic evocation of the Arcadian world.

1. Burton Fredericksen was the first to suggest the connection of the Pasadena painting to this 1801 sale (e-mail to Carol Togneri, 2 September 2009, NSM). The seller(s) at the time of the sale are still unknown.

2. Fredericksen noted that the dimensions given in the Kamermans sale of 1825 were in fact centimeters rather than the Dutch *duim* (2.6 cm). According to Hofstede de Groot 1907–28, vol. 9 (1926), no. 221, Arnoldus Lamme was a painter and art dealer/agent.

3. The Higginson sale catalogue notes that this painting was from the Boursault collection. According to J. Smith 1829–42, suppl. vol. 9 (1842), p. 604, no. 34, Henry Artaria was buying for Higginson at the Boursault sale. Artaria was the author of the 1842 catalogue of the Higginson collection and presumably its curator.

4. According to a copy of the sale catalogue annotated by Lord Northwick, formerly at Northwick Park Library, now at Yale University; a photocopy of the catalogue was consulted at the GRI.

5. John Hickman was one of the principals responsible for a private contract sale (no date) at the Great Room (later Cox's Museum), Spring Gardens, London, in which there were a number of paintings by Berchem described only as "landscape, cattle and figures." One painting, no. 239, described as *Cattle and Figures*, may be the painting he bought from the Higginson sale. A photocopy of the annotated sale catalogue at the National Gallery, London, is at the GRI. Subsequent Hickman auctions at Foster and Son and Christie's in 1847 and 1856 also include Berchem landscapes, but none of these can be definitively connected with the painting catalogued here.

6. See discussion of Berchem's late paintings in Schaar 1958, pp. 102f., and Biesboer 2006, especially pp. 28–32.

7. The prints executed by Jan Sadeler (1550–1600), Aegidius Sadeler, and Raphaël Sadeler (1561–1628) after a series of works from Jacopo Bassano's later period were particularly influential for Netherlandish painters. Berchem may also have known Bassano's painting, which Van Mander 1604, fol. 180, noted having seen in the Amsterdam collection of Joan Ycket (Jan Nicket). Three versions of the painting are known, of which that in the National Gallery of Art, Washington, DC, and that in the Accademia di San Luca, Rome (cut slightly at bottom), are considered to be autograph. The print by Aegidius Sadeler is also known in two versions: One was struck in reverse from a painting in the Gerolamo Giusti collection in Verona (Hollstein 1949–2010, vols. 21–22, no. 31), and a second engraving, which bears the inscription "Sadeler excudit Venetijs," was struck in the same direction as the painting.

8. On Berchem as a draftsman, see Schatborn 1974 and Stefes 2006.

9. See Biesboer 2006, p. 35.

10. Paris, Musée du Louvre, Départment des arts graphiques, inv. 22452 recto.

11. Illustrated in Schatborn 1974, fig. 15.

12. See Washington 1988.

13. For the development of the pastoral in the Netherlands, see Kettering 1982 and Utrecht/Frankfurt/Luxembourg 1993. Regarding court patronage, see also The Hague 1997b. On the Bamboccianti, see Cologne/Utrecht 1991 and Briganti, Trezzani, and Laureati 1983.

5

After Nicolaes Berchem

Dutch
Haarlem 1621/22–1683 Amsterdam

Evening Landscape with Tower and Figures and a Distant View of Mount Soratte, Rome

Late 17th/early 18th century[1]

Inscribed on boulder at lower right: "Berchem"
Oil on canvas, 80 × 94½ in. (203.2 × 240 cm)
Norton Simon Art Foundation, M.1977.11.P

Provenance
[Leggatt Bros., London, ca 1935].[2] Arthur Hamilton Lee (1868–1947), Viscount Lee of Fareham, London, in 1936, given? to;[3] Samuel Courtauld (1876–1947), London, in 1945.[4] Richard A. Butler (1902–1982), Gatcombe Park, Gloucester, by 1952 and until at least 1958.[5] [Thomas Agnew & Sons, London, sold 1977 to]; Norton Simon Art Foundation.

Exhibited
London 1952–53, no. 612, lent by Butler; on loan, Henry Art Gallery, University of Washington, Seattle, 1977–78.

References
Cooper 1954, p. 183, no. 239, as in the collection of the Rt. Hon. R. A. Butler, M.P., London, erroneously citing the provenance of a Berchem *Evening Landscape* in the Bute Collection, Scotland, passing through Leggatt, Lee of Fareham, to Courtauld; Schaar 1958, pp. 87–89, 98, as in the R. A. Butler Collection, England, and erroneously identifying it as Hofstede de Groot 1907–28, vol. 9 (1926), no. 495, as in the Bute Collection painting; Weston 1978; S. Campbell 2010, p. 405, no. 1423, ill.

Technical Notes
The original support is a twill-weave canvas lined to a plain-weave canvas with the tacking edges cut off. Pressure from lining has accentuated the surface textures from the two canvas weaves. A strong pattern of horizontal cracking suggests that at one time the painting may have been removed from a stretcher and rolled; perhaps the goal of lining was to reduce planar distortion. The white ground is of medium thickness. No underpainting or underdrawing is evident. The paint is generally opaque, in moderate to thin layers, applied directly over the ground. The condition of the painting is fair. Extensive solvent abrasion is found in the lower central part of the painting, where the three figures and the various animals have been seriously damaged. Treatment was undertaken in 1980 to ameliorate the condition problems, specifically to remove a darkened varnish and old retouching. Much damage had been concealed by the toned varnish, and cleaning left these areas very much in evidence. There are broad areas of repainting in the donkey, the landscape at the lower center, and the tree foliage at the middle right, but overall, restoration was inadequate, damages were not repaired well, and the painting's appearance is poor. Ultraviolet-light examination reveals an uneven synthetic-resin varnish; the surface is patchy and rather powdery.

With more than half of the enormous canvas dedicated to the sky, the rush of dark clouds, echoed by the feathery branches of two trees blowing in the foreground, gives the landscape a romantic mood and draws the viewer's eye toward the distant horizon, where a single summit rises before a broad expanse of mountains. Light filtering through the clouds picks out details across the landscape. In the foreground, idealized rustic travelers in contemporary Italian costumes halt to adjust the pack of a mule. Rather than dominating the composition, they are merely decorative staffage, providing anecdotal detail and compositional emphasis. The overall impression of an Italian landscape, with the distinctive Mount Soratte isolated in the distant right next to a lake, possibly Lake Bracciano, is undermined by the incongruous appearance of a Dutch windmill in the left middle distance.[6]

Painting in the studio, a seventeenth-century artist relied on drawings of actual landscapes and figures, his imagination, and his recollection of works by other artists. A prolific draftsman, Nicolaes Berchem repeated and adapted figure drawings in many of his compositions. A drawing in pen and bister wash relates closely to the primary group of idealized rustic figures in *Evening Landscape*, but the landscape and specific details differ.[7] Rather than a study for this painting, it was apparently made for an engraving by Johannes Visscher (1636–after 1692) that reproduces the drawing in reverse (fig. 5a).[8]

The Pasadena painting replicates both the composition and the scale of *An Extensive Wooded Landscape with Peasants on a Path*, a painting that has been in the Bute Collection since at least 1799 (fig. 5b).[9] Eckard Schaar considered what he thought was the Bute painting to be one of Berchem's largest paintings—indeed, one of the largest landscapes produced by a Dutch painter in the seventeenth century—and among the artist's transitional pictures of the late 1660s.[10] Dating it ca. 1670, he noted that the decorative effect of the trees in the foreground recalls the influence of Jan Both (1618–1652) on Berchem's paintings of the 1650s but that the view from a high point across the flat land to the distant mountains anticipates Berchem's paintings of the 1670s.[11]

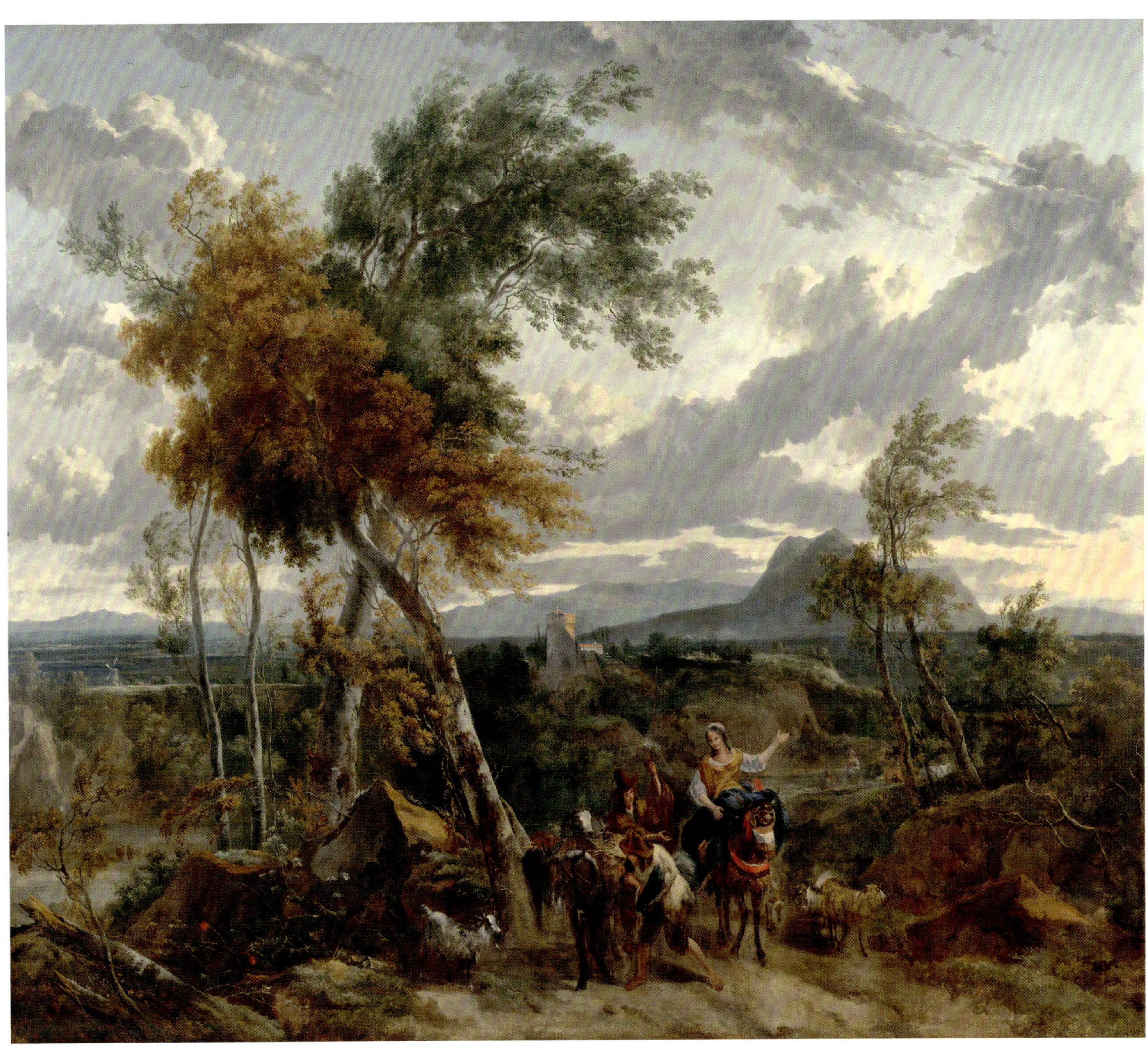

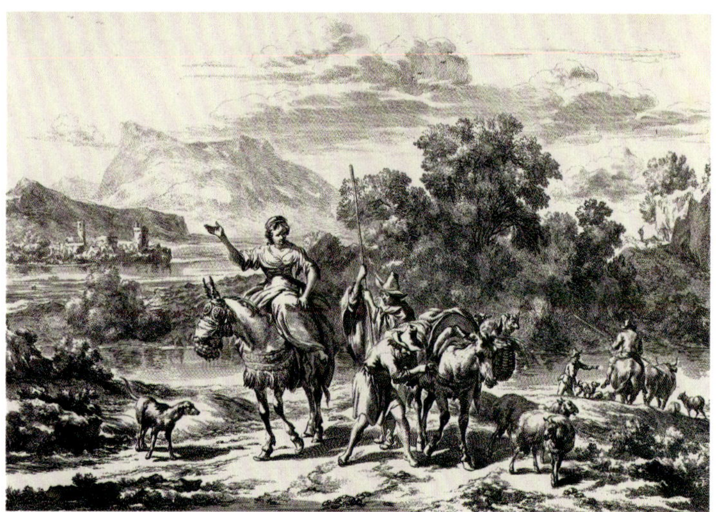

Fig. 5a. Johannes Visscher, after Nicolaes Berchem, *Shepherds and a Young Woman on a Donkey*, 1670, etching, 10⅛ × 14⅛ in. (25.8 × 35.9 cm), Rijksmuseum, Amsterdam.

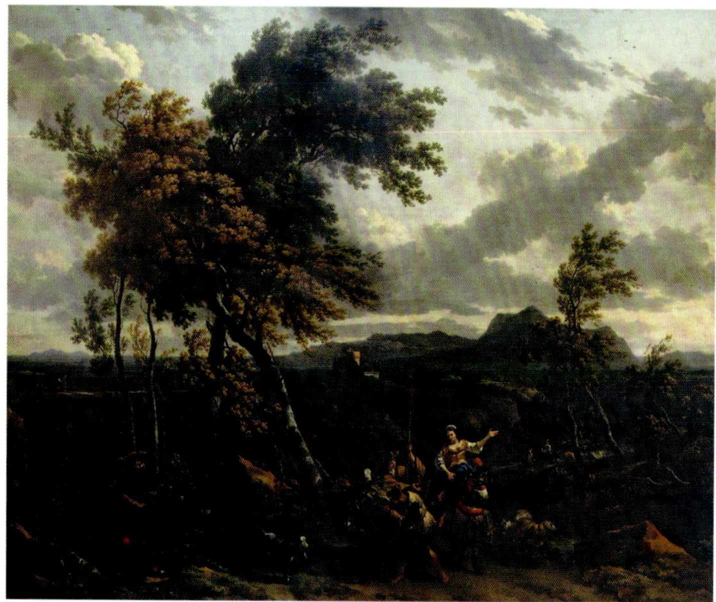

Fig. 5b. Nicolaes Berchem, *An Extensive Wooded Landscape with Peasants on a Path*, ca. 1670, oil on canvas, 81 × 94 in. (205.7 × 238.8 cm), The Bute Collection at Mount Stuart, Isle of Bute.

The taste for large-scale landscapes that developed in the Netherlands and Italy during the 1640s was influenced by—among other factors—the building of larger homes with greater expanses of wall area. Berchem's earliest panoramic landscapes date from the early 1650s, but his monumental landscapes begin more than a decade later. In the mid-eighteenth century, the Bute painting hung above the dining room fireplace in the home of the famous Amsterdam collector Gerrit Braamcamp (1699–1771). Berchem may have painted it to hang in a similar location in the home of his original patron, but it is also possible that he intended the painting to hang lower on a wall.[12] In *Het Groot Schilderboek* (Amsterdam, 1707), the artist-theoretician Gerard de Lairesse (1640–1711) recommended that landscapes be hung at a level so that the eye meets the horizon.[13] According to De Lairesse, landscapes—especially large ones—should appear as if one were looking through an open window, with the depth of the windowsill suggested by the width of the painting's frame.[14]

Since 1952, when the Pasadena painting was exhibited by Richard Butler at the Royal Academy of Arts in London as having come from the Bute Collection, its provenance has been confused with that of the Bute painting and the attribution accepted.[15] The extensive damage caused by chemical abrasion throughout the Pasadena painting (see Technical Notes) makes its relationship to Berchem and to the Bute painting difficult to assess. The figure group in the Pasadena version is particularly disfigured by abrasion and later overpainting. A large, yet reduced, contemporary version of the Bute painting signed by the Utrecht painter Willem de Heusch (before 1625–1692) attests to the fame of the original.[16] The large scale of the Pasadena painting, which is convincingly inscribed and appears to have been well executed, suggests it was painted on commission, perhaps as a replica by the artist or, like the painting by De Heusch, a large-scale copy by an artist working in the late seventeenth or early eighteenth century, when Berchem was at the height of his international popularity.[17] Without additional documentation, however, the questions of the painting's origin and attribution remain unresolved.

1. Because it is uncertain whether the painting is by Berchem, or more likely after him, it is impossible to precisely date this work. Berchem was incredibly popular during the eighteenth century, a period when prints after his work circulated and were copied widely. His genre scenes were also used to decorate Sèvres porcelain. On the seventeenth-century attitude toward making and collecting copies, see Franken 2005, pp. 180–89.

2. Cooper 1954, p. 183, no. 239. In an email to the author dated 25 April 2000, Anthony Crichton-Stuart kindly shared the entry for the Berchem in Francis Harvey's manuscript catalogue of the Bute Collection [n.d., but probably late 1930s; Mount Stuart, Scotland], which notes, "A reproduction of this picture was recently sold by Mssrs. Leggetts [*sic*]." According to Sir Hugh Leggatt, there are no extant records for this period, when the business was run by his father.

3. According to Cooper 1954, p. 183, no. 239. Regarding Viscount Lee of Fareham, see Herrmann [1972] 1999, pp. 394f. Statesman, benefactor, and patron of the arts, Lee served as a member of Parliament, minister of agriculture, personal secretary to Lloyd George, and First

Lord of the Admiralty. In 1917 Lee gave his house Chequers and its contents to the British nation for use as a country residence for the prime minister. Lee built a second collection, which he donated to public institutions in England and Canada. With his friend Samuel Courtauld, who shared his belief in the need for an institute for training scholars in art, Lee established what is today the Courtauld Institute, to which each bequeathed his collection. According to Cooper 1954, p. 183, no. 239, this painting was first owned by Lee of Fareham and then passed to Courtauld. The Lee of Fareham papers at the Courtauld Institute do not mention the painting.

4. Regarding Courtauld, see Cooper 1954 and Herrmann [1972] 1999, pp. 383f. Cooper 1954, p. 183, no. 239, identifies this painting as that which was formerly in the Bute Collection and notes that it was with Leggatt in 1935 and later in the collections of Viscount Lee of Fareham and Courtauld.

5. Richard Austen Butler, Baron Butler of Saffron Walden, served as a Conservative member of Parliament for Saffron Walden from 1929 to 1965; see *DNB* 1992, vol. 1, p. 421. Butler and his wife apparently acquired a number of drawings and paintings from Courtauld. See Cooper 1954.

6. The isolated form of the three-peaked, 2,267-foot Mount Soratte, located in the Roman *campagna* just north of Rome, appears as a landmark in landscapes by Jan Asselijn (ca. 1610–1652) and others. The tower in the middle distance is a common feature of Berchem's landscapes and may or may not be based on a real site.

7. Nicolaes Berchem, pen and bister with bister wash, 9½ × 13¾ in. (24.1 × 34.9 cm), present location unknown. According to an annotated copy of the sale catalogue at the GRI, Colnaghi bought the drawing at the sale of Jacques Arnal, Toulouse (Sotheby's, London, 24 February 1925, no. 9).

8. Johannes Visscher, *A Girl Riding a Mule* (Hollstein 1949–2010, vol. 41 [1992], p. 82, no. 114).

9. The Bute painting, which remains in the Bute Collection at Mount Stuart on the Isle of Bute, Scotland, is 81 × 94 in. It is presumed that John Stuart (1713–1792), 3rd Earl of Bute (or his son, John Stuart [1744–1814], 1st Marquess of Bute), acquired the painting before 1799, when it appeared in the catalogue of his estate at Luton. It had previously belonged to the famous collection of Gerrit Braamcamp, Amsterdam, who had purchased it from the Hendrik Oortman sale, Amsterdam, 9 January 1749; the painting was sold in Amsterdam from the Braamcamp estate on 31 July 1771, lot 17, to Pieter (Pierre) Fouquet. Although it has not been possible to examine it, we are grateful to Jessica Insley, curator of the Mount Stuart Trust, for clarifying many details associated with the Bute painting. See J. Smith 1829–42, vol. 5, no. 250; Hofstede de Groot 1907–28, vol. 9 (1926), p. 192, no. 495; Waagen 1854, vol. 3, p. 479 (Berchem no. 1); Luton MS catalogue 1799, p. 16. We are grateful to Anthony Crichton-Stuart for his help in distinguishing the two paintings and their previously confused provenances (Crichton-Stuart to the author, 11 May 2000), and to Andrew McLean at the Bute Archives at Mount Stuart. Regarding the Bute Collection, see F. Russell 2004.

10. Schaar was actually referring to the Pasadena painting, which was then in the Butler Collection and incorrectly assumed to have been in the Bute Collection.

11. Schaar 1958, p. 87, notes the similarity to Jan van Scorel's *Baptism in the Jordan* (Frans Hals Museum, Haarlem), which Berchem could have seen in the Janskerk, Haarlem; see M. Friedländer 1967–76, no. 317, pl. 173.

12. Bille 1961, vol. 2, p. 75.

13. De Lairesse [1707] 1738, bk. 4, p. 204.

14. De Lairesse [1707] 1738, bk. 4, p. 205.

15. An undated annotation in the personal journal of Ellis Waterhouse (GRI), who had seen the painting in the Bute Collection in 1934, indicates that he believed the painting had been sold from that collection and later belonged to Butler, who exhibited it at the Royal Academy of Arts, London, in 1952, with a provenance that included the Bute Collection and that of Samuel Courtauld.

16. Willem de Heusch, *Italian Landscape with Travelers*; 121 × 105 cm; signed lower left: "Wilhelm de Heusch." It was in the collection of Dr. Guglielmo Maccaferri, Bologna, 1986, and illustrated in Salerno 1977–80, vol. 2, p. 787, no. 139.4.

17. Regarding the popularity of Berchem's paintings in the eighteenth century, see Seelig 2006. See also Spieth 2018 and Altes 2003. It is also possible, though less convincing, that the Pasadena version is a copy done when the Bute painting was exhibited in London at the British Institution or the Bethnal Green Branch Museum. See London 1847, no. 65 (lent by the Marquess of Bute); and London 1854, no. 4 or 10 (both lent by the Marquess of Bute, who owned at least three paintings attributed to Berchem). See London 1882–83, p. 74, no. 249; and "Marquis of Bute" 1883, p. 24.

6

Jan van Bijlert

Dutch
Utrecht 1597/98–1671 Utrecht

Mars Vigilant (Man in Armor Holding a Pike)

ca. 1630–35

Signed, upper right:
"Jv [superimposed] bijlert: *Fe:*"
Oil on canvas, 33 × 26⅝ in. (83.8 × 67.6 cm)
Norton Simon Art Foundation, M.1978.18.P

Provenance
[Colnaghi, London, and Edward Speelman Ltd., London, by 1974, sold 1975 to];[1] [Schaeffer Galleries, New York, stock no. 2826; sold 1977 to]; [Robert Noortman Gallery, London, sold 1978 to]; Norton Simon Art Foundation.

Exhibited
New York 1974–75, no. 112, ill., lent by Edward Speelman Ltd.; on loan, Princeton University Art Museum, Princeton, NJ, 1978.

References
Crombie 1978, p. 432; Nicolson 1979, p. 28, fig. 207; Utrecht 1980, p. 7, fig. 7; Pasadena 1980, p. 53, ill.; P. Sutton 1986, p. 332; Utrecht/Braunschweig 1986–87, p. 137; De Meyere 1986–87, p. 353, fig. 20; Pasadena 1989, p. 58, ill.; Nicolson/Vertova 1990, vol. 1, p. 73, vol. 2, ill. 1313; Huys Janssen 1994, pp. 47n9, 168f., no. 98, ill. 13; Huys Janssen 1998, pp. 140f., no. 109, pl. 64; S. Campbell 2010, p. 416, no. 1524, ill.

Copy
Oil on canvas, 83 × 64.5 cm
Inscribed, lower right: "J. Bijlert"
Palazzo della Magnifica Communità di Fiemme, Pinacoteca, Cavalese (Trentino)[2]

Technical Notes
The support is a plain-weave medium-weight canvas. It has been lined with the original edges cut off; cusped threads on the original canvas are visible at the top, bottom, and right sides. The smooth ground is white. Microscopic examination of the surface reveals layers of underpainting that extend only under specific portions of the composition. There is a rose-beige underpainting beneath the gray background color. The yellow plume of the helmet was underpainted with black, and black underpainting seems to have been used beneath the flesh tones. The opaque paint is deftly brushed, with crisp outlines. X-radiography reveals a change on the back of the proper right shoulder, where a crest in shadow replaced an area of dense white that was originally beneath it. The paint is generally well preserved. Although the lining has slightly smoothed the paint profile, the contours of colors remain well defined. Traces of light red overlie the modulated yellows of the plume and sash, suggesting these elements were once a brighter orange. Numerous pinpoint losses visible in the background, especially to the left of the head, are old flake losses. Retouching was done in at least two campaigns: Older retouching, beneath the varnish, can be seen in the background at the upper and lower right side, as well as in some broader toning to the right of the figure. More recent retouching is in the yellow plume, the hand holding the pike, and the orange sash. There is none in the face and very little in the figure. Ultraviolet-light examination confirms the varnish is a natural resin, rather thinly applied.

His back toward the viewer, a gray-bearded soldier twists around and stares suspiciously at us over his right shoulder, his gaze intensified by a shadow cast across his eyes by his helmet. The twisting pose silhouetted against the light background is cut by the limits of the picture, bringing the three-quarter-length figure dramatically close. This kind of staged, confrontational pose was employed by Jan van Bijlert during the late 1620s and early 1630s and reflects his involvement with the Dutch Caravaggesque painters, who, like Van Bijlert, had recently returned to Utrecht from Italy.[3]

The soldier's theatrical pose and engraved suit of armor argue against this painting's being a portrait of a contemporary officer and in favor of its being a representation of a type or a historical personage.[4] The elaborate yellow-orange sash and blue and yellow-orange feathers that ornament the black armor refer specifically to the forces of the United Provinces of the Netherlands, which the Princes of Orange led against the armies of the Spanish king during the Eighty Years' War (1568–1648).[5] Similarly dressed and armed soldiers appear in illustrations in *Wapenhandelinghe*, the practical book of military instruction for the use of weapons that Jacob de Gheyn II (1565–1629) published in 1607 for Maurits (1567–1625), the Prince of Orange and Nassau, who as stadtholder of the Netherlands was captain general of the army and the navy.[6] In plate 20 (fig. 6a), De Gheyn illustrated a pike bearer striking a pose similar to that of the soldier in Van Bijlert's painting: The soldier's left hand holds the pike near the sharp end, his left elbow is next to his waist, and his right hand supports the pike at his waist on the opposite side so that that elbow extends

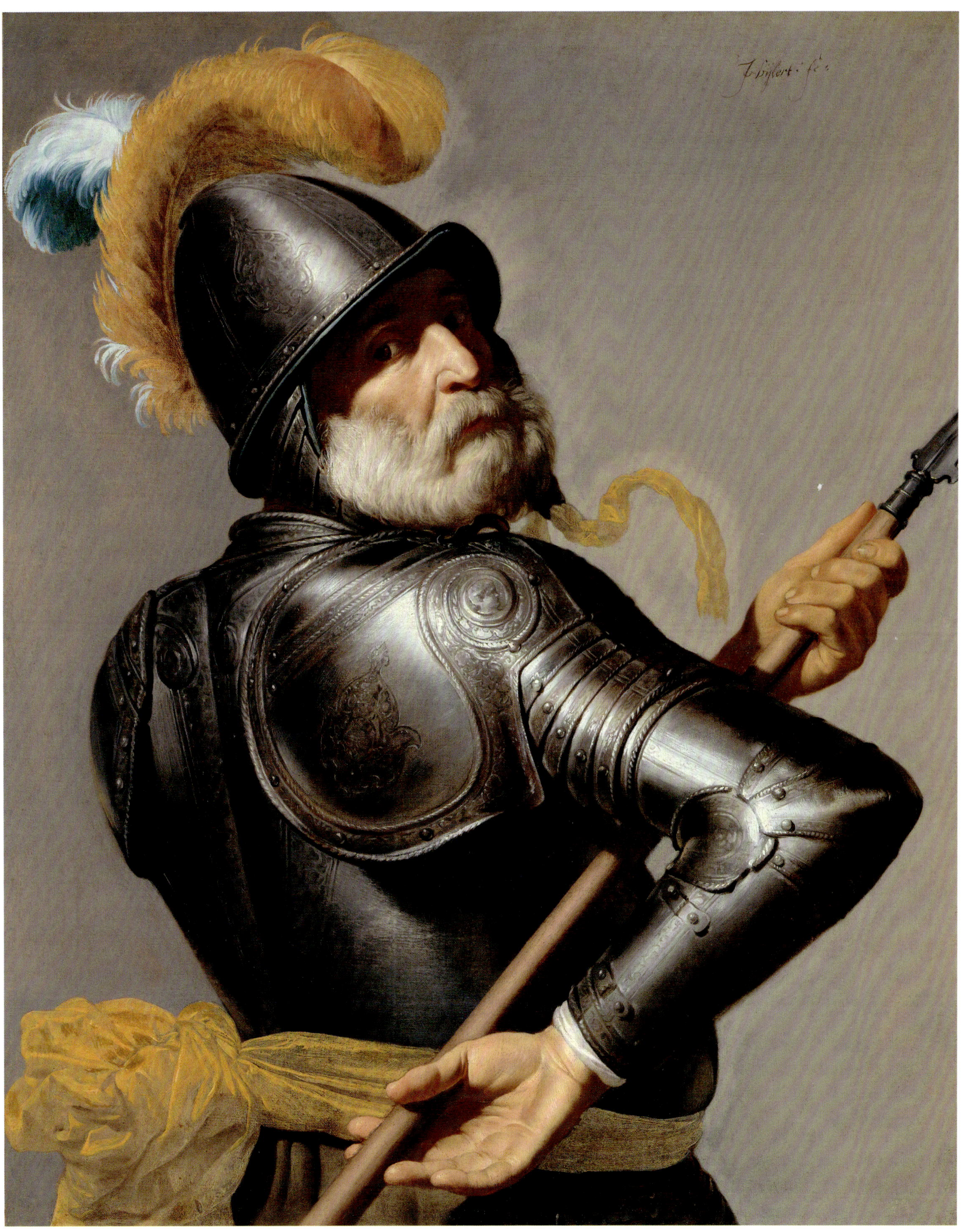

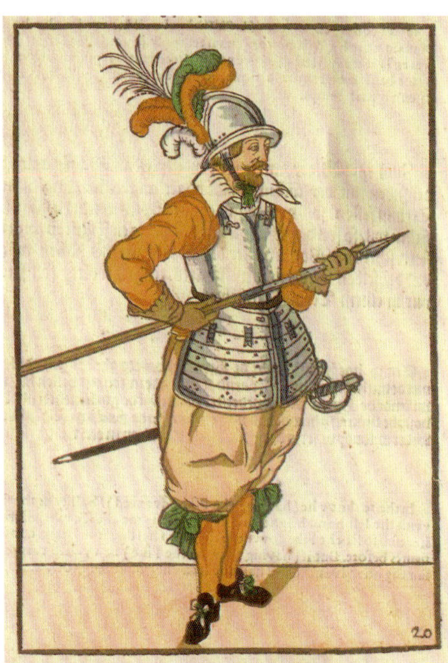

Fig. 6a. Jacob de Gheyn II, *A Pike Bearer*, engraving, from *Wapenhandelinghe*, 1607, (93-B10703) Getty Research Institute, Los Angeles.

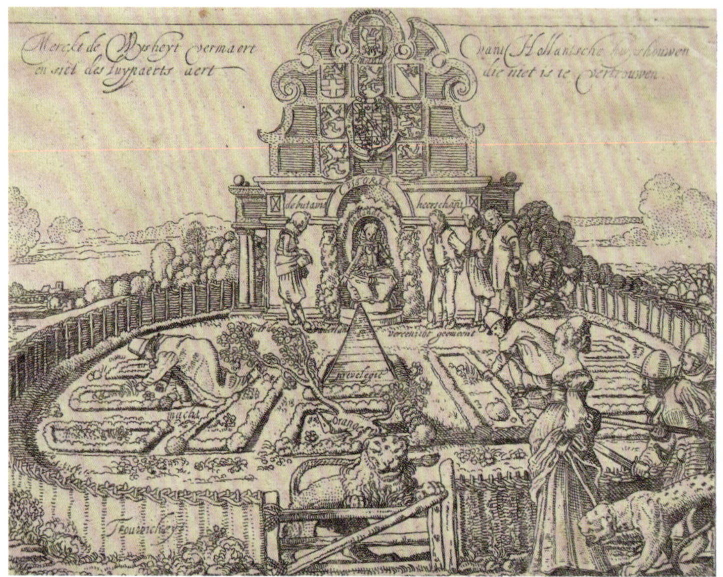

Fig. 6c. Willem Pietersz. Buytewech, *Allegory of the Deceitfulness of Spain and the Liberty and Prosperity of the Dutch Republic*, ca. 1615, engraving, 5½ × 7¼ in. (14.1 × 18.4 cm), Rijksmuseum, Amsterdam.

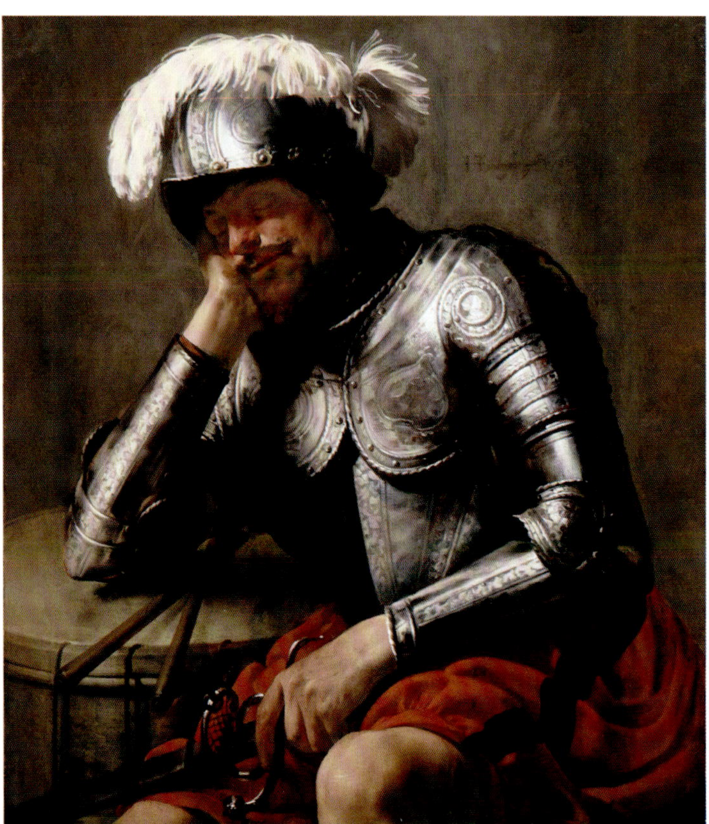

Fig. 6b. Hendrick ter Brugghen, *Mars Asleep*, 1629, oil on panel, 41⅞ × 36½ in. (106.5 × 92.8 cm), Centraal Museum, Utrecht.

outward. According to the English commentary accompanying De Gheyn's print in the 1619 edition of the book published in Zutphen with French, German, Dutch, and English texts: "Standing at a port at the marching in or out of any men, he shall hold the pike at the point, like this figure shows."[7] According to De Gheyn, the posture assumed by the figure in the print and in Van Bijlert's painting enabled the soldier to react quickly to defend himself against unexpected danger.

The finely crafted armor the soldier wears in the Pasadena painting also appears in Van Bijlert's painting *Mars Overpowered by Cupid*, ca. 1630 (Chrysler Museum, Norfolk, VA), and in his print *Mars in Armor*.[8] The armor—which was made in Milan about 1570, apparently after a Pisan model[9]—had probably previously been owned by Utrecht Caravaggist painter Hendrick ter Brugghen (1588–1629), who represented it in two paintings: *Mars Asleep* (fig. 6b) and *Trik-trak Players* (1627; Minneapolis Institute of Arts).[10] Van Bijlert may have acquired the suit of armor after Ter Brugghen's death in 1629, suggesting that the Pasadena painting should be dated in the early 1630s. This date is also suggested by the iconography of the painting, which appears to represent Mars vigilant.[11]

Van Bijlert's soldier is physically similar to the soldier represented sleeping on his drum in Ter Brugghen's *Mars Asleep*. Two poems written about Ter Brugghen's painting clearly identify that image as Mars, more specifically as a representation of peace.[12] Painted shortly after the conclusion of the Twelve Years' Truce (1609–21) between Spain and the United Provinces and the installation of Maurits's brother Frederik Hendrik (1584–1647) as the new stadtholder in 1625, Ter Brugghen's painting is a plea for the renewal of peace.[13]

Paul Huys Janssen hypothesizes that Van Bijlert, who often executed paintings as pairs, intended the Pasadena painting to hang with a pendant, but he does not suggest what its subject would have been.[14] Venus, the goddess of love, was frequently paired with the god of war. In contemporary paintings and in a pair of prints, Van Bijlert represented the seductive goddess disarming Mars as a metaphor for peace.[15] In the Pasadena painting, however, the soldier is armed. Addressing the viewer directly, he may never have had a pendant and hung alone, not as a victim of love, but as a defiant defender of the Dutch Republic.

In representing Mars as the vigilant god of war, ready to defend native soil, the Pasadena painting is a statement of the country's military preparedness. The theme of vigilance is also present in *Allegory of the Deceitfulness of Spain and the Liberty and Prosperity of the Dutch Republic* by Willem Pietersz. Buytewech (1591–1624; fig. 6c): While Mars sleeps, a rampant lion covered with the hundred eyes of Argus, the mythical shepherd, guards the gate to the Dutch Garden against the approach of the two-faced Spanish woman with a leopard.[16] Van Bijlert's painting, like Buytewech's print, proclaims the country's military preparedness and warns would-be aggressors against underestimating the strength of the Netherlands in times of peace, while admonishing the Dutch to remain alert to the deceit of those who would conquer their homeland.

Vigilance was very much on the minds of the Dutch around 1630. The United Provinces of the Netherlands had gained the upper hand militarily with their victory at 's-Hertogenbosch in September 1629. From 1629 to 1631, the Spanish government was determined to establish a new truce with the Dutch as well as with the English. Spain's efforts were, however, met with suspicion by Frederik Hendrik and the States General; likewise, Spain's appeal to Charles I of England (1600–1649) for a separate agreement was fiercely and cleverly fought by the English royal princess Elizabeth (1596–1662), exiled queen of Bohemia, who was living in The Hague as a guest of the Dutch government.[17]

Van Bijlert may have painted *Mars Vigilant* for a patron in The Hague, the home of the States General and the Dutch court, where the war policy of the country was determined and where half-length figures by Utrecht painters were avidly collected.[18] At the center of the court was Frederik Hendrik, who as captain-general of the navy and the army was personally credited with preserving Dutch liberty through his constant vigilance.[19] Themes of military preparedness characterize numerous paintings listed in the inventories made of Frederik Hendrik's collection during the summer of 1632.[20] Although both Frederik Hendrik and the exiled king and queen of Bohemia owned paintings by Van Bijlert, there is no evidence that the Pasadena painting ever belonged to either collection.

1. Schaeffer Galleries files in the GRI note that the painting was purchased from Colnaghi and Speelman in December 1975.

2. Huys Janssen 1998, p. 141.

3. De Meyere 1986–87, p. 353, suggests *Mars Vigilant* was painted shortly after Ter Brugghen's *Mars Asleep* (fig. 6b). Huys Janssen 1998, no. 109, dates the painting 1630–40.

4. The painting has been known since at least 1974 until now as *Portrait of an Officer in Armor*.

5. See Technical Notes above. I am grateful to John Griswold for discovering that there are traces of red over the yellow paint that indicate that the sash and feathers were originally orange.

6. De Gheyn I [1607] 1971, pt. 3: "Derde deel: 'Corte onderwijsinghe op de figuerlijcke afbeeldinghe, belanghende t'recht ghebruyck, van al t'ghene een Soldaet int handelen vande Spies noodich is"; noted by Huys Janssen 1994, p. 169.

7. De Gheyn II 1619, pl. 20; noted by Huys Janssen 1994, p. 169. Based on the English text but modernized for clarity.

8. Hollstein 1949–2010, vol. 16, p. 147, no. 191, ill.; Huys Janssen 1994, no. P-3.

9. Leonard Slatkes credits the identification of the armor to Dr. Helmut Nickel, Department of Arms and Armor at the Metropolitan Museum of Art, New York, who had studied the painting (probably when it was exhibited at the Metropolitan in 1975). See Utrecht/Braunschweig 1986–87, p. 137. See also Gamber 1958, pp. 104–20; and Van der Sloot 1959, pp. 99–124, esp. 114f.

10. Huys Janssen 1998, p. 141, notes that Dirck van Baburen (ca. 1595–1624) also included the suit of armor in his 1623 *Procurer* in Würzburg. Ter Brugghen may have acquired the suit of armor after Van Baburen's death the following year. See Nicolson 1958, A-67, fig. 84.

11. Huys Janssen 1994, p. 168, dated it 1625–35, but Huys Janssen 1998, p. 141, dated it 1630–40.

12. Utrecht 1980, passim.

13. For the truce and the pictorial theme of the sleeping Mars, see Utrecht 1980.

14. Huys Janssen 1994, p. 47n9. For a discussion of Van Bijlert's interest in painting pairs, see P. Sutton 1989a, pp. 4–16.

15. P. Sutton 1989a, pp. 6ff., figs. 7–8. The prints were published in Van de Passe 1643–44.

16. See Haverkamp-Begemann 1959, pp. 14, 170f., no. 17. The soldier sleeping at the side of the Maid of Holland within the enclosed Dutch Garden is an allegorical reference to the Netherlands and to the Twelve Years' Truce.

17. Elizabeth, who was married to Frederick, Prince of the Palatinate and exiled King of Bohemia, realized that if her brother, King Charles I of England, signed a separate peace with Spain, then it would eliminate any hope her sons had of reclaiming their German patrimony. See A. Walsh 1994, pp. 228–31.

18. The aggressive policy was largely pushed by the nobility, who stood to gain from war. In contrast, in Amsterdam, where the merchants were concerned with furthering their worldwide trade opportunities, there was greater interest in establishing peace with Spain.

19. Frederik Hendrik was viewed by his contemporaries as continuing the efforts of Willem I (1533–1584), who had led the United Provinces of the Netherlands away from the Spanish. The members of the House of Orange were thereafter regarded as the defenders of the religious and political freedom of the Dutch and were often portrayed wearing armor. See Janson 1982, especially pp. 131f.

20. A. Walsh 1994, pp. 231f.

7

Cornelis Bisschop

Dutch
Dordrecht 1630–1674 Dordrecht

Bathsheba

Early 1660s

Oil on panel, 15¼ × 13¼ in. (38.7 × 33.7 cm)
The Norton Simon Foundation, F.1969.45.P

Provenance
Stefan Auspitz von Artenegg (1869–1945), Vienna, sold 1931 through;[1] [Galerie Sanct Lucas, Vienna, to]; Daniel George van Beuningen (1877–1955), Rotterdam, consigned 1932 to;[2] [Kurt Walter Bachstitz Gallery, The Hague, as Nicolaes Maes].[3] Hans Ludwig Larsen (1892–1937), Noordwijk and Wassenaar;[4] Mrs. S. Larsen-Menzel (1911–2001), Wassenaar (later Mrs. Frank E. Brower, New York), sold 14 January 1943 to;[5] Erhard Göpel (1906–1966), sold 1 March 1943 to; Hans Posse (1879–1942) for; Führermuseum, Linz, no. 2774; recovered and returned to Dutch government (sale, Frederik Muller, Amsterdam, 19 March 1951, lot 52, ill., as Nicolaes Maes, *La Baigneuse*);[6] [Martin B. Asscher, London, 1953]. [Walter Andreas Hofer (1893–1971), Berlin, 1953].[7] Ch. van Spaendonck, Tilburg. [Kunsthandel Gebr. Douwes, Amsterdam, in 1968, as Nicolaes Maes, sold 1969 to]; The Norton Simon Foundation.

Exhibited
London 1932, no. 18, as Nicolaes Maes; on loan, Stedelijk Museum De Lakenhal, Leiden, 1939, lent by H. L. Larsen; on loan, Royal Academy of Arts, London, 1952; London 1953, no. 52, as Nicolaes Maes, lent by Martin B. Asscher, Esq.; Amsterdam 1968, as Nicolaes Maes; Montreal/Toronto 1969, no. 96; on loan, Phoenix Art Museum, 1970; on loan, Los Angeles County Museum of Art, 1974.

References
Chamot 1932, p. 563; Sumowski 1956–57, p. 264, fig. 60;[8] Haverkamp-Begemann 1969, p. 288, cat. 96;[9] Judson 1969, p. 704, no. 96; Sumowski 1983–93, vol. 3, pp. 1962, 1965n77, 1989, ill.;[10] Sluijter 1998, p. 99n88; Schwarz 2004, p. 156, no. xxiv/17; Ducos 2006, pp. 21f., ill.; Sluijter 2006, pp. 72, 366, fig. 364, ill.; S. Campbell 2010, p. 329, no. 701, ill.

Technical Notes
The support, a vertically grained oak panel, may have been a single board that subsequently cracked. The split near the center extends from the top to the bottom edge. The panel has been cradled and probably thinned. The first layer of preparation is a thin white ground. A second, dark-gray layer is evident throughout the painting, especially in the blue sky at top right, beneath cracks in the light paint. Microscopic examination of the surface did not reveal underdrawing. The paint is generally opaque, yet the dark underpainting provides some tonality to the flesh tones of Bathsheba and especially to the buildings and sky at the upper right. Paint was applied fluidly, mostly wet-into-wet, with some layering. The falling water at the left side and the tasseled cordage on the red drapery at bottom center were loosely brushed over nearly dry paint. Contours are sometimes rather blurred, an effect partly due to abrasion and thinning of the upper layer. A change is evident above the proper left forearm, where a lighter form seems to have been painted originally. Some of the brushmarking in the red robe in the foreground and the white drape across Bathsheba's thigh is unrelated to the final painting and indicates changes by the artist. Minor abrasion has occurred in various areas. Retouching is located in the vertical split that passes through Bathsheba's neck, shoulder, back, arm, and the white cloth beneath her. Retouching in the sky at the upper right covers contraction cracks. Ultraviolet-light examination shows fluorescence consistent with a synthetic-resin varnish, thickly applied.

The second book of Samuel recounts the story of Bathsheba, the beautiful wife of Uriah the Hittite.[11] One evening, while walking on the roof of his palace, King David spied Bathsheba bathing and sent a servant with a letter to bid her come to him. The painting represents Bathsheba seated on the edge of a fountain, reading the letter. The shadowy form of the female messenger stands at the edge of the wooded glen that encloses Bathsheba; in the distance, David appears on the balcony of his palace. Bathsheba's attention is absorbed by the letter she holds in her right hand. It is a critical moment of decision, the outcome of which is anxiously awaited by the king and the servant. According to the biblical narrative, Bathsheba went to David and conceived a child, which ultimately would lead David to order her husband, Uriah, sent into battle, where the king knew he would be killed.[12]

To seventeenth-century viewers, the story of Bathsheba exemplified the dangers of the sense of sight and its evil consequences of lust and adultery. Jacob Cats (1577–1660) identified these concerns in his popular 1625 book on marriage, *Houwelyck*: "Oh! Even David succumbed to sin, not only by being aroused, but really making love. And behold! It was a beautiful woman washing herself who fired this evil lust."[13] Bathsheba was, understandably, a popular subject of sermons. The fact that David, the Old Testament example of piety and strength, lost control of his senses upon seeing Bathsheba emphasized the danger of visual seduction. Menno Simons (1496–1561), the founder of the Mennonite

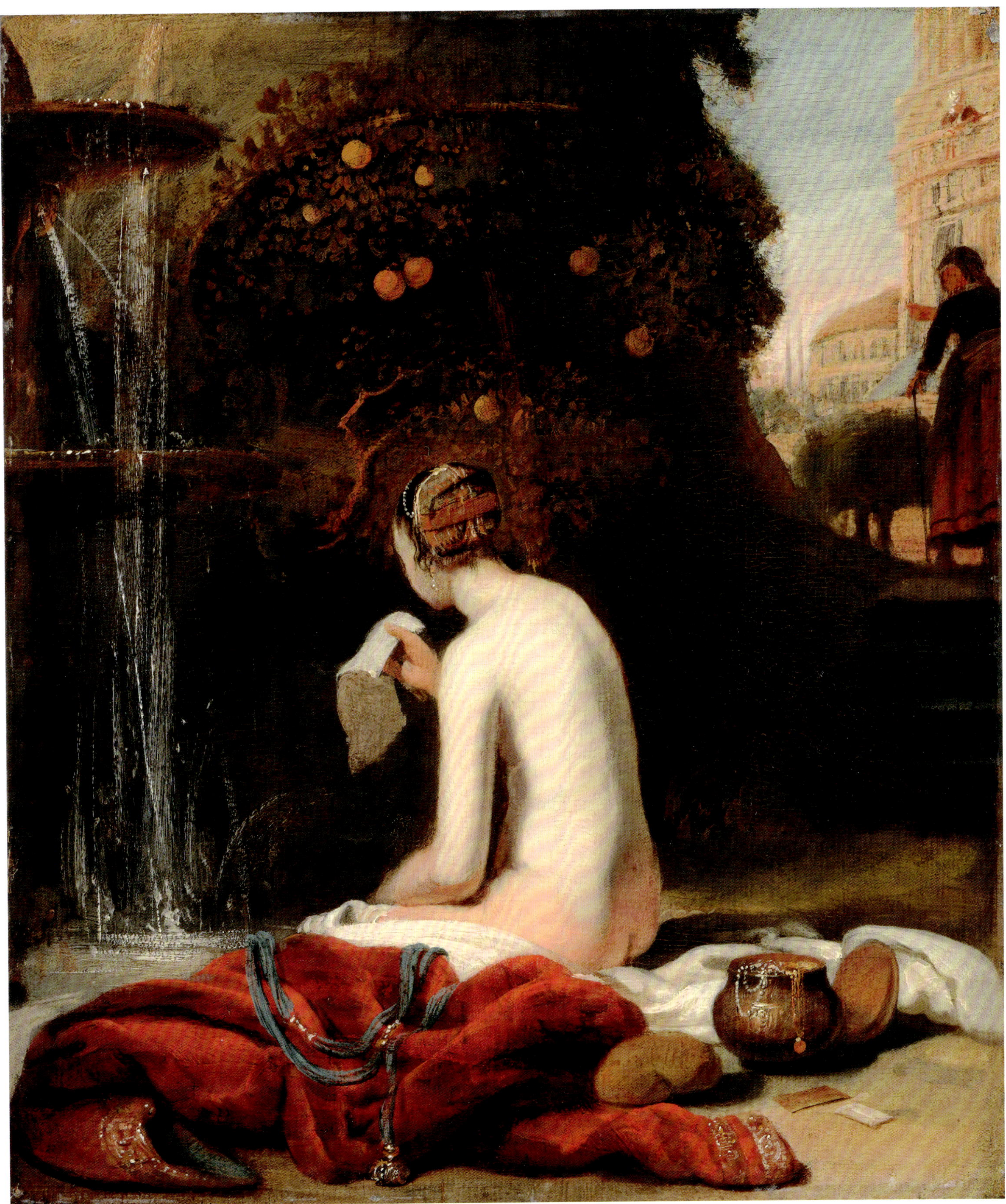

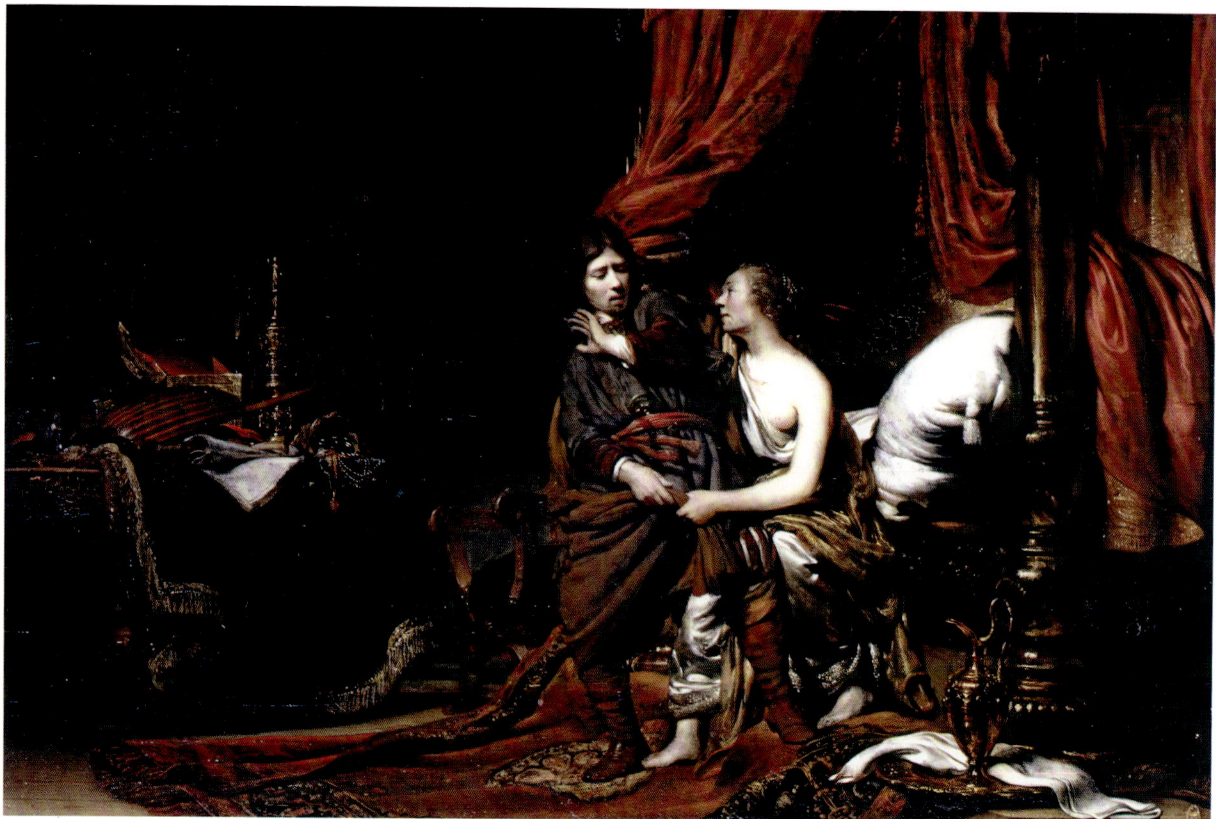

Fig. 7a. Cornelis Bisschop, *Joseph and Potiphar's Wife*, 1664, oil on panel, 24½ × 36⅜ in. (62.4 × 92.4 cm), Stiftung Museum Kunst Palast, Düsseldorf.

sect, devoted a sermon to the story as an example of the progression of sin and evil that stem from lust. For Simons, this human failing was grounds for excommunication.[14] In the present painting, the artist emphasized Bathsheba's sensuous allure by representing her nude body warmed by the red glow reflected from the richly ornamented clothes she has discarded on the ground beside her. Her exotic coiffure and the ornate metalwork further involve the viewer in the moral dilemma posed by the story.

First published as a work by Nicolaes Maes (1634–1693) in 1932, *Bathsheba* was included in the 1969 exhibition *Rembrandt and His Pupils* as an early work of Maes from about 1655, presumably because the coloring and broad handling of paint with soft shadows and gentle light resemble the early genre and history paintings of Maes, such as *Abraham Dismissing Hagar and Ishmael*, dated 1653, and *The Lacemaker* (ca. 1656; both Metropolitan Museum of Art, New York).[15] In a review of the 1969 exhibition, however, Richard Judson rejected the attribution to Maes but offered no alternative.[16] Lyckle De Vries questioned the attribution to Maes when he visited the Norton Simon collection in 1971 and wondered if the work might be by Cornelis Bisschop. Burton Fredericksen also suggested in 1976 that the picture was more typical of Bisschop.[17] In 1983 Werner Sumowski rejected his earlier acceptance of the painting as a work by Maes, commenting that neither the painting's quality nor its subject fit into Maes's oeuvre.[18] In reattributing the painting to Bisschop, a close follower of Maes, Sumowski pointed out how the figures of the old woman and the nude set against a dark rock and tree recall Bisschop's *Contest between Marsyas and Apollo* in the Alfred Bader Collection (Agnes Etherington Art Centre, Kingston, ON).[19] Sumowski placed the Bader and Pasadena works within a group Bisschop painted during the early 1660s, including *Joseph and Potiphar's Wife* (fig. 7a) and *Pilate Washing His Hands* (Bob Jones University Gallery of Sacred Art, Greenville, NC).[20] The broadly defined folds of drapery, especially the sleeve of the robe in the lower left of *Bathsheba*, are similar to the fall of drapery in *Joseph and Potiphar's Wife*.

The lack of anatomical definition in the figure of Bathsheba also resembles that in other nudes by Bisschop.[21] The emphasis on the smooth contours of her body—the line following the arc of her neck and back, the slope of her forward shoulder, and the soft muscles of her almost tubular arm—is like that of the seminude woman in *Joseph and Potiphar's Wife* and the figure of the slumbering Argus in *Mercury and Argus* (1659; Dordrechts Museum).[22] As in these paintings, reflected light defines the shadows of the arms and outlines the contour of Bathsheba's chest and stomach, relieving the dark shadow cast by her arm against her body.[23]

Bisschop probably based the figure of Bathsheba on a study of a nude model.[24] The pose and modeling of the nude, especially the treatment of light along the inner arm, are similar to those of a nude woman seated on a chair in a painting now attributed to Bisschop.[25] Bathsheba shares with this figure the oblique positioning of her back to the viewer, the elaborately braided coiffure, and the description of the shadows on her back and flaccid arms. Both paintings emphasize the nape of the woman's neck and the gentle fall of her shoulder, qualities also emphasized in Bisschop's *The Concert* (formerly collection of A. Mensing, Amsterdam), which is signed at the lower left: "C. Busschop f."[26]

1. See Chamot 1932; Borenius 1932, pp. 287f.; and Lillie 2003, pp. 112–36. The collection, formed during the first thirty years of the twentieth century, included more than 2,143 pictures and objects of art. Van Beuningen 1954 recounts the story of his acquisition of the collection of Stefan von Auspitz, who was president of the Österreichische Kreditanstalt, the principal bank in Austria. The collapse of the bank in 1932 created a major national crisis, resulting in the Austrian government's taking over the bank and personal property of Auspitz and the other directors. Van Beuningen (see note 2, below), who considered the Auspitz collection one of the two greatest collections in Austria, rushed to Vienna and in two days acquired 2,143 objects.

2. Daniel George van Beuningen was a merchant, industrialist, and shipping magnate as well as an art collector and major contributor to the Museum Boijmans, Rotterdam. Having purchased the Auspitz collection en bloc, Van Beuningen selected the masterpieces for himself and within two years sold 120 objects from the collection. The paintings were probably consigned to the Bachstitz Gallery.

3. Agnew in London 1932 identifies Bachstitz as the lender. In his review of the exhibition at Agnew's in 1932, Chamot 1932, p. 563, notes that "now the bulk of his [Auspitz's] collection is for sale."

4. According to London 1953b, Larsen was active as a collector during the 1930s. An inventory of his collection made after his November 1937 death mentions this painting in the *huiskamer* (living room). The collection was bequeathed to his children and sold on their behalf.

5. According to Ekkart et al. 1999–2004, vol. 3 (2002), pp. 283f., Mrs. Larsen lent part of the collection to the Stedelijk Museum De Lakenhal, Leiden, on 6 July 1939. In 1943 the Verwalter (administrator) Mr. M. H. H. Franssen ordered the Larsen paintings brought from the museum to the auction house Van Marle & Bignell, The Hague. The paintings were to be included in a public sale 25 January 1943. Before the sale, however, a number of paintings—including the Pasadena painting, as no. 48—were withdrawn and sold privately to Erhard Göpel; those paintings appear only in the draft, not in the official version of the catalogue. Göpel purchased the painting with the intention of selling it to Hitler for the Führermuseum, Linz. The painting appears as no. 17 in volume 24 of the notebooks prepared for Hitler's consideration (Schwarz 2004, p. 156) and on the Coblenz Lists of works of art identified by the Munich Central Collecting Point as intended for Hitler's planned museum (copies at offices of the Herkomst Gezocht, The Hague): "Munich #10552, Linz #2774. 1.3.1943 aus der beschlagen. Slg. Larsen für hfl.75.000. Zus in den nachfolgenden 11, gem. über Dr. Franssen den Haag, LFXXV1/46/244."

Following the war, the painting was returned to the Netherlands: transport records (State Archives, The Hague), "XIV USGA 3301, H. 2774"; White card (State Archives, The Hague) no. 3975. Documents in the Stichting Nederlandsch Kunstbezit and the Nederlandsch Beheersinstituut reveal that the Dutch authorities determined that the recuperated paintings could be returned to the Larsen heirs in return for repayment to Göpel of the money the family had received from the sale plus 2.75 percent of the appraised value at the time of the contribution. The additional sum was to cover costs incurred by the government. After lengthy negotiations, on 23 July 1947 B. P. Gomperts, the executor of the Larsen estate, refused restitution and the paintings reverted to the government.

6. The sale took place 13–19 March 1951. Lot 52 notes that there are remnants of a signature no longer visible.

7. Eduard Plietzsch to Walter Andreas Hofer, 18 September [19]53 (NSM). Before becoming Reichsmarshall Hermann Goering's private curator in 1937, Hofer was a small-time dealer in Berlin. His wife was a restorer who had worked previously for Duveen Brothers, New York. See Nicholas 1994, passim.

8. Sumowski 1956–57 incorrectly cites it as his no. 62 rather than 60 and notes that it doubtless goes back to Rembrandt's chalk study (Benesch/Benesch 1973, no. 192; coll. Koenigs, Rotterdam), which Sumowski incorrectly cites as his (Sumowski's) fig. 64 rather than fig. 61 (Benesch/Benesch 1973, no. 193, coll. Wendland, Lugano).

9. Haverkamp-Begemann 1969 mistakenly remarks that the lower part of the figure was originally behind the clothes in the foreground.

10. Sumowski 1983–93, vol. 3, p. 1965n77, includes in the provenance of the Pasadena painting Joseph Borsu, Brussels (sale, Galerie Georges Giroux, Brussels, 13 May 1929, lot 19, attributed to Govaert Flinck), but the illustrated catalogue of that sale notes that the painting of a very similar composition was on canvas and measured 56 × 46 cm.

11. 2 Samuel 11.

12. For a discussion of the moral attached to the theme during the seventeenth century, see cat. 86.

13. Cats [1625] 1712, p. 393; trans. from Sluijter 1998, p. 77.

14. Simons 1956, pp. 982–84.

15. Chamot 1932. Among those who accepted the attribution was Eduard Plietzsch: "Ich kenne das Bild schon seit langer Zeit und sah es zuletzt in London. Die Zuschreibung an Nicolaes Maes halte ich für überzeugend und absolut sicher" (Plietzsch to Hofer, 18 September [19]53 [NSM]).

16. Judson 1969, p. 704.

17. J. Paul Getty Museum curator Burton B. Fredericksen to Darryl Isley, 26 May 1976 (NSM).

18. Sumowski 1956–57, p. 281, as *Susanna* by Maes, in the trade, exhibited as no. 52 in London 1953b; Sumowski 1983–93, vol. 3, p. 1962. The Bader Collection is now at Agnes Etherington Art Centre, Queen's University, Kingston, ON.

19. Sumowski 1983–93, vol. 3, p. 1962.

20. Sumowski 1983–93, vol. 3, no. 426, pp. 900f., color pl. In an email to Emily Talbot dated 15 August 2023, Rebekah Cobb, Collections Support/Contract Registrar at the Bob Jones University Museum and Gallery, stated that the painting *Christ before Pilate* is currently attributed to Constantijn Daniel van Renesse, based on the signature "CAR" on the lower left of the column base.

21. A replica of the painting attributed to Govaert Flinck (1615–1660) and described as being on canvas and measuring 56 × 46 cm was formerly in the collection of Joseph Borsu (sale, Galerie Georges Giroux, Brussels, 13 May 1929, lot 19, ill.). Although the attribution of the Borsu painting to Flinck is difficult to assess from the old photograph, the nude body of Bathsheba appears to be more muscular than that of the figure in Pasadena and thus more typical of Flinck than Bisschop. The pose is also similar to a painting of *Susanna Spied on by the Elders*, attributed to the studio of Rembrandt and possibly Rembrandt (panel, 49.6 × 37.8 cm, Staatlichemuseen zu Berlin, Gemäldegalerie inv./cat. no. 813B).

22. *Joseph and Potiphar's Wife* is signed and dated on the edge of the table: "Corn. Bisschop 1664." Concerning *Mercury and Argus* (canvas, 99 × 126.5 cm), see Brière-Misme 1950, p. 143, fig. 2. According to Brière-Misme 1950, p. 145n1, the painting is signed and dated, below and to the right of Argus: "C. Bisschop. 165[9?]."

23. This method of shading appears to have been used by members of the Rembrandt circle. See the similar description of an arm in Rembrandt's drawing *Female Nude Seated* (Museum Boijmans Van Beuningen, Rotterdam; Benesch/Benesch 1973, vol. 5, no. 1121, fig. 1417).

24. Sketching from a nude model was routine in Rembrandt's "academy," in which Bisschop's teacher Ferdinand Bol had participated. Similar poses are found in the drawings of artists who participated in Rembrandt's academy as well as in drawings by Rembrandt himself, such as *Studio with a Model* (Benesch/Benesch 1973, vol. 5, no. 1161, fig. 1458).

25. The painting was in the collection of Bruce Ingram (1877–1963) in 1950, when it was exhibited in *Some Dutch Cabinet Paintings of the 17th Century*, Museum and Art Gallery, Birmingham, as no. 29, a work by Pieter de Hooch (panel, 29.8 × 25.4 cm).

26. About 1660 a number of artists working in Amsterdam (Bol et al.) were fascinated with the portrayal of female figures from the rear, which made it possible to emphasize the graceful line of the neck and shoulders. Concerning *The Concert*, see Sumowski 1983–93, vol. 3, p. 1962; and Brière-Misme 1950, pp. 179–80, 182, fig. 3. Brière-Misme notes that *The Concert* resembles a sketch in which the same person is studied from different angles. The same model, who may have been the artist's wife, also appears in four *vanitas* paintings and may have been the model for Bathsheba. The author does not, however, mention the Pasadena painting.

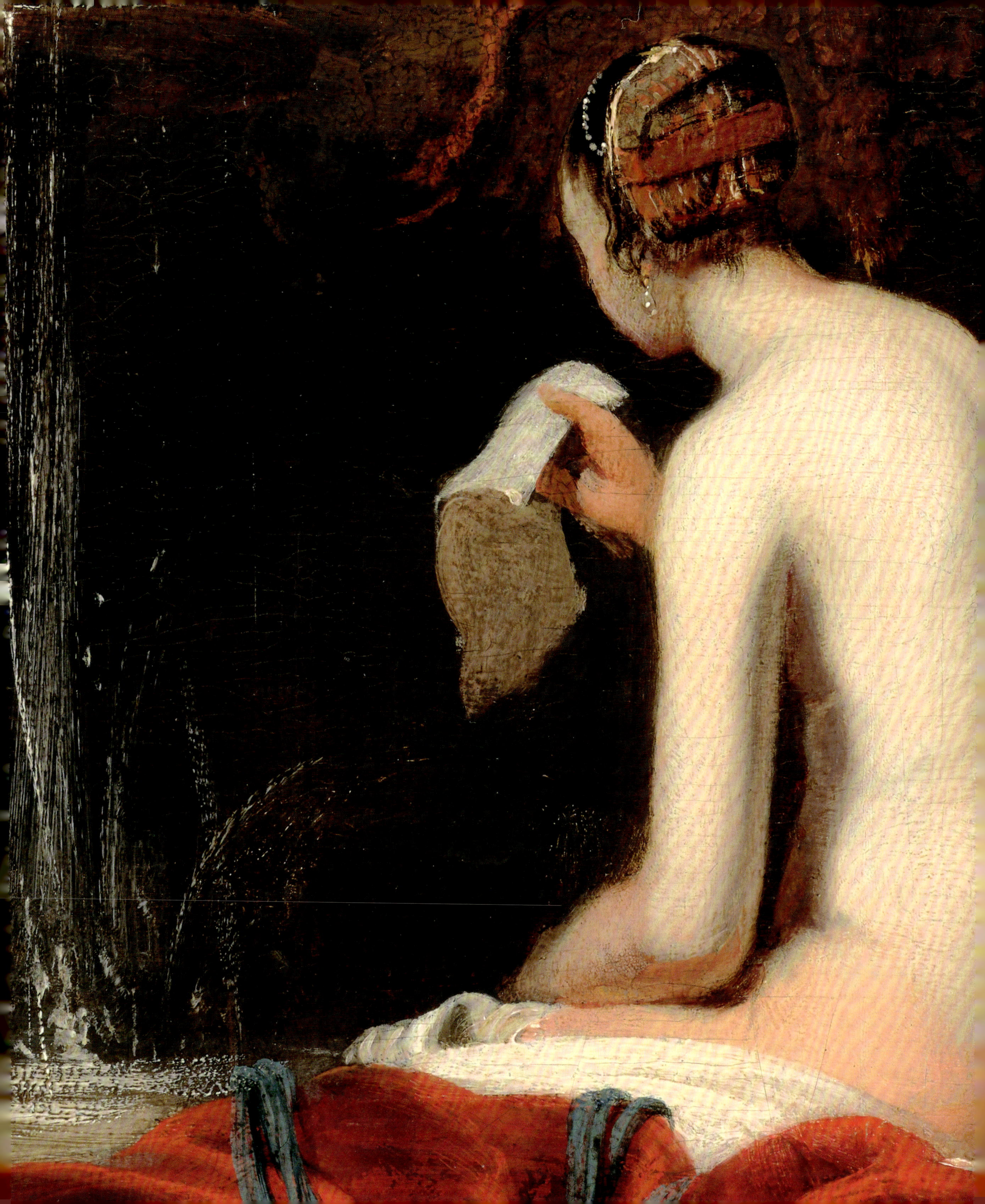

8

Circle of Ambrosius Bosschaert I

Dutch
Antwerp 1573–1621 The Hague

Large Bouquet in a Wan-Li Vase with a Gilt Mount

ca. 1618–28

Oil on panel, 31½ × 21½ in. (80 × 54.6 cm)
Norton Simon Art Foundation, M.1976.10.P

Provenance
Gustave Maes (1851–1904),[1] Lokeren, Belgium, to; Mme Gustave Maes, Lokeren, Belgium (estate sale, Brussels, Galerie Fievez, 10–11 November 1920, lot 29, ill., as Ambroise Brueghel). [Kunsthandel Gebr. Douwes, Amsterdam, sold 1972 to]; Norton Simon, Los Angeles, gift 1976 to; Norton Simon Art Foundation.

Exhibited
Delft 1972, p. 121, lent by Kunsthandel Gebr. Douwes; on loan, Phoenix Art Museum, October 1972–January 1973.

References
Bol 1960, p. 60, no. 11; Pasadena 1980, p. 49, ill.; Kahr 1982, pp. 191f., fig. 146; Bertram 1983, p. 46, fig. 5.8; Pasadena 1989, p. 70, ill.; S. Campbell 2010, p. 345, no. 857, ill.

Technical Notes
The support is a thin, vertically grained oak panel with beveled edges at the top and bottom. There is a white ground. Although close inspection shows some overlapping of leaf and petal edges, the artist generally painted each blossom, leaf, and stem separately, delicately building up opaque and transparent layers directly from the white ground. Some shadowy, peripheral flowers and greenery were painted over the black background. While such an approach suggests the artist relied on a well-established underdrawing, microscopic examination revealed no signs of one; future infrared examination may resolve this question. An X-radiograph reinforces how none of the primary flowers, leaves, and stems are superimposed and exposes no pentimenti. Paint thickness varies, with some flowers painted in a single layer of floating, liquid paint. In the blue iris, the contours are fairly well defined, but the paint has no distinct brushstrokes, modulations are hazy, and the thin paint is a suspension of pigment particles in medium. The white lily is rendered with thicker, opaque paint. The chrysanthemum at the lower left side is more defined, with a sense of actual brushwork: almost stippled with short dabs of yellow arranged over the base color of alizarin. The blue pigment in the vase may be smalt; high magnification picks up the glass-like characteristic of the pigment particles. The medium is highly transparent, with the light blues and darker blues differing only by density. With magnification, the black paint of the background reveals tiny dots of loss, possibly indicating that the black was especially vulnerable to solvents. By contrast, the flowers are quite well preserved. The butterfly at center right has four rather large paint losses in the wings that expose the ground; the losses escape notice because they appear to be a part of the pattern of the wings. The frequent small drying cracks coinciding with the contour of a blossom or leaf may be related to the artist's sequence of paint layers. Retouching is rather widespread and frequently discolored; much of it seems to be unnecessary. Scattered through the background in addition to numerous vertical lines in the upper right background, the retouching strengthens shadows around the sides of the vase. Retouching on a vertical crack at the left side is especially noticeable where it passes through the white lily. Less obvious are flake losses in the center of the white iris, barely visible under milky white overpaint. The glossy, natural-resin varnish is extremely thick and completely obscures brushmarking.

Large Bouquet in a Wan-Li Vase with a Gilt Mount represents an imaginary bouquet of spring and summer flowers displayed in a blue-and-white export porcelain vase made in China for the European market and mounted on a high, gadrooned gilt base embossed with foliate scrolls.[2] A crown imperial surmounts the tall, symmetrical bouquet that includes a stem of white Madonna lilies, a large blue iris, and tulips, as well as a red rose. Smaller flowers, including tulips, fritillary, columbine, roses, and carnations, compose the more compact lower half of the bouquet.[3] A butterfly appears to have landed on a cream-colored tulip flamed with red that lies on the ledge as a caterpillar inches along its stem. On the right, the twig of a briar rose and a second flower, its leaf extending over the ledge, visually balance the fallen tulip.

The selection of rare and exotic flowers—the crown imperial, tulips, and iris, among other blossoms—reflects the contemporary interest among scientists, courtiers, and amateurs in new species of plants imported from Asia, Africa, and the

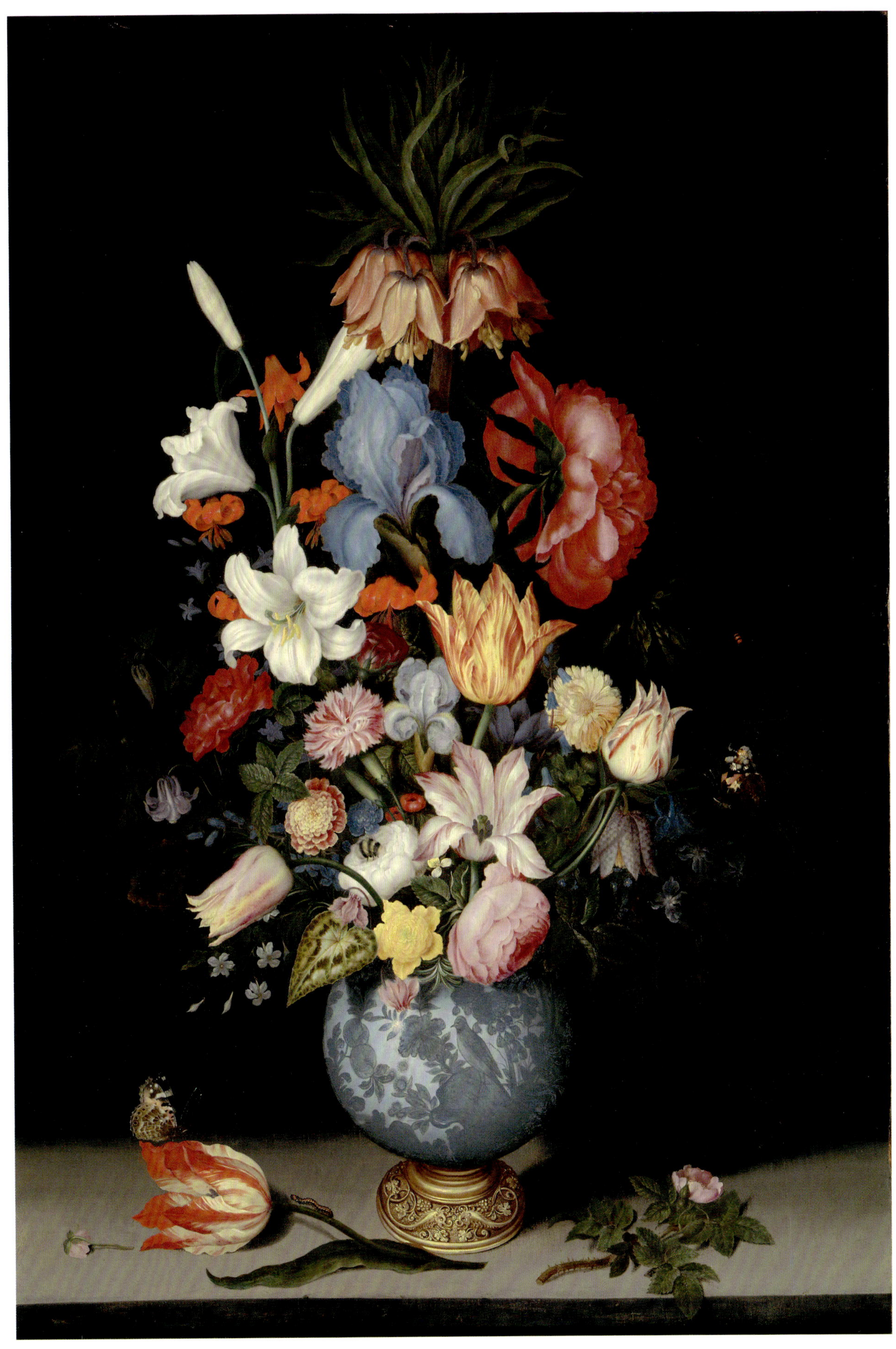

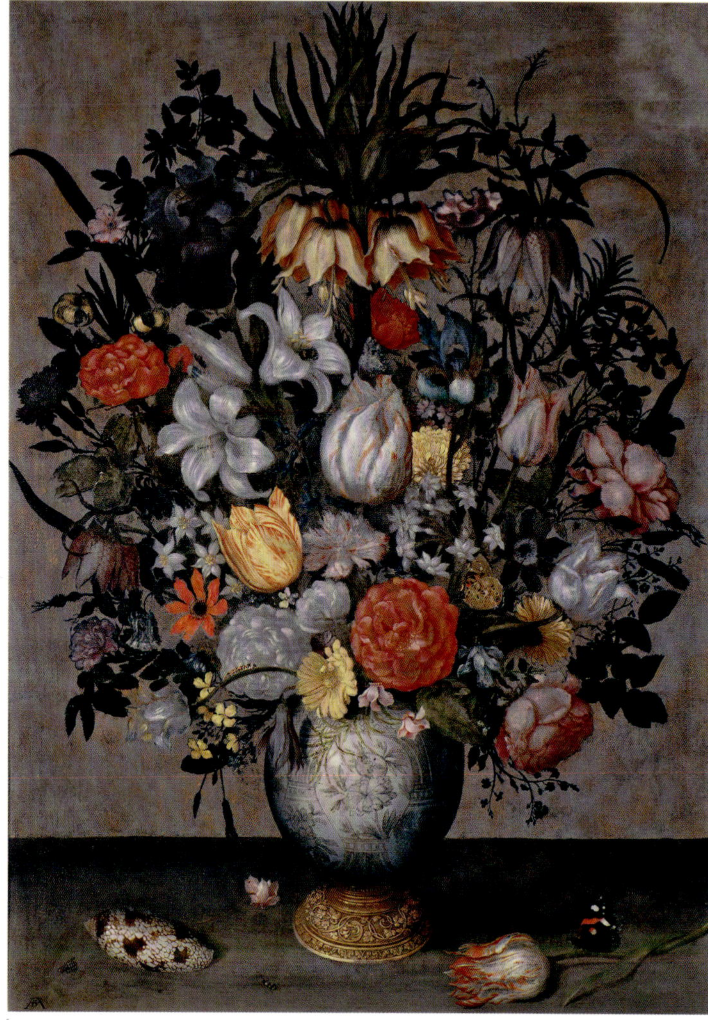

Fig. 8a. Ambrosius Bosschaert I, *Chinese Vase with Flowers, Shells, and Insects*, ca. 1609, oil on copper, 27 × 20 in. (68.6 × 50.8 cm), Museo Nacional Thyssen-Bornemisza, Madrid.

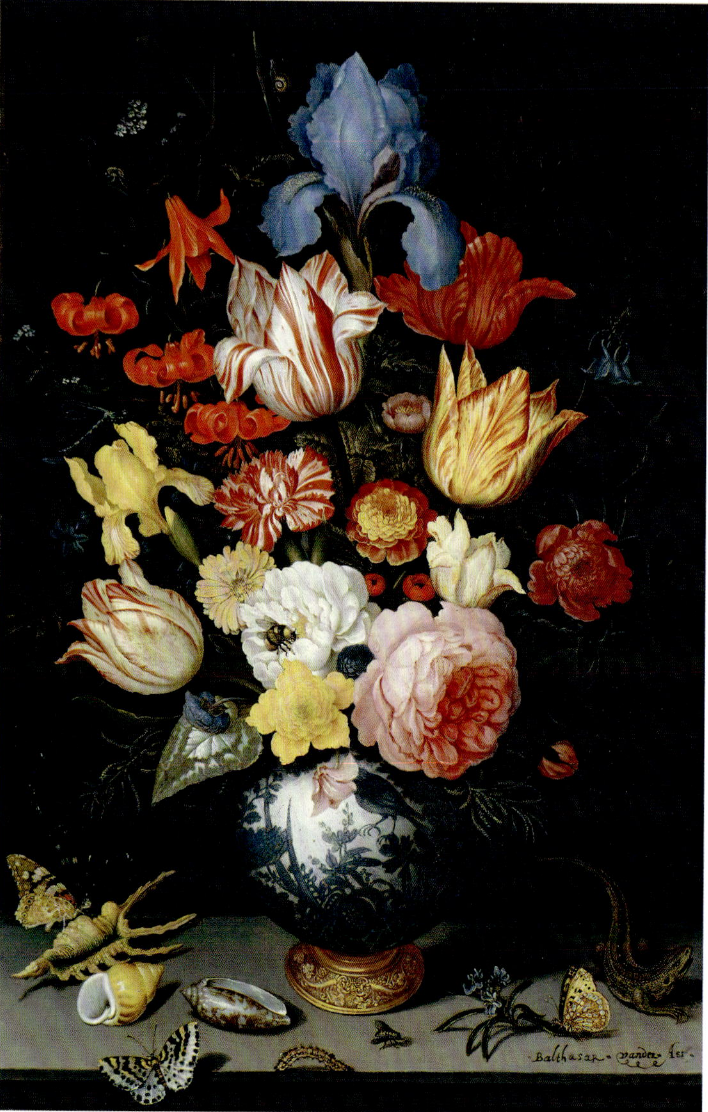

Fig. 8b. Balthasar van der Ast, *Flowers in a Chinese Vase*, 1628, oil on panel, 20 ¼ × 13 in. (51.6 × 33.1 cm), Museo Nacional Thyssen-Bornemisza, Madrid.

Americas and introduced into European gardens. Middelburg, where still lifes of realistically portrayed flowers were produced by Ambrosius Bosschaert I and others beginning in the early seventeenth century, was home to a number of collectors of exotic plants and gardens.[4] In contrast to medieval gardens, in which plants were grown for medicinal purposes, seventeenth-century gardens—like the famous one founded in 1593 at the University of Leiden by Carolus Clusius (Charles de l'Écluse; 1526–1609)—were essentially extensions of Kunst- und Wunderkamern, collections of rare plants intended for scientific study.[5] The shift in interest is reflected by the rise in realistic drawings of flora and fauna represented naturalistically as three-dimensional forms. While some illustrations, such as those in the Norton Simon Museum's beautiful tulip book (cat. 24), seem to have been intended essentially as catalogues to advertise a merchant's stock, others—such as that commissioned by the prince bishop of Echstätt, Johann Konrad von Gemmingen (ca. 1560–1612)—were produced to document a celebrated collection.[6]

According to the title page of *Hortus Eystettensis* (1613), Gemmingen understood the garden and the book to be living or pictorial versions of Psalm 150, a tribute to the Creator of all things.[7] Like Gemmingen, seventeenth-century viewers would have delighted in the beauty and realism of the rare flowers and the insects that inhabit them and would have appreciated them as expressions of God's greatness.[8] They would also have appreciated the imported blue-and-white porcelain vase, prized for its rarity, and for the artist's skill in portraying it and composing the convincing bouquet.[9] The artist's ability to render the realistic impression of the delicate blossoms, insects, and dew drops would have recalled Pliny's famous story of Zeuxis, who painted with such skill that he was able to fool the birds that flew to his still life in search of fruit.[10] The carefully crafted image would, furthermore, have been admired for its ability to preserve the

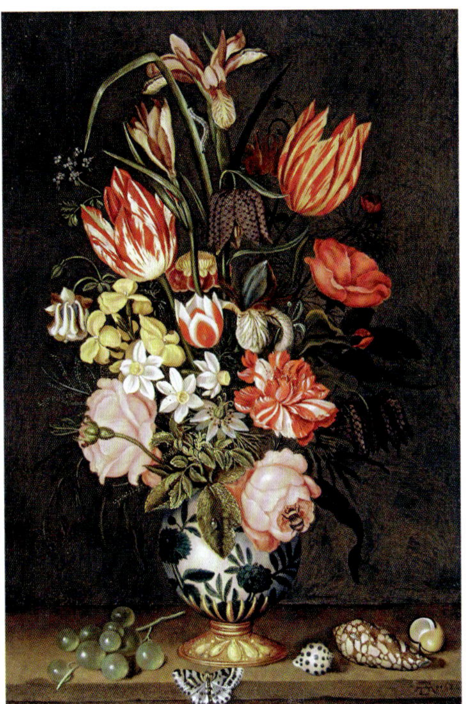

Fig. 8c. Ambrosius Bosschaert II and Johannes Bosschaert, *A Bouquet of Flowers in a Wan-Li Vase Surrounded by Some Shells, Grapes, and a Butterfly*, 1626, oil on panel, 18 ⅞ × 13 ⅜ in. (48 × 34 cm), private collection, Belgium, courtesy of Douwes Fine Art (since 1770), Amsterdam.

beauty of the flowers and suggestions of fragrance through the dark winter days.

Large Bouquet in a Wan-Li Vase with a Gilt Mount is neither signed nor dated. It was sold as a work by Ambrosius Brueghel (1617–1675) in 1920, but since at least 1960 it has been attributed to Ambrosius Bosschaert I.[11] The layering of transparent glazes containing relatively little pigment to produce the satin-like surfaces of the flowers resembles Bosschaert's characteristic technique. Specific details, such as the caterpillar crawling on the stem of the tulip and the plump bumblebee are also found in his documented work. Despite the painting's general similarities to the works of Bosschaert, weaknesses in execution suggest that it is not an autograph work of the master. The flowers, particularly those in the upper part of the bouquet, are stiff and, on close inspection, lack the depth of layering and surety of description typical of the artist. The awkward relationship of the vase to both the flowers and the mount, as well as of the mount to the table, also compare unfavorably with that in Bosschaert's painting now in Madrid (fig. 8a).

Rather than Ambrosius Bosschaert I, *Large Bouquet in a Wan-Li Vase with a Gilt Mount* was probably painted by a follower who was familiar with the master's late still lifes. The tall, narrow proportions of the Pasadena painting, with its single dominant flower at the top, are similar to those of Bosschaert's *Still Life with Flowers in a Vase*, signed and dated 1620 (Nationalmuseum, Stockholm). In place of the refined design of flowers or pomegranates that typically decorate Bosschaert's vases, a bird motif appears on the vase in the Pasadena painting, as it more frequently does in paintings by his brother-in-law Balthasar van der Ast (1593/94–1657).[12] Fred Meijer has suggested that the Pasadena painting may be an early work by Van der Ast, executed ca. 1618–1619, before he had fully developed his own individual style (see cat. 3).[13] The Pasadena composition shares with Van der Ast's painting dated 1628 (fig. 8b) many similar flowers and details, including the porcelain vase with a central bird and floral motif and the gilt base with a foliate pattern. A comparison of the two, however, demonstrates the technical weaknesses of the former: The decoration of the vase is coarser and the definition of flowers and leaves is stiffer and less accomplished in the Pasadena painting.

Although these observations may reflect differences in the dates of execution and/or condition, they may also suggest that *Large Bouquet in a Wan-Li Vase with a Gilt Mount* was painted by another artist, possibly one of Bosschaert's sons who studied with their uncle in Utrecht but imitated their father's late technique and compositions in their paintings of the mid- to late 1620s. A large painting of a bouquet in a gilt-mounted Wan-li vase, signed with a monogram and dated 1626 by Ambrosius Bosschaert II (1609–1645; fig. 8c), for example, shares with the Pasadena painting the tall, narrow proportions; the stiff compact lower half of the bouquet; and its slightly asymmetrical shape.[14]

1. Gustave Maes was a coal dealer and art collector. He donated his archaeological collection, including many pieces from Egypt, to the Stadsmuseum Lokeren.

2. The term *Wan-li* specifically refers to porcelain wares produced in China during the late Ming period during the reign of Emperor Wanli (1573–1620) but is often used more broadly to refer to blue-and-white ceramics imported from East Asia that appear in European paintings. Kraak porcelain, which was made in China specifically for export to the European market, was often based on designs and models sent by European merchants. The term *kraak* derived from the large cargo ships, or carracks, that transported the porcelain and other goods from Asia. The addition of a European gilt mount would have increased the porcelain's value; see Weststeijn 2022, pp. 436–76.

3. Bol 1960, p. 60, no. 11, identifies the flowers in the bouquet.

4. See Pennisi 2007 regarding Middelburg as a city of highly developed floral culture for the origin of Bosschaert's still lifes.

5. Tubular plants, including both tulips and the crown imperial, originally cultivated in Persian and Turkish regions, were first brought from Constantinople to the imperial medicinal herb garden in Vienna. They were introduced to Leiden in 1593. By 1610 tulips were highly coveted for their remarkable variability, and by 1633 collectors were paying such exorbitant prices

for individual bulbs that people spoke of "tulip-mania." See Bol 1960, p. 2; and Pavord 1999.

6. Gemmingen had live flowers from his garden sent in boxes each week to artists, who made watercolor drawings that were later translated into prints showing the various stages of a flower. The large prints, which were arranged in the album according to the seasons in which the flowers bloomed, were published in Nuremberg in 1613 as *Hortus Eystettensis*. The final publication was sold in two versions, either black-and-white or hand-colored. See Barker 1994, p. 16.

7. Barker 1994, p. 13.

8. Because of the brevity of their life and beauty, flowers have often been associated with transience and vanity. Porcelain could be interpreted similarly. This association may be implicit in many seventeenth-century flower still lifes, but it is not the direct meaning without specific iconographic clues. It is, for example, explicit in Jacques de Gheyn's *Vanitas Still Life*, 1603 (Metropolitan Museum of Art, New York), which includes a single tulip in a vase with Spanish coins, a skull, and a bubble. An inscription on a still life of a flower in a glass attributed to Jan Brueghel I (formerly with Richard Green, London) includes a cartouche, which makes the association clear. De Jongh 1982, p. 37n12; see also no. IV on p. 31. On imported porcelain, see Weststeijn 2022, pp. 452–53.

9. Blue-and-white porcelain was imported from East Asia by the Dutch East India Company (Vereenigde Oostindische Compagnie) en masse. Although variations of kraakware vases appear in paintings by Bosschaert, Van der Ast, and others in their circle, the cost of such an object was prohibitively expensive for many, if not most, artists, who probably relied on drawings of the popular decorative motifs rather than painting directly from an object. The desire for blue-and-white porcelain in the Dutch Republic, and Europe more broadly, spawned entire industries of export goods in Asia. The domestic production of blue-and-white pottery known as delftware provided an affordable alternative for people of various classes. See Weststeijn 2022.

10. Pliny 1967, vol. 9, p. 309 (35.34.65).

11. Bol 1960, p. 60, no. 11. A crude replica of the painting (panel, 87.6 × 62.3 cm) said to be monogrammed *Å* and dated *1645*, but not fully described, was attributed by Sam Segal to A[ndries] Daneels (active ca. 1599) in the catalogue of the sale at Christie's New York, 11 January 1989, and reattributed to Bartholomeus Assteyn (1607–ca. 1667) in the catalogue of D. Koetser Gallery, Zurich, 1990/91, no. 1. The attribution to Assteyn was repeated in the catalogue of R. Smeets Gallery, Milan, 1991/92, no. 1.

12. Segal 1984, p. 49, makes the distinction between the vases of the two artists, noting that Bosschaert's are generally decorated with flowers of pomegranates, while Van der Ast's vases are usually decorated with a bird or grasshopper.

13. During a visit to the Norton Simon Museum on 20 September 2000, Fred Meijer, then curator of seventeenth-century paintings at RKD, verbally agreed with the attribution of the painting to the workshop of Ambrosius Bosschaert I. In April 2011 he suggested the possibility that it was an early work of Van der Ast (NSM).

14. Segal 1984, pp. 65–69, fig. 19. In comments made in spring 2011, Walter Liedtke, then curator of Dutch and Flemish paintings at the Metropolitan Museum of Art, New York, supported the attribution to Ambrosius II, but Fred Meijer rejected it in favor of Van der Ast.

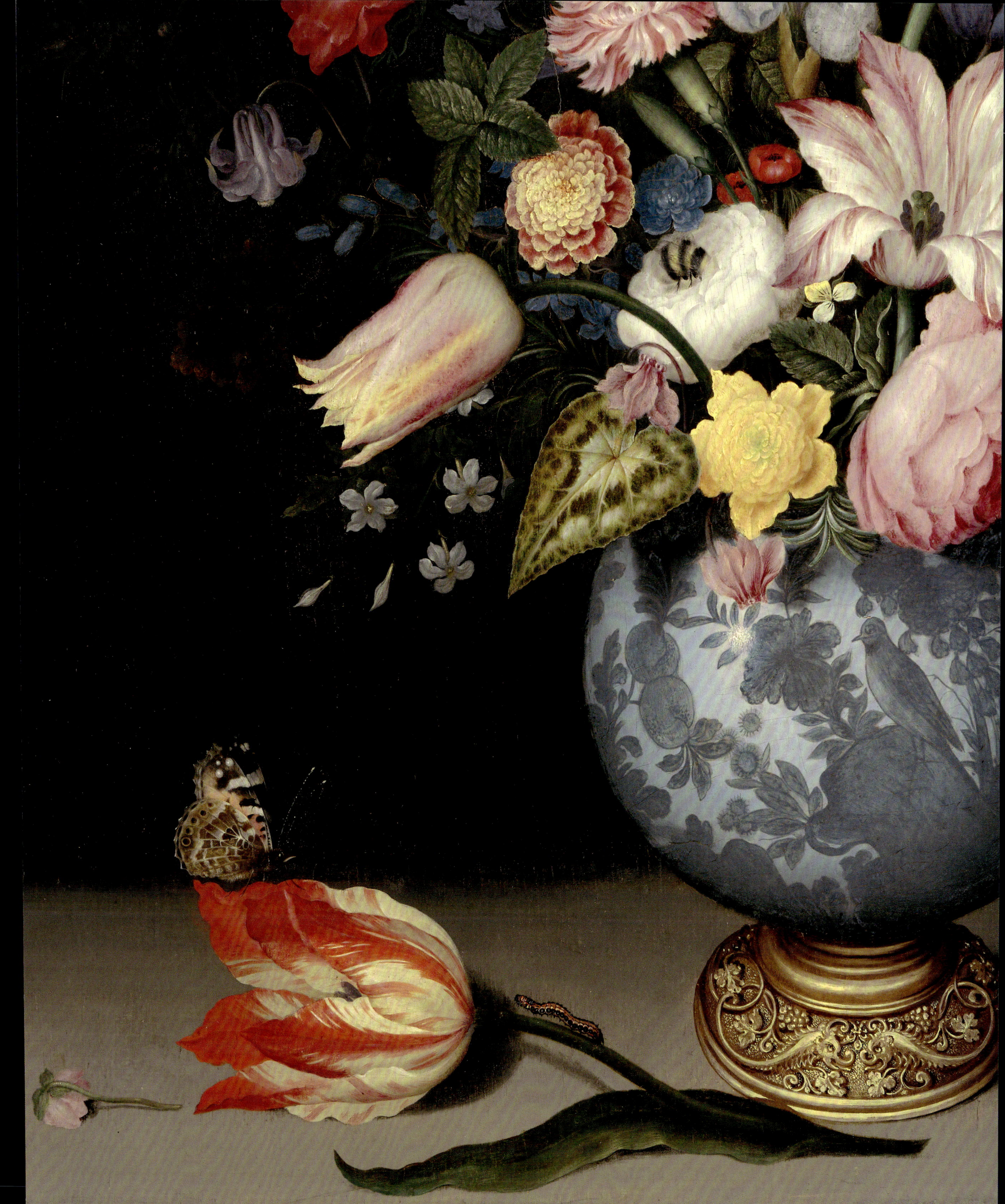

9

Circle of Ambrosius Bosschaert I

Dutch
Antwerp 1573–1621 The Hague

and

Jan Brueghel II

Flemish
Antwerp 1601–1678 Antwerp

Flowers in a Glass Beaker

ca. 1620

Monogrammed lower right: "AB" or "*PB*" (fig. 9a)
Oil on copper, 12½ × 9⅛ in. (31.8 × 23.2 cm)
The Norton Simon Foundation, F.1973.26.P

Provenance
Camille, Count du Chastel de la Howarderie (1827–1880), Brussels, in 1873, by descent to; Albert, Count du Chastel de la Howarderie (1857–1946), Brussels, as Abraham Brueghel, to his daughter; Thérèse du Chastel de la Howarderie (1889–1924), Brussels, who in 1912 married Boniface Bernard Marcel de Castellane, Marquis de Castellane-Esparron (1884–1951), by descent to her son; Albert de Castellane-Esperron (1924–1991), Brussels. [Kunsthandel P. De Boer, Switzerland, by 1956, consigned 1963 to]; [Kunsthandel P. De Boer, Amsterdam, sold 1963/64 to]; Heinrich Becker (d. 1975), Dortmund, sold 1973 through; [G. Cramer Oudekunst, The Hague, to]; The Norton Simon Foundation.

Exhibited
Brussels 1873, no. 224, as Abraham Brueghel, lent by Count C. du Chastel; Amsterdam 1963, no. 3, ill.; Laren 1963, no. 26, lent by a private collector; on loan, Princeton University Art Museum, Princeton, NJ, 9 October 1973–17 July 1974.

References
Bol 1960, p. 62, no. 19, pl. 13, pp. 23, 31, 87, as Ambrosius Bosschaert I, coll. Count Albert de Castellane; Fritz 1967, no. 55; Pasadena 1980, p. 50, ill.; Pasadena 1989, p. 69, ill.; Gaskell 1990, p. 50n10; S. Campbell 2010, p. 459, no. 780, ill.

Technical Notes
The support, a thin copper panel, is somewhat flexible. The ground is white; brushstrokes that are barely visible at certain angles seem to be related to the ground layer rather than the paint layer. Some areas were partially underdrawn in black paint: For example, a visible black outline surrounds the pink-and-white carnation at the center as well as the white rose at the bottom of the arrangement. The artist employed both opaque and semitransparent paint, with fine handling of tiny brushstrokes. The insects and smallest flowers are rendered with nearly transparent paint in layers, while the larger flowers are executed in thicker paint, blended directly. Pentimenti are seen in the leftmost contour of the pink-and-white tulip at the left upper center and surrounding the red-and-white tulip at the upper right. The green pigments may have undergone a change; leaves at the lower left of the bouquet are semitransparent, with almost no color. Microscopic examination reveals the thinly painted monogram to be a bit worn, consistent with other thinly painted dark lines, such as the shadows under the nearby flowers, both in the thickness of the lines and in the color. In general, the painting has survived well. Each brushstroke remains crisp and complete with contours intact. The painting was cleaned by Marco Grassi in 1974. Several areas of retouching near the bottom have discolored and are now rather conspicuous. The varnish is a clear natural resin; older darkened varnish remnants remain in crevices.

Flowers in a Glass Beaker is characteristic of the small, tightly painted "portraits" of flowers introduced and popularized by Jan Brueghel I (1568–1625) and Ambrosius Bosschaert I in the first decades of the seventeenth century.[1] The colorful bouquets of realistically portrayed exotic and local flowers reflected and appealed to the contemporary interest in botany and gardening shared by scholars and the educated public responding to the arrival in the Netherlands of flower bulbs and plants from the Levant and Asia.[2] Painted with apparent scientific accuracy, the still lifes include insects, often shells, and petals that have dropped onto the ledge. Artists composed the aesthetically appealing bouquets from drawings and watercolors of directly observed individual flowers, as well as from prints published in the popular florilegiums of Emanuel Sweerts (1552–1612), Crispijn van de Passe I (ca. 1565–1637), and others.[3] Artists often repeated motifs from their own paintings along with those borrowed from paintings by other artists, especially Brueghel.

In the Pasadena painting, a balanced bouquet of evenly lit flowers in a glass beaker decorated with raspberry prunts

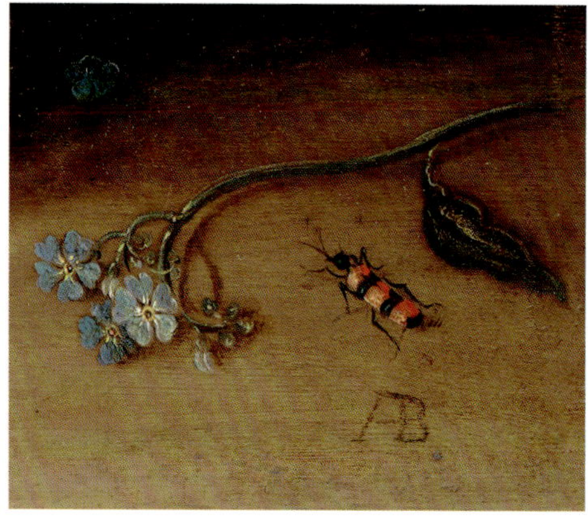

Fig. 9a. Detail of artist's monogram.

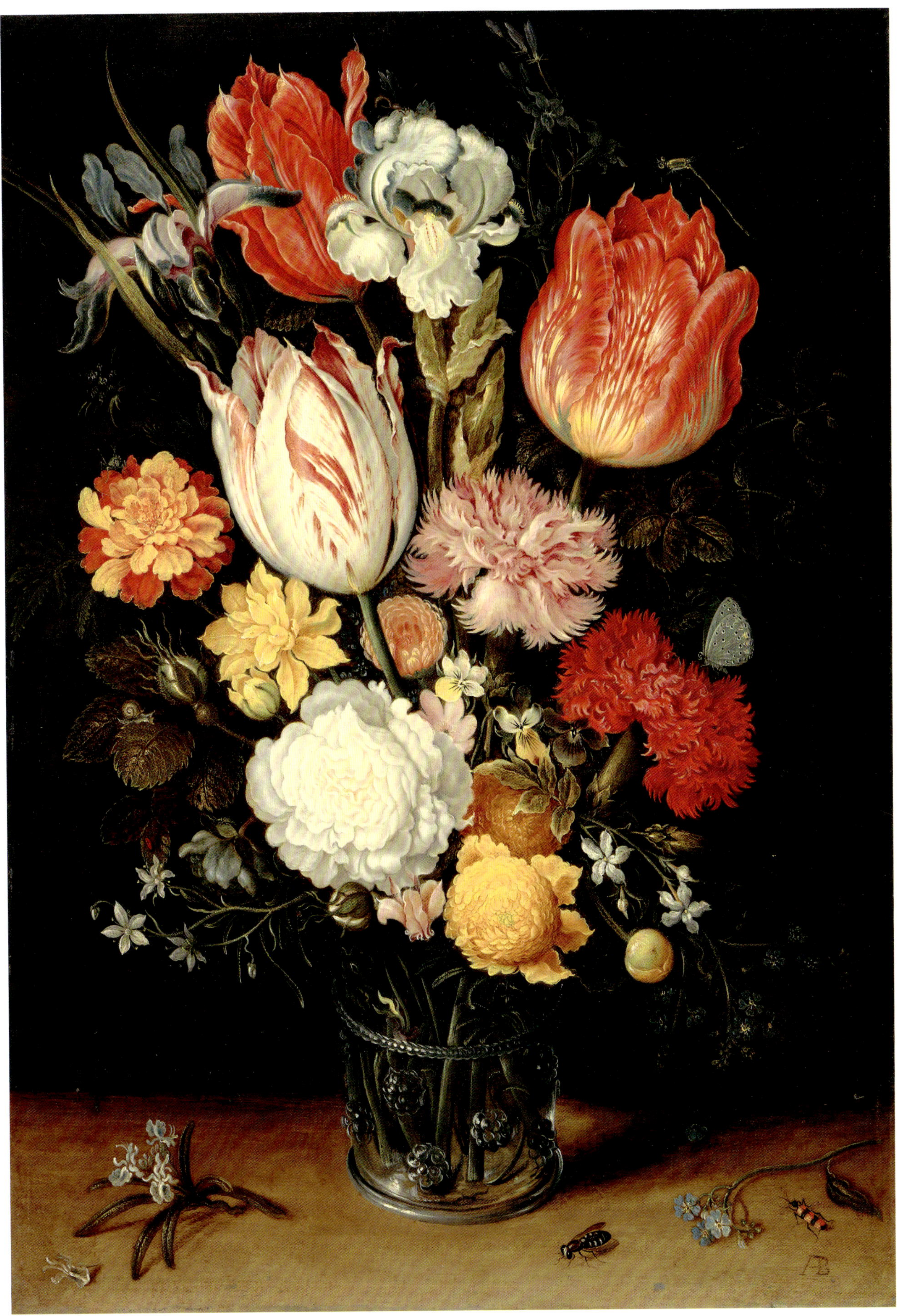

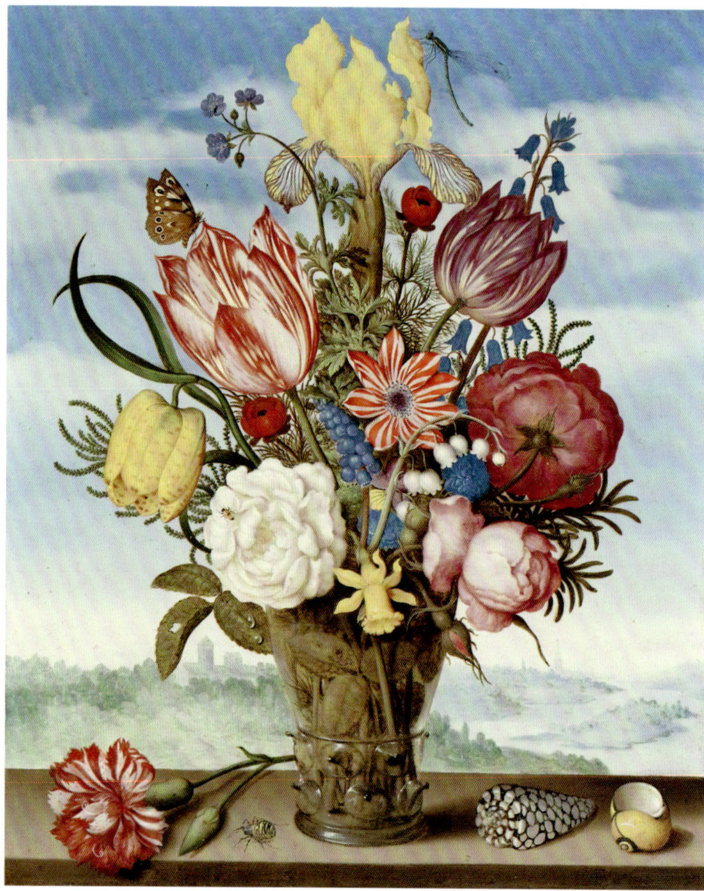

Fig. 9b. Ambrosius Bosschaert I, *Bouquet of Flowers on a Ledge*, 1619, oil on copper, 11 × 9 in. (27.9 × 22.8 cm), Los Angeles County Museum of Art.

rests on an undefined surface against a black background.[4] Painted on copper, the details and individual primary colors of each flower are carefully defined.[5] The bouquet is a conceit combining flowers that bloom in the spring and summer. Tulips and irises dominate the bouquet, which includes a lilac-blue rampion, a white tulip flamed with red, a French marigold (yellow with orange-brown), a double-flowered daffodil, another marigold, carnations of red and red-and-white, a pink cyclamen, a white rose, and a radiant yellow ranunculus. A few smaller flowers, including forget-me-nots, wild violets, and saxifrage, fill out the arrangement.[6] The flowers, which are in their prime, are shown in full, with only slight overlapping; the stems and leaves are visible through the green glass of the beaker. Small sprigs of flowers, which appear to have fallen from the bouquet, lie on the table, where a large black fly and a black-and-red striped beetle crawl. Other creatures—a butterfly, a grasshopper, a praying mantis, and a snail—inhabit the bouquet itself.

Until 1960 *Flowers in a Glass Beaker* was attributed to the son of Jan Brueghel II, Abraham Brueghel (1631–1690), who spent his career in Italy. In *The Bosschaert Dynasty*, published in 1960, Laurens Bol reattributed the Pasadena painting to Ambrosius Bosschaert I.[7] Although he questioned the signature, which he suggested may have been added by a later hand, he accepted the painting as a late work by Bosschaert.[8] It is not known if Bol ever saw the Pasadena painting. Comparison of *Flowers in a Glass Beaker* with well-preserved paintings securely attributed to Bosschaert reveals significant differences in technique, composition, and floral vocabulary. In his accepted works—such as *Flower Still Life in a Basket*, signed and dated 1614 (J. Paul Getty Museum, Los Angeles), and *Bouquet of Flowers on a Ledge*, signed and dated 1619 (fig. 9b; Los Angeles County Museum of Art)—Bosschaert carefully crafted his flowers with an orderly layering of paint and glazes applied to a prepared copper plate with brushstrokes that seem to melt away to suggest the sheen of fine satin.[9]

The artist of the Pasadena painting, however, used small parallel brushstrokes to create the effect of a hard enamel surface. In the rendering of the tulips and iris, in particular, line approaches a mannered independence unknown in the work of Bosschaert: A yellow line, for example, follows the active outline of the red tulip in the upper left, while elsewhere lines emphasize the scalloped edges of an iris and sharply define volumes. The composition of *Flowers in a Glass Beaker* and the structure of the bouquet also set it apart from similar still lifes by Bosschaert. In his accepted paintings, such as *Bouquet in an Arched Window* (1620; Mauritshuis, The Hague) and *Bouquet of Flowers on a Ledge*, the front edge of the table is defined, and a dominant flower is placed on the axis of the symmetrical bouquet. In the Pasadena painting, however, the edge of the table on which the bouquet rests is not defined, and there is no dominant central flower; the red tulip and the pink-and-steel-blue iris to the left of center mark the upper end of a visual diagonal.

As noted by Bol, the floral vocabulary of the still life is derived from Jan Brueghel I, Bosschaert's influential contemporary in Antwerp. The irises and the top two tulips in the Pasadena painting appear in the same form in a number of paintings by Brueghel, most notably the *Flower Still Life* he sent to Cardinal Federico Borromeo in 1606, destined for his Pinacoteca Ambrosiana in Milan (fig. 9c). The sprig of rosemary on the lower left and the red-and-black beetle in the Pasadena painting also appear on the lower right in the Milan painting, of which other versions and copies must have been known in the Netherlands.[10] The glass beaker with raspberry prunts under an applied crinkled glass thread is also more frequently found in paintings associated with Brueghel than with Bosschaert. The handling of paint, which approximates the impression of enamel, is, however, not typical of Brueghel, who painted more freely, combining thin strokes of opaque paint with glazes, twisting the brush at the end of his strokes to accent the edges of his flowers.

During the early and mid-seventeenth century, a number of artists borrowed motifs from Jan Brueghel I for inclusion in their own still lifes, complicating the attribution of

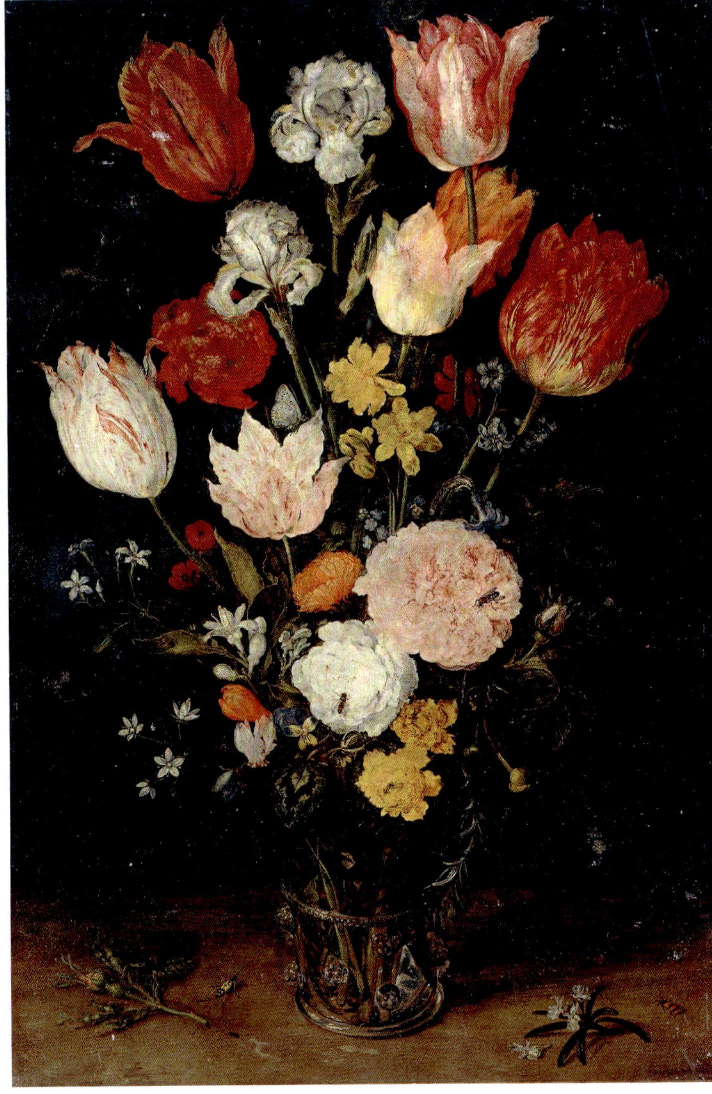

Fig. 9c. Jan Brueghel I, *Flower Still Life*, 1606, oil on copper, 16 15/16 × 11 13/16 in. (43 × 30 cm), Ambrosiana, Milan.

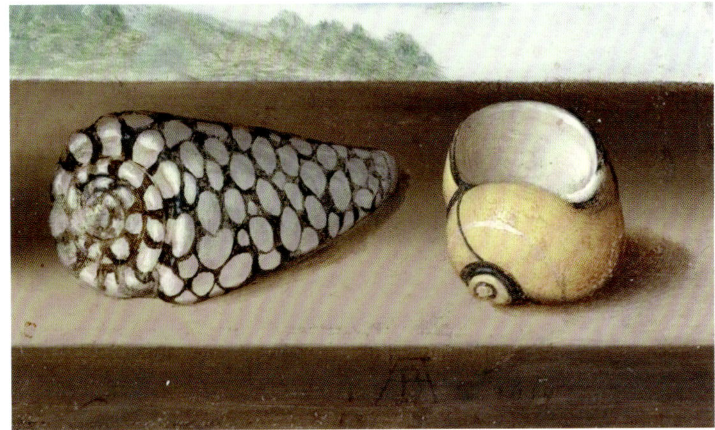

Fig. 9d. Detail of *Bouquet of Flowers on a Ledge* (fig. 9b).

Flowers in a Glass Beaker. The *AB* monogram (fig. 9a) on the lower right of the Pasadena panel, which Bol thought was a later addition, is actually part of the original paint, but it is not by Ambrosius Bosschaert, who signed his paintings with a square Gothic *A* enclosing a small *B* (fig. 9d).[11] The thin and somewhat carelessly painted monogram on *Flowers in a Glass Beaker* appears to be either an *A* and a *B* joined side by side or possibly an *F* or a *P* and a *B* joined so that the loop of the *P* overlaps or abuts the upper loop of the *B*. The latter is somewhat similar to the monogram of Peter Binoit (ca. 1590/93–1632), who signed his paintings *P/B* and often incorporated details from Brueghel's flower still lifes, but his paintings differ in tonality and character from the Pasadena painting.[12]

Flowers in a Glass Beaker was painted by an accomplished artist with knowledge of the popular work of Bosschaert and Brueghel.[13] The even lighting and firm definition of flowers with primary colors and outlines reflect the style of Bosschaert and suggest a date ca. 1620. The inclusion of elements from Brueghel's paintings testifies to the popularity and availability of his works, undoubtedly afforded by workshop copies. Repetition of elements from Brueghel's paintings in works by Bosschaert suggest that he not only knew and admired Brueghel's paintings, but also made copies that he kept in his workshop as models for himself and other artists in his orbit.[14]

From at least 1873 until 1967, *Flowers in a Glass Beaker* was paired with a still life of roses surmounted by a partially open red-and-cream tulip.[15] The similarly described glass beaker rests on a ledge on which a butterfly is perched. Although both still lifes are on copper with identical dimensions, the paintings were probably not conceived as a pair, nor painted by the same hand. *Still Life with Roses*, which is signed on the left side of the ledge with Bosschaert's typical monograph, appears from the illustration in the catalogue of the Heinrich Becker Collection (no. 56) to be painted in a manner more consistent with that of the Getty and LACMA paintings but different from the technique used in *Flowers in a Glass Beaker*. The pairing of the Pasadena painting with the one depicting roses in a vase may have originated with a dealer or collector during the eighteenth century, when it was popular, especially in France, to hang paintings as pendants.

1. Regarding the genesis of the floral still life and the relationship of Brueghel and Bosschaert, see De Clippel and Van der Linden 2015–16.

2. Regarding the importance for Bosschaert of the highly developed floral culture in Middelburg, see Pennisi 2007 and Bol 1960, especially pp. 14–33.

3. Emmanuel Sweerts, *Florilegium* (Frankfurt, 1612); and Crispijn van de Passe I, *Hortus floridus* (1614).

4. Raspberry prunts were created by drops of molten glass applied to the body of the vessel and impressed with a raspberry pattern of raised dots.

5. For more on oil paintings on copper, see Phoenix 1999.

6. Bol 1960, p. 62, inventories the flowers.

7. Bol 1960, pp. 23, 62.

8. The discussion of the Pasadena painting in Bol 1960, p. 23, includes a closely related unsigned painting that had been exhibited in London by the Tooth gallery in 1940, when it was attributed to Ambrose Brueghel. That painting is illustrated on the cover of the exhibition catalogue *Contrasts and Affinities: Four Centuries of Flower Painting*, Arthur Tooth & Sons Ltd., London, 16 March–6 April 1939, no. 26, *Flowers in a Vase with Butterflies and Other Insects* (oil on copper, 26¼ × 19½ in.). The bouquets are essentially identical, although in the Tooth painting, the sprig of rosemary in the left foreground is replaced by a fallen tulip. Bol groups both paintings with *A Vase of Flowers*, ca. 1609, signed with Bosschaert's monogram in the lower left (oil on copper, 37.5 × 25 cm; Ashmolean Museum, Oxford, inv. No. WA 1940.2.15).

9. A. Walsh 2019b, cat. 4, pp. 46–53.

10. Bol 1960, p. 87, notes that the detail of the sprig of rosemary also appears in a painting by Bosschaert's follower Balthasar van der Ast (1593/94–1667), *Flowers in a Chinese Vase* (Museo Nacional Thyssen-Bornemisza, Madrid).

11. The form was perhaps intended to recall the monogram used by the much revered Albrecht Dürer (1471–1523).

12. See, for example, *Still Life with Flowers and Fruit*, oil on copper, 72 × 52 cm, signed "P B," Skokloster Castle, Sweden. Two paintings in the National Gallery of Art, Washington, DC, *Still Life with Tulips* and *Still Life with Iris* (each oil on copper, 24.13 × 19.05 cm), are signed "PB / 1623." The "PB" stands for Peter Binoit, who was born in Cologne, was a student of Daniel Soreau (1554–1619), and later worked in Hanau in the circle of Isaak Soreau (1604–after 1645). See Bott 2001, pp. 48–93.

13. In his review of this catalogue entry in 2011, Fred Meijer wrote that the painting is "related to some still lifes by Abrosius [*sic*] Bosschaert from around 1610 . . . which have clearly been influenced by Jan Brueghel I's flower pieces from the first decade of the 17th century" (NSM). Meijer also pointed out that Sam Segal attributed the Pasadena still life to a "Pseudo-Bosschaert" in 1999 (See RKDimages, https://rkd.nl/en/explore/images/184560). As of 2020, the RKD identified the painting as "Anonymous Netherlander, after ca. 1620, or Pseudo Bosschaert."

14. Although Bol 1960, p. 22, doubted that Brueghel and Bosschaert ever met, recently discovered archival documents strongly suggest that they probably did meet in Antwerp and/or Middelburg and that Bosschaert, in his capacity as an art dealer, may have acted as an agent for Brueghel's paintings. See De Clippel and Van der Linden 2015–16.

15. Both paintings were in the collection of Count Camille du Chastel de la Howarderie when they were included as nos. 224 and 226, attributed to Abraham Brueghel, in Brussels 1873. No. 226 is described as: "Fleurs. Dans un verre sur une tablette de marbre, un bouquet où les roses dominent un papilon. Signé à droite des mêmes initiales que le tableau no. 224 mais autrement formées." The catalogue describes the monogram of no. 226 as an *A* like the one in Dürer's signature but enclosing a *B*. Both paintings appear together again as Ambrosius Bosschaert, in Fritz 1967, nos. 55 and 56, the catalogue of the Heinrich Becker Collection, Dortmund, in which it is suggested that the paintings were painted as pendants.

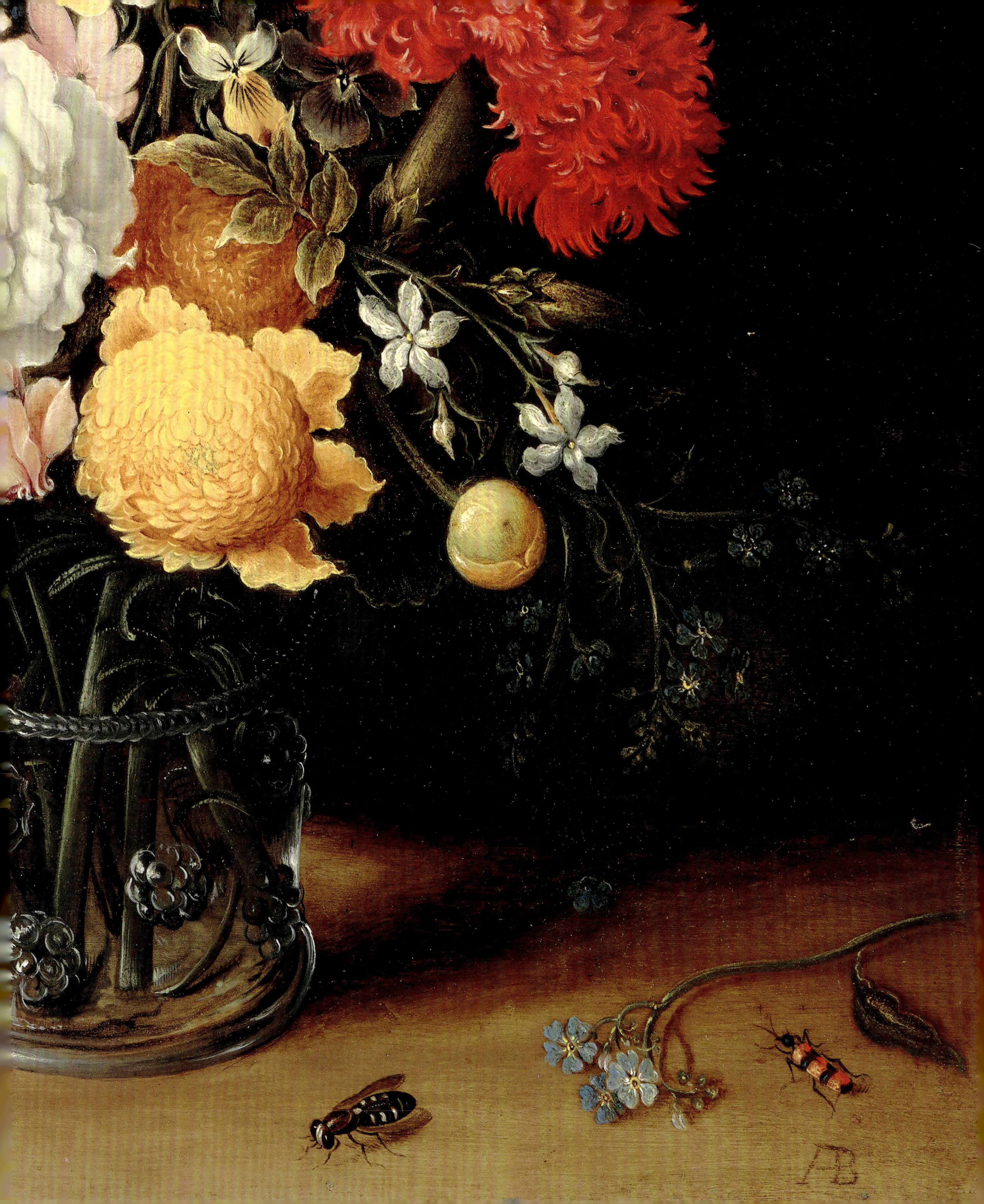

10

Workshop of Albrecht Bouts

Netherlandish
Louvain ca. 1452/55–1549 Louvain

The Penitence of Saint Jerome

1500–25

Oil on panel, 16⅛ × 17¾ in. (41 × 45.1 cm)
Norton Simon Art Foundation, M.2009.2.P

Provenance
The Rev. E. F. Egan, England, in 1891, by descent to his grandniece; Mrs. Elizabeth Mepham (sale, Sotheby's, London, 2 December 1964, lot 101, ill., sold to); [Julius Weitzner, London, sold to]; [Hallsborough Gallery, London, sold 1969 to]; The Norton Simon Foundation, transferred 2009 to; Norton Simon Art Foundation.

Exhibited
London 1891, no. 139, as "Flemish School (XVth Cent.), Saint Jerome, 15½ × 16½ [in.]"; on loan, Phoenix Art Museum, 18 August–15 December 1969; on loan, Los Angeles County Museum of Art, 16 December 1969–26 November 1974.

References
Friedmann 1980, pp. 86f., fig. 69; Pasadena 1989, p. 23, ill.; Stroo et al. 1996–2013, vol. 3 (2001), p. 162, fig. 82; Pasadena 2003, p. 38, ill.; S. Campbell 2010, p. 324, no. 658, ill.; Henderiks 2011, p. 323, cat. 274, ill.; Wolfthal and Metzger 2014, pp. 32–45, color pl. and details.

Technical Notes
The uncradled support, a horizontally grained oak panel, was made from two boards, joined 5¾ inches from the bottom. The panel has a deep bevel at each side. A crack that originates at the left side, approximately 3 inches from the bottom, is tightly closed. The ground was applied while the panel was in a frame, as indicated by barbes at each edge where unpainted margins are exposed. There may be two ground layers, as viewed along the left edge. The lower layer is light tan, and the upper layer is cream-colored. Examination with infrared reflectography reveals the painting to be completely underdrawn.[1] The paint was applied with crisply rendered details in enamel-like colors. Smoothly brushed in a highly finished handling, the paint shows no evidence of abrasion. It is densely cracked, however, and the slightly raised edges have become a dominant characteristic of the surface texture. There have been at least two campaigns of retouching. In the most recent, minor paint losses along the edge of the crack were filled and retouched. Older retouching in the sky at the top left corner, at the left end of the bottom edge, and in the red hat probably compensates for flake losses. The several varnish layers include synthetic resin applied in 1984, as well as an older natural-resin varnish that has yellowed noticeably.

For medieval theologians and Renaissance humanists, Jerome (ca. 342–420), one of the Latin fathers of the Church and the translator of the Vulgate, represented the ideal of the true scholar. Jerome fled Rome in search of the ascetic life of a hermit. He described his new life in a letter to Eustochium, a female disciple: "When I was living in the desert, in the vast solitude which gives to hermits a savage dwelling-place . . . I had no companions but scorpions and wild beasts . . . . [T]he fires of lust kept bubbling up before me when my flesh was as good as dead. Helpless, I cast myself at the feet of Jesus . . . . I remember how I often cried aloud

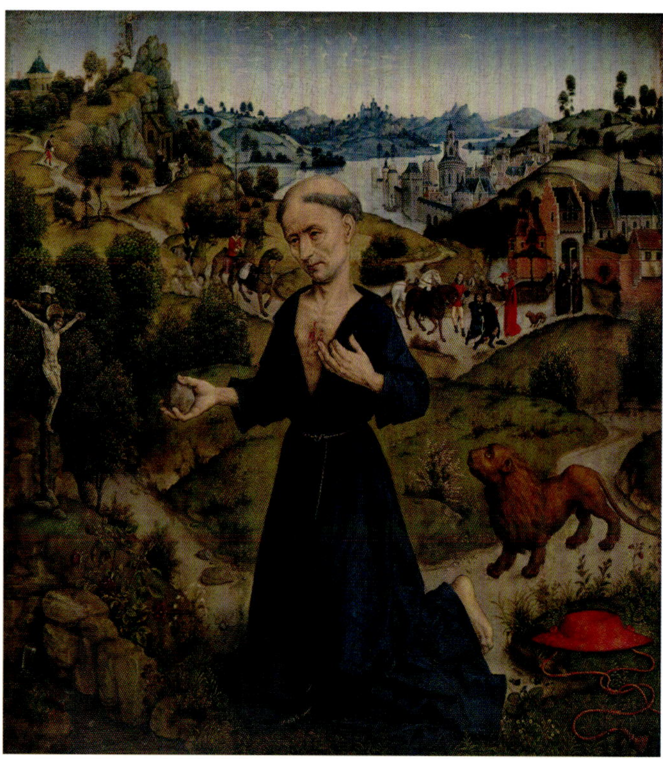

Fig. 10a. Albrecht Bouts, *The Penitence of Saint Jerome*, ca. 1480, oil on panel, 16⅜ × 14⅞ in. (41.6 × 37.8 cm), inv. 3134, Musées Royaux des Beaux-Arts de Belgique, Brussels.

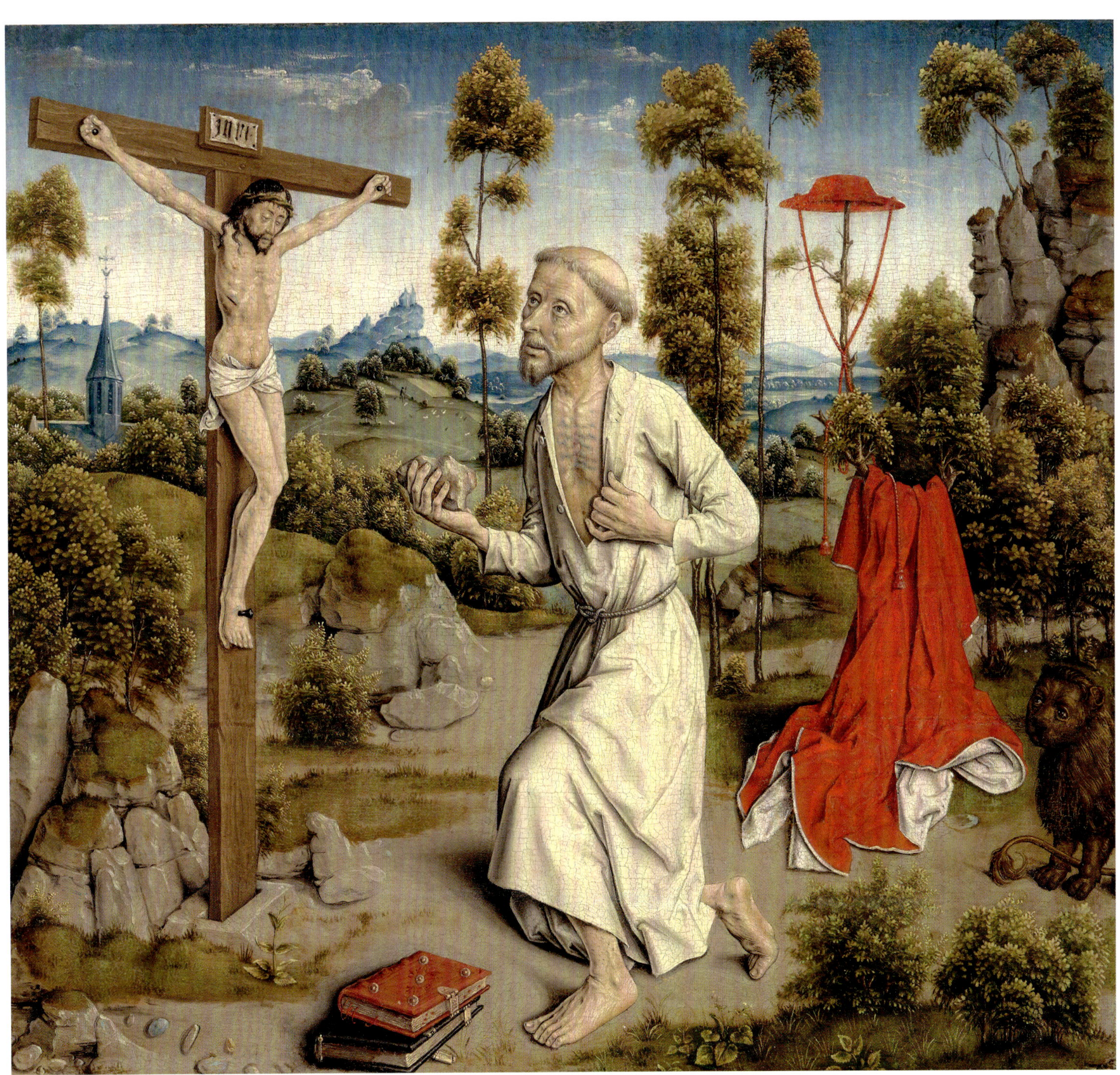

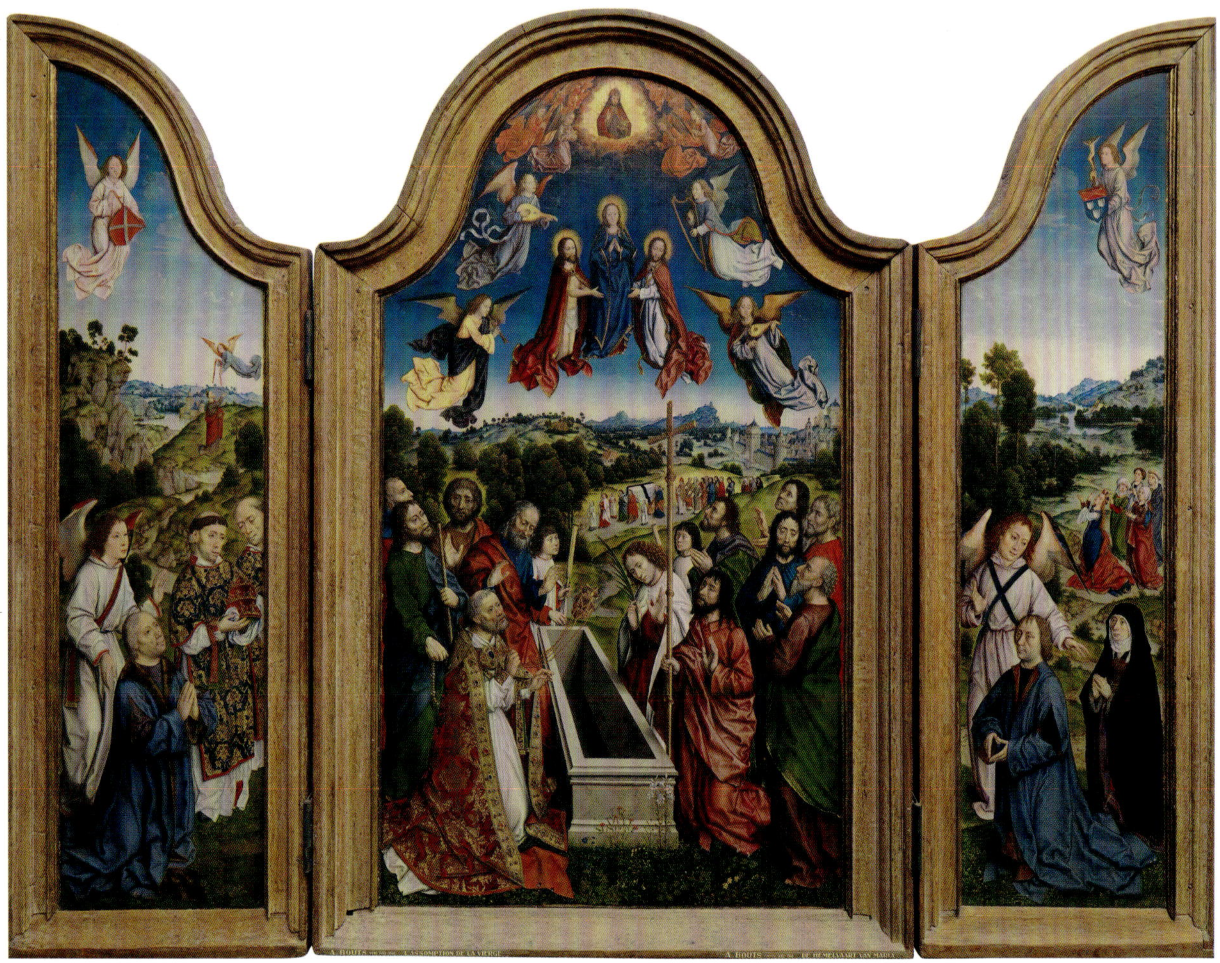

Fig. 10b. Albrecht Bouts, *Triptych of the Assumption of the Virgin*, 1495–1500, oil on panel, 73¼ × 42⅝ in. (186.2 × 108.5 cm), inv. 574, Musées Royaux des Beaux-Arts de Belgique, Brussels.

all night till the break of day and ceased not from beating my breast till tranquility returned at the chiding of the Lord."[2]

Depictions of the penitence of Saint Jerome were little known before about 1400, when the subject first appeared in paintings in Florence, inspired by the publication of a widely read book on the life of the saint by Giovanni Andrea (ca. 1270/75–1348), professor of canon law at the University of Bologne.[3]

The Penitence of Saint Jerome, probably painted during the first quarter of the sixteenth century, represents Saint Jerome, with tears streaming down his face, kneeling before a crucifix constructed of planed wood, the figure of Christ painted to appear as alive. Two leather-bound, metal-studded volumes on the ground at his feet refer to his work as the translator of the Gospels from Greek and Hebrew into Latin; the discarded crimson robes and hat hanging from a spindly tree refer to his role as cardinal.[4] Jerome wears rough, light gray robes tied at the waist with a leather cord in the manner of the habit adopted by the Hieronymites (the followers of Jerome) in 1460. Watching quietly on the far right side of the painting is the lion that became Jerome's faithful companion after the saint removed a thorn from its paw.[5] Stretching beyond the immediate foreground, the extensive landscape terminating in a castle or walled town atop a distant hill refers to his exile, while the steeple of a Netherlandish Gothic church in the middle ground refers to Jerome's contribution to the teachings of the Church.[6] Typical of northern representations of the subject, a verdant landscape has replaced the arid scenery of Italian examples.

The small size and character of the Pasadena *Penitence of Saint Jerome*, which emphasizes personal understanding of the Passion, suggest that it was painted for private devotion. Meditation on the Passion of Christ had been widely practiced since the early fourteenth century, particularly by the Hieronymites.[7] Prayers addressed to Saint Jerome reflect what petitioners imagined him to be saying and thinking as he knelt before the crucifix. Recorded in books of prayer, the most common of these prayers asked for the virtues that Jerome was supposed to have possessed: "humility, chastity, patience, firm faith, and a 'clear understanding of what we must know to do God's will.'"[8]

The Pasadena panel agrees in general terms with a group of small devotional paintings of the subject attributed to Albrecht Bouts and his workshop.[9] Common to these paintings are the broad forehead and narrow chin of the tonsured saint who rends his robes with his left hand and holds a rock in his right as he kneels before a small crucifix in the foreground beyond which stretches a lush, hilly landscape. The lion and discarded cardinal's hat and robe are nearby. In some versions, most notably that in Brussels (fig. 10a), which Valentine Henderiks believes to be an early autograph work painted by Albrecht Bouts ca. 1475, additional scenes of the life of the saint appear in the distant landscape.[10] The Pasadena painting lacks these secondary scenes and differs from the other versions in specific details. It alone represents Jerome as he appears in Florentine paintings—in the light gray robes and leather belt worn by the Hieronymite order rather than in the dark robe worn by the saint in northern depictions, suggesting that the painting may have been intended for an Italian client.[11] The Pasadena saint is also older, his hair grayed and bearded face wizened; rather than kneeling on both knees, his left foot is flat on the ground so that he partially stands. The cross is also distinct. Constructed of planed wood and placed into a flat rectangular stone, it differs from the typical rough logs supported by rocks seen in the Brussels version.[12] The diversity of style, quality, and details among these paintings probably reflects Bouts's extensive workshop and numerous followers.[13]

Bouts's oeuvre is complicated by his exceptionally long life and his employment of an active workshop.[14] Only one work, the *Triptych of the Assumption of the Virgin* in Brussels (fig. 10b), is securely attributed to him on the basis of documents.[15] Comparison of the Pasadena *Penitence of Saint Jerome* with the *Assumption* reveals certain similarities but ultimately suggests that it was painted by a workshop member rather than the master himself. Similar to the figures in the accepted altarpieces, the Pasadena Saint Jerome appears to stand precariously on the tilted foreground, while overlapping, rounded forms of hills, rocks, and bushes suggest the natural progression into the distant landscape. The bony, finely drawn face and body of the saint and the deep folds of drapery generally reflect the style of Bouts, but the sharply modeled, crisp description of forms contrasts with the softer, more subtle modeling of the figures in the *Assumption*.[16] In the Pasadena painting, the artist has reduced the highlights on the face, hands, feet, and rocks to abstract white strokes that contribute to the overall impression of brittleness that distinguishes the painting from Bouts's autograph works.[17]

1. Wolfthal and Metzger 2014, pp. 35f., fig. 4.

2. Erasmus 1992, p. 159. Jerome wrote the letter to Eustochium, a disciple who left Rome for Jerusalem with her mother and joined Jerome near the Church of the Nativity in Bethlehem. The editors of Erasmus 1992, p. 155, observe, "Although addressed as a letter to Eustochium, it is in fact a treatise of virginity as a way of life and on the pitfalls and vices that block that path." The letter was also reproduced in Jacobus da Voragine's enduringly popular hagiographic compilation from 1265, *The Golden Legend*. Wolfthal and Metzger 2014, 41.

3. See Meiss 1974. Before 1300 Jerome was known and represented primarily as a father and Doctor of the Church. The subject's popularity continued to increase in northern Europe after the publication of Erasmus's nine-volume edition of the saint's life and complete works, printed in Basel in 1516 by Johannes Froben, with a variety of other writings, a letter of dedication, a life of Jerome, and indices. Revised editions were published in 1524–26 and 1533–34 and followed by a number of reprints. See Erasmus 1992.

4. Jerome was a humble priest and monk who refused all rank. He was elevated posthumously to cardinal, an office created only after his death. See Rice 1985, pp. 35–37.

5. Regarding the legend of the lion, see Rice 1985, pp. 37ff.

6. According to Rice 1985, p. 76, "The contrast of *civitas* and wilderness, of the walled towns on the horizon and Jerome's rocky retreat, is strongly marked, at once a literal illustration of the eremitical impulse in Hieronymite spirituality and a metaphor for the separation from the world that the penitent has won by his ascetic practices and for the truer freedom of a soul naked and alone with God."

7. Rice 1985, p. 79, observes that after the Hieronymites broke their fasts, "'their most delicate food' was meditation on the Passion. They beat themselves 'per la memoria della passione di Cristo.'"

8. Rice 1985, p. 81.

9. Wolfthal and Metzger 2014, p. 41.

10. I am grateful to Dr. Henderiks for sharing her opinions about this painting with me in an email of 3 May 2011. See also Stroo et al. 1996–2013, vol. 2 (2001), pp. 156–64; and Henderiks 2011, p. 323, cat. 274.

11. In an email to Carol Togneri dated February 2, 2011, Maryan Ainsworth raised the possibility that the painting could have been commissioned by or meant for an Italian client (NSM). Wolfthal and Metzger 2014, p. 43, while noting that the depiction of the saint in light robes was uncommon in northern imagery, say Jan Gossaert (ca. 1472–1532) and Simon Bening (ca. 1483–1561) painted him in this way.

12. The cross composed of planed wood set into a flat stone block also appears in Rogier van der Weyden's depictions of the Crucifixion, such as *The Crucifixion, with the Virgin and Saint John the Evangelist Mourning*, ca. 1460 (Philadelphia Museum of Art).

13. Although the compositions differ in many ways, the bony facial type of Saint Jerome in the Pasadena painting—broad forehead and narrow chin—recalls that in a drawing after a lost painting of the penitent Saint Jerome by Albrecht's father, Dieric Bouts (ca. 1410–1475; Kupferstichkabinett, Staatliche Museen, Berlin, attributed to Master of the Drapery Studies). See Stroo et al. 1996–2013, vol. 2 (2001), p. 162, fig. 81.

14. See discussion in Stroo et al. 1996–2013, vol. 2 (2001), pp. 156–65. See Henderiks 2006, where she defines Albrecht's style and the influences of both his father and Hugo van der Goes in his work. See also Henderiks 2011, p. 323, cat. 274.

15. Regarding the *Assumption of the Virgin*, see W. M. Staring 1947, pp. 182–88; Wéra 1951; and Dechamps 1977a and 1977b.

16. Compare, for example, the faces of the bearded men on the far right side of the central panel of the Brussels *Assumption* and the saint in the Pasadena painting. See Wolfthal and Metzger 2014, p. 44.

17. I am grateful to Maryan Ainsworth for sharing her observations regarding these differences.

11

Dieric Bouts

Netherlandish
Haarlem ca. 1410–1475 Louvain

The Resurrection

ca. 1455

Distemper on linen, 35⅜ × 29¼ in.
(89.9 × 74.3 cm)
The Norton Simon Foundation, F.1980.1.P

Provenance

Probably Foscari family, Venice and Vienna, ca. 1810, to;[1] Count Diego Guicciardi [1756–1837], Vienna, by descent to;[2] Guicciardi family, Milan, in 1858–after 1860, by descent to; Vittorio Melzi, Milan, by 1872.[3] [Matthiesen, London, 1946]. Private collection, London (sale, Sotheby's, London, 16 April 1980, lot 114, sold to);[4] The Norton Simon Foundation.

Exhibited

Milan 1872a, no. 38 as "Luca d'Olanda (?) [a.k.a. Lucas van Leyden]," lent by Vittorio Melzi.

References

Perhaps Eastlake 1858–60: pt. 1, Milan, 1858, pt. 3, Milan, 1860; Milan 1872b, p. 8, no. 38; Davies 1953, pp. 26f.; Brussels/Delft 1957–58, p. 20; M. Friedländer 1967–76, vol. 3 (1968), pp. 76, 89n81, and addendum 116, pl. 122; Davies 1968, p. 16; *La Chronique des arts* 1980, p. 30, no. 161; Reynolds 1980, pp. 19–21, fig. 1; Vandenbroeck 1982, p. 42, no. 24; Brooks 1985; Getty 1985; Duret-Robert 1986, p. 87; J. Walsh 1986, pp. 214f. J.-L. Bordeaux 1986, p. 37; Bomford, Roy, and Smith 1986, pp. 41, 45f., 51, fig. 6; Zeri 1987, vol. 2, pp. 591f.; Eisler 1988, pp. 193, 195, 201n3; Fredericksen 1988, no. 16; Leonard, Preusser, and Rothe 1988, pp. 517, 520; Van Miegroet 1988, pp. 95f., 102, 105f.; Marijnissen 1988, pp. 112f.; Koch 1988, pp. 514–16, figs. 8, 12; Wolfthal 1989, pp. 38–41, fig. 60; Brown 1989; Pasadena 1989, pp. 22f.; Villers 1991, p. 258; Dunkerton et al. 1991, pp. 296f.; Massing 1991, p. 693; Bauman and Liedtke 1992, pp. 63, 319, fig. 127; Sander 1992, pp. 152f., no. 32; Van Miegroet 1992a, p. 63; Eeckhout 1992–93, p. 31; Humfrey 1993, pp. 159f., 184, 330n95; Belting and Kruse 1994, pp. 204, 208–11; Harbison 1995, pp. 63, 65, fig. 37; Fredericksen and Jaffé 1997, p. 42; Lucco 1997, pp. 199f., 202; Muchnic 1998, pp. 186f., 242, ill.; Fahy 1998–99, p. 74; L. Campbell 1998, pp. 42, 44, 45nn31–32, 50, figs. 2, 5; Smeyers 1998, p. 96, 100, 102; Aikema 1999, p. 83; Aikema and Brown 1999, p. 177n11; Dunkerton 1999, p. 94; Rohlmann 1999, p. 41; Stroo et al. 1996–2013, vol. 2 (1999), pp. 113–15, 118f., 122n54, 122n57, fig. 49; Kirsch and Levenson 2000, p. 115; Los Angeles 2001, p. 109; Allen et al. 2003, p. 40; Pasadena 2003, p. 37, ill.; Christiansen 2004, pp. 37–39; Lucco 2004, pp. 82f.; Nuttall 2004, pp. 188–90; Snyder, Silver, and Luttikhuizen 2005, pp. 147f.; Périer-d'leteren 2006, pp. 162–77; Stourton 2007, p. 127; Woods 2007, pp. 93, 295n78; S. Nash 2008, pp. 101f.; Zirpolo 2008, fig. 15; New York 2009, p. 14; B. G. Lane 2009, pp. 74f.; S. Campbell 2010, pp. 192, fig. 1, 193–95, 204, 223, 430, no. 1646, ill.; Badstübner 2011, p. 368; Silver 2011, pp. 250, 252; Fajt, Franzen, and Knüvener 2011, ill. 322; Nuttall 2013, pp. 24f., 109; Wolfthal and Metzger 2014, pp. 47–87, figs. 2, 5f., 9f., 12, 17f., 20, 22, 24f., 27f., 39, 41; Rosenauer 2016, pp. 15–16; Los Angeles 2017, fig. 3, pp. 17, 18, 106; Rutherglen 2017, pp. 17–27, figs. 13, 16–20; Muchnic 2019, pp. 131, 202–03, 255.

Technical Notes

A delicate and rare example of a *tüchlein* painting, *The Resurrection* is inherently fragile yet beautifully preserved.[5] Physical evidence and recent technical data support the association of *The Resurrection* with *The Entombment* in the National Gallery, London (fig. 11b); the two canvases are the same size and share a weave match indicating that they were cut from the same bolt of fabric.[6] This new data shows that *The Annunciation* in the J. Paul Getty Museum (fig. 11a), which is slightly smaller in size, has a similar thread count but does not share the same weave match with the other two paintings.[7] All three canvases are unprimed and painted on a fine-weave linen, which was likely to have been bleached prior to painting.[8] It has been suggested that the white color of the bleached canvas may have played a part in the painting process by intentionally being incorporated into the composition, especially in the flesh tones and lighter hues.[9] Exposure to light may have accelerated the oxidization of the canvas threads, resulting in the darkening of the exposed canvas nubs and giving the surface of the painting, especially in the lightly painted areas, a speckled appearance. The tacking edges are present and have been painted reddish brown to form a border to the image of *The Resurrection* that is believed to further link it to *The Entombment* and *The Annunciation*.[10]

The canvas was prepared by sizing with animal glue, omitting a conventional ground layer; onto this surface the initial outline for the composition was drawn.[11] Infrared (IR) examination revealed soft, blurry diagonal lines, starting below the top corners and above the lower corners, suggesting they would have intersected at the center to form a large X if continued. Parallel lines, previously concealed by paper tape, demarcate the lateral edges of the image and assisted in the placement of form. Reduction of the painted contours is indicative of Bouts, and this is revealed in the IR reflectogram, where the preparatory outline of the composition and subsequent modifications made by the artist become apparent. The torso, legs, and feet of the recumbent guard in the foreground had been drawn higher than they were painted; the hat of the seated guard on the left was initially larger; Christ's drapery swirls to the left and below its painted form. His blessing fingers and his foot were reduced in size compared to their underdrawn position; similarly, the wings of the angel were drawn slightly larger than the finished painted version. The lid of the sarcophagus was sketched at a different time at a more vertical angle than it was painted. Trees (to the left of Christ's elbow) initially outlined were never painted. A cluster of underdrawing in the form of lines on the face of the sarcophagus to the right of

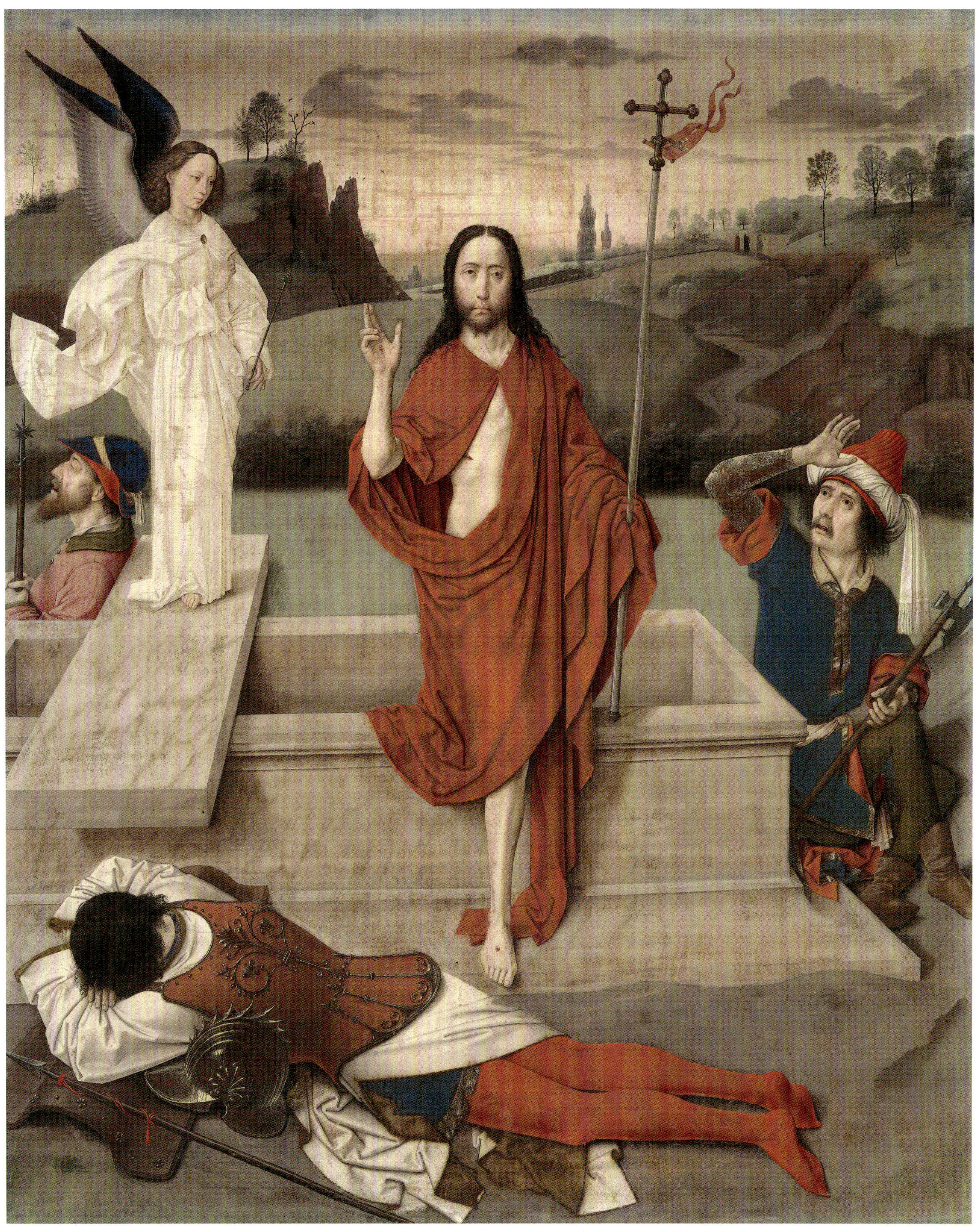

Christ's drapery was never painted; what might have been intended is unclear. The material used by the artist for the underdrawing was not identified, but its visibility in IR suggests it to be carbon based, possibly graphite.[12]

X-radiography reveals only a slight change in the left foot of the prostrate soldier, which was originally pointing down in a more vertical position. X-radiography has also assisted in the possible identification of certain pigments used by the artist. The paint is composed of pigments in a glue-based medium, a technique known as distemper and one that is inherently fragile. Certain pigments, such as chalk, when bound in glue maintain their hue. If bound in oil, chalk would become transparent. Unlike lead white or vermilion, chalk is less radio opaque and appears dark on an X-radiograph. The same can be said for iron oxide, a pigment that, like vermilion, is commonly used for red paint.[13] For example, close study shows the possible use of chalk in the scarf wrapped around the hat of the figure on the far right of the composition, as it appears dark in the X-radiograph; his red hat is white in the X-radiograph, suggesting the use of vermilion. In contrast, the red turnover of this figure's sleeves is dark in the X-radiograph, suggesting the use of red lead. No analysis has been carried out on the painting to confirm these observations.

The paint was applied with small brushes in a subtle and crisp manner showing refined handling; details and modeling were added after the color was applied. Its thin application has made it susceptible to abrasion, but it could also have been applied in this manner to utilize the white of the bleached linen support.

Animal glue is thought to be the adhesive used to attach the finely woven canvas to the reverse of the support of *The Resurrection* (a similar lining canvas has been found on *The Annunciation* and *The Entombment*), presumably to repair a small tear at the top right corner and a small hole at the lower left. The lining could also have served to protect the fourteen small holes (which have since been filled and retouched) across the top of the painting, below the present tacking edge. These holes are possibly from an early system of framing in which the linen was not stretched but attached to a panel with nails.[14] A reverse image of the red and blue passages in the composition can be found stained on the lining canvas support, which has been stretched onto a pine stretcher. It is thought that the glue medium used for the more coarsely ground pigments for these colors may have wicked through the original canvas, resulting in the transfer of sections of the composition onto the back of the lining canvas.[15] A dark stain at the bottom right corner appears to be from old moisture damage that occurred prior to lining.

Several causes have contributed to changes in the appearance of the painting. The thin paint surface is somewhat worn, exposing the nubs of the canvas weave, especially in the foreground; the fibers of the canvas have oxidized and become brown in color; the initial color of the paint has faded (strips across the upper and lower edges and along the right, possibly protected by the rabbet of a former frame, have remained brighter); and dust and dirt have accumulated onto the unvarnished surface. Small paint losses such as those in Christ's red banner and the blue collar and white tunic of the prostrate soldier are from past flaking. Notwithstanding these conditions, the painting is very well preserved, especially taking into account that, miraculously, the paint surface has escaped receiving a varnish coating since its inception over five hundred years ago. —*Devi Ormond*

Painted between 1450 and 1460, *The Resurrection* exhibits the delicacy of forms, clarity of composition, and harmony of colors for which paintings by Dieric Bouts are known. The frozen serenity of Christ's image is complemented by the lyricism of the landscape, which stretches into the distance beyond the low hedge at the edge of the burial grounds. The towers of a distant city rise above the horizon between a rocky cliff on the left and the gentle rolling hills on the right. The silhouettes of tall, spindly trees and wispy clouds animate the sky. Now discolored from exposure to light and dirt, the sky was originally a colorful display of pinks and blues, which is still evident along the upper border, where the canvas was protected by a previous frame. The soft, fluid transitions in the distant landscape suggest that Bouts painted this area while the canvas was wet, a technique recommended by the Italian writer and painter Cennino Cennini (ca. 1370–ca. 1440).[16] The sharp, linear definition of the figures and the architectural forms of the tomb, however, suggest that Bouts painted these areas when the canvas was dry.[17]

The Pasadena painting generally follows the iconography for the depiction of the Resurrection that was established by the mid-fifteenth century and incorporates elements from associated stories in the Bible.[18] Christ, wearing a long red mantle, occupies the center of the composition. Facing forward, he steps out of the open tomb, his right hand raised in blessing and his left hand, hidden beneath the red garment, holding a processional cross with a red swallow-tailed pennant ornamented with a cross. To the left of Christ, standing on the lid of the open sarcophagus and looking directly at him, is the diminutive figure of an angel, dressed in an alb, a full-length white linen garment tied at the waist.[19] Over the alb, the angel wears a piece of white cloth as a cope; fastened at the chest by a metal buckle known as a morse, the cope billows out behind the angel as if the appearance of Christ was accompanied by a gust of wind.[20] Copes were worn by all clerics in the sanctuary, especially in Flanders. Maurice McNamee has demonstrated that in early Netherlandish depictions of the life of Christ, angels were dressed in the alb and cope to identify them as subministers assisting during performance of the mass.[21] Viewers would have recognized the Eucharistic significance of Bouts's choice of liturgical garment, which emphasized that Christ, who appears here with the processional cross, was the celebrant assisted by the subminister angel.

McNamee has suggested the iconographic influence of contemporary passion plays performed by the clergy, particularly Franciscans, in the celebration of Easter.[22] The dramatic gestures and costumes of the different figures in the Pasadena *Resurrection* do seem to reflect theatrical performances. Holding a staff in his left hand, the angel raises his right hand in a gesture of blessing mimicking that of Christ. Three soldiers surround the tomb: Two have fallen asleep, one lies prone in the foreground, separating Christ from the viewer, and another, who leans against the lid of the tomb next to the angel, drops his head back, his eyes closed in heavy sleep as he clutches a pike in his hands.[23] The third soldier, however, responds dramatically to Christ's appearance, holding his hand up in a rhetorical gesture of surprise and fear.

The individualized expressions of the soldiers distinguish them from the hieratic image of Christ and the frozen serenity of the angel. Bouts emphasized this distinction by contrasting the colorful and ornate costumes of the soldiers with the simple attire of the heavenly figures. As in other paintings by the artist, the costumes provide important decorative interest, introducing areas of saturated color (now somewhat faded) and suggestions of texture that animate the composition. The soldier sleeping prone in the foreground wears a contemporary costume: a fitted, carved-leather cuirass over a white fur-lined tunic, beneath which can be seen the fringed skirt of his doublet and his crimson hose worn without shoes; next to him lie his spear and helmet. The burgonet with jagged "teeth" down the center is typical of those worn in Italian theatrical performances and festivals rather than in combat. Bouts could have taken the design for the helmet from a contemporary print.

Bouts also used clothing to characterize certain figures. Two of the soldiers wear historical costumes incorporating conventions specifically associated with Semitic people.[24] The bearded soldier near the angel wears a red leather-collared jacket fastened with three buttons and a soft blue felt hat with red lining and a gold-colored band; the mustachioed guard to the right of the tomb wears a conical red turban trimmed with white and a sashed, long, dark blue-green tunic trimmed with woven gold metal tape and red cuffs.[25] Beneath his tunic, the soldier wears a doublet with tight-fitting sleeves of red velvet with brocade worked in gold thread.

The earliest documentation of the Pasadena painting dates to 1872, when it was exhibited at the Palazzo Brera, Milan, as no. 38, *The Resurrection* by "Luca d'Olanda (?)," lent by Vittorio Melzi.[26] Two other paintings, also attributed to "Luca d'Olanda (?)" were exhibited as no. 39, *Adoration of the Magi*, lent by Paolo Guicciardi (now private collection, Switzerland), and no. 40, *The Annunciation* (now in the Getty), lent by Giuseppe Casanova (fig. 11a).[27] A label with the title of the 1872 exhibition attached to the back of *The Annunciation* confirms the association of these paintings with the exhibition.[28] Although the three paintings were owned by different collectors, all of the lenders were descendants of Diego Guicciardi.[29]

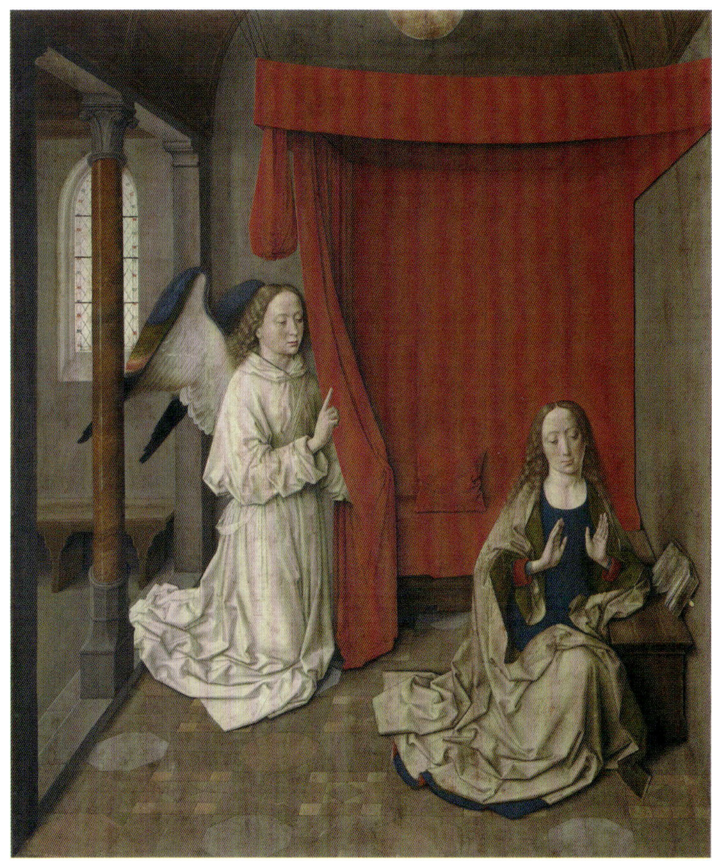

Fig. 11a. Dieric Bouts, *The Annunciation*, ca. 1450–55, distemper on linen, 35 7/16 × 29 3/8 in. (90 × 74.6 cm), J. Paul Getty Museum, Los Angeles.

In 1858 and again in 1860, Charles Lock Eastlake (1793–1865) noted four Netherlandish paintings on linen in the Guicciardi collection, Milan.[30] In 1858 he identified the paintings, which he attributed to Rogier van der Weyden (ca. 1399–1464), as *The Annunciation*, *The Adoration*, *The Presentation*, and *The Deposition from the Cross* and noted that the last was being offered for sale. Two years later when Eastlake revisited the Guicciardi collection, he identified two of these "four drawings or pictures in tempera by Rogier van der Weyden" as *The Entombment* and its pendant, *The Adoration of the Kings*, and noted "the other two are said to be the *Crucifixion* and the *Annunciation*." Eastlake purchased *The Entombment* (fig. 11b) for the National Gallery, London, in 1860. This has been presumed to be the same painting he identified two years earlier as *The Deposition*. Eastlake

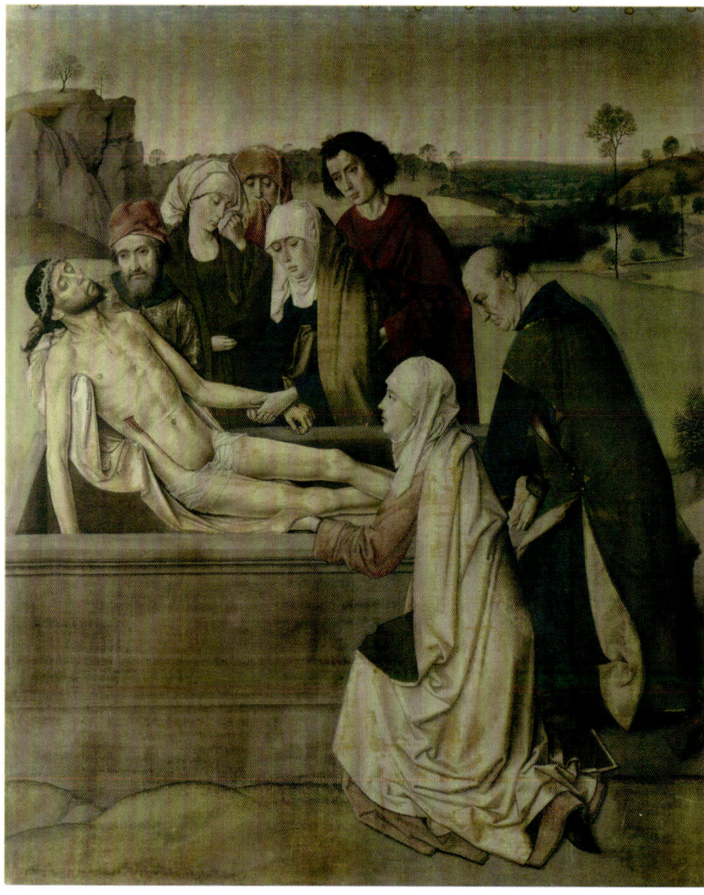

Fig. 11b. Dieric Bouts, *The Entombment*, 1450s, glue tempera on linen, 34½ × 29 in. (87.5 × 73.6 cm), The National Gallery, London.

makes no specific mention of *The Resurrection* in either 1858 or 1860. Wolfthal believes that the Pasadena painting may have been the work he refers to in 1860 as *The Crucifixion* and that his confusion may have come from never having seen the painting, which already may have been in the possession of another family member.[31] It is also possible, however, that because *The Resurrection* was in another residence, Eastlake may not have known of its existence and may have been referring to another unidentified painting. Stroo et al. tentatively suggest that the paintings may actually have been part of a larger group, which would have included scenes from the Passion on the interior wings surrounding the central image of the Crucifixion and scenes from the life of Christ on the exterior.[32]

Physical evidence and technical data support the association of *The Resurrection* with the same series as *The Entombment* and *The Annunciation* and place it in the same collection before 1860, when Eastlake acquired *The Entombment* for the National Gallery.[33] The three canvases also appear to have been prepared in an identical manner and to share the common characteristic of a relatively wide, reddish-brown painted border. They were also relined before 1860 in the same manner, with fine-weave linen over pine stretchers. The extreme edges of the canvases were covered with paper tape.

Details of composition also link the four canvases of similar size. *The Entombment* and *The Resurrection* are organized around the tomb, placed parallel to the picture plane. Likewise, the lost *Adoration* and *The Annunciation* are compositionally related. The most striking similarity among the paintings is the motif of the hands hidden beneath drapery—the left hand of Christ in *The Resurrection* and that of the angel of *The Annunciation*, hidden within the curtain; the hand of Nicodemus beneath the cloth supporting Christ in *The Entombment* and that of Joseph standing behind the Madonna in *The Adoration*. Although critics have used this detail in *The Annunciation* to discredit the painting's authenticity, other scholars have associated the gesture with an ancient sign of reverence in the presence of the divine, which was used in early Christian imagery.[34]

Assuming that the original altarpiece was limited to the four individual paintings owned by Guicciardi descendants, scholars have suggested that the four canvases originally formed the wings of a polyptych: *The Annunciation* in the upper left wing, with *The Adoration* below it; on the right wing, *The Entombment* in the upper register and *The Resurrection* below it.[35] The central image was presumably a Crucifixion, either sculpted or painted. The painting most frequently cited as a possible central image is *The Crucifixion* by Dieric Bouts in Brussels (fig. 11c). Badly damaged, it is painted in distemper on canvas and approximately twice as wide and twice as high as *The Resurrection* and the other individual canvases.[36] Some scholars have suggested that this was the painting that Eastlake saw in the Guicciardi collection.[37] Other scholars, including Stroo et al. and Wolfthal, are less convinced. Noting that the provenance of *The Crucifixion* extends back only to 1928, when it was in the Benedictine Saint Mary's Abbey in Colwich, Staffordshire, England, Stroo et al. observe that if *The Crucifixion* was among those large paintings given to the abbey in 1848, then it cannot have been the one Eastlake saw in the Guicciardi collection in 1858.[38]

Wolfthal cautions against assuming that all extant early canvases are necessarily related to one another.[39] *The Resurrection* and *The Entombment*, which have been identified as having been cut from the same bolt of linen, are intimately linked in style and technique as well as the subject of Christ's Passion. Although also painted on fine linen, *The Annunciation*, which relates to the cycle of Christ's infancy, does not share the same weave as the two Passion canvases and is slightly smaller. *The Adoration* is more loosely connected to the other three.[40] Wolfthal argues against including the Brussels *Crucifixion*, which she considers of inferior quality because it lacks the same relining stretchers, nail holes, and the reddish-brown border and brighter colors along the edges that characterize the other canvases.[41] Significantly, the canvas support of *The Crucifixion* is also more coarsely woven than that of the other paintings. Wolfthal and Metzger conclude, "It is highly unlikely that the five canvases formed a winged altarpiece."[42] In addition to the physical differences, they point out that it was very rare for an early Netherlandish altarpiece to mix scenes of Christ's infancy and Passion on the interior wings of an altarpiece, adding that "no documents or surviving examples attest to any fifteenth-century Netherlandish altarpiece that was painted entirely on linen."[43]

The similarity of style and iconography of the Pasadena painting to the representation of the Resurrection on the right wing of Bouts's Passion Altarpiece, dated 1450–58 (Capilla Real de Granada), suggests that the artist painted the Pasadena *Resurrection* about the same time.[44] In suggesting this date, Lorne Campbell notes the strong influence of Rogier van der Weyden's paintings, particularly the Miraflores Altarpiece (Staatliche Museen Preußischer Kulturbesitz, Berlin), probably from the 1430s, and *The Descent from the Cross* (Museo Nacional del Prado, Madrid), finished by 1443.[45]

A date before 1460 is also suggested by the influence the Pasadena painting had on artists in Venice. Lorne Campbell observes that the landscape background of *The Resurrection* appears to have inspired the distant landscape on the left of *The Transfiguration*, ca. 1460 (Museo Correr, Venice) and the sunrise in *Agony in the Garden* of about 1465 (National Gallery, London), both by Giovanni Bellini (1431/36–1516).[46] Other authors have recognized that Bouts's painting also directly and indirectly informed the narrative interpretation of the Resurrection theme by Bellini.[47] Of particular note are the cloud-streaked sunrise and the billowing shroud of Christ in Bellini's Resurrection Altarpiece painted in 1475–79 for San Michele di Murano, Venice (Staatliche Museen Preußischer Kulturbesitz, Berlin). The Pasadena painting as well as the Brussels *Crucifixion* may also have inspired Andrea Mantegna (1430/31–1506) when he painted the predella panels of the San Zeno Altarpiece (Verona) in 1456–59.[48] Campbell notes further similarities between the soldier second from the right in Mantegna's *Resurrection* (Tours) and the soldier on the right of Bouts's *Resurrection* and between the apostle on the left in Mantegna's *Agony in the Garden* (Tours) and the soldier in the foreground of Bouts's *Resurrection*.[49]

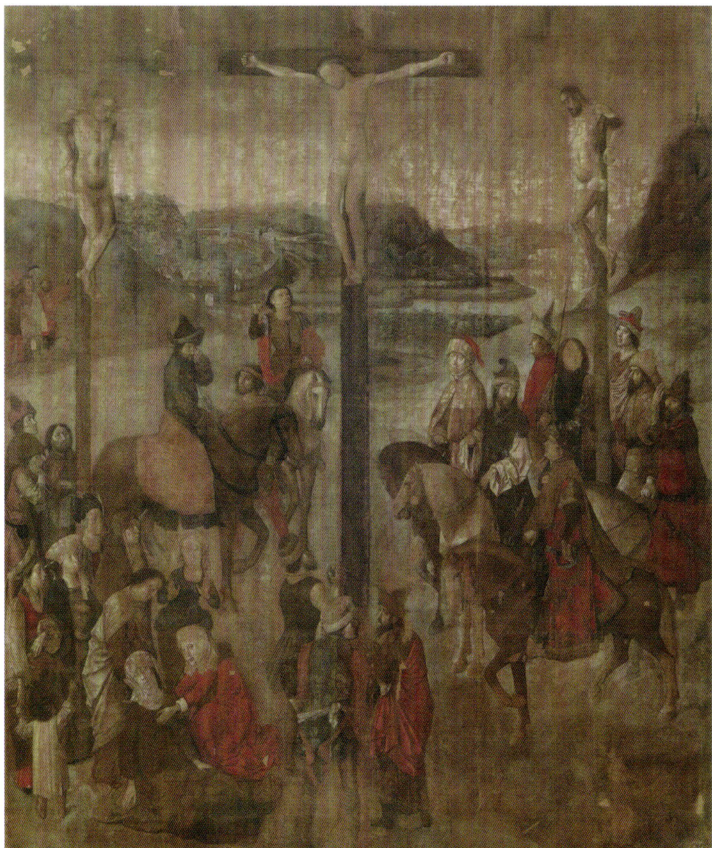

Fig. 11c. Dieric Bouts, *The Crucifixion*, ca. 1450–60, tempera on linen, 71½ × 61 7/16 in. (181.5 × 153.5 cm), inv. 8181, Musées Royaux des Beaux-Arts de Belgique, Brussels.

The apparent influence of *The Resurrection* on paintings produced by Venetian artists in the late 1450s and 1460s suggests that the painting was in Venice by ca. 1455. Eastlake stated that Diego Guicciardi, whose descendants owned the paintings in 1858, had acquired them in Vienna at the beginning of the nineteenth century and that they had originally been in the possession of the Foscaris, one of the great families of Venice, which during the eighteenth century had ties to Vienna.[50] In 1765 Francesco Foscari (1704–1790) served as Venetian ambassador to Vienna, and between 1783 and 1790 his son Federico (a.k.a. Ferigo) Foscari (1732–1811) was Venetian ambassador to St. Petersburg, spending some of that time in Vienna. Federico squandered his fortune and may have sold the paintings to pay off his debts.[51]

The painting may have been acquired by an earlier relative, Francesco Foscari (1373–1457), who was doge of Venice between 1423 and 1457, when he was forced to abdicate his position. He died shortly thereafter and was buried in an elaborate tomb in the chancel of the Franciscan church Santa Maria Gloriosa dei Frari in Venice. Unfortunately, little is known of Foscari's art patronage. In 1452 he purchased at auction a magnificent Gothic palace on the Grand Canal, which was renovated during the following years.[52] It is possible that Foscari or a member of his family commissioned or merely purchased the paintings by Bouts, perhaps including other now lost canvases, for the decoration of his impressive palace. It would not have been unusual for a member of the Foscari family to have purchased Flemish canvases (*panno fiandrescho*) during the fifteenth century, when these paintings were very popular in Italy.[53] Wolfthal notes documentary evidence that Flemish canvases were present in Venetian collections.[54] Lightweight and readily folded or rolled, the thinly painted canvases could be transported more easily than bulkier panel paintings. Once the paintings reached their destination, local craftsmen would have prepared frames and stretched the canvases and arranged them according to the owner's direction.[55]

The influence of the paintings on other artists suggests, however, that they were hung in a more public space, possibly a secular building or a church. Wolfthal has noted a possible connection between the Franciscan order and the use of linen for altarpieces.[56] Francesco Foscari, who had ties to the Franciscan order, or another member of the family, may have acquired the paintings for placement in their chapel in Venice. The fact that that the polyptych was later dismantled, taken to Vienna, and eventually sold to Guicciardi at the beginning of the nineteenth century may indicate, however, that it had remained a domestic possession of the family. The original number and placement of the paintings and their display in a row or as an altarpiece combining infancy and Passion scenes surrounding a central image remain unresolved questions. Further research in the archives of the Foscari family and the Franciscan order may provide additional information regarding the early history of the paintings.

1. Eastlake 1858–60 in Davies 1953, p. 27, and Avery-Quash 2011, vol. 1, pp. 416 [f. 19r], 539 [f. 2r]. The Foscari family was originally from Venice.

2. Eastlake 1858–60 in Davies 1953, p. 27, and Avery-Quash 2011, vol. 1, pp. 416 [f. 19r] 539 [f. 2r]. This painting appears to have been one of the four paintings Eastlake reported knowing about in the Guicciardi collection, Milan. According to Eastlake the paintings "originally in the possession of the Foscari family, found their way to Vienna, where Guizzardi [*sic*], envoy from Milan, purchased them early in the present century." L. Campbell 1998, p. 38, citing sources, identifies Diego Guicciardi, who in 1814 was said to have been raised in Vienna. In 1816, Guicciardi himself stated that he had been on five occasions Valtelline envoy to the court of Vienna. His missions were in 1786, 1787, 1791, 1793, and from September 1814 to April 1815. Guicciardi settled in Milan and died there.

3. Vittorio Melzi was the nephew of Diego Melzi, whose mother, Eleanora, was a daughter of Diego Guicciardi (L. Campbell 1998, p. 45n32).

4. Brooks 1985 cites the New York dealer Eugene V. Thaw, part of the dealer consortium that sold *The Annunciation* by Bouts to the J. Paul Getty Museum: "According to Thaw, the *Annunciation* [came] from the same collection in which [Derek] Johns, while [employed by] Sotheby's in 1980, discovered the *Resurrection*." The Getty notes the source of its painting as "Private Collection (Germany and/or Switzerland)."

5. Dubois et al. 1997. *Tüchlein* is a term used to describe pigments bound in a water-based medium, such as animal glue, on a sized, unprimed canvas.

6. See Johnson, Metzger, and Wolfthal 2017, p. 44. The average vertical thread density is 18.9 (th/cm), and the horizontal thread density is 17.6 (th/cm). See Wolfthal and Metzger 2014, p. 56.

7. *The Annunciation* has a similar thread count but is not from the same bolt of canvas. Johnson, Metzger, and Wolfthal 2017, p. 44. This research using computational analysis has refined the study carried out by Bomford, Roy, and Smith 1986, p. 45; Leonard, Preusser, and Rothe 1988, p. 517, mistakenly observes, "The thread counts for the *Annunciation*, the *Entombment* and the *Resurrection* are identical."

8. Bomford, Roy, and Smith 1986, p. 44; and Leonard, Preusser, and Rothe 1988, p. 517, have had fibers analyzed from the canvases of *The Entombment* and *The Annunciation*. Flax was identified, confirming that they are both painted on linen. By association through the weave match, *The Resurrection* is also believed to be linen.

9. See Heydenreich 2008, pp. 32–35, for more information on the bleaching processes of early Netherlandish canvas.

10. The border of *The Annunciation* is cooler and darker in tone than those found on the other two canvases. See Johnson, Metzger, and Wolfthal 2017, p. 43.

11. Through implication, it is believed that, since the canvases of *The Entombment* and *The Resurrection* were cut from the same bolt of fabric, they were both prepared with a size layer prior to painting. See Bomford, Roy, and Smith 1986, p. 44.

12. It is worth noting that ultraviolet illumination of both *The Entombment* (Bomford, Roy, and Smith 1986, p. 46) and *The Annunciation* (Leonard, Preusser, and Rothe 1988, p. 520) revealed underdrawing not visible in normal light or in infrared light. No underdrawing was visible in ultraviolet illumination when examining *The Resurrection*.

13. This is also dependent on the thickness of the paint layers. In *The Resurrection*, the paint is thinly applied consistently throughout.

14. The tack holes on *The Resurrection* are similar to those on *The Entombment* and *The Annunciation*. They are within the strip of the composition that has remained unaltered by light, suggesting that it was hidden by a frame, which possibly indicates that the canvas was originally attached to a panel by nails through a frame. Wolfthal 1989 observes on p. 82 that no Early Netherlandish stretchers are preserved and on pp. 27f. notes that there is general agreement that stretchers in the modern sense were not used to display paintings on canvas. Marijnissen 1988, p. 112n12, observes, "Little is known about the early stretchers. The cusping . . . is physical evidence of stretching, but this does not mean that the mounting of the discussed paintings was done on stretchers." On pp. 113f. the author suggests that there may have been a lost tradition of gluing canvases on panels, noting, however, that the method is technically disputable and does not mean that all canvases were glued. He cites the excellent condition of the Getty *Annunciation* as evidence that it was never stuck on panel. Leonard, Preusser, and Rothe 1988, p. 520, fig. 33, agree that stretchers as we know them were not used for the display of paintings. They propose that canvases were attached by hammering nails through the frame. This theory is supported by Johnson, Metzger, and Wolfthal 2017, pp. 40–41. The type of lining, the stretchers, and the same band of paint protected from light exposure by the rabbet of a frame coupled with a similar state of preservation suggest that the three works shared the same provenance for a period of time. See Wolfthal and Metzger 2014, p. 52.

15. This reverse image was also found on the verso of *The Entombment* and *The Annunciation*; see Bomford, Roy, and Smith 1986, p. 45; and Leonard, Preusser, and Rothe 1988, p. 520.

16. *Il libro dell'arte* (MS, 1390), trans. and notes by D. V. Thompson Jr., 1933; MS edited by F. Brunello, published in Cennini 1971.

17. Regarding the technique of distemper painting on canvas, see Wolfthal 1989, pp. 23–29. On Bouts specifically, see Bomford, Roy, and Smith 1986, passim; Marijnissen 1988; and Van Miegroet 1988. Villers 1991, p. 258, contends that Wolfthal made some "basic errors" in discussing the technique of painting on canvas during this period. Specifically, he notes that she misunderstood the technique advocated by Cennino Cennini, which Villers defines as different from the technique used by the Early Netherlandish painters.

18. Bouts represented the event in similar iconographic terms on the wings of at least two altarpieces: Bayerische Staatsgemäldesammlungen,

Munich (M. Friedländer 1967–76, vol. 3 [1968], no. 20, pl. 35), and Capilla Real de Granada (M. Friedländer 1967–76, vol. 3 [1968], no. 2a, pl. 6). To accommodate the tall, thin format of these wings—and possibly also for stylistic reasons—Bouts placed the sarcophagus in each panel on a diagonal.

19. McNamee 1998, p. 229.

20. Sandra Rosenbaum, formerly curator-in-charge of the Doris Stein Research Center for Costume and Textiles, Department of Costume and Textiles, Los Angeles County Museum of Art, has pointed out that, unlike the typical cope, which was semicircular in shape, this garment appears to be a square wrap. I am grateful to Rosenbaum for her analysis of the costumes in this painting.

21. McNamee 1998, pp. 214f.

22. See McNamee 1972; McNamee 1998, passim; and Madou 1998, pp. 196–203. For references to evidence linking the Franciscans to the production of religious drama, see Van Miegroet 1988, p. 100n44.

23. Only the Gospel of Matthew mentions the soldiers Pilate had assigned to guard the tomb.

24. Although often equated with Jews alone, the term refers to a group of languages, including Hebrew and Arabic, and to the people who traditionally speak them.

25. Davenport 1948, vol. 1, p. 181, illustrates a thirteenth-century Spanish manuscript on chess that depicts Semitic people wearing collared and buttoned coats. The rough, tall, pointed hat is referred to as a "Tartar" by Newton 1999, p. 93.

26. The attribution of the Pasadena painting to Bouts was first made by Nicole Veronée-Verhaegen in M. Friedländer 1967–76, vol. 3 (1968).

27. On *Adoration of the Magi* see Wolfthal and Metzger 2014, p. 77, fig. 45; and Johnson, Metzger, and Wolfthal 2017, pp. 37, 39–40, fig. 6.

28. Wolfthal 1989, pp. 204, no. 4, 204n1, according to information from the J. Paul Getty Museum; Davies 1953, pp. 26f. The frame of *The Annunciation* bore a handwritten label reading, "Bolletta N. 21 Sigr. Conte Diego Melzi." Beneath this label was another printed label: "Comitato esecutivo esposizione arte antica 427 III/I."

29. L. Campbell 1998, p. 45n32, was the first to identify the familial relationship of the lenders (see note 3 above). Casanova lived at the same address as the Melzi (Koch 1988, p. 509n1).

30. Excerpts from Eastlake's notebooks were first published in Davies 1953, p. 27, docs. 1–2. Eastlake was a British painter, collector, writer, and Keeper of the National Gallery from 1843 to 1847.

31. Wolfthal 1989, pp. 39f.

32. Stroo et al. 1996–2013, vol. 2 (2001), p. 122n49.

33. The technical data was gathered by the Getty Museum in defense of the authenticity of *The Annunciation* and the museum's acquisition of it. The controversy—sparked in the press by the dealer Alain Tarica, who charged that the painting was a forgery—focused on what was perceived to be the painting's unusual iconography and the seeming technical incongruity of the straight surface lines and the weave of the linen, which was distorted when stretched. For Tarica's objections, see Duret-Robert 1986; rebuffed by J.-L. Bordeaux 1986, Marijnissen 1988, Van Miegroet 1988, and Leonard, Preusser, and Rothe 1988.

34. Van Miegroet 1988, p. 102, who cites Andersson 1985, p. 134.

35. This reconstruction was first proposed by Bomford, Roy, and Smith 1986, p. 41, and diagrammed by J.-L. Bordeaux 1986, p. 38. The proposal has been repeated by, among others, Van Miegroet 1988; Marijnissen 1988, fig. 14; and Koch 1988, p. 514. See also Stroo et al. 1996–2013, vol. 2 (2001), p. 122n49.

36. See Masschelein-Kleiner et al. 1978–79.

37. Regarding the Brussels painting, see Stroo et al. 1996–2013, vol. 2 (2001), pp. 106–22; Brussels/Delft 1957–58, p. 20, discusses the Brussels *Crucifixion* in the context of the paintings Eastlake saw but observes that the style of the Brussels painting "is more archaic" than the painting in London. See also references cited in note 18 above.

38. Stroo et al. 1996–2013, vol. 2 (2001), p. 113.

39. Wolfthal 1989, p. 40.

40. Johnson, Metzger, and Wolfthal 2017, p. 44; Wolfthal and Metzger 2014, p. 80.

41. All these points may relate to the poor preservation of the canvas. Recent scientific examination of *The Crucifixion* has, in fact, revealed that there are no real traces of a painted border. Rather, according to Stroo et al. 1996–2013, vol. 2 (2001), p. 109, "A small number of blackish traces along the upper and lower edges are perhaps due to various deteriorations which the canvas has suffered . . . and do not necessarily indicate that it originally had a black border." See also Masschelein-Kleiner et al. 1978–79.

42. Wolfthal and Metzger 2014, p. 80. This point is repeated in Johnson, Metzger, and Wolfthal 2017, p. 40.

43. Wolfthal and Metzger 2014, p. 80. Previously, in rejecting the idea that *The Crucifixion* or another canvas formed the center of the presumed altarpiece, Wolfthal 1989, p. 40, briefly considered the possibility that the four paintings formed an altarpiece of four equal parts. Her conclusion, however, was that it is more likely that *The Resurrection* and the other canvases served as wings for an altarpiece, the center of which was a wooden sculpture or an oil painting on panel. She based her conclusions both on the familiar combination of panel wings with sculptural centers and on her research, which has found more documentation of altarpieces that combine media than of altarpieces constructed completely of canvas.

44. There are two replicas of Bouts's Passion Altarpiece: Colegio del Patriarca (Corpus Christi), Valencia (M. Friedländer 1967–76, vol. 3 [1968], no. 2); and Capilla Real de Granada (M. Friedländer 1967–76, vol. 3 [1968], no. 2a); Friedländer illustrates both in pl. 3. Wolfthal 1989, p. 41, observes, "The type and pose of Christ, the angel standing on the tomb, the trees and clouds dramatically silhouetted against [the] sky are typical of Bouts' early style." Wolfthal and Metzger 2014, p. 74, fig. 43, illustrates the Granada panel, which is the right wing of a triptych.

45. L. Campbell 1998, p. 44, dates the polyptych between 1440 and 1464, noting that it was probably painted in the 1450s.

46. L. Campbell 1998, p. 44.

47. Lucco 1997, pp. 199f., 202; Lucco 2004, p. 82f.; Aikema 1999, p. 83; Aikema and Brown 1999, p. 177n11; Christiansen 2004, pp 37–39; Rutherglen 2017, pp. 17–25; and Los Angeles 2017, pp. 17–18, figs. 3–4.

48. L. Campbell 1998, p 44. Mantegna also painted on canvas.

49. L. Campbell 1998, p. 45n50. For the pictures in Tours, see Tietze-Conrat 1955, pls. 41–42.

50. Wolfthal 1989, p. 39.

51. L. Campbell 1998, p. 44.

52. Regarding Foscari, see L. Campbell 1998, pp. 44, 45n43–45. See also Hazlitt 1900, vol. 2, pp. 49ff.; and Lauritzen 1978, pp. 98f.

53. The Medici, for example, owned twenty Netherlandish canvas paintings. Wolfthal notes that Denucé 1931–49 cites numerous examples of tempera paintings on canvas (*waterschilderdoeken*) sent abroad by Flemish merchants (Wolfthal 1989, pp. 18–19).

54. Wolfthal 1989, p. 19.

55. This procedure may explain the function of the reddish-brown painted borders around the canvases: indications to the frame maker of the dimensions of the painting (see also discussion in note 14 above). The nail holes are within the actual painted area of the Passion scenes but within the border of *The Annunciation*. This may support the suggestion by Stroo that the Passion scenes were located on the interior of the wings, and the scenes from the life of Christ were displayed on the exterior (Stroo et al. 1996–2013, vol. 2 (2001), p. 122n49). If the frame of the altarpiece was constructed in Italy, then the requirements of the frame may have demanded reducing the size of the paintings on the interior but not on the exterior.

56. Wolfthal 1989, pp. 5, 19, 36, 41, 62–63.

12

Salomon de Bray

Dutch
Amsterdam 1597–1664 Haarlem

The Expulsion of Hagar and Ishmael

1662

Signed and dated lower left: "SD Bray 1662" (*SD* in ligature)
Oil on panel, 21⅜ × 18⅝ in. (54.3 × 47.3 cm)
Norton Simon Art Foundation, M.1979.45.P

Provenance

Anonymous (sale, Ghent, Goesin-Verhaeghe, 30 April 1776, lot 45, sold for *f*2.1). Jan Jansz. Gildemeester (1744–1799), Amsterdam[1] (sale, Van der Schley . . . Pruyssenaar, Amsterdam, 11 June 1800, as lot 26, "Agar repudiée [panel, 21 × 19 pouces] Abraham dans une attitude imposant, les yeux elevés vers le ciel, benit son fils Ismaël agenoullé devant lui, tandis que Agar, les yeux baignés de larmes, descend les dégrés de la maison. Sara se montre dans la porte. Ce tableau a beaucoup de force, la touche en est belle, & la couleur savant," sold to [or bought in by]); [Philippus van der Schley]. Possibly L. C. Sommers (sale, Hôtel Bullion, Paris, 14 January 1805, lot 12, "Abraham renvoyant Sara [*sic*] et Ismaël. Vigoureux et piquant comme s'il étoit de Rembrandt.").[2] Probably Edward Solly (1776–1844), London and Berlin (sale, Christie's, London, 8 June 1819, lot 90 as "Abraham Blessing Ismael and Sending away Hagar," bought in at £19 5s.).[3] Probably anonymous (sale, G. Stanley, London, 13 April 1824, lot 94, sold for £16 5s.). Mr. Tate of Leicester Square, London[4] (sale, Foster and Son, London, 27–28 February 1833, lot 208 as "Abraham dismissing Hagar," sold for £6 10s. to); Crayor or Craig or Craigg. [Martin Asscher, London, before 1970].[5] "Property of a Lady" (sale, Christie's, London, 8 December 1967, lot 44, sold for 1,155 guineas to); Fitzalan-Howard. Anonymous[6] (sale, Sotheby's, London, 25 June 1969, lot 66, sold for £2,000 to); Simoni. Anonymous (sale, Christie's, London, 12 March 1976, lot 96, sold to); Norton Simon, gift 1979 to; Norton Simon Art Foundation.

References

Hamann 1936, p. 548n1; Moltke 1938–39, p. 379, cat. 3, as formerly Jan Gildemeester; Pasadena 1989, p. 64, ill.; Giltaij and Lammertse 2001, pp. 368, 371, 392n15; Sellin 2006, pp. 111f., fig. 26; Lammertse 2008, pp. 13, 15, fig. 9; S. Campbell 2010, p. 392, no. 1303, ill.; I. Q. van Regteren Altena catalogue, pt. IV (sale, Christie's, Amsterdam, 13 May 2015, p. 116, lot 187, fig. 1).

Technical Notes

The support, a vertically grained oak panel ¼ inch thick at the edges, was made from a single piece. The uncradled reverse appears to be in its original condition; all edges have been hand beveled. The thin, pale beige ground that covers the panel was toned with a light brown imprimatura. Sketchy brushstrokes at the bottom right corner expose these layers. Infrared reflectography carried out by Yvonne Szafran in 1999 revealed a fully developed underdrawing worked directly on the panel, with significant changes in the rendering of Hagar's head. She originally looked up, her gaze directed at Abraham, and may have worn a headdress. The eyes of the maid were also reworked in the underdrawing. The rich, moderately thick, opaque oil paint was directly applied with strong, firm handling. Occasionally, where the paint has become more transparent with age, the underdrawing is partially visible, such as in the face and fingers of Abraham. Brushwork is looser in the secondary areas of the walls and steps; a slight amount of texture is present in the small strokes and dabs of tree foliage. The paint is very well preserved, with no evidence of abrasion or damage, although magnification reveals several tiny flake losses. The relatively large amount of retouching in the sky at upper right seems to be compensation for an area of drying cracks. More recent retouching is found in a few small losses at the edges. UV fluorescence suggests a thick, even, natural-resin varnish, although file notes indicate a synthetic resin (MS2A).

The story of Abraham's dismissal of Hagar is told in Genesis 21:14. Beyond childbearing age, Sarah encouraged her elderly husband, Abraham, the patriarch of the Israelites, to take Hagar, her Egyptian maidservant, as his concubine. In time, Hagar delivered a son, Ishmael. Later, Sarah herself miraculously bore Abraham a son, Isaac, whom God announced would inherit the covenant made between God and Abraham. After Isaac's birth, Sarah insisted that Abraham expel the proud Hagar and the illegitimate Ishmael; Abraham reluctantly agreed when God told him to obey. The following morning Abraham took bread and a skin of water, which he placed on Hagar's shoulder, and sent her and their son away.

The expulsion of Hagar and Ishmael was a popular story among members of the Dutch Reformed Church because it could be used to illustrate a number of moral lessons, including the necessity of faith and obedience to God's will.[7] Both the clergy and popular literature made the story a vehicle for the promotion of family structure and values. John Calvin (1509–1564), a leading French theologian during the Protestant Reformation, condemned Hagar's pride, while blaming Sarah for disrupting domestic harmony, for it was she who had lost faith in God.[8] Abraham was likewise culpable because his loss of faith had led him to enter an adulterous relationship. The Dutch poet, moralist, and statesman Jacob Cats (1577–1660) cited the story in 1655, warning young women of the sin of pride, which brought about Hagar's fall.

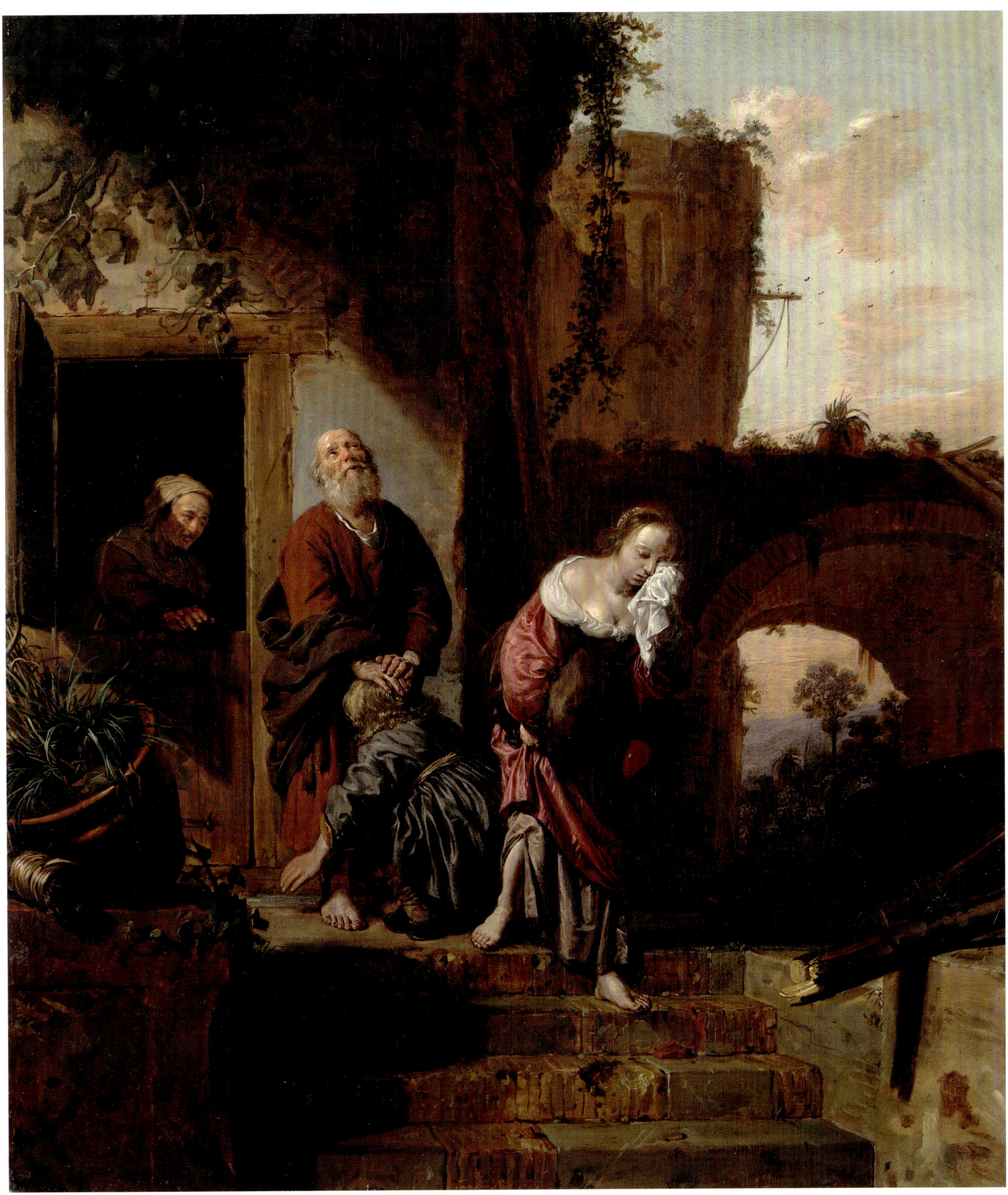

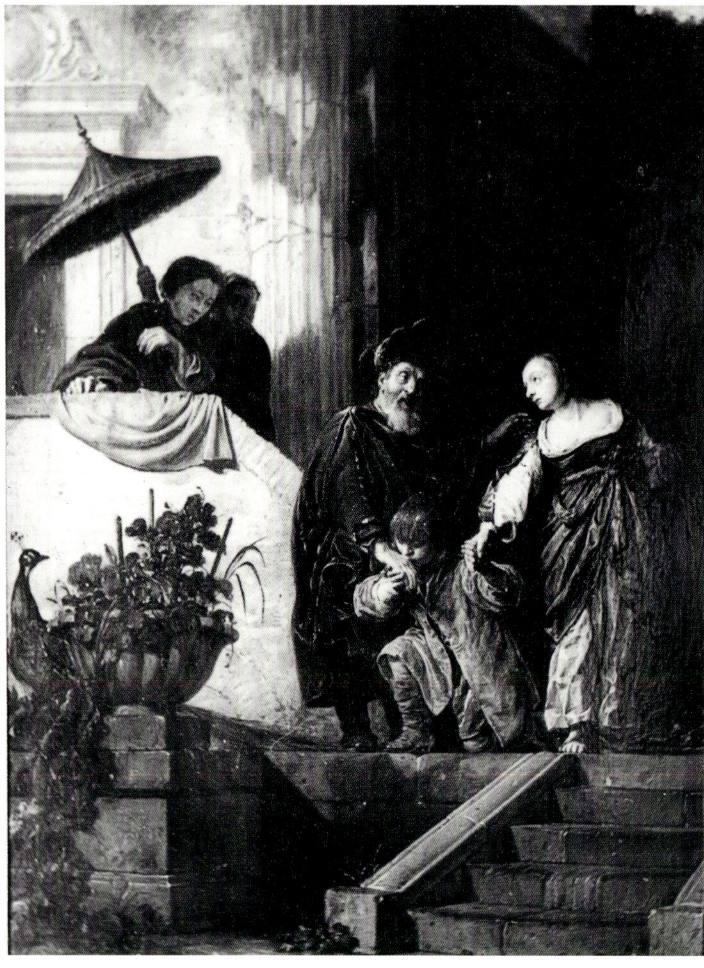

Fig. 12a. Salomon de Bray, *The Expulsion of Hagar and Ishmael*, 1656, oil on panel, 25 × 18½ in. (63.5 × 47 cm), Regional Picture Gallery, Tver.

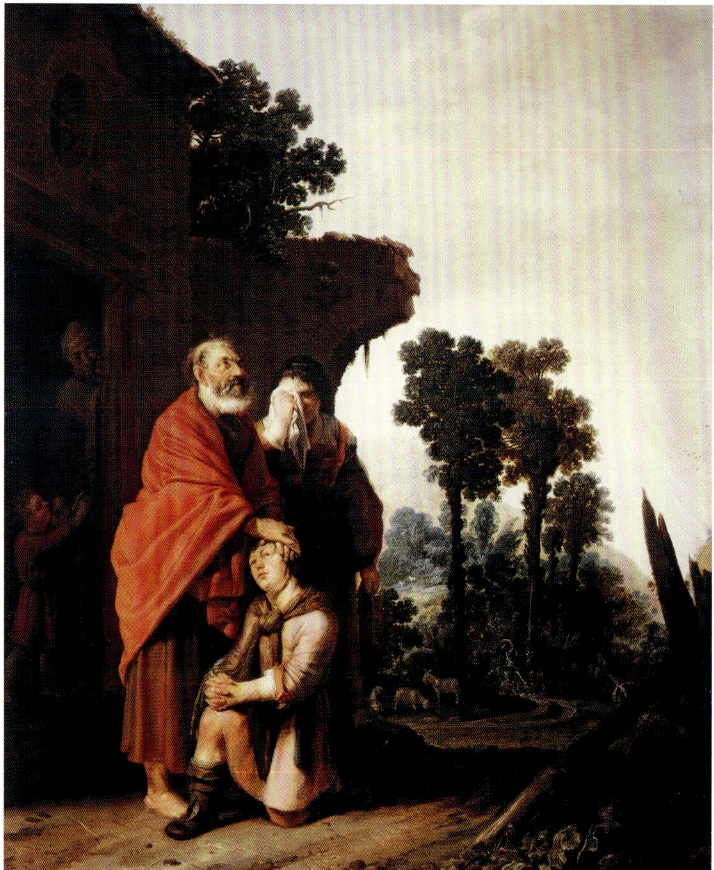

Fig. 12b. Salomon de Bray, *The Expulsion of Hagar and Ishmael*, 1633, oil on panel, 23⅜ × 19¾ in. (59.2 × 50.1 cm), private collection, photo courtesy of Johnny van Haeften Gallery, London.

The dismissal of Hagar and Ishmael, therefore, was not only a test of Abraham's obedience to God but also a restoration of family order and domestic harmony.[9]

During his late career Salomon de Bray painted several episodes of the story, including *The Expulsion of Hagar and Ishmael*, dated 1656 (fig. 12a), and the Pasadena painting of 1662. He had painted the expulsion at least once before, in a work signed and dated 1633 (fig. 12b) that shows Abraham at the entrance to his house with his hands on the head of Ishmael as Hagar weeps and Sarah and her young son, Isaac, stand in the doorway; the mountainous landscape into which Hagar and Ismael are banished is visible on the right.[10] In both of the later versions of the story, De Bray set the scene on the steps of a grand brick house, to the right of which is an arch overgrown with vegetation. The differences between the two late paintings, executed six years apart, demonstrate the artist's increasing emphasis on the psychological drama among the characters. The earlier and slightly larger painting is closely related to a popular etching published by Rembrandt in 1637.[11] In the Pasadena painting, which in many ways returns to his painting of 1633, De Bray transferred the dramatic emphasis to Abraham's anguishing psychological struggle: To obey God's command, he must banish his first-born son. In this tightly painted composition, executed in sumptuous shades of bronze, the elderly patriarch joins his hands in a gesture of blessing on the head of his young, disinherited son, who kneels before him. De Bray compositionally expressed the strong emotional ties between father and son by continuing the diagonal line of Abraham's arms across the kneeling boy's back and by Ishmael's outstretched arms, which prepare to embrace the legs of his father.

By carefully orchestrating the postures of the figures, De Bray emphasized the conflict and psychological pain of the separation. Hagar, a young woman, barefoot and wearing a loose bodice open at the neck to reveal her cleavage, holds a handkerchief to her weeping eyes with her left hand.[12] As she begins to descend the stairs, she leans forward, her head cast down. Still compositionally connected to her son and Abraham by the line of her uplifted hem, she appears to be tearing away from Abraham, who throws his head back in anguish. Sarah, the true protagonist, completes the drama: Standing behind Abraham, with her hand on the door, she appears poised to push it open, countering Abraham's resistance and propelling Hagar forward. A shaft of light from an

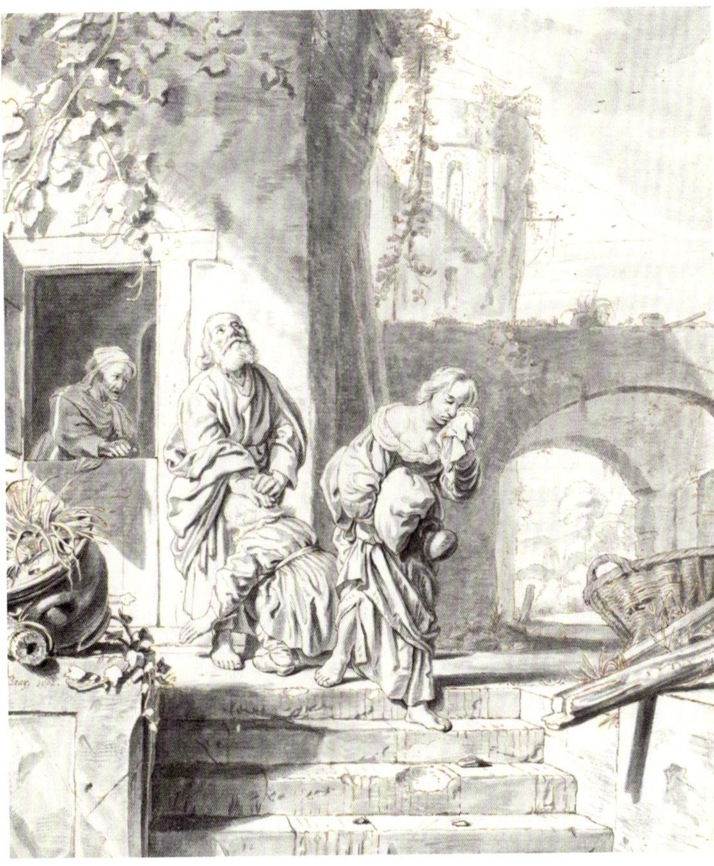

Fig. 12c. Salomon de Bray, *Expulsion of Hagar and Ishmael*, 1662, ink and wash, 11 7⁄16 × 9 3⁄8 in. (28.9 × 23.5 cm), private collection, Europe.

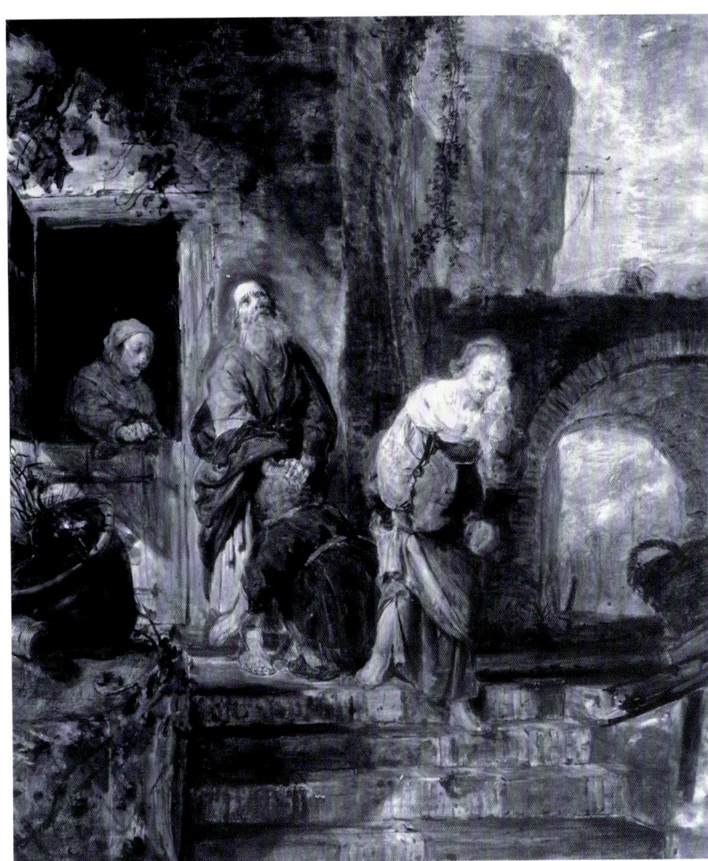

Fig. 12d. Infrared photograph of *The Expulsion of Hagar and Ishmael* (cat. 12), image courtesy of J. Paul Getty Museum, Los Angeles.

unseen source beyond the upper left falls across the wall of the house, following the major diagonal line connecting the figures of Sarah with those of Abraham, Ishmael, and Hagar. The painting is full of small details that reinforce the theme of rupture and breakage: Even the potted plants outside the front door of the house are thrown down in disarray.

A drawing signed and dated 1662 by De Bray (fig. 12c) replicates the Pasadena painting exactly.[13] Both Richard Hamann and Joachim Wolfgang von Moltke considered the pen, ink, and wash drawing to have been made in preparation for the painting.[14] The lively underdrawing revealed through infrared reflectography (fig. 12d) indicates, however, that the artist worked directly on the panel rather than from a precise preliminary drawing.[15] The finished quality of the drawing suggests it was made as a copy of the Norton Simon painting rather than a study for it. Stylistically similar drawings correspond to other paintings by De Bray from the 1660s; in each case the refined drawing repeats the exact composition and details of the painting, including the placement of the signatures and dates.[16] The existence of a number of these finished drawings suggests that the artist himself or his workshop made these as a record of his production.[17]

1. Jan Gildemeester was an Amsterdam merchant and served as consul for Portugal in the Netherlands. See De Bruyn Kops 1965.

2. For a discussion of the L. C. Sommers sale, as well as the preceding sale of 1776, see Getty Provenance Index (cited hereafter as GPI), Sales Catalogs F-85 and B-A2936.

3. Edward Solly was one of five brothers engaged in a highly successful family firm in London active in the trade of Baltic timber. Shortly after 1800 Solly moved first to Sweden and later settled in Berlin, where he began collecting art ca. 1810. By 1820 his collection numbered approximately 3,000 paintings. Facing bankruptcy, Solly in 1821 sold much of his collection to the Royal Gallery, Berlin. Moving back to London, he formed a second collection and became an art dealer. Although he owned a number of Dutch paintings, he was not particularly interested in those from the seventeenth century. Regarding Solly, see Herrmann 1967–68, summarized in Herrmann [1972] 1999, pp. 202–08.

4. Probably William King Tate, who is listed as a "Modeller" and a pawnbroker in Leicester Square in Robson's *Directory* in 1831, 1833, and 1834 (Robson 1819–).

5. According to an annotation on the mount of a photograph of the painting at the Witt Library, London, stamped 1971. Martin Asscher was active as a dealer from at least the early 1920s through at least the early 1950s.

6. An unidentified member of the extended family of the Duke of Norfolk.

7. Hamann 1936 identified more than one hundred examples of the theme of the dismissal of Hagar in the work of Rembrandt and his pupils during the mid-seventeenth century. A 1613 painting by Jacob Pynas (1592–1650; Aachen, Suermondt-Museum) and Rembrandt's etching of 1637 were important prototypes.

8. For an expanded discussion of Calvin's views on Hagar, see Thompson 1997, pp. 220–23.

9. See Sellin 2006, passim.

10. Christie's, London, 16 December 1998, lot 22. The 1633 painting draws on both Pieter Lastman's (1583–1633) influential painting dated 1612 (Hamburg, Kunsthalle), which sets the scene of Abraham blessing Ishmael and Hagar weeping in a landscape, and a painting dated 1614 by Jan Pynas (1581–1631), which includes the house and Sarah at the door on the left and the open landscape on the right but no contact between Abraham and Ishmael (private collection, the Netherlands; see Sellin 2006, p. 122, fig. 31).

11. Bartsch 1797, vol. 1, p. 31, no. 30.

12. Hamann 1936 suggests that Hagar's gesture of holding a handkerchief to her eyes to express her sadness was initiated by Lastman.

13. Moltke 1938–39, pp. 343, 394f., no. Z-2, fig. 31. With thanks to Benjamin Peronnet, who, when head of the Old Master Drawings Departments at Christie's, pointed out the sale of this drawing at Christie's, Amsterdam, 13 May 2015, lot 187; and to Stijn Alsteens, international head of Old Master Drawings at Christie's, Paris, for providing useful information about the drawing in 2023.

14. Hamann 1936, p. 548n1; and Moltke 1938–39, p. 379.

15. Thanks to Yvonne Szafran, conservator of paintings, J. Paul Getty Museum, for her examination and analysis of the painting with infrared reflectography in 1999.

16. For one of these paintings, *Jacob and Rachel at the Well* (signed and dated 1660; 90 × 156 cm; Musée de la Chartreuse, Douai), there is both a finished drawing (pen and brown ink with gray wash; signed and dated 1660; 18.2 × 31.2 cm; Kunsthalle, Hamburg: Bernt 1957–58, no. 127) and a second, more loosely handled drawing, dated 1659 (Städelsches Museum, Frankfurt), which is closely related to the painting but differs significantly in details and composition. The relationship of the Frankfurt drawing to the Douai painting is typical of a preparatory drawing. At least one finished drawing by De Bray, *Adoration of the Shepherds* (signed and dated 1628; Kunsthandel Gebr. Douwes, Amsterdam, 1972, no. 676), is scored for transfer to an unidentified painting.

17. See Giltaij and Lammertse 2001 and Lammertse 2008.

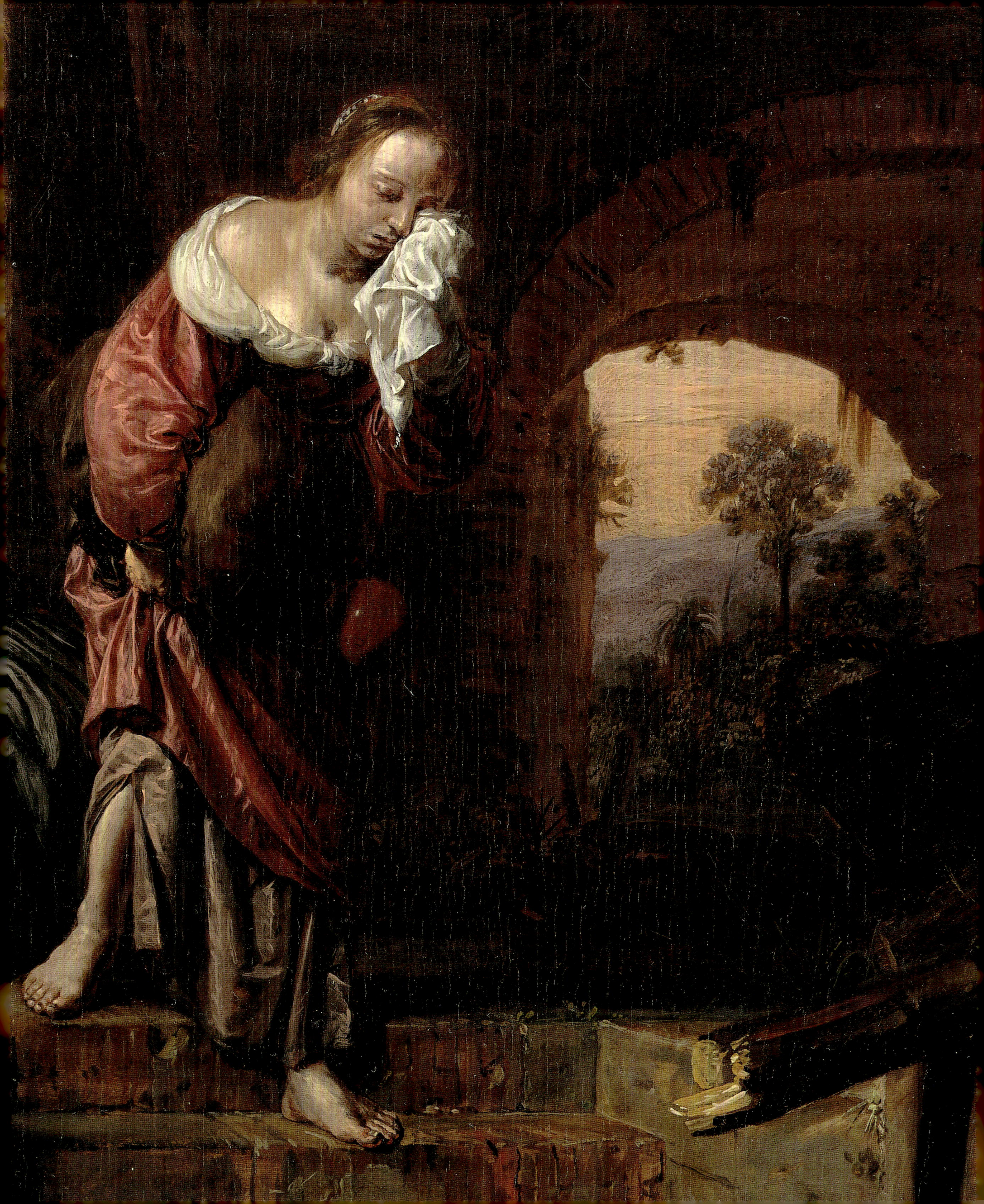

13

Quiringh Gerritsz. van Brekelenkam

Dutch
Zwammerdam? after 1620–after 1668 Leiden

The Shoemaker's Shop

ca. 1660

Signed with monogram on platform riser to right of center: "QvB"
Oil on panel, height: left side, 23⅛ in. (58.7 cm); right side, 23⅜ in. (59.4 cm); width: 32½ in. (82.6 cm)
Norton Simon Art Foundation, M.1977.28.P

Provenance
George Kinnaird, 7th Lord Kinnaird (1754–1805),[1] London (sale, Christie's, London, 7 May 1806, lot 35, sold to);[2] Woodburn. Possibly Anonymous (sale, Squibb, London, 14 March 1811, lot 107, sold for £22 1s.).[3] Possibly Thyssen, Amsterdam (sale, Christie's, London, 21 January 1854, lot 68, sold to);[4] Terry. Adolph B. H. Goldschmidt (1838–1918), Cavenham Park (sale, Christie's, London, 26 May 1922, lot 37, sold to); [P. & D. Colnaghi and H. M. Clark, London, stock no. A1094, sold 1922 to]; Tancred Borenius (1885–1948), London.[5] Dr. Hans Wertmuller (sale, Christie's, London, 26 June 1964, lot 155, ill., sold for 750 guineas to); Joseph. Anonymous (sale, Christie's, London, 2 July 1976, lot 51, ill., sold to);[6] [Galerie Julia Kraus, Paris, sold 1977 through]; [Essoldo Fine Arts Ltd., London, to]; Norton Simon Art Foundation.

Exhibited
On loan, Henry Art Gallery, University of Washington, Seattle, 22 December 1977–3 October 1978.

References
Pasadena 1980, p. 52, ill.; Sumowski 1983–93, vol. 1, pp. 501, 503n24, 511, 673 (no. 383), and 674 (no. 386), ill.; Philadelphia/Berlin/London 1984, p. xlii, fig. 62; P. Sutton 1986, pp. 218, 318; Pasadena 1989, p. 77, ill.; Lasius 1989, pp. 149, 150, 160n53, fig. 4; Lasius 1992, p. 92, no. 42, pl. 7; Lasius 1996, p. 96; Stichting Geschiedschrijving Holland 2002, p. 229, fig. 93; Kettering 2007, pp. 694–714, fig. 16; S. Campbell 2010, p. 412, no. 1487, ill.; Seelig 2010, p. 68; Baer 2015, p. 297n47.

Technical Notes
The support is a horizontally grained oak panel; the right edge was cut not quite straight. All edges were hand-beveled on the reverse. A horizontal crack that extends from side to side approximately 12 inches from the bottom has been repaired with four "butterfly" inserts. Matching wood grain seen in the X-radiograph, plus thin brown paint on the reverse that was present before the butterfly inserts were made, suggest this is a later repair rather than an original join. The thin cream-colored ground permits saw cuts and wood grain on the front surface to remain evident. A rose-beige underpainting is visible throughout the gray wall of the background where thin paint allows it to show through and at contours where two colors almost meet. Although microscopic examination and infrared reflectography did not reveal underdrawing, gradual changes in transparency of the white paint in the head scarf of the kneeling woman at right now reveal some dark strokes of paint below, which may indicate a preliminary painted sketch. The painting was executed with fluidly brushed paint, applied directly in much of the composition using a limited palette of warm browns, warm gray, white, and black. More liquid paint depicts the floor, objects under the table, the post at lower left, and the wall beneath the open window. The artist used subtle differences of hue to indicate shadow and depth on the left side of the scene. The right side of the composition has slightly more detail in the objects and figures that receive light from the window. The paint is generally very well preserved. The painting was selectively cleaned in an undocumented treatment, leaving older, thicker varnish in the lower portion of the painting. The scattered retouching found throughout seems to have no purpose.

In 1567 the Italian merchant and writer Lodovico Guicciardini (1521–1589) noted, "The people of the Low Countries are very hard-working, diligent, inventive, and have a ready wit. They are a nation of merchants and are skilled in all forms of commerce, such that the prosperity of the country is founded largely on trade and industry."[7] Nearly a century after Guicciardini made these observations, Quiringh Gerritsz. van Brekelenkam extolled the work ethic of the Dutch people in his paintings.[8]

The Shoemaker's Shop is one of at least fourteen versions of the subject that Van Brekelenkam painted between about 1653 and 1660.[9] In the Pasadena painting, which Angelika Lasius dates to about 1660, an old man, surrounded by the tools and products of his trade, sits at his workbench in a tidy workshop.[10] With the shoe on which he has been working still in his lap, he lights a clay pipe from a brazier. A woman leans over the windowsill into the shop; the coins in her hand indicate that she is a customer waiting to pay for services.[11] Behind the shoemaker, a second, older woman, probably the shoemaker's wife, draws beer into a tankard from a wooden keg bearing an image of a unicorn, likely indicating the brewer's mark.[12] On the floor in the foreground are cooking utensils, including a strainer used for cleaning fish.[13] A crockery jug fitted with a metal funnel stands on the edge of the wooden platform, a structure that served a practical

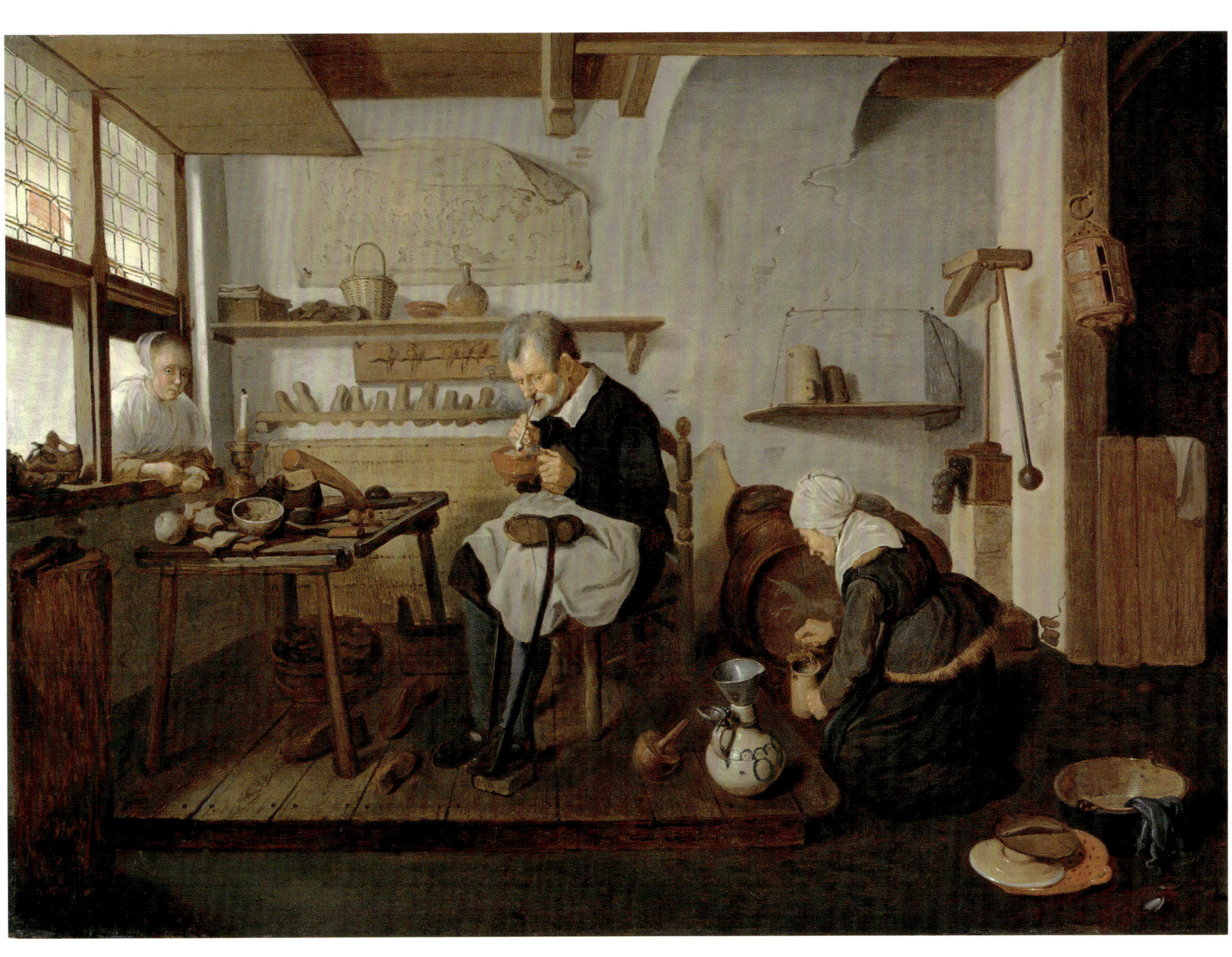

purpose by protecting the shoemaker from the cold floor and artistically helps to create the sense of a tangible, three-dimensional space.

Van Brekelenkam's paintings of shoemakers, tailors, spinners, and other professions helped to establish a new genre in Dutch painting during the mid-seventeenth century.[14] Popular prints representing people engaged in various trades, which were published in books or as series in Germany and the Netherlands beginning in the sixteenth century, were important precedents for these works. The most famous of these is Joost Amman's *Eygentliche Beschreibung aller Stände* (Exact Description of All Ranks; Frankfurt, 1568), known throughout Europe as the *Ständebuch*. Each of Amman's woodcuts represents the workshop activities of a different profession; a short descriptive text written by Hans Sachs (1494–1576) describes the activity, its usefulness, and products. Other prints and books from the period illustrate themes of labor and diligence.[15] The character and popularity of these prints reflect the improved value attached to labor by an increasingly capitalistic and urban society, which recognized that middle-class prosperity depended on hard work.

Van Brekelenkam's selection of incident and detail in *The Shoemaker's Shop* is very similar to that in Amman's print of the shoemaker (fig. 13a). Each image represents the assembly of shoes and a woman, presumably a customer, who leans through a window where shoes are displayed. Each artist included accurate details specific to the craft, perhaps guided by one of the technical treatises the shoemakers' guild used for training.[16] On the back wall in *The Shoemaker's Shop* are awls used to punch leather for sewing and the wooden lasts used as forms to make shoes. A stirrup stretching from beneath the shoemaker's foot over his knee holds the shoe steady while he sews. A large bend of stretched leather leans against the wall behind the cask of beer, and in the left foreground a log stands on end, on which the shoemaker beats components of shoes with the flat-faced hammer lying on top. The water pump against the right wall and the bucket under the table were used to temper the leather.

Here, as in most of his works of this genre, Van Brekelenkam expanded the traditional iconography of the prints to include the activity of a woman. Kneeling behind the shoemaker, the wife draws beer from a keg into a tankard, which she has taken from the shelf above her.[17] The firm, refined brushstrokes characteristic of the Leiden *fijnschilders* (fine painters) distinguish the jug from the broadly applied, thin, milky washes of paint used throughout the rest of the painting. The emphasis given the jug suggests that the woman at the window is waiting for it to be filled rather than for the shoemaker, who lights his pipe. A closely related painting by Van Brekelenkam sold in 1914 was described as representing a boy counting out money while the shoemaker smokes and a woman pours beer from a jug.[18] The *rekening bord* (accounting board) and the shelf of regulated measuring tankards in the Pasadena painting suggest that a tavern lies beyond the half door on the right, where the chimney of a fireplace and a jug in a niche can be vaguely discerned.[19]

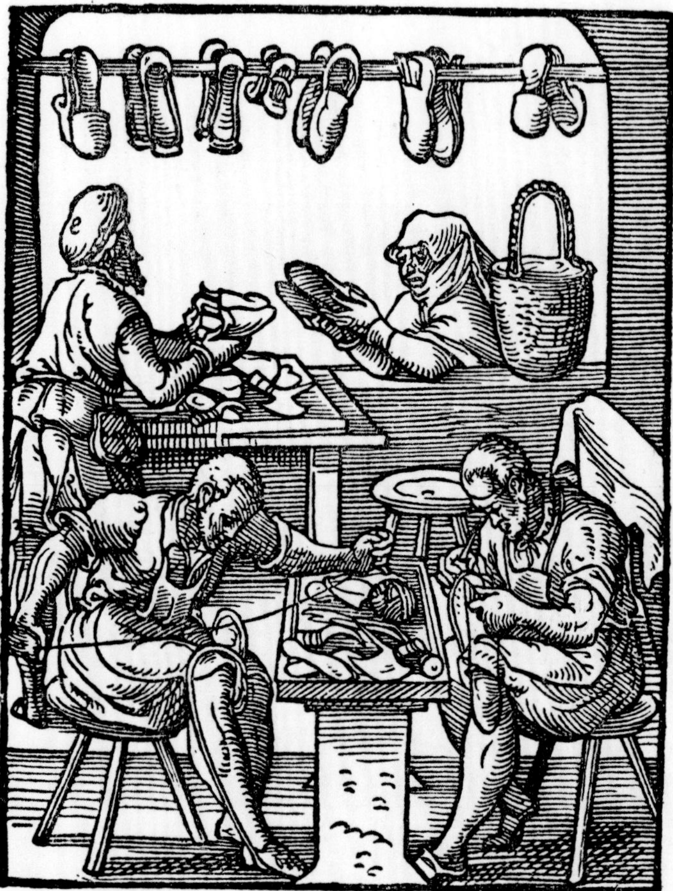

Fig. 13a. Joost Amman, *The Shoemaker*, etching, from *Ständebuch*, 1568, (84-B32492) Getty Research Institute, Los Angeles.

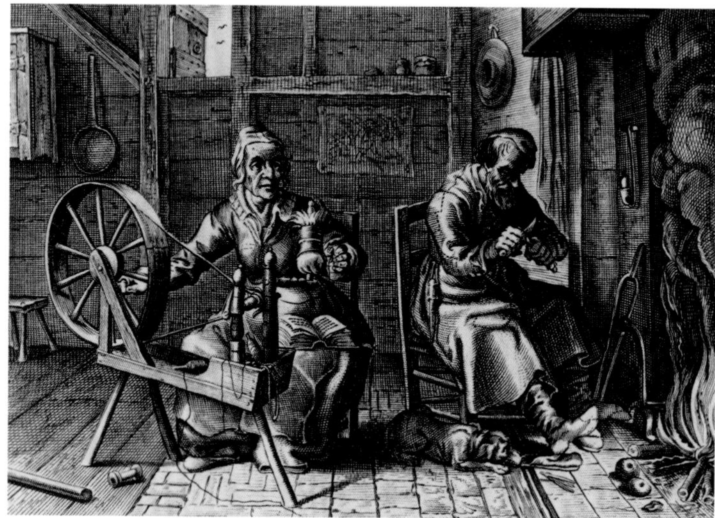

Fig. 13b. Johan de Brune, *Emblemata of Zinne-werck*, 1624, no. 318, (93-B10197c.2) Getty Research Institute, Los Angeles.

It is unlikely that Van Brekelenkam meant the image of the shoemaker interrupting his work to light a clay pipe as a negative example of laziness and inattention to business. Throughout his oeuvre, Van Brekelenkam praised the virtue of hard work as exemplified by artisans and housewives; negative exempla are absent from his oeuvre. Therefore, if the customer in the Pasadena painting is actually waiting for the older woman to fill her stoneware jug with beer, then the image of the shoemaker taking a deserved break to light a pipe would refer to a popular proverb recommending that the shoemaker keep to his last and not concern himself with other people's business.[20]

The artist, influenced by the tradition of *vanitas* iconography in Leiden, may nevertheless have intended to invoke the popular association of smoking with the brevity of human life, reminding the viewer of the vanity of earthly interests. Other details in the painting may also be connected with *vanitas*, such as the unlit candle on the worktable and the accounting board.[21] Protestant theologians, who believed that one's life on earth is transient and that true life comes only after death, stressed diligence and hard work as outward signs that one was among the elect of God, destined to enjoy eternal life. For Catholics, who rejected the concept of predestination, hard work was a way of pleasing God and earning his rewards. In either case, the shoemaker and his wife, like the elderly couple in an emblem from Johan de Brune's *Emblemata of Zinne-werck* (fig. 13b), are illustrative of hard work.[22]

Like paintings of spinning and tailor shops, trades specifically associated with Leiden's dominant textile industry, paintings of shoemakers also praised the local economy. According to the city historian Jan Jansz. Orlers, during the mid-seventeenth century Leiden was well known for the exceptionally high quality of the shoes it produced in greater quantity than its competitors.[23] The map tacked to the back wall of the Pasadena painting, showing Holland and West Frieseland (oriented with west on top), identifies the shoemaker and his wife as Dutch, a people Guicciardini and others praised as the foundation of the prosperity of the northern Netherlands.[24] Outside the shop window, a faintly seen flag bearing the crossed keys of Leiden specifically identifies this morally exemplary couple as citizens of Van Brekelenkam's own city.

1. A banker and art collector who, with Thomas More Slade and others, was one of the major purchasers of the Dutch and Flemish paintings from the Orleans collection in 1792.

2. Dimensions given in a handwritten annotation from a copy of the catalogue at the New York Public Library indicate size and support as "2 ¾ 2 P", or 2 ¾ feet × 2 feet, panel. While there are many references in late eighteenth- and early nineteenth-century sale catalogues to paintings by Van Brekelenkam of cobblers and shoemakers, the dimensions given here make this identification a possibility. Additionally, on the back of the panel is an old label with the letter "K," which may refer to Lord Kinnaird, the seller at this auction.

3. Described as "An Interior View of a Cobler's [*sic*] Habitation. The sagacious Master is reluming his comforting Pipe by the Embers of a Chafing-dish, while his industrious Helpmate prepares a temperate and wholesome Repast. Highly finished and characteristic. . . ." The identification of this painting with that in Pasadena is questioned because, although cooking utensils are present in the Pasadena painting, the woman is pouring beer rather than preparing food.

4. According to the catalogue of the Wertmuller sale (Christie's, London, 26 June 1964, lot. 51). The description "Interior, with a cobbler at work, and two females" could also refer to Lasius 1992, no. 43.

5. According to Colnaghi records. Tancred Borenius was a Finnish art historian, dealer, and archaeologist who was active in England. The painting does not appear in any of Borenius's sales.

6. The catalogue includes in the provenance of the painting: Rev. M. M. P. Mealey, Belmont, Bath, [sale] Christie's, June 11, 1870, lot 108, 15½ guineas, Adolph Goldsmith [*sic*], Cavenham Park." Lasius 1992, probably based on the 1976 sale entry, includes the 1870 sale in the provenance of the Pasadena painting. The 1870 sale catalogue description of the painting as "An Interior of a Shoemaker's Shop" is, however, too imprecise to conclude it is the Pasadena painting. The painting sold in 1870 was purchased by Enthoven.

7. Guicciardini [1567] 1612, p. 28; English translation from Veldman 1992, p. 227.

8. Kettering 2007, pp. 701–04.

9. The prototype, dated 1653, represents a shoemaker alone in his workshop (Lasius 1992, no. 33; also Lasius 1989, fig. 1).

10. Lasius 1989, no. 42.

11. The motif of the customer also appears in Lasius 1992, nos. 43 (*Shoemaker and Woman Scraping Carrots*, location unknown) and 44 (*The Shoemaker*, Musée de Picardie, Amiens).

12. Lasius 1992, nos. 40 and 41; Hochstrasser 2007, 56.

13. For an example of a seventeenth-century crockery fish strainer, or colander, see Museum Boijmans Van Beuningen, Rotterdam, inv. no. 50492.

14. Gerard ter Borch (1617–1681), Caspar Netscher (1635/36–1684), Jan Victors (1619/20–1676 or later), among others, also painted scenes of farriers, knife grinders, etc., but they did not make it their major subject. Paintings of the professions were known in antiquity. In *Natural History* (35.37.112–113), Pliny the Elder recounts how Piraeicus "painted barbers' shops and cobblers' stalls, asses, viands and the like, consequently receiving a Greek name meaning 'painter of sordid subjects'; in these however he gives exquisite pleasure, and indeed they fetched bigger prices than the largest works of many masters." The professions probably continued to be represented on shop signs, now lost, but they are most commonly found in the context of allegorical or religious images in manuscripts, stained glass, and prints. Manuscript illuminations include images of people working, particularly at rural occupations, as allegories of the different times of year and of the elements.

15. See Veldman 1992.

16. The man in the left foreground of the Amman print sews, and the one opposite appears to be using an awl to make holes for sewing.

17. During the seventeenth century, beer was recommended as a drink for both adults and children and could be purchased by housewives

from local taverns. Schama 1987b, pp. 172, 174, notes that these domestic casks were filled by peripatetic "tappers."

18. Arthur Grenfell, Esq. (sale, Christie's, London, 26 June 1914, lot 7, "The Cobbler's Shop. In the center is seated the cobbler, lighting his pipe at a pot of embers; beside him stands a boy counting out some money, while the shoemaker's wife kneels on the ground and draws beer from a cask; on the right are seen the cobbler's tools on a bench standing before an open window").

19. According to Moes 1910, p. 574, but otherwise undocumented, Van Brekelenkam acquired a license to sell beer and brandy after his second marriage in 1656.

20. During the early seventeenth century, smoking, which had been introduced by English sailors, was associated with the lower classes and social deviance. By the 1660s, however, smoking for pleasure had become socially acceptable, even among the burgher class; an order on the misuse of tobacco passed by the regents of Gouda in 1668 noted that workmen, guild members, and even children were seen with pipes. The same order stipulated that men were not to smoke at work except during specific rest periods, implying that this, too, had become commonplace. See Gaskell 1987, pp. 117–37, esp. p. 135. The positive association is expressed by the proverb "Schoenmaker, hou je (of blijf) bij je leest, bemoei je niet met zaken waar je geen verstand van hebt" (Shoemaker, keep to your last, don't concern yourself with things of which you have no understanding). According to Jones 1996, the origin of the proverb, which became popular in the Netherlands in the sixteenth century, was Pliny, *Natural History*, 35.36.85: "A shoemaker in his criticism must not go beyond the sandal." Likewise, moderate beer consumption during this period was seen as useful for "sustaining virtuous work"; see Hochstrasser 2007, 52.

21. *Rekening* (accounting) slates, which are common features of tavern scenes, also appear in representations of artisan workshops. See, for example, Van Brekelenkam's *Tailor Shop*, ca. 1660 (Rheinisches Landesmuseum, Bonn; Lasius 1992, no. 52). The inclusion of this detail could allude to taking inventory of one's life.

22. The caption explains that the humble couple represented in the emblem pleases God by their piety and hard work as craftspeople while they await their reward in Heaven. According to de Brune's explanation, nearing the end of their lives, the elderly couple acutely recognize the virtues of simplicity and spiritual strength. See De Brune 1970, p. 318.

23. Orlers 1641, p. 262. The discussion of shoemakers is included in a section devoted to handwork other than linen manufacture. Orlers devotes more attention to the description of shoemaking in this paragraph than to the activities of any of the other guilds.

24. The map may represent a free rendering of Balthasar Florisz. van Berckenrode's map published by William Jansz. Blaeu (1571–1638). The inclusion of the cartouche in the lower center of the map and the unelaborated borders may, however, indicate that Van Brekelenkam's model was the original map published in 1620 by Van Berckenrode, of which no originals exist. See Welu 1975, pp. 530f., fig. 2. Regarding the use of maps in genre paintings for political associations, see Hedinger 1986 and Hedinger 1987.

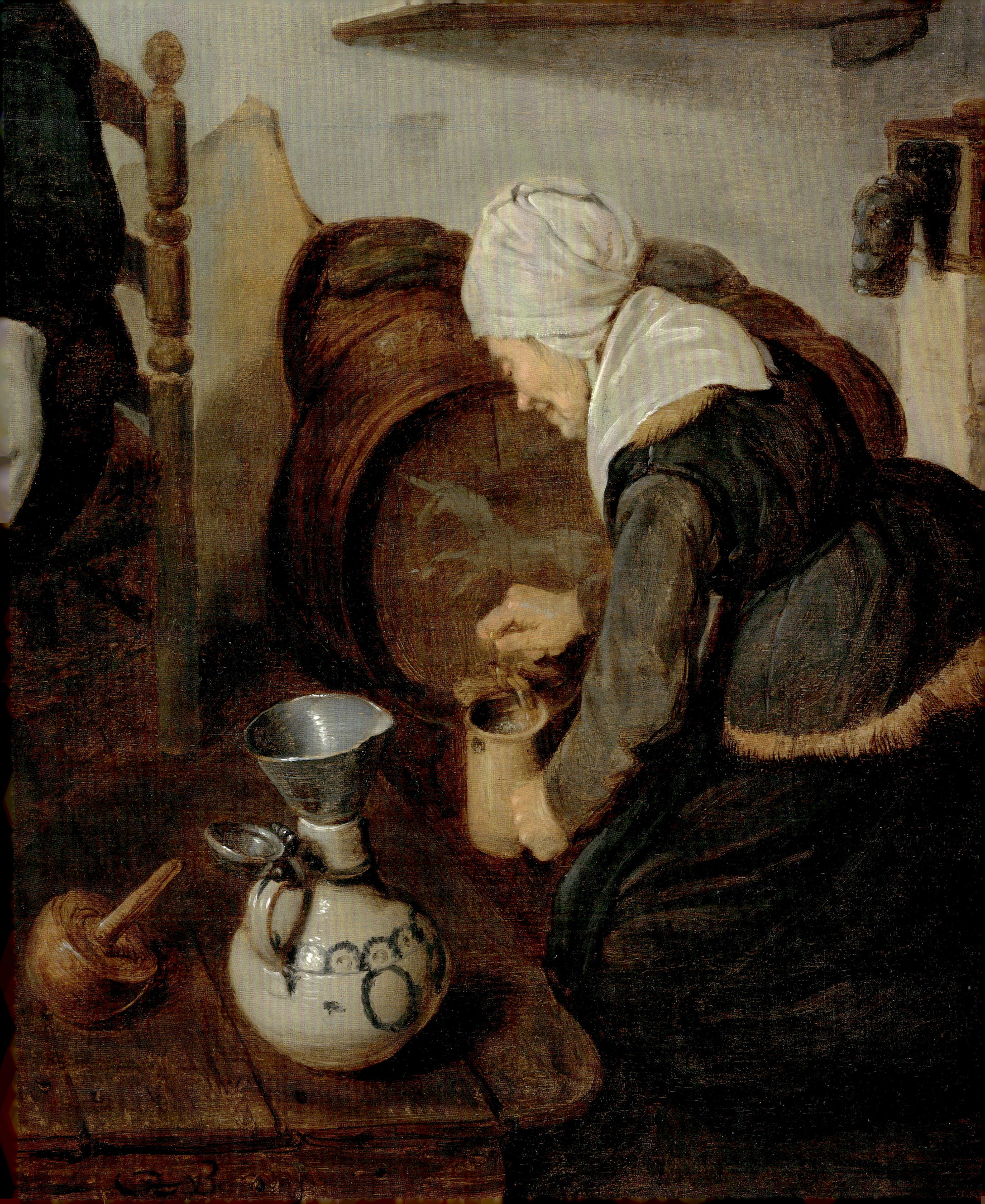

14

Jan Brueghel II

Flemish
Antwerp 1601–1678 Antwerp

Flowers in a Gilt Tazza

ca. 1620

Oil on panel, 21¾ × 16¾ in. (55.3 × 42.6 cm)
The Norton Simon Foundation, F.1972.13.P

Provenance
Maria Luisa de Alcocer Moreno (1910–1976), wife of Pedro Cortina y Mauri (1908–1993).[1] Private collection (sale, Palais Galliera, Paris, 7 December 1971, lot 6, as "Atelier de Jan Brueghel de Velours"). [MAHLA, Zurich, consigned 25 May 1972 to];[2] [Newhouse Gallery, New York, sold 25 May 1972 to]; The Norton Simon Foundation.

Exhibited
On loan, Allen Memorial Art Museum, Oberlin, 22 May 1972–8 May 1973; on loan, Los Angeles County Museum of Art, 9 May 1973–26 November 1974; on loan, Phoenix Art Museum, 21 November 1980–19 May 1981.

References
Ertz 1979, pp. 531n379, 602, as copy? (of painting by Jan Brueghel I); Pasadena 1980, p. 50, ill.; Ertz 1984, p. 449, no. 285, ill., as ca. 1620; Delft/Cambridge/Fort Worth 1988, pp. 100, 214n10, ill. 6.2, as private collection, Spain, autograph version of original 1612 painting (Ertz 1979, no. 269); Pasadena 1989, p. 70, ill.; Ertz 1997, pp. 290, 292, fig. 2, as Jan Brueghel II; Pasadena 2003, p. 62, ill., as Jan Brueghel I; S. Campbell 2010, p. 338, no. 786, ill.; Zanotti and Iacoviello 2015, pp. 295, 305, 307, 310–11, 316–17, fig. 6.

Technical Notes
The panel is composed of two vertically grained oak boards with the join in the approximate center of the panel. All edges are beveled. X-radiography reveals two splines placed across the vertical join that are not visible on either the reverse or the front. A moderately thick layer of warm white ground covers the join completely. X-radiography shows the ground was applied with vigorous brushstrokes in all directions. These diagonal strokes are discernible with normal vision in the foreground, through the thin paint used for the gray table. The interior or base color within the floral arrangement is medium brown, left in reserve as the black background was painted around it. Paint was applied directly with no evidence of underdrawing or underpainting. The clear and vibrant colors were applied in a fairly liquid consistency. Several flower colors are nearly transparent when viewed with the microscope. The golden tones of the tazza were created by the layering of yellow and ochre paint applied directly over the black. There is a slight amount of surface texture in the decoration of the tazza, and X-radiography indicates that the artist reworked the stem and the base. Pentimenti visible beneath the thinly applied gray paint in the foreground correspond with the findings of the X-radiography and indicate that the base was originally larger. There also may have been an additional flower at the lower right. The paint is extremely well preserved. There is very little retouching, in small scattered spots. A dent at the top left must have been present before the paint and ground were applied, as magnification reveals no disturbance to the paint layer. Ultraviolet-light examination indicates an aged synthetic-resin varnish.[3]

Silhouetted against a black background animated by a butterfly, an informal, colorful bouquet of delicate flowers overflows the flat bowl (*plaquette*) of an expensive gilt tazza elevated by an elegantly wrought stem.[4] Rather than the rare and exotic blossoms displayed in many early still lifes, such as *Flowers in a Glass Beaker* (cat. 9), the image includes wild and cultivated flowers, including roses, carnations, forget-me-nots, apple blossoms, and pansies that were common to the Netherlands. In this, the painting reflects actual practice in the Netherlands, where during the summer months wealthy households often displayed cut flowers in silver baskets or, as here, in gilt tazzas.[5]

The position and colors of the flowers produce a harmonious composition in depth. The larger flowers—three roses as well as a red-and-white carnation—appear in the center of the bouquet. Two bright red poppy anemones placed on either end of a visual diagonal that passes through the bouquet emphasize the dynamic cascade of barberry blossoms falling over the edge of the tazza. Small, delicate flowers and stems that weave in and out of the bouquet, at times partially concealing other blossoms, contribute to the impression of three-dimensional depth within the flat surface of the panel.[6]

Flowers in a Gilt Tazza is one of a number of paintings produced by members of the workshop of Jan Brueghel I (1568–1625) that were based on an original composition by the master.[7] The Pasadena painting is a particularly close variant of a painting by Brueghel (fig. 14a), which Klaus Ertz dates about 1612 and Matthias Winner dates ca. 1618.[8] The particular arrangement of flowers in the bowl of the tazza and other details are, however, closest to a drawing inscribed

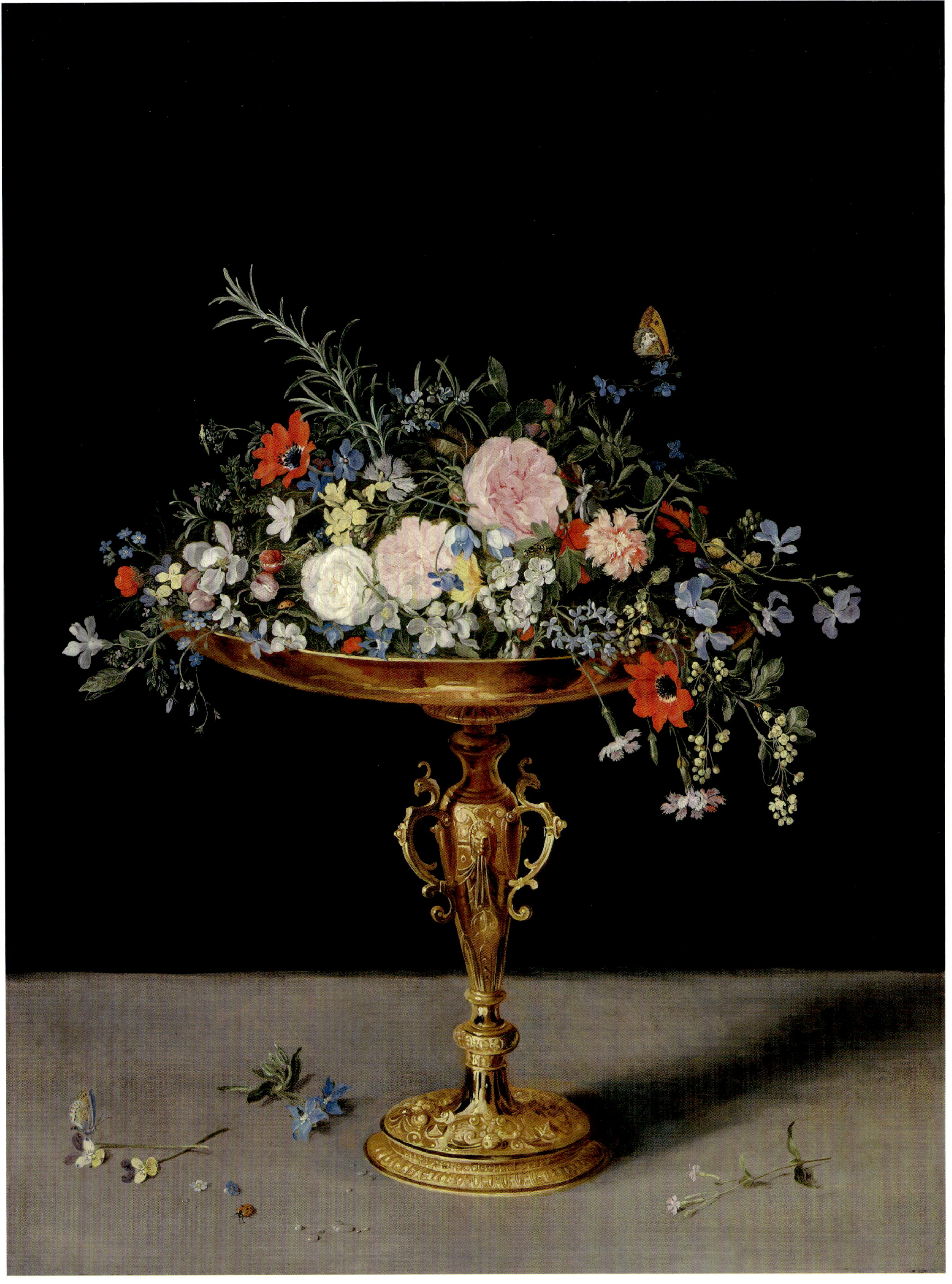

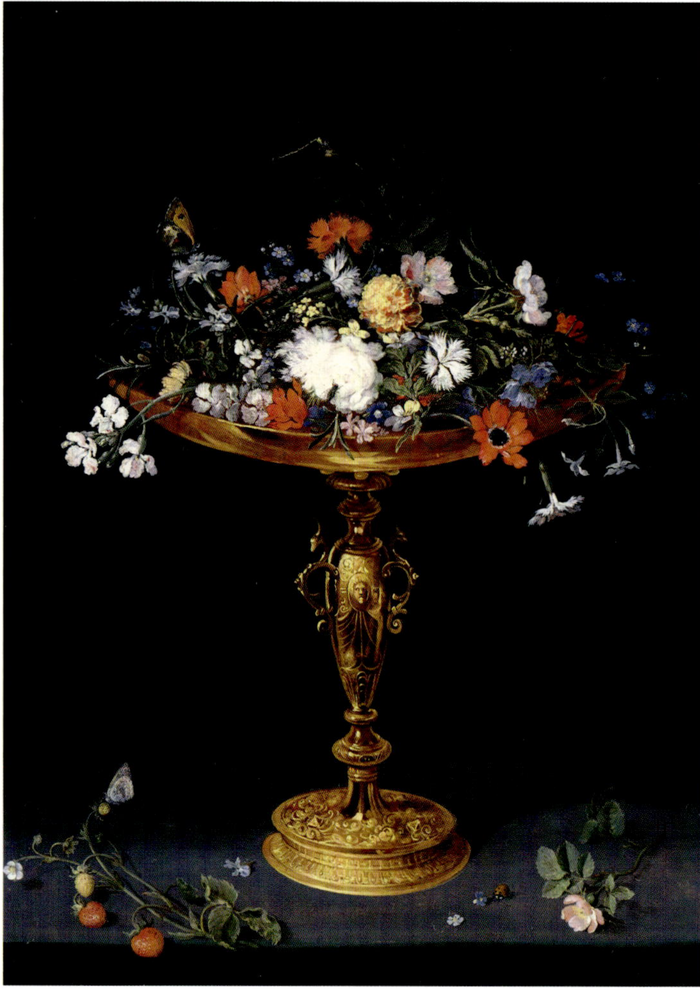

Fig. 14a. Jan Brueghel I, *Flowers in a Golden Tazza*, 1612, oil on panel, 18½ × 13⅞ in. (47 × 35 cm), private collection, photo courtesy of Noortman Master Paintings, Maastricht.

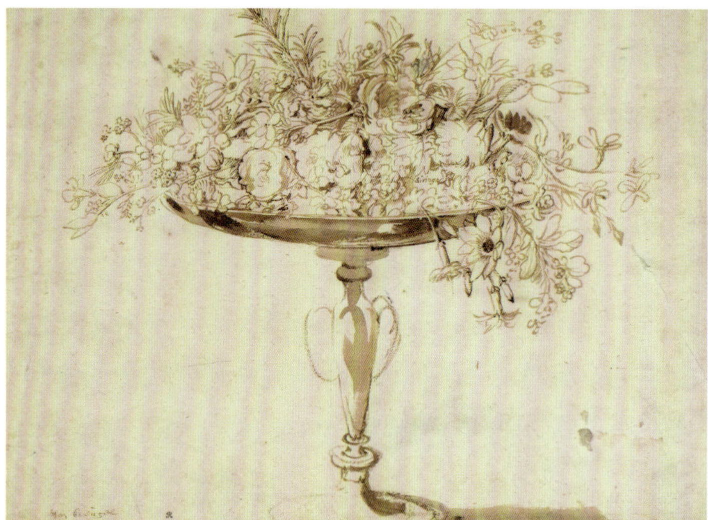

Fig. 14b. Jan Brueghel I, *Flowers in a Tazza*, 1583–1625, pen and brown ink with brown wash, 11 × 14¾ in. (27.9 × 37.4 cm), British Museum, Department of Prints and Drawings, London.

"Jan Bruegel" (fig. 14b) formerly attributed to Jan Brueghel I but now rejected as his work.[9]

The high quality of the Pasadena painting supports Klaus Ertz's attribution of it to Jan Brueghel II.[10] The artist worked from the age of ten in his father's active studio, acquiring the technical proficiency to enable him to make close copies of his father's works to satisfy the demands of the elder artist's many admirers. An early date, before his trip to Italy in 1624, is suggested by the younger artist's use of his father's characteristic method of preparing the panel with a layer of streaky white ground.[11] The high degree of technical skill demonstrated in the painting also suggests an earlier date, since Jan Brueghel II's style gradually moved away from that of his father. Using a technique like his father's, the artist rendered the flowers with thin, almost transparent paint that thickens at the edges of forms where the brush twists. He applied fluid, bright yellow paint over dark gold to suggest the reflections of light on the decoration of the gilt tazza rather than to define its exact design.

Correspondence between Jan Brueghel I and Cardinal Federico Borromeo (1564–1631), a patron of both father and son, reveals an appreciation for the capacity of paintings to preserve the beauty and freshness of blooms long after the actual flowers have withered and died.[12] In a letter written in 1606 to the cardinal's agent Bianchi, Brueghel described the flower piece he completed for Borromeo, painted entirely from life: "I have invested all my skill in this picture. I do not believe that so many rare and different flowers have ever been painted before, nor rendered so painstakingly: It will be a fine sight in the winter. Some of the colors are very close to the real thing."[13] Borromeo clearly appreciated the details with which Brueghel animated his flower pieces: "Butterflies flutter around, one feels the freshness of the plants, shells are scattered on the ground."[14] Jan Brueghel II's *Flowers in a Gilt Tazza* is thus a tour de force demonstrating the artist's ability to suggest through paint the fleeting images of fresh flowers, a fluttering butterfly, and waterdrops, which he undoubtedly saw as a challenge for verisimilitude.

1. Cortina y Mauri was Spanish consul general to Paris, 1955–58, and Spanish ambassador to France from 1966. The painting's previous provenance is suggested by a torn paper strip pasted to the top back of the panel, on which is a partial inscription written in what appears to be late nineteenth–early twentieth-century European script: "Domi Am . . . Duque." It is highly likely that the private collector who was selling at the 1971 Palais Galleria sale was Don Pedro's wife.

2. MAHLA, Zurich, was the name used by the New York dealer Frederick Mont.

3. Brueghel represented a typical Renaissance tazza: a simple shallow drinking cup with a domed foot and a baluster stem, the vase-shaped knob of which is decorated with a grotesque design. Freestanding volutes ending in griffin heads flank the stem. The foot of the cup is typically covered with bunches of fruit and festoons, and the rim of the foot is gadrooned. Gans and Duyvené de Wit-Klinkhamer 1961, p. 13.

4. Thornton 1978, pp. 265f. Tazzas were particularly fashionable in the Netherlands during the sixteenth century, when they were popular christening gifts. Like *pronk* goblets, they were filled with wine and passed around as a sign of friendship. They could also be filled with sweetmeats, pastry, and fruit as well as flowers. See Gans and Duyvené de Wit-Klinkhamer 1961, p. 81.

5. For the identification of the various flowers in the Pasadena painting, see Zanotti and Iacoviello 2015.

6. Taylor 1995, p. 112. This technique for suggesting depth was introduced during the first decade of the seventeenth century by either Ambrosius Bosschaert (1573–1621) or Roelandt Savery (1576–1639), contemporaries of Jan Brueghel I, and continued to be followed throughout the century. In 1707, by which time it had become general practice, Gerard de Lairesse (1640–1711) advised artists to place the larger flowers in the center, reducing the size of the flowers as the eye moves toward the perimeter of the bouquet. Warm colors should be placed in the center of the composition, and cool colors at the back, a device Paul Taylor terms "chiaroscuro of hue," which ideally creates a "hemisphere which gradually rounds."

7. Regarding the Brueghel workshops, see Van den Brink 2001 and Paderborn 2015.

8. Ertz 1979, pp. 360, 602, no. 269, ill.; Ertz 1997, no. 87, pp. 290–92; Winner 1961, p. 235.

9. Hind 1915–32, vol. 2 (1923), p. 94, no. 10, pl. xlvii; see also Ertz 1979, pp. 288f., fig. 358. For the rejection of the attribution to Jan Brueghel I, see Gerszi et al. 2019, p. 108. See also "Curator's comments," British Museum website, accessed 13 October 2023, https://www.britishmuseum.org/collection/object/P_1895-0915-1012.

10. Ertz 1984, p. 449, no. 285, ill.

11. Groen and Murray 1991, p. 151.

12. Brenninkmeijer-De Rooij 1996, pp. 60, 70.

13. English translation of passage from F. Borromeo, *Musaeum* (1625) in Brenninkmeijer-De Rooij 1996, p. 50.

14. Brenninkmeijer-De Rooij 1996, p. 60.

15

Pieter Claesz.

Dutch
Berchem 1596/97–1660 Haarlem

Still Life with Rummer

1645/48

Signed with monogram and dated, middle left: "PC 1645[8?]" (fig. 15a)
Oil on panel, 12 ¼ × 15 ¾ in. (31.1 × 40 cm)
Norton Simon Foundation, F.1972.39.P

Provenance
Ekenberg, purchased 1918, by descent to his son; Otto Ekenberg (sale, Sotheby's, London, 24 March 1971, lot 6, as *Still Life with a Lemon*, 1648, sold to); [H. Terry-Engell, London]. [Kunsthandel Gebr. Douwes, Amsterdam, in 1971, as 1645; sold 1972 to]; The Norton Simon Foundation.

Exhibited
Amsterdam 1971, no. 1, cover ill.; on loan, Phoenix Art Museum, 22 September 1972–17 April 1973; on loan, Los Angeles County Museum of Art, 17 May 1973–2 October 1974; Claremont 1974, 5 November–3 December.

References
Vroom 1980–99, vol. 2 (1980), no. 124, as 1645; Brunner-Bulst 2004, p. 279, no. 128; Valls 2005, ill., under entry for no. 5 as a pendant; S. Campbell 2010, pp. 141, 345, no. 850, ill.

Technical Notes
The support, a horizontally grained oak panel made in a single piece, retains its original state; it has not been cradled. The reverse has hand-beveled edges at the left, right, and bottom sides. A thin crack originates at the left side between the monogram and the date. The white ground is thin, leaving the darker lines of wood grain slightly perceptible in the background. Paint was applied in varied thicknesses. In the background a soft atmospheric quality was created with thinly applied paint, smoothly brushed and blended with no distinct brushstrokes. The lemon skins were painted with a thicker, almost viscous paint; the brushmarking creates a "dimpled" surface, suggesting that the paint was dabbed on with a small brush. Highlights in the glass rummer are opaque and creamy; the white cloth is painted with fluid brushstrokes of rich paint. A change in contour at the left edge of the table has become visible due to the increased transparency of the gray-blue paint. Minor abrasion is evident in thin glazes, such as in the pewter plate, the overturned cup, and the shadows at the bottom right corner. There are numerous tiny paint losses in the white cloth. The painting was cleaned prior to entering the collection. Residues of old varnish remain in the depressions of the paint surface, conspicuous in the wine glass, the lemon skins, and the white cloth, and along the bottom edge as well. Apart from retouching in the white cloth, which is from a more recent campaign, older retouching consists of a few small, scattered spots in the background. Ultraviolet-light examination indicates a thin, synthetic-resin varnish, only slightly discolored.

Employing a low horizon that assumes a close perspective, Pieter Claesz. portrayed an intimate view of a table from which he seems to have just pushed back his chair. A large rummer of beer anchors the diagonally arranged composition. The seemingly casual placement of the rummer, the tulip glass of red wine, the overturned gilt cup (*avond-maals beker*), the ebony and mother-of-pearl knife, and the pretzels echo the diagonal line of light cast onto the back wall from the upper left. Reflections of windows in the bowl of the rummer identify the source of the light, with which Claesz. modeled the three-dimensional forms. The low vantage point, which makes the objects appear to overlap, convincingly creates the impression of depth within the composition, while the rumpled white linen cloth that hangs over the edge of the table and is cut by the lower frame seemingly presses forward into the viewer's space. Placed on the cloth so that its highlighted rim faces forward, a foreshortened pewter plate supports a partially peeled lemon. Reflections of the lemon on the plate and on the cup, as well as cast shadows, contribute to the compositional unity of the still life. The same light glances off the edges of the vessels, picking out the embossing on the cup and the glass prunts on the stem of the rummer, while differentiating the different parts of the lemon: the nubbly peel, the soft white inner lining of the skin, and the moist fruit.

Characteristic of the monochrome still lifes painted in Haarlem during the 1630s and 1640s by Pieter Claesz. and Pieter Claesz. Heda (1593/94–1680/82)—which departed from the brightly colored still lifes composed of multiple layers of opaque paint and glazes—*Still Life with Rummer* is

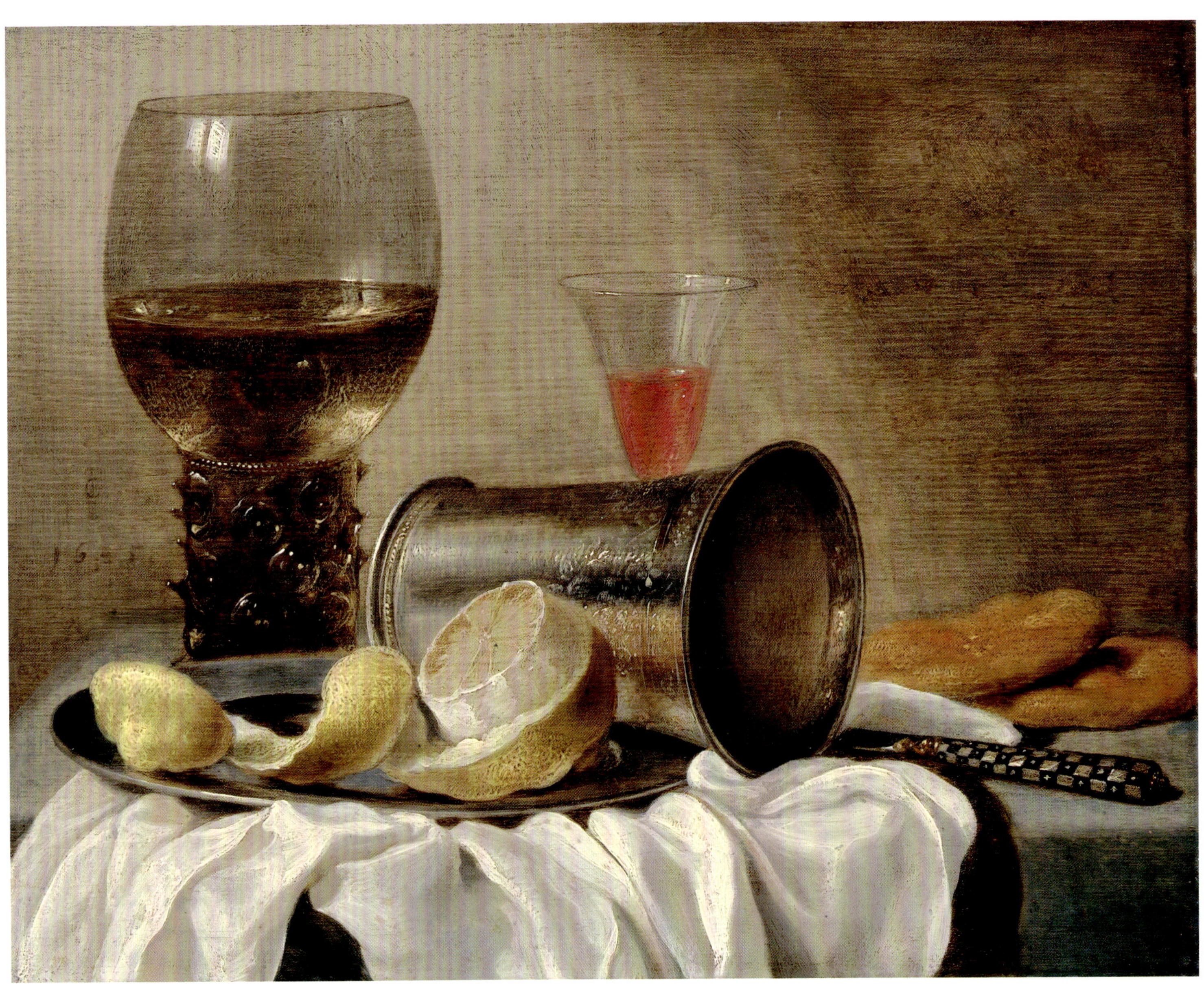

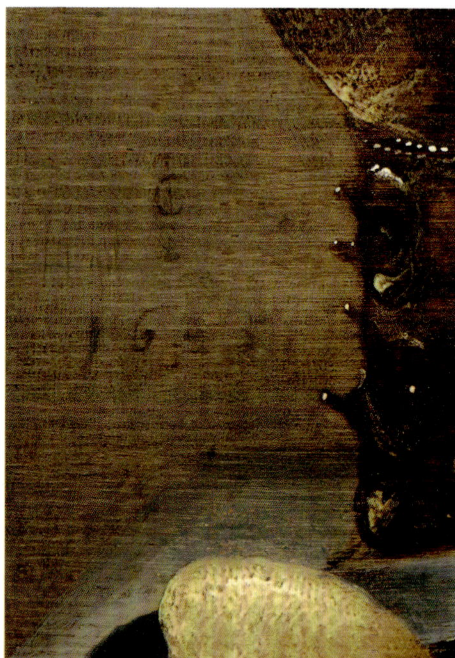

Fig. 15a. Detail of artist's monogram.

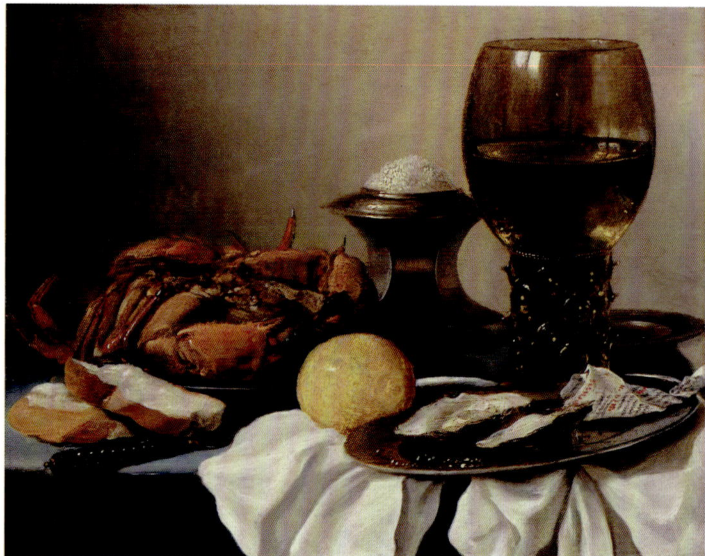

Fig. 15b. Pieter Claesz., *A Still Life of a Crab on a Pewter Plate, a Salt Cellar, a Roemer, a Knife, a Lemon, and Two Oysters on a Pewter Plate, All Resting on a Draped Table*, ca. 1645, oil on panel, 12¼ × 15¾ in. (31 × 40 cm), private collection, image courtesy of Rafael Valls Ltd., London.

composed of toned films of paint applied over a thinly prepared panel that allows the grain of the wood to show. Using a limited palette of tones of ochre, sienna, and umber, with gray and subtle accents of the rose-colored wine and shadowed pretzels and the yellow lemon, Pieter Claesz. suggested the effect of an overall atmosphere through which the composition is viewed. The technique and effect, as well as the organizational device of a diagonal, are similar to those employed in contemporary landscapes by Jan van Goyen (1596–1656), Salomon van Ruysdael (1600/03–1670), and others (see cats. 27, 80, and 81).

Still Life with Rummer is closely related in composition and details to a number of Claesz.'s paintings from the 1640s in which he repeated specific objects. As Zirka Filipczak has pointed out, the fact that these objects are represented from different perspectives as well as in different combinations suggests that Claesz. did not rely solely on preparatory drawings but also often painted directly from objects.[1] With the actual objects before him on a table, as in Jan Miense Molenaer's (1610/11–1668) *A Painter in His Workshop* (fig. 58a), he could easily manipulate the elements into endless variations. When perishable elements such as oysters, crabs, or fruit are included in the still life, however, Claesz. must have used drawings. Other details, such as the reflection of the windows in the rummer, represent popular conventions that reappear in his other paintings as well as in work by both his contemporaries and his predecessors.[2]

From at least 1918 until 1971 *Still Life with Rummer* hung as a pendant with *A Still Life of a Crab on a Pewter Plate, a Salt Cellar, a Roemer, a Knife, a Lemon, and Two Oysters on a Pewter Plate, All Resting on a Draped Table* (fig. 15b).[3] Although pendants were often composed by collectors rather than by artists, particularly during the eighteenth century, the similar dimensions and the formal relationship of the two compositions suggest that Claesz. could have painted them to hang together as pendants. Placed side by side, with *Still Life with Rummer* to the left, they appear as a continuous composition, viewed from the same vantage point and framed on either side by the same large rummer. In front of the rummer in each painting, a pewter plate rests on a white napkin. In place of the overturned gilt cup, *A Still Life of a Crab on a Pewter Plate* includes a cooked crab and a hexagonal diabolo salt cellar, probably pewter. A knife extends slightly over the forward edge of the table, creating a diagonal line pointing into the composition, as it does in *Still Life with Rummer*. Repeated curves and ovals create rhythmic harmony and coherent compositions within each painting that in turn relate each to the other.

The two paintings also seem to be thematically integrated. Taken together, the paintings offer a complete and sumptuous repast. *A Still Life of a Crab on a Pewter Plate*, in particular, includes costly items such as crab and oysters, the mound of salt, and the paper cone spilling pepper onto the pewter plate. The gilt cup and lemon imported from the Mediterranean portrayed in *Still Life with Rummer* also allude to the meals enjoyed by prosperous burghers.[4] Although contemporary viewers may have read in the compositions lingering references to *vanitas*, it is more appropriate to see them as presentation pieces. Rather than moral lessons, their primary appeal was certainly the sensual quality of their quiet harmony of color, light, form, and texture. Like a display of expensive artifacts, these images of a sumptuous meal allude to the comfort and wealth of the owners, who would have displayed them in the reception rooms of their homes. As such, they are forerunners of the large showpiece still lifes (*pronk stilleven*) of Jan Davidsz. de Heem (1606–1683/84), Willem Kalf (1619–1693), and Abraham van Beyeren (1620–1690) that openly celebrate Dutch prosperity and abundance.

1. Filipczak 1995, pp. 71–73.

2. Bergström 1970.

3. According to the 1971 sale catalogue, Otto Ekenberg's father had purchased lot 6 in 1918 together with lot 7, *A Still Life of a Crab on a Pewter Plate, a Salt Cellar, a Roemer, a Knife, a Lemon, and Two Oysters on a Pewter Plate, All Resting on a Draped Table*. The paintings were sold in 1971 with a copy of a certificate from Dr. Ingvar Bergström, dated 1970, who knew of only one other instance of pendants by Claesz., which he said had been exhibited in the National Museum, Warsaw (Warsaw 1939, nos. 23–24, ills. pp. 13–14). These two paintings, each of which measured 47.3 × 63.2 cm, were then owned by Edwarda Raczynshiego, Warsaw, but disappeared during World War II. Vroom 1980–99, vol. 2, nos. 105 and 106, p. 31, also lists a pair in the Museum of Fine Arts, Boston, dated 1642 (Brunner-Bulst 2004, nos. 112 and 113). He lists the Pasadena painting as no. 124 but does not mention *A Still Life of a Crab on a Pewter Plate*, which was sold at Sotheby's, New York, 27 May 2004, lot 18, where it was bought by the dealer Rafael Valls Ltd., London (Valls 2005, no. 5). It was sold to a private collector in 2010.

4. Along with cloves, nutmeg, and mace, pepper was an expensive foreign spice that had to be imported into the Netherlands from the East Indies. See Hochstrasser 2007.

16

Cornelis Cornelisz. van Haarlem

Dutch
Haarlem 1562–1638 Haarlem

Mars and Venus

1599

Signed with monogram and dated, on front of lower step, center: "CH ā 1599"[1]
Oil on copper, 22 1/16 × 17 5/8 in. (56.0 cm × 44.8 cm)
Norton Simon Art Foundation, M.2010.1.25.P

Provenance
Wilhelmus van Velthuyzen (sale, Philippus Losel, Rotterdam, 15 April 1751, lot 47).[2] Hendrik Verschuuring (d. 1769) The Hague, by 1752 (sale, Stephanus Rietmulder, The Hague, 17 September 1770, lot 75).[3] Jan Lucas van der Dussen (sale, Jan Slebes Hendriksz. et al., Amsterdam, 31 October 1774, lot 19, sold for ƒ110 to);[4] [Cornelis Ploos van Amstel (1726–1798), Amsterdam].[5] Probably anonymous (sale, Van Campen, Amsterdam, 25 January 1830, lot 29, sold to);[6] Esser. Possibly Sagan Collection and by descent to;[7] Friedrich Wilhelm Konstantin (1801–1869), Prince of Hohenzollern-Hechingen, Löwenberg-Schlesien, inventory 1858, no. 18.[8] [Galerie Fritz Gurlitt Berlin—after 1955 known as Galerie Wolfgang Gurlitt, Munich—by 1935 (sale, Lempertz, Cologne, 18 November 1965, lot 64, sold for DM 3,000 to)][9]; Ruax [Raux] for?;[10] [Adolphe Stein, Paris, by 1966].[11] [Ksth. P. de Boer, Amsterdam, sold 1967 to]; Heinrich Becker, Dortmund, sold 1973 through; [G. Cramer Oudekunst, The Hague, to]; Norton Simon, bequest 1993 to; Jennifer Jones Simon Art Trust, bequest 27 September 2010 to; Norton Simon Art Foundation.

Exhibited
Munich 1962, no. 30, ill.; Amsterdam 1966–67, no. 10, ill.; on loan, Henry Art Gallery, University of Washington, Seattle, 26 September 1973–11 February 1974.

References
Hohenzollern-Hechingen [1859], no. 123;[12] Parthey 1863–64, vol. 1 (1863), p. 676, no. 18; Stechow 1935, p. 84, ill. 11; Rolf 1967, no. 31; Pasadena 1980, p. 37, ill.; Sluijter 1986, pp. 38, 237, 378n38-2, 500n237-3; P. Sutton 1986, p. 215; Muchnic 1998, p. 126; Van Thiel 1999, no. 182, pl. 151, pp. 118, 129, 173, 196, 365; S. Campbell 2010, p. 359, no. 982, ill.; Muchnic 2019, p. 118.

Related Work
Reversed copy?, oil on panel, 53 × 38 cm; present location unknown, formerly Gallery Vitale Bloch, Paris, 1954. Van Thiel 1999, p. 365, pl. 152: "Either a work by an anonymous painter, who used the motifs occurring in cat. 182 [Pasadena] but arranged them differently, or a copy after a lost original."

Technical Notes
The support is a thin copper panel. Microscopic examination reveals that the surface was lightly scratched overall to provide "tooth." Instead of a glue-chalk ground layer, the ground consists of two thin layers of fairly liquid oil paint: the first layer smoothly brushed, and the second (upper) layer applied by stippling, or sponging. Because of contact with the copper, the oil in the ground has produced a pale green color. The color of the ground does not have a chromatic effect, but its slightly pebbled texture is an important element of the entire painting. The artist left margins around the painted image, with the ground layers exposed where they extend to the edges of the panel. Paint handling is varied. Areas of shadow on the figures have been applied softly in thin glazes. In contrast, the draperies of the canopy and cushion are fluid, opaque, and strongly brushed. In general, the painting is in stable condition. Small flake losses have occurred, but adhesion of paint to copper is good. Abrasion is found throughout the painting, but it is especially pronounced in the figures at the center right. It is probable that glazes have been removed in prior cleaning, such as the proper right shoulder of Mars, where the textured ground is evident through the paint layer, as well as the proper left shoulder of Venus. Retouching is located primarily in the figure of the woman kneeling at bottom right, the woman standing at center right, the rising mist at the right side, and a few other scattered spots. It covers the flake losses, and in other instances it strengthens thinly painted areas. The natural-resin varnish has a uniform gloss and saturates the colors adequately, though it is yellowed.

Her eyes cast upward, Venus lies seductively beneath the canopy of a sumptuously cushioned bed as a maidservant wearing a diaphanous blouse and jewelry fastens Cestia around her midriff; the famed girdle was reputed to make both mortal and immortal women sexually irresistible. Hovering above, putti, including Venus's mischievous son Cupid, scatter flowers over her in reference to Flora, with whom the goddess of love was often identified. A nude maidservant kneels on a dark-green velvet cushion to unlace Venus's sandals, while a nude youth helps the ruddy, mustachioed Mars remove his garments. The powerful Roman god of war has already discarded his weapons—his sword and helmet lie abandoned on the floor, while his sacred shield, Ancile, and his halberd have become the playthings of putti.

Both Homer (*Odyssey*, 8.266–365) and Ovid (*Metamorphoses*, 4.171–89) related the story of the love affair of Mars and Venus, but only Homer, speaking through a minstrel at the palace of King Alcinous, recounts their actual tryst.[13] Venus, the wife of Vulcan, the blacksmith of the gods, fell in

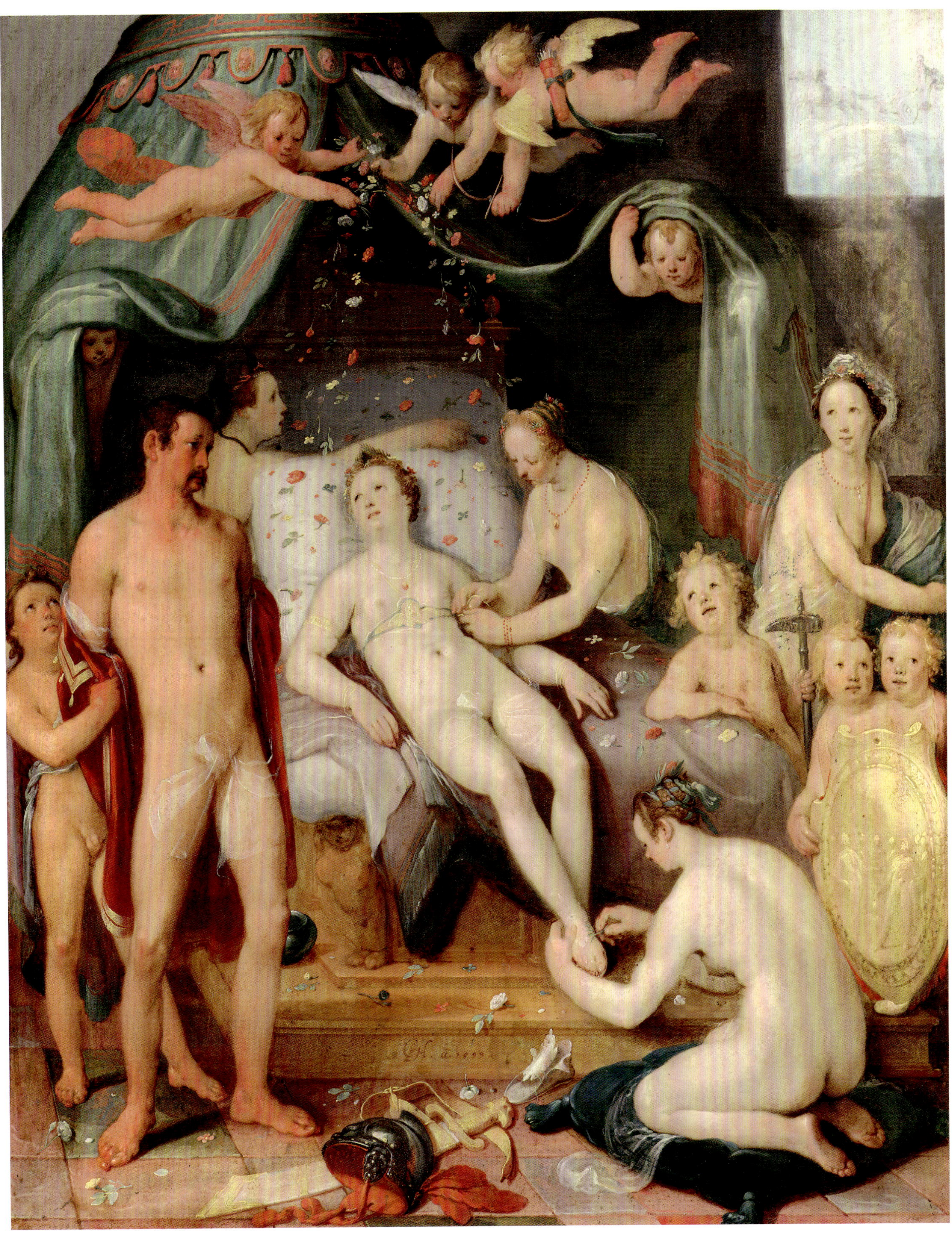

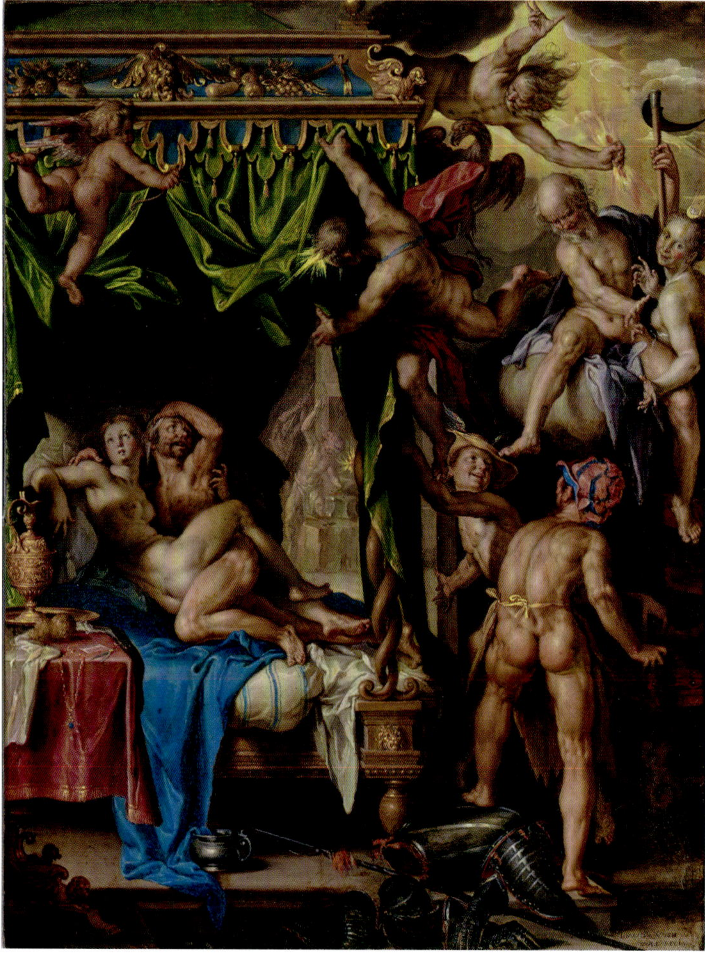

Fig. 16a. Joachim Wtewael, *Mars and Venus Surprised by Vulcan*, 1606–10, oil on copper, 8 × 6⅛ in. (20.3 × 15.5 cm), J. Paul Getty Museum, Los Angeles.

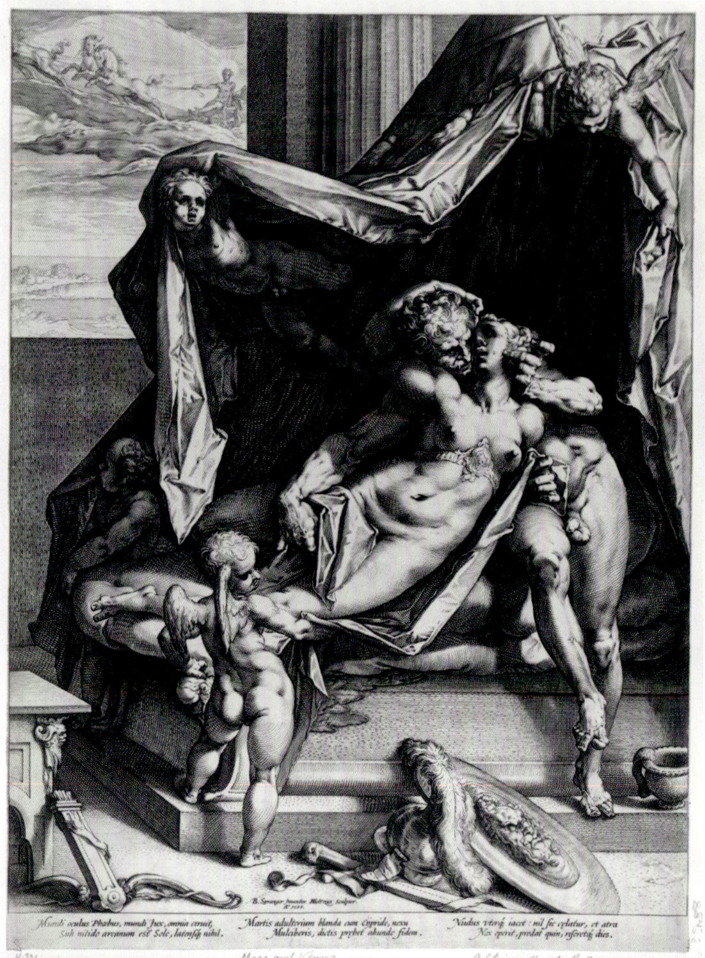

Fig. 16b. Hendrick Goltzius, *Mars and Venus*, 1588, engraving, 17⅜ × 12 15⁄16 in. (44.1 × 32.9 cm), Philadelphia Museum of Art: The Muriel and Philip Berman Gift, 1985.

love with Mars and lay with him in Vulcan's palace. The next morning, while making his daily journey through the sky, the sun-god Helios spied the two lovers and informed the cuckolded husband of his wife's infidelity. Ovid, through the voice of Leuconoe, describes Vulcan's reaction: "Vulcan dropped whatever he was doing and made a net with such fine links of bronze no eye could see the mesh: no woolen thread was ever so delicate . . . and then he spread it over the bed, and when the lovers came there again, the husband's cunning art caught them and held them fast, and there they were held in each other's arms, and Vulcan, Lord of Lemnos, opened wide the ivory doors and called the gods to come and see."[14]

Cornelis Cornelisz. van Haarlem painted *Mars and Venus* in 1599.[15] At the end of the sixteenth and beginning of the seventeenth centuries, stories of the loves of the gods were popular among the Dutch literary elite, enjoyed as much for their erotic content as for their literary references. Among Cornelis's Dutch contemporaries, the favorite scene from the story of Mars and Venus was the dramatic moment when the unsuspecting couple, locked in an embrace, is surprised by Vulcan and mocked by the other gods. Two engravings of the subject by Cornelis's colleague, the Haarlem printmaker/painter Hendrick Goltzius (1558–1617), inspired numerous contemporary prints and paintings, including *Mars and Venus Surprised by Vulcan* by Joachim Wtewael (1566–1638; fig. 16a).[16] In these Mannerist images, Venus and Mars lounge naked on a bed, their elongated bodies gracefully entwined in the shallow space in which Mars's armor is strewn carelessly across the floor. Cornelis, who would have known both works by his friend, seems to have been most interested in Goltzius's print of 1588 (fig. 16b), in which putti lift the canopy of the bed and Helios can be seen through the window riding his chariot across the sky.

In her monograph on Wtewael's *Mars and Venus Surprised by Vulcan*, Anne Lowenthal discusses the tension the artist maintains between indulgence and retribution, inviting the viewer's vicarious involvement in both the coupling and its consequences.[17] She observes that contemporary moralists considered erotic imagery dangerous: As the Dutch humanist Dirck Volkertsz. Coornhert (1522–1590), who was Goltzius's teacher, remarked in 1568, "Contemplating pictures of 'a naked Venus' produce 'fiery impurity, burning desire and hot

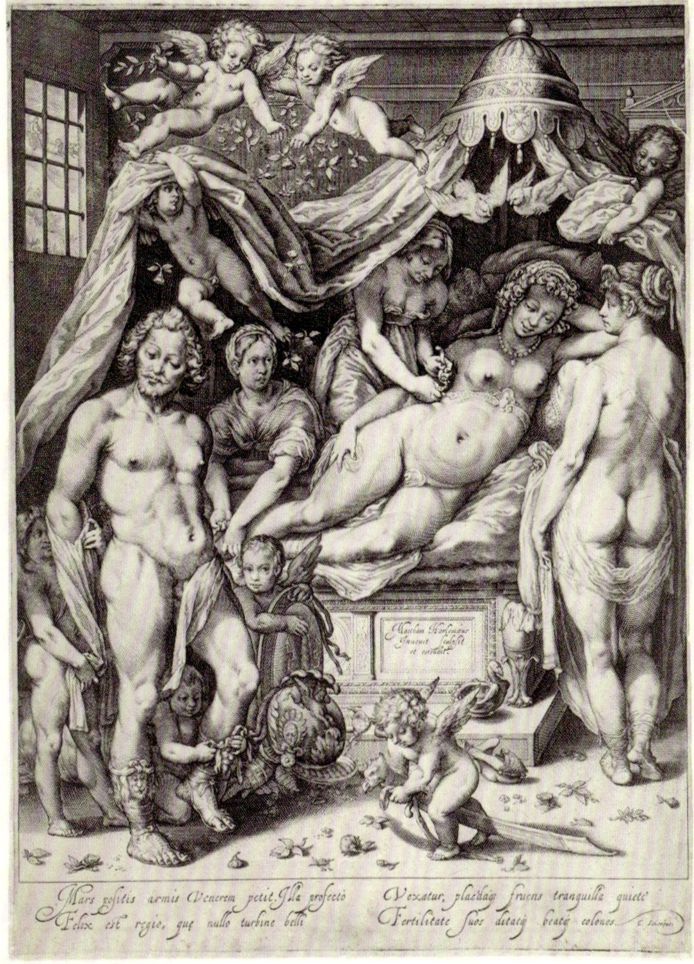

Fig. 16c. Jacob Matham, *Mars and Venus*, 1599–1600, engraving, 18 ½ × 13 ⅝ in. (47 × 34.6 cm), Rijksmuseum, Amsterdam.

passion.'"[18] Jacob Cats (1577–1660) was more emphatic in 1625 when he cautioned readers to avoid lewd pictures and not to be moved by them, "for even in art lies evil."[19] As Lowenthal points out, theorists of rhetoric realized, however, that pictures with an appeal to the senses could also serve a didactic function. The artist's goal was to captivate his audience through the sensual image, but not to seduce it.[20] According to Karel van Mander (1548–1606), who together with Goltzius and Cornelis founded the Haarlem academy, the lesson to be learned from the shame of Mars and Venus is that those who abandon God to follow lustful ways come to shame.[21]

Like Wtewael, Cornelis in *Mars and Venus* appealed to the viewer's delight in witnessing the erotic scene in which Venus's nude body is displayed in an open, frontal pose he frequently used.[22] Cornelis, however, muted the overt eroticism of Wtewael's version and depicted an earlier moment of the story, when Mars and Venus prepare for their sexual liaison. His still brightly colored figures originally rendered by means of layers of glazes, now somewhat abraded, have more natural proportions and postures than their mannered predecessors. Cornelis's choice of moment and composition is closely related to an undated engraving of *Mars and Venus* (fig. 16c) by the Haarlem artist Jacob Matham (1571–1631), the stepson and pupil of Goltzius and thus within Cornelis's intellectual and artistic circle.[23] Although the relationship of the two images is unclear, the more robust figures in the undated engraving by the younger artist suggest it postdates Cornelis's painting of 1599. An engraving by Matham after Paulus Moreelse (1571–1638), dated 1607, repeats and expands the composition in reverse, suggesting that the image was well known.[24]

Cornelis's selection of the scene portrayed in the Pasadena painting suggests that his concern was not with the harsh moralizing attached to the discovery of the lovers. The only reference to the consequences of their acts is the view through the window of Helios as he rides his chariot across the morning sky.[25] Here, it is Mars subdued by the power of love. His weapons cast down, Mars is no longer the ferocious warrior: rather, his body, like Venus's, appears to be without physical strength. Clues to the iconographic significance of Cornelis's erotically charged painting are found in the Latin inscription on Matham's engraving, which refers to the power of love over war and anger and proffers this as a guide for rulers: "As soon as Mars had removed the weapons, he longed for Venus. That truly is a fortunate realm, which is not plagued by the chaos of war and peacefully and quietly is able to enjoy leisure, the fecundity of the family, and the prosperity of its inhabitants."[26]

Like Matham's print, Cornelis's painting uses erotic content to make an appeal for peace. In 1599, the date of the painting, Spain and her representatives in the Southern Netherlands, the Archdukes Albert and Isabella, launched a remarkable peace initiative that gave hope that the devastating war between Spain and the United Netherlands would soon end.[27] War had ravaged the countryside, disrupting trade and commerce as well as personal contentment and safety. In Haarlem, where the memory of the long siege of 1572–73 was still bitter, the idea of peace was particularly welcome. Matham's print, and by extension Cornelis's painting, recommend peace as the preferred alternative to war. The inscription on Matham's print reiterates the theme, stressing the familiar argument that peace brings prosperity, security, and contentment.[28] It is not surprising that Cornelis's numerous other versions of the theme of Mars succumbing to the powers of love date from the period around the Twelve Years' Truce between Spain and the United Netherlands, 1609–21.[29]

1. The $\bar{a}$ in the signature is an abbreviation for the Latin word *anno*, meaning "year," which is also written as @. There appears to be no evidence that the $\bar{a}$ in Cornelis's signature was inscribed in a circle, but the straight line likely refers to it.

2. The title page of the catalogue describes the deceased Wilhelmus van Velthuyzen as an art connoisseur. The collection included paintings by Italian as well as Netherlandish masters. The two previous numbers in the sale were 45, *Venus and Mercury* by Goltzius, and 46, *Ganymede* by Rembrandt.

3. The title page of the sale catalogue notes that the paintings were collected over many years by the deceased Mr. Verschuuring, commissioner of finance for the state of Holland, etc. Rolf 1967, no. 31, cites the sale and notes that the painting was included in *Catalogue Hendrik Verschuring* [*sic*] (The Hague, 1752), which suggests that Verschuuring acquired the painting from the sale of the Velthuyzen collection or shortly thereafter.

4. The title page of the sale catalogue notes that the deceased Mr. Van der Dussen had been "Meesterknaap van Gooyland en onderhoorige Heerlykheden, enz." The sale of the large collection was divided into three parts. A copy of the catalogue in the RKD identifies the buyer of lot 19 as "Ploos," undoubtedly Cornelis Ploos van Amstel, who was also one of the brokers (*makelaars*) listed for the sale with Slebes et al.

5. Cornelis Ploos van Amstel was a Dutch timber merchant who is known as a collector (especially of drawings), printmaker and publisher, draftsman, and art theorist. He was director of the academy of drawings in Amsterdam and developed a printing technique that closely mimics the appearance of drawings. Cornelis Cornelisz. van Haarlem's painting was not included in the posthumous sale of Ploos van Amstel's collection. Although he may have sold it anonymously in another sale, it is possible that Ploos van Amstel, whose name often appears as a broker of Amsterdam sales, was buying in or acting as an agent for a collector when he was listed as the buyer of the painting in 1774. Regarding Ploos van Amstel, see Laurentius, Niemeijer, and Ploos van Amstel 1980.

6. First suggested by Rolf 1967, no. 31, and restated by Van Thiel 1999, no. 182, who identifies the buyer.

7. Many of the paintings in the Hohenzollern-Hechingen Collection, Löwenberg, came from the Sagan Collection through Dorothea von Medem and Duke Peter von Kurland (d. 1800), since 1795 "Standesherr auf Sagan in Slesien," whose second daughter, Pauline (1782–1845), was the mother of Friedrich Wilhelm Konstantin, Prince of Hohenzollern-Hechingen. I am grateful to Dr. Petra Mandt, Wallraf-Richartz Museum, Cologne, for providing information on this collection in email correspondence on 22 January 2002 (NSM). See Holst 1938, pp. 570f., where he notes that the manuscript of the catalogue of the Sagan Collection made by Professor Keller, Berlin, in 1846, was then in his possession, and a printed copy of the catalogue (published in 1849) was in the Sagan library. The collection included approximately five hundred paintings. According to Holst, after 1846 the Sagan Gallery was greatly reduced by inheritance. An 1855 printed catalogue of the collection (Sagan library, Berlin) included considerably fewer paintings, many of the most valuable having passed to the second daughter.

8. Prince Friedrich Wilhelm Konstantin succeeded his father in 1838. Parthey 1863–64, vol. 1, p. 676, identifies the painting as no. 18 of an inventory dated 1858. Holst 1938, p. 572, notes that a catalogue of the collection made in 1859 includes many well-known works from the Sagan Collection (see Hohenzollern-Hechingen [1859]). Following the war of 1870–71, the best pieces from Löwenberg were sold privately; others were later sold at an auction at Lepke, Berlin, 1–9 October 1913 (sale no. 1687) under the name of "Graf R." [Rotenburg, Schlesisch-Nettkow]. The rest of the collection remained in the various residences in Schlesien.

9. According to Stechow 1935, p. 84, fig. 11. Fritz Gurlitt (1854–1893) was a dealer and publisher. In 1880 he founded Galerie Fritz Gurlitt, which his son Wolfgang Gurlitt (1888–1965) continued under his name following his father's death. During the Nazi era, like his cousin the art historian and art dealer Hildebrant Gurlitt, Wolfgang Gurlitt was involved in the sale of degenerate art and the purchase of works for Hitler's planned museum in Linz. In 1943 Galerie Fritz Gurlitt in Berlin was destroyed by bombs, and the business closed. Wolfgang Gurlitt moved to Bad Ausee and continued to run his publishing operation. In 1946 he gained Austrian citizenship and from 1946 to 1956 was director of the Neue Galerie der Stadt Linz. Galerie Wolfgang Gurlitt opened in Munich in 1955 and closed in 1977. Galerie Fritz Gurlitt was a promoter of German contemporary artists and was the first to exhibit works by the French Impressionists in Germany. In 1937 Wolfgang Gurlitt donated 1,533 glass negatives to the Deutsche Dokumentationszentrum für Kunstgeschichte-Bildarchiv Foto Marburg (DDK). The negatives document artworks exhibited by, sold through, or used for promotional purposes by Galerie Fritz Gurlitt, as well as images of interior design projects. No written documentation accompanies this archive, although some of the photographs are dated between 1914 and 1928. In her article on this collection of negatives, Sonja Feßel suggests that Wolfgang Gurlitt ceased using photographic documentation by the end of the 1920s. Feßel 2016, pp. 8–22, esp. 18. The glass negative of cat. 16 is undated, so it cannot be documented as being in the Gurlitt collection before 1935. We are grateful to DDK archivist Annette Otterbach for confirming this information.

10. According to an annotated copy of the catalogue at the GRI; not mentioned by Van Thiel 1999. Raux may have been acting as an agent for Stein or represent a code name for the collector/dealer.

11. According to Van Thiel 1999, no. 182.

12. I am grateful to Dr. Petra Mandt, Wallraf-Richartz Museum, Cologne (22 January 2002, NSM), for identifying this catalogue.

13. Both works were well-known to Cornelis and his learned contemporaries in Haarlem. The first Dutch translation of the *Odyssey* was published in Haarlem in 1561 by Dirck Volkertsz. Coornhert as *De dolinghe van Ulyss*. Karel van Mander included his commentary on Ovid's *Metamorphoses*, "Wtlegghingh op den Metamorphosis Pub. Ovidij Nasants," in *Het Schilderboek*, published in Haarlem in 1604.

14. Sluijter 1986, p. 372n38-2.

15. An inventory dated 3 August 1684 of the estate of Aeltie Pieters. Begga (d. 8 June 1684), the granddaughter of Cornelis, mentions in the *voorhuis*, "Een schilderij van Mr. Cornelis van Haerlem uijtbeeldende Mars en Venus" (Biesboer 2001, pp. 270–74, no. 58; GPI, Archival Inventory N-4330, Item 0058). Because Cornelis painted the subject more than once, however, it is uncertain whether the Pasadena painting was that in the 1684 inventory. The painting does not appear in the 1639 inventory made of Cornelis's estate after his death (Bredius and Hirschmann 1921, p. 98, no 18).

Aeltie Pieters. Begga was the widow of Willem Claesz. Stam. Her mother, Maria Cornelisdr. (bapt. 27 February 1611, Amsterdam), who was married to Pieter Jansz. Begeyn (Begga), was the illegitimate daughter of Cornelis. Aeltie appears to have inherited paintings, drawings, and prints by Cornelis through her mother and/or her brother, the painter Cornelis Bega (1631/32–1664). The inventory made of Aeltie's estate includes numerous works by both Cornelis van Haarlem and Bega. A second inventory, dated 18 November 1684 (Biesboer 2001, p. 275), includes one unidentified painting by Bega and all the drawings and prints left by Cornelis van Haarlem and Bega ("Alle de prenten en teijckeninge bij Mr. Cornelis van Haerlem en Cornelis Begga naergelaten").

16. Both engravings owe a debt to Bartholomeus Spranger (1546–1611). The work in Hollstein 1949–2010, vol. 8 (1952), no. 137, dated 1585, is after Goltzius's own design but is strongly influenced by Spranger (see Mielke 1979, pp. 23f., no. 2; and Hendrix 1992). Goltzius himself attributed the design of Hollstein 1949–2010, vol. 8 (1952), no. 321, dated 1588, to Spranger (see Mielke 1979, pp. 27f., no. 7, ill.).

17. Lowenthal 1995, p. 17.

18. Lowenthal 1995, p. 17, quotes from Coornhert [1586] 1942, p. 31. Regarding contemporary attitudes to images of nudes, see Sluijter 1991–92, pp. 337–96.

19. Lowenthal 1995, p. 17.

20. Lowenthal 1995, p. 17.

21. Lowenthal 1995, p. 20, citing Van Mander 1604, fols. 39r and 39v.

22. See, for example, the figure of Oenone in Cornelis's painting *Paris with Oenone* (London, Collection Larsen; Van Thiel 1999, cat. no. 154) and Venus in his *Mars and Venus* (Landesmuseum, Hanover).

23. Hollstein 1949–2010, vol. 11 (1955), p. 228, no. 213; Hollstein 1993–, vol. 16 (2007), pt. 2, pp. 91, 94, no. 187, ill.). Matham claimed to have invented, drawn, and engraved the print. Baumstark 1974, p. 179 and pp. 226f., nos. 401 and 404, suggests, however, that Matham was probably inspired by a drawing of the subject by Rosso Fiorentino (1495–1540; Louvre, Paris), apparently made in Venice for Pietro Aretino (1492–1556) but possibly sent to Francis I of France. The influence of Rosso's image probably came via one of the prints made after the drawing. See Bartsch 1978–, vol. 28, under Jacopo Caraglio, B. 51 (87); p. 181 of the text volume tentatively reattributes the print to Binck.

24. Hollstein 1949–2010, vol. 11 (1955), p. 227, no. 205; Hollstein 1993–, vol. 16 (2007), pt. 2, pp. 91, 187, no. 186, ill.

25. The area between the turning maidservant on the far right and the window, which appears to represent smoke, is actually an area of abrasion.

26. “Mars positis armis Venerem petit. Illa profecto / Felix est regio, quæ nullo turbine belli / Vexatur, placidaque fruens tranquilla quiete / Fertilitate suos ditatque beatosque colonos.” English translation based on German translation in Baumstark 1974, p. 180. On page 227n405, Baumstark notes that the author of the inscription was the humanist Cornelius van Schoon (“Schonaeuse”; 1540–1611), who was head of the Latin school in Haarlem from 1575.

27. See Israel 1995, pp. 254ff.

28. See Baumstark 1974, pp. 180f.

29. Van Thiel 1999, nos. 183–192, records ten other versions of the story of Venus and the disarmed Mars, all but one of which date before 1628. On the theme of the passive Mars as a reference to peace, see Utrecht 1980.

17, 18

Lucas Cranach I

German
Kronach 1472–1553 Weimar

Adam

ca. 1530

Signed on trunk of tree, lower right, with artist's coat of arms (fig. 17a)
Oil on panel, height: left side, 73¾ in. (187.3 cm); right side, 74⅛ in. (188.3 cm);
width: top, 27⅜ in. (69.5 cm); bottom, 27½ in. (69.9 cm)
Norton Simon Art Foundation, M.1971.1.P

Eve

ca. 1530

Oil on panel, height: left side, 74¼ in. (188.6 cm); right side, 73⅞ in. (187.6 cm);
width: top and bottom, 27¼ in. (69.2 cm)
Norton Simon Art Foundation, M.1991.1.P

Provenance

Said to have been in the Stroganoff Collection.[1] Located in the Church of the Holy Trinity, Kiev, from around 1919, transferred June 1927 to;[2] Lavra Reserve Museum, Kiev, inv. no. 11,390, as "[single] picture of Adam and Eve with defects," unattributed, transferred 1928 to;[3] Museum of Art, Ukrainian Academy of Sciences, Kiev,[4] inv. no. 5741, as single, cradled panel, 1.87 × 1.405 m, removed by Soviet government 29 September 1929 to the Antiquariat Leningrad[5] (sale [Stroganoff Collection], Rudolph Lepke's Kunst-Auctions-Haus, Berlin, 12–13 May 1931, nos. 44–45; sold for 47,000 Reichsmarks to);[6] [Jacques Goudstikker (1897–1940), Amsterdam,[7] appropriated 1940 through]; [Alois Miedl (1903–1990), Amsterdam to];[8] Reichsmarshall Hermann Goering (1893–1946), Berlin;[9] recovered 1945 by Allied Forces and transferred to; Stichting Nederlands Kunstbezit, inv. nos. NK 1693 (*Adam*) and NK 1694 (*Eve*);[10] claimed 1962 by and transferred 1966 to Commander George Stroganoff Scherbatoff (1898–1976), New York and Connecticut, and sold 1970 (*Eve*) and 1971 (*Adam*) through; [Spencer A. Samuels & Co. Ltd., New York, to]; Norton Simon Art Foundation (*Adam*) and The Norton Simon Foundation (*Eve*), the latter transferred in 1991 to; Norton Simon Art Foundation.[11]

Exhibited

Amsterdam 1936b, no. 35; on loan, National Gallery of Art, Washington, DC, 26 February 1971–15 November 1972; Princeton 1972–74, no 5; Los Angeles 2024.

References

Ghilarov 1929, passim;[12] Schmidt 1931, pp. 194f., English summary pp. 35f., ill., as in the Museum of Art, Ukrainian Academy of Science; M. Friedländer and Rosenberg 1932, p. 60, no. 164, ill., as with Goudstikker; Steadman 1972, no. 5, pp. 32f., p. 33, ill., detail, *Eve*, p. 26; Seldis 1972, ill. p. 25; M. Friedländer and Rosenberg 1978, p. 108, no. 195, ill.; Pasadena 1980, p. 35, ill.; Koerner 1985, pp. 84, 88, fig. 14; Venema 1986, p. 603, nos. 32–33; Pasadena 1989, pp. 31, 32, ill.; Bonnet 1994, pp. 144f., figs. A 89–A 90; Muchnic 1998, pp. 179–83; Hollander 1998, p. 255; Yeide, Akinsha, and Walsh 2001, pp. 135–37; Schoen 2001, p. 200, as about 1530, p. 288n100 (*Adam*); Jager 2001, pp. 151–70; Pasadena 2003, p. 41, ill.; Odom and Salmond 2009, pp. 119–27, 135n63; Yeide 2009, pp. 71f., nos. A356–A357; S. Campbell 2010, pp. 115, 119, 333, no. 734 (*Eve*), 334, no. 742 (*Adam*), ill.; Muchnic 2019, pp. 196–99, 315–17; Cranach Digital Archive n.d.

Technical Notes

Painting Supports

The primary painting support consists of two large, previously cradled limewood panels, each comprised of seven individual boards in vertical orientation and grain structure. The individual boards vary in width and have numerous imperfections such as knots, some of which were cut out and replaced with inserts at the time of the panel construction.[13] Three small original inserts are present in the *Eve* panel, located to the left of her forehead, above the head of the serpent, and along the left edge of the panel, in the tree. At the upper right of the *Adam* painting, a large non-original wood insert measuring 8½ by 4 inches was set diagonally into the panel, replacing a portion of Adam's forehead and hair and a small amount of background detail. Numerous knots and imperfections in the *Adam* panel were not replaced with inserts, and they now feature somewhat prominently on the painting surface. While the preparation of the painting supports using seven individual boards for each panel is not unusual, it is surprising to find so many knots and imperfections, since a construction employing a greater number of narrow boards typically avoided the imperfections found in wider boards. The thickness of the limewood supports presently averages about ¼ inch. The original thickness of the panels can be estimated based on the partial dowel holes that can be found along the right edge of *Adam*—matching corresponding dowel holes along the left edge of *Eve*. When the old heavy cradles were applied (before 1919), the original panels were thinned, leaving about half of the dowel holes intact, therefore it can be assumed that the original panel thickness ranged from ⅜ to ½ inch. The dowels served to align and connect the two individual panels when displayed as one continuous composition, though there is no evidence to support the theory that *Adam* and *Eve* were originally constructed using one large single panel that was later cut in half; they were instead likely conceived as two separate panels. Both panels had suffered extensive damages along the bottom edges that were later cut out and filled with wooden inserts in a cross-grain direction. These damages were likely caused by prolonged exposure to moisture and

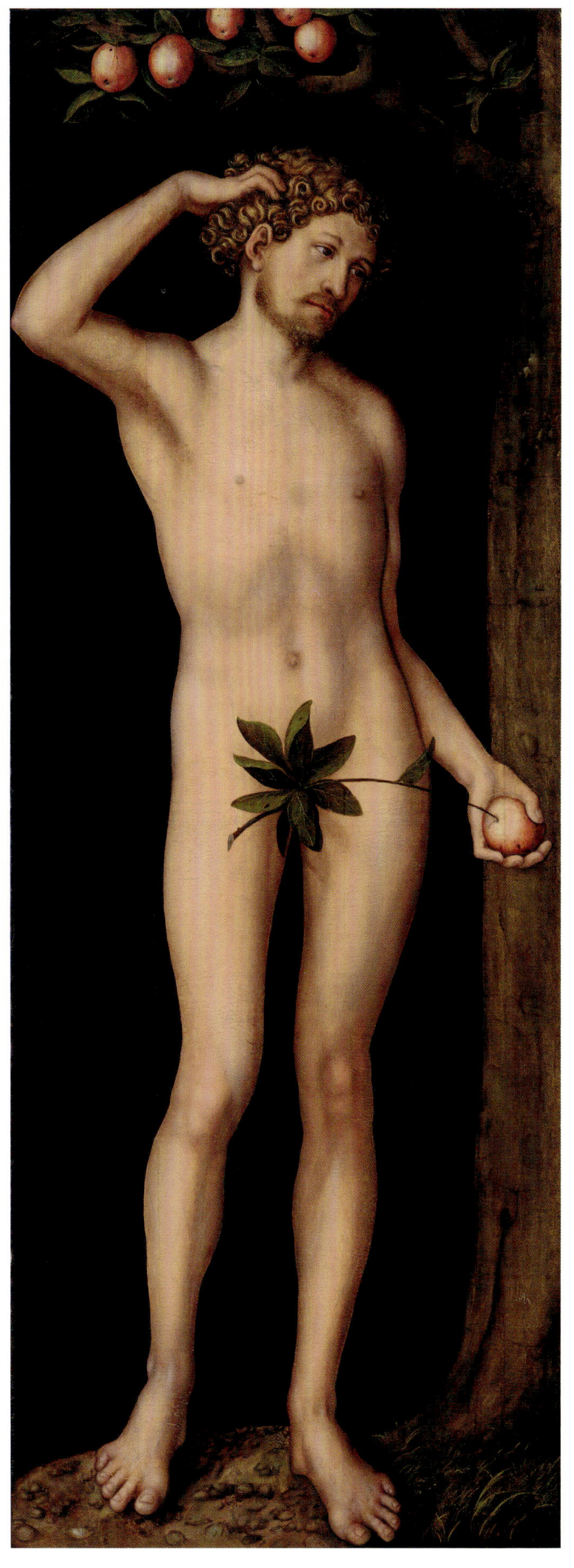
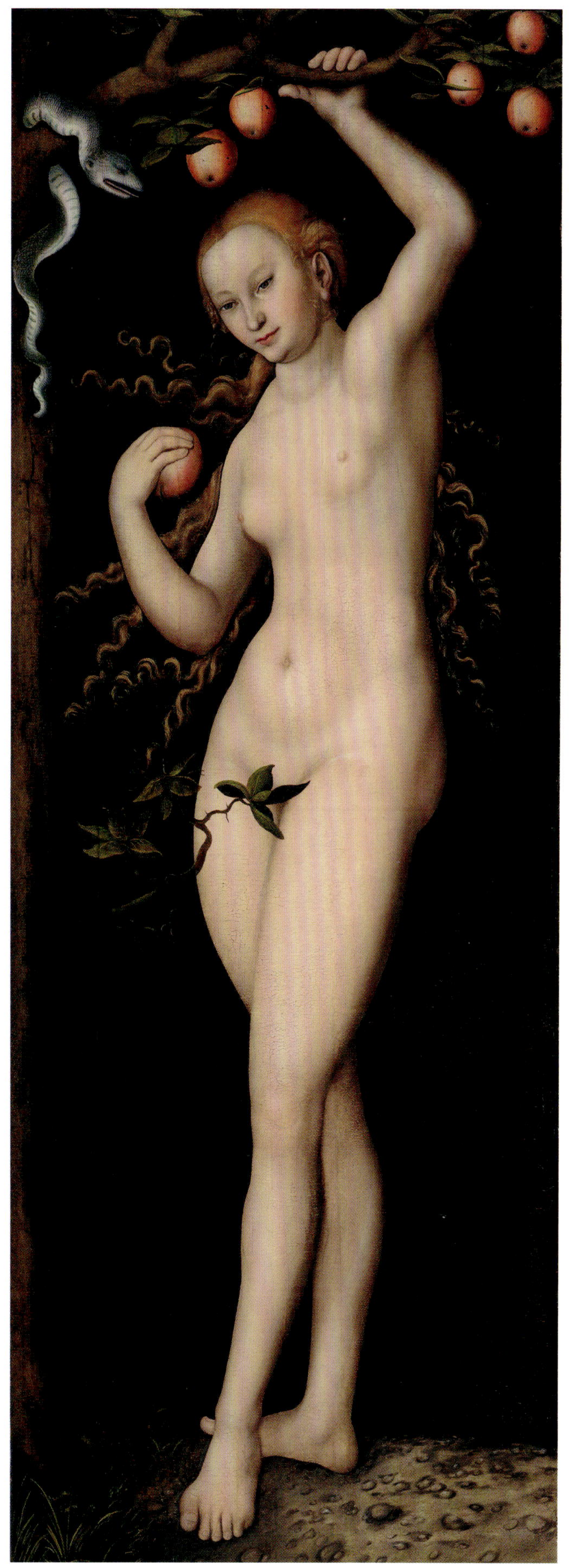

were furthermore associated with tunneling from insect infestation along the bottom of the panels.

The heavy cradle caused numerous long vertical splits to develop over time in both panels, resulting in a distinct "washboard" effect with a strong cross-grain warp of the individual boards. X-radiography examination elucidates other details of the process of the original construction and preparation of the panel supports. The panels were hand-planed in a horizontal direction, perpendicular to the vertically butt-joined boards. The planed panels were then reinforced with "werg," a fibrous material adhered across the surface to strengthen the joins and to cover imperfections in the wood.[14] Such material in Cranach's paintings often consisted of hemp fibers, flax fibers, or horsehair, among other materials. The fibers were adhered to the panel surface using animal glue and subsequently covered by the gesso ground. Frequently observed in Cranach's panel paintings, the gesso ground and paint layers often develop mechanical cracks following the direction of individual fibers beneath, and this can also be observed in the present *Adam* and *Eve*. An exposed area of the fibrous material in one of the many old paint losses was identified under 300x magnification as sinew, made from connective tissue such as tendons from various animals.[15]

Paint Application

Macro-X-radiograph-fluorescence scanning (performed by Douglas MacLennan of the Getty Conservation Institute) was carried out across the *Eve* panel, paying particular attention to the figure to better understand Cranach's materials and painting technique. The thinly painted flesh tones contain mostly lead with some mercury, likely lead white and vermilion. Facial features contain a little copper, perhaps present as azurite. XRF mapping also reveals multiple adjustments to Eve's body, suggesting that contours and positions of her arms were subtly adjusted during painting. A zinc- and potassium-rich outline is present around most of the figure, suggesting the use of potassium zinc sulfate, commonly referred to as zinc vitriol or white vitriol, added as a drier.[16] Zinc sulfate has been previously identified in Cranach's *Portrait of Johannes Feige* and *Portrait of a Woman* (both National Gallery, London).[17] This painted outline also contains iron and manganese, likely present as an umber. Eve's auburn hair contains mostly iron and mercury, but highlights also contain lead and tin, probably present as lead tin yellow. The fig leaves contain copper, lead, and tin, suggesting a mixture of lead tin yellow with a copper blue or green pigment. The snake is painted with a copper blue pigment, likely azurite, with details painted using a black pigment. Examination aided by X-radiography as well as visual examination with a stereomicroscope informed the likely painting sequence. First, a very thin umber wash was broadly applied, outlining the figures. Cranach then indicated key features in the figure, such as general outlines, navel, position of the kneecaps, and certain muscle groups using relatively fluid paint with a narrow brush. The buildup of the flesh tones in very thin layers then followed, likely beginning with a warm mid-tone and slowly building the features in the figures, letting each layer dry thoroughly, with the highlights applied last. The result is an extremely subtle and beautiful effect, with the passages of lights and shadows seemingly melting together, and no individual brushstrokes discernible. The flesh tones extend beyond the outlines of the underdrawing, allowing for revisions during the painting process, since the next step involved application of the nearly black background that was then used to redefine the borders of the figure. The black paint is always on top of the flesh tones, creating a silhouetting effect, a prominent feature in many of Cranach's paintings. Other features, such as the tree and the apples, were likely painted after the central figures, basically suggesting a paint application sequence from the center outward.

Conservation Treatment

A comprehensive conservation treatment was performed between 2021 and 2024 addressing both structural as well as aesthetic issues. Old restorations and considerably yellowed and discolored varnishes were removed, revealing numerous old damages, paint losses, and abrasions, most of which were quite old. A few damages—such as a large, irregularly shaped paint-and-gesso loss above Adam's extended hand—appeared to be of a more recent date, possibly caused during recovery of the paintings in the summer of 1945. There are several deep circular holes about 1 cm in diameter, with the most prominent one located to the right of Eve's elbow. Removal of the old wax fills revealed what can only be described as a crater, with the wood fibers of the panel support pulverized. Two of the small round holes visible across the panel were analyzed by XRF. The results of the scans show that both holes contain an enrichment of iron, lead, mercury, and titanium.[18]

The structural treatment was performed by two experts who specialize in large-scale wooden supports: George Bisacca, conservator emeritus at the Metropolitan Museum of Art, New York; and José de la Fuente, conservator of panel paintings at the Museo Nacional del Prado, Madrid. Bisacca and De la Fuente initiated the complex process of removing the cradle from each panel and attaching a new support system of their own design. After surgically detaching the cradles, they painstakingly filled every one of the minute cracks in the seven discrete planks of wood that comprise each of the panels, then fitted all crevices with perfectly shaped wedges using wood of the same density as that used by Cranach. This process reestablished consistent strength and a gentle natural curvature in each panel.

A large wooden insert near Adam's forehead posed particular challenges to the process. Inserted at an oblique angle relative to the overall grain direction, the insert had been the site of repeated repair, paint loss, and restoration, at one point being completely surfaced with a wax putty and repainted. Bisacca and De la Fuente created a new insert for this area by laminating together correctly oriented pieces of antique linden wood and shaping them to match the curvature of the panel. The final stage of their work involved creating a new support system to replace the cradles. For this, Bisacca and De la Fuente designed a highly specialized strainer—a framework constructed to match the nuanced curvature of the panels, then secured to an adjustable spring system. This innovation enables the strainer to respond to infinitesimal movements in the wood while providing physical support.

The removal of the oxidized and discolored varnishes and old retouching yielded Cranach's original subtle color palette and restored the sense of space and depth in the picture. Abrasions were revealed to be concentrated primarily along joined boards, impacting mostly the black background. Paint losses that required major reconstruction concerned Adam's forehead and hair, the big toe of his proper left foot, as well as the fingertips of Eve's proper left hand grasping the tree branch, and the tips of the toes of her proper left foot. For the reconstruction of Adam's forehead and locks, Cranach's *Adam* (1528; oil on panel) now at the Gallerie degli Uffizi, Florence, was used as a model and involved projecting a photograph of the pertinent passage onto the paint loss.[19]

After isolating and resaturating the surface with dilute damar resin, the deeper losses of paint were in-filled with traditional gesso and in-painted with Gamblin conservation colors. A spray application of dilute damar served as the final protective layer. —*Ulrich Birkmaier*

Adam and Eve appear before their fall from God's grace, which occurred when they succumbed to the serpent's temptation to defy God's command and ate an apple from the Tree of the Knowledge of Good and Evil.[20] They stand unashamed and do not hide their nakedness: rather, leafy branches fortuitously cover their genitals, preserving their modesty. Eve's upraised arm, however, seems to celebrate her nudity, inviting the viewer's gaze with her coy, though averted, glance.

Between 1510 and 1540, Lucas Cranach I is estimated by one author to have depicted Adam and Eve more than fifty times, using at least eighteen formats.[21] His first monumental paintings of the subject with life-size figures date from the late 1520s, when he employed an active workshop. Signed on the lower right of the Adam panel with a crowned, winged serpent—Cranach's coat of arms (fig. 17a)—the Pasadena panels, each isolating a single, life-size figure in separate but interrelated spaces, compare stylistically and iconographically to documented paintings by Cranach from the late 1520s and early 1530s. Particularly closely related are *Adam and Eve* in the Gallerie degli Uffizi, Florence, signed and dated 1528, and the pair in the Gemäldegalerie Alte Meister, Dresden, signed and dated 1531.[22] The elegant, graceful lines created by the crisp contours and smooth surfaces of the subtly modeled figures of Adam and Eve silhouetted against a solid black background are typical of Cranach's paintings from this period, as are the preliminary sketches visible beneath the flesh areas of the figures indicating the basic contours and areas of general shading.

Fig. 17a. Detail of artist's coat of arms.

Cranach's inspiration for the series of paintings of Adam and Eve was two works by Albrecht Dürer (1471–1528): his famous engraving of 1504 (fig. 17b), which had introduced the classical canon of human proportion to northern artists, and his paintings of 1507 (figs. 17c–d), which established the model for life-size nudes set against black backgrounds in individual panels.[23] Dürer's model for Adam was the famous ancient statue of Apollo known as the *Apollo Belvedere*, and for Eve, an ancient statue of Venus. Cranach's Eve is a composite of Dürer's figures from 1504 and 1507.[24] Although clearly derived from Dürer's 1504 print, Cranach's Adam lacks the strong, masculine anatomy of Dürer's example, and the figure's light beard depends on the northern brand of naturalism rather than on the classical images that inspired Dürer's depiction of the clean-faced Adam. Cranach's orientation to the emerging Mannerist style of the North is also evident in the continuous, elastic contours and the preference for a soft, lyrical mood rather than the stiff movements and highly articulated anatomy of Dürer's 1504 print. Typical of his paintings from the late 1520s, Cranach seems to have delighted in the decorative play of the spiraling curls of Eve's golden hair against the black background, echoed by the serpentine form of the snake coiled around the branch above her.[25]

Cranach, who probably never traveled to Italy, adopted the composition and proportions from Dürer's print but eliminated the numerous iconographic details, placing his figures

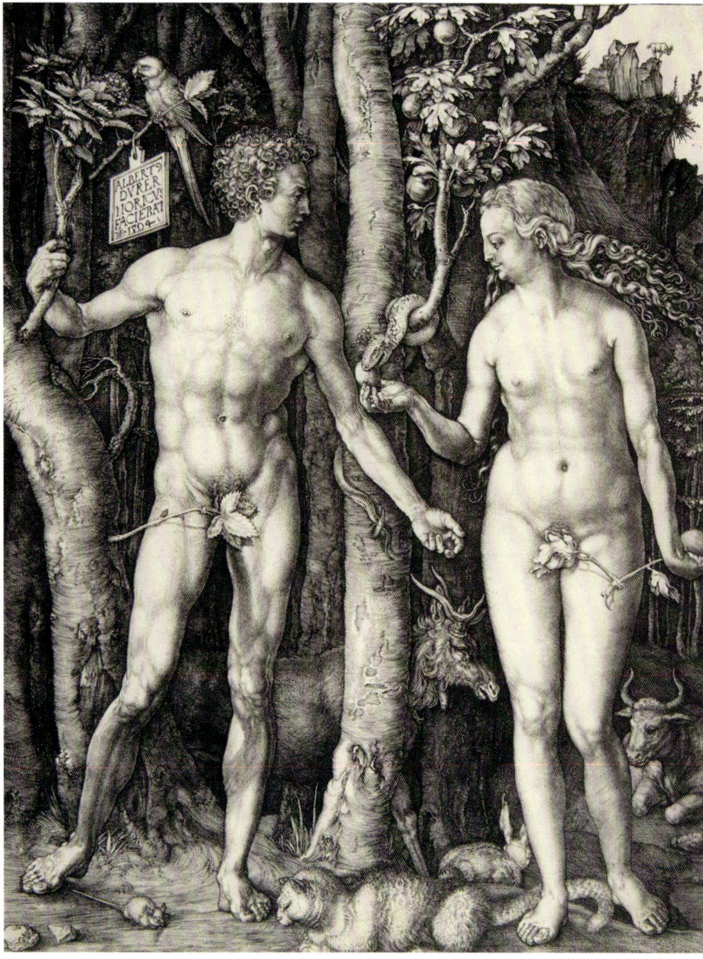

Fig. 17b. Albrecht Dürer, *Adam and Eve*, 1504, engraving, 9 7/8 × 7 7/8 in. (25.1 × 20 cm), The Metropolitan Museum of Art, New York.

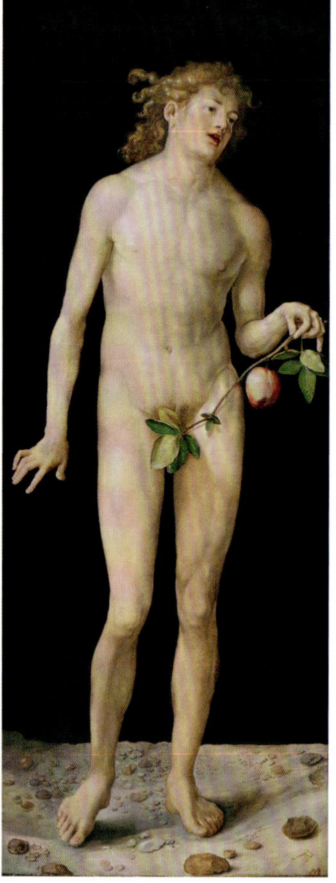

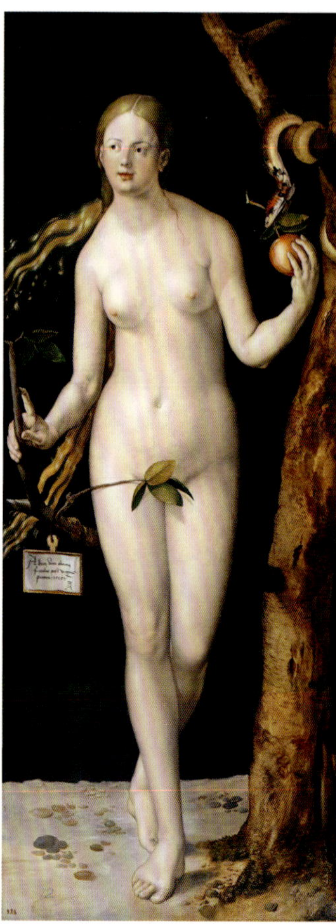

Fig. 17c. Albrecht Dürer, *Adam*, 1507, oil on panel, 82 3/8 × 31 7/8 in. (209 × 81 cm), (P002177), Museo Nacional del Prado, Madrid.

Fig. 17d. Albrecht Dürer, *Eve*, 1507, oil on panel, 82 3/8 × 31 7/8 in. (209 × 80 cm), (P002178), Museo Nacional del Prado, Madrid.

on a simple, pebbled ground, and silhouetting them against a black background that accentuates their sinuous forms.[26] In contrast to Dürer's 1507 composition, Cranach retained the central position of the tree, which he divided between the two panels. He further emphasized the continuity of space by the gestures of the figures: Adam's right arm raised to scratch his head reflects Eve's gesture of grasping the branch with her left hand. Eve's right arm appears poised to place the apple in Adam's extended hand and complete the compositional circle, which ties the two panels together. The placement of her left leg across her right suggests movement and reinforces the presumption that the action will be completed.[27]

Cranach may have intended the seductive quality of the beautiful, sensuous nudes in these monumental paintings to encourage viewers to contemplate their own mortality and personal responsibility. The nature of original sin and the origin of death were actively debated at the Saxon Court, where Cranach served as court painter to Frederick the Wise, Elector of Saxony (1463–1525), for more than twenty-five years. According to Martin Luther (1483–1546), who was Cranach's personal friend, human mortality, as distinct from the death of animals, had a specific historical origin in the sin of Adam. Viewers' attraction to Cranach's nudes—like those by his contemporary Hans Baldung Grien (1484/85–1545)—confirms their susceptibility to desire and thus their descent from Adam.[28] Viewers, reflecting Luther's call for personal responsibility, are thus challenged, as were Adam and Eve, to resist temptation.[29]

The original commission and intended purpose of the Pasadena paintings is not known. Before 1919, when they were discovered in the Church of the Holy Trinity in Kiev, they had reportedly hung as a single work of art in the vestibule and not on the altar.[30] At least one pair of large panels by Cranach representing Adam and Eve (Kunsthistorisches Museum, Vienna)[31] originally did serve as the outer wings of an altarpiece, the reverse of which depict figures of the Man of Sorrows and the mourning Virgin Mary, considered the typological antitypes of Adam and Eve.[32] The larger dimensions of the Pasadena paintings, which are each approximately twenty inches taller and six inches wider than the Vienna panels, suggests they served a different purpose.[33] The format and scale of the Pasadena paintings are similar to the monumental paintings of heroines from classical and biblical history, particularly Lucretia and Judith, that Cranach painted for wealthy members of the court circle to hang in special "cabinets of nudes" reserved for the patron's private enjoyment.[34] Like these, Pasadena's monumental nude figures of Adam and Eve were most likely painted for a member of the Saxon court and at some point relocated to the Church of the Holy Trinity in Kiev. Today, hanging in the galleries of the Norton Simon Museum, the beautiful, nearly life-size figures that survived two world wars and an untold early history hang as independent works of art, admired as two of the most important examples by this iconic German Renaissance artist.

1. The panels were referenced by Commander George Stroganoff as belonging to the Stroganoff family before they fled Russia during the Bolshevik Revolution (Yeide, Akinsha, and Walsh 2001, p. 135; and "Reminiscences of George Stroganoff-Scherbatoff, 1974," interview by Marc Raeff, individual interviews oral history collection, Columbia University). However, the paintings do not appear in earlier references to the Stroganoff collection, including Stroganoff 1800 or Waagen [1864] 1870.

2. Ghilarov 1929, p. 3, notes that the paintings (then joined as one panel) were found under the stairs to the belfry of the Church of the Holy Trinity in Vasyl'kivska Street in Kiev by an official of the Lavra Reserve Museum, V. G. Ishchenko, the commissioner for requisitioning valuable works of art from churches. According to Ishchenko, the painting was half-buried under piles of debris in the church, and it took up to two hours to extract it. Ghilarov 1929, p. 4, notes that they were unable to find out how and when the picture came to the Church of the Holy Trinity. Clergyman Steshenko, who had been senior priest at the church since 1919, reported that the painting[s] had hung in the vestibule of the church, "not as an icon—a sacred image—but as a decoration, a work on a religious topic." Ghilarov notes further that according to P. P. Kurinnyi, director of the Lavra Reserve Museum, the picture was sent to the Church of the Holy Trinity together with other cultural property during the liquidation of regiment churches by those military units that were operating in Galychina (a.k.a. Galicia, the area around Lvov/Lemberg/Lviv), but there is no evidence to support this. See letter dated 6 October 2002 from Alexei Ghilarov, Moscow, grandson of Sergei Alekseevich Ghilarov (1887–1946), senior researcher at the Museum of Art, Ukrainian Academy of Sciences, Kiev (NSM).

3. Ghilarov 1929, p. 3; and Schmidt 1931, p. 194. The so-called Anti-Religious Museum located in the Kievo-Pecherskaia Lavra Monastery was the repository for cultural property the Bolshevik government confiscated from various Kiev churches. See Yeide, Akinsha, and Walsh 2001, p. 136.

4. According to Yeide, Akinsha, and Walsh 2001, p. 136, the Museum of Art, Ukrainian Academy of Sciences, was formerly the Khanenko Museum and is now known as the Kiev Museum of Western and Oriental Art. Ghilarov 1929 is the earliest-known publication of the paintings and the first to publish them as by the hand of Cranach. Ghilarov states on pp. 5ff. that the paintings were restored and separated into the original format of two separate panels while at the Academy of Sciences.

5. According to Yeide, Akinsha, and Walsh 2001, pp. 136f. the museum was visited on 16 August 1929 by "a commission of the People's Commissariat of Enlightenment of Ukraine and the 'Gostorg'—the state trade organization responsible for the sale of the museum collection abroad—which authorized the sale of the Cranach *Adam* and *Eve*. Despite protests from museum curators, on 29 September the paintings were sent to the office of the 'Antiquariat' in Leningrad, a collecting point for artworks destined to be sold abroad."

6. The Cranach panels were offered for sale by the Soviet government. The introduction to the auction catalogue notes that the sale included the collection formed by Count Aleksandr Stroganov (1733–1811) with additions by Sergei Stroganov (1794–1882) and part of the collection of Count Pavel Stroganov (1774–1817). Some versions of this catalogue contain an addendum, stating that a number of the paintings in the sale (including the two panels discussed here) came from other Russian collections. The auction was contested by the Stroganoff family as well as other families that had fled the revolution in 1917. For a detailed description of this auction, see Odom and Salmond 2009, pp. 119–27, 135n63.

7. Rotterdam 1936–37, nos. 8–9, ill.; 1940 inv. nos. 2721 and 2722.

8. The Jewish art dealer Jacques Goudstikker died from a fall on a boat fleeing from the Germans on 15 May 1940. Goering purchased the contents of Goudstikker's studio, and the German banker Alois Miedl purchased the real estate. After the war, what could be recovered of the Goudstikker collection was returned to the Dutch government. On Goudstikker, see Hollander 2009 and P. Sutton et al. 2008, published in connection with an exhibition including many of the restituted paintings. For Miedl, see Fiebig 2020. The paintings restituted to the heirs of Goudstikker by the Dutch government were sold in a series of auctions held in various locations by Christie's in 2007.

9. Catalogued by the Office of Fine Arts, US State Department, for the Munich Central Collecting Point (Ardelia Hall Collection 1946–51; microform copy, GRI, roll 7). The records identify *Adam* as "5258 / Berchtesgaden" and *Eve* as "5260 / Berchtesgaden." Both had belonged to Goering and bore identifying marks indicating they had come from Goudstikker: *Adam*, "G 460 A" and *Eve*, "G460 B / Goudstikker." The records note "id. acc. to Photo of Goering Coll."

10. Royal Decree E-133 (20 October 1944). The operative legal opinion relating to this part of the history of the panels is available in Von Saher v. Norton Simon Museum of Art at Pasadena, 897 F.3d 1141 (9th Cir. 2018), cert. denied 139 S. Ct. 2616 (2019) (". . . the Court concludes that . . . the Dutch State owned the Cranachs when it transferred the paintings to Stroganoff in 1966.").

11. After a lengthy litigation initiated by the daughter-in-law of Jacques Goudstikker in 2007, the Ninth Circuit Court of Appeals unanimously affirmed on 30 July 2018 summary judgment in favor of the Norton Simon Art Foundation as having proper title to both *Adam* and *Eve* by Cranach. The US Supreme Court denied review. *Von Saher*, 897 F.3d 1141.

12. An English translation of the original Ukrainian text was commissioned by the Norton Simon Museum (NSM).

13. In keeping with the Cranach studio practice described by Heydenreich 2007b.

14. Heydenreich 2007b, p. 70.

15. Kühnen and Herm 2016 summarizes a study of ten objects, altarpieces, and panel paintings (including two *Adam* and *Eve* panels by Cranach now in Dresden) with protein fibers that were conclusively identified as sinew from connective tissue.

16. Spring 2017.

17. Foister 2015.

18. The unique physical appearance of the holes or craters suggest that they were caused by relatively high-velocity impact, and the presence of iron, lead, mercury, and titanium would suggest that the damages were caused by bullets.

19. The head of the Uffizi Adam in particular is very close to the Norton Simon version, which suggests that they were both based on the same preparatory drawing or cartoon.

20. Genesis 3.

21. Heydenreich 2007a, p. 19. Bonnet 1994, p. 143, suggests Cranach depicted the subject more than thirty times. See also M. Friedländer and Rosenberg 1978; the Cranach Digital Archive n.d.; the Getty Photo Study Collection; and the Witt Library at the Courtauld Institute of Art.

22. The Florence panels measure 172 × 61 cm and 167 × 61 cm (inv. 1890, nos. 1459–58), and the Dresden panels are each 170 × 70 cm (inv. nos. 1911–12). See also *Venus and Cupid as the Honey Thief*, 1531, 170 × 73 cm, Galleria Borghese, Rome.

23. For discussion of Dürer's panels, see Schoen 2001. Schoen suggests that Cranach must have known Dürer's paintings by 1508/09, when he painted *Venus and Cupid* (Hermitage, St. Petersburg), which measures 213 × 102 cm.

24. Cranach's earlier depictions of Eve reflect the posture of Eve in Dürer's print. Here, however, the representation of Eve with her left leg crossed in front of the right appears to have been influenced by Dürer's painting, although the pose remains more static.

25. Cranach derived from Dürer this abstracted play of Eve's locks and Adam's tightly coiled hair.

26. The Pasadena paintings also depart from Cranach's engraving *Adam and Eve*, dated 1509 (Hollstein 1954–2019, vol. 7 [1964], p. 10, no. 1), which sets the figures within a landscape surrounded by stags and other animals as Adam, seated under the apple tree, eats an apple and Eve reaches for another. The print is a clear derivation of Dürer's 1504 print of the *Fall of Man* (Hollstein 1954–2019, vol. 7 (1964), p. 5, no. 1), in which the artist included carefully selected animals to refer to the four humors: the cat was associated with choleric, the rabbit with sanguine, the ox with phlegmatic, and the elk with melancholic. See Panofsky 2005, pp. 84f.

27. The motif of Adam scratching his head was first used by Cranach in 1526 for *Adam and Eve* (Courtauld Institute Galleries, London; see M. Friedländer and Rosenberg 1978, no. 191). The combination of that motif and that of Eve extending her straight leg across her back leg appear in paintings datable to the late 1520s–1530. In addition to the Courtauld painting, see, for example, *Adam and Eve*, dated 1528, Gallerie degli Uffizi, Florence (M. Friedländer and Rosenberg 1978, no. 194).

28. According to Koerner 1985, p. 77, "Luther's emphasis on the catastrophic origin of human mortality, of its particular historical and human cause, is linked to his notion of individual, human responsibility in regard to sin and to salvation through Faith."

29. Koerner 1985, p. 80.

30. See notes 1 and 3 above.

31. Inv. nos. 861 and 861 A. Each panel measures 137 × 43 cm and is thus considerably smaller than the Pasadena paintings.

32. Bonnet 1994, p. 148n20. Jan van Eyck (ca. 1390–1441) was the first northern artist to monumentalize the figures of Adam and Eve on the Ghent Altarpiece. Before that, Adam and Eve were depicted in scenes of Paradise and the Fall.

33. There is no evidence that the Pasadena panels were ever painted on the reverse and served as the wings of an altarpiece when they were planed down and backed by a single cradle before 1919. See Technical Notes.

34. Bonnet 1994, pp. 147f., no. 43, cites a description in Meinhart's *Dialogues* (1507) of the Castle Wittenberg, which was built by Frederick III, Elector of Saxony (1463–1535), between 1490 and 1509 and is more fully described in Matsche 1994. Like *Adam* and *Eve*, these women, usually ornamented with jewelry, stand either nude or wrapped in transparent drapery on a pebbled ground against a solid black background. See, for example, Cranach, *Venus and Cupid* (167 × 62 cm; Gemäldegalerie, Berlin, inv. no. 14594) as well as *Lucretia* (1624; Alte Pinakothek, Munich). Two paintings attributed to Cranach and datable to after 1537—*Lucretia* (lucascranach.org/en/DE_SKD-Lost_1916-1) and *Judith* (lucascranach.org/en/DE_SKD-Lost_1916-2), formerly in the Gemäldegalerie Alte Meister, Dresden (each 172 × 64 cm; lost 1945)—hung together in the Kunstkammer, Dresden, from at least 1595. The similarity of compositions and dimensions of these paintings suggests that Cranach and his studio may have produced series of these historical women to be hung together.

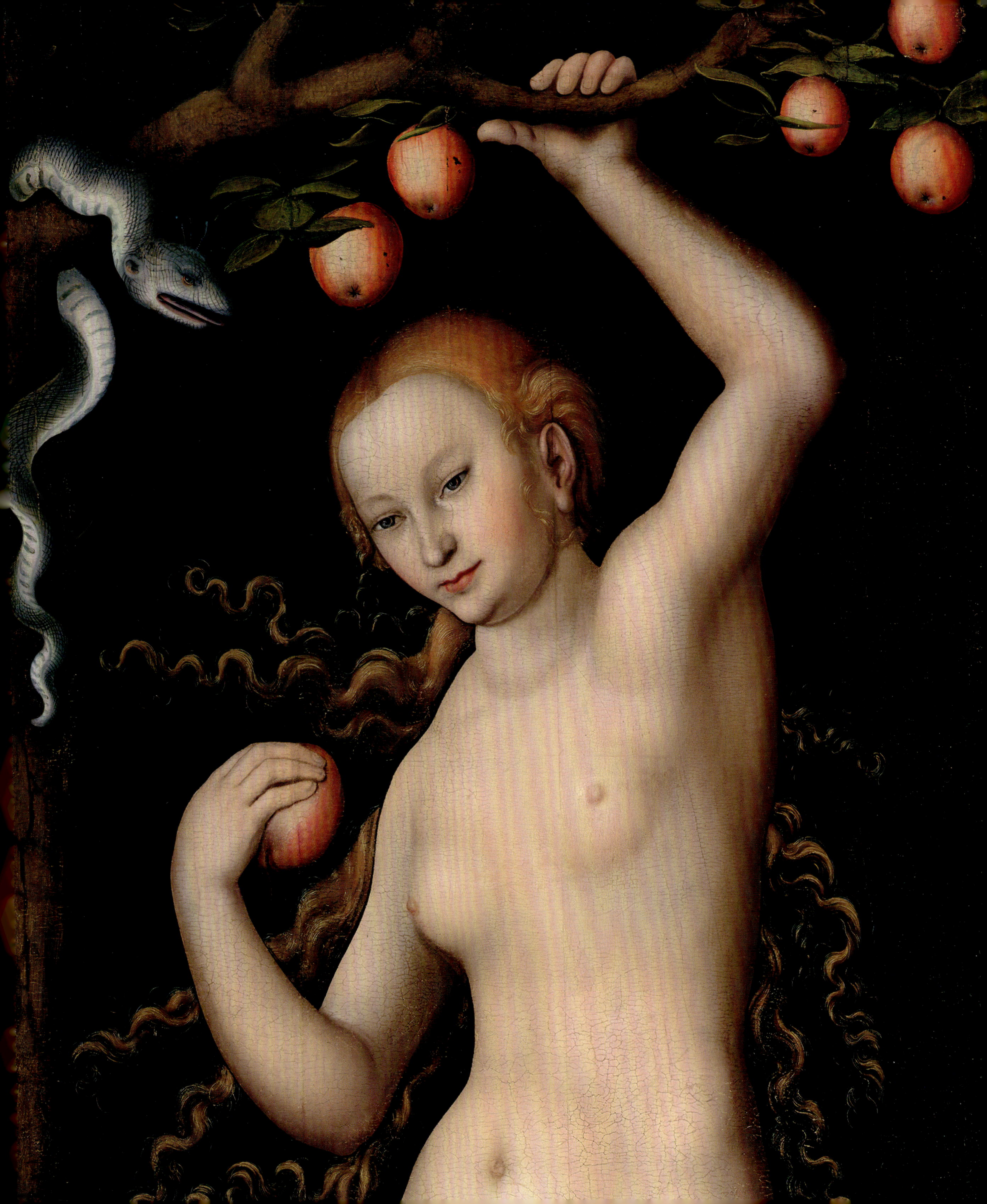

19

Possibly John de Critz I

English, of Flemish origin
Antwerp 1551/52–1642 London

Portrait of a Woman

ca. 1605–10

Oil on canvas, 71 × 39 in. (180.3 × 99.1 cm)
The Norton Simon Foundation, F.1965.1.027.P

Provenance
Stanford White (1853–1906), New York (sale, American Art Association, New York, 4 April 1907, lot 110, ill., as Federico Zuccaro, *Portrait of Mary Tudor*.[1] [Meredith Galleries, New York, sold June 1945 to]; [Duveen Brothers Inc., New York, sold 1964 to]; The Norton Simon Foundation.

Exhibited
New York 1946a; Richmond 1957; New York 1964, no. 10, ill., as Marcus Geeraerts; on loan, Metropolitan Museum of Art, New York, 30 December 1965–16 April 1973; on loan, Dorothy Chandler Pavilion, Los Angeles, 10 May 1973–30 March 1984.

References
"Selected Old Masters" 1946, p. 8; Breuning 1946, p. 7; Frankfurter 1946, pp. 34f., ill.; Douglas 1951, pp. 163, 165f., ill., "Thought to be *Lady Arabella Stuart*: M. Gheeraerts, Jr."; La Farge 1959a, p. 12, ill.; Strong 1969a, p. 266, no. 253, ill., attributed to John de Critz; Arnold 1985, p. 12, no. 60; S. Campbell 2010, p. 443, no. D25, ill.

Technical Notes
The support, a plain-weave canvas, is lined, with most of the original tacking margins retained. The ground is white. Small bumps and the overall surface texture suggest that it was not a perfectly smooth layer and was at least partly applied in broad strokes with a trowel or large spatula. Infrared reflectography shows underpainting throughout, drawn with fluid delineating strokes and some staccato hatch marks, for example, at the proper right hand and upper folds of the skirt. The broad structure of the dress, including the ribbon ties and scalloped edges of the lace collar and bodice, and figure are thus established. The paint has suffered extensive damage. X-radiography indicates that the original canvas has no major tears, although there are numerous small holes along the top edge. In addition to old losses of paint and ground across the bottom edge, solvent abrasion has also occurred throughout, removing or dramatically thinning layers of paint or glazes. Little of the original paint handling seems to be intact, and many areas, such as the green cloth at the left side, are now difficult to read. Ultraviolet light shows retouching to be extensive, located in the woman's proper left hand, the chest, throat, a large area on the proper left side of the chin, and additional spots in the face. Although there are broad areas of toning in the skirt, and in much of the background at the center left, reintegration was insufficient. A synthetic-resin varnish imparts even gloss.

This full-length portrait of a young woman dressed in an elaborate costume and facing three-quarters left, with the knuckles of her right hand resting on a table covered with green velvet, probably depicts a member of the English court from the first decade of the seventeenth century. Unfortunately, the poor condition of the Pasadena painting, which appears to have lost important surface subtleties from overcleaning, has made it particularly difficult to attribute it with confidence to any one of the closely related painters affiliated with the English court. When the portrait was sold at auction in 1907 it bore an attribution to Federico Zuccaro (1540/42–1609), an Italian painter who traveled in 1574 to the Netherlands, Spain, and England, where he painted portraits of members of the court. In 1951 Robert Langton Douglas published the painting as a work by Marcus Geeraerts II (ca. 1561–1635), a Flemish-born painter to the court of James I (r. 1603–25); in 1969 Roy Strong reattributed it to Geeraerts's brother-in-law, the court painter John de Critz I.[2] Jessica David, senior conservator of paintings at the Yale Center for British Art, recently indicated that, based on having seen many infrared images of both De Critz and Gheeraerts, she supports the attribution of the Pasadena portrait to De Critz. She noted in particular the intelligent gaze of the sitter and the staccato, cursory strokes and hatching of the underpainting.[3]

The artist's delight in decorative detail is characteristic of the first decade of the seventeenth century. The carefully described box pattern of the starched needlepoint lace is repeated throughout her costume and in the woven pattern of the rush matting on which she stands. Needlepoint lace frames her low-cut neckline and forms the cuffs of her dress as well as the stiffly starched open fan-shaped ruff lined with a flat linen collar. The elegant lace ruff, which attaches to the front of the dress just above a row of pearl buttons and rises in back above the shoulders, frames the woman's face, while her dark brown hair sweeps in short swirls over the matching starched box-patterned lace "crown" that encircles her head.

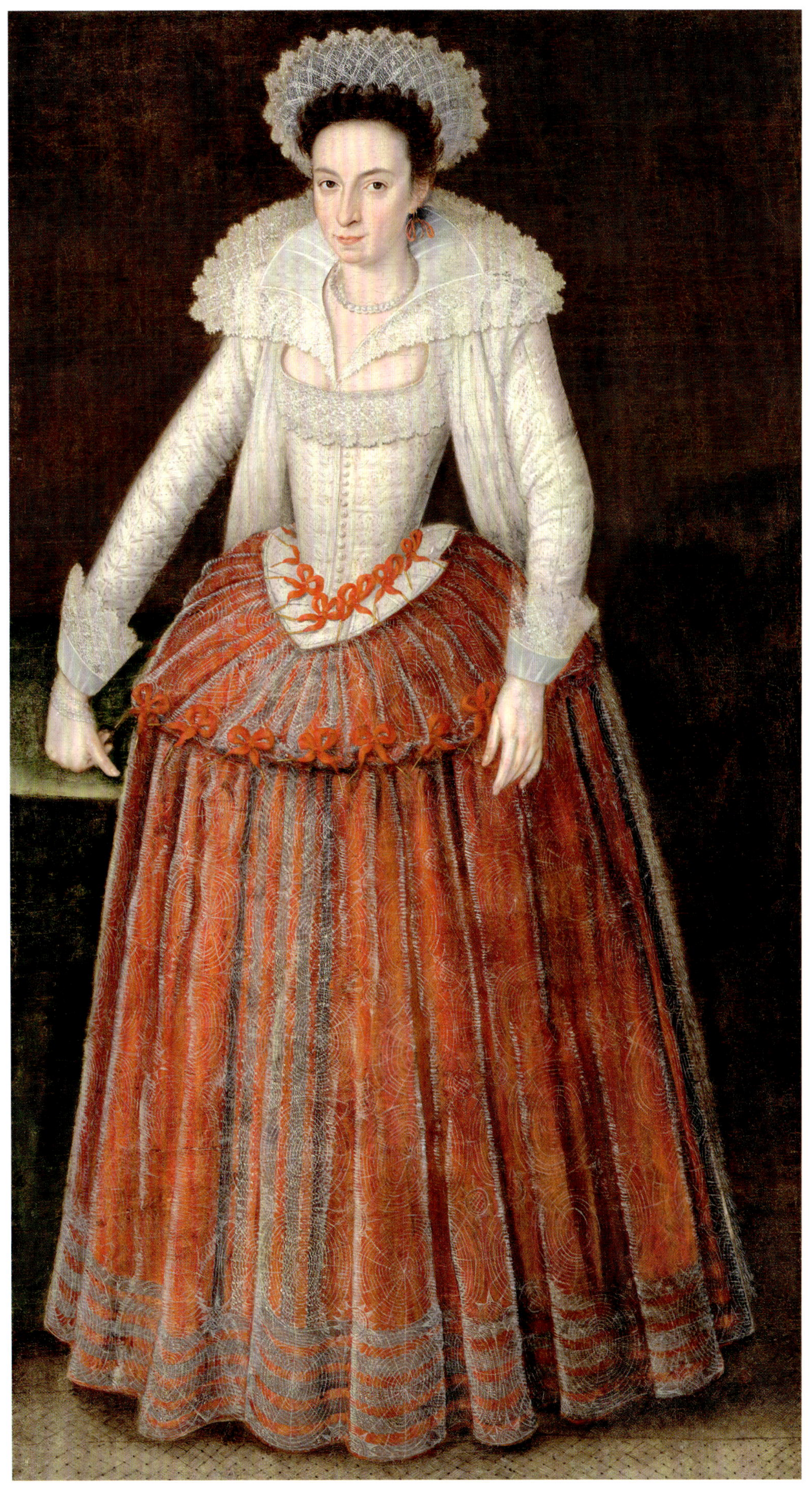

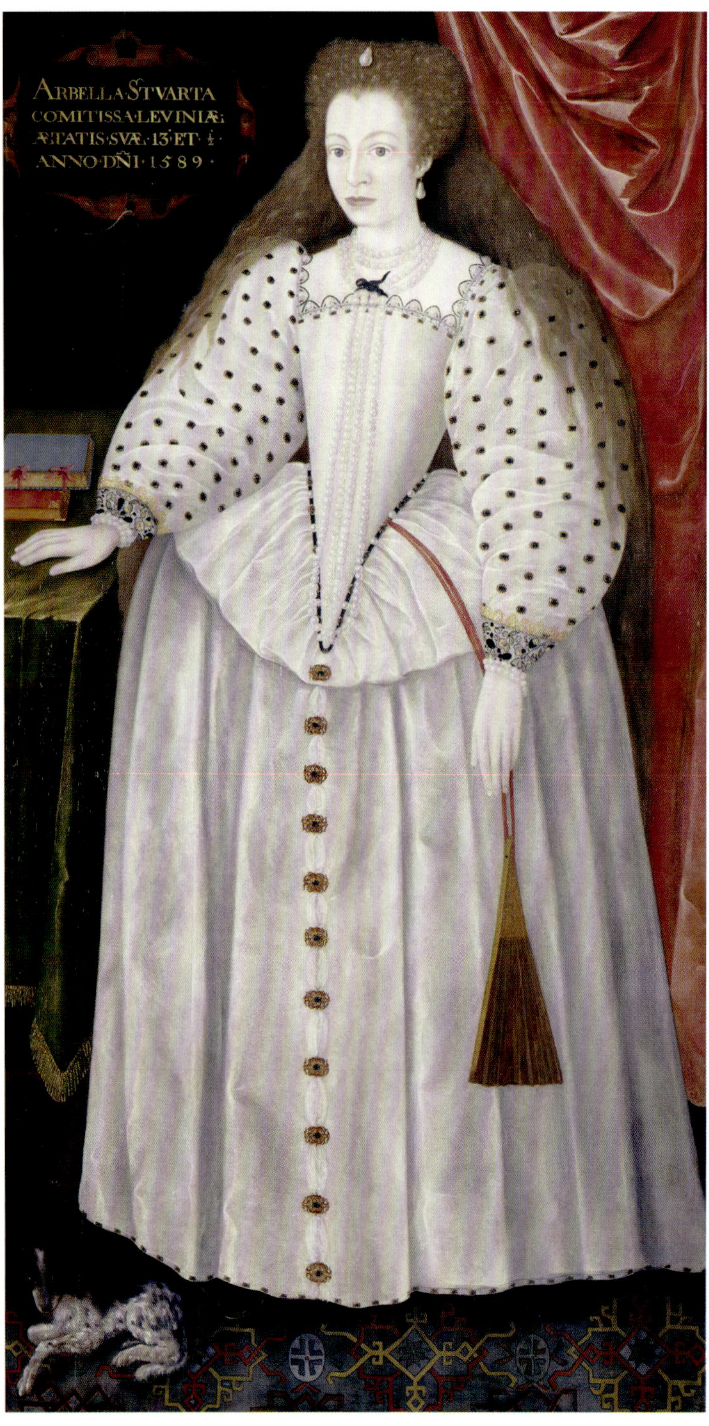

Fig. 19a. Possibly Rowland Lockey, after British (English) School, *Lady Arabella Stuart, Later Duchess of Somerset (1575–1615), aged 13½*, 1598 (inscribed)–1599, oil on oak panel, 63½ × 33 in. (161.3 × 83.8 cm), National Trust, Hardwick Hall, Derbyshire.

In comparison with the lace, her jewelry is modest, restricted to a pearl choker necklace, a three-stranded pearl bracelet, and a double-loop earring through which a narrow red ribbon is drawn.

The dress—a significant reduction of the enormous farthingales and excessive ornament of dresses worn at the court of Elizabeth I (r. 1558–1603)—is nevertheless an expensive and stylish costume.[4] The skirt is its most remarkable feature, reflecting the delight in the exotic and fantastic as well as the contemporary interest in scientific observation of natural phenomena. Probably made from red velvet, it is covered with silk *mezza mandolina*: woven netting with a white lace spiderweb pattern. An English farthingale gives a soft, rounded shape to the skirt, which is tucked up and pinned to produce a decorative flounce with red bows on the edges. The tight, fitted shape of the bodice, which was made from white satin damask with a bar pattern and trimmed with red bows at the waist, was a popular adaptation of the fashionable doublet worn by men.[5]

The identity of the sitter, who appears to be in her twenties, is unknown. Robert Langton Douglas identified her as Arabella Stuart (1575–1615), a cousin of Elizabeth I who stood second in line to the throne after James.[6] The only secure portrait of Arabella Stuart is that painted by an unknown artist when she was thirteen (fig. 19a). Following her secret marriage in 1610 to William Seymour, heir to the royal Suffolk line, King James had both her and her husband arrested. Arabella died in the Tower of London in 1615. A relatively obscure courtier in her own day, she became a tragic figure of romantic biographers during the nineteenth century, when, as Roy Strong points out, her name was attached to "almost any portrait of a lady of the late 16th and early 17th centuries."[7] Although Roy Strong calls the portrait *Unknown Lady*, ca. 1605–10, it can be assumed that the woman was associated with the court of James I: Only members of this affluent and influential class could afford full-length, life-size portraits and elegant, expensive costumes.[8]

1. A photograph published in the sale catalogue shows the painting hanging in the drawing room of White's residence at 119 East Twenty-First Street in New York. Stanford White was a principle partner in the influential architectural firm McKim, Mead & White. Among his most important works was the design of the arch at Washington Square in New York.

2. Strong 1969a, no. 253. Although no signed or securely attributed portraits by De Critz are known, Strong has identified a small group of portraits that are stylistically related to those attributable to De Critz on the basis of strong circumstantial evidence. Strong 1969a, pp. 259–68.

3. I am grateful to John Griswold, head of conservation and installations, Norton Simon Museum, for sharing his summary report of his conversation with Jessica David.

4. Farthingales were large, stiffened structures placed under the skirt to push it out and enlarge the profile of a woman's lower body.

5. I am grateful to Sandra Rosenbaum, former curator-in-charge of the Doris Stein Research Center for Costume and Textiles at the Los Angeles County Museum of Art, for her valuable help in understanding and describing this costume. The interpretation of the white fabric that hangs from the sitter's shoulders and passes under her arms to the back and reappears on the edge of her skirt is confusing. The explanation may be that they were references to hanging sleeves, which in the sixteenth century hung from the shoulder on either side of a full sleeve. By the early seventeenth century, when the fashion was fitted sleeves, hanging sleeves were purely decorative.

6. Douglas 1951, pp. 165f. Arabella Stuart was the daughter of Charles Stuart, Earl of Lenox, whose maternal grandmother was Margaret, the eldest sister of Henry VIII. Regarding Arabella Stuart, see *DNB* [1921–22] 1973, vol. 1, p. 525; and Strong 1969b, pp. 302ff.

7. Strong 1969b, p. 303. On p. 304, Strong notes that much of the confusion seems to come from the conflicting appearance of the sitter in the authentic portraits of Arabella Stuart and the romantic image created by nineteenth-century biographers.

8. Strong 1969a, no. 253. Strong notes that his no. 252 (North Carolina Museum of Art, Raleigh), which he also attributes to De Critz, is "called Arabella Stuart," presumably because of its similarity to the authentic portrait of Arabella Stuart at age thirteen (Hardwick Hall, National Trust).

20

Aelbert Cuyp

Dutch
Dordrecht 1620–1691 Dordrecht

Evening in the Meadows

ca. 1650

Signed, lower right corner on smaller rock: "A. cuijp."
Oil on canvas, 41½ × 54⅝ in. (105.4 × 138.8 cm)
The Norton Simon Foundation, F.1970.07.P

Provenance

Johan van der Linden van Slingeland (1701–1782), Dordrecht (sale by his heirs, Yver, Dordrecht, 22 August 1785, lot 81, sold for ƒ1,007 to);[1] [Pieter Fouquet Jr. (1729–1800), Amsterdam, sold to];[2] [Jean-Baptiste Pierre Lebrun (1748–1813), Paris (sale, Paris, 11 April 1791, lot 49, sold for F 5,150 to)];[3] François-Antoine Robit (ca. 1762–1815), Paris (sale, Joseph-Alexandre Lebrun, Paris, 6 December 1800, lot 58, sale cancelled);[4] François-Antoine Robit, Paris (sale, Alexandre Joseph Paillet, Delaroche, Paris, 11 May 1801, lot 28, sold for F 10,100 to); [Guillaume-Jean Constantin (1755–1816), Paris, for];[5] [Michael Bryan (1757–1821), London, private contract sale, exh. 6 November 1801–31 May 1802, lot 56, as from Robit, sold for 1,000 guineas to)];[6] Sir Simon H. Clarke, 9th Bart. (1764–1832), Oakhill, Hertfordshire (sale, Artaria, London, 8 May 1840, lot 105, sold for £955 10s. to);[7] [Artaria, London, for];[8] Sir Samuel Scott, Bart.; until after 1860.[9] [D. Katz, Dieren, sold 1934 to]; Cornelis Johannes Karel van Aalst (1866–1939), Huis-te-Hoevelaken, the Netherlands,[10] by descent to his grandson; N. J. van Aalst, Huis-te-Hoevelaken, sold 1970 through; [G. Cramer, The Hague, to]; The Norton Simon Foundation.

Exhibited

London 1829, no. 25, lent by Sir Simon H. Clarke, Bart.; London 1860, no. 75, as lent by Samuel Scott, Esq.; Haarlem 1934, no. 54, lent by Dr. C. J. K. van Aalst; Arnhem 1953, no. 16; Delft 1967, n.pag., exhibited by G. Cramer; Tokyo/Kyoto 1968–69, no. 17; Richmond 1970–72; on loan, Los Angeles County Museum of Art, 22 April 1972–26 November 1974.

References

Buchanan 1824, vol. 2, pp. 43f. no. 20, 68, no. 56; J. Smith 1829–42, vol. 5 (1834), p. 292, no. 21, as location unknown, p. 304, no. 70, as coll. the late Sir Simon Clarke, Bart., and vol. 9 (1842), p. 651, no. 9, as bought by Mr. Artaria from 1840 Clarke sale for Sir S. Scott, Bart. Blanc 1857–58, vol. 2, pp. 129, 191; G. H. Veth 1884, p. 286, no. 81; Hofstede de Groot 1908–27, vol. 2 (1909), no. 367, provenance confused with painting formerly in the Weber collection; Moltke 1939, p. 100, pl. xxiii; Valentiner 1939, p. xiv, as "from his great romantic period"; "Notable Works of Art" 1966, p. 652, suppl., p. vii, pl. 7;[11] Cramer 1966–67, p. 3, ill.; Cramer 1968a, p. 11, ill.; Reiss 1975, pp. 207, 212, lists painting in "Appendix D, Slingeland Sale, 1785," where he calls it "doubtful" though gives "Art Trade 1956" as last location; Dordrecht 1977, p. 122n6; J. G. van Gelder 1977, p. 122n6; Müllenmeister 1978–81, vol. 1, p. 54, no. 105, ill.; Pasadena 1980, p. 60, ill.; Edwards 1982, p. 499, no. 28;[12] P. Sutton 1986, p. 218; Pasadena 1989, p. 60, ill.; Chong 1992, vol. 1, pp. 353f. no. 112, vol. 2, p. 129, ill.; Edwards 1996, p. 300, no. 28; Washington/London/Amsterdam 2001, p. 231, ill.; Pasadena 2003, p. 58, ill.; S. Campbell 2010, p. 332, no. 726, ill.

Related Work

Anonymous, eighteenth-century copy, canvas, 101 × 138 cm, signed lower right (Chong 1992, C64); present location unknown. Provenance: [Dorus Hermsen, The Hague (The Hague 1922b, no. 10, ill.)]. Anonymous (sale, Mak van Waay, Amsterdam, 28 January 1941, no. 6, as "Aelbert Cuyp?," ill., sold for ƒ2,250 to); V. d. Linde, Rotterdam for; Gemäldegalerie, Danzig [stored near Hamburg in 1945]. Missing since 1945. References: Drost 1943, p. 14; Tomkiewicz 1950, p. 56, no. 127, pl. 122.

Technical Notes

The plain-weave canvas has been lined with the original tacking edges removed. In the upper left quadrant, a short horizontal tear has been repaired. The smoothly applied ground is a light reddish-brown color, visible in the fissures of wider cracks and at the top edge. There is no evidence of underdrawing. Opaque, rich paint was applied directly over the ground, with colors blended on the palette and applied wet-into-wet. The slight profile of brushmarking has been smoothed and incorporated into weave transference from the lining. At the upper right, a pentimento at the back side of the cow on the hilltop indicates a slightly changed position of the rear right leg and the tail. The paint is fairly well preserved, with only minor problems, most of them related to chromatic distortions caused by a prior restoration. Cleaning was uneven, leaving residues of dirt and darkened varnish visible in some areas of lighter colors and causing abrasion in other parts of the sky and clouds. The extensive retouching, located primarily in the sky, was often applied as rather broad areas of toning. It does not appear always to be covering abrasion but may have been an effort to compensate for uneven cleaning. Its discoloration gives a mottled look to the sky. A dense network of thin, spidery, light-colored lines visible in the foreground and middle ground in the green areas of the painting appears to be fractured varnish overlying very thin cracks in the paint. The visual effect is one of cloudiness, especially in the hillside at the right. Overall the varnish has discolored to yellow-gray.

On the banks of a river, a Dutch milkmaid squats next to a cow, dwarfed by its enormous bulk; two other cows silhouetted on a nearby hill look out across the river. Aelbert Cuyp consciously accentuated the monumentality of the cow by employing a low vantage point that juxtaposes the bucolic scene in the foreground against the deep view across the river with sailboats and men standing on a dock to distant towers lost in the mist. Long shadows and reflections on the cattle, blades of grass, and distant sails suggest the setting

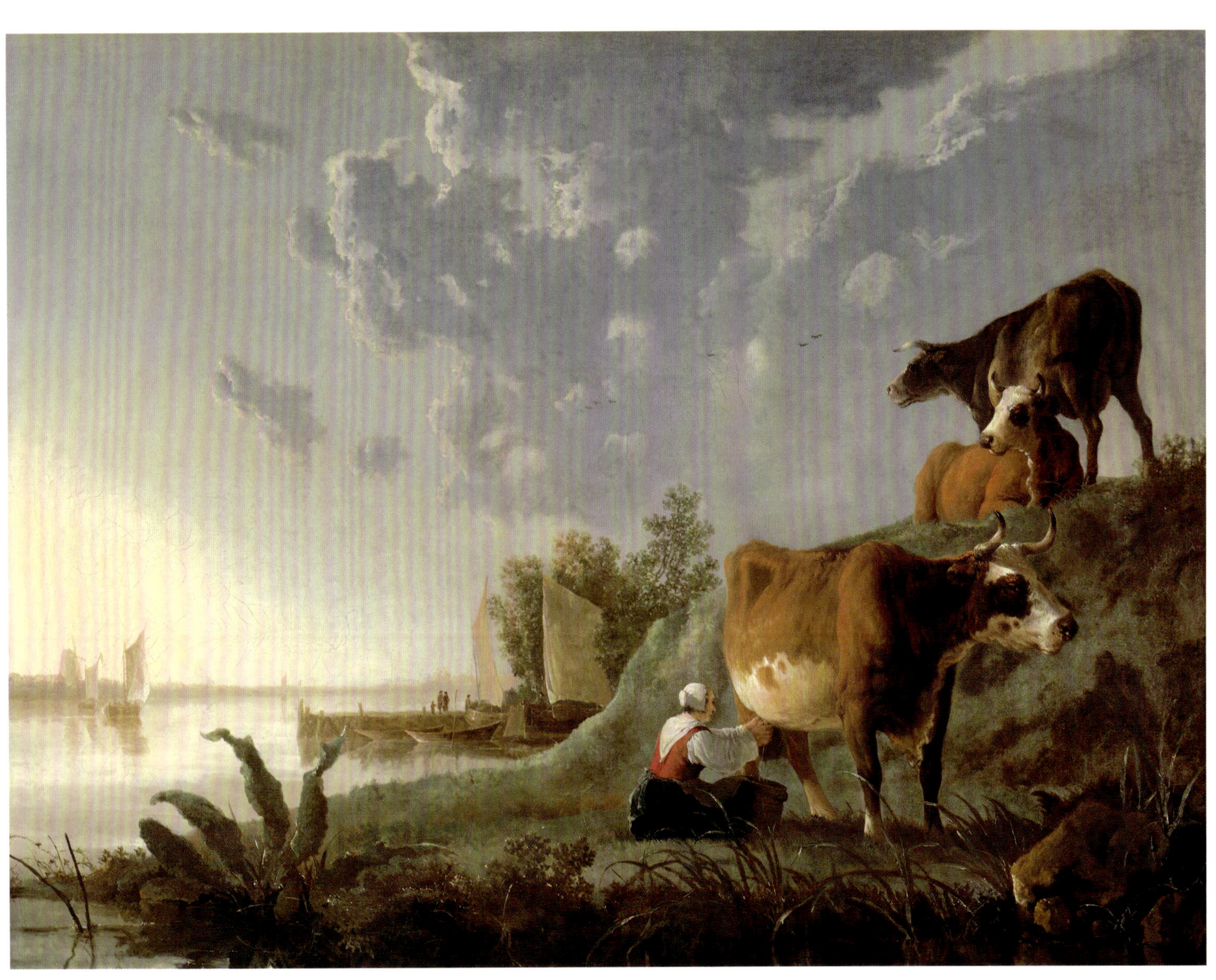

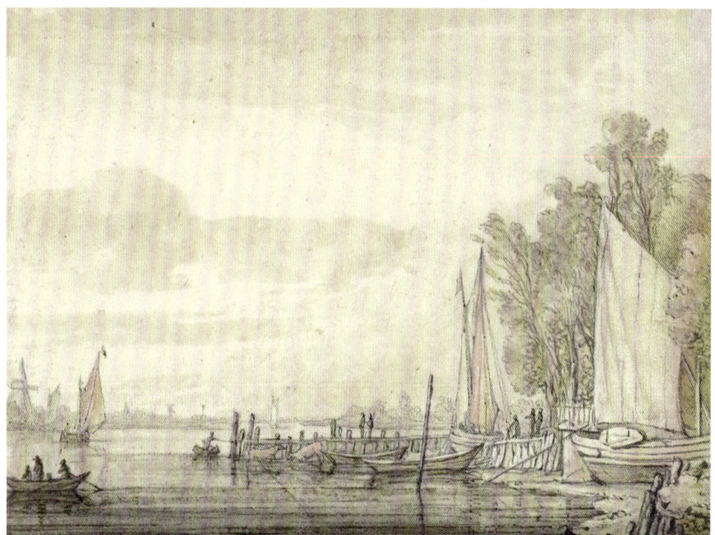

Fig. 20a. Aelbert Cuyp, *Boats at a Pier on a River*, ca. 1641–42, black chalk, pen and ink heightened with white, 5 ¾ × 7 11⁄16 in. (14.6 × 19.5 cm), Rijksmuseum, Amsterdam.

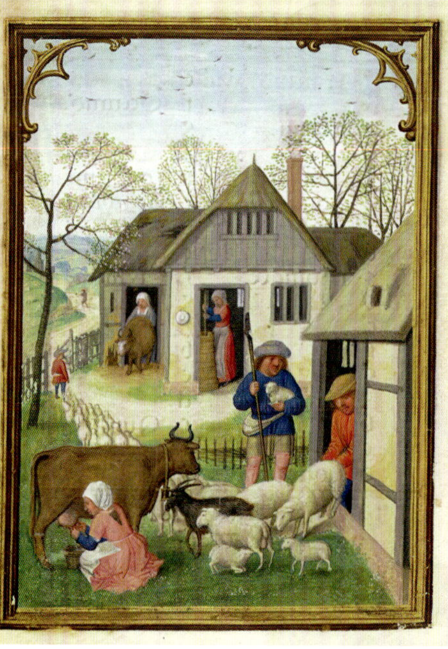

Fig. 20b. Simon Bening, *April*, from the *Da Costa Hours*, ca. 1515, vellum, The Morgan Library & Museum, New York.

sun and the diffused atmosphere of mist rising from the water. A prolific draftsman, Cuyp based the background of this painting on a washed chalk drawing he made in the vicinity of Alblasserdam and Ijsselmonde (fig. 20a). Already in this youthful drawing, years before the probable date of the painting, Cuyp had captured the effect of shimmering light reflected on the river that also characterizes this work.

The warm, golden atmosphere, the long shadows of the setting sun, and the mist rising on the river in *Evening in the Meadows* suggest Cuyp painted this large canvas about 1650, close in date to his *View of Dordrecht* (National Gallery, London) and *Herdsmen and Their Cattle at a Bridge* (Museo Nacional Thyssen-Bornemisza, Madrid). In the late 1640s and early 1650s Cuyp turned away from the monochromatic paintings of his early career and, under the influence of the Italianate landscapes of the Utrecht painter Jan Both (1618–1652) and other artists who had been to Italy, developed a style sensitive to the effects of light, color, and clarity of form. Adopting many of the techniques of these Italianate painters, Cuyp reduced details and introduced a warm, pervasive light to create images of an idyllic countryside, portraying the different times of day through the naturalistic representation of atmospheric conditions and light effects.[13] Unlike the Italianate painters, however, Cuyp never departed from the local Dutch scene, which remained the subject of his paintings throughout his career.

Evening in the Meadows draws on the popular tradition of milkmaids and cattle as metaphors for earth, fertility, and spring, associations that would have been familiar to the artist's contemporaries.[14] The image of the milkmaid and cow was an oft-used analogy for spring (fig. 20b), but here the enormous proportions of the cow relative to the milkmaid suggest that Cuyp also intended it to refer to the fecundity of the earth, specifically the Netherlands. In *Het Schilderboek* (1604), Karel van Mander wrote, "The Earth was also previously represented by the cow. . . . If one . . . desires to represent the Earth as one of the four elements, because it is a massive animal, the cow is appropriate."[15] The association is also specifically made in a print by Cornelis Bloemaert II (ca. 1603–1692) after Abraham Bloemaert (1566–1651) entitled *Terra [Earth]*, which represents a Dutch milkmaid with two cows and a sheep in a pasture with a basket of fruit in the foreground (fig. 20c).[16]

In the seventeenth century, Holland had a far-reaching reputation for producing large, healthy cattle, whose production of milk far exceeded in quantity and quality that of

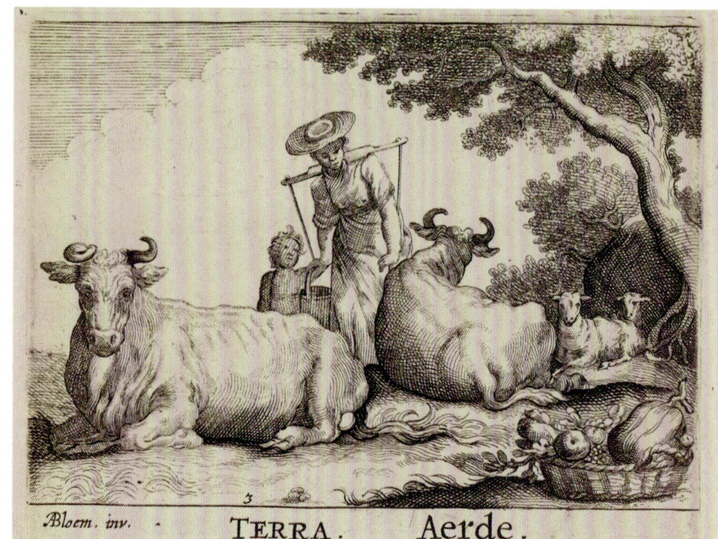

Fig. 20c. Cornelis Bloemaert II after Abraham Bloemaert, *Terra [Earth]*, 1640–77, engraving, 3 ¾ × 4 ⅞ in. (9.6 × 12.3 cm), British Museum, Department of Prints and Drawings, London.

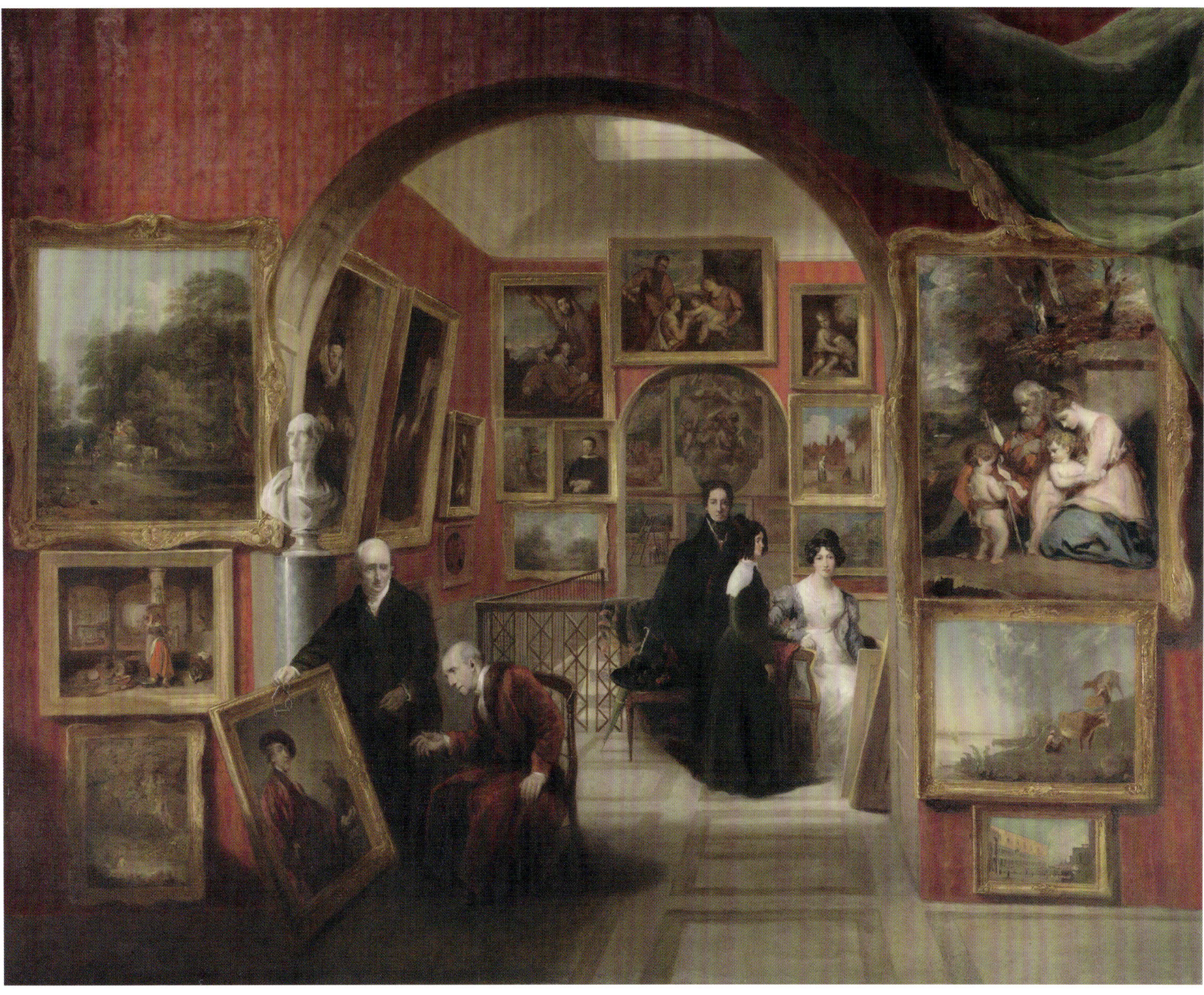

Fig. 20d. John Scarlett Davis, *The Interior of the British Institution Gallery*, 1829, oil on canvas, 44½ × 56 in. (113 × 142.4 cm), Yale Center for British Art, Paul Mellon Collection, New Haven.

cows elsewhere in Europe.[17] In 1636 a Dutch historian noted with pride that Holland had three products that surpassed those of the rest of the world and brought the country great fame and profit: herring and other netted fish; horses, oxen, cattle, and sheep; and butter, cheese, and other dairy products, which were shipped in great quantities throughout the world.[18] Representing one of the major industries of the Netherlands, the Dutch milk cow was a popular symbol of the Netherlands itself, which prospered during times of peace but suffered during periods of conflict, when fishing, trade, and agriculture were disrupted.[19] One side of a coin struck by Westfriesland in 1609 to commemorate the signing of the truce with Spain, for example, represents a woman milking a cow in a farmyard encircled by the inscription "Aridi Spes Fida Coloni" (The sure hope of the industrious farmer).[20] The Dutch milkmaid also appears as an emblem of prosperity on the hem of the Dutch maid's skirt in *Allegory of the Blossoming of the Republic of the United Netherlands during the Stadhoudership of Prince Maurits* by Jan Tengnagel (ca. 1584–1635; Museum Prinsenhof, Delft).[21]

Painted within a few years of the conclusion of the long war with Spain, *Evening in the Meadows* celebrates the prosperity of the country at peace, alluded to by the warm southern light and the bucolic subject featuring the Dutch milk cow in the context of fishing and transport, important areas of commerce for the Netherlands as a whole and Dordrecht specifically. The celebratory nature and relatively large scale and format of *Evening in the Meadows* suggest that it was painted on commission to hang over the mantelpiece in the patron's home. The original patron of the painting has not been identified but undoubtedly was a member of the wealthy Dordrecht burgher class for whom Cuyp worked almost exclusively.

In the nineteenth century, *Evening in the Meadows* was in the collection of Sir Simon H. Clarke, Bart., who lent the painting to its first documented exhibition in 1829. The exhibition was recorded in a painting by the British painter John Scarlett Davis (1804–1845), who placed the Cuyp painting in the lower right of the foreground (fig. 20d).

1. According to Chong 2001, p. 42, who calls Johan van der Linden van Slingeland "the most important collector of Cuyp's paintings, in any era." Van Slingeland, a Dordrecht iron dealer and mintmaster, owned ten major works by Cuyp by 1752 and forty-one in 1785.

2. Pieter Fouquet Jr. was a publisher and print dealer in Amsterdam. Lebrun bought a number of works from the Van Slingeland sale through Fouquet. See Lebrun 1792–96.

3. Blanc 1857–58, vol. 2, p. 129, identified the buyer as "Rubes," possibly misreading the annotation.

4. Lugt 1938–87, vol. 1, no. 11058, cites another Robit sale, undated. Burton Fredericksen, former director of the Getty Provenance Index, notes that the catalogue must predate the sale of May 1801 but also has much in common with Lebrun's catalogue of 6 December 1800. It was probably the first version of the 1801 catalogue. The catalogue of the 1800 sale describes the painting in reverse. According to J. Smith 1829–42, vol. 9 (suppl.), p. ix, "The best writers of the French catalogues of pictures" employed the terms "right" and "left" to refer to the picture and not the spectator.

5. An annotated copy of the sale catalogue at the RKD identifies Constantin as the buyer. Guillaume-Jean Constantin (Constantine) was a picture dealer in Paris, a member of the commission entrusted by Napoleon with organizing the Louvre as a museum, and the appointed Garde des Tableaux of Josephine's picture gallery at Malmaison (December 1807). Regarding Paillet, see Edwards 1996. Edwards discusses the Robit sale; on p. 299, no. 28, she lists *Evening in the Meadows* among "the major paintings" in the sale.

6. Constantin was apparently buying at the Robit sale for Michael Bryan, an important art dealer in London from 1798 to 1804. From 1781 to 1790 Bryan had lived in Flanders, where he was an agent for his brother's wool trade and also acted as a buyer for paintings. Buchanan 1824, vol. 2, pp. 35ff., notes that Bryan purchased the majority of the finest paintings from the Robit sale with the support of Sir Simon Clarke and G. Hibbert, Esq. Bryan worked primarily through private contract sales, exhibiting the paintings in his gallery in Pall Mall for several months before completing their sale.

7. Chong 1992, p. 353, suggests that Clarke probably reserved the painting before the 1801 Bryan sale. Since Clarke was one of the primary backers of Bryan's acquisition of the Robit paintings, he probably had an arrangement to take the profits from his investment in paintings. The Pasadena painting was certainly in the Clarke collection by 1829 when it was shown at the British Institution.

8. J. Smith 1829–42, vol. 9 (1842), p. 651, no. 9.

9. J. Smith 1829–42, vol. 9 (1842), p. 651, no. 9, and London 1860, no. 75.

10. C. J. K. van Aalst was a banker and president-director of Nederlandsche Handel-Maatschappij, N.V.

11. "With the exception of the Rijksmuseum's acquisition last year of a large Cuyp [inv. No. A4118] . . . no comparable work by the artist has come on to the market in recent years. . . . The picture originally came from England in the early 1930s, and De Groot records it under No. 367 . . . but confuses it with another work in the Weber collection. It was stored for almost thirty years in a bank safe and has now been cleaned by a restorer of the Mauritshuis, Mr. J. C. Traas" ("Notable Works of Art" 1966, p. 652, suppl., p. vii, pl. 7).

12. Edwards calls the painting ex-Weber, noting that the painting was last known in 1967, when it was in the art trade (G. Cramer, The Hague). Her reference to Weber indicates her reliance on the confused provenance in Hofstede de Groot 1908–27, vol. 2 (1909), no. 367.

13. Sandrart [1675] 1925, p. 183, notes that Pieter van Laer (1599–after 1642) as well as Jan Both and Andries Both (1611/12–1641), leaders of the northern painters in Rome, painted the different times of the day as well as of the year.

14. In the Netherlands, cattle were traditionally kept in barns during the winter and released in the spring. Because there was no threat of wolves in the Netherlands, throughout the spring and summer cattle remained in the meadows, where the milkmaids went to milk them. For an extensive discussion of the significance of seventeenth-century cattle paintings, see A. Walsh 1985, pp. 247ff.

15. "D'aerde was oock voormaels uytghebeeldt met de koe . . . Als men oock uytbeeldt de Aerde in een der vier hooft-stoffen wort haer daerom en om dat het een swaer aerdsch Dier is de koe by ghevoeght." Van Mander 1604, fol. 125a.

16. Bearing the inscription "Terra," the engraving by Cornelis Bloemaert II (Hollstein 1949–2010, vol. 2, no. 239) is after a drawing from the 1620s by Abraham Bloemaert (Roethlisberger and Bok 1993, vol. 1, p. 230, no. 295; vol. 2, fig. 431). Likewise, the representation of a cattle market in a print by Jan van de Velde (1593–1641) after a drawing dated 1622 by Willem Pietersz. Buytewech (1591–1624; see Franken and Van der Kellen 1883, p. 77, no. 141) is recognized as an allegory of Earth only because of the inscription praising the fecundity of the land.

17. J. de Vries 1974, p. 138.

18. Van Gouthoeven 1636, p. 6, quoted in Hengeveld 1865–70, vol. 2, p. 30.

19. Dutch markets, trading mostly with Denmark, Sweden, Holstein, Spain, and Portugal, were closed when Dutch ships were attacked and the ships normally used for transporting butter and cheese were confiscated for the movement of troops. In 1586 the Earl of Leicester forbade the export of cheese and butter from the Noorderkwartier and a number of ships loaded for Spain and Portugal had to be unloaded (Hengeveld 1865–70, vol. 2, p. 26).

20. The reverse of the coin shows a ship under full sail on a calm sea with the inscription "Verrit turbida nauta aequora 1609" (The sailor sweeps the restless seas). The coin was restruck eight years later. See G. van Loon 1723, vol. 2, pp. 54f. The Scheepvaart Museum, Amsterdam, has a second version of the coin dated 1617. Van Loon interpreted the coin as a celebration of Dutch prosperity.

21. The other scenes include a woman churning butter and a man carrying cheese. There are also references within the painting to the products of the sea and sailing fleets. See H. Schneider 1921, p. 25, no. 13, ill. 5.

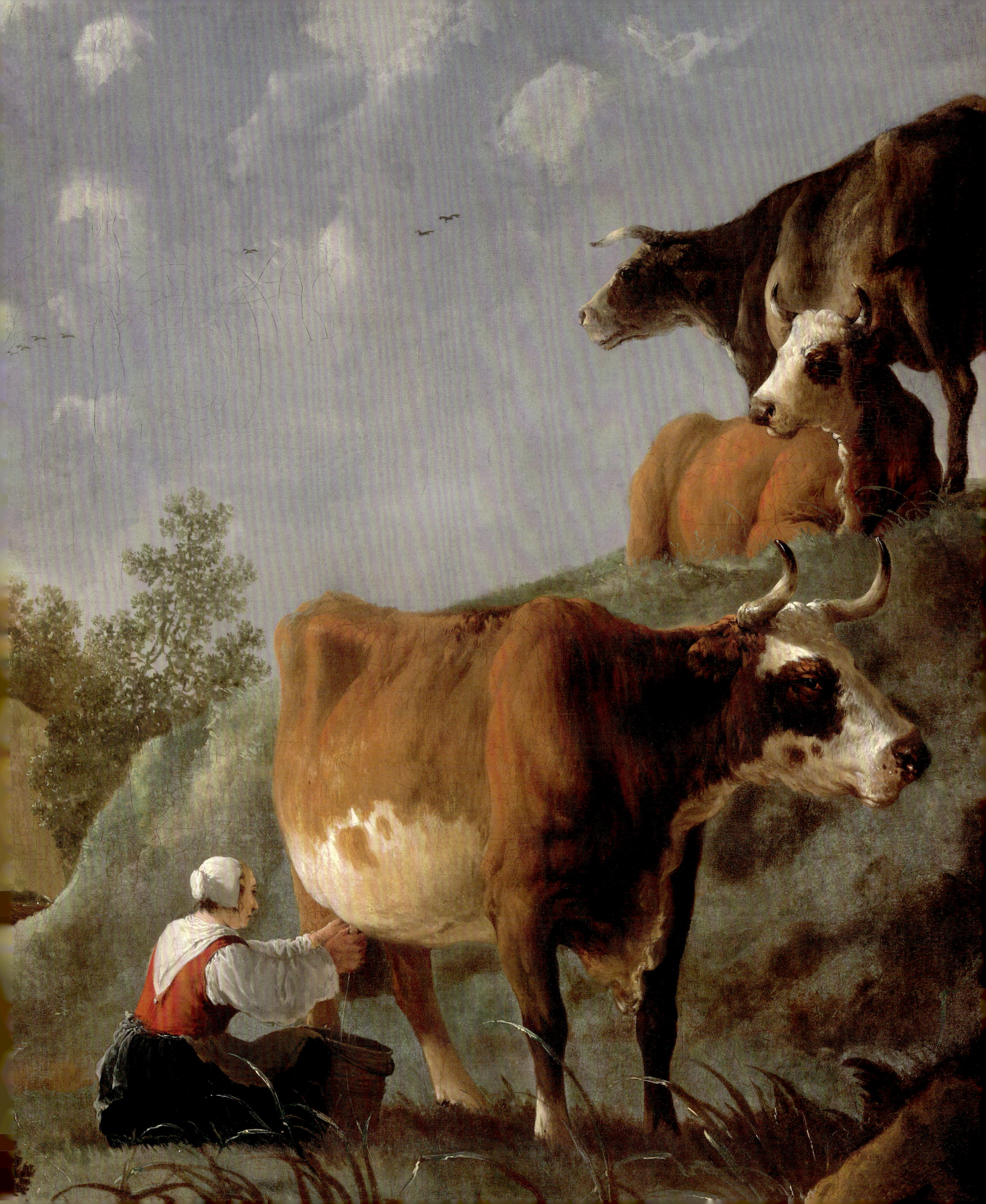

21

Gerard David

Netherlandish
Oudewater ca. 1460–1523 Bruges

The Coronation of the Virgin, Maria in Sole

ca. 1515

Oil on oak panel, 28 × 21½ in. (71.1 × 54.6 cm)
The Norton Simon Foundation, F.1965.1.017.P

Provenance

Prince Juan de Bourbon, Count of Montizon (1822–1887), Madrid.[1] Count Santa Maria, probably Sr. D. Matías Muntadas y Rovira, Count de Santa María de Sans (1854–1927), Madrid, sold through;[2] [Ali (Allen) Loebl,[3] Paris, sold half share in July 1935 and then his own half share in January 1936 to]; [Duveen Brothers Inc., New York, stock nos. 29697, 29844, 30108, sold 1964 to]; The Norton Simon Foundation.

Exhibited

Long-term loan to Museo Nacional del Prado, Madrid;[4] Detroit 1941, no. 15, ill., lent by Duveen; New York 1942b, p. 62, no. 19; New York 1946b, no. 3, ill.; Bruges 1949, no. 19; Indianapolis 1950, no. 20; London 1953–54, no. 125; Bordeaux 1954, no. 24; London, ON, 1957, n.pag.; Bruges 1960, no. 60; Detroit 1960, no. 48; New York 1964, no. 4, ill.; on loan, Cleveland Museum of Art, 10 January 1967–23 September 1969; on loan, Los Angeles County Museum of Art, 24 September 1969–13 September 1972; Houston 1972–74.

References

Destrée 1923, pp. 356, 360; M. Friedländer 1924–37, vol. 14 (suppl.), p. 106; Richardson 1941, p. 18; Douglas 1946, pp. 161–63; J. G. van Gelder 1949, pp. 253f.; Chaban-Delmas 1954, p. 5; Marlier 1957, p. 181; Fahy 1969, p. 192; M. Friedländer 1967–76, vol. 6b (1971) pp. 112, suppl. 254, pl. 252, as "Now in the County Museum of Art, Los Angeles"; D. Sutton 1979, pp. 40f., no. 10; Morse 1979, p. 91; Mundy 1980, p. 38; Pasadena 1980, p. 33, ill.; Ainsworth 1988, p. 529, no. 5; Ainsworth 1989, pp. 21–24, 37n38, figs. 20–23; Van Miegroet 1989, pp. 256–63, 265n81, 265nn91–92, 306–07, no. 41, figs. 248, 251–53; Pasadena 1989, p. 24, ill.; Ainsworth 1990b, p. 652; Van Miegroet 1992b, p. 94; Ainsworth 1993, p. 20, pls. 5–7; Sander 1997, pp. 167–69; Muchnic 1998, p. 79; Bruges 1998, p. 49, fig. 21 (as *The Glorification of the Virgin [Deipara Virgo]*); New York 1998–99, pp. 20–31, 45–48, 55n76, 96, 275, 320, figs. 28, 31, 37, 59; Pasadena 2003, p. 39, ill.; S. Campbell 2010, p. 442, no. D13, ill.; Wolfthal and Metzger 2014, pp. 104–21, figs. 1, 5–10.

Related Works

- Copy after Gerard David, *The Madonna and Child, Crowned by Two Angels and Adored by Four Saints*, panel, 28½ × 21½ in. (69 × 54 cm). Described in Detroit 1960, p. 191, no. 48, as "a late, exact copy of this composition." The catalogue notes that there is a photograph of the painting at the RKD. This is probably the copy sold at the Count Greffuhle sale, Paris, 27 July 1937, lot 58: Van Miegroet 1989, p. 306, no. 41a (photograph of the painting at the RKD; no. 88241).
- Copy with variations, 28 × 21 cm. Present location unknown. Photograph stamped "Foto Gasparini, Genova" (GRI) came from the files of Julius Weitzner. The crude handling and outlines suggest it is a Spanish or possibly South American copy. The copyist elaborated the background with clouds and added two angels, one hovering on either side of the Virgin.
- Copy after Gerard David, *Virgin and Child with Saints*. Sold, Hôtel Drouot, Paris, 26 April 1993, lot 4; formerly with Kaethe Perls Gallerie, Paris. Wolfthal and Metzger 2014, p. 115, describe the painting as representing two saints and measuring 72 × 49 cm. A photograph at the RKD (no. 50651) indicates that the painting represents only the two inner saints but also includes the hands of the two outer saints.
- Illumination attributed to Simon Bening (ca. 1483–1561), Ms. Cod. Lat 23637 clm. 41. Staatsbibliothek, Munich. Marlier 1957, p. 179, pl. xli; Van Miegroet 1989, pp. 306f.
- Attributed to Ambrosius Benson (d. before 1550), ca. 1530. Panel, 132 × 108 cm. Koninklijk Museum voor Schone Kunsten, Antwerp. Marlier 1957, pp. 180–83; Van Miegroet 1989, pp. 306f. (See fig. 21a.)
- Attributed to the Master of the Holy Blood (1480–1525). Panel, 94.5 × 117 cm; wings each 96 × 53 cm. Sint-Jacobskerk, Bruges. M. Friedländer 1967–76, vol. 9 (1973), no. 195; Van Miegroet 1989, pp. 306f., fig. 250.
- Attributed to Jan Provoost (1462/65–1529). Canvas (transferred from wood), 203 × 151 cm. Hermitage, St. Petersburg. M. Friedländer 1967–76, vol. 9 (1973), no. 177; Van Miegroet 1989, pp. 306f.

Technical Notes

The painting was executed on an oak panel composed of two vertically grained boards; the join is located 7¼ inches from the right edge. The panel was probably thinned before the heavy cradle was attached. Unpainted margins at each edge, and the presence of a barbe where the ground is slightly built up, indicates that the panel was prepared while in a frame. The moderately thick ground masks the wood's texture, providing a smooth surface. Infrared reflectography reveals a fully developed underdrawing, with tonal variations and cross-hatching for shadowed portions.[5] The folds of the Virgin's drapery were redrawn. In the first underdrawing, her outer cape was open, revealing the simple vertical folds of the robe. This was later redrawn so that her cape would sweep from right to left, under the crescent moon. The lines of the restruck contours are heavier and darker than the original drawing lines. The later drawing appears to skip over a rough surface, an effect that may indicate an aqueous material imperfectly adhered to an oily painted layer. The position of the crescent moon at the bottom of the painting was originally slightly lower at its left side. The paint is thinly layered in a highly refined technique. Flesh tones are smoothly blended with subtle shading. The rays of the aureole were depicted with mordant gilding, of which only traces remain. A significant amount of damage in the right third of the panel is shown by both infrared reflectography and X-radiography. The damaged area corresponds to the right board. A slight amount of abrasion has occurred throughout the rest of the painting.

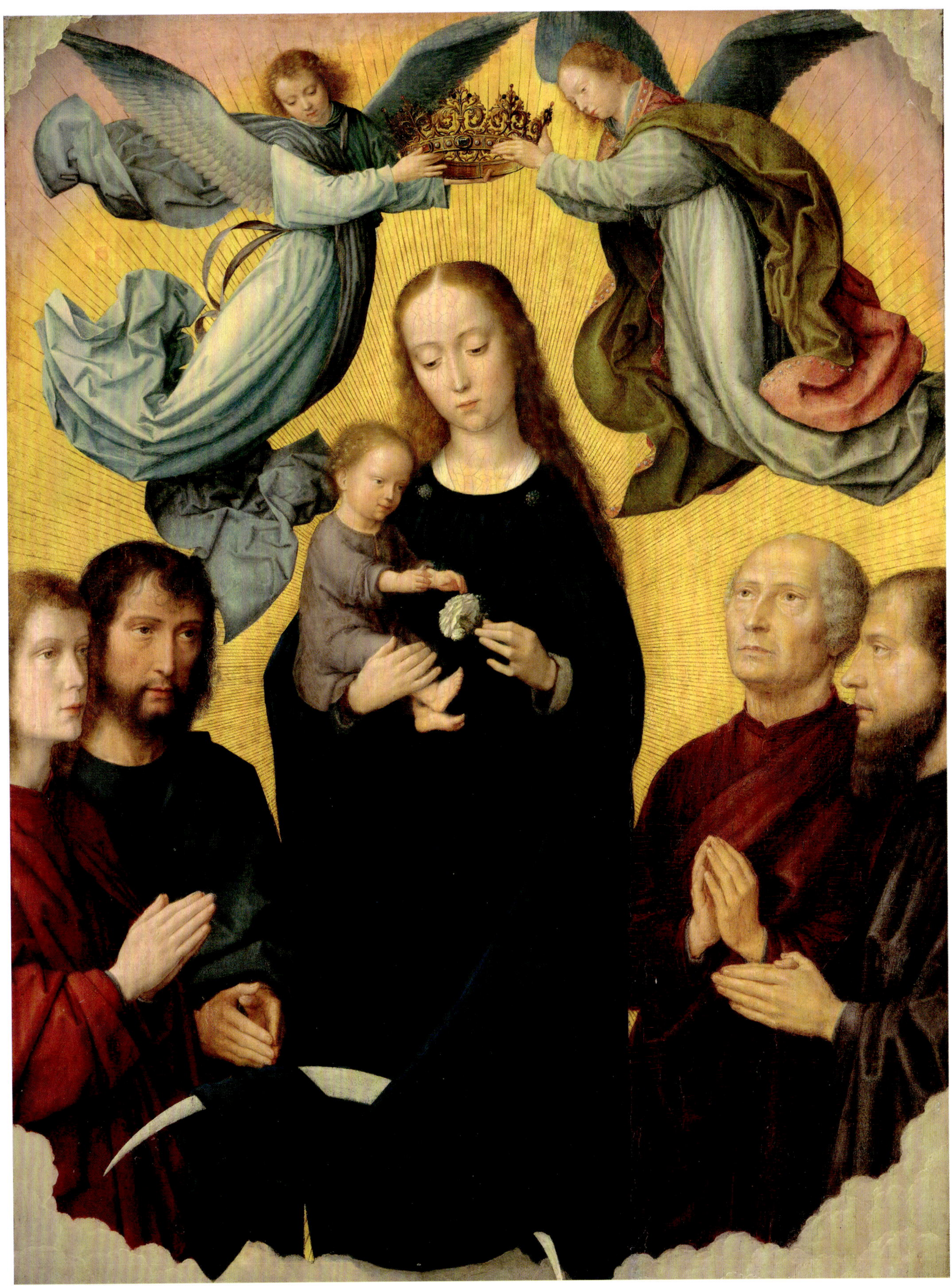

The restoration of the image at the right side of the painting was carefully done with extensive retouching and glazing. The natural-resin varnish is quite yellowed.[6]

Gerard David represents the Virgin Mary as the combined image of the Queen of Heaven crowned by two angels and the Woman of the Apocalypse, described in Revelation 12:1 as being "clothed with the sun, and the moon under her feet, and upon her head a crown of twelve stars." Puffs of clouds in the upper corners and across the bottom of the panel suggest the heavens, and the gold background, the brilliant sun. Surrounding her four men appear in positions of prayer.

The identification of the Virgin Mary with the anonymous Woman of the Apocalypse, the so-called *Signum Magnum* (Great Sign), originated in the twelfth century. In David's time, the Maria in Sole, by which the merged image became known, was used to represent both the Madonna of the Rosary—a Dominican theme—and the Immaculate Conception of the Virgin, a Franciscan one.[7] In the Pasadena painting, the Virgin holds a white rose out to the Christ Child. A rose without thorns was an established symbol of the purity of the Virgin and thus a reference to the Immaculate Conception, the belief that the Virgin had been born without original sin. By representing the Christ Child reaching for the rose with two hands, David extends the meaning to include Christ's miraculous conception.[8]

David's devotional image is closely related to abbreviated images of the Virgin and Child in sixteenth-century prayer books and block prints,[9] which were often accompanied by a prayer and the promise (attributed to Pope Sixtus IV [r. 1471–84]) that those who prayed before the image would be granted an indulgence from the torments of purgatory lasting eleven thousand years.[10] This image of the Immaculate Conception ultimately derives from representations of the Tree of Jesse, which outlines the lineage of the Virgin Mary and Christ.[11]

Sensitive to the natural behavior of children and to human relationships, David represented a restless child kicking with excitement as he reaches for the white rose held by his mother—a youthful, tender Madonna, her head dropped in meditation on the Passion.[12] David's mastery of sfumato, the technique of softening the definition of forms so they appear to be seen through atmosphere, contributes to the melancholy tenderness of the appealing devotional image. Set against the gold background, incised with lines to suggest the rays of the sun, this very human Virgin appears both regal and heavenly, having the power necessary to intercede on behalf of those who ask for her help.

The identities of the four men standing next to the Virgin are disputed.[13] They have been identified both as the four Latin Fathers of the Church[14] and the four Evangelists.[15] Hans van Miegroet has proposed another interpretation based on comparing the David painting with a now

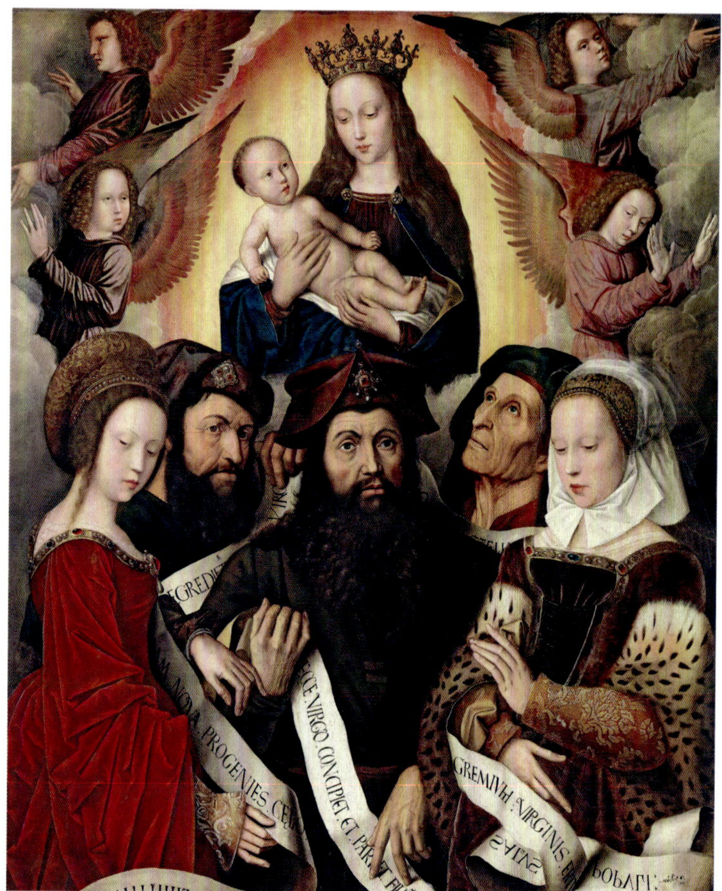

Fig. 21a. Ambrosius Benson, *Deipara Virgo*, 1530, oil on panel, 51⅝ × 42½ in. (131 × 108 cm), Koninklijk Museum voor Schone Kunsten, Antwerp.

lost composition by Hugo van der Goes (1440–1482), *Deipara Virgo Foretold by the Prophets and the Sibyls*.[16] That work, which in David's time was in the Mechelen (Malines) residence of the humanist Hieronymus Busleyden (ca. 1470–1517), is known from Busleyden's written description as well as by a copy painted by Ambrosius Benson (fig. 21a).[17] There are more witnesses in Hugo's tightly packed painting than in David's; among them are sibyls and prophets, each identified by banderoles. On the basis of this comparison, Van Miegroet recognizes the smooth-faced man on the far left in David's painting as a familiar "type" he used for John the Evangelist, generally credited with being the author of the book of Revelation in which the vision of the Virgin is described. Van Miegroet identifies the man in a dark blue robe standing next to John as the prophet Balaam and the somewhat older man with a beard seen in profile at the far right as the prophet Isaiah. Both Balaam and Isaiah were Old Testament prophets who anticipated the coming of Christ.[18] Van Miegroet's suggestion that the bald older man is a portrait of the donor is disputed by Maryan Ainsworth, who notes that it would be inappropriate for a donor to be represented on the same scale and level as saints.[19] Ainsworth suggests that the two figures on the left are Gerard David's personal saints, John the Evangelist and

John the Baptist. The others, she suggests, may be saints of a particular order.[20] David's direct dependence on Hugo's painting can also be questioned given the popularity of the image in contemporary prints and prayer books.

The Coronation of the Virgin has generally been dated after 1500. Van Miegroet and Ainsworth suggest a date of ca. 1515 or later, at the end of the artist's career. The painting's subtle handling of form, sensitive rendering of character, and especially the use of Leonardesque sfumato are all characteristic of David's mature late style.[21]

The small scale of the painting and its subject suggest it was probably made for private devotions. The painting came from a descendant of the Spanish royal family, and at least one copy appears to have derived from Spain. As the major port of the Netherlands until the mid-sixteenth century, Bruges had close ties with Spain and was home to numerous Spanish merchants. It is possible that David painted the Pasadena panel for a wealthy Spanish patron in the Netherlands or Spain, who may have presented it to a member of the royal household. The gold background and regal image of the Virgin could even indicate that its royal history extends back to the time of its creation, a period when the Holy Roman Emperor Charles V (r. 1519–56), following the lead of his grandparents King Ferdinand II of Aragon (r. 1479–1516) and Queen Isabella (r. 1469–1504), was an ardent promoter of the popular cult of the Immaculate Conception.[22]

1. Robert Langton Douglas (1864–1951, who worked for Duveen Brothers and often contributed to the writing for their presentation dossiers) on 21 November 1945 described the painting as "formerly in the collection of a Spanish prince, Juan de Bourbon, it was exhibited for many years in the Prado" (GRI, Duveen Archive, Box 235, f.11). Prince Juan was the son of Ferdinand VII, king of Spain (r. 1808, 1813–33) and grandson of Charles IV, king of Spain from 1788 until his abdication in 1808.

2. GRI, Duveen Archive, Box 30, New York Stockbook (21), no. 29844, notes that the painting came from the collection of Count Santa Maria, Madrid. Sr. D. Matias Muntadas y Rovira, Conde de Santa María de Sans, had a large collection of fourteenth- and fifteenth-century religious paintings and sculpture, both Catalan and Flemish. The introduction to a catalogue of his collection published in 1931 (which does not include this painting) notes that the collection had been dispersed. Part of his collection is now in the Museu Nacional d'Art de Catalunya, Barcelona.

3. Ali Loebl was Franz Kleinberger's nephew and served as director the Paris office of Kleinberger & Co.

4. According to New York 1946b.

5. On David's underdrawings, see Ainsworth 1998, pp. 20–31, 45–48, 55n76, 96, 275, figs. 28, 31, 37.

6. See Wolfthal and Metzger 2014, pp. 104–21, for technical details and illustrations. The Pasadena painting is probably the same work represented in a photograph in the Max Friedländer archive at the RKD (no. 50649): "After Gerard David, *Virgin and Child, Crowned by Two Angels and Surrounded by Four Saints*, first half of the 16th century, panel, 69 × 52 cm, London/Paris/New York, Duveen Bros." The painting repeats the composition of the Pasadena painting, including the clouds, but represents the bald, clean-shaven saint closest to the Virgin on the lower right of the Pasadena painting with hair and a beard. The drapery of the angel in the upper right as well as other areas also appear to have been overpainted. Friedländer annotated the back of the photograph with "Duveen/publ. Douglas/1946."

On another photograph in the archive, Friedländer wrote that the work was in the collection "Prinz v. Bourbon, Paris/1905 off." On the back of the same photograph, he noted that the painting had been heavily overpainted and cleaned in 1935 (RKD). Evidence from X-radiographs of the Pasadena painting indicated that it was badly damaged on the right side. Duveen, which purchased a half share of the painting from the Parisian dealer Ali Loebl in 1935 and another half share from him in January 1936, may have been responsible for some of the restoration of the painting. In a 1994 Getty Survey record (NSM), Andrea Rothe, paintings conservator at the Getty Museum, who was not aware of the documents in the Duveen archive, conjectured that the damaged right third was probably restored by conservator William Suhr (1896–1984) and recommended, as it was so beautifully done, that this restoration should be preserved.

7. Ringbom 1962 and Stratton 1994.

8. For a discussion of the cult of the Immaculate Conception and Sixtus IV's adding the feast of the Immaculate Conception to the church calendar in 1476, see Van Miegroet 1989, p. 259.

9. See, for example, Marten Schongauer's (ca. 1435/50–1491) engraving *The Madonna and Child Clothed with the Sun and on the Crescent Moon, Her Crown Held by Two Angels*, ca. 1470 (Bartsch [1854–70] 1970, vol. 6, p. 73, no. 31).

10. Van Miegroet 1992b, p. 94, no. 23.

11. The iconography of the Immaculate Conception evolved gradually, finally settling in the seventeenth century on the image of the Virgin standing on a crescent moon, her arms crossed over her chest. Prior to the sixteenth century, however, the Immaculate Conception was often represented by the embrace of Joachim and Anna, Mary's elderly parents, at the gates of Jerusalem or by the Tree of Jesse.

12. Detroit 1960, p. 191, no. 48, notes the similarity of the Virgin holding a rose and David's *Virgin of the Rose* (Colegiata del Sacromonte, Granada).

13. Ainsworth 1989, p. 20, figs. 5–7, notes the different methods David used for the underdrawings of the figures of the two men on the left and the robe of the Virgin. She suggests that the "extremely meticulous and careful" drawing of the men, which presents a "fully resolved form and modeling in brush and a black pigment," indicates the artist's reliance on a preliminary drawing on paper. The underdrawing of the Virgin's robes, however, is in a "crumbly" medium (probably black chalk) and shows that the artist continued to work out his ideas on the panel. See the discussion by Cathy Metzger in Wolfthal and Metzger 2014, p. 111 and fig. 8 on p. 113.

14. This identification was made by Douglas 1946, p. 161, and by Brockwell in London 1953–54, p. 40, no. 125. Douglas also considered the men to be portraits. The four Latin Fathers of the Church are Saint Ambrose, usually dressed as a bishop; Saint Augustine, also dressed as a bishop; Saint Gregory, portrayed as a pope; and Saint Jerome, who is depicted as an old man, sometimes with the hat and crimson robes of a cardinal.

15. Detroit 1960, p. 191, no. 48, notes that "the Saints in this painting wear the simple tunic and robe usually worn by Christ's apostles and disciples. Their facial characteristics also correspond to the traditional way in which the four Evangelists are represented, especially the two unbearded figures. The one at the extreme left seems to be Saint John and the one on the right resembles Saint Luke as he appears, for example, in the painting by Rogier van der Weyden preserved in the Museum of Fine Arts, Boston."

16. Van Miegroet 1989, pp. 257f.

17. Destrée 1926. Regarding these sources and other known copies of the painting, see Van Miegroet 1989, pp. 257–58.

18. Numbers 24:17: "There shall come a Star out of Jacob, and a Scepter shall rise out of Israel." Isaiah 11:1: "There shall come forth a rod out of the stem of Jesse and a Branch shall grow out of his roots."

19. Van Miegroet 1989, p. 259. Maryan Ainsworth, 1999, personal communication with the author.

20. Ainsworth, personal communication with the author.

21. Van Miegroet 1989, p. 306; Ainsworth 1998, p. 45.

22. Stratton 1994, pp. 4, 35ff. Isabella and Ferdinand, the Reyes Católicos, founders of the Franciscan Order of the Conception in Toledo, were important for the propagation of the cult of the Immaculate Conception. Charles V was the first member of the Confraternity of the Immaculate Conception in Toledo. During the sixteenth century, countless family chapels in Spain were dedicated to the Virgin of the Immaculate Conception.

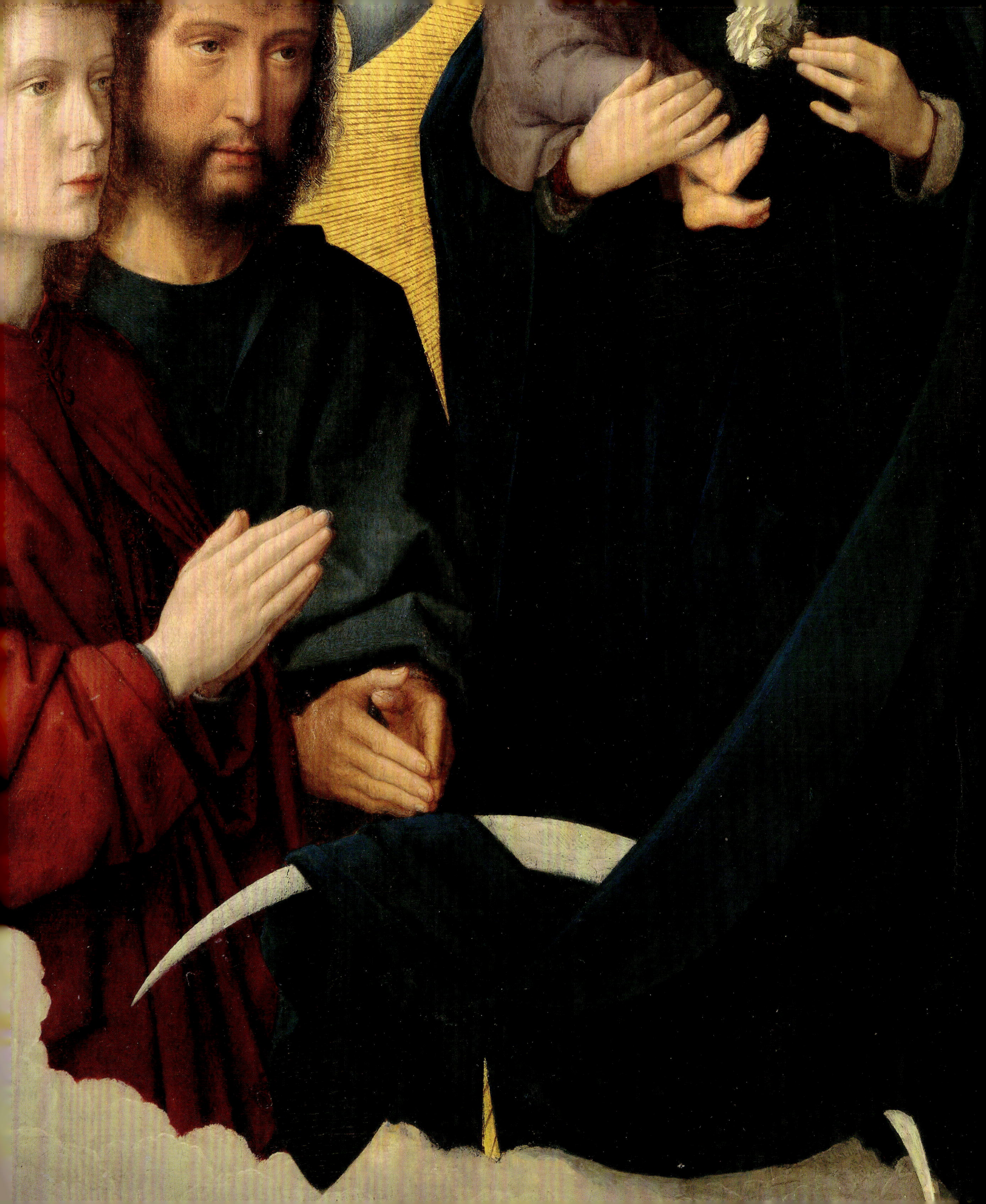

22

Gerrit Dou

Dutch
Leiden 1613–1675 Leiden

Portrait of a Woman

ca. 1645

Oil on oval panel, 19 ⅜ × 15 ¼ in. (49.2 × 38.7 cm)
The Norton Simon Foundation, F.1969.43.P

Provenance
Marquis de Forbin-Janson, Paris (sale, Hôtel Drouot, Paris, 3 December 1906, lot 24, ill., sold with lot 25, *Portrait d'un gentilhomme* [fig. 22b], for F 15,700 to); Depri.[1] Mej. C. Brunner, Paris.[2] Anonymous (sale, Hôtel Drouot, Paris, 17 June 1910, lot 12, ill., sold for F 14,200 to); [E. Singer, Paris, to];[3] Madame Singer, Paris (sale, Palais Galliera, Paris, 14 December 1960, lot 65, pl. xxxiv, sold for F 10,800 to); A. Baude, Paris.[4] [Frederick Mont and Bruno Meissner, Zurich, the latter consigned his half 21 April 1969 to]; [Newhouse Galleries, New York (consignment no. 61197, stock no. 18281), sold 1969 to];[5] The Norton Simon Foundation.

Exhibited
On loan, Phoenix Art Museum, 21 January–7 May 1970; on loan, Los Angeles County Museum of Art, 8 May 1970–26 November 1974.

References
Hofstede de Groot 1908–27, vol. 1 (1908), p. 459, no. 372; W. Martin 1913, p. 49, as ca. 1635/40, Singer Collection, Paris; Pasadena 1980, p. 52, ill.; Sumowski 1983–93, vol. 1, pp. 536, 597, no. 300, ill.; P. Sutton 1986, p. 216; Pasadena 1989, p. 83, ill.; Baer 1990, no. 35b, p. 39; Lilian 2007, pp. 18–20; S. Campbell 2010, p. 328, no. 698, ill.; Surh and Rahusen 2017/2020.

Technical Notes
The oval support is a vertically grained oak panel. The conspicuous striation of the surface could be from a brush application of the ground, but it is more likely that its thinness allows the texture of wood grain to remain prominent. The warm red-brown color of the ground influences the tonality of both the background and the figure. A painted black line at the back edge of her collar appears to be an initial guide to the position of the figure. No other underdrawing was found. Paint was applied smoothly, with meticulous attention to details such as lace, jewelry, and fabrics. Only a few examples of layered paint were noted in the dark-gray paint surrounding the proper right hand and the head. Dou left reserves for the white cuffs and collar, brushing the black paint of the dress up to the edges, then brushing the thin white paint of the fabric and lace over the layer below. Microscopic examination reveals a change in the proper right cuff. It originally was wider, and the first version of the scalloped lace edge is becoming faintly evident beneath the black paint. Minor abrasion is located in the shadow behind the sitter's neck, at the back edge of her collar, and in the yellow neck chain. The hair also is slightly abraded. The background, the draped curtain, and the tablecloth have clouded or mottled colors that signify a change from the original appearance of the paint; the cause may have been a partial removal or damage to glazes in cleaning. In previous treatment, varnish was removed from the flesh tones and from the white collar and cuffs. The minimal retouching is located at the back of the collar, in the proper left cheek, in the forehead, and at the center of the skirt at the bottom edge. Ultraviolet-light examination indicates an aged synthetic varnish, likely with added wax. The varnish has discolored to a slightly opaque gray and saturates poorly.

A demure woman, shown in three-quarter view facing toward the viewer's left, turns her gaze outward; her right hand rests near a leather-bound book with silver locks and corners standing upright on a table covered with a reddish-brown cloth. The book is undoubtedly the *Statensbijbel*, the Dutch translation of the Bible authorized by the Synod of the Reformed Church and States General, published in Leiden in 1637. Together, the curtain draped over the Bible and a similar curtain swag on the right enclose the woman's space and focus attention on the holy text. On the table, in the shadows behind the Bible, is a wooden strongbox covered in tooled leather and ornamented with iron hardware. Hidden in the shadows of the curtain on the left is a column with the relief of a putto, a detail that Gerrit Dou included in other paintings, including *The Young Mother* from 1658 (fig. 22a).

In addition to these costly possessions, the unidentified woman's clothing, influenced by the conservative styles current about 1640, suggests that she was a member of the burgher class in Leiden, where Dou was a leading painter. The sitter, her hair swept back in a chignon and covered by a simple cap, wears a black dress with a low, square neckline that reveals her linen chemise. A flat cambric kerchief trimmed with lace represents the contemporary fashion that had replaced the outdated mill ruff. Vestiges of an earlier fashion are, however, still evident in her long, narrow sleeves with cone-shaped, lace-trimmed linen cuffs and especially her stomacher, embroidered in gold thread.[6] Except for

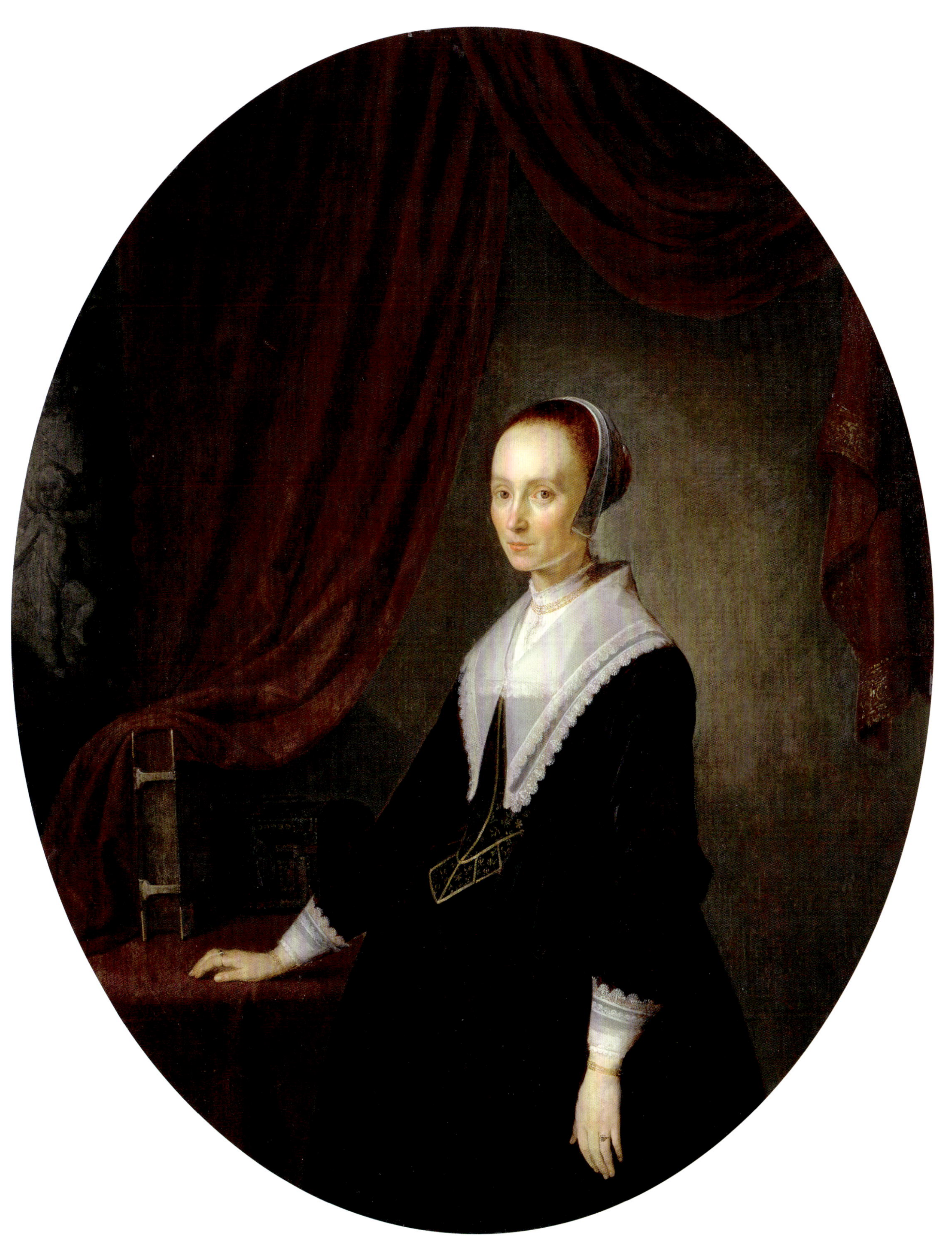

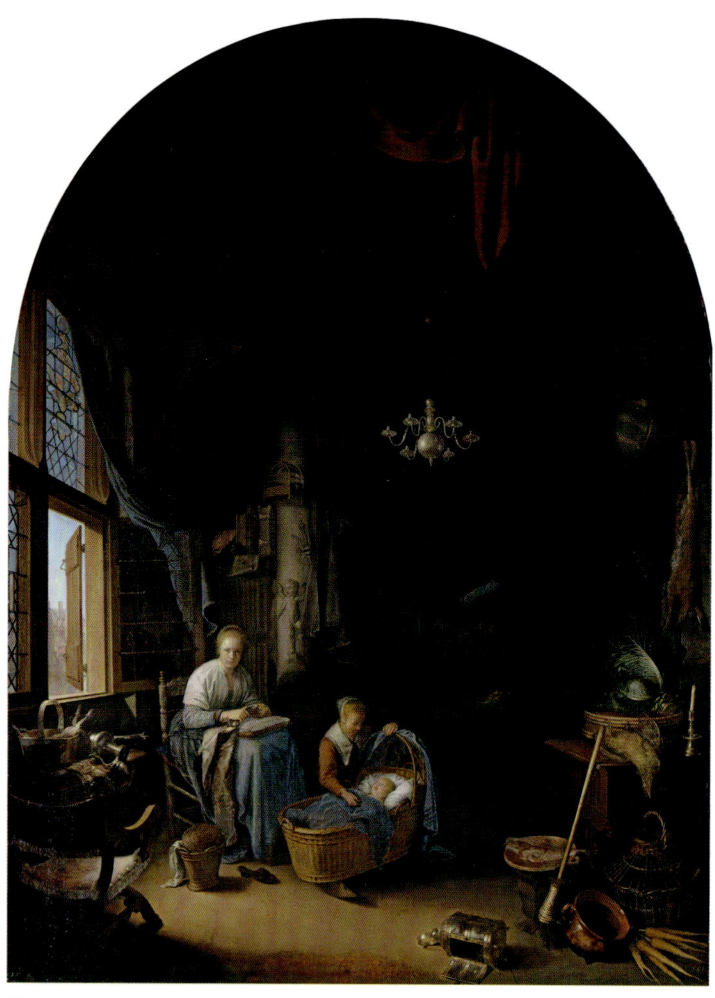

Fig. 22a. Gerrit Dou, *The Young Mother*, 1658, oil on panel, 29 × 21¾ in. (73.7 × 55.5 cm), Mauritshuis, The Hague.

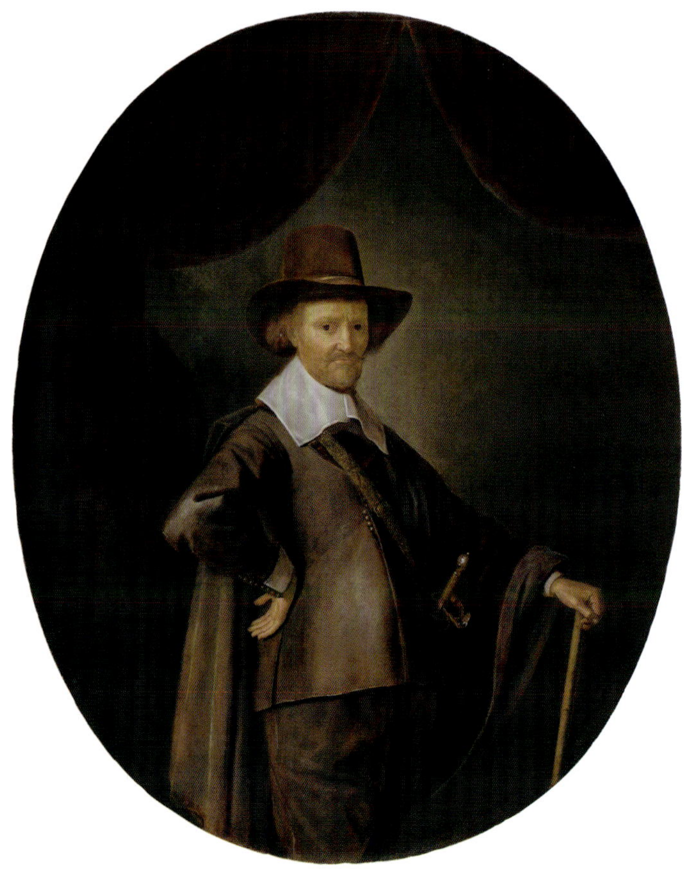

Fig. 22b. Gerrit Dou, *Portrait of a Gentleman with a Walking Stick*, ca. 1645, oil on oval panel, 19⅜ × 15⅝ in. (49.2 × 39.7 cm), The Leiden Collection, New York.

these elements of lace and embroidery, the woman's only accessories are the gold "choker" she wears around her short, standing collar, a gold bracelet on each wrist, and gold rings—the one on the forefinger of her right hand indicating that she is married.

Dou defined his sitter's features and costume with the precision and refinement of a miniaturist. There is virtually no evidence of brushwork in her face: only the long, graceful fingers of her hands reveal tiny brushstrokes of flesh-colored paint. To create the effect of the lace on the collar and cuffs, Dou used small, thin strokes of white paint over black.

Portrait of a Woman was painted ca. 1645[7] as a pendant to a portrait of the sitter's husband, *Portrait of a Gentleman with a Walking Stick*, signed "Gdov" (fig. 22b).[8] Painted at approximately the same time, the portraits were together in 1910, when they were sold to separate buyers. The two oval panels have almost identical dimensions, and the scale of the diminutive figures corresponds. The reddish-brown background and drapes that frame each figure create the impression that the two share a common space as if part of a single composition.[9] As is typical with portrait pairs, the two figures relate compositionally to each other: The arc formed by the husband's extended left hand is met and continued by the wife's right hand, which rests on the table beside her. The concave curve of her stomacher similarly appears to greet the convex line of the husband's stomach.

Adopting traditional conventions for marriage portraits, Dou used his sitter's sober pose and demeanor, emphasized by the gentle slope of her shoulders, to define her social position and to suggest the ideal of *tranquillitas*, the restraint of emotions. Seen here, the woman's realm is the home; her tranquility comes from her piety, which is proclaimed by the prominence of the Bible next to her right hand. Her love for and devotion to her husband are testified to by Cupid and the strongbox. By contrast, her husband belongs to the world beyond the home. Standing with his right arm akimbo and wearing a fashionable black hat with a high crown and a burgundy-plum wool suit and cloak, he exudes confidence. With a rapier hanging from an embroidered strap that crosses his shoulders, he grasps a walking stick and is posed as an officer of one of the local militias.[10]

The three-quarter-length format Dou used to portray this wealthy burgher couple had been traditionally reserved for the portraits of sovereigns. Especially for the new class of nonregent patrons, such formal portraits represented the social, economic, and political status to which they aspired.[11] The small-scale format of the Pasadena portrait suggests the influence not only of Thomas de Keyser (1596/97–1667), who had established the vogue for small-scale portraits in Amsterdam during the 1620s, but also of the many diminutive copies made of life-size portraits of members of the English court.[12] Dou, in fact, often repeated in his portraits postures found in these monumental court paintings. In selecting the poses and small-scale, three-quarter-length format, therefore, Dou combined the status of the court portrait with the interpretive message of the marriage portrait, representing the Dutch burghers as proud and powerful yet firmly grounded by faith and family.

1. According to the annotation in a copy of the sale catalogue at the GRI, the name is Depri. Carol Togneri suggests that the buyer at this 1906 sale may actually have been M. Depret, Bellevu (Seine), Villa Joliette Allée Pompadour, who was an anonymous seller at the 1910 Hôtel Drouot sale.

2. Presumably identical with Galerie Charles Brunner, active in Paris ca. 1920. The painting was not included in the sale of Mej. C. Brunner's estate, Dordrecht, A. Mak, 4–6 April 1922.

3. According to W. Martin 1913, p. 49.

4. According to a dossier produced by the Newhouse Galleries, New York, at the time of the painting's acquisition (NSM).

5. Newhouse stock card indicates that Frederick Mont held half interest in the painting.

6. Du Mortier 1989, pp. 47f. From ca. 1615, this kind of stomacher, known as a *borst*, was embroidered with multicolored silk, gold, silver, and pearls. Later, the style was to have it embroidered with black on black.

7. Baer 1990, p. 198, no. 35, dates both the Pasadena painting and its pendant (*Portrait of a Gentleman with a Walking Stick*) to ca. 1640–44 on the basis of the character of the portraits and the costumes. In support of this dating, Baer compares the wooden quality of the hands of the man in *Portrait of a Gentleman with a Walking Stick* to that in *Portrait of a Man* (Baer 1990, no. 36; Hermitage, St. Petersburg), which she dates to the same years. Based on the details of her dress, however, Marieke de Winkel dates *Portrait of a Woman* to 1645 (Surh and Rahusen 2017/2020, p. 5n5).

8. Dou's *Portrait of a Gentleman with a Walking Stick* is addressed in Baer 1990, no. 35a: as *Portrait of a Man*, ca. 1645(?). Oval panel, 49.2 × 39.7 cm (19¼ x 15⅝ in.), signed at right, *Gdov* (in ligature). The Leiden Collection, New York, GD-113. Provenance: Collection, Marquis de Forbin-Janson, Paris (sale, Hôtel Drouot, Paris, 3 December 1906, lot 25); Baron von Goldschmidt Rothschild, Frankfurt; anonymous (sale, Hôtel Drouot, Paris, 17 June 1910, lot 13); Kunsthandel Gebr. Douwes, Amsterdam, 1928; R. Semmel, Berlin (sale, Frederik Muller, Amsterdam, 21 November 1933, lot 11); Geus van den Heuvel (sale, Sotheby Mak van Waay, Amsterdam, 26–27 April 1976, lot 12). [Solomon Lilian Gallery, Amsterdam, sold 2007 to]; Leiden Gallery, New York.

9. According to Surh and Rahusen 2017/2020, infrared reflectography of *Portrait of a Gentleman with a Walking Stick* indicates that, like the Pasadena portrait, there was originally a second drapery swag on the right. The infrared reflectography also reveals that the background of the male portrait originally included architectural details.

10. The husband also interacts both physically and psychologically with the viewer. Standing, facing right, he turns to address the spectator; with his right hand on his hip, his elbow protrudes forward into the viewer's space, while his left hand grasps the top of the walking cane. This pose, which was adopted in the Netherlands by the early seventeenth century, closely resembles *Standing Officer with Walking Stick*, no. 3/10, by Salomon Savery (1594–1678), from his series *Gewapende officieren en soldaten* (Armed Officers and Soldiers), ca. 1630–35; see Surh and Rahusen 2017/20, p. 3, fig. 1.

11. In the portraits by Dou and the Amsterdam painters Thomas de Keyser, Nicolaes Eliasz., called Pickenoy (1590/91–1654/56), and to some extent Cornelis van der Voort (ca. 1576–1624), the elaborate settings of the sixteenth century gave way to plain backgrounds and only a minimum of auxiliary elements: a chair, a table, and/or a curtain—familiar attributes in court portraits. The austere simplicity of these burgher portraits focuses greater attention on the sitters and imbues them with a sense of formality and sophistication.

12. Adams 1985, vol. 1, pp. 206–09. Dou and De Keyser also shared a similar concern for precise details and smooth surfaces.

23

Karel Dujardin

Dutch
Amsterdam 1626–1678 Venice

The Denial of Peter

Probably 1667

Signed top edge, right of center: "K DU JARDIN F / 16 . . . 7"[1]
Oil on canvas, 47⅛ × 41¼ in. (119.7 × 104.8 cm)
Norton Simon Art Foundation, M.1975.16.P

Provenance

Probably in the collection of the artist at the time of his wife's death in 1678, inv. 19–24 October 1678, Amsterdam, "[in the studio] Een groot schilderij zijnde Petrus met een meit en een soldaat."[2] Probably Jacob Cromhout (1652–1708), Amsterdam,[3] or Jasper Loskart (sale, Zomer, Amsterdam, 7–8 May 1709, lot 4, "Daar Petrus bekent werd van de Dienst maagd van, Carel du Jardin").[4] Possibly Nicolaes Nieuhoff, Amsterdam.[5] François Tronchin des Délices (1704–1798), Geneva, by 1780[6] (sale, exp. Constantin and c.p. Boileau, Paris, 23 March 1801, lot 44, "Le Reniement de S. Pierre, composition de cinq figures grandes comme nature, vues jusqu'aux genoux. T. Haut 44 pouc. Larg. 38 pouc. 9 lign."; sold or bought in for F 200 to/by); [Guillame-Jean Constantin (1755–1816), Paris].[7] John Walter III (1818–1894), Bearwood, by 1868,[8] by descent to; John Walter IV (1873–1968), Harcourt House (sale, Sotheby's, London, 10 June 1942, lot 45, sold to); Welker.[9] Henri Bredius (d. 1972), London, by descent to;[10] "Bredius Heirs," Haarlem, sold 1975 through; [G. Cramer Oude Kunst, The Hague to]; Norton Simon Art Foundation.

Exhibited

Leeds 1868, no. 895, lent by J. Walter, Esq.; Delft 1975, p. 82, ill., lent by Cramer; on loan, Krannert Art Museum, University of Illinois Urbana-Champaign, 3 January–2 August 1977.

References

Tronchin 1780, p. 61; Skinner 1781, vol. 2, p. 39; J. Smith 1829–42, vol. 5 (1834), p. 242, no. 28; "Bearwood" 1884; "Bearwood" n.d.; Bredius 1906, p. 226; Hofstede de Groot 1907–28, vol. 9 (1926), p. 301, nos. 19a, 20, 20a; Brochhagen 1958, pp. 67ff.; Geneva 1974, p. 53, no. 108, ill.; 1975; Cramer 1975, no. 7, ill.; "Cramer" 1975; "Current and Forthcoming Exhibitions" 1975; Pasadena 1980, p. 58, ill.; P. Sutton 1986, p. 219; P. Sutton 1990, p. 108; Kilian 1993, pp. 30, 109f., 112, 372f., no. 88, pl. 88; Broos 1997, pp. 221, 224, 225n21, 225n36; Kilian 2005, pp. 36, 66–67, 70n61, 192–93, no. 92, pl. 74; Amsterdam 2007, p. 19; S. Campbell 2010, p. 389, no. 1277, ill.

Related Works

- Drawing: H. A. Lammers, Kampiraai KP J. Africa, ca. 1978. (Photocopy in Rijksprentenkabinet and the RKD). Annotated: "Reminiscence d'un tableau de Karl Dujardin, par Mr N. Châtelaine 1788." On the back, in the same handwriting: "Ce croquis a fait partie de la collection de feu Mr le Cte Fédor Golowkin. / Le tableau original était dans la galerie du Procureur Général Tronchin à Genève. —Cabinet qui fut acheté par Catherine II & qui périt dans La Baltique."[11] Kilian 2005, p. 193, describes the drawing: "Peter at the left, half-length seated at a table. The maid is in the middle facing left, finger raised, next to her is a boy. At the right in the distance is a doorway framing the figure of a servant. All figures shown half-length. Composition horizontal. The moment shown appears to be the first denial of Peter (Matthew 26:69–70)." Kilian speculates that the differences in composition between the drawing and the actual painting may be because the drawing was made from memory.
- Copy: Erick Wilkes (or Van den Weerelt).[12] Canvas, 52⅜ × 43¾ in. (133 × 111 cm). Formerly Burgerweeshuis (Sociaal-Agogisch Centrum het Burgerweeshuis), Amsterdam, inv. no. B. 4852. References: I. H. van Eeghen 1952, p. 124; Brochhagen 1958, p. 69n248; Blankert et al. 1975–79, p. 95, no. 123, ill. (since 1978 no longer in the collection); Kilian 2005, pp. 36, 193, notes that the painting includes "landscape, wall and sky at upper left which is not visible in Pasadena painting."

Technical Notes

The primary support, a plain-weave canvas, carries an old lining; the original tacking edges were cut off. X-radiography reveals cusped threads at the left, right, and bottom edges. The top edge may have been trimmed because of damages before lining, as the X-radiograph reveals a considerable amount of paint loss across it. The signature is located in this damaged area, resulting in loss to the upper half of most of the letters and to some of the numbers from the date painted beneath. Weave transference from lining pressure has exaggerated the canvas texture, formerly masked by the white ground, which appears to be of moderate thickness. There is a rose-beige imprimatura applied on top of the ground layer, visible in the sky at upper left, where it is exposed by abrasions in the blue paint of the sky. The central figures in the painting have strongly modeled forms executed in rich opaque paint applied directly with rather broad handling. Contours are generally soft and somewhat indistinct. The paint is abraded at the edges of numerous cracks, most probably by cleaning. Much of Saint Peter's halo has been removed, and the blue in his robe appears to have been altered. The painting received a great amount of retouching and some areas of repainting, such as the woman's white sleeve. Recent cleaning removed a thick glossy varnish and the old discolored retouching, improving the overall tonality of the work and allowing it to be read as a unified composition. *—Rosamond Westmoreland with Devi Ormond*

After the Last Supper, Jesus and his disciples went to the Mount of Olives; there, Jesus prophesied that before the cock crowed the next morning, Peter, his most devoted disciple, would deny him three times.[13] That night soldiers arrested Jesus and brought him for questioning before Caiaphas, the high priest. Peter followed but remained in the courtyard. When a maid servant approached him and said, "You were with Jesus the Galilean," Peter denied he

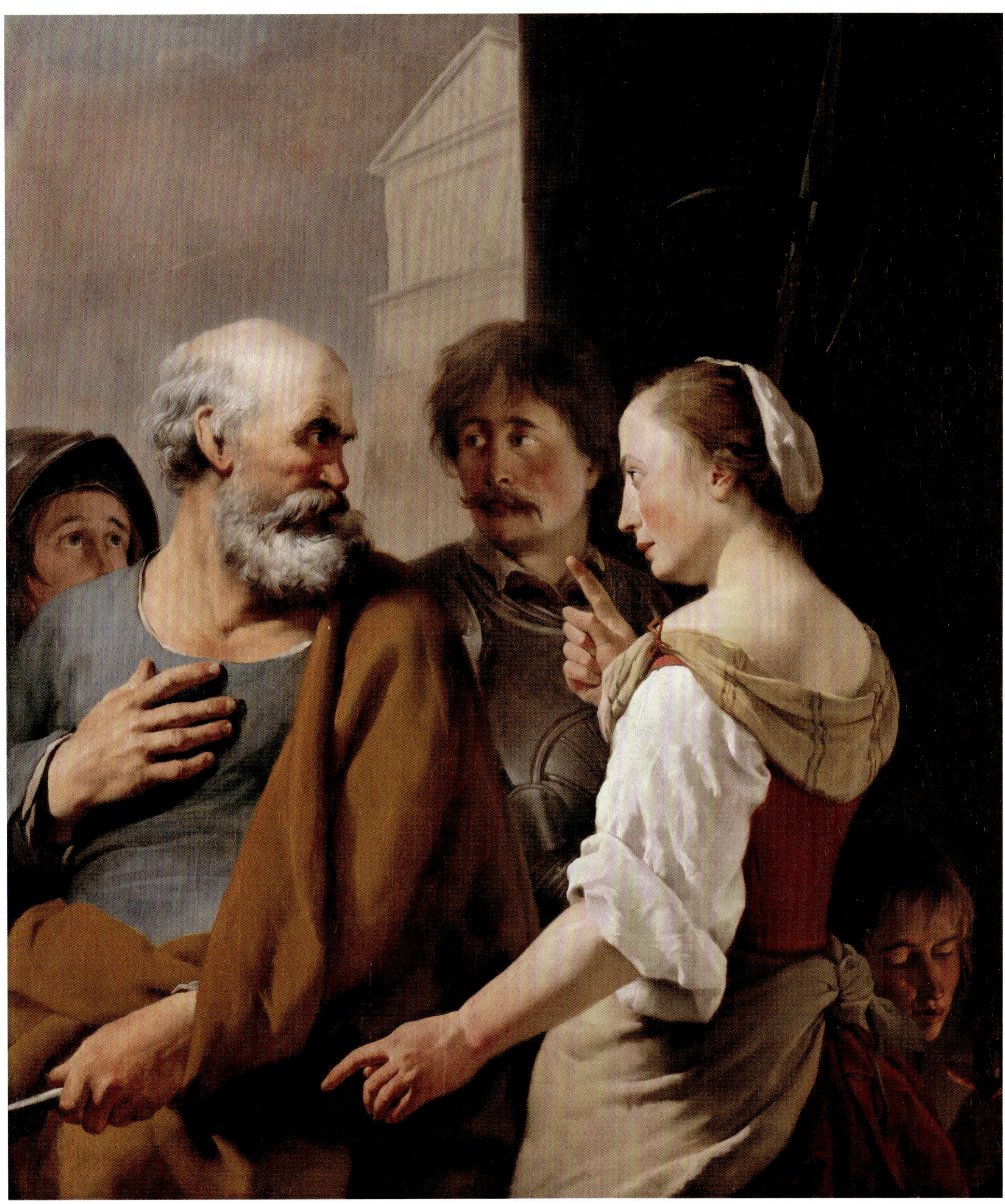

knew him.[14] Later that night, "when he [Peter] went out to the entrance, another servant girl saw him, and she said to the bystanders, 'This man was with Jesus of Nazareth.' And again he denied it with an oath, 'I do not know the man.'"[15] For a third time that night, Peter was confronted by people standing outside the high priest's house, but again Peter denied knowing Jesus; after the third denial, he heard the crowing of the cock and recalled with sorrow Jesus's prediction.[16]

The outdoor daylight setting of the dramatic scene of the maid pointing toward Peter, who holds his right hand over his heart as if swearing an oath, identifies the subject of Karel Dujardin's painting as the second betrayal of Jesus by Peter. Light from an undisclosed source models and separates the carefully rendered classical figures of Peter and the maid from the minor figures of the two soldiers, who stand behind them in shadow.[17] The blond tonality suggestive of the approaching dawn modulates Peter's dark blue tunic and burnt orange cloak and the combination of buff, yellow, and dark peach of the maidservant's costume, set off by a brilliant white sleeve.

Dujardin probably painted *The Denial of Peter* about 1667.[18] Although best known for his bucolic, light-filled landscapes populated by domestic cattle and Arcadian shepherds, Dujardin produced large-scale history paintings in the classical mode following his return to Amsterdam from The Hague in 1659. In keeping with the style that dominated art in Amsterdam and The Hague during the 1660s, Dujardin's painting incorporates elements from both the Utrecht Caravaggists and the Haarlem Classicists as well as from Flemish, French, and Italian art.

Dujardin's depiction of the Denial of Peter as a tense scene of personal conflict reveals his familiarity with and interest in the work of Caravaggio (1571–1610) and his followers, known as the Caravaggists, who frequently treated the theme as a nighttime scene.[19] As in Caravaggio's *The Denial of Saint Peter* (fig. 23a), Dujardin used the active play of expression and gesture to create dramatic tension, which he heightened by crowding the three-quarter-length figures together in the shallow foreground, cutting off the body of Peter on the left.[20] A famous, now lost painting by Caravaggio, known only by Pietro Bellori's (1613–1696) description, was particularly influential for the Caravaggists: "In Naples his *Denial of Saint Peter* in the Sacristy of S. Martino is considered to be one of Caravaggio's best works. Here the servant-girl points to Saint Peter, who, turning around, opens his hands in the act of denying Christ; the painting is a night scene in which one sees various figures warming their hands at a fire."[21] Dujardin, who is not known to have traveled to Italy before 1675, could only have known Caravaggio's original through the work of others.

Gerrit van Honthorst (1592–1656), the most important of the Utrecht Caravaggists who returned to the Netherlands from Rome in 1620, painted at least three versions of the

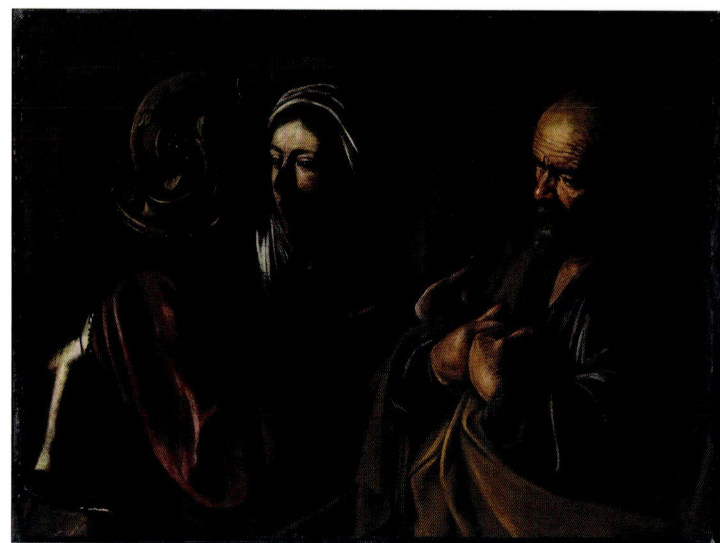

Fig. 23a. Caravaggio, *The Denial of Saint Peter*, 1610, oil on canvas, 37 × 49⅜ in. (94 × 125.4 cm), The Metropolitan Museum of Art, New York.

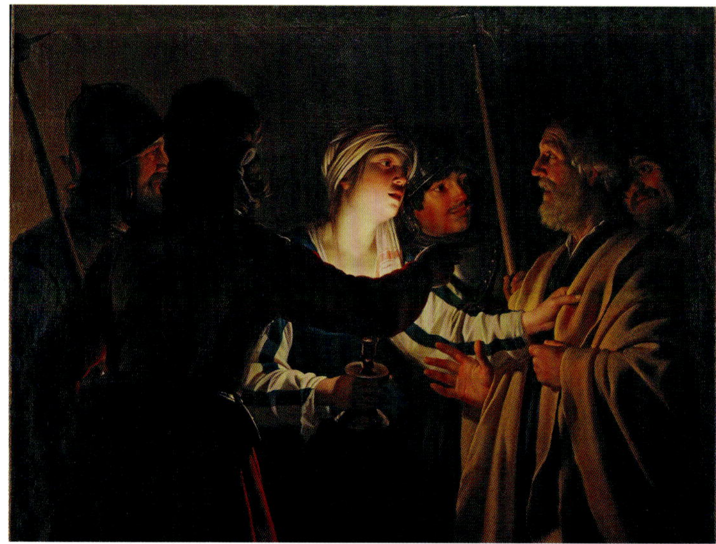

Fig. 23b. Gerrit van Honthorst, *The Denial of St. Peter*, ca. 1623, oil on canvas, 43½ × 57 in. (110.5 × 144.8 cm), Minneapolis Institute of Art, The Putnam Dana McMillan Fund.

Denial of Peter, which suggest his direct knowledge of the painting praised by Bellori as well as other versions of the subject by Caravaggio.[22] Dujardin's depiction of full forms frozen by dramatic tension and the tight composition are similar to those in Honthorst's *Denial of St. Peter* (fig. 23b) painted in the Netherlands ca. 1623. The relationship of the maid confronting Peter and the soldier between them who turns toward the disciple recalls the central group in Honthorst's painting in reverse. The second soldier who wears a helmet and peers over the shoulder of Peter in the Pasadena painting does not appear in Honthorst's horizontal version, which also includes two soldiers next to the maid. The most significant difference between the two paintings is Dujardin's focus of the central event in a vertical

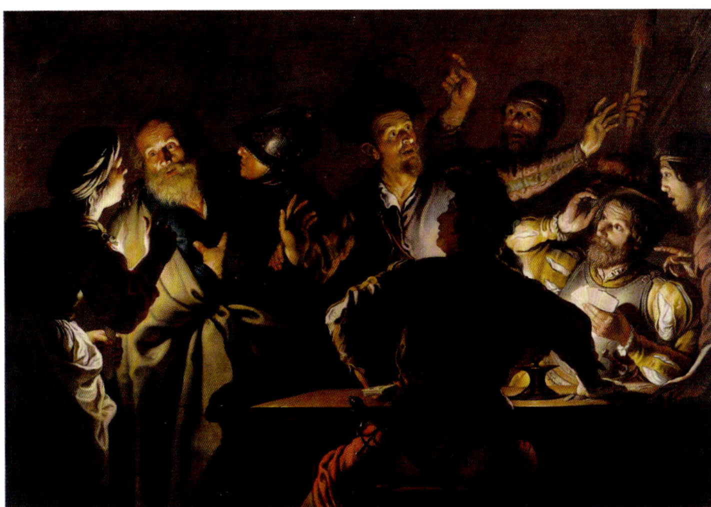

Fig. 23c. Gerard Seghers, *The Denial of St. Peter*, ca. 1620–25, oil on canvas, 68 × 89½ in. (172.7 × 227.3 cm), North Carolina Museum of Art, Raleigh, Purchased with funds from the State of North Carolina, 52.9.112.

composition and his light palette rather than the nocturnal setting illuminated by artificial light, which was preferred by the Caravaggists.

The nighttime portrayal of the betrayal of Peter was the specialty of the Flemish Caravaggist Gerard Seghers (1591–1651), whose popular work Dujardin would have known.[23] In addition to the original paintings, Seghers's compositions were known through reproductive prints and copies. One of the most influential was a horizontal composition known in several versions, the original of which is thought to be that in the collection of the North Carolina Museum of Art, Raleigh (fig. 23c). The evening scene portrays the maid confronting Peter, who is restrained by a soldier dressed in armor. Five other figures gathered around a table react to the maid's accusation. The painting, which was in a private collection in Antwerp in 1638,[24] is also known from prints by S. à Bolswert (1586–1659), one of which reverses the composition so that the confrontation occurs on the right rather than the left. A print by P. Daret (1604–1673; Albertina, Vienna) that reproduces the three major figures from the horizontal composition in a tightly compressed vertical composition is similar to Dujardin's portrayal of the scene.

Dujardin's *Denial of Peter* was influenced by the precedents of Caravaggio and the Caravaggists, like Honthorst and Seghers, but it probably did not have a single model. Instead, Dujardin established his own successful solution. Rejecting the dramatic nighttime setting, which by then was no longer fashionable, and reflecting the classical style of artists active in Amsterdam, Haarlem, and The Hague, Dujardin chose a lighter, subdued palette and focused his composition by crisply rendering details and texture.[25] The restraint and elegance suggested by Dujardin's clearly defined contours, smooth surfaces, and well-articulated gestures transform the subject from an active narrative into a tense, psychological drama that focuses on the emotional conflict of Peter.

1. Kilian 1993, p. 353, notes that Dujardin typically signed his religious and historical subjects with capital letters. Getty paintings conservator Devi Ormond notes in her technical report that "the date appears to read 16 . . . 7?"

2. The inventory covers the possessions of Suzanna van Royen, noted as the deceased wife of "Carel du Gardijn, the art painter who is out of the country." Suzanna was buried in Amsterdam on 17 October 1678, eight days following the burial of the artist in Venice on 9 October 1678. The inventory is published by Bredius 1906, pp. 224ff., and referenced by Brochhagen 1957, p. 67n245; Kilian 2005, pp. 107–12, doc. 105, publishes the inventory with an English translation. As evidence that the Pasadena painting is the one mentioned in Dujardin's inventory, Kilian 2005, p. 36, cites a copy of the painting made for the Burgerweeshuis, Amsterdam (see related works in Kilian 2005, pp. 96, 103, and note 12 below).

3. Jacob Cromhout (Cromhoult) was the son of a wealthy Catholic merchant family in Amsterdam. His father, Jacob (1608–1669), married to Margretha Wuytiers, commissioned the famous Cromhout houses at Herengracht 364, 366, 368, and 374, which were designed and built by Philips Vingboons around 1660–62. Jacob Cromhout II studied law in Leiden, married Catrina Wuytiers in 1675, and later inherited his father's house, Herengracht 364. See I. H. van Eeghen 1966; and I. H. van Eeghen et al. 1976, p. 520.

4. Hoet 1752–70, vol. 1, pp. 131–33, included only thirty-seven of the actual 200 lots in the sale; among those omitted was lot no. 4. A full copy of the catalogue of this sale is in the collection of the RKD.

5. According to J. Smith 1829–42, vol. 5 (1834), p. 242, no. 28, who notes that the canvas measured 111.5 × 96.3 cm. The painting does not, however, appear in the catalogue of Nieuhoff's sale, Van der Schley, De Winter & Yver, Amsterdam, 14 April 1777, in which there are three other paintings by Dujardin, including a self-portrait.

6. Tronchin 1780, p. 61 (catalogue of the second collection). Skinner 1781, vol. 2, p. 39, identified the owner of the painting as Tronchin (see introduction to Geneva 1974). Kilian 1993, p. 372, quoting Tronchin 1780, says:

> Le reniement de St. Pierre: la servante de Caïphe vue par le dos et la tête de profil; le premier doigt de la main droite élevé, & le bras gauche étendu dans l'attitude d'apostropher St. Pierre pour lui faire avouer qu'il connoît J.C. St. Pierre, vu de face et la tête de profil, la main gauche sortent de sa draperie & la droite sur sa poitrine, & dans ce mouvement d'affirmer qu'il ne le connoît point. Entre St. Pierre et la servante est un soldat en cuirasse; il a une moustache & les cheveux épais; il fixe St. Pierre derrière qui est un autre soldat en casque. Au coin de la composition est un garçon éclairé par la lueur du feu; il est derrière la servante. St. Pierre est vêtu de bleu sous une draperie jaune; la servante est en manches de chemise corset & cotillon rouges; un tablier noué par derrière, et un mouchoir de col rayé. Figures de grandeur naturelle jusqu'aux genoux. Ce tableau, très capital, est peut être l'unique qui existe de ce maître au figures grandes comme nature. Il ne laisse rien à désirer dans toutes ces parties. Composition, expression, couleur, fini, effet, tout y est supérieurement beau; & de faire regretter qu'il ne se soit pas fixé á un genre où il s'est montré tout au moins l'égal des plus grands maîtres.

Tronchin, who was councillor of state for the Republic of Geneva, assembled his second collection after selling his first collection to Catherine II of Russia in 1770.

7. The *commisseur-priseur* of the sale was Constantin, an art dealer in Paris. The painting may, therefore, actually have been bought in.

8. John Walter [I] (1739–1812) founded the London *Times* in 1785. According to Waagen [1857] 1970, p. 294, most of the collection was acquired by John Walter [II] (1776–1847). Because neither Waagen 1854 nor Waagen [1857] 1970 mention Dujardin's painting, it probably entered the collection later. In 1868 the painting was exhibited at Leeds by John Walter III, who inherited and rebuilt the original home on the Bearwood estate (Sindelsham, Berkshire) between 1865 and 1871. The house was used during World War I as a Canadian army convalescent hospital. John Walter IV sold Bearwood in 1919; it was first put up for sale in 1911 but failed to find a buyer. Today it is known as Reddam House, Berkshire, a coed independent school. The painting is mentioned in two manuscript catalogues of pictures at Bearwood, which were made for insurance—one dated 14 February 1884 and the other undated (copies of the MSS are at the GRI).

9. According to a copy of Hofstede de Groot 1907–28 annotated by Ellis K. Waterhouse (GRI), the painting was bought in at £92. The GRI possesses an annotated copy of the 1942 sale that indicates "Welker" as the buyer, which may be a mistake for the bought-in name "Walter." Geneva 1974 illustrates the picture but notes that its location is unknown, although it also mentions that a very similar painting was sold with the Walter collection in London at Sotheby's 10 June 1942, no. 45.

10. I am grateful to Pieter Biesboer for properly identifying Henri Bredius, who was originally from the Netherlands and lived in London from about 1932.

11. The annotation, which dates the drawing by N. Châtelaine to 1788, therefore probably does not concern an otherwise unknown painting in Tronchin's first collection, which was sold to Catherine II in 1770, but the Pasadena painting, which was in Tronchin's second collection.

12. I. H. van Eeghen 1952, p. 124, attributes this painting and another after Dujardin's *Paul Healing a Man Who Could Not Walk* (Rijksmuseum, Amsterdam) to Erick Wilkes (or Van der Weerelt), an orphan in the care of the Burgerweeshuis, which paid for his study with Dujardin in 1668–72 and made a payment to Wilkes in 1672. No other works by his hand are known. See also Amsterdam 2007, p. 19.

13. Mark 14:66–77; John 13:38; Matthew 26:34.

14. Matthew 26:69–70.

15. Matthew 26:71–72; Kilian 2005, p. 193: The story is also told in John 18:15–27; Mark 14:66–72; and Luke 22:55–61.

16. The Gospels vary in the specifics of the story of Peter's denial of Christ. Matthew relates that Peter was addressed twice by a woman and once by a man, whereas Luke records that he was addressed once by a woman and twice by servants.

17. See Kilian 2005, pp. 63ff. On p. 66, she observes: "The compactness of the composition [of the Pasadena painting] is achieved by focusing on Peter and the maid, first by illuminating them more brightly than the other figures, and second through the wonderful interplay of hands and gestures. Here Du Jardin's [*sic*] style is close to tendencies found in Haarlem classicism, with finely painted details and rather smooth facture reminiscent of De Bray, for instance. The colour is similar to that in earlier works."

18. Kilian 2005, pp. 66, 70. The features of the maid in the Pasadena painting are close to those of Mary in the *Return of the Holy Family from Egypt* (Detroit Institute of Arts), dated 1662. On p. 187, Kilian includes the Pasadena painting in a series of similarly conceived pictures originating in the 1660s, including *Hagar and Ishmael in the Wilderness* (Ringling Museum of Art, Sarasota), *Paul Healing a Man Who Could Not Walk* (Rijksmuseum, Amsterdam), and *The Conversion of Saul* (National Gallery, London).

19. See Nicolson 1971. Regarding the treatment of the subject by Rembrandt, see Henkel 1934 and Judson 1964.

20. The presence of cusping only on the left, bottom, and right sides indicates that the painting was trimmed and that Dujardin thus intended the figures to appear compressed in a narrow space. See Technical Notes.

21. "Si tiene in Napoli frà suoi quadri megliori la negatione di San Pietro nella Sagrestia di San Martino, figuratovi l'Ancella, che addita Pietro, el quale volgesi con le mani aperte, in atto di negar Christo; ed è colorito à lume notturno, con altre figure, che si scaldano al fuoco." Pietro Bellori, *Le vite de' pittori, scultori et architetti moderni* (1672), quoted in W. Friedländer 1955, p. 242, English trans. p. 250.

22. See Judson and Ekkart 1999, pp. 75–79, nos. 54–56. pls. 19–20, 20a–c, 21, color pls. iii and iv.

23. Nicolson 1971, fig. 19: *Denial of St. Peter*, described as a copy after a lost original by Seghers, canvas, 86 × 123 cm, when sold by Hôtel Drouot, Paris, 26 February 1934.

24. See Bieneck 1992, p. 140–45. The North Carolina painting is no. A12; Bolswert's engraving is A12a; Daret's engraving is A14.

25. Dujardin's only reference to the candlelight effects of the Caravaggists is the face of the boy, which glows from an unseen light source in the shadows of the lower right corner.

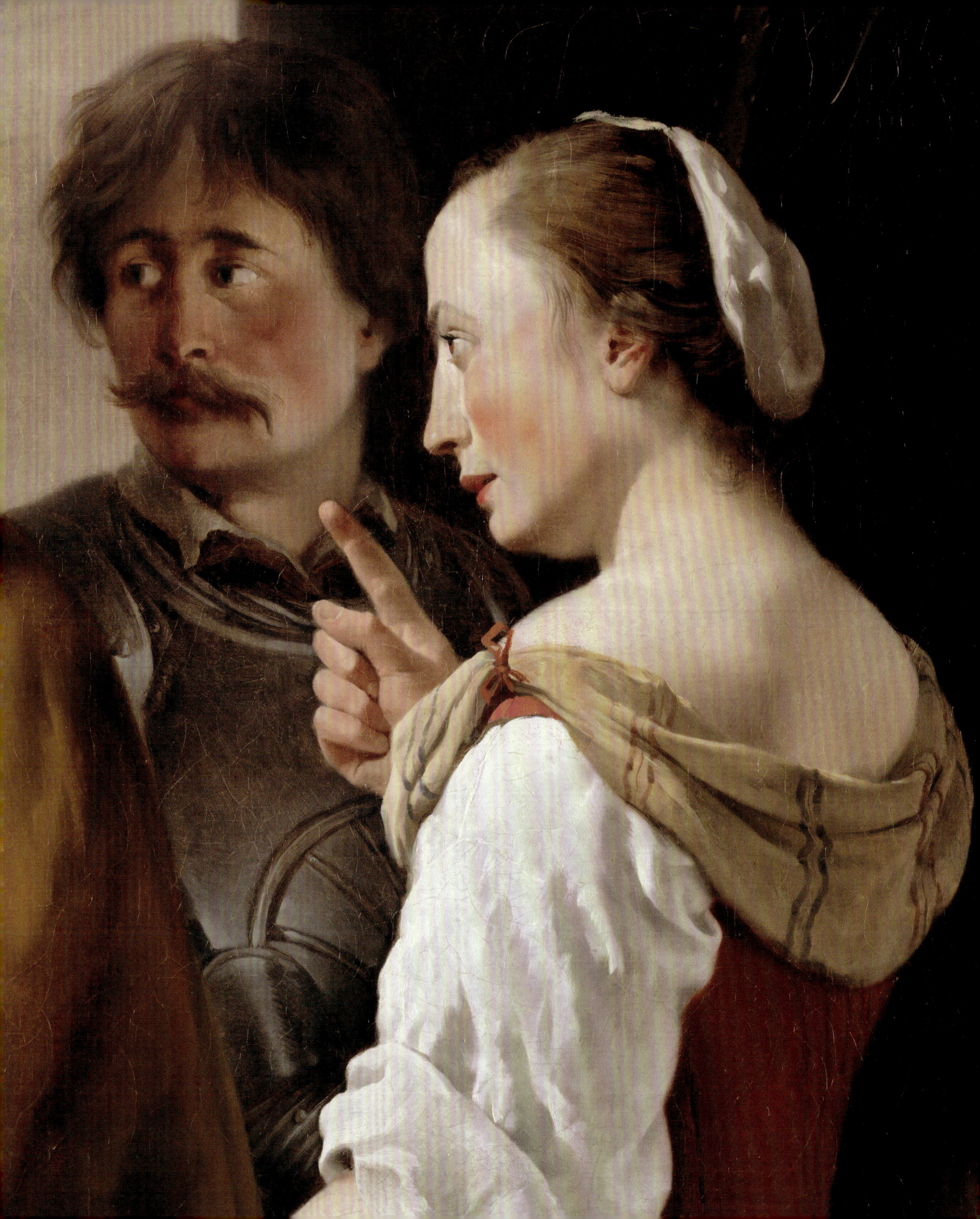

24

A Tulip Book

Dutch, ca. 1640s

Inscriptions: Folios include names of tulip specimens in brown ink at the lower left or right; page numbers are in brown ink at the top right corner
Gouache, watercolor, and pencil on paper, 12⅛ × 7⅞ in. (30.8 × 20 cm)
Norton Simon Art Foundation, M.1974.08.001–158.D

Provenance
Probably Simon Voorhelm (1685–1759), Haarlem, by descent to his brother;[1] Joris Voorhelm (1712–1787), Haarlem, by descent to his daughter;[2] Catharina Voorhelm Schneevoogt (1742–1800), Haarlem, by descent to her son;[3] George Voorhelm Schneevoogt (1775–1850), sold by 1837 to; Ernst Heinrich Krelage (1786–1855), Haarlem; Krelage Botanical Library, Haarlem (sale, International Antiquariaat [Menno Hertzberger & Co.], Amsterdam, 30 March 1948, lot 274);[4] Van Tubergen Tulip Nurseries, Haarlem (sale, Sotheby's, London, 27 June 1974, lot 119); Norton Simon Art Foundation.

Exhibited
Haarlem 1974, no. 59c; Los Angeles 2023–24.

References
Krelage 1942, pp. 57 [as Tulip Book B], 59, 202, no. 61; Pasadena 2003, pp. 158f., ill.; Willemse 2005, p. 36; S. Campbell 2010, pp. 168–69, 367, figs. 5–6, no. 1060, ill.

Technical Notes
The supports are medium-weight handmade laid papers. Irregularly shaped slubs scattered throughout indicate linen as the composition; brown fibrous inclusions are remnants of the flax. Three different watermarks (foolscap, crozier, fleur de lys) are visible on more than half the folios. The sheets were sized with gelatin, providing a desirable substrate for the watercolor technique. They are trimmed on all four sides. The left edges are somewhat uneven as a result of disbanding. Terre verte, or green earth, is visible on the top, right, and bottom edges and may have served as a bole for gilding, though no evidence of this remains. The paper is generally in good condition except for scattered discoloration, foxing, and cockling. The watercolor medium, made in house by the artists or their assistants, is a mixture of pigments. Glossy touches apparent under magnification suggest gum arabic as a binder. When crackling and crazing is evident, it mainly occurs in the red colors where particularly rich mixtures of pigment and gum arabic occur. Occasional pencil outlines on the flowers indicate the sketches laid down by the painter.
—*Lisa Forman and Mark Watters*

First cultivated in Central Asia around 1000 CE, tulips—the signature flower of the Ottoman Empire—were introduced to Europe by traders to the Levant during the late sixteenth century. They first entered scientific and courtly gardens, where they were grown and studied along with newly discovered plants and flowers from Asia, Africa, and the Americas. Scientists, collectors, and courtiers throughout Europe eagerly sought and exchanged written and visual information about new species of plants and actual specimens for their gardens. Among the most famous of these botanical gardens was that established at the University of Leiden by Carolus Clusius (Charles de l'Écluse; 1526–1609). Clusius, who assumed the newly established position of Horti Praefectus at the university in 1593, was largely responsible for popularizing the tulip in the Netherlands.[5] Distinct from the medieval gardens in which plants were grown for medicinal purposes, these botanical gardens were extensions of *Kunst-* and *Wunderkammern* that collected examples of the most exotic and rare specimens from art and nature.

The unique and mysterious ability of a tulip bulb to produce different blossoms from year to year, a characteristic now attributed to a virus, made these flowers among the most prized possessions of collectors and the most speculative purchases. In 1623, when the average annual income in the Netherlands was 150 guilders, a single bulb of the highly prized *Semper Augustus* sold for 1,000 guilders. By 1637, when bulbs were traded on the stock exchanges in Amsterdam, Rotterdam, and Haarlem among other towns in the Dutch Republic and "Tulipomania" had overtaken the country, the price had risen to 10,000 guilders, equivalent to the cost of a house on a canal in the center of Amsterdam with gardens and a coach house.[6] In the same year, however, the market crashed, and many speculators, including the artist Jan van Goyen (1596–1656), were financially ruined. Nevertheless, the fascination with tulips and other flowers continued throughout the century.

The Norton Simon's watercolors once formed part of a *tulpenboek*, or tulip book. Painted on laid paper, the 158 flower portraits were originally bound in an album. A single variety of tulip is illustrated on each page, accompanied by

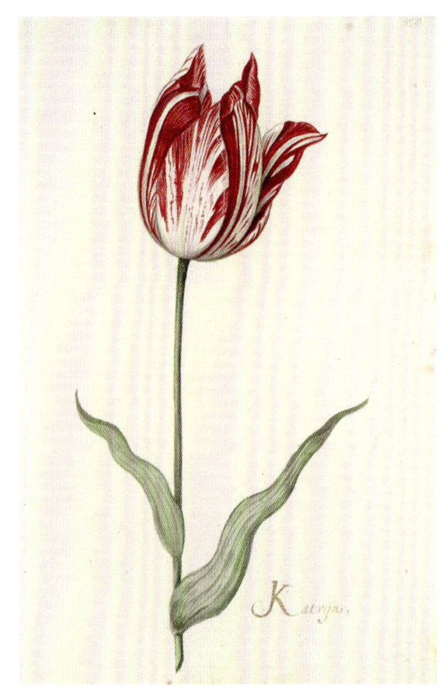
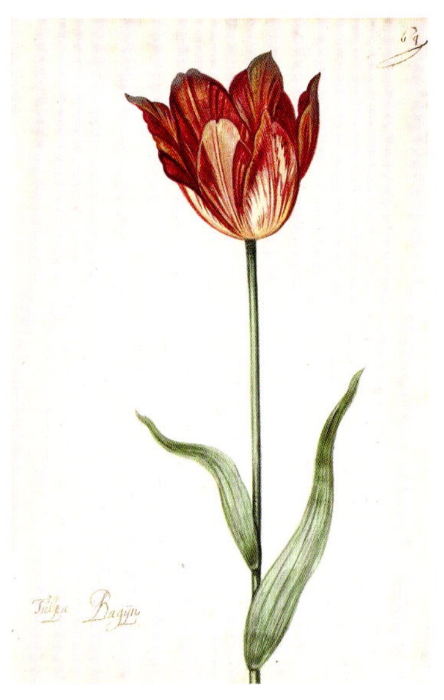
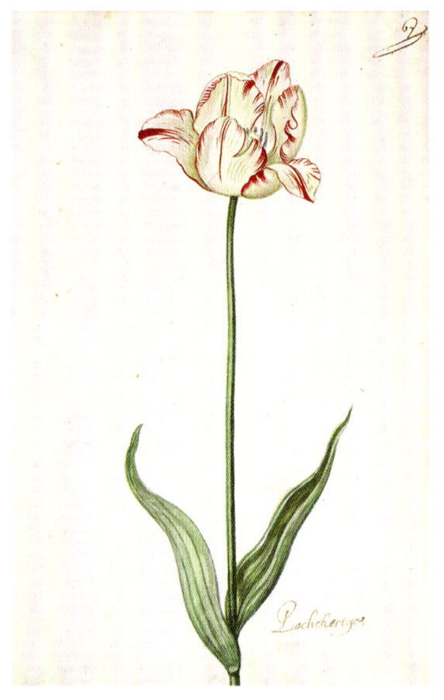
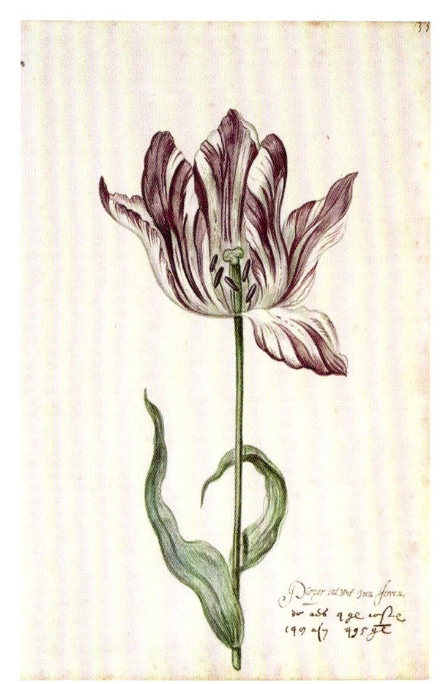
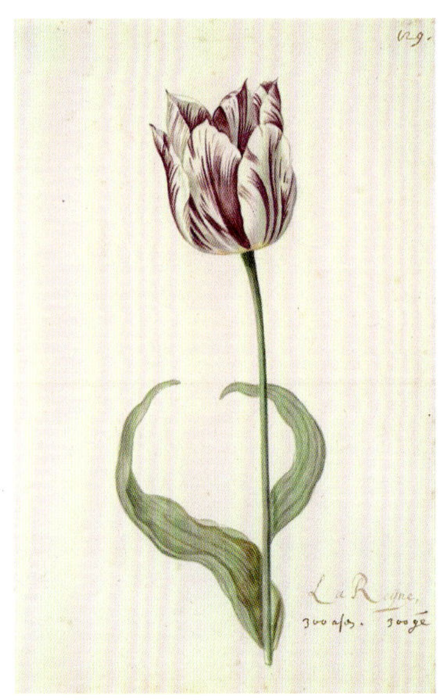
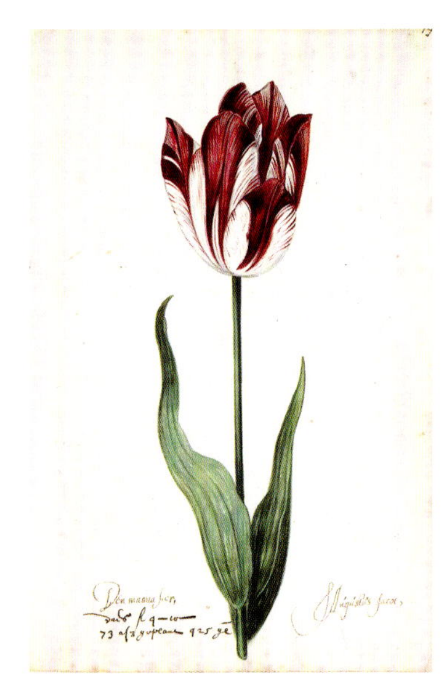
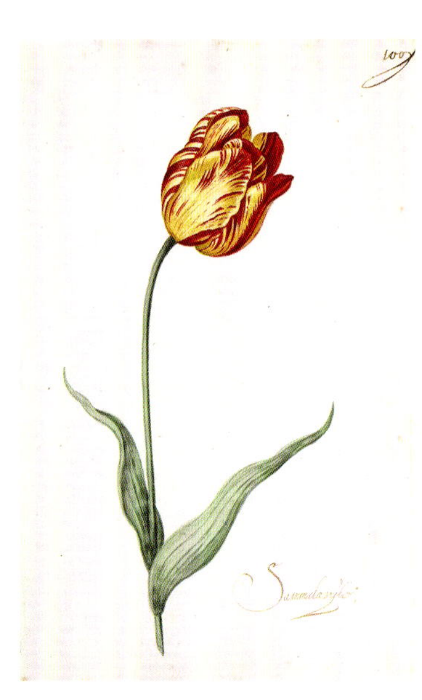
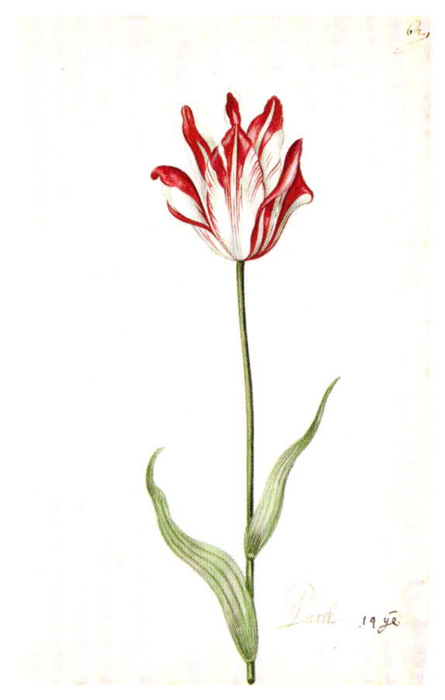
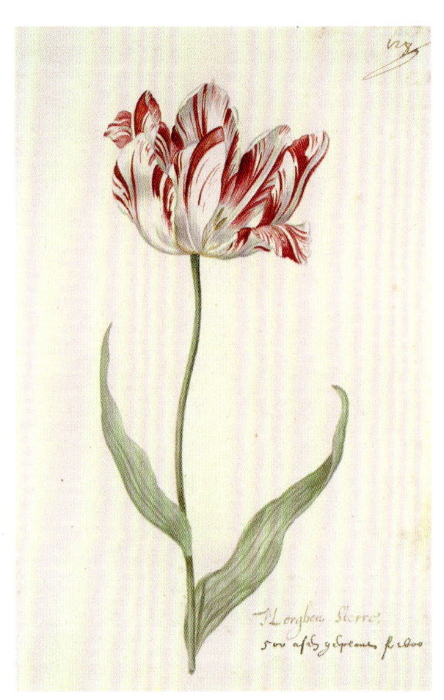
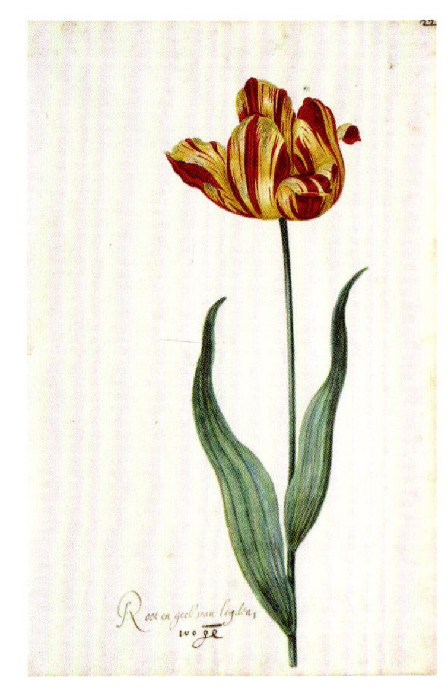
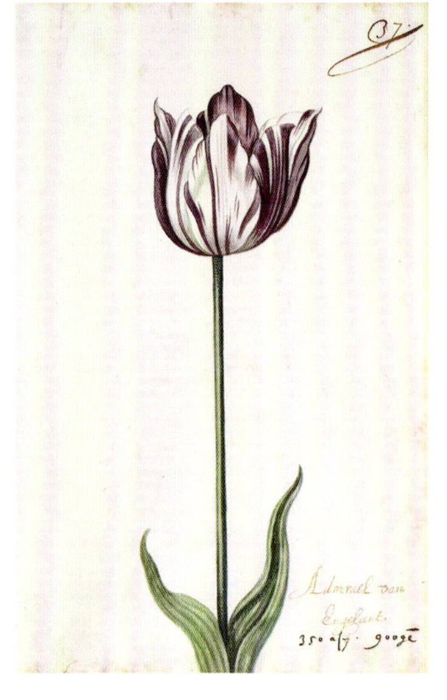
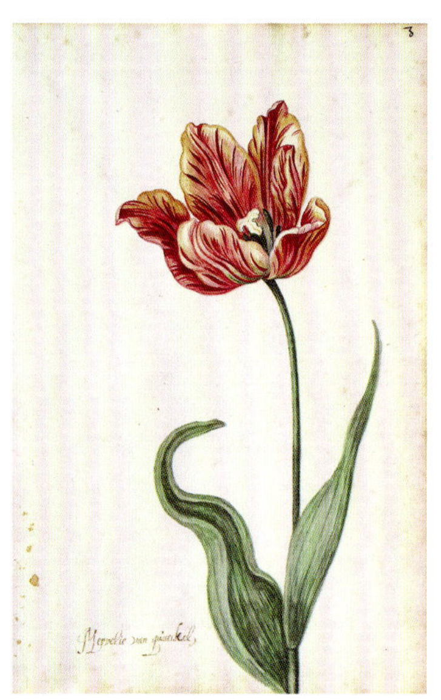

its popular name penned in a flourishing cursive script. The names of the tulips tended to be popular and well known, often associated with towns, military heroes, or figures from antiquity. Some were named in honor of growers and owners.[7] A few folios bear secondary inscriptions in Dutch that record the price and weight of each tulip bulb depicted. In the example of *Admirael Der Admiraels de Gouda*, four rows of text and numerals are visible directly under the tulip's name (fig. 24a). The numerals document the weight of the bulb, in *asen*, at different stages of its maturity, followed by the bulb's monetary value at that weight noted in guilders.[8] Heavier, generally more mature bulbs offered greater likelihood of a successful bloom in the spring and were therefore more costly.

Each tulip is depicted with great attention to the detail of its calyces, petal formation, and coloring. The contours of the petals are delineated with graphite and then filled in with gouache. Those tulips featuring petals that open outward or that appear to turn in space are further articulated in gray wash to enhance their physicality (fig. 24b). The taxonomic requirements of these flower portraits produced a high degree of conformity, which complicates their attribution to a specific artist. The album also includes copies that were either made by the artists themselves while working from the model or copied after another image to which they had access. Two portraits of the *Semper Augustus* in this album, for example, are copies after the same flower from the *Tulpenboek Brandemandus* in Delft.[9] At least two painter-illustrators contributed to the Pasadena album. One hand is characterized by tight, linear descriptions of the petals and the sparing application of the gouache medium; the disposition of his tulips tends toward rigidity. By comparison, the flowers illustrated by the second artist are animated and take up more space on the page. This artist's relatively painterly application of color is especially notable in the "broken" flowers, those varieties characterized by streaks of vivid color that create mosaiclike patterns on the petals. Similar variations are noticeable in the description of the foliage and leaves.[10]

Related to florilegia, botanical books in which woodcuts or drawings record details of various plants, tulip books played a practical role in this period of acute interest in the flower.[11] The majority of the approximately fifty tulip books known today date from the mid-1630s to 1650, coinciding with the height of the Dutch tulip bulb trade. Considering that a single bulb could fetch hundreds and even thousands of guilders during this period and that more than 600 varieties were known, it is not surprising that accurate and detailed descriptions of the blooms were considered crucial.

Tulip books, as well as those manuscripts that also included other rare flowers, were designed to appeal to various audiences. While some were used to advertise a merchant's stock, others from some of Holland's most

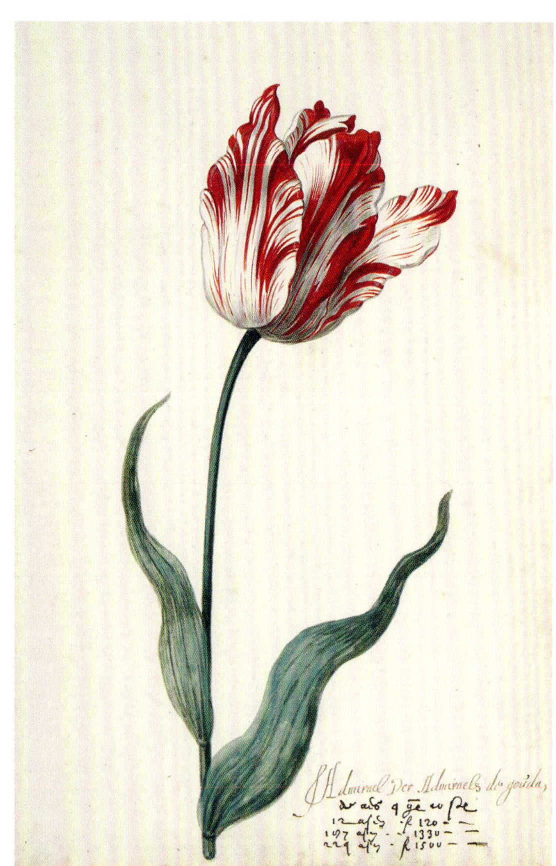

Fig. 24a. *Admirael Der Admiraels de Gouda*, sheet from cat. 24.

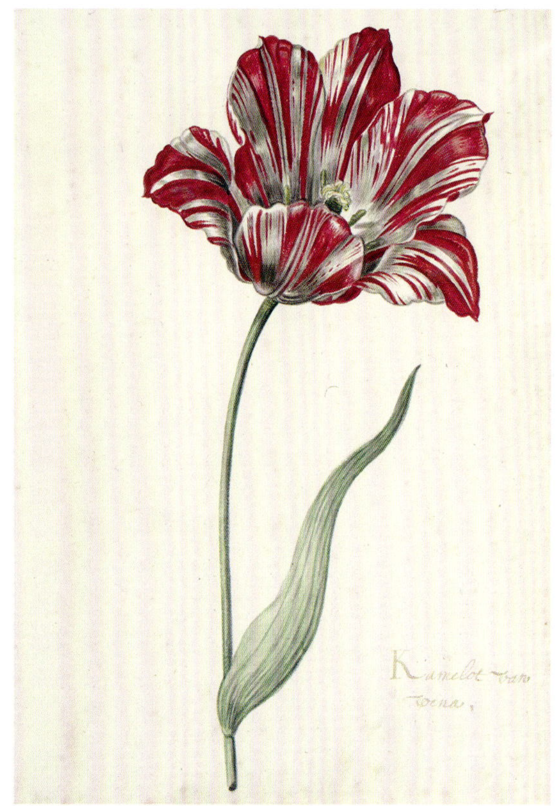

Fig. 24b. *Kamelot Van Wena*, sheet from cat. 24.

accomplished artists, including Anthony Claesz. (1607–1649) and Pieter Holsteyn II (1614–1673), and the German artist Jacob Marrel (1613/14–1681) were commissioned by aristocrats and wealthy burghers seeking to celebrate the beauty and diversity of their horticultural collections.[12] Johann Konrad von Gemmingen (1561–1612), Prince Bishop of Eichstätt, for example, had boxes of live flowers from his garden sent every week to artists, who made accurate watercolor drawings of them. The drawings were later translated into prints showing the various stages of a flower and published both in black-and-white and color editions as *Hortus Eystettensis* (Nuremberg, 1613).[13]

The provenance of this beautiful tulip book, connected to two of the most prestigious nurseries active in the Netherlands from the seventeenth to the early twentieth centuries, adds credence to its function. Simon Voorhelm, the likely first owner of the watercolors, was a third-generation nurseryman born into a family of growers founded by his grandfather Dirck in 1648 (the decade that coincides with the date of these watercolors). Simon expanded the business and the bulb exports of the Voorhelm Nursery, even capitalizing on the early eighteenth-century hyacinthmania much as his grandfather did with the tulipmania a century earlier. The other candidate for first owner is also connected to the Voorhelm interests. In 1706, Simon acquired a garden business called the Bloem Tuyn on the Kleine Houtweg of Haarlem. The acquisition included the botanical drawings and watercolors of the previous owner, whose identity is unknown.[14]

George Voorhelm Schneevoogt, a scholar and art collector, inherited the nursery and its library from his mother, Catherine, around 1800. By this date the nursery's tulips were widely known to gardeners and considered among the most beautiful in Europe. Nevertheless, his business suffered from competition with other growers who offered lower-priced bulbs. In 1837 he sold the nursery and its assets to Ernst Heinrich Krelage, a neighbor and fellow nurseryman on the Kleine Houtweg.[15] Most of Krelage's catalogues were bequeathed to the University of Wageningen in 1916. His botanical library was auctioned in Amsterdam in 1948.

The museum's now disassembled manuscript containing 158 folios of hand-colored drawings of tulips—a collaboration of two or more artists, painted on paper rather than vellum, and bearing market-related annotations—would have served commercial and horticultural interests. As an illustrated inventory, it could be shown to prospective customers during the months when the flowers were not in bloom. Later it could be used as a reference book or simply enjoyed as a collection of drawings. —*Gloria Williams Sander*

1. Simon Voorhelm was a third-generation nurseryman in the family business founded by his grandfather Dirck around 1648. See note 13 below.

2. Joris Voorhelm wrote a treatise on the hyacinth, published in Haarlem in 1752. It attracted such attention that it was translated into English, French, Italian, and German. An English-language copy is located in the Hunt Library, Carnegie Mellon University, Pittsburgh. See W. Roberts 1935.

3. In 1770 Catherina married Gottfried Schneevoogt (1744–1802), who became a partner in her family's nursery firm, which continued to operate on the Kleine Houtweg as Voorhelm & Schneevoogt. Pieter Biesboer clarified this line of descent in email correspondence with the author, 15 March 2011 (NSM).

4. This sale has traditionally been associated with the provenance of these watercolors. The lot description contains errors concerning the number of folios in the volume (151 rather than 158) and the support (vellum rather than paper), though it does mention the single watercolor of a pink (carnation) found in the Pasadena book. It also dates the watercolors later: 1667–74.

5. Clusius had previously established the Imperial Botanic Garden in Vienna and served as adviser to Wilhelm IV, Landgrave of Hesse (r. 1569–92). He was the author of *Rariorum aliquot Stipium*, a book about the flora of the Iberian Peninsula, and was responsible for introducing and distributing many new plants from Africa, the Americas, and especially from Asia.

6. The high price of the beautiful *Semper Augustus*, characterized by blood-red flames and streaks on its white petals, was at least partially due to the control of the rare bulbs by Adriaen Pauw (1581–1653), the grand pensionary of Amsterdam from 1631 to 1636, who grew only *Semper Augustus* on his estate in Heemstede and jealously guarded its propagation. His son was, notably, Dutch consul in Turkey. Pavord 1999, p. 133.

7. Goldgar 2007, pp. 109ff.

8. The Dutch *asen* was a unit of measurement designed specifically for the weighing of tulip bulbs. One *asen* equals approximately 1/20 gram or 1/5 ounce.

9. The *Semper Augustus* is illustrated on pp. 2 and 30 of the museum's manuscript. The *Brandemandus* tulip book is in the Museum Prinsenhof Delft, inv. no. PDT 178. See Segal 1992, p. 17, for illustrations. Because the relationship of these two manuscripts is not known, it is not clear which drawing was the primary illustration or if both were possibly based on the same model.

10. The artists who illustrated this album undoubtedly contributed to other tulip books as well. Krelage 1942, p. 57, sees evidence of this in various tulip books from the Krelage Collection at the University of Wageningen and in tulip books at the Utrecht University Library, the Gemeentearchief in Delft, and the Stichtung Hortus Bulborum in Limmen. The Pasadena book contains watercolors that resemble tulips painted by Anthony Claesz., but comparing these works under the proper circumstances has yet to be undertaken. See Segal 1987c; according to his classifications, the more linearly described tulips are closer to Claesz.

11. The most famous of these were *Hortus Floridus* (Utrecht, 1614) by Crispijn van de Passe II (ca. 1597–ca. 1670), and *Florilegium* (Frankfurt, 1612), a catalogue without text published by Emmanuel Sweerts (1552–1612) to advertise plants for sale at the Frankfurt fair. Sweerts was an Amsterdam merchant of rare bulbs, shells, and other exotica. The realistic illustrations in seventeenth-century stock books and albums contrast dramatically with medieval herbals. The earlier texts, which describe the properties of medicinal plants, were accompanied by two-dimensional woodcut illustrations drawn from pressed rather than fresh flowers.

12. The finest books were painted on vellum and were signed by the artist. Owning and

maintaining a garden in seventeenth-century Holland was a luxury. Such exclusive circumstances further contributed to establishing the tulip as a status symbol—i.e., the quantity and quality of tulips in a garden reflected the status of the grower who provided them and the gardener who cultivated them. See Segal 1987c, for comparisons among Marrel, Claesz., and Holsteyn. Marrel painted the illustrations for two books: one dated 1639, now in the Print Room, Rijksmuseum, Amsterdam, inv. No. RP-T-1959-266, and one dated 1634, in the Oak Spring Library, Upperville, VA. See Tomasi 1997, no. 73. A tulip book in the Frans Hals Museum, Haarlem, fols. 29–30, thought to have been painted in its entirety by Judith Leyster (1609–1660), in fact bears only two pages known to be by her hand.

13. Regarding Gemmingen, see Barker 1994 and Reithmeier 2010. The albums consisted of large prints arranged according to the seasons in which the flowers bloomed. The final publication was available in either a black-and-white or hand-colored edition. In 1613 a black-and-white copy sold for ƒ35; a hand-colored version cost ƒ500 (Barker 1994, p. 16).

14. My thanks to Pieter Biesboer, who discovered this information conducting research on the Krelage Archives housed in the Noord-Hollands Archief, Haarlem.

15. At the time of liquidation, Voorhelm & Schneevoogt housed a considerable library of horticultural books, pamphlets, tulip books, and watercolors acquired over the previous two centuries. Provenance for the Pasadena tulip book may be traced back, circumstantially, to the Voorhelm family of nurserymen. See the introduction to the 1948 International Antiquariaat/Menno Hertzberger & Co. auction catalogue mentioned above; Willemse 2005, pp. 198–200; and Biesboer correspondence cited in note 3 above. Portions of George Voorhelm Schneevoogt's personal collection are conserved in the Noord-Hollands Archief and Teylers Museum in Haarlem.

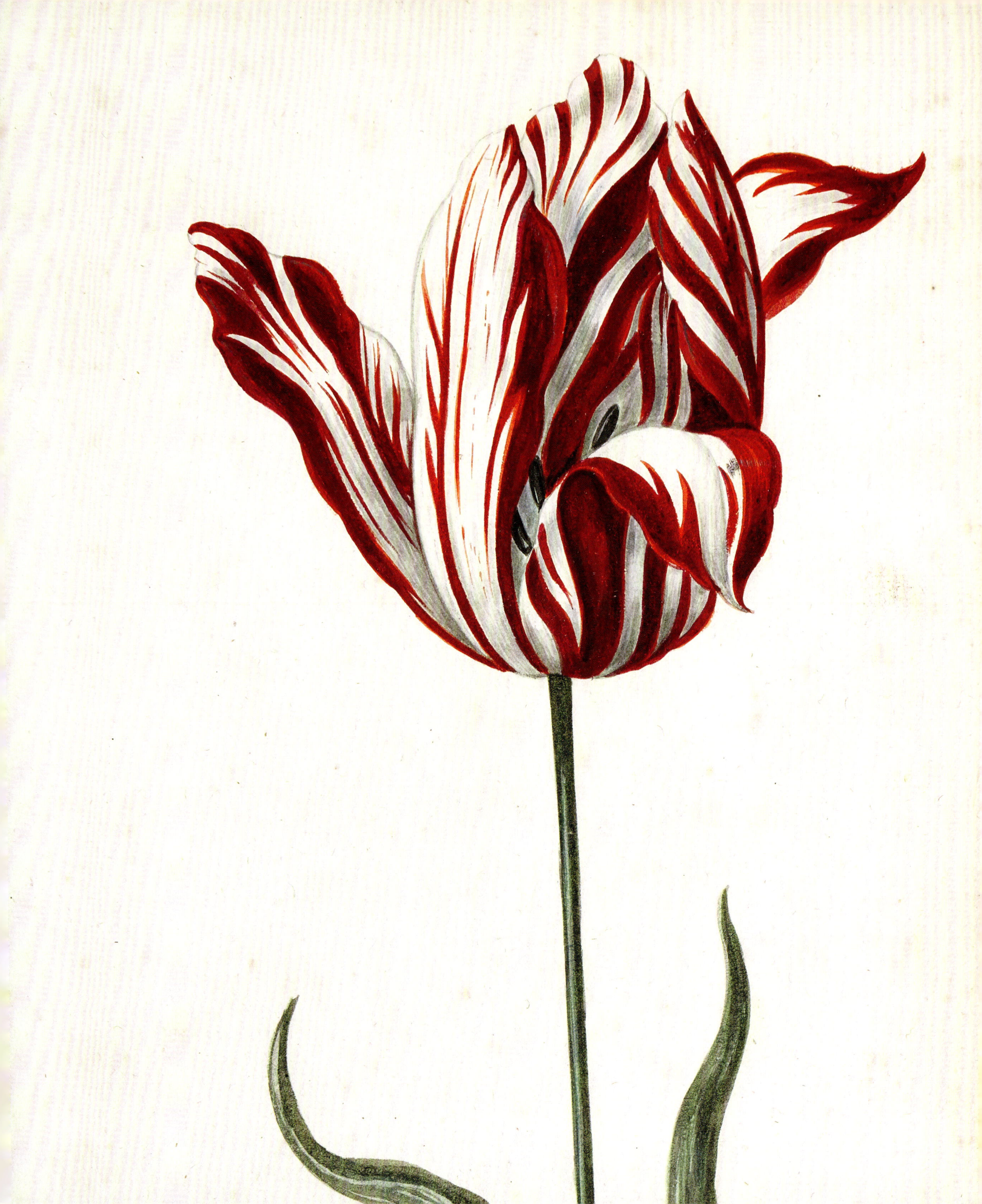

25

Workshop of Cornelis Engebrechtsz. (?)

Netherlandish
Leiden? 1460/65–1527 Leiden

The Adoration of the Magi
ca. 1520

Oil on panel, triptych, wings open: 18¾ × 26⅞ in. (47.6 × 68.3 cm); left and right wings: 16¼ × 4½ in. (41.3 × 11.4 cm); wings closed: 18¾ × 13⅜ in. (47.6 × 34 cm)
The Norton Simon Foundation, F.1968.11.05.P

Provenance
Morris I. Kaplan (1913–2011), Chicago (sale, Sotheby's, London, 12 June 1968, lot 36, sold to);[1] The Norton Simon Foundation.[2]

Exhibited
On loan, Brooklyn Museum, 8 August 1968–6 October 1969; on loan, Los Angeles County Museum of Art, late 1969–18 September 1972; Houston 1972–74.

References
Gibson 1977, pp. 169f., 247f., no. 35; S. Campbell 2010, p. 302, no. 475, ill.; Filedt Kok et al. 2014, pp. 134–36, figs. 131–32, no. 4, as workshop of Cornelis Engebrechtsz. (?).

Technical Notes
The small folding altarpiece is in the form of a triptych, with each wing attached to the central panel with two hinges. Each of the three vertically grained oak panels has an engaged frame. X-radiography confirms that the three panels are of closely similar wood. Painted surfaces were carved into the front of the panels, leaving a raised molding, later gilded. The lower edges of the panels are flat sloped sills and were left ungilded. The reverse of all three panels was left flat. The exterior left and right wings are painted, each with a saint (fig. 25a); the exterior central panel was left unpainted, retaining its original surface. The surfaces that were to be painted, as well as the engaged frames, were prepared with a moderately thick white ground that covers the wood grain. The frames were further prepared with bole before gilding. The paintings on the interior of the triptych skillfully depict many details of costume, such as jewels and embroidered fabrics. Flesh tones are smoothly blended. Figures and landscape in the distant backgrounds are also crisply painted but in lighter colors. The artist used a limited palette on the exterior wings and portrayed simplified surroundings, possibly as an allusion to statues in a niche. The tiny flake losses that are found throughout primarily follow the wood grain, a result of the expansion and contraction of the wood. Abrasion is relatively minor. Infrared reflectography reveals extensive underdrawing, both to provide contour lines and to depict volume via cross-hatching (figs. 25b–c). Several pentimenti have become evident in the left wing, probably because of increasing transparency of the aging oil medium: the horizon is now visible behind the slightly transparent horses and riders, and the facial features of the donor seem to be very slightly different. In the painting of the right wing, the artist slightly changed the proper left arm of Saint Ursula, raising the position of the forearm slightly and widening the black cuff of her garment. The angle of the arrow was also changed; the original position of the feathered end was once higher. The triptych was conserved in 2008 by Rosamond Westmoreland, at which time darkened varnishes, including an aged synthetic resin, were removed from the gilding and the paintings, and losses were filled and retouched.

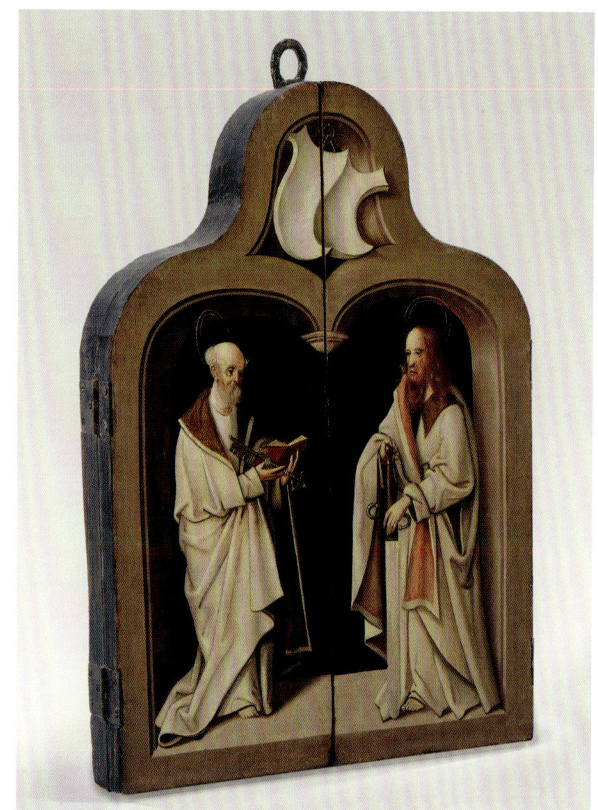

Fig. 25a. Closed triptych.

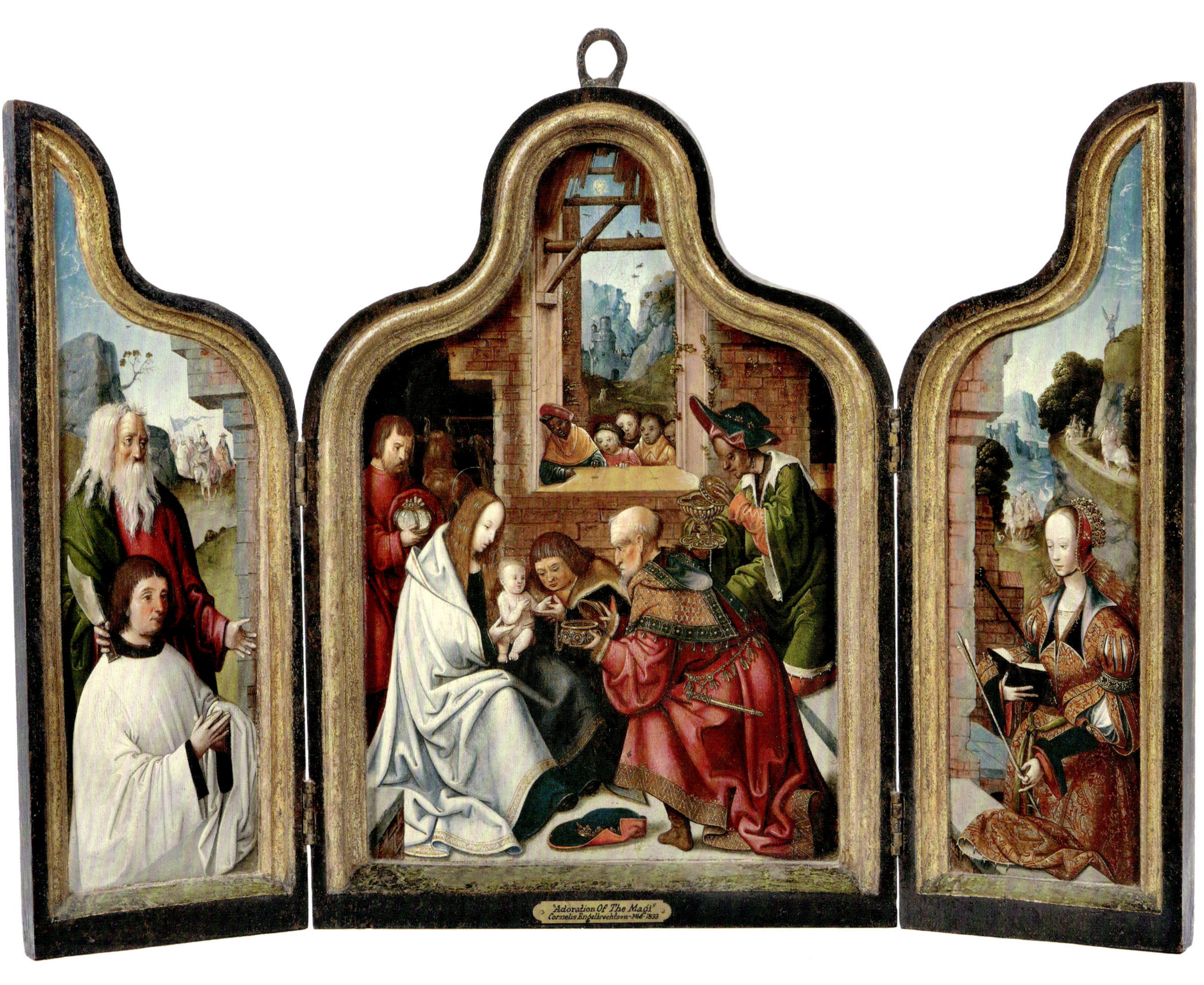
"Adoration Of The Magi"
Cornelis Engelbrechtsen-1468-1533

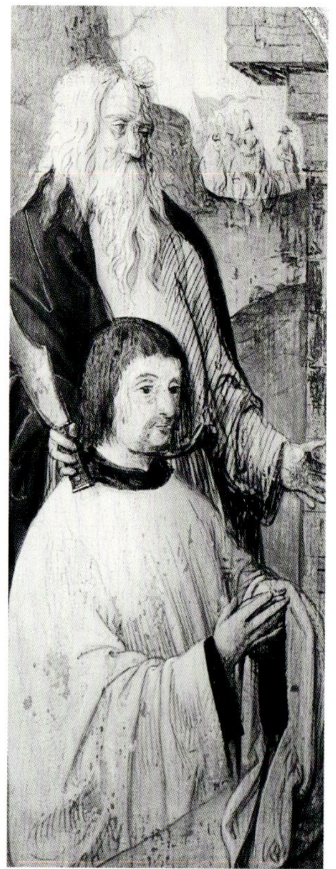

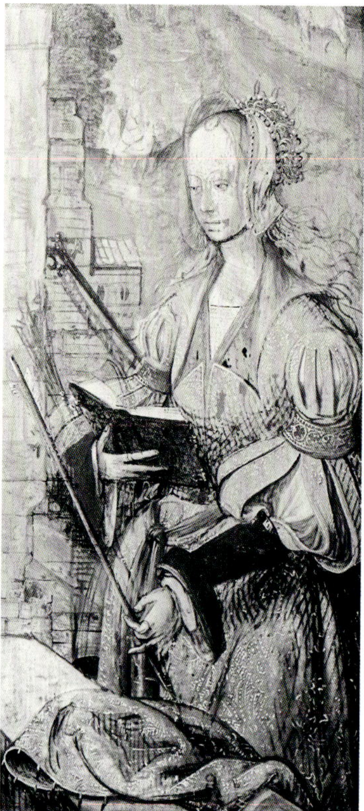

Fig. 25b. Infrared photograph of left wing.

Fig. 25c. Infrared photograph of right wing.

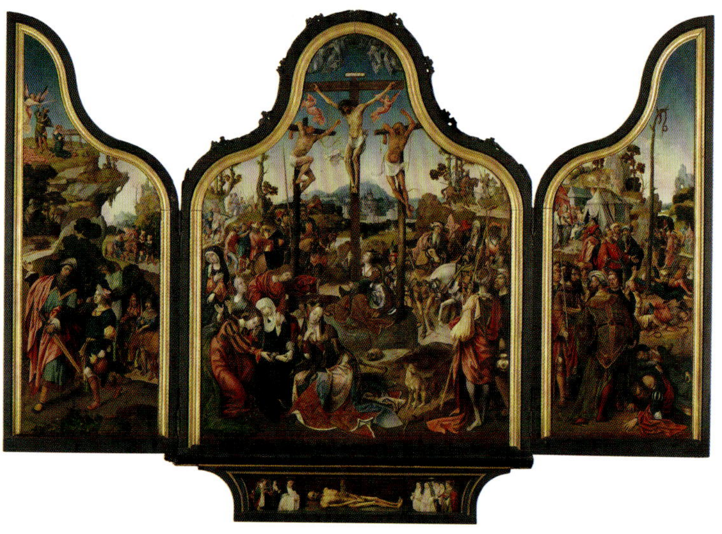

Fig. 25d. Cornelis Engebrechtsz., *Triptych with the Crucifixion of Christ*, ca. 1515–17, oil on panel, inv. nr. S 93, Museum de Lakenhal, Leiden.

Except during times of prayer, this small altarpiece intended for personal devotions would have remained shut so that one saw, on the closed exterior wings, only Saints Peter and Paul standing within Gothic arches (fig. 25a).[3] As the joint founders of the Christian Church, Peter, representing the Jews, and Paul, representing the Gentiles, introduce *The Adoration of the Magi* depicted on the central panel of the open altar. The event takes place among ruins rather than in a rustic stable, a reference to the *Golden Legend* (1260s) of Jacobus de Voragine (ca. 1230–1298), which recounts that when Christ was born, the Ara Pacis in Rome collapsed, marking the end of the old order and the inauguration of the new.[4] A subject associated with the universal acceptance of Christ as the manifestation of God in the flesh, the three Magi—Caspar, Melchior, and Balthazar—were believed to have traveled from India, Persia, and Africa, respectively, bringing with them expensive gifts for the Christ Child.[5] Following late medieval visual conventions, the men in the Pasadena altarpiece are represented as three different ages: Melchior, the oldest, has a white beard; Caspar, the youngest, has a smooth, beardless face; and Balthazar, a Black African, is presumably middle-aged.[6]

The three panels of the interior of the altarpiece are linked by the small narrative scenes of the journey of the Magi through the distant landscape depicted in the wings.[7] The miraculous star leading them to the nativity of the Christ Child is visible through the window, where four children observe the Adoration. The pilgrim badges on the hats of two of the children recall pilgrimages to holy sites that parallel the journey of the Magi, while their varying skin tones suggest they originate from different parts of the known world. On the right wing, Saint Ursula, dressed in contemporary costume and holding the arrow of her martyrdom, reads from an open prayer book, separated by a wall from the central scene. On the left wing, an elderly man with flowing white hair and beard, holding a knife, stands in the position of the patron saint of a man, presumed to represent the donor, who kneels before him, dressed in vestments appropriate for saying mass.[8]

The presence of Saint Ursula on the Pasadena triptych suggests that the painting may have been executed for a religious order or another patron within the bishopric of Cologne, which in the sixteenth century extended into the Netherlands. According to the *Golden Legend*, Ursula was killed by an arrow in Cologne, where she and her entourage of eleven thousand maidens had stopped on their return from a pilgrimage to Rome.[9] Ursula, who was particularly associated with convents, was a popular saint throughout the bishopric of Cologne. As the repository of the relics of the Magi, Cologne was also a pilgrimage destination.[10]

As is typical of many small fifteenth- and sixteenth-century paintings, the panels and frames of each section of the Pasadena triptych formed a single construction. Chisel

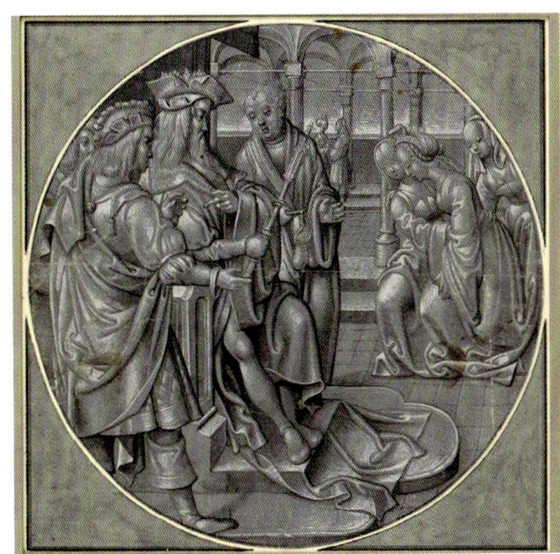

Fig. 25e. Cornelis Engebrechtsz., *Esther before Ahasuerus*, pen and brush in gray ink, heightened with white on gray paper, diameter 8 13/16 in. (22.4 cm), Albertina, Vienna.

marks suggest that the three panels were cut together to assure the same outside contours. While the outside surfaces of the panel are flat, the interiors are carved to produce the effect of moldings surrounding the flat painted surfaces.[11] Van Asperen de Boer discovered that early sixteenth-century frames were originally quite colorful, often painted to resemble marble. Since the frame was conceived as an integral part of the painting, its color and texture were thus important components of the painting's overall aesthetic effect.[12] Without more extensive scientific investigation, the original appearance of the frame of the triptych can only be conjectured. It appears, however, that the interior molding of the top and sides of the frames next to the painted scenes were originally gilded but that the lower ledges were painted dark green. The flat sections forming the outer frame, including the sides of the triptych, were a brown or a brownish-red, probably matching the warm brown of the painted arch surrounding the niches on the exterior wings.

In 1937 Max Friedländer attributed this small altarpiece to the Leiden painter Cornelis Engebrechtsz.[13] In his biography of the artist, Karel van Mander referred to a badly damaged large canvas representing the three kings that hung in Leiden's town hall.[14] Now lost, the painting is Engebrechtsz.'s only major exploration of the subject. It is impossible to know how the composition of the Pasadena triptych reflects that of the large town hall *Adoration*, which would have had a complex organization. The shape and format of the small Pasadena triptych are related to the monumental altarpiece of the Crucifixion that Engebrechtsz. painted for the Mariënpoel Convent outside Leiden (fig. 25d).[15] It is probable that the Engebrechtsz. workshop produced small altarpieces intended for private devotion that reflected the composition of the important, large painting and were sold on the open market. However, surprisingly, a 1515/25 *Adoration of the Magi* (Art Institute of Chicago), which is larger and finer than the Pasadena altarpiece, is the only other painting of the subject attributed to the Engebrechtsz. workshop.[16]

The association of the Pasadena altarpiece with Engebrechtsz. is supported by the similarity of individual figures to those in documented works by the artist. The figure on the far left of Engebrechtsz.'s *Christ Taking Leave of His Mother* (Rijksmuseum, Amsterdam), for example, echoes the long, oval shape of Saint Ursula's face framed by an exotic hat, which narrows from the broad, rounded forehead to her chin; the oval shape is repeated in her sharply defined eyes.[17] The long, bony faces and long, sharp noses—especially the cheekbones of the elderly saint in the left wing as well as of the Magi Melchior and Balthazar—also recall similar figures in Engebrechtsz.'s paintings.[18] The crisply defined collar and sleeves of the ornate brocaded costumes of Ursula and Melchior furthermore recall figures in Engebrechtsz.'s later paintings in which the influence of the Antwerp Mannerists is evident, suggesting a date after 1510.

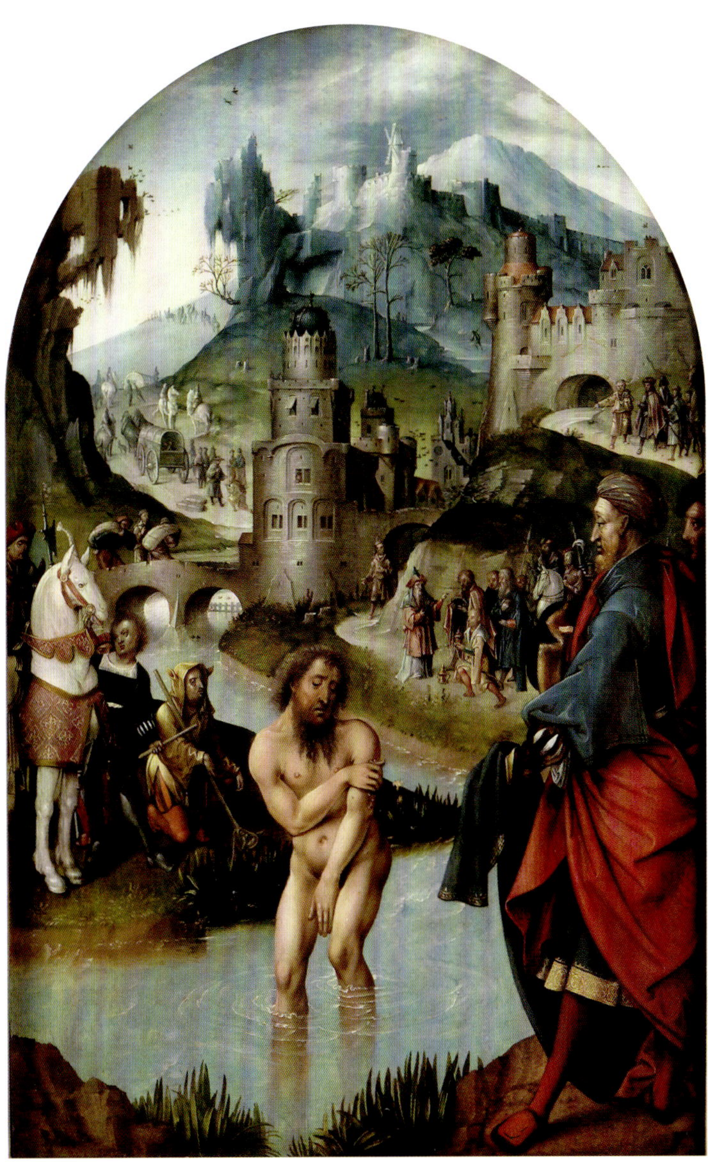

Fig. 25f. Cornelis Engebrechtsz., *Naamen Bathing in the Jordan*, central panel of *Triptych with the Healing of Naamen*, 1520/25, oil on oak panel, 23 1/4 × 14 15/16 in. (59 × 34 cm), Kunsthistorisches Museum, Vienna.

In 1977 Walter Gibson attributed the Pasadena altarpiece to "Hand B," an artist working in Engebrechtsz.'s studio rather than to the master himself.[19] Within this group, Gibson considered the Pasadena altarpiece to be closest to two drawings depicting the story of Esther in the Albertina, Vienna.[20] Gibson compared the head of the Virgin Mary to that of Esther in *Esther before Ahasuerus* (fig. 25e) and the head of the saint on the left wing (whom he identified as Saint Bartholomew) to those in the *Triumph of Mordecai*. He noted especially the similarity of the narrow profiles of Mary, Melchior, and Balthasar and the angular folds of the robes of the Virgin and of Peter and Paul. In contrast to Engebrechtsz.'s documented paintings, which show his concern for rendering volume through light and shade, however, the Pasadena triptych features folds of drapery that are simpler and without a sure sense of three-dimensional form.

Infrared reflectography, not available to Gibson in 1977, provides access to the underdrawing of the Pasadena altarpiece (figs. 25b–c), much of which is visible to the naked eye.[21] Jan Piet Filedt Kok believes that Engebrechtsz. may have executed at least part of the underdrawing but engaged the workshop to carry it out, comparing it to the *Triptych with the Healing of Naamen* (fig. 25f) and *Lamentation with Donors and Saints* (Alte Pinakothek, Munich).[22] Drawn in ink with either a brush or a pen, the first stage of the Pasadena underdrawing combines contour lines and a system of parallel hatchings. A series of short, slightly curved parallel strokes are drawn across the folds with cross-hatching in the deeper folds.[23] The final stage of the drawing consists of parallel diagonal hatchings that cut across figures without consideration of folds of drapery or forms of the body to suggest shadows.[24] Particularly characteristic of Engebrechtsz. is the single loop that defines the cheekbones of the bearded saint in the left wing in the Pasadena altarpiece.[25]

Although the overall impression of the underdrawing agrees with documented works by Engebrechtsz., the limited concern for three-dimensional form and cruder handling of the drawing and finished painting suggest that the triptych is the product of his workshop with minimal intervention from the master. The workshop production is also suggested by the two uninscribed shields on the exterior wing above the saints. The rapid spread of private devotion as well as the trade in indulgences and associated pilgrimages during the fifteenth century created a strong demand for small devotional images and triptychs; in response, by the first quarter of the sixteenth century many workshops in the Netherlands emphasized serial production of small altarpieces for the open market.[26] Cornelis Engebrechtsz. employed a workshop in Leiden that involved his three sons, among others, who continued to work even after the master's death.

1. Advertised in *Apollo* 87 (May 1968), p. cxvii, ill. Kaplan was a prominent businessman and philanthropist.

2. The painting may have been in Amsterdam in 1937, when Max Friedländer wrote an authentication for it (although he also is known to have written expertises based on photographs). In 1957 Ernst Buchner (b. 1892), curator of the Alte Pinakothek, Munich, inscribed the back of a photograph of the painting (which he said he had examined in person) attributing it to Engebrechtsz.: "Dr. Ernst Buchner, Munich, Passin 30 × 1957."

3. Defined by light and shadow, the saints appear to be fully rounded figures within a Gothic niche. The exterior wings of Engebrechtsz.'s *Lamentation* (Museum De Lakenhal, Leiden) represent four saints in similar but more elaborate niches.

4. Sanfuentes Echeverría 2023, p. 290.

5. The Adoration of the Magi is traditionally celebrated on the feast of the Epiphany, January 6. The Magi were specifically associated with the Gentiles, whereas the shepherds were associated with the Jews. The eldest Magus, Melchior, offers a gift of gold. Balthasar, the dark-skinned Magus dressed in green, kneels behind Caspar, the youngest Magus, who kisses the baby's left hand. This motif is related to that of the Magi kissing the Christ Child's feet, which became a feature of scenes of the Adoration in the fourteenth century.

6. Olaya Sanfuentes Echeverría, Kristen Collins, and Bryan Keene have shown that after European colonization in the Americas, a representation of Balthazar as an Indigenous person representing Brazil was incorporated into an altarpiece for Viseu Cathedral, Portugal, dated 1500–06, and suggest that the figure of Caspar, who kneels to kiss the hand of the Christ Child, was also meant to be an Indigenous person (Sanfuentes Echeverría 2023, pp. 294, 300; Collins and Keene 2022, p. 86, fig. 86). They contend that his straight hair and light-brown skin, as well as his smooth face, were signifiers of Indigenousness. However, in the Viseu altarpiece, Balthazar, who is typically represented as an African, is shown wearing contemporary European clothes, suggesting that he is one of the Indigenous people brought to Europe as "specimens"; a feathered headdress clearly identifies him as such. Contemporary prints of American Indigenous people represent men of status with feathers. In the Viseu altarpiece, Caspar, the Magus who stands on the left, is clean shaven, a reference to his youth, and wears a hairstyle similar to that of Caspar in the Pasadena altarpiece. Although the Viseu altarpiece is an interesting document of the encounter of Europe with the Indigenous population of America, this author believes it is unlikely that the person who created the small workshop altarpiece for the open market in Leiden would have made such a bold departure from traditional iconography.

7. Matthew 2 is the only book in the Bible to tell the story of the Magi, who came from the east, following a star in search of the king of the Jews. The story was substantially amplified by later accounts, especially the *Golden Legend*. Directed by Herod's officials to go to Bethlehem, the Magi, accompanied by a large entourage and, following the star, arrived at the stable where the holy family had taken shelter. On the interior of the right wing of the present work, a group of travelers has stopped on the hill and points to an angel standing on the summit. A walled city in the distance alludes to Jerusalem. Gibson 1977, p. 248, notes that the motif of the angel appears in reverse in *The Adoration of the Magi* attributed to the workshop of Cornelis Engebrechtsz. (1515/25; Art Institute of Chicago).

8. Gibson 1977, p. 170, identifies the elderly man as Saint Simon, but on p. 247, no. 35, he identifies him as Saint Bartholomew, the identification accepted in Filedt Kok et al. 2014, p. 136 and

entry no. 4. Saint Simon Zelotes is sometimes considered one of the shepherds to whom the angel announced the birth of Christ. Following the Crucifixion, he preached the Gospel throughout Syria and Mesopotamia. He is represented with a large saw or a cross, references to the two versions of his martyrdom. Mentioned only by name in the New Testament, Saint Bartholomew is known from the *Golden Legend*, which describes his missionary journey to India and his death in Armenia by being flayed alive. He is typically portrayed as a middle-aged man with a knife. The combination of the man's flowing white beard and hair does not, however, agree with the traditional representation of either saint. The Old Testament patriarch Abraham is typically represented with a long white beard and knife, a reference to the sacrifice of Isaac. Although there is no known precedent, his presence in this context could refer to the continuation of the Old Law through Christ.

9. Saint Ursula was killed when she refused to marry the leader of the Huns, who had besieged the city of Cologne.

10. The relics, which were discovered outside Milan, were transferred in 1164 by Reinald von Dassel to Cologne, where they were housed in an elaborate shrine. The increased popularity of the subject of the Magi in literature and art can be attributed to these events. See J. Braun 1928.

11. See Van Asperen de Boer 1975, p. 77, with additional references at p. 77n3. Marette 1961, pp. 123–26, discusses the construction of these panels. The width of the original plank restricted this technique to small panels. An alternate method, used on larger panels and sometimes on small ones, was a grooved frame into which the panel was fitted. The frames and panels constructed according to either method were similarly prepared as a unit before being painted. The practice of painting panel and frame as an integral unit is illustrated in *Saint Luke Painting the Virgin and Child*, ca. 1530, attributed to Quentin Metsys (1465/66–1530; National Gallery, London).

12. Van Asperen de Boer 1975, p. 84 and passim.

13. Certificate dated Amsterdam, 26 IX [September] 37 (NSM).

14. Van Mander/Miedema 1994–99, vol. 1, pp. 100f. (fol. 210v): "In the same town hall [in Leiden], there is also a large canvas in watercolour [tempera] by Cornelis with large figures representing the Three Kings in which is to be seen an imposing, elevated manner of composition and drapery, so that it is easy to see that Lucas van Leijden learned from or trained after his work. But this piece is badly decayed, which on account of its craftsmanship is a great pity."

15. *The Lamentation* triptych (a.k.a. *The Seven Sorrows of the Virgin*, ca. 1508–10), and *The Crucifixion* triptych (ca. 1515–17; both Museum De Lakenhal, Leiden) are the only extant works mentioned by Van Mander. Regarding Engebrechtsz.'s employment of assistants in a workshop, see Filedt Kok et al. 2014, pp. 19ff.

16. This is supported by the two blank shields on the exterior and by the figure of the donor, who appears somewhat generic both in the underdrawing and in the painting. Van Asperen de Boer and Wheelock 1973, p. 73, note that underdrawings of the heads of donors are frequently cursory, suggesting that the master would paint the portraits and leave the rest of the painting to assistants. Filedt Kok 1999, p. 27, notes that the faces of the donors in *Lamentation with Donors and Saints* (Alte Pinakothek, Munich) are not underdrawn in detail but only indicated as ovals. He assumes that these were to have been painted from life. Gibson 1977, p. 169, notes that the generalized features of the nuns in *Christ on Golgotha* (Koninklijk Museum voor Schone Kunsten, Antwerp) and *Christ Crowned with Thorns* (Staatliche Museum, Berlin) "can hardly represent specific portraits, but probably stand for the whole community at Mariënpoel, very much as the nuns in the predella of the *Crucifixion* Triptych."

17. The figure of Ursula is also similar to the kneeling figure of Mary Magdalene in the same painting; Van Asperen de Boer and Wheelock 1973, fig. 4.

18. Compare, for example, the face of the saint and that of Emperor Constantine in Engebrechtsz.'s *Constantine and Helen* (Alte Pinakothek, Munich). The profile of Melchior is virtually identical to that of the elderly man standing to the right in Engebrechtsz.'s *Descent from the Cross* in Ghent.

19. Gibson 1977, pp. 161–221, identifies four groups of stylistically related works that are difficult to attribute to specific artists. In his biography of Engebrechtsz., Karel van Mander mentions five pupils: Lucas van Leyden, Aert Claesz. (a.k.a. Aertgen van Leyden), and Engebrechtsz.'s three sons, Pieter, Cornelis, and Lucas (Van Mander/Miedema 1994–99). Among the paintings Gibson attributes to Hand B are *Christ on Golgotha* (Koninklijk Museum voor Schone Kunsten, Antwerp), *Christ Crowned with Thorns* (Staatliche Museum, Berlin), and two drawings in the Albertina, Vienna.

20. Gibson 1977, pp. 168–70. See also Benesch 1928, nos. 58 (*Esther before Ahasuerus*, inv. no. 7794) and 59 (*The Triumph of Mordecai*, inv. no. 7795), pl. 18. Regarding these drawings, Gibson 1977, p. 168, notes:

> Although very close to Engebrechtsz. in many respects, they differ from him chiefly in the hard, labored execution and in the awkward draftsmanship that occasionally results in such details as the clumsily foreshortened figure of the soldier on the right in the Antwerp panel and the excessively thin profiles in the Albertina drawings. The graceful rhythms of Engebrechtsz.'s figure poses and drapery have been transformed into harsh angularities; characteristic of all the works are the hard crumpled folds assumed by the drapery as it puckers along the sleeve or falls to the floor, as in the robes of the donatrices at Antwerp and Berlin.

21. The infrared photographs made by Maryan Ainsworth are cited by Filedt Kok et al. 2014. Regarding the underdrawings in the paintings by Engebrechtsz., see Van Asperen de Boer and Wheelock 1973 and Filedt Kok 1999.

22. Jan Piet Filedt Kok, email to the author, 25 October 2002 (NSM), and in conversation in Amsterdam, 1 March 2004. For a general discussion of this theory, see Filedt Kok 1999. The central panel of the Naamen altarpiece, dated ca. 1520 (Kunsthistorisches Museum, Vienna), measures 59 × 38 cm; each of the wings is 59 × 17 cm. The *Lamentation* (Alte Pinakothek, Munich) measures 115 × 124 cm.

23. In her summary report of her infrared study of the altarpiece (NSM), Maryan Ainsworth noted that the underdrawing appeared to be executed in pen and ink. Van Asperen de Boer and Wheelock 1973, pp. 75, 79f., 79n52, report that samples indicate that Engebrechtsz. used a brush and black aqueous paint to sketch the underdrawings of the *Crucifixion* and *Lamentation* altarpieces in Leiden. Filedt Kok 1999, p. 21, notes that a similar technique was used for Engebrechtsz.'s *Emperor Constantine and His Mother Helena* (Alte Pinakothek, Munich), but on pp. 23–25 notes that he has also discovered underdrawings done in black chalk.

24. See, for example, the proper left arm and chest of the figure of Saint Bartholomew and the wall of the ruined stable.

25. Van Asperen de Boer and Wheelock 1973, p. 71, fig. 6.

26. Small triptychs with the Adoration were particularly popular in Bruges. For an interesting discussion of copies and the production of small triptychs and devotional paintings based on common prototypes in Antwerp workshops, see Van den Brink 2001.

26

Jan (Johannes) Fyt

Flemish
Antwerp 1611–1661 Antwerp

Still Life with a Red Curtain

ca. 1660

Signed on ledge at left center: ". . . hnes Fyt"
Oil on canvas, 43 × 62⅞ in. (109.2 × 159.7 cm)
The Norton Simon Foundation, F.1972.36.3.P

Provenance
Probably Richard Sutton (1821–1875), 4th Baronet of Lexington, in 1863, by descent to his grandson;[1] Sir Robert V. Sutton (1897–1971), 8th Baronet of Lexington, Wincanton, Somerset (estate sale, Christie's, London, 29 January 1971, lot 61, sold to); [Edward Speelman Ltd., London, sold 1972 to]; The Norton Simon Foundation.

Exhibited
Possibly London 1863, no. 72, as *Dead Game, etc.*, lent by Richard Sutton;[2] Houston 1972–74.

References
Graves [1913–15] 1970, vol. 1, p. 367; Greindl 1983, p. 349, no. 83;[3] S. Campbell 2010, pp. 141, 344, no. 844, ill.

Technical Notes
The original support, a plain-weave canvas, has been lined with wax, with the original tacking edges removed. No cusping is visible at any edge. A hole in the upper right was repaired by the lining. The thin, cream-colored ground was covered with a translucent red-brown imprimatura. X-radiography shows that Fyt drew with dense white paint on the colored imprimatura to establish the lightest tones, building upon them with both strokes of opaque color and colored glazes. The latter is especially apparent in the red cloth. The background was thinly painted in a broad application of subtle color. The central elements of the still life were executed in thick, opaque paint applied with a small brush, creating complex surfaces that are very descriptive. Rich paint mimics the texture of fur, feathers, and straw. Though brushmarking may have been slightly smoothed by lining pressure, it remains an important part of the rich surface in the rabbits, ducks, cat, and fowl. Magnification reveals extensive abrasion in the dark background. The white cloth has been cleaned aggressively, leaving the paint thinned and rather bright. There is a great amount of retouching carefully applied here, perhaps excessively. Ultraviolet light reveals the varnish to be a thin, aged synthetic resin.

Still Life with a Red Curtain is typical of the medium-sized canvases Jan Fyt painted throughout his career concurrently with smaller panel paintings and large-scale still lifes. In this carefully arranged composition, the central axis of which is marked by a hare suspended by its hind leg, Fyt displays on a tabletop a rather modest kill, including another hare, two ducks, and a basket with song birds and a bittern. Brought close to the picture plane, the composition recalls the early, relatively small still lifes by Frans Snyders (1579–1657) as well as details in the older master's more baroque larders and market scenes in which game is represented in the context of other foodstuffs and often costly Chinese import ware to create an atmosphere of wealth and abundance.[4]

Trained in Snyders's workshop, Fyt was strongly influenced by his teacher well into his career. A pen-and-ink drawing signed and dated by Fyt in 1660 (GRI Photo Archive) suggests that, following Snyders's practice, he drew a compositional sketch in preparation for the Pasadena painting.[5] The hare suspended by its back leg was a favorite device of Snyders, who sometimes replaced it with a deer. The brilliant red cloth and sharp white linen beneath the dead game in Fyt's painting are also standard elements of Snyders's still lifes, although Fyt's coloration and technique diverge sharply from that of his model.[6] In contrast to Snyders's relatively evenly lit and brightly colored compositions, *Still Life with a Red Curtain* has a muted tonality. Rather than the smooth brushstrokes and glazes Snyders used to suggest the translucence of grapes and flesh, Fyt characteristically painted parallel strokes of different colors over heavy impasto, suggesting the distinct textures of the fur, feathers, and basket and imparting to them a sense of depth as well as surface.

While referring to Snyders as a model, Fyt abstracted and developed elements from the older master's painting to create a new genre of still life representing the trophy of a hunt. *Still Life with a Red Curtain* is particularly closely related to Snyders's painting *Small Game and a Cat* (fig. 26a). In both, dead game is displayed on a table set against a stone wall and stalked by a cat. In Snyders's painting, the cat is on the window ledge in the upper right corner of the painting, while in Fyt's painting, the cat has already advanced to the tabletop and come nose to beak with the prey. Both paintings also include a view to the outside—Snyders's through a window, Fyt's through a doorway—but the different views

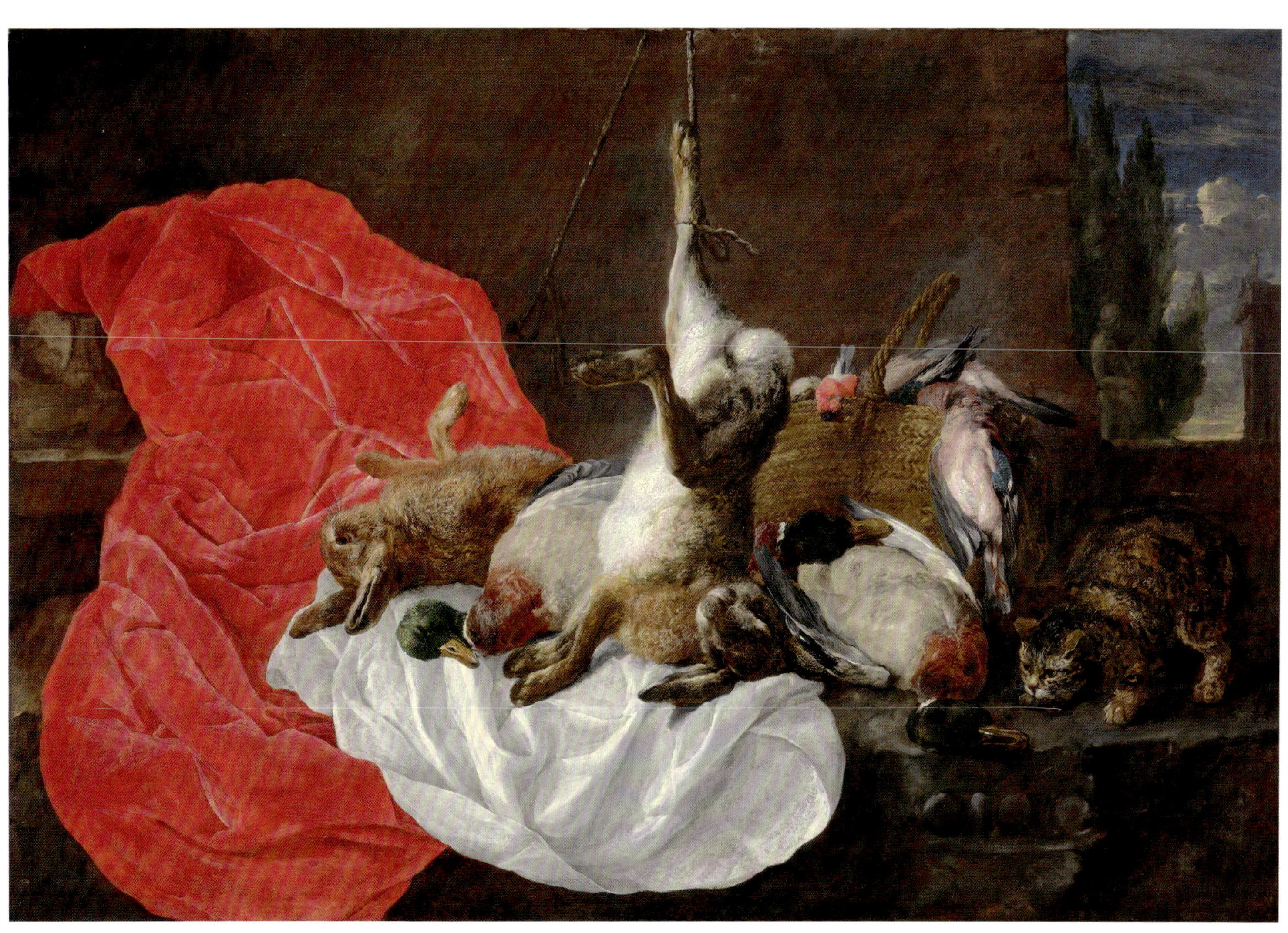

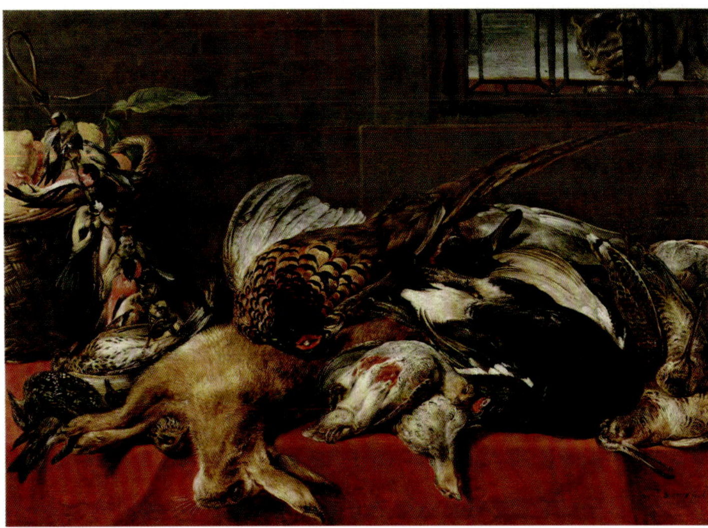

Fig. 26a. Frans Snyders, *Small Game and a Cat*, ca. 1640–50, oil on panel, 29½ × 42⅛ in. (75 × 107 cm), Kunsthistorisches Museum, Vienna.

define the two paintings' subtle differences of emphasis. Whereas Snyders's game is already on a formal table covered by a red cloth, Fyt's game appears to have been casually deposited on a table by someone who has just returned from hunting. In the background, through the open doorway, is a stone statue behind which tall trees are set against a clouded evening sky and, on the far right, the silhouette of a building. Referring to the country estate on which the game was caught, this vignette points ahead to the elegant, large-scale trophy still lifes of Jan Weenix (1642–1719), such as *Still Life with a Hare and Birds* (fig. 26b).

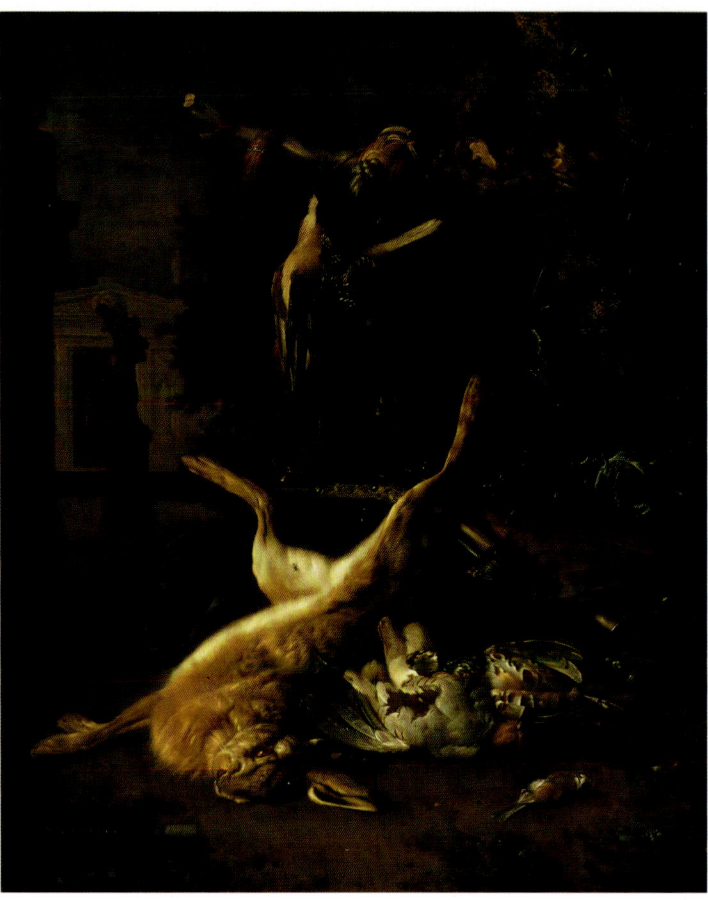

Fig. 26b. Jan Weenix, *Still Life with a Hare and Birds*, late 17th century, oil on canvas, 50 15/16 × 41⅞ in. (129.4 × 106.4 cm), Philadelphia Museum of Art.

Hunting was traditionally the prerogative of the nobility of Europe. By the mid-seventeenth century, however, as larger numbers of wealthy merchants joined the ranks of owners of landed estates, hunting privileges appear to have been extended beyond the original limits. The rising popularity of the "gamepiece" during this period suggests that these paintings were desired not only by those who actually participated in the sport but also by those who wanted to associate themselves with it.

1. *DNB* [1921–22] 1973, vol. 19, pp. 182f.; Richard Sutton (1798–1855), 2nd Baronet of Lexington and the father of Richard Sutton, 4th Baronet of Lexington, was one of the wealthiest men in England and an ardent lover of the chase. The elder man became master of foxhounds in 1822 and master of the Burton Hunt in Lincolnshire.

2. This could also be a reference to the painting by Fyt that was lot 62 in the 29 January 1971 sale of the Sutton collection, described as *A Turkey, a Peacock, Rabbits and Pigeons in a Landscape* (38½ × 53½ in. [96.5 × 135.9 cm]).

3. Included among a list of signed works with reference to the 1971 sale. Not included in the 1956 edition of Greindl's book.

4. See, for example, the painting attributed to Fyt, *A Still Life with Fruit, Dead Game and a Parrot*, late 1640s (National Gallery, London; NG6335).

5. Greindl 1983 lists only five drawings by Fyt, including this one. On p. 106, she notes that she knows of only two paintings that correspond to Fyt's compositional drawings, neither of which is the Pasadena painting. Although there are differences between the two works, it is possible—because Fyt signed and dated the drawing 1660—that the quickly sketched drawing in ink may have been made by the artist to record the composition of *Still Life with a Red Curtain*.

6. Ben Johnson, formerly head of conservation at the Los Angeles County Museum of Art, observed (undated remarks, NSM): "A noteworthy compositional change in the red drapery at the left. The relationship between the bright white and the rich red obviously was a point of concern for the artist in working out the composition."

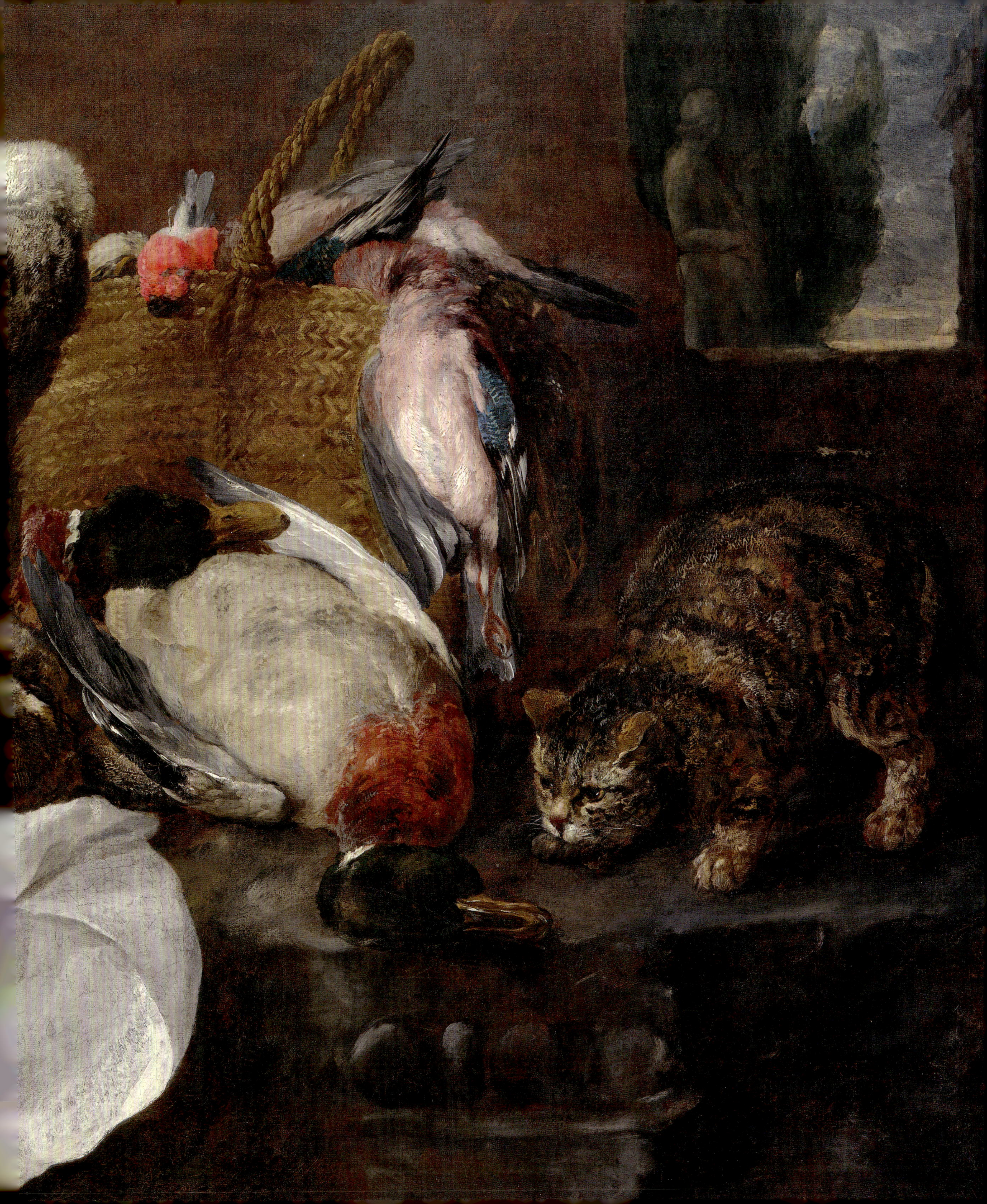

27

Jan van Goyen

Dutch
Leiden 1596–1656 The Hague

River Landscape with a Village Church

1642

Signed with monogram and dated on the side of the ferry boat: "VG 1642"
Oil on panel, 12 × 15⅛ in. (30.5 × 38.4 cm)
The Norton Simon Foundation, F.1969.49.P

Provenance

Paul Randon de Boisset (1708–1776), Paris[1] (sale, Pierre Remy, Paris, 27 February 1777, lot 41, sold for F 906 to); "le d^c de Choiseul" or "le vic^te de Choiseul."[2] Louis-Robert de Saint-Victor (1738–1822), Rouen[3] (sale, Roux, Paris, 26 November 1822, lot 429, sold for F 130).[4] Gustav Rothan (1822–1890), Paris by 1873[5] (sale, Georges Petit, Paris, 29 May 1890, lot 47, ill. with print, sold for F 4,900 to); Goldschmidt.[6] Anonymous (sale, Sotheby's, London, 26 March 1969, lot 25, sold to); [Edward Speelman Ltd., London, sold 1969 to]; The Norton Simon Foundation.

Exhibited

Paris, 3rd Exposition Universelle, 1878, no. 123, lent by Rothan; on loan, Phoenix Art Museum, 8 January–28 April 1970; Houston 1972–74.

References

Mantz 1873, pt. 1, p. 288; Hofstede de Groot 1908–27, vol. 8 (1927), pp. 157, 176, nos. 631a, 677;[7] MacLaren 1960, p. 136 (as in Rothan sale); Beck 1972–87, vol. 1, p. 111, no. 313, vol. 2, p. 228, no. 481; Pasadena 1980, p. 65, ill.; P. Sutton 1986, p. 218; Pasadena 1989, p. 68, ill.; S. Campbell 2010, p. 330, no. 710, ill.

Technical Notes

The support is a horizontally grained oak panel; the left, right, and bottom edges are beveled. Narrow wood strips have been glued to each side. A thin crack originates at the left edge, near the top. The white ground is quite thin, barely covering the wood grain. A rose-beige layer was then applied, visible in the sky and water. The painting was executed with a limited palette, using smoothly brushed thin paint. In the sky the rose-colored underpainting is almost exposed, creating a veil of soft color. The tree foliage and figures were painted with short, deft brushstrokes with dabs of color mixed on the palette; a single short stroke often contains two colors. Darker areas in the left foreground are rendered with golden-brown glazes; areas of color abut each other without overlapping. At the lower right, two fingerprints were pressed into the paint; although they are not distinct from every angle, they can be seen in raking light. The paint is in exceptionally good condition. Prior cleaning left small amounts of darkened varnish in the tree foliage. Scattered retouching is primarily in the sky. Across the top edge there is an unexplained narrow margin of old varnish, visible in both ultraviolet and normal light. Ultraviolet-light examination indicates a thin synthetic-resin varnish overall.

By 1642, the date of *River Landscape with a Village Church*, Jan van Goyen was recognized as one of the masters of the tonal landscape. Introduced and developed during the late 1620s and employed through the 1640s by Van Goyen, Salomon van Ruysdael (1600/03–1670), Pieter de Molijn (1595–1661), and others, tonal landscapes depict scenes of the local Dutch countryside using a palette limited to tones of browns, soft greens, and gray-blue rendered with fluid, loosely applied paint and glazes.[8] Often monochromatic, these paintings were referred to by contemporaries as *grisailles* (*graeuwtjen*), rather than by their subject.[9]

River Landscape with a Village Church is painted on an oak panel covered by a thin layer of light-colored ground that is virtually transparent, allowing the grain of the panel to show through, imparting a subtle overall texture to the painting.[10] Dark, calligraphic lines—visible with infrared light and in places with the naked eye—reveal that Van Goyen freely sketched his composition directly on the panel, probably between the ground layer and the thin tinted priming layer. The fluid quality of the sketch recalls Van Goyen's many drawings of the Dutch landscape and its inhabitants. In areas of the painting in which he wished to suggest shadow, he omitted pigment and applied a glaze of unpigmented medium, through which the pink tone of the panel and calligraphic lines of the sketch are visible. In areas of more definition, the artist used a combination of thin, opaque washes in tones of green, gray, and brown paint and a variety of short, lively strokes of thin paint; to suggest leaves, he used a small, soft brush, which he twisted as he stroked, leaving more paint on one side than the other. Throughout, the pink tone of the panel and subtle texture of the wood grain show through the thin washes and glazes, adding to the visual effect of an enveloping atmosphere.

In addition to the subtle handling of paint, Van Goyen achieved a sense of compositional unity by employing a low horizon and confining all the elements of his painting within a receding compositional "wedge." The river format, which he first adopted during the early 1630s, is perfectly suited to this new aesthetic. In *River Landscape with a Village Church* the riverbank defines the lower diagonal of the wedge. The

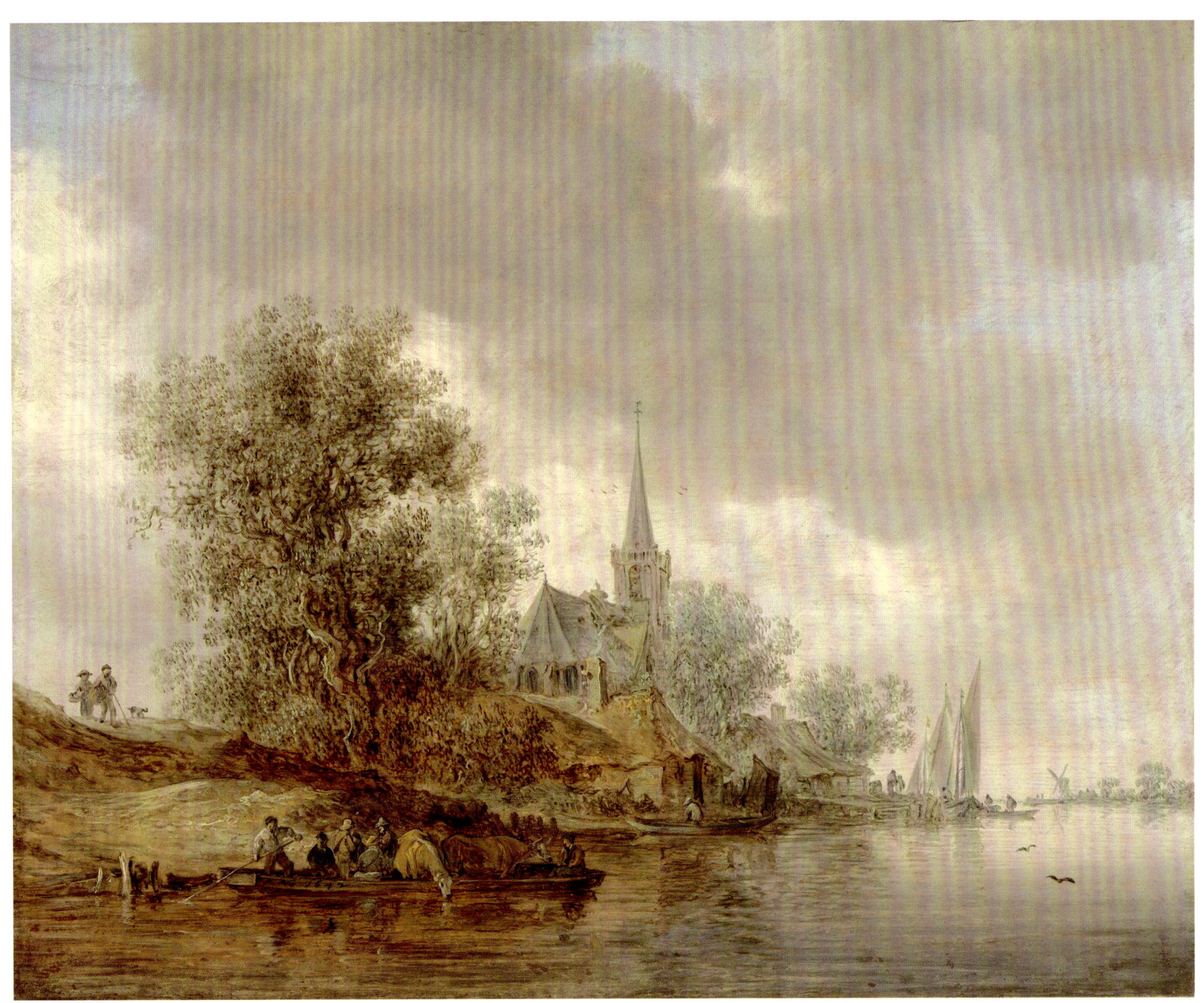

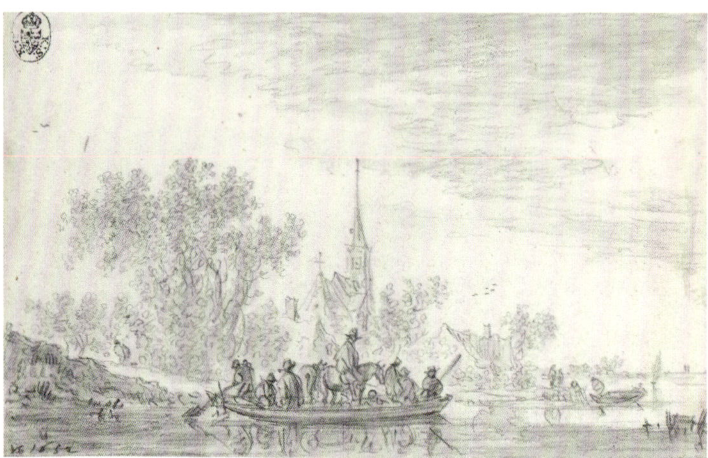

Fig. 27a. Jan van Goyen, *Village Behind Trees by the Water, Ferry with People*, 1652, black chalk and gray wash, 4 11/16 × 7 11/16 in. (11.9 × 19.5 cm), Kupferstich-Kabinett, Staatliche Kunstsammlungen Dresden.

shoreline meanders from the lower left of the painting to the dramatically low horizon, visually drawn toward the distant right by the windmill. A second receding diagonal, suggested by the tall tree on the left, the church steeple, and the delicately rendered sails of the boats, forms the upper line of the compositional wedge. Dark clouds animate the broad expanse of sky and accent the dramatic rush into depth. This movement is checked by the careful placement of the ferry. A man standing in the stern of the ferry strains against the resistance of the long pole dug into the river bottom as he pushes off from shore. This implied horizontal movement and the dark gray washes, which appear to represent the water's reflection of the brooding clouds, visually anchor the composition.

In the Pasadena painting, as in all Van Goyen's landscapes, the narrative elements are incidental to the landscape and dominated by it. Here, the ferry boat, laden with people and cattle, departs from a simple mooring near a village church. Rounding the top of the dune at the left and silhouetted against the sky, a couple and a dog walk toward the ferry; she carries a basket, and he walks with a stick. The rural travelers appear to be either going to or returning from market, where cattle and other goods were sold or traded.

River Landscape with a Village Church is closely related to a black chalk drawing by Van Goyen dated 1652 (fig. 27a), suggesting that both works incorporate details of a specific location.[11] Van Goyen represents the same church from a similar vantage point, and the drawing includes a ferry that transports a man on horseback and other figures across the river, corresponding to that in the Pasadena painting.[12] The Pasadena painting and possibly the drawing were perhaps based on an early, now lost drawing that Van Goyen, a prolific draftsman, made of an actual site and then elaborated in his studio.[13]

Wolfgang Stechow has suggested that the church in this composition resembled the village churches in Overschie, Ouderkerk, and Jaarsveld (Yaersvelt).[14] The silhouette and specific details of the building in Van Goyen's painting particularly resemble the church at Jaarsveld as it appears in a print (no. 181) from Abraham Rademaker's (1675–1735) 1725 series of topographical prints of the Netherlands, *Kabinet van nederlandsche outheden en gezichten*.[15] It also resembles the church that Beck identifies as that at Jaarsveld in *Ferry with Three Cattle and Six Passengers*, signed and dated by Van Goyen in 1653 (Louvre, Paris).[16] Jaarsveld is located on the north shore of the River Lek, which flows from the east, past Rheenen and Rotterdam, before emptying into the sea. Van Goyen painted many views of Rheenen and would have passed Jaarsveld en route. Rademaker notes that Jaarsveld is located opposite the larger town of Ameide, with which it was probably linked by a ferry similar to that represented by Van Goyen, Ruysdael, and Rademaker.[17]

Van Goyen began to represent topographical subjects more frequently during the 1640s before tapering off during the 1650s. Similar scenes of the Dutch countryside and cities appear on the borders of contemporary maps of the United Netherlands as well as in Anthonie van der Croos's (1606/07–1662/63) composite painting *Views of The Hague, with Twenty Scenes in the Neighborhood*, signed and dated 1663 (Gemeentemuseum, The Hague). Like these and Claes Jansz. Visscher's (1587–1652) series of prints of casual views around Haarlem and elsewhere, Van Goyen's incidental scenes of the Dutch countryside, such as the Pasadena painting, were popular among contemporary Dutch burghers. They enjoyed identifying landmarks and found in the bucolic scenes of the prosperous local landscape sources of spiritual peace and refreshment from the stress of the city as well as expressions of pride in the prosperity and political felicity of the Netherlands.[18]

1. Pierre-Louis-Paul Randon de Boisset held the lucrative position of receveur général des finances of Lyon. He applied his enormous fortune to acquire one of the richest libraries of his time and a famous collection of paintings, sculptures, porcelains, prints, and furnishings. In 1766 Randon de Boisset traveled to Holland and Flanders accompanied by the painter François Boucher (1703–1770). Clement de Ris 1877, p. 367, however, contends that the most beautiful Dutch and Flemish paintings in his collection were acquired at sales in Paris. See A. Walsh 1996.

2. It is unclear which Choiseul was the buyer. Clement de Ris 1877, p. 379, notes that among the major buyers at the sale were the king of France, the Duc de Choiseul-Praslin, and M. de Choiseul. In the annotated catalogue of the sale in the GRI, the buyer appears to be "le dc de Choiseul." The annotations of two copies of the catalogue included in the RKD microfiche archive, however, appear to identify the collector as "le cmte de Choiseul" and "le Victe." Étienne-François, duc de Choiseul (1719–1785) had accumulated a large art collection of French and northern works by the time he was forced to sell a large portion of his paintings in 1772. His son, Jacques-Philippe, duc de Choiseul-Stainville (1727–1789), was also a collector, and lot 1 of his sale on 23 November 1789 has two paintings by Van Goyen, both river scenes on wood, measuring 14 *pouces* (inches) high by 19 *pouces* wide. Beyond these two collectors, the buyer at the Randon de Boisset sale may have been either Renaud César, duc de Choiseul-Praslin (1735–1791), or his son Antoine Choiseul-Praslin (1756–1808).

3. Louis-Robert de Saint-Victor was counselor at the Parliament of Normandy and, like his father, president of the Chambre des Comptes, Aides et Finances of Rouen. He was a distinguished magistrate, known for his erudition and intelligence, and a member of numerous academies. He had one of the richest collections in the province, which he kept at his Hôtel Bouvreuil at Rouen. The sale of November 1822, held nine months after his death, contained ten paintings by Van Goyen. See Ratouis de Limay 1913, vol. 7, pp. 422–39.

4. The catalogue was prepared by Pierre Roux, who is described as an artist and "appreciator" of works of art.

5. See also Mantz 1873. The introduction to the 1890 sale of Rothan's collection (p. x) notes that the French diplomat and historian was one of the major admirers of Van Goyen in Paris and that Van Goyen was his favorite artist.

6. Possibly Salomon Goldschmidt, who was selling in Paris in 1888/90; Leopold Goldschmidt, who was active ca. 1900; or M. G. Goldschmidt, who seems to have been active at the same time. The painting has not, however, been identified in any of their sales or collection catalogues.

7. Hofstede de Groot 1908–27, vol. 8 (1927), p. 176, suggests that no. 677 is "possibly identical" with no. 821, then owned by Arthur Kay, Glasgow. Beck 1972–87, vol. 2, p. 388, no. 866, identifies the Kay painting as a different painting that is actually dated 1647.

8. On the techniques of early Dutch landscape painters, see Gifford 1983, Bomford 1986, and Gifford 1995; see also note 11 below.

9. For example, the 10 October 1668 posthumous inventory of the possessions of the painter Jan Miense Molenaer (ca. 1610/11–1668) records "een graeuwtje van Jan van Goyen," no. 73 in the "schildercamer" (Bredius 1915–22, vol. 1, p. 5).

10. The ground is probably composed of chalk and oil, which becomes transparent. Regarding Van Goyen's technique, see Gifford 1996. On ground layers in seventeenth-century painting, see Hout 1998.

11. Hofstede de Groot 1908–27, vol. 8 (1927), p. 176, no. 677, notes that "according to a named sketch in a sketchbook by Van Goyen in the possession of the art historian/museum director/collector A[braham] Bredius [1855–1946], the church is that of Overschie." Beck 1972–87, vol. 1, p. 71, however, notes that the misleading annotations are by a later hand and require correcting. See also Beck 1972–87, vol. 1, p. 268, nos. 845/55 and /57. The intact sketchbook (Collection Joseph O. Kronig, Monaco) has 109 sketches, which Beck 1972–87, vol. 1, p. 265, notes were drawn during Van Goyen's wanderings in the neighborhood of The Hague or northward toward Haarlem.

12. Beck 1972–87, no. 313: black chalk, gray wash, 119 × 195 cm; signed left: "VG 1652."

13. Salomon van Ruysdael may also have represented the same location in two paintings: *River Scene with Duck Shooting*, dated 1663 (with Terry-Engell Gallery, London, 1965), appears to represent the same church from a similar angle but from a more distant vantage point; and *River Landscape with a Ferry*, 1650 (Los Angeles County Museum of Art) appears to represent the same church from the opposite direction. See Los Angeles/Boston/New York 1981–82, pp. 88ff., no. 22, fig. 3; see also A. Walsh 2019b, pp. 166–69.

14. An unpublished note by Wolfgang Stechow credits these suggestions to Hans Ulrich Beck (NSM). Hofstede de Groot 1908–27, vol. 8 (1927), no. 631a, was the first to make the suggestion in print that the scene represents Overschie.

15. Rademaker 1725; see also nos. 182 and 183.

16. Beck 1972–87, vol. 1, no. 567.

17. Rademaker 1725, no. 182, based on a drawing of 1610.

18. See Levesque 1994.

28

Dirck Hals

Dutch
Haarlem 1591–1656 Haarlem

A Fiddler

ca. 1629

Oil on panel, 14 ¾ × 12 in. (37.5 × 30.5 cm)
The Norton Simon Foundation, F.1969.42.1.P

Provenance[1]
Private collection, the Netherlands; [A. van der Meer, Amsterdam, sold 1969 to]; The Norton Simon Foundation.

Exhibited
On loan, Phoenix Art Museum, 8 January–28 April 1970; on loan, Los Angeles County Museum of Art, 29 April 1970–13 September 1972; Houston 1972–74.

References
Van der Meer 1969, no. 20, as School of Haarlem, 17th century; Pasadena 1980, p. 53, ill., as School of Haarlem; Pasadena 1989, p. 76, ill., as School of Haarlem, Dutch, 17th century; Bogendorf Rupprath 2003, pp. 23–24, fig. 179, as Dirck Hals; Senenko 2009, p. 170, as Dirck Hals; S. Campbell 2010, p. 328, no. 696, ill.

Technical Notes
The cradled oak support consists of a single board with a vertical grain. The lighter color of the reverse as compared to the sides suggests that the panel was thinned before the cradle was attached. The ground is a warm pinkish-beige. Infrared examination shows that the toe of the proper right shoe was moved slightly. A faint shadow at the top and right sides of the black hat seems to be a pentimento indicating the slight change in its position. Paint is smoothly brushed in a fairly thin consistency, with details of costume rendered crisply. The thinly painted, monochromatic background is influenced by the ground color. Brushmarking, found in the shoe bows and small flourishes of thicker paint, is minimal. For the most part, the painting is well preserved except for minor abrasion in the face and the hat. Other small losses or mechanical abrasions are confined to the edges. There is a moderate amount of retouching in the background, rather arbitrarily applied, with no evident cause. It has discolored enough to be noticeable. The glossy, natural-resin varnish has yellowed.

A young man, his left leg crossed over his extended right leg at the knee, leans back in his chair as he plays the fiddle. A songbook lies open on the table next to him. The fiddler wears the festive costume of a stylish young Dutch man of the late 1620s and early 1630s: a medium-brown fitted doublet with pointed waistline and peplum, slashed in the bodice and upper sleeves to reveal the white silk lining; matching loose breeches with a row of buttons down the side seam extend to just below the knee, where they are fastened with knee bands. Decorative silk sashes serve as garters for the colorful, probably silk hose and as ties for the shoes. Like the slashed doublet, the white silk *nestles* that hang from his waist are echoes of the previous century, when they were used to secure the breeches to the doublet; by the seventeenth century, however, hooks were used, and the *nestles*, when they appear, were purely decorative. A white linen shirt with simple white cuffs, a flat scalloped collar, and a black wide-brimmed hat tilted at an angle over his forehead complete his costume.[2] The long, soft, loopy folds of the trousers, which have no reference to the underlying forms, create an impression of precarious imbalance that is increased by the diagonals of his black hat, his right arm, and his bent left leg.

A Fiddler, which is unsigned, was formerly attributed generically to "Haarlem School" but can be confidently attributed to Dirck Hals on the basis of technique and the specific figure type.[3] The definition of drapery without reference to underlying forms and especially the play of superficial reflections on the fiddler's hose, sashes, and on his hands are typical of Dirck Hals's technique, which resembles, on a much smaller scale, the animated brushwork of his older brother Frans Hals (1582/83–1666). The specific figure of the fiddler appears in works signed by Dirck Hals, including *Elegant Company Playing Music in an Interior* (fig. 28a).[4] The long wooden bench that extends from behind the fiddler to the right is also found in a painting by Dirck Hals that was on the market in 1984.[5]

The reappearance of specific motifs in Dirck Hals's paintings indicates that he made and kept drawings or sketches of stock images for use in his compositions, varying them slightly to suit the context.[6] Peter Schatborn has identified a group of grisaille oil sketches on paper that appear to have been prepared for this purpose.[7] Among these is a sketch of a seated fiddler (fig. 28b), signed and dated on the wall to the right of the figure's knees: "DH [in monogram] / 1629."[8] The costume and pose resemble those in the Pasadena painting with some differences. In the sketch, for example, the fiddler's proper left leg is fully extended rather than crossed over his right leg, he holds his proper left elbow high rather than dropped, and his right arm and hand are at an angle.

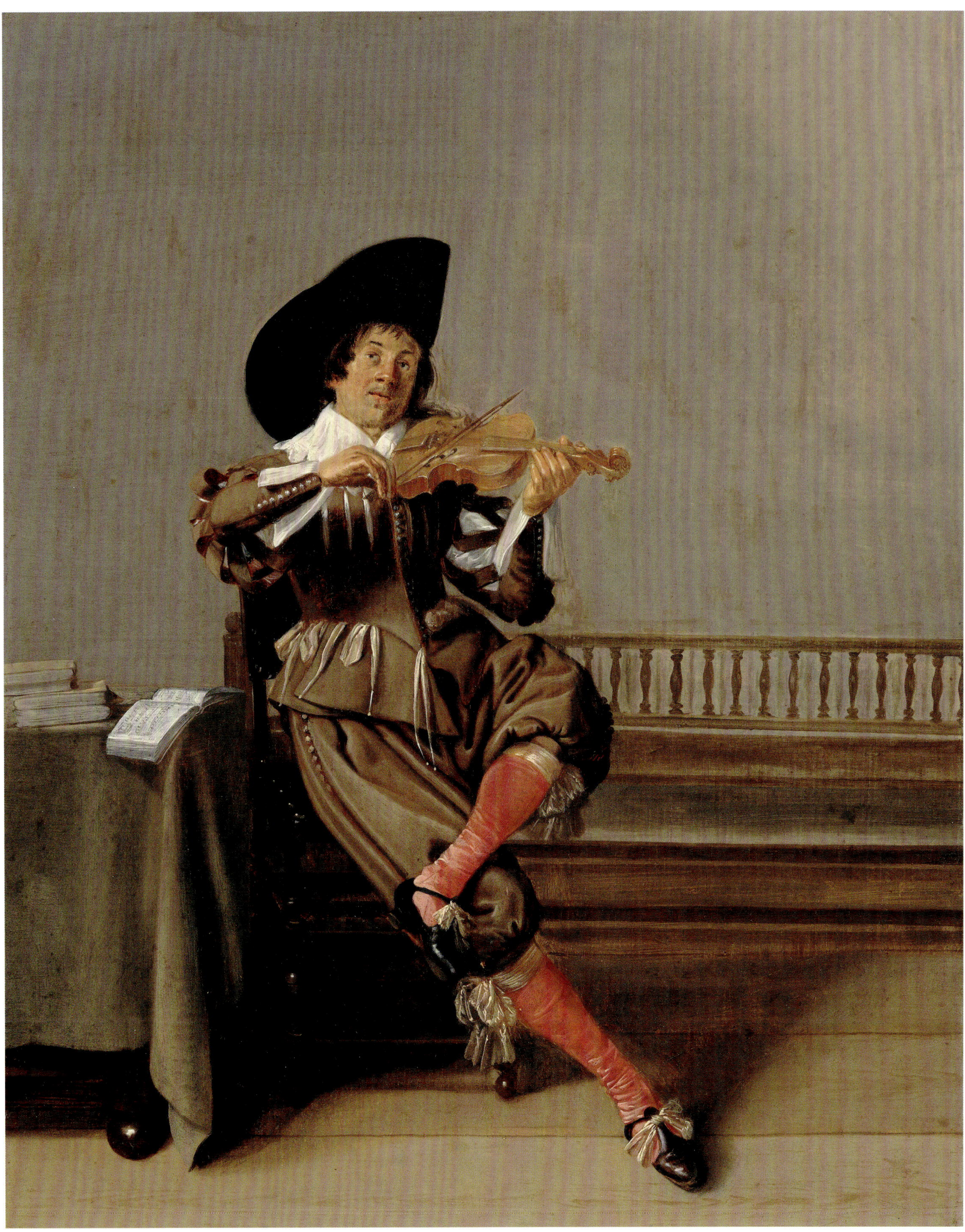

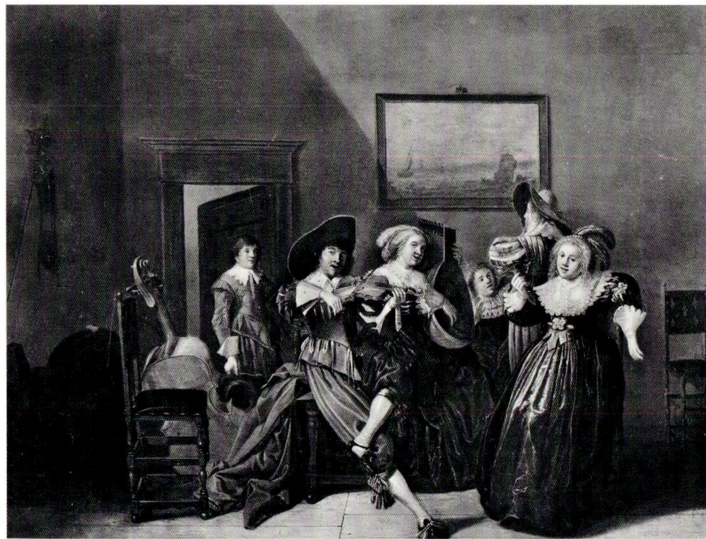

Fig. 28a. Dirck Hals, *Elegant Company Playing Music in an Interior*, ca. 1630, oil on panel, 18½ × 25¼ in. (47 × 64 cm), present location unknown; photograph courtesy Collection Rijksbureau voor Kunsthistorische Documentatie (RKD), The Hague.

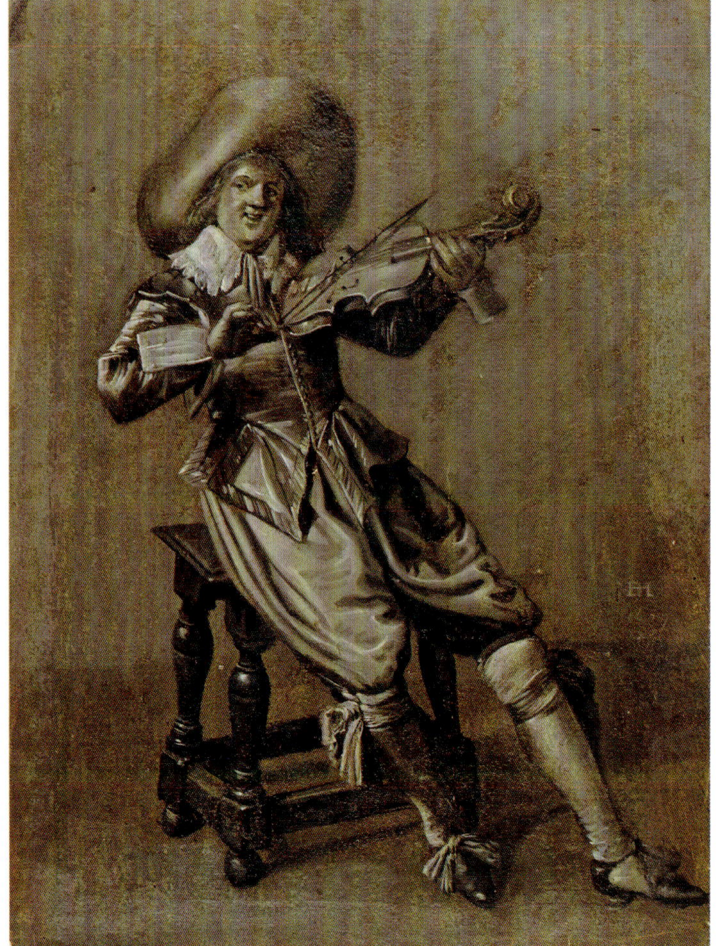

Fig. 28b. Dirck Hals, *A Seated Man Playing the Violin*, 1629, grisaille oil sketch on paper, 8½ × 6⁷⁄₁₆ in. (21.5 × 16.4 cm), Fitzwilliam Museum, Cambridge.

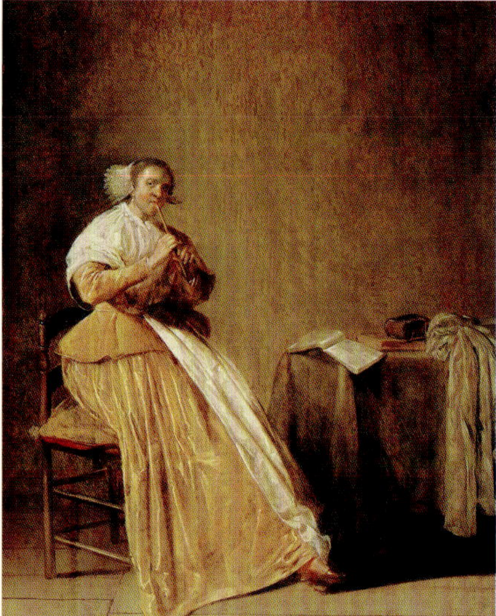

Fig. 28c. Dirck Hals, *Woman Playing a Flute*, 1630, oil on panel, 14⅝ × 11⁷⁄₁₆ in. (37 × 29 cm), Frans Hals Museum, Haarlem.

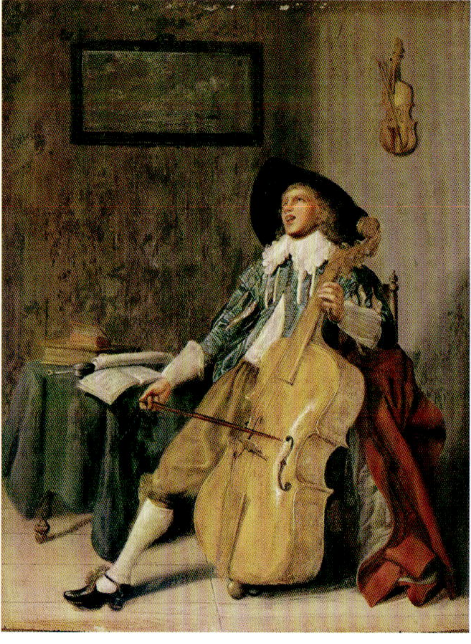

Fig. 28d. Dirck Hals, *The Soloist*, ca. 1633, oil on panel, 15 × 11¹³⁄₁₆ in. (38 × 30 cm), Gemäldegalerie der Akademie der bildenden Künste, Vienna.

A Fiddler belongs to a group of small-format genre scenes of single figures that Hals painted in the early 1630s. His palette of brown, ochre, and gray contributes to the paintings' quiet, contemplative mood.[9] Among this group of upright paintings of similar dimensions are three of single musicians seated in simply defined interiors next to a draped table with a simple still life of books and sometimes additional objects: *Woman Playing a Flute*, signed and dated 1630 (fig. 28c), *The Lute Player* (location unknown), and *The Soloist* (fig. 28d).[10] The pose and costume of the man in *A Fiddler* are particularly close to those of the musician in the latter. The similarity of size, composition, tonality, scale, poses, and subject suggests that Hals, who is known to have conceived of paintings in series and groups, may have painted *A Fiddler* as part of a larger grouping that could have included one or more of the other paintings.[11] The 1668 inventory of Hals's contemporary Jan Miense Molenaer (1610/11–1668), for example, lists four paintings of single musicians in the *voorhuis* (entrance hall) of his home.[12]

By the 1630s the violin was a popular instrument in the Netherlands, used as accompaniment for both dancing and singing. The subdued demeanors and fashionable costumes of the musicians portrayed in *A Fiddler* and the other single-figure paintings—as well as those in Hals's merry-company scenes who are shown accompanying singing—suggest that the musicians were members of the burgher class rather than hired entertainers.[13] Indeed, in his book *The Courtier*, first published in 1528 and known by various editions in the Netherlands during the seventeenth century, Baldassare Castiglione (1478–1529) recommended the violin as the most suitable musical instrument for a gentleman.[14] Since the fabled contest between Marsyas and Apollo known from antiquity, string instruments had been considered superior to wind instruments; especially in the context of singing and other instruments, they were often used as references to harmony and, thus, reason. Like merry-company scenes, therefore, these paintings of individual musicians may still have retained some associations with love and harmony.[15]

1. A painting described as "The Fiddler" by Frans Hals appeared at two sales at Foster and Son, London, 10 August 1831, lot 92 (seller Ballingale, bought in at £1.2), and 30 January 1832, lot 22 (anonymous seller, bought in at 24s. [shillings]). The low prices suggest the paintings were small.

2. Du Mortier 1989, pp. 53–54. According to Du Mortier, p. 59n81, "A *nestle* was a band or tape ending in a needle or tag to allow it to be passed through an opening." Typically, the scallops of a linen collar would have been formed by bobbin lace. See the example illustrated and discussed in Du Mortier et al. 2016, no. 6; that volume also illustrates and discusses breeches in no. 3. For an interesting discussion of costume and its place in Dutch society during the 1620s and 1630s, see B. Roberts 2012.

3. In reattributing *A Fiddler*, I have greatly benefited from conversations with Cynthia Kortenhorst-von Bogendorf Rupprath prior to the publication of her 2003 article on the Pasadena painting and several other related works attributable to Hals: Bogendorf Rupprath 2003, pp. 23–24, fig. 179. Other scholars, including Wolfgang Stechow (unpub. MSS, NSM) and Christopher Brown (informal remarks made in the Norton Simon Museum in 1984), also previously suggested the attribution to Hals. Marijke C. de Kinkelder, Department of Old Netherlandish Painting, RKD, The Hague (letter dated 15 March 1995, NSM), rejected the previous attribution to Pieter Codde (1599–1678) and considers it an early work by Hals dating from the mid-1620s. Her opinion was also based on discussions with Kortenhorst-von Bogendorf Rupprath.

4. Another is *A Music Party* (panel, 43.5 × 55 cm; Pushkin Museum, Moscow, no. 575). According to the RKD mount, the painting, which was with Müllenmeister, Soningen, in 1965, is signed and painted on a panel measuring 47 × 64 cm (*Weltkunst*, 9 September 1965, p. 766). Closely related figures also appear in paintings formerly on the art market attributed to Hals: *An Interior with a Jovial Company* (panel, 13½ × 11¾ in.), sale, Sotheby's, London, 8 July 1981, no. 29; and *Musical Company* (panel, 35.2 × 50.7 cm), Galerie International, The Hague, ca. 1930. Kortenhorst-von Bogendorf Rupprath has also noted the similarity of the figure in the Pasadena painting to those in two other works: one sold at Spek, Bad Kissingen, 22 May 1964, lot 171, as Jan Miense Molenaer (panel, 40 × 63 cm); and another in the background right of a painting at Wawel Castle, Kraków, inv. no. 14, as Dirck Hals (panel, 45 × 71.6 cm; published in Białostocki and Walicki 1955, no. 304, as Willem Hals).

5. Sale, Sotheby's, London, 16 May 1984, lot 38 (RKD photo no. 170831). Kortenhorst-von Bogendorf Rupprath was the first to notice this comparison.

6. It is also possible that Hals owned sketches and/or paintings of works by Willem Pietersz. Buytewech (1591–1624) from which his own images clearly derive. See discussion in Trnek 1992, p. 163.

7. Schatborn 1973.

8. On the verso of the sketch is written in seventeenth-century handwriting: "de jonge Hals fecit" and either 1609 or 1619; in ink: "de jonge Hals" (the young Hals). Schatborn 1973, p. 107, no. 6, fig. 10.

9. Plietzsch 1956, p. 194, was the first to identify this group. The two paintings he discussed from the Jaffé Collection, Berlin, are now in the Clark Art Institute, Williamstown, MA (see note 11 below). Also among this group of small paintings is *Seated Woman with a Letter*, signed with a monogram and dated 1633 (Philadelphia Museum of Art, no. 434). See Philadelphia/Berlin/London 1984, p. 207.

10. Regarding Hals's single figures, see Nehlsen-Marten 2003, pp. 175ff. *The Lute Player* is represented as fig. 202. Regarding *The Soloist*, see Trnek 1992, pp. 162–66.

11. In addition to a series on the senses, Hals painted at least one pair of paintings of children—*Children Playing with a Cat* and *Children Playing Cards* (the latter dated 1631; both in the Clark Art Institute, Williamstown, MA). See Haarlem/Worcester 1993, pp. 266–73. Trnek 1992, p. 166n12, notes that Bode suggested that *The Soloist* was a pendant of *The Lute Player*, dated 1626, formerly in the Gsell Collection.

12. See Bredius 1915, p. 3, nos. (12–15): "(12) Een Luytslager van syn huysvrou; (13) Een vroutge met een Cyter van Molenaer; (14) Een vroutge met een tangetje van Molenaer; (15) Een vroutge op de Clauwe Cimbael spelende van Molenaer" ([12] A lute player by his wife [the artist Judith Leyster]; [13] A woman with a cittern by Molenaer; [14] A woman with tongs [?] by Molenaer; [15] A woman playing the harpsichord by Molenaer).

13. B. Roberts 2012. Other indications that the musician was probably a member of the burgher class is that he is seated and holds his instrument in the correct position on his shoulder, whereas dance musicians generally stood and held the violin against their chest and gripped the short bow with the thumb positioned under the bow hair. See Haarlem/Worcester 1993, p. 371. Regarding the history of the violin, Kortenhorst-von Bogendorf Rupprath 1993, p. 373n3, refers the reader to Sadie 1980, vol. 19, pp. 876f.; see also Winternitz 1967.

14. Castiglione 1561, p. 108, quoted in Haarlem/Worcester 1993, p. 373n2. Among the Dutch editions is Balthasar Castiglione, *De Volmaeckte Hovelinck* (Amsterdam, 1662). Cornelis Saftleven (1607–1681) undoubtedly knew this association when within a single composition he portrayed himself and his younger brother Herman Saftleven (1609–1685) seated next to each other in their studio, one playing a violin and the other a cittern: *The Duet*, oil on panel, 43 × 53 cm (Gemäldegalerie der Akademie der bildenden Künste, Vienna). Trnek 1992, p. 163, interprets the painting "as an expression of harmony, not only between music and painting in general, but also between the brothers themselves." See Minneapolis/Houston/San Diego 1985, p. 88.

15. Trnek 1992, p. 163, suggests that the presence of the calm seascape behind the cellist in *The Soloist* is a reference to harmonious love. The author suggests that the concept of *vanitas* and the transitory nature of all pleasures, often associated with the merry-company scenes, are inherent in the scene because of the fleeting and transitory quality of the music.

29

Frans Hals

Dutch
Antwerp 1582/83–1666 Haarlem

Portrait of a Young Man, formerly called *Jan van de Cappelle*

1650–55

Signed with monogram, lower right: "FH"
Oil on canvas, 26 5⁄8 × 20 in. (67.6 × 50.8 cm)
Norton Simon Art Foundation, M.1972.4.P

Provenance
Rodolphe Kann (1845–1905), Paris by 1900, by descent to his nephew;[1] Edouard Kann (1873–1927), sold 1907 to; [Duveen Brothers, London, until after 1909];[2] Arthur M. Grenfell (1873–1958), Roehampton, Surrey, sold 1913 to; [M. Knoedler & Co., Paris, stock no. 5661,[3] as "Hals's *Portrait of a Young Man* from the Rodolphe Kann collection," sold 1913 to]; George Eastman (1854–1932), New York.[4] [Duveen Brothers, New York]. J. M. Stettenheim, New York, by 1923 until at least 1942;[5] [Kurt M. Stern, New York, sold 7 December 1953 to];[6] [Wildenstein & Co., New York, sold 1961 to]; Norton Simon, gift 1972 to; Norton Simon Art Foundation.

Exhibited
Detroit 1935, no. 48, ill.; New York 1940, no. 83;[7] New York 1942b, pp. 44–45, no. 26, ill., as lent by Mr. I. M. Stettenheim, New York, and formerly having belonged to Arthur Grenfell; Los Angeles 1965; San Francisco/Toledo/Boston 1966–67, no. 19; on loan, Los Angeles County Museum of Art, 20 January 1971–28 February 1972; on loan, Virginia Museum of Fine Arts, Richmond, 15 January 1973–16 December 1974; on loan, Chrysler Museum, Norfolk, VA, 31 October 1980–21 July 1981.

References
Bode 1900, vol. 1, pp. xii–xiii, no. 50; Glück 1900, p. 89; E. Michel 1901, p. 389; Marguillier 1903, pp. 30–31, ill.; Bode 1907, vol. 1, pp. 44f., no. 42, ill.; Nicolle 1908, p. 199; Moes 1909, p. 106, no. 147;[8] Hofstede de Groot 1908–27, vol. 3 (1910), p. 86, no. 301; Péladan 1912, p. 148; Bode 1914, vol. 2, p. 65, no. 239, pl. 151b; Valentiner 1921a, p. 241, ill.; Valentiner 1923a, p. 254, ill.; Dülberg 1930, p. 200; Valentiner 1936b, no. 98, ill.; Trivas 1941, p. 58, no. 101, pl. 132; Valentiner 1941, pp. 292–95, figs. 15, 17 (det.); Slive 1970–74, vol. 1 (1970), p. 190, vol. 2 (1970), pl. 311, vol. 3 (1974), p. 103, no. 200; Grimm 1972, p. 205, no. 133; Grimm and Montagni 1974, pp. 105f., no. 177; McCleery 1974, p. 10; Gerson 1976, pp. 165f., pl. A; Pasadena 1980, p. 38, ill.; D. W. S. 1981, p. [5], ill.; P. Sutton 1986, p. 216, fig. 313; Pasadena 1989, p. 81, ill.; Muchnic 1998, p. 44; Pasadena 2003, p. 70, ill.; S. Campbell 2010, pp. 30–31, 34–35, 37, 44, 256, fig. 12, no. 93, ill.; Slive 2014, pp. 308–09, 335, pl. 189; Grimm 2023–24.

Technical Notes
The original support, a plain-weave canvas of moderate weight, has been lined, with the original tacking edges cut off. A tear in the sleeve at the bottom left corner has been repaired. A moderately thick white ground covers the canvas texture. The opaque, rich paint was handled with broad, energetic brushstrokes. Fast strokes were used to lay down highlights, shadows, and the modeling of the face and hands. Two quick strokes of yellow in the proper right sleeve appear vibrant in the subdued palette. Hals employed some thin layering to achieve certain colors. For example, the ochre-fawn-colored jacket was painted over a black layer. The background color was warmed with a reddish-brown underpainting. The hands were modeled by leaving spaces between the fingers and exposing the black paint beneath. X-radiography shows that Hals made a slight change, raising the shoulder seam of the proper right sleeve. Previous restorations have altered the paint significantly. Lining has flattened the paint surface; microscopic examination reveals the tops of the white highlights to be mashed or melted. Cleaning has left extensive severe abrasion, which has diminished the depth and crispness of the dark colors and has left shadows thinned. Glazes have been removed in the background at the right side, leaving this area difficult to read. Retouching is located around all four edges, in the jacket (including the large tear at lower left), in the proper right cheek, under the chin, in the proper left cheek, below the proper left eye, and in numerous small spots of the background. Although overall the synthetic-resin varnish appears only slightly discolored, remnants of darkened varnish remain in the recesses of brushstrokes.

Seen in three-quarters view with his gaze directed toward the viewer, the sitter forms a visual triangle anchored by the lower corners of the painting. The placement of his proper left hand in the center foreground, aligned with the lower edge of the frame, contributes to the sense of both the figure's stability and its three-dimensional form.[9] The restrained pose appears to constrict the sitter within the boundaries of the picture. The Pasadena painting is thinly painted but combines areas of bold, spirited brushwork and vivid contrasts of light and shadow with more delicately painted areas, such as the face. This combination suggests that Frans Hals painted the portrait ca. 1650–55, a period of transition during which he was developing the style of his late works.[10] According to Seymour Slive, in Hals's later paintings the paint is thinner and the touch broader, the artist deliberately suppressing detail while increasing emphasis on character and mood. In addition, Hals's later works generally tend to be darker and the blacks richer and more dominant.

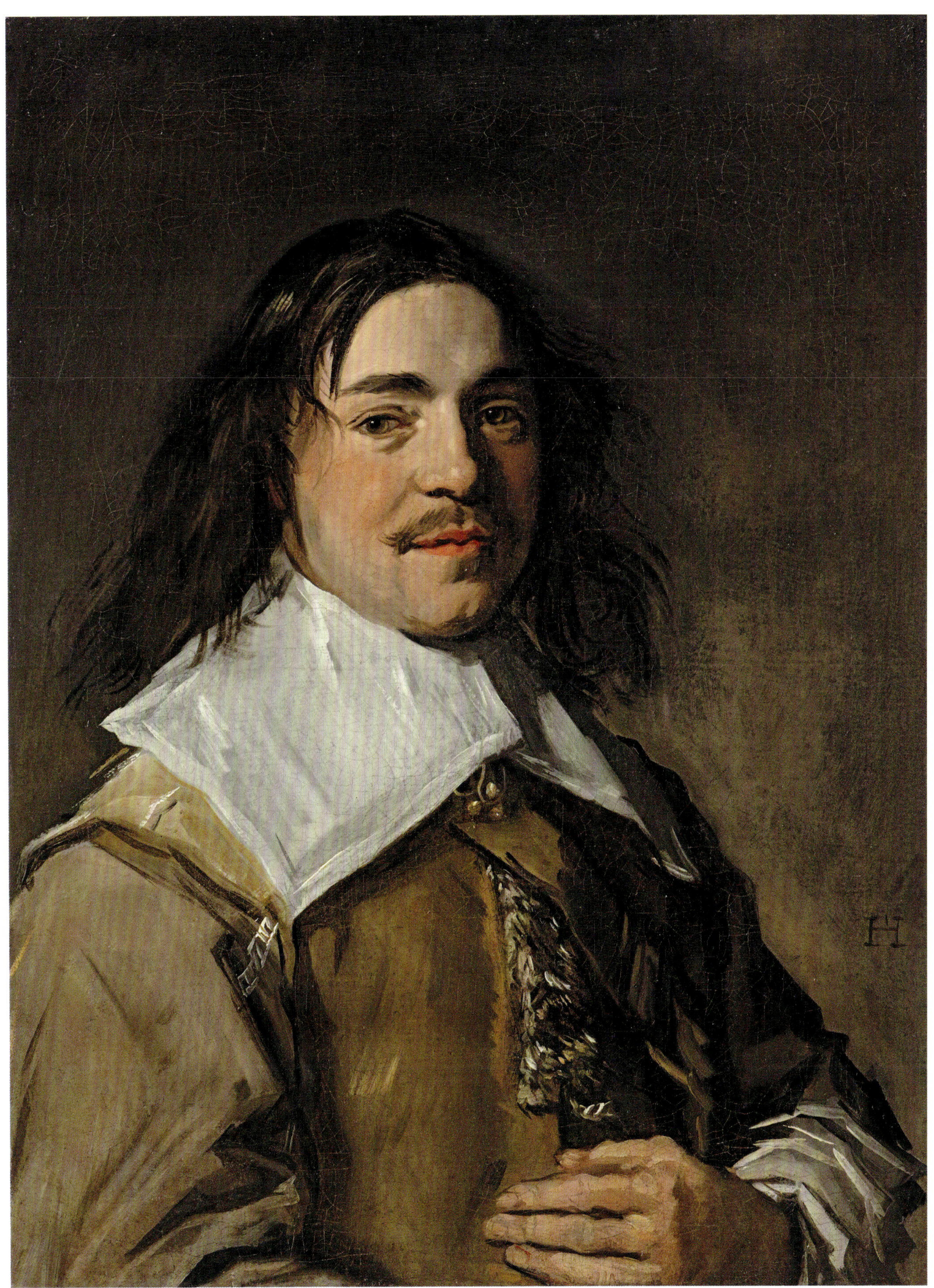

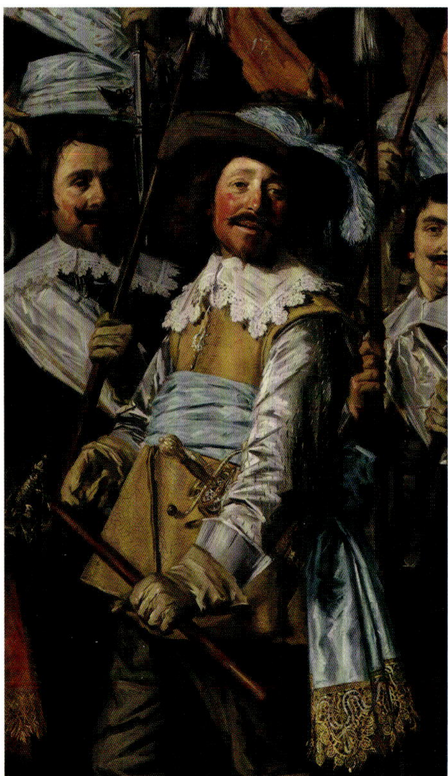

Fig. 29a. Frans Hals, detail of central figure from *Officers and Subalterns of the St. George Civic Guard*, 1639, oil on canvas, 85 ⅞ × 165 ¾ in. (218 × 421 cm), Frans Hals Museum, Haarlem.

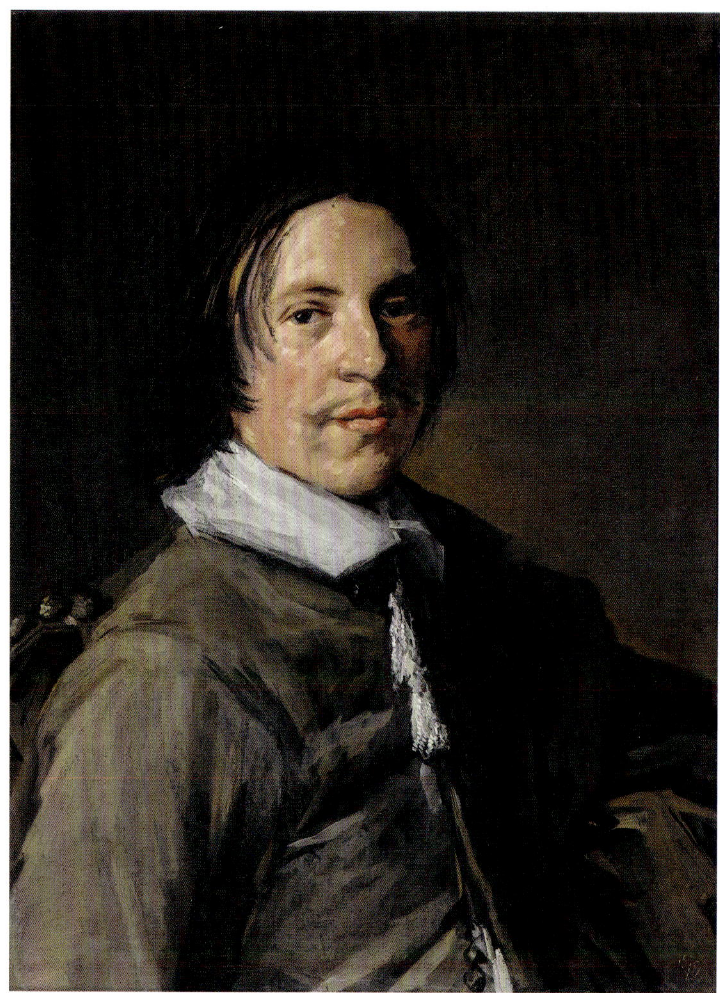

Fig. 29b. Frans Hals, *Vincent Laurensz. van der Vinne*, ca. 1655–60, oil on canvas, 25 ½ × 19 ¼ in. (64.7 × 48.9 cm), Art Gallery of Ontario, Toronto, bequest of Frank P. Wood, 1955.

Deep olive greens and dark grays increasingly replace the ochre and silver-gray backgrounds of his earlier works.

Hals painted the background of the Pasadena portrait in a greenish-gray over gray-ochre warmed by the reddish-brown underpaint, which complements the sitter's ochre jacket shaded with black. He wears a leather jerkin, or *kolder*, similar to that worn by the central figure in Hals's *Officers and Subalterns of the St. George Civic Guard* (fig. 29a).[11] Intended as a protective garment for soldiers, horsemen, and sailors, *kolders* were generally made of buffalo hide. A strap of similar color crosses diagonally from his proper right shoulder to his waist and probably, as Pieter Biesboer has suggested, would have supported an ammunition pouch.[12] A broad, flat linen collar tied in front with tassels covers the sitter's shoulders.[13] What appears to be a pentimento to the right of the man's head suggests that he originally wore a hat over his stylishly long, loose hair, which would have complemented the lines of his face and costume.[14] Hals's original plan to include a hat may explain the somewhat awkward gesture of the sitter's left hand, which appears to finger his jacket opening but may originally have been planned to hold a glove, as the sitter does in *De Heer Bodolphe* (Yale University Art Gallery, New Haven).

The sitter's identity remains a mystery. In 1921 Wilhelm Valentiner suggested that it represented the same man Hals portrayed in a portrait later identified as the Haarlem painter Vincent Laurensz. van der Vinne (1628–1702; fig. 29b).[15] Subsequently, Valentiner—referring to a portrait in the Frick Collection, New York, which was then thought to be by Rembrandt—proposed that the sitter was the famous Haarlem marine painter Jan van de Cappelle (1626–1679), who owned nine paintings by Hals, including a portrait of himself.[16] Subsequent scholars, including both Seymour Slive and Margaretta Russell, author of a monograph on Van de Cappelle, have rejected this identification but put forth no other.[17] In the absence of a specific identification, it can, however, be assumed that the sitter was connected with one of the militia companies in Haarlem that turned to Frans Hals for their portraits.

1. Rodolphe Kann began collecting paintings and decorative arts objects in about 1880, creating one of the most important turn-of-the-century collections in France. Among the most significant paintings in his collection were Vermeer's *Girl Asleep* (Metropolitan Museum of Art, New York), Ghirlandaio's *Portrait of Giovanna Tornabuoni* (Museo Nacional Thyssen-Bornemisza, Madrid), and *Aristotle with the Bust of Homer* (Metropolitan Museum of Art, New York), one of eleven works by Rembrandt owned by Kann. Rodolphe Kann's brother Maurice (1839–1906) was also an important collector who at one time owned the Norton Simon Museum's painting *Three Great Trees in a Mountainous Landscape with a River* (cat. 78) by Jacob van Ruisdael (1628/29–1682). The brothers, whose vast fortune derived from diamond and gold mines in South Africa, lived in adjacent mansions in Paris, with the second floor of each house reserved for the display of their art collections; connecting doors made it possible to join the areas into a single large gallery. Maurice's son Edouard inherited the collections of both Rodolphe and Maurice. See Glück 1900, E. Michel 1901, Marguillier 1903, Bode 1907, Nicolle 1908, and Prévost-Marcilhacy 2022.

2. Duveen Brothers purchased the Rodolphe Kann collection for F 21 million (reported in the American press as $5 million) on 6 August 1907. Fowles 1976, p. 36, notes that "Joseph [Duveen] and Nathan Wildenstein were occupied throughout the whole of the summer of 1907 negotiating the purchase of the Rodolphe Kann Collection." Wildenstein & Co., which financed 25 percent of the purchase and shared in the profits, was also paid a 1 percent commission by Kann for acting as the agent for the sale (GRI, Duveen Archive, box 257, folder 2). For a chatty description of the events surrounding this transaction, see Fowles 1976, pp. 36ff.

3. Also New York stock no. 13261 and older stock nos. for London (4547) and again New York (11820).

4. George Eastman founded the Eastman Kodak Company in 1892.

5. This is probably Isadore M. Stettenheim, who was born in Germany in 1855 and became a naturalized citizen of the United States in 1890. The Pasadena painting was not included in the 16 December 1950 sale of the Stettenheim collection at Kende Gallery, New York.

6. With thanks to Joseph Baillio, Wildenstein & Co., for providing this information in his letter of 26 June 2002 (NSM).

7. Identified as this painting in New York 1942b.

8. Moes lists two paintings, each titled "Portrait d'homme," as with Duveen Brothers, Paris. New York 1942b, p. 44, no. 26, identifies the Simon painting as no. 137. Moes, however, notes that that painting is dated 1643. No. 147, without date, is thus probably the Pasadena painting.

9. The painting may have been cut along the left edge, increasing the sense of constriction. In his last years, Hals tended to push his figures toward the edges of his pictures to achieve more monumental effects, but even then he generally put space around them.

10. Slive 1970–74, vol. 1 (1970), p. 182. Regarding the dating of the Pasadena portrait, Hofstede de Groot 1908–27, vol. 3 (1910), p. 86, no. 301, suggests ca. 1640; Valentiner 1921a, no. 254, and Valentiner 1936a, no. 98, suggest ca. 1650; Trivas 1941, no. 101, suggests no earlier than 1655, which is also the opinion of Slive 1970–74, vol. 3 (1974), p. 103, no. 200, who suggests 1655–60. Grimm 1972, no. 133, suggests 1645–46. Pieter Biesboer, then curator of the Frans Hals Museum (in conversation with the author, Pasadena, December 1995), stated that the painting should be dated in the early 1650s because of the mixture of roughly and smoothly painted passages. Grimm 2023–24 dates the Pasadena painting to 1650–52 but attributes it to the workshop of Frans Hals or "possibly Frans Hals (II)."

11. This figure was painted by Pieter Codde (1599–1678), who took over the unfinished commission from Hals ca. 1633. Regarding the leather *kolder*, see Du Mortier 1989, p. 55, with additional references. Du Mortier et al. 2016, pp. 30f. illustrates and discusses a similar leather *kolder* worn by Hendrick Casimir I (1612–1640), Count of Nassau Dietz and Stadtholder of Friesland, in July 1640, when he was killed in battle by a bullet. In battle, the *kolder* would have been worn over a padded layer; a metal cuirass added additional protection. Leather *kolders* were sleeveless. In the Pasadena portrait, as well as in *Officers and Subalterns of the St. George Civic Guard*, the sleeves appear to be made of the same material as the *kolder*. The *kolder* worn by Casimir is in the collection of the Rijksmuseum, Amsterdam.

12. Pieter Biesboer, personal communication with the author, 29 October 2007.

13. Flat collars, which replaced stiff, starched millstone ruffs, came increasingly into fashion, especially among the younger people, after the 1630s. See Kinderen-Besier 1950, pp. 170–71.

14. Long hair became popular once the stiff millstone ruffs were replaced by flat collars, but the trend engendered considerable controversy. The "Dispute of the Locks," a heated debate among various Protestant congregations, began in 1640, when several church councils, including that of Haarlem, protested the untended hair of many men, which they considered against the teachings of the Bible. In 1643, for example, Jacobus Borstius (1612–1680), a popular preacher in Dordrecht, delivered a "sermon on long hair, with reference to I Corinthians XI:14"; a physician, Johan van Beverwijk (1594–1647), considered the issue from another point of view when he wrote a treatise on "whether hair is animate and truly nourished." For a further discussion of this issue, see Du Mortier 1989, pp. 55f.

15. Valentiner 1921a, p. 253; Slive 1970–74, no. 203 (Art Gallery of Ontario, Toronto; inv. 54/32).

16. Valentiner 1941, p. 292. The inventory of Van de Cappelle's collection, which was made at the time of his death in 1679 (Bredius 1892, p. 32), notes, "Een dito Conterfeijtsel [sijnde den Overleden] van Frans Hals" (Another portrait [being the deceased], by Frans Hals). Van de Cappelle's inventory also mentions painted portraits of the artist by Rembrandt and Gerbrand van den Eeckhout (1621–1674), as well as a copy of a portrait drawing by Jan van Noordt (ca. 1620–ca. 1675).

17. Slive 1970–74, vol. 1 (1970), p. 190, notes that the Frick portrait is no longer considered a work by Rembrandt and "the similarity between the two models [is] unconvincing." See also Margaretta Russell, letter dated 4 January 1996 (NSM).

30

Jan Davidsz. de Heem

Dutch
Utrecht 1606–1683/84 Antwerp

Vase of Flowers

Mid-1670s

Signed and dated on ledge (abraded): "[J.] D. D. Heem/16[??]"
Oil on canvas, 26½ × 21¾ in. (67.3 × 55.3 cm)
The Norton Simon Foundation, F.1973.06.P

Provenance
Possibly Daniel Marsbag or Herr C*** (sale, Ploos van Amstel et al., Amsterdam, 30 October 1775, lot 36, "Een fles met eenige Bloemen, op een steene tafel, waarby een Oranje-Appel legt. Zeer natuurlijk en uitvoerig geschilderd op Doek, h. 24 b 20 duim").[1] Possibly Pieter Loquet (1700–1782), Amsterdam (sale, Ph. van der Schley, Amsterdam, 22 September 1783, lot 131, "Een Glaaze geribde Fles, staande op een Steene Tafel, gevult met diversche soorten van Bloemen en Vrugten, als een takje met een Oranje-Appel en bladeren; witte en roode Roozen, Iriassen, Tulpen en andre Bloemen. Op de tafel legt een takje met Kruys en Aalbezien, en verders eenige vliegende Cappelletjes, dit stuck is kragtig en tevens uitvoerig gepenseelt. h. 26 v. 21 d Doek," sold for 106 guilders to); [Fouquet]. Possibly Auguste-Louis-César-Hippolyte-Théodore de Lespinasse de Langeac (1759–1814), Comte d'Ariet (sale, Paris, 14–15 December 1808, lot 38, "Très-beau Bouquet de fleurs et de fruits artistement groupés dans une Carafe de verre bleu, posée sur une Table de pierre. Divers Insectes répandus sur les Fleurs, ajoutent, par leur précieuse et étonnante vérité, à la richesse de ce Morceau brillant et du plus agréable détail, que nous présentons ici comme un Morceau de choix dans son genre. Sur toile, haut 28, larg. 22 p.," not sold).[2] Colonel Alfred Henry Hudson (1850–1946), Wick House, Pershore, Worcestershire. [William Hallsborough Gallery, London, sold 1971 to]; [Paul Rosenberg & Co., New York, stock no. 6410-2686, sold 1973 to]; The Norton Simon Foundation.

Exhibited
On loan, Phoenix Museum of Art, 7 February–6 July 1973; on loan, Los Angeles County Museum of Art, 9 July 1973–26 November 1974.

References
Pasadena 1980, p. 49, ill.; P. Sutton 1986, p. 215, as Jan Davidsz. de Heem; Segal 1987a, pp. 32–33n4; Segal 1987b, p. 48, as Jan Davidsz. de Heem; Pasadena 1989, p. 71, ill.; Utrecht/Braunschweig 1991, p. 191, fig. 33c, as falsely signed Jan Davidsz. de Heem, reattributed to Jan Jansz. de Heem; Wheelock 1995, p. 106, as Jan Davidsz. de Heem; Muchnic 1998; Pasadena 2003, p. 63, ill.; S. Campbell 2010, p. 352, no. 926, ill.; F. G. Meijer 2012, p. 9; F. G. Meijer 2016, pt. 1, pp. 276–77, color pl. p. 276, pt. 2, pp. 302–03, no. 269, color pl.

Technical Notes
The plain-weave canvas has been lined with the original tacking edges cut off. Cusping on all sides indicates that the original compositional dimensions were unchanged. The smooth ground is red-brown. Areas of underpainting were not positively identified, but a rose-brown color surrounds several of the flowers in the upper part of the arrangement, which may have been an area left in reserve during the application of the black background color. The same color also appears beneath the gray of the stone ledge. Thin layers of opaque paint were precisely applied in meticulous detail; highly finished flowers have crisp contours and clear colors. Glazes were also employed. Several areas of color, such as the large green leaf over the pink hibiscus at the center, are nearly transparent. Magnification reveals some leaves and blossoms with distinct dark contours that may have been underdrawn. Overall the paint is in excellent condition, with minimal losses (the flowers in particular are beautifully preserved). The stone ledge in the lower portion of the painting and the lower background exhibit some minor abrasion. The visible remnants of the signature and date appear to be part of the original paint; fine drying cracks exposing some white ground pass through both the stone background and the inscription; some darker gray-black areas may be later strengthening.

Characteristic of Dutch flower pieces from the second half of the seventeenth century, *Vase of Flowers* portrays a dynamic, baroque arrangement of voluptuous flowers in full bloom overflowing a ribbed vase of blue glass placed on a dark gray stone parapet. In addition to roses, tulips, hollyhocks, a blue iris, African marigold, and morning glories, the arrangement includes an orange and a sprig of peas on the lower left balanced on the right by two red peonies drooping under their own weight. Gooseberries, red currants, and the sprig of peas extend over the stone, and butterflies fluttering around the blossoms and a snail crawling across the cold stone enliven the composition and contribute to the illusion of pictorial depth against an undefined black background.

By carefully considering the position and color of each flower within the bouquet and controlling the light, Jan Davidsz. de Heem created the impression of a fully rounded bouquet. The brightest elements—the pink and white roses, the orange, and the peonies—appear in the foreground; the darker, less lively blue-purple iris and dark green foliage are positioned on the perimeter of the bouquet. Light cast from the upper left interacts with the flowers, modeling them and casting shadows of one flower onto another to define their relationships within the bouquet. Layers of thin glazes colored with only minimum pigment subtly model the flowers,

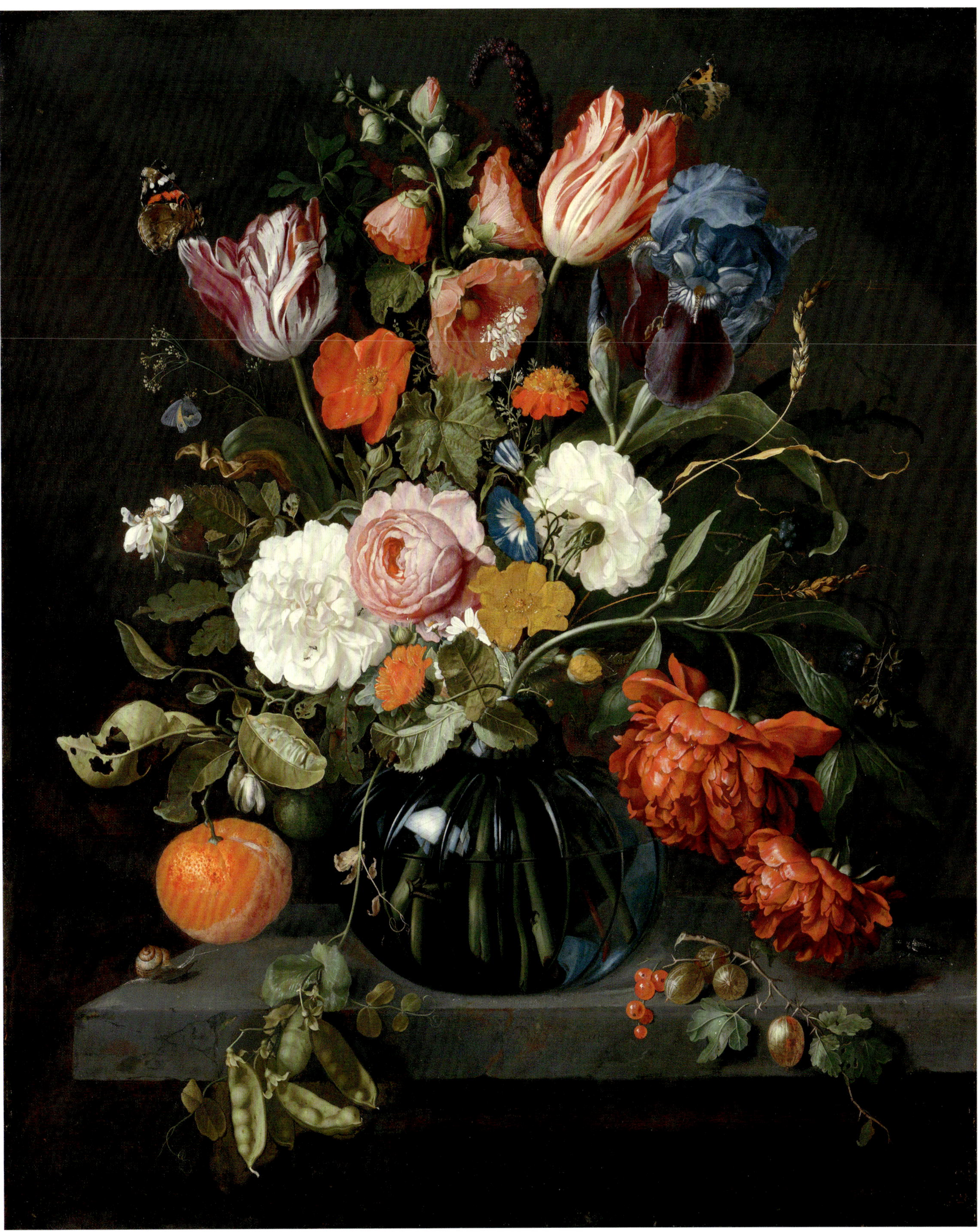

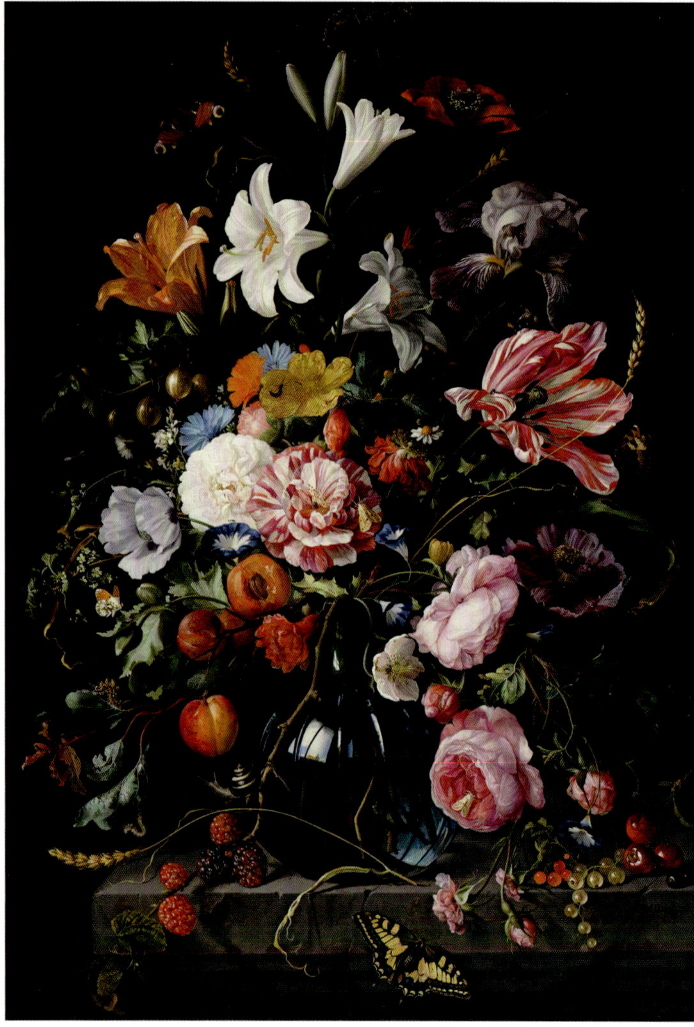

Fig. 30a. Jan Davidsz. de Heem, *Vase with Flowers*, ca. 1670, oil on canvas, 29 ¼ × 20 ¾ in. (74.2 × 52.6 cm), Mauritshuis, The Hague.

creating the illusion of depth and volume while rendering the effect of a hard, porcelain surface. To define the lower petals of the large iris, for example, De Heem applied thin blue glazes over a red base to create the beautiful purple hue.

While scholars have generally accepted the Pasadena painting as an autograph work by Jan Davidsz. de Heem, the badly damaged signature and date written across the front of the stone parapet—the *J* is almost completely gone and the last two digits of the date are indistinct—have led to questions about the attribution. Both the signature and the date, however, appear to be part of the original paint and approximate the form that De Heem used to sign a document in 1683.

In his 2016 monograph and catalogue raisonné of the work of De Heem, Fred Meijer accepts the Pasadena painting but notes that it is "a strange amalgam of De Heem motifs, many of high quality, but also of deviating elements," suggesting that the artist may have left the still life unfinished, after which it was completed by another hand. He dismisses the previous reading of the damaged date as 1654, objecting that "De Heem did not produce any elaborate flower pieces in the first half of the 1650s." A date in the early to mid-1670s appears preferable. Certain motifs and the handling, he notes, are closer to the artist's flower still lifes of the early 1670s. Details such as the ribbed glass vase, the red admiral butterfly, and the curly leaf of the stalk of wheat, for example, are characteristic of De Heem's paintings of the early 1670s, including *Vase with Flowers* (fig. 30a).[3] Other details, such as the pea pods, peonies, white roses, iris, gooseberries, and leaves of the orange are also found in De Heem's late works, although here they appear more opaque and "waxy."[4] Two intersecting diagonals define the relatively open composition of the Pasadena painting, visually connecting the orange on the lower left to the tulip on the upper right and the two red peonies at the lower right to the tulip at the upper left. Two white roses and one pink dominate the center of the bouquet. Many of De Heem's flower pieces are defined by a diagonal arrangement of flowers extending from the lower left to upper right, with a dense group of flowers at center; other paintings that Meijer dates ca. 1673/74 feature a compositional organization of intersecting diagonals that form a visual "X" in which a red peony also appears on the lower right.[5]

The visual pleasure derived from De Heem's sumptuous image, with its elegant and realistic details, would have been appreciated by many in the seventeenth century as a celebration of the endless variety of God's creation.[6] The transitory beauty of flowers, hastened by the ants and snail that have already bored holes in the leaves, was often associated with *vanitas*; however, one could also regard still lifes of flowers and fruit as a way of preserving nature.[7] Cardinal Federico Borromeo (1564–1631), who was a devoted patron of Jan Brueghel I (1568–1625) and owned one of his monumental flower still lifes, wrote about the sensual pleasures of regarding a flower painting, remarking how painted flowers could outlast the ephemeral flowers of summer and provide delight in the winter, when the grand flower bouquets that decorated the houses in summer had long since faded.

In several of his flower paintings, such as *Still Life with Crucifix and Skull* (Alte Pinakothek, Munich) and *Memento Mori* (Gemäldegalerie Alte Meister, Dresden), De Heem introduced specific religious and *vanitas* references;[8] in others, such as *Vivat Oraenge* (Paleis Het Loo, Apeldoorn), he made overt reference to political events.[9] The prominent inclusion of an orange in the Pasadena still life, a detail that begins to appear in De Heem's paintings only after his return to Utrecht from Antwerp ca. 1660, may, as Fred Meijer has suggested, also have been a reference to the House of Orange and the contemporary efforts by the Orangist Party to restore the office of stadtholder to the young prince, William of Orange (1650–1702).[10]

1. F. G. Meijer 2016, pt. 2, p. 303, calculates the dimensions to be equivalent to 61 × 51 cm and questions if they represent the sight size.

2. According to F. G. Meijer 2016, pt. 2, p. 303, the painting was withdrawn.

3. A similar vase also appears in a painting sold by Christie's, London, 5 July 2007, lot 70, and now in a private collection. See F. G. Meijer 2016, no. 247.

4. F. G. Meijer 2016, pt. 1, pp. 276–77.

5. These include F. G. Meijer 2016, pt. 2, nos. A 247 (*A Bouquet of Flowers in a Green, Globular Glass Vase*, not signed, oil on canvas, 70.5 × 48 cm, private collection); A 251 (*Flowers in a Blue, Ribbed Glass Bottle on a Marble Pedestal*, not signed, oil on canvas, 94.6 × 73 cm, private collection, Europe); and A 248 (*A Bouquet of Flowers in a Rich Glass Goblet upon a Stone Pedestal in Front of a Niche*, signed lower center "J. D. De Heem R," oil on canvas, 100.3 × 76.2 cm, private collection, United States).

6. Fundamental to capturing these pleasures was the artist's ability to represent reality in paint so exactly that it is impossible to distinguish art from artifice. For De Heem and his contemporaries, the challenge was established by Pliny's famous story of Zeuxis, the ancient painter who was able to paint a bowl of fruit so realistically that even the birds were fooled and tried to peck at the fruit.

7. Gaskell 1990, no. 13, notes that "the lack of specificity suggests that [De Heem's *Flowers in a Glass Vase* (Museo Nacional Thyssen-Bornemisza, Madrid), a painting similar to the Pasadena painting] . . . might have been purposefully contrived so as not to have been subject to interpretative closure. That is, a contemporary viewer inclined to seek religious or *vanitas* significance in this work might justifiably do so, whilst those who sought rather to delight in the skill of the painter in emulating the variety of nature in the depiction of vegetable and insect life might with equal justification confine their attention to a consideration of this quality."

8. See Utrecht/Braunschweig 1991, no. 31, pp. 191–93. The Munich still life, which was painted by De Heem in 1645 and reworked by Nicolaes van Veerendael (1640–1691) probably during the late 1660s, includes a piece of paper with an inscription that admonishes the viewer (in translation): "But one does not turn to look at the most beautiful flower of all." Placed directly below the crucifix, the moral message of the inscription identifies the watch, the empty shell, and the skull as additional references to transience and the need to focus on the meaning of Christ's life and death if one hopes to achieve salvation.

9. Van Haeften 2003, no. 17, ill. (entry by Meredith M. Hale).

10. See F. G. Meijer 2016, pt. 1, pp. 28, 260, 268. Meijer notes that during De Heem's period in Antwerp he made work with Roman Catholic associations. De Heem's references to the House of Orange begin to appear during the 1660s after his return to the Netherlands. The late 1660s and 1670s, as William III approached his eighteenth birthday, was a period of a political power struggle between the republican Dutch States Party and the Orangists, who sought to install the young prince as stadtholder, effectively the leader of the country; the position had been vacant since the death of Willem II in 1650, one week before the birth of his son and heir. In 1672, while engaged in war with France and England, the States General appointed William III stadtholder. In 1689, after the English Parliament declared that King James had abdicated the throne, William and Mary, his wife and cousin (both were grandchildren of Charles I), were appointed joint monarchs.

31

Maarten van Heemskerck

Dutch
Heemskerck 1498–1574 Haarlem

Allegory of Nature

1567

Signed on banderole, upper right: "MARTEN VAN HEEMSKERCK FECIT" (fig. 31a)
Inscribed on base of the center statue: "NAT/VRA/1567"
Oil on panel, 14 3/8 × 63 in. (36.5 × 160 cm)
The Norton Simon Foundation, F.1973.20.P

Provenance
Paul van Zuylen (1873–1956), Liège, in 1910, by descent to his nephew; Baron Albert van Zuylen (1916–2008), Liège (sale, Christie's, London, 29 June 1973, lot 40, ill.; sold to); [Cyril Humphries,[1] London, sold 1973 to]; The Norton Simon Foundation.

Exhibited
Liège 1910, no. 226, lent by Paul van Zuylen, Liège; on loan, Henry Art Gallery, University of Washington, Seattle, 25 July 1973–28 May 1974.

References
Preibisz 1911, pp. 75, 106, no. 35; Hoogewerff 1936–47, vol. 4 (1941–42), pp. 383ff., vol. 5, p. 158; Weston 1974a; Gerson 1976, p. 163; Grosshans 1980, pp. 137, 246–49, no. 101, ill., as with a London dealer; P. Sutton 1986, p. 215; Harrison 1987, pp. 917–27, no. 101; Pasadena 1989, pp. 34–35, ill.; Veldman 1996, pp. 128–39, figs. 1, 3, 4, 8; Muchnic 1998, pp. 125–26; Slim 1997, pp. 8f., 13ff.; Slim 1998–2002, pp. 188f.; S. Campbell 2010, pp. 357, 971, ill.; Veldman 2019, pp. 43ff., fig. 5.

Technical Notes
The support, a single board with a dense horizontal grain, possibly linden wood, has unbeveled edges. Apart from a thin strip of wood screwed to the bottom edge of the panel, there appear to be no modifications. Several cracks in the panel follow the grain. A long crack originating at the center of the left side was repaired in 1984. A crack at the upper right is slightly opened but appears to be stable. Unpainted edges at the left and right sides suggest that the panel was originally set into a supporting frame or other structure such as an overdoor. The smooth white ground is moderately thick. Paint was applied with fluid handling and rather loosely brushed in the larger elements of the composition. Details of faces and costumes were rendered in minute detail once the broad areas had dried. The painting's pale aspect was previously attributed to overcleaning, but that conclusion is incorrect. The probable use of white lead in combination with a fugitive red pigment (though not confirmed by analysis in this case) might explain the fading of some flesh tones and other light-colored areas. The large edifice in the left background has distinct, crisp edges, as do columns, capitals, balustrades, and sculptures, exhibiting paint that is undamaged albeit changed. Darker greens, blue-green, and brown have retained their color. There are numerous examples of the paint having become transparent, such as the small figures at the water's edge, behind the picnic party, and the tiny figures at the lower level of the fountain. The mountain range in the central background has become almost imperceptible. Scattered abrasion is minor; some thin glazes appear somewhat worn. Incomplete cleaning during a previous restoration left dark residues throughout the painting. There is very little retouching apart from an area surrounding the crack at the center right. The varnish, which appears to be an aged synthetic resin, imparts a gray hue.

Dated 1567, *Allegory of Nature* is one of the few landscapes and among the last paintings Maarten van Heemskerck made before his death in 1574. The long, narrow composition depicts a fantasy landscape focused on an island shrine of the multibreasted Diana of Ephesus, or Artemis, the Greco-Roman goddess of nature and fertility, here identified as Natura. Overhead, four genii fly toward the statue bearing oblations of ears of corn, flowers, a cornucopia, a torch, and a flaming brazier. A fifth genius on the right holds a fluttering banderole with Van Heemskerck's signature (fig. 31a). To the left and behind the statue is a classical city, now appearing as if sketched in tones of thin white paint. A similar technique defines the distant mountains in pastel colors (see Technical Notes).

In the left foreground (fig. 31b), a courtier, painted in stronger, brighter pinks, greens, and yellows, sits on the ground next to a scantily dressed woman playing the lute. A songbook is open on his lap as he sings and taps the *tactus*, or beat of a

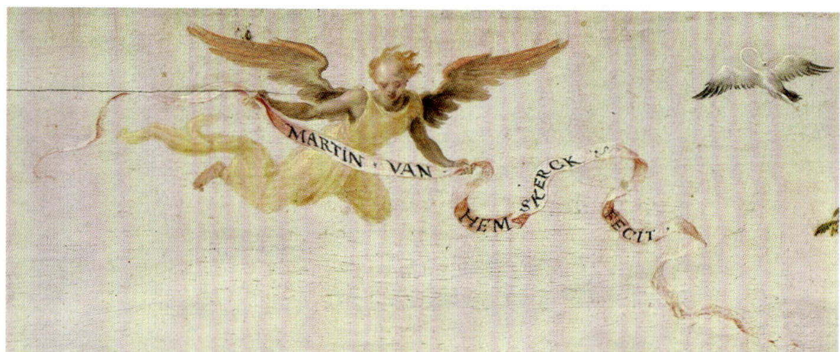

Fig. 31a. Detail of artist's signature.

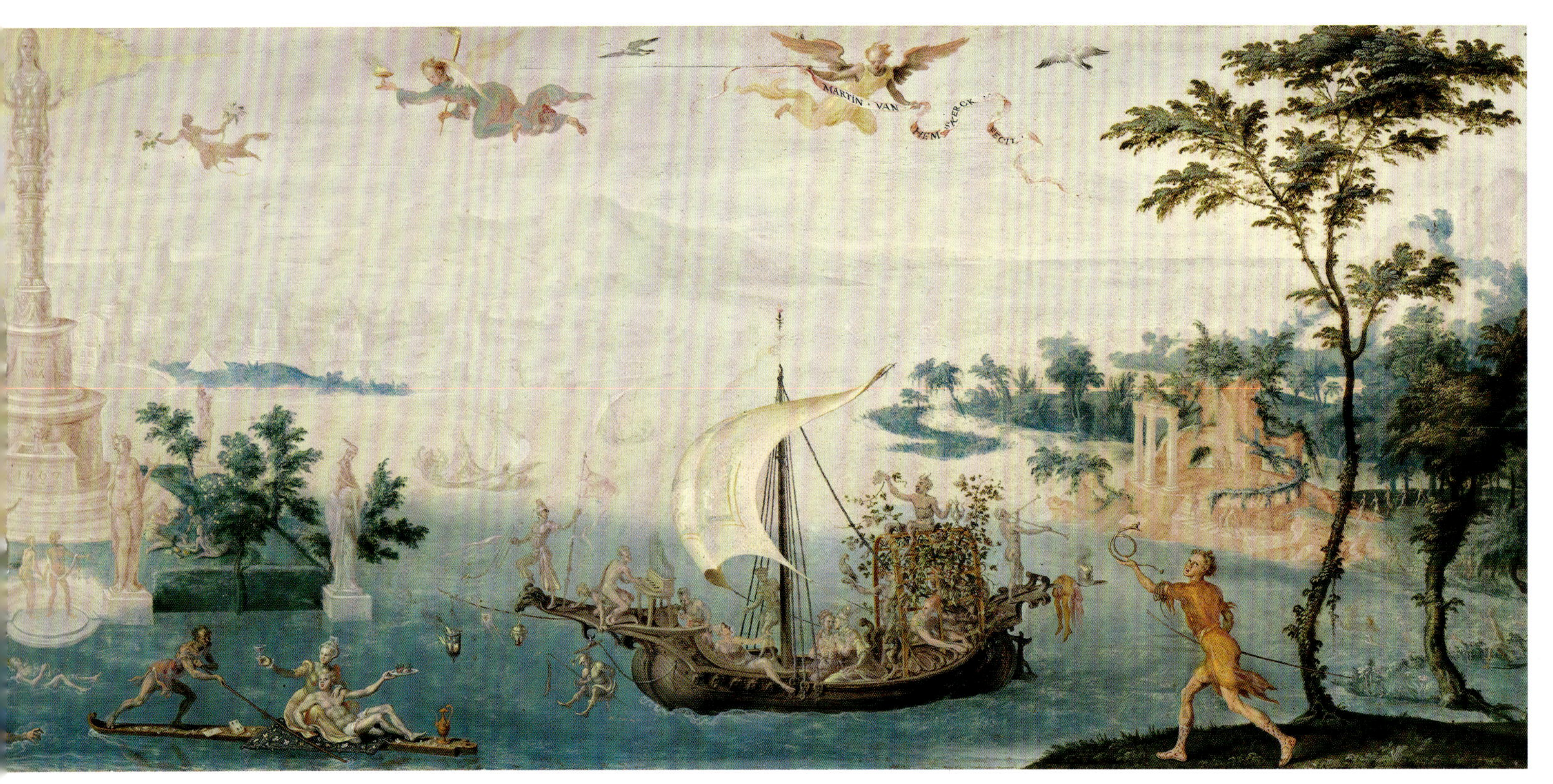
MARTIN · VAN
HEM·SKERCK
FECIT

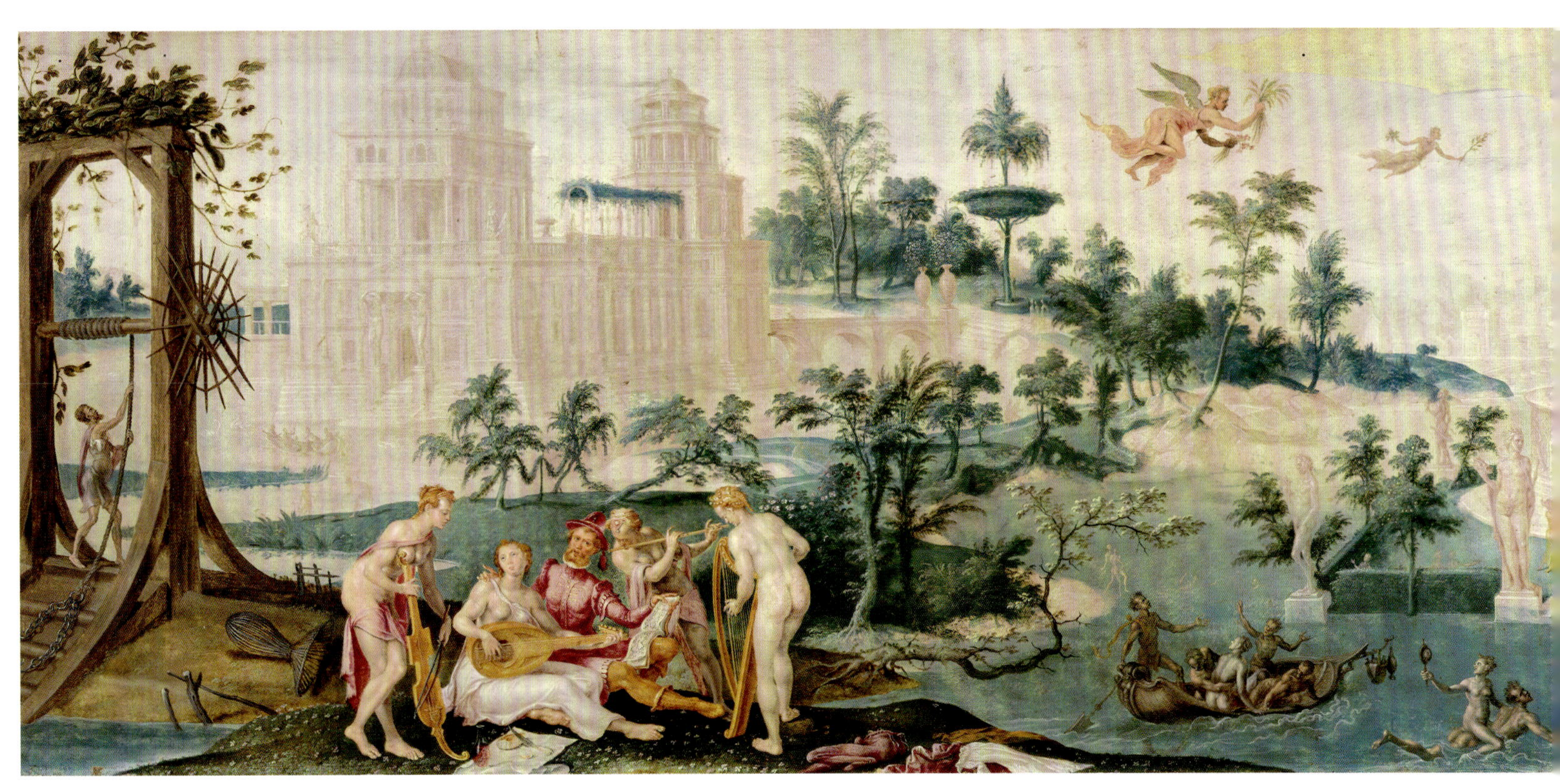

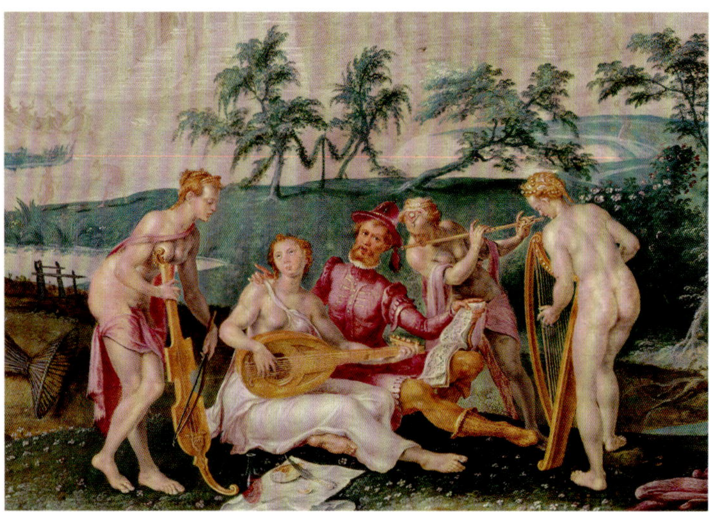

Fig. 31b. Detail of musical group.

song, with the index finger of his right hand on the shoulder of the lute player. She looks toward the standing woman on the left who plays a *viol de fantasie*, an imaginary version of a viol, a bowed stringed instrument. Two other nude or partially nude female musicians stand to the right of the courtier; one plays a flute, which is realistically rendered but, like the *viol de fantaisie*, the musician is represented playing the instrument in reverse of the traditional technique.[2] The second woman plays a twelve-string frame harp. On the ground to the left of the musicians is a fish trap, beyond which is a winch used to move boats from one body of water to another.

On the right side of the painting, a sixteenth-century galleon sails toward the statue of Natura (fig. 31c). Near the stern, well-dressed couples drink and lounge under a grape arbor on which a satyr sits with a barrel of grapes and a pitcher of wine. On the stern itself, a nude man stands and plays a double *alos*, or double reed pipe, the sole classical instrument represented on the ship.[3] On the bow, a nude man seated on the back of a nude woman on all fours plays a small, portable "positive" organ, powered by a putto blowing into a bladder beneath the organ.[4] A man standing on the bowsprit blows an S-shaped trumpet, while another man dressed as a fool swings from the raised anchor below.[5] On a spit of land in the right foreground of the composition, a man blows a horn, announcing a stag hunt on the distant right shore (fig. 31d).

Since 1973, when The Norton Simon Foundation purchased *Allegory of Nature* and placed it on public exhibition for the first time since 1910, several authors have addressed the meaning of the painting's complex iconography.[6] Wallace Weston, curator of the Henry Art Gallery, University of Washington, Seattle, where the painting was on loan in 1973–74, interpreted the painting as an allegory of nature set in a garden of love. In this reading, the four statues surrounding Diana of Ephesus represent the planets, and the figures at the entrance to the island represent day and night.[7] He associates Diana with the planet Venus and the people frolicking in the water surrounding the island as her children and suggests that the green tones and the ship with lovers, including a falconer, refer to seasonal iconography, specifically that for the month of May.[8] The fool perched on the anchor of the ship who relieves himself into the water warns of the foolishness of those who overindulge in sensual self-gratification. Weston's interpretation, however, does not fully explain the iconography and interpret details such as the ship, which appears to be a Spanish galleon, or the hunt, which does not involve a falcon but rather the pursuit of a stag.

In an extensive article published in 1996, Ilja Veldman proposes a reading of the painting as a moral choice between good and bad senses, a reflection of the struggle within man of common sense (*ratio*) and sensuality (*sensualitas*). She believes that the statues surrounding Natura represent neither the planets nor the elements but the four seasons, as Harrison suggested in 1988.[9] In the Pasadena painting, the gifts brought by the flying genii to the goddess emphasize the importance of the four seasons, an essential part of Nature. Their offerings, which correspond to the attributes of the four statues, are all connected with fertility.[10] To support her theory, she notes that the attributes of the statues match those in Van Heemskerck's depiction of the four seasons in his print series of 1563.[11]

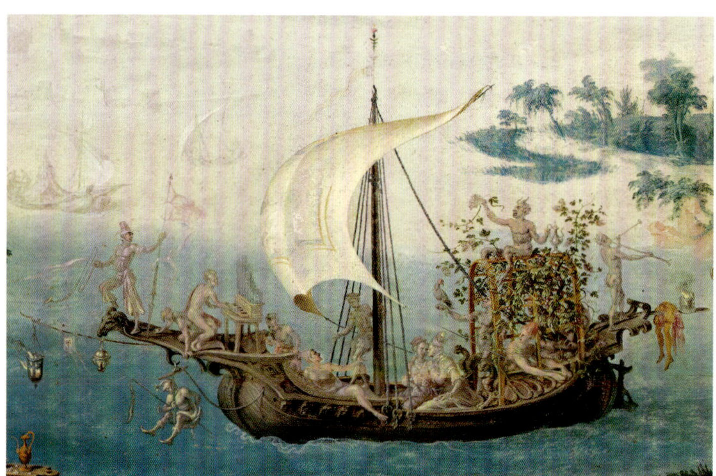

Fig. 31c. Detail of galleon.

In the water in front of the statue of Natura, couples indulge in sensual pleasures, which individually refer to the various senses.[12] The passengers and crew of the galleon, meanwhile, have abandoned themselves completely to sensuality. On the basis of the fool perched on an anchor and the large bell hanging from the ram's head at the bow, Veldman identifies this as the Ship of Fools, an ancient allegory warning of human moral and intellectual weakness.[13] She notes that this combination of human folly and the improper use of the senses—the "real evildoers"—also appears in satirically moralistic literature of the fifteenth and sixteenth centuries, specifically in an allegorical tract written in 1498 by the south

Netherlandish humanist Jodocus Badius Ascensius (d. 1535) that stated, "Stultiiferae naves sensus animosque trahentes / mortis in exitium" (Ships of fools that drag senses and souls / to death and ruin).[14]

Veldman aptly points out that both cosmic forces—common sense and sensuality—are natural. In the relatively larger and brighter group of musicians on the left, she recognizes a positive reference to the tempering of human nature. Although similar in some ways to Van Heemskerck's print of the Prodigal Son from 1562, this is not the Prodigal Son with sex workers indulging in the sensual pleasures of drink and flesh but a serious group of musicians and muses.[15] As Veldman notes, "Seen from this viewpoint, the group making music in the Pasadena picture can be interpreted in a positive light, as an exhortation to practice the arts in order to temper and regulate human nature so as to avoid excesses of the kind taking place in and on the water."[16] The sixteenth-century author Natale Comes (*Mythologiae*, 1551) noted that "for those who study, the musical, poetic skills are not in the habit of being simply lustful or inhuman, since leisure and ignorance encourage vice, but the acquisition of knowledge leads to virtue."[17] Indeed, music has a long association with reason because of its mathematical basis.[18] Veldman concludes that both the painting's fantastical Greco-Roman setting and its emphasis on the senses and rationality embody the humanism genre.[19]

Beyond these iconographic readings of the painting, there are several important details that suggest the artist was addressing a political dimension related to the disturbing events of 1566 and 1567. The year 1567, the date Van Heemskerck inscribed on the base of the statue of Natura, was the year the Duke of Alva (1507–1582) assumed the position of governor-general of the seventeen states of the Netherlands. He had been sent from Spain to the Netherlands to suppress the uprisings and desecration of Catholic churches, which had begun the previous year in opposition to the oppressive policies of the Roman Catholic Church enforced by the Spanish overlords. Responding to the increasingly unstable situation, Alva imposed even harsher punishments to maintain order and ensure the supremacy of Catholicism in the Netherlands. The result was greater persecution and terror throughout the region.

The details of *Allegory of Nature* suggest that Van Heemskerck was making a political statement about these turbulent and terrifying events. In 1565 he had begun publishing a series of prints engraved by Dirck Volkertsz. Coornhert (1522–1590) showing enraged men wielding hammers and axes to destroy idolatrous temples and statues. In the Pasadena painting, dated 1567, the double-headed eagle on the flag suspended from the bowsprit of the galleon identifies the Ship of Fools and its courtier passengers with the Habsburgs—and, thus, with the dreaded Spanish regime. As the ship moves toward the left, it is followed by the stag hunt, a prerogative of the nobility and a familiar metaphor for war.[20] In this context, the musical group on the left represents peace, the rational alternative to war.[21]

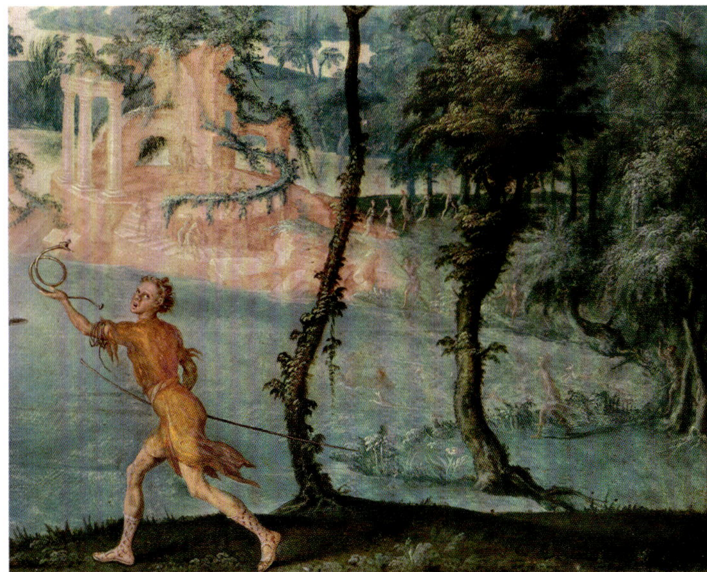

Fig. 31d. Detail of hunters.

Van Heemskerck understood Nature in terms of the philosophy of the Stoics, which extols Nature as Supreme Reason. A philosophy arising in Rome during the first century out of the need to find solace in times of disruption and conflict, Stoicism was revived in the sixteenth century by intellectuals such as Erasmus (1466–1536) and Justus Lipsius (1547–1606), who sought to reconcile the ancient pagan philosophy with Christianity, viewing Nature as an expression of the Divine organized in accordance with principles of human reason. The aim of such Christian Stoicism was to lead an ethical life, defined as living according to Nature, which follows the cycles of the seasons and of day and night. Van Heemskerck and the writer and engraver Coornhert were among the leading Dutch intellectuals interested in the revival of Stoicism, which marked a reorientation away from the emphasis on theological themes to the study of man and of nature without specific reference to God.[22]

The references to contemporary events expand Veldman's interpretation into a political metaphor, which equates the repression the Spanish imposed in 1567 with *sensualitas* and the musicians with peace and reason. The Ship of Fools, which flies the Habsburg flag, and the metaphorical stag hunt clearly threaten peace. The prominence of the statue of Natura surrounded by references to the cycles of life and situated between war and peace suggests that the humanist Van Heemskerck sought solace from the threat of impending war in the Stoic concept of Nature as Supreme Reason. The placement of the date on the base of the statue seems to accentuate the reference.[23] *Allegory of Nature* appears to represent Van Heemskerck's resolve and acceptance of war as part of Nature's order.

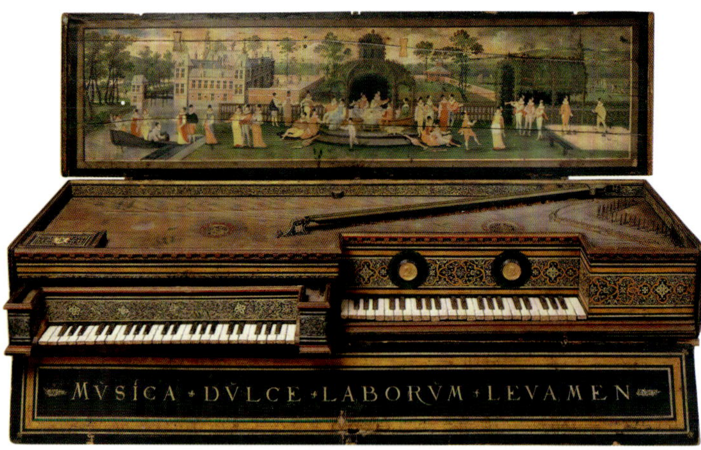

Fig. 31e. Hans Ruckers I, *Double Virginal*, 1581, Chordophone-Zither-plucked-virginal (pine, beech, poplar, mahogany, paint, gesso, metal, parchment, brass), 19½ × 71¾ in. (49.5 × 182.2 cm), The Metropolitan Museum of Art, New York.

The original function of the oblong panel is not known. Weston suggested that *Allegory of Nature* was originally painted as a cover for a double virginal, a harpsicord with two separate keyboards. He based his theory on the musical subject of the painting and the similarity of it to the cover of a double virginal made in Antwerp by Hans Ruckers I (ca. 1545–1594) in 1581 (fig. 31e).[24] This theory does not, however, appear to be substantiated by either the physical condition of the panel or the iconographical content of the image.

Typically, the iconography of musical instruments includes idyllic scenes, often with people playing music, but never with negative or moralizing content. The portrayal of the Ship of Fools would, therefore, be unusual. Laurence Liben, curator of musical instruments at the Metropolitan Museum of Art, recently pointed out that the panel does not exhibit the typical characteristics of a Flemish virginal lid, which were usually constructed of a single panel painted with a scene on the interior and with marbleizing on the exterior. The interior scene was usually bordered by a painted frame, and the panel was hinged to the actual instrument along the bottom edge of the lid.[25] None of these expected characteristics is present on the Pasadena painting. There is no evidence of the panel having been attached to hinges; the painting extends to the upper and lower edges of the panel but not to the right and left sides, where there is an unpainted margin of wood approximately ⅜ inch wide. The back of the panel is painted with a simple layer of reddish-brown paint over which there is a light coat of brown paint.[26] This suggests that Van Heemskerck painted *Allegory of Nature* not as the cover of a virginal but for another purpose.

Paintings, particularly landscapes, with similar proportions were popular from the mid-sixteenth into the seventeenth century. They were typically hung high in rooms as overdoors, mantel decoration, or part of a frieze. The unpainted side margins of the Pasadena painting suggest that the unbeveled panel was inserted into a grooved frame on the sides. This may indicate that that the painting was not originally displayed in an independent frame but was instead framed by the molding of a room, perhaps on a fireplace.[27]

The painting's provenance offers an intriguing explanation for the panel's origins. The first known reference to *Allegory of Nature* was in 1910, when it was exhibited in Liège as the property of Paul van Zuylen, a resident of that city. The painting remained in the possession of the Barons Van Zuylen van Nyevelt until 1973, when it was sold at auction in London. In 1567, the date of the painting, Willem van Zuylen van Nyevelt, Lord of Bergambacht en Aartsberge (1538–1608), played an important role in the Dutch resistance and uprising against the Spanish, which was led by William I (1533–1584), Prince of Orange and Count of Nassau and from 1572 stadtholder of the United Provinces of the Netherlands. As a close friend of William I, Van Zuylen was a member of the Alliance of Noblemen that petitioned Margaret of Parma (1522–1586), Habsburg regent of the Netherlands (r. 1559–67) on 5 April 1566. He was later identified by the Duke of Alva and the Council of Troubles (1567–74) as being the leader of the iconoclasts in Utrecht, Culenborg, Vianen, and Asperen. Van Zuylen fled the Netherlands in 1568, and his goods were confiscated. He was later able to return and reassume an important political role.[28] It is tempting to consider that Willem van Zuylen commissioned Van Heemskerck to paint *Allegory of Nature*. In addition to being a soldier, he was a respected intellectual who shared the philosophical as well as political views of Coornhert and Van Heemskerck, whom he probably knew. The presence of the painting in the residence of the Van Zuylen family since the sixteenth century, particularly if it were installed in the paneling, would help explain its not having been known before 1910. Additional research into the Van Zuylen family may further elucidate the provenance of the painting and thus its iconography.

1. Noted as "C. Hughes" in the sale summary.

2. In correspondence with the Museum (22 January 1997, NSM), H. Colin Slim, professor emeritus of music, University of California, Irvine, identified the instrument, explaining that the lute has eight strings, four pegs, and eight frets. It should have double courses of strings, but here it does not. Although Slim found that Van Heemskerck painted very detailed, readable, and recognizable music scores in other paintings, the sheet music in this painting is stylized and does not represent actual music. Slim 1997 identified the instrument as a *viol de fantaisie* and noted that the woman is playing it in reverse of the usual technique; it is typically held and fingered by the left hand and bowed with the right. The artist was probably taking artistic license so that the figures would contribute to the unity of the composition. The instrument, which appears in other paintings by Heemskerck, is also inaccurate in that it has five pegs but only three strings and three frets.

3. Noted by Slim, who questioned why Heemskerck included a single classical instrument (22 January 1997, NSM).

4. Slim identified the positive organ, which lies on a table when played (22 January 1997, NSM). Tintoretto (1519–1594) included a positive organ in two paintings representing *Contest between the Muses and Pierians*: In one version, a Muse blows the positive organ (Museo di Castelvecchio, Verona); in the other, a near-naked man provides the wind source (Bayerische Staatsgemäldesammlungen, Munich). See Weddigen 1984, ills. pp. 77, 87. I am grateful to Slim for directing me to this information.

5. Grosshans 1980, p. 247, calls him a herald; Slim suggested that he is the ship's captain (22 January 1997, NSM).

6. Weston 1974a; Harrison 1987; Veldman 1996.

7. The ancients considered the sanctuary of Diana of the Ephesians—in Ephesus, in what is now Turkey—to be one of the Seven Wonders of the World. In 1570 Van Heemskerck reconstructed these monuments for a series of engravings: Hollstein 1949–2010, vol. 8, p. 245, nos. 357–64. The drawings, dated 1570, are in the Witt Collection, Courtauld Institute, London.

8. Weston 1974a. Grosshans 1980, p. 248; and Harrison 1987, pp. 921f., repeat this idea.

9. Veldman 1996, pp. 130–32; Harrison 1987, pp. 421f.; Grosshans 1980, p. 248, suggests they represent the four elements.

10. As Veldman points out, "The four seasons are an essential aspect of Nature in this painting. The importance of this unchanging annual cycle . . . is underscored by the gifts that the genii are bringing the goddess of Nature." Veldman 1996, p. 132.

11. Veldman 1996, p. 132. Hollstein 1949–2010, vol. 8, p. 245, nos. 538–41. The idea derived from Ovid, *Metamorphoses* 2:27–30. Regarding the iconography, see Veldman 1980.

12. Veldman 1996, p. 136.

13. Grosshans 1980 and Harrison 1987 also make this association. Regarding the influence of Sebastian Brant's (1458–1521) satire *Ship of Fools* (1494), see Veldman 1986.

14. Veldman 1996, p. 134. The book was illustrated by six woodcuts, each with a rowboat: Adam and Eve were in one; each of the other rowboats had figures referring to one of the five senses.

15. Veldman 1996, pp. 136–38, elaborates her comparison. Slim (September 1998, NSM), however, countered her identification of the man, noting that his costume is virtually identical to that of the Prodigal Son (Grosshans 1980, pl. 121).

16. Veldman 1996, p. 138. See also Veldman 2019, pp. 43f., where she notes the placement, behind and to the left of the musicians, of a large, wicker fish trap: "A well-known symbol of the trap in which human beings easily find themselves when captured in the crafty schemes of the other sex."

17. Veldman 1996, p. 138, cites Veldman 1985, p. 40.

18. See, for example, the inscription on a print by Coornhert that refers to harmony in terms of moderation and reason: "When the senses hark to reason's measure, and when that measure restrains all free will, then there is nothing sweeter than that harmony." Veldman 1996, p. 139; see also Slim 1993.

19. Veldman 1996, p. 139.

20. Because of its emphasis on arms and horsemanship, hunting was considered ideal training for war. See Rosand 1969, p. 38.

21. At the end of the sixteenth century, a favorite metaphor for peace as a rational alternative to war was the story of Orpheus, who convinced the animals to live in peace not through brute force but through the sound of his lyre. See Langedijk 1976, pp. 33–52.

22. In 1586 Coornhert published *Zedekunst, dat is Wellevenskunste* (Ethics, that is the Art of Living Well). Coornhert offered a didactic guide based on his own philosophy of Erasmian Christianity with a strong element of Stoicism. The major figure in the revival of Stoicism in the Netherlands was Justus Lipsius (professor of history at the University of Leyden, 1579–92), who sought to accommodate ancient pagan philosophy with Christianity. His major work, *De Constantia* (1589), provided a new structure for the comprehension of the world. The chief aim of Lipsius's Christian Stoicism was to lead an ethical life. He defined a moral life as living according to Nature, which he equated with God, Supreme Reason. Fundamental to one's understanding of the moral life was an understanding of Nature or God, which could be learned by study and examination of the real world.

23. Because the date is separate from the artist's name and placed in such a prominent position, it is possible it was meant as an historical reference rather than the date the artist completed the painting.

24. Weston 1974a. Veldman 1996, p. 139, accepts this suggestion, if only in passing.

25. Weston misinterpreted the construction of the virginal lid in the Metropolitan Museum. He assumed that the painting was set into the frame, but the frame is actually painted on the panel itself. The dimensions of the Pasadena panel are also inappropriate for the lid of a virginal.

26. The date of this coat of paint is unknown and could have been added later.

27. Two vertical stripes, one on either end of the back, appear to have been made by strips of wood previously glued to the back of the panel. It is possible that these, in turn, were glued or otherwise attached to a wall.

28. Regarding Willem van Zuylen, see Molhuysen and Blok 1911–37, vol. 3 (1914), cols. 1526f., and Gaillard 1863, pt. 1, pp. 66–70.

32

Maarten van Heemskerck

Dutch
Heemskerck 1498–1574 Haarlem

Boaz, His Kinsman, and the Elders at the Gate

1549

Signed, lower left, in brown ink: ". Martinus . Heemskerck ."
Dated, lower left, in brown ink: "1549"

Inscribed, lower right, in brown ink, by a seventeenth-century hand: "Marten Hemskerck 3."
Brown ink over black chalk, partially squared in black chalk, partially incised, on off-white antique laid paper, 11¼ × 16 15⁄16 in. (28.6 × 43 cm)
Norton Simon Art Foundation, M.1975.24.D

Provenance
Anonymous [Sotheby's, London, 27 June 1974, lot 153, sold to]; Norton Simon, deeded 30 December 1975 to; Norton Simon Art Foundation.

Exhibited
On loan, Henry Art Gallery, University of Washington, Seattle, 9 August 1974–12 December 1974.

References
Hollstein 1993–, vol. 1, pt. 1, p. 90, under no. 91; S. Campbell 2010, p. 368, no. 1061; "Curator's comments," British Museum website, accessed October 13, 2023, https://www.britishmuseum.org/collection/object/P_1949-0709-42.

Technical Notes
The support is a sheet of off-white laid paper attached overall to a sheet of antique laid paper with a watermark of a later date. The design is drawn in pen and brown ink over a black chalk underdrawing, with the left half of the composition squared in black chalk. The design is incised for transfer (visible using raking light, most clearly on the foremost of the large columns in the left foreground and the pyramid in the right distance). The incised lines are difficult to see as a result of flattening from pressure during the lining process. There is a small edge tear at the left lower edge as well as two small holes at the lower right edge from framing nails, brown spots from glue or oil near the right edge, and a touch of red chalk near the top edge as indications of the sheet's further use. Glue residue from a previous mounting remains on the original support, causing mild distortion at the corners. The brown ink shows signs of fading overall consistent with use and the age of the drawing.

The prolific Haarlem master Maarten van Heemskerck had a long and successful career as a painter of altarpieces and other religious pictures, as well as portraits, allegories, and mythological scenes (see cat. 31). Hardly less significant than Van Heemskerck's achievement as a painter is the oeuvre of some six hundred etchings and engravings made by specialist printmakers from his designs.[1] From an early date these widely circulated images formed the basis of his international reputation. Giorgio Vasari (1511–1574) mentioned the numerous prints made after Van Heemskerck's compositions in the 1568 edition of his *Lives*, and in 1604 the Dutch biographer and art theorist Karel van Mander (1548–1606) wrote: "He was a very good designer, yes: a man who, in a manner of speaking, filled the world with his inventions. . . . There would be no end of it if one wanted to relate how many prints have already been published by him."[2] A few of the prints are after paintings, but the vast majority reproduce detailed pen-and-ink drawings. Hundreds of these have survived, and they, too, have long commanded the admiration of scholars and collectors. Neatly executed with clearly defined contours and sharp, distinct parallel lines and cross-hatchings for shading, they provided easily translatable models for the printmakers who copied them onto copper plates. In Van Mander's account, Van Heemskerck "had a very subtle manner of drawing with the pen, and was very precise in shading, with a deft, light way of handling."[3] The first of his collaborators was Dirck Volkertsz. Coornhert (1522–1590), an engraver and moral philosopher with whom Van Heemskerck worked from 1548 to 1559. Initially, they probably copublished their prints in Haarlem, but from 1553 onward most were issued in Antwerp by Hieronymus Cock (1518–1570) and marketed there by Cock and the printer-publisher Christoffel Plantijn (1520–1589).[4] Later, the Antwerp master Philips Galle (1537–1612), among others, engraved and published Van Heemskerck's compositions, which he continued to design into the 1570s. Many were produced in series, including Old and New Testament narrative cycles, devotional imagery, mythological scenes, and allegorical subjects.[5]

Boaz, His Kinsman, and the Elders at the Gate served as the model for the right-hand plate of an exceptionally large two-plate etching by Coornhert, where it is reproduced in reverse and virtually identical in size (fig. 32a).[6] The print is signed by both Heemskerck and Coornhert and dated 1550, a year later than the drawing. An inscription next to the signatures on the print—"rüth. 2."—cites chapter 2 of the biblical book of Ruth, where the narrative begins. Impressive in size and teeming with antiquarian detail, the Pasadena drawing

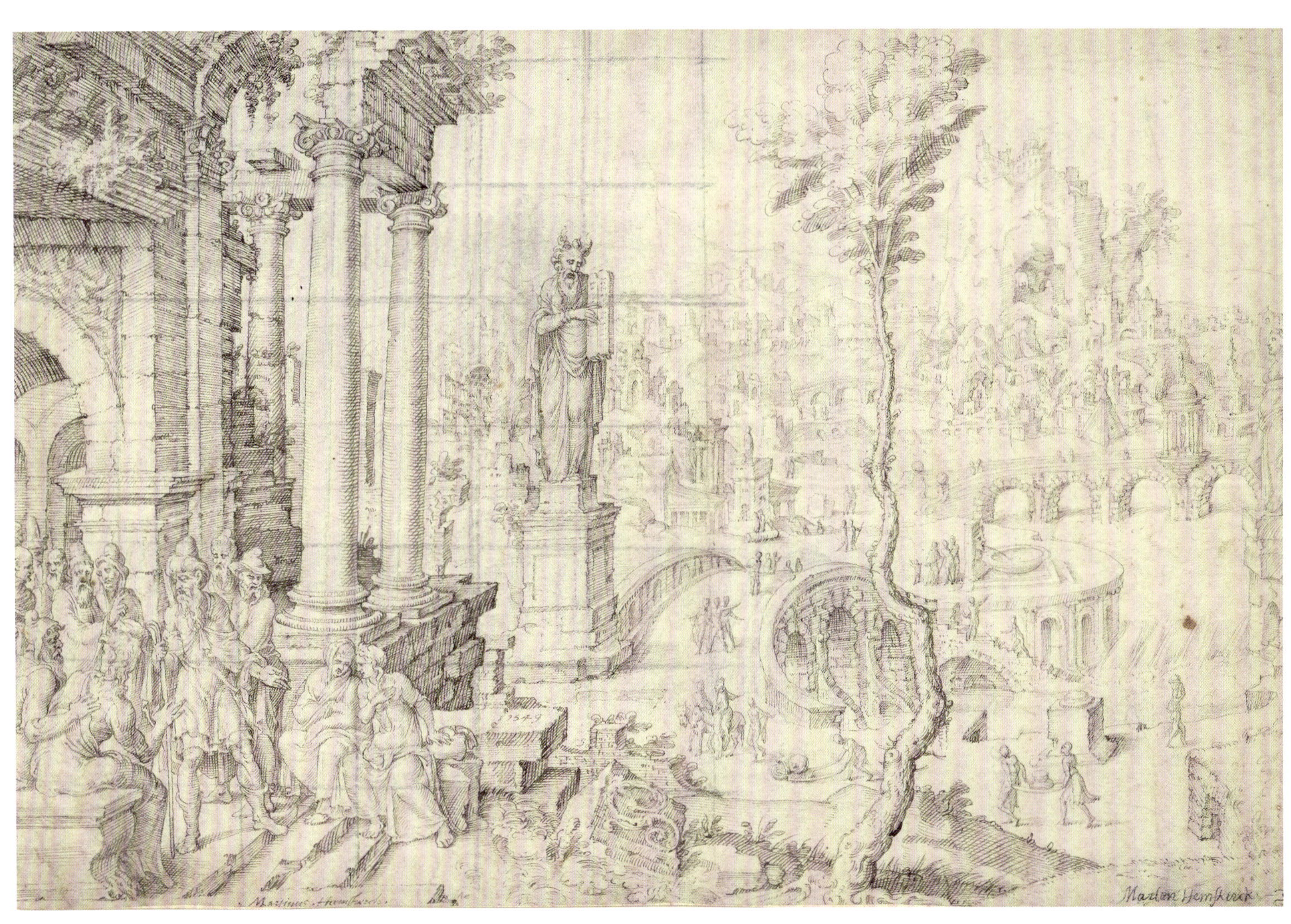

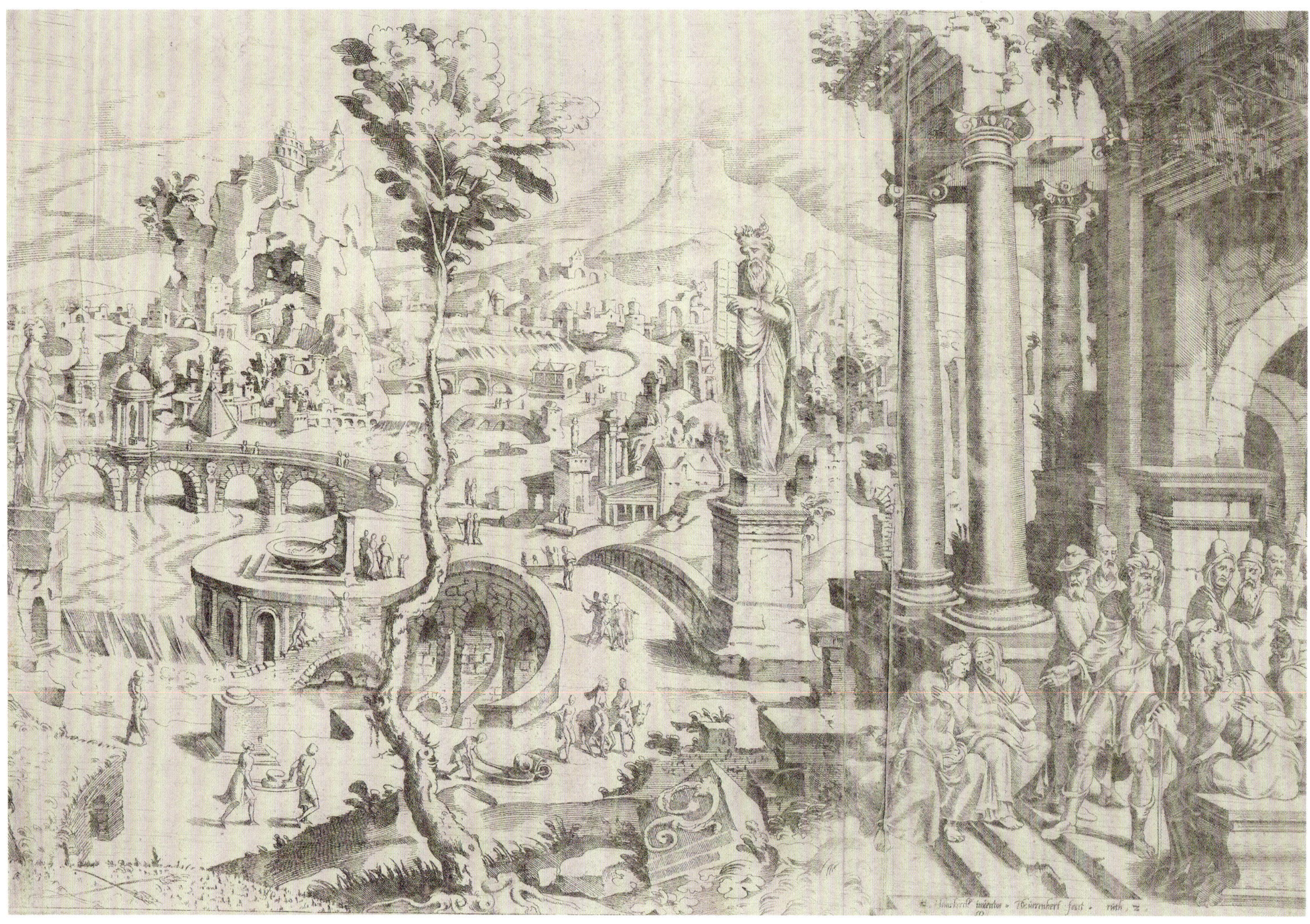

Fig. 32a. Dirk Volkertsz. Coornhert, after Maarten van Heemskerck, *Boaz and Ruth*, 1550, engraving and etching, right plate: 11⅛ × 28¼ in. (28.2 × 42.5 cm), British Museum, London.

is an outstanding example of Van Heemskerk's work of this kind. He must have prepared a model of the same dimensions for the left-hand plate, but it has not come to light.

Following his customary practice, Van Heemskerck started work on the sheet by sketching the outlines of the composition in black chalk. Only a few of these lines—for example, the original contour of the bridge railing in the center middle ground—are now visible to the unaided eye. With a sharp pen and ink, he worked up the details and shading over this preliminary sketch in a manner consistent with that of other early models for prints.[7] The left half of the sheet, which includes the figures essential to the narrative and the densely worked architectural details in the foreground, was squared in black chalk. The majority of the models Van Heemskerck provided to Coornhert in the late 1540s were partially squared or squared overall, so the presence of the grid here conforms to other technical evidence of their collaboration.[8] The contours of the finished composition have been impressed with a stylus to trace the design onto the etching ground. It is unclear why, in this and other early models for prints, the drawings were both incised and squared. Squaring usually served to facilitate the transfer of a design to a larger or smaller support, but these were intended to be reproduced in their original size, a result best obtained by tracing the composition directly onto the plate. Later designs by Van Heemskerck for prints, including those produced by Coornhert after 1550, were nearly always incised, but not squared.[9]

The large etching summarizes in two episodes the nadir and redemption of Ruth's fortunes (Ruth 1–4). In a time of famine, Naomi and her husband, Elimelech, left Bethlehem and settled in Moab. Their two sons married Moabite women, Ruth and Orpah, but when Elimelech and both sons died, Naomi and her daughters-in-law were left destitute. While Naomi resolved to return to her late husband's kinsmen in Bethlehem, she urged the young widows to remain with their Moabite families. Ruth refused, insisting on accompanying Naomi and adopting her people and her God. They arrived during the barley harvest, and Naomi sent Ruth to glean in fields owned by Boaz, a wealthy relative of Elimelech. The left plate shows Ruth stooping to glean in the center foreground, while the harvest proceeds in the distance. Standing to the left of her, Boaz, aware of Ruth's reputation as a virtuous woman who remained faithful to Naomi, instructs his foreman to allow her to glean in his fields and share the food and drink distributed to the other harvesters. In the right plate (which reverses the Norton Simon drawing), Boaz has gathered ten elders at the city gate of Bethlehem to witness his negotiation with another kinsman for the right to purchase land that had belonged to Elimelech and marry Ruth. Naomi and Ruth sit to the side while Boaz, in the center of the group of men, completes the transaction and one of the elders raises his hand in blessing. Boaz and Ruth had a son, who was a direct ancestor of both King David and Jesus of Nazareth.

After working in Haarlem in the late 1520s with Jan van Scorel (1495–1562), Van Heemskerck—like Van Scorel before him—traveled to Rome, where he remained about four years (1532–36/37). There he drew assiduously from ancient architecture and sculpture, studied the works of Raphael, Michelangelo, and Giulio Romano, and developed the dynamic Italianate manner and antiquarian sophistication that he cultivated for the rest of his life. The muscular, athletically poised figure of Ruth bending to glean among the unbound stalks in the left plate of the etching unmistakably reflects his study of Michelangelo. As exhaustively analyzed by Arthur J. DiFuria, the landscape in the two-plate etching combines reminiscences of drawings Van Heemskerck made of Roman architectural remains with invented structures based on his memories of the city's ancient ruins. The result is a wholly imaginary setting for a narrative that takes place, not in Rome, but in Bethlehem, with only a prominent statue of Moses atop a column to hint at the biblical source.[10] As DiFuria explains, even when the text he illustrated prescribed a definite locale, Van Heemskerck resorted to such "fictive, Rome-inspired" spaces in his print designs. In so doing, he did not intend to disassociate the visual setting from the text. The imaginary landscapes inspired by Van Heemskerck's knowledge of ancient Rome provided his histories with an adaptable, nonspecific stage that flaunted his capacity for invention to a sixteenth-century humanist audience steeped in the culture of antiquity.[11] —*William W. Robinson and Nancy E. Yocco*

1. Ilja Veldman in Hollstein 1993–, vol. 1, passim.

2. Van Mander/Miedema 1994–99, vol. 1, p. 245, vol. 4, p. 79n120.

3. Van Mander/Miedema 1994–99, vol. 1, p. 246.

4. Ilja M. Veldman in Haarlem 1986b, p. 14.

5. Haarlem 1986a, pp. 14–15.

6. Dirk Volkertsz. Coornhert, after Maarten van Heemskerck, *Boaz and Ruth*, engraving and etching, two plates, 1550; 287 × 428 mm (left), 283 × 425 mm (right). London, British Museum, inv. Nos. 1949,0709.42 (left) and 1949,0709.43 (right). Hollstein 1993–, vol. 1, pt. 1, pp. 90–91, no. 90.

7. Compare Garff 1971, nos. 1–31.

8. Of the thirty-one drawings datable to 1548 and 1549 in the Statens Museum for Kunst, Copenhagen, nearly all of which were engraved by Coornhert, nineteen or twenty show traces of squaring in black chalk. Garff 1971, nos. 1, 5–21, 22(?), and 24.

9. See, for example, the Copenhagen drawings, Garff 1971, nos. 32–135.

10. DiFuria 2017, pp. 410–14; and DiFuria 2019, pp. 193, 195, 212–15.

11. DiFuria 2019, pp. 192, 214–15.

33

Jan van der Heyden

Dutch
Gorinchem 1637–1712 Amsterdam

Townscape with Gothic Church

ca. 1670

Oil on panel, 13 3/8 × 15 3/4 in. (34 × 40 cm)
Norton Simon Art Foundation, M.1982.1.2.P

Provenance
Pieter van Winter (1745–1807), Amsterdam, bequeathed to his daughter;[1] Anna Louisa Agatha (Annewies) van Loon-van Winter (1793–1877), bequeathed 1877 to;[2] her children, sold 1877 to;[3] Edmond James (1845–1934), Baron de Rothschild, Paris and Château Rothschild, Boulogne-Billancourt, Hauts-de-Seine, by descent to his daughter; Miriam Caroline Alexandrine Rothschild (1884–1965), Château Rothschild, Boulogne-Billancourt, Hauts-de-Seine, confiscated 1940 by the Einsatzstab Reichsleiter Rosenberg, ERR no. R857,[4] stored at Altaussee, no. 212/32; recovered by Allied forces and transported to the Munich Central Collecting Point, inv. no. 218. Restituted to the Rothschild family, presumably before May 1946.[5] Max Wassermann, Paris, 1967. [E. V. Thaw & Co., New York, sold 1982 to]; Norton Simon Art Foundation.

Exhibited
Paris 1911, p. 13, no. 69, lent by Baron Edmond de Rothschild.

References
J. Smith 1829–42, vol. 5, no. 119; Eastlake 1858–60, 30 October 1860, pt. III, p. 19; Dayot 1912a, p. 130, no. 70, ill. op. p. 46; Hofstede de Groot 1908–27, vol. 8 (1927), p. 379, no. 163;[6] Wagner 1971, p. 85, no. 80; Sluijter 1973, pp. 2, 249, fig. 5;[7] Pasadena 1989, p. 66, ill.; Priem 1997, pp. 220, no. 71, 227; Sutton 2006, p. 49, fig. 42; Greenwich/Amsterdam 2006–07, p. 49, fig. 42; S. Campbell 2010, p. 435, no. 1688, ill., Avery-Quash 2011, vol. 1, p. 550 [f. 19r].

Technical Notes
The original support is a horizontally grained oak panel, the bottom edge of which has a wide bevel unlike the plain-cut sides and top. The original panel is set into a flush-fitting, one-piece frame, cut from a slightly larger oak panel of matching grain and thickness, save for broadly beveled edges. The original panel was let into a cut-out depression in the face of this frame, which is open in the center. An X-radiograph shows the sides of the original panel were thinned along a vertically cut incision from the back, approximately one inch from the edge, to form a lap joint with the corresponding depression in the frame. The top and bottom edges of the original panel were not thinned and remain visible on the recto and verso. Adhesive residue, possibly animal glue, is seen in all joints between the panel and frame. All edges of the original panel bear remnants of aged brown-paper tape on the verso, confirming that the painting was at one time shown in its original smaller size without the supplemental support. A tightly mended split extending horizontally across the verso of the original panel below the centerline, with several other incomplete horizontal cracks above it at left, suggest the stabilizing intent of the added frame.

The painting extends to the four edges of the original panel; the surrounding margins, approximately a half inch wide, are created by the support frame. The original panel was prepared with a white ground in a smooth, thin layer. The borders created by the added panel have a smooth white ground that is slightly thicker. A rose-beige underpainting, visible throughout the sky, provides the mid-tone in the large clouds at the upper right as well as in the distant buildings at the right. The highly finished scene is meticulously rendered. Details of architecture, including the pointing of brick masonry, were drawn with a very fine brush and liquid paint having low viscosity; tree leaves are tiny globules of dark green paint. The blue sky and the thin gray clouds were painted with extremely thin washes over the rose underpainting; however, this area may have been thinned to some degree by solvent abrasion. Paint on the borders appears to have been partially scraped away, supporting a theory that the added panel was adapted from a previous use. In some places, thin, sketchy paint appears to have been applied with the intention of continuing design elements of the painting. In addition to retouching in the upper right sky, which probably covers abrasion, retouching of smaller losses is located along the upper edge and the right edge, where the join of the secondary panel meets the original, in small losses to the left of the church spire, and along the lower left side. Ultraviolet-light examination indicates the clear, thinly applied varnish is a natural resin.

Townscape with Gothic Church is one of the most appealing of the many realistic views and "capriccios"—architectural fantasies composed of elements fabricated, at least partially, from existing buildings—of Amsterdam and other cities and country estates that Jan van der Heyden painted during the second half of the seventeenth century. Typical of his topographical paintings, *Townscape with Gothic Church* portrays the quiet, early hours of an ideal summer day. Far

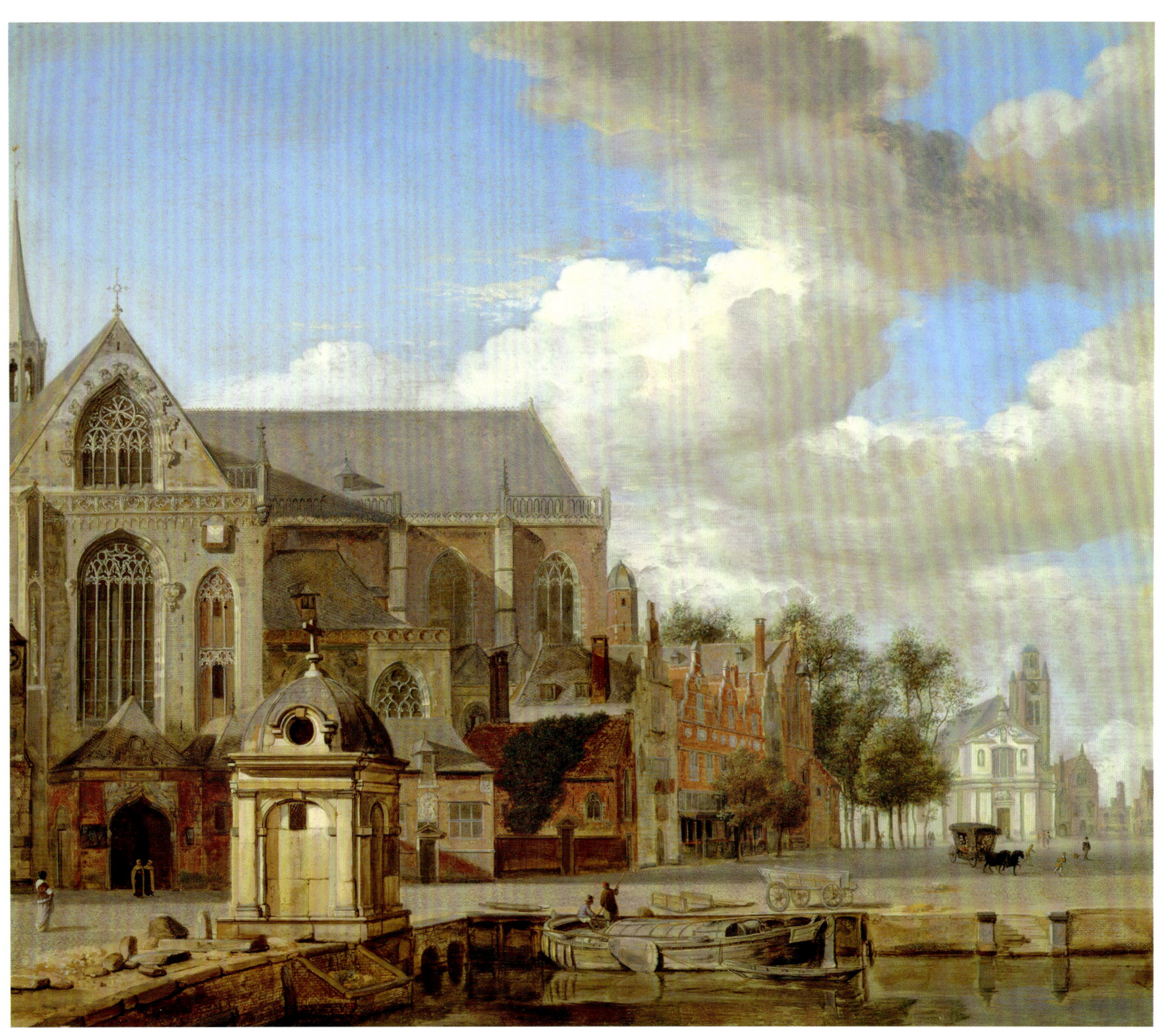

removed from the reality of overcrowded cities, the clean, peaceful scene recalls the positive descriptions of cities, villages, and even streets in contemporary poems that reflect the optimism that followed the peace with Spain in 1648.[8] With increased security in the countryside came an enthusiasm for travel and an interest in maps, guidebooks, and travelers' accounts, as well as topographical images of distant and local scenes.[9] Like maps, prints, and modern postcards, the painted views of Dutch and neighboring cities by Jan van der Heyden and his contemporaries Gerard Houckgeest (ca. 1600–1661) and Gerrit Adriaensz. Berckheyde (1638–1698) celebrated landmarks of historical and cultural interest for travelers and local citizens.[10]

Assuming a low vantage point, Van der Heyden represents a casual view of a large Gothic church situated on a town square bounded by a canal, at the end of which is a small domed building surmounted by a cross. In the distant right, a carriage crosses a cobblestone square with a church, the facade of which includes niches with sculptures reminiscent of Italian Baroque churches. A limited number of carefully placed figures—a woman walking on the left, two priests outside the entrance to the church, another two men on the boat in the foreground, and a passing carriage—subtly animate and help to integrate the scene without detracting from the architectural forms. Although Van der Heyden's prints on firefighting reveal his ability to render figures in motion, his friend and frequent collaborator Adriaen van de Velde (1636–1672) was probably responsible for the carefully placed and clearly articulated figures.[11]

The organization of the scene along a diagonal that extends from the end of the canal on the left past the row of houses to the distant sunlit church testifies to Van der Heyden's knowledge of the principles of perspective as illustrated in books by Sebastiano Serlio (1475–1554) and others.[12] Van der Heyden achieved the illusion of an integrated space by combining the consistent perspective with an equally controlled rendering of light and shadow. By limiting the range of subtly varied tones of ochres, grays, and red and manipulating sunlight and shadow, Van der Heyden suggested a pervasive atmosphere that modulates the delicate brushstrokes used to render details. Skillfully, he described the texture of the mortar between the bricks, the tracery of windows, and the costumes of passengers in the passing coach without distorting the perspective or the overall balance of the individual details or composition. Arnold Houbraken (1660–1719), his earliest biographer, marveled at Van der Heyden's technique, noting that he drew from life and later executed the scene on panel, painting every little stone in the building so minutely that one could clearly see the mortar in the grooves in the foreground as well as the background and taking into account the diminishing scale of the stones according to the reduction in size of the buildings.[13]

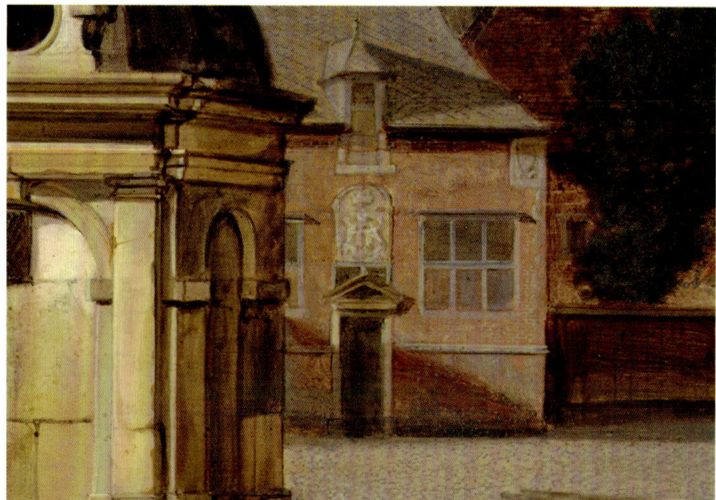

Fig. 33a. Detail of church with Amsterdam coat of arms.

The Gothic church in this painting is based on the Nieuwe Kerk in Amsterdam; indeed, the city crest appears on the wall above the side door to the church seen to the right of the domed building (fig. 33a). Located on the Dam in Amsterdam next to the recently completed City Hall (now the Royal Palace), the Nieuwe Kerk, which served a Calvinist congregation, was originally consecrated in 1410 as a Roman Catholic church dedicated to the Virgin Mary and Saint Catherine. Severely damaged by fire in 1645, the Nieuwe Kerk was represented accurately by Van der Heyden in a number of paintings, including *Dam Square in Amsterdam against City Hall and Nieuwe Kerk* (fig. 33b) and *Dam Square in Amsterdam*, ca. 1668 (Amsterdam Museum), both of which appear to have been based on the same drawing.

Comparison of the church in the Pasadena painting with that represented in the paintings in Basel and Amsterdam, as well as contemporary prints recording the historical appearance of the Nieuwe Kerk, reveals how Van der Heyden manipulated the appearance of the church and fabricated the setting.[14] *Townscape with Gothic Church* represents the church in reverse, suggesting that Van der Heyden used a counterproof of the drawing he employed for earlier paintings.[15] In addition to reversing the orientation of the building, Van der Heyden also changed the fenestration of the building, substituting two windows separated by a decorative frieze and defined by different tracery for the actual single window that reaches the full height of the transept above which is a sundial (fig. 33c).

The square structure at the foot of the canal resembles the small storage buildings or pump houses located along the side of canals. The unusual use of hard stone, as well as the domed roof, however, set it apart from these utilitarian structures. The cross that surmounts the dome suggests that it is a shrine that has fallen into disrepair. The similarity of the construction material and square form of the domed building recall the general characteristics of the Beckeneelhuisje.

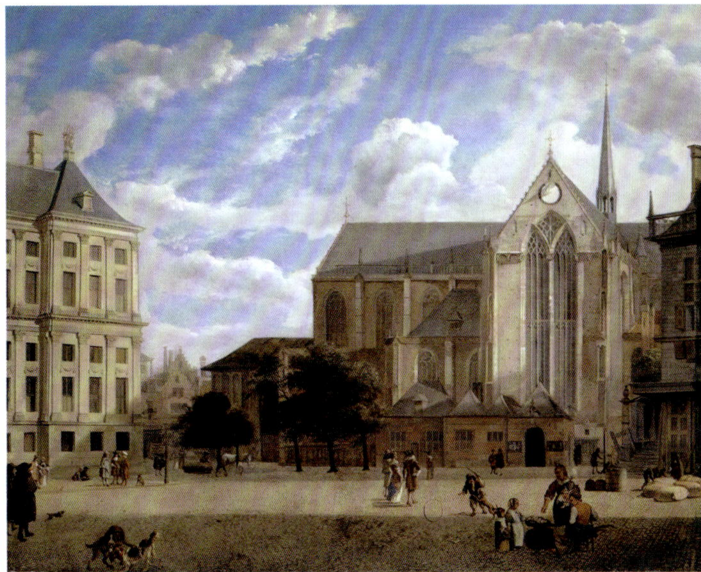

Fig. 33b. Jan van der Heyden, *Dam Square in Amsterdam against City Hall and Nieuwe Kerk*, ca. 1670, oil on oak, 17 ⅝ × 21 ¼ in. (44.9 × 56 cm), Kunstmuseum Basel, legacy of Max Geldner, Basel 1958.

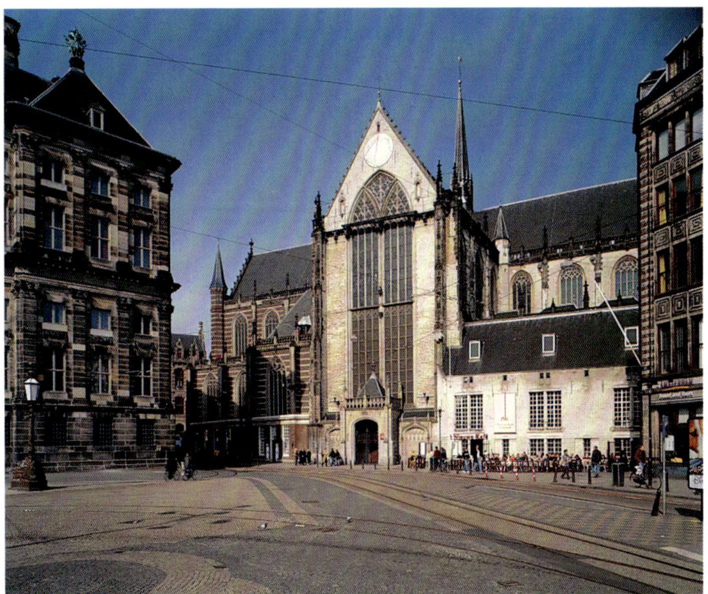

Fig. 33c. Exterior of the Nieuwe Kerk, Amsterdam, photograph courtesy of Erik and Petra Hesmerg.

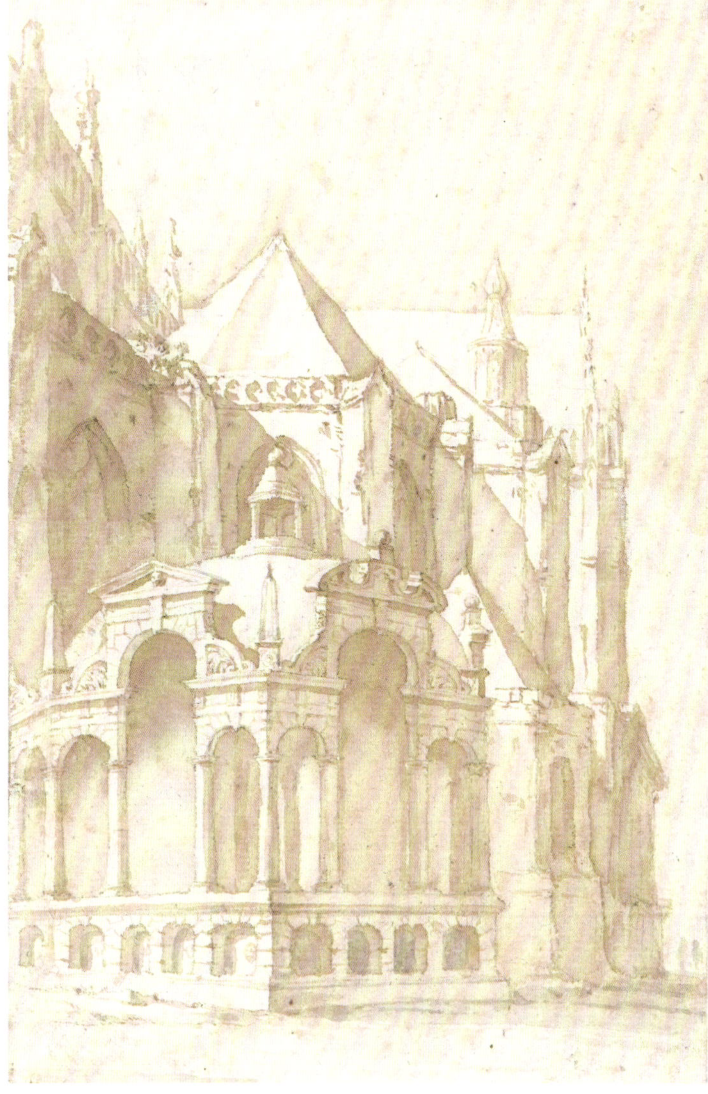

Fig. 33d. Jan de Bisschop, *Beckeneelhuisje aan de Nieuwe Kerk te Amsterdam*, 1648, paper and chalk, 5 ⅞ × 3 ⅞ in. (15 × 9.3 cm), Rijksmuseum, Amsterdam.

Designed by Joost Jansz. Bilhamer (1521–1590) and built in 1560 next to the northeast corner of the Nieuwe Kerk, this small building, which collapsed in 1656, was described by the Amsterdam historian Jan Wagenaar as a templelike structure constructed of attractive hardstone.[16] A drawing of the Beckeneelhuisje by Jan de Bisschop (1628–1671) dated 1648 (fig. 33d) represents it as a domed square building with pedimented niches in the center of each side and arched colonnades on the corners; a lantern surmounts the dome.[17] Although Van der Heyden's building is significantly simplified, its square, cube-like form and domed roof constructed of hardstone, both of which were unfamiliar, if not unique, in the Netherlands, suggest that he was thinking of the destroyed landmark when he included it in the Pasadena painting.

In contriving *Townscape with Gothic Church*, Jan van der Heyden was neither concerned with historical accuracy nor with telling a story. Rather, as in *The Herengracht, Amsterdam, from the Leliegracht* (Los Angeles County Museum of Art) and other paintings, he referred simply to the mundane activities of a city. His primary interest appears to have been to use architecture as the building blocks of his composition and as a vehicle for the description of light that glides over the surfaces of buildings, roads, and water, defining different textures and creating a sense of atmosphere as it guides the viewer through the fanciful city. Referring to what must have been a vast repertoire of drawings, he selected buildings that suited his needs for the composition without concern for their actual identities or associations. The Beckeneelhuisje, for example, was not a temple or a shrine but the place where the church placed the unclaimed human bones when they cleared tombs. By neither referring to an actual place or historical event, *Townscape with Gothic Church* engages the visual appeal of an ideal, well-ordered, prosperous city filled with sunlight.

1. Pieter van Winter was a trader in indigo and a man of letters who lived in Saxenburg House at 224 Keizersgracht (now part of the Pulitzer Hotel). Priem 1997, p. 220, no. 71. The collection of Pieter van Winter was to be divided among his three children at his death.

2. Of Pieter van Winter's heirs, only the sisters Anna Louisa Agatha and Lucretia Johanna wanted the paintings, so they divided the collection among themselves according to desired objects and value. In 1815 the Pasadena painting, with figures by Adriaen van de Velde (1636–1672), was valued at 1,000 guilders; see Priem 1997, p. 227. Anna Louisa Agatha was married to Jonkheer Willem van Loon (1790–1847), who also inherited part of their collection from his family. John Smith saw the Van Loon/Van Winter Collection in 1825, when the paintings were housed in the Van Loon residence at 499 Herengracht (J. Smith 1829–42, vol. 5, no. 119). See The Hague/San Francisco 1990, pp. 153f., 295f.

3. After a visit on 30 October 1860 to the Van Loon collection, Charles Eastlake described the painting in his diary: "V. der Heyden—A good specimen—A church—A little water in foreground. 1-3½ w. w-1½ h. wood." Eastlake 1858–60, p. 19r, and Avery-Quash 2011, vol. 1, p. 550. Gustave (1829–1911), Baron de Rothschild, paid the Van Loon family a half million guilders for the majority of the collection, which was to be divided between himself and other members of the Rothschild family; see Michael Hall to Carol Togneri, emails, 14 June 2005 and 10 April 2021 (NSM); see also The Hague/San Francisco 1990, p. 196.

4. The reverse of the ERR card notes, "Sichergestellt im Luftschutzkeller der Alexandrine Rothschild, Boulogne s.s."

5. Michael Hall to Carol Togneri, email, 10 April 2021 (NSM; see note 3).

6. Hofstede de Groot 1908–27, vol. 8 (1927), p. 379, no. 163, identifies it as "*The Choir of a Church*, 14 × 18 inches. The Gothic church may be the Nieuwe Kerk, Amsterdam, but surroundings are fanciful. Possibly identical with Hofstede de Groot 171a, *View of Town in Brabant* with figures by A. van de Velde; 14 × 16½ inches."

7. Figs. 5 and 8 in Sluijter 1973 are reversed. Therefore, when Sluijter notes "Het Duitse stadsgezicht dat de St. Pantaleon in Keulen en de St. Martin in Emmerik combineert (cat. nr. 64) (afb. 5)," he is actually referring to fig. 8, which was sold at Sotheby's, London, 6 December 1972, no. 32 and is Wagner 1971, no. 64.

8. Constantijn Huygens wrote a number of poems about various Dutch cities and towns, including Valckenburg, Loosduinen, Scheveningen, Rijswijk, 's-Gravenzande, and The Hague. See Huygens 1892–99, vol. 2, pp. 66ff.

9. With *Civitates orbis terrarum* (1581), Georg Braun and Frans Hogenberg published the first uniform collection of plans and views of cities from around the world; see Braun and Hogenberg [1618–23] 1966. They were followed by Joan Blaeu's *Toonneel der steden van de vereenighde Nederlanden, met hare Beschrijvingen* and *Toonneel der steden van 's konings Nederlanden, met hare Beschrijvingen*; see Blaeu 1649. Limited to plans and distant views, these popular atlases were often annotated with prints and drawings of specific places, people, and things. Large, elaborate wall maps like that of Pieter van de Kerre of 1611 (Sutro Library, San Francisco) incorporate images of plants, animals, and sailing vessels as well as mythological, historical, and contemporary figures within the actual maps and vignettes of cities, costumed figures, and national heroes—rulers, explorers, and geographers—in the borders of the most elaborate examples. Unfortunately, few of the large maps, which were produced in large numbers during the seventeenth century, have survived into this century. See Welu 1991, pp. 110f.; and Schilder and Welu 1980.

10. The 1632 inventory of the stadtholder Frederik Hendrik's collection at his palace Noordeinde (Drossaers and Lunsingh Scheurleer 1974–76, vol. 147, pp. 202f.) reveals how he displayed these paintings for political effect.

11. On the issue of collaborations, see P. Sutton 2006–07, pp. 56f.

12. Serlio [1611] 1980, with bk. 2 containing discussion on perspective. Regarding Van der Heyden's knowledge of perspective, see P. Sutton 2006–07, pp. 63–72.

13. Houbraken [1753] 1976, vol. 3, p. 81, based on a translation from Wallert 2006–07, p. 98. Houbraken suspected that the artist had "invented a means whereby . . . he could accomplish things that seem impossible with the customary ways of painting."

14. See, for example, the print by an anonymous artist after Pieter Hendriksz. Schut (ca. 1618–after 1660): Rijksmuseum, Amsterdam, no. RP-P-AO-23-14A.

15. The west end, rather than the apse, appears on the right, and the three small structures with pitched roofs, including the entrance to the south transept, extend toward the right rather than left.

16. See Wagenaar [1760–67] 1971–72. Also known as the "dead bones house" (*doodsbeenderenhuisje*), it was the place where human bones were kept after graves were cleared. I am grateful to Carolyn Mensing, Trineke Thorig, and Ilona van Tuinen at the Rijksprentenkabinet and Leonora van Sloten at the Rembrandthuis for their help in directing me to information about the Beckeneelhuisje.

17. Brush in brown and gray, black chalk on paper, 150 × 93 mm.

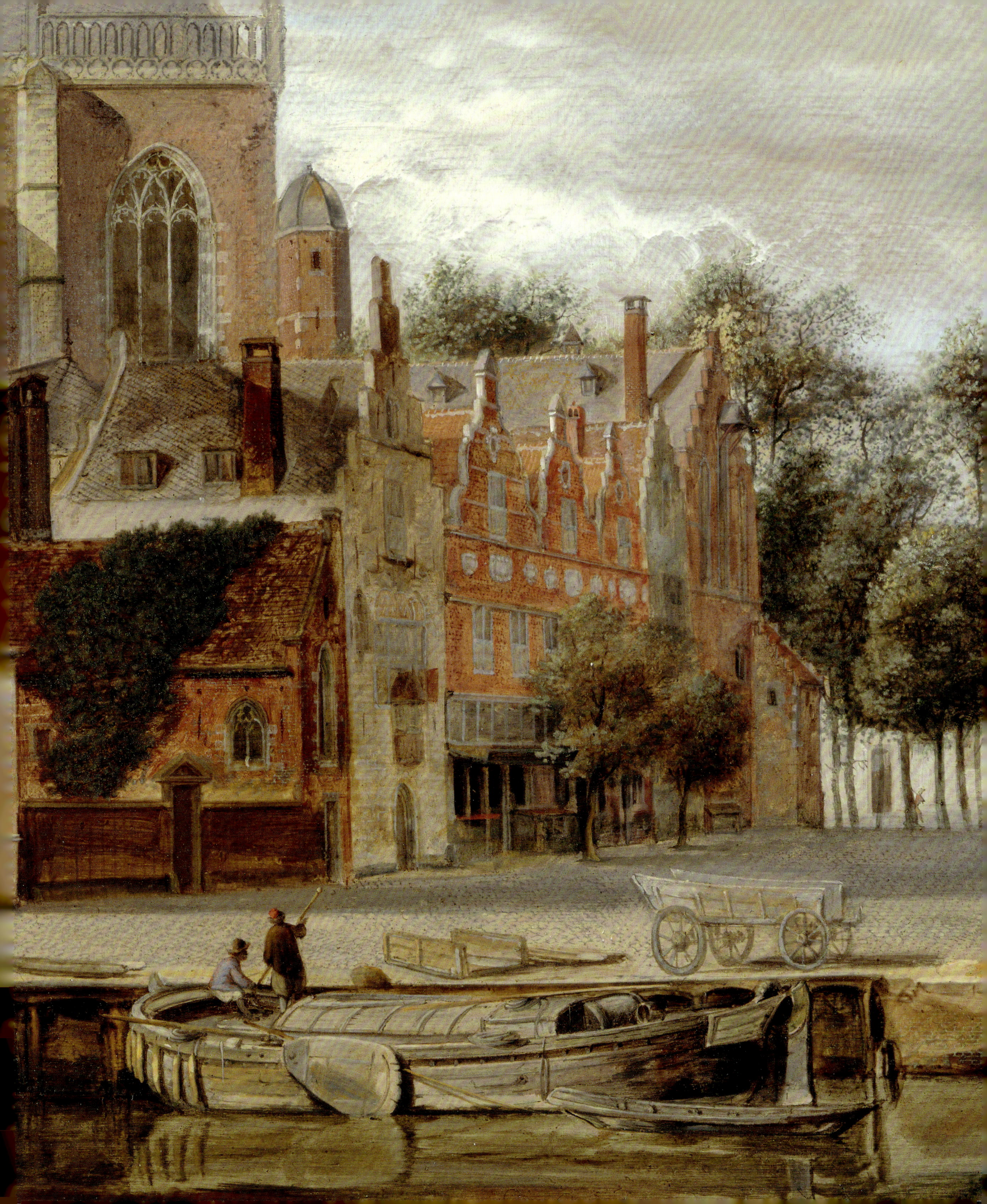

34

Jan van der Heyden

Dutch
Gorinchem 1637–1712 Amsterdam

Library Interior with Still Life

ca. 1710/11

Signed and dated on the base of the torchier: "J v D Heyden/ [oud 73]"[1]
Oil on canvas, 26¾ × 22½ in. (68 × 57.2 cm)
The Norton Simon Foundation, F.1972.17.P

Provenance
Huybert Ketelaar, Amsterdam (estate sale, Hendrik de Winter & Jan Yver, Amsterdam, 19 June 1776, no. 88, as "Een Studeer Kamer; op Doek, h. 27¾, br. 25 duim, Op een Marmere Tafel, bedekt met een Tapyt, zyn geplaast twee Globens, en een opengeslagen Boek; ziende men verder een Kabinet, en een Kas met Boeken. Dit alles is zeer fraay en uitvoerig gepenceelt").[2] Probably Marcus van Arp, Amsterdam (sale, Diederiks, Amsterdam, March 1812, lot 30, as "Een Binnenvertrek waarin een Tafel met een Tapyt bedekt, waarop een opengeslagen Boek en twee Globes, ter zyde ziet men in een Boekenkast en in de Schoorsteen een Bybelsche Ordonnantie; uitvoerig gepenseeld, oud 74 jaren").[3] Anonymous (sale, Frederik Muller & Cie., Amsterdam, 28 November 1906, lot 283, as anonymous master "portant la signature de J. v. D. Heyden," canvas 68 × 57 cm; sold to);[4] Cornelis Gerardus 't Hooft (1866–1936), Amsterdam, probably sold 1922 to;[5] [J. Goudstikker, Amsterdam, sold (share?) 1927 to];[6] [Thomas Agnew & Sons, London, stock no. 6741, sold 1935 to];[7] John Hugh Smith, London (sale, Christie's, London, 21 July 1944, lot 95, withdrawn).[8] Anonymous [J. Hugh Smith] (sale, Christie's, London, 1 December 1944, lot 93, bought in by Cullum).[9] [Thomas Agnew & Sons, London]. Private collection, London (sale, Christie's, London, 29 November 1968, lot 73; sold for 7,500 guineas to); [Walter Feilchenfeldt, Zurich;[10] sold 1972 to]; The Norton Simon Foundation.

Exhibited
Rotterdam 1922–23, no. 39; The Hague 1922a,[11] p. 11, no. 43; The Hague 1926, p. 36, no. 92; Rotterdam 1926, no. 46; The Hague 1928–29, no. 14;[12] Amsterdam 1933, no. 150; Amsterdam 1937, no. 31, as "*Stilleven*, doek, 76 × 63.5 cm. Voluit getekend met de toevoeging 'oud 73 jaar,' HdG 332, Particuliere Engelsche Verzameling [John Hugh Smith]"; on loan, Phoenix Art Museum, 5 June 1972–17 April 1973; on loan, Los Angeles County Museum of Art, 17 May 1973–26 November 1974.

References
Bredius 1912, ill. p. [132]; Hooft 1912, pp. 12f.; W. Martin and Moes 1912, no. 12, ill.; Bode 1915, p. 186; Bode 1919, p. 287; Bode 1923, p. 287; Hofstede de Groot 1908–27, vol. 8 (1927), p. 421, no. 332, as from the "Vrancken" Collection; Vorenkamp 1933, p. 110; Rózsaffy 1931–34, pp. 166, 169, fig. 2, 170; H. C. Smith 1944, p. 285, fig. 3; Bode/Plietzsch 1958, p. 369; Wagner 1971, no. 218, pp. 114, 178;[13] Thornton 1978, pp. 306–11, fig. 300, 396n99, 414; Pasadena 1980, p. 51, ill.; P. Sutton 1986, p. 219; Pasadena 1989, p. 82, ill.; Gaskell 1990, pp. 302–05, fig. 1; Greenwich/Amsterdam 2006–07, pp. 39, 206, fig. 1; S. Campbell 2010, p. 340, no. 800, ill.

Technical Notes
The fine plain-weave canvas has been lined, with the original tacking edges cut off. The thin warm-white ground layer does not cover the canvas texture completely. Above it, a medium-brown layer of opaque paint is often visible at the edges or contours of objects and in the back wall, beneath the gray paint where it has been exposed by abrasion. The smoothly applied paint was brushed directly over the medium-brown layer, which is apparently present everywhere except under the open book. Here, the white ground was employed as the foundation for the brightly illuminated pages. Objects and surfaces throughout the interior scene were described meticulously. Transparent brown paint brushed in thin lines depicts the wood grain in floor planks. Delicate shading and tiny lines of lettering were painted on the spines of the books. Black and red paints depict the tortoiseshell veneer of the cabinet drawers. The artist gave careful attention to the information on the globes and the title page of the open book. Though the painting reads well, the work is generally not well preserved, and there is extensive paint loss throughout. X-radiography reveals a large number of losses, but it is not clear whether they relate to tears or damages to the support or to poor adhesion of paint to the support. There is a large amount of solvent damage. For example, thin brown shadows below the table cover are noticeably abraded, as are the glazes in the table cover itself. The black of the cabinet is quite worn. Retouching was done in at least two campaigns; the larger, known repairs are completely masked by the varnish. Later retouching, also covered by the varnish but visible with ultraviolet light, was done in small dabs and strokes. The natural-resin varnish is moderately yellowed.

Library Interior with Still Life is one of three closely related paintings Jan van der Heyden executed during the last two or three years of his life. Diverging from the more conventional *vanitas* still lifes in niches that he painted early in his career (see, for example, that in the Akademie der bildenden Künste, Vienna), these innovative compositions fuse still-life painting with scenes of elegant interiors.[14] The Pasadena painting shares with the examples in both Madrid (fig. 34a) and Budapest (fig. 34b) a general arrangement and specific details, such as the red table rug, the open book, and the globes, but other details map to only one or the other of them.[15]

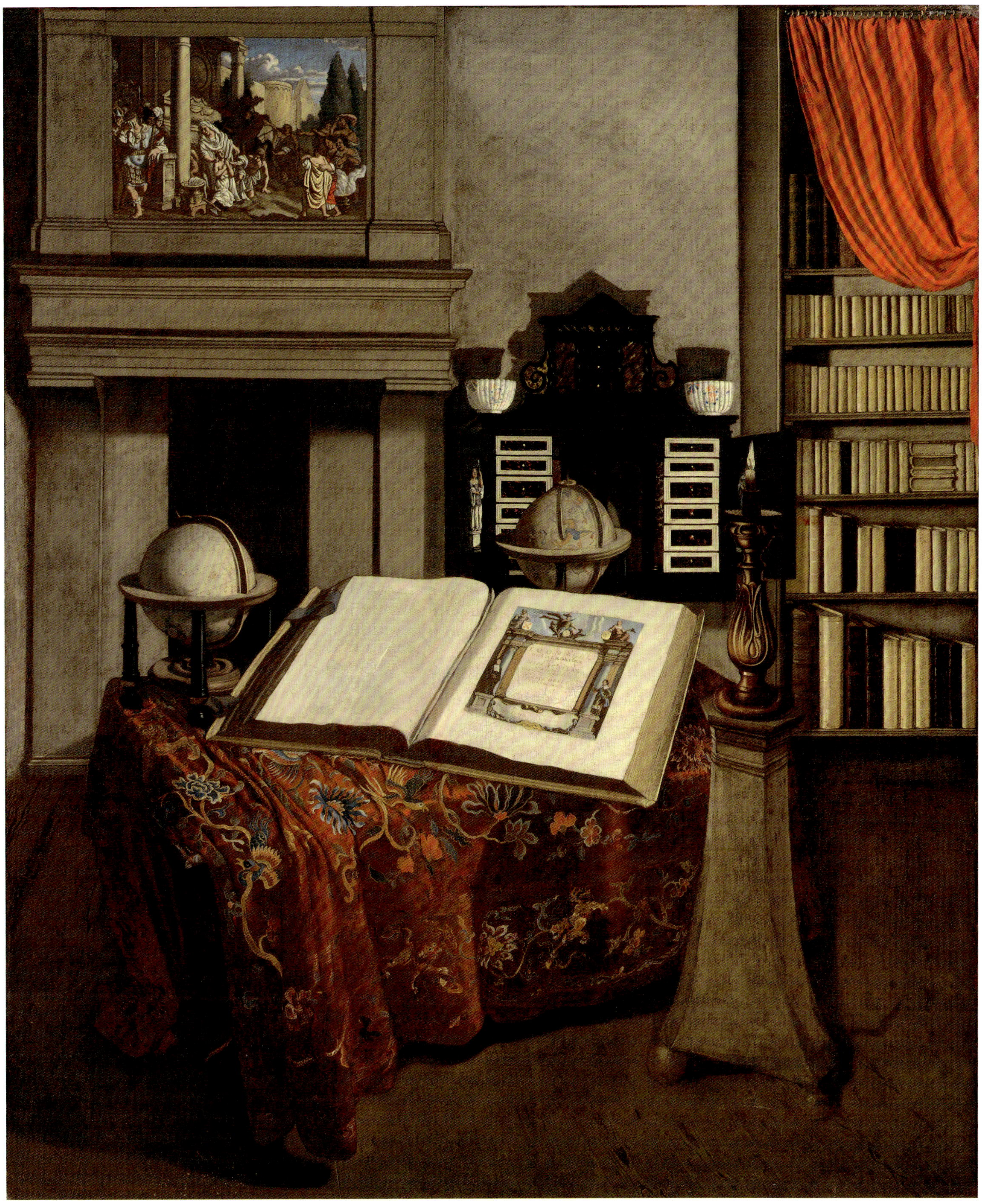

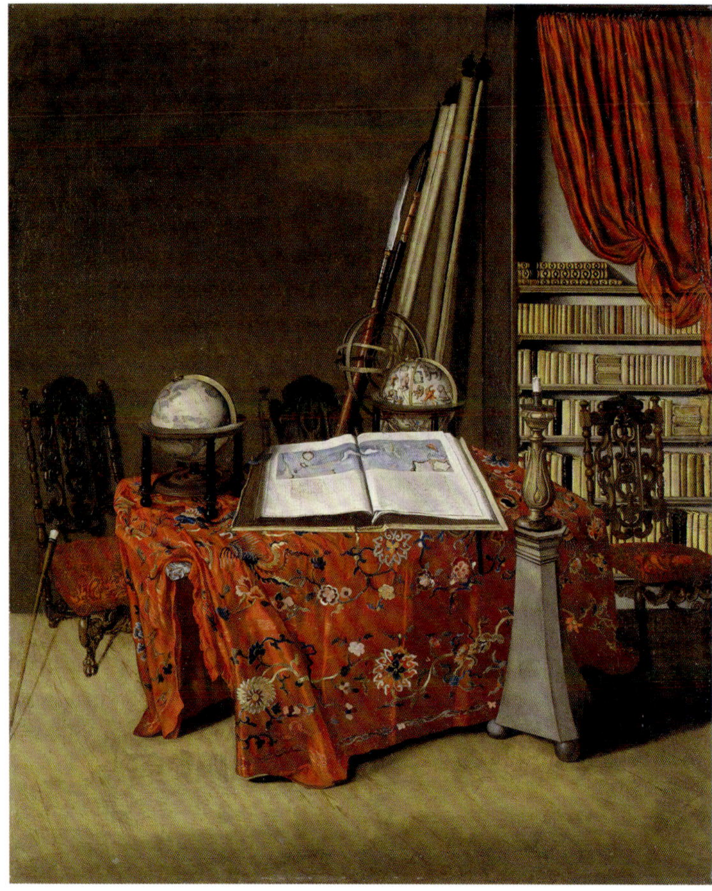

Fig. 34a. Jan van der Heyden, *Corner of a Library*, ca. 1711, oil on canvas, 30 5/16 × 25 in. (77 × 63.5 cm), Museo Nacional Thyssen-Bornemisza, Madrid.

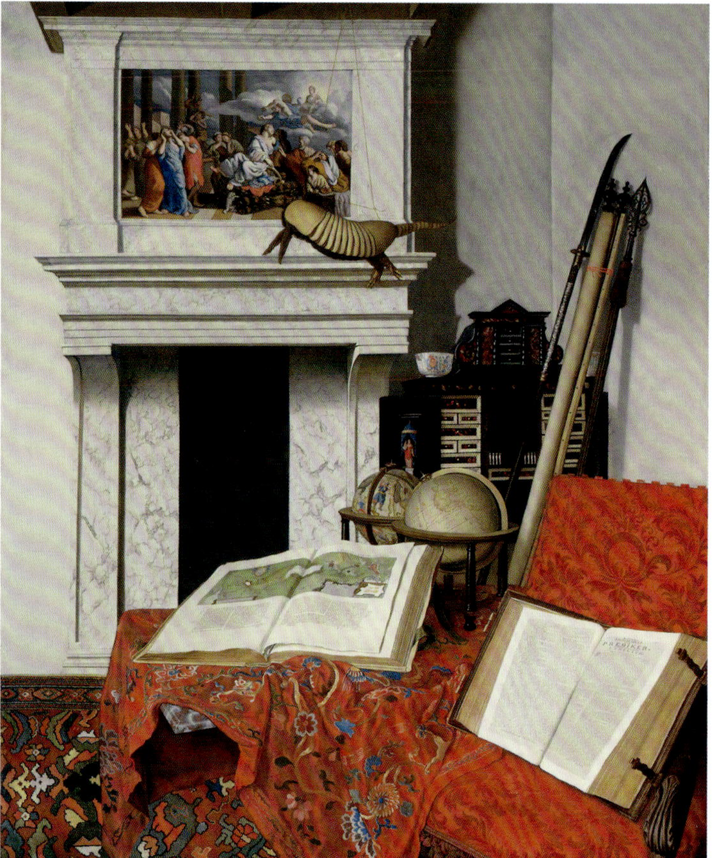

Fig. 34b. Jan van der Heyden, *Room Corner with Rarities*, 1712, oil on canvas, 29 ½ × 25 in. (75 × 63.5 cm), Szépművészeti Múzeum, Budapest.

In *Library Interior with Still Life*, a bookshelf filled with classic texts serves as a backdrop for a marble table covered with a sumptuous red Chinese silk textile embroidered with birds and plants on which a portable desk supports a large open book.[16] Van der Heyden's painstaking lettering on the elaborate title page of the book identifies it as the second volume of part one of the 1642 Dutch edition of *Toonneel des Aerdrijkx, ofte Nieuw Atlas* (Theatre of the World, or the New Atlas), which included maps relating to Germany and immediately adjacent territories.[17] This atlas—originally published in Amsterdam in 1635 by Willem Jansz. Blaeu (1571–1638) as *Theatrum Orbis Terrarum* followed by numerous publications in four languages—was the most expensive book printed in the seventeenth century; a hand-colored edition of the atlas cost the equivalent of the annual income of a middle-class burgher. Into these large tomes collectors typically inserted drawings and prints that related to the information printed in the atlas itself. Together, the atlas and the celestial and terrestrial globes, which may also have been made by Blaeu, represent a microcosm of the universe. Prized possessions, they attest to both the intellectual and the social status of the owner and may also reflect something of the interests of the prosperous artist himself, whose estate included a large number of books: 26 folio volumes, 16 unbound, 38 in-quarto, 119 in-octavo, and duodecimo and others unbound.[18]

The Pasadena painting and its variants are closely related to the intellectual portraits of men in their studies that became increasingly popular during the second half of the seventeenth century. Known now only from a lithograph (fig. 34c), *The Scholar*, attributed to Nicolaes Maes (1634–1693), for example, depicts a young man seated in a study before a table with open books and writing utensils. A bookcase is visible behind him, and on the floor are a globe and two books, one of which is titled "atlas."[19] Most often identified in the inventories of jurists, doctors, and ministers, studies were places for retreat and work, usually located on an upper floor of a house and sparsely furnished.[20] Seventeenth-century inventories suggest that these studies were primarily workspaces and only occasionally used to store a collection.[21]

Van der Heyden's late still lifes include references to not only contemplation but also the active life of a man of the world, represented here by the atlas as well as objects collected from around the world that would typically have been displayed in a cabinet of curiosities: an armadillo from the Americas in the Budapest painting and rolled maps and Japanese halberds in the painting in Madrid.[22]

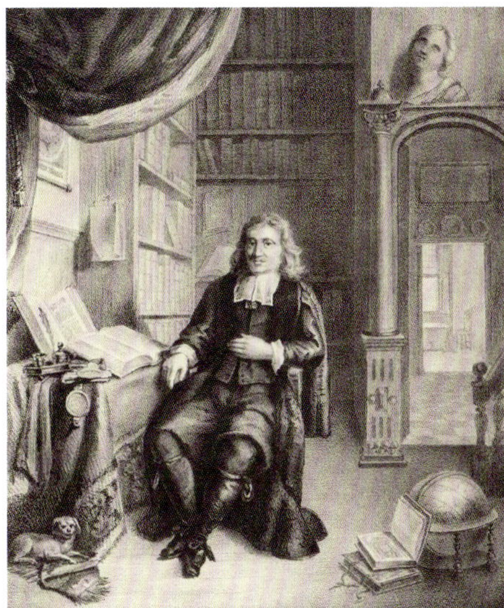

Fig. 34c. E. de Loose, after Nicolaes Maes, *The Scholar (1656)*, 1828–29, lithograph, 8¼ × 7 in. (20.7 × 17.5 cm), The British Museum, London.

The ebony cabinet decorated with tortoiseshell and ivory inlays that appears in both the Pasadena and the Budapest works was probably similar to those made by Van der Heyden's grandfather to protect and display rarities.[23] The twelve small drawers on the interior would have held precious objects such as coins and shells. The central niche, which appears to be empty here, was often fitted with mirrors to reflect a prized object. An unidentified figure holding a palm appears on the inside of the open left door of the cabinet. Two imported Japanese kakiemon bowls and a pedimented box rest on the top of the cabinets in both Pasadena and Budapest.

Van der Heyden based the painting of an ancient sacrifice that appears above the marble mantelpiece in the Pasadena composition on a well-known etching published in 1667 after a design by the Amsterdam artist and theoretical writer Gerard de Lairesse (1640–1711).[24] The legend on the second state of the print published by Nicolaes Visscher II (1618–1709) identifies the subject as the sacrifice of Polyxena by Pyrrhus on the grave of Achilles, a popular story of tragic love.[25] An old inscription on a drawing at the Rijksmuseum, Amsterdam, specifically identifies De Lairesse's print as an illustration of a scene from the tragedy *Polyxena* by Ludolf Smids (1649–1720).[26] R. P. Claude du Molinet (1620–1687) included a painting of a classical subject in a series of prints representing the library of the Monastery of Saint-Geneviève in Paris (1692), suggesting that such images, like sculptures, coins, and texts from antiquity, were admired as indications of ancient cultures.[27]

Van der Heyden's still lifes were likely viewed as objects of luxury and curiosity themselves. This is suggested by the primary print from Du Molinet's series, which represents above a fireplace a large still-life painting of a print or scroll displayed on an imported carpet thrown over a balustrade.[28] One suspects that Van der Heyden's three related paintings, with their references to exotic foreign places and societies, would have particularly appealed to directors of the Dutch East India Company and other collectors. It is unclear, however, to what extent the variations in the three still lifes are significant. The terrestrial globe included in the Budapest painting, for example, is turned so that the viewer sees South America, the origin of the armadillo suspended from the ceiling. Joan Blaeu's *Atlas Maior* of 1665, however, is opened to show the fortifications marking the separation of the Northern and Southern Netherlands during the Eighty Years' War, and Japanese pikes and rolled maps rest against a wall next to an ebony cabinet. In the Pasadena painting, Van der Heyden included pieces of fine Japanese porcelain and orients the terrestrial globe toward southern Asia, but he also includes the volume of Blaeu's book that concerns German territories. Painted at the end of his life, each of them signed not with a date but with the artist's age, these late still lifes may also have had particular meaning for Van der Heyden himself. The lit candle that illuminates the scene in the Pasadena painting (dated when the artist was seventy-three) suggests that Van der Heyden may have intended this painting to serve as a metaphor for learning or, literally, enlightenment. Both the Madrid and the Budapest canvases, created after the Pasadena painting, contain allusions to *vanitas*. In the Madrid image, a candle is extinguished—a traditional reference to *vanitas*—while in the foreground of the Budapest painting the Bible is opened to Ecclesiastes 1:2: "Vanity, vanity, all is vanity."[29]

1. Van der Heyden's age (*oud*), which is no longer legible, has been read as both 73 and 74. See Wagner 1971, no. 218; Rózsaffy 1931–34 notes that the number is 73.

2. Hofstede de Groot confused the provenances of the Pasadena painting (no. 332) with the other versions. He associated the Ketelaar sale with a version of the subject in Budapest, although the dimensions—27¾ × 25 *duim* (1 *duim* = about 1 inch)—are closer to those of the Pasadena painting than to similar works in Madrid (30 5/16 × 25 in.; fig. 34a) or Budapest (29½ × 25 in.; fig. 34b). The identification of the Ketelaar painting and the Pasadena version is reinforced by the mention of a cabinet, which does not appear in the Madrid version, and bookshelves, which do not appear in the Budapest version.

3. With thanks to Burton Fredericksen, who identified this painting in a unique, incomplete copy of the sale catalogue at the Bibliotheek, Koninklijk Museum voor Schone Kunsten, Antwerp. The exact date of the sale in March 1812 is unknown, but the description is almost certainly that of the Pasadena painting. B. Fredericksen, email to Carol Togneri, 19 September 2008 (NSM). See also GPI, Sales Catalog N-227.

4. The two-day sale included the portraits from the gallery of the family v. I. v. D., the collection of Mr. H. C. Du Bois of The Hague, and others. This painting was included in the second day without identification of the owner. GRI has a copy of this sale annotated by Ellis Waterhouse, where he identifies the family v. I. v. D. as "Van Iddekinge van Drogenhorst."

5. W. Martin and Moes 1912, no. 12, ill. Rotterdam 1926 also mentions Hooft in the provenance of

this painting. Hooft most likely sold the painting directly to Goudstikker, who mentioned in The Hague 1922a that the painting was with Hooft until 1922.

6. The painting appears in two subsequent exhibitions by Goudstikker—one in The Hague in 1928 and one in Amsterdam in 1933—which may indicate that the gallery retained partial ownership of it. The Pasadena painting was no. 150 in the 1933 exhibition of still lifes organized by Goudstikker for the benefit of the Rembrandt Fund (see Exhibited). No. 149 in that exhibition, *De bibliotheek*, canvas, 77 × 63.5 cm, is the painting currently in the Museo Nacional Thyssen-Bornemisza, Madrid. See Gaskell 1990, pp. 302–05, no. 66, ill.

7. Advertisement, *Art News* 26, no. 17 (28 January 1928): p. 2.

8. The entry in the annotated catalogue at the GRI has been crossed out with ink, suggesting that the lot was withdrawn.

9. According to Christie's clerk's copy. Illustrated in H. C. Smith 1944, p. 285.

10. The painting was cleaned in London by Johannes Hell after Feilchenfeldt acquired it. It may have been at this time that the black paint that covered the wall behind the ebony chest (evident in the photograph of the painting published in the catalogue of the Goudstikker exhibition: Rotterdam 1926) was removed, revealing the strong shadows cast by the bowls.

11. The Goudstikker catalogues, beginning in 1922, incorrectly identify the painting as Smith vol. 5, no. 390, which in 1834 was in the Vrancken collection, Flanders, and is now in Budapest. The dimensions mentioned in the Goudstikker catalogues (76 × 63.5 cm) apparently derived from Smith (2 ft. 6 in. × 2 ft. 1 in., or 76.2 × 63.5 cm) rather than the object itself. The mention of a painting after De Lairesse above the fireplace in the still life confirms the correct association of these exhibitions with the Pasadena painting, which is the only version to include this detail.

12. Wagner 1971, p. 114, no. 218.

13. Wagner 1971, p. 114, no. 218, dismisses Hofstede de Groot's assumption that the painting came from the collection of Francken [Vrancken]; she believes that the Francken painting is identical to that now in the Museo Nacional Thyssen-Bornemisza, Madrid (Wagner 1971, no. 219); this is accepted by Gaskell 1990 and by the present author.

14. Regarding the Vienna painting, see Trnek 1992, pp. 190–96, no. 64, ill., and Greenwich/Amsterdam 2006–07, pp. 180–83, no. 29, color pl.

15. See Gaskell 1990, pp. 302–05, no. 66, ill.; and Cologne/Utrecht 1987, pp. 84f., no. 20, ill.

16. The background is badly abraded but it is still possible to decipher the names of Homer and other ancient writers on the spines of the books.

17. See Koeman [1663] 1970.

18. Bredius 1912, p. 137; cited by Gaskell 1990, p. 304n9.

19. Other significant details include a classical head over the door, a seal hanging from a document on this table, a picture over his desk, a dog, and a curtain. See Van der Veen 2000, p. 160, fig. 15.

20. According to Van der Veen 2000, however, in the seventeenth century the portrayal of a man in a study was a convention rather than an indication of his erudition, since the inventories of many of these men include only a few books.

21. Van der Veen 2000, p. 149, notes that, with rare exceptions, inventories reveal that these simply furnished workspaces did not include storage cabinets or collections of rarities, which were often displayed throughout the house.

22. More than forty collections of rarities have been documented in Amsterdam during the late seventeenth and early eighteenth centuries. Traditionally the property of Renaissance princes, in the Northern Netherlands they were owned by wealthy merchants and scholars, most of whom were associated with the Dutch East India Company. As the international market for curiosities, Amsterdam provided a particularly advantageous and stimulating environment for local collectors, who corresponded and exchanged gifts of exotic and scientific objects, drawings, prints, and books with connoisseurs throughout Europe. The proliferation of travel literature during the second half of the seventeenth century further attests to the intellectual pleasure these collectors took in actual and vicarious travel to exotic places. See Hanover/Raleigh/Atlanta 1991 and Amsterdam 1992.

23. Jan Cornelisz. Munster (1580–1652) was an ebony worker or cabinet maker in Utrecht. See I. H. van Eeghen 1973, pp. 29–36. The cabinet, which also appears in Van der Heyden's painting in Budapest, may have belonged to the artist.

24. First identified by Hofstede de Groot 1908–27, vol. 8 (1927), p. 421, no. 332. Hollstein 1949–2010, vol. 11, no. 52, 30.3 × 38.7 cm. See Roy 1992, pp. 416f., no. G. 9. The first state of the print is signed: "Gerardus Lairesse inventor, fecit. et exudit Amsterdami."

25. Roy 1992, p. 416, no. G. 9. P. C. Hooft (1581–1647) and Samuel Coster (1579–1665) had previously written plays about the tragic couple. In exchange for the lifting of the siege of Troy, Achilles was offered the hand of Polyxena, the daughter of Priam, king of Troy. Achilles fell in love with the young princess at first sight and fell prey to a plot to kill him. Asked by Polyxena to make an offering at the altar of Apollo, Achilles was killed as he knelt at the altar by an arrow shot by Polyxena's brother Paris and guided by Apollo. Following the victory of the Greeks, Achilles's ghost returned and demanded that Polyxena be sacrificed on his grave.

26. Roy 1992, p. 416, no. G. 4. Van der Heyden also included a painting of a classical scene in his Budapest painting (Wagner 1971, no. 217). There, the painting within the painting is based on a print by G. C. Testa (ca. 1630–1655) after the painting *The Death of Dido* by Pietro Testa (1611–1650). According to Peter Sutton in Greenwich/Amsterdam 2006–07, p. 208, "In the seventeenth century the subject was interpreted as a parable about the fugitive nature of love."

27. Published in Paris in 1692, Du Molinet's prints represent the cabinet of curiosities at one end of the library of the Monastery of Sainte-Geneviève in Paris. See Thornton 1978, ills. 291–94. Nicholas Witsen (1641–1717), a director of the Dutch East India Company, lamented that knowledge about the cultures of newly encountered societies was sadly not the concern of the Dutch East India Company, which remained focused on material objects. Witsen, who hosted Peter I of Russia (r. 1682–1725) and other dignitaries at his home in Amsterdam, was a prominent collector. In 1687 he published a map and in 1692 *Noord en Oost Tartaryen. . .* (2 vols., Amsterdam), the first book on north and east Tartary (comprising the northern parts of Europe and Asia), in which he described and compared the language, religion, customs, and homes of the region. See Amsterdam 1992, pp. 156f., passim.

28. On a visit to the Norton Simon Museum on 4 March 1981, Arthur K. Wheelock suggested that because of the unusual perspective in the painting, it might have been used in conjunction with a piece of furniture. Collector's cabinets did sometimes have painted doors, although these are generally painted on wood rather than, as here, on canvas. On painted art cabinets, see Th. H. Lunsingh Scheurleer 1973. Although most of these cabinets are now lost, many were apparently decorated with allegorical figures painted on panel *en grisaille*.

29. For a discussion of the late still lifes, with particular focus on the Madrid painting, see Greenwich/Amsterdam 2006–07, no. 38, p. 206, where the Pasadena painting is mentioned as having been done in the artist's seventy-fourth year. Although the date has been abraded, it appears to be "73."

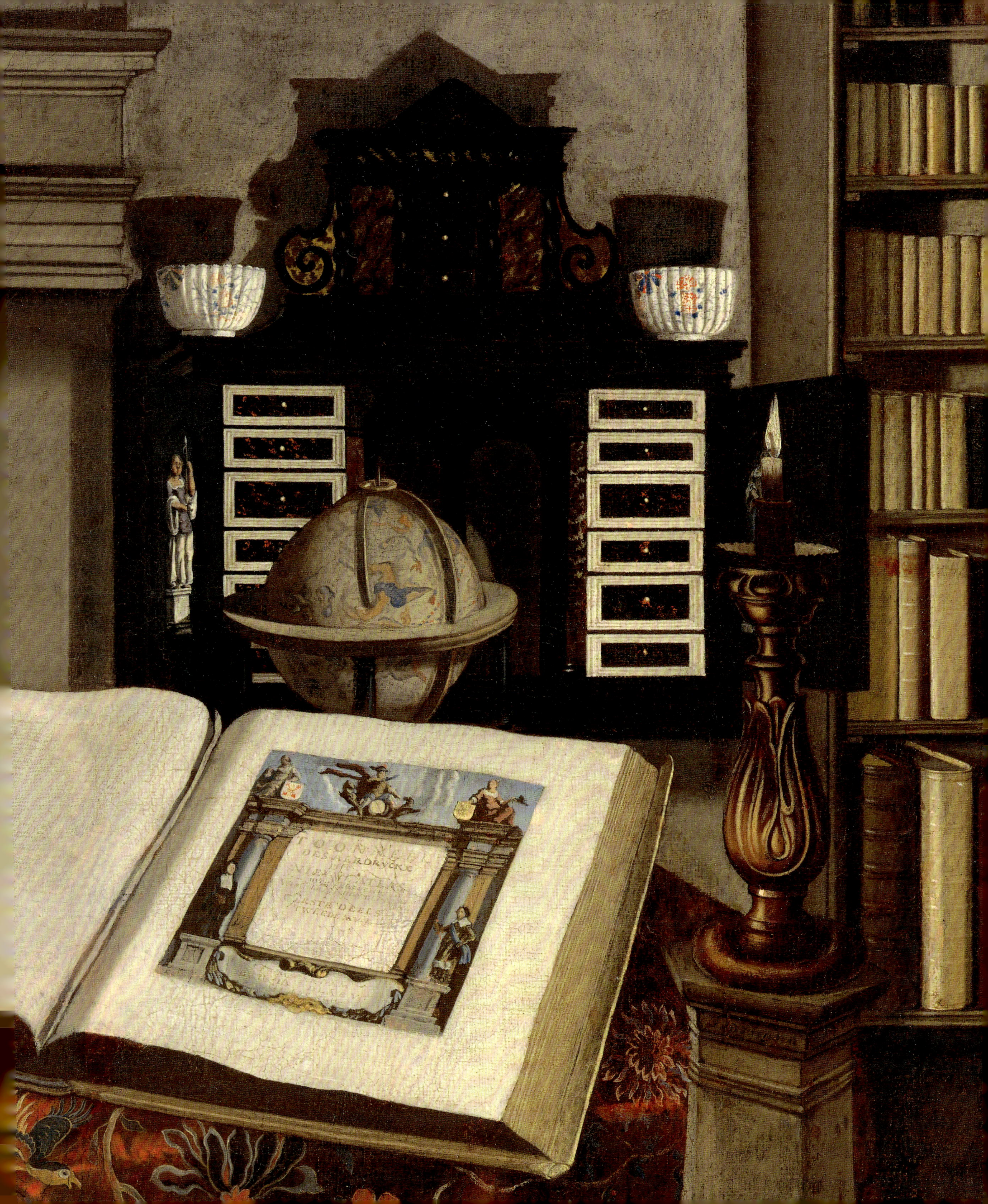
DES AERDRYCKS

35

Gerard Hoet I

Dutch
Zaltbommel 1648–1733 The Hague

Mercury and Herse,
formerly known as
Festival in Honor of Mercury
ca. 1710

Signed, lower right on fountain: "G. Hoet"
Norton Simon Art Foundation, M.1979.51.P
Oil on copper, 22 3⁄16 × 26 3⁄4 in. (56.4 × 67.9 cm)

Provenance
Idestam family, Revel [Tallinn], Estonia. Sesemann, St. Petersburg. James Whittick-Kunau, Helsinki.[1] [Svensk-Engelska Konstgalleriet, Stockholm, sold May 1937]. Anonymous (sale, Sotheby's, London, 10 July 1974, lot 92, sold to); The Norton Simon Collection, gift 1979 to; Norton Simon Art Foundation.[2]

Exhibited
On loan, Henry Art Gallery, University of Washington, Seattle, 12 August–9 December 1974.

References
Sluijter 1986, pp. 63, 402n63-1; P. Sutton 1986, p. 219; S. Campbell 2010, p. 368, no. 1069, ill.

Related Work
A *Mercury and Herse*, signed "G. H." lower right, was at Sotheby's, London, 8 July 1999, lot 114, listed as an oil on copper, 22 × 27 in.; 56.5 × 68.5 cm.[3]

Technical Notes
The support, a heavy copper plate, appears to be in its original state. Raking light reveals scattered shallow undulations and very small dents on the surface that predate the application of paint. The medium-gray ground was toned with an opaque rose-beige layer that provides a warm tonality through the thinly painted blue sky. The opaque paint was smoothly blended in controlled brushwork. The paint is generally well preserved, having suffered a minor amount of solvent abrasion in the darker areas. Adhesion of the paint and ground to the copper support is good, while numerous losses scattered along all edges are probably related to frame abrasion. Undocumented prior cleaning was selective. Examination with ultraviolet light shows a patchwork of materials. Some areas of thick, natural-resin varnish remain in the lower right quadrant, with remnants of it elsewhere, especially in the lower right. The exception is the sky, where there are no traces of varnish. Retouching has been done throughout, often for the purpose of strengthening contours. The varnish, though not noticeably discolored, is degraded and does not saturate well; it has also become brittle and is fractured into tiny cracks.

During the late seventeenth century, mythological subjects enjoyed a revival in the art and literature of the Netherlands.[4] Artists turned to the *Odyssey* of Homer and to Virgil's *Aeneid* for many of their subjects. By far the most popular source, however, was the *Metamorphoses* by the Roman poet Ovid (43 BCE–17/18 CE), the many illustrated editions of which provided artists with particularly valuable sources of inspiration. *Mercury and Herse*, painted by Gerard Hoet I in about 1710, depicts an event related in *Metamorphoses* 2:708–31: One day as Mercury, messenger to the gods, flew over Athens, he noticed a procession of young maidens returning from a festival in honor of the goddess Minerva, to whose temple they had brought gifts in baskets wreathed with flowers. Spying Herse, the loveliest of all the maidens, Mercury was filled with desire. Clutching the caduceus in his right hand and wearing his winged sandals, he confidently flew down without donning a disguise and asked Herse to be with him.[5]

In the Pasadena painting, Mercury hovers over Herse and her two sisters, who are part of a long procession leading from the aqueduct in the left distance to a fountain in

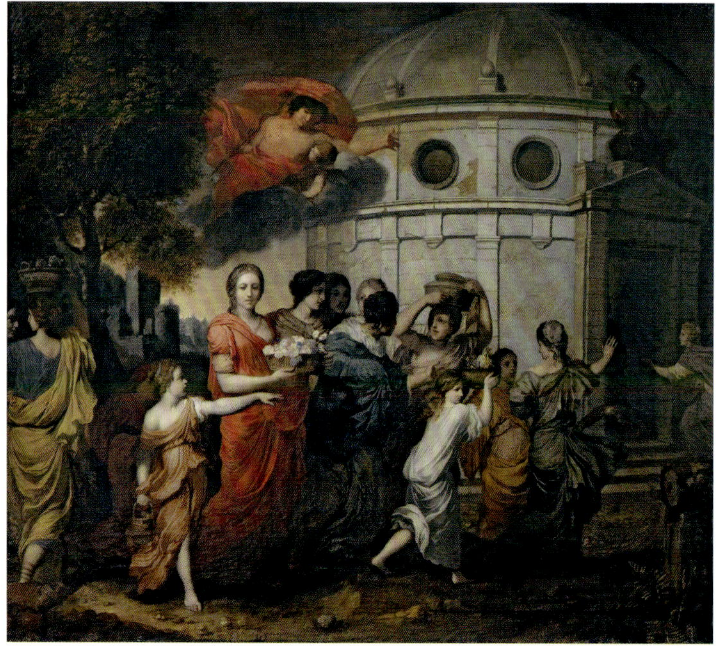

Fig. 35a. Gerard de Lairesse, *Mercury and Herse*, ca. 1662, oil on canvas, 20 7⁄8 × 27 1⁄8 in. (53 × 69 cm), Latvian National Museum of Art, Riga.

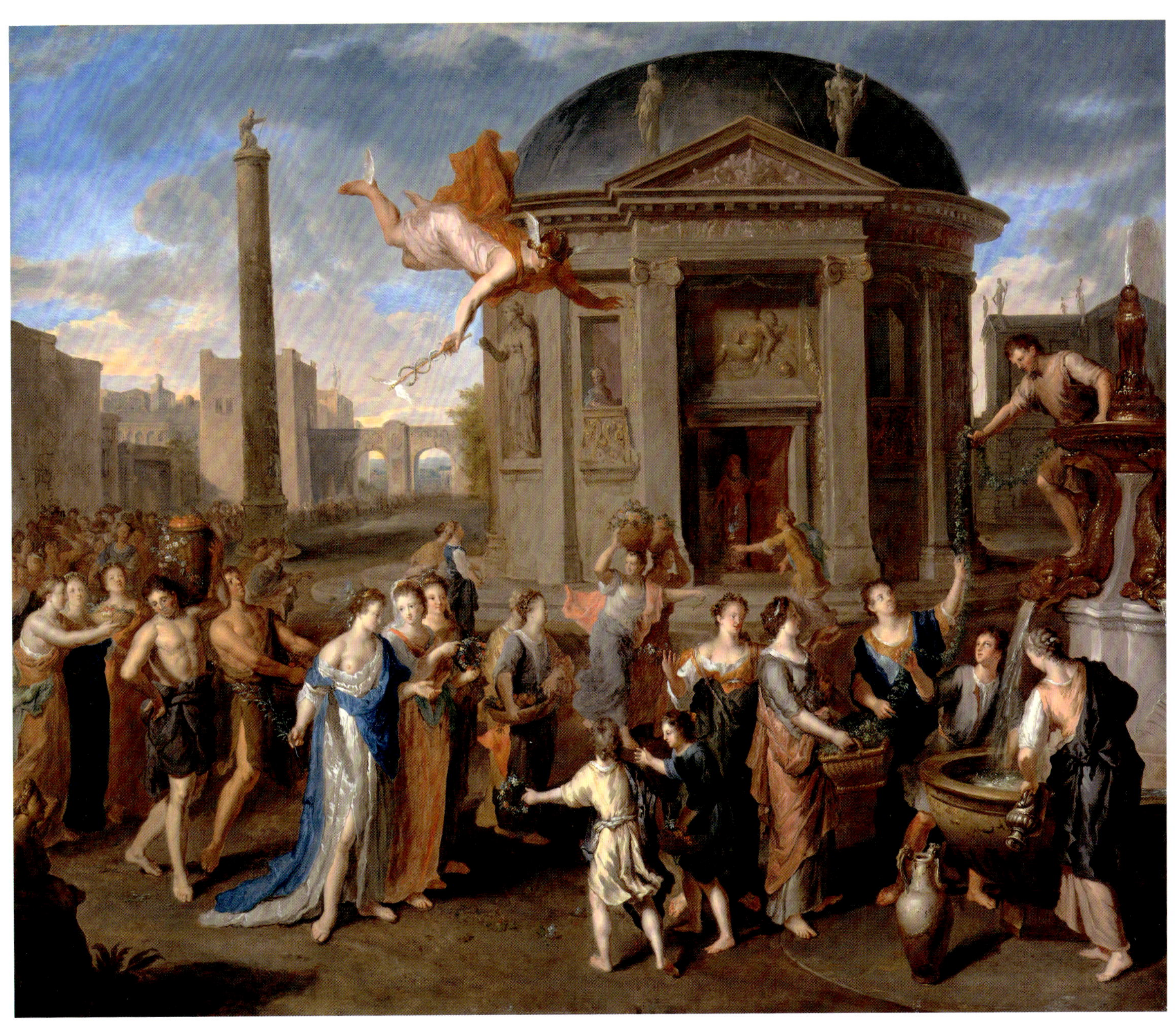

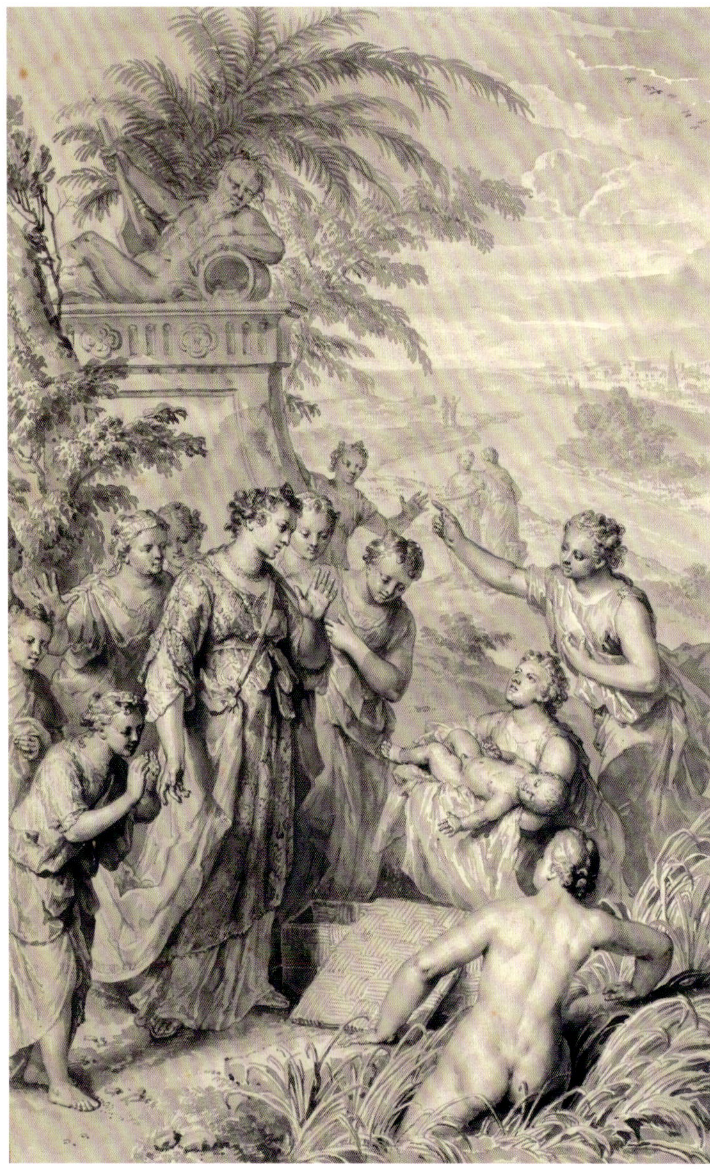

Fig. 35b. Gerard Hoet I, *The Finding of Moses*, ca. 1700–05, pen and ink, 12 13/16 × 8 1/4 in. (32.5 × 21 cm), Museum Boijmans Van Beuningen, Rotterdam.

front of the circular temple of Minerva, goddess of wisdom. Clothed in a pseudoclassical gown that drops off one shoulder to reveal her right breast, Herse stands in the foreground to the left of center, clutching a branch in her hand. Others in the procession hold flower wreaths and baskets of flowers. This scene of the maidens going to the temple anticipates Ovid's account of their return.

Rather than illustrating the written text, Hoet was apparently following the precedent set by sixteenth-century published illustrations of the story as well as early seventeenth-century paintings by the so-called "Pre-Rembrandtists."[6] While Hoet probably knew these works, the central scene and specific motifs of his painting suggest the influence of a painting of the same subject datable to about 1662 by the contemporary Flemish/Dutch painter and theorist Gerard de Lairesse (1640–1711; fig. 35a). A comparison of the two works identifies not only Hoet's source of inspiration but also his distinctive style and interpretation. In choosing a subject not actually described in the literature, Hoet reflects De Lairesse's attitude toward artists' freedom in selecting an incident in a story. In contrast to historiographers, who must tell a story sequentially, De Lairesse argued that "a painter . . . has a greater liberty of choice since it is indifferent to him whether he falls upon the beginning, middle or end of a story; and therefore sometimes begins where he pleases; picking out of the story what best suits his intention; either what went before now is in action, or must be in consequence."[7]

A circular temple dominates the compositions of both Hoet and De Lairesse, as it does many of the earlier examples of the subject. The form of the temple, which was—at least generally—inspired by the Pantheon in Rome, and the central placement of the structures link the two paintings.[8] Hoet, however, reoriented the entrance to the temple so that the door is parallel to the picture plane rather than at an angle and changed other architectural details. Hoet also adopted specific figures from De Lairesse, such as the figure of the woman with her left arm extended as she rushes from the right side of the composition toward the door of the temple. The figures of the two women with baskets on their heads standing apart from the main procession on the central axis of Hoet's painting derive from the single figure of a woman holding a basket on her head in De Lairesse's painting; the two-handed gesture of De Lairesse's figure is divided between Hoet's figures, each of whom holds her basket with only one hand. In another adaptation, Hoet created a more convincing image of Mercury hovering over Herse by turning De Lairesse's figure of the god so that his body faces the earth and his wand extends over the maidens.

In making compositional and narrative changes to De Lairesse's compact, classical composition with its clear narrative, Hoet created a busier, more theatrical scene. The higher vantage point of his painting places the viewer farther away from the events so that the figures appear relatively small and insubstantial, an impression increased by the fussy treatment of the draperies and the abundance of gesturing. The higher viewpoint also meant that Hoet could expand the scene to incorporate the city landscape through which the long procession winds forward from the distant left, where a prominent column similar to Trajan's Column, as well as an aqueduct and other buildings, suggest ancient Rome.

Author of a book on figure drawing, Hoet used individual studies to prepare his composition.[9] Herse, for example, can be recognized in a fully clothed woman in a compositional sketch *The Finding of Moses* (fig. 35b), suggesting that it was based on this same work. Many of the drawings in Hoet's book reflect the influence of sculpture from antiquity, and both male and female figures appear to have been based on male models, explaining the somewhat androgynous character of some of his women. As in the paintings, the musculature of the figures in his drawings is often ill defined, their proportions somewhat elongated and doll-like, and their motions exaggerated.

Hoet's theatrical portrayal of *Mercury and Herse*, with its emphasis on the procession, was undoubtedly appreciated by his patrons for its evocation of ancient ritual and festivities, in which they had a growing interest.[10] Many of Hoet's popular paintings were intended to be hung together with related subjects. There is, however, no evidence that *Mercury and Herse* had either a pendant or was part of a series.

1. The Estonia, St. Petersburg, and Helsinki collections are mentioned on the Svensk-Engelska Konstgalleriet label on the reverse of the painting.

2. A number of descriptions of paintings appeared in early French and British auctions that may be the Pasadena painting. We list those sales here:

- Bonneuil and others (sale, Paris, 6 February 1816, lot 71, "Mercure voltigeant autour des jeunes filles d'Athènes, dans le moment oú, chargée d'offrandes, ells se rendent au temple de Minerve, aperçoit Hersé et en deviant amoureux. Cette peinture est une de celles qui flattent les yeux par leur amabilité," sold for F 99.6).
- Bonneuil or Delamotte (sale, Paris, 30 September 1816, lot 1, "Mercure voltigeant autour des jeunes filles d'Athènes, dans le moment oú, chargée d'offrandes, ells se rendent au Temple de Minerve, aperçoit Hersée, et en deviant amoureux. Ce Tableau est une de ceux qui flattent les yeux par leurs compositions agréables et la grâce de l'exécution," sold for F 66).
- Melrose Hall, Wandsworth, Surrey (sale, London, Farebrother, 14 July 1824, lot 34, "Procession to a Fountain with Mercury Attending," sold for £18 7s.).

3. With thanks to Anne Woollett, curator of paintings at the J. Paul Getty Museum, for bringing this to our attention in an email of 16 March 2009.

4. The previous period of significant interest in mythology among Dutch artists was from 1590 to 1620. As Sluijter 1986, p. 55, points out, the numerous translations of the works of Ovid, Virgil, and Homer after 1590 are clear evidence of an expanded interest in mythology.

5. This is one of the two most commonly represented scenes from the story. The second scene, not known to have been represented by Hoet, represents a later event when Mercury enters Herse's chamber. In that scene Aglauros, one of Herse's sisters who was consumed with envy and tried to prevent Mercury from entering the chamber, is shown on the ground at Mercury's feet, where she has fallen after being touched by his wand and turned into black stone, the color of her thoughts. Herse starts back in surprise. An alternate version shows Aglauros jealously peering around a curtain at the couch where the lovers embrace.

6. The most influential of these works was a painting, now lost, of Mercury and Herse by Adam Elsheimer (1578–1610), known only by a print by Wenceslaus Hollar (1607–1677). See Sluijter 1986, pp. 62 and 401n62-8.

7. De Lairesse [1707] 1738, p. 82.

8. The connection with the Pantheon is particularly evident in De Lairesse's painting, which repeats the pilasters and cornice as well as the circular windows of the drum and reduces the porch to a portal. In his painting, Hoet essentially eliminated the drum and enlarged the pilasters, which now reach to the cornice. The added and enlarged windows of the temple in Hoet's painting reflect Renaissance style. Compare the temple in Perugino's *Giving of the Keys to Saint Peter* (1481, fresco; Sistine Chapel, Vatican) and Raphael's *Marriage of the Virgin* (1504; Pinacoteca di Brera, Milan), the latter influenced by Bramante's *Tempietto*. Roy 1992, p. 190, and no. P.2., notes that De Lairesse had already used this edifice in his painting *Palès*, dated 1662.

9. Hoet 1713.

10. See the scene of an ancient ritual after a painting by De Lairesse displayed as an overmantel in Jan van der Heyden's painting *Library Interior with Still Life* (cat. 34).

36

Gerard Hoet I

Dutch
Zaltbommel 1648–1733 The Hague

Paris Presenting Helen at the Court of Priam, formerly known as *Achilles Taking Brisais Back to Her Parents*

Early 18th century

Signed, center right: "G. Hoet"
Oil on copper, 22 3⁄16 × 26 3⁄4 in. (56.4 × 68 cm)
Norton Simon Art Foundation, M.1976.04.P

Provenance
Estate of Graf Rudolf Széchényi (1862–1928),[1] Budapest (?) (sale, Dorotheum, Vienna, 4–6 June 1930, lot 217, ill. 11). Possibly anonymous (sale, Kende, Vienna, 13–14 December 1933, lot 264, as Historische Szene aus dem alten Rom, copper, 57 × 68 cm). [Silvano Lodi, Munich, sold 1966 to]; [Dr. Walter Feilchenfeldt (b. 1939), Zurich, sold 1976 to]; Norton Simon Art Foundation.

Exhibited
On loan, Phoenix Art Museum, 30 March–20 July 1976.

References
P. Sutton 1986, p. 219; S. Campbell 2010, p. 393, no. 1314, ill.

Related Works

- A second version of the painting formerly belonged to Mr. and Mrs. Otto-O'Méara,[2] Brussels (sale, Galerie Georges Giroux, Brussels, 15–17 October 1928, lot 50a, *Paris présente Hélène à la cour de Priam*, copper, 54.5 × 66.5 cm, signed at center). Lot 50b, *Pyrrhus enlève Astyanax des bras de sa mere*, also signed by Hoet, is painted on a copper plate with the same dimensions as lot 50a (see fig. 36b). Both paintings apparently remained together and were sold as a pair at Sotheby's, London, 28 October 1987, lot 106. *Pyrrhus* may be identical with a painting of that subject by Hoet in the Warnant Collection, Belgium (an undated photograph at the RKD cites the O'Méara sale and notes that the painting is signed and on copper, 54.5 × 66.5 cm).
- A third version of the painting on canvas was formerly in the collection of C. F. Toyne, Esq. (sale, Christie's, London, 21 July 1972, lot 103, *The Reception by an Emperor and His Court of an Ambassador Bearing Gifts* [canvas?] 21 × 25 in. [53.3 × 63.5 cm], sold to "Van Harften" [Haeften?]). This is also probably the painting, of the same subject and format, sold at Christie's, London, 24 July 1987, lot 2, as "attributed to Gerard Hoet,"[3] and Christie's, New York, 15 April 2008, lot 63.
- Copy attributed to William Hamilton, *The Family of Darius before Alexander*, 17 × 32 in. (43.2 × 81.3 cm) (sale, Christie's, London, 24 July 1987, lot 193).

Technical Notes
The support is a heavy copper plate, approximately 1⁄16 inch thick. Shallow depressions and undulations over the entire surface, revealed by raking light, appear to predate the application of paint. Although the ground is difficult to access because losses at the edges are generally of both paint and ground, it appears to be a warm medium gray, with perhaps a second ground consisting of a dark-brown layer above it. Tiny particles of undetermined material are dispersed in it, contributing to a pervasive texture throughout the painting. Paint was directly applied and blended wet-into-wet. The figures were clearly and convincingly rendered with deft brushwork of rich, fairly liquid paint. Modeling of the flesh tones is simple, but features were sharply drawn. Tiny blobs of white create the decorative elements of Paris's tunic and knife handle. Brushmarking is slight but can be seen, especially in the longer brushstrokes of the garments. The principal figures were painted in slightly more vibrant colors; the background (ships at the center right, sculpture under the arch) was rendered in muted colors with crisp contours. Overall the paint is well preserved. Retouching is minor, located in several spots around the perimeter and some small areas at the outside edge of the architecture at upper right. The brittle, natural-resin varnish is densely crazed in some areas, abraded at the edges, and no longer saturates well.

Paris Presenting Helen at the Court of Priam is a well-preserved painting on copper, which retains the slick surface and color as originally painted by Gerard Hoet, one of the preeminent Dutch painters of classical subjects in a classical style. The figures and narrative are clearly defined according to concepts of *affetti*—the communication of emotions through gesture and movement—as well as the carefully considered use of light and color to clarify and enhance the forms. Costumes and architecture provide a context that alludes to the ancient past.

The works of Gerard de Lairesse (1640–1711), Hoet's slightly older contemporary, frequently served as the compositional and thematic inspiration for Hoet's work, and De Lairesse's *Het Groot Schilderboek* (The Great Painting Book; Amsterdam, 1707) provided its theoretical underpinning. The Pasadena composition is adapted from De Lairesse's *The Landing of Helen Led by Paris at the Palace of Priam, in Troy*, ca. 1685/90 (fig. 36a).[4] As if stepping back from De Lairesse's scene, Hoet reduced the scale of the figures so that the main characters no longer dominate. He also rearranged the buildings in the background so that they present a flat

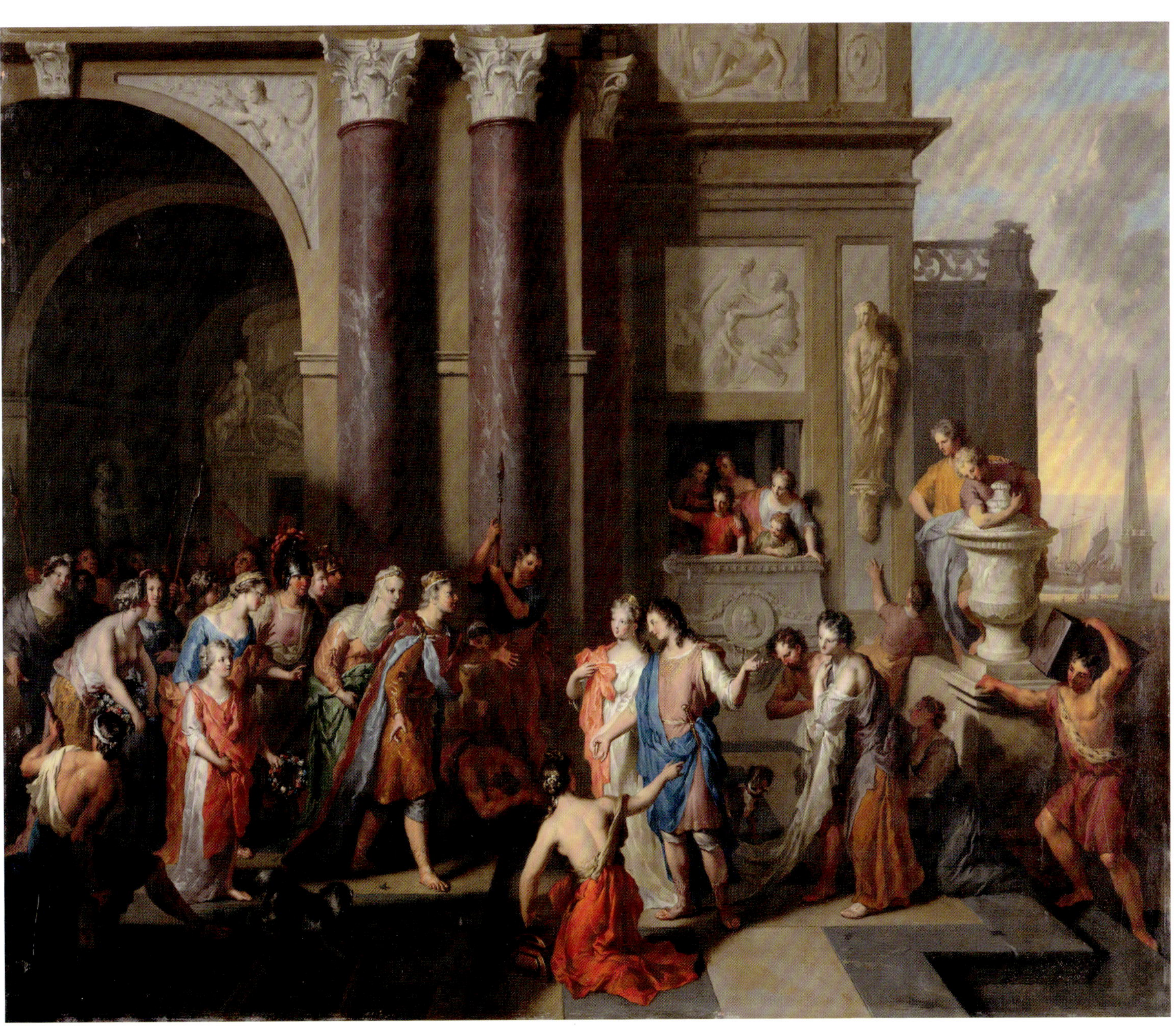

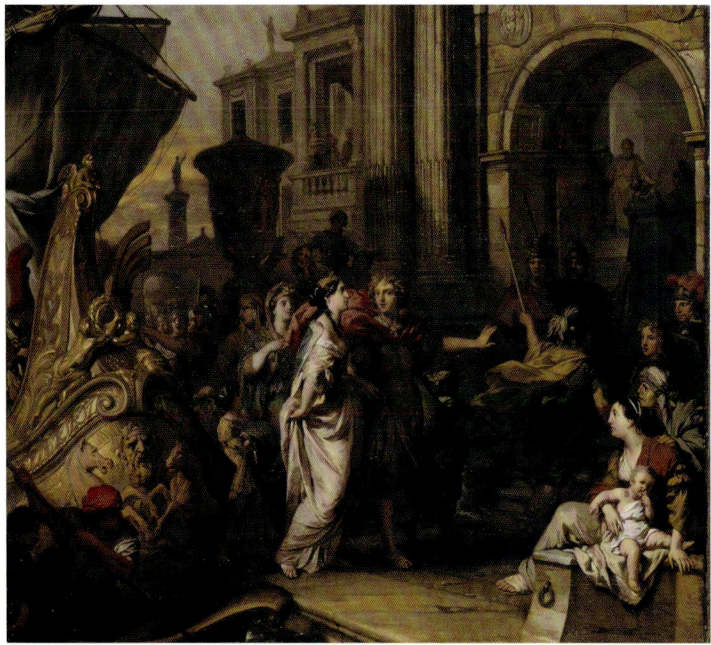

Fig. 36a. Gerard de Lairesse, *The Landing of Helen Led by Paris at the Palace of Priam, in Troy*, ca. 1685/90, oil on canvas, 23 5/8 × 26 5/8 in. (60 × 67.5 cm), Musée du Louvre, Paris.

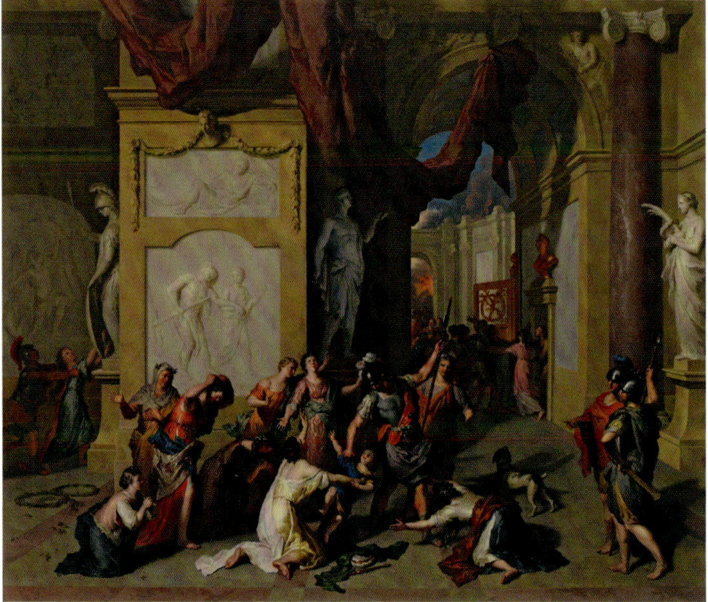

Fig. 36b. Gerard Hoet I, *Pyrrhus Snatching Astyanax from the Arms of His Mother*, 1680, oil on copper, 22 3/8 × 26 3/4 in. (56.6 × 68 cm), Gemäldegalerie Alte Meister, Museumslandschaft Hessen Kassel.

backdrop parallel to the picture plane rather than serving as stage flats to suggest recession into depth.

To fill the larger foreground space, Hoet introduced additional figures and a dominant architectural form. According to *Het Groot Schilderboek*, it is necessary to fill large compositions with "anything that will entertain the eye, since small figures, in a large compass, are not of themselves capable of doing it: [therefore] the ornaments ought to be large, in order to create broad lights; yet these ornaments must not be so monstrous as some have them. . . . [W]e should always bring together such parts or objects as neither lessen the figures nor cause any obstructions in the composition."[5] To maintain the classical unity of a painting, De Lairesse advocated that a painter focus on only a single passion and divide large histories into several pictures. He rejected as "unnatural" pictures in which the same person is represented more than once.[6] Of the two versions of the *Arrival of Paris and Helen* by De Lairesse and Hoet, De Lairesse's more closely follows the tenets of the "natural" picture, for it isolates Helen and Paris in the spotlight at the center of the composition, where the height of the figures is half that of the canvas. In Hoet's painting, on the other hand, the figures are one-third of the height of the composition, and the focus on them is diluted by the addition of the crowd streaming out of the palace as well as by the men bearing boxes from the ships moored in the distant harbor. Rather than Paris and Helen, the compositional focus of Hoet's painting is the space between the two groups, across which the king extends his hand in welcome.

The story of Paris presenting Helen at the Court of Priam derives from the epic tales of the Trojan War.[7] Returning with Helen and the booty he had stolen from Menelaus, king of Sparta, Paris is greeted at the entrance to the palace by his father, Priam, king of Troy, and his mother, Hecuba. Neither the *Iliad* nor the *Odyssey*, which take up the story of the ten-year Trojan War in its last year, gives an account of the return of Paris to his native city. Indeed, although it is often referred to as the event that precipitated the Trojan War, the abduction of Helen, the wife of Menelaus, is not actually described in any of the Trojan epics. The fullest surviving early account of the events surrounding the abduction of Helen and Paris's return is the *Diary of the Trojan War*, presumed to have been written by Dictys, a Greek soldier who fought at Troy and made first-hand reports of the war.[8] According to Dictys, Paris fell in love with Helen while he was the guest of her husband at Sparta. Taking advantage of the king's absence, Paris wooed and carried off Helen as well as considerable treasure from the king's coffers. Sailing toward Troy, they were forced by bad weather to land first on Cyprus and then in Phoenicia, where the king of the Sidonians greeted them warmly. Paris, however, again took advantage of the kindness and trust of his host, killing him in his sleep and pillaging the city before setting sail. After a fierce battle, Paris and his companions returned to Troy with their captured treasure. Word of Paris's misdeeds, however, angered his family and the people of Troy, who feared retaliation.[9] According to Dictys, "Upon his arrival, all of the people showed their disgust at what he had done; some cursed the evil precedent he had set; others bewailed the injustice Menelaus had suffered. And finally, disgusted and angry, they raised a revolt."[10]

The anger with which the Trojans greeted Paris and Helen is not evident in Hoet's painting, which celebrates the arrival of the guests—crowds, including many women who bear wreaths and baskets of flowers, surge forward from the entrance and lean out of the windows of the palace. A crowned couple, presumably the king and queen, lead the crowd and extend a gesture of welcome. Hoet's image, like De Lairesse's, was probably derived from the popular description of Paris's homecoming given by Raoul Lefèvre (active 1460) in *Recueil des histoires de Troie* (1460):

> There came forth of the town King Priamus, with a great company of Noblemen, and received his Children and his friends with great joy, and came to Helen, and bowed so courteously to her, and welcomed her honourably. And when they came nigh the City, they found great joy all the night, throughout all the City, for these tidings. And the next morning, Paris by consent of his father, wedded Helen in the Temple of Pallace and the feast was lengthened throughout all the City for the space of eight days.[11]

In 1930, when the painting first appeared on the market, it was sold together with another painting by Hoet, *Mythological Scene. The Abduction of a Boy*.[12] It is now known as *Pyrrhus Snatching Astyanax from the Arms of His Mother* (fig. 36b), a subject related to the history of Troy and Priam.[13] The two works, both of which are painted on copper panels with the same dimensions and with matching perspectives and proportions, were probably originally intended to hang together, either as a pair or with three or four other paintings showing scenes from the Trojan War.

1. The foremost member of this important aristocratic family was Count Istvan Széchényi (1791–1860), a champion of the modernization of Hungarian economic, social, and intellectual life and a leader of the moderate liberal group in the Hungarian Diet. His father, Count Ferenc Széchényi, formed an important collection of Hungarian books and manuscripts at the end of the eighteenth century, which he gave to the people of Hungary in 1802 and which became the foundation of the National Széchényi Library in Budapest.

2. According to the sale catalogue, her maiden name was Moselli.

3. The provenance includes the O'Méara sale, but this must be incorrect because the painting in the O'Méara sale was on copper, not canvas.

4. Canvas, 60 × 67.5 cm; monogrammed in upper left. Roy 1992, no. P.176, questions the subject of De Lairesse's painting.

5. De Lairesse [1707] 1738, p. 77.

6. De Lairesse [1707] 1738, p. 83.

7. The earliest known reference to the Pasadena painting, the Dorotheum auction catalogue of 1930, identified it only as "Mythologische Szene, Empfang eines fürstlichen Hochzeitspaares" (Mythological Scene. Reception of a Princely Couple). In 1928, however, the subject of a second version of the painting (see Related Works) was identified as *Paris Presenting Helen at the Court of Priam*. P. Sutton 1986, p. 219, refers to the painting as *Achilles Taking Brisais Back to Her Parents*.

8. See Dictys 1966. It is now generally agreed that Dictys is fictive and that the text was written in Greek in the first century CE. Nevertheless, the text, which was translated into Latin in the fourth century, was enormously popular and influential for later adaptations in the Middle Ages and Renaissance.

9. At his birth, it was prophesied that Paris, the son of Priam, king of Troy, would bring ruin upon Troy. Paris was consequently left exposed to die on slopes of Mount Ida but was rescued and raised by shepherds.

10. Dictys 1966, p. 26.

11. Taken from the English translation of Lefèvre 1676, bk. 3, ch. 3, p. 23. First published in 1460, the book was translated into several languages and widely read throughout Europe.

12. Estate of Graf Rudolf Széchényi, Budapest (?) (sale, Dorotheum, Vienna, 4–6 June 1930, lot 218, Hoet, *Mythologische Szene. Entführung eines Knaben*, oil on copper, 57 × 68 cm). The painting (now called *Pyrrhus Taking Astyanax from the Arms of his Mother*) was acquired by the Gemäldegalerie Alte Meiser, Kassel, in December 2004. Dr. Gregor J. M. Weber, email to Gloria Williams Sander, 22 July 2005 (NSM).

13. See description under Related Works.

37

After Hans Holbein II

German
Augsburg 1497/98–1543 London

Sir Bryan Tuke

Mid-17th century

Inscribed: back wall, top (interrupted by hat): "BRIANVS TVKE, MILES, ANO ETATIS SVÆ.LVII [line over date]"; back wall, center (interrupted by body): "• DROIT ET AVANT •"; on paper lower left: "NVNQVID NON PAVCITAS DIERVM. / MEORVM FINIETVR BREVI:"[1]
Oil on panel, 19 ½ × 15 ⅜ in. (49.5 × 39.1 cm)
The Norton Simon Foundation, F.1965.1.030.P

Provenance
Robert Sidney (1649–1702), Viscount Lisle, after 1698 4th Earl of Leicester, in 1678, by descent to his son and heir; Philip (1676–1705), 5th Earl of Leicester, by descent to his brother; John (1680–1737), 6th Earl of Leicester, by descent to his brother; Jocelyn (1692– 1743), 7th Earl of Leicester;[2] by descent to the heirs of Thomas Pelham;[3] John Thomas Townshend (1764–1831), 2nd Viscount Sydney,[4] by descent to John Robert Townshend (1805–1890), 3rd Viscount Sydney of St. Leonards, by descent to his wife; Lady Emily Caroline, by descent to her husband's nephew;[5] Robert Marsham-Townshend (1834–1914)[6] (estate sale of the Sydney Collection, Frognal, Chislehurst, Kent, Knight, Frank & Rutley, London, 7 June 1915, lot 11, sold to);[7] Hugh Blaker (1875–1936), London,[8] sold 1921/23 to;[9] [Duveen Brothers, London and New York, sold by 1927 to]; Elisabeth Severance Prentiss (1865–1944), Cleveland,[10] bequeathed 1944 to; Cleveland Museum of Art (acc. no. 44.85), sold 1959 to;[11] [Duveen Brothers, New York, stock no. 30330, sold 1964 to]; The Norton Simon Foundation.

Exhibited[12]
Cleveland 1936, no. 191, pl. xliv (lent by Elisabeth Severance Prentiss); Cleveland 1944, no. 7, pl. v; on loan, Wadsworth Atheneum, Hartford; 15 March 1965–23 March 1968; on loan, Minneapolis Institute of Art, 1 April –31 October 1968; on loan, Los Angeles County Museum of Art, 18 July 1969–23 August 1972; on loan, Dorothy Chandler Pavilion, Los Angeles, 10 May 1973–3 October 1977.

References
Evelyn 1906, vol. 3, p. 18; Tatlock 1923, as property of Hugh Blaker; Vaughan 1927, pt. 1, p. 23; pt. 2, p. 67, ill.; Kuhn 1936, p. 80, no. 352, pl. lxxii;[13] Schmid 1948, vol. 2, p. 386;[14] Urquhart 1948, pp. 2–4; Ganz 1950, p. 219; Ganz 1956, p. 234;[15] Blaker and Urquhart 1963, pp. 295, 298n11;[16] Hand 1980, pp. 38f., fig. 5; Rowlands 1985, p. 145, no. 64b; Washington 1993, pp. 95, 96n26;[17] Yeide, Akinsha, and Walsh 2001, pp. 30–32; S. Campbell 2010, p. 443, no. D27, ill.

Technical Notes
The uncradled oak panel consists of two vertically grained boards with a tightly closed join. There are shallow bevels on the top and bottom edges. The panel has a slight cross-grain convex warp. The cream-colored ground is a smooth layer of medium thickness. A light red underpainting is visible in a space between the contour of the black hat and the green paint of the background, as well as in several losses at the left edge. Although infrared reflectography and microscopic examination of the surface did not reveal underdrawing, it appears that the outlines of the figure were incised before paint was applied. The portrait is executed in opaque paint, much of it applied wet-into-wet. The face is smoothly blended. Traces of gold leaf are found on the jeweled cross, the sleeve fabric, the round button, and the lettering of the inscription. The paint layer has a very fine crackle overall. Before the painting entered the collection, varnish was reduced over the lighter colors. Retouching is located in scattered spots throughout, with larger areas of toning in the proper left hand and fingers, the proper left cheek/jowl, and the pupil of the proper right eye. Some strengthening of shadows in the black robe has also occurred. The thick natural-resin varnish is yellowed and cloudy with an uneven surface.

Identified by the inscription above his head, Bryan Tuke (d. 1545), age fifty-seven, wears a loose black mantle with fur collar and "cloth of gold" sleeves (woven gold and black threads) over a close-fitting black jacket fastened by a gold button at the throat. A soft black cap with ear flaps cuts a sharp silhouette against the green background. In his left hand Tuke clutches leather gloves, an indicator of his social standing. On a heavy gold chain, an honorary gift, hangs a weighty jeweled cross.[18]

Sir Bryan Tuke was an important official at the court of Henry VIII (r. 1509–47). By 1516 he was a Knight of the King's Body and the following year was appointed Governor of the King's Posts, England's first postmaster general. His career advanced rapidly as he served as secretary to Cardinal Thomas Wolsey (ca. 1471–1530), French secretary to Henry VIII, and clerk of Parliament. Surviving the political crisis of the 1530s, when Henry VIII broke with Rome, Tuke served as sheriff of Essex and Hertfordshire in 1533. Three years later, as secretary and treasurer of the royal household, a position

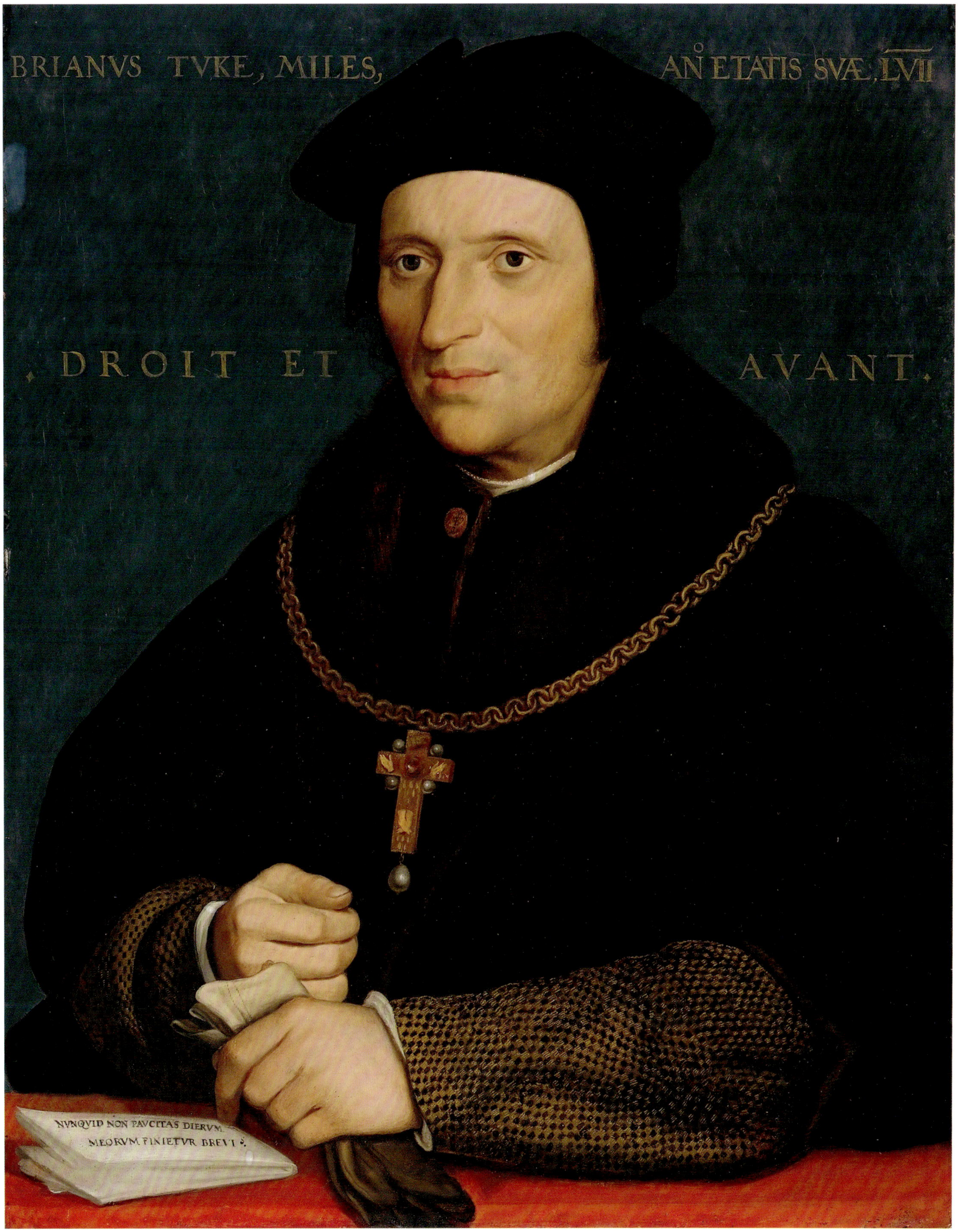

BRIANVS TVKE, MILES,
AN° ETATIS SVÆ, LVII
. DROIT ET AVANT .
NVNQVID NON PAVCITAS DIERVM
MEORVM FINIETVR BREVI ?

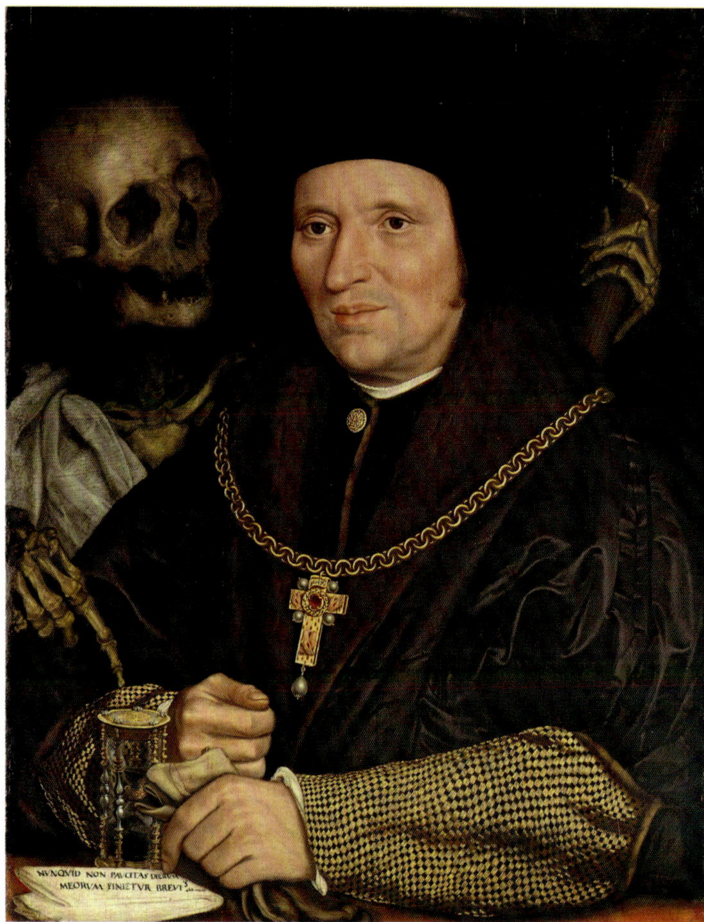

Fig. 37a. Attributed to Hans Holbein II, *Portrait of Sir Bryan Tuke*, after 1537, oil on oak panel, 18 ⅞ × 15 in. (48 × 38 cm), Alte Pinakothek, Bayerische Staatsgemäldesammlungen, Munich.

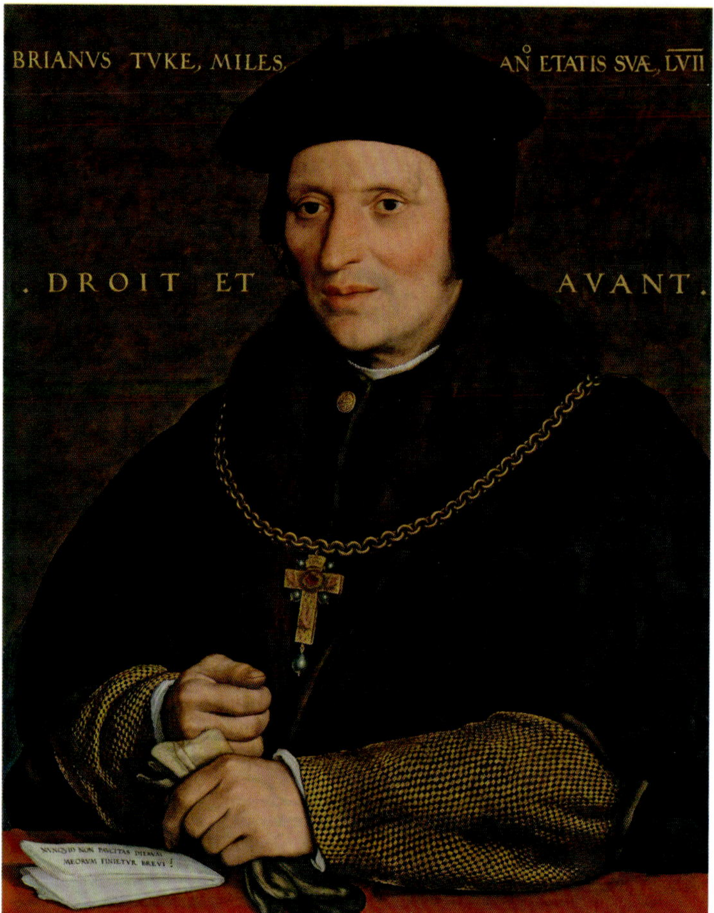

Fig. 37b. Hans Holbein II, *Sir Bryan Tuke*, ca. 1527/28 or ca. 1532/34, oil on panel, 19 ⅜ × 15 ⅛ in. (49.1 × 38.5 cm), National Gallery of Art, Washington, DC, Andrew W. Mellon Collection.

he held until his death, he paid the salary of Hans Holbein when he served as court painter to Henry VIII.[19] In addition to his official court functions, Tuke was an important member of the intellectual circle around Sir Thomas More (1478–1535) and was regarded as an eloquent communicator in the written and spoken word and a skilled cryptographer.[20] In recognition of his service to the crown, Tuke was deeded the manors of South Weald, Layer Marney, Thorpe, and East Lee in Essex. He died at Layer Marney on 16 October 1545 and was buried in the church of Saint Margaret Lothbury, London.

Although it was conceived to portray his public image, the portrait reveals, as John Hand has demonstrated, something of Tuke's personal side.[21] The sitter's family motto, "Droit et Avant" (Upright and Forward), is inscribed across the background. On the table is a folded piece of paper with an inscription taken from the book of Job (10:20) as found in the Latin Vulgate. In translation, it asks "Are not my days numbered?" As Hand has suggested, this reference to Job's suffering and the vanity of earthly life may very well reflect the fact that between 5 June and 14 July 1528 Tuke was gravely ill and presumably contemplated his own death. The concept of *vanitas* is emphasized in a version of the portrait in the Alte Pinakothek, Munich, in which a skeleton hovers over the proper right shoulder of the sitter, pointing to an hourglass on the ledge next to Tuke's hands (fig. 37a).

The Pasadena painting is one of six extant versions of the portrait of Tuke.[22] The primary version is generally believed to be that in the National Gallery of Art, Washington, DC (fig. 37b).[23] Five of the six versions, including that in the National Gallery, have virtually the same dimensions as the Pasadena painting. All but one is painted on panel. Only the painting in Munich includes specific references to *vanitas*. Most authors date the primary version ca. 1527/28, at the end of Holbein's first English period; other authors, however, date it well into his second period in England, ca. 1532/34. John Hand favors a date in the first part of the second English period, a date supported by dendrochronological analysis of the Washington painting.[24]

Evidence from the Pasadena panel indicates that it postdates by almost a century the artist's death in 1543 in London from the plague and thus cannot be autograph, nor can it have been painted in the artist's workshop.[25] According to John Fletcher of the Research Laboratory for Archaeology and the History of Art, Oxford University, who examined the

Pasadena portrait in October 1979 at the National Gallery of Art, Washington, DC, the tree from which the Pasadena panel was cut was felled in 1616, indicating a date of 1620–35 for the earliest use of the panel.[26] Such late copies of Holbein's portraits were apparently made to satisfy the demand of descendants of the sitters as well as interest on the part of the English court in assembling collections of portraits of famous people. At times the commissioning of a copy may also have reflected the patron's desire to identify politically with the royalist cause.

Using infrared reflectography to compare the underdrawings of portraits attributed to Holbein with related preparatory drawings, Maryan Ainsworth of the Metropolitan Museum of Art, New York, and Susan Foister of the National Gallery, London, determined that Holbein made use of patterns, which he kept in his workshop.[27] These full-size drawings were sometimes pricked, or pounced, along the major lines of the figure and placed against a prepared panel; using a gauze ball filled with chalk or charcoal to dust the back of the drawing, the artist transferred the basic design to the panel. The lines were then reinforced with brushstrokes of wash. In other paintings, Holbein placed a paper blackened on one side between the drawing and the panel and used a stylus to incise the drawing and transfer the image to the panel. After Holbein's death, many of his portrait drawings were bound together in what became known as the "Greate Booke."[28] Other drawings, however, were apparently in circulation in painters' studios; many of them were probably copies produced from the original drawings by the same process used to transfer images to panels.[29]

No drawings for the Tuke portrait are known, but the multiple copies, which agree in detail and size, indicate that a drawing was made and used both within Holbein's workshop and later.[30] Infrared examination of the Pasadena version reveals no underdrawing, although recent examination suggested that the major outlines of the figure had been incised, indicating the use of a cartoon. Additional studies and comparison of the infrared photographs of this painting with that in Washington are required to determine how the two paintings are related and if they were based on a common portrait pattern.[31]

The provenance of the Pasadena version can be traced back to 25 August 1678, when John Evelyn noted having seen the portrait at the home of Lord Lisle: "Lord Lisle . . . son to the Earl of Leicester . . . has divers first rate pictures, above all, that of Sir Brian Tuke, by Holbein."[32] In 1678 Lord Lisle was Robert Sidney, later 4th Earl of Leicester, whom King William III summoned to the House of Lords in 1689 as Baron Sidney of Penshurst.[33] The painting then passed by descent to John Robert Townshend, third and last Viscount Sydney of St. Leonards and Baron Sydney of Chislehurst (1805–1890), who died without direct heirs. Following his death, his wife gave the painting to his nephew Robert Marsham Townshend, following whose death in 1914 the painting was put up for auction.[34]

On 15 June 1915, eight days after the sale of Holbein's *Sir Bryan Tuke* in London, H. S. Marsham-Townsend wrote to Hugh Blaker, the purchaser of the painting: "In reply to your enquiries about picture [*sic*] of 'Sir Bryan Tuke,' the picture has probably always been in the family, as the Tukes were ancestors, and the motto 'Droit et Avant' is our present motto."[35] Although no direct genealogical relationship has been identified, a personal connection between the two families is supported by the inclusion in the sale of the Sydney collection in 1915 of a portrait by an unidentified artist of "Charles Tuke, at the age of 23, 1546 (panel, 11 × 10 in.)," Bryan Tuke's second son.[36]

1. The top dot of the colon is continued as a sloping *S*. The cross Tuke wears in the Pasadena painting does not include the "INRI" inscription at the top, which appears in the Washington version (fig. 37b).

2. A fourth brother had died in 1728, so following the death of Jocelyn, the title became extinct.

3. Thomas Pelham (1650–1711/12), 4th Baronet and 1st Baron Pelham, was the son of John Pelham, 1st Viscount Sydney, and Lucy, the daughter of Robert Sidney, 2nd Earl of Leicester. The similarity of the names Sidney and Sydney is coincidental.

4. John Thomas Townshend was the great-grandson of Charles Townshend (1674–1738) and Elisabeth Pelham (d. 1711), the daughter of Thomas Pelham.

5. Lady Emily Caroline, who was the daughter of Henry William (Paget), 1st Marquess of Anglesey, married John Robert Townshend in 1832.

6. The Marsham, Townshend, and Sydney families, living in Kent, were related through various marriages. Robert Marsham Townshend was the son and heir of Mary Elizabeth Townshend (1794–1847), sister of John Robert Townshend, 3rd Viscount Sydney (1805–1890). Mary Elizabeth Townshend was the second wife of Charles Marsham, 2nd Earl of Romney (1777–1845).

7. In his diary entry for 17 April 1921 [Blaker and Urquhart 1963, p. 295], Hugh Blaker notes, "I bought [Holbein's *Portrait of Sir Bryan Tuke*] at a tragic sale of the Sydney family in Kent. The Marsham-Townsends [*sic*], I think? Had never left the ancestral homes of Kent. . . ."

8. Hugh Blaker, Isleworth, was trained as an art student in Antwerp. As a connoisseur of paintings at the beginning of the twentieth century, he advised the sisters of David Davies, later Lord Davies, in forming a collection of paintings, which was in the Art Gallery of the National Museum of Wales by 1963. Among his favorite paintings was *An Old Woman* ("*The Ugly Duchess*"), ca. 1513, by Quentin Metsys (1465/66–1530), which his sister gave to the National Gallery, London, following his death. See Urquhart 1948, pp. 2–4; and Blaker and Urquhart 1963, p. 294.

9. Blaker and Urquhart 1963, p. 295 (entry for 17 April 1921), notes: "Duveens are negotiating for it, and Langton Douglas, as well. So it looks healthy. . . ." Paul Ganz, in a letter dated 27 July 1921 to Duveen Brothers (NSM), refers to his having examined the painting, which Duveen was considering for purchase. He notes, "This portrait of Sir Bryan is a genuine work by Hans Holbein the Younger, painted during his first

stay in England. It has suffered by overcleaning, losing some of the glazes which Holbein used to paint on the first couch of varnish. Neverless [*sic*] the condition of the picture is a good one, considering the marvelous state of the right hand, the black cloth, the golden sleeves and the gloves—Tuke's portrait in the old Pinakotheque at Munich was copied after this picture, before it was cleaned—so all the details lost are to be seen in the copy." Ganz calls the Washington painting, formerly in Lady Guest's collection, "A replica by Holbein himself." The sale of the painting to Duveen may have been protracted, since Ganz did not write an official letter of authentication for Duveen until 1923 (NSM).

10. Elisabeth Severance Prentiss was one of the Cleveland Museum of Art's earliest and most important benefactors. In 1916, as Mrs. Dudley P. Allen, she presented the Cleveland Museum of Art with a series of eight tapestries depicting the story of Dido and Aeneas. See introduction to Cleveland 1944.

11. For correspondence regarding the sale, see GRI, Duveen Archive, Box 328, F-3.

12. In his letter of 27 July 1921 to Duveen (NSM), Ganz notes that he would like to include this painting in a forthcoming "exhibition of primitives in Zurich." That exhibition has not been identified.

13. As collection of Mr. and Mrs. Prentiss. Kuhn dates the painting ca. 1526–28 and calls it "a less fine version of Number 351," now National Gallery of Art, Washington, DC.

14. "Die Einfachkeit der Komposition, die geschlossene Wirkung der Heute bekannten Bildnisse von Sir Bryan Tuke in Washington und in Cleveland sprechen nicht für die Zeit des ersten englishen Aufenthaltes, obgleich außere Gründe die Entstehung in diesen Jahren wahrscheinlich machen. Verwandte Kompositionen kommen in der Zeit zwischen 1532 und 1536 mehrfach vor. Die Eigenart der letzten Arbeiten zeigt die Komposition noch nicht. Ein endgültiges Urteil ohne Kenntnis des Originals wäre wohl allzu gewagt."

15. As at the Cleveland Museum of Art, discussed in relation to no. 51, the Washington version, as "a second version, also of good quality, which in 1678 belonged to Lord l'Isle."

16. The reference here to the Norton Simon Foundation's painting as formerly in the Cleveland Museum of Art and now with Messrs. Duveen, New York, is presumably that of the editor of the 1963 article, since in 1936, the actual date of the diary, the painting belonged to Elisabeth Severance Prentiss.

17. John Hand suggests it may be the painting seen by Evelyn although he includes Lisle in the provenance of the National Gallery version; see Washington 1993, p. 95n4.

18. Hand 1980, pp. 41–47, describes the cross at length as ornamented with pearls and a jewel at the crossing to represent the Five Wounds of Christ.

19. See "Vertue's Note Book A.b. (British Museum Add. MSS 23,069)," in "Vertue Note Books. Volume I," special issue, *The Volume of the Walpole Society* 18 (1929–30): pp. 9–60, cited by Washington 1993, p. 94.

20. See Washington 1993, p. 95n12.

21. Washington 1993, pp. 94f.

22. Washington 1993, p. 96nn26–30. Known versions include: National Gallery of Art, Washington, DC, inv. No. 1937.1.65 (oak, 49.1 × 38.5 cm); Alte Pinakothek, Munich, inv. No. 737 (oak, 49.5 × 38.5 cm); with Atelier Helvetica, Konstanz, 1980 (oak, 49 × 39.5 cm); Sir Anthony Tuke, Wherwell, Hampshire (canvas, 48.3 × 36.9 cm); and Nicholas Tuke, Hastings, East Sussex (mahogany, 94 × 63.5 cm). Note 30 reviews references to other versions of the painting not now identified. In the expertises written for Duveen Bros., Max Friedländer, 20 March 1921, considered the Pasadena version an autograph replica of the painting then in the possession of Mrs. Guest of Inwood (now National Gallery of Art, Washington, DC); Paul Ganz, 7 September 1923, wrote, "This finely conserved picture is in its eminent qualities certainly a genuine work by Hans Holbein the younger, and a most important addition to his works of the first stay in England" (NSM).

23. See Washington 1993, pp. 91–97.

24. For discussion of the date, see Hand 1980, p. 36n6; and Washington 1993, p. 94.

25. The existence of numerous copies of Holbein's portraits suggests that he maintained a workshop with assistants. After 1529, however, noncitizens were allowed to set up new workshops in London only if they became English nationals or denizens, and then they could employ only English apprentices. There is no record of Holbein's ever becoming a denizen or obtaining privileges—although, as in other countries at the time, his association with the court would have made him exempt from the regulations of the guilds.

26. John Fletcher, correspondence in NSM. John Fletcher was in Washington, DC, to study the National Gallery of Art's version of the Tuke portrait.

27. Ainsworth 1990a, Ainsworth 1991, and Foister 1993.

28. This is possibly the one mentioned in the 1547 inventory of Edward VI as "Itm A booke of paternes for phiosioneamyes." British Library, Harleian MS. 1419A, fol. 157r., cited by Ainsworth 1990a, p. 173. See also Foister 1983, p. 12.

29. Ainsworth 1990a, passim.

30. According to Foister 1993, p. 121, "Portraits were being produced in sixteenth-century England using patterns at least once removed from Holbein's drawings, as well as drawings themselves."

31. Foister 1993, p. 118, points out that when a pattern was used, examination of the underdrawings reveals the exact correspondence of the major features of the figure. Techniques used by later artists to transfer an image often differ from those used by Holbein himself. Underdrawings of portraits by Holbein or his workshop typically are limited to crisp, schematic lines used to define the features of the face: the line where the two lips meet, the eyebrows, nose, etc. There is no attempt to indicate how light falls on the form. According to Foister, the presence of hatching and the absence of brush drawing in the underdrawing remove a painting from Holbein's immediate circle.

32. Evelyn 1906, p. 18. In an expertise written for Duveen Brothers in 1923, Paul Ganz noted, "The present picture rediscovered recently must be the portrait mentioned in Evelyn's diary under the date of August 27th 1678, as being in the possession of Lord Lisle, the son of Lord Leicester" (NSM). See also Ganz 1950.

33. Lord Lisle is the name traditionally taken by the heir of the Earl of Leicester.

34. See note 6 above.

35. Copy from Duveen Brothers (NSM).

36. Knight, Frank & Rutley 1915, lot 8. *DNB* [1921–22] 1973, vol. 19, p. 1222, notes that Charles Tuke died soon after the death of his father in 1545. He, thus, apparently died shortly after the original painting was completed.

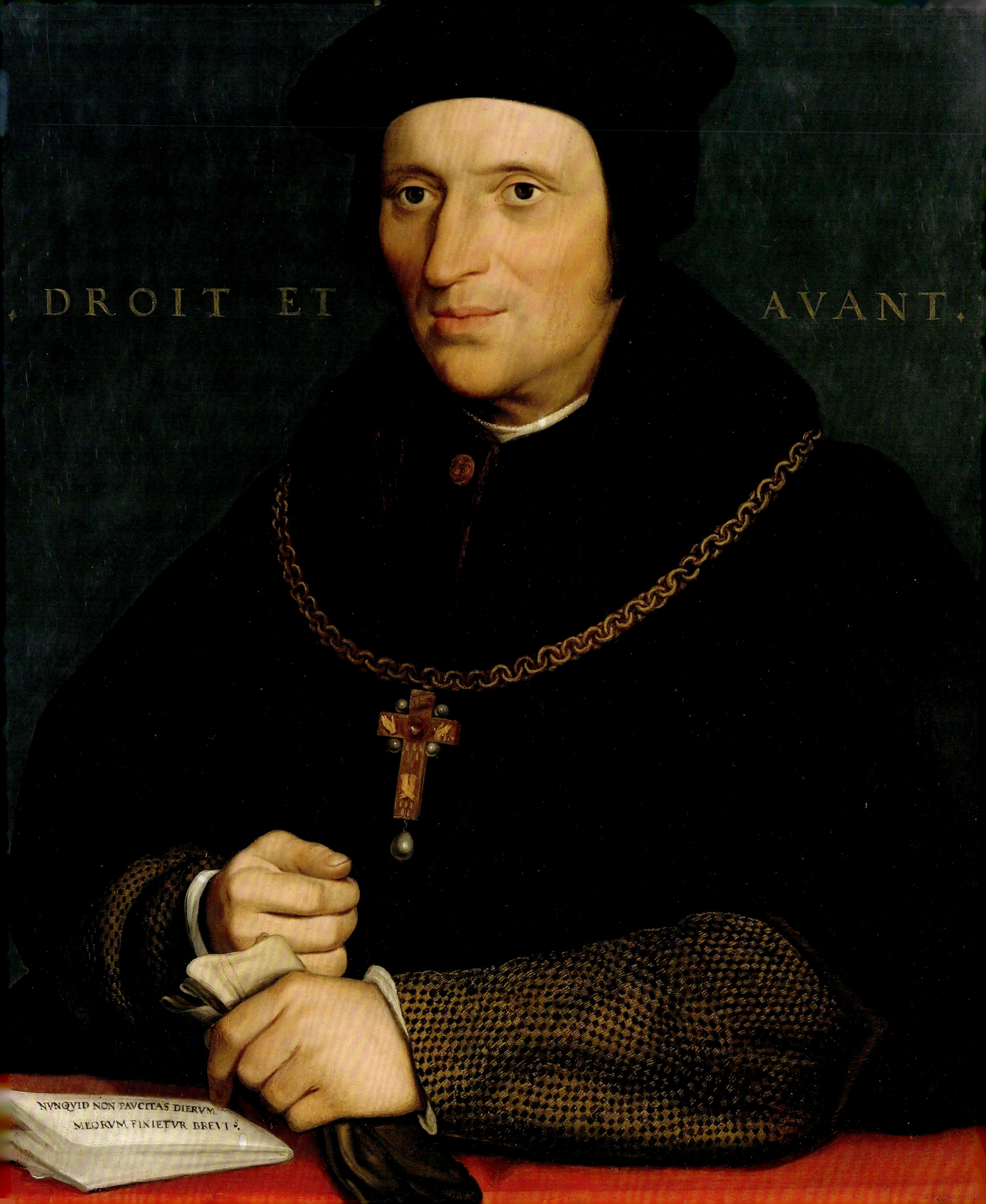

. DROIT ET AVANT .
NVNQVID NON PAVCITAS DIERVM
MEORVM FINIETVR BREVI.

38

Jan Baptist Huysmans

Flemish
Antwerp 1654–1716 Antwerp

A Wooded Italianate Landscape

1690

Signed and dated, lower center: "JBHuÿSmanS. Je.f. 1690" (*JBH* in ligature)
Oil on canvas, 67⅝ × 95¾ in. (171.8 × 243.2 cm)
Norton Simon Art Foundation, M.1982.7.2.P

Provenance
[Victor Spark (1898–1991), New York, stock no. S5254, 1967 until after 1970.][1] Charles Bradley. Anonymous (sale, Christie's, New York, 9 January 1981, lot 178, sold to); Norton Simon National Institute, Washington, DC, sold 1982 to;[2] Norton Simon Art Foundation.

Exhibited
On loan, Henry Art Gallery, University of Washington, Seattle, 21 May 1981–16 March 1983.

Reference
S. Campbell 2010, p. 433, no. 1668, ill.

Technical Notes
The plain-weave canvas has been lined, with the original tacking edges removed. Cusped threads at the edges indicate that the dimensions of the painting are probably unchanged. The ground is a light reddish-brown, occasionally left exposed to serve as a warm middle tone. The opaque paint is rich and often thickly applied in heavy brushstrokes. The landscape elements were executed in a more sketch-like handling. Although probably diminished by lining, a considerable amount of brushmarking remains. X-radiographs do not clearly reveal losses, although the large amount of retouching suggests there have been many. Abrasion, though widespread, has not compromised the image. Retouching includes a significant amount of strengthened contours throughout the immediate and middle foreground. A large area of overpaint is located in the bottom center immediately below the signature. In the group of five women at the lower left, the second and third from the right have a large amount of retouching. Immediately above them are five diagonal lines of thick overpaint, easily seen in raking light because of differences in texture. A prior restoration selectively removed varnish from the sky and clouds. The natural-resin varnish is moderately discolored.

Signed and dated 1690, *A Wooded Italianate Landscape* is typical of the romantic landscapes that Jan Baptist Huysmans and his brother and teacher Cornelis Huysmans (1648–1727) painted at the close of the seventeenth century. Integrating the traditions of Flemish landscape with the dramatic scenes painted by the Italian Salvator Rosa (1615–1673) and the Frenchman Gaspard Dughet (1615–1675), the painting pulsates with light passing through trees, picking out figures and ruins in its path. The grandeur of the wooded terrain beneath dramatic skies overwhelms the pastoral figures, who animate the landscape without commanding it.

In *A Wooded Italianate Landscape*, monumental trees cut by the bounds of the painting frame a deep, central view across a flat landscape to the distant mountain range. Huysmans divided the composition into three zones, marking the progression into depth as if it were a stage set: Trees, architecture, and hills jut into the painting from the sides like stage flats, guiding the viewer's eye into and through the scene following a zig-zag pattern of paths, overlapping hillocks, and trees. Areas of light and dark help to define the space. A shaft of sunlight breaking through the clouds spotlights a sandy bank on the left, transforming it into a scar in the verdant hillside. The sandy bank, a detail often included by both Huysmans brothers and perhaps derived from Jacob van Ruisdael (1628/29–1682), creates a compositional focal point. Softer light illuminates pastoral figures dressed in deep blue and lavender who gather flowers and converse among themselves near a river. Beyond them, other figures come and go along a shaded path. From there the viewer's attention quickly moves through the painting following the flickering light, which illuminates ancient ruins, wayside temples, and billowing clouds, as well as details of the white bark of tree trunks and broken branches scarred with red that are also found in landscapes by Ruisdael.

From the example of his brother Cornelis's paintings (fig. 38a), Jan Baptist Huysmans derived the basic compositional scheme of his fantastic Italianate landscape as well as the autumnal palette and the alternating play of clear, golden light with shadowy patches of undergrowth. Both artists combined zones of barren, eroded earth with wooded areas, recalling the work of the Flemish painter Jacques d'Artois (1613–1686), except that the surroundings are more open and less densely wooded, the handling more painterly, and the colors livelier. The portrayal of rugged, dramatic nature animated by contrasts of light and dark reflect the influence of Rosa, whose untamed landscapes

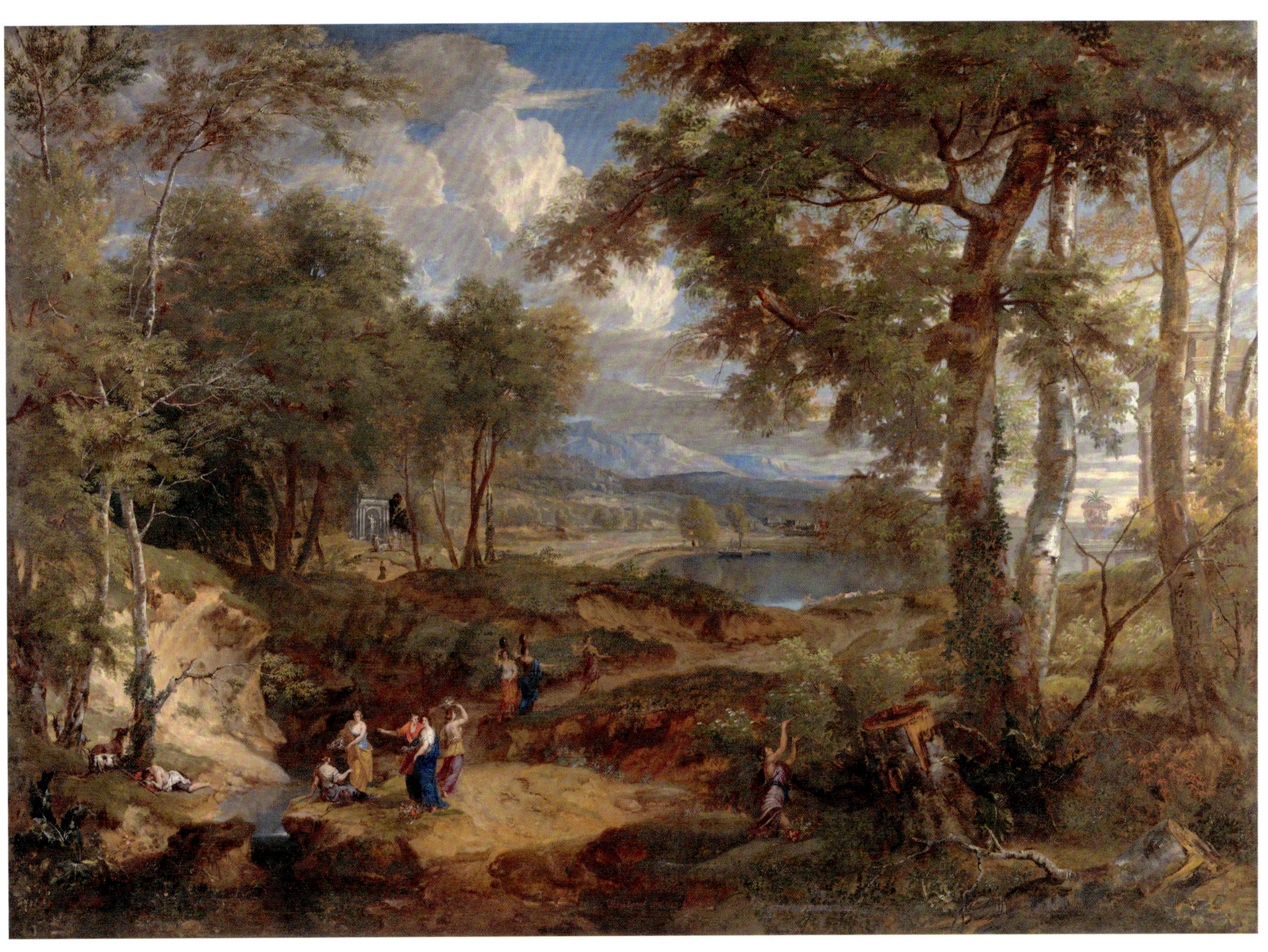

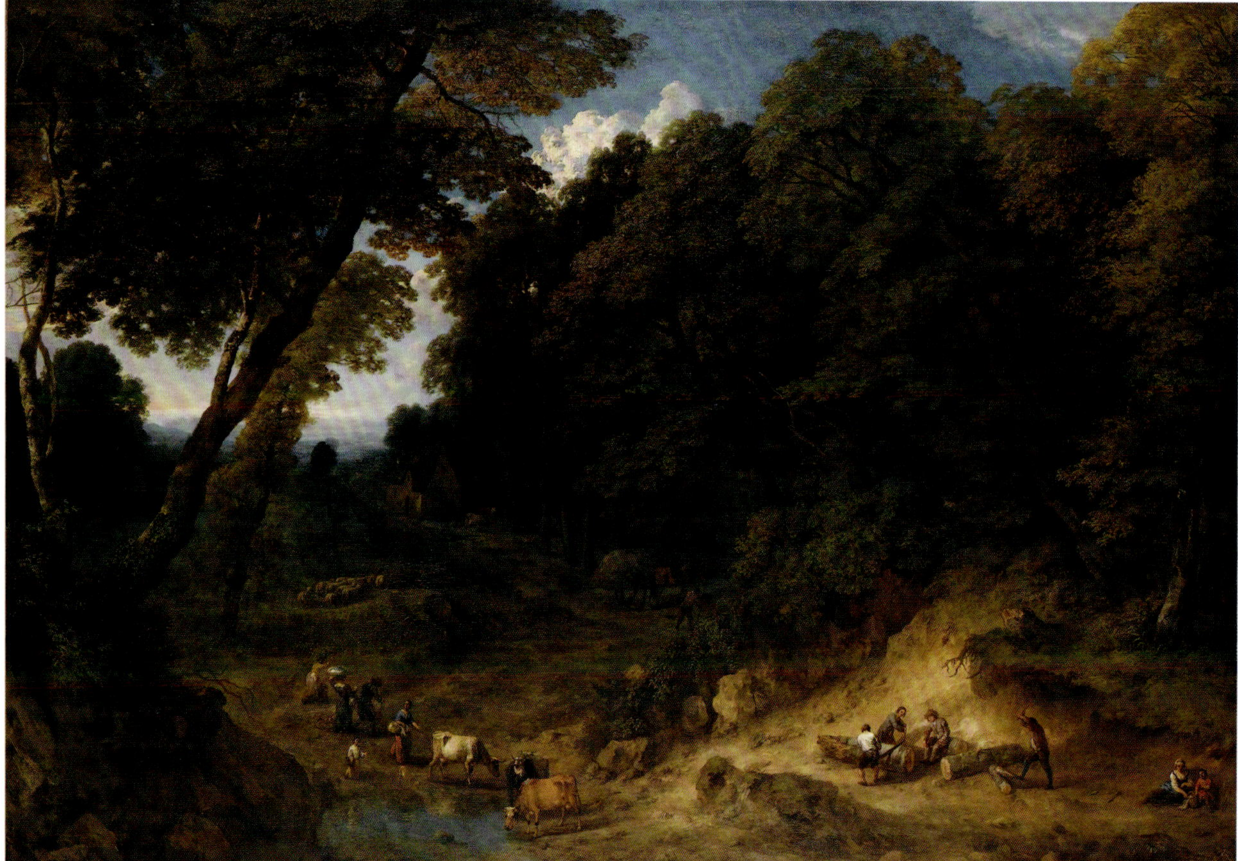

Fig. 38a. Cornelis Huysmans, *Forest Edge with Lumberjacks*, 17th–18th century, oil on canvas, 63 × 91 in. (160 × 231 cm), Musée du Louvre, Paris.

were well known in the north. Unlike the work of his brother, however, *A Wooded Italianate Landscape* is flatter and more enclosed by trees. The distant landscape also appears more agitated. Jan Baptist Huysmans's choice of Arcadian figures also distinguishes his landscape from those of his brother, who often combined Italianate scenes with animals and figures derived from prints and/or paintings by the Dutch painters Nicolaes Berchem (1621/22–1683) and Paulus Potter (1625–1654) as well as the Flemish painter Jan Siberechts (1627–1703).

The large scale of *A Wooded Italianate Landscape* reflects the influence of earlier Dutch Italianate landscape painters including Berchem and Jan Both (ca. 1618–1652) and suggests that it was painted on commission to decorate a grand house. The painting would have hung either over the fireplace or, more probably, on a wall so as to seem to offer a view through a window. In *Het Groot Schilderboek* (The Great Painting Book), published in Amsterdam in 1707, the artist and theoretician Gerard de Lairesse (1640–1711) recommended that landscapes be hung at a level so that the eye meets the horizon. In his opinion, landscapes, especially large ones, should appear as if one were looking through an open window, the depth of the windowsill indicated by the width of the painting's frame.[3]

1. Spark sent a photograph of the painting to the RKD in 1970.

2. The Norton Simon National Institute was created 5 February 1981 and dissolved on 31 January 1986.

3. De Lairesse [1707] 1738, pp. 204–05.

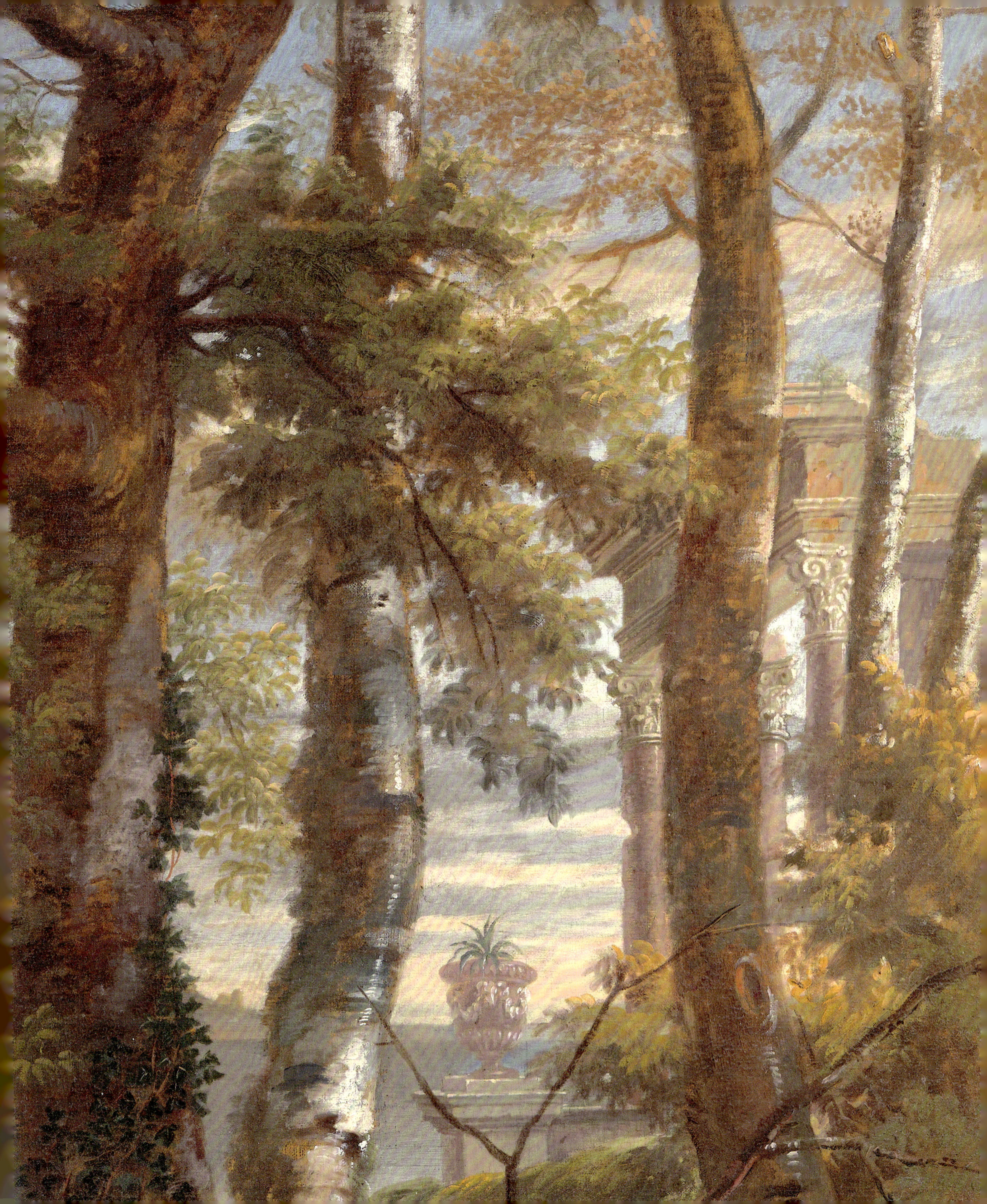

39

Adriaen Isenbrant

Netherlandish
Antwerp? ca. 1480–1551 Bruges

Young Man with a Rosary

ca. 1518

Oil on panel transferred to canvas and later transferred to panel, 16 ¾ × 12 ½ in. (42.6 × 31.8 cm)
The Norton Simon Foundation, F.1965.1.032.P

Provenance
[Paul Cassirer, Berlin, in 1921]; [Lucerne Fine Art Co. (a.k.a. Böhler and Steinmeyer, Lucerne), sold 1923 to]; [Kleinberger Gallery, New York, stock no. 15569, as on panel, sold 10 December 1923 for $6,250 to];[1] Albert J. Kobler (1876–1936), New York, by descent to his wife; Mignon Sommers Kobler, New York (m. 27 December 1941 to Edward A. Westfall), by descent to her sons;[2] A. John Kobler and Jason Sommers Kobler, sold 16 October 1947 to;[3] [Duveen Brothers, New York, sold 1964 to]; The Norton Simon Foundation.

Exhibited
New York 1929, no. 70, ill., lent by Albert J. Kobler; New York 1946b, nos. 13–14 (detail), ill., as lent by Mrs. Edward A. Westfall; New York 1964, no. 8, ill.

References
M. Friedländer 1928, pp. 4, ill., 6 (English summary by C. C. H. Drechsel, p. 3);[4] "Kleinberger/Flemish Primitives" 1929, p. 5; "Kleinberger/Flemish Show" 1929, p. 12, no. 70; Burrows 1929, p. 9; Noe 1930, p. 39; M. Friedländer 1924–37, vol. 11 (1933), p. 140, no. 219; M. Friedländer 1967–76, vol. 11 (1974), p. 92, no. 219, pl. 151;[5] S. Campbell 2010, p. 446, no. D60, ill.

Technical Notes
Records indicate that the painting was originally executed on panel. By the time of its acquisition in 1964 the painting had been transferred to canvas in an undocumented treatment. It was removed from the canvas support in 1978 and mounted on a new oak panel with an attached cradle. The white ground is of undetermined thickness and may not be the original preparation layer. Microscopic examination revealed no underdrawing. The paint, significantly altered, appears to have been moderately thin originally. The surface, which has been badly affected by the transfers, is covered with small bumps and pits. The extent of losses or damaged paint was not documented. Retouching is extensive. The moderately thick varnish appears to be a wax-modified natural resin, although ultraviolet-light examination yields an unfamiliar dark blue-green fluorescence.

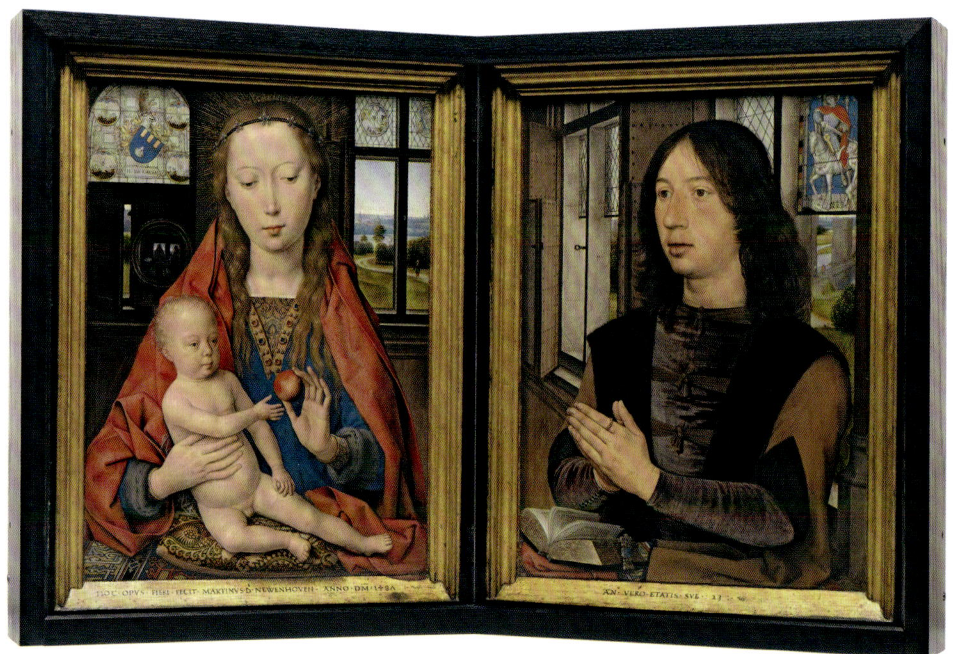

Fig. 39a. Hans Memling, *Diptych of Maarten van Nieuwenhove*, 1487, oil on panel, 20 ½ × 16 ⅜ in. (52 × 41.5 cm), Musea Brugge: Museum Sint-Janshospitaal, Bruges.

Rather than an independent portrait, this bust-length depiction of a well-dressed young man originally formed the right wing of a diptych, as in *Diptych of Maarten van Nieuwenhove* by Hans Memling (ca. 1430/40–1494; fig. 39a).[6] When the diptych was open, the man would have faced a devotional image, probably that of the Virgin with the Christ Child—more specifically the Virgin of the Rosary—to whom he would appear to be repeating prayers as he fingers the coral beads of a rosary, attached to which are at least two bells (fig. 39b). The sitter's expensive costume, including a black hat with a notched rim, and his short hair identify him as a member of the wealthy burgher class of Bruges. He wears a sleeveless robe with a black fur collar over a brown square-neck tunic trimmed with a band of black, probably intended to represent fur or velvet.[7] The brown sleeves, which would have been attached to the bodice by ties at

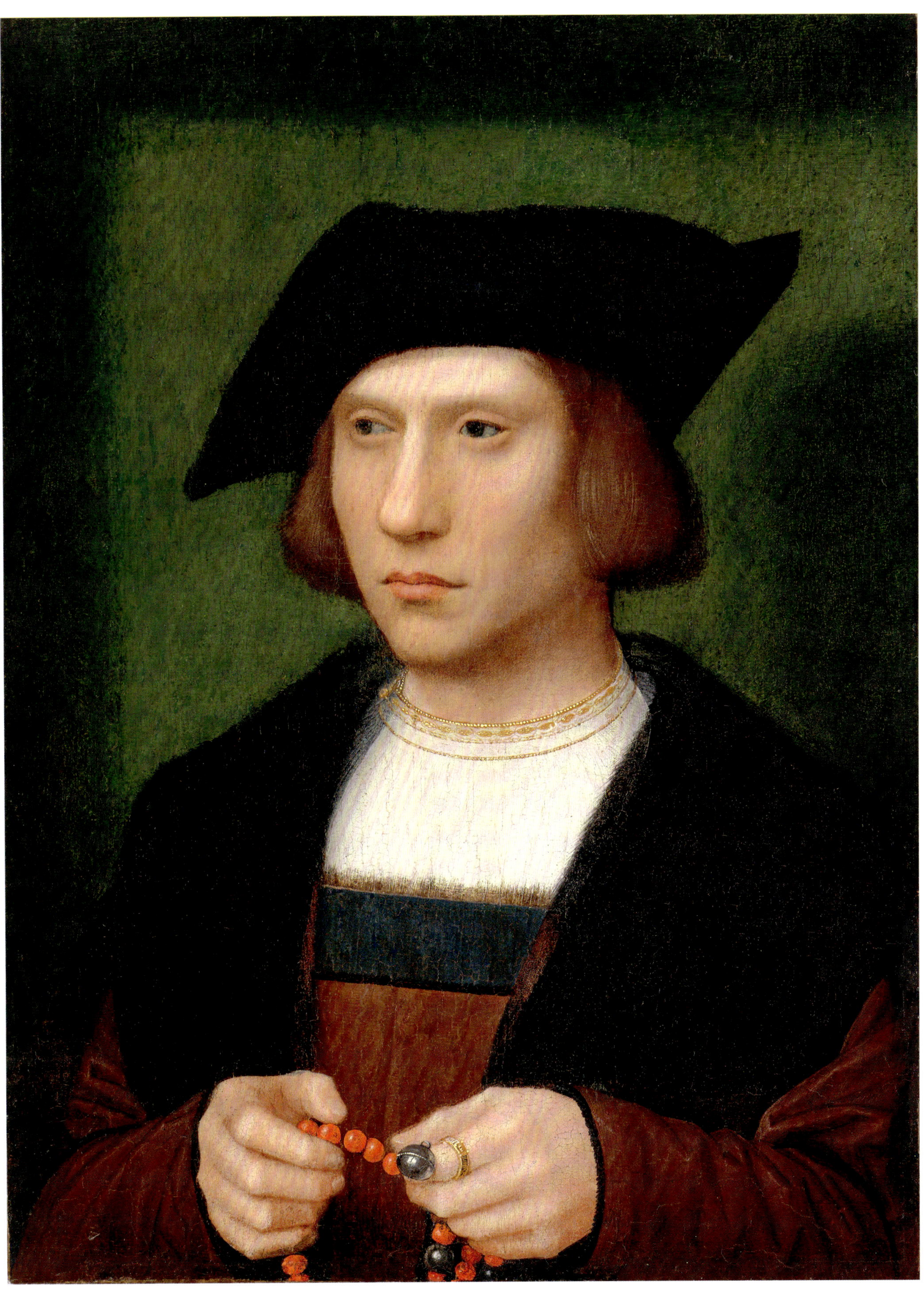

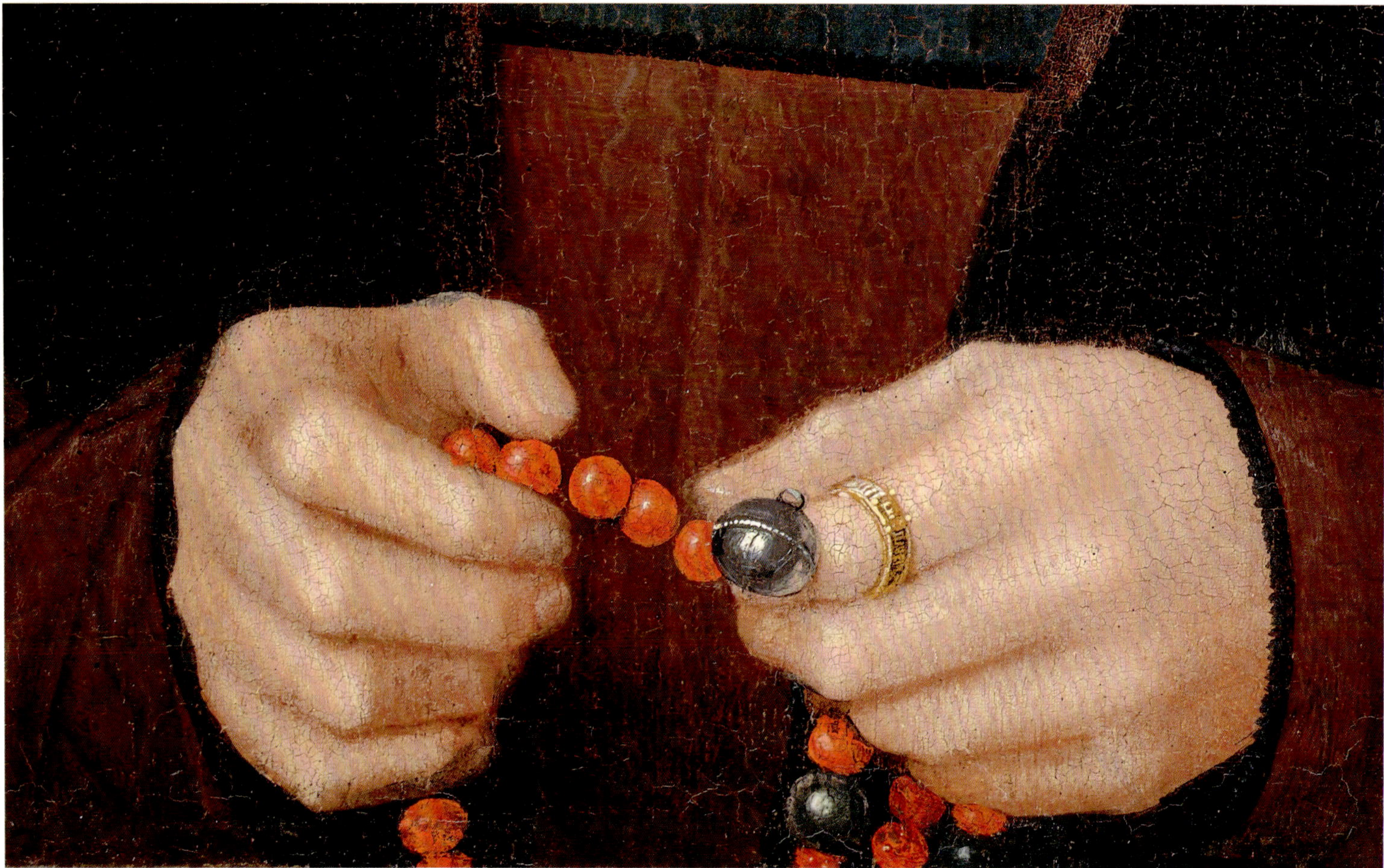

Fig. 39b. Detail of rosary bells.

the shoulders, appear to belong to the tunic. The robe has either nonfunctional sleeves that hang behind or simple slit openings. Beneath his tunic he wears a shirt of white cambric linen gathered by gold embroidery at the neckline. The donor's coat of arms may have decorated the reverse of the original panel, which was lost when the painting was transferred to canvas.[8]

Attributions to Isenbrant are problematic because of the lack of paintings securely attributed to him and the consequent confusion of his oeuvre with works by his contemporaries.[9] The composition and enigmatic personality of the sitter in the Pasadena painting is typical of Netherlandish donor portraits of the fifteenth and sixteenth centuries that relied on standard models. In 1928 Max Friedländer published *Young Man with a Rosary* among a group of portraits he identified as the work of Adriaen Isenbrant.[10] Friedländer's attribution to the artist has remained unchallenged by subsequent authors, although the similarity to works by Ambrosius Benson (1495/1500–1550) has been noted.[11] The sculptural definition of forms, frozen gaze, and abstract placement of the sharply silhouetted figure against a green background defined by shadows cast from both the frame and the figure are characteristic of portraits attributed to Isenbrant.[12] Damage caused to the Pasadena portrait as the result of the early transfer of the painting from panel to canvas and back to panel makes it difficult to judge the subtleties of style that could aid in the attribution of the painting; nevertheless, *Young Man with a Rosary* appears closer to Isenbrant's warmer tonality and subtler transitions between light and dark than to Benson's style.

1. According to the Kleinberger stock card, Department of European Paintings, Metropolitan Museum of Art, New York.

2. New York 1946b, no. 13.

3. The painting was exhibited by Duveen in 1946, but a letter from Duveen Brothers to John S. Kobler dated 16 October 1947 concerns the gallery's purchase of the painting. For lengthy correspondence between A. J. Kobler and Duveen, as well as Kobler's two sons and Duveen, see GRI, Duveen Archive, Box 256, file 17, and Box 474, files 1–8.

4. As owned by Böhler and Steinmeyer, Lucerne. The painting actually then belonged to Kobler. According to Kleinberger stock no. 15,569 (Kleinberger records, Metropolitan Museum of Art, New York), Friedländer authenticated a photograph of the painting on 30 July 1923, when it still belonged to Böhler and Steinmeyer, with whom Kleinberger often worked in partnership.

5. M. Friedländer 1967–76 notes, "In 1964 on the art market, New York [Duveen]: transferred to canvas."

6. According to convention, if the portrait was intended to hang as a pendant to a portrait of the man's wife, then it would have been oriented to face either forward or toward the viewer's right.

7. The texture of the black band appears to be flat, but the upper edge is feathered as if fur. Although the band does not appear to have been overpainted significantly, the panel has suffered abrasion in this area. I am grateful to Sandra Rosenbaum, formerly curator-in-charge of the Doris Stein Research Center for Costume and Textiles, Department of Costume and Textiles, Los Angeles County Museum of Art, for her help in defining the parts of this costume. The standard source book for costume in this period is Scott 1986.

8. Any painting on the reverse of the panel was lost when the painting was transferred from panel to canvas. The painting was transferred from canvas to a new panel by Marco Grassi in 1978–79.

9. See Wilson 1995 for a discussion of the problem of defining Isenbrant's oeuvre.

10. M. Friedländer 1928, p. 4.

11. See comments by the restorer William Suhr and Theodore Rousseau, curator of European paintings at the Metropolitan Museum of Art, New York (NSM). See also note from "BB" [Bernard Berenson], New York, to E. F. [Edward Fowles, owner of Duveen Brothers], Paris, 6 March 1953: "(Prof. Coremans was here on March 6th)—With regard to the ISENBRANDT, though he did not think it was by him, he nevertheless considered it a wonderful picture and far superior to its illustration, to any photographs he had seen. I did not tell him that the picture had only recently been cleaned, but he was most enthusiastic about it and kept commenting on how much better it was than the photographs he had seen in Brussels." (GRI, Duveen Archive, box 256, file 17).

12. For the stylistic similarities between Isenbrant and Benson, see Wilson 1995, p. 4. Benson's portraits, in which the sitter often addresses the viewer, are generally more lifelike and animated and the postures of his sitters are more varied than Isenbrant's.

40

Jacob Jordaens

Flemish
Antwerp 1593–1678 Antwerp

and

Jan Wildens

Flemish
Antwerp 1585/86–1653 Antwerp

Mercury and Argus

Early 1640s

Oil on canvas, 47¾ × 72¾ in. (121.3 × 184.8 cm)
The Norton Simon Foundation, F.1976.01.P

Provenance
Possibly [Jaques de Roore (1686–1747), The Hague (sale, Hendrik Verheyden, The Hague, 4 September 1747, no. 79, "Een ditto [Capitaal] landschap, door ditto [Jaques Jordaans], verbeelt Mercurius en Argus, h. 3 v, 10 d.; br. 6 v 2 duim. 21—0")].[1] Possibly [David Jetswaart (Ietswaart; 1691–1749), Amsterdam (sale, Amsterdam, 22 April 1749, no. 102, "Een stuk daar Mercurius Argus het Hoofd af wil slaan, met verscheide Beesten door Jordaans, h. 4 v, br. 6 v. 6 d. 31—0")].[2] Possibly Capello[3] (sale, Amsterdam, 6 May 1767, no. 58, "Een fray Landschap, geordineert met de Historie daar Mercurius Argus, die in een slaapende Actie legt, het Hoofdt afkliest, en teffens Jo. Verloft; met verder Hoornvee daar by, door Jacques Jordaans, van zyn allerbeste tydt, op doek; hoek; hoog 52, breet 71 duimen. 102—0")]. Anonymous, Antwerp, to; Major Whitlock (d. by 1802), Dublin, to;[4] Alexander Mangin (1732–1802), Dublin, or William Ashford (ca. 1746–1824), Dublin (sale, James Vallance, Dublin, 9 May 1803, lot 116).[5] Margaret Talbot (1740–1834), from 1831, 1st Baroness Talbot of Malahide, Dublin,[6] by 1815, by descent to; Milo John Talbot (1912–1973), 7th Baron Talbot of Malahide, Dublin, by descent to his sister; the Hon. Rose Maud Talbot (1915–2009), Malahide Castle[7] (sale, Christie's, London, 2 April 1976, lot 62, ill., sold to); The Norton Simon Foundation.

Exhibited
Dublin 1815, p. 4, no. 32, as *Landscape, with Mercury, Argus and Io* by Van Uden and Jordaens, lent by Mrs. Talbot.

References
Hussey 1947, p. 762, fig. 5; Millar 1953, no. 110;[8] Adler 1980, p. 116, no. G119, fig. 154; Pasadena 1980, p. 48, ill.; Pasadena 1989, p. 60, ill.; Stewart 1990–95, vol. 2, p. 370; S. Campbell 2010, p. 393, no. 1316, ill.

Technical Notes
The plain-weave canvas is lined with the original tacking edges removed. A white ground is visible at various edges of cracks and small losses in the paint layer. There also appears to be a rose-beige underpainting. While this layer seems to be present beneath much of the darker tones of the foreground and trees, it is not seen beneath the lighter tones of the sky. In the foreground and the middle ground, paint was broadly applied in thin washes of greens and browns. Tree leaves were dabbed on quickly over the sky; the tree trunks were painted more densely. The figures and cattle were painted with more robust opaque paint, possibly over already established landscape details; this remains to be confirmed by X-radiography. In 1976 the painting suffered water damage during shipment, as the painting and its lining canvas remained wet for an unspecified time. The varnish was severely blanched, and paint was damaged by leaching of the oil medium, particularly in glazes in the right half of the painting and much of the foreground. The reversal of the damage was successful in that the painting retains its impressive presence. Microscopic examination of the surface, however, reveals alteration of the original texture and characteristics of the paint. Lining pressure compressed the paint profile, and weave transference accentuated the canvas texture. Pinpoint losses are found scattered throughout, and the edges of cracks are abraded. Residues of dark varnish left in the depressions of the canvas weave are adjacent to abraded paint. Some brushstrokes are discontinuous, leaving fractured or interrupted dark glazes in the foreground and the deeper shadows lacking their original depth. Retouching was executed in broad areas of toning, in combination with more localized strengthening of darks and shadows. The varnish is a thin, evenly applied natural resin.

This painting depicts a moment of high tension in the story of Mercury and Argus (Ovid, *Metamorphoses* 1:568–721). Sent by Jupiter to retrieve the maiden Io, whom jealous Juno has transformed into a white heifer and placed under the guard of Argus, Mercury lulls the old shepherd to sleep with the sound of his pipe; a moment later he will strike off Argus's head with his sword. Although the image contains no reference to the hundred eyes that covered the body of the vigilant shepherd, it does include Mercury's winged hat, sword sheath, and caduceus, which the messenger has cast to the ground to avoid recognition by Argus.

Sold as a work by Jacob Jordaens and Jan Wildens in 1803, *Mercury and Argus* was exhibited in 1815 as a work by Jordaens and Lucas van Uden (1595–1672), the latter an artist closely associated with Wildens.[9] Since its rediscovery in 1976, however, the Arcadian landscape setting of the painting has been firmly reattributed to the more accomplished artist Jan Wildens and the figures to Jacob Jordaens.[10] Specific elements and the general composition of the landscape are similar to a pen, bister, and indigo-wash drawing by Wildens

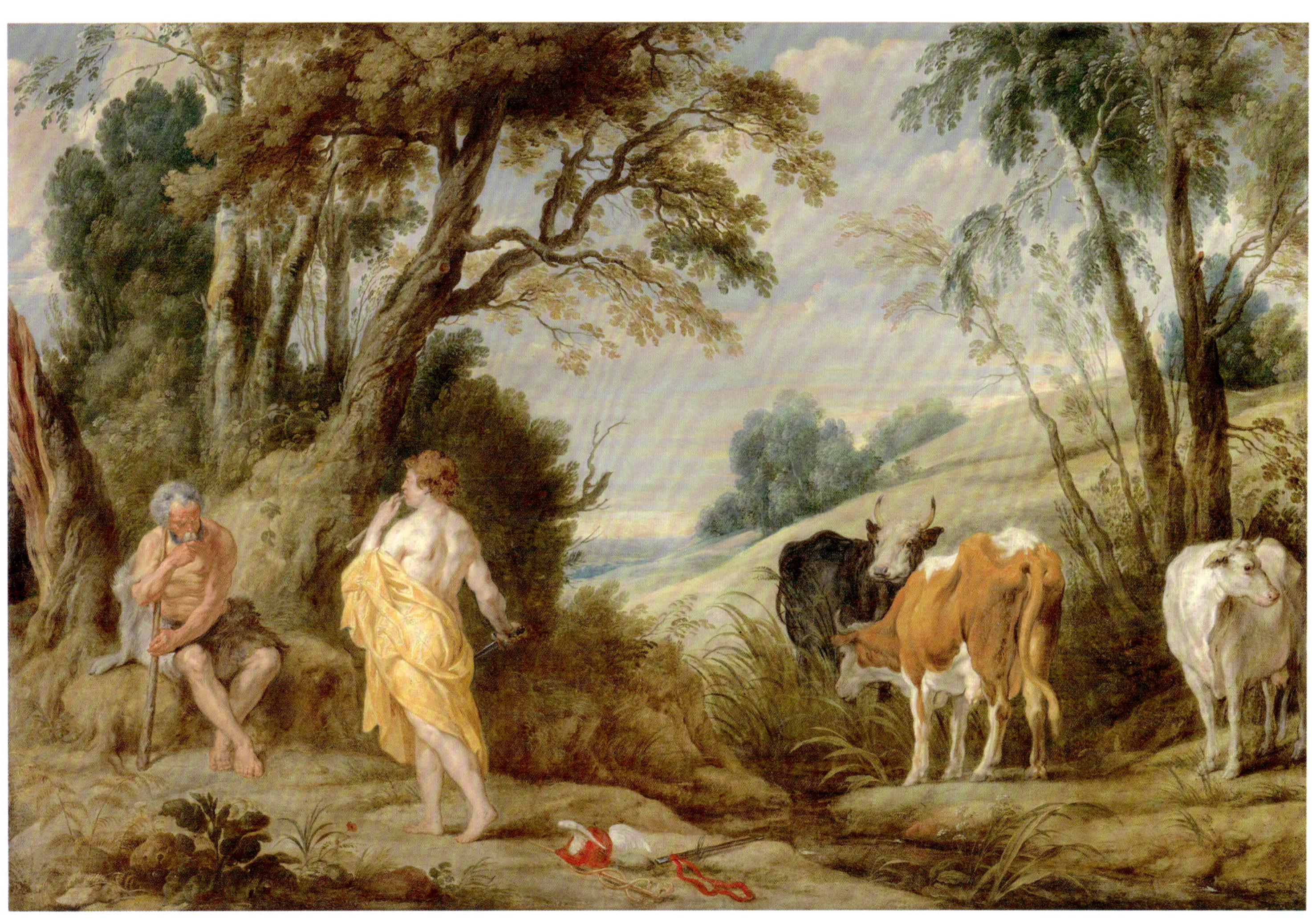

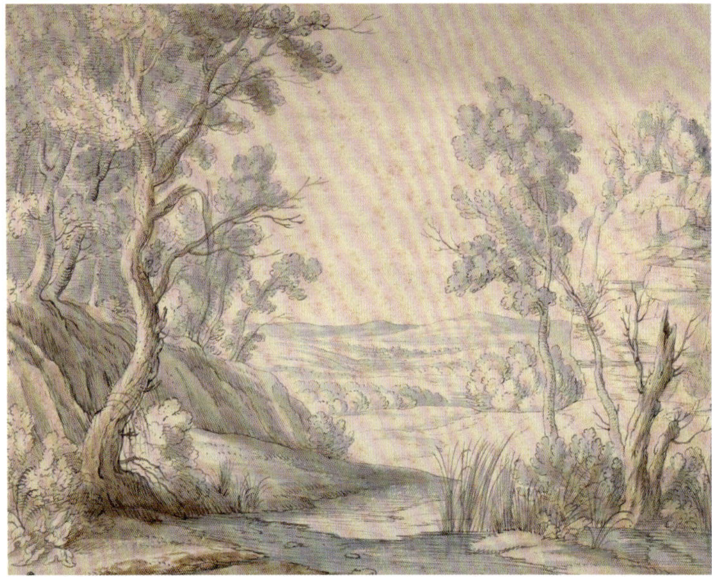

Fig. 40a. Jan Wildens, *Landscape*, n.d., pen, bister, washed with blue, 9 × 12¼ in. (22.8 × 31.2 cm), Musée du Louvre, Paris.

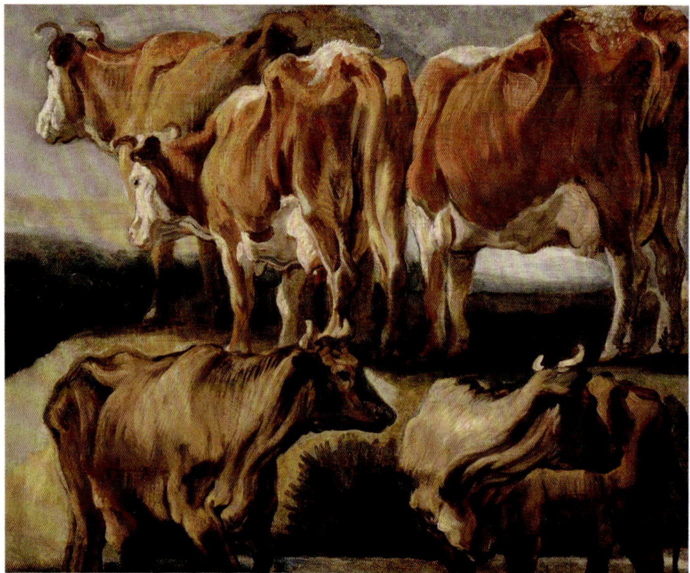

Fig. 40b. Jacob Jordaens, *Study of Five Cattle*, early 1620s, oil on canvas, 26⅛ × 31⅞ in. (66.5 × 81 cm), Palais des Beaux-Arts, Lille.

in the Louvre (fig. 40a). Both share a lyrical quality created by the light, arching forms of the feathery trees and grasses that frame the central view. Notations in early inventories indicate that Jordaens himself also painted independent landscapes.[11] His collaboration with Wildens and other landscape painters, therefore, was undoubtedly intended to increase the efficiency of his production.[12] Following the deaths of Rubens in 1640 and Anthony van Dyck in 1641, Jordaens became the most sought-after painter in the popular Flemish tradition. Collaboration was a common practice in large workshops, where individual artists specialized in one of the genres. Both Jordaens and Wildens had worked as independent artists in Rubens's Antwerp studio; Wildens painted landscape backgrounds for Rubens from about 1616 to 1620 as well as for other artists throughout his career.

The procedure followed by Jordaens and Wildens in executing the Pasadena painting is not immediately evident since landscape elements appear both under and over the figures. Although it is possible that Jordaens followed the traditional method of sketching the figure composition on the primed canvas after which Wildens executed the landscape, leaving the area for the figures in reserve, it appears more likely that Jordaens, who was familiar with Wildens's rather standard landscape compositions, simply requested a landscape of a certain size and composition. The inventory of Jan Wildens's son, the painter Jeremias Wildens (1621–1653), lists numerous landscapes "after the old Wildens," many of which are mentioned as being "unstaffed," suggesting that they may have been painted on speculation.[13] In the case of such a prominent artist as Jordaens and the large scale of this painting, however, it is probable that Wildens painted the landscape according to Jordaens's specifications and that Jordaens then added the figures. Either Wildens or Jordaens would then have painted the blades of grass and other details that overlap the animals.

Mercury and Argus is related to a number of drawings by Jordaens, which the artist and his assistants used in various paintings over a period of years. An oil sketch of five cattle in the Palais des Beaux-Arts, Lille, datable to the early 1620s (fig. 40b), is closely related to the two cattle on the right of the Pasadena painting. The sketch, which has been generally associated with other versions of the subject by Jordaens, represents two cows drawn from different angles.[14] The oil sketch is divided into two registers: The cow in the middle of the upper register is an almost exact replica of the central cow seen from the rear in the Pasadena painting. The two cattle in the lower register of the sketch are closely related—in terms of both the fluid description of the sinewy bodies and the "pinched" noses of the animals—to the white cow that twists its neck to look beyond the right edge of the painting. The combination of the passive central cow and the alert bull behind her appears in an oil sketch attributed to Jordaens[15] and again in a thematically and compositionally related painting, *Mercury and Battus* in the Museum Boijmans Van Beuningen, Rotterdam (fig. 40c).[16]

The Rotterdam painting is a variant of the Pasadena composition. The landscapes differ significantly, but the figures are closely related. The appearance, posture, and gesture of the younger man are virtually the same in both works, but whereas in the Pasadena painting he holds a pipe to his mouth and carries a sword in his right hand, in the Rotterdam example he holds nothing in the left hand and a walking stick or shepherd's staff in his right hand.[17] The old man is also very similar in both paintings, but whereas in the Pasadena version the shepherd sits, in the Rotterdam painting he stands. Despite employing similar figures, the two compositions

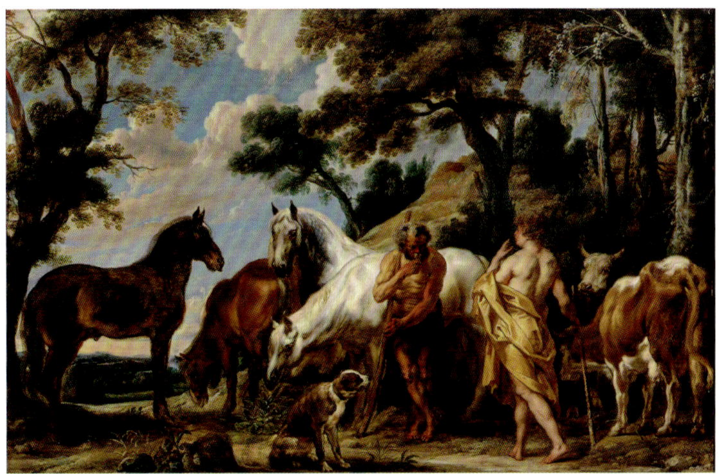

Fig. 40c. Jacob Jordaens, *Mercury and Battus*, 1635–40, oil on panel, 31½ × 43¼ in. (80 × 110 cm), Museum Boijmans Van Beuningen, Rotterdam.

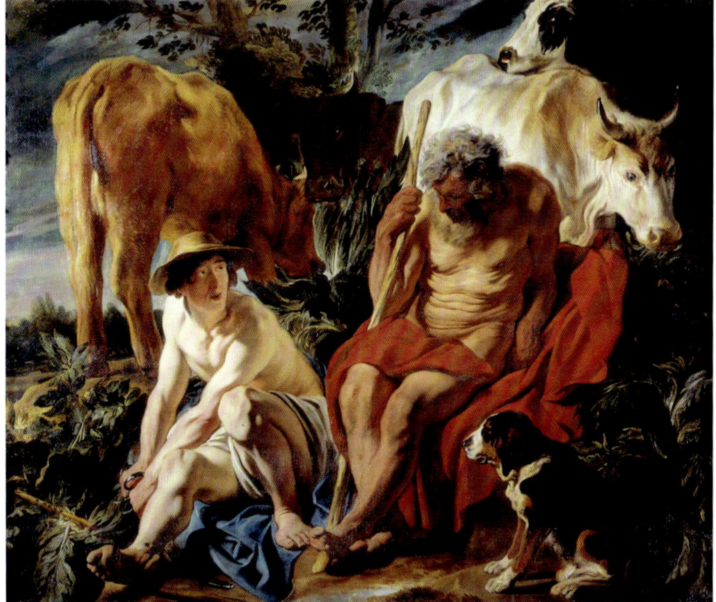

Fig. 40d. Jacob Jordaens, *Mercury and Argus*, 1625, oil on canvas, 79½ × 94⅞ in. (202 × 241 cm), Musée des Beaux-Arts, Lyon.

depict different stories. The inclusion of horses in the Rotterdam painting identifies it as a representation of the story of Mercury and Battus, a shepherd who was turned into stone for telling Apollo that Mercury had stolen his herd.[18]

Max Rooses attributed thirty-one versions of the story of Mercury and Argus to Jacob Jordaens, not including the present painting, which was unknown to him.[19] The Pasadena painting differs significantly in its choice of incident, landscape setting, and handling of paint from Jordaens's best known version of the subject in the Musée des Beaux-Arts, Lyon (fig. 40d). In the Lyon example, both protagonists sit side by side on a clump of ground in the foreground; Mercury cautiously reaches across his body for his sword to slay the sleeping Argus. The tight confinement of the figures within the frame visually reinforces the psychological tension of the dramatic moment. The Pasadena painting depicts the previous scene in the story in an Arcadian landscape: Mercury, having subdued Argus with the soothing sound of the pipe, moves easily across the landscape toward the slumbering shepherd. The differences between the Lyon and Pasadena paintings are characteristic of the compositional and stylistic changes that took place in Jordaens's work between the early 1620s and the 1640s. Typical of paintings produced in Antwerp during the first decades of the seventeenth century, the figures in the Lyon *Mercury and Argus* are firmly modeled and dominate the foreground, with little description of landscape. The hard enamel surfaces of Jordaens's early figures create the effect of reflected light. In the Pasadena painting, by comparison, local colors are reduced, and both the figures and the landscape are loosely rendered. The resulting atmospheric effect unifies rather than accentuates individual forms. These stylistic characteristics support a date in the early to mid-1640s, when, under the influence of Rubens and the Venetian landscape tradition, both Jordaens and Wildens turned to a looser handling of paint to describe lighter, feathery foliage and more elegant figures and poses such as Jordaens's figure of Mercury.[20]

The subject of Mercury and Argus was popular during the early seventeenth century and especially the 1640s. In his commentary on the *Metamorphoses* of Ovid, *Wtlegghingh op den Metamorphosis Pub. Ovidij Nasonis. . .* , published in Haarlem in 1604, the Dutch artist, chronicler, and theorist Karel van Mander (1548–1606) associated the story of Mercury and Argus with the need to guard one's virtue. The inscription on an engraving by Schelte Bolswert (ca. 1586–1659) after a later, enlarged variation of Jordaens's Lyon composition repeats this association.[21] The closing line declares, "Chastity is the guardian of virtue, and just like many-eyed Argus, perishes heeding the dictates of love."

Typical of seventeenth-century imagery, however, the story of Mercury and Argus could also be adapted to other interpretations based on the underlying theme of vigilance. Significantly, the majority of Jordaens's representations of the story of Mercury and Argus are dated or datable to the 1640s, a period of high anxiety in both the northern and the southern Netherlands as ending the war between the Dutch Republic and Spain was discussed, culminating in the signing of the Peace of Münster in 1648.[22] To celebrate the peace, the city of Amsterdam erected a *tableau vivant* representing the story of Mercury and Argus. A commemorative broadsheet of the event associates the story with the need to remain vigilant even in times of peace, a popular theme during the period of the Twelve Years' Truce (1609–21) and again during the 1640s, when many feared that the declaration of peace would leave them, like Argus, vulnerable to outside attack.[23]

While Jordaens and his patron may have intended to convey the theme of vigilance to the viewer, the greater emphasis on the Arcadian landscape than on the figures and the resulting detachment of the viewer from the drama of the scene also suggests that the aesthetic appeal of the romantic Arcadian landscape staffed with graceful, mythological figures, was at least equally important.

1. Hoet 1752–70, vol. 2, p. 206.

2. Hoet 1752–70, vol. 2, p. 245.

3. Hoet 1752–70, vol. 2, p. 588. The sale was identified only as "een voornaam Liefhebber," but Hoet [p. 583] notes parenthetically "zynde, zo men zegt, den Heer Capello."

4. According to the 1803 sale catalogue, "Mercury and Argus, Cows, &c. Jordaens and Wildens. This most capital Picture is in the highest preservation, possesses all the excellencies of these masters, was brought from Antwerp to that well known judge of Pictures, the late Major Whitlock. It has frequently been enquired after and regretted by the admirers of Painting in that city." Major Whitlock is unidentified.

5. The sale catalogue does not identify the seller of individual lots. Alexander Mangin was an important official in Dublin, where his father and uncle had emigrated from Haarlem in 1715. Mangin's important collection of drawings and prints was sold in London 29 March 1810. The catalogue notes that he sometimes engaged agents to assist him in collecting, among whom were Mr. Crone in Italy and Mr. Greenwood in Holland (see Lugt 1956, p. 240). William Ashford was a landscape painter born in Birmingham, England. In 1764 he went to Ireland and settled in Dublin, where he was known for his paintings of Irish country houses (see Moore-Gwyn 2007).

6. The lender to the 1815 exhibition is identified only as Mrs. Talbot. Margaret Talbot (née O'Reilly), by then the widow of Richard Talbot (ca. 1736–1788), was created 1st Baroness of Talbot of Malahide in 1831. The couple were the parents of eight sons and seven daughters.

7. A photograph of the small drawing room at Malahide Castle, reproduced by Hussey 1947, p. 762, fig. 5, shows the painting hanging high on the wall to the left of the fireplace.

8. Cited by Adler 1980, p. 116.

9. On Van Uden, see Adler 1980, pp. 17ff.; Thiery 1986, pp. 167–74; and Cologne/Antwerp/Vienna 1992, pp. 454–55.

10. Adler 1980, p. 116.

11. The 1678 inventory of the estate of the painter Erasmus Quellinus II (1607–1678), for example, notes "een lantschapken van Jordaens" (a landscape by Jordaens); Denucé 1932, p. 275.

12. The inventory of Jordaens's sister Anna, who died in 1668, mentions "een stuck van Momper, door d'Heer Jordaens gestoffert" (a piece by Momper, with staffage by Mr. Jordaens); Denucé 1932, p. 251.

13. See, for example, no. 147: "Noch een Lantschap, ongestoffeert, naer Wildens" (Another landscape, without figures, after Wildens); Denucé 1932, p. 158.

14. Although the sketch appears to have been drawn directly from life, it probably represents the artist's reworking of images recorded first in chalk, possibly on a portable, reusable pad. See Van de Wetering 1991.

15. *Two Oxen* [*sic*] *with Two Men Before an Altar*, oil sketch on wood, 47 × 54 cm (the current location is unknown; it was with Hans Wendland, Lugano, in 1931); see Berlin 1931, no. 47, pl. 18.

16. The Rotterdam painting (oil on panel, 80 × 110 cm) is on long-term loan from the Rijksdienst voor Beeldende Kunst, The Hague, inv. NK 2626, to the Museum Boijmans Van Beuningen, Rotterdam.

17. Jordaens may have based the figure of Mercury in both paintings on a statue of Mercury by Quellinus that belonged to Rubens and is recorded in drawings made by Jordaens (Harvard Art Museums, Cambridge, and Museum Plantin Moretus, Antwerp). The striding pose of Mercury, however, suggests the ultimate inspiration was the Apollo Belvedere, a Roman copy of a Greek original, that was well known to Rubens, who employed its posture in his paintings. Jordaens may have adapted the pose from a drawing or painting by Rubens or another artist, or he may have made his own studies of a sculpture based on the antique. A stone statue of Mercury is listed in the inventory of the *groote neercamer* (large downstairs room) of Jeremias Wildens's home in 1653; see Denucé 1932, p. 154.

18. The relatively weak description of the animals in the Rotterdam painting and the figure of Mercury differ significantly from the Pasadena painting and may indicate that the Rotterdam painting was at least partially a product of the workshop of Jordaens. See Rotterdam 1990, pp. 52–53, no. 9.

19. Rooses 1908, p. 277.

20. Adler 1980, p. 116. The graceful pose of Mercury (see note 17 above) is similar, for example, to that of Bacchus in *Bacchus and Ariadne*, ca. late 1640s (Museum of Fine Arts, Boston).

21. Hollstein 1949–2010, vol. 3, no. 5.

22. Following the peace, and perhaps earlier, Jordaens worked on commissions in the Dutch Republic, most notably the decoration of the Oranjezaal, the magnificent series of paintings in the ballroom of the palace Huis ten Bos, The Hague, painted between 1648 and 1652,

23. Three stages were erected and six different sets of *tableaux vivants* were designed by the playwright Samuel Coster (1579–1665); Gerard Brandt (1626–1685), a playwright, poet, and historian; and Jan Vos (1610–1667), also a poet and playwright. The Mercury and Argus stage was designed by Coster, who was also responsible for the text beneath the print. See Snoep 1975, pp. 77f., for a general discussion of the celebration and p. 81 for a discussion of Mercury and Argus. The print of Mercury and Argus is also discussed by Van de Waal 1952, vol. 1, p. 22.

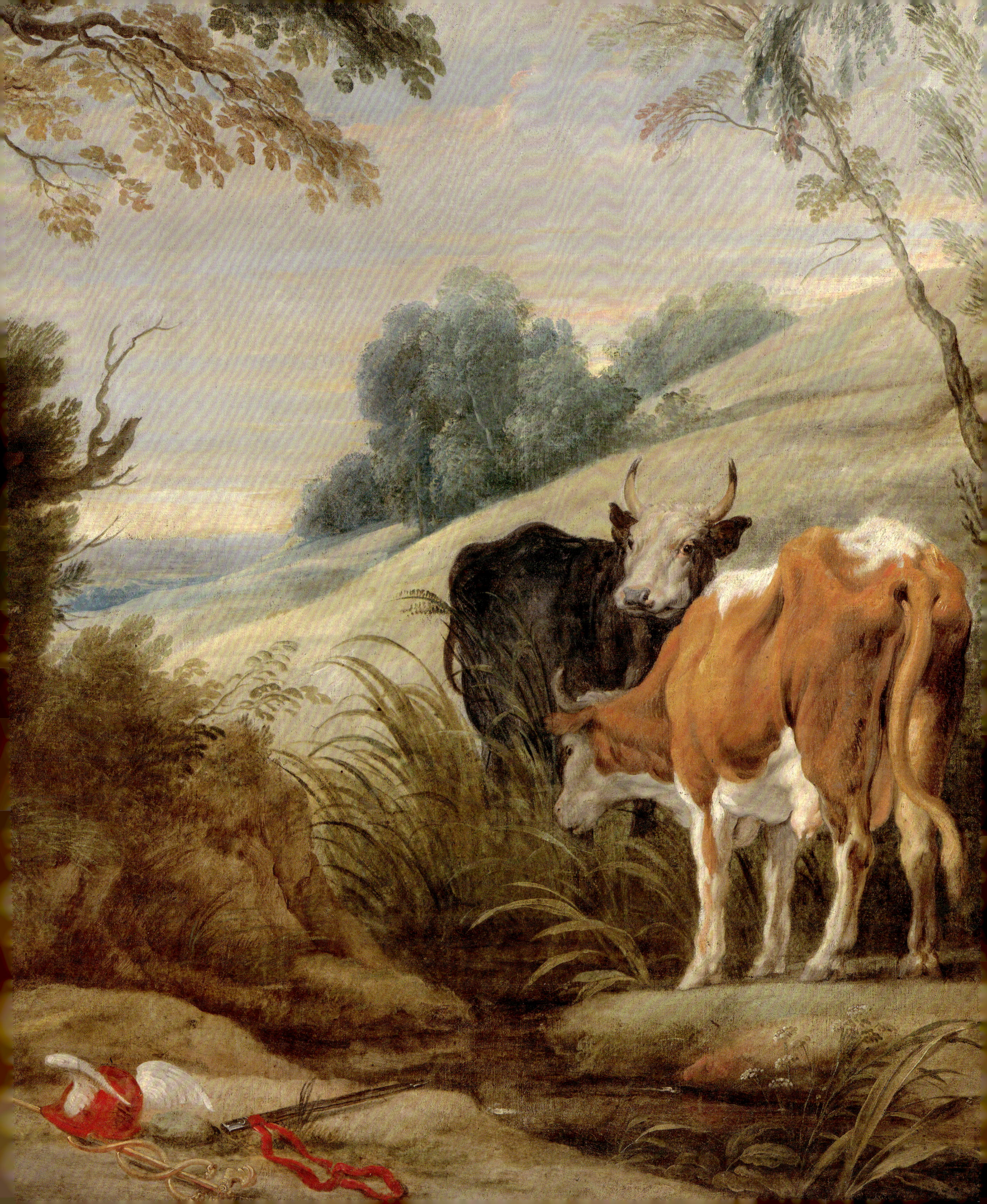

41

Attributed to Justus Juncker

German
Mainz 1703–1767 Frankfurt

Sportsmen in a Tavern

ca. 1735

Oil on canvas, 9 × 14½ in. (22.9 × 36.8 cm)
Norton Simon Art Foundation, M.1982.7.1.P

Provenance
Anonymous (sale, Christie's, New York, 9 January 1981, lot 131, sold to); Norton Simon National Institute, Washington, DC,[1] sold 1982 to; Norton Simon Art Foundation.

Exhibited
On loan, Henry Art Gallery, University of Washington, Seattle, 21 May 1981—16 March 1983.

Reference
S. Campbell 2010, p. 433, no. 1669.

Technical Notes
The painting is executed on a lined plain-weave canvas. The thin smooth ground is white. It appears that the artist first drew the figures with dark-brown paint. In the figure of the seated man at the right, for example, the strong dark outline of his proper left shoulder and hand are at the edges of the painted form. The paint is rather thin and smoothly brushed, filling in the drawn figures and the details of the interior. Abrasion is minor; the edges of cracks are rather worn. However, black lines and details such as window mullions, posters on the wall, and the gun barrel remain crisp and vivid. Retouching is minimal and occurs only in a few scattered spots. The painting was cleaned in 1981 by Gertrud Blumel, New York. Ultraviolet light indicates a thin, synthetic-resin varnish.

Attributed to Justus Juncker, a German artist trained in Frankfurt in the style of the seventeenth-century Dutch artists and later active in England, *Sportsmen in a Tavern* was probably painted in the second quarter of the eighteenth century. Meticulously painted, the fluid chiaroscuro modeling of the figures and solid overall light and dark construction of the composition rendered in soft, golden, gray-brown tones are typical of Juncker's small-scale genre scenes, such as *Interior with a Man Seated before a Table Smoking a Pipe*, signed and dated 1752.[2]

The subject, costumes, and setting of *Sportsmen in a Tavern* suggest that it represents an English country inn frequented by a cross-section of the local population. Seated next to a long wood table, a bailiff smokes a pipe as he leans back in his chair. His responsibilities as groundskeeper of an estate are indicated by the game bag at his waist, the rifle on the long table, and the hunting dog resting quietly on the floor next to him. At the far end of the table, another man sits before the window and smokes a clay pipe. His clothes are somewhat more formal, suggesting that he is a townsman. Seated at the left next to the fireplace, a third man with a pipe dangling from his mouth and tankard in his hand appears more disheveled in dress and attitude.

The Pasadena painting appears to be the best of several versions of the composition, including an anonymous glass mezzotint (fig. 41a). Each version repeats the general composition but differs subtly in the placement of the dog and the description of the broadsheets tacked to the wall, as well as other details. None of the paintings agrees exactly with the mezzotint. A painting formerly in the collection of Paul Mellon is closest but inferior to the Pasadena painting in handling.[3] Another version of the composition was sold in London in 1986 as a pair with *Card Players at a Table and a Man Drinking by a Window in a Tavern*.[4] Juncker's composition of *Sportsmen in a Tavern* continued to be popular in England into the late eighteenth century, when George Morland (1763–1804) painted

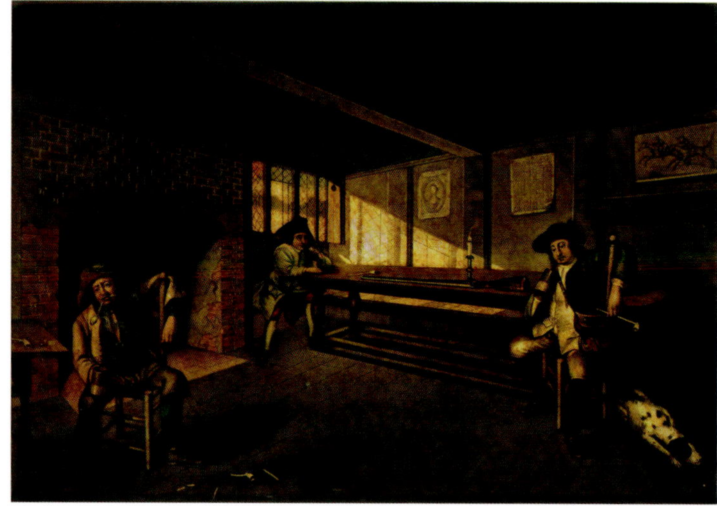

Fig. 41a. British, glass color print depicting the interior of a tavern with three men drinking, ca. 1715, mezzotint printed on glass, 9 7⁄16 × 13¾ in. (24 × 34.9 cm), Victoria and Albert Museum, London.

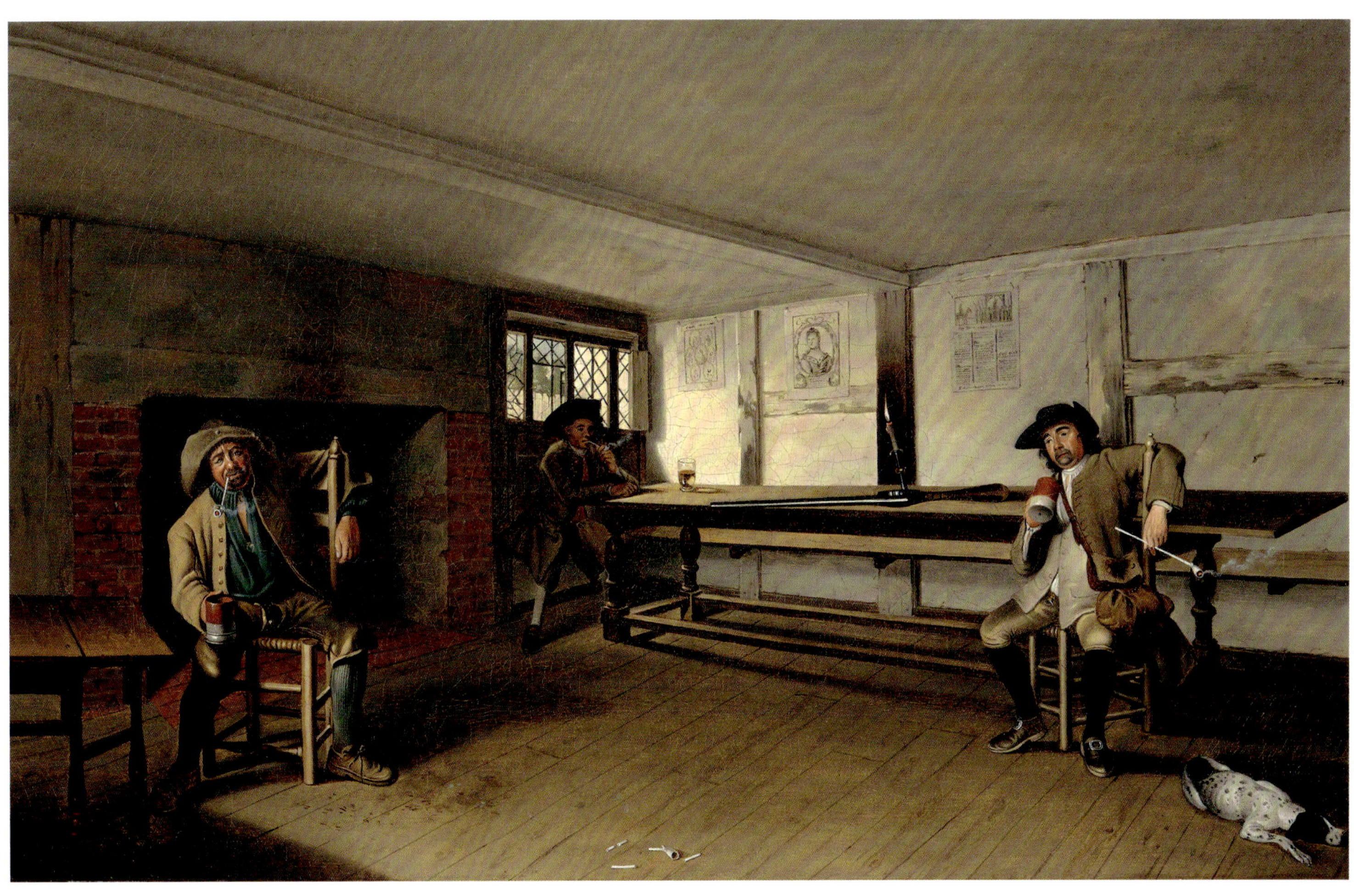

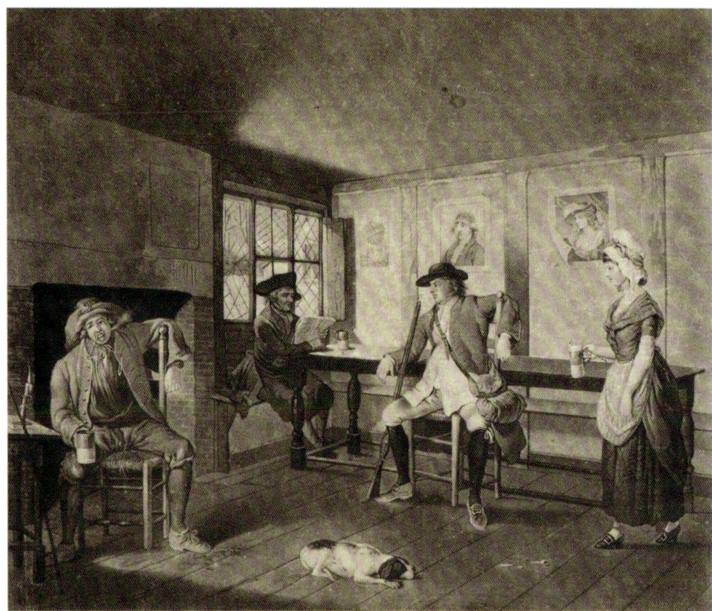

Fig. 41b. William Ward, after George Morland, *Sportsman's Hall*, 1788, mezzotint on paper, 14 11⁄16 × 17 in. (37.3 × 43.3 cm), The British Museum, London.

his now lost *Sportsman's Hall*, reproduced by William Ward (1766–1826) in a mezzotint dated 1788 (fig. 41b).[5]

The selection of broadsheets tacked to the back wall in the different versions is intriguing and perhaps significant. Both the mezzotint and the Pasadena painting represent the same portrait engraving in the center of the wall. The broadsheets on either side of the central image, however, differ in the two versions. The Pasadena painting depicts on the left a broadsheet with six medallion portraits around a central portrait—probably a genealogical diagram—and on the right a broadsheet with a horseman and other figures gathered around a scaffold; in the mezzotint, an advertisement and a broadsheet with a race between two horses appear on the wall.

The mezzotint identifies the portrait of the woman in the central broadsheet as Queen Anne (1665–1714), the daughter of James II, who succeeded William III and reigned as queen of England, Scotland, and Ireland from 1702 until her death in 1714. The popular bust-length image was based on a portrait of the queen by Sir Godfrey Kneller (1646–1723) that was reproduced in prints by multiple artists and published in numerous texts.[6] The inclusion of the print in the Pasadena painting supports the assumption that the paintings were produced in England or at least for an English market. Images of country life were particularly sought after in the eighteenth century by members of the English upper classes, who built country homes for retreat and recreation. Relaxation of the restrictions on hunting, which formerly limited the sport to noblemen, led to the popularity of hunting among a wider society.[7]

The publication of the portrait print of Queen Anne related to the Pasadena painting has been dated ca. 1715, probably based on the death of Anne in 1714. The costumes worn by the men—the long vests, the close-fitting sleeves, the wide skirts of the jackets, and the rounded toes of the shoes—indicate, however, that the Pasadena painting and the other versions of the image were produced in the 1730s, by which time England was ruled by George II (1683–1760), the son of Anne's Hanoverian successor.[8]

The outdated broadsheets suggest that the image may have referred to specific political events or ideas. Between 1702 and 1713 England was engaged in Queen Anne's War (1702–13), the War of Spanish Succession fought in America. Throughout the war, Anne countered the Whig party in England and actively sought an end to hostilities, which was eventually established by the Peace of Utrecht in 1713. Her successor, George I, however, supported the Whigs and pursued an aggressive foreign policy until his death in 1727, when his son George II succeeded him. The early years of George II's reign (until the War of the Austrian Succession in 1742 and the Jacobite uprising in 1745–46) were tranquil and notably prosperous. Against this background, it may be possible that this image of a hunter resting was a reference to the current peace.

1. The Norton Simon National Institute was created 5 February 1981 and dissolved on 31 January 1986.

2. Sale, Sotheby's Olympia, London, 10 December 2002, lot 396.

3. Sold from the Paul Mellon Collection (Sotheby's, London, 18 November 1981, lot 130) as English School, 18th century, *A Sportsman Drinking in an Inn*, panel, 25.5 × 38 cm (10 × 15 in.). According to Egerton 1978, p. 36, no. 38, the painting was purchased from Sabin Galleries, London, 1966.

4. Formerly in the collection of the duke of Leeds, Hornby Castle, sold London, Christie's, 11 December 1986, lot 38, as by Justus Juncker, *A Sportsman and Two Other Figures in a Tavern*, oil on copper, 21.3 × 29.4 cm (8 ¾ × 11 ½ in.), as a pair with *Card Players at a Table and a Man Drinking by a Window in a Tavern*, oil on copper, 22.9 × 29.4 cm (9 × 11 ½ in.).

5. Frankau 1904, pp. 266f., no. 272. The connection of the mezzotint to Morland's painting was first made in Egerton 1978, pp. 36f., no. 38. Timothy Williams, of Timothy Williams Fine Art, London, recently suggested that Moreland's painting may be that sold as William Redmore Bigg (1755–1828), *Sportsman Drinking in a Tavern*, canvas, 61 × 73 cm. The higher quality of the painting by Bigg than the print by Ward suggests that it was not based on the print but that the print followed the painting.

6. The print appears to represent a hand-colored engraving that was included as no. 108 in vol. 1 of the *Atlas Royal* commissioned by Augustus the Strong, Prince Elector of Saxony, and published in Amsterdam in 1707. The engraving, which may be by Pieter van Gunst (1654–1724) and not actually commissioned by Augustus, was probably circulated widely in England.

7. See Bermingham 1986. Mezzotints were also particularly popular in England during the eighteenth century.

8. I am grateful to Sandra Rosenbaum, formerly curator-in-charge of the Doris Stein Research Center for Costume and Textiles, Department of Costume and Textiles, Los Angeles County Museum of Art, for identifying and dating the costumes.

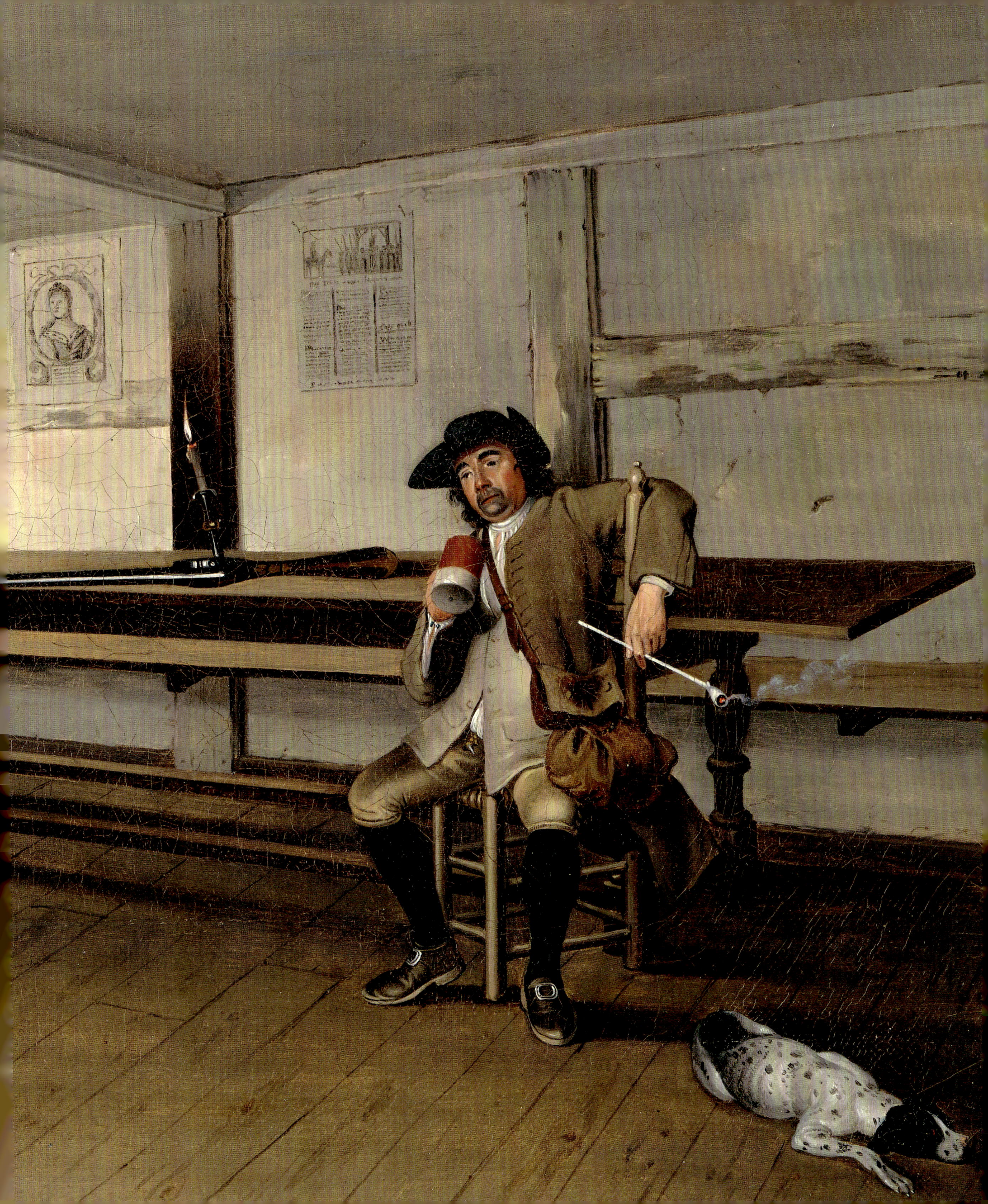

42, 43

Follower of Jan van Kessel I

Flemish
Antwerp 1626–1679 Antwerp

Still Life with Fruit and Vase of Flowers

ca. 1670–75

Oil on copper, 7 × 9 in. (17.8 × 22.9 cm)
Norton Simon Art Foundation, M.1984.3.1.P

Still Life with Fruit and a Bird

ca. 1670–75

Oil on copper, 7 × 9 in. (17.8 × 22.9 cm)
Norton Simon Art Foundation, M.1984.3.2.P

Provenance

Franz Joseph II (1906–1989), Prince of Liechtenstein, Schloss Feldsberg, Valtice, Czechoslovakia, from at least 1930,[1] transferred 1944 to Vaduz, Liechtenstein, sold 2 April 1984 to;[2] [Galerie Nathan, Zurich, consigned or sold to];[3] [Galerie Sanct Lucas, Vienna, sold 1984 to]; Norton Simon Art Foundation.

Exhibited

Vienna 1984–85, nos. 19–20, as "aus hocharistokratische Besitz."

References

S. Campbell 2010, p. 439, no. 1720A–B, ill.; Ertz and Nitze-Ertz 2012, M.1984.3.2: pp. 15–17, color pl. 9, 138, 428, no. 111; M.1984.3.1: pp. 18–19, color pl. 11, 138, 444, no. 162, as Jan van Kessel II.

Technical Notes

Still Life with Fruit and Vase of Flowers

The support is a thin copper panel. There is no ground layer. The background was painted very thinly with a near-transparent brown. At the right side of the blue-and-white plate, there is a blue-brown layer of underpaint beneath the grapes. The artist employed both opaque paint and semi-transparent glazes, all smoothly brushed with crisp, clear contours. Scattered tiny flake losses, visible with magnification, were probably caused by the lack of a ground layer. A moderate amount of retouching covers some of the losses. Ultraviolet-light fluorescence suggests the same thin natural-resin varnish brushed on both panels.

Still Life with Fruit and a Bird

The thin copper panel has several shallow deformations at the center of the bottom edge; the top right, bottom right, and lower left corners have creases from having been bent. Microscopic examination of the surface provided no evidence of a ground layer. The paint is generally quite thin, often consisting of glazes brushed with crisp clear outlines. The background was painted very thinly with a near-transparent brown. The grapes to the left of the plate were painted over a light rose-gray layer. In the lighter and more thickly painted colors, the paint is densely cracked. There are tiny flake losses throughout the panel that expose the copper support. The painting has been previously cleaned, although little spots of incompletely removed dark varnish remain, an example of which is the speckled appearance of the light-green grapes. Extensive retouching is mostly in the background and the foreground. The thin natural-resin varnish was applied with a brush.

The identical dimensions, similar compositions, and common provenances of these two paintings suggest that they have been together since their creation and were intended to be seen together. Resembling miniaturized versions of still lifes by Frans Snyders (1579–1657) and Jacob van Hulsdonck (1582–1647), each composition painted on a small copper panel represents a wood table laid with a platter of grapes, apples, and other autumn fruit set against a light-colored background. The front edge of the table is visible in each painting. In *Still Life with Fruit and Vase of Flowers*, the plate is blue-and-white Chinese export porcelain, while in *Still Life with Fruit and a Bird* it is a white pottery plate with a scalloped rim. The plates lie to the left of the central axis, balanced on the right by vegetables and fruit lying on the table, carefully orchestrated to unify the compositions. In *Still Life with Fruit and Vase of Flowers*, the left rear corner of the table is visible and light is cast from an unseen source at the upper left. In *Still Life with Fruit and a Bird,* the boundaries of the table are undefined and the light source is from the upper left.

The original context for these small copper panels is not known. The earliest reference to them is 1930, when they were hanging together in the servants' quarters at Schloss Feldsberg, the residence of the princes of Liechtenstein in what is now the Czech Republic from the fourteenth century until 1939. The panels may have been painted to hang as a single pair, but they may also have formed part of a larger decorative painting similar in format to the composite

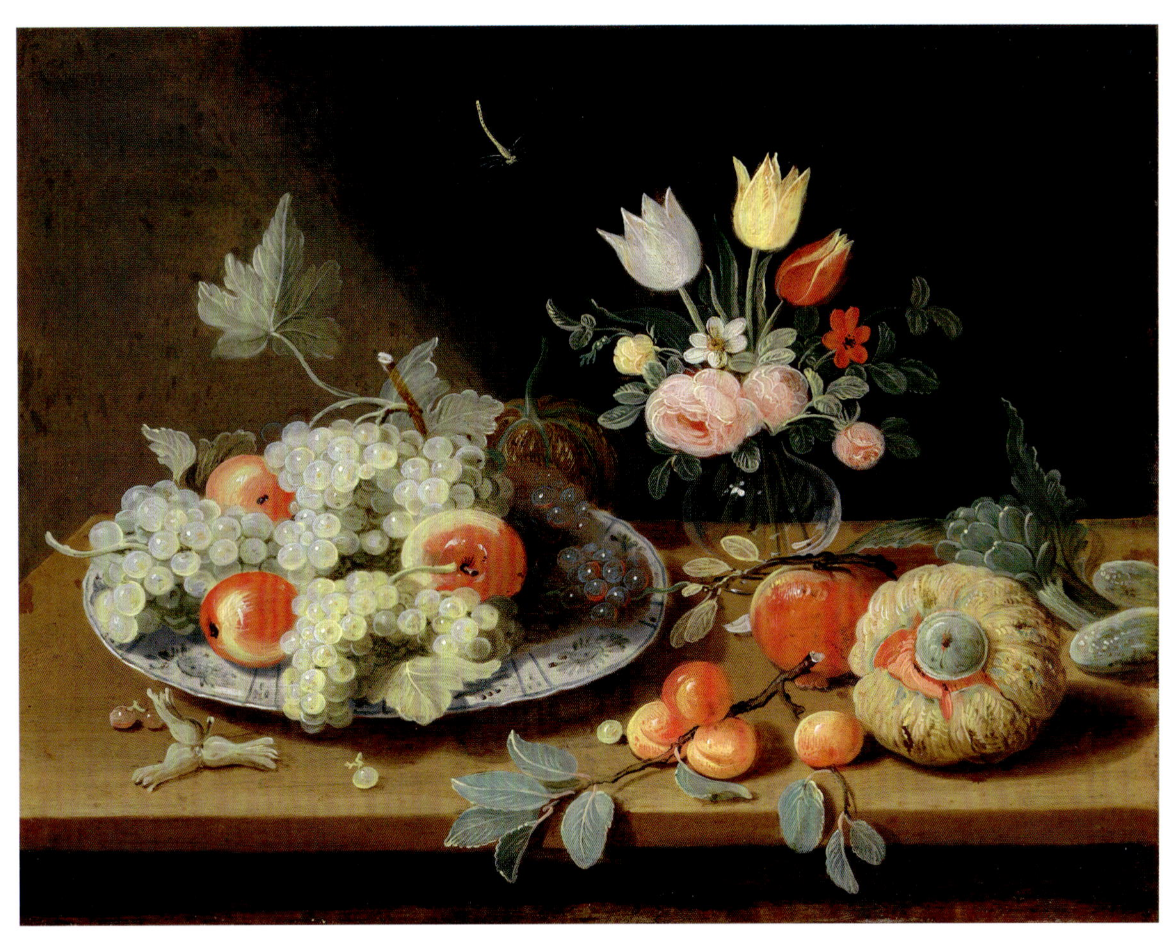

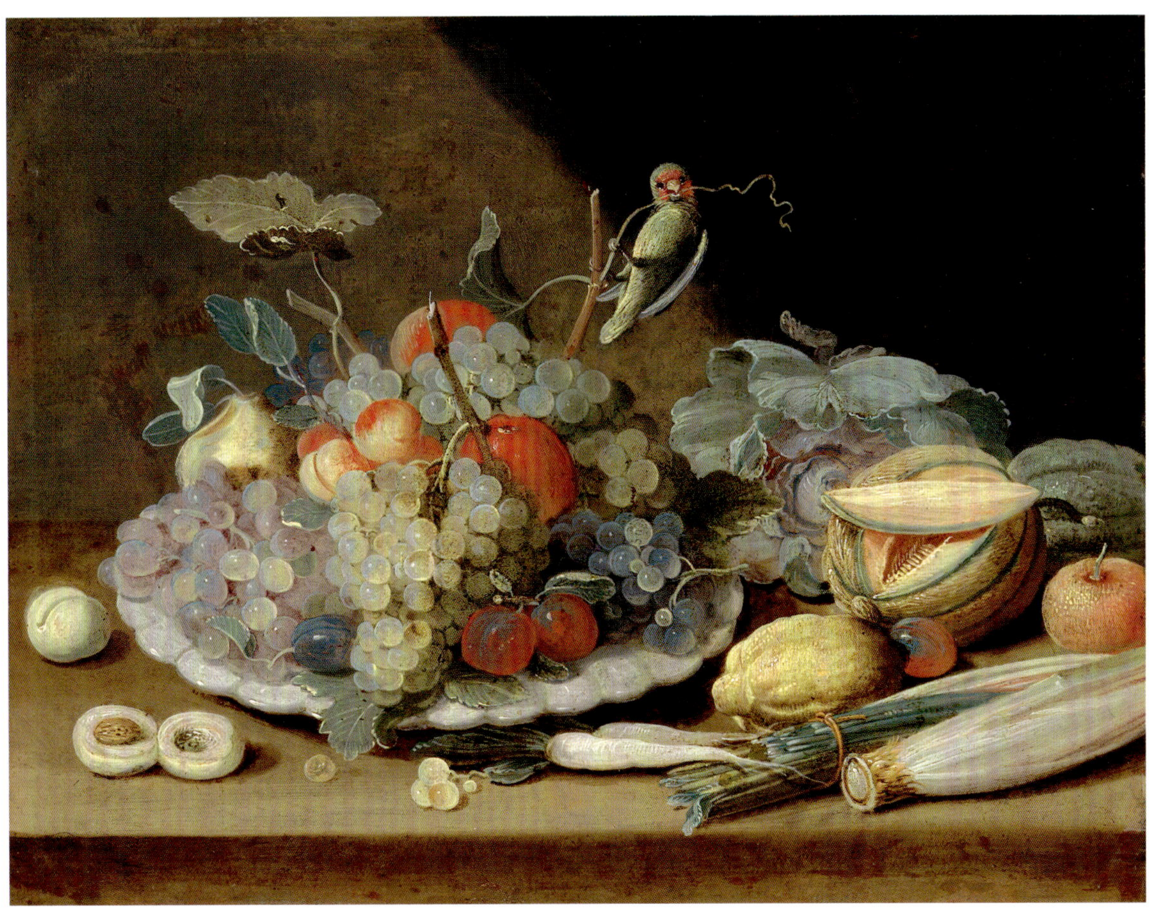

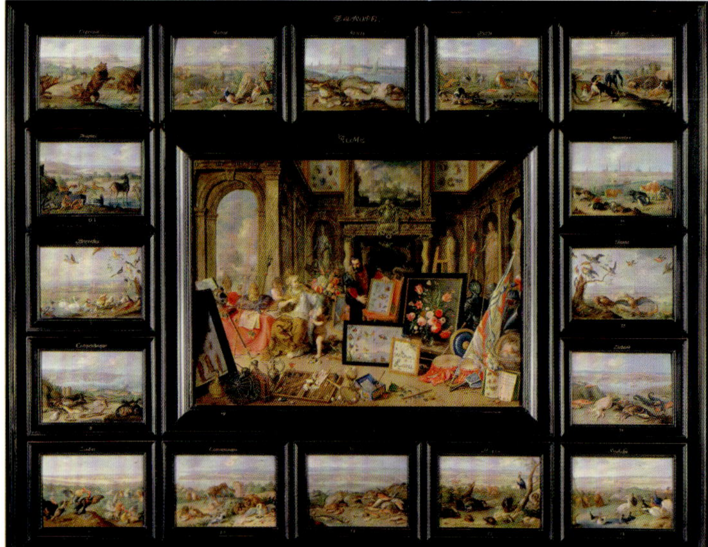

Fig. 42a. Jan van Kessel I, *The Four Continents: Europe*, 1664, oil on copper, 19 × 26 7⁄16 in. (48.4 × 67.1 cm), Alte Pinakothek, Bayerische Staatsgemäldesammlungen, Munich.

paintings of the four parts of the world by Jan van Kessel I (fig. 42a)[4] as well as to that of a group of panels formerly in the collection of the Earl of Craven, where they were attributed to Van Kessel (fig. 42b).[5] Although the Craven paintings have been dismantled, their original arrangement has been convincingly reconstructed: eight panels, each 12.5 × 29 cm and representing a nosegay of flowers lying casually on a table, surround a larger painting of a formal bouquet in a glass vase set on the front left corner of a table. The front corner of the table is visible on the left in the four paintings to the left of the central image and on the right in the four paintings to its right. A number of still lifes of tabletops with fruit and vegetables painted on copper panels with the same dimensions as the Pasadena paintings have been identified.[6] In some of these paintings, the corner of the table is on the left; in others it is on the right, suggesting that they originally may have been arranged in similar groups.

The Norton Simon Art Foundation acquired the paintings in 1984 as works by Jan van Kessel I, who is known for his realistic still lifes of flowers and produce, especially arrangements of insects, shells, and flowers displayed like scientific specimens on light, bluish-green backgrounds. Although the subjects, compositions, formats, and tonality of these paintings reflect Van Kessel's style and his Flemish heritage, the summary quality of the brushwork, particularly of the flowers, differs significantly from the artist's documented works, in which there are traces of the influence of the elegantly refined and crisp still lifes of Daniel Seghers (1590–1661).[7] The faulty perspective of the Pasadena paintings, which also lack Van Kessel's typical concern for the illusion of reality, suggest they were probably executed by a follower rather than by the master himself. The large number of similar small paintings attributed to the artist that exhibit a range of quality indicate that Van Kessel worked with assistants and had a number of followers who imitated his work.[8] Two of his sons, Jan II (1654–1708) and Ferdinand (1648–1696), made signed copies of his paintings and also worked independently in his manner but with a much looser and less accomplished technique.[9]

In their 2012 monograph on the Van Kessels, Klaus Ertz and Christa Nitze-Ertz, who originally attributed the paintings to Jan I, include them among a group of paintings they attribute to Jan II. Noting the difficulty of attributing paintings to specific members of the Van Kessel circle, however, they acknowledge that paintings they attribute to Jan II may be confused with work by others in the circle. Only a few paintings by Jan II and only one—*Allegory of Europe* (Kunsthistorisches Museum, Vienna)—by Ferdinand can be securely attributed to either artist. Without additional documentation, it is not possible to specify who within the group of known and anonymous followers of Jan van Kessel I painted the Pasadena panels.[10]

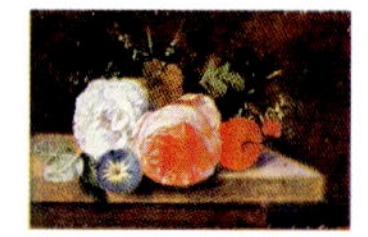

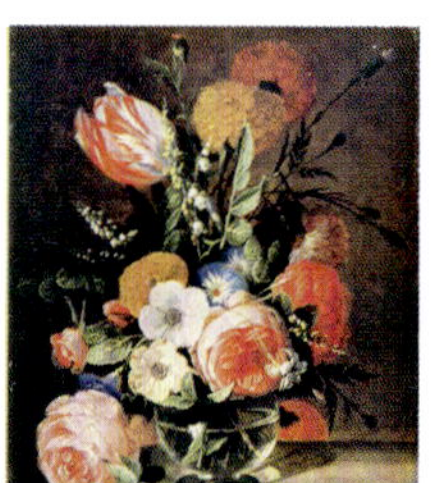

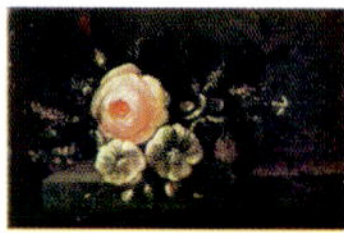
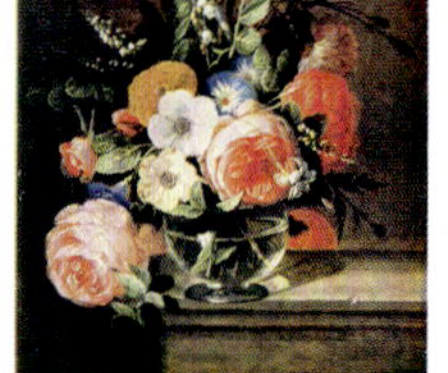
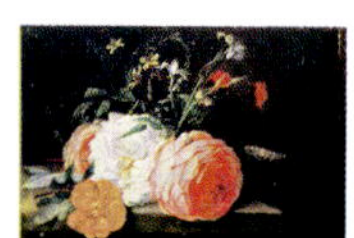
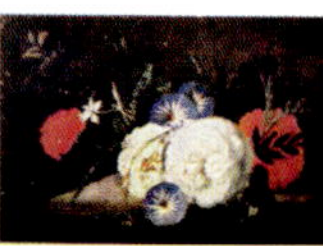
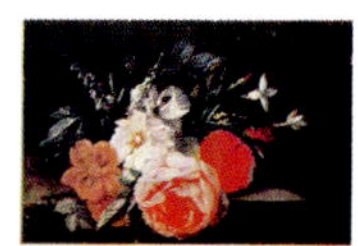

Fig. 42b. Reconstruction of the Craven panels' arrangement with paintings attributed to Jan van Kessel I, center panel: 11 3⁄4 × 9 in. (29.9 × 22.9 cm), surrounding panels: 4 7⁄8 × 7 1⁄2 in. (12.4 × 19.1 cm), sold Leonard Koetser Gallery, 7 April–31 May 1967, London, lot 5, location unknown, image courtesy of Koetser Gallery.

1. The House of Liechtenstein acquired Feldsberg in 1394; it remained its residence until 1939, when the Nazis seized it. Stickers on the reverse of the paintings identify *Still Life with Fruit and a Bird* as "Schloss Feldsberg, inv. no. 1440," and *Still Life with Fruit and a Vase of Flowers* as "Schloss Feldsberg, inv. no. 1439." According to Dr. Arthur Stoegmann, Archiv und Historische Bibliothek, Liechtenstein Museum, Die Fürstlichen Sammlungen, Vienna (emails, 8 and 15 April 2011, NSM), the numbers correspond to paintings recorded at Schloss Feldsberg in an inventory of artworks made in Czechoslovakia about 1930 by the Fürstliche Zentraldirektion, Olmütz, the central agency for the administration of the Czech properties of the princely house. Numbers 1439 and 1440 are included in "Objekt Nr. 174 Dienerzimmer mit Wandnischenbettkasten." Although mentioned as painted on wood, the descriptions agree with the Pasadena paintings: "[Nr.]1439, Ölgemälde auf Holz von Unbekannt; Stillleben, auf einem Tisch ein Teller mit Weintrauben und Birnen, daneben ein Blumenstrauß in einem Glas, eine Melone und Pfirsiche 17:22. [Nr.]1440, Ölgemälde auf Holz von Unbekannt; Stillleben, auf einem Tisch ein Teller mit Weintrauben u. anderem Obst, daneben verschiedenes Gemüse, auf dem Stengeleiner Weintraube sitz ein kleiner grüner Papagei. 16:22." The paintings also appear in an inventory of Schloss Feldsberg ca. 1940.

2. According to Stoegmann, a list of works of art that were sold "refers to both paintings as being painted by Jan van Kessel I on copper. 1439 is described [in translation] as still life with fruits and flowers, 17:22 cm.; 1440 is described as still life with fruits, 16.5:22 cm. Annotations added to the entries of both paintings state that they had been brought from Feldsberg to Vaduz [Castle] in 1944 and that they were sold to the 'Galerie Nathan' in Zürich on the 2nd of April 1984."

3. Eva Metelka, writing on behalf of Roman Herzig of Galerie Sanct Lucas, email to Carol Togneri, 23 March 2004, states that the two paintings "were acquired by us in exchange directly from the Princes of Liechtenstein" (NSM). The contradiction may be explained if Galerie Nathan was acting on behalf of Galerie Sanct Lucas.

4. The dimensions of the Pasadena paintings are similar to those of the sixteen copper panels that border the central images of the Van Kessel *Four Continents* (fig. 42a). Each of the border panels measures 14.5 × 21 cm. See Munich 1973.

5. Exhibited by L. Koetser Ltd., London, Spring 1967, no. 5. Fred Meijer (email, 19 April 2011, NSM) rejects the attribution of the ex-Craven group of paintings to Van Kessel in favor of Hieronymus Galle I (1625–after 1679).

6. Among the panels that may have been part of this group or a similar series based on the dimensions, perspective, portrayal of the table, and specific handling and details are *Still Life with Basket of Fruit and Parrot*, where the far left corner is visible (copper, 16.5 × 21.6 cm, exh., Brian Koetser Gallery, London, March–May 1966); *Still Life with Vase of Flowers, Basket of Fruit, Squirrel and Parrot*, near right corner visible (called the pendant of *Still Life with Basket of Fruit and Parrot*; copper, 16.5 × 21.6 cm, exh., Brian Koetser Gallery, London, March–May 1966); *Still Life with Fruit and Monkey*, far right corner visible (copper, 16.8 × 21.8 cm, sale, Palais Galliera, Paris, 23 November 1972, no. 39); *Still Life with Basket of Fruit*, far right corner visible (copper, 6 ¾ × 8 ¾ in., exh., Brian Koetser Gallery, London, April–June 1963); *Still Life with Plate of Grapes*, no visible corners (copper, 6 ¾ × 8 ¾ in., exh., Brian Koetser Gallery, London, April–June 1963); *Still Life with Tazza*, far right corner visible (copper, 6 ½ × 8 ½ in., exh., Brian Koetser Gallery, London, Spring 1964); and *Fruit Still Life with Flowers* (copper, 16.8 × 21.9 cm, sale, Kunsthaus Lempertz, Cologne, 20–22 November 1986, no. 88).

7. The nervous and rapid brushwork, leaving ribbons of color along the edges of the thinly applied paint, is reminiscent of Jan Brueghel II (1601–1678), Van Kessel's uncle and teacher. The still lifes, furthermore, appear to be miniaturizations of details—for example, the sliced melon, grape leaves, and the bird—taken from the large kitchen and larder paintings by Frans Snyders and Cornelis de Vos (ca. 1584–1651; see cat. 83).

8. According to Fred Meijer (April 2011, NSM):

> These panels belong to a large group of anonymous still lifes, traditionally (at least since the 20th c.) associated with Jan van Kessel and provisionally catalogued in the RKD files as studio of Jan van Kessel the Elder. There is no evidence, however, that they can be connected with Van Kessel. [Not one] of the many examples is signed. The majority [are] on copper, the few on panel are not on oak, but on what appears to be walnut, a panel used in southern Europe and very rarely in the north. The whole group may be by an artist (or studio, since there appear to be differences in handling within the group) working in Italy, perhaps of Flemish origin.

His association of the paintings with Italy derives from the Italian provenance of many of the paintings.

9. Jan II spent most of his career in Spain, where he worked for the Spanish court. Ferdinand, who lived primarily in Breda, served as court painter to the king of Poland, for whom he painted a copy of his father's famous *Allegory of the Four Parts of the World* (Alte Pinakothek, Munich) and other paintings. See Schütz 2002, pp. 102–05.

10. Ertz and Nitze-Ertz 2012, pp. 9–10, 13–15.

44

Follower of Jan van Kessel I

Flemish
Antwerp 1626–1679 Antwerp

Still Life with Fruit

ca. 1675

Oil on copper, 5¼ × 6½ in. (13.3 × 16.5 cm)
The Norton Simon Foundation, F.1969.42.2.P

Provenance
Private collection, the Netherlands, sold to; [A. van der Meer, Amsterdam, sold 21 November 1969 to]; The Norton Simon Foundation.

Exhibited
On loan, Phoenix Art Museum, 23 January–28 April 1970; on loan, Los Angeles County Museum of Art, May–July 1972; Houston 1972–74; Lang Art Gallery, Scripps College, Claremont, CA, 5 November–3 December 1974, no. 12, ill.

References
Van der Meer 1969, no. 16, ill.; S. Campbell 2010, p. 328, no. 697, ill.; Ertz and Nitze-Ertz 2012, pp. 138, 141, color pl. 136, 442, no. 156, as Jan van Kessel II.

Technical Notes
The thin copper support has gentle planar distortions throughout as well as crumpled corners at the upper and lower right. A thin warm gray ground layer covers the copper. No underpainting is evident. Paint was applied with very refined brushwork, and each object in the still life was defined with crisp contours. Thin opaque layers were sometimes modified by transparent glazes on top, such as in the grapes. Intermittent smaller losses of ground and paint are found throughout the painting, as are several isolated areas of paint damage, the cause of which is unclear. Solvent abrasion is evident in the thin blue glazes. The small losses have generally been retouched without any fill material. The painting was superficially cleaned in 1985 to remove surface dirt. The yellowed natural-resin varnish has a granular character.

Still Life with Fruit is characteristic of the small still lifes on copper painted by Jan van Kessel I and his followers, which recall the larger still lifes painted in Antwerp by Jacob van Hulsdonck (1582–1647) and others. In this painting a white pottery plate filled with three varieties of grapes and other fruit lies on a table covered by a coral-colored cloth. A half walnut shell, a few loose grapes, and hazelnuts appear to have fallen from the plate onto the table. The flat leaves and grapevine, the only elements to break the profile of the fruit, animate the upper third of the composition and emphasize the horizontal line of the plate and table. Employing a technique characteristic of Flemish still-life painters, especially Jan Brueghel II (1601–1678) and Frans Snyders (1579–1657) and their followers, including Van Kessel, the artist applied paint rapidly in thin glazes so that the paint pooled around the perimeter of the forms like a loose outline, creating the impression that the grapes have translucent skins.

Although smaller and compositionally oriented around the central axis, the subject and style of *Still Life with Fruit* closely resemble those of *Still Life with Fruits and Bird* and *Still Life with Fruit and Vase of Flowers* (cats. 42 and 43). Like them, *Still Life with Fruit* was previously attributed to Van Kessel, who is known for his still lifes of flowers and fruit and especially his detailed renderings of insects displayed as if scientific specimens. This still life, however, lacks Van Kessel's characteristic precision and refinement. The definition of the plate and fruit, especially the highlights on the grapes, is less detailed and more mechanical, suggesting that *Still Life with Fruit* was painted by a follower rather than by the master himself. In their 2012 monograph on the Van Kessels, Klaus Ertz and Christa Nitze-Ertz attribute the painting to Jan van Kessel II. Admitting the difficulty of attributing paintings to the different members of the Van Kessel family and workshop, they acknowledge that some of the paintings they include as works by Jan II may be by followers.[1]

The small size and relative simplicity of *Still Life with Fruit* may indicate that it was painted as part of a decorative arrangement of similar copper panels, perhaps forming a border surrounding a central vertical panel with a still life of fruit.[2] However, the large number and range in quality of these compositions suggests that *Still Life with Fruit* may have been produced as an independent work to satisfy a popular market for miniaturized still lifes in the tradition of Snyders, Van Hulsdonck, and other artists active in Antwerp.[3]

1. Ertz and Nitze-Ertz 2012, pp. 9, 13–17.

2. See cats. 42 and 43 for discussion.

3. See cats. 42 and 43, note 8, for Fred Meijer's comments regarding the group of small still lifes on copper and panel that he believes are incorrectly associated with Jan van Kessel.

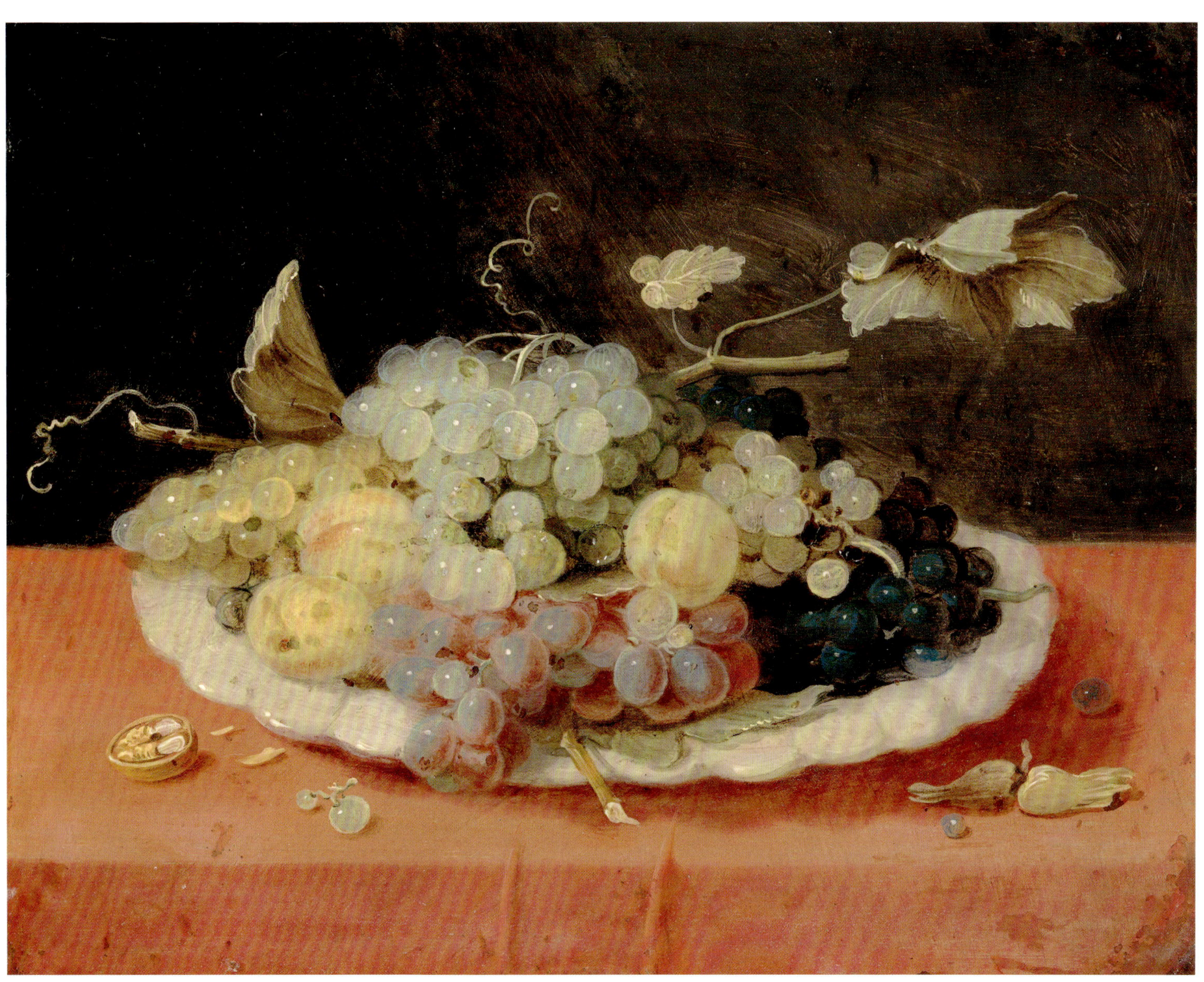

45

Thomas de Keyser

Dutch
Amsterdam 1596/97–1667 Amsterdam

Dirck van Wissel and His Son Jacob

1631

Signed, on left foot of table: "TDK" (*T, D* as part of stem, and superimposed *K* in ligature)
Dated on pediment above door, under coat of arms: "Ano 1631"[1]
Oil on panel, 25 × 19¼ in. (63.5 × 48.9 cm)
The Norton Simon Foundation, F.1968.11.09.P

Provenance
Gerald Maunsell Gamul Farmer Wilshere (1898–1972), The Frythe, Welwyn, Hertfordshire (sale, Sotheby's, London, 21 October 1942, lot 92, to);[2] [W. Duits, London, stock no. 7516, sold 6 October 1943 to]; [Frost & Reed, London]. John C. Myer Jr.; Ashland, OH, sold February 1955 to; [Newhouse Galleries, New York, stock no. 15614, sold February 1957 to]; Morris I. Kaplan, Chicago (estate sale, Sotheby's, London, 12 June 1968, lot 58, to); [A. K. Armytage for]; The Norton Simon Foundation.

Exhibited
Chicago 1961, n.pag., lent by Mr. and Mrs. Morris Kaplan; on loan, Brooklyn Museum, 1 August 1968–31 January 1969; on loan, Los Angeles County Museum of Art, 16 July 1969–26 November 1974.

References
Sotheby's 1968, p. 39, ill.; Paris 1970, p. 120; Bénézit 1976, vol. 6, p. 206; Pasadena 1980, p. 52, ill.; Adams 1985, vol. 1, pp. 255–60, vol. 3, pp. 65ff., no. 35; P. Sutton 1986, pp. 216, 312, ill.; Pasadena 1989, p. 76, ill.; Liedtke 2007, vol. 1, p. 402; S. Campbell 2010, pp. 90, 302, no. 474, ill.; Adams 2020, pp. 15–21.

Technical Notes
The support is a vertically grained oak panel ⅜ inch thick. The left and right edges are beveled. Rough chisel furrows and other tool marks on the reverse suggest that the original surface is intact. The panel was prepared with a thin warm-white ground. A light golden-brown imprimatura is evident throughout the painting—for example, in the upper left background. The paint is very well preserved. Although the picture is relatively smoothly painted overall, brushmarking is visible throughout. The artist deftly handled opaque rich paint to portray a wide variety of materials. The background was painted with looser handling and larger brushstrokes, quickly applied. Delicate modulations of light versus shadow in the man's doublet serve to model the form. Lace was depicted with tiny drips and dribbles of dense white paint applied with a very fine brush. The squares of the floor were directly brushed freehand over the golden-brown imprimatura. Retouching is minimal, confined to possible strengthening of shadows in the man's fingers, below the sleeve in his proper right hand, and the shadow surrounding his chin. Records note the use of a ketone-based synthetic-resin varnish, but ultraviolet light indicates a natural resin. While the varnish is not significantly discolored, it appears slightly cloudy and does not saturate well. An undocumented selective cleaning left a considerable amount of older, discolored varnish remaining in areas that are yellow-gold in tone, such as both chairs and the cloth covering the table.

Poised between the privacy of the home and the public arena of the street, a stylishly dressed man stands next to a table and directs attention to a boy, presumably his son, who stands nearby. The carefully described ornamental gilt leather wall covering, the broad oak frieze, and the elegantly carved doorframe of the well-appointed room create an impression of wealth and status, reinforced by the plush velvet chair cushions, heavily fringed green tablecloth, and the family crest—two red wings on a neutral field—at the peak of the door's pediment. The attention to architectural detail recalls the early training in architecture Thomas de Keyser received from his father, Hendrik de Keyser (1565–1621).

The Pasadena painting is one of a number of small-scale, full-length portraits of elegantly dressed figures in architecturally grand surroundings that De Keyser painted during the late 1620s and early 1630s. Probably inspired by the small-scale replicas of portraits of Charles I of England (r. 1625–49) and his court then circulating in The Hague,[3] De Keyser adopted the full-length format and attributes of international court portraiture for the portrayal of Amsterdam's patricians.[4] As in his prototypes, in the Pasadena painting De Keyser represented his figures standing beside a table covered with a sumptuous green velvet cloth fringed in gold; here, a fashionable wide-brimmed hat replaces the crown or helmet represented in traditional images of kings and noblemen.

Rather than the reserved black clothing worn by Amsterdam's regents before about 1650, the gentleman in De Keyser's

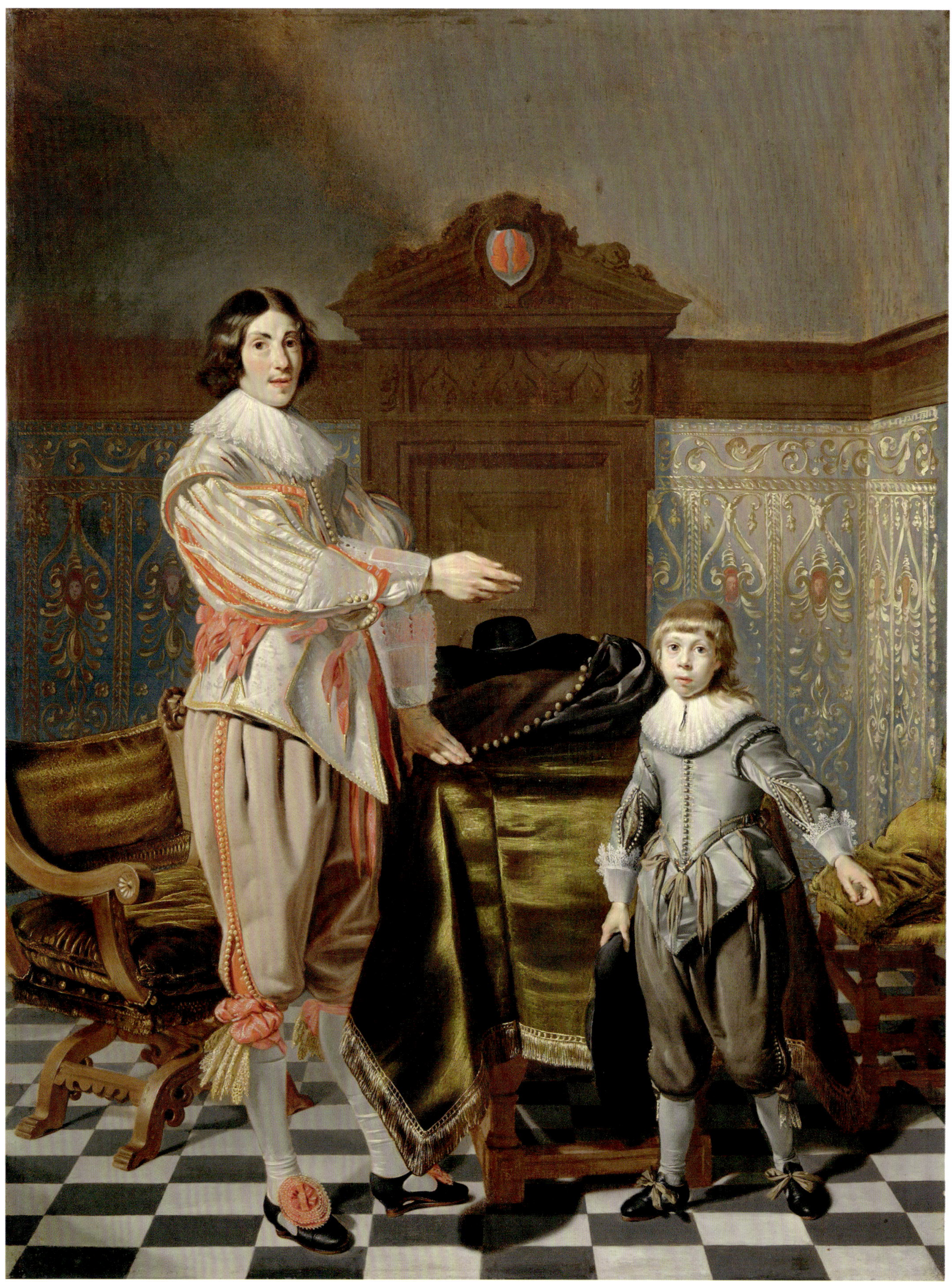

portrait is fashionably dressed in a long doublet of white silk with trapezoidal skirts trimmed with gold and red; the sleeves of the doublet are slashed to reveal a linen shirt, the wide laced cuffs of which are visible at his wrists; a soft linen ruff is at his neck.[5] The red silk ties at the waist of his doublet were used to fasten his light-brown leg-of-mutton breeches. Matching gold lace garters and red bows tie the breeches just below the knee and above the expensive silk hose; matching rosettes on the front of his shoes complete his costume. The boy wears a version of his father's attire in blue silk. Inspired by French fashion, the clothes worn by De Keyser's sitters represent international court taste.[6]

The elaborate costumes present questions regarding the sitters' identities. The crest with two red bird wings belongs to the Van Wissel family.[7] On this basis, F. G. L. O. Kretschmar, of the Central Bureau voor Genealogie of the Iconographisch Bureau of the Netherlands, identified the sitters as Dirck van Wissel (ca. 1594–1643) and his eldest son, Jacob (1624–1680), who would have been approximately thirty-seven and seven years old, respectively, in 1631.[8] Karen Schaffers-Bodenhausen, Kretschmar's successor as director of the Iconographisch Bureau, questioned this identification, objecting that the "youthful manner" and "flamboyant costume" of the father is "decidedly different from the way a married citizen of Amsterdam of thirty-seven years of age would have been painted in 1631."[9] Additional biographical information about Dirck van Wissel published by Ann Jensen Adams suggests that the sitters' colorful silk attire may have been a reference to Dirck's profession.[10] Born in Haarlem, Van Wissel was by 1617, at the age of 23, living in Amsterdam and trading in colored silk. In 1622 he married Catharina Rombouts (1596–1649), the orphaned daughter of a wealthy cloth dyer. They would have at least eight children, of which five lived to adulthood.[11] In 1631, the year he commissioned De Keyser to paint his portrait with his eldest surviving son and heir, Jacob, Dirck van Wissel built his home, "Het Huis te Merwe," at Keizersgracht 128, a neighborhood of wealthy and powerful men. De Keyser, whom Adams suggests Van Wissel met through his brother-in-law Jacob Rombouts, lived nearby.[12]

A closely related portrait of a father and son on copper attributed to De Keyser shares the basic composition and details of the Pasadena painting, including the figure of the man identified as Dirck van Wissel (fig. 45a).[13] In place of the young boy, however, a toddler sits on the table covered by a colorful Persian rug. The right hand of the man, which in the Pasadena painting directs attention to his seven-year-old son, drapes a long red-coral necklace across the chest of the child like a sash. The gesture, which is met by the child's tiny hand tenderly touching his father's, as well as the child's square collar indicate that it is a boy; a girl would have worn the familiar talisman as a necklace.[14] By comparison with the Pasadena painting, the figure of the man with the

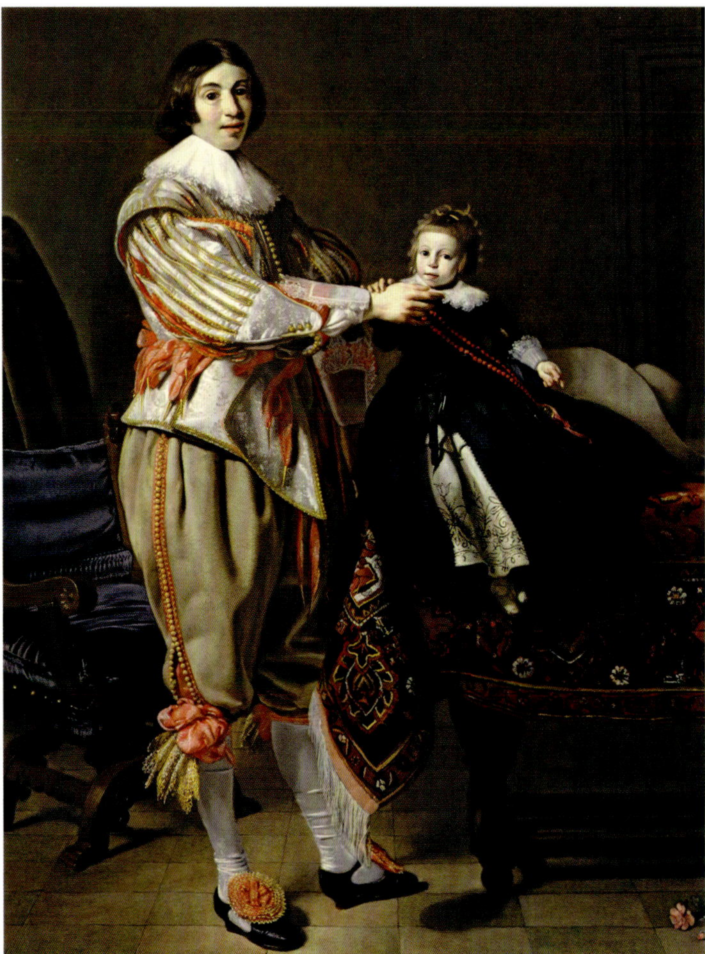

Fig. 45a. Thomas de Keyser, *Portrait of a Gentleman and His Son*, 1625/26, oil on copper, 19½ × 16⅝ in. (50 × 42 cm), private collection, photo courtesy of Otto Naumann Ltd., New York.

toddler appears considerably younger; his face is softer, and he lacks the small moustache evident in the 1631 painting. The costume, which is identical to that in the Pasadena painting, is also somewhat less skillfully rendered; the buttons for example, are placed too far to the side, and the suggestion of the man's right leg beneath the full drapery of his pants is unconvincing. If this is an early portrait of Dirck van Wissel and his son Jacob, then it would date to late 1625 or 1626.

Adams suggests that, rather than an earlier portrait by De Keyser showing Jacob as a child of one or one and a half years old, the portrait of the father with a toddler represents another child. She posits that work was painted by Henry Stone (1616–1653), De Keyser's nephew, who worked in his studio from 1633 to 1638.[15] Since no other male child of Dirck van Wissel would have been the appropriate age when Stone was in Amsterdam, however, she proposes that the boy represents the couple's first-born child, Dirck, who was buried on 16 September 1623, three months after his baptism at the Nieuwe Kerk, Amsterdam, was recorded on 6 June 1623. The fallen carnation to which the child points with his left hand would thus be a reference to his death.[16] The description of the man's face and handling of the costume in the second version are less skilled than in the Pasadena portrait, suggesting a possible copyist. Yet the sensitive expression and detail of the child in this version imply that rather than an imagined portrait of an infant who died at least ten years earlier, the portrait represents a directly observed child. Both issues of the identity of the toddler and the relationship of the copper version to that in Pasadena remain elusive.

The similar costume in both portraits of Dirck van Wissel, one of which portrays him as a younger man, may indicate the existence of an earlier, now lost, marriage portrait of Dirck and Catharina that served as the model.[17] In that hypothetical portrait, painted about 1622, the date of their marriage, for which his elegant attire would have been acceptable, Dirck's rhetorical gesture would have introduced his wife. In the Pasadena portrait painted nine years later, De Keyser updated Dirck's appearance by adding a moustache and references to his prosperity by portraying him and his son in an elegant room. With walls covered in expensive gilded leather, an elegantly carved doorframe, and black-and-white tiled floor, the room undoubtedly reflected the taste of his new home on the Keizersgracht, which was valued at 24,000 gulden in 1631, the year of the painting.[18] Standing in front of the family crest prominently displayed above the door, Dirck van Wessel's gesture pointing to Jacob, who extends the gesture with his proper left hand, celebrates the proud father's faith in his eldest son to carry on his legacy.[19]

1. The escutcheon separates "Ano" from the date.

2. The sales catalogue notes that the paintings in this sale had "been in the Wilshere family for very many years."

3. Adams 1985, vol. 1, pp. 209f. In a letter to Sir Dudley Carleton, English ambassador to The Hague, dated 18 August 1618, the painter Daniël Mijtens I (ca. 1590–ca. 1647) refers to a copy of a portrait of Thomas Howard, Earl of Arundel, and his wife, which he had made "in a small forme" at Arundel's request.

4. In 1548 the Portuguese humanist and court painter Francisco de Holanda (1517–1584) noted in the introduction to his treatise on portrait painting that few people merited the honor of portrayal and thus immortality: "Illustrious princes, kings and emperors, princesses and queens of virtue and wisdom, men famous in arms, art and letters, or of singular liberality and virtue, 'and nobody else at all'" (Woodall 1990, p. 34). By the second quarter of the seventeenth century, when De Keyser painted popular portraits of the regents of Amsterdam, the propriety of who could be portrayed in portraiture had been further expanded and redefined to reflect the republican society of the United Netherlands.

5. See Rotterdam 1977, p. 29, no. 79, Crispijn van de Passe II, *Gui-Michel le Jay and His Family*, ca. 1628/29. According to Woodall 1990, p. 45, this distinction in costume had broader social and political implications: "The Amsterdam elite generally failed to adopt the courtly modes during the 1630s and 1640s not because it rejected the idea of a noble ruling class, but because it was engaged in a power struggle with the court at The Hague which necessitated maintaining a distinctive identity."

6. In De Keyser's contemporary *Portrait of a Gentleman*, dated 1632 (Louvre, Paris), for example, the wealthy Amsterdam gentleman is dressed in a similar suit cut in the French style but rendered in black silk. See London/The Hague 2007, p. 152, no. 35.

7. Adams 1985, vol. 3, pp. 65f. The crest is reproduced in Rolland 1967, vol. 6, pl. clxxxi.

8. Information communicated to Ann Jensen Adams and recorded by her in Adams 1985, vol. 3, pp. 65f.

9. Karen Schaffers-Bodenhausen, letter dated 18 June 1987 (NSM). It was unconventional for a father to be portrayed with only his eldest son. It is more common that family portraits represent the sons of the family with the father and the daughters and male infants with the mother, either in one painting or two. See, for example, the rather crude portraits by Jacob van Campen (active in Franeker, ca. 1634–46) of a *Father and Son and Mother and Daughter* of 1646, Fries Museum, Leeuwarden.

10. Adams 2020, pp. 15, 17.

11. In addition to Jacob, Dirck van Wissel and his wife, Catharina, were the parents of Dirck (1626–1634), Johannes (b. 1628), twins Eduwart (1629–1661) and Willem (1629–1678), and Maria (1631–1667), all of whom were alive in 1631. Their daughter, Anna, was born the following year in 1632. As noted in the text, their first-born child, Dirck, died as an infant in 1623. An unidentified child of the couple was buried in the Westerkerk, Amsterdam, on 12 January 1633. (Adams 2020, pp. 19, 21n34).

12. Adams 2020, pp. 17–18.

13. Purchased at a sale in Paris in 1997, the previously unrecorded portrait (with Newhouse Galleries, then Otto Naumann, New York, in 2004–09; sold Sotheby's, New York, 29 January 2009, lot 139) is painted on copper, 50 × 42 cm (19½ × 16⅝ in.) and bears traces of a monogram and date on the table leg at lower right: "[. . .] DK[?] 16[. . .]."

14. Adams 2020, p. 19.

15. Adams 2020, p. 19. In the caption for the painting, which appears as her fig. 2, Adams attributes the painting to "Henry Stone & Thomas de Keyser" and titles it *Portrait of Dirck van Wissel and One of His Sons, Possibly the Eldest, the Already-in-1623 Deceased Dirck*. She dates it ca. 1633–38. Liedtke 2007, vol. 1, p. 402, previously suggested that the painting on copper is later than the Pasadena painting and that the toddler is a girl. The costume of the toddler could have been worn by either sex but, as Adams points out, the square collar indicates it is a boy.

16. The baby's gesture is emphasized by the diagonal line of the red-coral beads, which serves as a talisman and to which his teether is attached.

17. De Keyser is known to have updated portraits, reusing some figures and replacing others. For the *Portrait of Frederick van Velthuysen and His Son Dirck* (1660), the artist appropriated the figure of the father, who was by then deceased, from an earlier portrait of Velthuysen and his first wife, replacing the figure of the wife, who was deceased, with that of his son from his second marriage.

18. Adams 2020, p. 18, estimates that this was equivalent to €241,000 in 2018.

19. Adams 1985, vol. 1, p. 260, notes that independent portraits of a man and his son were "relatively rare," and that dynastic pride was more often expressed in portraits of men and their grandsons. As an example, she cites Anthony van Dyck's portrait *Thomas Howard, Earl of Arundel with His Grandson Lord Maltravers* (ca. 1635, Arundel Castle, coll. Duke of Norfolk).

46, 47

Thomas de Keyser or follower

Dutch
Amsterdam 1596/97–1667 Amsterdam

Portrait of a Man

ca. 1637

Oil on panel, 18 3/8 × 15 7/8 in. (46.7 × 40.3 cm)
The Norton Simon Foundation, F.1972.15.3.1.P

Portrait of a Woman

1637

Dated upper left: "A.No: 1637."
Oil on panel, 18 × 15 1/2 in. (45.7 × 39.4 cm)
The Norton Simon Foundation, F.1972.15.3.2.P

Provenance

Neffert.[1] De Jonge, Paris, in 1911/12. Albert Dubosc du Haire (sale, Hôtel Drouot, Paris, 5 December 1947, lots 27 [man], 28 [woman]). [Edward Speelman Ltd., London, by 1951, sold 1972 to]; The Norton Simon Foundation.

Exhibited

Paris 1911, nos. 77 (man), 78 (woman); London 1953a, no. 4; on loan, Allen Memorial Art Museum, Oberlin, 1 June 1972–8 May 1973; on loan, Los Angeles County Museum of Art, 9 May 1973–26 November 1974.

References

Oldenbourg 1911, nos. 114 (man), 115 (woman); W. Martin 1911, pp. 250 (man), 251 (woman), ills.; Dayot 1912a, p. 133, nos. 80 (man), 81 (woman), ill.; Adams 1985, vol. 3, pp. 238–39, nos. R-12 (man), R-13 (woman); P. Sutton 1986, p. 216; S. Campbell 2010, p. 339, nos. 789A–B, ill.; Speelman 2022, p. 126.

Technical Notes

Portrait of a Man
The vertically grained oak panel has been thinned and cradled. The smoothly applied white ground is moderately thin and does not completely cover the texture of the wood. There is a warm-brown imprimatura visible in the jacket as well as at the juncture of the proper right wrist and the cuff. Opaque rich paint was deftly applied. The black-on-black design of the jacket was done by applying deep gray in irregular shapes over the imprimatura, then painting cross-hatchings in black paint over the gray. X-radiography reveals that an additional book was originally placed on the table at the right, behind the visible books. The paint is generally well preserved. Scattered areas of minor abrasion are noticeable in the black suit; the edges of the white lace and the adjoining black have been disturbed slightly. In a prior undocumented restoration, selective cleaning reduced the varnish over the face, hands, collar and cuffs, and objects on the table. Small residues of darkened varnish remain in the recesses of brushstrokes in the cuffs and collar and to a lesser extent in the face. Ultraviolet light indicates a natural-resin varnish.

Portrait of a Woman
The support is a vertically grained oak panel. The absence of beveled edges or tool marks on the reverse suggests that the panel was thinned before a cradle was added. A split at the right side that extends from the top edge to the bottom edge is tightly closed. The white ground is moderately thin, leaving the wood texture evident. A golden-brown imprimatura is apparent in several areas: for example, around the woman's bonnet and hair and around her proper right shoulder. The artist used opaque, fairly rich paint in a direct application blended wet-into-wet for much of the painting except for the tablecloth, which was rendered in semitransparent paint. X-radiography shows that the features of the face were originally slightly different, with the mouth more firmly V-shaped and the lips compressed. Cleaning in a prior treatment left small residues of dark varnish in the depressions of the brushstrokes in the face, collar, and cuffs, creating a slightly speckled effect. Small flake losses have been retouched in the white collar along fine vertical cracks. Across the sitter's proper left shoulder, where the split in the panel goes through the collar, the paint has been damaged and the retouching is visible, underlying the thick natural-resin varnish.

Conceived to hang as pendants, these panels represent the sitters seated on opposite sides of tables so that they appear—despite the mismatched perspectives—to occupy the same space and to address each other as well as the viewer. The small-scale format that merges portraiture and genre, placing the sitters in the context of their home or study, was introduced during the 1620s in Amsterdam by Thomas de Keyser and adopted by, among others, Pieter Codde (1599–1678), whose portraits of the Amsterdam

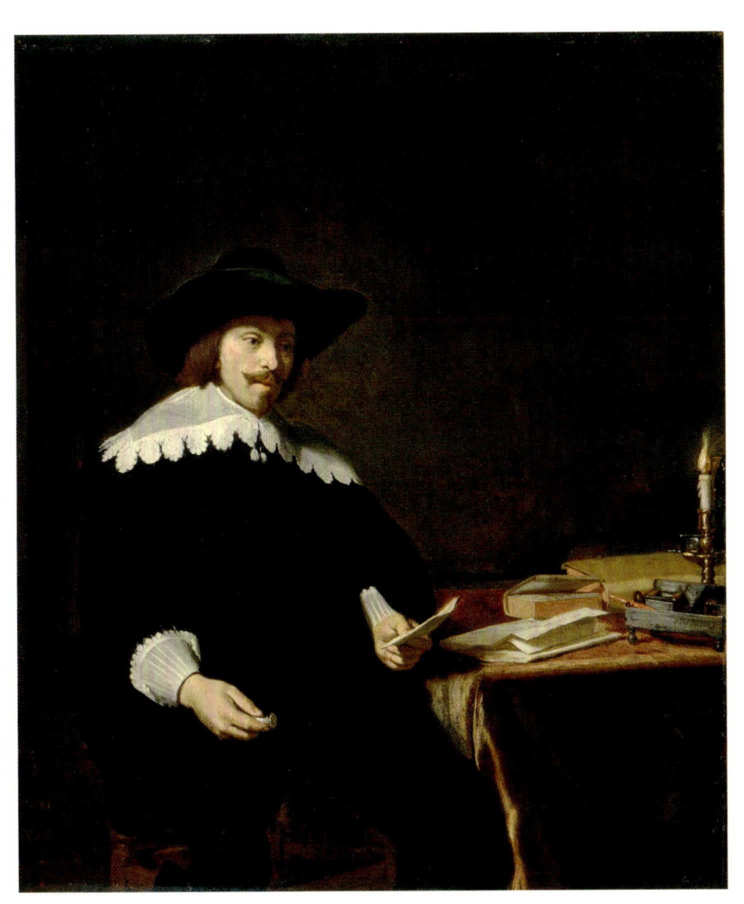

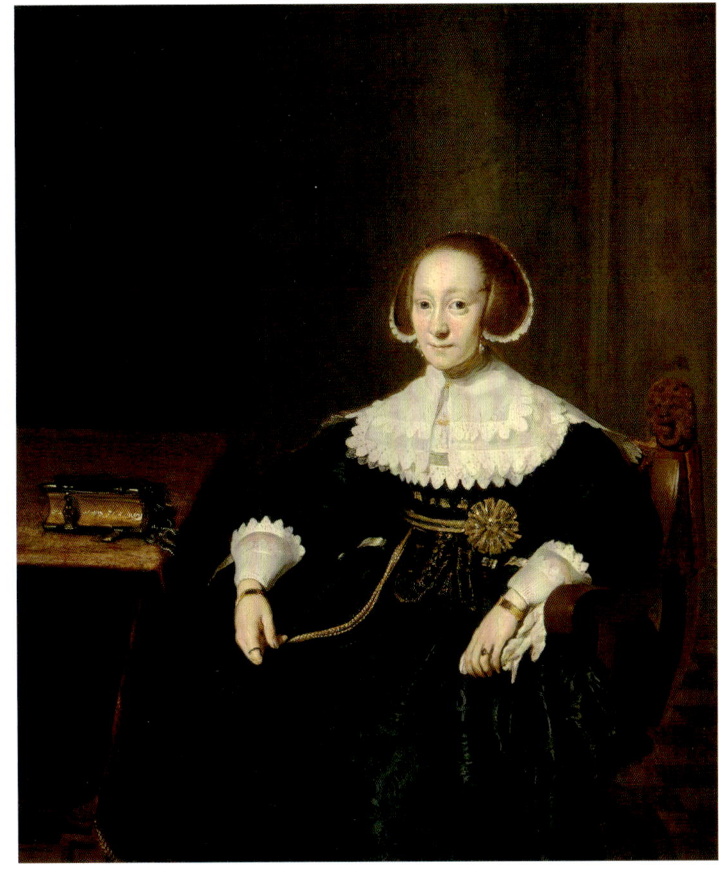

schoolmaster and writer Hendrick Meurs (1603–1639) and his wife, Judith Kotermans, share the aspects of the poses and iconography of the Pasadena portraits (see figs. 46a and 46b). The unidentified sitters in the Pasadena panels were, like Codde's sitters, probably members of Amsterdam's burgher class, which by the mid-1630s provided a growing market for portraits. Even on this relatively small scale, portraits were important status symbols through which the sitters expressed their public personae.

In the Pasadena paintings, the sitters wear fashionable sober black clothing with white lace trim. The black-on-black diamond pattern of the man's close-fitting jacket and trousers appears in numerous portraits painted in Amsterdam during the late 1630s. Black silk garters tied in simple bows support the man's black hose. His pleated, white "cambric" cuffs, made from tightly woven plain linen, are modestly trimmed with a narrow band of lace, but the flat collar is trimmed with the more expensive lace also worn by his wife. The multilayered fine cambric collar trimmed with heavy lace worn flat against the bodice of the woman's black silk brocade dress was the height of fashion in Amsterdam during the mid- and late 1630s, marking a break from the short-lived restraints imposed by the sumptuary laws at the beginning of the decade.[2] Attached to the band worn around her fashionably high-waist dress and shortened stomacher, she wears an ornamental rosette formed from fabric ribbon woven with gold threads.[3] Her "cap" is actually a form around which her own hair is smoothed and then backed with cambric and lace; from her ears, or more likely from the headband itself, hang pear-shaped pearl earrings, which had become popular with the disappearance of the cumbersome ruffs. A decorative hairpin is stuck between the hair band and the left side of her face, and a choker of gold-colored beads is visible at her neck. With her right hand she holds a fan made of feathers set in a mount of metal or wood (often ebony) and suspended from the waistband by a cord or chain.[4] Popular since the beginning of the seventeenth century, fans were particularly associated with status, as were handkerchiefs.[5]

Typical of the period, *Portrait of a Woman* emphasizes the wife's domestic role and relationship to her husband. Her steady gaze and the self-possession with which she occupies her chair suggest the value of her position in the household as the wife of a successful burgher. In the contemporary pair of portraits by Pieter Codde, known through engravings by Paulus Pontius (1603–1658), the love that the writer Hendrick Meurs felt for his wife, Judith Kotermans, is evident in the inscription by Joost van den Vondel (1587–1679) that surrounds her printed image: "Here is the likeness of Judith Kotermans / who brightens Meurs's heart with friendly sparks / His spirited quill thrives on that ogling / When she shuts her eyes he lives without luster" (fig. 46b).[6] A wife's piety was also important to visualize in such portraits, as in *Portrait of a Woman* by Gerrit Dou (1613–1675; cat. 22). Here, it is alluded to by the leather-

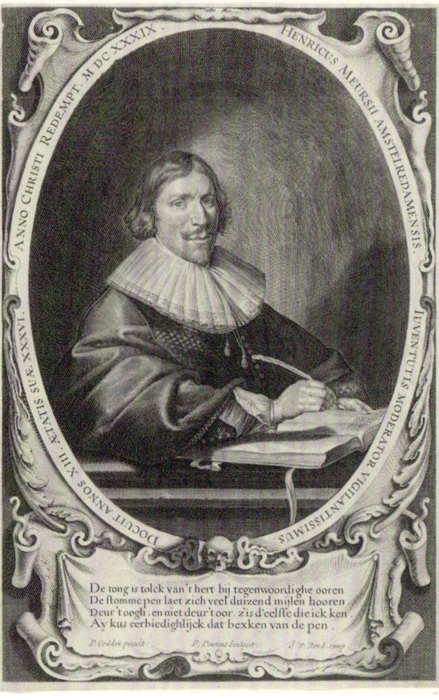

Fig. 46a. Paulus Pontius, after Pieter Codde, *Portrait of Hendrick Meurs*, 1639, engraving, 13 ⅛ × 9 in. (33.4 × 22.9 cm), Rijksmuseum, Amsterdam.

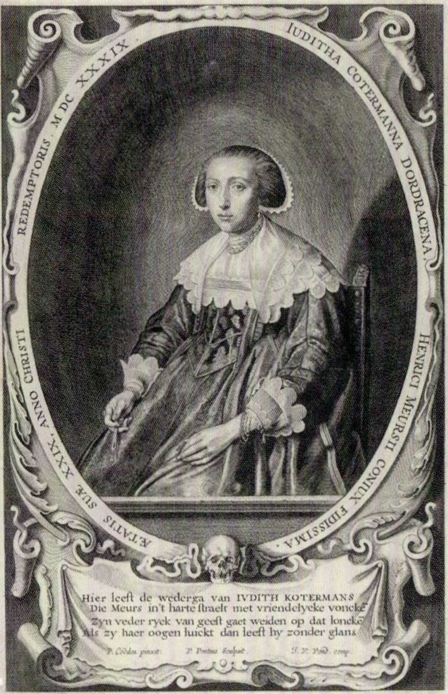

Fig. 46b. Paulus Pontius, after Pieter Codde, *Portrait of Judith Kotermans*, 1639, engraving on paper, 13 ½ × 8 ⅞ in. (34.3 × 22.7 cm), Rijksmuseum, Amsterdam.

bound Bible on the table, ornamented with metal fittings and a gold chain by which it could be suspended from her belt.

In addition to alluding to his responsibilities as a husband, *Portrait of a Man* suggests the sitter's life beyond the home. Wearing a hat and cape, he is seated at a table strewn with books and papers. A candle and a small tray with writing utensils lie on the table. Holding a folded sheet of paper in his left hand and a seal in his right, he appears to have just drafted and sealed a letter for posting. During the 1630s portraits of men writing at their desks or handling letters enjoyed particular popularity among Amsterdam burghers.[7] The best-known example of this genre is De Keyser's 1627 portrait of the statesman-scholar Constantijn Huygens (1596–1687) seated at his writing desk and turning to receive a letter from a young man (Rijksmuseum, Amsterdam).[8] Rather than references to scholarly interests, as in the portrait of Huygens, portraits such as the Pasadena *Portrait of a Man* and *Portrait of Hendrick Meurs* (fig. 46a) reflect the sitters' desire to be represented as sophisticated men of the world and active correspondents. Indeed, letter writing was not only a necessity but also a popular pastime. The inscription on the portrait of Meurs, who was known as an "artful writer" (*kunstig schoonschrijver*), refers to the power of the written word, which can be heard across thousands of miles, whereas the human voice can only be heard by those who are present.[9]

The attribution to De Keyser in this pair of portraits dates from at least 1911, when the paintings were exhibited in Paris and Rudolf Oldenbourg published his monograph on De Keyser. Ann Jensen Adams rejected the attribution to De Keyser in 1985 but offered no alternative artist. In common with portraits by De Keyser, the eyes of the sitters appear round with large pupils, and the eye sockets are well defined. The description of costume, the iconographic and compositional types of the portraits, as well as the proportions and character of the paintings are clearly related to the work of De Keyser. The handling of paint—particularly the lace and other details—and perspective, however, are less accomplished than that of other works securely attributed to De Keyser, suggesting that the portraits may have been painted by another artist working in Amsterdam during the late 1630s under the influence of De Keyser and Codde.[10]

1. According to Dayot 1912a, p. 17.

2. Similar costumes appear in contemporary portraits by Amsterdam artists, notably Pieter Codde. This may be compared to the elegant variation worn by Maria Trip in Rembrandt's famous portrait in the Rijksmuseum. A low, square-cut neckline was usually covered with a cambric neckerchief, or *neerstich*, which was often edged with lace. Over this was worn the kerchief. Both the neckerchief and the kerchief were fastened at the front with a linen cord tied in a bow. The bows, which were originally functional, became purely ornamental. In the present portrait of the woman, the gold strands that can be seen in the opening of the collar may represent these ornamental ribbons, which were often woven from gold and silver thread or multicolored silk. See Du Mortier 1989, pp. 45–52.

3. By this time the stomacher had lost its low waistline and no longer protruded. Rather, it was worn fairly short, ending in a small, pointed peplum.

4. First introduced in the second quarter of the sixteenth century, fans gained popularity with the growing influence of French style in the Netherlands during the early seventeenth century. Folding fans from China were less common at this time. Regarding fans see Du Mortier 2010.

5. De Winkel 2006, p. 79, with additional references (p. 79n106) to Braun-Ronsdorf 1967, pp. 20ff.; Peri 1992, p. 10; and Haarlem 1986a, p. 112.

6. The inscription on Pontius's print after Codde's portrait of Judith Kotermans reads: "Hier leeft de wederga van IVDITH KOTERMANS / Die Meurs in't harte straelt met vriendelycke voncke[n] / Zyn veder ryck van geest gaet weiden op dat loncke[n]. /Als zy haer oogen luickt dan leeft hy zonder glans." The original painting was with Appleby Bros., London, June 1963, as Thomas de Keyser, *Portrait of a Lady*, oil on panel, 24 × 19 in.

7. The iconographic prototypes for these paintings were the representations of the Apostles writing the Gospels and the scenes of Saint Jerome in his study. The image of a man seated at a desk became popular for the portrayal of secular portraits during the sixteenth century.

8. For a discussion of De Keyser's portrait of Huygens, see Adams 1985, vol. 1, pp. 117–48, and more recently, London/The Hague 2007, pp. 150f., no. 34.

9. "De tong is tolck van't hart bij tegenwoordighe ooren / De stomme pen laet zich veel duizend mijlen hooren, / Deur't oogh; en niet deur't oor. Z'is d'eelste die ick ken. / Ay kus eerbiedighlijck dat bexken van de pen." I am grateful to Dane Reeb for identifying the passage by the Dutch playwright and poet Joost van den Vondel. See Van den Vondel 1927–40, vol. 3 (1627–1640), p. 796. In Codde's portrait, Meurs appears to have been interrupted from writing in an open book. Hatless and draped in either a cape or dressing gown worn over his street clothes, he assumes the traditional appearance of a scholar in his study.

10. For example, the woman and table are viewed from different vantage points. The disparity between the perspectives in the two paintings when seen together, however, is also found in De Keyser's *Portrait d'un homme assis près d'une table*, ca. 1632, at the Musée du Louvre and its pendant in Berlin. See London/The Hague 2007, nos. 35–36.

48

Attributed to Jan Lievens

Dutch
Leiden 1607–1674 Amsterdam

Young Man with Red Beret

ca. 1629–30

Oil on panel, original panel: 25¼ × 17½ in. (64.1 × 44.5 cm);[1] with additions: 27¼ × 20¾ in. (69.2 × 52.7 cm)
Norton Simon Art Foundation, M.1997.1.1.P

Provenance

Napoléon-Louis (1811–1898), 3rd Duke of Talleyrand-Périgord, Duke of Valençay et Sagan, Paris and Château de Valençay (sale, Galerie Georges Petit, Paris, 2 December 1899, no. 49; as signed Rembrant [*sic*]; sold for F9,000 to);[2] [Charles Sedelmeyer, Paris (sale, Ch. Sedelmeyer, Paris, 25 May 1907, lot 158, as Rembrandt, *Portrait of the Artist*, ill.; sold for F 126,000 to)];[3] [Schnell for]; Henri-Georges Heugel (1844–1918), Paris, by descent to;[4] Mme Heugel (née Gordon-Creed) and their son Jacques Heugel (1890–1979), Paris, sold ca. 1955/56 to; [Heim Gallery, Paris]. Collection Sikorsky, Hamburg.[5] Possibly Gustav Schimert, Munich.[6] [Acquavella Galleries, New York, sold in 1961 to]; Mrs. Stuart H. Ingersoll (née Elinor Dorrance), New York and Newport, RI (estate sale, Christie's, New York, 12 January 1978, lot 79, as Lievens, sold to); Norton Simon, bequest 1993 to; Jennifer Jones Simon Art Trust, gift 1997 to; Norton Simon Art Foundation.

Exhibited

On loan, Henry Art Gallery, University of Washington, Seattle, 25 January–4 October 1978.

References

J. Smith 1829–42, vol. 7 (1836), pp. 107, 150, 154, nos. 292,[7] 448, 473;[8] Dutuit 1885, pp. 62, 66, no. 261;[9] Bode and Hofstede de Groot 1897–1906, vol. 8 (suppl., 1905–06), pp. 37, 96, no. 567, ill., as Rembrandt; Sedelmeyer 1906, p. 38, no. 30, ill., as Rembrandt; Hofstede de Groot 1906, p. 27, no. 28b, as "not by the hand of Rembrandt but closest to Jan Lievens"; Saint-Groux 1907, pp. 17, 19, ill., as Rembrandt; Valentiner 1908, p. 145, ill., as Rembrandt, ca. 1633, panel, 67.5 × 52.5 cm; Hofstede de Groot 1908–27, vol. 6 (1916), p. 227, no. 431, as Rembrandt, ca. 1633, oak, 27 × 21 in., and p. 385, no. 838, "Sm. 448—[possibly identical with no. 431]";[10] Valentiner 1921c, p. 145, ill., as Rembrandt, ca. 1633, panel, 67.5 × 52.5 cm; Bauch 1926, pp. 30, 85, no. 90, pl. 20, as Backer, ca. 1635; Kauffmann 1926, pp. 245f., as Rembrandt; Hollstein 1949–2010, vol. 10, p. 46, no. 14;[11] Gerson 1973b, pp. 175, 208, pl. 42, ill., as Lievens; Bauch 1973, p. 218, as Lievens; *Corpus* 1982, pp. 25–26, 28, 49f., ill., as Circle of Rembrandt; Sumowski 1983–93, vol. 1, pp. 198, 245, no. 42, ill., as Backer; Brejon de Lavergnée 1994, p. 229, fig. 22;[12] Amsterdam/Aachen 2008, pp. 112f.; S. Campbell 2010, pp. 185, 186, 189n30, 414, no. 1501, fig. 11, ill.; Schnackenburg 2016, p. 469, R7.

Technical Notes

The original support is a vertically grained hardwood panel. The top corners of the painting are separate pieces of wood, possibly repairs of damages or flaws in the panel. The wood grain at the left corner matches the rest of the panel; the right corner does not. Both corner pieces are held by the addition of a veneer to the reverse as well as a cradle. Narrow wood strips were then attached to the sides of the panel and painted, but not with the intention of continuing the image of the portrait. (The borders are not visible when the painting is framed.) The smoothly applied ground is white. Above the ground is a light golden-brown layer visible beneath the sgraffito at the proper left shoulder, in the embroidered collar, near the spine of the feather, within the looser brushwork in the coat, and in the beret, where gaps in the brushwork of the beaded decoration expose it. The paint is exceptionally well preserved. The artist has handled it rather freely in the hair, coat, and feather; the face has a smooth blending of flesh tones. Both opaque and semitransparent paints are evident. He employed sgraffito to depict tendrils of hair where the thicker, opaque background paint meets the near-transparent paint at the outer contour of the hair. The background paint appears to be uninterrupted as it continues over the joins of the triangular additions at the top corners. Retouching is located in a long crack at the left side, the join of the top left triangle, the entire top right triangle, and much of the added borders. Retouching within the figure consists only of several small dots in the cap, hair, beard, and face. The painting was restored by Mario Modestini in the late 1950s. The present varnish, likely a synthetic resin over the older, natural-resin varnish, saturates poorly and is becoming slightly cloudy.

Dressed in a dark red cloak richly ornamented with gold brocade and closed with three buttons, a lightly bearded young man with long, wavy hair wears a soft, red velvet beret decorated with a band of pearls and a feather plume. The gold chain just visible beneath his parted cloak and the delicate green scarf woven with gold threads and wrapped around the gathered neck of his white shirt create an exotic impression that distinguishes the sitter from conservative Dutch burghers and suggests that he is an artist.

Rembrandt and artists in his circle often portrayed themselves and other artists wearing similar costumes. Marieke de Winkel has demonstrated that this clothing combines references to the historic past—the beret or bonnet, fashionable in the early sixteenth century—with objects and clothing sourced from distant regions, such as the African ostrich feather and thin transparent scarf with gold threads, a garment frequently imported by the East India Company.[13] The sitter in the Pasadena painting is dressed, for example, in a

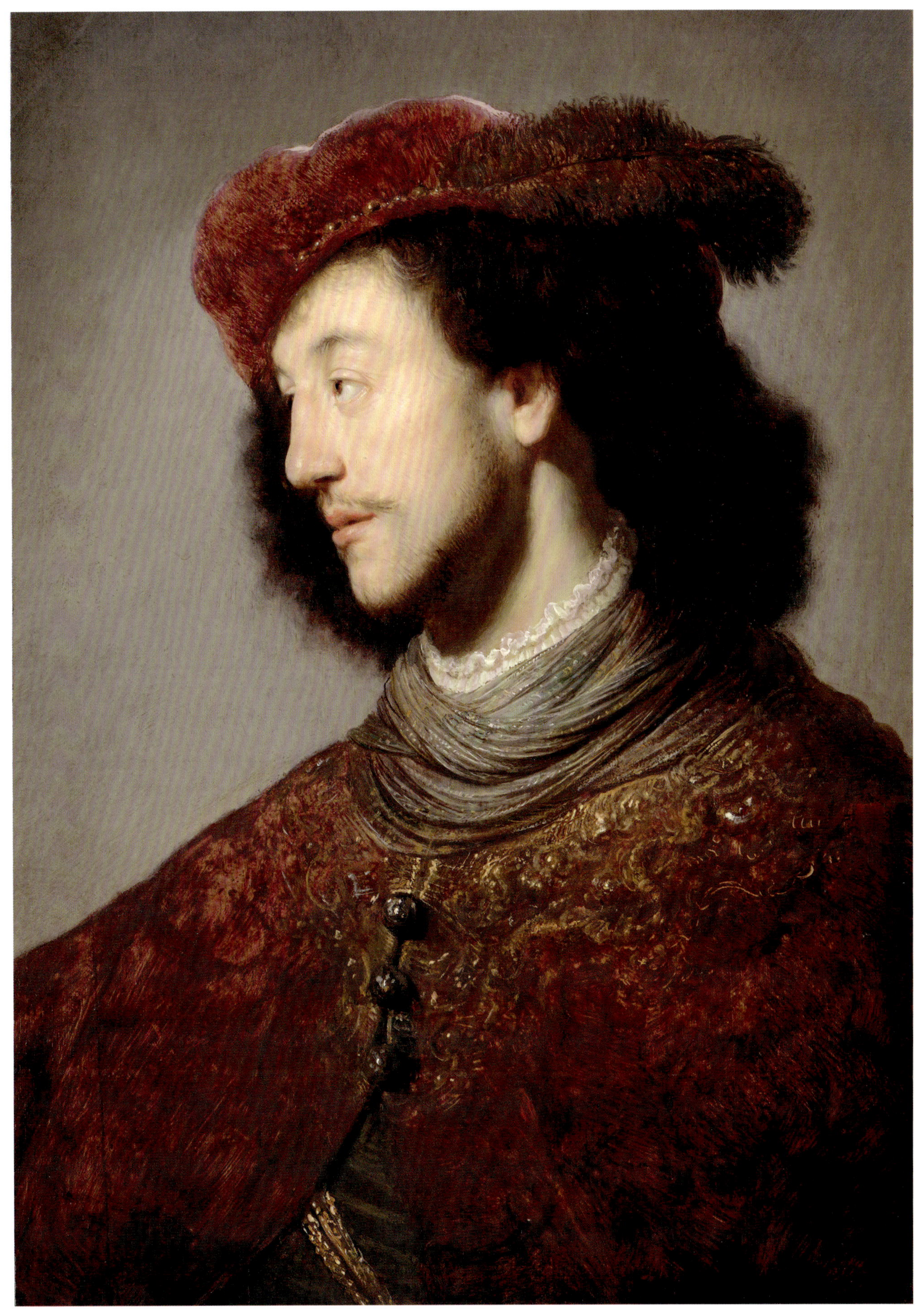

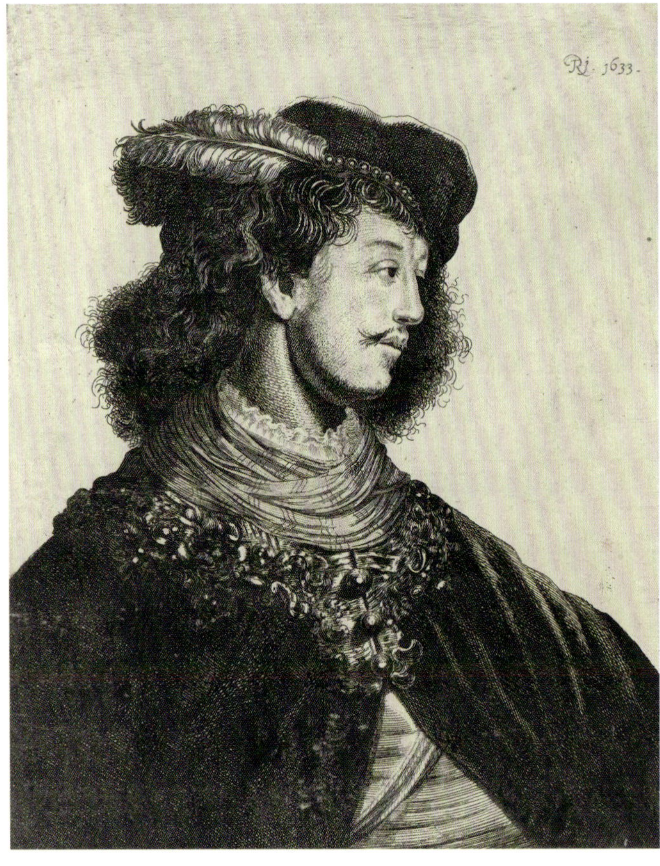

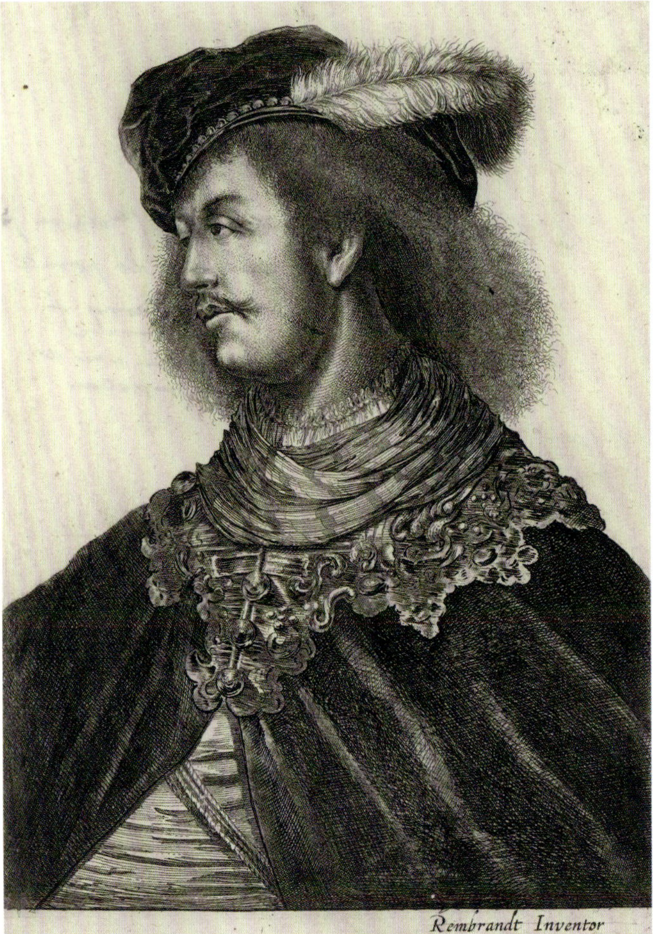

manner similar to Rembrandt in his self-portrait of ca. 1629 (Isabella Stewart Gardner Museum, Boston). In the Boston painting, however, the gold chain draped over Rembrandt's shoulders is composed of several strands worn diagonally across the sitter's chest in a manner consistent with the gold chain artists such as Rubens, Anthony van Dyck (1599–1641), and others received as a mark of honor.[14]

The identity of the sitter represented in *Young Man with Red Beret* is unknown. The painting was probably not intended as a *contrefeijtsel*, a portrait made to record the likeness of a specific individual, but as a *tronie,* a study of a head or a bust of an interesting type often used for history paintings.[15] Profile poses were used for both commissioned portraits, such as Rembrandt's 1632 *Portrait of Amalia von Solms*, the wife of the Stadtholder Frederik Hendrik (Musée Jacquemart-André, Paris), and for *tronies* of figures who often wear sumptuous, fanciful costumes without attributes or setting.[16] It appears most likely that *Young Man with Red Beret* was painted from an individual but also appreciated, and perhaps sold, as a *tronie*. An etching after this painting by Willem van der Leeuw (1603–ca. 1665) does not identify the subject (fig. 48a), while an etching by Salomon Savery (1594–1678) has been associated with the biblical patriarch Joseph (fig. 48b).[17]

The production of *tronies* was an integral part of the training of Rembrandt and the artists in his circle. In his autobiography of 1629–31, Constantijn Huygens (1596–1687), poet and counselor to the prince of Orange, praises Rembrandt for his skill in rendering emotion and expression, the apparent goal of painting *tronies*.[18] An inventory of Rembrandt's possessions reveals that, in addition to works painted by the artist himself and by others after his work, he also owned *tronies* by his contemporaries such as Adriaen Brouwer (1605/06–1638) and by, or more likely after, revered Old Masters such as Jan van Eyck (ca. 1390–1441) and Raphael (1483–1520).[19] The frequent inclusion of the term *tronie* in seventeenth-century inventories indicates that these paintings were also sold and appreciated as independent works of art, hung in prominent places in collectors' homes.[20]

Young Man with Red Beret relates to the *tronies* and self-portraits Rembrandt produced in the early 1630s, particularly his undated early self-portrait in the Gardner Museum. These paintings have in common subjects wearing wistful expressions and full heads of hair as well as similarities in costume. However, in contrast to Rembrandt's subtle, atmospheric rendering, where shadow obscures half the face, the profile view of the head and concern with detail in the Pasadena painting

Fig. 48a. Willem van der Leeuw, *Portrait of an Unknown Young Man with Beret*, 1633–35, etching, 8 3/8 × 6 3/8 in. (21.3 × 16.2 cm), Rijksmuseum, Amsterdam.

Fig. 48b. Salomon Savery, *Portrait of a Young Man with a Beret with a Feather on His Head* after *Young Man with Red Beret*, ca. 1633, etching, 7 1/2 × 5 1/2 in. (19.1 × 13.9 cm), Rijksmuseum, Amsterdam.

create a harder, psychologically more remote image. Rather than an active pattern of brushstrokes that appear to model the form of the face in Rembrandt's portraits, here the sitter's face is described by a pattern of fine brushstrokes applied in a diagonal direction. The sitter's clothing appears flat without any indication of the underlying form.

The attribution of *Young Man with Red Beret* has long been a matter of debate. The painting was for many years attributed to Rembrandt on the basis of Savery's etching (fig. 48b).[21] This print, which renders the image in proper orientation to the painting and bears the inscription "Rembt. Invent." ("Rembrandt Inventor"), was probably a copy of the etching traditionally attributed to Van der Leeuw (fig. 48a).[22] In 1906 Cornelis Hofstede de Groot read the monogram in the upper right corner of the Van der Leeuw print as "R.j.," which he interpreted as "Rembrandt inventor."[23] The Rembrandt Research Project, however, reads the "strange monogram" as "JRi/1633" and suggests that it may have been misread previously as a Rembrandt monogram. It notes that "the hardly Rembrandtesque impression that the clothing and expression of the young man makes [in the print] is borne out by the [Pasadena] painting, which probably served as the model."[24] The prints made after the painting indicate that the painting was cut on the left side, possibly removing the signature.

Hofstede de Groot was the first Rembrandt scholar to express doubt about the attribution of *Young Man with Red Beret*, noting in 1906 that the painting is closest to Jan Lievens. By the time of the publication of his revised edition of Smith's catalogue in 1916, however, Hofstede de Groot again believed that Rembrandt was the author. Ten years later Kurt Bauch attributed the painting to Jacob Adriensz. Backer (1608–1651), dating it about 1635. In 1973 Horst Gerson returned the attribution to Lievens and, according to Sumowski, convinced Bauch to reject his earlier attribution of the painting to Backer. Sumowski, however, rejected the attribution to Lievens and again attributed the painting to Backer and dated it ca. 1640, when Backer's paintings demonstrate a high degree of quality.[25]

Following a visit to the Norton Simon Museum in June 2006, Bernhard Schnackenburg remarked that the Pasadena painting is closer to Backer than Lievens. Schnackenburg explained that the painting is "much too colorful for Lievens, who uses at this time, 1630/31, only a few pale colors, as in the Getty's portrait" of *Prince Charles Louis of the Palatinate with His Tutor Wolrad von Plessen in Historical Dress* (1631). He also noted that Lievens typically defined the faces, hands, clothing, and background of his *tronies* using broad brushstrokes to apply paint in a variety of thicknesses. In *Young Man with Red Beret*, tight brushstrokes of heavily applied paint sweep over and around the eye and down the face. The light contrasts are also stronger and the expression too lively for Lievens, according to Schnackenburg. Yet, he noted, "But if it would be by Lievens it must be dated not 1629/30 but a little bit later, 1630/31."[26]

Peter van den Brink, who visited the Norton Simon Museum in November 2007 to examine the painting, rejected the attribution to either Lievens or Backer. He agreed with this author that the broad, fluid handling of paint and soft forms, which are typical of Backer throughout his career, are absent in *Young Man with Red Beret*, which relies on the development of detail with a fine brush and at times the incised lines of the butt end of a brush to emphasize the decorative detail of the cloak. In his monographic catalogue of Backer in 2008, Van den Brink again rejected the attribution to Backer.[27]

Rather than Backer, Van den Brink suggests that *Young Man with a Red Beret* is by Isaac de Jouderville (1613–1648), Rembrandt's apprentice in Leiden in 1630–31.[28] In his 2016 monograph on Jan Lievens, Schnackenburg rejects the attribution to Lievens and accepts Van den Brink's attribution to Jouderville. He refers the reader to *Bust of a Young Man* (National Gallery of Ireland, Dublin), the only securely signed painting by Jouderville.[29] A comparison of the Pasadena painting with that in Dublin, however, reveals significant differences. In the Dublin painting Jouderville, in imitation of Rembrandt, applied paint thinly, allowing the ground color to show through the upper layers, whereas the artist of *Young Man with Red Beret* painted with tight brushstrokes and thick paint that covers the ground. The attention to detail is also different. Jouderville described the sitter's full hair in general terms without definition of individual strands; the sitter in the Pasadena painting has similar full hair, but the artist painted with a thin brush and the butt end of the brush to define individual strands of hair and to emphasize the texture of the embroidery on the proper left shoulder. The description of the sitters' scarves is also different. On the Dublin painting, abstracted highlights are hard and precise dots of color that only broadly describe the fabric, while in the Pasadena painting the highlights are more delicate and accurately follow the individual folds of the thin fabric.

Other stylistic characteristics of *Young Man with Red Beret*, however, relate to Lievens's paintings. Lievens, more than other artists, represented figures in profile and used the butt end of the brush to scratch into the paint, a technique only used by Lievens and Rembrandt ca. 1628.[30] The gray tonality is similar to that of Lievens's *Portrait of Constantijn Huygens* (1628/29; Musée de la Chartreuse, Douai, on loan to the Rijksmuseum, Amsterdam), *Bust of an Old Woman (Rembrandt's Mother?)*, ca. 1630 (Royal Collection, Windsor Castle), and *Old Man* (fig. 48c). In both the Vienna and the Pasadena paintings, the artist described the reflection of light on the top of the beret and used the butt of the brush to inscribe lines into the surface of the paint—in the beard of the old man and the decorative pattern of the young man's cloak, respectively. Similar sgrafitti also appear in a profile bust of a young man in a cap, signed with

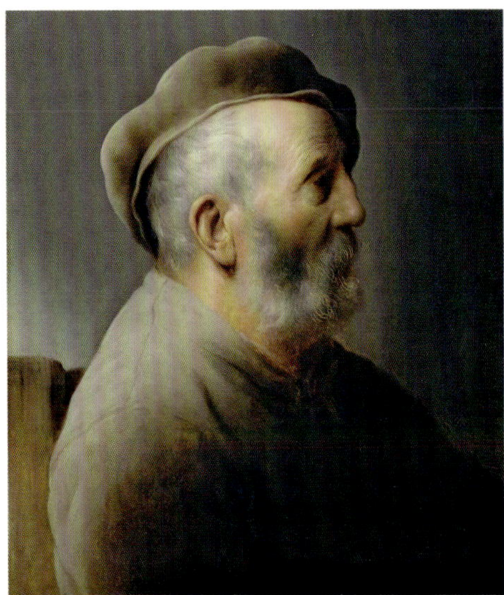

Fig. 48c. Jan Lievens, *Old Man*, ca. 1625/26, oil on panel, 20⅞ × 18½ in. (53 × 47 cm), Kunsthistorisches Museum, Vienna.

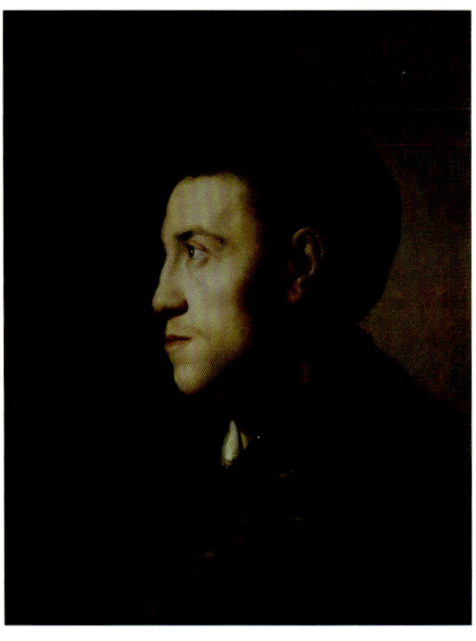

Fig. 48d. Jan Lievens, *Head of a Young Man with a Cap*, ca. 1630, oil on panel, 25 × 19½ in. (63.5 × 49.5 cm), private collection, image courtesy of Jean-Luc Baroni Ltd., London.

Lievens's monogram "IL," formerly with the London dealer Jean-Luc Baroni (fig. 48d), which also shares other details with the Pasadena, Vienna, and Windsor paintings.[31]

The upper and lower lids of the subject's eye are defined in these paintings with a fine but strong arching line accentuating the round shape of the underlying eyeball. Red suggests the canthus of the eye, which is obscured from actual view. The delicate rendering of the mouth is also similar—sharply defined by lines over which a delicate wash of red is applied. Similar attributes are found in the profile description of the young prince in *Prince Charles Louis of the Palatinate with His Tutor Wolrad von Plessen in Historical Dress* (J. Paul Getty Museum, Los Angeles), signed with a monogram and dated 1631; there, however, the more subtle modeling and coloring of the faces and the elaborate gold robe and dramatic lighting reveal the different demands of a court portrait.

As the history of attribution of the Pasadena painting indicates, there remains confusion regarding many of the early paintings attributable to Rembrandt's circle, including *Young Man with Red Beret*, which tentatively retains an attribution to Jan Lievens while recognizing valid questions. The oddly flat appearance of the sitter's costume that reveals nothing of the underlying form and the somewhat abstract shadow of his face, for example, are distinctive characteristics sometimes associated with Jouderville.[32] The limited number of works securely attributed to Jouderville, however, compounds the difficulty of distinguishing his paintings from those produced in Leiden by other artists, especially Lievens, during the late 1620s/early 1630s. The fact that Jouderville was Rembrandt's student during these years has perhaps resulted in the presumption that he was responsible for this and other paintings. The tight, somewhat fussy attention to detail, despite the date of 1633 inscribed on Van der Leeuw's print, suggests that the Pasadena painting dates from the late 1620s, no later than 1631, when both Lievens and Jouderville were still working in close proximity to Rembrandt in Leiden. Between 1632 and 1644 Lievens lived in London and Antwerp, where he was strongly influenced by the work of Van Dyck. His later work painted in the international Baroque style after his return to Amsterdam in 1644 bears little resemblance to the tight handling of his *tronies* and early portrait of Huygens. It is not surprising, therefore, that in 1654—the date Savery's print was published in *De Grooten Emblemata Sacra* by Jan Philipsz. Schabaelje in Amsterdam—the Pasadena painting was attributed to the internationally praised Rembrandt, who was known for the production of *tronies*.

1. Seventeenth-century etchings made after the painting suggest that several inches may have been cut from the panel on the left. Sumowski 1983–93, vol. 1, p. 198, mentions a copy of the Pasadena painting in oval format that was in a Dutch private collection in 1940. It is possible that this is actually the Pasadena painting in its previously altered state. The painting was restored in the 1950s. The presence of added wood strips on the sides of the panel precludes confirmation that the panel has been trimmed (see Technical Notes).

2. Many of the paintings in this 1899 auction originally came from the collection of the Sagan family at Kurland, which had become the property of the French princes of Talleyrand through marriage. The Sagan collection included Netherlandish paintings of the seventeenth century as well as German and Italian Baroque painters. The ducal gallery at Kurland was created by Duke Peter (d. 1800), who in 1785 became Standesherr auf Sagan in Schlesien. Holst 1938, p. 570, refers to a manuscript catalogue of the Sagan collection made in 1846 by Professor Keller, Berlin, then in his possession, as well as printed catalogues from 1846 and 1855. The latter revealed that the collection, which had numbered at least five hundred paintings, had already been reduced significantly by inheritance.

3. "Quelques Bons Prix Obtenus à la vente Sedelmeyer; Le 'Portrait de Rembrandt' par Lui-Même a Eté Adjugé 126,000 Francs," undated newspaper clipping (NSM).

4. Henri-Georges Heugel was the head of Heugel et Fils, a major music publishing house founded in 1839 by his father, Jacques Léopold Heugel (1815–1883), and continued by his son Jacques. The firm was sold in 1980 to Éditions Alphonse Leduc. In correspondence dated 30 July 2004 to Carol Togneri, François Heugel, the grandson of Henri-Georges, confirmed that the Pasadena painting was purchased at the Sedelmeyer sale. He added that it hung in his father's office in Paris, 76, avenue Marceau (NSM).

5. This is probably Hans Carl Sikorski (1899–1972), founder in 1935 of Sikorski Music Publishing, Germany's largest music publishing group. His son, Hans Wilfred Sikorski (b. ca. 1926), succeeded his father as head of the firm, with headquarters in Hamburg.

6. Correspondence from Richard G. Leslie, 19 May 1981 (NSM), where he suggests this additional owner. Schimert is presumably Gustav Christian Schimert (1910–1990) of Munich, who in 1959 married Editha Gabrielle Anna, Prinzessin von Bayern. (The father of Gustav C. Schimert was Gustav J. Schimert [1877–1955.]) While the Schimert provenance has not been confirmed, it may have been he who owned the painting after it was in the Sikorski collection in Hamburg (see note 5).

7. Smith says that the painting is dated 1633, but he probably got this from Willem van der Leeuw's print (see fig. 48a), which he calls an anonymous engraving. It is very likely that the author had not actually seen the painting, for which he gives no location, and that he only knew it from the print.

8. No. 292 described from an anonymous print and no. 473 described from the print (presumably that by Salomon Savery; see main text) that is inscribed "Rembt. Invent."

9. Listed among portraits of unknown sitters, dated 1633, owner unknown.

10. "The original is lost. Described by Sm[ith] from a print by W. de Leeuw."

11. The Willem van der Leeuw print (see fig. 48a) is described as after the painting in the Sedelmeyer collection.

12. Brejon de Lavergnée 1994 cites the painting as no. 76, "Rembrandt, *Autoportrait*," in the 1912 catalogue of the collection of Henri Heugel, Paris.

13. De Winkel 2005, pp. 60–68. De Winkel 2006, p. 255, notes, "Such shawls are frequently referred to in artist's inventories as *sluyers*, or veils. . . . Imported by the East India Company, in great quantities, these pieces were never worn around the neck in the East but utilized as sashes to cinch the caftan." Regarding "Oriental" fashions and objects in Dutch art, see Philipp 2020.

14. See De Winkel 2005, p. 63, for a discussion of the significance of the gold chain worn either over the shoulders, as in Rembrandt's self-portrait, or across the chest. Held 1969, p. 35, notes that "the ancient custom of giving a special reward in the form of a golden chain was revived in the Renaissance and widely practiced in the seventeenth century. . . . The chain . . . fulfilled two functions: . . . financial reward, and . . . a rather spectacular demonstration of recognition in high quarters."

15. The term is derived from the Old French word *troigne*, meaning "expression" or "face." Sixteenth-century artists, such as the Flemish painter Frans Floris I (ca. 1519–1570), also apparently used *tronies* in the production of their large history paintings. Many of these earlier paintings and drawings were presumably destroyed over time. It is perhaps significant that they were preserved in the seventeenth century. Regarding *tronies*, see L. de Vries 1989, pp. 185–202.

16. See, for example, Rembrandt's *Young Woman with a Fan* (1632; National Museum of Sweden, Stockholm) and *Young Man in a Turban* (1631; Royal Collection, Windsor Castle).

17. Schabaelje 1654. It is unclear exactly whom the print was intended to represent.

18. Huygens 1629–31.

19. Rather than the work of earlier artists, these *tronies* were probably copies made by Rembrandt or other artists to record interesting figures and expressions. Seventeenth-century references to *tronies* made *naer het leven* (from life) may refer to the practice of copying from another work of art as well as to indicate that those paintings were made directly after the living model rather than *van het gheest* (from the imagination). The inventory of Rembrandt's collection made in Amsterdam 25–26 July 1656 is published by Strauss and Van der Meulen 1979, pp. 295–382, and also by the GPI, Archival Inventory N-1848.

20. For example, the inventory of Jacoba van Horne and Dr. Hermanus van Friessem, Amsterdam (GPI, Archival Inventory N-192, 30 November 1697) mentions as item no. 14 a *tronie* by Jan Lievens hung in a round frame in the inner room of their home ("een tronie, boven met een ronde lijst door d'oude Jan Lievens").

21. The engraving is inscribed below the image at right "Rembrandt Inventor." (Hollstein 1949–2010, vol. 24, p. 68, no. 141). *Corpus* 1982, p. 49, and British Museum, no. 2006.U.1064, consider Savery's print, which reproduces the painting in its proper orientation, to be a copy of the print attributed to Willem van der Leeuw (fig. 48a). Hollstein 1949–2010, vol. 24, p. 68, no. 141, considers the print attributed to Van der Leeuw to be a copy of Savery's print.

22. *Bust of a Young Man with Neckerchief and Feathered Cap*, inscribed (upper right), "Rj 1633" (Hollstein 1949–2010, vol. 10, p. 46, no. 14). Van der Leeuw worked in Antwerp and is best known for his reproductive prints after Rubens.

23. Hofstede de Groot 1906, p. 27, no. 28a.

24. *Corpus* 1982, p. 49. The Rembrandt Research Project cites other examples in which attributions on seventeenth-century prints assign authorship to Rembrandt and other significant artists as a way of promoting sales. "As in the case of De Leeuw's [*sic*] print after Dou, it is apparent that Rembrandt's name here covers an invention looked on as representing his style."

25. Sumowski 1983–93, vol. 1, p. 198, notes that the painting reflects Rembrandt's style ca. 1633 after both artists had left Leiden. He compares the Pasadena painting to Backer's *Self-Portrait in Blue Cloak with a Beret* (formerly Ronald Cook Collection, London; Sumowski 1983–93, vol. 1, fig. 40), *Young Man with Cloak and Beret, the Right Hand in a Glove* (Martin von Wagner-Museum, Würzburg), and *Woman with Pearls in Her Hair, Profile Left* (Alte Pinakothek, Munich).

26. Bernhard Schnackenburg, email to the author, 20 March 2007 (NSM). Schnackenburg visited the Museum in the course of researching his book on Lievens (Schnackenburg 2016).

27. Amsterdam/Aachen 2008.

28. In Amsterdam/Aachen 2008, pp. 112f., no. C30, Van den Brink rejects the attribution not only to Backer but also to Lievens, noting, "Quite honestly it seems to me that Jouderville is still the best choice. Lloyd De Witt holds the same opinion." For Ernst van de Wetering's contribution on Isaac de Jouderville, see Van de Wetering 1983 as well as Amsterdam 1983, pp. 178–81.

29. Schnackenburg 2016, p. 469, R7: "The figure type and the brightly coloured palette of the painting of ca. 1630 differ distinctly from Lievens's style."

30. Christopher Brown suggested a Lievens attribution in conversation with the author in 1983.

31. Lievens's monogram is described as an *L* in Washington/Milwaukee/Amsterdam 2008, p. 108.

32. Van de Wetering 1983. See note 28 above.

49

Jan Lievens

Dutch
Leiden 1607–1674 Amsterdam

Panoramic Landscape

1640

Signed and dated, lower left: "iL: fecit: 1640"[1]
Oil on panel, 15¼ × 19½ in. (38.7 × 49.5 cm)
The Norton Simon Foundation, F.1974.2.P

Provenance
Private collection, France, sold to; [Mahla, Zurich (Frederick Mont), consigned by 1973 to];[2] [Newhouse Galleries, New York, consignment no. 61677, stock no. 18810, half interest with Frederick Mont, New York, sold 1974 to]; The Norton Simon Foundation.

Exhibited
On loan, Cleveland Museum of Art, 27 February–15 December 1974.

References
Pasadena 1980, p. 62, ill.; Sumowski 1983–93, vol. 4, pp. 2879, 2887n75, 2925, ill.; C. Schneider 1984, pp. 15f., fig. 9; P. Sutton 1986, p. 218; Pasadena 1989, p. 67, ill.; C. Schneider 1990, pp. 156–59, fig. 123; Pasadena 2003, p. 59, ill.; Washington/Milwaukee/Amsterdam 2008, p. 292, no. 42, note 1; Weller 2009, pp. 118f., fig. 27A; S. Campbell 2010, p. 362, no. 1007, ill.

Technical Notes
The support is a horizontally grained oak panel made from two boards, a fact revealed by slight differences in level on the reverse. The panel is uncradled, and the reverse retains its original surface. The four edges have been beveled in differing widths. On the front of the panel at the lower left, three round dents in the wood are covered by the paint and the ground, indicating that they already existed when the artist began to work. The white ground is moderately thick. Horizontal striations in the surface texture could be from a brush application of the ground layer. The sky is underpainted with dark gray, which influences the dramatic character of the clouds. The paint and ground extend to all edges, and the paint thickness is varied. The landscape was created in numerous layers, using opaque but rather liquid paint, semitransparent glazes, and light-colored scumbles. Although many contours are blurred or rubbed, in the lighter-colored wall of the city, as well as some of the buildings beyond, the brushstrokes are more clearly defined. The middle ground consists of thicker, more opaque paint, and in this area drying cracks expose lighter underlayers. The artist made several changes, some of which are discernible in the paint profile, where brushmarking from lower layers remains visible through reworked areas. A pentimento of a tall, dark spire in the left tower is visible beneath a cloud. At the right side, a triangular shape of thin light-brown paint partially obscures other shapes beneath it. X-radiography faintly records the underlying horizontal brushwork, but not the fawn-colored alteration. Overall, the painting is very well preserved, with only minor retouching located along the left edge and in a thin horizontal line in the upper left sky. Ultraviolet-light examination suggests an aged synthetic-resin varnish.

Viewed from a distance, across dunes and an undefined body of water, a walled city is nestled into the shadow of the mountains on the edge of a broad, flat valley. The low horizon emphasizes the breadth of the landscape, which stretches far into the distance. Shrouded in mist, the rugged mountains are balanced compositionally by the clouds that mount toward the right. Light dramatically animates the landscape, focusing attention on the gateway to the city. In the shadows of the foreground, fishermen and goats are silhouetted against the water; to the right stand a small house and trees. Vague smaller figures walk across the dunes toward the gateway, their forms having faded into the brighter paint.[3] The large cathedral with a single square tower, the castle on the hill at the left, and the pentimento of a Gothic spire beneath the square tower of the church to the left of the cathedral suggest that the landscape represents an imagined foreign place.[4]

The painting is signed and dated on the lower left *iL* and *1640*;[5] the monogram is the same as that Jan Lievens used to sign the portrait of *Prince Charles Louis of the Palatinate with His Tutor Wolrad von Plessen in Historical Dress* (J. Paul Getty Museum, Los Angeles) and *Head of a Young Man with a Cap* (see fig. 48d). Nevertheless, scholars have questioned the attribution of the Pasadena landscape to Lievens because the technique and vista of *Panoramic Landscape* differ significantly from the richly colored and freely painted landscapes that Lievens executed under the influence of Adriaen Brouwer (1605/06–1638) and Rubens after his move to Antwerp in 1635.[6] Werner Sumowski, who seems to accept the date, dismisses the signature and attributes *Panoramic Landscape* to Jacob de Villeers (1616–1667), an artist who worked with Rembrandt in Amsterdam in 1640.[7] He compares the painting to landscapes signed by Villeers in Dresden and

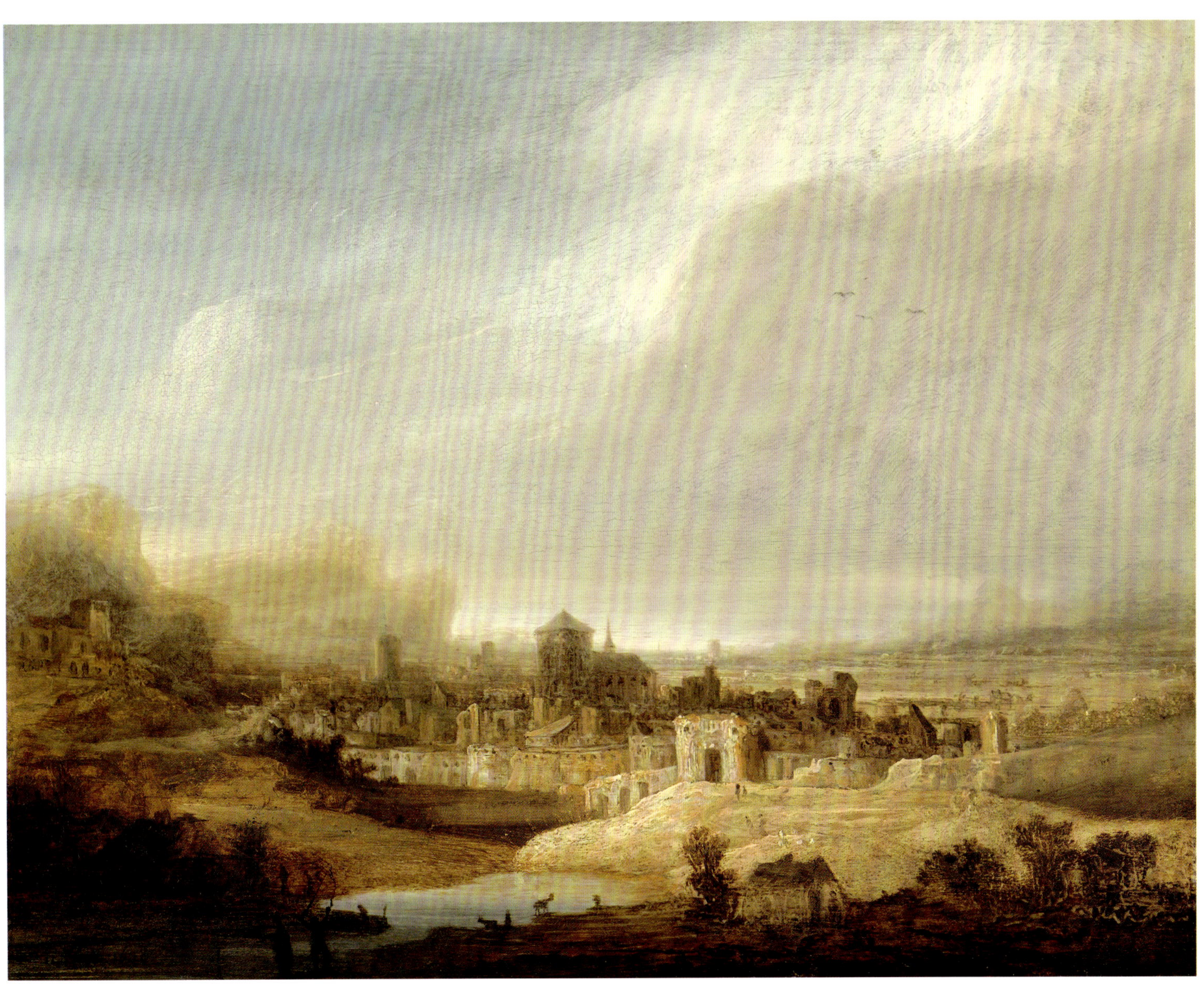

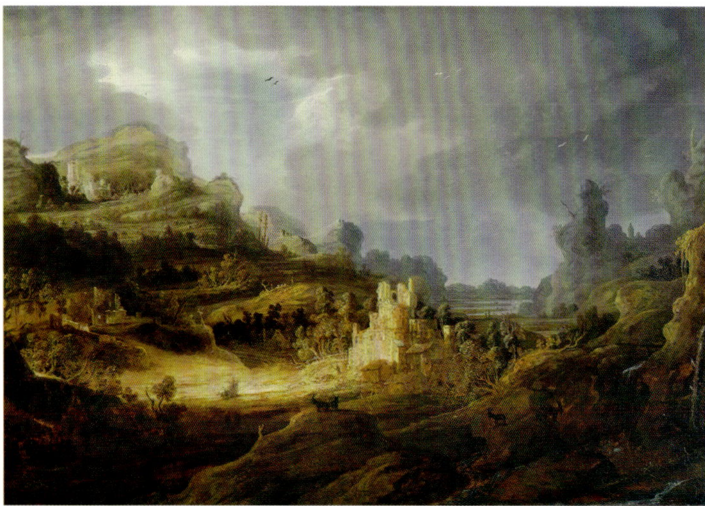

Fig. 49a. Jan Lievens, *Fantastic Landscape*, ca. 1643–45, oil on cradled panel, 34 ⅞ × 50 ½ in. (88.6 × 130.8 cm), North Carolina Museum of Art, Raleigh, gift of Morton D. May, GL.59.3.1.

one formerly in the collection of Dr. Alfred Bader in Milwaukee, placing *Panoramic Landscape* among a group of paintings he considers to be of higher quality.[8]

Cynthia Schneider, who was able to examine the painting carefully and discuss it with conservators, accepts the authenticity of both the monogram and the date, which appear to be part of the original paint surface but to have been abraded by cleaning.[9] The date has been particularly compromised. Schneider considers *Panoramic Landscape* a key work painted by Lievens under the influence of Rembrandt's contemporary fantastic landscapes, such as *Stormy Landscape* (Herzog Anton Ulrich Museum, Braunschweig), which combine exotic details with idyllic references to the local landscape. She suggests that Lievens could have seen the revolutionary landscapes by his old friend Rembrandt in 1639 when he traveled from Antwerp to the Dutch Republic on business.[10]

Lievens shared Rembrandt's affection for the work of Hercules Seghers (1589/90–ca. 1638). The influence of Seghers's evocative landscapes of rugged mountains shrouded in clouds and mist suggestive of changing weather can be recognized in *Panoramic Landscape*. Lievens differed from Rembrandt, however, in his use of a more traditional color scheme, which defines the landscape in terms of three atmospheric zones proceeding from a dark brown foreground to a light horizon. Lievens's sky, like that of his contemporaries in Haarlem and Antwerp, retains color, whereas in Rembrandt's landscapes dark areas of brown tone control the entire composition. Rather than Rembrandt's assertive brushwork and juxtaposition of thinly and thickly painted areas, Lievens's technique is tight and wiry, consisting of layers of fine, superimposed strokes combined with glazes.

In *Panoramic Landscape*, Lievens painted the shadowy foreground in freely applied dark brown glazes, creating a dramatic contrast with the area of brilliant light rendered with more thickly painted ochres and white scumble.[11] Here, as in *Fantastic Landscape* (fig. 49a), Lievens provided a transition between the two zones by the placement of the black silhouettes of animated fishermen in the immediate foreground and the animals farther back. This pictorial device, as well as the relatively unusual subject of fishing, are also found in Lievens's drawings, such as that of a man fishing (fig. 49b), which is inscribed on the lower right: "J. Lievisse Fec: ."[12]

On the basis of *Panoramic Landscape,* Schneider attributes two other paintings to Lievens: *Landscape with a Church* (Duchess of Alba Collection, Madrid), formerly attributed to Rembrandt, and *Fantastic Landscape*, in which the distant mountains on the left and general composition resemble the Pasadena painting.[13] In her opinion, the landscapes "help to clarify [Lievens's] distinctive combination of Flemish landscape traditions with those of Rembrandt and Seghers."[14] In particular, *Panoramic Landscape* and *Fantastic Landscape* share "similarities of conception, execution and even individual motifs."[15]

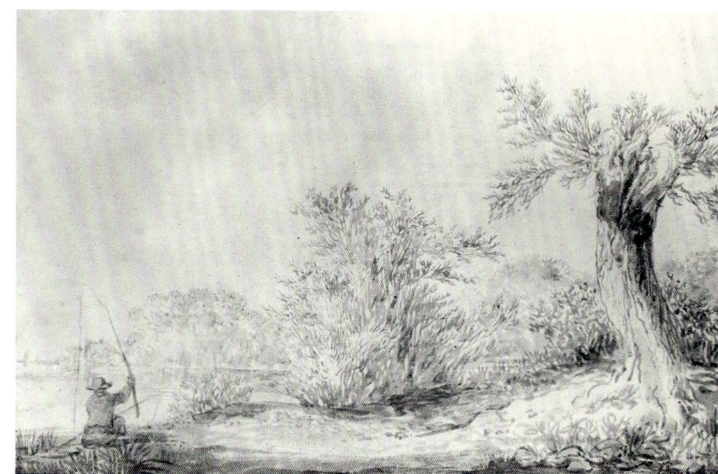

Fig. 49b. Jan Lievens, *A Man Fishing in a River*, brush and brown wash, 8 ¼ × 12 9/16 in. (20.9 × 31.9 cm), sold Sotheby's, London, 28 March 1968, lot 92, location unknown, image courtesy of Sotheby's.

1. The first letter may originally have been an *I*. Microscopic examination of the signature suggests that abrasion has broken the line.

2. Mahla was the name of Frederick Mont's firm in Zurich through which he acquired paintings. Before fleeing under the Nazi threat, Mont (né Mondschein) was active as a dealer in Vienna, working with Galerie Sanct Lucas. After the war he worked closely with the New York art dealer Clyde Newhouse. Mont had knowledge of and access to numerous collections in Europe but relied on Newhouse to finance the acquisitions. The two dealers typically divided the profits.

3. The lower right corner of the panel appears to have been abraded, creating vague references to the original forms.

4. The single, large tower on the west end of the cathedral may also have replaced two square towers, but this is difficult to discern.

5. See note 1 above. The signature was first noted by Frederick Mont and Clyde Newhouse.

6. See H. Schneider/Ekkart 1973, pp. 57–64, 161–68, no. 300-36; Jacob 1979; and Sumowski 1983–93, vol. 3, pp. 1769f., 1812–16.

7. Sumowski 1983–93, vol. 4, p. 2879.

8. Sumowski 1983–93, vol. 4, p. 2879, figs. 2929–30. Each has a signature in the lower right corner of the painting: "J. de Villeers."

9. Cynthia Schneider participated in a series of conversations and correspondence about the painting ca. 1987/88 with Nancy Purinton of the Norton Simon Museum and Mark Leonard, then paintings conservator, J. Paul Getty Museum. Their observations have been confirmed by Rosamond Westmoreland (see Technical Notes).

10. C. Schneider 1990, pp. 156–59. Arthur K. Wheelock in Washington/Milwaukee/Amsterdam 2008, p. 292, no. 42, note 1, supports her theory.

11. Lievens employed a variety of techniques: The active movement of brown oily paint at the left looks as if he used his finger; the hill on the left was originally defined by dark-brown paint then enlarged and overpainted with milky gray-green paint, which now makes the forms appear amorphous. He used combinations of glazes and washes of opaque light green throughout.

12. The manner in which sketchy figures are silhouetted against the light in the painting is similar to Lievens's drawings. Lievens's calligraphic pen drawings use washes and line to "color" and shade forms. See Hessisches Landesmuseum Darmstadt, inv. No. AE 743.

13. Sumowski 1983–93, vol. 4, p. 2879, also notes the similarity between the Raleigh and Pasadena paintings but attributes both to Villeers. See also Weller 2009, pp. 116–20.

14. C. Schneider 1990, p. 156.

15. C. Schneider 1990, pp. 157f., oil on panel, 88.6 × 128.2 cm. Her attribution to Lievens of the unsigned Madrid painting, which was formerly attributed to Rembrandt (Br. 446; oil on wood, 42 × 60 cm) is, however, brought into question by the similarity of the motif of the rider and footman in the lower left corner to that in a similar location in *Mountain Landscape with Waterfall* (Dr. Alfred Bader Collection, Milwaukee), which Sumowski 1983–93, vol. 4, pp. 2879, 2929, ill., notes is signed "J. de Villeers." The perspective also differs from the Pasadena painting.

50

Nicolaes Maes

Dutch
Dordrecht 1634–1693 Amsterdam

Dordrecht Family in an Interior

ca. 1656[1]

Oil on canvas, 44¼ × 47⅝ in. (112.4 × 121 cm)
The Norton Simon Foundation, F.1972.15.2.P

Provenance
Anonymous (sale, Lebrun, Paris, 16 April 1811, lot 78, sold for F 300 to);[2] [Royer, Paris]. Probably "A late distinguished Marshal of France" (sale, Stanley, London, 11 June 1816, lot 28).[3] John Evans-Freke (1765–1845), 6th Baron Carbery, Laxton Hall, Northamptonshire, by 1824,[4] by descent to; Algernon William George Evans-Freke (1868–1898), 9th Baron Carbery, Castle Freke, County Cork, Ireland, by descent to his wife; Mary (1867–1949), Lady Carbery,[5] Castle Freke, County Cork, Ireland (sale, Christie's, London, 4 March 1921, no. 29, signed and dated 1656, bought-in by Taylor for £3,000),[6] by descent to her son; Christopher Sandford (1902–1983), Eye Manor, Leominster, Hertfordshire (sale, Sotheby's, London, 5 July 1967, no. 35, ill., sold for £5,800 to); [Daan H. Cevat, London]. John William Middendorf II (b. 1924), New York and The Hague, by exchange ca. 1971 to; [Edward Speelman Ltd., London, sold 1972 to]; The Norton Simon Foundation.

Exhibited[7]
London 1929b, p. 165, no. 349, as signed and dated 1656, lent by Mary, Lady Carbery;[8] on loan, Allen Memorial Art Museum, Oberlin, 1 June 1972–3 May 1973; on loan, Los Angeles County Museum of Art, 9 May 1973–27 November 1974.

References
Neale 1824–29, vol. 1, n.pag.; A. Staring 1965, pp. 169–71, 179, fig. 1; Gerson 1976, p. 164, fig. 6; Pasadena 1980, p. 52, ill.; Sumowski 1983–93, vol. 3, pp. 1960–61, 1964n43, no. 1439, p. 2165, ill.; P. Sutton 1986, pp. 216ff.; Gaskell 1990, p. 170n2, fig. 1; Pasadena 1989, p. 83, ill.; W. W. Robinson 1993, pp. 101f.; W. W. Robinson 1996, p. 255, no. A-51, as *A Family of Zwijndrecht*; Krempel 2000, pp. 65f., 103, 286, no. A23, ill.;[9] Hochstrasser 2007, p. 146, fig. 80; Weller 2009, p. 124, fig. 28A; S. Campbell 2010, pp. 141, 339, no. 790, ill.; The Hague/London 2019–20, pp. 17, 20, fig. 12.

Technical Notes
The original support is a medium-weight plain-weave canvas that has been lined, with the original tacking edges cut off. X-radiography reveals eight damages in the original canvas, located primarily in the left, right, and center background, all well repaired by the lining. The cream-colored ground is thick enough to mask the canvas weave and provide a smooth surface. A reddish-brown underpainting is visible in the shadowed side of the man's face and in the chair leg at the lower right, where the artist left it exposed. Other compositional elements were blocked in with light brown, visible around the father's head, around the center child's shoulders and arms, and beneath the father's proper left wrist. Black underpainting is beneath the floor. Paint was applied in thin opaque layers with somewhat softened edges. The faces are finely modeled with cool gray shadows smoothly blended into opaque flesh tones. Dark-brown paint was used for contours and shaded lines under chins, beneath cuffs, and between fingers. Details of the rather somber interior are quite simple apart from the blue-and-white porcelain on the shelf at the upper right. The distant view out the window is suggested in broad, light colors. As he developed the composition Maes made several changes that are revealed with infrared examination: The infant's proper right sleeve was originally wider. The back of the chair at the right was originally higher, and the scrolled left arm appears to have been added later, after the infant's dress was completed. The original shape of the mother's white collar was slightly wider. The proper right arm of the child at the far left was changed; increased transparency of the paint allows the father's shoe to be partly visible beside her skirt. Before the painting entered the collection, it was selectively cleaned to remove varnish from the flesh tones and the white areas of the painting. The chromatic relationships now seem somewhat out of balance. Dark paint has been abraded in many shadows, and abrasion in the shadow beneath the fruit basket makes this area somewhat difficult to read. Several repairs were retouched, including a large damage in the window frame, a large loss to the right of the man's head, a small loss at center left in the dark background, a small loss to the right of the mother's head, and a large loss in the mother's red skirt. The synthetic-resin varnish imparts an uneven cloudiness in the darker areas.

Dordrecht Family in an Interior, painted ca. 1656, is Nicolaes Maes's earliest known family portrait and among the first portraits he painted in Dordrecht after his return by December 1653 from Amsterdam, where he had trained in Rembrandt's studio. Painted with the same palette of black and white with brick red, ochre, and gray details that he used for his contemporary history and genre subjects, Maes's conservative early portraits present soberly dressed, upper-middle-class burghers of Dordrecht in terms of their personal and social iconography.[10]

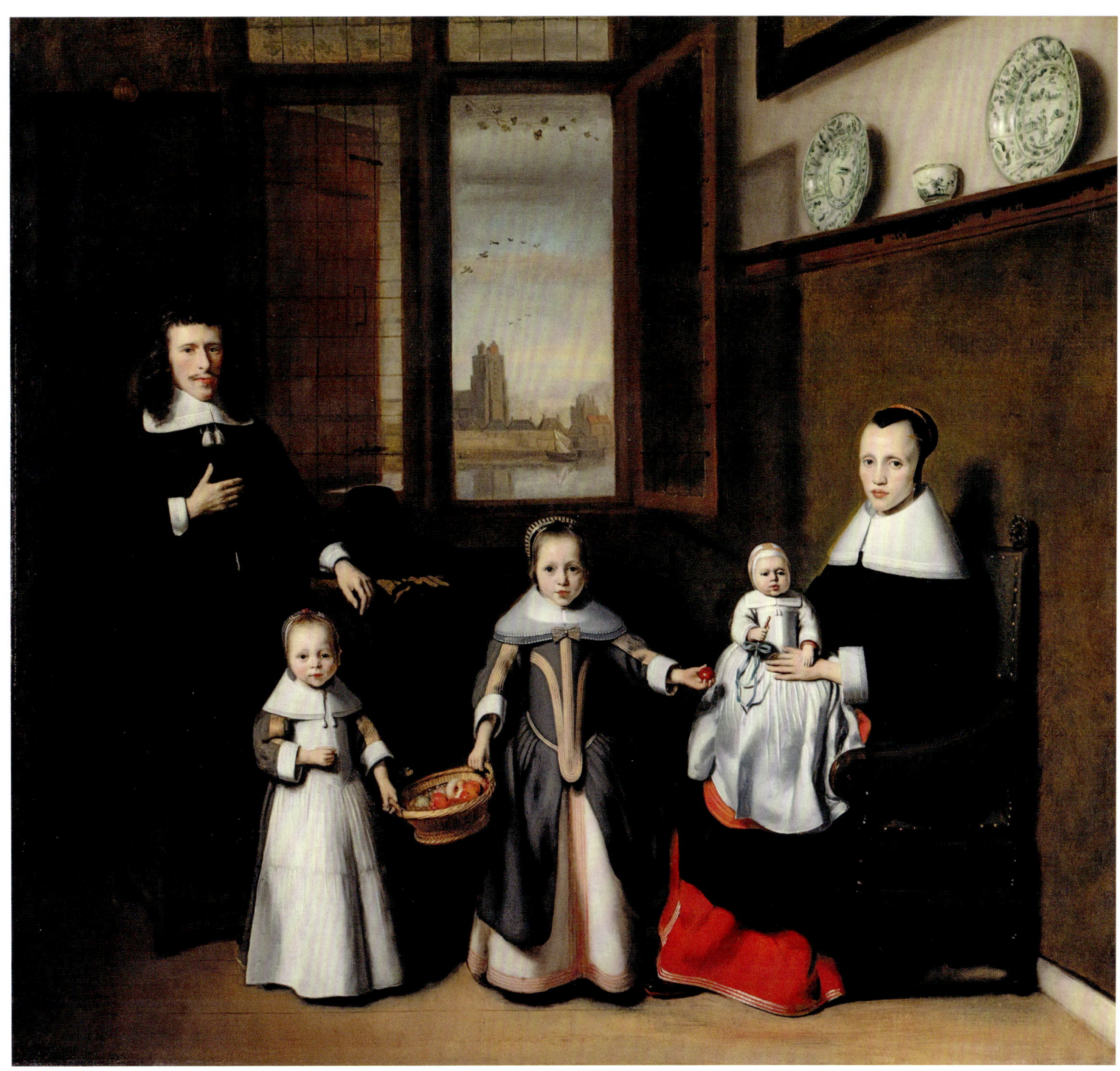

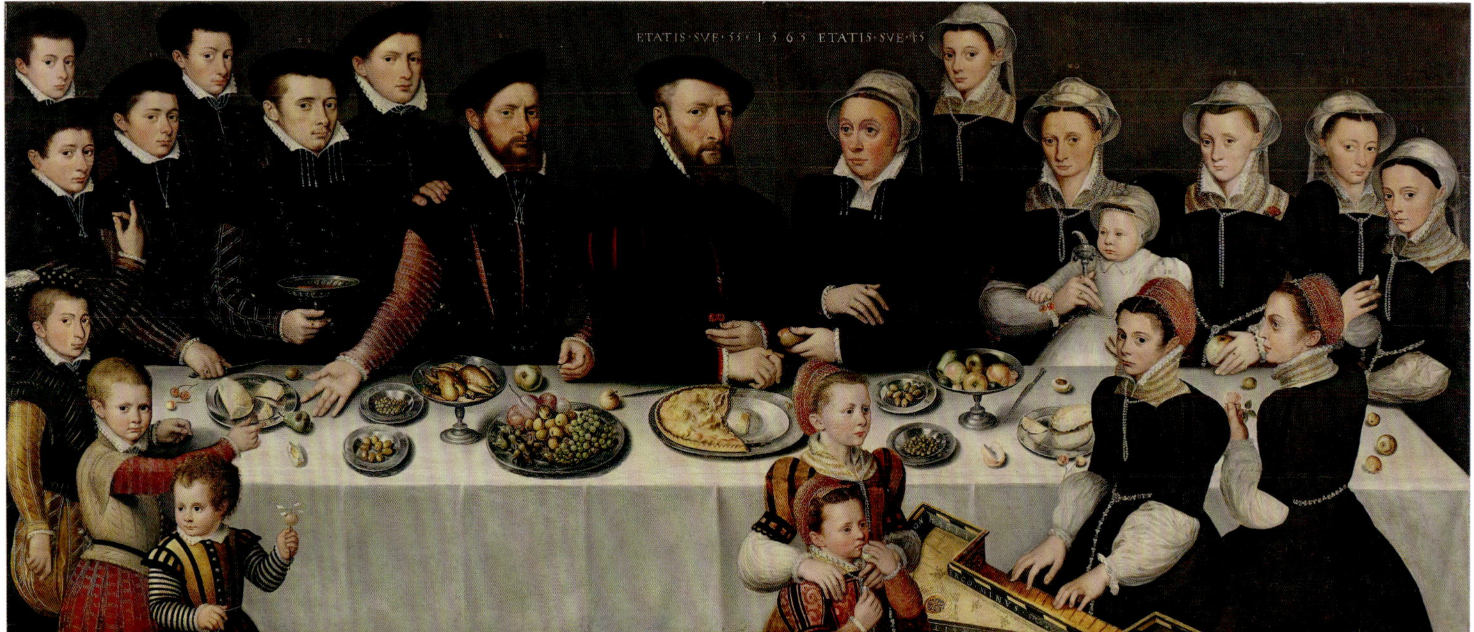

Fig. 50a. Formerly attributed to Cornelis de Zeeuw, *Pierre de Moucheron (1508–67), His Wife Isabeau de Gerbier, Their Eighteen Children, Their Son-in-Law Allard de la Dale, and Their First Grandchild*, 1563, oil on panel, 42½ × 96⅞ in. (108 × 246 cm), Rijksmuseum, Amsterdam.

Maes derived the format of this portrait from the sixteenth-century tradition of portraying families seated behind a table in an undefined space, exemplified by the Antwerp School portrait of the De Moucheron family in the Rijksmuseum, Amsterdam, dated 1563 (fig. 50a). Painted almost one hundred years later, the Pasadena portrait looks as if it is taking place in a room of the family home. Maes has moved the table to the background and given the basket of fruit to the two older children, making it the compositional and iconographical link in a chain that stretches from the father on the left, through the children, to the mother on the right. Chiaroscuro light effects contribute to the fluid integration of forms and space. Light from an unseen source in the upper left flows around the carefully orchestrated figures, rippling in and out of the folds of their dresses and casting the shadow of the open window onto the side wall.

Maes defined the relationship of the sitters in terms of traditional iconographic references to marriage and the family. Seated to the viewer's left, the father holds his right hand over his heart, a gesture used in marriage portraits to indicate his commitment to the union.[11] The tall, brimmed beaver hat, which Dutchmen wore indoors during the seventeenth century, and the gloves resting on the table were references to social status.[12] The infant seated on the lap of the woman signifies her maternal role within the family. Although the figures are still somewhat stiffly posed, the portrait represents a new informality and attitude toward the family. Foreign visitors to the United Netherlands often remarked on the Dutch respect for the institution of marriage and their love of their children. This is reflected in contemporary advice books on marriage, such as Jacob Cats's enormously popular *Houwelyck* (Marriage), published in 1625.[13] Typical of his early portraits, Maes portrayed his subjects with unusual sensitivity. His subtle suggestion of the innocence of the young children recalls the tender, intimate scenes of mothers and children in his contemporary genre pieces, such as *The Lacemaker* (ca. 1656; Metropolitan Museum of Art, New York).

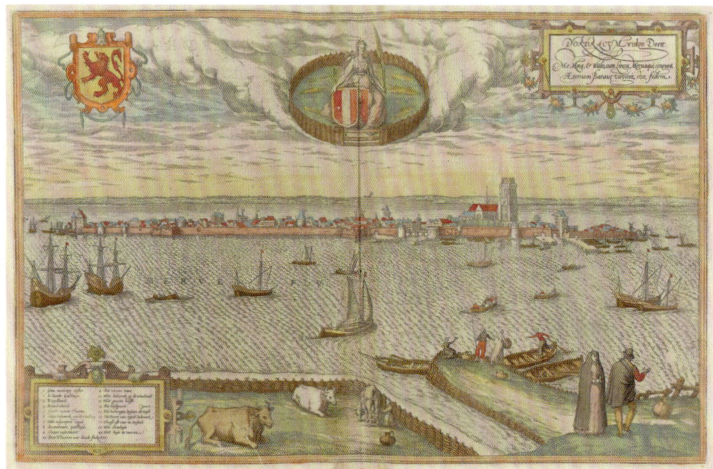

Fig. 50b. *View of Dordrecht,* detail from Georg Braun and Franz Hogenberg, *Civitates Orbis Terrarum (Towns of the World),* Cologne, 1575, The New York Public Library.

Other details in the *Dordrecht Family in an Interior* relate to the traditional iconography of sixteenth-century portraits. Beginning about 1590, Dutch family portraits incorporated motifs derived from the Bible and referred to in church sermons to emphasize the sanctity and importance of the family. Psalms 1, 127, and 128, which concern the fertility of the family and refer to children as the fruit of marriage, were particularly important.[14] According to Psalm 1:3, the God-fearing man "is like a tree planted by streams of water that yields its fruit in its season, and its leaf does not wither. In all that he does, he prospers." Psalm 127:3 refers to children as "the fruit of the womb," and Psalm 128:3 explains, "Your wife will be like a fruitful vine within your house; your children will be like olive shoots around your table."[15]

In the Pasadena portrait, Maes subtly incorporated the biblical references without disturbing the realism of the setting or the natural behavior of the sitters: The fruit held by the children symbolizes the fertility of the family, the vine across the upper part of the window is a reference to the mother's fertility, and the river outside the window may be a reference to the fruitfulness and prosperity of the father. In addition to identifying the location of the family's residence, the view of the church around which the family gathers completes the iconography by referring to the central focus of the family in the church. Other details, such as the blue-and-white Chinese export porcelain plates and the small bowl displayed on the shelf above the mother, a reference to trade with the Dutch East Indies, were commonly found in middle-class houses by 1650 and here appear to be primarily decorative.[16] The scallop shell that conceals the nail from which the valuable mirror is hung is an unexplained detail.[17]

The parents wear conservative black wool clothes, which remained popular with residents of Dordrecht long after their counterparts in Amsterdam and The Hague adopted the more elegant French style of dress.[18] During the seventeenth century, children dressed as miniature adults, and until the age of about seven boys as well as girls wore skirts.[19] Here the two older children can be identified as girls on the basis of the similarity of their funnel-shaped collars to that of their mother and the tradition of representing girls with baskets. The baby's flat collar, which is similar to the father's, probably indicates that he is a boy.[20] The girls wear gray dresses trimmed with soft red-and-gold braid and caps that allow strands of their soft blond hair to drift down. The younger girl still wears a long white apron to protect her skirt. The older girl, however, wears a simple stomacher and white wool underskirt trimmed with braid similar to her mother's. The baby, dressed in a long white gown with a fitted bodice and a warm red underskirt, holds a *rinkelbel*, a small rattle tied to his waist by a blue silk ribbon.

The identity of the family is not known. Staring noted that the use of smooth planks rather than paneling as wall covering suggests the family was middle class rather than wealthy. Following seventeenth-century portrait convention, the view through the open window to the Grote Kerk and Vuilpoort in Dordrecht identifies the family as residents of that important port city. Located at the confluence of the River Maas to the north and the Scheldt to the south, it was a major gateway to Zeeland and North Brabant in the Spanish Netherlands.[21] The view is from the northwest, roughly from the location of Zwijndrecht, the rural community situated across the Maas from Dordrecht, where in the mid-seventeenth century a number of wealthy families from the city owned estates (fig. 50b). This view, which emphasizes the wooden bulwark that protected the land reclaimed from the water, was published in 1575 in *Civitates Orbis Terrarum*, the great city atlas published in Cologne by Georg Braun (1542–1622) and Franz Hogenberg (ca. 1540–ca. 1590) and repeated in the panorama of the city painted by Adam Willaerts (1577–1664) in 1629 and hung in the city hall (Dordrechts Museum).

Dordrecht Family in an Interior was first recorded in a French sale in 1811. This portrait, like so many Dutch paintings, probably had fallen victim to marauding French troops, who took it to Paris. Until then, it undoubtedly hung over the mantelpiece in the home of the descendants of the sitters in Dordrecht, the intended testament to the family's moral as well as physical heritage.

1. The 1929 catalogue of the exhibition at the Royal Academy notes that the painting was signed and dated 1656. Although the 1921 Lady Carbery sale catalogue also mentions the date, no signature or date is now visible.

2. Many of the paintings in this sale came from the August 1810 Smeth van Alphen sale; this painting was, however, not included in that earlier sale.

3. The title page of the catalogue states that the paintings in the sale were "the intended ornaments to the gallery of a late distinguished marshal of France." The similar wording in the title here and in Neale's description of paintings he saw at Laxton Hall in 1824 (see note 4 below) further suggest that this is the same painting.

4. Neale 1824–29, vol. 1, n.pag., mentions "A Burgomaster and Family" by Maes among the principal pictures at Laxton Hall, where it was exhibited in the library.

5. The English author Mary Carbery, née Mary Vanessa Toulmin, was married first to Algernon William George Evans-Freke (1868–1898), 9th Baron Carbery. Following his death, she married Prof. Arthur Wellesley Sandford. Her son John Evans-Freke (1892–1970), 10th Baron Carbery, died without issue and was succeeded by his nephew, Peter Ralfe Harrington Evans-Freke (1920–2012). Christopher Sandford was the eldest son of Mary Carbery's second marriage.

6. Castle Freke was bought by the Freke family in the seventeenth century. In the late 1780s Sir John Evans-Freke, later 6th Baron Carbery, built a new house. Gutted by fire in 1910, the house was rebuilt and sold after World War I, probably precipitating the 1921 auction.

7. A card attached to the back of the painting bears the registration number 103 for an unidentified exhibition at the Royal Academy, London. The exhibition probably dates after 1912, the terminus of Graves [1913–15] 1970.

8. London 1929a says that a false signature and date were removed when the picture was cleaned after the exhibition. A. Staring 1965, p. 169n2, notes the commemorative catalogue's statement about the signature and offers Sturla Gudlaugsson's probable theory that the original, but faint, signature had been reinforced and was later misunderstood as false and removed.

W. W. Robinson 1996, p. 255, no. A-51, accepts the date of 1656 as appropriate for the painting.

9. Krempel mistakenly proposes that the painting was sold from the estate of E. J. de Court van Valkenswaard, Dordrecht (1784–1846) (sale, Van Geluk en Mak van Waay, Dordrecht, 12–14 April 1847). Neale 1824–29, vol. 1, n.pag., identifies the painting as in the Carbery collection by 1824.

10. Regarding Maes's early portraits, see W. W. Robinson 1993 and 1996 and A. Staring 1965. Maes's portrait *Interior with Husband and Wife and Infant* (location unknown; see Krempel 2000, no. D46) is close to the Pasadena painting in terms of color, pose, setting, and treatment of space and detail.

11. See D. R. Smith 1982, pp. 72–81. Another popular gesture referring to marriage commitment was clasped hands, especially the right hands, which Maes included in *The Cuijter Family* (1659; North Carolina Museum of Art, Raleigh).

12. De Winkel 2006, pp. 87, 160. English and German travelers remarked that Dutch men kept their hats on indoors, during meals, in company, and even in church. Regarding beaver hats, which were made from beaver pelts imported from the Americas, see Brook 2008, pp. 42ff.

13. Schama 1987b, p. 485, notes that visitors were surprised by the affection shown by parents to children.

14. See Bedaux 1987, pp. 150–68.

15. The King James Version translates the first part of this passage as "Thy wife shall be as a fruitful vine by the sides of thine house." I am grateful to William Robinson for bringing this to my attention. For an analysis of grapes, vines, and biblical symbolism in seventeenth-century portraiture, see Bedaux 1987, pp. 150–68.

16. The specific kraakware depicted in this painting, which dates to the Ming dynasty, Chongzhen reign, ca. 1635–40, is identified in Canepa 2019, p. 265.

17. Large mirrors such as this were extremely valuable, often appraised at more than paintings. Scallop shells, a traditional reference to one's pilgrimage to Santiago da Campostella, Spain, were not a common device used in the family crests of the major families of Dordrecht reproduced in Balen 1677, vol. 2.

18. See Groeneweg 1995, pp. 199–251. The standing funnel-shaped collar, which created the desired impression of sloping shoulders, came into fashion about 1640. The husband wears a short black jacket, the lower buttons of which have been left fashionably undone. Although fashion called for the newer cylindrical breeches introduced by the French to go with the short doublet, he wears the old-fashioned style of breeches tied below the knee with black garters. His shoulder-length, unrestrained hair, which had been opposed by various Protestant factions in the early and mid-1640s, was generally accepted by the 1650s. See Du Mortier 1989, pp. 55f.

19. On the determination of the sex of children portrayed in portraits, see Amsterdam 1977; Kuus 1994, pp. 6–13, 57f.; and Kuus 2000, pp. 78–82.

20. Pieter Biesboer kindly brought this distinction to my attention.

21. A. Staring 1965, pp. 170f., who mistakenly considered the point of view rather than the view being recorded as significant, sought to identify the family among the sheriffs and preachers of Zwijndrecht between 1650 and 1660 but was unable to come to a conclusion. W. W. Robinson 1996 repeats the identification but does not explore the idea.

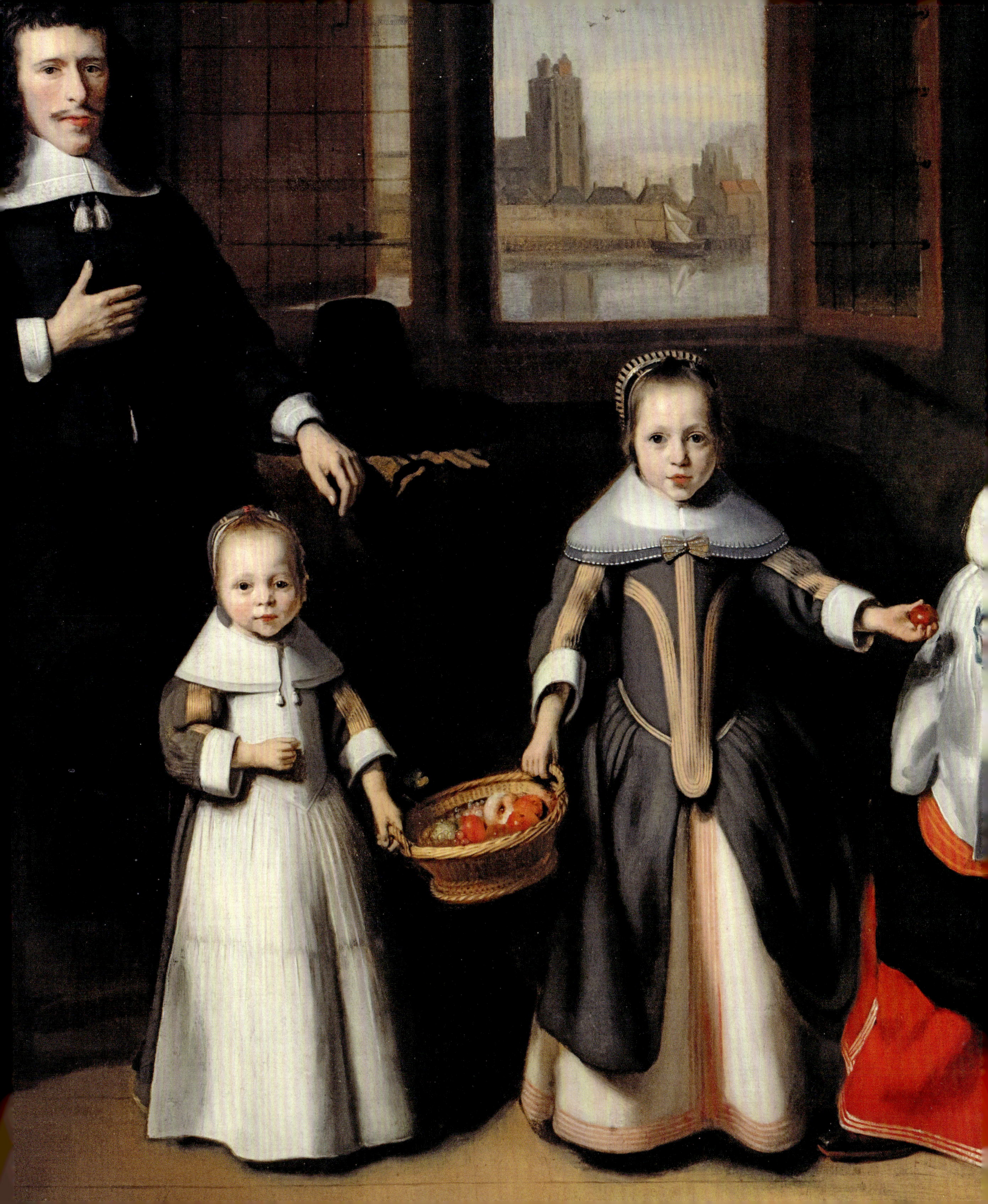

51, 52

Nicolaes Maes

Dutch
Dordrecht 1634–1693 Amsterdam

Portrait of Dirck Fredericksz. Alewijn

ca. mid-1670s[1]

Signed lower right, outside of the painted oval: "MAES"
Oil on rectangular panel, 17 11⁄16 × 12 ½ in. (45 × 31.8 cm)
The Norton Simon Foundation, F.1972.43.3.1.P

Portrait of Agatha Bicker

ca. mid-1670s[2]

Oil on panel, 17 3⁄8 × 12 ½ in. (44.1 × 31.8 cm)
The Norton Simon Foundation, F.1972.43.3.2.P

Provenance

The sitters, by descent to their son; Dirck Dircksz. Alewijn (1682–1742), by descent to;[3] Dirck M. Alewijn (sale, Roos, Amsterdam, 16 December 1885, nos. 32 [Dirck] and 33 [Agatha], sold together for ƒ480 to);[4] [Van Nulck].[5] W. H. Blaauw, Amsterdam, by 1892 until after 1916.[6] Cornelis Johannes Karel van Aalst (1866–1939), Hoevelaken, by descent to his son; Dr. N. J. van Aalst, sold 1972 through; [G. Cramer Oude Kunst, The Hague, to]; The Norton Simon Foundation.

Exhibited

On loan, Virginia Museum of Fine Arts, Richmond, 27 September 1972–16 December 1974.

References

D. C. Meijer 1886, part 1, p. 337; Moes 1892–1905, vol. 1 (1892), nos. 124.2 (Dirck), 651.1 (Agatha);[7] Hofstede de Groot 1908–27, vol. 6 (1916), pp. 514f., nos. 131 (Dirck), 132 (Agatha); Moltke 1939, p. 186, pl. xliv (Dirck) p. 190, pl. xlv (Agatha); Sumowski 1983–93, vol. 3, p. 2031, no. 1414, ill., p. 2140 (Dirck), p. 2141, no. 1415, ill., and p. 2237 (re. no. 1550) (Agatha); Dudok van Heel 2008, p. 600, figs. 440 (Dirck), 441 (Agatha); S. Campbell 2010, pp. 141, 345, no. 859A–B, ill.; A. Walsh 2019b, p. 98.

Technical Notes

Portrait of Dirck Fredericksz. Alewijn

The support is a vertically grained oak panel made from a single board. Rough chisel marks on the reverse suggest that this is the original state. Each edge has been hand-beveled, and the width and depth of each one differs from the others. The smooth pale-beige ground was applied as a thin layer, leaving the texture of the wood discernible. A dark-brown underpaint is beneath the orange clouds at the right and also surrounds the central oval. The artist used both opaque and transparent paint, applied with a moderately loose handling. Textured, wavy hair is rendered with distinct brushstrokes of opaque paint over a thin light-brown layer. Some details of costume such as the clasp and chain were painted with delicate drops of thick paint. Although the painting is generally well preserved, small areas of abrasion and loss exist. Small flake losses of paint and ground in both eyes are vertically oriented, following the wood grain. Shadows to the side of the proper left eye are abraded, as is the area to the right of the hair. The shadow under the nose and along the proper left side of the face is rather worn. Abrasion in the clouds at the right background follows the grain and exposes the dark underlayer. The paint overall has a fine, dense craquelure, becoming less pronounced in the area surrounding the oval. Examination with ultraviolet light indicates that varnish, likely a natural resin with a possible wax component, was removed from the face and white shirt in an unrecorded treatment. There is a small amount of retouching in the neck and the shadow under the white collar. Although it is not noticeably discolored, the varnish is brittle and crazed, resulting in a somewhat cloudy appearance.

Portrait of Agatha Bicker

The vertically grained panel consists of a single board, of which the top, right, and bottom edges are beveled. Examination of the reverse of the panel and that of its pendant disclosed that tool marks were quite different. The male portrait has pronounced vertical furrows from a chisel; the female portrait is considerably smoother. The depth of beveling is also quite different. The thin white ground leaves the surface texture of the panel visible. A warm golden-brown underpainting was used for a reserve beneath the figure, seen at the outer edges of the hair and above the shoulders. The rich, moderately thick paint was fluidly applied. The thickness and direction of brushstrokes indicate that the area surrounding the oval was painted after the background color was applied. A minor amount of abrasion can be seen in the eyes, but otherwise the painting remains very well preserved. Shortly before entering the collection, the painting was selectively cleaned; varnish was removed from above the figure but not the background. Minor retouches are located in the neck above the pearls, the chest, and the shoulder.

For more than two hundred years, Nicolaes Maes's elegant portraits of Agatha Bicker (1647–1716) and her husband Dirck Fredericksz. Alewijn (1644–1687), members of two of the most prominent regent families in Amsterdam, hung

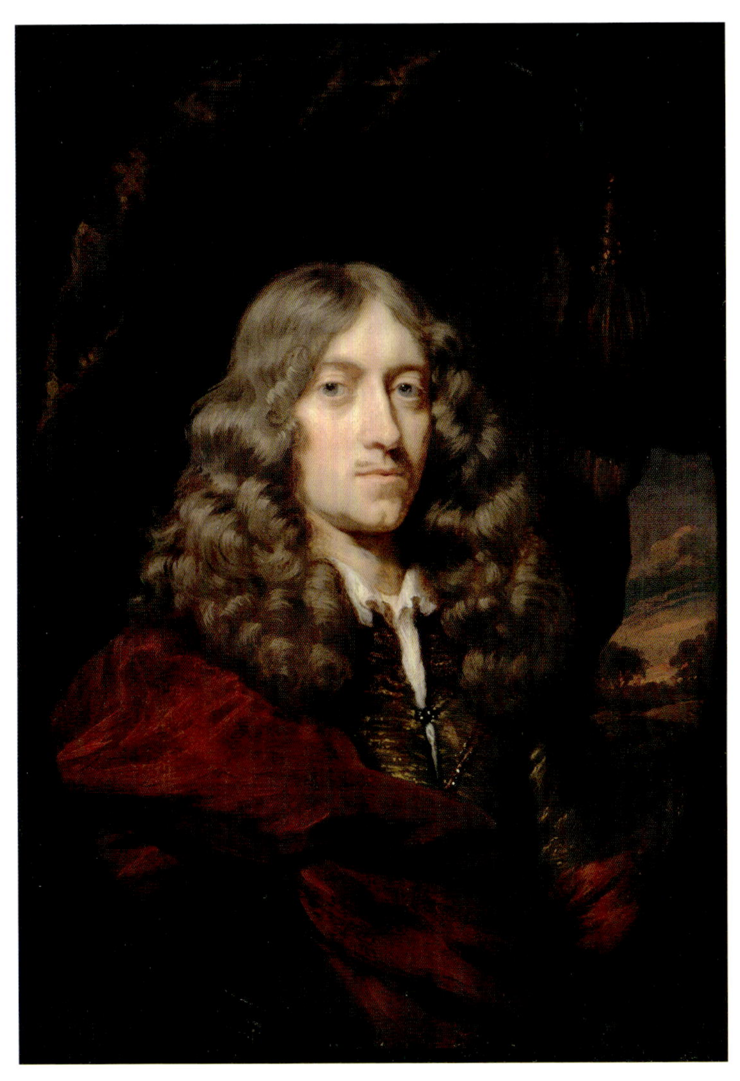
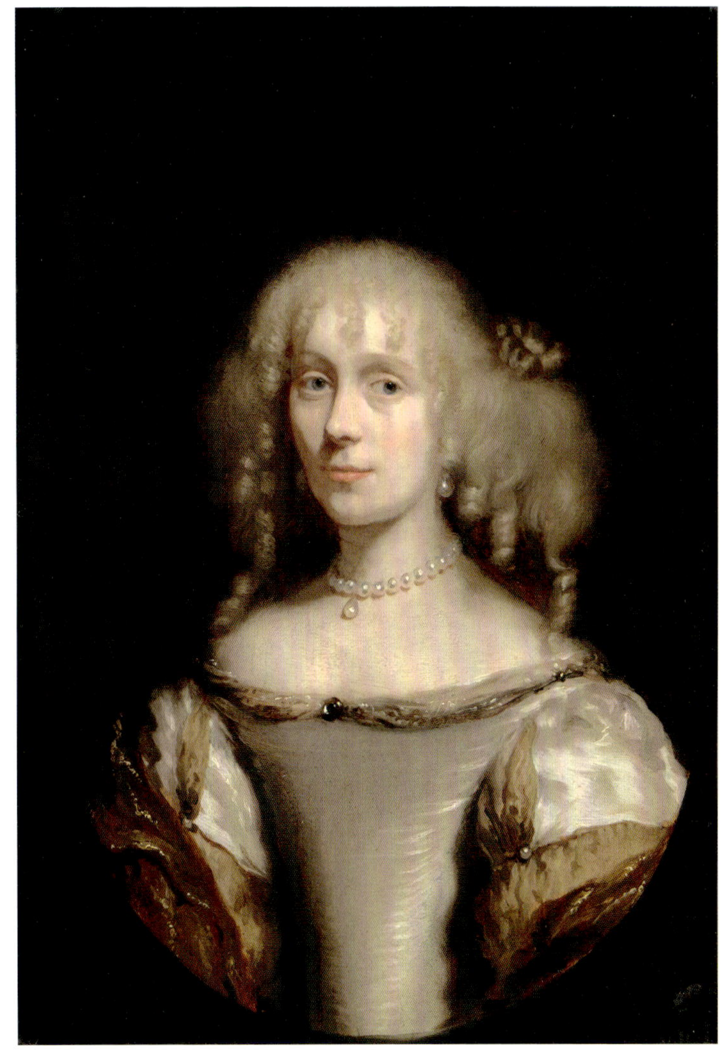

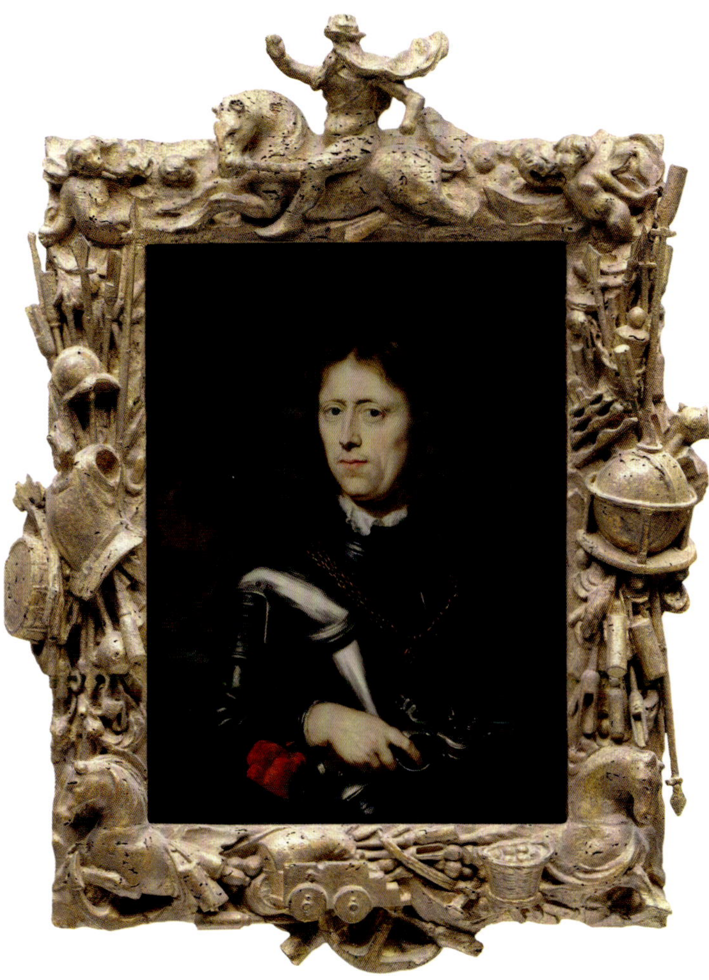

Fig. 51a. Nicolaes Maes, *Admiral Jacob Binkes*, 1676, oil on canvas, 17 ¼ × 12 ⅞ in. (43.8 × 32.7 cm), The Metropolitan Museum of Art, New York.

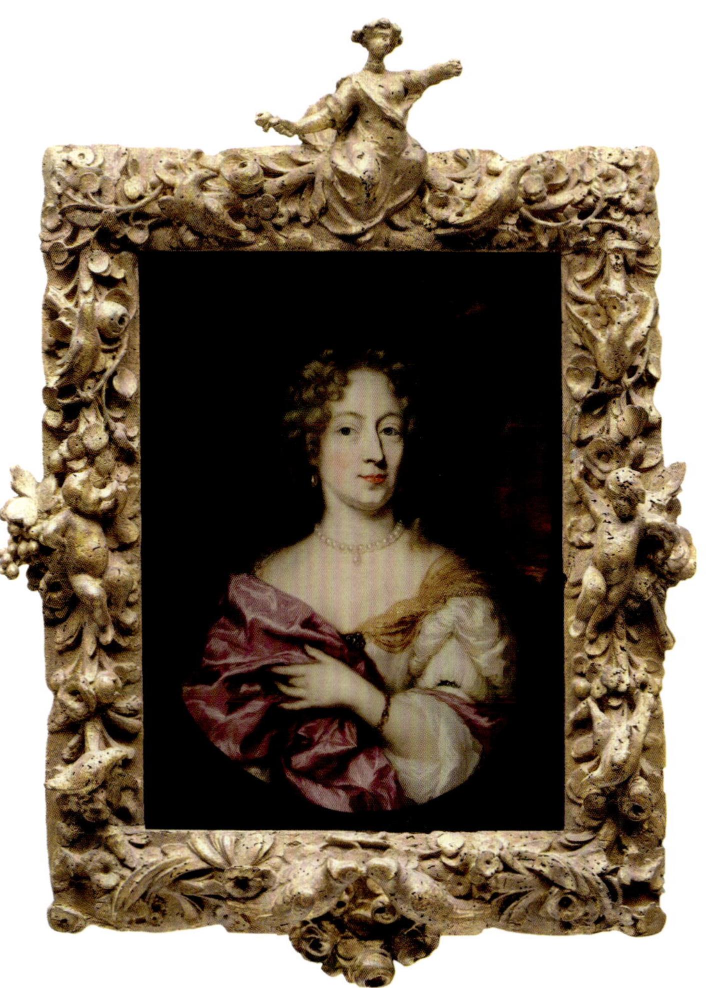

Fig. 51b. Nicolaes Maes, *Ingena Rotterdam (died 1704), Betrothed of Admiral Jacob Binkes*, 1676, oil on canvas, 17 ¼ × 13 in. (43.8 × 33 cm), The Metropolitan Museum of Art, New York.

together in the Alewijn family's portrait gallery. In December 1885 the entire collection of family portraits was sold in Amsterdam. Representing over three hundred years of family history, the collection included seventeenth-century portraits of the extended family by Paulus Moreelse (1571–1638), Thomas de Keyser (1596/97–1667), Dirck Santvoort (ca. 1610–1680), and Maes, among others. These included a full-length portrait identified as Dirck Alewijn as a child and attributed to Jacob Gerritsz. Cuyp (1594–1652) and framed pastel portraits of Dirck and Agatha by Wallerant Vaillant (1612–1677).[8] In his review of the sale for *De Gids,* D. C. Meijer Jr. lamented the dispersal of the collection, which he wished had been acquired as a whole by a Dutch public museum, noting the unique opportunity such collections give the historian to see a portrait and family in context.[9]

Dirck was the son of Frederick Dircksz. Alewijn (1603–1665) and his second wife (m. 1640), Eva Jacobsdr. Bicker (1609–1665).[10] Dirck Fredericksz. was named for his paternal grandfather, Dirck (1571–1637), who had amassed a large fortune as a successful linen merchant in business with Balthasar Jacot, the husband of his half-sister. The elder Dirck Alewijn had been among the private investors in the first major land reclamation project to drain the Beemster, an inland lake in the Norderkwartier, north of Amsterdam. The project was a major economic success and deeded considerable property to Alewijn. In 1630 the senior Dirck became the first member of his family to hold the important office of *hoofdingeland* of the Beemster.[11] In the same year he purchased for ƒ32,000 a stately house occupying a double lot on the east side of the Herengracht (no. 182), which passed at his death to his son Frederick. The large double house built in 1615 in the style of Hendrik de Keyser (1565–1621) was known as the Sonnewyzer Huis (Sundial House). Educated at the University of Leiden, Dirck Fredericksz.'s father, Frederick, later joined the family linen business and established an art collection.[12] He was the first member of his family to be accepted as a regent of Amsterdam, serving as a member of the city council from 1657 to 1665 and as sheriff from 1658 to 1662, a position that ranked second only to that of burgomaster in the city government.[13]

Following his father's death in 1665, Dirck Fredericksz. inherited the Sonnewyzer Huis, which appears on the far left in Jan van der Heyden's (1637–1712) painting *The Herengracht, Amsterdam, Viewed from the Leliegracht* (Los Angeles County Museum of Art).[14] Dirck also inherited Vredenburg, the classically inspired country estate his father had built ca. 1640 in the Beemster.[15] In 1674 the younger man's wealth was assessed at ƒ250,000.[16] Like his father and grandfather before him, Dirck also served as both *hoofdingeland* and *hoogheemraad* (chief dike reeve) of the Beemster, powerful positions that gave him control over the dikes.[17] Unlike his forebears, however, he appears to have been less involved with civic affairs in Amsterdam, where his name appears only a few times among the lists of government officials: lieutenant of the civic guard in 1670 and church warden (*kerkmeester*) of the Nieuwe Kerk in 1681. His absence from city rosters may be at least partially attributable to his early death in 1687 at the age of forty-three.[18] His wife, Agatha, continued to live in the Amsterdam home until her death in 1716; the following year her children sold the property for ƒ65,800 to Gerrit van Oosten de Jonge.[19] The family apparently retained the country house in the Beemster, where the gallery of family portraits may have hung.

Married in 1667, Agatha and Dirck were first cousins. Her father, Hendrik Jacobsz. Bicker (1615–1654), was the brother of Dirck's mother, Eva Jacobsdr. Bicker; and her mother was Eva Geelvinck (1619–1698), the sister of the first wife of Dirck's father. The sisters were the daughters of the merchant Jan Cornelisz. Geelvinck (1579–1651), who was elected burgomaster of Amsterdam twelve times between 1626 and 1647.[20] Hendrik Bicker was captain of the Amsterdam civic guard.

Between 1627 and 1650 the Bicker family, led by Agatha's grandfather Andries Bicker, held the position of "magnificat," the term used for the leading burgomaster of Amsterdam and his family. Together with the De Graeff family, with whom they were related through marriage, the Bickers were major forces in the politics of Amsterdam and the United Netherlands throughout much of the seventeenth century. Johan de Witt (1625–1672), the grand pensionary of Holland between 1650 and 1672, consolidated his power with his 1655 marriage to Wendela Bicker (1635–1668), the daughter of burgomaster Jan Bicker and niece of the powerful burgomaster Cornelis de Graeff. De Witt's fall from favor in 1672 also marked the end of the family's leading role in the country's politics. Nicolaes Maes portrayed both Wendela Bicker and Johan de Witt (Dordrechts Museum) in 1657. Although following their marriage the couple lived primarily in The Hague, it is possible that De Witt, a native of Dordrecht, helped the artist to establish his initial network of patrons in Amsterdam and introduced Maes to Wendela's cousin Agatha and her husband, Dirck.

Nicolaes Maes probably painted the Pasadena portraits shortly after his arrival in Amsterdam in about 1673/74.[21] In

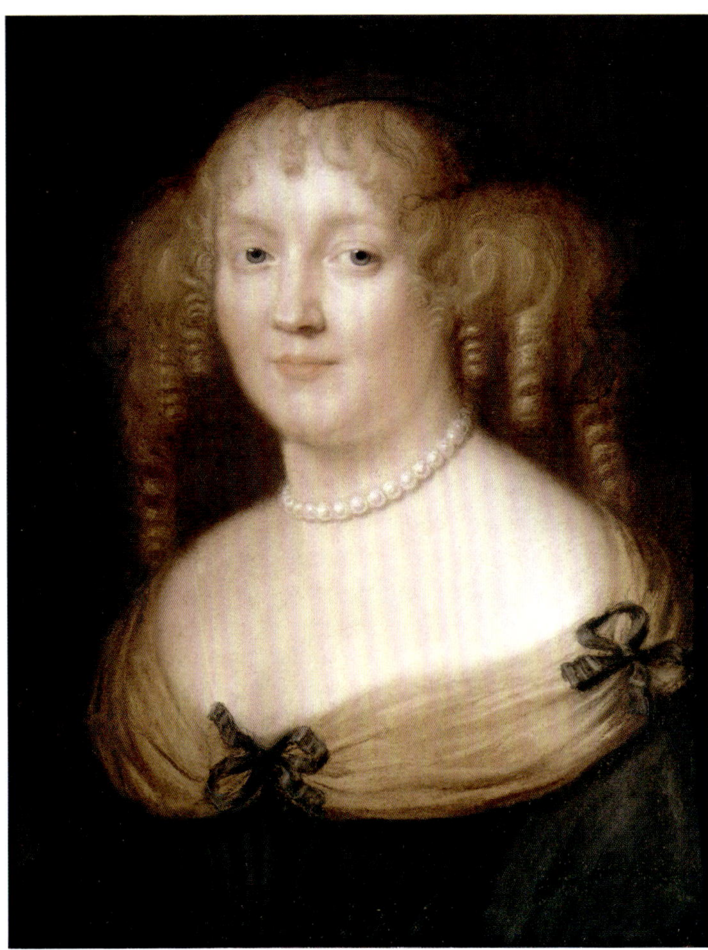

Fig. 52a. Robert Nanteuil, *Portrait de Madame de Sévigné*, 1665–75, pastel, 20½ × 16⅞ in. (52 × 42.8 cm), Musée Carnavalet, Paris.

Amsterdam, Maes turned away from the life-size format of his Dordrecht portraits, adopting a more modest scale for Dirck and Agatha, who are depicted within the painted ovals of individual rectangular panels. By placing his signature outside the oval in Dirck's portrait, Maes indicated that he intended that the painted "frame" be visible, as in the contemporary portraits *Admiral Jacob Binkes* (see fig. 51a) and *Ingena Rotterdam (died 1704), Betrothed of Admiral Jacob Binkes* (fig. 51b), which remain in their original elaborately carved rectangular frames.[22] Following the established formula for portraits of couples, Maes portrayed Dirck on the viewer's left, his body turned toward his wife, who turns to him from the privacy of her own panel. Both sitters address the viewer, but not each other; confined to a bust-length format that omits the hands, they make no overt signal across the frames to address each other directly.

The portraits of Dirck and Agatha illustrate the looser brushstrokes and fractured light that accompanied the greater elegance of Maes's later portraits, which were strongly influenced by the court portraits of Anthony van Dyck (1599–1641). Following his example, Maes sought to represent his subjects according to the seventeenth-century ideal of refined, emotionally restrained members of the leisure class. Dirck is elegantly dressed.[23] Coiffed in a long, flowing, brown wig and sporting a narrow mustache, he wears a tight-fitting jacket closed by a "frog," which opens slightly at the neck to reveal a casual shirt. A full red cape wraps around him, creating the desired image of a man of culture and position, properly restrained in his demeanor. Maes makes no reference to Alewijn's profession as a linen merchant. Rather he adopts a popular device Van Dyck used to refer to the sitter's possession of property. Dirck appears against a brown brocade curtain with thick fringe that has been lifted to reveal a view through an open window to a wooded landscape at sunset, undoubtedly a reference to his property in the Beemster.[24] Landscapes and motifs such as fountains, potted plants, and columns, which became prominent features in Maes's portraits during the 1670s, reflect the desire of many Amsterdam merchants, such as the Alewijns, to identify with the landed gentry.

Maes depicts Agatha Bicker against a neutral dark background that emphasizes the elegant beauty of her fine features. Probably painted in the mid-1670s, it is typical of the society portraits Maes painted in Amsterdam, where he increasingly eschewed capturing likeness in favor of portraying icons of wealth and sophistication. The subject is dressed in high fashion: the tight, figure-flattening bodice of her expensive white silk dress contrasts with the dress's full, billowy sleeves of matching white silk trimmed with contrasting silk. A fashionable shawl drapes over her arms. Agatha's blond hair hangs in ringlets above her shoulders in a stylish *coiffure à la Sévigné*, named after the famous French belletrist who is shown wearing this hairstyle in a portrait by Robert Nanteuil (1623–1678; fig. 52a).[25] In contrast to the severe hair style of the women in earlier portraits, such as those by Gerrit Dou (1613–1675) and Johannes Cornelisz. Verspronck (1601/03–1662; see cats. 22 and 95), the *coiffure à la Sévigné*, which had many variations, was intended to move freely, regardless of the support it received from hairpieces or stiffening agents; pearls, jewels, ribbons, and silk commonly ornamented the hair. Often, as is probably the case with Agatha's coiffure, three short, artificial curls hung over the forehead. Here on her proper left side, Agatha wears a bow—apparently constructed of her own hair—to lift her coiffure up above her shoulders. Large drop pearls hang from her ears and from the pearl choker. Smaller pearls ornament the sleeves and décolleté of her dress. As traditional references to chastity, Agatha's pearls identify her as an affluent member of Amsterdam's sophisticated patriciate.

1. Sumowski 1983–93, vol. 3, no. 1414.

2. Sumowski 1983–93, vol. 3, no. 1415.

3. According to D. C. Meijer 1886, p. 338, the family portrait gallery passed from the sitters to Dirck Dircksz. Alewijn, who married Bregtje Looten in 1717.

4. Three separate inventory stickers from the Alewijn family are on the reverse of each panel.

5. Van Nulck was a *makelaar* (broker) according to the annotated catalogue of the sale, now in the Ryerson and Burnham Libraries, Art Institute of Chicago.

6. Hofstede de Groot 1908–27, vol. 6 (1916), no. 131. Not included in the sale of H. S. Blaauw, 4 July 1924, Christie's, London, but possibly sold at about the same time.

7. Moes 1892–1905, vol. 1, p. 77, no. 651.1, incorrectly identifies the painting, which was then with W. H. Blaauw, Amsterdam, as a portrait of Margaretha Bicker (1647–1716), wife of Dirck Alewijn.

8. Vaillant's portraits of Dirck and Agatha (two individual portraits included as lot 99) were part of a suite of fifteen framed portraits in pastel. Lot 15 of the sale, attributed to Jacob Gerritse [*sic*] Cuyp and identified as Dirck Fredericksz. as a child (panel, 107 × 76 cm), is now attributed to Santvoort and datable, according to Rudolf Ekkart, to 1641–44 (communication to Lawrence Steigrad based on a transparency; Steigrad, email to the author, 12 December 2006, NSM). If correct, that date would eliminate the possibility that the portrait (with Lawrence Steigrad, New York, in 2006) represents Dirck Fredericksz., who was born in 1644. The portrait probably represents Dirck's first cousin Abraham Abrahamsz. Alewijn, who was born in 1639. This identification is supported by two similarly sized portraits of children (each 122 × 89 cm) by Santvoort that were included in the sale as lots 79–80. The sale catalogue incorrectly identifies the children as Martinus and Anna Alewijn, children of Dirck and Agatha. Those portraits (Rijksmuseum, Amsterdam, inv. nos. A1310 and A1311), dated 1644, are now identified as Martinus (b. 1634) and Clara, children of Abraham Dircksz. Alewijn and siblings of Abraham Abrahamsz. Lot 42, identified as busts of Dirck and Agatha by Michiel Jansz. van Mierevelt (1567–1641), also appears to be misidentified. Since Mierevelt died in 1641, three years before the birth of Dirck Fredericksz., the portrait must represent another sitter, possibly Dirck Fredericksz.'s grandfather Dirck, who died in 1637.

9. D. C. Meijer 1886 reflected the growing anxiety among many Dutch nationalists. Led by Victor de Steurs (1845–1916), they saw their artistic patrimony slipping away to foreign lands. Meijer noted, with some satisfaction, however, that this auction was spared the greatest sadness of many sales: the purchase of the best pieces by foreign collectors. He would undoubtedly be chagrined to find the paintings living in California.

10. Portraits of Frederick Alewijn (Rijksmuseum, Amsterdam; Moes 1892–1905, vol. 1 [1892], p. 16, no. 126) and Eva (D. C. Meyer Jr. collection, Amsterdam, 1892; Moes 1892–1905, vol. 1 [1892], p. 75, no. 636) by Santvoort were included in the Alewijn sale in 1885.

11. The *hoofdingeland* was a large property owner and member of the water board who represented the landowners within the territory of a water board. Van Tielhof and Van Dam 2006, p. 264.

12. Both the Alewijn and the Bicker families were collectors. The inventory of the Frederick Alewijn collection made at the time of the death in 1665 (GPI, Archival Inventory N-2349) includes among 106 items a *tronie* of a Turk by Rembrandt in the "*groote sael*" and three prints by Rembrandt in the room where his son Dirck slept. A portrait signed and dated by Jan Miense Molenaer (1610/11–1668) in 1637 (Rijksmuseum, Amsterdam, no. 1635 A2) represents many members of the Van Loon, Alewijn, and Geelvinck families.

13. D. C. Meijer 1886, p. 334.

14. See A. Walsh 2019b, pp. 96–100; and I. H. van Eeghen et al. 1976, pp. 460f.

15. Elias [1903–05] 1963, vol. 1, p. 498, notes that the house was built according to the design of Philips Vingboons (1617/18–1678). It was actually Pieter Jansz Post (1608–1699), however, who received the commission for which both he

and Vingboons, among others, submitted plans (Rem 2004). The house and estate are illustrated in Zandvliet 2006, p. 306.

16. Elias [1903–05] 1963, vol. 1, p. 498, 504, n.b., cites [Amsterdam City Archive] Quohier 1674, fol. 392v.

17. Elias [1903–05] 1963, vol. 1, p. 498.

18. D. C. Meijer 1886, p. 337.

19. Agatha and Dirck had four children: Eva, who married Jacob Jan de Bakker (GPI, Archival Inventory N-1266), Frederick (1676–1724), Dirck (1682–1742), and Anna, who married Jacob Faas. Frederick lived alternately on the Keizersgracht and the Heerengracht in Amsterdam and inherited the country house Vreden Burg in the Beemster. Following his death in 1724, the estate passed to his brother Dirck, who married Bregje Loten (1692–1760). The Alewijn sale of 1885 included two portraits of children in pastoral costumes, which D. C. Meijer 1886, p. 137, thought dated no earlier than 1675; the boy's portrait, which was reportedly signed Santvoort (probably Abraham), was bought by the Amsterdam dealer Muller. Meijer suggested incorrectly that the children represented the cousins Martinus and Anna; see note 8 above.

20. D. C. Meijer 1886, p. 337. Companion portraits of Hendrik Bicker and Eva Geelvinck by Joachim von Sandrart (1606–1688), dated 1639, were given as part of the Bicker bequest to the City of Amsterdam in 1877. They were placed on loan at the Rijksmuseum in 1881 (nos. 2119–20).

21. The appraisal of Dirck's wealth in 1674 (see note 15 above) may signal an important event in his life, which may also have been the reason the couple commissioned Maes to paint their portraits at this time.

22. Liedtke 2007, vol. 1, pp. 446–49, nos. 113–14.

23. In addition to an art collection (see note 12 above), Dirck's 1637 will includes expensive clothes that he left to his sons Frederick and Abraham as well as to his wife. See Moes 1911.

24. Sandrart portrayed Agatha Bicker's parents, Hendrik Bicker and Eva Geelvinck, with similar backgrounds but on a much larger scale in two stylish portraits dated 1639 (Rijksmuseum, Amsterdam).

25. Kinderen-Besier 1950, pp. 190f.

53

Jan Massys

South Netherlandish
Antwerp ca. 1509–1575 Antwerp

Susanna and the Elders

1564

Signed and dated on the socle to the left: "IOANNES MASSIIS PINGEBAT • 1564 •"
Oil on panel, 42 × 77½ in. (106.7 × 196.9 cm)
Norton Simon Art Foundation, M.2005.2.P

Provenance
Possibly Maria Rave, widow of Peter Danijs, Antwerp, cited in an inventory dated 8 November 1672.[1] Possibly Jan Gillis (d. 1681), Antwerp, cited in an inventory dated 28–30 July 1682.[2] Probably Jean Baptiste Du Bois (sale, Pierre de Goesin, Ghent, 21 September 1776, as Quentin Metsys).[3] Anonymous (sale, Hôtel Drouot, Paris, 13 November 1922, lot 9, ill., sold to); M. and Mme. René Kieffer, Paris[4] (estate sale, Hôtel George V, Paris, 29 May 1969, lot 91, ill., sold to); [Sylvia Blatas/Galerie René Drouet, Paris for]; The Norton Simon Foundation, transferred 2005 to the Norton Simon Art Foundation.

Exhibited
On loan, Brooklyn Museum, 19 March–21 June 1970; on loan, Los Angeles County Museum of Art, 22 June 1970–26 November 1974.

References
Wescher 1930, p. 227; M. Friedländer 1924–37, vol. 13 (1936), p. 142, no. 14a; De Mirimonde 1962, pp. 550, 563n13; Brussels 1963, p. 135 (mentioned under no. 161); Scaff 1970, p. 278; M. Friedländer 1967–76, vol. 13 (1975), p. 75, fig. 14a; Gerson 1976, p. 163; Pasadena 1980, p. 37, ill.; Pasadena 1989, p. 34, ill.; Buijnsters-Smets 1995, pp. 60, 81f., 144–45, 210f., no. 47, ill.; S. Campbell 2010, p. 321, no. 636, ill.

Technical Notes
The large uncradled oak panel consists of four horizontally grained boards. Although the joins are tightly closed and flush on the front, they are slightly offset on the reverse to accommodate the varied thicknesses of the boards. The top and bottom edges are not beveled. What appear to be two small incised designs may be related to the panel maker. The smooth ground layer is white. At the left and right edges, there is a ¼-inch margin of exposed wood on the front; a groove was cut where the paint and ground stop. A thin rose-brown tint covers the ground, visible at the upper left and upper right in the sky, around the architectural elements, and around the feet of the two young women, among other places. Increased paint transparency reveals underdrawing in several places: in the leg and foot of the young woman at the far right; in the cheek of the same woman; here and there in Susanna's robe; and in the domed building at the upper right. The paint extends to the top and bottom edges. Thin, liquid, luminous glazes were employed in the robes of the two young women and the cloudy sky. More robust, opaque paint was blended for the smoothly modeled figures. Tree leaves were painted in dark brown with several greens delicately dotted in opaque dabs of color. Finely detailed, enamel-like paint was used for the foliage and flowers of the background. The pale yellow highlights in the women's hair are isolated delicate lines painted wet-over-dry. Some white highlights are like beads of color on the surface. The cloudy appearance of the paint in Susanna's cloak, especially noticeable where it is over dark, shadowed areas in the folds, was not explained with microscopic examination; the condition may be related to the fading of a pigment. The paint is generally quite well preserved. There are a few tiny scattered flake losses that for the most part have been left alone. Undocumented restoration included partial cleaning to reduce varnish over the flesh tones. Retouching is minimal; most of it is in tiny strokes in the elder's red cloak at the left side and at the bottom right corner. The woman second from the right has more recent retouching in broader strokes in the folds of the proper right sleeve and skirt of her dress. The present varnish is likely an aged synthetic resin.

The book of Daniel tells the story of Susanna, the beautiful and pious wife of a rich Jewish man living in exile in Babylon, who was walking through her husband's orchard when two "elders of the people" noticed her.[5] These lecherous old men spied on Susanna when she later returned to the orchard to bathe. When her two maids departed to fetch oil for her bath, the men became bolder, making indecent propositions and threatening her with disgrace should she refuse them. Finally her cries drove them off. To avenge themselves, however, the men claimed that they had caught Susanna with a young man. Charged with adultery, she was condemned to death. At the last moment, however, Daniel, who suspected their deceit, questioned each man separately and uncovered their lie, whereupon the elders were put to death.

Jan Massys painted three versions of the story of Susanna; this version, dated 1564, is the second and the most successful. In his first treatment of the theme, painted in 1556, the two elders accost the protesting Susanna (fig. 53a).[6] Massys emphasized her entrapment by employing a vertical composition that visually constrains her. The Pasadena painting and the closely related version in Brussels (fig. 53b) dated 1567 represent an earlier moment in the story: The beautiful Susanna, unaware of the presence of the two older

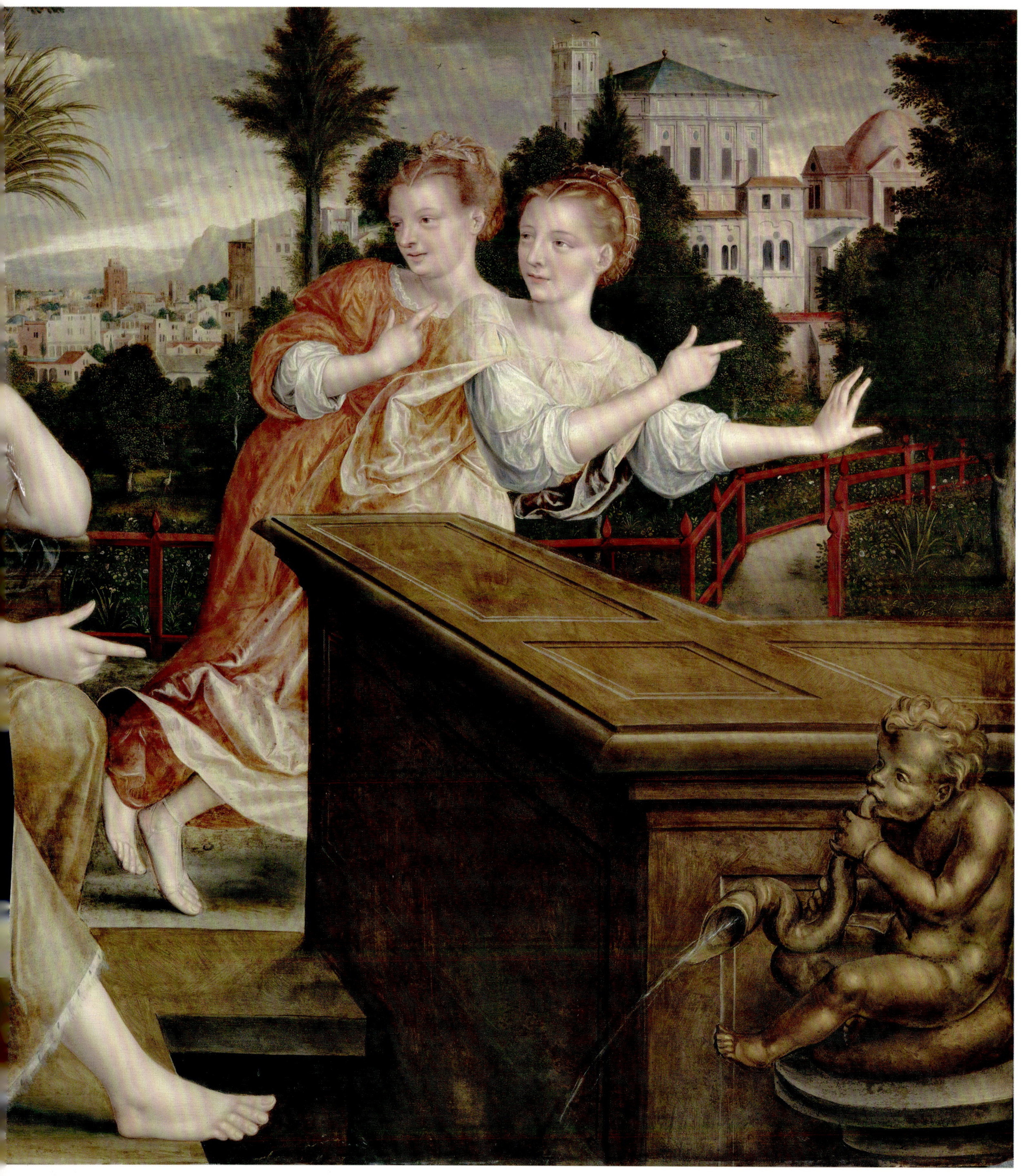

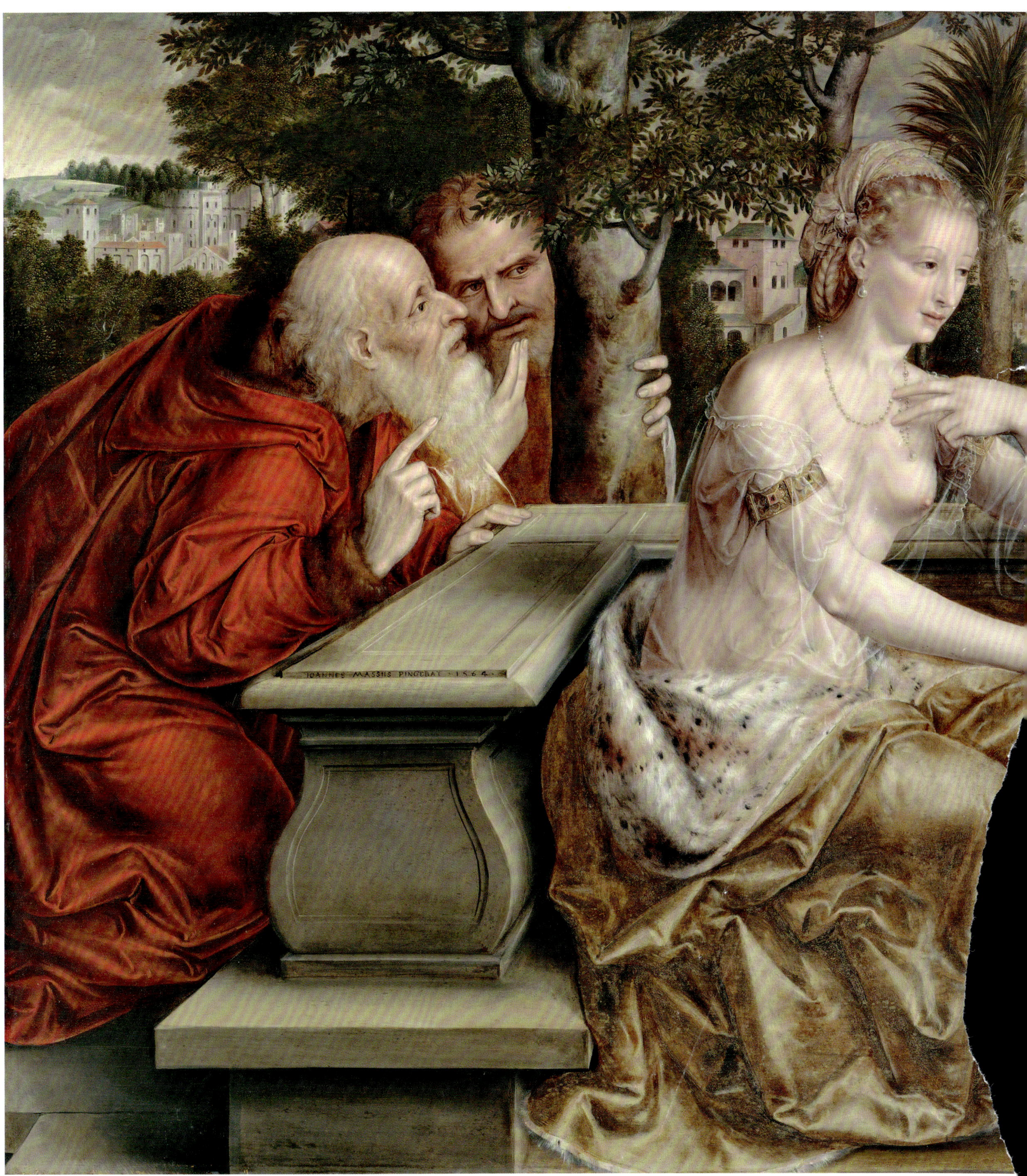
IOANNES MASSIIS PINGEBAT · 1564 ·

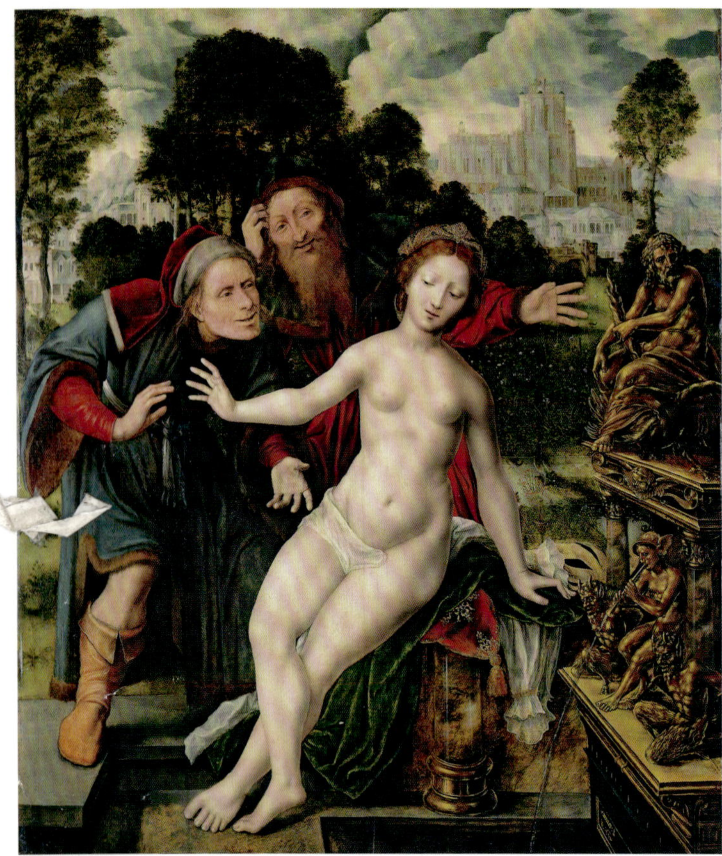

Fig. 53a. Jan Massys, *Susanna and the Elders*, 1556, oil on panel, 51⅝ × 43¾ in. (131.2 × 111.2 cm), private collection.

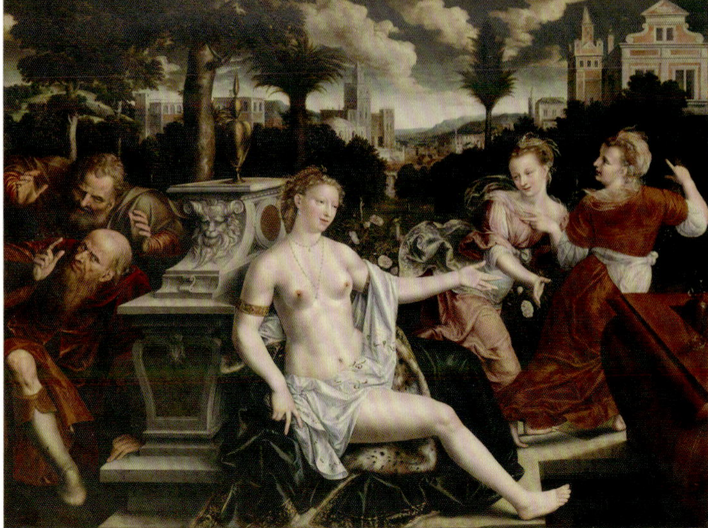

Fig. 53b. Jan Massys, *Susanna and the Elders*, 1567, oil on panel, 63¾ × 87⅜ in. (162 × 222 cm), inv. 2548, Musées Royaux des Beaux-Arts de Belgique, Brussels.

men who crouch next to the wall behind her, sends her maids to retrieve oils for her bath. The horizontal format of these paintings suggests the continuity of the narrative, which will climax at a later moment.

In the Pasadena painting Massys confines the monumental figures to the shallow foreground, set against the backdrop of a landscape defined by palm trees and architecture inspired by Italian Renaissance prototypes. The painting lacks a consistent perspective but is integrated by the relationship of the fluid, rhythmic organization of the background and the movement and dramatic gestures of the figures in the foreground that it echoes.

Massys drew on the naturalistic tradition of the northern Renaissance for the lascivious old men but turns to the mannered style of Fontainebleau for the figures of Susanna and her maids.[7] The elegant, seminude Susanna—her rich robe dropped to her waist and her upper torso covered with only a thin, transparent veil revealing the jewels that adorn her body and hair—reflects the taste of the French court, which preferred mythological and bath scenes with female nudes or seminudes.[8] In contrast to the later, dramatically elongated and elegant figures of the second style of Fontainebleau, inspired by the Italian painter Primaticcio (1504–1570), Massys's Susanna is defined according to a natural canon of proportion, which was characteristic of Fontainebleau ca. 1550 but unknown in northern painting before its introduction by Massys. Susanna is typical of Massys's females: She possesses an oval face with a long, classical nose; slanted, sharply outlined eyes; gold-highlighted hair; and an oyster-white complexion. Crisp outlines—rather than the soft modeling with which his father, Quentin Metsys (1465/66–1530), defined his figures—contribute to the sense of refined elegance, which is extended by the mannered gestures and elegant, long, bony hands.

Massys's portrayal of the biblical heroine Susanna reflects the growing acceptance of nude images of virtuous women from the Bible. Around 1500 there was a notable expansion of subjects representing nude women, initially in the south but increasingly in the art of the north.[9] While most of them were represented in the context of mythological or allegorical subjects, there were also numerous examples of biblical figures, especially Susanna, Bathsheba, and Eve, whose nudity is described in the Bible. Renaissance writers commonly employed women from the Old and New Testaments, as well as from classical history, as examples of moral behavior for contemporary women.[10] The story of Susanna, who was admired as an example of chastity and for choosing death rather than dishonor, however, is limited to a few plays and minor works, where it is often used to emphasize that "those who trust in God will not be betrayed."[11] Reflecting this association, paintings depicting the story of Susanna often appeared in medieval and early Renaissance courtrooms to remind judges and litigants of their respective rights, duties, and responsibilities.[12]

The erotic quality of the Pasadena painting, however, suggests that Massys's primary intention was to provide aesthetic, sensual pleasure rather than to give moral instruction. The elegant, partially nude Susanna is a provocative image. Massys represented the moment of heightened anticipation when her maids depart, leaving Susanna vulnerable to the advances of the duplicitous old men who lie in wait. Such erotically charged paintings would have been inappropriate for public display except in bath houses or taverns—or in the bedroom of a private patron.

1. Duverger 1984–2009, vol. 9, p. 406: "Noch eene schilderije schoustuck [chimneypiece] van Susanna met de twee Boeven oock geschildert door Jan Metsijs." Burton Fredericksen brought this inventory to the attention of Carol Togneri in an email dated 9 August 2004 (NSM).

2. Denucé 1932, p. 307, estate inv., 28–30 July 1682, by the notary Ant. Herreyns, mentions "historie van Susanna" by Jan Massys. The introduction to the inventory mentions that Jan Gillis, silversmith, died 10 November 1681 in "de Spiegel" on the Grote Markt, Antwerp. Buijnsters-Smets 1995, p. 220, cat. 54, without supporting evidence, mentions the inventory in association with the provenance of the version in Brussels, which by the end of the seventeenth century was in the collection of Storp in Münster. The fact that the inventory was made in Antwerp ten years after the inventory of Maria Rave in 1672 suggests that the painting belonging to Gillis could also refer to the Pasadena painting.

3. The auction catalogue identifies the seller as "Jean-Baptiste Du Bois, en son vivant Echevin de la Ville de Gand." The painting is described as "een Schoon Stuck representerende Susanna met de boeven," on panel and measuring "Haut 3½ pieds, large 6½ pieds," which translates to 107 × 198 cm, nearly identical with the Pasadena panel. The Brussels panel is 162 × 222 cm, and the dimensions of the upright panel sold at Christie's in 2016 are 131.5 × 111.4 cm. The information about the Du Bois sale was sent by Burton Fredericksen in an email dated 27 March 2010 (NSM).

4. René Kieffer (1876–1963) was a publisher, bookbinder, and bookseller in Paris.

5. The story of Susanna and the elders, considered part of the canon of the Roman Catholic Church, is regarded as apocryphal by Protestants and not included in the English Standard Version. It can be found in Daniel 13:1–62 in the Douay-Rheims 1899 American edition.

6. Present location unknown. It was last sold at Christie's, New York, 14 April 2016, lot 136. Its earliest history of ownership was with Sedelmeyer in Paris in 1905 and the Heugel collection in Paris in 1930. See Buijnsters-Smets 1995, cat. 29, pp. 175–77.

7. Los Angeles 2018, p. 362.

8. For a discussion of Christian nudes in the French tradition from the fifteenth century, such as Bathsheba, see Los Angeles 2018, pp. 28–30.

9. For more on the northern tradition of nudity in art, see Nuttall 2012, pp. 311–13.

10. Buijnsters-Smets 1995, p. 72. These texts reflect, in fact, a new attitude toward women and the relationship between men and women, which evolved during the early sixteenth century. In 1523 the Spanish writer Juan Luis Vives (1493–1540) published *De Institutione Feminae Christianae*, his influential text on the education and proper upbringing of women, followed in 1527 by *Christiani matrimonii institutio*, in which Erasmus (1466–1536) upheld the institution of marriage and extolled the positive qualities of women. Much of the discussion regarding the role of women was led by Protestants, who rejected the teachings of Augustine and the doctrines of the Roman Catholic Church, which elevated celibacy above marriage. Luther considered marriage not a sacrament but a natural circumstance of man, of which sexuality was an important part.

11. Buijnsters-Smets 1995, pp. 79f. During the Middle Ages, reflecting the traditional Jewish regard of Susanna as an example of marital fidelity, the chaste Susanna was considered a prefiguration of the Virgin Mary and thus was a symbol of the Church.

12. See De Ridder 1989, pp. 82–87. Although a relatively rare subject in Italy during the early sixteenth century, when it did appear, the story of Susanna was depicted as part of suites of allegories of justice intended as decorations for civic halls or loggias where magistrates pronounced judgments. See Rearick 1978, pp. 339f., 342n16.

54

Master of the Mansi Magdalen

Netherlandish
Antwerp, active ca. 1510–25

The Lamentation

Early 16th century

Oil on panel, 21¼ × 25¼ in. (54 × 64 cm)
The Norton Simon Foundation, F.1972.43.2.P

Provenance
Possibly Jan-Baptiste de Navigheer (sale, Coninck, Ypres, 19 April 1809, lot 40).[1] Jakob Johann Nepomuk Lyversberg (1761–1834), Cologne, by descent to his daughter[2]; Maria Eva von Geyr (née Lyversberg), by 1840, by descent to; Haan family, ca. 1900, by descent to; Frau Dr. Christine Virnich (née Haan), Bonn (sale, Lempertz, Cologne, 26 May 1971, lot 11). [G. Cramer, The Hague, sold 1972 to]; The Norton Simon Foundation.

Exhibited
Düsseldorf 1904, no. 164, as follower of Quentin Metsys, lent by "Frau witwe Dr. Virnich"; Brussels 1977, no. 361.

References
Noël 1837, p. 3, no. 24, as *Schoreel* [*sic*]; Clemen 1905, p. 224, no. 8, fig. 149, as School of Quentin Metsys; M. Friedländer 1915, pp. 8, 10, no. 3, fig. 2; Förster 1931, pp. 90f., fig. 51; Held 1931, p. 69; M. Friedländer 1967–76, vol. 7 (1971), pp. 46, fig. 91; Wolfthal 1989, pp. 21, 74, no. 66, fig. 17; Cologne 1995, pp. 204, 575f., no. 176; Kier and Zehnder 1998, p. 217; S. Campbell 2010, p. 345, no. 860, ill.

Technical Notes
The uncradled support is a horizontally grained oak panel made from two boards of approximately equal width, with a glued join. The reverse retains its original surface and toolmarks. On the front, the four sides have ¼-inch margins that are unprimed and unpainted, suggesting that the painting was once part of an altarpiece or other framed construction. The presence of a barbe indicates the panel was installed in the framework before the ground was applied. The smooth ground, an off-white or buff color, is of medium thickness, leaving the texture of the horizontal grain slightly evident. Microscopic examination of the surface did not reveal underdrawing. The paint was applied in small, well-defined brushstrokes applied directly over the ground, which is occasionally revealed through tiny gaps in the brushwork. X-radiography reveals a third hand located at center right, below the two visible hands of Mary. The hand, now completely painted over, seems to be an early position of Mary's right hand, palm up, fingers slightly curled. The artist combined opaque paint in the flesh tones with layering of semitransparent, jewel-colored glazes in the garments. Paint that appears under the microscope to be thin and smoothly applied nonetheless has very distinct, crisp contours, especially clear when viewed in raking light. There is discernible brushmarking throughout. The paint layer has almost no cracking, other than a limited area of very thin horizontal cracks in Christ's proper right thigh. The paint is generally well preserved. There is no evidence of solvent abrasion; however, prior cleaning left noticeable residues of dark varnish in the recesses of brushwork. The muddy quality of the deeply shadowed folds in the cloth beneath Christ is at least partly due to incomplete cleaning. The Virgin's cloak has been retouched along the join and over areas of loss in the knee. Other small areas of retouching are located in Christ's torso, stomach, and proper left thigh and in the chest of Mary Magdalene at center. The glossy varnish, an aged synthetic resin, is not appreciably discolored. Residues of darkened older varnish are particularly conspicuous along the lower edge and in the white cloth.

In this scene of the Lamentation, six mourners crowd around the body of the dead Christ, who is displayed horizontally across the foreground of the composition. The tightly confined space emphasizes the grief shared by the Virgin and her attendants, who respond to the broken body of Christ with a variety of expressions. The stoic figure of Nicodemus appears in profile on the far left cradling a container of salve. Next to him Joseph of Arimathea, portrayed with wide, reddened eyes, supports the shoulders of the dead Christ as he looks out toward the viewer with an expression of restrained grief. Behind the Magdalene and Virgin Mary, who quietly cast their eyes down toward the body of Christ as tears run down their faces, another woman holds her hand to her face as she weeps. His head tilted back as if to fit within the panel, John the Evangelist stands behind the Virgin, gently supporting her left arm; his furrowed brow, strained expression, and tears reveal his anguish.

Although nothing certain is known about this painting's whereabouts prior to the nineteenth century, in 1837 it was in the Lyversberg collection in Cologne.[3] Formed by Jakob Johann Nepomuk Lyversberg (1761–1834), a tobacco and wine merchant, the collection included an extraordinary group of devotional paintings that had been removed from churches and monasteries during the Napoleonic upheavals and

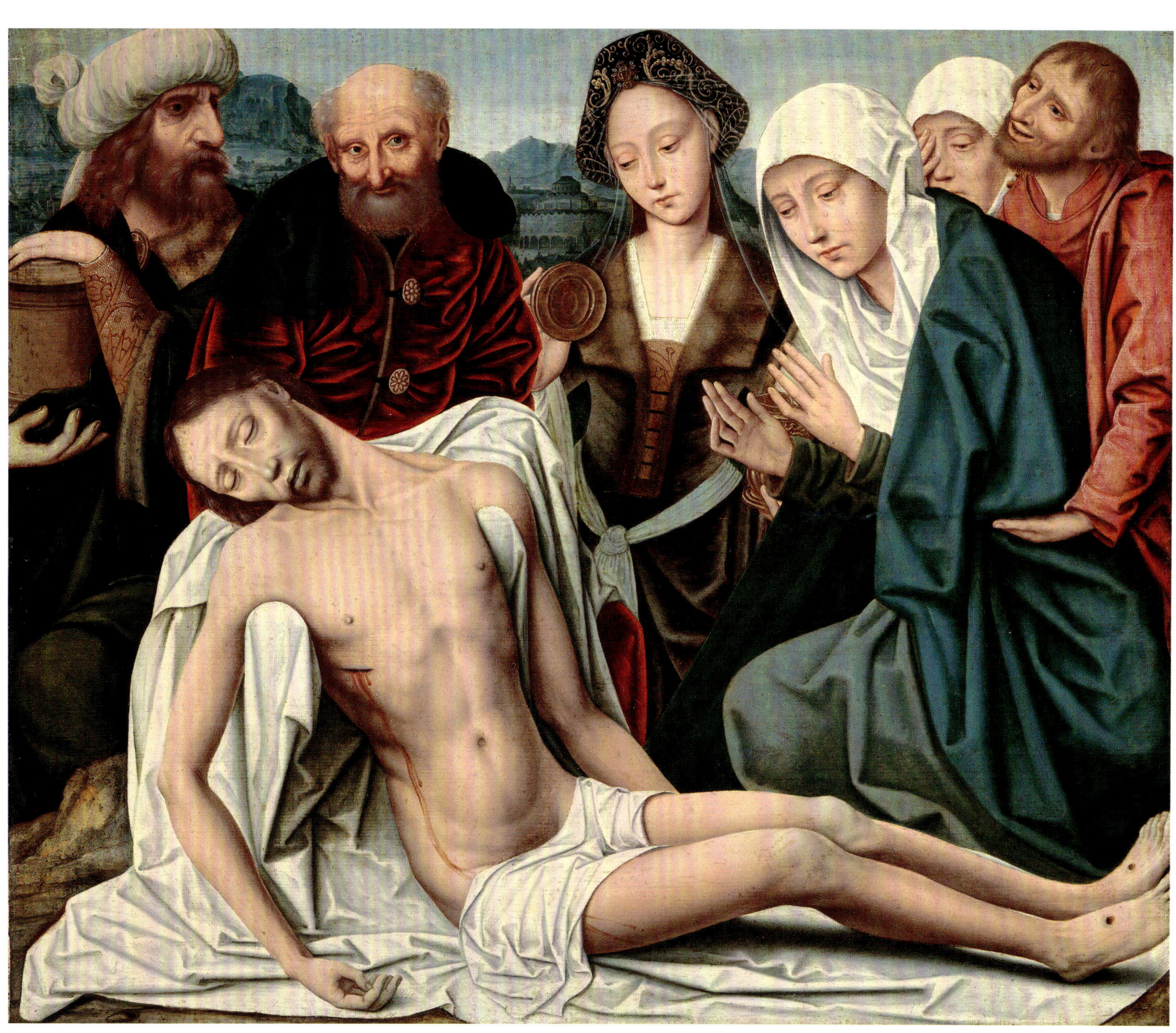

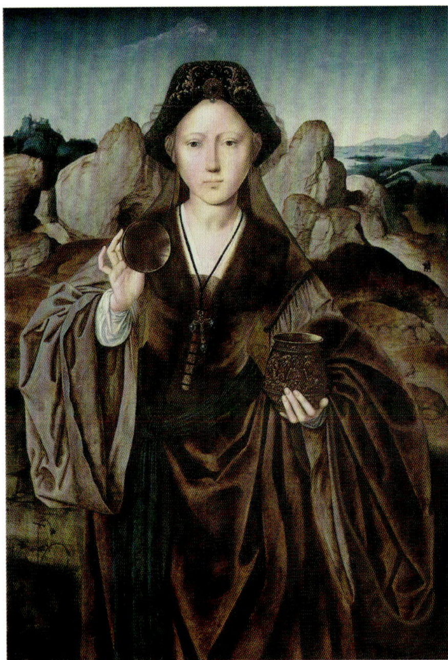

Fig. 54a. Master of the Mansi Magdalen, *Mary Magdalene*, after 1525, oil on panel, 32 × 22⅝ in. (81.5 × 57.5 cm), Gemäldegalerie, Staatliche Museen, Berlin.

consisted of works by German, Dutch, and Flemish artists, some rare and others unknown, but all remarkable for their fine quality. The Pasadena painting remained with the Lyversberg family until it was sold at public auction in 1971. Over the course of the 150 years or more that it was in the Lyversberg collection, *The Lamentation* was variously attributed to Jan van Scorel (1495–1562), Quentin Metsys (1465/66–1530), Jan Massys (ca. 1509–1575), and, finally, to an anonymous follower of Metsys's known as the Master of the Mansi Magdalen. Fewer than two dozen paintings have now been attributed to the hand of this unidentified artist, whose sobriquet derives from a painting that depicts Mary Magdalene (fig. 54a) formerly in the collection of Giovanni Battista Mansi of Lucca and today in the Gemäldegalerie, Berlin.

Max Friedländer was the first to attribute the Pasadena painting to the Master of the Mansi Magdalen, who was active in Antwerp between 1510 and 1525.[4] Strongly influenced by Quentin Metsys, to whom he may have been apprenticed, some of his paintings also indicate his knowledge of the graphic work of Albrecht Dürer (1471–1528), Albrecht Altdorfer (ca. 1480–1538), and Marcantonio Raimondi (ca. 1470/82–1527/34). Friedländer described the main characteristics of the Master of the Mansi Magdalen's style, noting that there were "three peculiarities" that distinguish the painter's hand: the rigidity of the monumental figures pushed to the frontal plane of the panel, a monochromatic palette, and a "curious relationship between figure and landscape."[5] This last point is particularly evident both in the Berlin painting, where craggy boulders encase the Magdalene's head, and in *Virgin and Child* at the Metropolitan Museum of Art, New York (fig. 54b), where the landscape assumes the role of Mary's mandorla. The landscape is less significant in the Pasadena painting, where the heads of the tightly

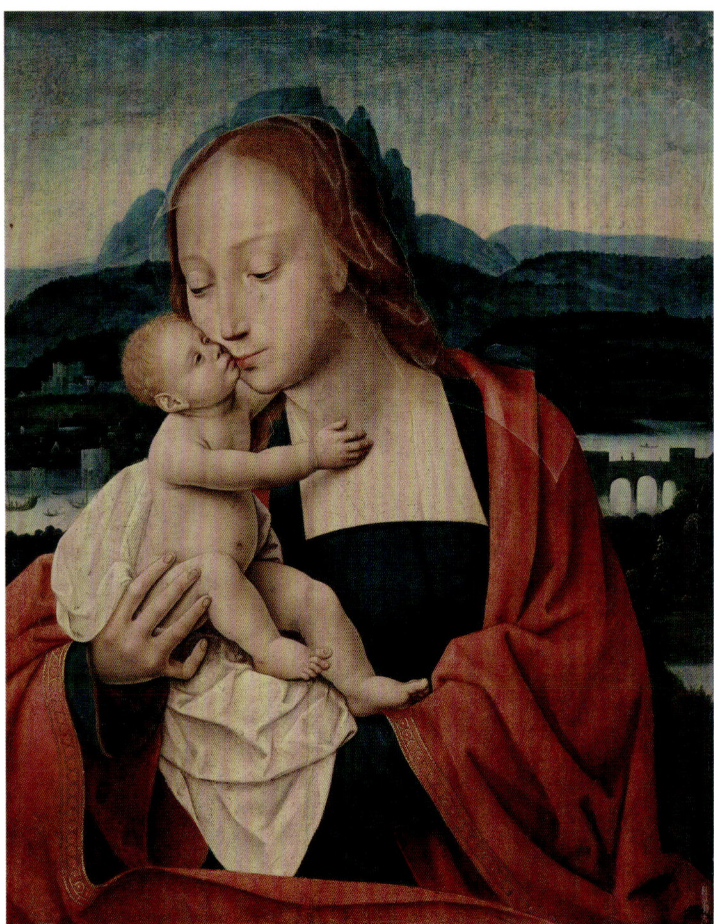

Fig. 54b. Master of the Mansi Magdalen, *Virgin and Child*, ca. 1500–25, oil on panel, 19⅛ × 15¼ in. (48.6 × 38.7 cm), The Metropolitan Museum of Art, New York.

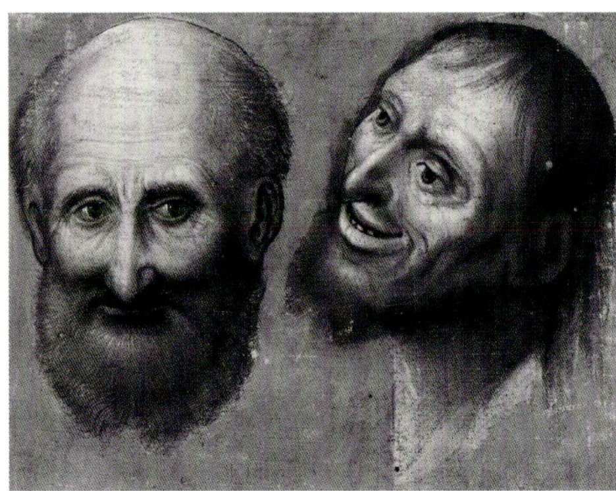

Fig. 54c. Master of the Mansi Magdalen, *Heads of Two Old Bearded Men*, ca. 1520, tempera on canvas, 5⅜ × 6½ in. (13.5 × 16.6 cm), Kupferstichkabinett, Staatliche Museen, Berlin.

compacted group of seven figures project above the narrow suggestion of distant mountains. In other ways, however, *The Lamentation* closely reflects the style of the Master of the Mansi Magdalen, particularly in the compressed arrangement of the figures in the immediate foreground of the panel and the muted palette. The figure of the Magdalene in the Pasadena painting also generally agrees with its counterpart in the Berlin picture, especially in her headdress and costume, as well as in the way she displays the lid of the unguent jar she holds in her left hand.[6]

The artist's additive manner of working from individual models based on other drawings, paintings, and prints is suggested by the mismatched proportions of his figures. Both John and Joseph of Arimathea appear proportionally smaller than the other figures; Joseph's arms, furthermore, would not be long enough to support Christ. A *tüchlein* sketch now in the Kupferstichkabinett, Staatliche Museen, Berlin (fig. 54c), is generally assumed to have served as a preliminary study for the heads of Joseph and John in the Pasadena panel, for which the artist reworked the exaggerated expressions to convey the pain felt by both men.[7] Ultimately, the individualistic, almost caricature-like faces and the emotional impact of the figures reveal the Master of the Mansi Magdalen's indebtedness to Quentin Metsys. —*Carol Togneri*

1. "N. S. détaché de sa Croix prêt à mettre au Tombeau, par Quintin Messis [*sic*], sur bois, haut 568 millimètres (21 pouces) large 642 millimètres (25 pouces). Les Figures ont beaucoup d'expression." Although the painting described in this sale has the exact dimensions of the Pasadena panel, its attribution to Metsys (not Scorel, as it was called in 1837 when in the Lyversburg collection) and the fact that it came from a sale in Ypres, Belgium, suggest that this may not be the same as the Pasadena painting. However, the auction was composed of objects owned by Jean-Baptiste de Navigheer, "Prêtre, ancien Chanoine gradué et Trésorier de la Cathédrale," which is very much in keeping with the type of sources Lyversberg was accessing to acquire his paintings. The reference to the sale and its contents comes from GPI, Sales Catalog B-150, lot 40.

2. The back of the panel bears a small white label with the number "24" written in ink. That number corresponds to the inventory number given in Noël 1837, which was prepared as a catalogue for an auction of the paintings in the Lyversberg collection. The sale did not take place, and instead the collection was divided among the children of Lyversberg. Matthias Joseph de Noël (1782–1849), the author of the catalogue, was the nephew of Jakob Johann Nepomuk Lyversberg. He was an artist as well as an art dealer whose early travels to tour churches and art collections were in part financed by his uncle. See Böhm 1980.

3. For a complete discussion and reconstruction of the collection assembled by Lyversberg, see Cologne 1995, pp. 193ff.; and Kier and Zehnder 1998, pp. 210–31.

4. M. Friedländer 1915, p. 10.

5. M. Friedländer 1967–76, vol. 7 (1971), p. 45. On p. 47 he mentions the possibility that the Master of the Mansi Magdalen is identical with Willem Muelenbroec, who was apprenticed to Metsys in 1501.

6. See also the painting attributed to the Master of the Mansi Magdalen that was restituted to the heirs of Jacques Goudstikker by the Bonnefantenmuseum, Maastricht; Greenwich/New York 2008–09, pp. 92–95, cat. 5. M. Friedländer 1967–76, vol. 7 (1971), p. 45, notes that this master based the Berlin *Mary Magdalene* on the *Sainte Madeleine* by Metsys in the Louvre; see Scaillíerez 2007, pp. 9ff.

7. Joseph's direct gaze at the viewer is interpreted as an "inappropriate smirk" by Friedländer and as "soulful restraint" by Held: M. Friedländer 1967–76, vol. 7 (1971), p. 46; Held 1931, p. 69.

55

Hans Memling

South Netherlandish
Seligenstadt ca. 1430/40–1494 Bruges

Christ Giving His Blessing

1478[1]

Oil on panel, 15⅛ × 11¼ in. (38.4 × 28.6 cm)
Norton Simon Art Foundation, M.1974.17.P

Provenance

Don Manuel II (1889–1932), King of Portugal (r. 1908–1910), Palácio das Necessidades, Lisbon, sold 1910 to; [Duveen Brothers, London and New York, sold 1927 to]; Dr. and Mrs. Alexander Hamilton Rice Jr.,[2] New York and Newport, RI, sold 1957 to; [M. Knoedler and Co., New York, stock no. A-6680, jointly owned with Pinakos Ltd., New York, sold 5 April 1964 to]; Norton Simon, Los Angeles, gift 1974 to; Norton Simon Art Foundation.

Exhibited

London 1927a, p. 31, no. 62, ill.; New York 1929, pp. 80f., no. 23, ill.; New York 1939a, no. 252, no. 13, ill. opp. p. 48, dated 1479–87; New York 1942b; Bruges 1960, no. 37, p. 150, ill. p. 102; Detroit 1960, no. 34, p. 154, ill. p. 102; Bruges 1994, no. 10, pp. 17, 66, 106, ill. p. 67.

References

Kronig 1910, p. 28, ill.; Longhi 1914, p. 212;[3] Tancred Borenius in London 1927b, p. 29, no. 62, pl. xxxiv; Alexandre 1927, pp. 61–67; M. Friedländer 1927, pp. 211–12; M. Friedländer 1924–37, vol. 6 (1928), p. 124, no. 39, pl. xxviii; "Kleinberger/Flemish Primitives" 1929; "Kleinberger/Flemish Show" 1929, p. 4, ill.; Vaughan 1929, p. 40, ill.; Vollmer 1930, p. 375; Frankfurter 1932, p. 22; New York 1939b, p. 10, no. 252, pl. 39; Lauts 1940, pp. 13f., 34; Winkler 1960, p. 314; Vaughan 1961, p. 295; Longhi 1961, p. 80;[4] Corti and Faggin 1969, p. 87, no. 5, ill.; M. Friedländer 1967–76, vol. 6a (1971), p. 51, no. 39, pl. 90; Białostocki 1976, pp. 313–20; Morse 1979; Pasadena 1980, p. 34, ill.; B. G. Lane 1980, p. 24, no. 38; Snow-Smith 1982, p. 75 passim, fig. 76; Castelfranchi Vegas 1984, p. 88; De Vos 1987, passim; Pasadena 1989, p. 23, ill.; Van Miegroet 1989, pp. 128, 133, 141n97, fig. 116; Bauman and Liedtke 1992, p. 354, fig. 354; De Vos 1994, pp. 142f., no. 27; Bruges 1994, pp. 17, 66–67, 106, no. 10; L. Campbell 1995a, p. 265; P. Sutton 1995, pp. 27f., 30, fig. 1; Buijsen 1996, pp. 65, 67, fig. 17; Padovanni et al. 1996, p. 171; Muchnic 1998, pp. 97f.; Dunkerton 1999, p. 98; Ginzburg 2001, pp. 10f.; Pasadena 2003, p. 36, ill.; New York 2004, p. 268; B. G. Lane 2009, pp. 111n14, 309, no. 62, fig. 248; S. Campbell 2010, pp. 58, fig. 8, 59f., 65, 271, no. 210, ill.; Kennedy and Nolan 2011, pp. 115f., fig. 50; Wolfthal and Metzger 2014, pp. 122–38; Ginzburg 2015, pp. 137–39; Los Angeles 2017, p. 106; Muchnic 2019, p. 321.

Technical Notes

The support is a vertically grained oak panel made from a single board. Two horizontal battens approximately one inch wide are glued to the reverse; the entire reverse including the battens has been covered with a thin chalky material, then painted, first with dark gray, then with brown paint. A vertical crack that originates at the left end of the top edge was repaired in 1961 by gluing a thin wood strip on the reverse. A short, near-diagonal crack or split originates at the lower end of the right edge; no repairs were made. The moderately thick white ground does not extend to the edges, indicating that the ground was applied while the panel was in a frame. Infrared reflectography reveals a complete underdrawing. The face and hair were not changed, but Memling made several small alterations as he worked out the placement of the hands and fingers. The paint was directly applied in thin, subtly blended layers with delicate shading. Fine lines of gold depict the aureole. Brushmarking faintly outlines the contour of the head and hair and very slightly around the hands. A pentimento is visible at the neckline of the robe, where the original line was higher. Pentimenti are visible also in the fingers, especially the index finger of the proper right hand. There is a fine, dense pattern of thin, branched cracks, especially visible in the flesh tones. Numerous paint losses from flaking have occurred. Solvent abrasion has damaged the delicate shadows of the flesh tones, most noticeably in the neck, areas at the outer contour of the hair, especially at the proper right side where the brown overlaps the blue-green background, and both eyes. At the proper right side, only one faint line of the gold rays of the aureole has survived. The painting was treated before acquisition, at which time a very dark coating was removed. Retouching does not fluoresce with ultraviolet light, possibly because it is masked by the thick synthetic-resin/wax varnish, but it can be identified with infrared examination.

Christ Giving His Blessing is one of Hans Memling's most captivating images, combining the hieratic qualities of a religious icon with the gentle humanity of his portraits. The date 1478, which was inscribed on an old frame (possibly original) formerly attached to the panel, has been generally accepted by scholars as appropriate for the Pasadena painting.[5] It is iconographically and compositionally similar to *Christ Blessing* in the Museum of Fine Arts, Boston (fig. 55a), which is still engaged in its original frame dated 1481. The more slender and ascetic figure of Christ in Boston suggests that it is a slightly later reprise of the Pasadena version.[6] As in Memling's *Portrait of a Man*, ca. 1480–90 (fig. 55b), here the youthful Christ appears to rest his hand on the lower edge of the frame, as if he were standing behind a window or a parapet. Christ confronts the viewer directly, his shoulders parallel to the picture plane, his eyes focused straight

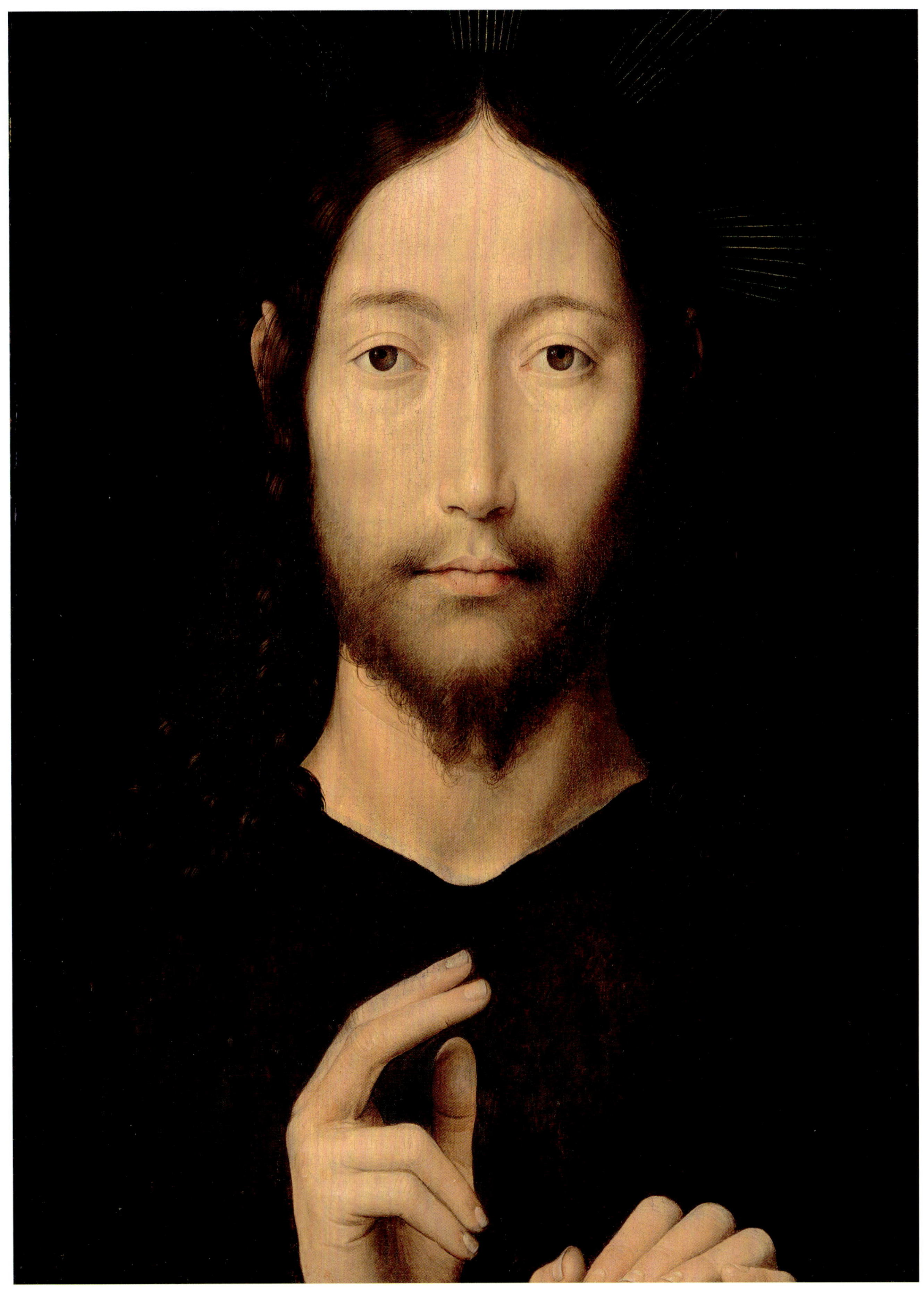

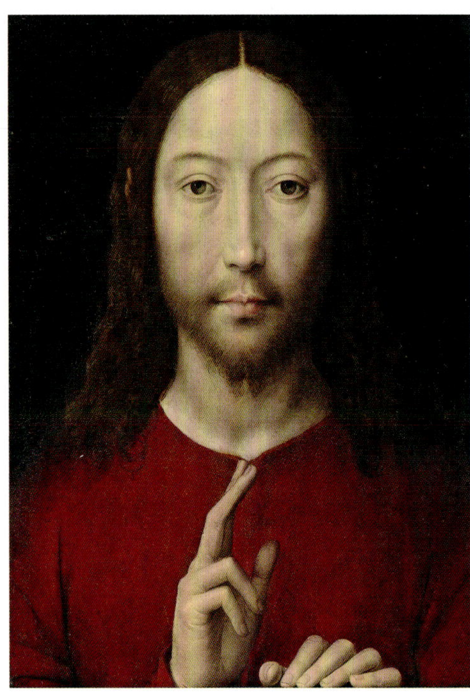

Fig. 55a. Hans Memling, *Christ Blessing*, 1481, oil on panel, 13 13⁄16 × 9 7⁄8 in. (35.1 × 25.1 cm), Museum of Fine Arts, Boston, bequest of William A. Coolidge, 1993.40.

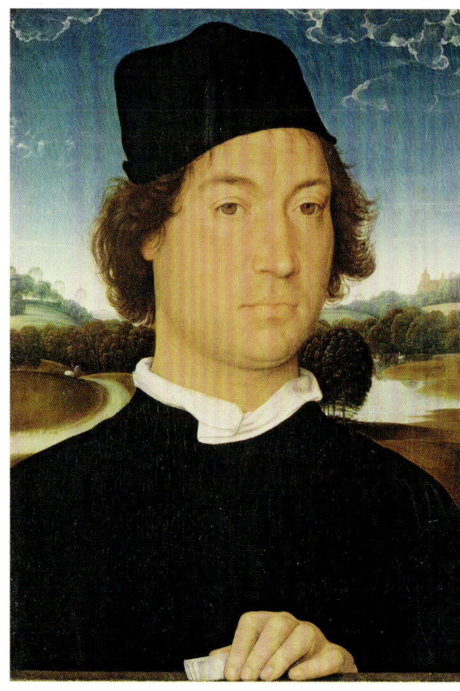

Fig. 55b. Hans Memling, *Portrait of a Man*, ca. 1480–90, oil on panel, 13 7⁄8 × 9 7⁄8 in. (35 × 25 cm), Gallerie degli Uffizi, Florence.

ahead. The face of Christ is similar to that in Memling's monumental altarpiece *Christ with the Musical Angels* (Koninklijk Museum voor Schone Kunsten, Antwerp). Although much earlier and less robust than the Antwerp painting, the features, the soft hair of the beard and mustache, and the fingers are all comparable.

The image of Christ in the Pasadena painting is a fusion of several iconographic types that were particularly popular with Flemish, German, and Italian painters during the late fifteenth and early sixteenth centuries. Memling's portrayal of Christ is essentially that of the "Holy Face," closely corresponding to a description in the so-called Lentulus Letter, an apocryphal document from no earlier than the thirteenth century that for many years was considered to have been written to the Roman Senate by Publius Lentulus. The document describes Christ as "having a reverend countenance which they that look upon may love and fear; having hair of the hue of an unripe hazelnut and smooth almost down to his ears . . . waving over his shoulders; having a parting at the middle of the head according to the fashion of the Nazarenes; a brow smooth and very calm, with a face without wrinkle or any blemish . . . ; having a full beard of the color of his hair, not long, but a little forked at the chin."[7]

Depictions of the Holy Face were popular in German and Netherlandish art from the fourteenth century onward. The prototype in the Netherlands is generally assumed to have been the *Holy Face* by Jan van Eyck (ca. 1390–1441) from the second quarter of the fifteenth century, which represents only the head of Christ without hands. It is known today only from copies, such as the faithful copy made in the seventeenth century in Bruges (fig. 55c).[8] In Memling's painting and in the Van Eyck copy, the head and shoulders of Christ appear in a fully frontal, traditional pose. Remnants of gold paint to the proper left of Christ's head in the Memling indicate the original presence of a gold aureole. This was probably less ornate than the floriated gold tripartite nimbus in the Bruges painting, in which a jeweled gold collar encircles Christ's neck.[9] In both examples the strict alignment of the parted hair, the nose, and the slightly separated beard create a strong vertical accent, which, when combined with the horizontal line created by the alignment of the eyes and lateral gold lines of the nimbus, suggests the form of the cross. In the Pasadena painting this is reinforced by the position of his raised hand, the thumb and fingertips of which are aligned with the central vertical axis. The immediate typological precursor is *Christ and the Virgin* (Philadelphia Museum of Art) by the Master of Flémalle (active ca. 1420–40), in which the fingers of the left hand similarly appear just above the edge of the lower frame.[10]

Memling's addition of the gesture of Christ blessing with his right hand incorporates the *Salvator Mundi* iconography of Christ the redeemer of the world as represented in the central panel of the *Braque Triptych* by Rogier van der Weyden (ca. 1399–1464; fig. 55d), which was ultimately derived from the Byzantine iconic image of Christ Pantocrator. In Rogier's famous altarpiece, where the half-length figures are set against a landscape, Christ assumes the traditional pose between the Virgin Mary and John the Evangelist. Holding the crossed orb in his left hand, Christ raises his right hand in a gesture of blessing similar to that in the Pasadena painting. Several authors have also suggested the importance of a lost version of the Holy Face by Rogier van der Weyden, the influence of which is thought to have extended to Antonello da Messina (ca. 1430–1479) in Italy.[11] Significantly, both Memling and Van der Weyden (in the *Braque Triptych*) represent

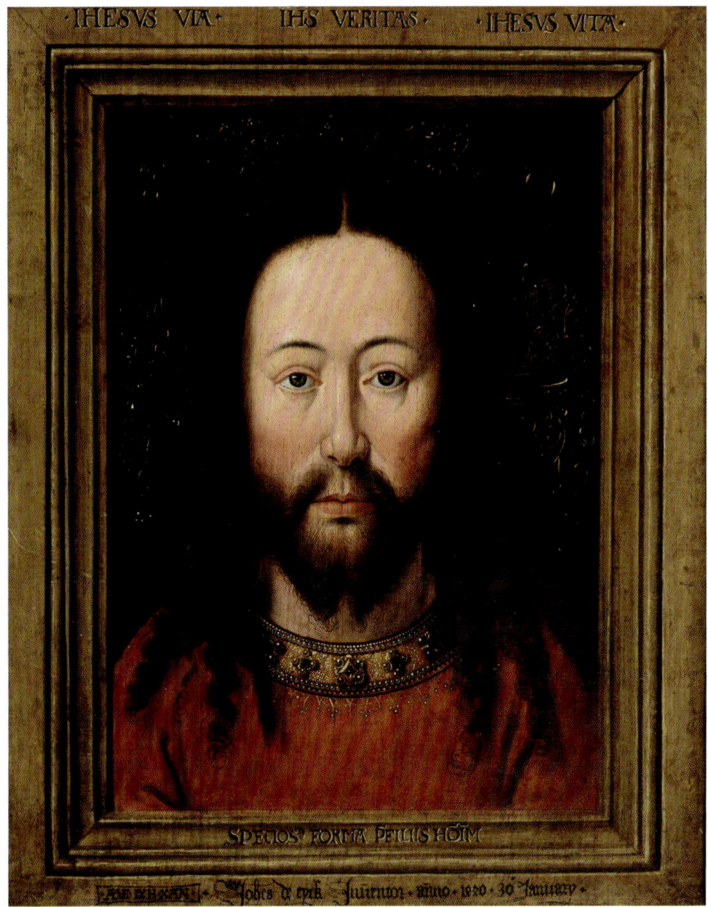

Fig. 55c. Early 17th-century copy after Jan van Eyck, *Christ as Salvator Mundi*, 1440, oil on panel, 12 ⅝ × 10 ¼ in. (32 × 26 cm), Stedelijke Musea Groeningemuseum, Bruges.

Christ in a humble robe rather than the jewel-necked robe in Van Eyck's painting.

The unblemished, peaceful appearance of Christ distinguishes these versions of the Holy Face from another popular representation, the so-called sudarium type, which includes the crown of thorns and often blood dripping down Christ's anguished face. This type refers to the sixth episode seen in the modern Stations of the Cross when Veronica wiped Christ's face as he carried the cross to Golgotha. The traditional image shows only the face of Christ with the crown of thorns;[12] however, popular fifteenth-century examples, such as the *Head of Christ* (Metropolitan Museum of Art, New York) by Petrus Christus (active 1444–75/76), ca. 1445, include the head, neck, and shoulders.[13] Both the Holy Face and the sudarium types are related to the cult of Veronica.[14]

Many of the depictions of the Holy Face/sudarium type were conceived as pendants to images of the Virgin Mary at prayer. A typical example is *Christ as the Man of Sorrows* (Palazzo Bianco, Genoa) and *The Virgin in Prayer* (private collection, United Kingdom), which originally formed the wings of a diptych by Memling.[15] In most of the paintings that hung as pendants, the images—like contemporary portraits—acknowledge each other by turning slightly in the direction of the other panel. No companion has ever been suggested for the Pasadena panel, and its iconic presentation suggests that it hung alone. Physical evidence of the original frame of the Boston version shows no evidence of having been hinged and supports the idea that the Pasadena *Christ Giving His Blessing* was likewise conceived as an independent work.

The rise of individual devotion and the cult of Veronica during the fifteenth century created a demand for small representations of the Holy Face. In response to the market's demand, Memling and his workshop produced numerous similar panels.[16] Examination of the Pasadena painting using infrared reflectography shows evidence of extensive underdrawing and reworking of the hands in both the underdrawing (fig. 55e) and the paint layer. This method of working directly on the panel is characteristic of Memling and distinguishes his authentic paintings from those of his workshop, which typically were worked up from patterns and show evidence of pouncing.[17]

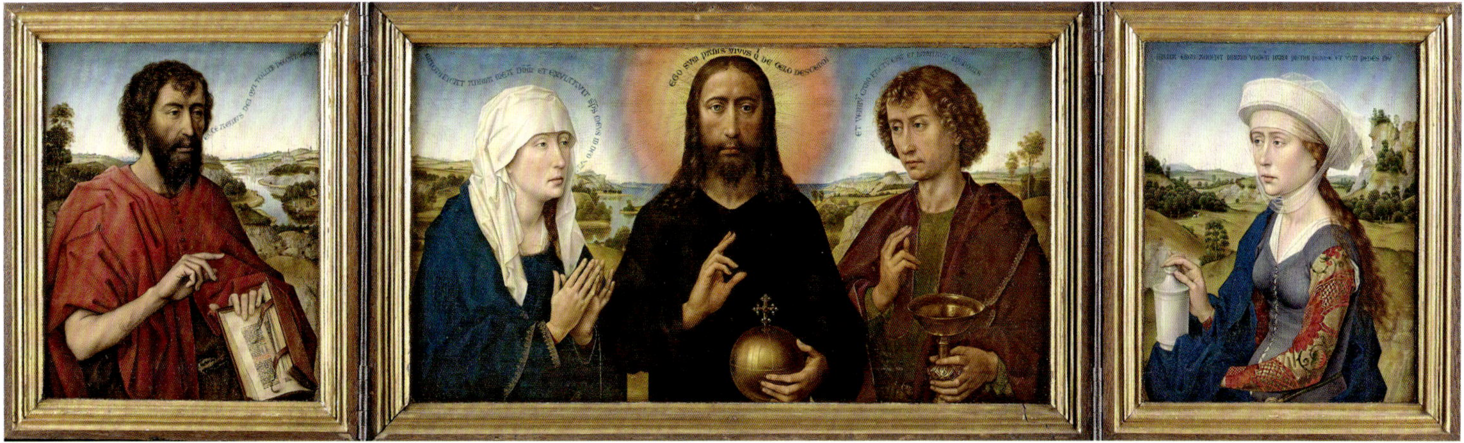

Fig. 55d. Rogier van der Weyden, *Braque Triptych*, 15th century, oil on wood, 16 ⅛ × 26 ¾ in. (41 × 68 cm), Musée du Louvre, Paris.

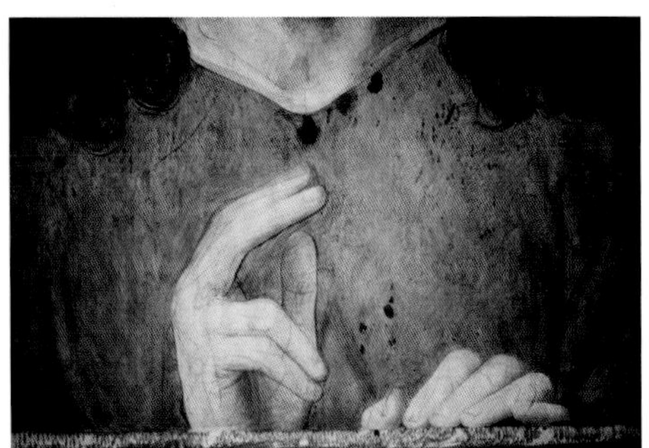

Fig. 55e. Infrared photograph of hands.

The high quality of *Christ Giving His Blessing*, painted when Memling was at the height of his career, as well as the use of mordant gilding for the aureole, indicate that it was an expensive work painted on commission rather than intended for the open market. The painting was unknown until 1910, when it was sold from the collection of King Manuel II of Portugal, a country that in the fifteenth century had strong political and economic ties to Bruges and an appreciation for Flemish paintings. Noting this, Diane Wolfthal and Cathy Metzger have proffered that a wealthy Portuguese collector, perhaps even King Alfonso V (1432–1481), commissioned the Pasadena painting for his personal devotions.[18]

1. Inscribed on "original" frame (see note 5) known from photograph in the Friedländer Archive at the RKD. The full inscription on the frame, as described by De Vos in Bruges 1994, p. 66, is top: "EGO – SVM – VIA – VERITAS – VITA"; bottom: "EGO – SVM – ALPHA – ET O[MEGA] – PRINCIPIV[M] – ET – FIN[I]S – 1478."

2. Dr. Alexander Hamilton Rice Jr. (1875–1956) was a physician, a professor of geography at Harvard University, and an explorer of the Amazon. In 1915 he married Eleanor Elkins Widener (d. 1937) of Philadelphia, the widow of George Dunton Widener (1861–1912), who with their son died on the Titanic. She was a socialite and philanthropist, remembered for her donation of the Widener Library to Harvard in memory of her son.

3. Longhi wrongly refers to the painting as in Antwerp.

4. Republication of Longhi 1914; it repeats mistaken provenance and also neglects to properly cite A. Hamilton Rice Jr. as owner.

5. M. Friedländer 1927, pp. 211f., notes that the painting was formerly in an old frame with the "important and credible date 1478." It has also been speculated, however, that the now lost frame may have been only eighteenth century. See also Bruges 1994, p. 66; and Wolfthal and Metzger 2014, p. 124.

6. Bruges 1994, p. 106, no. 24, considers the Boston painting "a reprise with slight variations of the Pasadena Christ." The frame is painted green, as is the background of the painting. There is extensive underdrawing and the hands were painted and then altered slightly after the red garment was painted. A third version rediscovered ca. 2010 represents a similar figure of Christ with dark clouds surrounding a gold sky and remnants of a radiating nimbus, ca. 1480–85 (promised gift, Los Angeles County Museum of Art; illustrated in catalogue of Old Masters, Sotheby's, New York, sale, 1 February 2013, lot 10).

7. Hand 1992, p. 10. Hand notes that a similar description in the *Vita Christi* composed in the fourteenth century by Ludolph of Saxony (d. 1378) was particularly popular in the Netherlands and Germany.

8. Panofsky 1958, vol. 1, pp. 187, 430, nos. 1, 4. Panofsky identified six replicas of the *Holy Face,* the most convincing having been in the Swinburne collection at Durham. Regarding Van Eyck's *Holy Face*, see Van Miegroet 1989, p. 128.

9. Although now difficult to see, London 1927a, p. 31, no. 62, ill., notes that the head of Christ in what is now the Pasadena painting was then encircled by a golden aureole.

10. The Master of Flémalle is generally believed to be Robert Campin (ca. 1375–1445).

11. Snow-Smith 1982, p. 75. Corti and Faggin 1969, no. 5, cite the possibility of the existence of a Van der Weyden prototype that preceded Memling's *Christ Giving His Blessing*. De Vos 1994, p. 66n3f, no. 27, considers this possible but notes that the existence of a Van der Weyden prototype has never been adequately demonstrated.

12. Hand 1992, pp. 7ff., discusses the derivation and evolution of this type. The type is related to the Man of Sorrows in which Christ wears a crown of thorns and displays his wounds.

13. Regarding the Metropolitan Museum's painting (60.71.1), see New York 1998–99, pp. 96f., no. 3, with additional references, including Upton 1990, pp. 56–59, 64f.; and Hand 1992, passim.

14. From the early thirteenth century, the sudarium of Veronica, the cloth on which the face of Christ was believed to have been imprinted when the saint wiped his face, was an increasingly important and powerful object of veneration. Housed in Saint Peter's in Rome, Veronica's veil with the imprint of the Holy Face was the first indulged image. Pope Innocent IV (ca. 1180–1254) granted an indulgence of forty days for saying the prayer "Ave facies praeclara" (Hail most beautiful face) and at least ten thousand days for reciting the prayer "Salve sancta facies" (All hail Holy Face) in front of the sudarium or a representation of it (Hand 1992, pp. 10–16). See also Bruges 1994, no. 72.

15. Buijsen 1996, pp. 57–69.

16. See Dijkstra 1990, pp. 9f. Dijkstra has shown that the production of copies from the fifteenth century onward was in response to the rapid spread of private worship and personal devotion and the trade in indulgences and the associated pilgrimages. Regarding the contemporary rise in indulgences related to the cult of Veronica, see Ringbom 1965, pp. 23f., cited with other references to indulgences in Hand 1992, p. 14, fig. 6, p. 17n18.

17. See Buijsen 1996, pp. 65, 67, fig. 17. Regarding Memling's technique, see Faries 1993, pp. 102f.; Ainsworth 1994; Périer-d'Ieteren 1994; L. Campbell 1995b; Borchert 1995. Regarding the Pasadena painting, see Wolfthal and Metzger 2014, pp. 127–34.

18. Wolfthal and Metzger 2014, pp. 134.

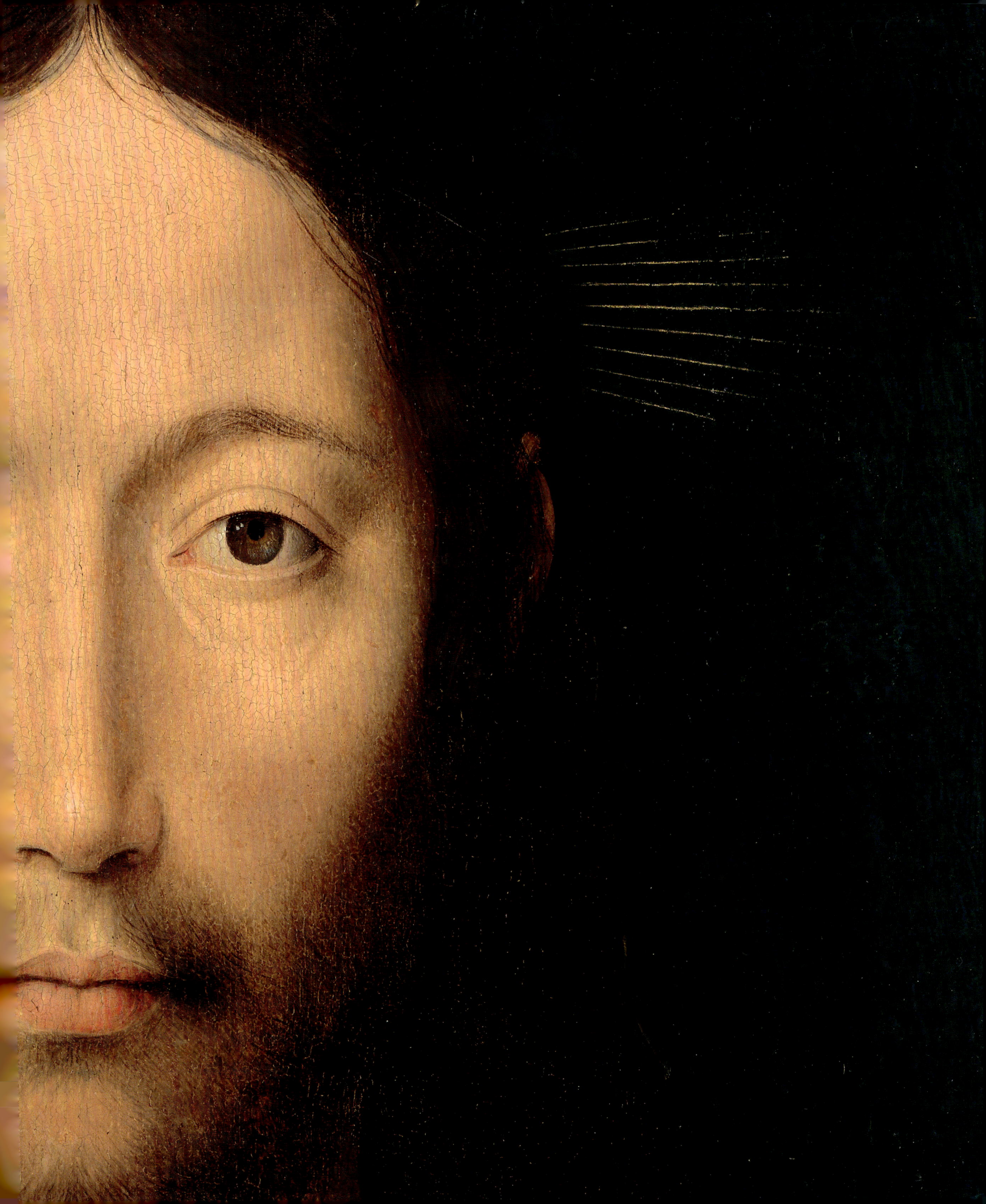

56

Gabriel Metsu

Dutch
Leiden 1629–1667 Amsterdam

Woman at Her Toilette

ca. 1659

Signed on music sheet at right: "G. Metsu"
Oil on panel, 25½ × 22¾ in. (64.8 × 57.8 cm)
The Norton Simon Foundation, F.1972.15.1.P

Provenance

Jonas Jonasz. Witsen (1676–1715), Amsterdam (sale, Zomer, Raket & Benoorden, Amsterdam, 31 March 1717, lot 53, "Een Juffer die gekamt werd, van Gabriel Metzu," sold for ƒ195).[1] Jacob van Leyen (sale, Amsterdam, 17 April 1720, lot 6, "Een Kamster in een Kamer [heele Beelden] van G. Metzu, extra puyk," sold for ƒ230). Joachim Rendorp (1728–1792), Amsterdam (sale, Philippus van der Schley et al., Amsterdam, 9–10 July 1794, lot 37, sold for ƒ275 to);[2] [Eberlein].[3] Corneille-Louis Reynders, Brussels (sale, L.-J. Nieuwenhuys and Louis de Man, Brussels, 8 August 1821, lot 64, sold for F20,000 to);[4] Sébastien Érard[5] (1752–1831), Château de la Muette, Passy (sale, Château de la Muette, Paris, 7 August 1832, lot 93, bought-in); Sébastien Érard, Château de la Muette, Passy (sale, Christie's, London, 22 June 1833, lot 34, sold for 245 guineas to); the Rev. W. Clowes.[6] John Rogers (sale, Christie's, London, 30 April–1 May, 1847, lot 187, sold for 270 guineas to); [Nieuwenhuys, London]. Marquise Théodule de Rhodes (sale, Le Roy, Petit, Paris, 30 May 1868, lot 9).[7] [E. H. Phillips, London, sold 1879 to];[8] Sir Francis Cook (1817–1901),[9] by descent to his grandson; Sir Herbert Frederick Cook (1869–1939), Doughty House, Richmond, by 1915, sold by Trustees of Sir Herbert Cook, 2 October 1944 to; [Thomas Agnew & Sons, London, stock no. 9012, and Edward Speelman Ltd., London, sold 1945 to]; Sir John Heathcote-Amory, 3rd Bart.; Tiverton (1894–1972), sold 1972 to; [Edward Speelman Ltd., London, sold 1972 to]; The Norton Simon Foundation.

Exhibited

London 1946, no. 5 (as 25¼ × 22¾ in.); King's Lynn 1958, no. 7; King's Lynn 1965, no. 12; Leiden 1966, no. 32; on loan, Allen Memorial Art Museum, Oberlin, 1 June 1972–8 May 1973; on loan, Los Angeles County Museum of Art, 9 May 1973–26 November 1974.

References

Hoet 1752–70, vol. 1 (1752), pp. 208, no. 53, and 246, no. 6; J. Smith 1829–42, vol. 4 (1833), p. 97, no. 74, as Érard sale 1832;[10] Blanc 1857–58, vol. 2, p. 395; Blanc 1861, vol. 1, p. 336; Hofstede de Groot 1908–27, vol. 1 (1908), nos. 88, 93a; Cook 1914, no. 284; Brockwell 1932, p. 45, no. 284 (132);[11] Schneede 1968, pp. 47, 51, fig. 6; Gudlaugsson 1968, pp. 24, 25nn22 and 40; F. W. Robinson 1974, pp. 49–50, 82, 85, 172, fig. 122; Pasadena 1980, p. 51, ill.; Philadelphia/Berlin/London 1984, p. 253n6; P. Sutton 1986, pp. 218, 341, fig. 319; Pasadena 1989, p. 82, ill.; P. Sutton 1990, p. 108, fig. 3; P. Sutton 1992, p. 123; Blankert 1995, p. 40, fig. 13; Lammertse 1998, p. 118; Van Heemstra 2000, p. 86; Pasadena 2003, p. 71, ill.; Danziger 2004, p. 448; S. Campbell 2010, p. 339, no. 791, ill.; Franits 2010, p. 71, fig. 87; Gifford 2010, p. 164, fig. 87; Roelofs 2010, pp. 110, 124n88 and 90; Du Mortier 2010, pp. 128–53, fig. 87; Waiboer 2012, pp. 40–44, 77, 91, 134, 180 (A-28).

Technical Notes

The vertically grained oak panel is a single board with beveled edges; the uncradled reverse retains the original tool marks. The thin white ground was evenly applied. A rose- or salmon-colored imprimatura covers the ground, imparting a unifying warm tone to the scene. The painting is smoothly brushed in opaque paint as well as thin glazes. The skilled handling depicts different types of materials and textures such as polished wood, silver, glass, tortoiseshell, feathers, and a tapestry cushion. At the upper left, the vibrant green window curtain was painted to appear translucent and dramatically backlit. X-radiograph fluorescence reveals that its brilliant effect was achieved with bits of silver leaf beneath a thin green copper-resinate glaze in the drapery and beneath the pale blue of the sky behind the open window shutter. Infrared reflectography discloses several changes in the composition. Metsu moved the canopy bed farther to the right along with the darkened archway and painted over a plate or similar object originally placed to the right of the blue-and-white Chinese porcelain behind the window. The chair at the lower left corner originally faced out, and the pattern of folds in the young woman's skirt has also shifted slightly. The painting has a significant amount of chemical abrasion. In the face, throat, and white cape of the young woman, the losses and discolored retouching impair the delicate brushwork and subtle coloring of these areas. Numerous glazed passages have been disturbed: in the white tablecloth, the rose-colored underpainting is visible beneath thin layers of white and gray, but losses of the upper layers have made it slightly difficult to read. Scattered retouching is fairly widespread and noticeable as a result of discoloration. The natural-resin varnish layer is thin, with no discoloration.
—*Rosamond Westmoreland with Devi Ormond*

Signed but not dated, *Woman at Her Toilette* was probably painted shortly after 1657, when Gabriel Metsu moved to Amsterdam.[12] As in his other paintings from this period, such as *A Musical Party* (fig. 56a), here Metsu carefully manipulated architecture, light, figures, and objects to create a coherent space that concentrates attention on the central subject. Metsu's oblique view of the corner of a room, defined by two walls, wooden floor, and coffered ceiling, is a compositional device often employed in contemporary paintings by Gerrit Dou (1613–1675) and his followers.[13] Metsu relieved the dark, enveloping atmosphere of the room with natural sunlight that passes through the open window and

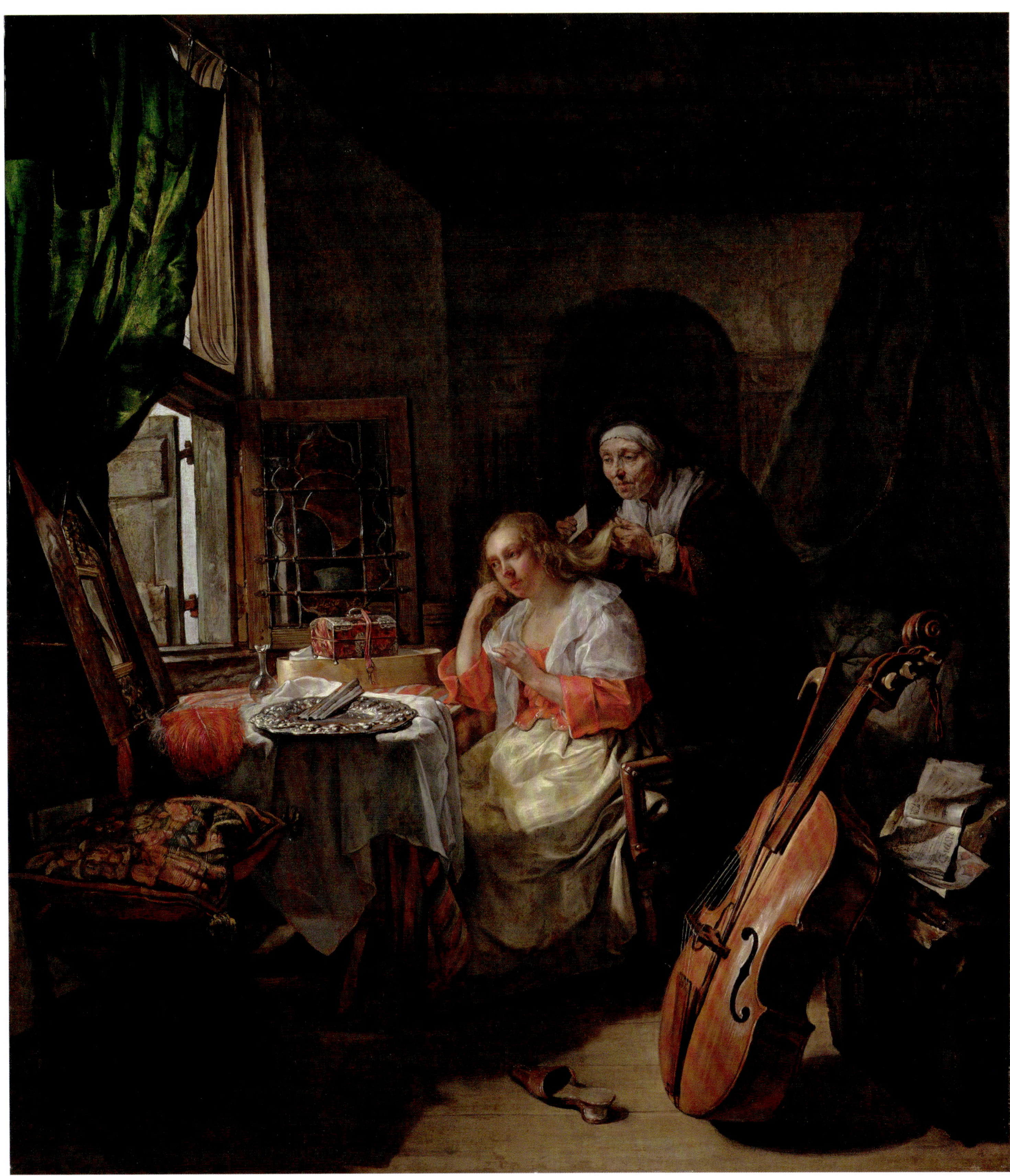

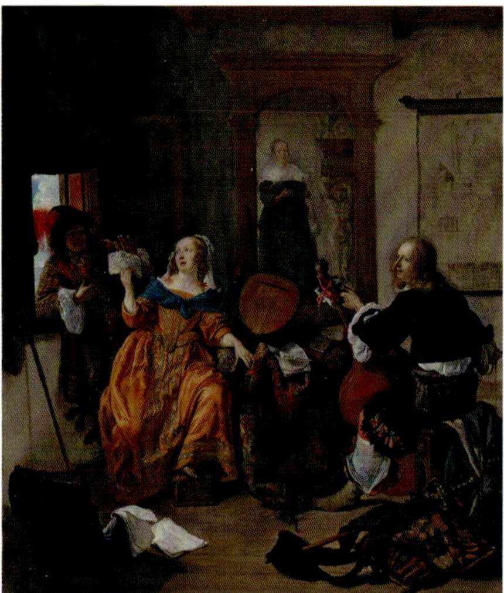

Fig. 56a. Gabriel Metsu, *A Musical Party*, 1659, oil on canvas, 24½ × 21⅜ in. (62.2 × 54.3 cm), The Metropolitan Museum of Art, New York.

over objects on the dressing table, illuminates the figure of the seated woman and the face of the maid, and finally comes to rest on the graceful form of the five-stringed violoncello leaning against a trunk in the lower right corner.[14] The passage of sunlight emphasizes the continuity of interior and exterior space, suggested by the leaded window, which opens into the room, and its shutter, which opens outward. Metsu introduced and framed the scene by positioning a "Spanish stool" (also known as a "back stool") with a tasseled tapestry cushion in the left foreground and the violoncello on the right. On the upper left is a green curtain, pulled back from the window by an expensive, molded-silver mirror encased in a protective wooden box with open doors. In the right background the tentlike canopy of the bed continues the line of the violoncello.

Related to the theme of Venus at her toilette, the subject of a woman engaged in such activity suited the quieter and more introspective character of Dutch paintings after 1650. Metsu and his contemporaries Gerard ter Borch (1617–1681), Frans van Mieris I (1635–1681), and Gerard Dou frequently represented the subject of a woman looking at herself in a mirror, either held in her hand or on a table; often she is elegantly attired in colorful satins. Metsu's *Young Woman at Her Toilette* (Wallace Collection, London), for example, depicts a modestly dressed young woman looking at herself in a mirror, a comb resting in her hand on the table. The artist drew on the viewer's familiarity with the positive associations of the mirror and comb with introspection and spiritual cleansing without specific reference to emblems.[15] More important was the way in which the focus of the woman's gaze draws the viewer to her unspoken thoughts.

In the Pasadena painting one is drawn into the shadowy interior by the light and by the pensive character of the woman who fingers a long strand of her hair as a maid quietly brushes her loose, blond hair. Once captivated by this intimate world, one gradually comprehends the scene and the luxurious details: the ostrich feather lying on the table next to the ornate silver plate on which rests a folded paper;[16] the jewelry casket of red tortoiseshell with silver mountings resting on top of a wooden box used to store a starched ruff; the Chinese bowl seen through the glass of the open window; the shoe on the floor, the violoncello, and the sheets of music set in the foreground against the backdrop of the canopy bed. The overstuffed tapestry cushion with four large tassels and the green curtain contribute to the impression of luxury and ease associated with high status.

The informal appearance of the young woman *en déshabillé*, the cast-off slipper, and the opened canopy of the bed distinguishes her from the proper housewife in Metsu's painting in the Wallace Collection, as well as from the woman with her maid represented in Dou's closely related painting, *A Young Woman at Her Toilet* (fig. 56b), and Ter Borch's *A Woman Having Her Hair Combed by a Maid*, ca. 1670 (The Leiden Collection, New York).[17] The prominent placement of the violoncello and the chair with the lush, distorted cushion in the foreground of Metsu's painting suggests, furthermore, the recent presence of a visitor. Music making could refer to both honest and illicit love: it was a metaphor for harmony, the companion of pleasure, and the balm for sorrow in allegories of love.[18]

Unlike his contemporaries Dou and Ter Borch, who represented elegant young women groomed by young maids, in the Pasadena painting Metsu juxtaposed a fashionable young woman with an older maid dressed in an outmoded costume. The contrast of youth and age, especially in the context of a mirror, which reflects truth, often alludes to the vanity of youth and "Superbia" (pride), one of the seven deadly sins.[19] In Jan Miense Molenaer's (1610/11–1668) *Allegory of Vanity* (fig. 56c) and Jacob Duck's (ca. 1600–1667) *Woman Playing a Theorbo* (Indianapolis Museum of Art), for example, beautifully dressed women are accompanied by an older woman. In each of these paintings, however, a skull, and in the latter an hourglass, clearly associate the painting with the theme of *vanitas*.[20] The attribution of the same meaning to Metsu's painting is unsupported by specific emblems. It must, therefore, remain a question whether, in the late 1650s, when emblematic readings of sophisticated paintings were on the wane if not outmoded and uncommon in his work, Metsu would have intended his painting to carry a negative warning.

Although the 1717 sale in Amsterdam refers to it only as "Een juffer die gekamt werd" (A woman having her hair combed), it is possible that the work would have been recognized as an allusion to a specific subject. Metsu's depiction of an old woman grooming the younger woman is strikingly similar to depictions of the Old Testament heroine Esther at her toilette painted by artists working in Amsterdam, especially in the circle of Rembrandt. Like Metsu's *Woman at Her Toilette*, Rembrandt's *Esther Preparing to Intercede with Ahasuerus*, dated 1637 (National Gallery of Canada, Ottawa) and in

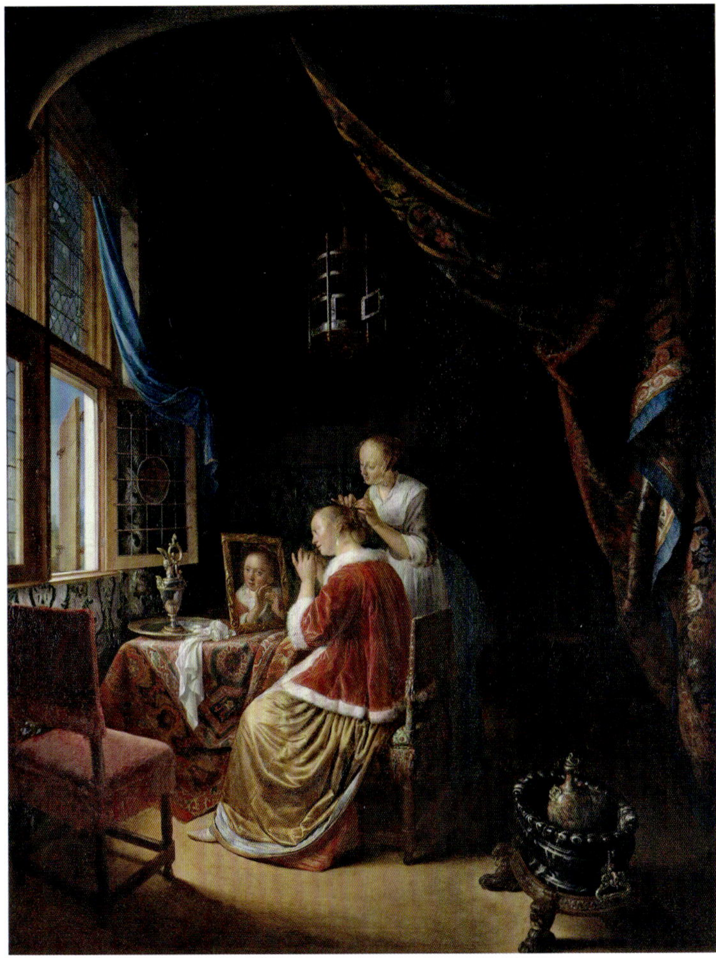

Fig. 56b. Gerard Dou, *A Young Woman at Her Toilet*, 1667, oil on panel, 22⅞ × 29¾ in. (58 × 75.5 cm), Museum Boijmans van Beuningen, Rotterdam.

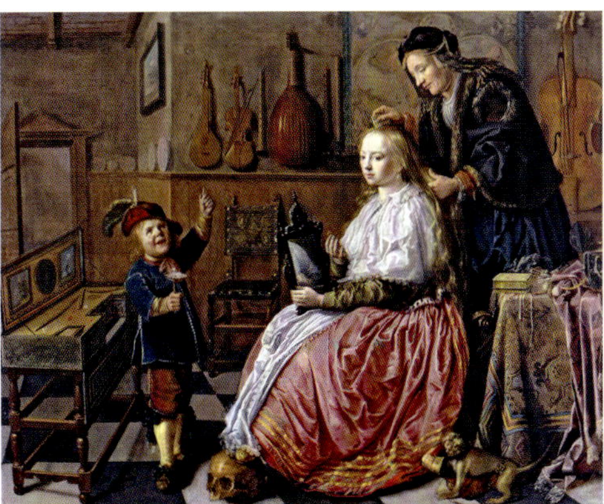

Fig. 56c. Jan Miense Molenaer, *Allegory of Vanity*, 1633, oil on canvas, 40¼ × 59 in. (102 × 127 cm), Toledo Museum of Art, Toledo, Purchased with funds from the Libbey Endowment, Gift of Edward Drummond Libbey.

particular Johannes van Noordt's (active 1621–52) *The Toilette of Esther* (fig. 56d) represent a beautiful, richly dressed young woman seated at her dressing table surrounded by objects of wealth and staring pensively as an older woman combs her hair.[21] Madlyn Kahr points out the significance of this motif for the story of Esther: "The part that her hair played in her self-abasement accounts for the artist's picturing her fully clad in her regal attire and having her hair groomed as the crowning touch in the reinstatement of her beauty."[22]

The story of Esther was very popular in literature and art during the seventeenth century in the Netherlands, where the heroine was admired as an example of fortitude, having triumphed through her piety.[23] Esther, a beautiful, young Jewish woman living under the domination of the Persians, was chosen by King Ahasueras to be his queen. Upon learning of a plot by the court official Haman to massacre all the Jews in the kingdom, Esther dressed herself in splendor to go to Ahasueras, even though to do so without an invitation was punishable by death.[24] The king listened to her plea and ordered Haman killed, thus sparing the Jews. The pensive quality of Metsu's young woman, like Rembrandt's and Van Noordt's, focuses attention on her inner mind and her decision to debase herself for the sake of her community. This intimate image seems to dominate the references to wealth and lovemaking, to which it is, nevertheless, related.

The display of expensive objects in the Pasadena painting is exceptional within Metsu's oeuvre, suggesting that in addition to creating a rich environment for his subject, these luxury items were intended to appeal to the tastes of a specific patron.[25] Metsu himself probably owned at least some of these objects, such as the richly lobed silver plate, the sculpted mirror encased in a box, the tasseled cushion, and the violoncello, which also appear in other paintings.[26]

The first known reference to the Pasadena painting is in 1717, when it was sold from the estate of Jonas Witsen, who held various positions in Amsterdam, lived on the south side of the Keizersgracht (today no. 674), and owned three plantations in Suriname. At the end of the seventeenth century the Witsens were one of the most powerful families in Amsterdam, instrumental in establishing and building trade with the West and East Indies as well as with Russia and China.[27] They were also significant collectors. Jonas Witsen's father, Jonas Cornelis Witsen (1647–1675), died before the birth of his only son. Jonas was adopted by his uncle Nicolaas Witsen (1641–1716), the famous burgomaster of Amsterdam, who had no surviving children.[28] It is possible that Jonas inherited the Pasadena painting and a painting by Metsu of a harpsichord player from his grandfather Cornelis Jan Witsen (1605–1669), a collector and important patron of the arts, sciences, and exploration.[29] Three other paintings by Metsu, including a self-portrait, were owned by Jonas's second cousin Lambert Witsen (1681–1746), who lived in the house at 327 Keizersgracht built by their grandfather Cornelis in 1660.[30] A contemporary described the house as filled with paintings, suggesting that Cornelis may have acquired the five paintings directly from Metsu.[31] The use of expensive silver to evoke sunlight behind the curtain in the Pasadena painting suggests it was commissioned.

The details of the Pasadena painting and perhaps the Old Testament story of Esther would have appealed to Cornelis Witsen. In 1659, the year before the completion of Witsen's new house on the Keizersgracht opposite the Schouwburg

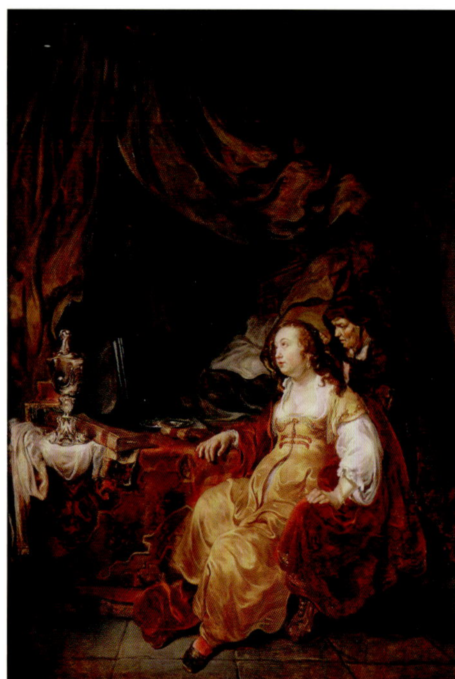

Fig. 56d. Johannes van Noordt, *The Toilette of Esther*, n.d., oil on panel, 41½ × 30¾ in. (105.5 × 78 cm), private collection, Europe.

theater, Johannes Serwouters (1623–ca. 1668) published the first edition of his play *Hester, of de Verlossing der Jooden* (Esther, or the Deliverance of the Jews). The figure of Esther as an exemplum of fortitude and civic virtue would have interested a community leader as well as his contemporaries who regarded political duty as a religious obligation. The inclusion of costly items also appears to reflect Witsen's specific interests and taste. The catalogue of the 1717 sale of his grandson Jonas's effects lists numerous musical instruments, including at least three "extraordinarily beautiful" viola da gambas, and many music books in all languages.[32] The sale also included several mirrors in boxes, four tapestry stool cushions, and three green curtains.[33] In 1790 the sale of the collection of Jonas Witsen's grandson, also named Jonas (1733–1788), which he had inherited from his father, Jonas (1705–1767), included wood boxes with silver mountings from the East Indies, perhaps like those displayed by Metsu. The small Chinese bowl seen through the glass of the opened window in Metsu's painting may refer to Cornelis Witsen's fascination with China,[34] while the prominently placed silver plate recalls the work of the famous silversmith Johannes Lutma (1584–1669), who made a profile sketch in black chalk of his patron Cornelis Witsen for a commemorative coin.[35]

1. Hoet 1752–70, vol. 1 (1752), p. 208; the sale, pp. 205–10, includes 119 lots. The large collection included paintings and rarities. A sale of his furnishings took place on 23 March 1717; see Chr. P. van Eeghen 1946. Roelofs 2010, pp. 110, 124nn88 and 90, does not mention the Witsen sale but suggests that the Pasadena painting was included in two other collections: Jacob Jacobsz. Hinlopen (1644–1705) and Debra Popta (1644–1700), estate, Amsterdam, 23 November–5 December 1705, "Een kemment Vrouwtje van Metzu"; and Johannes Smit (d. 1720), estate, February 1720, Amsterdam, "Een Kamstertje van Metsu." The first reference seems to indicate that the woman herself is combing her hair and the second reference is to a chambermaid, whereas the Witsen catalogue says that she is being combed, indicating the presence of a second woman. The Van Leyen sale mentions that the figures are full size. The separation of the Smit and Van Leyen sales by no more than two months and the differences in descriptions suggest that there may have been different paintings on the market. Metsu painted at least one other work that represents the subject of a woman combing her hair. In *Young Woman at Her Toilet* (Wallace Collection, London) a woman sits at a dressing table holding a comb in her right hand as she stares into a mirror. She is represented alone and close up so that the viewer sees her only from the knees up. The Pasadena painting is Metsu's only painting of the subject with full-length figures.

2. Joachim Rendorp was Vrijheer van Marquette and incumbent burgomaster of Amsterdam. See Molhuysen and Blok 1911–37, vol. 10 (1937), pp. 799ff.

3. Probably one of the brokers for the sale, Johannis Eberlein.

4. The entry mistakenly notes the painting is on canvas. Buchanan 1824, vol. 1, pp. 349ff., mentions visiting Reynders's collection in Brussels in 1817. Corneille-Louis Reynders may have been the man by that name who was born in 1755 and later served as consul of Spain in Amsterdam and died in Cleve.

5. Sébastien Érard was a famous maker of pianofortes and harpsichords with a factory in England. Buchanan 1824, vol. 2, pp. 189f., notes that Érard formed a small collection of high-quality Flemish and Dutch pictures and that he shipped many to England. See A. de Vries 1981.

6. Cited by Hofstede de Groot 1908–27, vol. 1 (1908), no. 88. This may be William Clowes (1780–1851), one of the founders of the Primitive Methodist Connexion in 1810.

7. An oval red-wax seal stamped "LE ROY" is attached to the back of the panel. Two other red wax seals are unidentifiable.

8. Cook 1914, no. 284, notes that the painting was bought in 1879 from E. H. Phillips.

9. Sir Francis Cook was the head of one of the great merchant houses of London. He acquired his first paintings as a young man in Italy and began collecting seriously ca. 1869 with the guidance of Sir Charles Robinson.

10. Smith's description of no. 74 matches the Pasadena painting, but he mistakenly notes that the scarlet negligee worn by the young woman is trimmed with ermine.

11. The author's description states, "On the floor near the violoncello is a slipper; on the right, a dog. Signed on an open book placed on the box." There is, however, no evidence of the dog in the Pasadena painting.

12. F. W. Robinson 1974, p. 49, dates it 1658. Schneede 1968, p. 47, dates it 1654–58.

13. See Liedtke 1988, pp. 100f.

14. With thanks to James Young, who identified this instrument in an email in 2005 (NSM).

15. Emblematically, a mirror could represent the sense of sight, referring either to vanity or to truth and inward reflection. Likewise, combing the hair was associated with both pride and mental and spiritual cleansing. Visscher 1614, pt. 1, no. 9, illustrates a comb for the adage "Purgat et ornat" (To cleanse and adorn). In 1632 Jacob Cats advised, "Comb, comb again and again, and not only the hair, but also that which lies hidden inside, to the innermost bone." Translated from Cats [1632] 1658, p. 173, by Otto Naumann in Philadelphia/Berlin/London 1984, p. 158.

16. Although letters are often included in scenes of a lady at her toilette, alluding to the story of Bathsheba or Esther, here the paper appears

to hold decorative "sticks," ornamented with red at the ends, used by women to hold their coiffures in place.

17. Gudlaugsson 1959–60, no. 234.

18. See Philadelphia/Berlin/London 1984, p. 344, no. 119. For discussion of music in art, see De Mirimonde 1966.

19. Schneede 1968, p. 51, refers to the depiction of sight in Abraham Bosse's (1602–1679) series of prints representing the five senses.

20. In addition to the skull beneath the younger woman's foot, the map of the world and the candle in the Molenaer painting refer to *vanitas*.

21. De Witt 2007, no. R12, pp. 228f.

22. Kahr 1966, p. 235.

23. Esther 1–10. See Kahr 1966, pp. 228–44. On p. 228n1, she lists among the literary works based on the book of Esther in the Dutch Republic during the seventeenth century the play *Esther, ofte 't Beeldt der Ghehoorsaamheid*, 1638, by the Amsterdam physician Nicolaes Fonteyn (b. ca. 1600); Jacob Cats's (1577–1660) poem *Vashti* in his *Toneel der mannelicke achtbaerheyt*, published in several editions, some illustrated, in the early seventeenth century; Jacobus Revius's (1586–1658) tragedy *Haman* (Deventer, 1630); and the popular and often reprinted play by Johannes Serwouters, *Hester, of de Verlossing der Jooden* (Amsterdam, 1659). Kahr also notes the frequent incidental references to the story of Esther in other writings.

24. The Apocrypha, which were included in the States-General Bible of 1637 as well as in earlier Protestant Bibles, vividly describe Esther's preparations. See Kahr 1966, p. 235.

25. The prominent portrayal of silver and the five-stringed violoncello probably appealed to the nineteenth-century collectors Corneille-Louis Reynders and Sébastien Érard. See note 5 above.

26. The plate reappears in Metsu's *Music Company* (National Trust, Waddesdon Manor, Aylesbury); the cushion in *The Music Party* (Metropolitan Museum of Art, New York); and the sculpted mirror in a box appears in a painting known only from an engraving by the French printmaker Pierre Charles Lévesque (1736–1812).

27. See Hart 1952.

28. Molhuysen and Blok 1911–37, vol. 4 (1918), pp. 1473, 1478; and Van der Aa 1852–78, vol. 7 (1852), p. 11. See also Rietbergen 1986, pp. 121–34, and note 2 above.

29. Jonas Jonasz. Witsen (1676–1715), Amsterdam (sale, Zomer, Raket & Benoorden, Amsterdam, 31 March 1717, lot 22: "Een Clavecimbael-Speelster van Gabriel Metzu, zeer fraei"). Regarding Cornelis Witsen, see Molhuysen and Blok 1911–37, vol. 4 (1918), p. 1471; and Amsterdam 1992, p. 156. Regarding some of his commissions of works of art and literature, see Blussé and Falkenburg 1987.

30. Lambert Witsen inherited the house from his father, Lambert Cornelisz. (1638–1697), the brother of Jonas Cornelisz. and Nicolaas Cornelisz. Witsen. Jonas Jonasz. Witsen was Lambert's only surviving male cousin, who could have shared in their grandfather's collection. Lambert Witsen's sale took place through Philippus van de Land, Amsterdam, 25 May 1746, and included no. 4, "Een Juffer met een satyne kleed aan, die met een Heer Musiceert, teder en puyk. Door Gabriël Metzu, h. 1 v. 4 en een half d., br. 1 v. 1 d.," sold for ƒ1010; no. 5 "Een Heer zittende te paart, die een glas wyn vool wert geschonken door een Juffer, en een Knegt die het paard vast hout voor een buyte plaats die te koop staat, deftig behandelt door denzelven, h. 2. v. 4 d., br. 1 v. 9. d.," sold for ƒ615; and no. 6 "Het Pourtrait van den vermaarde Konst-schilder Gabriël Metzu, door hem zelfs geschildert, h. 6 en een half d., br. 5 d.," sold for ƒ40.

31. Van Gent 2012, p. 44. Cornelis Witsen's collection included allegorical paintings on the ceiling as well as paintings, sculpture, and medals. Jan Vos (1610–1667) dedicated several poems to the collection, including poems praising the portraits of Cornelis Witsen and his wife, Katrina Opsy, by Bartholomeus van der Helst (1613–1670) and a marble bust by Erasmus Quellinus I (1584–1640; Vos 1726, vol. 1, pp. 264–65). Vos also described the allegorical paintings by M. Bloem on the ceiling of Witsen's house (Vos 1726, vol. 1, pp. 377–70), but does not mention other paintings.

32. Sale, 1717, lots 5–7: "Een ditto [Extraordinaire schooner] Fiool de Gamba." There were also ten violins, an extraordinarily beautiful bass violin, three guitars, flutes, a harpsichord by Andreas Ruckers (1578–after 1645), etc.

33. The mirrors in boxes were listed as no. 41, "1 Toiletspiegel in Verlakte Lyst met Doosen, etc."; no. 42, "1 Compleet zwart met Goud Verlakt Toilet met Spiegel, doosen en toebehooren"; and no. 43, "1 Rood ditto met ditto, als boven." No. 80 mentions four cushions: "4 Genaajde Stoelkussens." The green curtains—no. 75, "3 Groene Casjanten Gordynen"—may have been particularly prized because of the value attached to green dye. A similarly backlit green curtain appears in Metsu's *Musical Party* (Metropolitan Museum of Art, New York); like the Pasadena painting, it is painted over metal leaf. See Technical Notes and Liedtke 2007, vol. 1, p. 456, where it is identified as gold leaf.

34. In 1655 Cornelis Witsen commissioned Johannes Nieuhof (1618–1671) to accompany the first Dutch legation to the Chinese emperor and record in drawings and writing everything he saw along the way. Elaborately illustrated and translated into French, English, German, and Latin, Nieuhof's travel log, *Het gezantschap der Neêrlandtsche Oost-Indische Compagnie* (Amsterdam, 1665), was responsible for stimulating the craze for chinoiserie and Chinese porcelain and lacquerwork. See Amsterdam 1992, pp. 167f., and Blussé and Falkenburg 1987.

35. See Hart 1952, pp. 88ff.

57

In the style of Daniël Mijtens I

Dutch
Delft ca. 1590–ca. 1647 The Hague

Portrait of a Young Noblewoman

ca. 1620

Oil on canvas, 77⅛ × 48½ in. (195.9 cm × 123.2 cm)
The Norton Simon Foundation, F.1965.1.042.P

Provenance
Stanford White (1853–1906), New York (sale, American Art Association, New York, 4–6 April 1907, lot 119, as Juan Carreño de Miranda). [Meredith Galleries, New York, sold 12 June 1945 to]; [Duveen Brothers, New York, as Mijtens, sold 1965 to]; The Norton Simon Foundation.

Exhibited
Richmond 1957; on loan, Metropolitan Museum of Art, New York, 30 December 1965–16 April 1973; on loan, Dorothy Chandler Pavilion, Los Angeles, 10 May 1973–30 March 1984.

References
Breuning 1946, p. 7; Douglas 1951, pp. 163, 165f., ill., "may represent a princess of the House of Brunswick"; La Farge 1959a; S. Campbell 2010, p. 444, no. D37, ill.

Technical Notes
The support is a plain-weave canvas with the original tacking edges removed. Several old tears were repaired by the lining. There is a thin white ground. Interventions from past treatments prevent identifying the layer structure, but there appears to be a dark underpainting in some areas. The paint, both thin and opaque, was smoothly brushed out and blended. The artist may have employed dark glazes for transparent shadows, but these have been removed, as well as much of the original paint in the background. The lace and embroidery of the dress probably was painted originally with impasto in those details, now compressed by the lining process. The volume of the drapery at the upper right side and the depth of the space at the upper left is difficult to read, as paint is severely abraded here. The background has been extensively toned and/or repainted, and there are numerous areas of retouching, including a tear at the woman's proper left hip and losses near her proper left shoulder, at the bottom right of the painting, scattered areas in the skirt, and at her proper right temple. A synthetic-resin varnish was applied in 1987.

This full-length portrait of an elaborately dressed young woman standing on a Persian carpet, her hand resting on a table draped with green velvet and gold fringe, is characteristic of the international style of court portraiture produced during the first quarter of the seventeenth century.[1] Sold in 1907 as a painting by the Spanish painter Juan Carreño de Miranda (1614–1685),[2] the portrait was published in 1951 as a work by Daniël Mijtens I, a Dutch painter active at the English court from 1618 to 1634.[3] The formal pose and the limited setting and scale of the portrait recall documented portraits by Mijtens, such as *Elizabeth, Queen of Bohemia* (fig. 57a).[4] Mijtens is further suggested by the gentle expression and soft transitions in the modeling of the figure. The description of the sitter's hands, however, is less delicate than that in his autograph portraits, pointing to the possibility that this is a product of his workshop or by another artist working in his style.

The formal pose and carefully described costume define the sitter's station in life rather than her individual character. The profusion of lace is the clearest indication that this is a woman of exceptional wealth and high status. During the seventeenth century, lace was often even more valuable than jewels. A treasured heirloom, it was to be passed on to future generations. The rich needle lace covering the bodice of the dress was probably adapted from one of the popular woodcut illustrations published by Cesare Vecellio (ca. 1521–1601) in *Corona delle nobili et virtuose donne* (Venice, 1593–1600).[5] Single white lace marguerites with red inner petals, probably intended to represent a flower known as a "crown of thorns," secure the lace of the bodice and ornament the sitter's shoulders (fig. 57b). Similar flowers form the waistband of a white apron with a drawnwork design of marguerites and borders of needlepoint lace. Red silk ornamented with silver embroidery and jewels and lined with white silk form full-length pendant sleeves hanging from her shoulders, while fitted dress sleeves of similarly decorated red silk extend to just below her elbows, terminating in deep double cuffs of needle lace. Fine silver chains wound several times around her lower arms form delicate bracelets. A relatively small ruff supported in the back by an underproper frames her face and softly coiffed brown hair.[6] A jeweled silver tiara and a stiffened band of lace ornament her hair. A pentimento

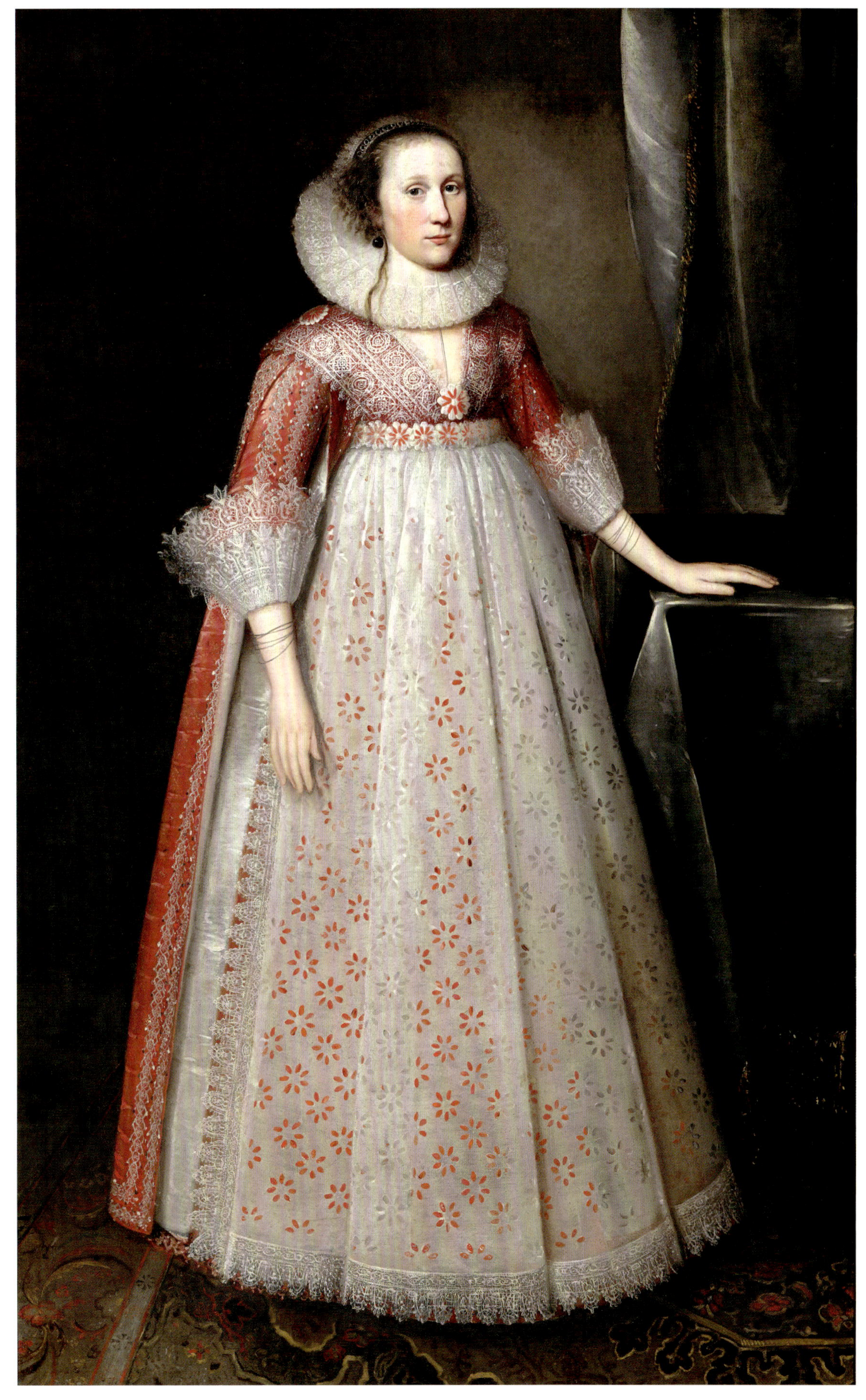

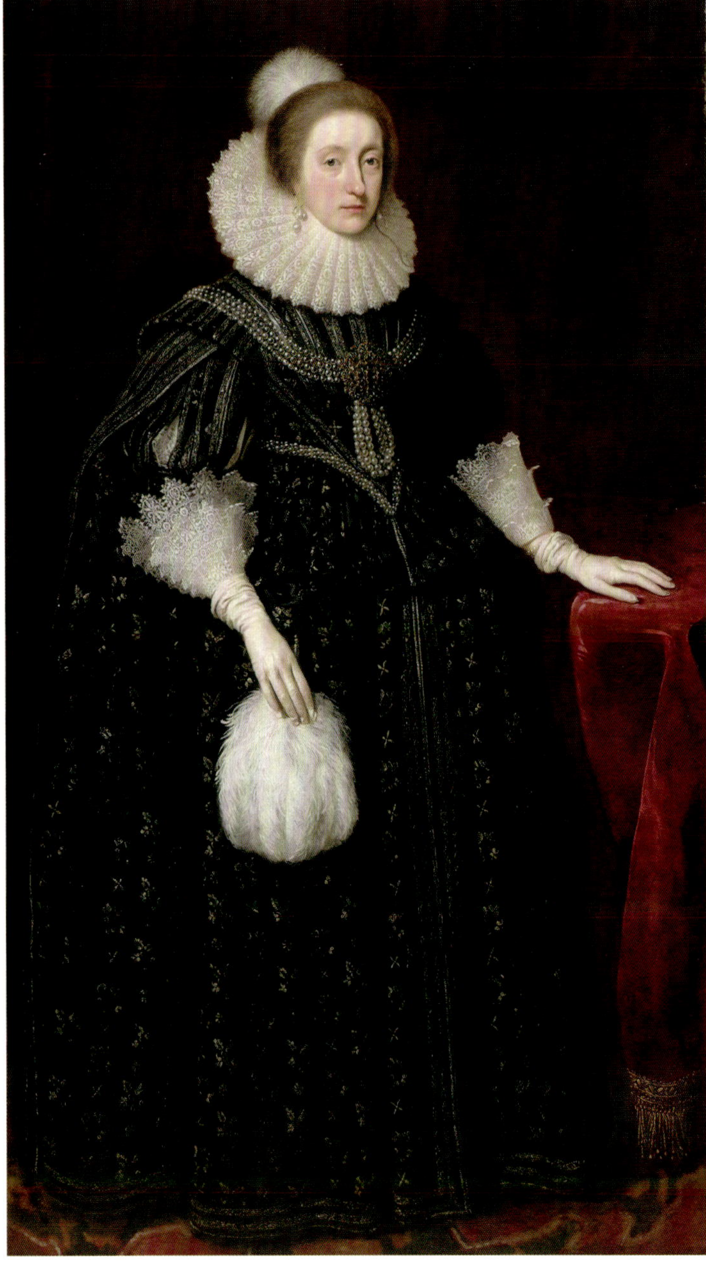

Fig. 57a. Daniël Mijtens I, *Elizabeth, Queen of Bohemia (1596–1662)*, 1626–before 7 March 1627?, oil on canvas, 77⅜ × 45 in. (196.4 × 114.4 cm), Royal Collection, London.

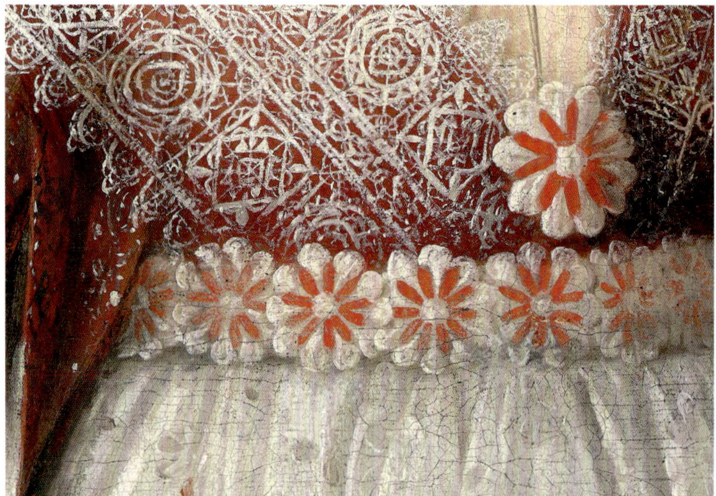

Fig. 57b. Detail of marguerites on dress.

suggests that a spray of ornamental flowers or berries originally may have fallen from her tiara on the viewer's right as in a portrait by Michiel Jansz. van Mierevelt (1567–1641) of *Amalia, Countess von Solms*, wife of the Dutch stadtholder Frederik Hendrik (1584–1647), Prince of Orange (ca. 1625; National Museum Het Loo Palace, Apeldoorn).[7]

The identity of the sitter is not known. The costume and coiffure of the woman in the Pasadena portrait were worn around 1620 by women at the court of James I (r. 1603–25) in London as well as in The Hague, where James's daughter Elizabeth Stuart (1596–1662) had taken refuge in 1620 with her husband, Frederick, the deposed King of Bohemia.[8] The single lock of hair hanging from the coif on one side was an affectation of Elizabeth Stuart, appearing in virtually all of her portraits from the 1620s and early 1630 as well as in portraits of members of her court.[9]

Details of the sitter's unusual costume may provide clues to her identity. The extensions of her lace cuffs, which are in the shape of tulips, may indicate a relationship with the Netherlands, while the overall lace pattern of marguerites may indicate that her name is Margaret.[10] The flower detail could also refer to Saint Margaret of Antioch, the virgin-martyr who was the patron saint of childbirth. In contrast to the tight-fitting bodices of dresses worn by contemporary women at the court, the high-waist style of the dress worn by the sitter may indicate that she is pregnant.[11]

1. Traces of gold paint beneath the roughly applied black paint in the background of the Pasadena painting may suggest that the painting originally had either a more elaborate setting or an inscription.

2. See Pérez Sánchez 1985 and Pérez Sánchez 1986.

3. Douglas 1951, p. 166, citing C. H. Collins Baker.

4. Both paintings are virtually the same size; the London painting (196.2 × 114.3 cm) is only slightly narrower than that in Pasadena.

5. Published in at least five volumes between 1593 and 1600, it served as the model book for lace throughout Europe during the seventeenth century. I am grateful to Sandra Rosenbaum, former curator-in-charge of the Doris Stein Research Center for Costume and Textiles, Los Angeles County Museum of Art, for her assistance in identifying and describing the costume of the sitter.

6. For a description of an underproper, also known as a whisk in England and a *suportasse* in France, see Bendall 2017.

7. See The Hague 1997a, p. 167, fig. 155.

8. See, for example, Mijtens (style of), *Anne Vanlore (d. 1625), first wife of Sir Charles A. M. Imare Caesar* (?), which is dated 1624 (Collection T. Cottrell-Dormes, Esq., Rousham House; photo consulted at the Witt Library, Courtauld Institute of Art, London), as well as Mijtens, *Lady Simon Clarke*, dated 1621 (Spink & Son, London; photo consulted at the Witt Library, Courtauld Institute of Art, London). The central sections of the aprons in both of these portraits are composed of horizontal panels of lace framed by wide borders of lace and narrower lace edges.

9. See, for example, Mijtens's portrait *Elizabeth Bassett, First Wife of William, Duke of Newcastle*, dated 1624 (Collection of the Duke of Portland), who wears a similar lock on her left side.

10. One possibility at the Dutch court is Margaretha Maria von Daun, Gravin van Falckenstein, married in 1616 to Walraven van Brederode, heer van Cloetingen, Vianen, Ameide en Noordeloos, who was knighted in 1618. Michiel Jansz. van Mierevelt painted her portrait in 1624 as a pendant to a portrait of her husband, who died in 1618 or 1619 when his horse fell on the ice (Van der Aa 1852–78, vol. 1 [1852], p. 389). Both portraits appear in the Heidelberg inventory of 1685 of the collection of the King and Queen of Bohemia. Hoogsteder 1986: Mierevelt's portrait of Margaretha is listed as HB XIII, 21. The pendant of her husband is R 89.

11. Portraits of pregnant women, often with exaggerated bumps, such as *Portrait of a Woman in Red*, 1620 (Tate Britain, London) by Marcus Gheeraerts II (1561/62–1636), were popular at the English court during this time, regarded as celebrations of the woman's fertility and the hoped-for birth of an heir, as well as recording for posterity the woman herself. See Hearn 2002, pp. 40–51.

58

Attributed to Jan Miense Molenaer

Dutch
Haarlem 1610/11–1668 Haarlem

Portrait of a Gentleman

Late 1630–35

Oil on panel, 32¾ × 23 in. (83.2 × 58.4 cm)
The Norton Simon Foundation, F.1972.52.P

Provenance
Senator Ferdinand Raphaël Bischoffsheim (1837–1909), Brussels and Paris, as attributed to Dirck Hals in 1886,[1] by descent to his granddaughter; Marie-Laure Henriette Bischoffsheim (1902–1970), Vicomtesse de Noailles, Paris, until at least 1947, as Thomas de Keyser.[2] [Galerie V(ictor) Mandl, Paris, as "Dutch, 17th century," consigned 1950 to];[3] [Kunsthandel Pieter de Boer, Amsterdam, as "Thomas de Keyser," returned to]; [Galerie V(ictor) Mandl, Paris].[4] [Wildenstein, Paris, in 1963, as Thomas de Keyser].[5] [Galerie Les Tourettes, Basel/Dr. Otto and Anne Wertheimer, Paris and Basel, as "Molenaer," by 1971, consigned June 1972 to]; [Schaeffer Galleries, New York, stock no. 2709, sold December 1972 to]; The Norton Simon Foundation.

Exhibited
Brussels 1886, no. 83;[6] on loan, Fogg Art Museum, Harvard University, Cambridge, 30 November 1972–4 December 1974.

References
Hymans 1886, p. 428, as Dirck Hals, illustrated p. 433 with an etching by M. A. Ronner; De Wyzewa and Perreau 1890, ill. p. 116, as attributed to Dirck Hals; P. Sutton 1986, p. 216, as Molenaer; Raleigh/Indianapolis/Manchester 2002–03, p. 93, fig. 3, "attributed to Jan Miense Molenaer"; Nehlsen-Marten 2003, p. 323, no. 413, ill. p. 419; S. Campbell 2010, p. 349, no. 892, ill.

Technical Notes
The support consists of a single vertically grained board, possibly oak. A vertical split at the right side has been repaired by attaching a second panel of the same dimensions and a cradle. The white ground is a thin layer that does not mask the texture of the wood grain. Microscopic examination did not reveal any underdrawing or underpainting. Paint was thinly applied in the monochromatic background in a glaze-like consistency. The face is finely modeled. Handling in the costume varies, with thin, almost sketchy brushwork in the suit and green stockings, while details of lace, braid, buttons, and ribbons are given texture with delicate drops and swirls of white paint applied with a small brush. Light colors such as the collar, glove, and flesh tones are heavier and more opaque. Prior cleaning resulted in abrasion of the thin, glazed passages, most evident under magnification. There is extensive retouching in the foreground and the left background and very little in the figure. The crack at the right side has been overpainted from top to bottom. An older, natural-resin varnish has been coated with a synthetic resin.

Dramatically lit, a man dressed in a brown ensemble including a hat, cloak, and gloves gestures with his gloved left hand as he turns to address the viewer. His posture, parted lips, and gesture animate the otherwise undescribed scene. This small, full-length portrait blends elements associated with both Haarlem and Amsterdam, where merry-company scenes and group portraits often include similar posing figures. Full-length portraits of any scale, however, were rare in Haarlem; Frans Hals (1582/83–1666) is known to have painted only one such work, *Willem van Heythuysen* (Bayerische Staatsgemäldesammlungen, Munich), and that on a grand scale. The production of small-scale paintings of single, full-length figures was centered in Amsterdam, where Pieter Codde (1599–1678) and Thomas de Keyser (1596/97–1667) popularized the genre during the 1620s and 1630s.[7] Other Amsterdam artists, most notably Pieter Jansz. Quast (1605/06–1647), also made popular paintings and drawings of cavaliers standing in dramatic, self-assured poses. Transformed into prints by Salomon Savery (1594–1678), these images were not intended to represent specific people but rather character types and costumes.[8]

The Norton Simon Foundation purchased *Portrait of a Gentleman* in 1972 as a work by Jan Miense Molenaer, based on an attribution made by J. G. van Gelder and supported by Seymour Slive.[9] The painting had previously been attributed to Dirck Hals (1591–1656) and to Thomas de Keyser.[10] Although the attribution to Molenaer, who began his career in Haarlem and moved to Amsterdam in 1636, has been questioned, it is tentatively accepted here and by Dennis Weller in the 2002 exhibition on Molenaer.[11] The presumption that Molenaer painted single, full-length portraits is suggested by the accomplished quality of his large group portraits, such as *The Wedding Portrait of Willem van Loon and Margaretha Bas*, 1637 (Museum Van Loon, Amsterdam). Commissioned by major Amsterdam patrons, these portraits suggest that Molenaer had a reputation for portraiture as well as for genre scenes. Molenaer's production of portraits is further suggested by the discovery, via infrared reflectography,

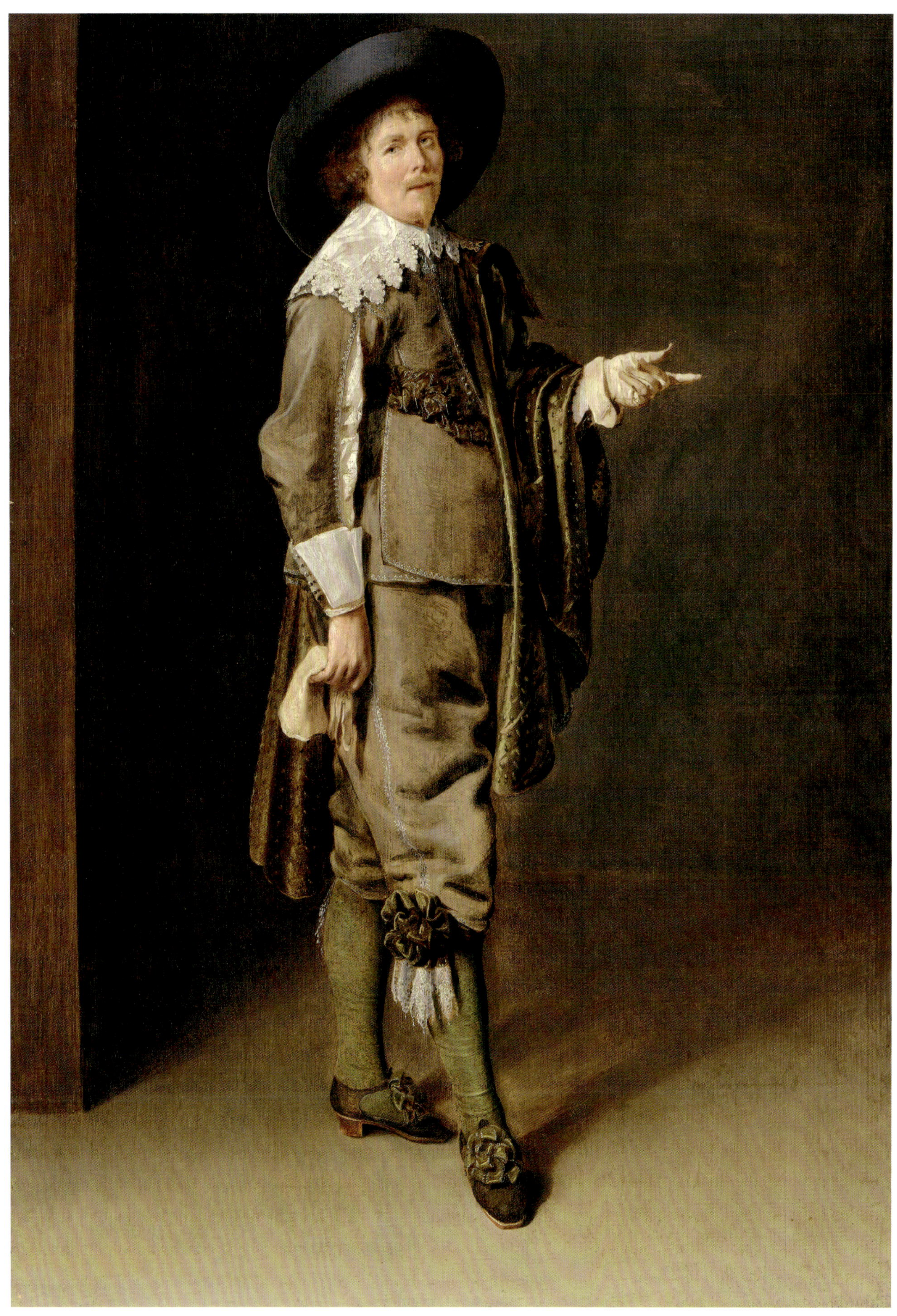

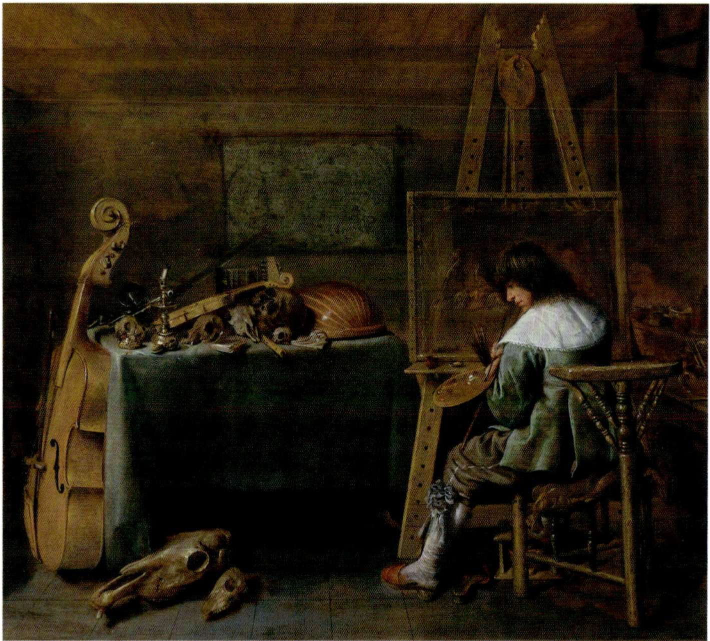

Fig. 58a. Jan Miense Molenaer, *A Painter in His Workshop*, 1630, oil on panel, 16 ½ × 18 ⅞ in. (42 × 48 cm), Museum Bredius, The Hague.

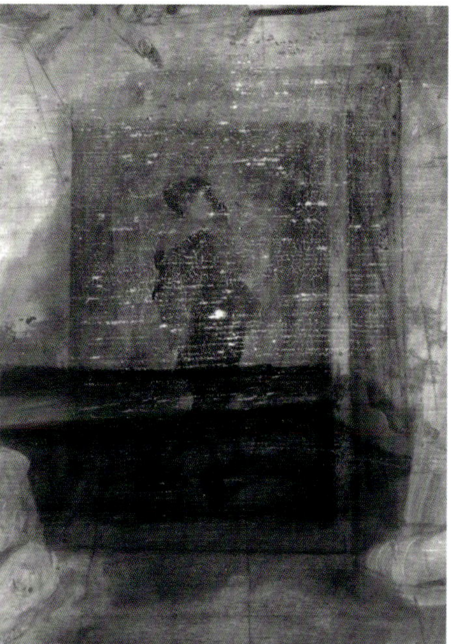

Fig. 58b. Infrared detail of fig. 58a showing painting leaning against table, RKD, The Hague.

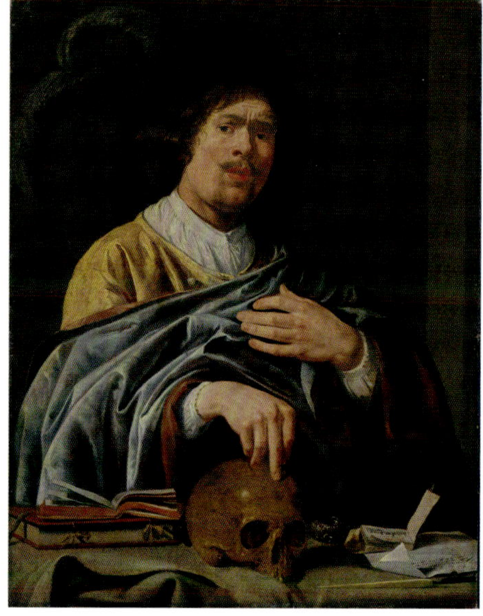

Fig. 58c. Jan Miense Molenaer, *Self-Portrait with Skull*, ca. 1639–40, oil on canvas, 34 ⅝ × 27 ⅛ in. (88 × 69 cm), Alte Pinakothek, Bayerische Staatsgemäldesammlungen, Munich.

that a similar painting of a standing man was originally included in *A Painter in His Workshop*, attributed to Molenaer (figs. 58a–b).[12]

The theatrical pose of the man in the Pasadena painting, the style and color of his costume, and the overall warm brown tonality are similar to portraits and genre paintings by Molenaer, such as *Allegory of Fidelity* (Virginia Museum of Fine Arts, Richmond) and the Van Loon wedding portrait.[13] The costume is that of a fashionable Dutch burgher, a citizen of the upwardly mobile bourgeoisie, in the mid- to late-1630s: brown doublet with slashed sleeves and flat, lace-trimmed collar and full breeches gathered below the knee and trimmed with green ribbons edged with gold. A collared cape made of matching brown fabric (probably wool) and lined with greenish satin woven in a lozenge design is draped over his left shoulder. Garters, one of the primary decorative accessories in the wardrobe of fashion-conscious men of wealth, fasten the close-fitting pea-green silk stockings just below the knee. Large rosettes made of the same green ribbon trimmed with gold and lace ornament the garters and shoes.

Despite these similarities to works by Molenaer, there are also differences. The brushstrokes in the Pasadena painting are more refined than the loose handling of paint typical of Molenaer's genre scenes. The description of the man's costume also differs from the way Molenaer typically described fabric with a broad "scribble of light" on the top edges of folds, a technique common to artists working in Haarlem around Dirck Hals. In the Pasadena painting, light highlights the folds only on the sleeve of the man's proper right arm. The trousers are defined by broad areas of shadows that suggest the realistic fall of fabric only generally.[14] Although these differences bring into question the attribution to Molenaer, they do not deny it. Rather, they probably reflect the demands of a formal portrait and suggest a date after Molenaer's move to Amsterdam in 1636, when Pieter Codde's smoothly applied paint and interest in cast shadows influenced his style.[15] Molenaer employed more refined brushwork and palette, for example, in the Van Loon wedding portrait.

Comparing this figure to that of the young man in *The Departure of the Prodigal Son* (private collection), Dennis Weller has suggested that the Pasadena painting may represent the Prodigal Son.[16] The pose and expression of *Portrait of a Gentleman*, however, are characteristic of contemporary small-scale, full-length portraits of single figures. Painted with little reference to setting, these portraits portray ambitious and increasingly wealthy Dutch burghers. The self-confident, even defiant, attitude of the Prodigal Son, who stands with his right arm akimbo, differs from the reserved character of the Pasadena sitter. Without attributes or additional evidence, identification of the man in the Pasadena painting as the Prodigal Son seems, therefore, less likely than the presumption that the painting is a portrait of a man who introduces his wife, whose portrait would have hung as a pendant on the viewer's right. The facial type and expression of the man in the Pasadena painting are, in fact, somewhat similar to Molenaer's own appearance in *Self-Portrait with Skull* (fig. 58c), suggesting that this might have been a portrait of the artist himself.

1. Hymans 1886, p. 431. The residence of Bischoffsheim is not noted, but the exhibition described by Hymans consisted of paintings owned by Belgians. Bischoffsheim, who was born and resided in Brussels and died in Pau, maintained a home in Paris on the Place des États-Unis. He owned a sizable collection of paintings.

2. According to the annotated mount of the photograph of the painting at the RKD. Marie-Laure Bischoffsheim inherited and lived in her grandfather's home in Paris. She and her husband, Charles, Vicomte de Noailles (1891–1981), were major patrons of modern art and design in France during the 1920s. Regarding Bischoffsheim and especially the Vicomte and Vicomtesse de Noailles, see Jullian 1964; see also Gee 2007 for additional bibliography.

3. Victor Mandl was a middleman for many people in France who were trying to sell pictures during and after World War II.

4. The DeBoer/Mandl provenance was relayed by Pieter de Boer, Amsterdam, in conversation with Cynthia Kortenhorst-von Bogendorf Rupprath, 1 May 2002.

5. RKD mount.

6. Unidentified retrospective exhibition of paintings in Brussels in 1886 noted by Hymans 1886.

7. See, for example, Codde's *Young Cavalier* (Ashmolean Museum, Oxford), signed and dated 1625, and *Portrait of a Married Couple* (Mauritshuis, The Hague), signed and dated 1634. Both Codde and De Keyser may have been trained by the Flemish portrait painter and dealer Barend van Someren (1572–1632), who had immigrated to Amsterdam and had business dealings with Frans Hals and others in Haarlem.

8. See Hollstein 1949–2010, vol. 24, p. 29, nos. 63ff.

9. Correspondence from Seymour Slive to the Wertheimers, May 1971 (Schaeffer Gallery records, GRI).

10. Based on the print published by Hymans 1886, Nehlsen-Martin 2003, pp. 234f., fig. 261, accepts the painting as a work by Dirck Hals, noting, "Der Habitus, die Kleidung und die Gesichtszüge des Kavaliers könnten eine Zuschreibung der Vorlage an Dirck Hals erlauben."

11. Raleigh/Indianapolis/Manchester 2002–03, p. 93. Christopher Brown in the Norton Simon Museum galleries, 1984, considered the handling too tight for Molenaer. Pieter Biesboer in the Norton Simon Museum galleries, 1995, and Cynthia Kortenhorst von-Bogendorf Rupprath, in conversation in The Hague, 1997, tentatively accepted the attribution to Molenaer.

12. See Buijsen 2001, pp. 22–25, figs. 1–6, especially p. 25, fig. 6. The painting within the painting stood on the floor, leaning against the table; it was probably painted out when the artist made adjustments to the table. The scale of the painting within the painting appears to have been similar to that of the Pasadena picture. Infrared reflectography was performed with a Hamamatsu C 2400-07 equipped with an N2606 IR vidicon, a Nikon Micro-Nikkor 1:2.8/55 mm lens, a Heliopan RG 850 (or RG 1000) filter, with a Lucius & Baer VM 1710 monitor (625 lines). Digitized documentation was done with a Meteor RCB framegrabber, 768 × 574 pixels, colorvision toolkit (Visualbasic). The IRR-assembly reproduced here was made with PanaVue ImageAssembler and Adobe Photoshop by Margreet Wolters.

13. Contemporary paintings by Codde are rendered, by contrast, in a gray tonality. See the discussion of Molenaer's theatricality in Westermann 2002–03.

14. Areas of shadow define the general shape of the breeches by suggesting the folds. In some places the folds appear to have been defined first by a line, which marks the deepest point of the shadow, a technique often used by draftsmen and engravers. See, for example, the pen-and-ink drawing on parchment by Gerrit Adriaensz. de Heer (1606–after 1652), *Portrait of a Man (Johannes Bogaert?)*, 1634 (Groninger Museum).

15. The treatment of shadows is, in fact, similar to that in Codde's *Portrait of a Painter Smoking at His Easel (Self-Portrait)* (Museum Boijmans Van Beuningen, Rotterdam) and in his famous painting of the melancholic young scholar in Lille, for which see New York 1992–93, no. 13, pp. 99–102.

16. Raleigh/Indianapolis/Manchester 2002–03, p. 93.

59

Aert van der Neer

Dutch
Gorinchem 1604–1677 Amsterdam

Soldiers and Villagers Leaving a Burning Village

1637

Signed and dated, lower right: "A • van der • Neer • 1637 •"

Oil on panel, 14 5/16 × 20 5/16 in. (36.4 × 51.6 cm)
Norton Simon Art Foundation, M.2010.1.87.P

Provenance
Anonymous (sale, Palais Galliera, Paris, 6 April 1976, lot 47, sold to); [Sylvia Blatas, Paris, for]; Norton Simon, Los Angeles (sale, Christie's, New York, 12 June 1981, lot 37, ill., unsold); Norton Simon, Los Angeles, bequest 1993 to; Jennifer Jones Simon Art Trust, Los Angeles, bequest 27 September 2010 to; Norton Simon Art Foundation.

Exhibited
On loan, New Orleans Museum of Art, 1976.

References
Bachmann 1982, pp. 22–23, ill. 7; Schulz 2002, pp. 28, 246, no. 461, ill. 81; S. Campbell 2010, p. 394, no. 1323, ill.

Technical Notes
The support, a horizontally grained oak panel, consists of a single board with shallow beveled edges. Conservation treatment in 1976 by Marco Grassi included cleaning to remove layers of varnish and overpaint, followed by careful retouching of the sky. A long horizontal crack near the bottom edge extending from the left to the right side was repaired in 1984 by George Bisacca and Giovanni Marussich, with Bernie Rabin finishing the inpainting. The thin, smooth ground is cream colored. The artist surrounded the painted image with a thinly painted medium-brown border at each edge of the panel. A portion of the lower end of the left edge shows a gap between the brown border and the blue sky that exposes the ground. There is a considerable amount of underdrawing in graphite, much of which is apparent with unassisted vision. For example, the church spire and the buildings to the left of it were completely underdrawn. X-radiography reveals several changes at the bottom left corner of the painting, including the addition of a brown horse. The front log was originally painted to extend farther to the left. To the left of the large trees, faint dark shapes of pentimenti are visible where the light sky was painted over lines of dark pigment. The artist employed near-liquid paint in very thin glazes in the large dark trees at the right. The light-colored elements (buildings, trees in the center and middle ground) were handled rather loosely; a quick shorthand was enough to render the figures. Multiple layers of very thin glazes in numerous colors achieve a soft atmospheric effect of fire and smoke. Overall, the paint is quite well preserved. There are minimal losses along the repaired crack. The present varnish is a synthetic resin.

Dated 1637, when Aert van der Neer was already in his mid-thirties, *Soldiers and Villagers Leaving a Burning Village* is among the artist's earliest known paintings.[1] The palette is limited to tones of ochre and pale white applied in thin washes of paint with accents of red and black. An amber-tinged cloud of smoke billowing from the ruins of a burning Gothic church establishes the tone of the painting. It also forms an important compositional element, arching over the ruined church and echoing the shape of the trees. Recalling the knotted trees painted by Alexander Kierincx (1600–1652), the trees reflect the light of the fire and serve as a repoussoir on the right side of the painting. Van der Neer described the glow of the fire on the weathered trunks by fluidly painting a mixture of dark brown pigment and glazes. This limited use of glazes is typical of Van der Neer's work until approximately 1642, after which he increasingly used them to create luminous effects.

Soldiers and Villagers Leaving a Burning Village is also Van der Neer's earliest known portrayal of fire, a subject he would treat on many occasions in his later career, when he excelled in rendering the effect of fractured light reflected on dramatically lit night landscapes. For these later paintings, Van der Neer probably took as a starting point Esaias van de Velde's (1587–1630) portrayals of Dutch towns engulfed by fire in which flames shoot into the night sky, illuminating buildings, landscape, and the people who watch or evacuate their possessions (fig. 59a). In contrast to the nighttime drama of these paintings, however, the Pasadena painting portrays the aftermath of a fire that has destroyed a church and still smolders the following morning.[2]

Van der Neer executed a complete underdrawing of the composition on the prepared panel before beginning to paint. The drawing, which is especially visible in the thinly painted architecture, indicates the form of the smoke and describes shadows as well as outlines. Van der Neer also appears to have sketched in the figures, although pentimenti reveal that he rethought their positions in the final painting.[3] The elegant, spindly dogs were, however, painted entirely

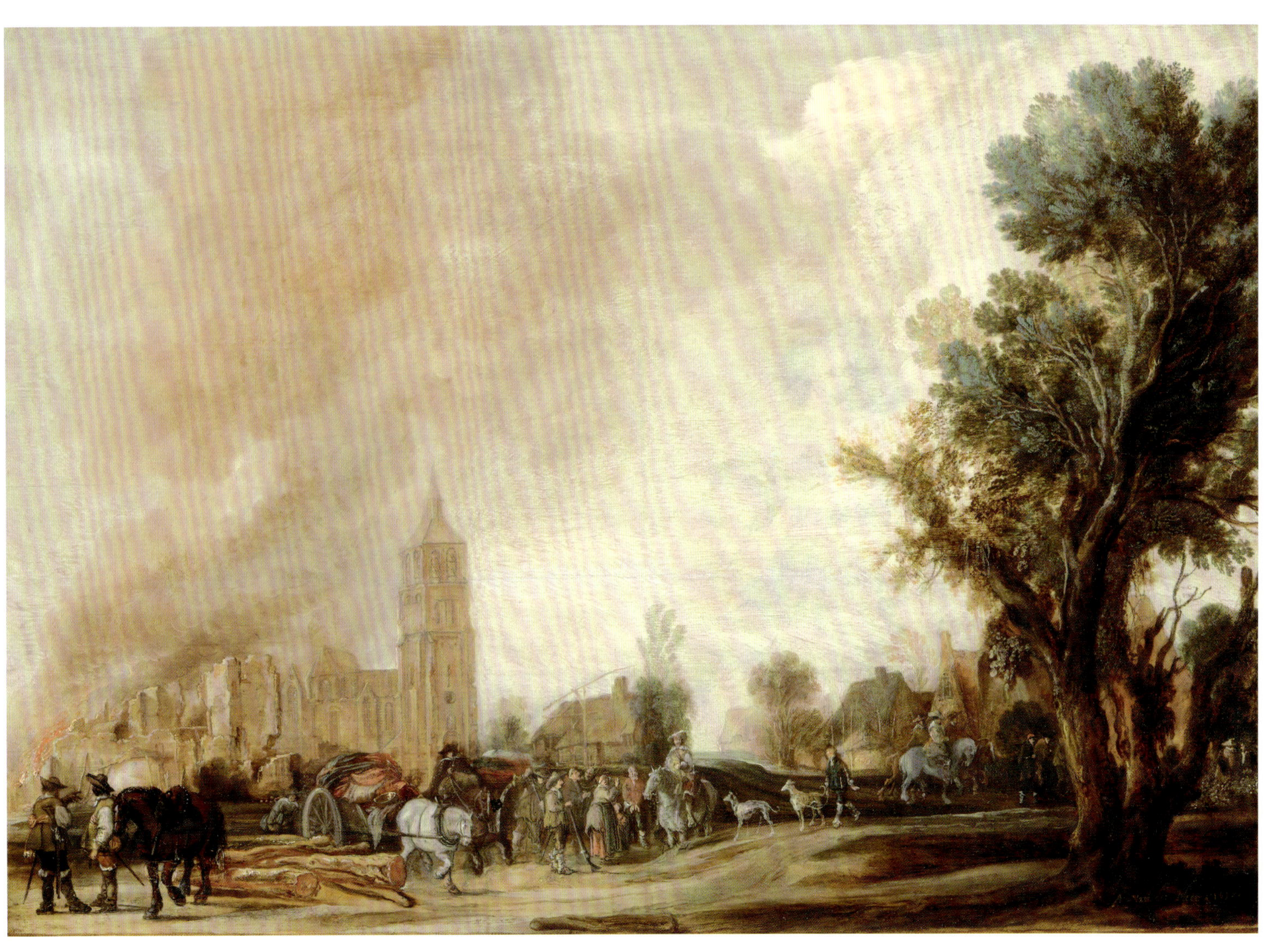

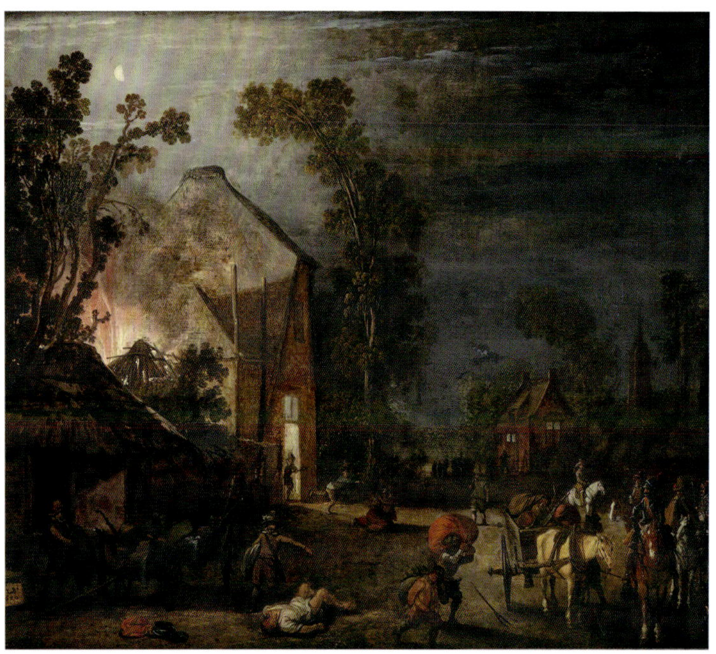

Fig. 59a. Esaias van de Velde, *A Village Looted at Night*, 1620, wood, 13¾ × 15½ in. (35 × 39.5 cm), Staatens Museum for Kunst, Copenhagen.

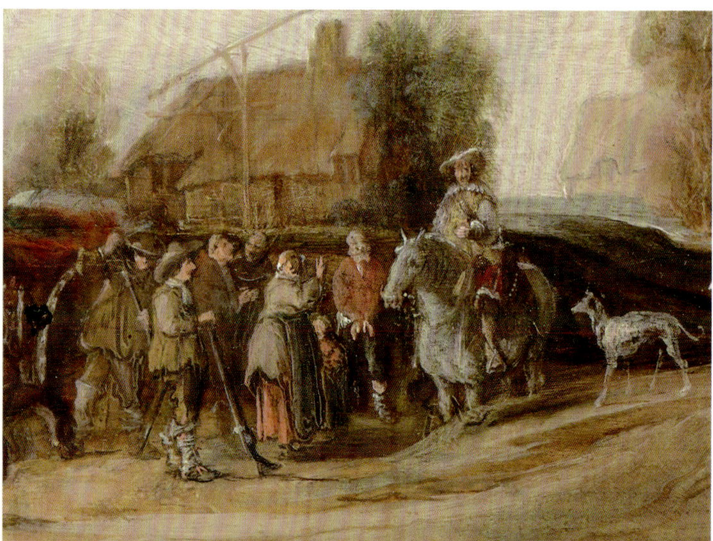

Fig. 59b. Detail of central group.

freehand with spontaneous, delicate lines that attest to the excellent condition of the painting.

Van der Neer depicted the primary figurative scene from a distance, separated from it by two soldiers who stand in the foreground left and whose significance becomes apparent only on close inspection of the central scenes set in the middle ground (fig. 59b). Employing free, calligraphic shorthand to describe the facial expressions and body language of the diminutive figures, Van der Neer skillfully captures the emotions of the agitated villagers who petition a gentleman on horseback, as well as the dejected postures of the manacled prisoners, whom the cavaliers drive off in the distant right.

The actions of the soldiers—driving a cart loaded with household goods away from the fire, cleaning their guns, or taking prisoners—and the seemingly desperate reactions of the townsfolk indicate that the soldiers are responsible for the conflagration. Van der Neer's painting recalls the genre of representations of cavalry battles and skirmishes, ambushes by soldiers and bandits, and images of soldiers relaxing in makeshift inns that were inspired by the turbulent experience of the Eighty Years' War (1568–1648). After the initiation of the Twelve Years' Truce in 1609, the maritime provinces, including Holland, were largely spared the violence they had suffered during the early years of the long war with Spain, but the continuing victimization of the inland countryside and the garrisoning of soldiers in the major cities served as reminders of the previous terror, even in areas where the war no longer raged.[4]

In its representation of peasants suffering at the hands of the army, *Soldiers and Villagers Leaving a Burning Village* is unique in Van der Neer's oeuvre. The petitioners recall those in paintings by Esaias van de Velde and others in which a man, hat in hand, kneels obsequiously before a finely dressed cavalier, presenting him with a ransom for people or cattle or to prove the payment of a *brandschat* or *sauvegarde*, purchased by individuals or communities as protection against violence.[5] In the Pasadena painting, however, it is not a man but an angry woman and at least one Franciscan monk who confront a gentleman on horseback.

The presence of the Franciscan monk in connection with the burning church suggests that Van der Neer may have been appealing to a specific Catholic audience and possibly referencing a specific historical event. Bachmann notes the resemblance of the tower of the ruined Gothic church to the 60-meter-high tower of Sint Janskerk (completed ca. 1570), the medieval church in Gorinchem (Gorcum) where Van der Neer lived before his move to Amsterdam in 1632.[6] The city, which until the late sixteenth century had two Catholic parishes and a Franciscan priory, had a history of difficult relations between Catholics and Protestants.[7] The harsh oppression of the Reformed Calvinist Church under the Spanish had been followed by suppression of the practice of Catholicism.[8] The most significant event occurred in 1572, six years after the iconoclastic storm (*beeldenstorm)* had swept through the Netherlands, leading to the destruction of icons and other Catholic images and monuments. In that year Gorinchem and Dordrecht fell to the Geuzen (Sea-beggars), a confederacy of Calvinist nobles—who were also adventurers and pirates—that opposed the Spanish rule of the Netherlands. Nineteen Franciscan monks in Gorinchem and additional Catholic clergymen were captured and cruelly tortured. A letter from the rebel leader, William of Orange (1533–1584), entreating those in authority to leave priests and members of religious orders unmolested failed to dissuade the Geuzen, and the nineteen "Martyrs of Gorcum" who refused to denounce their faith and the pope were hanged by Protestant troops.[9]

Whether the Pasadena painting refers to this infamous event or more generally to the sufferings of the Catholic community, it highlights the role of the elegantly attired gentleman on horseback who is confronted by the distraught petitioners. In contrast to related works by Van de Velde and others, here the man appears to be a local nobleman rather than an officer. Accompanied by a footman and greyhounds (the ownership of which was restricted to the nobility), he appears to be returning from, or going to, the hunt, uninvolved with the violent activity that preceded his arrival.[10] He may be a reference to one of the influential families in Gorinchem who remained Catholic and helped to curb authorities. Until 1650, the lord over the town of Gorinchem and the surrounding countryside was Jacob van Paffenrode (ca. 1591–1652), whom the stadtholder Prince Maurits (1567–1625) had installed as *drost* in 1617, following the death of Roelof van Arkel (1565–1616).[11] As lord of the town and surrounding countryside, it would have been to him that people took their complaints and requests. In his biography of the artist, Arnold Houbraken mentions that Aert van der Neer worked in his youth as a manager for the Lord of Arkel, *drost* of Gorkum.[12] It is possible, therefore, that in the Pasadena painting the artist was making a reference to the benevolence of his former employer and possibly to a specific historical event. The sympathy for the past suffering of Catholics may also reflect the greater tolerance of Catholicism in the Dutch Republic after 1632, when the States General accepted, if reluctantly, Frederik Hendrik's (r. 1625–47) petition to permit the practice of the Catholic religion in all places that fell to the States General in that year.[13]

1. According to Bachmann 1975, p. 215, the earliest landscape by Van der Neer with a date is *Landscape with a Farmhouse* (with Pieter de Boer, Amsterdam, 1972), dated 1633. However, Schulz 2002, no. 1065, fig. 75, color pl. 23, calls the 1633 painting (now in a private collection) a collaboration of Van der Neer and Joachim Govertsz. Camphuysen (ca. 1601–1659).

2. A similar daytime scene of a fire is portrayed in *Soldiers Plundering a Village*, attributed to Pieter Post (oil on canvas, 77.5 × 112 cm), formerly J. Paul Getty Museum, Los Angeles.

3. The figure of the soldier leading the horse and cart on the left has been adjusted.

4. Citizens were often forced to house and feed soldiers and to work for them without pay; they were also subjected to plunder and robbery by (the often unpaid) soldiers, mutineers, and bandits who roamed the countryside. On the suffering of the countryside, see Parker 2004; Gutmann 1980; and Fishman 1982, pp. 2–33. Although officially opposed by the authorities and discussed in numerous contemporary pamphlets, abuses of country folk occurred. During the 1590s Prince Maurits initiated reforms of the military code, which were later expanded; these reforms included rules of behavior toward farmers and hostages. See Gutmann 1980, pp. 54–71; and Van Maarseveen 1998, pp. 159–63.

5. See, for example, Willem Cornelisz. Duyster (ca. 1598–1635), *Prisoners before an Office* (Kunsthalle, Hamburg), and Pieter Jansz. Quast (1605/06–1647), *Scene in a Guardhouse* (Fine Art Museum, Krasnodar). A related scene is found among David Vinckboons's (1576–ca. 1632) series of paintings and prints *Troubles of Peasants*. See Czobor 1963, pp. 150–59, ills. 8–9; and Fishman 1982, pp. 31ff. In *Peasant Sorrow* (Rijksmuseum, Amsterdam), Vinckboons depicts the brutality the army inflicted on the citizenry.

6. The tower is the only section of the original church that remains today.

7. The city was besieged throughout its history. In at least one instance, in 1389, it was almost reduced to ashes. See Rademaker 1725, no. 157.

8. Tissink and De Wit 1987, pp. 16–17. Catholics were reduced to second-class citizens, unable to practice their religion openly or to hold public office, although many continued to practice secretly, served after 1601 by itinerant priests.

9. Van Peer 1971, no. 50. Hanged 9 July 1572, the Martyrs of Gorcum were beatified 14 November 1675 and canonized 29 June 1865.

10. Van der Neer represented a similarly attired gentleman on horseback accompanied by a page with a hawk and dogs in *Landscape with a Faulkner and a Horseman on a Country Road; in the Background a Castle*, 1641, long-term loan from the Rijksdienst Beeldende Kunst, The Hague, to the Museum De Lakenhal, Leiden (Schulz 2002, no. 393, fig. 92).

11. Israel 1995, p. 704. *Drosten* and *baljuws* were the key rural magistrates, appointed traditionally by the stadtholder.

12. Houbraken 1718–21, vol. 3 (1721), p. 172.

13. Israel 1995, p. 536. The relaxation of restrictions against Catholics was connected with the desire to open peace negotiations with the Spanish Netherlands in 1632. From this point on, a greater tolerance of Catholicism spread to other regions in the Dutch Republic, so much so that by 1637 a pamphleteer lamented the open toleration of Catholicism.

60

Aert van der Neer

Dutch
Gorinchem 1604–1677 Amsterdam

Winter Scene with Figures Playing Kolf

1655–60

Signed with monogram, lower right on plank: "A V D N" (*V* and *D* superimposed over *A* and *N*)[1]
Oil on canvas, 22 ¾ × 30 ¾ in. (57.8 × 78.1 cm)
The Norton Simon Foundation, F.1972.35.P

Provenance
Charles William Mills (1865–1919), 2nd Baron Hillingdon, Camelford House, Park Lane, London, by 1891,[2] by descent to his son; Arthur Robert Mills (1891–1952), 3rd Baron Hillingdon, Camelford House, Park Lane, London, by descent to his son; Charles Hedworth Mills (1922–1978), 4th Baron Hillingdon (sale, Christie's, London, 7 July 1972, lot 18; sold for 80,000 guineas to);[3] [Edward Speelman Ltd., London; sold 1972 to]; The Norton Simon Foundation.

Exhibited
On loan, Metropolitan Museum of Art, New York, 30 August 1972–19 December 1973; on loan, Princeton University Art Museum, Princeton, NJ, 2 May 1974–17 July 1974.

References
Harding and Harding 1891, p. 21; Pasadena 1980, p. 60, ill.; P. Sutton 1986, p. 218; Pasadena 1989, p. 66, ill.; Schulz 2002, pp. 85, 138, no. 45, ill. 22; S. Campbell 2010, pp. 141, 344, no. 843, ill.

Technical Notes
The support is a plain-weave lined canvas. Very small bits of the original tacking edges remain at the left, right, and bottom edges. The ground layer, which appears to be a warm white, is difficult to isolate because of accumulated old varnishes remaining at the edges. The artist modified the ground color with a dark gray underpainting in the sky, where it is visible at the top edge and intermittently in the light clouds. A golden light brown is under and around the houses at the center right, extending down to the bottom right corner, across the bottom of the painting, and over to the lower left quadrant. At the center of the left edge, both a white and then a gray layer are above the creamy ground color. The sky was scumbled in a thicker, more opaque paint. The remainder of the painting was done in thin washes and translucent glazes, depicting the reflected light in the ice, with fine lines of brown, black, and white paint creating the details of the houses in the village. Van der Neer made numerous changes as he painted, eliminating some figures by painting them out, even changing one to a tree stump in the center foreground. As cleaning has thinned most black areas, it is sometimes difficult to distinguish the original intent. At the right, pentimenti of two standing figures are now partially covered by horizontal strokes of white paint. Above them are two figures—one kneeling, one standing—who are also partially covered by white paint. Subsequently, the increasing transparency of the oil paint revealed the pentimenti, which were perhaps misinterpreted and often abraded. One area of altered paint is inexplicable: the sky at upper right, where countless tiny losses in the form of minute "pits" in the upper light gray layer reveal the dark underpainting. The painting was cleaned and varnished with a thin synthetic resin in 1972 before entering the collection. Retouching is limited to a relatively small area in the sky at the upper right.

Winter Scene with Figures Playing Kolf is a classic example of Aert van der Neer's best paintings, the true subject of which is the way the light of the sun, the moon, or a fire, refracted by clouds and the moist atmosphere, reflects on a neutral landscape.[4] His figures provide anecdotal interest but, like the landscape, function primarily as vehicles for color and light.

The high quality of *Winter Scene with Figures Playing Kolf* suggests a date of 1655–60, the strongest period of the artist's career. Typical of Van der Neer's mature paintings, the large composition is organized around a central body of water; here the frozen water is bordered on the left by the thatched houses of a village and on the right by a less densely populated community of cottages. Rather than a canal, with relatively straight shorelines, Van der Neer represented a meandering river with irregular boundaries, swampy areas, and minor estuaries. Clumps of grass, logs, and fences protrude from the ice at various points, preventing the kind of broad sweep across the ice represented in earlier winter landscapes by Hendrick Avercamp (1585–1634; fig. 60a) and others. Tall trees, denuded by winter, form a coulisse on the left side of the painting; guided by the figures bundled against the wind, the viewer visually moves into the landscape toward the area of brightest light just to the right of center, where two men play *kolf*, a popular antecedent of modern golf, and then back to the horizon. The alignment of

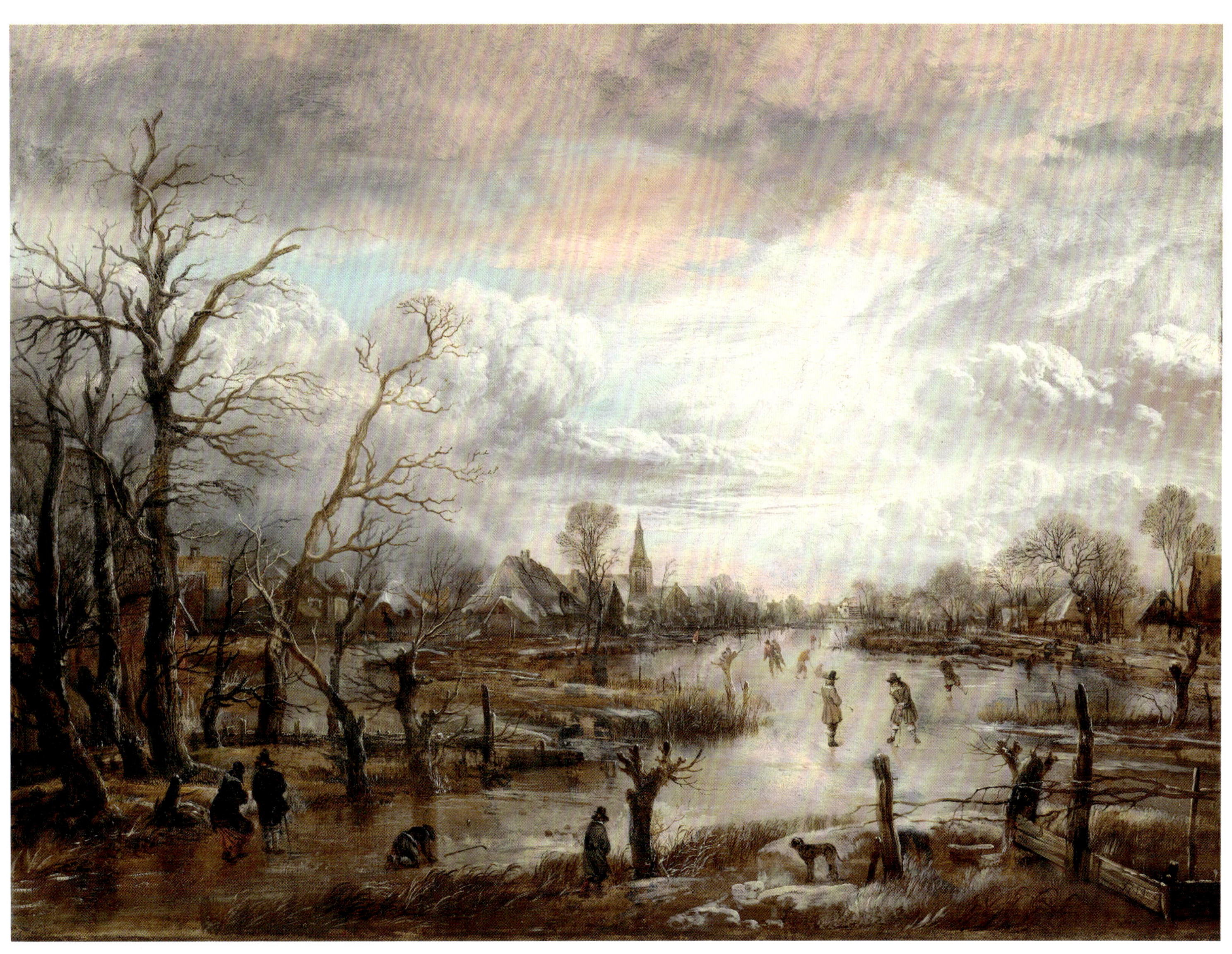

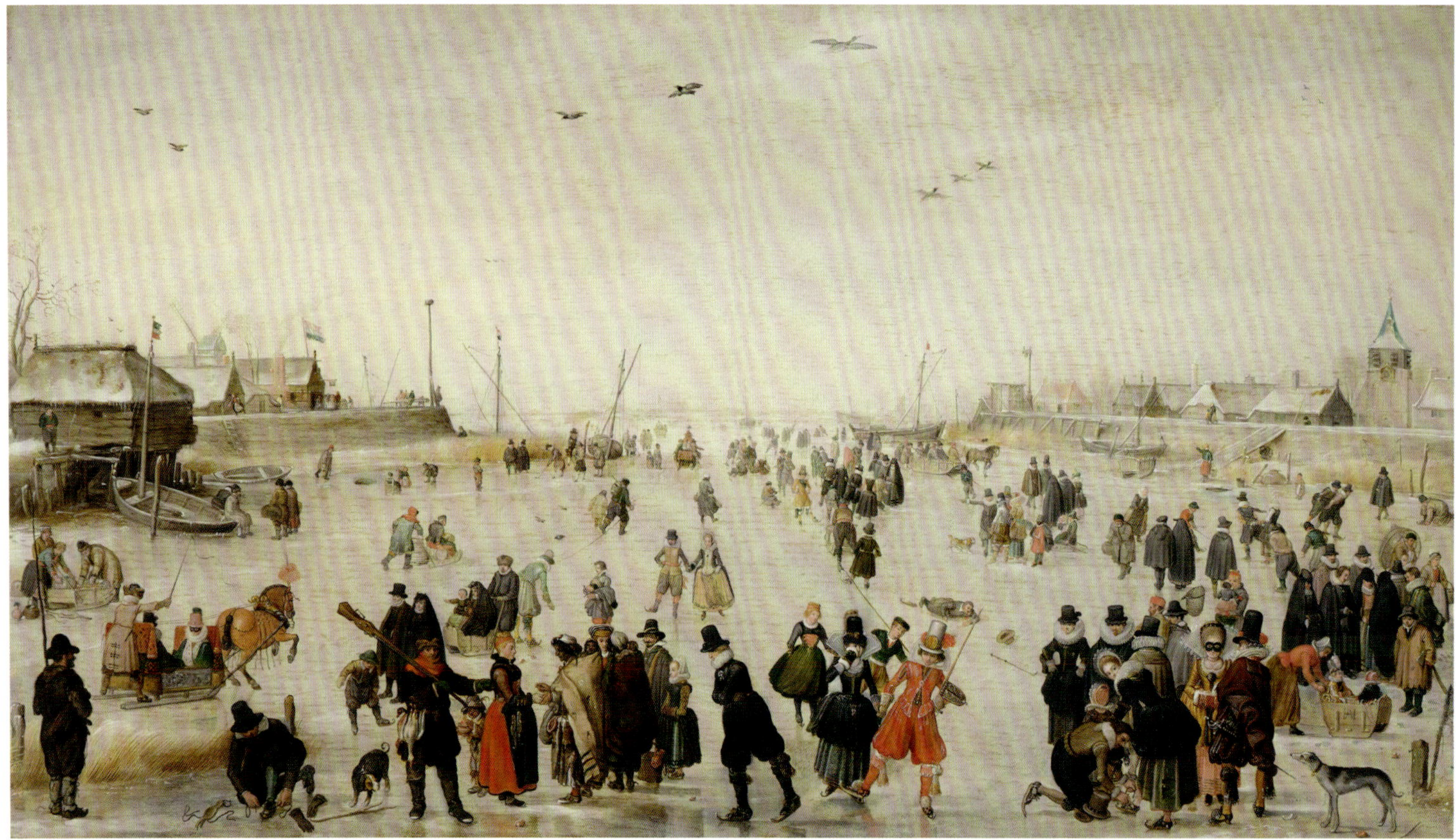

Fig. 60a. Hendrick Avercamp, *Winter Scene on a Frozen Canal*, ca. 1620, oil on panel, 14½ × 25¾ in. (36.8 × 65.4 cm), Los Angeles County Museum of Art.

the weathered tree stump with the spire of the village church marks the central axis of the painting and connects the foreground and the distance. Van der Neer's subtle arrangement of figures and other elements, such as the diagonal placement of the low fence in the right foreground, contributes to the cohesiveness of the composition.

Van der Neer employed a complex technique to create the impression of an enveloping atmosphere and light that seems to radiate from within the picture. Thin washes of color combine with translucent glazes and fine lines of brown, black, and white paint to suggest the barren winter landscape. Here, the setting sun, obscured by a combination of billowing, cumulus clouds and high, thin cirrus clouds with scumbles of white paint, transforms the steely gray winter sky into a luminous, if subtle, display of color: pink, blue, and gray mixed with ample amounts of white. Van der Neer's greatest achievement is the way in which he suggested the reflection of the colors of the sky on the snow- and ice-covered landscape by combining thin washes of color ranging from gray to white over and sometimes under brown glazes. Areas of dark-brown and black as well as white provide accents throughout the painting.

Van der Neer distributed broken areas of light and color to suggest the interrelationship of sky and landscape. Light affects various segments of the landscape in different ways. The brightest area of the painting is the right side, where white paint follows the edges of trees, the road, and logs to suggest the effect of light reflected on the ice. Thin lines of black, brown, and white sketched over the ochre undertone of the canvas describe distant cottages and trees. In the most delicate areas, the artist appears to have used a brush the width of only a few hairs to sketch his forms quickly but deftly in freehand.

On the dominant left side of the composition, the warmer, reddish-orange tone suggests the reflection of indirect light on the houses, trees, and earth. Using thin black lines over darker-toned glazes to define the thatch and general structure of the buildings, Van der Neer added small dots of reddish-orange and white along the peaks of the roofs to emphasize the most brilliant highlights. Softer areas of pink suggest the reflected glow of the rosy areas of the sky on the snow-covered roof of the large house closest to the church. A dark wedge-shaped cloud, which appears to have moved in from the left behind these buildings, accentuates the feeling of a bitterly cold winter day, broken by these glimmers of reflected light.

To suggest the atmospheric effect of decreased visual perception of distant objects, the artist varied his application of paint, using coarse brushstrokes to apply the underlayers of paint at the horizon. The irregular surface breaks up the fine lines applied over it, producing a convincing impression of atmosphere. Van der Neer's portrayal of the haze produced when barren branches are viewed against the winter sky further testifies to his keen observation of atmospheric effects. To achieve this, he softly blurred the grayish background paint—possibly with his finger—before painting the delicate branches of the trees.[5]

The figures provide anecdotal references to the season, continuing the rich tradition first established in the calendar pages of medieval manuscripts.[6] The physical response of a couple walking carefully along the frozen ice, buffeted by the wind blowing from behind them, suggests the cold temperatures. In a similar way, the two men playing *kolf*, which could be played on land or ice with two or four players, represent an activity of the season.[7] Building on these anecdotal details, Van der Neer's control of light and color captured the impression of a crisp winter day.

1. According to Bachmann 1982, p. 25, this is the monogram Van der Neer employed after about 1640. Van der Neer signed *Soldiers and Villagers Leaving a Burning Village* (cat. 59), dated 1637, with a full signature.

2. Harding and Harding 1891 record the presence of the painting at Camelford House, "in the morning room." With thanks to Charles Sebag-Montefiore for verifying in 2002 the inclusion of this picture in this rare publication.

3. Sold by the trustees of his estate. According to Anthony Speelman, the buyer noted on the Kunsthandel Gebr. Douwes photo mount at the GRI, "G. Henderson," was buying for Speelman.

4. Regarding Van der Neer's color, see Bachmann 1982, pp. 93–98; and Kauffmann 1923.

5. Zeldenrust 1983 discusses the technique Van der Neer used in painting *River Landscape by Moonlight*, dated 1645 (Rijksmuseum, Amsterdam), noting his use of his fingers for similar effects. Van der Neer does not, however, appear to have used an incised instrument to relieve the color of the underpaint for highlights in the Pasadena painting as he did in the Amsterdam painting.

6. See The Hague 2001–02, pp. 36ff; Stechow 1968a, pp. 82–100.

7. Van Hengel 1990; and The Hague 2001–02, p. 26. *Kolf* originated in the thirteenth century but became a rage in the seventeenth century, suddenly dropping off in popularity ca. 1700. It was played outdoors on the ground—sometimes on streets or in public squares—or, in winter, on the ice. The players would either set up a pole as their target or choose an existing landmark or object. The goal of the match was to reach the chosen point in the least number of strokes.

61

Jacob Ochtervelt

Dutch
Rotterdam 1634–1682 Amsterdam

Family Portrait

ca. 1670–72

Signed over door center right: "Jac. Ochtervelt"
Oil on canvas, 36⅛ × 31⅛ in. (91.8 × 79.1 cm)
The Norton Simon Foundation, F.1969.12.P

Provenance

Émile Pereire (1800–1875) and Isaac Pereire (1806–1880), Paris (sale, Charles Pillet, Paris, 6–9 March 1872, lot 167, as Jacques Uchtervelt, sold for F3,000 to);[1] [Charles Sedelmeyer, Paris and Vienna (sale, Künstlerhaus, Vienna, 20–21 December 1872, lot 128, ill. with etching by [P. E.] Le Rat [1849–1892], bought in for ƒ1,700)].[2] [Ehrich Galleries, New York, sold 1913 to];[3] Mrs. Whitelaw Reid [née Elizabeth Mills] (1858–1931), Ophir Hall, Purchase, NY (estate sale, Purchase, NY,[4] American Art Association/Anderson Galleries, 14–18 May 1935, lot 1175, sold for $1,550 to); [Julius H. Weitzner, New York, sold 1936 to]; John H. McFadden Jr., Philadelphia, gift 1951 to;[5] Philadelphia Museum of Art (sale, Parke-Bernet Galleries, New York, 29 February 1956, lot 11).[6] [Altona Company, Vaduz, consigned November 1958 to]; [Kunsthandel P. de Boer, Amsterdam, returned after summer 1959 to]; [Altona Company, Vaduz]. Dr. Herbert Girardet (1910–1972), Kettwig.[7] [Kunsthandel Gebr. Douwes, Amsterdam, inv. no. 8320, in 1967].[8] [H. Shickman Gallery, New York, by 1967, sold 1969 to]; The Norton Simon Foundation.

Exhibited

Amsterdam 1958–59, ill.; Amsterdam 1959, ill.; New York 1967, no. 9, ill.; on loan, Phoenix Art Museum, 18 August–20 November 1969; Oakland 1969, no. 9, ill.; on loan, Los Angeles County Museum of Art, 8 January 1970–26 November 1974.

References

Moes 1892–1905, vol. 2 (1905), pp. 60, 62, no. 4803/39, p. 605, no. 9095, p. 608, note to no. 51; "In the Galleries" 1909, ill. p. xvii; Valentiner 1924, p. 274; Weitzner 1936, no. 15, ill.; Plietzsch 1937, pp. 370–72; Plietzsch 1960, p. 66; Donahue 1969, p. 52; Kuretsky 1971, vol. 1, no. 99, pp. 164f., 325f., vol. 2, ill. 99, as Los Angeles County Museum of Art; P. Sutton 1978, p. 169n1; Kuretsky 1979, pp. 43, 81, no. 66, fig. 157; Kuretsky 2000, p. 236; S. Campbell 2010, p. 322, no. 642, ill.; Ekkart 2011, vol. 1, p. 188, no. 62.

Technical Notes

The support is a medium-weight, plain-weave canvas, lined, with the original edges removed. There are no cusped threads at the edges. Two damages to the original canvas—a complex tear in the upper right background and a small hole in the upper left background—were repaired by the lining. The ground may be dark gray, although the dark layer could also be underpainting. The artist used both opaque and thin paint. The faces are delicately modeled with soft gray shading. The woman's white satin dress was painted wet-into-wet in soft-edged and subtle glazes; tiny drops of thick white paint create the embroidered borders. Her brooch was painted with white and gray dots over a black reserve. The little girl's dress was painted with bold red and orange patterns over a dark-gray layer. Abrasion is minor, though fairly widespread. It is not clear what the original appearance of the little girl's hair may have been; it appears that there were once two hair ornaments at either side. The woman's hair has also been abraded, and the long curls in front of her shoulders are very worn. Ultraviolet light indicates that varnish over the woman's figure and the other two faces was reduced or removed in an undocumented treatment. An early campaign of retouching was rather broadly applied: the upper right background around the tear, the top left corner, the central background to the right of the woman's head, and small dots in the woman's white dress. More recent retouching on top of the varnish is found primarily at the edges. The varnish, a synthetic resin, is not appreciably discolored.

Skillfully integrating genre painting and portraiture, Jacob Ochtervelt created a sumptuous image of formal elegance that reflects the aristocratic ideals and social ambitions of his patrician subjects. Influenced by the fashions of the French court, they shared the values of Louis XIV's France—"the regulation of the passions, reasonableness, decorum, subtle communication through wordless expressions and gestures, polish, and gallantry."[9] The artist contributed to the sense of refinement by restricting detail to within the major forms, which he emphasizes with clear, rhythmic lines: the graceful arch of the man's silhouetted belly and the shoulders of the woman, as well as the leading strings of the child. The family, placed close to the foreground, forms a stable pyramid dominated by the father, who stands at an oblique angle facing his wife. The strong architectonic quality of the Pasadena painting suggests a date slightly later than Ochtervelt's more loosely organized and casually posed *Portrait of a Family* of 1670 (fig. 61a). The refined costumes and figure types and the lighting in the Pasadena painting also compare to the artist's *Tric-trac Players* of 1671 (Museum der bildenden Künste, Leipzig).[10]

The family poses in the main room of an elegant home decorated in the classical style of the late seventeenth century. The focal point of the room is a monumental fireplace

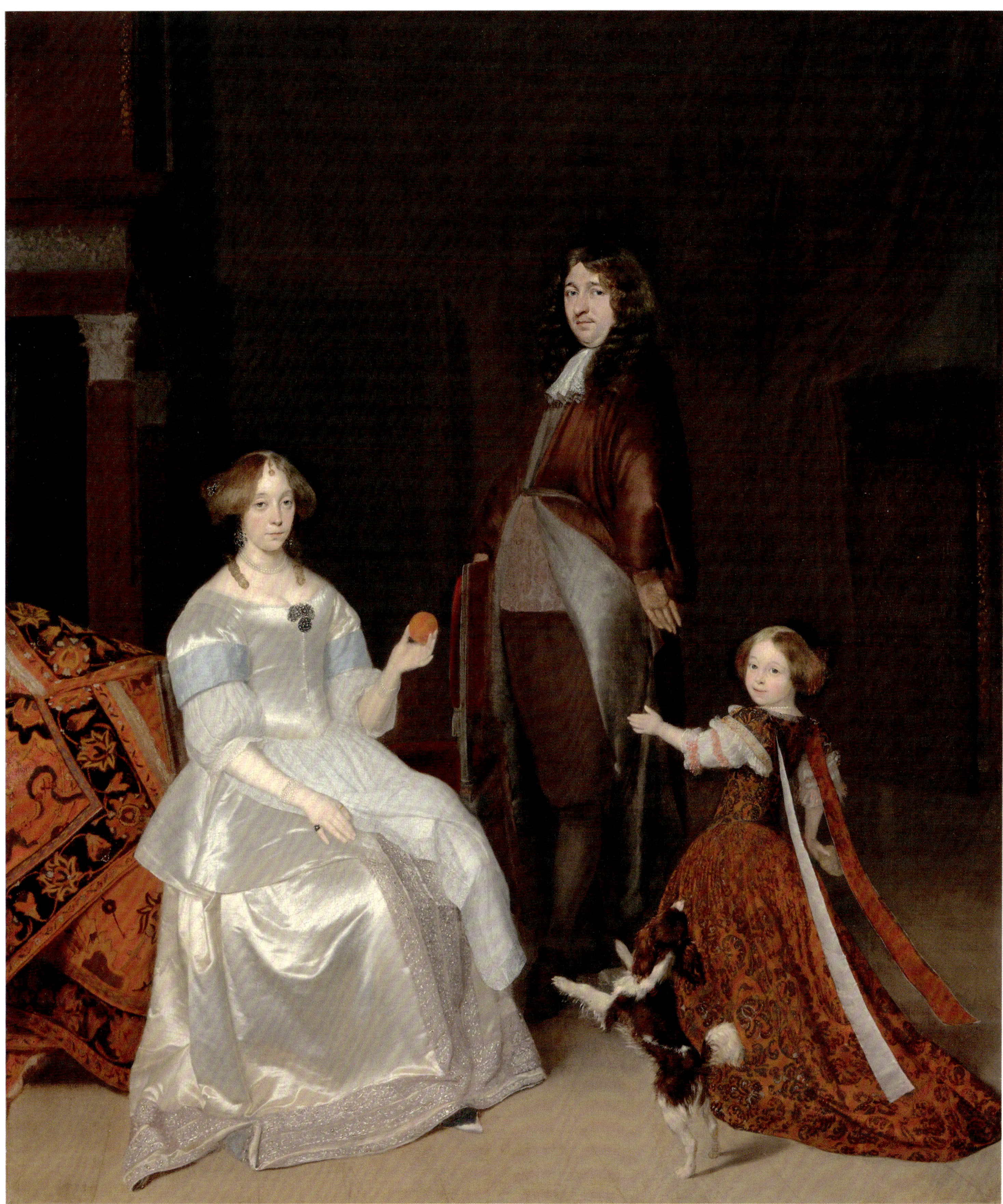

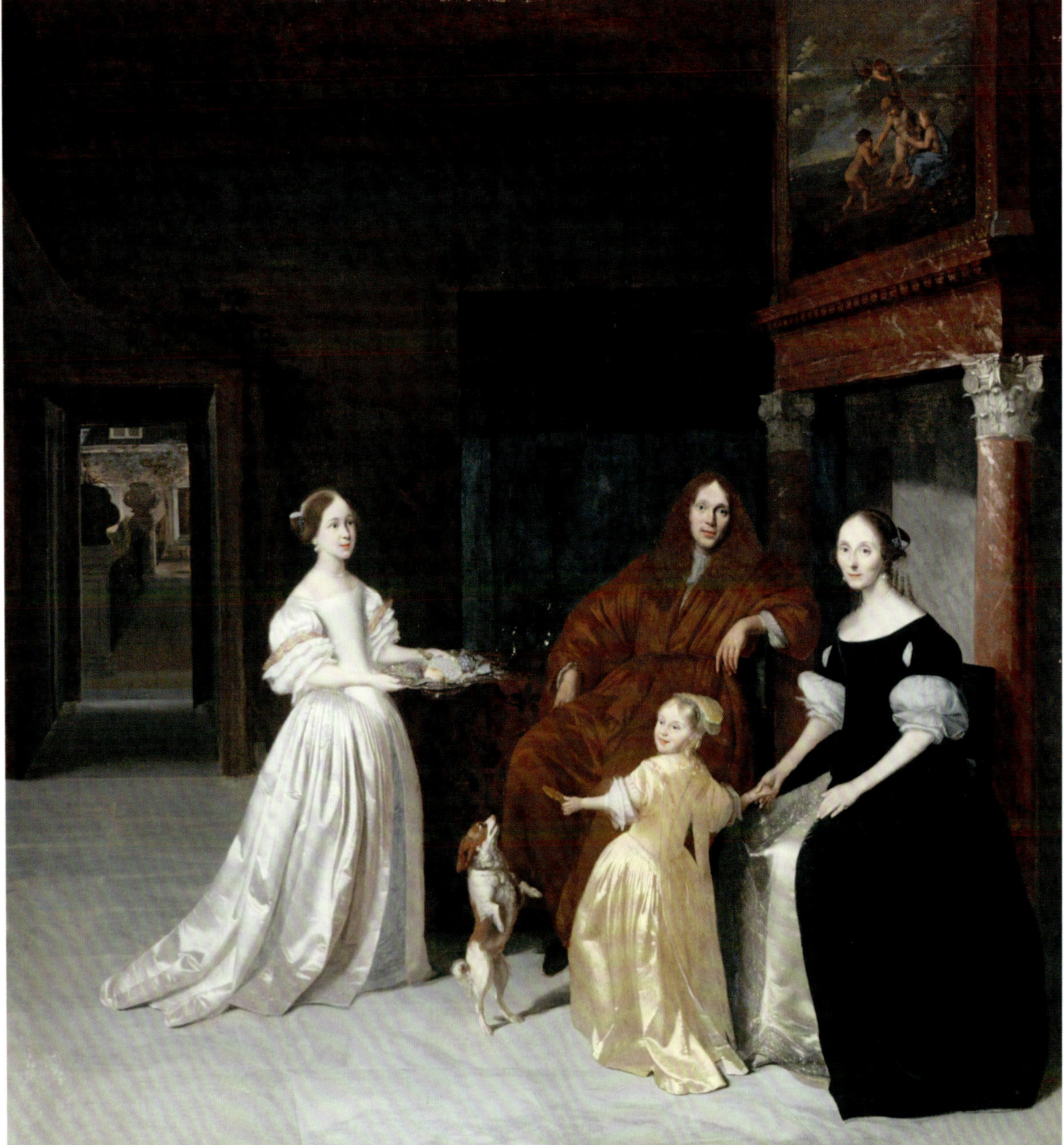

Fig. 61a. Jacob Ochtervelt, *Portrait of a Family*, 1670, oil on canvas, 38 × 35⅞ in. (96.5 × 91 cm), Szépművészeti Múseum, Budapest.

seen from the side. Freestanding smooth, rounded columns with Corinthian capitals support the mantelpiece's massive frieze, above which can be seen the edge of the gilded and carved frame of a painting.[11] The setting is strongly reminiscent of paintings by Gerard ter Borch (1617–1681), such as *Curiosity* and *A Young Woman at Her Toilet with a Maid* (Metropolitan Museum of Art, New York), indicating his influence on the younger artist. Ter Borch probably also influenced Ochtervelt's rendering of form and texture. Enveloping the background of his painting in warm gray-brown shadow, Ochtervelt bathed his figures in light, rendering the rich textures with delightful detail: the woman's shimmering white silk dress embroidered with silver thread; the soft red velvet of the Dutch farthingale chair; and the plush Anatolian carpet.[12]

The fashionably dressed gentleman in the Pasadena painting wears a long, flowing brown wig. At his neck is a loosely pleated *bef*, or *rabat*, of heavy Venetian lace.[13] Standing with his left hand at his hip, he proudly displays his full-length brown silk kimono lined with gray and belted at the waist, beneath which is a red-and-gold brocade vest and matching brown knee breeches and hose. Japanese kimonos such as this were fashionable among Dutch patricians during the second half of the seventeenth century, when they were considered exotic and modish leisurewear for the home.[14] Kimonos were the traditional gift presented by the Japanese shogun to the head of the Dutch East India Company and his entourage after signing the annual contract granting the company exclusive right to trade with Japan. By the second half of the seventeenth century they were manufactured specifically for European export through the Dutch East India Company. Once in Holland, kimonos were reassembled in the "Dutch style" and sold through the East India House. Made of quilted silk, they were warm and comfortable.

In contrast to the smooth silk of her husband's kimono, the hem and front panel of the woman's elegant white satin dress are richly embroidered with silver thread.[15] Quilted shoulders and light blue satin cuffs high on the sleeves add interest to the outfit, which shimmers with light. Her jewelry ensemble consists of a tri-lobed brooch, earrings, rings, and hair ornament of diamonds set in silver foil.[16] A triple-strand choker and bracelets of small pearls complete her jewelry. Like her husband, who has replaced his formal, "public" jacket with his kimono, she protects her expensive dress with a fine linen apron, indicating that she, too, is enjoying the pleasures of her home rather than participating in public affairs.

The domestic context of this sophisticated couple is emphasized by the child, whose active pose enlivens an otherwise static image: With the train of the dress dragging and the training ribbons flying behind, the child appears to have just entered the room chased by a lively spaniel. The child wears a long black-on-red brocade dress, which would have been an appropriate costume for either young girls or boys up to the age of six or seven. Adriaen Hanneman's (ca. 1601–1671) *Portrait of Prince William III (1650–1702)* as a three- or four-year-old child (Rijksmuseum, Amsterdam), for example, represents the Prince of Orange, the future king of England, wearing a similar costume and assuming a similar pose with a dog. The short lacy white sleeves and ribbons of the dress suggest, however, that the child in Ochtervelt's portrait is a girl. The remnants of red on either side of the head were probably originally hair ribbons. Square hats and hats trimmed with feathers, such as that worn by Prince William III in Hanneman's portrait, always signify that the sitter is a boy, whereas ribbons and jewels in the hair indicate girls.[17]

The informality of Ochtervelt's painting reflects the unique emphasis Dutch society placed on domestic intimacy and children and the recognition of the importance of a nurturing home life. Dogs included in genre scenes and family portraits are often references to learning. Ochtervelt represented children training dogs in several of his family portraits, including one of 1670 in Budapest and one of 1663 in the Fogg Museum, Harvard Art Museums. Typically, a young child teaches a dog, usually a small spaniel, to dance or sit on its hind legs.[18] In contrast to paintings in which the dog is clearly responding to instruction, however, in the Pasadena painting the dog leaps up in a very undisciplined manner, apparently excited by the child's entry into the room.[19] With an extended left hand, the child reaches toward an orange held by her mother. A popular reference to fertility, an orange was also included in Ochtervelt's *Family Portrait* (1664?; Wadsworth Atheneum, Hartford, CT).[20]

The former identification of the sitters as the Prince of Orange and his family is unsupported.[21] The style of the portrait, as well as the portrayal of the gentleman in a kimono, suggests that the unidentified sitters were wealthy patricians living in one of the centers of the Dutch East Indies trade—probably Rotterdam, where the artist resided until at least 1672 before moving to Amsterdam, where he is first documented in 1674.[22] Rudi Ekkart has identified ten double and group portraits, most of which he believes Ochtervelt painted in Rotterdam between 1660 and the mid-1670s: "Of the portrayals of family groups, the one in Budapest [fig. 61a] and the near contemporary painting in Pasadena are among the artist's more mature works in which he disposed his models in a balanced and elegant composition." The Budapest painting, which includes an elegant fireplace and a man wearing a kimono, he notes, also repeats the figure of the girl with her left hand extended over a dog.[23]

1. Thoré 1864 makes no reference to the painting in his comprehensive article about the Pereire collection, suggesting that the painting was acquired after that date. The brothers Émile and Isaac Pereire amassed a great fortune during the last decade of Louis-Philippe's reign (1830–48), when they, with the Rothschilds, developed the railway system of northeastern France. In 1852 they founded the enormously influential Crédit Foncier. The Pereire collection, which consisted of paintings from all schools, hung in the *hôtel* the brothers built on rue du Faubourg-Saint-Honoré, Paris. With the advice of the art historian and critic Théophile Thoré (1807–1869), who wrote under the name of William Burger, the brothers acquired paintings from sales of famous collections, including Mecklenburg, Patureau, Rhoné, Piérard, Countess Lehon, Prince Demidoff, Lord Northwick, and the Duke of Pembroke. The brothers sold the collection in 1872 as a result of a financial debacle toward the end of the Second Empire. See Haskell 1976, pp. 83ff.

2. According to an annotated copy of the catalogue at the GRI. The second digit of the price is ambiguous.

3. According to the 1935 sale catalogue. Whitelaw Reid (1837–1912) was an American politician and newspaper editor who, among other positions, served as ambassador to France and the United Kingdom. His death in 1912 confirms that it was his wife who acquired the painting from Ehrich Galleries in 1913.

4. The sale took place on the premises of Ophir Hall, Purchase, NY, the Whitelaw Reid estate.

5. John H. McFadden Jr.'s father made his fortune brokering cotton following the Civil War. John Sr. (1850–1921) was part of a group of men who pushed for the establishment of the Philadelphia Museum of Art. He left his collection of mostly English portraits and landscapes to the museum. John Jr. donated additional paintings to the museum during the 1940s and 1950s.

6. A note within the entry regarding lot 11 refers to a manuscript certificate by W. R. Valentiner,

dated 24 May 1935, that would be given to the purchaser. According to the same note, "In [the certificate, Valentiner] states that the composition is one of Ochtervelt's rare portrait paintings, delicate in color and in a fine state of preservation."

7. According to annotations on the back of the photograph mount from Kunsthandel Gebr. Douwes, Amsterdam (GRI).

8. According to the photograph mount from Kunsthandel Gebr. Douwes, Amsterdam (GRI).

9. See Franits 1995, with references to additional sources.

10. Kuretsky 1979, p. 43.

11. In the shadowy background there is a large bed enclosed by heavy curtains, over which a landscape painting may have originally hung. The painting, which is no longer visible, appears in the print made by Paul-Edme Lerat (1849–1892) in 1872. To the right, a portière has been pulled back to reveal a view through a partially open door to an unidentified gilded, carved molding.

12. Noted for their bold patterns and limited colors, these rugs were manufactured in large numbers in Anatolia (Turkey) for export to Europe, where they were especially admired by the Dutch after the mid-seventeenth century. See Ydema 1991, pp. 99ff.; and Thornton 1978, p. 109, who distinguish these from the more refined Persian rugs, which had more subtle designs and were usually larger.

13. See Kinderen-Besier 1950, p. 214. After about 1675 the *bef* went out of fashion, replaced by the cravat.

14. During the seventeenth century, the Dutch referred to a kimono as *Japonsche rock*, *Japonsche tabbaerd*, *samaer*, or *japon*. The Dutch also took gifts to the shogun, who would send specific requests for items he wished to receive from Europe, such as velvet and especially telescopes, magnifying glasses, and terrestrial and celestial globes. See Lubberhuizen-van Gelder 1947–49.

15. Ochtervelt represented the same dress in *Lutist with Tric-trac Players* (Wallraf-Richartz-Museum, Cologne). During the seventeenth century, kimonos were most often made of smooth silk; only later was embroidered silk preferred. Lubberhuizen-van Gelder 1947–49, 62 (1947), p. 145.

16. A similar jewelry ensemble is worn by a woman in Michiel van Musscher's (1645–1705) *Sinfonia*, dated 1671 (Detroit Institute of Arts).

17. On the determination of the sex of children portrayed in portraits, see Kuus 1994, pp. 6–13, 57f.; and Kuus 2000.

18. See Bedaux 1990, pp. 109–69. The significance of the motif is explained by the engraving for *Maeghde-Wapen* (maiden arms) in Jacob Cats's (1577–1660) influential book on marriage and family, *Houwelyck* (1625), in which the begging dog is paired with a girl who personifies *leer-sucht* (willingness to learn). Bedaux relates this metaphor and the contemporary attitude toward education, which considered the proper training and discipline of the child to be essential to the formation of the adult. The Dutch system was based on Plutarch's three-part theory of education: natural aptitude, instruction, and practice.

19. The dog may also be a reference to the "natural" state of the child herself. A biscuit, with which children usually tempt dogs to obey, is barely visible in the child's lowered right hand on her far side.

20. Early photographs and an etching after the painting reveal that what now appears as an orange orb originally represented an orange. The stem and leaves disappeared (probably during cleaning) before the Norton Simon Foundation acquired the painting in 1969.

21. The former identification of the sitters as Prince William of Orange and his family was made on the basis of the orange held by the mother. Historically, however, it cannot represent either Willem II or his son William III (1650–1702), both of whom were known as the Prince of Orange. Willem II, who was born in 1625 and succeeded his father Frederik Hendrik (1584–1647) to the powerful position of stadtholder and commander of the army in 1647, died suddenly in 1650, shortly before the birth of his first child. That child, William III, married his cousin Princess Mary Stuart (1662–1694) in 1677; they were crowned king and queen of England in 1689 but had no children.

22. Partially in response to the influx of immigrants from the Southern Netherlands, Rotterdam had experienced significant growth during the late sixteenth and early seventeenth centuries and had become a major port for world trade, as well as for herring and brewing. The city hosted the admiralty for the Maas region (as of 1597), one of the six chambers of the Dutch East India Company (as of 1605), and a branch of the Dutch West India Company.

23. Ekkart 2011, pp. 188 and 190, related to no. 62.

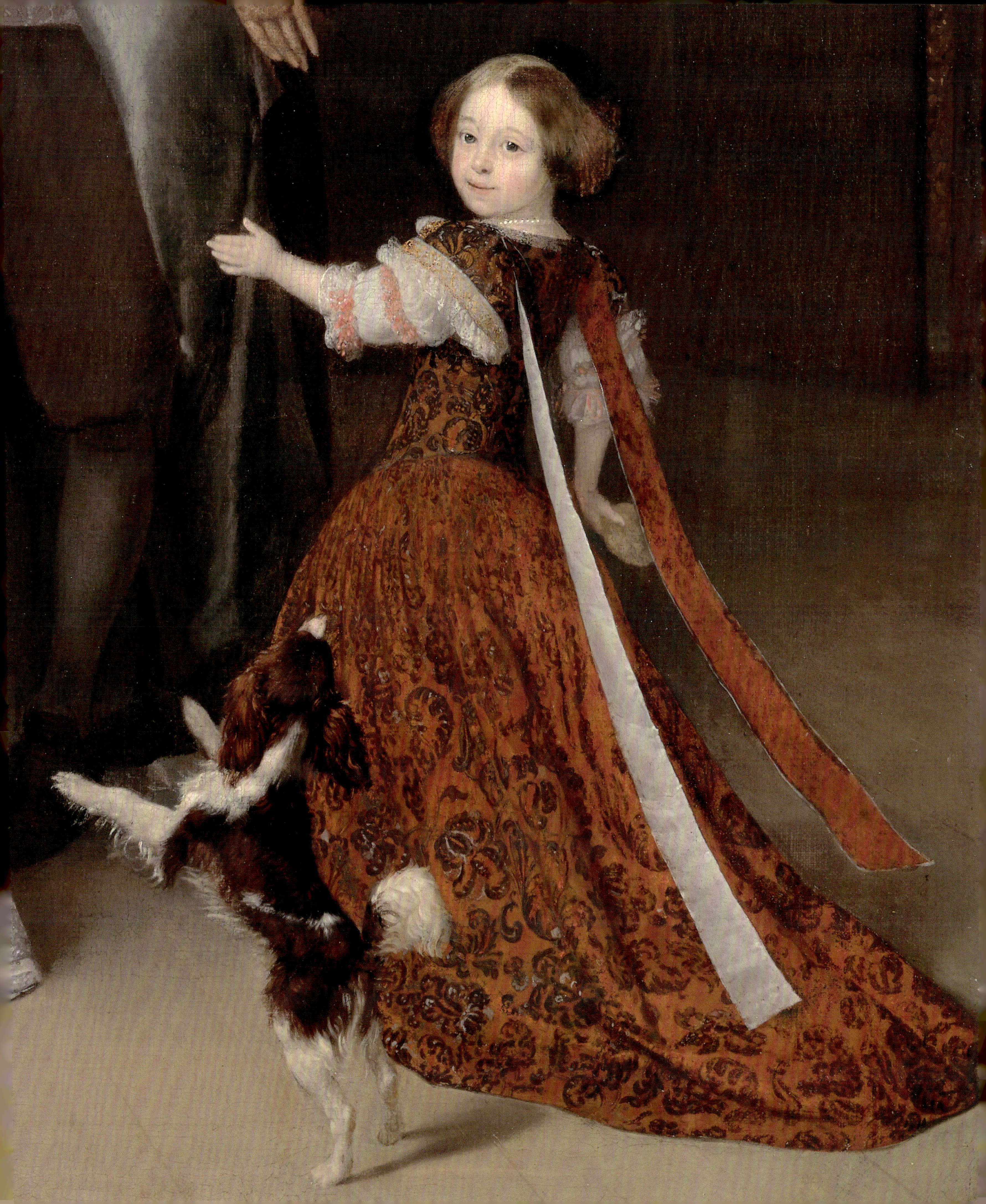

62

Adriaen van Ostade

Dutch
Haarlem 1610–1685 Haarlem

Carousing Peasants

ca. 1636

Signed behind tipped-over three-legged stool, lower right: "Av. ostad"[1]
Oil on panel, 16 ½ × 23 ⅛ in. (41.9 × 58.7 cm)
The Norton Simon Foundation, F.1972.14.P

Provenance
Possibly George Cornwall Legh (1804–1877), High Legh Hall, Knutsford, Cheshire, by descent to his son;[2] Lt. Col. Henry Cornwall Legh (1839–1904), High Legh Hall, Knutsford, Cheshire. L. Venau, Paris, sold 3 February 1909 to;[3] [Galerie F. Kleinberger, Paris, stock no. 8616, sold 27 April 1909 to]; August de Ridder (1836/37–1911), Schloss Schönburg, Frankfurt, returned 1910 to; [E. M. Sperling, Galerie F. Kleinberger, Paris,[4] sold 1924 to]; Marczell von Nemes[5] (1866–1930), Budapest (sale, Frederik Muller, Munich, 16 June 1931, lot 56, pl. 25, sold for 8,200 Reichsmarks). Private collection, Switzerland. [Galerie Nathan, Zurich, consigned half shares June 1971 to]; [Schaeffer Galleries, New York, stock no. 2678, sold 30 May 1972 to]; The Norton Simon Foundation.

Exhibited
Paris 1911, no. 104; New York 1913, p. 10, fig. 39; on loan, Allen Memorial Art Museum, Oberlin, 1 June 1972–8 May 1973; on loan, Los Angeles County Museum of Art, 9 May 1973–26 November 1974.

References
Hofstede de Groot 1908–27, vol. 3 (1910), p. 316, no. 575; W. Martin 1911, p. 246; Dayot 1911, p. 62, ill.; Dayot 1912a, pp. 51, ill., 141, no. 113;[6] Dayot 1912b, p. 194, ill.; New York 1913, p. 10, ill. 39;[7] Pasadena 1980, p. 60, ill.; P. Sutton 1986, p. 218; S. Campbell 2010, p. 338, no. 787, ill.

Technical Notes
The support is an oak panel made from two horizontally grained boards, with a horizontal join 6 inches from the top. X-radiography shows the upper board with a slightly more open grain. The lower board is split 3 ½ inches from the bottom. The panel was cradled after having been thinned to its present ⅛-inch thickness. A thin white ground, which leaves the wood grain evident, was toned with a thin light-brown imprimatura. Although microscopic examination does not reveal underdrawing, an infrared photograph in the curatorial file clearly shows the figures in the right background, one climbing a ladder and others occupied at the hearth. The thinly painted, nearly monochromatic background is sketchy. Objects in the foreground, such as the jug, were carefully observed and fully modeled. The figures occupying the central foreground were rendered with opaque paint in a livelier palette, yet brushmarking is generally faint. The paint is very well preserved overall. Some undocumented selective cleaning reduced varnish in the figures and the light portion of the foreground. Filling material that covers the splits may be excessive; its surface is quite smooth, which makes both of the repairs very obvious. Retouching in the background to the right of center strengthens several shadowed lines. Ultraviolet light indicates an aged synthetic-resin varnish overall.

Carousing Peasants is one of a number of paintings dating from the 1630s in which Adriaen van Ostade uses dramatic lighting to focus attention on a small group of peasants partying in a dusky, rustic interior.[8] Clay pipes and vessels of beer suggest that overindulgence is the cause of the good-natured but unrestrained behavior. The exaggerated, caricatured features and gestures of the peasants, their rustic surroundings, and compositional diagonals contribute to the general impression of noise and confusion. As in paintings by his brother Isack van Ostade (1621–1649), a young child observes the activity, here of the frivolity of the inebriated adults, while in the dusky background on the right a woman tends a pot over the fire as others converse and

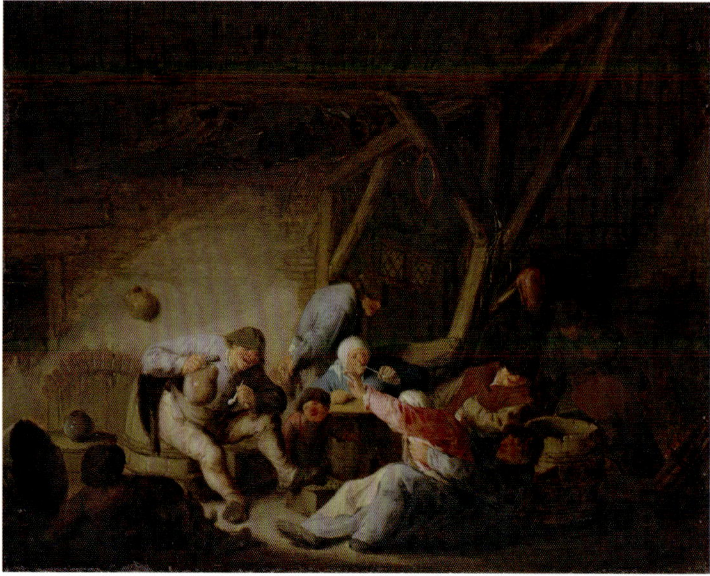

Fig. 62a. Adriaen van Ostade, *Men and Women in a Barn Interior*, 1635, oil on panel, 11 7⁄16 × 14 ¼ in. (29.1 × 36.3 cm), Alte Pinakothek, Bayerische Staatsgemäldesammlungen, Munich.

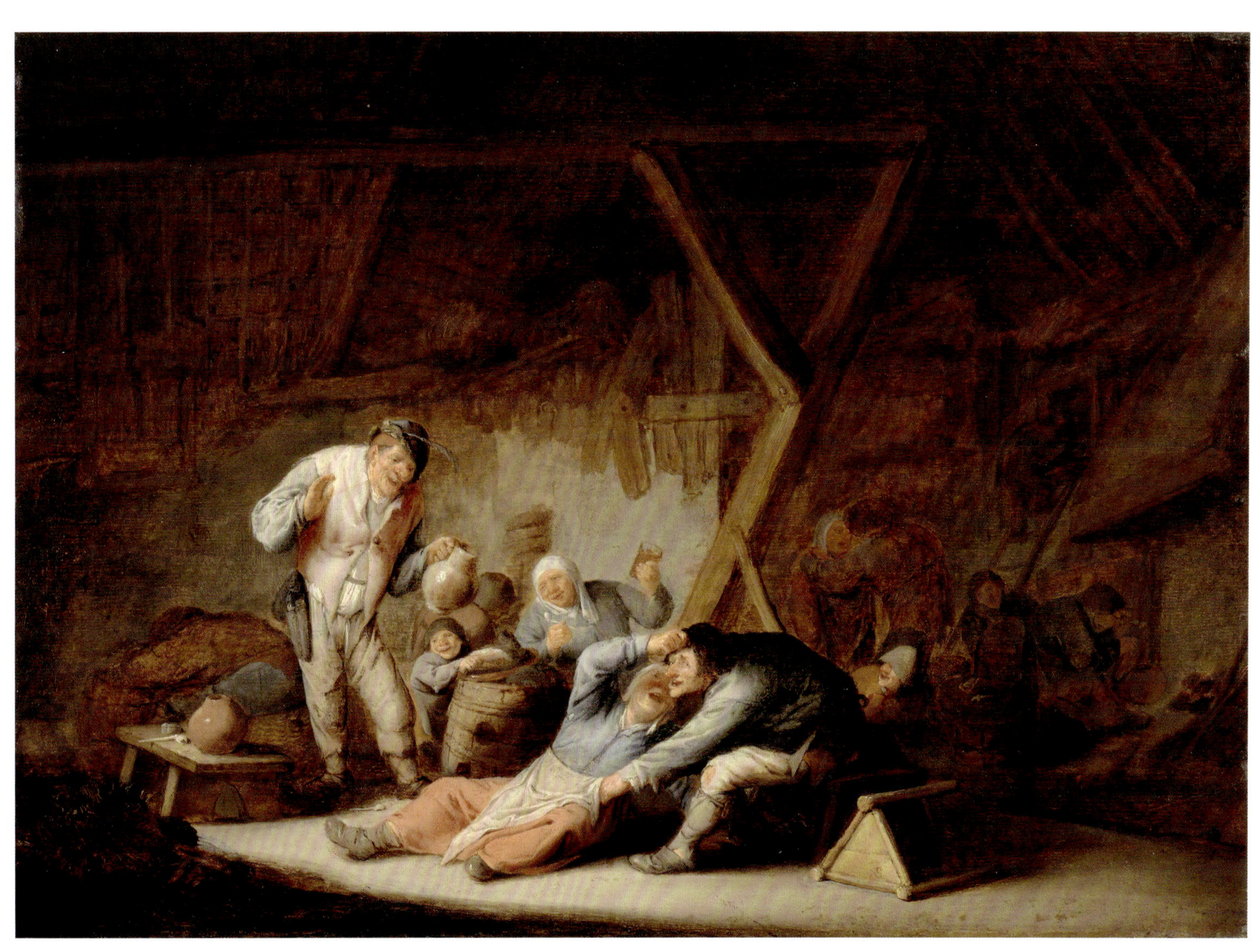

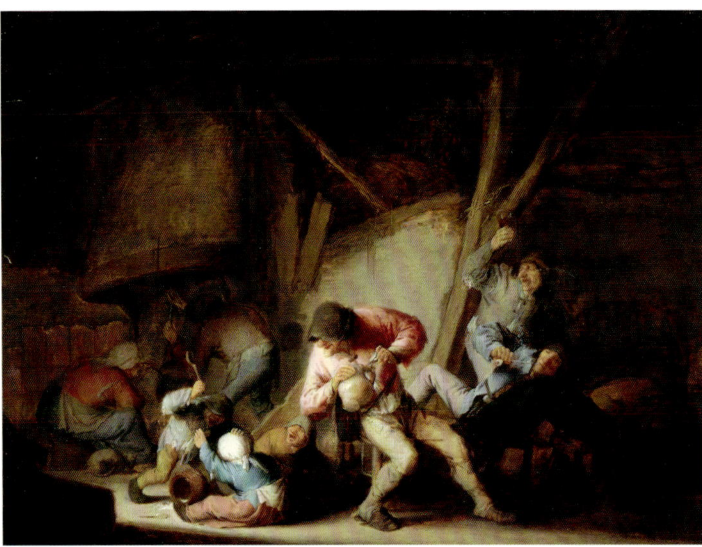

Fig. 62b. Adriaen van Ostade, *Drinking Figures and Crying Children*, 1634, oil on panel, 12 ¼ × 16 ¾ in. (31.1 × 42.6 cm), Sarah Campbell Blaffer Foundation, Houston.

undertake chores. Only the person seated next to the woman at the fire seems to notice the activity in the foreground.

The Pasadena painting is particularly close in subject and general composition to *Men and Women in a Barn Interior* (fig. 62a) and *Drinking Figures and Crying Children* (fig. 62b). The repetition of a number of very closely related details and especially the similar definition of space in the Pasadena and Munich paintings suggest that Van Ostade painted them at approximately the same time but slightly later than the Houston painting. Dated 1634, *Drinking Figures and Crying Children* is characteristic of the artist's earliest paintings, such as *Peasants Playing Cards* (Hermitage, St. Petersburg), in which the secondary figures, though pushed to the shadowy background, remain essentially part of the primary group. In the Munich and Pasadena paintings, as well as in other works from the later 1630s, the space is more clearly defined, with the secondary figures submerged in a darker, deeper space to the side, separated from the figures in the bright foreground by a Y-shaped support and a short wall.[9]

Van Ostade's use of dramatic facial and physical expression to portray a small group of peasants at a point of heightened emotion links him to his slightly older contemporary, the Flemish painter Adriaen Brouwer (1605/06–1638).[10] Like Brouwer, Van Ostade employed loose brushwork to increase the sense of physical and emotional transience and a cool, delicate palette of light blues and grays with pale pinks to relieve his primary figures, who are cast in bright light, from the more thinly painted brown tones of the shadowy background. Both artists were probably influenced by the strong characterizations in Rembrandt's early beggar prints and the dramatic lighting effects of his early paintings, such as *Christ at Emmaus* (1631; Musée Jacquemart André, Paris).[11]

Reminiscent of the rowdy, uncontrolled peasants who drink, fight, or freely celebrate with dance and romance in *Boeren Geselschap*, published by the Dutch playwright Gerbrand Adriaensz. Bredero (1585–1618) in 1622, the primary intention of Van Ostade's paintings was to entertain.[12] His patrons probably responded to paintings such as *Carousing Peasants* with amusement rather than contempt or mocking humor. The caption (in translation) of a print after Pieter Bruegel I (ca. 1525–1569), *Kermis at Hoboken*, ca. 1559, "Let the peasants have their kermis," suggests that raucous behavior portrayed in sixteenth-century prints and paintings was recognized as characteristic of a certain social class and condoned, especially within the context of the yearly church celebration. For seventeenth-century viewers, Bredero's and Van Ostade's humorous portrayals of the unrestrained behavior and rustic habits of peasants, which drew on familiar clichés and stereotypes, served as an entertaining foil for sophisticated society.[13]

By the mid-1640s, approximately ten years after painting *Carousing Peasants*, Van Ostade shifted away from the portrayal of boisterous, rustic peasants to that of respectable, middle-class farmers and urban dwellers who gather quietly outside well-kept cottage doors and in tidy, evenly lit interiors. Similar to Salomon van Ruysdael's (1600/03–1670) contemporaneous *Halt in Front of an Inn* of 1643 (cat. 81), beginning in the 1640s Van Ostade's employment of a more detailed, refined technique for the portrayal of respectable rural folk reveals a new, idealized respect for life in the country far from the stresses of the overcrowded cities.[14]

1. The signature, which is very faint, appears to have been painted in white or gray paint with a very thin brush. The "v" is formed from the lower right side of the "A."

2. According to Bode in New York 1913, p. 52, no. 39. This is the son of Rev. Henry Cornwall Legh (1811–1847). Carter 1905 mentions that the collection, especially the collection of portraits, was formed gradually by various members of the family, but "it was . . . the late Mr. George Cornwall Legh [1804–1877] who collected, not only fine and rare paintings, but [also] every class of work of art . . . in his travels abroad." Carter does not mention the present painting among those at High Legh Hall, suggesting that it had already left the collection by 1905.

3. Beginning with Hofstede de Groot, the name has been incorrectly cited as "Venon." According to the Kleinberger stock card for the painting (Metropolitan Museum of Art, New York) and noted in their catalogues, however, "L. Venau" sold the painting to Kleinberger, Paris, 3 February 1909.

4. Paris 1911, p. 5, mentions that the paintings in the exhibition are for private sale at the Kleinberger galleries in Paris and New York. The entry for the Pasadena painting mentions the exhibition at the Jeu de Paume and therefore postdates that.

5. The *Scène de cabaret* by Van Ostade mentioned by Dacier 1913, p. 460, was not the Pasadena painting but another painting sold from the Marczell von Nemes Collection as lot 59 (ill.), 17–18 June 1913, Galerie Manzi-Joyant, Paris. Marczell von Nemes was a Hungarian financier, art collector, and art dealer.

6. The book was published by the Paris dealers Georges Petit and F. Kleinberger and included paintings exhibited the previous year at the Jeu de Paume. The owner of the Pasadena painting was listed as M. Sperling, Paris, who was director of Kleinberger's New York office.

7. Although included in New York 1913, the painting had already been returned to Kleinberger before De Ridder's death. In the introduction to New York 1913, Wilhelm von Bode mentions that the original edition of the book was published shortly before De Ridder's death on 13 May 1911.

8. The rustic setting in *Carousing Peasants* was probably not meant to represent an independent structure specifically designated as an inn but the living area of a *langhuis*, which may have served as an informal public house. The most common form of rural dwelling in Holland during the early seventeenth century, the *langhuis* was a long, thatched building divided into a front room and a long, open area behind it that housed the farmer's family and, in winter, animals as well. The family quarters were toward the front of the back area and were dominated, as in this painting, by a large fireplace in the wall that divided the living area from the front room. The area above the front room was used for storage and reached by a ladder such as that on which the man stands to the left of the fireplace. For a contemporary tourist's description of a farmer's dwelling, see John Locke's Journal, 28 August 1685 (Bodleian Library, MS Locke, f. 8), reprinted in Van Strien 1993, p. 319 (where it is erroneously cited as MS Locke, f. 9).

9. Schnackenburg 1970, pp. 158ff.

10. Houbraken [1753] 1976, vol. 1, pp. 320, 347, reported that Brouwer and Van Ostade were fellow students in Haarlem of Frans Hals (1582/83–1666). Brouwer may have been in Haarlem in 1621 before he traveled to Amsterdam in 1625, and he was in Haarlem between 1626 and 1631, when he returned to Flanders. Brouwer's training with Hals has, however, been questioned by later scholars.

11. Schnackenburg 1970, pp. 159f., 165f.

12. Hessel Miedema and Keith Moxey have argued that scenes of rowdy peasants were meant as moralizing examples of negative behavior, foils for civilized society, while Svetlana Alpers has countered that they were simply comic images meant to entertain sophisticated audiences at the expense of the peasant. See Alpers 1975–76; Miedema 1977; Miedema 1981; Moxey 1981–82; A. Walsh 1997; Westermann 2002–03; and Ebert 2011, especially pp. 147–51.

13. In his biography of Van Ostade, Arnold Houbraken (1660–1719) praised the artist as a witty observer of peasant life. Houbraken 1718–21, vol. 1, p. 247.

14. In addition to oil paintings, Van Ostade produced beautiful colored drawings and etchings of subjects related to his paintings.

63

Isack van Ostade

Dutch
Haarlem 1621–1649 Haarlem

Peasants Outside a Farmhouse Butchering a Pig

1641

Signed and dated, lower left: "Isack van Ostade / 1641"
Oil on panel, 19 ⅛ × 25 ½ in. (48.6 × 64.8 cm)
The Norton Simon Foundation, F.1969.44.P

Provenance[1]
Anonymous (sale, de Winter, Yver, Amsterdam, 7 August 1776, lot 112; sold for ƒ31). Sir William Robert Williams (1860–1903), Bart. Upcott, Barnstable (estate sale, Christie's, London, 28 November 1903, lot 35; sold for £73 10s. to); [Martin Colnaghi, London].[2] Rt. Hon. John Frederic (1902–1982), 2nd Baron Gretton, Stapleford Park, Leicestershire (sale, Christie's, London, 27 June 1952, lot 106, "signed and dated 164[?]"; sold for £420).[3] Private collection, the Netherlands. Anonymous (sale, Arne Bruun Rasmussen, Copenhagen, 16–29 May 1968, lot 215, ill.). [A. van der Meer, Amsterdam, sold 1969 to]; The Norton Simon Foundation.

Exhibited
On loan, Phoenix Art Museum, 8 January–29 April 1970; on loan, Los Angeles County Museum of Art, 1 May 1970–26 November 1974.

References
Hofstede de Groot 1908–27, vol. 3 (1910), p. 483, no. 153gg, p. 487, no. 159; Van der Meer 1969, no. 19, cover, ill.; Pasadena 1980, pp. 39, 60, ill.; P. Sutton 1986, p. 218; Pasadena 1989, p. 76, ill.; Kaufman 1995, vol. 1, pp. 118ff., 207f., 288f., no. 19, vol. 2, p. 458, fig. 19; S. Campbell 2010, p. 329, no. 700, ill.

Technical Notes
The uncradled oak support consists of two horizontally grained boards. The left and right edges are widely beveled, the bottom has a narrow bevel, and the top edge has none. The panel has a major crack extending from side to side, located 4 inches from the bottom; it has been treated and is stable. The thin white ground leaves the wood grain evident. A rose-beige layer covering the ground is influential in the overall tone. It often shows through the sky, owing to the increasing transparency of the blue oil paint, which also was thinned and abraded during a previous cleaning. Much of the background and the immediate foreground were loosely sketched with thin ochres and browns. The figures in the center were painted with more opaque and vivid colors. Faces have just a few strokes of color and almost no modeling. The light blue of the sky, applied with a nearly dry brush, shows through the tree branches and leaves, as they also have become more transparent. A slight amount of texture is present in the foliage and details of the farmhouse; the artist used thicker blobs of white paint to emphasize the mortar between the bricks, the pig's innards, and occasional articles of clothing. There are numerous tiny losses of paint and ground throughout that appear to have been caused by flaking.

Because of the predominantly thin application of paint in mainly earth, umber, and ochre colors, neither X-radiography nor infrared reflectography revealed any major compositional changes. However, during the 2015 conservation treatment, it was noted that damaged areas, most notably along the join, had been excessively retouched, concealing the original paint. The most compelling example of this was found in the lower left corner, where a man seated on a stool was located above the artist's signature (fig. 63a). Careful cleaning of this area revealed a pristine original paint layer that had been overpainted, probably in the nineteenth or early twentieth century, to conceal the original subject, which an owner or dealer considered distasteful. Removal of the overpaint revealed that the stool and the trousers of the squatting figure had been added to Van Ostade's original figure of the man, with his buttocks uncovered, defecating rather than sitting idly watching the slaughter of a pig (fig. 63b).[4] Treatment of the painting in 1986 selectively removed darkened, yellowed, and rather gritty varnish, artificially spotlighting the figural group and farmhouse facade. Full removal of the old varnish and retouching has helped to reestablish the correct tonal balance of the scene. *—Devi Ormond*

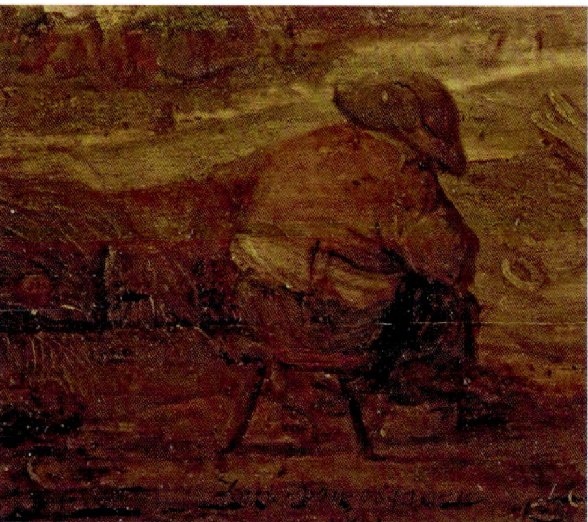

Fig. 63a. Detail of painting before cleaning.

Signed and dated 1641, *Peasants Outside a Farmhouse Butchering a Pig* is one of Isack van Ostade's earliest exterior scenes.[5] It is closely related in handling and subject

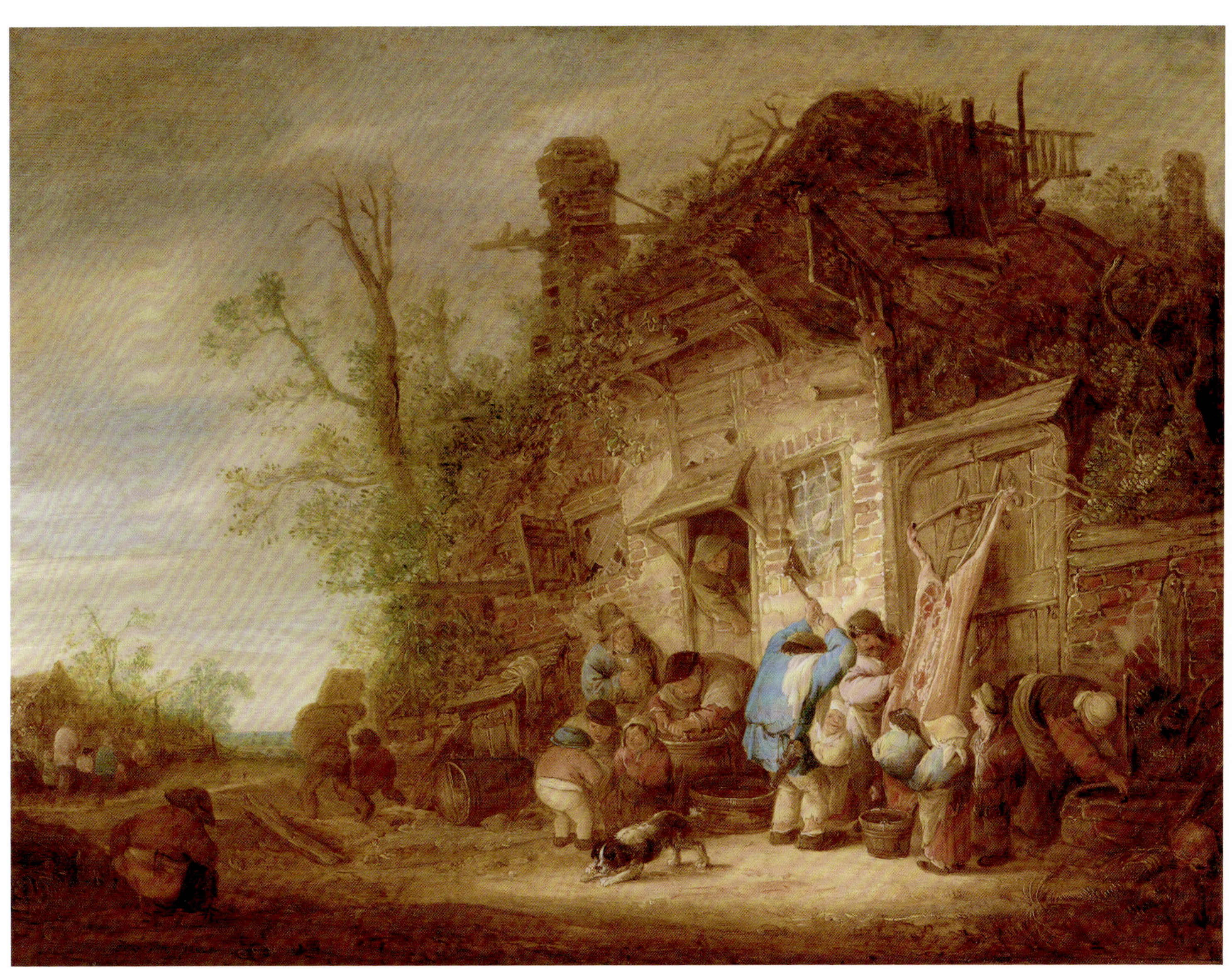

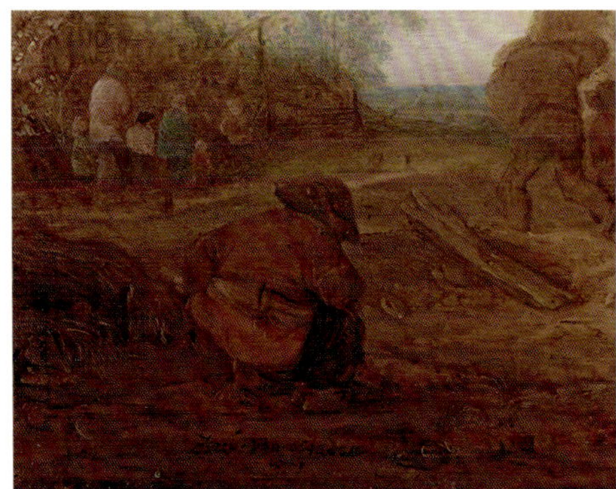

Fig. 63b. Detail of painting after cleaning.

to the artist's *Rural Scenery in front of a Farm House*, also dated 1641 (fig. 63c).[6] Freely brushed in thin, monochromatic tones of ochre, umber, and earth, the Pasadena painting is an important work of the artist's short career. While still closely related to the manner of his older brother and artistic mentor Adriaen (cat. 62), it already demonstrates signs of the younger man's nascent personal style. Like Adriaen, Isack's primary interest was in the figural subject of the painting in which children play active roles as observers of the adult world. Isack's distinctive personal style is, however, already present in the landscape setting and the detailed description of the physical environment of the scene: the texture of the splintered wood, the broken windows, and the thatched roof overgrown with grass and vines and cluttered with branches and debris. Thick impasto captures the actual feel of the mortar in the crumbling brick wall.

In contrast to the early paintings by his brother, which invite laughter, Isack van Ostade's paintings portray a positive image of peasants, highlighting their peaceful, inwardly controlled and moral character rather than bawdy excesses.[7] His industrious, responsible peasants provide physical sustenance and education for their offspring. In the Pasadena painting, as children watch, a farmer raises his ax to butcher a pig suspended from the side of the house by its hind legs, an annual event of early winter (fig. 63d).[8] Since the late Middle Ages and Renaissance, the humble plowman had been associated with industriousness, moderation, and integrity.[9] As such, he was included in allegorical images of peace, diligence, and hope. Isack van Ostade's positive image of rural life reflects the contemporary revival of interest in the *Georgics*, Virgil's first-century poem on farming that emphasizes the practical, rustic aspects of the author's native landscape and introduced descriptions of realistic detail.[10] Interest in the *Georgics* was part of a general positive assessment of those who live a simple life according to the cycles of nature expressed by contemporary authors interested in neo-Stoic philosophy.[11] Writers such as the statesman and poet Constantijn Huygens (1596–1687), who extolled the pleasures and benefits of the countryside in his poem *Hofwijk* (1653), considered the peasant a virtuous example for sophisticated man, who had strayed from nature and God and been corrupted

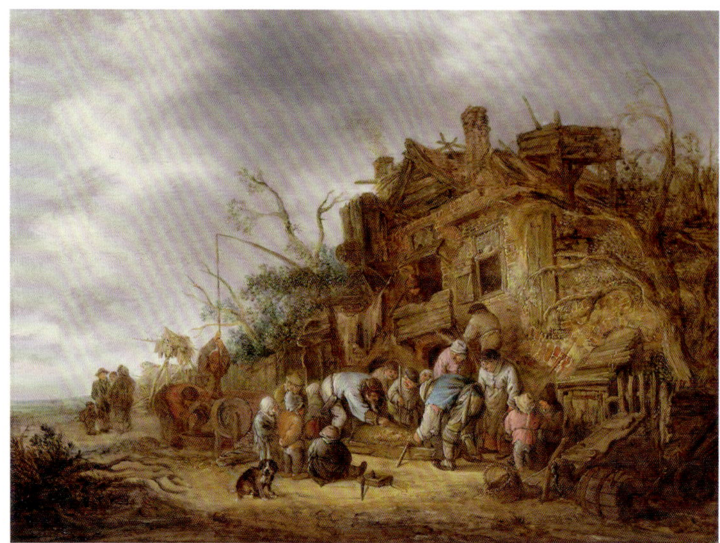

Fig. 63c. Isack van Ostade, *Rural Scenery in front of a Farm House*, 1641, oil on panel, 18 15/16 × 25 1/4 in. (48 × 64 cm), location unknown (sold Auktionshaus im Kinsky, 2015), photograph courtesy of Auktionshaus im Kinsky GmbH, Vienna.

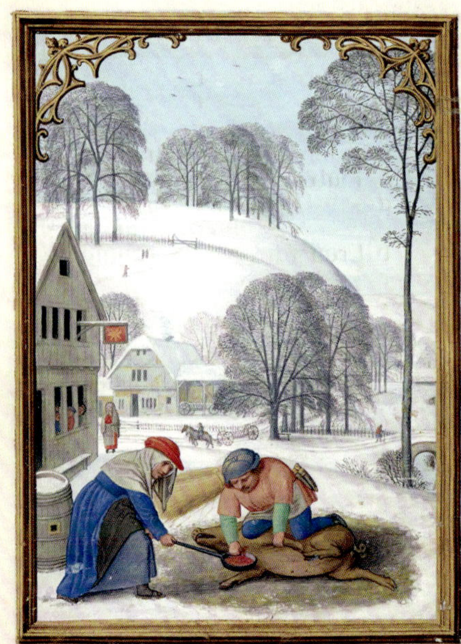

Fig. 63d. Simon Bening, *Pig Slaughter, The Month of December*, from the *Da Costa Hours*, ca. 1515, vellum, The Morgan Library & Museum, New York.

by the "artificiality and backbiting" of the cities.[12] According to the title page to a set of prints designed by Abraham Bloemaert (1566–1651) and engraved by Boetius Adams Bolswert (1580–1633) in 1614: "Most happy is he and truly blessed is the one who may spend his years free of burgher cares, content to live under the thatched roof of his hut; his spirit does not become entangled in complications, he does not wrestle with a vacillating heart, but he looks at the yellow corn or the ripe apples of the tree or he drives his gleaming cow towards the meadow which he may call his own. When his wife happily takes her part in the work, most happy is he and the highest measure blessed."[13]

In *Peasants Outside a Farmhouse Butchering a Pig*, the ramshackle cottage, tattered clothes, and even the rounded forms of Isack's figures—which recall Pieter Bruegel I's (ca. 1525–1569) peasants in *Haystacks* (Metropolitan Museum of Art, New York)—emphasize their close ties to the earth. This association is expressed by the inscription on a print by Isack's contemporary Herman Saftleven (1609–1685), which recounts how the farmer comes from the earth and will eventually return to it.[14] In this context, the man squatting in the left foreground, who was recently revealed to be defecating rather than seated on a three-legged stool watching the butchering of a pig (figs. 63a–b)—like similar figures in paintings and prints by fellow artists, including Paulus Potter's (1625–1654) *Peasant on the Dung Heap* (1651; Staatliches Museum Schwerin)—was not intended as a negative or comedic statement but was, rather, another reference to peasants living a simple, natural life guided by instinct.[15]

1. The back of the painting bears the following: "22" printed on paper, from a French entry in an unidentified sale catalogue, "108" written on the back, and a red-wax seal.

2. An annotated copy of the 1903 auction catalogue at the GRI identifies the buyer as "M. Col." According to Burton Fredericksen, this is Martin Colnaghi, who was buying separately from the firm of P. & D. Colnaghi. There is no reference to this painting in the archives of P. & D. Colnaghi (GRI, microfiche copy of files).

3. Christie's stencil "306KC" for this sale appears on the back of the painting.

4. Adelaide Izat, conservator at the Royal Collection (personal communication with the author), discovered a similar situation in 2015 when overpaint was removed on another painting by Isack van Ostade in the Royal Collection, *A Village Fair with Church Behind* (1643): a figure on the right of the composition was originally depicted as defecating behind bushes. The location of the figure and his forward-facing position in that composition is not, however, quite as obvious as in the Pasadena painting. The detail in the Royal Collection painting is believed to have been painted over in the early twentieth century. Another example of the discovery of a defecating figure beneath later overpaint is Jan Steen's (ca. 1626–1679) *Peasants Merrymaking Outside an Inn*, ca. 1676 (previously *Fair at Warmond*; The Leiden Collection, New York; JS-108). Removal of overpaint revealed that the squatting woman in the foreground was originally represented defecating, similar to Rembrandt's etching *Woman Urinating* of 1631 (Rijksmuseum, Amsterdam; RP-P-OB-637). Kloek 2017/2020–.

5. The previous year Isack van Ostade had painted *Peasant Interior with a Slaughtered Pig* (Alte Pinakothek, Munich). He repeated the subject of the slaughtered pig hanging by its feet inside a barn in other paintings.

6. Kaufman 1995, no. 20 (Hofstede de Groot 1908–27, vol 3 [1910], no. 153ggg); with Richard Green Fine Paintings, 1976.

7. During the early 1640s, Adriaen van Ostade rejected his early images of raucous peasants and thereafter portrayed only peaceful gatherings of respectable farmers and villagers, often emphasizing family life.

8. Calendar pages of early Netherlandish manuscripts and prints provided seventeenth-century artists with the richest source of images of the countryside. By the early seventeenth century, allegories, which were essentially limited to prints, were primarily represented as genre scenes—active, multi-figured compositions camouflaged as realistic representations of the countryside. For descriptions of pig slaughtering and the use of various animal parts in food, see Barnes and Rose 2002, pp. 18, 96–97.

9. See Veldman 1992.

10. Karel van Mander's 1597 translation of Virgil's Latin text into Dutch made the *Georgics* widely available.

11. The primary figure in the revival of Stoic philosophy in the late sixteenth century was Justus Lipsius (1547–1606). In 1589 Lipsius published *De Constantia* out of what he called a need for support during the sufferings of wars. The chief aim of his Christian Stoicism was to lead a good or ethical life, which he defined as living according to Nature. He equated Nature to God, Supreme Reason. To understand the moral life, he advocated studying and examining the natural world. One cannot control fortune, but by understanding Nature, both universally and within oneself, he contended, one could accept fortune as part of God's plan. See A. Walsh 1985, pp. 295–338, for a discussion of this attitude in relationship to the revival of Stoic philosophy and the interest in the *Georgics* of Virgil.

12. See also Gibson 2000, pp. 117–40.

13. Quoted from the English translation by Kettering 1974, p. 164n8.

14. Bartsch [1854–1870] 1970, vol. 1, p. 164, no. 26. The plate is signed at the lower right with Saftleven's monogram and dated 1646. The lower margin includes the Latin inscription "Terra factus homo terram proscindit arator. . . ."

15. See Seelig 2010, pp. 192–94. The addition of the cock crowing behind the squatting peasant and the pink sky in Potter's painting, furthermore, place the scene at dawn. Similar figures appear in other contemporary Dutch landscapes, including *The Beach at Scheveningen*, by Adriaen van de Velde (1636–1672), 1670 (Los Angeles County Museum of Art; M.2009.106.14), where a bare-bottomed man squats in the background behind the beached boat directly below the church steeple. See A. Walsh 2019b, pp. 182–87.

64

Georg Pencz

German

Breslau ca. 1500–1550 Leipzig

Sleeping Female Nude, Vanitas

1544

Signed on candle snuffer in niche with monogram: "PG"; dated on wall to left of niche: "1544"
Oil on canvas, 36 7⁄8 × 68 7⁄8 in. (93.7 × 174.9 cm)
The Norton Simon Foundation, F.1982.2.1.P

Provenance
Private collection, southern France; [Christophe Bernoulli (1897–1981), Basel, to]; [Kate Perls (1889–1945), Paris, by 1936(?),[1] possibly owned in partnership with Richard Goetz by 1944?]; [Perls Galleries, New York, consigned 28 December 1945 to]; [Schaeffer Galleries, New York, stock no. 1074, returned April 1951 to]; [Perls Galleries, New York]. Anonymous (sale, Sotheby's, London, 22 June 1960, lot 57, sold to); Johnson. [Bernoulli, sold February 1969 for $2,000 to];[2] [Schaeffer Galleries, New York, half share Perls, stock no. 2586, sold May 1973 to]; Norton Simon, gift 1982 to; The Norton Simon Foundation.[3]

Exhibited
New York 1939c, no. 8;[4] Nuremberg 1952, p. 15, no. C-9, as *Ruhende Venus*, dated 1543, private collection; on loan, Phoenix Art Museum, 1 June–10 September 1973.

References
Hadeln 1923; Wescher 1936, pp. 34, 280f., ill.; Frankfurter 1939, p. 11, ill.; Breuning 1939, p. 298, ill.; J. W. Lane 1939, pp. 298f., ill.; Upjohn 1939, pp. 133f., ill.; Baldass 1940, p. 254; Gmelin 1961, pp. 106–08, 286, no. 24; Gmelin 1966, pp. 66–67, 86f., 89, no. 24, fig. 38; Gmelin 1968, pp. 247–48; Osten and Vey 1969, pp. 234, 281, 362n5, ill.; Osten 1973, p. 253; Pasadena 1980, p. 37, ill.; Pasadena 1989, p. 34, ill.; Jestaz 2007, p. 372, fig. 296; Ekserdjian 2007, p. 201; S. Campbell 2010, p. 353, no. 936, ill.; Dyballa 2015, pp. 146–48, 155, 196, 342–43, no. G6, 417, ill.

Technical Notes
The support, a fine plain-weave canvas, has undergone extensive repairs. The original edges of the painting have not survived, and it is not known to what extent portions of the edges were lost. The restoration is easily distinguished by means of X-radiography. In treatment before the painting entered the collection, inserts of canvas were attached along all four edges of the painting and secured by lining. There are also five various damages to the original support, including a complex tear near the top left corner, and another tear at the lower right. All repairs are stable and in plane. The white ground was smoothly applied. Microscopic examination of the surface offers no clear evidence of underpainting. Information noted in the X-radiograph, however, suggests that the artist covered the ground with a dark layer and then painted the figure and the pillow completely in white or a similarly dense pigment. The paint is thin and smoothly applied in a highly finished technique. Paint in the figure was applied in thin, subtly blended, smooth strokes. Finer details such as tiny wisps of hair and eyelashes were drawn with delicate lines of dark paint. The glaze of the red bedcover is glassy and finely cracked. Pinpoint flake losses have occurred throughout; while many of them have been carefully retouched, others are still visible in the lighter areas. There is a significant amount of loss in the woman's face and chest. Abrasion is widespread; shadowed areas and transitional tones have been thinned, and contours are abraded. UV light reveals extensive retouching and an aged synthetic-resin varnish.

Georg Pencz's nearly life-size female nude shown asleep on a bench derives from early sixteenth-century German and Italian prototypes but represents a new, provocative subject that both appeals to sexual desire and warns viewers of the vanity of earthly life. A popular woodcut illustration *Naiad-Venus Observed by Satyrs* (fig. 64a), published in *Hypnerotomachia Poliphili*, was particularly influential in developing the theme of the sleeping Venus in both Germany and Italy.[5] The print refers to a famous ancient fountain, beneath which was a statue of a sleeping guardian nymph.[6] According to a rumor that circulated toward the end of the fifteenth century, an inscription on the front of the fountain warned the wanderer not to disturb the nymph.[7] Originally the fountain was believed to have been located on the banks of the Danube, but during the sixteenth century various Renaissance gardens claimed to possess the original.[8] Both Albrecht Dürer (1471–1528) and Lucas Cranach I (1472–1553) refer to the tradition in several of their works: Dürer in a drawing datable to about 1510 (Albertina, Vienna), and Cranach in several versions of *Nymph of the Spring* in which cartouches refer to the fountain, the earliest example being dated 1518 (Museum der bildenden Künste, Leipzig).[9]

The position of the reclining nude in Pencz's painting—her extended left leg crossed over the right—is similar to those derived from the *Hypnerotomachia* woodcut and the Bernard de Montfaucon (1655–1741) engraving of a fountain nymph formerly in the garden of the Palazzo Colocci, Rome (fig. 64b).[10] As in these examples, the figure's left hand rests on her thigh. Pencz differs from this tradition, however, in placing the

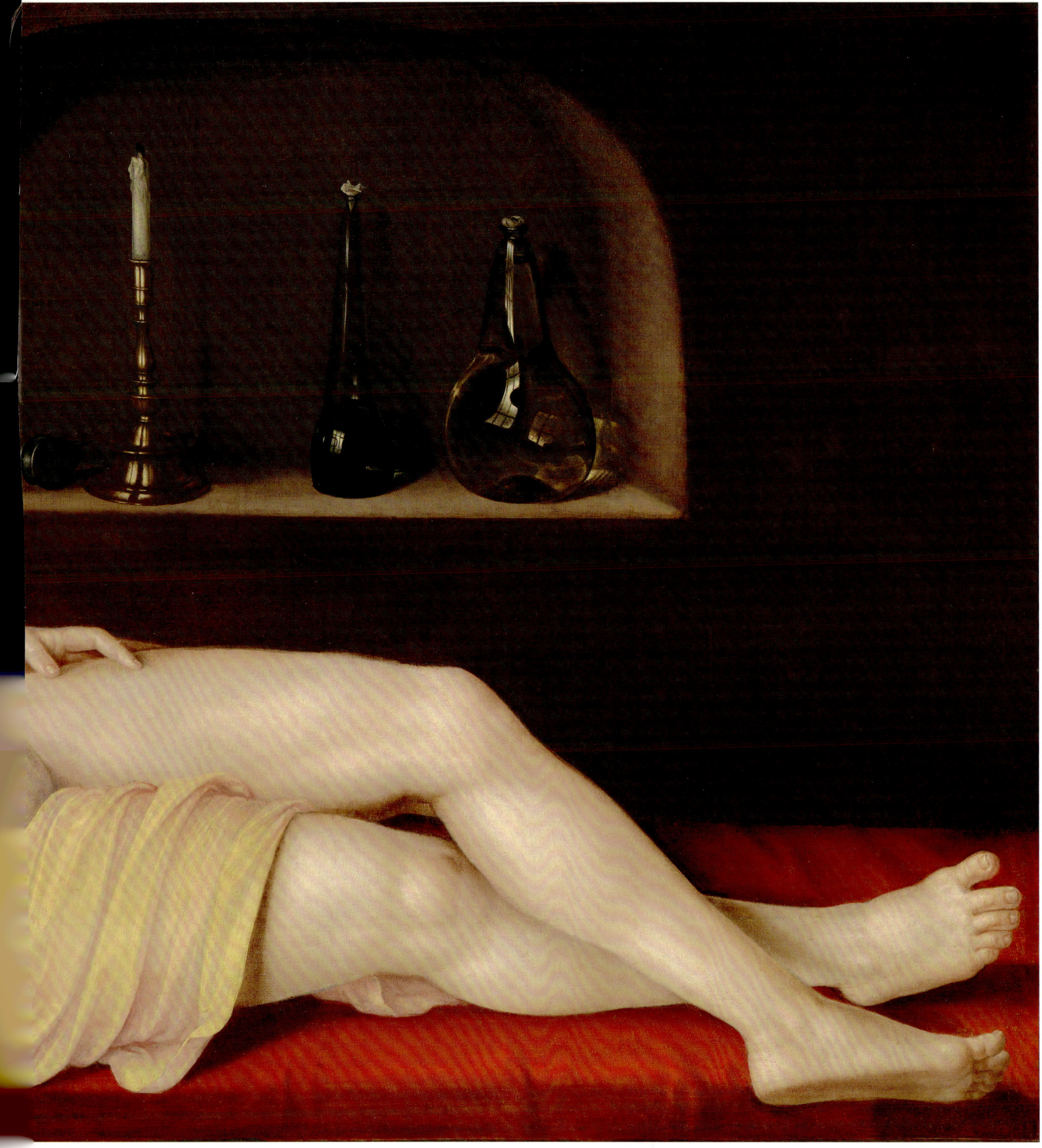

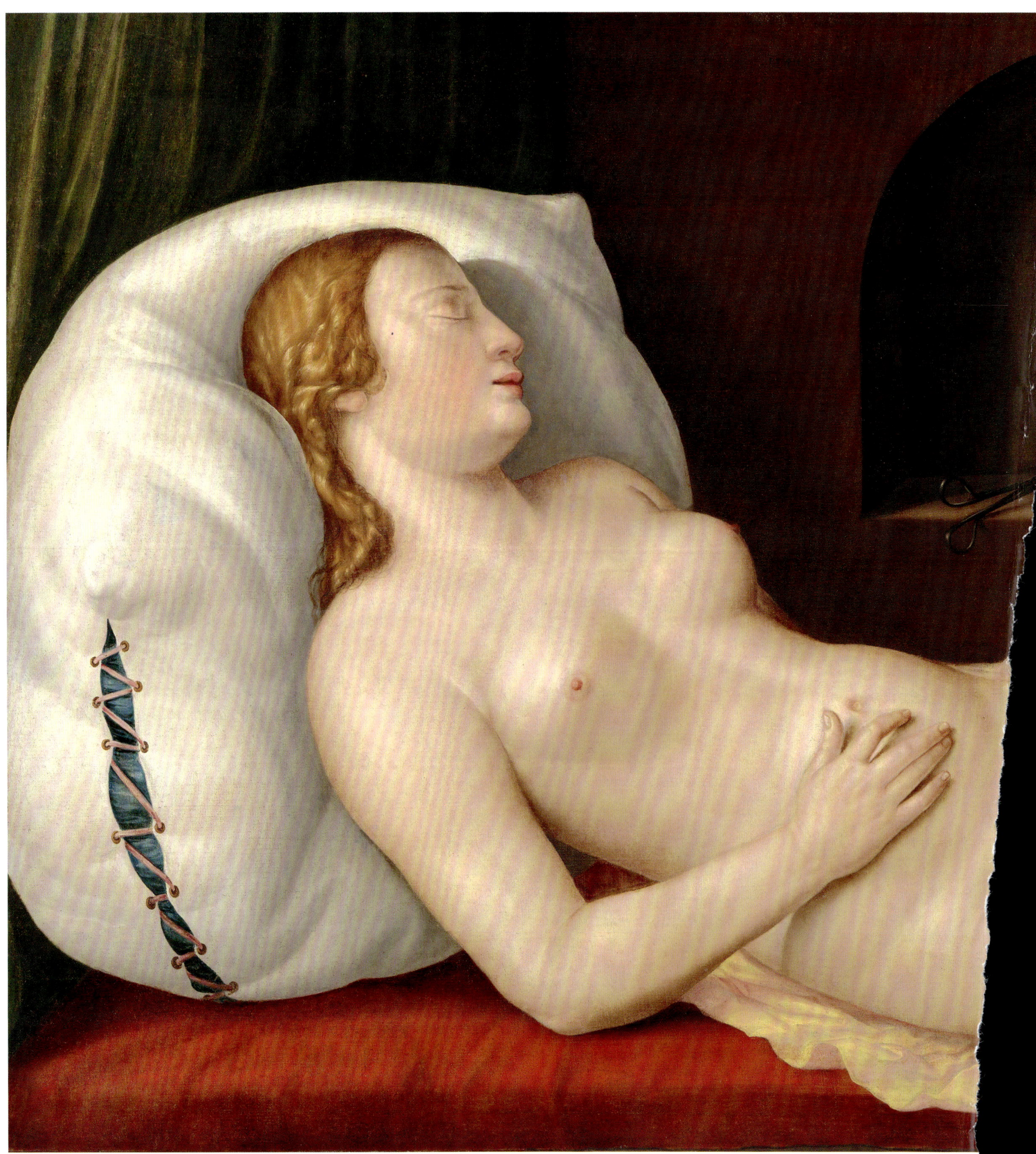

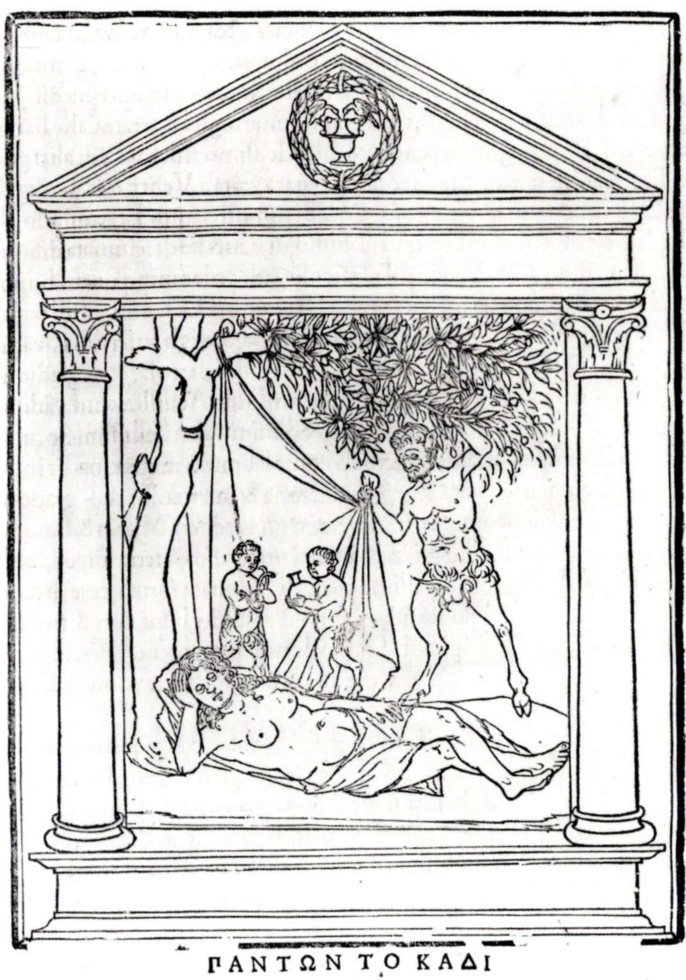

Fig. 64a. *Naiad-Venus Observed by Satyrs*, woodcut, from *Hypnerotomachia Poliphili* (Venice, 1499), Getty Research Institute, Los Angeles.

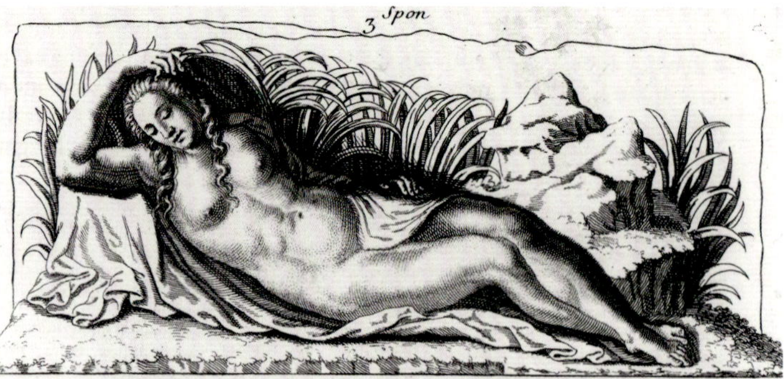

Fig. 64b. Bernard de Montfaucon, *Fountain Nymph*, from *L'antiquité expliquée et représentée en figures* (Paris: Chez Florentin Delaulne, 1719), engraving, Getty Research Institute, Los Angeles.

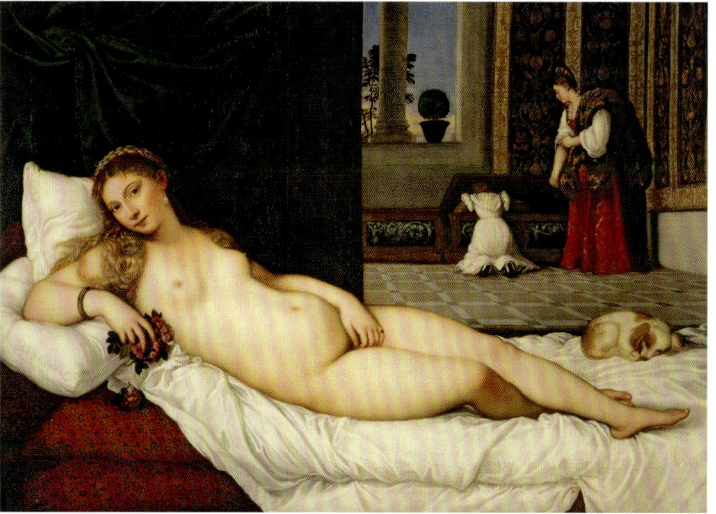

Fig. 64c. Titian, *Venus of Urbino*, 1538, oil on canvas, 46 7/8 × 65 in. (119 × 165 cm), Gallerie degli Uffizi, Florence.

woman's right arm on her belly rather than over or supporting her head, the traditional Roman pose of sleep adopted by the German and Italian portrayals of the subject. Pencz also turns her face away so that it appears in profile and she assumes a more relaxed pose, oblivious to presence of the viewer.

The large scale and details of the Pasadena painting suggest that Pencz, who traveled to Italy in the 1520s, was also influenced by Italian paintings, possibly the large *Sleeping Venus* (ca. 1510, Gemäldegalerie, Dresden) begun by Giorgione (1477–1510) but finished by Titian (ca. 1488–1576). This masterpiece of Venetian painting represents Venus asleep in a landscape, propped up by an overstuffed pillow, her right arm encircling her head, and her left hand cupped provocatively over her pubic area. The interior setting and elaborately plaited golden hair of Pencz's sleeping subject suggest that he also knew, possibly through copies, later versions of Titian's treatment of the theme, including the *Venus of Urbino* (fig. 64c).[11] Like Titian's Venuses, Pencz's nude reclines on a draped bench in a contemporary interior.[12] His emphasis on contour—which renders a cool, dispassionate figure—is aesthetically tied to the Roman tradition of Giulio Romano (1499?–1546), whose work Pencz knew through his travels, and the popular prints of Marcantonio Raimondi (ca. 1470/82–1527/34).[13]

Pencz manipulated the body and composition to create an erotic, seductive image.[14] Supported by a voluptuous pillow with suggestive stitching, the life-size figure is brought so close to the picture plane that her foot appears to extend beyond the edge of the bench into the viewer's space. Pencz placed the woman so that we look down on her belly, our attention drawn by the encircling gesture of the right arm echoed by the yellow drapery, which reveals rather than conceals, and reinforced by the placement of the left hand and the candle on the shelf of the niche.[15] Realistic details, particularly the description of pubic hair, emphasize our intimate proximity. Pencz has transformed the popular views of Venus sleeping in a landscape, secretly observed by satyrs, into a contemporary woman in a contemporary setting. By isolating the nude and eliminating the narrative elements of the story, Pencz placed the viewer in the highly charged role of a satyr uncovering the seductive sleeper.

Erotic images, usually presented in terms of the loves of the gods and antics of nymphs and satyrs, were popular in Renaissance court circles.[16] The earliest known paintings of a reclining figure of Venus are a pair of late quattrocento Florentine marriage chests called cassones, where the goddess is observed by a clothed mortal, the groom.[17] Venus sleeping or resting was, in fact, traditionally associated with weddings. Claudius (ca. 370–ca. 404), the last of the Roman poets, began an epithalamium, a poem or song dedicated to newlyweds, with a description of Venus asleep.[18] Following his example, Renaissance writers began songs glorifying love—sung by young men and maidens before the bridal chamber—with a description of Venus either sleeping or resting in her garden after the departure of Mars.[19]

During the Renaissance, paintings of reclining nudes displayed in bedrooms and baths were understood to represent courtesans.[20] The reclining posture of even clothed figures was generally associated with moral laxity, and pillows were common references to luxury and indolence. The yellow drapery across the woman's leg in Pencz's painting would have specifically identified her as a courtesan.[21] Until the mid-sixteenth century, brothels were officially sanctioned and controlled in virtually all German cities; they were often operated by town councils, religious houses, and even bishops. Women in this industry were restricted in their public behavior and required to be instantly identifiable by wearing yellow.[22]

The literate patron of Pencz's painting, almost certainly a man, would have recognized the allusions to classical precedents while delighting in the seductive subject. He would also have recognized Pencz's reference to traditional northern admonitions to think about one's own mortality.[23] Prominently placed in the niche behind the figure, the extinguished candle and snuffer reinforce the association of the sleeping figure with death. The sleeping woman lying on a bench in front of a niche parallel to the picture plane recalls contemporary memorials, dating back to the medieval period, in which the effigy of the deceased person is presented like Christ laid on the altar. The theme of *vanitas* or memento mori was often invoked in the prints by Barthel Beham (1502–1540) and Sebald Beham (1500–1550), Pencz's compatriots in Nuremberg. In *Death and the Maiden* of 1547, for example, Sebald Beham represented a winged figure of death embracing the nude figure of a young woman; the inscription reads "OMNEM IN HOMINE VENVSTATEM MORS ABOLET" (Death abolishes all human beauty).[24] In Sebald Beham's seductive *Death and the Sleeping Woman*, the relationship to Pencz's painting is even more striking.[25] Like Sebald Beham's print, the Pasadena painting seduces viewers with the beauty and the erotic pleasure of the sleeping nude but then cautions them that life on earth is only transitory and that one must think about eternal life.[26]

1. Wescher 1936, p. 280: "Aus dem südfranzösischen Besitz neu aufgetauchten Bild, das sich gegenwärtig im Pariser Handel befindet." That Parisian dealer is possibly Kate Perls, who had purchased the painting at an unknown date from the Basel dealer, Christophe Bernoulli. This information comes from the "Memorandum of Agreement" dated 6 March 1946 between Klaus G. Perls and Frank R. and Thomas A. Perls in settling the estate of their mother, Kate Perls. See box 1, folder 16, page 4 of this legal document in the Frank Perls papers and Frank Perls Gallery records, ca. 1920–83, bulk 1949–75, Archives of American Art, Smithsonian Institution. A photograph of the Pencz shown hanging in the New York studio of Richard Goetz in 1944 is in the Perls Gallery records, 1937–97, Archives of American Art, Smithsonian Institution, box 75, file 47. In this photo, the Pencz hangs near Jacopo Tintoretto's (1519–1594) *Tarquin and Lucretia*, which was in the Goetz collection by 1939 and now belongs to the Art Institute of Chicago.

2. Bernoulli was probably acting as an agent at this point. Schaeffer documents indicate that Bernoulli was paid a commission of $1,000 on 24 January 1973.

3. Dyballa 2015, p. 343, refers to a painting identified as by Hans Holbein II (1497/98–1543) mentioned in the 1621 inventory of the collection of Emperor Rudolf II (r. 1583–1612) in Prague: "Ein nachend Weib liegend auf einen bett, von Holbein." She notes there is no known work by Holbein that fits that description, but her conclusion that it might refer to the Pasadena painting by Pencz remains speculative. Paintings particularly close in spirit, detail, and scale to Pencz's nude of 1544 were painted by younger artists working at the imperial court later in the century. Two paintings of recumbent, nearly life-size female nudes (Kunsthistorisches Museum, Vienna, and Musée des beaux-arts, Dijon) painted as pendants by Dirk de Quade van Ravesteyn (ca. 1576–1612) for the Habsburg court suggest the popularity of these images in German courts, particularly after the middle of the sixteenth century. See Kaufmann 1988, pp. 224–25, ill.; Lawner 1987, p. 135.

4. The catalogue lists the lender as R. M. Coe, which was likely a printer's mistake.

5. The significance of the print for Giorgione's Dresden painting was first discussed in a lecture, "Titian and Pietro Aretino," given by Fritz Saxl at the Warburg Institute in May 1935 (Saxl 1957, pp. 72ff.). See general discussion of subject in Meiss 1966. The posture of the woman ultimately depends on ancient Roman prototypes, notably a second-century marble sculpture *Sleeping Ariadne* (Vatican Museum, Rome).

6. The ancient Greeks represented the goddess of a spring as a nymph asleep with her arm over an urn. See, for example, *Sleeping Nymph*, a Roman copy of a Greek original (Vatican Museum; Kurz 1953, fig. 23b). These images, in turn, were adapted from those of the prostrate Maenad. See Kurz 1953, p. 171, which dates the drawing ca. 1514.

7. Kurz 1953, p. 171, gives the text of the epigram, which was included in almost all epigraphical syllogai thereafter.

8. Kurz 1953, pp. 172f.

9. Museo Nacional Thyssen-Bornemisza, Madrid; Staatliche Museen, Kassel; Gemäldegalerie Alte Meister, Dresden (GK19); and the Metropolitan Museum of Art, New York (1975.1.136). Kurz 1953, p. 176, remarks that many scholars have noted that Cranach was inspired by Giorgione's *Venus*. Regarding Cranach's Venuses, see Talbot 1987.

10. De Montfaucon 1719, vol. 1, pt. 2, pl. 220.

11. The classical pose of the reclining nude is most often associated with the sleeping Ariadne discovered by Bacchus on Naxos. Images on ancient Roman topazes, however, indicate

that Venus was also represented as a reclining nude in both art and literature during antiquity. Anderson 1980, p. 337, suggests that these gemstones were important sources for artists in Venice, where there were no monumental ancient sculptures. In identifying the ancient tradition of representing the sleeping Venus, Anderson consciously contradicts Meiss 1966, p. 348, who had asserted that Venus was never shown lying asleep in Graeco-Roman art. Anderson points out that the ancients also represented Rhea and Silvia as well as various nymphs as reclining nudes. In antiquity, the Greek word *anapauomenai* was used to designate these pictures of women at rest.

12. Regarding Titian's Venuses, see Goffen 1997.

13. A similar image appears in Raimondi's own engraving *Cleopatra* (Bartsch [1854–70], 1970, vol. 14, p. 162, no. 199). Gmelin 1966, p. 87, compares the Pasadena painting stylistically to Raimondi's etching *Morbetto: Plague of Phrygia* (Bartsch [1854–70] 1970, vol. 14, p. 314, no. 417).

14. Baldass 1940, p. 554, noted the similarity of the Pasadena painting to the erotic *Venus* (Contini Collection, Florence) by Titian's follower Bernardino Licinio (ca. 1490–after 1549). Licinio's nude is, however, more provocative.

15. Note especially the suggestive placement of the candle above the figure's hand and crotch and the bulbous forms of the bottles. Vessels were often used as metaphors for the uterus. Peter W. Parshall (unpublished correspondence, 12 January 1989, NSM) suggests that "the bottles would certainly imply urine and hence pregnancy (or illness)."

16. See Levy 1988, pp. 40–53. For discussion of the imperial court at the end of the sixteenth century, see Kaufmann 1985, pp. 29–46.

17. Anderson 1980, p. 341, citing Wind 1967, p. 143n7, pls. 44–45.

18. Anderson 1980, p. 338.

19. Venus is usually surrounded by *amori*, and her slumber is always disturbed by Cupid, who arrives with arms to spur his mother to action. She attends weddings as the patroness of marriage. See Anderson 1980, p. 338.

20. By clothing his figures only in expensive jewelry and hats, Cranach connected these provocative nudes in landscapes with contemporary courtesans. See Levy 1988, pp. 40ff.

21. Anderson 1980, p. 103.

22. For a fascinating look at this underside of German society in the age of Luther, see Wiesner 1986, pp. 97–109.

23. According to Levy 1988, p. 40, "Both the earlier images and many in the sixteenth-century were informed by a moralizing, satirical, or didactic spirit that is largely absent from the erotic engravings of the Behams. Instead, the prints of the Behams reinterpreted the subjects to create works that were self-conscious quotations of the artistic past intended to delight a visually literate audience and were frankly—and primarily—erotic." Sebald Beham and his younger brother, Barthel Beham, were born in Nuremberg and possibly trained by Dürer. In 1525, together with their colleague Georg Pencz, they were expelled from Nuremberg for their professed agnostic beliefs. See biographical sketches in Lawrence 1988, pp. 221–24.

24. Bartsch [1854–70] 1970, vol. 8, p. 99, no. 150.

25. Dated 1548 (Bartsch [1854–70] 1970, vol. 8, pp. 97f., no. 146; Pauli 1911, no. 147), it is a copy in reverse of Barthel Beham (Bartsch [1854–70] 1970, vol. 8, p. 58, no. 41; Pauli 1911, no. 39). Regarding these and other prints by Beham, Pencz, and the other "German Little Masters," see Lawrence 1988, specifically pp. 160–65. See also Barthel Beham's *Vanitas*, 1540 (Hamburger Kunsthalle), which represents a nude woman standing on a stone plinth with the figure of death and a child next to a sleeping (dead) nude woman. Beham referred to three biblical passages that compare human flesh to the grass, which will wither, and beauty to the flower, which will fade (Isaiah 40:68; Psalms 103:14–16; and Peter I, 1:24). A variation of the theme is Hans Mielich (1516–1573), *Vanitas*, dated 1536 (Städtliche Museum, Regensburg), which represents a naked infant sleeping supported by a pillow on a ledge through which can be seen a view of the cloisters of Saint Emmeram's Abbey in Regensburg. Between his legs is an hourglass, a traditional symbol of *vanitas*.

26. Sebald Beham's *Death and the Sleeping Woman* includes, on the bottom right, the inscription "O. DIE STUND IST AUS" (The hour has come).

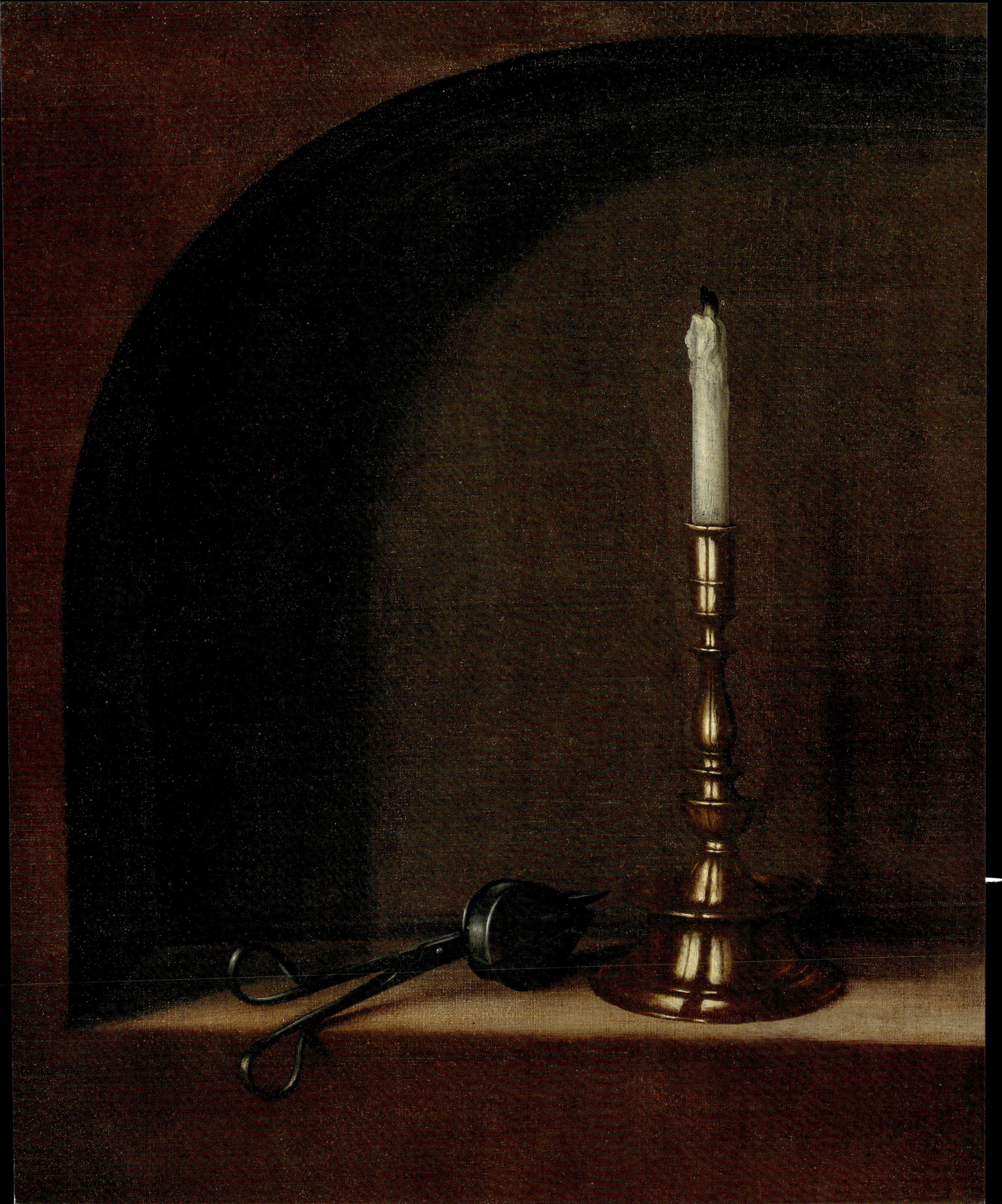

65

Rembrandt Harmensz. van Rijn

Dutch
Leyden 1606–1669 Amsterdam

Portrait of a Bearded Man in a Wide-Brimmed Hat, Probably Jacob Jacobsz. van Couwenhoven (1592–1661)[1]

1633

Signed and dated, center right: "Rembrandt f 1633"
Inscribed with monogram, middle left: "AET 41"
Oil on oval panel (cradled), 27½ × 21½ in. (69.9 × 54.6 cm)
Norton Simon Art Foundation, M.1977.31.P

Provenance
Probably William Lygon (1782–1823), 2nd Earl Beauchamp, Madresfield Court, Great Malvern, Worcestershire, by inheritance to;[2] Sir Frederick Lygon (1830–1891), 6th Earl Beauchamp, by 1889, by inheritance to his son; Sir William Lygon (1872–1938), 7th Earl Beauchamp, Madresfield Court, Great Malvern, Worcestershire, sold with its pendant 1909 to; [M. Knoedler & Co., London, stock no. 4642, and New York, stock no. 11944, owned with P. & D. Colnaghi, London, sold January 1911 to]; Henry Clay Frick (1849–1919), New York, traded back October 1911 to Knoedler, sold May 1912 to; William Henry Moore (1848–1939), New York, by inheritance to his wife; Ada W. Small (Mrs. William Henry Moore, d. 1955), New York, by descent to their son; Edward S. Moore, New York (estate sale, Sotheby's, London, 23 March 1960, lot 67, sold to); [Thomas Agnew & Sons, London, sold to]; Baron H. Thyssen-Bornemisza, Lugano, until after 1971. [E. V. Thaw & Co. Inc., New York, sold 1977 to]; Norton Simon Art Foundation.

Exhibited
New York 1915, no. 11, as dated 1634; on loan, Yale University Art Gallery, New Haven, June 1956–January 1960; on loan, St. Louis Art Museum, 14 June–22 November 1977; on loan, J. B. Speed Art Museum, Louisville, 22 November 1977–10 January 1978.

References
Madresfield [1889], p. 26, no. 78 or 80;[3] Arundel 1909, no. 13; Hofstede de Groot 1908–27, vol. 6 (1916), p. 360, no. 769; Valentiner 1921b, pp. xviii, pl. 30, no. 33, ill.; Valentiner 1923b, pp. xxii, 32, no. 37, ill.; Benesch 1935, p. 14;[4] Bredius 1935, no. 177, ill.; Heinemann 1958–64, no. 345a; Bauch 1966, no. 365, ill., erroneously as "formerly Lugano, Baron Thyssen-Bornemisza Coll."; Bredius/Gerson 1969, pp. 151, 562, no. 177, ill.; Heinemann 1969, vol. 1, p. 281, no. 259, vol. 2, pl. 141; Heinemann 1971, vol. 1, pp. 323f., no. 259, vol. 2, pl. 141; Schlégl and Berkes 1971, pp. 64f., ill.; "A Bearded Man" 1977, p. 135, ill.; "Acquisitions" 1978, p. 351, ill.; Slive 1979, pp. 3ff., figs. 2, 4; Pasadena 1980, p. 56, ill.; Schwartz 1985, p. 153, no. 140, ill.; *Corpus* 1986, pp. 440–44, A86; P. Sutton 1986, p. 217; Tümpel 1986, p. 428; Pasadena 1989, p. 78, ill.; Slatkes 1992, p. 214, no. 122, ill., as Rembrandt; Tümpel 1993, pp. 88, 432, 462, no. A84, ill.; Muchnic 1998, p. 65; Wright 2001, pp. 188, 202, ill.; Pasadena 2003, p. 68, ill.; Van der Veen 2003, passim; Wolleswinkel 2005, no. 6; Indianapolis 2006, p. 36, fig. 14; Woollett 2009, p. 27, no. 10; S. Campbell 2010, pp. 221, 223, 412, no. 1489, ill.; Bailey et al. 2011, pp. 18f.; Van de Wetering 2017, pt. 1, p. 198, ill., pt. 2, p. 537, no. 119a; Manuth, De Winkel, and Van Leeuwen 2019, pp. 86, 657–58; Dudok van Heel 2020b, pp. 137–38; Ekkart and Van den Donk 2021, pp. 148f.

Technical Notes
The support is an oak panel made in a single piece. The slightly irregular contour of the oval corresponds to the historical conjecture that it was cut down from a rectangular format. This theory is based on traces of beveling on the sides of the pendant portrait panel in the collection of the Speed Art Museum, Louisville.[5] Both panels have been thinned, adhered to a second mahogany panel of the same dimensions, and similarly cradled. The wood texture is visible through the thin off-white or beige ground. A thin medium-brown underpainting lies beneath the black areas, in the shadow across the forehead, and in the shaded portion of the face, where the form is modeled with small, unrefined brushstrokes. There is light salmon underpainting beneath the white ruff and the background, visible at the center right, likely created by the addition of white to the wet brown underpainting. The paint and ground layers, which extend to all edges, are generally very well preserved. Rembrandt employed the optical contrasts of cool opaque green-gray and transparent warm red-brown to enliven the modeling of the face. The underpainting was occasionally left exposed as transitional mid-tones in the face. The minimal amount of detail in the black coat is achieved by the brushwork. The strong suggestion of form in the ruff is created by the alternation of warm and cool grays. The hat brim at the far right remains inside the reserve left for it as well as at the right side of the crown. Shadows are created with semitransparent paint; the thickest, most opaque paint provides highlights. Brushmarking is minimal, primarily over the proper right shoulder of the coat, in the underside of the hat, and in the eyes, eyebrows, mustache, and beard. X-radiography indicates that the position of the proper right shoulder was altered, painted slightly lower in the final state. The painting was selectively cleaned in the face and ruff in an undocumented treatment before acquisition. There is minor abrasion in the black coat and the left side of the hat. Small abrasions around the mouth and eyes are distracting. Old retouching at the center of the right edge may be covering

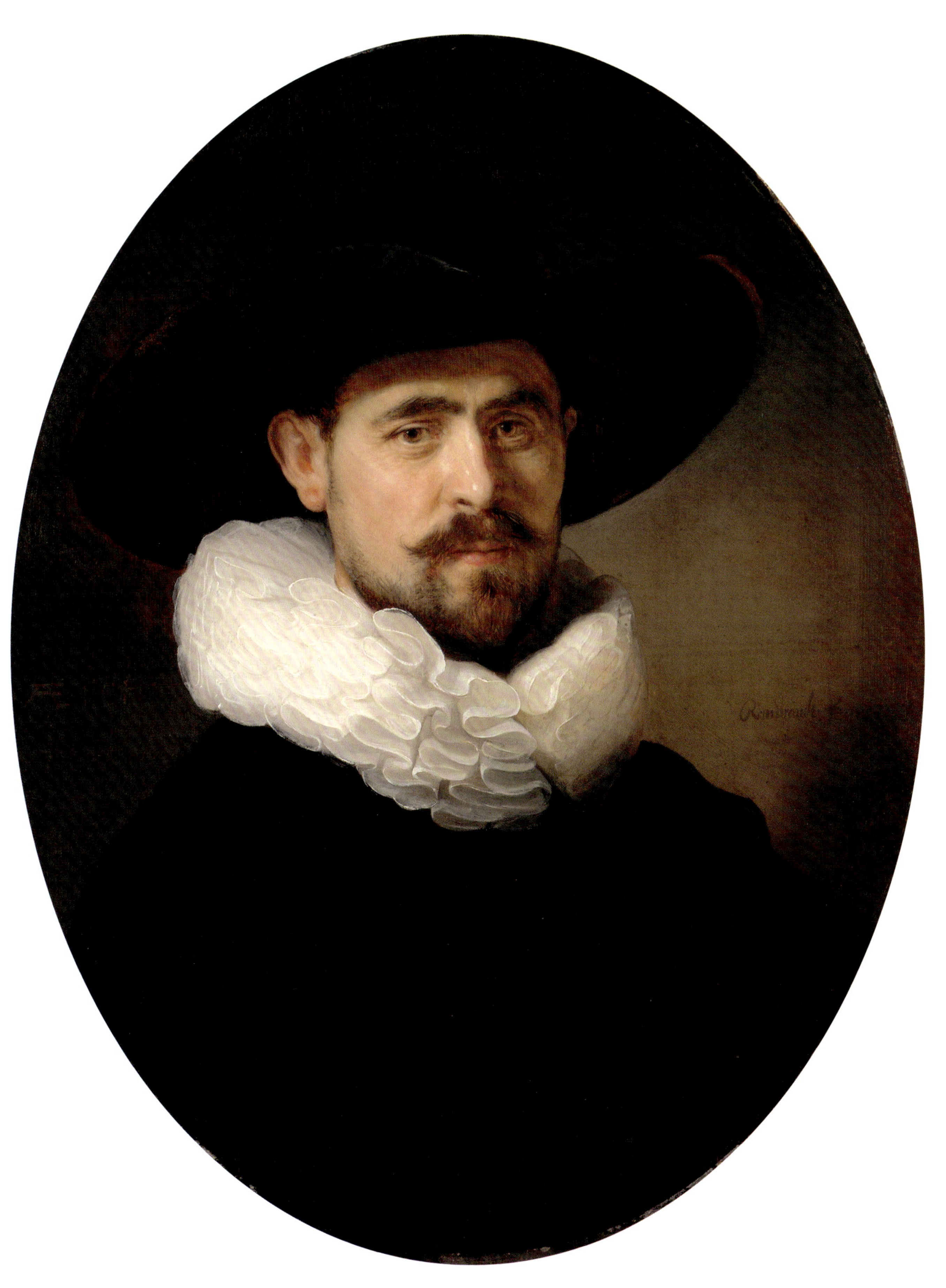

abrasion in the background. The synthetic-resin varnish is not noticeably discolored, but it does not saturate well.

Dated 1633, *Portrait of a Bearded Man in a Wide-Brimmed Hat, Probably Jacob Jacobsz. van Couwenhoven* is one of a group of bust portraits Rembrandt painted during the 1630s, when the artist transformed the fashionable oval format into a new type of dynamic composition.[6] Omitting the sitter's hands and any reference to setting, the image focuses attention on the sitter's face framed by the voluptuous white ruff and the wide brim of his black hat. The undulating line of the brim and the large loops of the ruff that encircles the sitter's neck create a striking impression of three-dimensional form and space. Rembrandt used light and shadow selectively to emphasize the sculptural quality of the sitter as well as to animate him. Light cast from the upper left illuminates the proper right side of the sitter's face but leaves the left side in partial shadow, rendered with abbreviated brushstrokes that allow the brown underpaint to show and serve as a middle tone. Reflections from the elaborate collar contribute to the lively play of light on his face, while the shadow cast on his forehead seamlessly integrates the hat and face. Rembrandt enlivened the background by applying gray paint over the medium-brown underpaint, varying the intensity and value of the gray. The darkest area is in the upper left; the lightest gray is to the right of the sitter, where an area of darker paint suggests the shadow of his head.

From at least 1889 until 1960, when the two paintings were sold to different buyers, the Pasadena portrait hung with *Portrait of a Forty-Year-Old Woman, Possibly Marretje Cornelisdr. van Grotewal* (fig. 65a).[7] The formal, bust-length portraits have similar proportions and are painted on oval panels with virtually the same dimensions.[8] Addressing the viewer from mirrored positions within separate panels, the sitters are compositionally bound together as if they occupy a continuous space with a common light source.[9] Typical of portraits conceived as pendants, the man is placed on the viewer's left and the woman, on the right. Light from the upper left that casts the male sitter in partial shadow fully illuminates the face of the female sitter.[10]

Rembrandt portrayed the sitter in the Pasadena portrait as a public figure who exhibits the ideals of sobriety and moderation that characterized the bourgeois values of the Dutch elite. Turned slightly to the right and looking toward the viewer, he wears a wide-brimmed black hat, a black cloak with velvet facings, and a loosely pleated ruff that encircles his neck.[11] Rembrandt emphasized the sitter's eyes by casting the shadow of the hat's wide brim as a straight line above his eyebrows, while the brows themselves cast the proper left eye into shadow and partially obscure the right eye as well. For Rembrandt, as for Karel van Mander (1548–1606) and others, the eyes revealed character and were thus the most important features of the face.

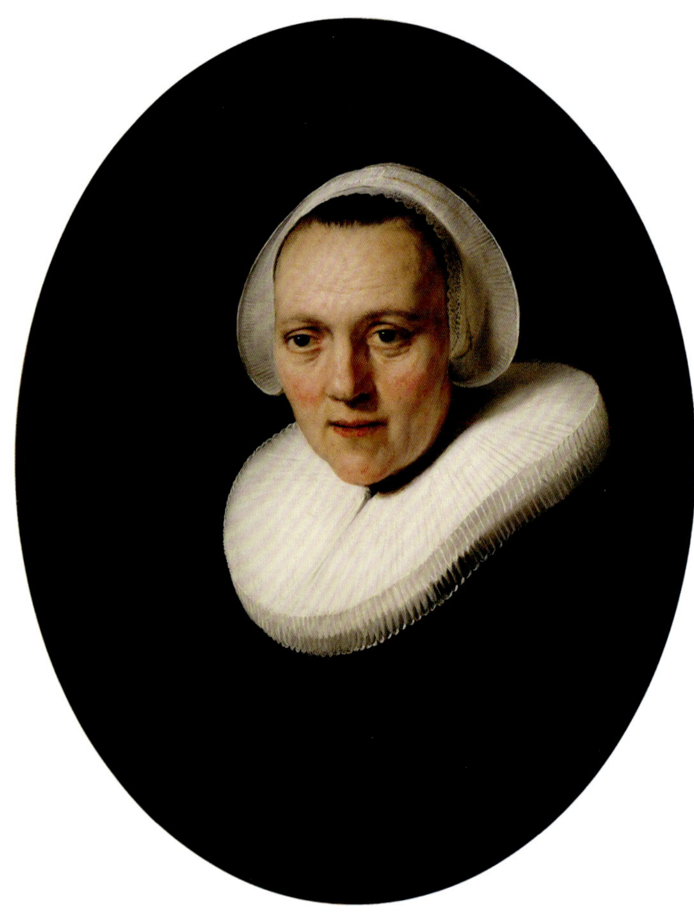

Fig. 65a. Rembrandt Harmensz. van Rijn, *Portrait of a Forty-Year-Old Woman, Possibly Marretje Cornelisdr. van Grotewal*, 1634, oil on panel, 27 × 21½ in. (68.5 × 54.5 cm), The Speed Art Museum, Louisville, purchased with funds contributed by individuals, corporations, and the entire community of Louisville, as well as the Commonwealth of Kentucky 1977.16.

By partially obscuring his features in shadow, Rembrandt portrayed the sitter as an enigmatic personality—one cannot fully grasp the details of his face, which appear transient. In contrast to the portrayal of her husband, light fully describes the female sitter's features, as well as her stiff ruff and the white cap that frames her pleasant face. Turning to directly address the viewer, the light subtly models the proper left side of her face and casts her cap in soft shadow. The beautiful delicate highlight that follows the rim of her cap contributes to the perception of volume and further animates the portrait.

Scholars have offered several suggestions for the identity of the couple represented in the Pasadena portrait and its pendant in Louisville, which were painted when Rembrandt was associated with the Amsterdam art dealer Hendrick Uylenburgh (ca. 1587–1661),[12] who helped him secure portrait commissions from members of the Mennonite community. In 2003 Jaap van der Veen proposed that the Pasadena portrait and its pendant represent Pieter Sijen (ca. 1592–1652) and his wife, Marretje Cornelisdr. van Gro[o]tewal (ca. 1593–1666), members, like Uylenburgh, of the Amsterdam Waterlander Mennonite congregation. In 1633 Sijen was forty-one and his wife was forty, the ages Rembrandt inscribed on the portraits. At the time of their marriage in 1613 Sijen inherited 12,000 guilders from his father's estate, upon which he built a sizable fortune as a linen merchant and investor. Van der Veen arrived at the names of the sitters while investigating the identity of "twee portrette van voorouders geschildert door Rembrant" (two portraits of ancestors painted by Rembrandt) in the 1703 inventory of the property of the linen merchant Pieter Pietersz. Sijen (1665–1706) of Gouda, the great-grandson and direct heir of the couple. Van der Veen notes that by using the term "voorouders" Pieter Pietersz. Sijen indicated that the sitters were his direct ancestors. Van der Veen suggests that Rembrandt was introduced to Pieter Sijen through Uylenburgh, who borrowed money from the merchant in 1639 and probably knew him as a fellow congregant.[13]

Alternately, E. J. Wolleswinkel suggests that the painting portrays the Mennonite preacher Cornelis Claesz. Anslo (1592–1646), whom Rembrandt represented speaking to a woman in a famous portrait dated 1641 (fig. 65b). Wolleswinkel notes that Pieter Pietersz. Sijen was related to the Anslo family through his grandmother Marretje Arents Bosch (1613–1662), the wife of Joris Pietersz. Sijen (1614–1666), Pieter Sijen's only child to survive to adulthood. Wolleswinkel observes that the sitters in Pasadena and Louisville portraits physically resemble the couple Rembrandt portrayed in 1641 and that Anslo was forty-one in 1633. However, the birth date of Anslo's wife, Aeltje Gerritsdr. Schouten (d. 1657), which has been cited as both 1589/90 and 1598, as well as the indirect line of inheritance, makes this suggestion doubtful.[14]

Marieke de Winkel dismisses the identification of the sitter in the Pasadena painting as either Pieter Sijen or Cornelis Claesz. Anslo, convincingly arguing that the elaborate, loosely pleated ruff, known as a *fraise à la confusion*, would have been inappropriate for a conservative Mennonite.[15] Similar ruffs are, significantly, worn by the sitters in Rembrandt's portraits of the preacher Dr. Johannes Wtenbogaert (1557–1644) (Rijksmuseum, Amsterdam) and Dirck Jansz. Pesser (1586–1651; fig. 65c), a wealthy brewer in Rotterdam. Both men were leaders in the Remonstrant Brotherhood, moderate Calvinists who broke away from the orthodox Calvinist church. De Winkel proposes that the Pasadena portrait represents the Rotterdam brewer Jacob Jacobsz. van Couwenhoven (1592–1661), who was married to Marritge Jansdr. Pesser (1593–1646), sister of Dirck Pesser. The ages of Van Couwenhoven and his wife agree with those Rembrandt inscribed on the portraits: In 1633 he was forty-one, and in 1634, the date on the female portrait in Louisville, she was forty or forty-one.

Jacob Jacobsz. van Couwenhoven, the son of Jacob Allertsz. van Couwenhoven, was baptized 29 June 1592 in Brielle.[16] Some members of the Van Couwenhoven family were involved in the herring business and held various positions in the municipal government of Brielle; others were prominent brewers in Rotterdam. In 1621 Jacob van Couwenhoven, who would become one of the wealthiest men in the Netherlands during the seventeenth century, founded De Twee Klimmende Leeuwen (The Two Climbing Lions) brewery on the Leuvenhaven in Rotterdam with the financial assistance of his brother-in-law Dammas Jansz. Pesser (1590–1670), the owner and operator of the Witte Leeuw (White Lion) brewery.[17] Another brother-in-law, Dirck Jansz. Pesser, was the owner of the Swarte Leeuw (Black Lion) brewery. The names of the three brothers-in-law often appear together in documents in Rotterdam, indicating their close personal and professional relationship through marriage and shared interests in business and religion.

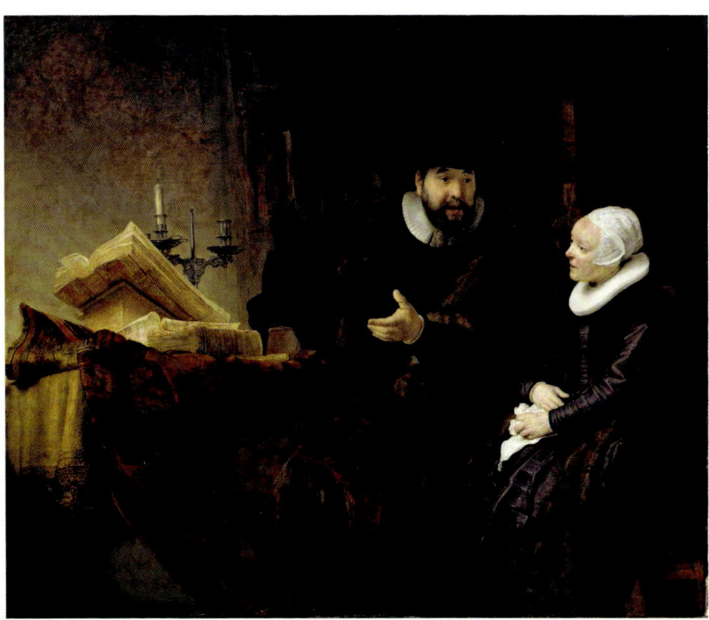

Fig. 65b. Rembrandt Harmensz. van Rijn, *Mennonite Preacher Cornelis Claesz. Anslo (1592–1646) and His Wife, Aeltje Gerritsdr. Schouten*, 1641, oil on canvas, 69⅜ × 89½ in. (176 × 210 cm), Gemäldegalerie, Staatliche Museen, Berlin.

Both the Van Couwenhoven and the Pesser families were prominent leaders of the Remonstrants, the moderate religious group that in 1610 had presented the officials of the orthodox Calvinist church with five articles of remonstrance calling for greater religious tolerance and revision of the doctrine of predestination.[18] In 1618 the Synod of Dort (Dordrecht) condemned the Remonstrants and sent many of their leaders, including relatives of the Van Couwenhoven and Pesser families, into exile. The stadtholder, Prince Maurits (1567–1625), who sided with the orthodox Calvinists, dismissed the libertine governments in the cities of Holland and Utrecht and forbade Remonstrants to gather. Following the closure of the Remonstrant church in Rotterdam, however, the congregation met secretly in the open fields and in the

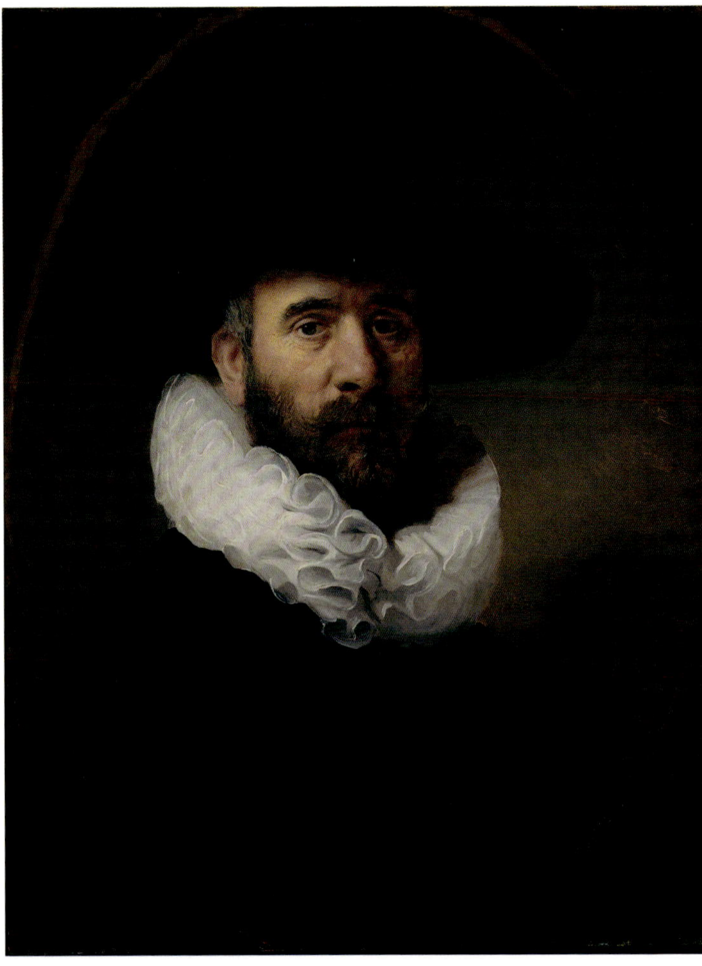

Fig. 65c. Rembrandt Harmensz. van Rijn, *Portrait of Dirck Jansz. Pesser*, ca. 1634, oil on wood panel, oval: 25 ½ × 19 ⅞ in. (64.8 × 50.5 cm), enlarged to rectangle: 27 ⅛ × 20 ⅞ in. (68.9 × 53 cm), Los Angeles County Museum of Art.

brewery of Jacob van Couwenhoven and the malt house owned by Dirck Pesser on the Wijnstraat. The meetings, which drew huge crowds, were often interrupted by violent conflicts with soldiers who plundered and brutalized the Remonstrants.[19] Jacob van Couwenhoven and his brothers-in-law were briefly arrested but then released. With the succession of the more liberal Frederik Hendrik (1584–1647) as stadtholder in 1625, the restrictions on the Remonstrants eased. In 1630, when Remonstrants could again openly practice their religion, the first large gathering was held in Rotterdam. Two years later Jacob van Couwenhoven and Dirck Pesser, together with other brewers, founded the Remonstrant church in a brewery on the Vissersdijk in Rotterdam.[20]

S. A. C. Dudok van Heel proposes that Rembrandt painted the portraits of both Jacob van Couwenhoven and Dirck Pesser in Amsterdam in April 1633.[21] Johannes Wtenbogaert, the celebrated elder leader of the Remonstrants who had resided with the Pessers in Rotterdam after his return from exile, probably introduced the two men to Rembrandt. According to his diary, on 13 April 1633 Wtenbogaert met with Rembrandt and posed for the monumental three-quarter-length portrait now in the Rijksmuseum.[22] Wtenbogaert, who lived in The Hague, was in Amsterdam for the large annual gathering of the Remonstrant Brotherhood held 2–21 April 1633. The date 1633 on the Pasadena painting suggests that the sitter, Jacob Jacobsz. van Couwenhoven, was also among the attendees at the Remonstrant gathering and sat for Rembrandt while in Amsterdam. Dudok van Heel proposes that the very similar oval portrait of Pesser, who likely accompanied his brother-in-law to Amsterdam for the conference, also sat for Rembrandt in Uylenburgh's studio.[23]

The format of the portraits of Jacob van Couwenhoven and Dirck Pesser indicate they were painted to hang with pendant portraits of their wives. The portraits of Marritge Jansdr. Pesser and Dirck Pesser's wife, Haesje Jacobsdr. van Cleyburgh (1583–1641), are dated 1634, one year later, indicating that they were probably painted when Rembrandt was in Rotterdam.[24] While there, Rembrandt also painted the portrait of the widow Aechje Claesdr. (1551–1636), the eighty-three-year-old matriarch of the Pesser family (National Gallery, London), which is painted on an oval panel similar in size to the portraits of the two couples. The frontal pose, which precludes a pendant, and her outdated clothes indicate her status as a widow.[25]

In 1647, the year Jacob van Couwenhoven sold De Twee Klimmende Leeuwen brewery for ƒ85,000, he and Marritge sat again for their portraits, this time by Bartholomeus van der Helst (1613–1670), then the most fashionable portrait painter in the Netherlands.[26] The crest of the Van Couwenhoven family on the frames of copies of the portraits at the Museum Rotterdam confirm the identities of the sitters.[27] In her monograph on the artist, Judith van Gent places the oval portraits among a group of eleven bust portraits Van der Helst painted in Rotterdam in 1646/47.[28] Seven of the sitters, including members of the Pesser-Van Couwenhoven family, were part of the powerful community of Remonstrant brewers.[29] Two portraits of previously unidentified sitters painted on oval panels with similar dimensions as the portraits of Jacob van Couwenhoven and Marritge Pesser were identified in 2014 as Marritge and Dirck's brother Dammas Jansz. Pesser (1590–1670) and his second wife, Dorothea Adriaensdr. Keijser (1599–1675).[30] The similarities of scale, pose, and the oval format of Van der Helst's portraits, which by 1647 was out of date, suggest that they may have been planned to hang with Rembrandt's portraits in a private family gallery or perhaps a community gallery honoring the history of the Pesser-Van Couwenhoven family and their contribution to the history of the Remonstrant Brotherhood and the city of Rotterdam.[31] The known provenances of the paintings do not, however, appear to support this.[32]

1. Jacob Jacobsz. Couwenhoven was Heer van de Oude en Nieuwe Struyten (Lord of Old and New Struyten). Oude en Nieuwe Struyten was originally a small polder, south and east of Hellevoetsluis, with Kanaal Voorne to the west and the Haringvliet to the south. It is almost due south of Brielle and southwest of Rotterdam. It is now covered by the Hellevoetsluis suburbs Wittenhoeck and De Struyten.

2. According to the preface to Madresfield [1889], "The collection of historical portraits was made by William Lygon, 2nd Earl Beauchamp (1782–1823) and enlarged by the addition of some portraits belonging to General Edward Lygon, which were removed from Spring Hill in 1861."

3. Madresfield [1889] notes that "78 [and] 80 Portraits, Rembrandt (signed)" hung in the Drawing Room.

4. This painting is not included in the reprint, Benesch/Benesch 1970.

5. The authors of the *Corpus* 1982–2011 note that there is "filling in of presumed beveling visible at left and right under the cradle . . . in the Louisville painting, suggesting that it may have been cut down from the original rectangular shape, leaving the only evidence of the original beveling on the side edges of the panel (*Corpus* 1986, p. 445). Examination of the Pasadena portrait may reveal similar evidence of the original beveling on the sides of the panel that were filled in when the painting was cradled. Thin pieces of wood inserted on the left and right sides of the Louisville panel are thicker in the center than at either side, suggesting that they were cut to match the variable depth of the bevel." According to John Griswold, who reviewed Rosamond Westmoreland's notes (NSM), the Pasadena panel was thinned to a uniform 0.7 cm. There are no traces of beveling or of thin inserts to compensate for variable depth due to beveling. Westmoreland speculated that this thinning was done to eliminate the beveling prior to cradling. Evidence of similar remnants of beveling on the left and right sides of the panel of Rembrandt's related portrait of Dirck Jansz. Pesser (Los Angeles County Museum of Art), however, suggests that the present twelve-sided panel was cut down from an original oval so that it could later be expanded into a rectangle format by the addition of wood fitted to the twelve flat sides. The unusual ten-sided panel of the pendant portrait of Pesser's wife, Haesje Jacobsdr. van Cleyburgh (Rijksmuseum, Amsterdam), suggests that it, too, was also cut, not from a rectangle but from an oval to be expanded later to a rectangle. This theory is supported by recognition that the majority of Rembrandt's bust portraits of the 1630s are ovals, not rectangles.

6. With the exception of Tümpel 1993, no. A84, ill. p. 88, who, without explanation, relegates the portrait to Rembrandt's workshop, scholars accept the portrait as an autograph work by Rembrandt.

7. According to its website, the Speed Art Museum has retained the previous identification of the sitter and her husband, Pieter Sijen. See discussion below. The female portrait is inscribed near center right "Rembrandt. *f* /1634" and near center left "Æ . . . S 40" (the zero is very thin). The Speed Art Museum purchased the portrait in 1977, the year it was exhibited at the Rijksmuseum, Amsterdam, lent by J. W. Middendorf II of New York, who had owned the painting since 1970. The painting had been purchased by a private collection in Manchester, England, at the 1960 sale of the Moore collection.

8. On the oval format of the portraits in terms of their condition, see note 5 above.

9. According to heraldic tradition, the man is positioned to the right of his wife, which places him on the viewer's left.

10. Woodall 1990, p. 42.

11. Manuth, De Winkel, and Van Leeuwen 2019, p. 657.

12. Regarding Van Uylenburgh, see Lammertse and Van der Veen 2006 and Dudok van Heel 2020a.

13. Van der Veen 2003, passim. Pieter Pietersz. Sijen, who had moved from Amsterdam to Gouda, made the inventory in 1703, when he was forced to sell his property to repay the loan he had received from the city of Gouda in 1702 to manufacture linen. Several sales of his property took place. On 16 June 1704 the sale of twenty-five paintings produced 795 guilders and 15 stuivers. Although the descriptions are summary, the total number of paintings agrees with that in the inventory. No names of buyers are noted but, as Van der Veen speculates, it is possible that a member of Sijen's family purchased the portraits. Following the sales, Pieter Pietersz. Sijen and his family moved to Moscow, where he died in 1706, shortly after the death of his wife. In 1720 their children are mentioned as heirs to one quarter of their grandmother's estate in Amsterdam.

14. Wolleswinkel 2005, no. 6.

15. Manuth, De Winkel, and Van Leeuwen 2019, p. 657.

16. Jan Dammasz. Pesser was married to Aechje Claesdr. (1551–1636), daughter of Claes Mathijsz. van der Horst and Marritgen Pietersdr. from Brielle, where members of her family were members of the local patriciate; Dudok van Heel 2006, p. 240. The Pesser family, which had occupied various important government positions in Rotterdam since at least 1524, were successful businessmen and tradesmen who had both wealth and property. Aechje and Jan Dammasz. had five children who lived to adulthood: Meijnsje (d. 1657), Dirck Jansz. (1586–1651), Dammas Jansz., Marritge, and Maertje (ca. 1595–1641).

17. Jacob van Couwenhoven's sister Maria (1591–1625) was Dammas Jansz. Pesser's first wife. Zandvliet 2006, pp. 353f., identifies Van Couwenhoven (1592–1661) as no. 216 of the 250 wealthiest people in the Netherlands during the seventeenth century. Regarding De Twee Klimmende Leeuwen, see Bijlsma 1911, who provides interesting history of the breweries in Rotterdam but does make some factual mistakes.

18. The best source of information about the history of the Remonstrant Brotherhood is Brandt [1720–23] 1979, vol. 4.

19. Brandt [1720–23] 1979, vol. 4, bk. 47, pp. 26–33.

20. Dudok van Heel 2006, p. 249.

21. Dudok van Heel 2020a, p. 80, revises his previous ideas: Dudok van Heel 1992, p. 15, assumed that Dirck Pesser and his wife, Haesje, traveled to Amsterdam to have their portraits painted but that the artist had gone to Rotterdam to paint the portrait of the eighty-three-year old widow, Aechje Claesdr. Pesser. Dudok van Heel 2006, p. 240, suggests that Rembrandt went to Rotterdam to paint the portrait of Aechje and then painted those of Dirck and Haesje while he was there. Manuth, De Winkel, and Van Leeuwen 2019, p. 657, were the first to suggest that Rembrandt painted Van Couwenhoven's portrait in Amsterdam and that the sitter invited the artist to come to Rotterdam the following year to paint the portraits of his wife, his mother-in-law, and his brother- and sister-in-law.

22. Wtenbogaert, considered one of the foremost champions of religious tolerance in the Netherlands, led the struggle against the more conservative Calvinists over questions of predestination and decision-making in the church. In 1610 Wtenbogaert drew up the "Remonstranti" that advocated unity in freedom. Regarding Rembrandt's portrait of Wtenbogaert, see Dudok van Heel 1994 and Kloek 1992. The fact that Rembrandt had only one short sitting to capture his likeness suggests to Dudok van Heel 2020a, p. 80, that the Remonstrant leader was in the city to attend the gathering of the Remonstrant Brotherhood.

23. Manuth, De Winkel, and Van Leeuwen 2019, p. 657, followed by Dudok van Heel 2020a, p. 80, reject the authenticity of the signature and date 1634 on the portrait of Dirck Pesser and suggest that they were copied after that on the portrait of Aechje. According to Joseph Fronek, head of paintings conservation, Los Angeles County Museum of Art, the signature looks fine but needs further study. He cannot confirm the date, the last two digits of which are difficult to read and may have had some restoration.

24. Rembrandt appeared before the notary Jan van Aller Andriessen on 22 July 1634: Rotterdam, Gemeente Archief, Notary Jan van Aller Andriessen, NA 13, fol. 290 r & v. See Strauss and Van der Meulen 1979, p. 112.

25. Dudok van Heel 1992 and Dudok van Heel 2006, pp. 238–51.

26. Van Gent 2012, pp. 193f., no. 38, *Jacob Jacobsz. van Couwenhoven (1592–1661)*, ca. 1647, oval panel, 68.6 × 55.9 cm, Toronto, private collection (2011); and no. 39, *Maritge Jansdr. Pesser (ca. 1593–1649)*, signed and dated, middle left, "B. van der helst / 1647 / Ae.ta.54," National Gallery of Ireland, Dublin, inv. no. 65.

27. Unidentified artist, seventeenth-century copies: *Jacob van Couwenhoven*, canvas, 71 × 56 cm, Museum Rotterdam, inv. no. 10513; *Marritge Jansdr. Pesser*, canvas, 71 × 56.5 cm, inscribed on reverse: "Maria Jans Pe[sser] / huisvrouw van J. Janse Couwenhove[n]." Both paintings came to the Museum Rotterdam from Bichon-van Ijsselmonde in 1936. Van Gent 2012, p. 194, notes that they were passed from the Van Couwenhoven family via Visch en Bichon, possibly related to Maria Jacobsdr. van Couwenhoven, who was married to Gerrit Willemsz. Visch (ca. 1627–1701) but had died by 1663.

28. Van Gent 2012, pp. 41–43.

29. Van Gent 2012, p. 42, identifies eight sitters: no. 30, Willem Allertsz. van Couwenhoven (1592–1659); no. 31, Aesje Cornelisdr. Briel, gezegd Welhouck (1597–1651); no. 32, Samuel van Lansbergen (1589–1669); no. 33, Maria Pietersdr. de Leest (?–1652); no. 38, Jacob Jacobsz. van Couwenhoven (1592–1661); no. 39, Maritge [*sic*] Jansdr. Pesser; no. 40, Aechte Cornelisdr. Briel, gezegd Welhouck (1587–1657); and no. 41, Cornelis Jansz. Hartigsvelt (1587–1641).

30. Lilian 2014, no. 6, pp. 36–43.

31. Manuth, De Winkel, and Van Leeuwen 2011, p. 657, without explaining their opinion. Van Gent 2012, p. 42, suggests that Van der Helst's portraits of Jacob van Couwenhoven and Marritge Pesser may be those mentioned among the family portraits in the 1683 inventory of Allaert Willemsz. van Couwenhoven, who was married to Elisabeth Jacobsdr. Van Couwenhoven, one of the daughters of the sitters.

32. The portraits of Dirck Pesser and Haesje van Cleyburgh passed to their only surviving child, Maria Dirxsdr. Pesser (d. 1675), who was married to Reynier van der Wolff (d. 1679), a wealthy brewer and art collector in Rotterdam. The last descendant known to have owned the portraits was Johan Salomon von Gersdorff (1718–1799). Dudok van Heel suggests that Rembrandt's portrait of Aechje Claesdr. was commissioned by her daughter Maertje Jansdr. Pesser (ca. 1595–1641), who was married to Ds. Simon Episcopius, professor of theology at the Remonstrant Seminary in Amsterdam. If this is accurate, then following Maertje Pesser's death without direct heirs, the portrait would have been inherited by one of her surviving sisters, either Meijnsje (d. 1657), who was married to the Remonstrant preacher Petrus Cupus in Rotterdam, or Marritge, the wife of Jacob van Couwenhoven. The portrait was included as lot 6 in the sale of paintings belonging to Klaas van Winkel (1710–1791) in Rotterdam on 20–21 October 1791. According to Dudok van Heel 2006, pp. 239, 265n9, Van Winkel was the chief collector of taxes in Rotterdam. See also The Hague/London 2007–08, p. 254, no. 55.

Rembrandt's portraits of Jacob van Couwenhoven and Marritge Pesser, as well as the portraits of the couple by Van der Helst, would have passed to one of the couple's (at least) six children, possibly soon after Marritge Pesser's death in 1649 and before Jacob van Couwenhoven married Antoinette Doudyns in 1650. In her will dated 3 January 1663 (Rotterdam, notary Jacobus Delphius, deed 121, pp. 438–41, inv. no. 362), Maria Jacobsdr. van Couwenhoven and her husband Gerrit Willemsz. Visch, who apparently had no children, mention as heirs her siblings, including Jacob Jacobsz. van Couwenhoven Jr.; Jan Jacobsz. van Couwenhoven (d. before 1663); Elisabeth Jacobsdr. van Couwenhoven, married to Allaert Willemsz. van Couwenhoven; Aechge Jacobsdr. van Couwenhoven (d. before 1663) married to Andries van Outshoren [?]; and Nicolaas van Couwenhoven. See also Van Gent 2012, p. 42.

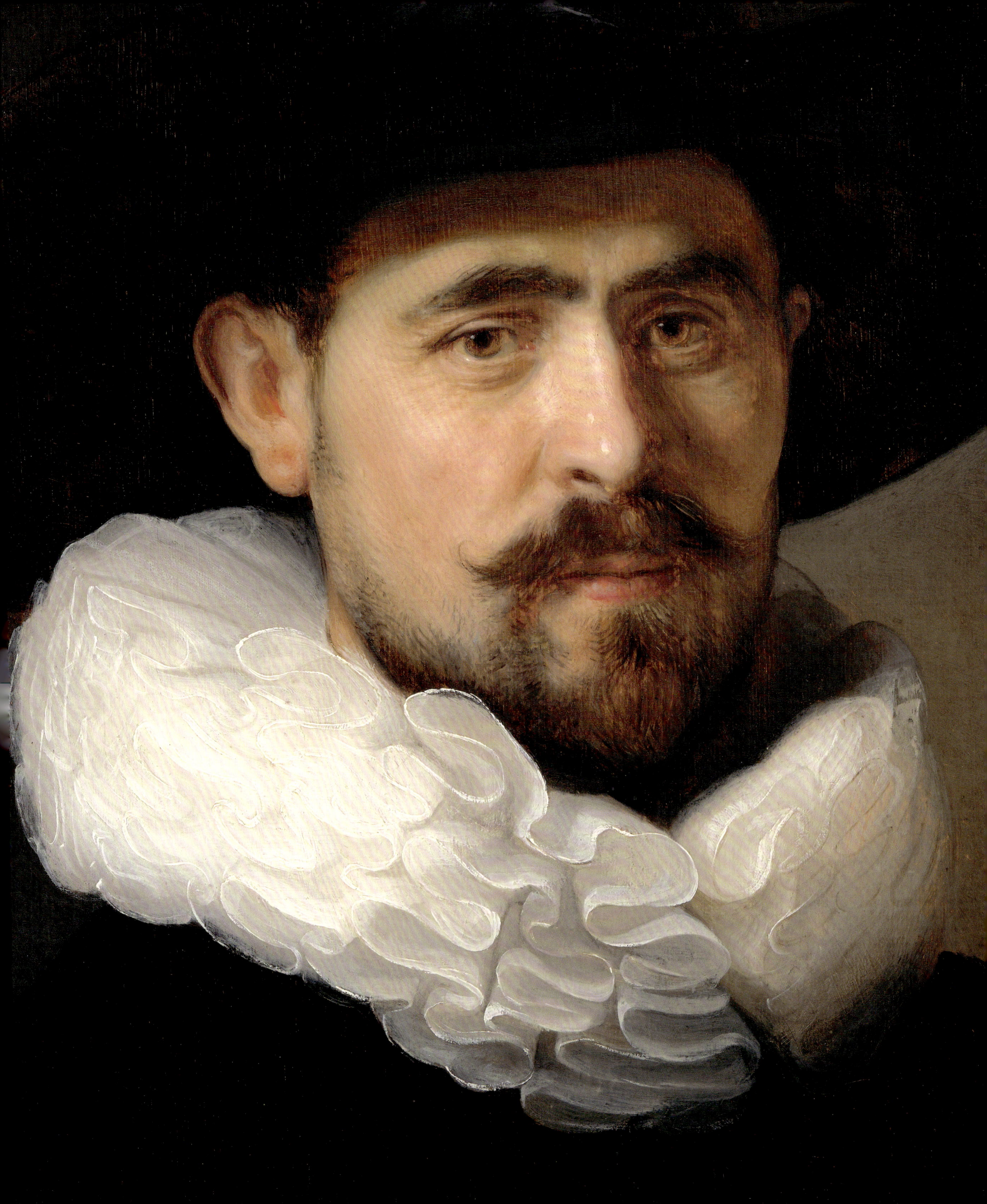

66

Rembrandt Harmensz. van Rijn

Dutch
Leyden 1606–1669 Amsterdam

Self-Portrait

ca. 1639

Inscribed and dated, center right: "Rembrandt F. 163[8 or 9]"
Oil on panel, 24 ⅞ × 19 ¾ in. (63.2 × 50.5 cm)
The Norton Simon Foundation, F.1969.18.P

Provenance

Mary Newport (née Wilbraham; 1661–1737), 2nd Countess of Bradford,[1] Weston Park, Stafford, in 1735 inv., case no. 3, item no. 25 "Rembrandt's head, by himself," by descent to her daughter;[2] Diana Newport Coote (1705–1766), 6th Countess of Mountrath, by descent to; George Damer (1746–1808), 2nd Earl of Dorchester, Milton Abbey, Dorsetshire, held in trust for his sister; Caroline (1752–1829), Lady Damer, Milton Abbey, Dorsetshire, by descent to her cousin; Henry John Ruben Dawson-Damer (1822–1889), 3rd Earl of Portarlington, Emo Court, Leix (sale, Christie's, London, 28 June 1879, no. 89, sold for £1,312 10s. to);[3] Albert Levy (ca. 1820–1883), London (sale, Christie's, London, 3 May 1884, no. 56, sold for £1,890 to);[4] [Martin Colnaghi, London, sold 1884 to];[5] Arthur Pemberton Heywood-Lonsdale (1835–1897), Shavington, Market Drayton, Shropshire, by descent to his son; H. Heywood-Lonsdale (1864–1930), Shavington, Market Drayton, Shropshire, by descent to his son; Lt. Col. Arthur Heywood-Lonsdale (1900–1976), Shavington, Market Drayton, Shropshire (sale, Christie's, London, 27 June 1969, no. 70, sold to); The Norton Simon Foundation.

Exhibited

Dublin 1853–54, p. 459, no. 208; Dublin 1865, p. 133, no. 12; Dublin 1872, p. 93, no. 127; London 1878, no. 98; London 1890, no. 61; London 1899, no. 64, as *Portrait of the Painter*, signed and dated "Rembrandt f. 1637 (?)"; London 1936–37, no. 67; London 1938, p. 64, no. 121; London 1949, no. 27; Edinburgh 1950, no. 9; Amsterdam 1952, no. 141; London 1952–53, no. 177; Stockholm 1956, no. 20; on loan, Walker Art Gallery, Liverpool, 1958–68; Chicago/Minneapolis/Detroit 1969, no. 6;[6] on loan, Los Angeles County Museum of Art, August–October 1969; on loan, Los Angeles County Museum of Art, 28 April 1970–November 1974; on loan, New Orleans Museum of Art, 15 November 1974–3 May 1975; on loan, Phoenix Art Museum, 21 November 1980–24 June 1981; on loan, Art Institute of Chicago, 3 March–6 June 2009.

References

Bode 1883, p. 246, as 1635 or 1638 (?); Dutuit 1885, p. 48, no. 142, p. 67, no. 142, as "Pontarlington" [*sic*]; Wurzbach 1886, no. 235; E. Michel 1893, p. 557, no. 432, as about 1635; Bode and Hofstede de Groot 1897–1906, vol. 3 (1899), no. 175, ill.; Moes 1892–1905, vol. 2 (1905), p. 313, no. 6693/35; Valentiner 1908, no. 241; Hofstede de Groot 1908–27, vol. 6 (1916), pp. 282f., no. 576; Tipping 1918, p. 115; Meldrum 1923, pp. 43, 193, pl. 186; Weisbach 1926, p. 85; Benesch 1935, p. 19; Bredius 1935, pl. 32, p. 3; H. E. van Gelder [1948], p. 28; J. G. van Gelder 1950, pp. 327f., as 1638/39; Pinder [1943] 1950, pp. 73, 76, ill.; Liverpool 1959, p. 9; Van Hall 1963, p. 268, no. 51;[7] Bauch 1966, p. 16, pl. 313, as about 1639; Gerson 1968, no. 229, as probably about 1638; Bredius/Gerson 1969, pp. 28, 549, no. 32, ill.; Benesch/Benesch 1970, p. 19; J. Nash 1972, no. 56; Johnson and Cairns 1972, p. 26, figs. 6–7, cover; Gerson 1976, pp. 164, 166, cover; Brown 1977, no. 54, ill.; Selleck 1977, p. 40, ill.; Fowkes 1978, p. 72, fig. 64; Brown 1979, pl. 16; Pasadena 1980, pp. 6, 54, ill.; White 1982, p. 112;[8] Wright 1982, pp. 27, 42, 132, pl. 64; Schwartz 1985, pp. 193, pl. 207, as ca. 1638; Tümpel 1986, pp. 204, 409, no. 166, ill.; Guillaud and Guillaud 1986, p. 625; P. Sutton 1986, p. 217; *Corpus* 1989, pp. 619–24, C97, as attr. to Carel Fabritius; Pasadena 1989, p. 81, ill.; Stewart 1990–95, vol. 1, pp. 594f.; Brown et al. 1991, p. 360; Slatkes 1991, p. 73, ill.;[9] Slatkes 1992, p. 384, no. 255, ill.; White 1992, p. 266; Liedtke 1995, p. 460n13; Liedtke 1997, pp. 43, 59, fig. 2–12; Muchnic 1998, pp. 157, 253; London/The Hague 1999, p. 176, no. 96, as "Rembrandt? c. 1641?"; Wright 2001, p. 202, pl. 333; Pasadena 2003, p. 66, ill.; Liedtke 2004, p. 62, fig. 7;[10] Corpus 2005, "Corrigenda" no. C-97, pp. 96, 242f., 249, 357f., 605–08, ills.; Woollett 2009, pp. 28–29; Fried 2010, p. 29, fig. 1.29; S. Campbell 2010, pp. 94–95, 101n59, 221, 223, 323, no. 654, ill.; Van de Wetering 2017, pt. 1, no. C-97, p. 269, ill., pt. 2, pp. 172, 567; Manuth and De Winkel 2019, pp. 102–03; Manuth, De Winkel, and Van Leeuwen 2019, pp. 101, 191, 608; Muchnic 2019, pp. 176, 265.

Technical Notes

The portrait is painted on an oak panel composed of three vertically grained boards.[11] A white preparation layer applied onto the panel is visible in some places along the edges and has been identified as consisting predominantly of calcium carbonate.[12] On top of this layer is an off-white/beige imprimatura paint layer in which lead white is the main pigment with lesser amounts of calcium carbonate and iron oxide earth(s).[13] This imprimatura layer can be seen in the shirt cuff at the proper left wrist, where the artist left it uncovered. No preliminary underdrawing is evident, but modifications made by the artist during the painting process were revealed during infrared examination of the painting (fig. 66a). For example, the sitter's garment has been changed: the present square-necked jerkin replaces a simple shirt that appears to have wrapped across his chest from right to left, overlapping to produce a V-shaped opening at the neck. The line of the present gold chain closely follows the line of the original shirt. As pointed out by Ernst van de Wetering, Rembrandt originally intended a larger, looser hat that extended diagonally on the lower left and upper right in a manner similar to that in a drawing in the Lehman Collection, New York. Infrared reflectography also revealed changes in the contours of the torso and face: the jaw line on the viewer's right was possibly broader, and the shape of the hair on the left has been changed. Also visible are some preliminary linear washes blocking in the forms and shadows, such as in the cheek and shoulder.

The paint consists of an oil medium applied with fluid handling with slight impasto visible in the gold chain, the

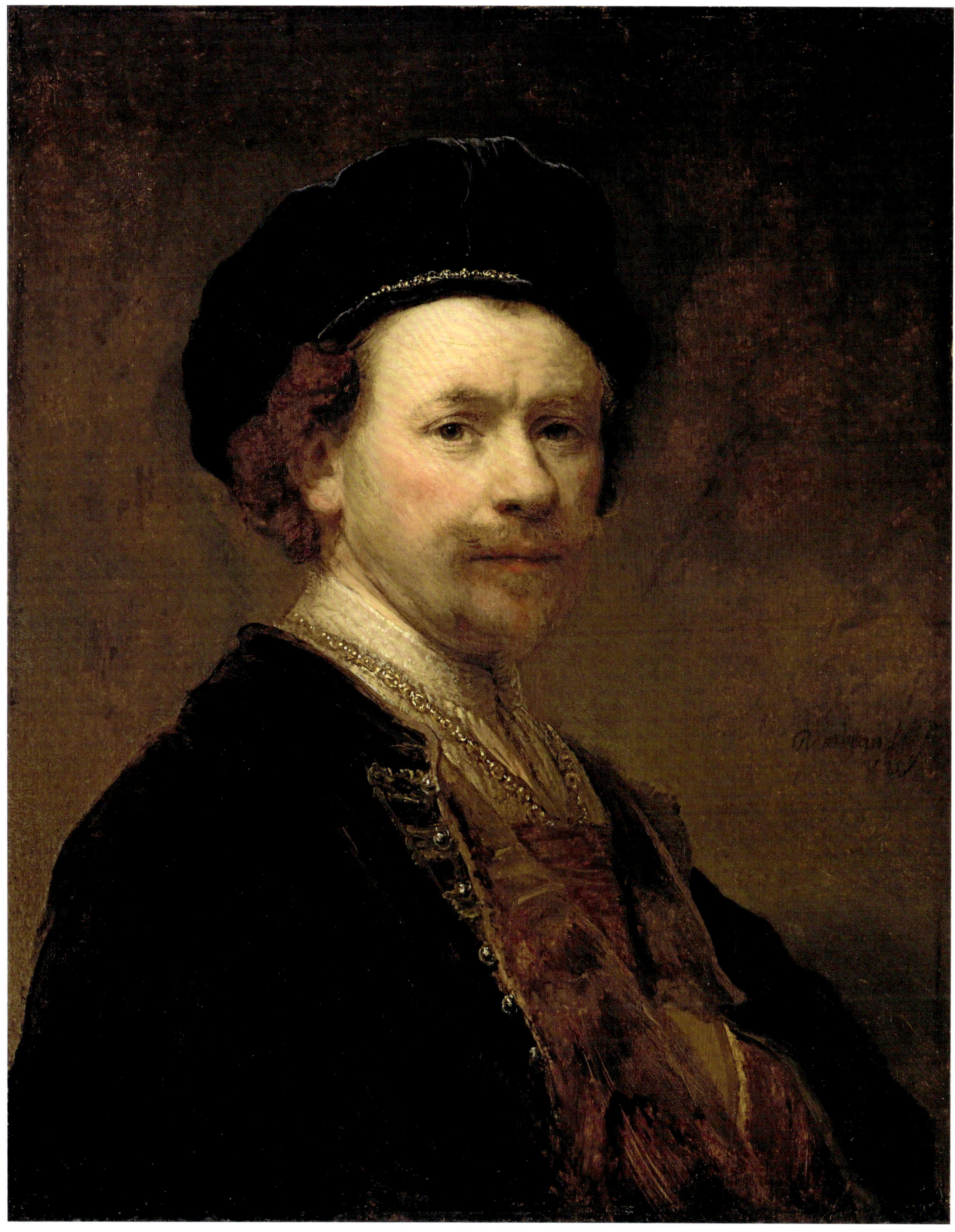

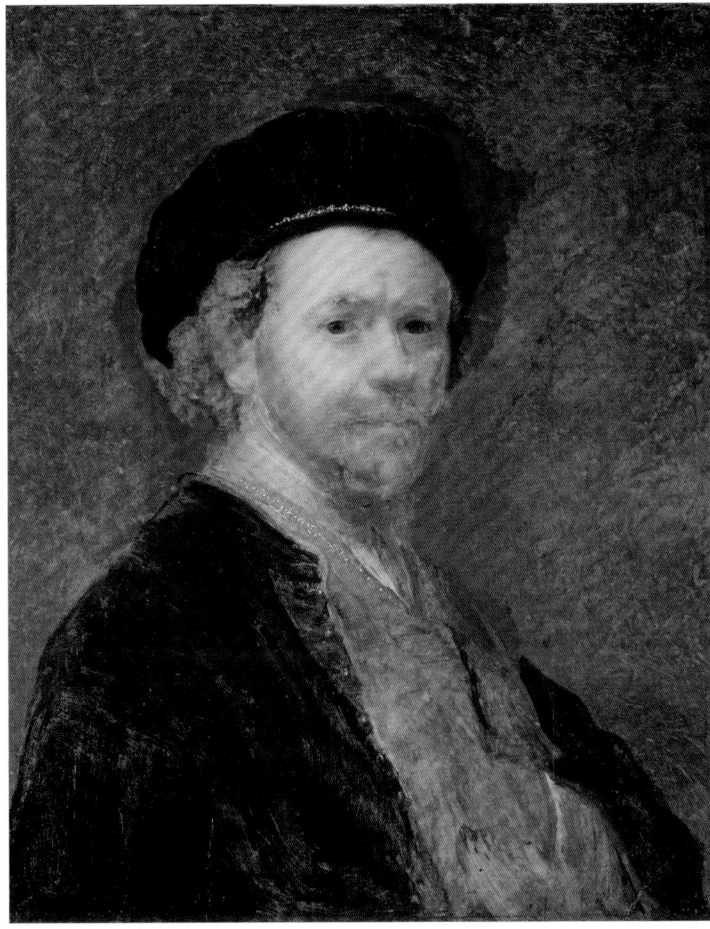

Fig. 66a. Infrared photograph of *Self-Portrait*, J. Paul Getty Museum, Los Angeles.

ornament on the hat, and the buttons on the jacket. Paint application varies in thickness from thin and translucent in the background to multiple layers of more opaque paint in the flesh tones. Noninvasive X-radiograph fluorescence analysis (XRF) was performed on the painting, giving elemental composition of each area studied.[14] XRF data suggest the presence of lead white, vermillion, lead tin yellow, iron oxide earths, possibly umber, possibly smalt in the hat, an unidentified copper blue or green, and extensive use of calcium. The palette is compatible with artists' materials available during Rembrandt's lifetime.

In 1989 the Rembrandt Research Project rejected the Pasadena *Self-Portrait* as an autograph work by Rembrandt and reattributed it to Carel Fabritius (1622–1654), ca. 1641.[15] The committee acknowledged the general "Rembrandtesque appearance of the work . . . in particular . . . the convincing plasticity achieved in some parts of the head such as the eye area on the left," but it pointed to the signature and the very elaborate painting of the face as atypical of Rembrandt, especially noting that the brushstrokes do not clearly relate to the forms they describe.[16] The authors were also concerned about the abrupt transitions from light flesh color to darker tints—on the left along the hair and below the ear and (less markedly) on the right side of the forehead and cheekbone.

Subsequent scholars have dismissed this negative assessment of the Pasadena *Self-Portrait* and its attribution to Fabritius.[17] Among them, Ernst van de Wetering, who served as a junior member of the Rembrandt Research Project in 1971 and later directed the project, reversed his opinion and in vol. 4 of *A Corpus of Rembrandt Paintings* devoted to the self-portraits (2005) published the Pasadena portrait as an autograph work by Rembrandt.[18] Critical to Van de Wetering's acceptance of the painting was his ability to study it out of the sealed Plexiglas climate box and to refer to X-radiographs and a microscope not available to the Rembrandt Research Project in 1971.[19] In 2017, having seen the Pasadena *Self-Portrait* in the J. Paul Getty Museum's conservation laboratory, after it had been cleaned and restored by Yvonne Szafran in 2012, Van de Wetering wrote, "Any doubt as to its authenticity disappeared."[20]

The 2012 cleaning of the painting selectively removed heavily discolored varnish layers and old retouching, which were concealing the subtle tonal relationships of the portrait. The removal of some of the old varnish also revealed the application of thicker opaque paint—found in the chain, white shirt, and highlighted portion of the face—juxtaposed with translucent paints in the shadows of the face and the red shirt. As Szafran observed, "The entire painting seems built on this combination, one kind of paint playing off the other, so characteristic of Rembrandt's technique."[21]

Close examination of the sitter's dark gray jacket using a stereomicroscope revealed an underlying dark black paint layer suggestive of the initial monochromatic dark paint application, which is indicative of Rembrandt's painting technique.[22] However, due to the sensitivity of the original dark gray paint in the jacket (applied on top of the monochrome layer) to solvent action, the older varnish was not removed from this area.[23] The disturbing retouching that created sudden shifts between light and dark in the flesh tones and hair noted by scholars to be atypical of the artist's hand was removed, revealing the original paint to be in remarkably good condition with subtle light/dark transitions intact.

In the flesh tones, it is difficult to decipher specific brushstrokes; paint appears to have been dabbed on, leaving crevices in the paint. Remnants of a red lake glaze found in these pits in the face suggest that a final layer consisting of a thin semitransparent glaze was applied and has since faded.[24] In the shadows on the face, the glazes seem to have developed a whitish crust, and the rich color is only visible, upon close examination, through cracks. This is especially noticeable under the microscope in the area around the nose, lips, mustache, and proper left side of the sitter's face.[25] Close study of the signature under high magnification showed that only part of the original signature survives with strengthening of the lettering and numbers carried out by a former restorer's hand.

A significant amount of abrasion to the original paint layer found beneath the varnish layers probably resulted from past cleaning. This, coupled with the increased transparency of the oil medium, the fading of red lakes, and the aging characteristics of some pigments, may have led to misinterpretation that resulted in repainting and heavy-handed retouching, altering the original appearance of the portrait. —*Devi Ormond*

This is one of more than seventy self-portraits Rembrandt created in various media throughout his life. They provide a history of his aging as well as his stylistic development. Many attempts have been made to associate the self-portraits with events in his life, although it is debatable whether one can or should see them as personal, psychological investigations rather than works motivated purely by the artist's desire to study human expressions and document his own changing physical image. Ernst van de Wetering suggested that Rembrandt (and his studio) may have produced self-portraits and portraits of the artist as commodities to satisfy the desire of art lovers to own images of the artist, which would also serve as examples of his style and skill.[26] These portraits of the artist—both by Rembrandt and by others in his studio—would have been kept on hand for sale to collectors.

Rembrandt sought to craft and market his own image to further his reputation.[27] In his etched *Self-Portrait in a Soft Hat and Embroidered Cloak*, dated 1631, the year he moved to Amsterdam, as well as in the oval self-portrait of the following year, now in Glasgow, Rembrandt portrayed himself in the white ruff and dark clothing of a sophisticated Amsterdam burgher.[28] In the Pasadena *Self-Portrait*, painted a year or two before the great self-portrait of 1640 (National Gallery, London),[29] Rembrandt identified with the revered artists of the northern Renaissance by arraying himself in the historical costume worn by Netherlandish artists a century earlier, ca. 1520–30: a black tabard lined with red and trimmed with gold frogs, a matching square-necked jerkin over a white smocked and ruched linen shirt, and a gold chain.[30] The black beret or bonnet, a typical sixteenth-century artist's attribute, was by the mid-seventeenth century a cliché signifying old-fashioned.[31] Rembrandt's point of reference for both the pose and the costume, as well as for his 1638 etching *Self-Portrait in Velvet Cap and Plume* (fig. 66b), was probably the engraved *Portrait of Jan Gossart* (fig. 66c) from the popular series of portraits of Netherlandish artists published in 1572 in Antwerp by the humanist Dominicus Lampsonius (1532–1599), *Pictorum aliquot celebrium Germaniae inferioris effigies*.[32] The three works share elements of costume and the gesture of the left hand either slipped into the tabard, as in the works by Rembrandt, or clutching it, as in the portrait of Gossaert (ca. 1472–1532).[33] Although this gesture can refer to sloth (one of the deadly sins) or to melancholy, here as in other portraits it probably refers to the concept of leisure, an appropriate attribute for a gentleman who proudly does not use his hands for work.[34]

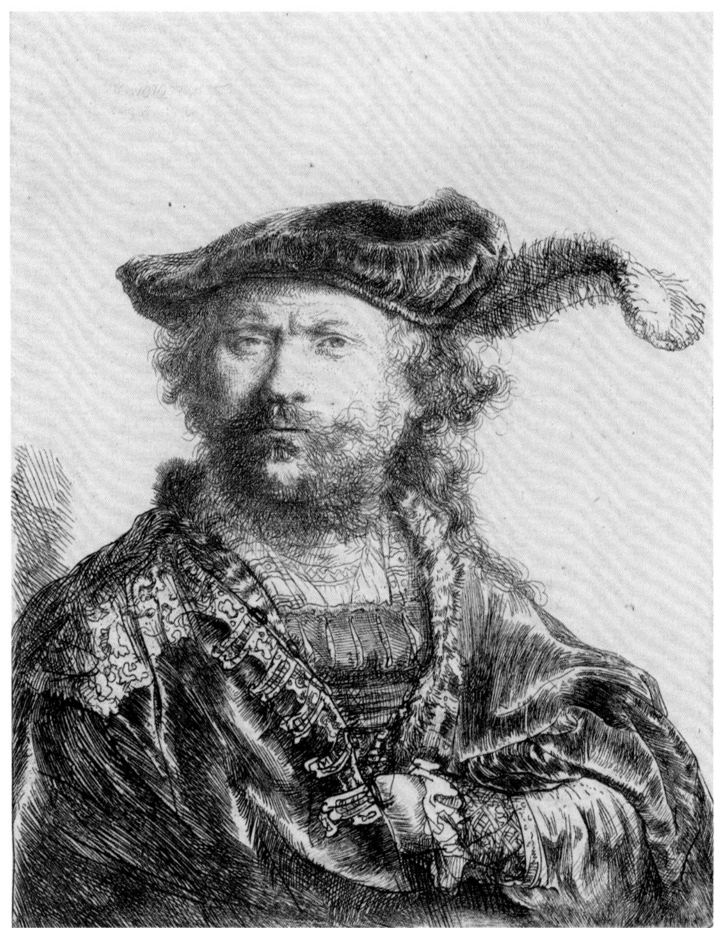

Fig. 66b. Rembrandt Harmensz. van Rijn, *Self-Portrait in Velvet Cap and Plume*, 1638, etching, 5⅜ × 4⅛ in. (13.7 × 10.5 cm), Amgueddfa Cenedlaethol Cymru–National Museum of Wales, Cardiff.

In both the etching and the Pasadena *Self-Portrait*, Rembrandt replaced the coat worn by Gossaert with a coat with frog closures. Marieke de Winkel notes that during the late 1620s and early 1630s, "frogging," derived from the military and ultimately from East Asian and Near Eastern dress, was fashionable in civilian attire in the Netherlands.[35] The fashion for decorative frogging was undoubtedly stimulated by the colorful Persian costumes worn by the embassy of Shah Abbas I (1587–1629) to the Netherlands in 1626. Leonard Slatkes has demonstrated the strong impression the embassy made on Rembrandt, who knew Eastern styles through costume books and was particularly interested in incorporating these themes in his work beginning in the mid-1630s.[36]

The inscription in the background to the right of the figure in the Pasadena *Self-Portrait* is poorly preserved; as stated in Technical Notes, "only part of the original signature survives with strengthening of the lettering and numbers carried out by a former restorer's hand." Van de Wetering—who observes that the date "163." appears to be "solely

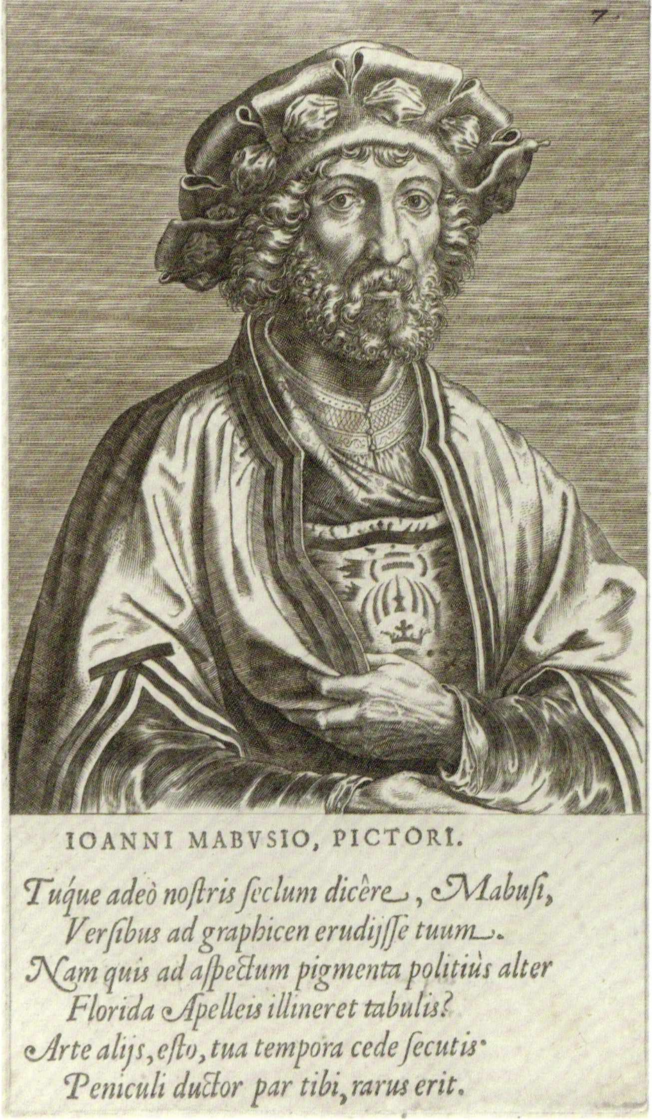

Fig. 66c. Johannes Wierix, *Portrait of Jan Gossart*, 1572, engraving on paper, 8 9⁄16 × 5 1⁄16 in. (21.9 × 12.9 cm), Rijksmuseum, Amsterdam.

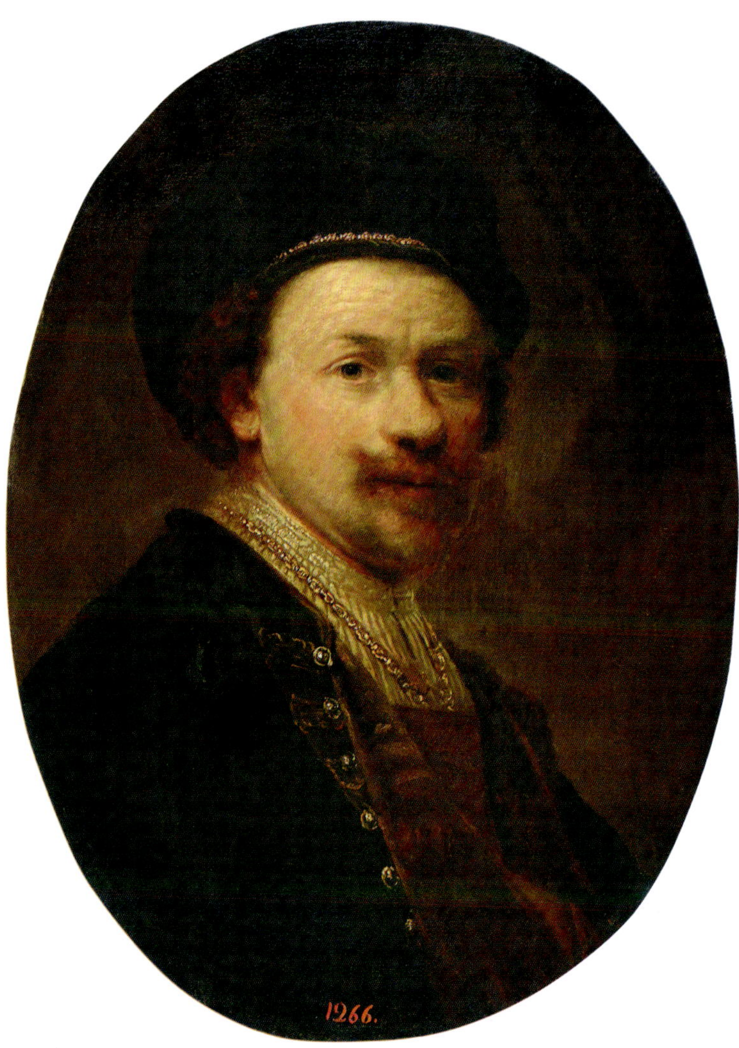

Fig. 66d. Rembrandt School, copy of *Self-Portrait*, n.d., oil on panel, 24 3⁄4 × 18 1⁄2 in. (63 × 47 cm), Museum of Western and Eastern Art, Odessa.

constituted by retouches which may cover remnants of an earlier inscription"—believes a date in the late 1630s, cited by most scholars, is appropriate.[37] Stylistically and thematically the Pasadena portrait fits well into a group of paintings datable to the late 1630s. Van de Wetering notes, "The subtle differentiation in the course of the contours of the torso . . . with an angular element indicating a collar or some other detail of apparel, exhibits a refinement characteristic of Rembrandt around 1640."[38] Common to his self-portraits of the late 1630s, when Rembrandt was searching for ways to convey his dignity as a painter, are the extended torso, the antiquarian costume, and the gold chain.[39] Rather than a reference to the ancient tradition of a patron bestowing gold chains on artists and thus an expression of his ambition, De Winkel suggests that Rembrandt included a gold chain as part of his historicizing costume based on fashionable dress at the beginning of the sixteenth century.[40]

The many copies of the Pasadena *Self-Portrait* indicate that it was well known by Rembrandt's contemporaries and artists of the following century. A self-portrait by Govaert Flinck (1615–1660) dated 1639 (National Gallery, London) in which the sitter wears nearly identical sixteenth-century clothing, including a large hat at an angle, may reflect the original conception of the Pasadena painting. Many of the copies, characterized by a taller beret and exaggerated facial features, however, may have actually been based on an oval painting now in Odessa (fig. 66d), which Catherine II (1729–1796) of Russia acquired in the late eighteenth century with the collection of the Comte de Baudouin (1715–1797).[41] Before his collection was sold, Baudouin had commissioned copies of the paintings, which were sold as such in a posthumous sale.[42] An etching made by the French artist J. B. Lesueur (active 18th century) attributes the Odessa painting to Flinck, an attribution that may reflect the Rembrandt student's popularity during the eighteenth century rather than any stylistic affinity or historical basis.[43]

The earliest known reference to the Pasadena *Self-Portrait* is 1735, when it appears in the inventory of Mary, Countess of Bradford, widow of Richard Newport (1644–1723), the 2nd Earl of Bradford. Mary probably inherited the Pasadena painting from her parents. The daughter and sole heir of Sir Thomas Wilbraham, Bart. (1630–1692) and Elizabeth Mytton (1632–1766), Mary had inherited Weston Park from her mother, through whose family the Weston estates had passed since at least the early fifteenth century. Elizabeth Mytton (known as Elizabeth Wilbraham after her marriage), considered by some to be the first female architect, designed and built a new house on the property in 1671.[44] Following their marriage in 1651, Elizabeth and Sir Thomas Wilbraham went on an extended honeymoon to Europe, traveling through Germany, Italy, and the Netherlands, where she studied with the architect Pieter Post (1608–1669). A three-quarter-length portrait of Elizabeth Mytton by Peter Lely (1618–1680) as a young woman in a yellow dress standing in a garden and fingering tulips (Weston Park) portrays her prior to her marriage and hung with portraits by Anthony van Dyck (1599–1641) and others at Weston Park. It is possible, if not probable, that Elizabeth and Thomas acquired the Pasadena *Self-Portrait* during their stay in the Netherlands, perhaps even when visiting Rembrandt's studio, and that Mary inherited it from her mother. The fact that the portrait passed by inheritance from Mary to her daughter suggests that it was her property. Mary's husband, Richard Newport, 2nd Earl of Bradford, is listed as the buyer of eleven paintings from the sale of Peter Lely's collection (Thompson, London, 18ff April 1682), one year after the couple married in 1681. Among his purchases was a self-portrait by Van Dyck, which may indicate his interest in self-portraits of artists, possibly inspired by the Rembrandt already in the collection.

1. Newport had inherited the Weston estates from her mother, included in which may have been Rembrandt's *Self-Portrait*.

2. I am grateful to Burton Fredericksen for extending the provenance and exhibition history of the painting between 1735 and 1878.

3. Hofstede de Groot 1908–27, vol. 6 (1916), p. 283, quotes the sale price as £1,312 10s.; Tipping 1918, p. 115, says the painting "sold at Christie's in 1878 [*sic*] for 1,250 guineas."

4. *Corpus* 1989, p. 624, cites a handwritten note in the RKD copy of the 1879 catalogue: "24 × 19 in. on panel. Some doubt its authenticity. Vosmaer appears never to have heard of it."

5. Liverpool 1959, p. 10; the buyer is annotated as "Colnaghi" in the GRI copy of 1884 sale catalogue.

6. Chicago/Minneapolis/Detroit 1969, no. 6, notes that the date has been read as 1633 and 1638.

7. Van Hall mentions an old replica of 1635 in the sale, R. Lepke, Berlin, 5 May 1914, no. 62, ill., and a copy dated 1634 in the sale of the H. O. Havemeyer Collection, American Association of Art, Anderson Galleries, New York, October 4, 1930, no. 102, ill.

8. White suggests that the slightly turned head seen in the X-radiograph of Rembrandt's *Self-Portrait with a Flat Hat* in the Royal Collection at Windsor Castle is a self-portrait based on the Pasadena painting.

9. Slatkes states that "the Norton Simon *Self-Portrait* . . . had never before been questioned (a single late-18th-century print labeled it Flinck). . . . I find no evidence, technical or other, that suggests the Norton Simon *Self-Portrait* is by anyone other than Rembrandt."

10. In his review of *Corpus* 1989, Liedtke 2004 writes that he agrees with Leonard Slatkes "that the plethora of new attributions to Carel Fabritius—previously a very rare artist—seems not only extreme, but in the case of the Simon picture [fig. 7] almost beyond belief."

11. In 2012 the painting underwent both structural and aesthetic conservation treatment to resolve the problem of the continuing stresses that were impacting the stability of the panel subsequently leading to paint loss. The wooden additions were removed and the panel immediately relaxed into an almost completely even plane; it was found to be completely intact, with original bevels on all four sides. The structural treatment was carried out by George Bisacca and Sue Ann Chui in August 2012; see Szafran 2014.

12. Analysis was carried out in February 2013 by Alan Phenix and Lynn Lee; see Phenix and Lee 2013, p. 5.

13. Phenix and Lee 2013, p. 5.

14. The presence of particular elements provides an indication of some of the pigments present and is not conclusive. XRF analysis is most successful at analyzing inorganic material and often provides confusing results as it reads all layers of a painting's structure.

15. *Corpus* 1989, p. 621, C97. The committee inspected the painting in 1971. See note 19 below.

16. *Corpus* 1989, p. 621: "The shape of the letters is, so far as these are clearly visible, inarticulate and so wide compared to those in authentic Rembrandt signatures that the authenticity of the inscription seems extremely doubtful."

17. Among others, Christopher Brown, who rejects the attribution to Fabritius, is convinced that the general Rembrandtesque quality and physical attributes of the portrait are consistent with autograph paintings by Rembrandt. P. Sutton 1986, p. 217, accepts the painting, which he calls "the great Self-Portrait of the lat[t]er half of the decade. Surprisingly, this work was attributed to . . . Flinck in an eighteenth-century engraving by Le Sueur. However, as Gerson has so astutely observed, Flinck was a saleroom favorite at that time . . . with the result that an astonishing variety of pictures were misattributed to him. Clearly there is no cause to doubt the authorship of this work." A letter from Egbert Haverkamp-Begemann to Norton Simon (NSM), 30 June 1969, states: "I should like to congratulate you on acquiring the Rembrandt Self-Portrait from the Heywood-Lonsdale Collection. I personally find it one of his most beautiful self-portraits. . . . I saw the painting last in 1956." Slatkes 1992, p. 384; Liedtke 1997, p. 43; and Liedtke 2004, p. 62, accept the attribution.

18. *Corpus* 2005. Van de Wetering examined the painting in the spring of 2001 and again in 2003. He had the opportunity at that time to consult X-radiographs and infrared photographs as well as to use a microscope and discuss the painting with the author (Amy Walsh) and conservators Rosamond Westmoreland (in 2001) and Joseph Fronek, chief conservator of paintings, Los Angeles County Museum of Art (in 2003). The author is grateful to the conservators and to Van de Wetering for our hours of discussion regarding the painting at that time and for Van de Wetering's sharing a draft of his entry for

Corpus 2005, written after his 2001 examination of the painting (NSM).

19. In *Corpus* 1989, p. 619, the authors note that they examined the painting "in good artificial light, in the frame and inside a climate-controlled Plexiglas box." X-radiographs of the painting that were made for Norton Simon by the conservation department at the Los Angeles County Museum of Art in 1974 were available to Van de Wetering during his later visits, when he also had use of a microscope, which had not been available to the original Rembrandt Research Project team.

20. Van de Wetering 2017, p. 567, discusses the previous concerns in context. He ultimately concludes, "The stylistic and technical characteristics of the Pasadena *Self-Portrait* described here and discussed in *Corpus IV Corrigenda* III C 97, when taken together, argue strongly in favour of the (re)attribution of this painting to Rembrandt."

21. Szafran 2014, p. 5: "Much has been written about Rembrandt's painting technique but there is still ongoing research focusing on his working methods and materials, and new findings continue to emerge as methods of analysis become more sophisticated. . . . The online Rembrandt Research Database also provides a rich material resource, some of which might indicate that Rembrandt's technique is not always straightforward."

22. Phenix and Lee 2013, p. 5. The use of bone black was indicated by the coincident abundance of calcium and phosphorus in the black pigment.

23. The sensitivity of the original paint in the dark gray jacket was investigated. The possible presence of Kassel earth, a pigment that is a poor drier, coupled with the result of past restorations may have caused this sensitivity to solvent action. Carbon black is the black pigment identified in this layer and large, ovoid fluorescent particles suggest the presence of starch, which may also explain the paint's sensitivity. No resin was found in the paint mixture. Szafran 2014, p. 2; Phenix and Lee 2013, p. 5.

24. Szafran 2014, p. 6: "Because these colors are organic in origin, they are not always stable; this can depend on the source of origin as well as the method of manufacture, among other things. They are typically sensitive to light (but not always) and they often fade, the fading most often being apparent where they have been thinly applied. Sometimes they develop crusts of whitish material as they age, disguising their original color below. They are difficult to identify analytically and evidence of Rembrandt's use of them is often circumspect, but is clearly evident in this painting."

25. Szafran 2014, p. 4. Numerous recent studies document similar examples of altered paint in other paintings by Rembrandt and his use of lakes is well documented. See Noble et al. 2012 and A. van Loon 2008.

26. Van de Wetering 2003, pp. 26–42, with additional bibliography, builds on ideas expressed by De Jongh 2001, esp. pp. 13–14. The numerous self-portraits and portraits of Rembrandt by others attest to the interest not only in Rembrandt but also in portraits of artists. By 1633 a self-portrait by Rembrandt was in the collection of Charles I of England (r. 1625–49), one of at least twelve self-portraits of artists displayed in adjoining rooms in the palace at Whitehall. This was probably the painting now in Liverpool, which dates from 1630/31. See Manuth 1999, pp. 46ff.; and London/The Hague 1999, no. 26, pp. 132ff., which summarize the evidence and cite further literature. The gallery of self-portraits that Cosimo III de' Medici (1642–1723) assembled and displayed in Florence also included a portrait of Rembrandt, which Cosimo may have acquired on one of his two trips to the Netherlands in 1667–68 and 1669. Such displays were popular during the late sixteenth and seventeenth centuries and parallel an interest in the biographies of artists and collections of artists' portraits exemplified by Vasari, Van Mander, and others as well as the published collections of portrait prints.

27. For an excellent discussion of Rembrandt's self-fashioning through dress, see De Winkel 2005.

28. Hollstein 1949–2010, vol. 19, no. 7; and Bredius/Gerson 1969, nos. 17 and 28. See also Chapman 1989.

29. This portrait is Rembrandt's ultimate claim to his dignity as an artist. In it, he identified with the great masters of the Italian High Renaissance by adopting the costume and pose of Raphael's (1483–1520) *Portrait of Baldassare Castiglione* (Louvre, Paris) and Titian's (ca. 1488–1576) supposed *Portrait of Ariosto* (National Gallery, London), both of which were in contemporary Amsterdam collections and also known through engraved reproductions.

30. Van de Wetering 2003, p. 6, notes that an almost identical costume is found in a painting from Rembrandt's studio that is now in Glasgow (Bredius/Gerson 1969, no. 28), which he considers a free variant after the Pasadena painting rather than a self-portrait by the master.

31. De Winkel 1999, pp. 68f.

32. The engraving, no. 7 from the series, is 219 × 129 mm. The extremely popular series was reissued four times before 1600. In 1610 Hendrick Hondius (1573–1649), an engraver and publisher in The Hague, increased from twenty-three to sixty-eight the number of portraits originally published by Lampsonius. See Manuth 1999, pp. 42f.

33. The same gesture appears in *Self-Portrait*, ca. 1635, pen and wash, in bister and Indian ink, 145 × 121 mm, Metropolitan Museum of Art, New York (Benesch/Benesch 1973, no. 434, fig. 525). London/The Hague 1999, no. 161, rejects the drawing as a self-portrait, stating that the authors see no resemblance to Rembrandt.

34. London/The Hague 1999, p. 166: "A slothful man hideth his hand in his bosom, and will not so much as bring it to his mouth again" (Proverbs 19:24). See also Koslow 1975, pp. 418–32.

35. De Winkel 2005, p. 48.

36. Slatkes 1983. Although Rembrandt's jacket is open rather than closed, as it is typically represented in costume illustrations, the reference to "Oriental" costume may also explain the original asymmetrical shape of the shirt and the peculiar shape of the hat as revealed in the infrared image of the Pasadena *Self-Portrait*. The hat, which resembles that in the Metropolitan Museum of Art drawing, where Rembrandt also wears a coat with frogging, is not only larger but also worn unusually low on the back of the head, bulging out and upward over his forehead on the viewer's right. Although it may have been similar to the brimmed hat worn in the 1660 *Self-Portrait* (Metropolitan Museum of Art, New York), in the context of the coat and shirt, it could also be seen as similar to turbans represented by Rembrandt in his drawing *Four Orientals Seated Beneath a Tree* (British Museum, London). Regarding Rubens's use of costume book illustrations of Turkish dress, see Kurz and Kurz 1972.

37. *Corpus* 2005, p. 608n6.

38. *Corpus* 2005, p. 608.

39. *Corpus* 2005, pp. 242f., 242–43n341. Rembrandt seems to have first introduced the detail of the gold chain in his Liverpool self-portrait of ca. 1630/31 (Bredius/Gerson 1969, no. 12). In several of the paintings, such as that in the Louvre dated 1633 (Bredius/Gerson 1969, no. 19), Rembrandt fingers the gold chain. In others, including the Pasadena painting, the chain merely hangs ceremoniously around the artist's neck.

40. Revived in the Renaissance and in the seventeenth century, the presentation of a gold chain was a familiar form of official praise and recognition of the wearer's accomplishments. Rembrandt, who never received a gold chain, made reference to the tradition in *Aristotle with the Bust of Homer* (Metropolitan Museum of Art, New York) and undoubtedly knew that Titian and Raphael as well as his contemporary Rubens had been so honored (De Winkel 2005, p. 63). De Winkel 2005, p. 69, says, in reference to Rembrandt's etched *Self-Portrait* (Hollstein 1949–2010, vol. 19, no. 7), "Another element through which Rembrandt indicates that he is dressed in the fashion of a century earlier is the chain with a cross that he wears over his shirt, which refers to the period before the Reformation." There is no indication of a cross in the Pasadena portrait.

41. In comparing it to the Pasadena portrait, *Corpus* 1989, p. 624, notes that the Odessa

painting "shows the figure on the same scale as the original in an oval, with a strong accent on the folds in the shirt collar and a beret standing slightly taller. These differences from the original recur in the print by Le Sueur . . . which was undoubtedly made after this copy." Silvain-Raphaël Baudouin was a French soldier, amateur printmaker, and collector. He appears to have assumed the title of "comte." In 1779 he sold 115 paintings from his collection to Catherine II. He had copies made of 92 of these.

42. F. L. Regnault, Paris, 4 May 1797: "No. 43: Idem [d'après Rembrandt]. Deux portraits; l'un Arminius, chef de secte, portant une robe noire avec rabat blanc, il est coëffée d'un chapeau rond à haute forme; l'autre, Rembrandt dans sa jeunesse, la tête couverte d'une bonnet plat, & vêtu d'un manteau à gros boutons: hauteur 23 pouces, sur 19 de large [62.1 × 51.3 cm]. T. de forme ovale." Present location unknown.

In addition to the Odessa painting and a copy sold by Baudouin, *Corpus* 1989, p. 624, notes the following copies: panel, 61.5 × 51 cm, dated 1635, formerly collection Grimaldi, Cadiz (sale, Frederik Muller, Amsterdam, 4 December 1912, lot 57, bought in for 17,000 guilders, and sale, Lepke, Berlin, 5 May 1914, lot 62, ill.), present location unknown; and panel, 64.6 × 51.7 cm, dated 1634, formerly Mrs. H. O. Havemeyer (sale, New York, 10 April 1930, lot 102, ill., for $4,500 to F. M. Hardy), present location unknown. A third copy, panel, 56 × 46.5 cm, attributed to Flinck, appeared in the sale, "Alte Kunst," Lempertz, Cologne, 11 November 1964, lot 57, pl. 65.

43. Print by Lesueur after painting in Odessa (reverse image). Inscribed in print "G. Flinck pinx" (left) and "J. B. le Sueur sculpt" (right). First noted by J. G. van Gelder 1950, esp. p. 328.

44. Olivar 2010, passim.

67

Rembrandt Harmensz. van Rijn

Dutch
Leyden 1606–1669 Amsterdam

Portrait of a Boy in Fancy Costume, formerly known as *Titus*

ca. 1655–60

Oil on canvas, 25½ × 22 in. (64.8 × 55.9 cm)
The Norton Simon Foundation, F.1965.2.P

Provenance

Private collection, near The Hague, sold to; Mr. Barker, sold ca. 1830 to;[1] George Spencer (1758–1834), 2nd Earl Spencer, Althorp, Northamptonshire, by descent to his son; John Charles (1782–1845), 3rd Earl Spencer, Althorp, Northamptonshire, by descent to his son; Frederick Spencer (1798–1857), 4th Earl Spencer, Althorp, Northamptonshire, by descent to his son; John Poyntz Spencer (1835–1910), 5th Earl Spencer, by descent to his brother; Charles Spencer (1857–1922), 6th Earl Spencer, Althorp, Northamptonshire, sold September 1915 to;[2] Herbert Frederick Cook (1868–1939, later Sir Herbert, 3rd Bart.), loaned to his father, Sir Frederick Lucas Cook (1844–1920), 2nd Bart. and Visconde de Monserrate in Portugal, Doughty House, Richmond, Surrey, returned 1920 to; Sir Herbert Frederick Cook (1868–1939), 3rd Bart., Doughty House, Richmond, Surrey, gift to his son; Sir Francis Ferdinand Maurice Cook (1907–1978), 4th Bart. and Visconde de Monserrate in Portugal, Le Coin, Jersey, C.I., gift to his seventh wife;[3] Dame Bridget Brenda Cook (1921–2018) (sale, Christie's, London, 19 March 1965, lot 105, sold to); The Norton Simon Foundation.

Exhibited

London 1867, no. 18, as "William, Prince of Orange, afterwards William III, as a Boy" (original sticker attached to back of stretcher); Dublin 1872, no. 80 (original sticker on back of stretcher); London 1895, no. 130; Amsterdam 1898, no. 95, pl. 29; London 1899, no. 30; London 1907, no. 60; London 1922, no. 13; London 1929b, no. 120; Toledo/Toronto 1944–45, no. 544, ill.; on loan, Fitzwilliam Museum, University of Cambridge, 1947–51; on loan, National Gallery of Art, Washington, DC, 28 May–5 December, 1965; on loan, Los Angeles County Museum of Art, December 1965–October 1966; San Francisco/Toledo/Boston 1966–67, no. 37, p. 73, color frontis.; on loan, Cleveland Museum of Art, 1 April 1967–23 March 1968; on loan, Minneapolis Institute of Arts, 1 April 1968–January 1969; on loan, Metropolitan Museum of Art, New York, January–August 1969; Amsterdam 1969, pp. 53, 68–69, no. 12, color pl.; on loan, Los Angeles County Museum of Art, January 1970–September 1972; on loan, Museum of Fine Arts, Houston, September 1972–December 1973; on loan, M. H. de Young Memorial Museum, San Francisco, December 1973–June 1974; on loan, Dallas Museum of Fine Arts, 3 September–20 October, 1974; on loan, National Gallery of Art, Washington, DC, 11 May–4 September 2007.

References

J. Smith 1829–42, vol. 7 (1836), p. 116, no. 318; Althorp House 1851, no. 129; Bode 1883, pp. 537, 578, no. 355; Dutuit 1885, pp. 48, 63, no. 335, provenance unknown, cites Bode's dating of the painting, 1658–60; Wurzbach 1886, p. 67, no. 24; E. Michel 1893, p. 555, no. 433; Bode and Hofstede de Groot 1897–1906, vol. 6 (1901), pp. 17, 112, no. 440, ill.; Valentiner 1908, p. 336; "Lord Spencer" 1911, p. 17, color pl.; Graves [1913–15] 1970, vol. 3 (1914), pp. 1009, 1014, 1017–18; Cook 1915, pp. vii, 73, 186f., no. 544, pl. xxvi; Hofstede de Groot 1908–27, vol. 6 (1916), pp. 248f., no. 489; Brockwell 1917, pp. 25f., fig. xv; Schmidt-Degener 1917, pp. 100–02, ill.;[4] Meldrum 1923, no. 343, p. 20, p. 138; Weisbach 1926, pp. 536, 629; Dangers 1928, pp. 16, 45;[5] Witt 1929, pp. 3–5, pl. 1; Chamot 1929a, p. 23; Chamot 1929b, p. 135; Van Regteren Altena 1929, pp. 118, 121, ill.; Bauch 1929, p. 18; Wilenski 1929, pp. 95f., pl. 50; London 1929a, p. 61, fig. 70; Brockwell 1932, p. 734, no. 544 (195), pl. xxiv; Bredius 1935, no. 119, ill.; Poortenaar [1940], p. 122; J. Veth 1941, no. 106, pp. 211ff., ill. 218; H. E. van Gelder 1942, pp. 21, 25, ill.; Wilenski 1945, p. 81, pl. 50; J. Rosenberg 1948, vol. 1, p. 220n21; Knuttel 1956, p. 170; J. Rosenberg 1964, p. 349n21; Bauch 1966, pp. 21, 36, 45, no. 410, ill.;[6] Los Angeles *Annual Report* 1968; Wallace 1968, p. 88, color pl.; Saarinen 1968; Gerson 1968, pp. 392f., 501, no. 319, ill.; Arpino and Lecaldano 1969, pp. 114–15, no. 303, ill., as 1653/54; Bredius/Gerson 1969, pp. 107, 557, no. 119, ill.; Christlieb 1969, pp. 50–60, ill.; Descargues 1969, pp. 2–3, color pl.; Gerson 1973a, p. 27;[7] Malraux 1974, vol. 2, pp. 274, 297, no. 171; Brown 1976, pp. 216–19; Rosenbaum 1982, pp. 62–63, ill.; Failing 1983, p. 20, ill.; Schwartz 1985, p. 309, no. 348, ill.; Koning 1986, p. 112, ill.; Tümpel 1986, pp. 269, 430, cat. A99, ill., as from Rembrandt's circle; Sebag-Montefiore 1988, p. 51; Bonafoux 1990, pp. 82–84; Herbert 1990; Grimm 1991, p. 104; Van Thiel 1992, pp. 30, 45, 88, no. 95, fig. 41, ill.; Slatkes 1992, p. 453, no. 300, ill.; Liedtke 1995, p. 136, no. 41; Sonnenburg 1995, p. 5, fig. 3; Van de Wetering 1997, pp. 202f., 205, 211, 290, fig. 265;[8] Manuth 1998, pp. 330f., 335n67, fig. 9; Muchnic 1998, ill., pp. 2–4, 86–95, 99, 124, 126, 185, 253; The Hague/London 1999, p. 176, cat. 56, as Rembrandt? ca. 1641?; Van de Wetering 2000, pp. 202f., 211, 290, fig. 265; Danziger 2004, pp. 454f., fig. 23; Braunschweig 2006, pp. 24f., fig. 9; Dibbits 2006, pp. 101–02, fig. 2; Wieseman 2010, pp. 99–100, 110, fig. 4, no. 11; S. Campbell 2010, pp. 66, 69, 70–75, 79–81, 101n46, 153, 206n7, 223, 277, no. 266, fig. 4, ill.; Bailey et al. 2011, pp. 21f.; Van de Wetering 2016, p. 270, fig. 247; Van de Wetering 2017, vol. 1, p. 368, pl. 243, vol. 2, p. 632, pl. 243; Manuth, De Winkel, and Van Leeuwen 2019, no. 302, pp. 378, 380, 440, 675, 696, 700, ill.; Muchnic 2019, pp. 3–6, 83–91, 94–95, 320–22.

Technical Notes

The primary support is a medium-weight plain-weave canvas. The original tacking edges have been cut off, and the edges are slightly irregular. Near the center of the right side, the trimmed edge abruptly interrupts full brushstrokes, indicating that that side has been cut down. An X-radiograph reveals no cusped threads at any side. The painting has been lined to a canvas with a pronounced weave and a great many slubs, the bumps of which have transferred to the front of the painting with the pressure of lining. Two old vertical tears, one originating at the top edge, slightly left of center, and the other originating at the bottom edge, left of center, were repaired by the lining. The ground is a dark color, possibly brown. There appears to be an opaque, medium-warm gray imprimatura covering the ground throughout, as seen in the lower left corner. The paint is an oil medium, applied in varied

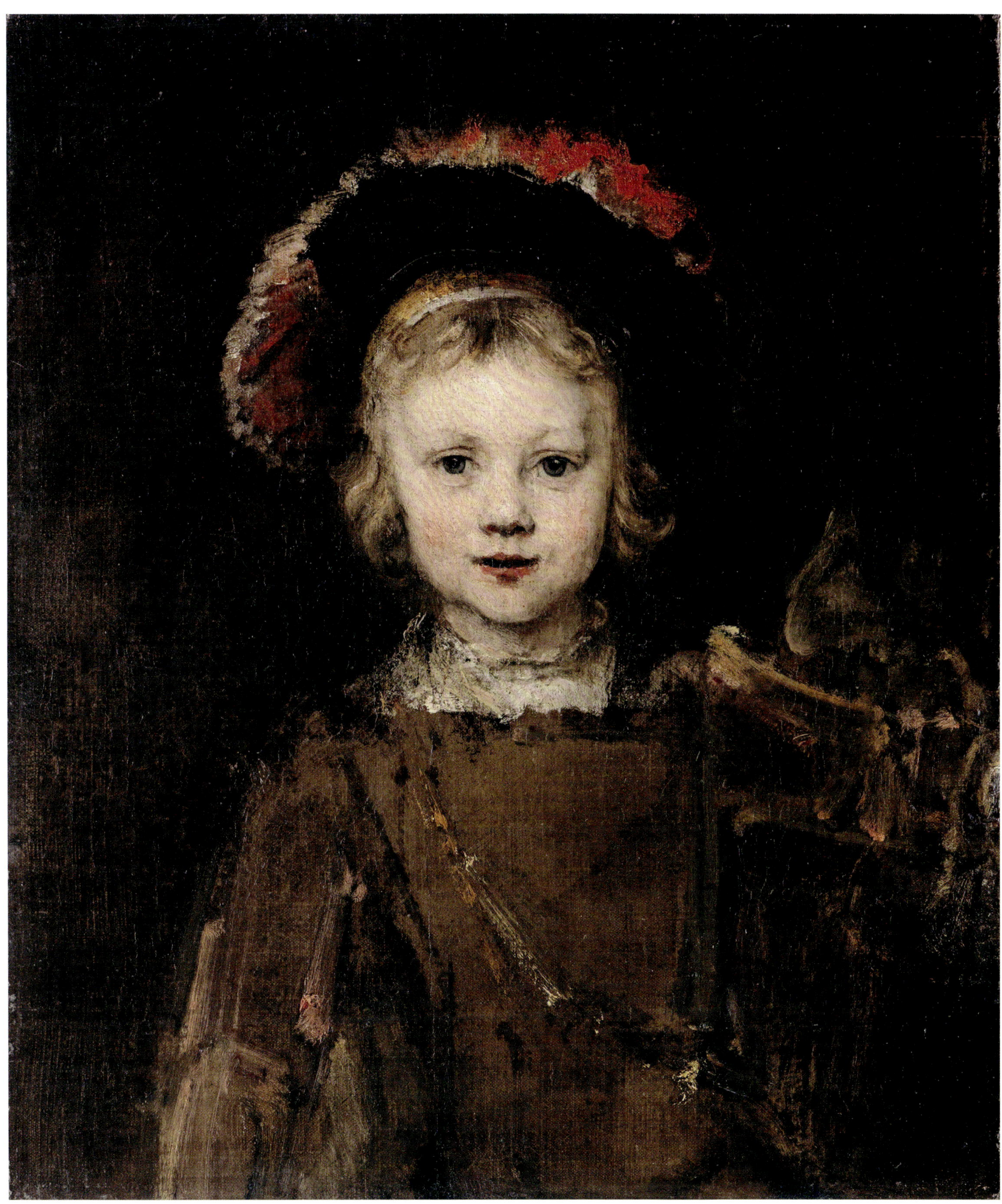

thicknesses and brushstrokes, with the face fully developed and the tunic painted rather loosely in broad strokes. Thin, rather fluid black brushstrokes first established the figure, as seen in and beneath the collar, with the background and mid-tones of the tunic and arms scrubbed in with translucent brown. The face is heavily worked in multiple layers, with a dark layer below the light-colored flesh; cracks in the light colors expose the dark ground, which extrudes into the cracks, suggesting that the preparatory layers may not have fully dried. The image is arresting yet has been altered considerably by past restoration. The proper right sleeve seems to have been abraded in cleaning, although it is difficult to discern what should be attributed to the unfinished state and what is a result of interventions. In the thick impastoed paint in the face, weave interference from lining has changed the paint profile noticeably. Brushstrokes in the white collar were probably more robust originally. Incomplete cleaning left residues of dark material in the recesses of brushstrokes, which are especially distracting in the face. The two vertical tears have been thickly overpainted in poorly matched color. Ultraviolet light provides almost no information about other retouching. The brittle, natural-resin varnish is fractured and moderately yellowed; it is also becoming slightly cloudy.

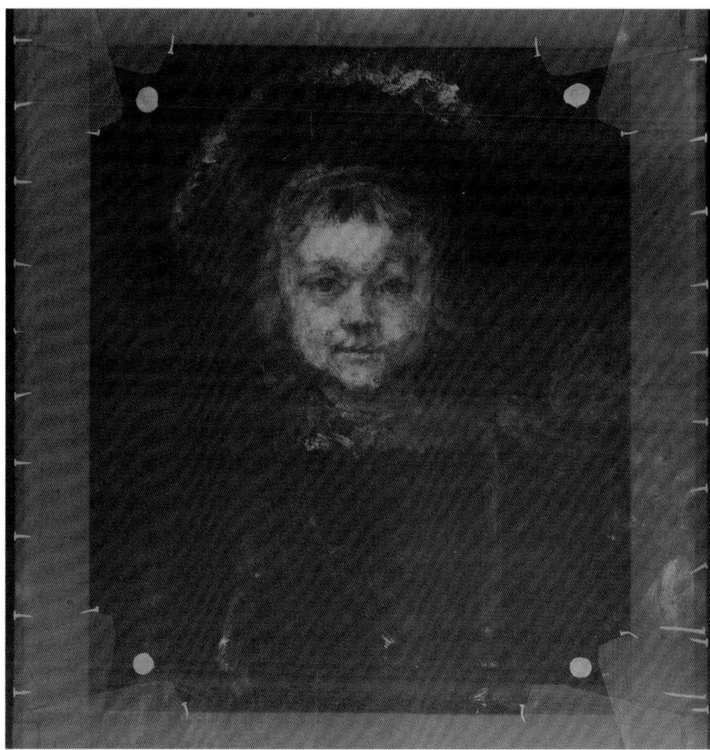

Fig. 67a. X-radiograph of *Portrait of a Boy in Fancy Costume*, image courtesy of National Gallery of Art, Painting Conservation Department, Washington, DC.

Appearing to be approximately five or six years old, the blond, blue-eyed boy in *Portrait of a Boy in Fancy Costume*, formerly known as *Titus*, addresses the viewer with his shoulders square to the picture plane. A black hat ornamented with a great, arching red plume encircles the soft blond curls that frame his face. Quick, broad strokes of black, gold, and white roughly define a square-necked tunic with sleeves worn over a white shirt visible only at the neck. A strap crosses the boy's chest from his proper right shoulder to the opposite hip. His extended proper left arm was cut when the canvas was cut on the right.[9] An area of vertical brushstrokes close to his side and below the proper left arm is similar to that on the opposite side and may suggest that the artist originally planned that a cape would hang from his shoulders down his back. The emphatic lines, especially the white line on top of his extended arm, support the idea that the artist rethought his original design. An amorphous, loosely painted area above the extended arm appears to continue across the sleeve. It has been interpreted as both a falcon and a monkey.[10]

This unfinished painting reveals Rembrandt's working procedure. After blocking out the form of the child in black paint over the warm gray imprimatura that covers the dark ground layer of the canvas and roughly scrubbing in the background with dark, translucent browns, the artist established the broad areas of light in the face with thick strokes of dense white paint. To give structure to the face, he deftly defined the nose and mouth by exposing the underlying tone and applying reddish-pink paint. Highlights appear on the forehead, cheeks, nose, chin, and eyelids. The detailed description of the face, including the eyes and the subtle blending of the face, was, however, left incomplete.

The very thick application of white paint on the boy's face, which appears as a solid mass in an X-radiograph (fig. 67a), has led some scholars to question the attribution to Rembrandt, who more typically applied paint with individual strokes as if he were modeling the form with paint.[11] A similar application of the white underpaint is found, however, in portraits where the face is seen in direct light. The resulting somewhat thick surface is found in other works of the late 1650s and early 1660s, including *An Elderly Man as Saint Paul*, probably 1659, and the *Portrait of Jacob Trip* (ca. 1661; both National Gallery, London), in which the faces are depicted with more shadow. The differences between these paintings and the Pasadena painting may be at least partially explained by the fact that the latter was left unfinished.

The frontal pose of the boy is found in a number of works painted by Rembrandt beginning in the 1640s.[12] These are commissioned portraits as well as *tronies*—studies of human expression or character—and historical subjects in which isolated figures with their shoulders square to the picture plane confront the viewer directly. While in many cases light falls from the side, casting part of the face in shadow, in other paintings—including that in Pasadena—the light falls from the front, fully illuminating the face. The effect is similar to that in portraits of women who traditionally face left into full light to address the portraits of their husbands. Perhaps in the case of this painting it was intended to suggest the child's innocence and openness.

In an article about the seventeenth-century fascination with the portraits of Hans Holbein II (1497/98–1543), Volker Manuth observes that *Portrait of a Boy in Fancy Costume* resembles what Rembrandt's contemporaries would have considered the characteristic Holbein portrait. Manuth renews an observation first noted by Schmidt-Degener and suggests that Rembrandt was influenced by Holbein's *Portrait of Edward VI as a Child* (fig. 67b), which was then part

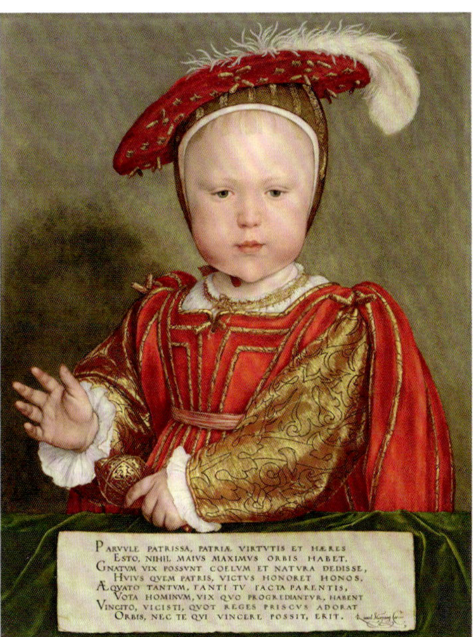

Fig. 67b. Hans Holbein II, *Portrait of Edward VI as a Child*, ca. 1538, oil on panel, 22 ⅜ × 17 5/16 in. (56.8 × 44 cm), National Gallery of Art, Washington, DC, Andrew W. Mellon Collection.

of the famous collection of paintings and drawings assembled by Thomas Howard (1585–1646), 14th Earl of Arundel, and known from a print by Wenceslaus Hollar (1607–1677).[13] Indeed, beyond the general similarity of the frontally posed figure, the square face in the Pasadena painting, with its delicately bowed mouth, knob-like chin, and broad forehead beneath a feather-trimmed cap, recalls that of the sixteenth-century portrait of the young English prince. The aristocratic costume of the boy in the Pasadena painting, with its square neck, high-cut shirt ruffed at the neck, and suggestion of a cape falling from his shoulders, also resembles that of the prince in Holbein's portrait. The combination of the dark feathered beret worn over his close-cropped coif further links the costume to sixteenth-century fashion.[14]

Throughout the nineteenth century, the Pasadena painting was known as a portrait of William III (1650–1702), Prince of Orange. The son of the Dutch stadtholder Willem II (1626–1650), Prince of Orange, and his wife, Mary Stuart (1631–1660; the daughter of Charles I of England), William III was born in November 1650, shortly after the death of his father. Rembrandt's choice of Holbein's portrait of the English Prince Edward as the model for his portrayal of the heir to the ambitious court at The Hague would certainly have been appropriate. Sporting a plumed felt hat and a strap across his chest, Rembrandt's boy—like the one in *A Boy with a Hawk and Leash*, painted by Jan van Noordt (ca. 1620–ca. 1675; fig. 67c)—wears the trappings of an aristocratic youth for whom hunting with a falcon would have been a prerogative.[15]

The identification of Rembrandt's portrait as William III seems, however, to have originated with a spurious tale recounted to the Earl of Spencer at the time of the painting's acquisition ca. 1830.[16] The seller, Mr. Barker, probably calculated that the painting's appeal and price would be enhanced by the identification of the sitter as the future King William of England, who would reign with his wife, Queen Mary. While he had executed several paintings for stadtholder Frederik Hendrik (1584–1647) early in his career, Christopher Brown notes there is no indication that Rembrandt maintained contact with the court after his move to Amsterdam in 1631.[17] Certainly in the so-called stadtholder-less period that followed the sudden death of Frederik Hendrik's son, Willem II, and occurred during the protectorate of the young prince, patronage by the court dropped significantly.

In 1901 Wilhelm Bode tentatively suggested that the Pasadena portrait represents Titus (1641–1668), Rembrandt's only child to survive infancy. The identification was accepted by Wilhelm Valentiner and continued throughout most of the twentieth century.[18] If this identification is correct, then the painting would be the earliest portrait of the boy who would eventually manage his father's financial affairs. Rembrandt painted Titus on several occasions: the one showing the fourteen-year-old youth seated at his desk, dated 1655 (fig. 67d), is considered the standard against which to judge other pretenders.[19] The shape of the face, mouth, and eyes in that work—as well as that in the portrait of the slightly older youth thought to be Titus in *Young Man in a Beret* (Wallace Collection, London)—generally agree with those of the boy in the Pasadena painting, who appears to be approximately eight years younger.

Opinions about the identity of the sitter hinge largely on the dating of the unfinished painting. Dutuit, citing Bode, dated the painting (which he identified as William III) as 1658/60; the catalogue of the 1898 Amsterdam exhibition (which rejected the identification of the sitter as the young prince) dates it 1655; in 1908 Valentiner (who identified the boy as Titus) dated the painting 1648.[20] It is unclear whether he based the identification on his stylistic attribution of the date and the age of the artist's son, or whether he based the date on his presumption that Rembrandt portrayed Titus. Subsequent scholars (led by Bauch and Gerson), however, generally date it on the basis of style to ca. 1654, when Titus was thirteen or fourteen.[21] According to the organizers of the Amsterdam exhibition in 1969, "The generous brushstroke and the coloring belong to a much later period."[22] In response, Christopher Brown argued that the authors did

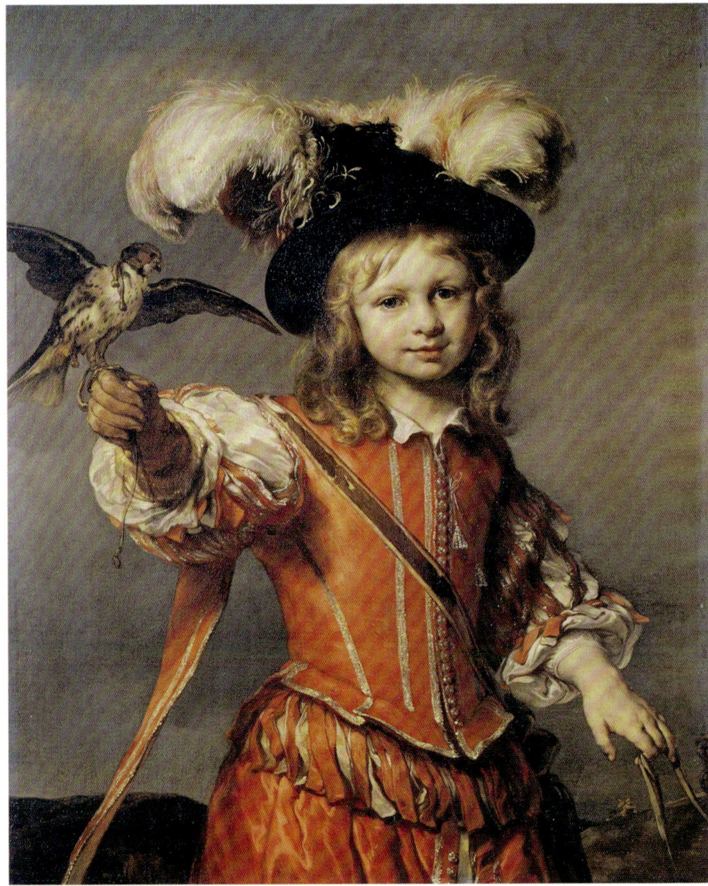

Fig. 67c. Jan van Noordt, *A Boy with a Hawk and Leash*, ca. 1655, oil on canvas, 32 7/16 × 25 15/16 in. (82.3 × 65.8 cm), The Wallace Collection, London.

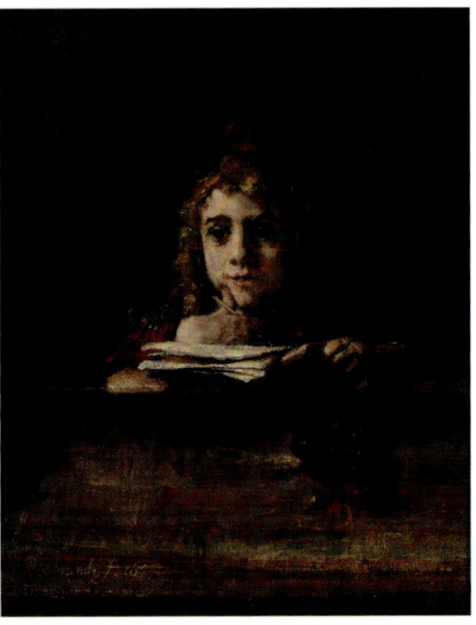

Fig. 67d. Rembrandt Harmensz. van Rijn, *Titus at His Desk*, 1655, oil on canvas, 30 1/4 × 24 3/4 in. (77 × 63 cm), Museum Boijmans Van Beuningen, Rotterdam.

not take into account that the painting was left unfinished. According to him, the "handling is comparable in detail, for example, to the *Young Girl Leaning on a Window-sill* . . . at Dulwich, which is dated 1645." Brown accordingly dates the painting to the late 1640s and seriously considers the sitter to be Titus, noting that the portrait "possesses a degree of tenderness and intimacy that runs counter to the idea of its being a state portrait, or even a formal portrait at all."[23] Ernst van de Wetering has returned the portrait to Rembrandt's late works, dating it ca. 1656 and comparing it stylistically to the 1659 *Moses Breaking the Tables of the Law* (Gemäldegalerie, Berlin) and *The Polish Rider*, ca. 1655 (Frick Collection, New York).[24] Volker Manuth dates it slightly later, ca. 1658.[25]

A date for the Pasadena painting in the mid- to late 1650s seems most appropriate stylistically and historically because of its reference to the portrait *Edward VI as a Child*. The Holbein painting was in the Arundel collection in Antwerp until at least 1650, when Wenceslaus Hollar made and dated his etching of it. Five years later, the painting appeared in the inventory in Amersfoort of the possessions of Arundel's widow and heir, Althea Talbot (1581–1654), Countess of Arundel, who had moved from Antwerp to the Netherlands to be near Elizabeth Stuart (1596–1662), the exiled Queen of Bohemia. Although it is likely that Rembrandt knew the painting only by reputation and from Hollar's etching after it, there is a possibility that he could have seen the actual portrait after the countess's death in Amsterdam in 1654.

Rather than a portrait of Titus, who was born in 1641, or William III, who was born in 1650, therefore, the Pasadena painting is probably either a portrait of another child in fancy dress, such as those by Jan van Noordt representing a youth as a falconer (see fig. 67c), or a *tronie*, painted as a figure type. The absence of cusping on all but the left side of the canvas, and the abrupt break in the brushwork describing the boy's proper left arm beyond the right edge of the canvas, suggest that Rembrandt cut the image of the boy from a larger composition.[26] Arthur Wheelock has proposed that the Pasadena portrait was cut from a large family portrait that Arnold Houbraken (1660–1719) mentioned Rembrandt abandoned when the patron objected to the inclusion of their recently deceased pet monkey.[27] Although it remains an intriguing theory, there is no evidence to support it.

Attracted to the popular portrait of the young prince by Holbein, which perhaps reminded him of his own son as a toddler, Rembrandt appears to have adapted the facial features and expression as well as the sixteenth-century costume from the earlier portrait to create his endearing image of an older child. Although he may have planned it as a portrait, he may merely have been developing an idea based on the Holbein example. This could explain the unfinished state of the painting and the unresolved definition of the object on the boy's arm, which does not agree with the proper practice of controlling or displaying a falcon, monkey, or other animal.[28]

As described in the introduction to this volume, Norton Simon's acquisition of Rembrandt's *Portrait of a Boy in Fancy Costume* in 1965 sent ripples through both the art world and the popular media. Regarded by many as one of the major works by Rembrandt still in private hands, the sale of the painting at Christie's, London, on 19 March 1965 was eagerly anticipated. Norton Simon was one of three serious bidders. Determined to acquire the painting, he concocted an elaborate system to bid, and the auctioneer, confused by Mr. Simon's early verbal bids, assumed that he was out when he fell silent. When the painting was knocked down to a competitor, Simon protested loudly, halting the sale and, ultimately, winning the prize.[29]

1. Brown 1976, p. 217, quotes an unpublished memorandum written by Lady Sarah Spencer (1838–1919), dated Saint Michael's Day, 1878, stating that the painting, which she knew as William III, Prince of Orange, was bought by "Mr. Barker, father of George Barker, the picture cleaner, who was often employed at A[lthorp]" from a farmer whom he met near The Hague and with whom he spent the night. The following day, in The Hague, a stranger saw Mr. Barker with the painting and identified the sitter as an ancestor. Only later did Barker learn that it was a portrait of the king. Lady Spencer reported that Barker discovered Rembrandt's signature. Returning to England, he told his story to Lavinia, Lady Spencer, who insisted on acquiring the painting.

2. The annotated catalogue of the 1965 Cook sale at the GRI notes, "May be identical with Head of a Child by Rembrandt which belonged to Earl Spencer as early as 1746." The confusion comes from Brockwell in Cook 1915, pp. 73 and 186, who identified the painting with that mentioned by Dibdin 1822, p. 275: "First Apartment, on the left hand, on reaching the top of the Great Staircase; opposite the bed: 'Head of a Young Man, in a green robe, by Rembrandt.'" As Brown 1976, p. 217, sorted it out, the Pasadena portrait "is not in the 1823 Althorp catalogue nor in the 'Aedes Althorpianae,' but it had arrived before 1834 as it is in that catalogue [the 1834 Althorp catalogue] as 'William III by Rembrandt.'"

3. Sir Francis's gift of the painting to his wife, who then wished to sell it, created a legal issue between Sir Francis and the trustees of a family settlement to which Sir Francis had a life interest. The court decided that Sir Francis was entitled to give the painting to his wife and that she could sell it and retain the profits for her own benefit. If the sale had been made by her husband, however, the proceeds would have become the property of the settlement.

4. Schmidt-Degener 1917 says it is unlikely a portrait of Titus, but rather a fantasy of Holbein's *Portrait of Prince Edward Tudor*.

5. Dangers 1928 has this as a work by Judith Leyster, who he says was the mother of Titus.

6. Bauch 1966 has this as *Titus van Rijn mit einem Falken (?)* and dates it 1653/54.

7. Gerson writes, "The *Titus* [*at His Desk*] portrait in the Boymans Museum may serve as a standard for a Rembrandt portrait of his son around 1655 [Br. 120]. . . . The *Titus* of the Norton Simon Collection [Br. 119] represents certainly another boy of another age. The attribution to Rembrandt seems acceptable notwithstanding some 'difficult to read' passages."

8. Van de Wetering 1997 has this as unfinished, ca. 1655/60, "I can see no reason to reject the painting."

9. See Technical Notes.

10. Bauch 1966, p. 21, says it is a falcon; Van Thiel in Amsterdam 1969, p. 68, identifies it as a monkey.

11. Tümpel 1986, p. 430, no. A99, attributes it to Rembrandt's circle. Koning 1986, p. 112, cites Hubert von Sonnenberg, then director of the Doerner Institute, Munich, as of the opinion that "*The Man with the Golden Helmet*, if not authentic, must be by a very good pupil of Rembrandt's—a better pupil, in his opinion, than the one who painted the so-called *Titus* (The Norton Simon Museum 'does not endorse the methods' of the research team)." Von Sonnenburg had examined the painting at the Metropolitan Museum of Art, New York, in 1969 when he was director of its paintings conservation laboratory.

12. In Rembrandt's three-quarter portrait *Agatha Bas*, dated 1641 (Bredius/Gerson 1969, no. 409; Royal Collection, Windsor Castle), for example, the subject stands with her proper left hand on the frame of a window through which she regards the viewer in a surprisingly direct manner.

13. Schmidt-Degener 1917, pp. 100f.; Manuth 1998, pp. 330–31, 334–35nn65–67, fig. 9.

14. Manuth, De Winkel, and Van Leeuwen 2019, p. 696, note that although the headgear is similar to that worn by the boy in Rembrandt's late family portrait in Braunschweig, "the combination of coif and beret points to the early sixteenth century."

15. By the second half of the seventeenth century, many wealthy members of the regent class who had acquired country estates also assumed the lifestyle and privileges previously limited to the landed aristocracy.

16. See note 1 above.

17. Brown 1976, p. 217.

18. Bode and Hofstede de Groot 1897–1906, vol. 6 (1901), pp. 17 and 112, no. 440; Valentiner 1908, p. 336.

19. The other generally accepted portraits of Titus include *Portrait of a Young Man Reading* (Kunsthistorisches Museum, Vienna), *Young Man in a Beret* (Wallace Collection, London), and *Portrait of Titus* (Louvre, Paris). Brown 1976, p. 219n4, lists others that have been considered portraits of Titus by Rembrandt but are not generally accepted.

20. Dutuit 1885, p. 48, no. 335; Bode 1883, pp. 537, 578, no. 355; Valentiner 1908, p. 336.

21. Bauch 1966, no. 410, as Titus, 1653; Gerson 1968, no. 319, as not 1640s, and therefore not Titus.

22. Amsterdam 1969, p. 68, no. 12.

23. Brown 1976, p. 218.

24. Van de Wetering 2016, p. 270.

25. Manuth, De Winkel, and Van Leeuwen 2019, p. 696.

26. An infrared photograph of the relined painting shows only minimal distortion of the canvas caused by stretching: Cusping, or at least weave distortion, appears only along the left—especially lower left—side, suggesting that the original canvas extended on the other three sides. Regarding Rembrandt's use of long strips of primed canvas from which individual canvases could be cut, see Van de Wetering 1997, p. 116.

27. Arthur Wheelock, unpublished manuscript (NSM), cites Houbraken 1718–21, part 1, pp. 259f. See also Slive 1953, p. 182.

28. A falcon was held on the left hand by the talons, not perched on the shoulder or upper arm. If the amorphous form in the Pasadena portrait were meant to represent a falcon, then the boy's arm would have had to be bent back at the elbow so that he could grasp the bird with his hand as in *A Boy with a Hawk and Leash* by Jan van Noordt (fig. 67c)—an unnaturally awkward pose. If the form were a monkey or perhaps a squirrel, then one would also expect that the sitter's hand would hold the chain that was generally attached to a band around the middle or neck of the animal. It is also possible that the diagonal lines across the arm may actually represent creases in the sleeve and that the amorphous object above the arm is a reference neither to a bird nor an animal but to furniture or architecture.

29. S. Campbell 2010, p. 72. After the sale, Norton Simon and the painting appeared on the cover of *Time* magazine, 4 June 1965.

68

Willem Reuter

Flemish
Brussels ca. 1642–1681 Rome

A Roman Market

ca. 1665–69

Signed vertically middle left margin: "JG^MO^/[R]EV/[T]ER"[1]
Oil on canvas, 47⅝ × 77 in. (121 × 195.6 cm)
Norton Simon Art Foundation, M.2010.1.207.P

Provenance
Anonymous (sale, Palais Galliera, Paris, 1 June 1967, lot 9, as Michelangelo Cerquozzi). [P. & D. Colnaghi, London, 1968]; [Herner-Wengraf Gallery, London, 1971, as Miel]. [P. & D. Colnaghi, London, as Miel, consigned to];[2] [Hoogsteder Gallery, The Hague, as Cerquozzi].[3] Dr. T. Praalder, the Netherlands (sale, Sotheby's, New York, 8 January 1981, lot 81, as Willem Reuter, sold to); Norton Simon, Los Angeles, bequest to; Jennifer Jones Simon Art Trust, bequest 27 September 2010 to; Norton Simon Art Foundation.

Exhibited
London 1968a, no. 14, ill., as Miel; London 1971b, no. 5, ill., as Miel.

References
Kren 1978, pp. 194, 218, nos. D15, D73; Trezzani 1983, pp. 327, 330–32, figs. 14.3–14.4 (detail); Trnek 1992, p. 323n7; S. Campbell 2010, p. 433, no. 1667, ill.; Gozzano 2015, p. 35, plate x, fig. 63 (detail).

Technical Notes
The twill-weave canvas has been lined, with the original tacking edges cut off. A small hole at the top center, a vertical tear that originates at the bottom center, and a hole in the lower right have been repaired. The off-white ground is moderately thick, smoothing the texture of the twill weave. The rich, opaque paint was directly applied, with crisply defined figures and objects in the expansive scene. The sky was painted with thinner paint and with some use of layering in shades of blue. X-radiography reveals a substantial amount of paint loss along the upper half of the right edge and at the lower portion of the left edge. Under high magnification, the thin blue paint in the sky reveals some unusual deterioration in the form of tiny pits, apparently unrelated to other conditions in this painting. There are also very small drying cracks in this layer. In a 1981 conservation treatment by Bernard Rabin, varnish was removed from the sky and part of the foreground. Some losses in the central foreground have been retouched in a perfunctory manner, with other minor retouching scattered throughout the sky. The synthetic varnish is recorded as both Acryloid B-67 and B-72.

A *Roman Market* is characteristic of paintings produced by an informal association of northern painters in Rome known as Bamboccianti in which small figures depict scenes of everyday life in and around Rome, essentially translating Dutch and Flemish subject matter into the Italian idiom.[4] Employing Caravaggesque chiaroscuro, the artists established a new and distinct Italian genre. The majority of the paintings by the Bamboccianti are small in scale, yet inventories and extant examples also document the existence of large paintings. Criticized for their base subjects and naturalism, paintings by the Bamboccianti were nevertheless widely accepted by the second half of the seventeenth century, when members of the Italian aristocracy and bourgeoisie were willing to pay high prices to acquire them.

Before 1978 *A Roman Market* was attributed at various times to the Italian painter Michelangelo Cerquozzi (1602–1660) and to the Flemish painter Jan Miel (1599–1664). Thomas Kren's attribution of this large work to the Flemish painter Willem Reuter is now confirmed by the identification of the signature written vertically along the left margin of the painting.[5] As Kren observed, the Pasadena painting relates closely to *Festival in the Piazza di Spagna, Rome* (fig. 68a)[6] and *Market Scene* (Galleria Spada, Rome).[7] In each painting a plaza surrounded by architecture forms the stage for a cross-section of Roman society separated into

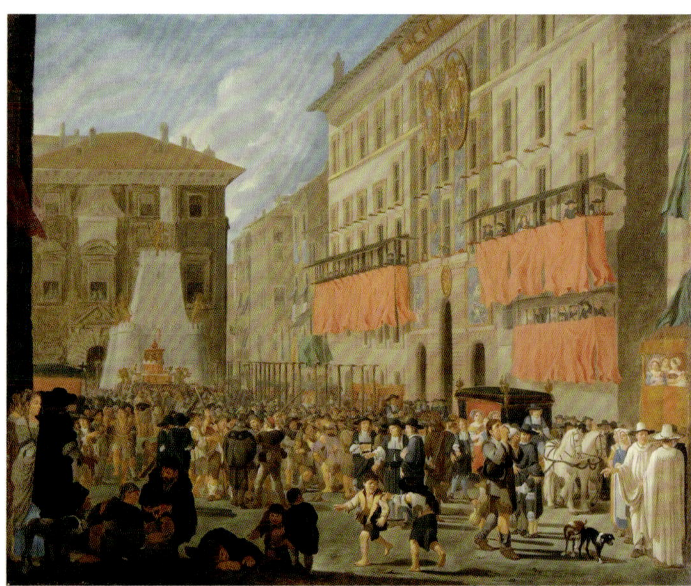

Fig. 68a. Willem Reuter, *Festival in the Piazza di Spagna, Rome*, after 1661, oil on canvas, 20⅛ × 29½ in. (51 × 75 cm), Gemäldegalerie der Akademie der bildenden Künste, Vienna.

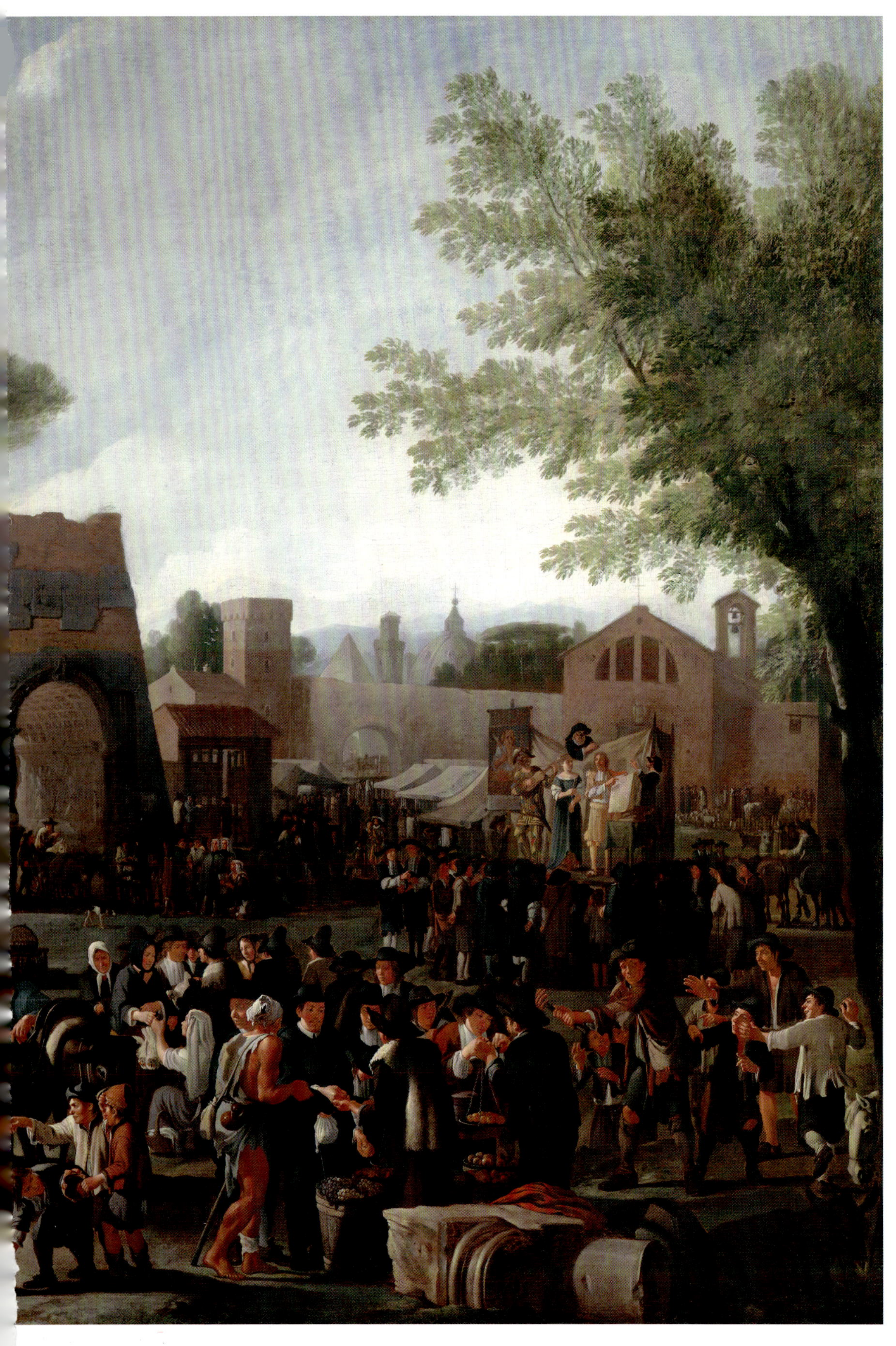

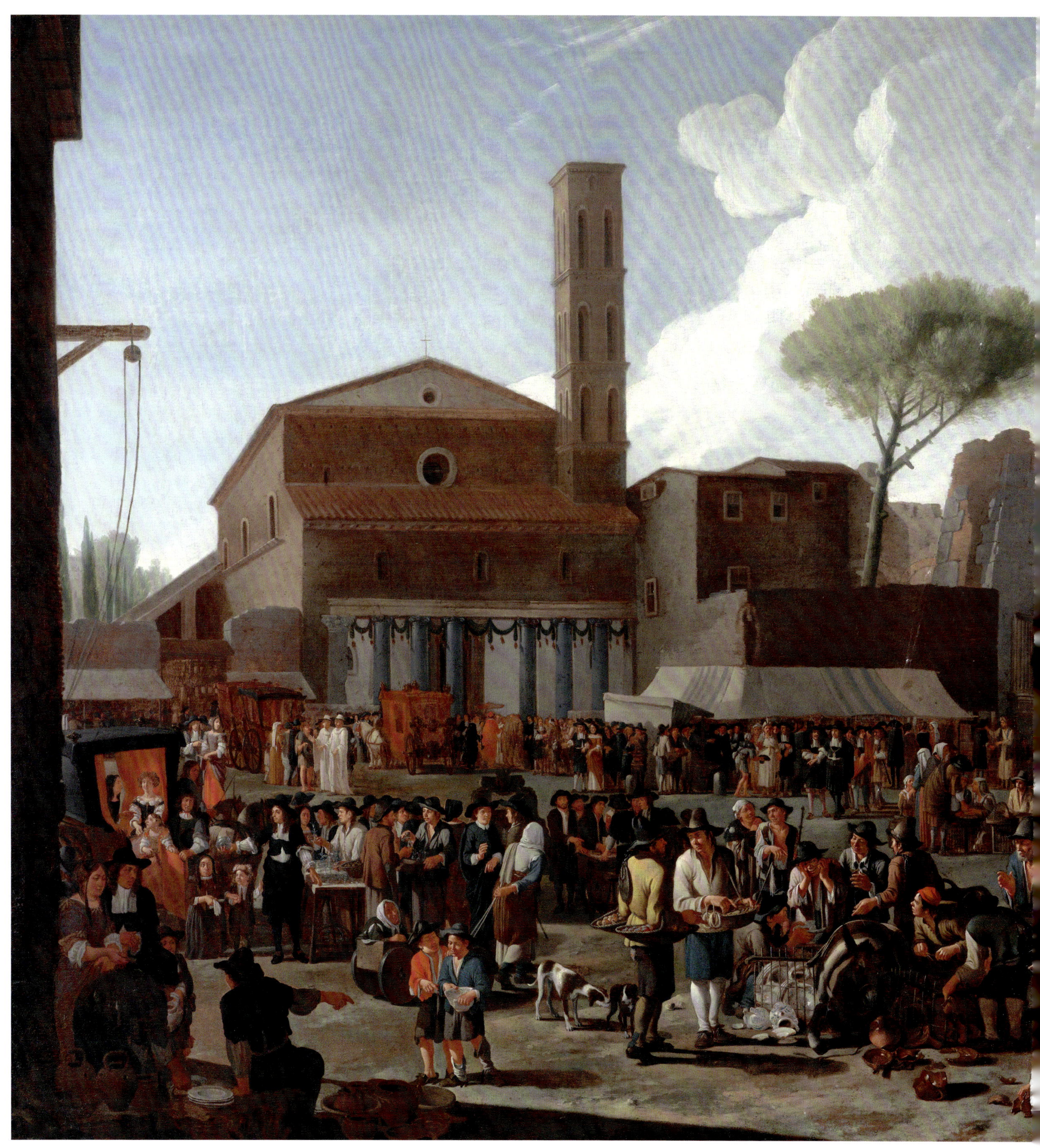

anecdotal vignettes but unified into a cohesive composition. The sculptural figures, individually defined by strong, raking light that casts long shadows on the ground, are reminiscent of the classically inspired figures of Michiel Sweerts (1618–1664), with whom Reuter probably studied. Reuter's figures are noteworthy for their expressive gestures and movements, which retain a quiet sobriety. The Pasadena painting includes stock figure types that reappear in Reuter's other paintings. The horse-drawn carriage with elegant female passengers, for example, also appears in *Festival in the Piazza di Spagna, Rome*.

The compositional structure of the Pasadena painting, with its broad, open piazza, differs significantly from that of the Vienna and Rome paintings, which include a central building in the middle ground and a sharply receding street on the right, reminiscent of perspective stage designs of the Renaissance employed by Jacques Callot (1592–1635).[8] The affection for Callot's beggars and vagrants among the Bamboccianti has often been mentioned. However, his stage designs and such popular prints as *The Fair at Xeuilley*,[9] *The Punishments*,[10] and *The Fair at Impruneta* (fig. 68b)[11] also influenced the development of larger paintings—composed of multiple anecdotal groups disposed on broad, open piazzas defined by architecture—in the second half of the seventeenth century.[12] Similarities between the Pasadena painting and *The Fair at Impruneta* suggest that Reuter adapted Callot's basic composition of the open square in front of a basilica framed in the foreground by a building on the left and tree on the right.[13] Reuter's device of placing silhouetted figures in the lower left corner next to a narrow section of wall also undoubtedly derived from Callot, who uses a similar device in many of his panoramic prints, including *The Palace Gardens at Nancy*, where the similarity to Reuter is particularly evident.[14]

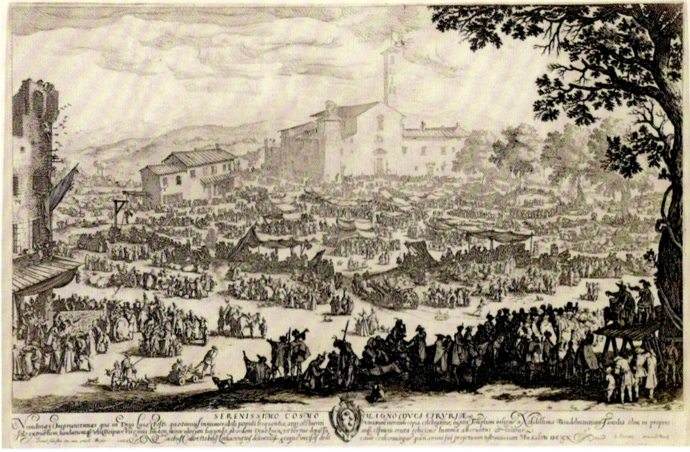

Fig. 68b. Jacques Callot, *The Fair at Impruneta*, 1622, etching, 16¾ × 26 in. (42.3 × 66.9 cm), Fine Arts Museums of San Francisco, Gift of Dr. Ludwig A. Emge.

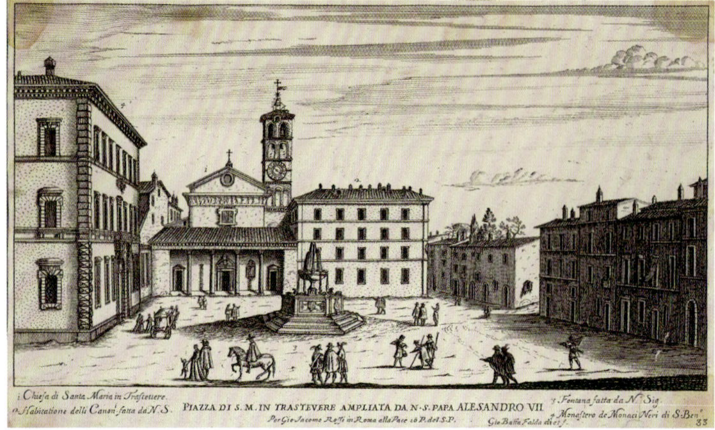

Fig. 68c. Giovanni Battista Falda, *Piazza di Santa Maria in Trastevere ampliata di N.S. Papa Alessandro VII*, 1665, etching, 6 11⁄16 × 11 1⁄16 in. (17 × 28.1 cm), British Museum, London.

Dating Reuter's paintings is problematic. Kren's notation that the Pasadena painting is dated 1669 is unsupported by its present appearance, which is signed but not dated.[15] *Festival in the Piazza di Spagna, Rome*, which is thought to represent the celebration in 1662 following the November 1661 birth of Carlos (1661–1700), later King Carlos II of Spain, may in fact have been painted later than the event.[16] Although it is probable that Reuter, who was born about 1642, was in Rome for several years before his 1672 marriage (the first evidence placing him in the city), the quality of the Vienna painting suggests a more experienced artist. A date for the Vienna and the Pasadena paintings in the mid- to late 1660s appears appropriate.

The Pasadena painting is a capriccio, incorporating references to familiar Roman landmarks brought together from different parts of the city and placed together in the fantastic setting: the church of Santa Maria in Trastevere with its medieval tower (fig. 68c) appears next to the Arch of Titus,[17] located in reality on the Via Sacra, southeast of the Forum; in the distant right, the dome of Saint Peter's Basilica is incongruously placed next to the Pyramid of Casius Cestino, which is actually located near the Porta San Paolo.[18] In the foreground, the broad, open plaza is alive with the bustling activity of a large Roman market, where vendors offer local and imported goods to a wide spectrum of the city's ever-changing population. Reuter represented every segment of Roman society. Significantly, the wealthy are relegated to the left and upper perimeters of the scene. On the left, next to an elegant carriage in which well-dressed women sit, a merchant selling silver vessels attempts to engage others of the group, who appear to be observers rather than actively involved in the market scene. Two roaming vendors chat, one with scales slung over his shoulder and shallow baskets of fruit, the other with a basket of taralli, southern Italian crackers formed from rings of dough.[19] Elsewhere Reuter showed Dominican clerics dressed in white and middle-class folk going about their business. Beggars, originally inspired by Callot's popular prints and common to works by the Bamboccianti, appear throughout the painting: a seminude man dressed in rags and leaning on a crutch begs, without response, from a well-dressed man paying for goods over a barrel of grapes. In the left distance another beggar approaches two Dominican priests, and in the center of the painting a third beggar approaches a Middle Eastern potentate, who bears striking resemblance to the figure on the frontispiece Callot designed for the play *Il Solimano*.[20] On the far right edge of the square, an acting troupe performs on a portable stage, while, amid the scattered ruins of Roman columns, street urchins fight and collect shards of pottery shattered when an overloaded mule collapsed and destroyed the vendor's wares.

Attempts to read iconographic meaning into individual elements of Bamboccianti painting are unconvincing.[21] More informative is the parallel interest in the world of the poor and the working classes shared by the contemporary literati. In *Povertà Contenta* (Contented Poverty), published in 1650, for example, Daniello Bartoli (1608–1685) draws a comparison between the rich, who are never content, and the contented poor. Nevertheless, although almsgiving is a frequent theme in Bamboccianti works, including the Pasadena painting, these works were not intended primarily as stimuli to moral behavior. Rather, like the famous etchings of Callot and paintings by Pieter Bruegel I (ca. 1525–1569), they were probably intended for the enjoyment of the members of the upper classes who would have delighted in their anecdotal complexity, observing at a distance, like the wealthy visitors on the left of the Pasadena painting, the activities of the Italian lower classes, whom Bartoli idealistically identified as content with their station in life.

1. I am grateful to Christopher Brown for identifying the missing letters, which made it possible to identify the inscription as Reuter's signature using the Italian form of his first name.

2. Colnaghi and Herner-Wengraf may have owned the painting together.

3. A letter dated 14 December 1988 from John Hoogsteder (NSM) notes that the firm had the painting on consignment and that it had come from Colnaghi.

4. The term derived from Il Bamboccio (the Ragdoll), the nickname of Pieter van Laer (1599–after 1642), the most influential member of the group, also known as the *Bentveughels* (Birds of a Feather). Originally from Haarlem, Van Laer was in Rome ca. 1625–ca. 1637, after which he returned to the Netherlands. The influence of Van Laer and the Bamboccianti continued in Rome and extended to the Netherlands and Flanders following Van Laer's departure.

5. Regarding the signature, see note 1, above. Kren 1978, p. 194, no. D15. Kren also reattributes to Reuter *Carnival Scene* (Collection Andrea Busiri Vici, Rome), which had been known as Michiel Sweerts. This attribution is, however, disputed by Trezzani 1983, p. 327n3.

6. See Trnek 1992, pp. 320ff.

7. Zeri 1954, p. 130, no. 107, ill., as Michiel Sweerts. See also Trnek 1992, p. 323n7.

8. See, for example, Callot's prints for the tragedy *Il Solimano* by Prospero Bonarelli (1580–1659) in Lieure [1924–27] 1969, nos. 364–68; and Meaume 1860, vol. 2, p. 207, nos. 436–39. The folded prints were inserted before each act of the play when it was published in 1620 in Florence by Cecconcelli. The play, which enjoyed great popularity in the seventeenth century, was a tragedy that took place at the Ottoman court of Suleiman the Magnificent (r. 1520–66). See Washington 1975, pp. 112–19, nos. 74–79.

9. Lieure [1924–27] 1969, no. 561; Meaume 1860, vol. 2, p. 295, no. 623.

10. Lieure [1924–27] 1969, no. 1402; Meaume 1860, vol. 2, p. 319, no. 665.

11. Lieure [1924–27] 1969, no. 361; Meaume 1860, vol. 2, p. 295, no. 621.

12. See also similar compositions in the work of Johannes Lingelbach (1622–1674) and Jan Miel (1599–1664).

13. Callot, who dedicated his famous etching to his patron Cosimo II de' Medici (1592–1621), Grand Duke of Tuscany, represented a panoramic view of the square in front of the church at Impruneta, the small Tuscan village where the celebration of the festival of Saint Luke, patron saint of painters, took place on 18 October each year.

14. Lieure [1924–27] 1969, no. 566; Meaume 1860, vol. 2, no. 622. Trnek 1992, p. 323, attributes Reuter's use of this device in the Vienna painting to the influence of Michiel Sweerts, who undoubtedly also knew the earlier etchings by Callot.

15. Kren 1978, p. 194n1, notes that Albert Blankert pointed this out to him. The reference to the date appears to derive from the catalogue of the 1971 Herner-Wengraf exhibition (London 1971b).

16. Carlos II was the son of Philip IV (1605–1665) of Spain and Mariana of Austria. He became king following his father's death. His mother served as regent from 1665 to 1675.

17. The slanted walls of the arch, which differ from the perpendicular walls of the actual Arch of Titus, are similar to the arch as it appears in paintings by Reuter's contemporary Niccolò Codazzi (ca. 1642–1693), a painter of architectural fantasies. In addition to the sloping sides, Codazzi depicted a single large broken fluted column on either side of the arch, similar to those in Reuter's painting. The historic arch has two narrower engaged columns to either side. See Marshall 1993, nos. NC 34, Niccolò Codazzi and Jacob de Heusch (1656/57–1701), *The Arch of Titus*, 1675–80 (Musée des Beaux-Arts, Bordeaux, inv. E 262; M6625); and NC 35, Niccolò Codazzi and Dirk (Theodor) Helmbreker (1633–1696), mid-1670s (private collection, Coral Gables, FL).

18. A similar church also appears as the setting for *Almsgiving in front of a Church* (private collection, Rome); Briganti, Trezzani, and Laureati 1983, no. 14.5, p. 333, ill. I thank Christopher Brown for identifying the church, the facade of which was restored in 1702 by Carlo Fontana (1634–1714). The present portico was added in the nineteenth century.

19. In describing this group, I benefited from Maggie Bell's label for the painting in the Norton Simon Museum's 2023 exhibition *All Consuming: Art and the Essence of Food*.

20. Washington 1975, p. 119, no. 79.

21. Trnek 1992, pp. 322f., has determined that the Vienna painting commemorates the celebrations that took place in the Piazza di Spagna to honor the birth of Spanish Prince Carlos on November 6, 1661. Other attempts to assign meaning to the choice of details have been rejected. See Brown 1992, p. 56, who rightly objects to contrived, symbolic readings of the paintings and recommends that one regard the subjects painted by the Bamboccianti in terms of their Flemish ancestry and the well-established northern tradition of representing peasant customs and rituals. See also Briganti 1983, p. 16, where he notes, "In a very few cases painters looked to religious subjects, narratives or fables . . . though certainly not to the patrimony of folk fables, the picaresque novel, the *commedia dell'arte*, or the heroico-comic poem of Tassoni . . . but instead to Tasso's epic and especially his tale of Erminia because of her rustic sojourn among the shepherds."

69

Peter Paul Rubens

Flemish
Siegen 1577–1640 Antwerp

Portrait of an Elderly Man, formerly known as ***Sebastian Münster***; copy after a 16th-century Flemish portrait attributed to Joos van Cleve (ca. 1485–1540/41)
ca. 1616

Oil on panel, 26 1/16 × 20 5/16 in. (66.2 × 51.6 cm)
The Norton Simon Foundation, F.1968.11.14.P

Provenance
Ladislaus Bloch, Vienna (sale, Frederik Muller, Amsterdam, 14 November 1905, lot 36, as a "presumed portrait of Sebastien Münster by a German master at the beginning of the sixteenth century,"[1] sold to); John G. Johnson (1841–1917), Philadelphia, 1905–12, given 1912 to; W[illiam]. P. Wilstach Collection,[2] Philadelphia Museum of Art[3] (sale, Samuel T. Freeman & Co., Philadelphia, 29–30 October 1954, lot 202, as attributed to Joos van Cleve, sold to); [Julius Weitzner (1896–1984), New York, until at least 1955]. Morris I. Kaplan (1913–2011), Chicago (sale, Sotheby's, London, 12 June 1968, lot 85, as *Sebastien Muenster* by Rubens after Joos van Cleve, sold to); The Norton Simon Foundation.

Exhibited
On loan, Brooklyn Museum, 1 August 1968–31 January 1969; on loan, Los Angeles County Museum of Art, 4 November 1969–18 January 1972.

References
Philadelphia 1922, p. 7, no. 17, pl. 3, as Joos van Cleve; M. Friedländer 1967–76, vol. 9a (1972), p. 68, no. 89a, pl. 103, as "old copy, location unknown"; Jaffé 1989, p. 218, no. 373, ill., as Rubens, ca. 1616; Pasadena 1989, p. 52, ill.; Hand 2004, no. 99.1;[4] Belkin 2009, vol. 1, pp. 200–01, vol. 2, fig. 268; S. Campbell 2010, p. 303, no. 482, ill.

Technical Notes
The cradled oak panel consists of a vertically grained board; all sides have been beveled. The smooth ground is white. Rubens then brushed on a medium-gray paint with strong diagonal brushstrokes, visible in the space reserved for the hands and the rolled paper. It is smoothly blended with no texture or brushmarking, but some light and dark striations from the broad strokes remain visible. The face was begun by toning the gray layer with very thin light brown, then adding pink to sketch in the cheeks and furrows in the forehead, lips, and nose in thin glazes. The whites of the eyes are almost completely unpainted, exposing the gray underpainting to the sides of the iris. Short hatching strokes depict the white beard stubble. The hands were painted with thicker applications of smoothly blended paint. Pentimenti surrounding portions of both hands indicate slight changes as Rubens worked. The white cuffs were the last deft strokes. The painting is very well preserved. Retouching is located in small scattered spots in the upper right background, small spots in the black robe, a larger area at the left side of the black hat, several broader areas at the bottom edge, below the proper left forearm, and a vertical line at the bottom left edge. The thick, natural-resin varnish over the light colors has been reduced, likely in the early twentieth century. Additional cleaning and perhaps revarnishing was performed at the Los Angeles County Museum of Art by Ben Johnson in February 1972.

The half-length figure of an elderly man seen in three-quarter view wears a black gown over a simple white linen shirt, visible at the neck and cuffs. The collar of the gown is folded back softly at the neck, revealing its black silk lining embroidered in black with tendrils. Between the white shirt and black gown is the beautifully rendered short stand-up collar of a black silk shirt closed by a double black string. The sitter wears a close-fitting black cap, typical of those worn during the second quarter of the sixteenth century.[5] The plain background is defined only by a dark border on the left and top, which suggests shadows cast by the frame onto the picture.

The attribution of *Portrait of an Elderly Man* to Rubens, which has been supported by Michael Jaffé and tentatively by Kristin Belkin, was first made by Julius Held in 1955.[6] The painting was called the work of an anonymous German master in 1905, and in 1922 it was attributed to the Flemish painter Joos van Cleve. Max Friedländer maintained the association with Joos van Cleve but called the Pasadena painting an anonymous early copy after his work in the Museo Nacional del Prado, Madrid (fig. 69a).[7] The sitter in the Madrid painting, which has also been attributed to Hans Holbein II (1497/98–1543), was formerly identified as the German cosmographer Sebastian Münster (d. 1552).[8] It is unclear when this identification was made. Comparison of the man in the Madrid and Pasadena portraits to the man represented in an undisputed portrait of Münster by Christoph Amberger (1505–1562; Gemäldegalerie, Berlin), however, suggests that they represent different sitters. Most significantly, in contrast

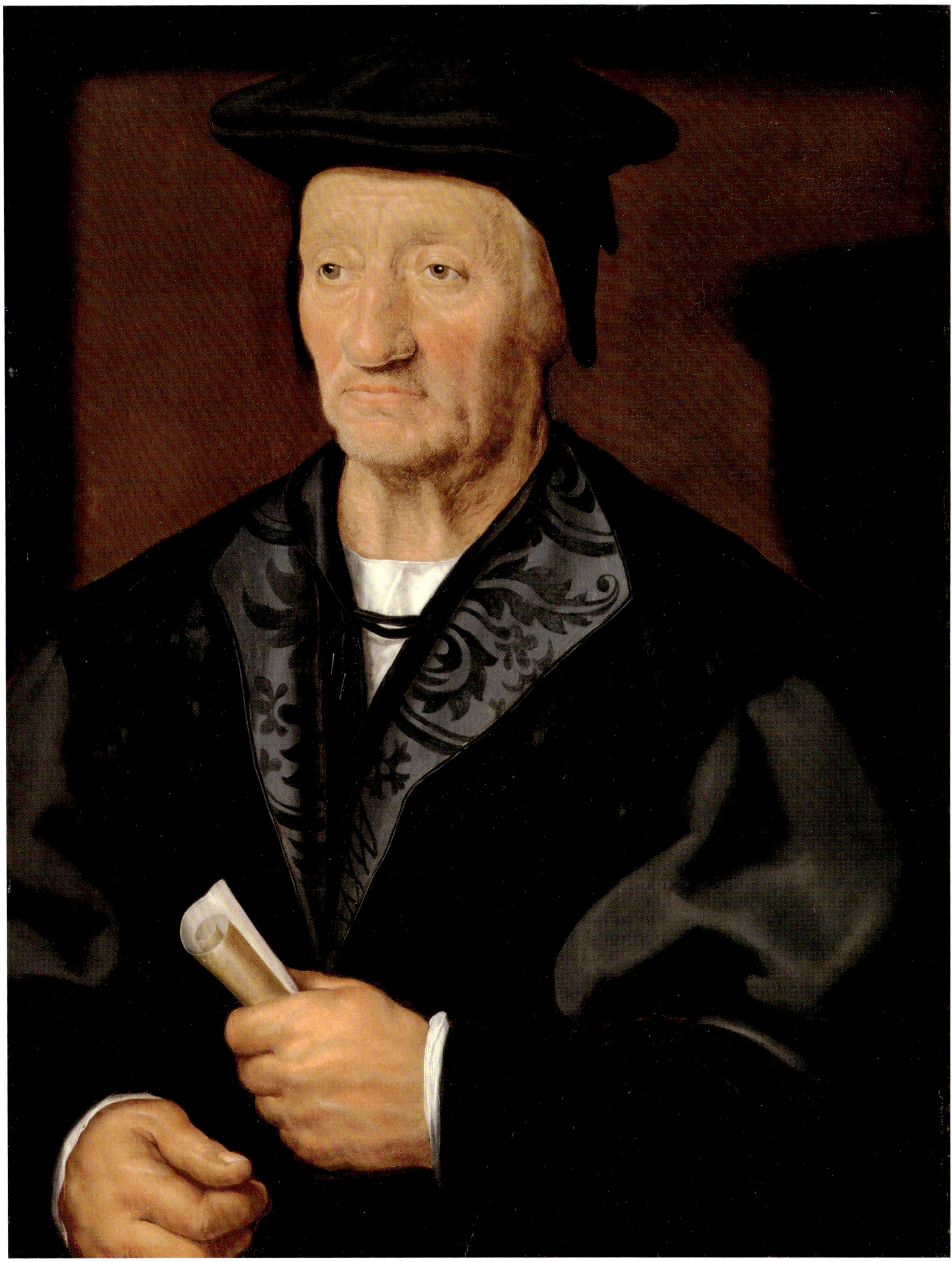

to Münster's appearance in the Berlin portrait, the sitter in the Madrid and Pasadena portraits has an enlarged nose characteristic of people suffering from rhinophyma.[9]

Rubens carefully followed the appearance of the sitter in his copy, while making slight changes. Most notably he somewhat reduced the size of the sitter's nose, altered the pattern of the embroidered tendrils on the left side of the collar (as seen by the viewer) and adjusted the position of the hands. In both the Pasadena and the Madrid paintings the sitter holds his hands at waist level; in his left hand, he holds a scrolled piece of parchment.[10] The hands in the Pasadena portrait, however, are slightly farther apart—probably, as Kristin Belkin has suggested, to accommodate the work's taller proportions.[11]

Rubens's handling of paint varies dramatically between the hands and the face, a discrepancy that may represent his attempt to imitate his model. The hands are painted in a manner consistent with Rubens's earliest paintings, where he constructed his forms with a heavy application of paint containing white lead over which he painted areas of color to produce the desired smooth, "plastic" surface. The appearance of the hands and the similar enamel-like rendering of the costume suggested to Julius Held and Kristin Belkin that Rubens painted the copy during his first Antwerp period, before leaving for Italy, thus ca. 1597–1600.[12]

A somewhat later date—Jaffé suggests ca. 1616—may be indicated by the treatment of the sitter's face, which is delicately sketched, with no evidence of underpainting in white lead. Rather, one can see the stroking of the light-brown imprimatura in a diagonal direction from the lower left to the upper right of the panel in a manner consistent with Rubens's sketches from the mid-1610s.[13] As in these sketches, the brown imprimatura forms the middle tone of the face. The sitter's features are delicately sketched with a fine brush, using short hatching strokes to define areas such as the contours of his throat. While some areas are left without further elaboration, the artist applied a thin film of pink over this sketch for the cheeks and washes of white for highlights. Delicate dashes of white on his chin suggest the stubble of his beard. The thin, grayish-white washes of paint used to define the sitter's hair have been absorbed by the brown tone so that the hair has essentially disappeared, leaving the discomfiting appearance of a man with a missing ear.

Rubens made copies of many sixteenth-century paintings both as records of expressions and as figure types for future reference and also to satisfy the popular demand for copies in Antwerp and throughout Europe.[14] There was an especially strong market for copies of contemporary and historical portraits, which was met by artists who made a specialty of painting copies. The painter Bernaert de Rijckere (1537–1590), for example, operated what Jeffrey Muller has described as a "factory," producing copies after popular originals in his large collection.[15] The portraits were collected by scholars and nobles for popular displays of "famous men";

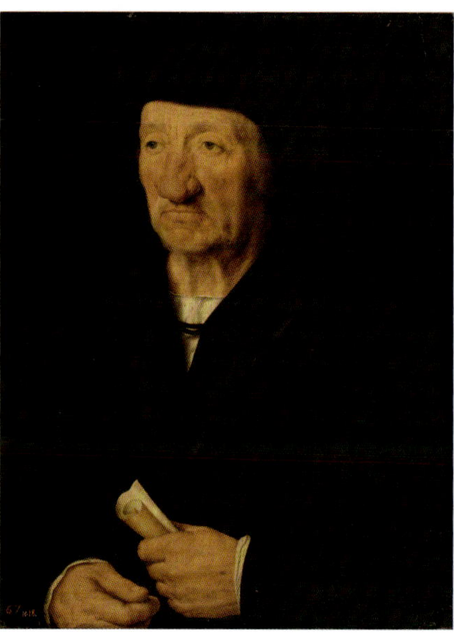

Fig. 69a. Joos van Cleve, *Portrait of an Old Man*, 1525–27, oil on panel, 24 3/8 × 18 1/2 in. (62 × 47 cm), (P002182), Museo Nacional del Prado, Madrid.

these collections could include scholars and soldiers as well as political figures, both past and present.[16]

Rubens must have had access to the Madrid portrait in order to paint the Pasadena painting, and he may even have owned it. The Madrid portrait was in Spain by 1666, when the royal inventory of the Alcázar identifies it as a panel by "Alberto Dulero," that is, Albrecht Dürer (1471–1528).[17] Philip IV (r. 1621–65), who died the previous year, was a great admirer of Rubens and had acquired a number of paintings from the posthumous sale of the collection of the Flemish painter-diplomat. Although the Madrid portrait does not appear among those paintings acquired for Philip IV directly from Rubens's estate in 1641, it could have been acquired at another time.[18] The painting, which is currently attributed to Joos van Cleve, was known as a work by Dürer until 1873.[19] The only painting by Dürer in the inventory of Rubens's collection made at the time of his death in 1640 is no. 175, identified as "Vn renard d'Albert Durer/A Son of Albert Durer."[20] The Madrid *Portrait of an Old Man* could not have been mistaken as the artist's son. It may, however, have been listed under a different name in Rubens's inventory, which includes a number of portraits attributed to sixteenth-century artists. Belkin, following Jaffé, suggests that the Madrid painting may be identical to that listed in the first catalogue (1640) of Rubens's collection as no. 225: "Vn pourtrait de Joos van Cleue, sur fond de bois/A picture by Joos van Cleue vppon a bord."[21] A stronger identification with the Madrid painting, however, appears to be no. 200 in Rubens's collection: "Un pourtrait d'un homme avec un grand nez, de Hemsen/The picture of a man with a great nose by Hemsen."[22] In addition to the physical appearance of the unidentified man with rhinophyma in the Madrid and Pasadena paintings, stylistically, it is conceivable that the latter could have been considered a work by Jan Sanders van Hemessen (ca. 1500–ca. 1566), who was revered as an Old Master in the seventeenth century.[23]

1. The sale catalogue also notes (in French) that "the painting recalls the work of Bartel Bruyn and of the school of Hans Holbein the Younger."

2. The Wilstach Collection was bequeathed to the city of Philadelphia in 1892. The museum formally acquired the collection in 1917.

3. Acc. W'12-1-13, as "Beke, Joost van der (called Van Cleve or Kleef)." According to the records of the registrar's office at the Philadelphia Museum of Art, the painting was on display in the first-floor galleries from about May 1937 until about March 1952.

4. I am grateful to Kristin Lohse Belkin and John Hand for sending me the manuscripts for their entries in advance of the publication of their books.

5. Belkin 2009, pp. 200f.

6. Certificate (apparently made at the request of Julius Weitzner, who then owned the painting) dated 15 February 1955 (copy in NSM). Jaffé 1989, p. 218, no. 373; Belkin 2009, pp. 200f.

7. M. Friedländer 1967–76, vol. 9, pt. 1, p. 68, no. 89a; Hand 2004, p. 174, no. 98.

8. The painting was still published as "attributed" to Hans Holbein II in Buendia 1993, p. 180.

9. Belkin 2009, pp. 200f.; and Ingelheim am Rhein 1988, p. 109, nos. 5, 13, b. The identification of the Amberger portrait is based on an inscription on the reverse of the panel, according to which the painting was done in 1552. Belkin points out that Münster is known to have visited the Netherlands (Louvain) only once, as a young man in 1607.

10. Pentimenti indicate that Rubens adjusted the placement of the hands and the parchment in the Pasadena portrait.

11. Belkin 2009, pp. 200f.

12. Julius Held, letter, 1955 (NSM); Belkin 2009. While noting that she is "not overwhelmingly confident as to Rubens's authorship," Belkin feels that it could be very early Rubens. In her opinion, "Jaffé's suggested date of ca. 1616 clearly is too late."

13. Presumably it is this observation that led Jaffé 1989 to date the painting ca. 1616.

14. See Stechow 1972b, pp. 23–44; J. M. Muller 1989, pp. 59f.; and Belkin 2009, pp. 200f.

15. J. M. Muller 1989, p. 60. Before Rubens built his collection, De Rijckere owned the most important collection in Antwerp. According to Muller, the primary function of his collection was to provide models for copies. The 1590 inventory of De Rijckere's collection included twenty-one "portraits of faces, copies," which Muller supposes were done after portraits by Cornelis van Cleve (1520–after 1570) and Willem Key (ca. 1515–1568), which also belonged to De Rijckere. J. M. Muller 1989, p. 60n56, also notes the example of the painter Abraham Matthys (d. 1649), whose inventory lists multiple copies of pictures.

16. In 1604 Antonio de Succa (d. 1621) bought a house in Antwerp in which he established a gallery with historical portraits. Many of these apparently served as models for a painted series of portraits of former rulers of the Spanish Netherlands, which he painted for the town hall of Antwerp. Similar dynastic displays were commissioned by private and especially noble clients, often supplementing collections of original paintings they already owned.

17. Martínez Leiva and Rodríguez Rebollo 2015, p. 452, no. 605, "Un retrato, des tres quartas de alto, poco más a menos, y de terzia poco más de alto, en tabla, de Alberto Dulero en sesenta ducados de plata . . . 660." The authors, pp. 452f., also publish excerpts from royal inventories through 1814. For the attribution to Holbein, see note 18 below.

18. Regarding the sale of Rubens's estate, see Génard [1865–66]. The group of twenty-nine paintings purchased by Don Francisco de Rochas for Phillip IV are listed on pp. 83–85. The majority of these are works by and after other artists, especially Italian artists. Prior to this purchase, on 24 June 1641, Phillip IV had purchased four paintings by Rubens himself (pp. 80f.) and had been sent a copy of the *Marriage of the Virgin Mary and Joseph* (p. 82).

19. In 1873 the attribution was changed to Hans Holbein II, the name by which it was known until John Hand included the painting as a work by Joos van Cleve, ca. 1535, in his catalogue raisonné of the artist: Hand 2004, p. 174, no. 98.

20. J. M. Muller 1989, p. 125.

21. Belkin 2009, pp. 200f.; Jaffé 1989, p. 218, no. 373; J. M. Muller 1989, p. 133, cat. 1, no. 225. It is unknown if Jaffé was aware of the history of the Madrid painting's attributions or was influenced by the current attribution to Joos van Cleve.

22. J. M. Muller 1989, p. 130, notes that the painting by Hemessen is lost.

23. Van Hemessen was active in Antwerp between 1519 and 1551, when he moved to Haarlem, where he died ca. 1566. Regarding Van Hemessen, see Wallen 1971. Wallen does not mention the Madrid painting.

70

Peter Paul Rubens

Flemish
Siegen 1577–1640 Antwerp

David Slaying Goliath

ca. 1615–17

Oil on canvas, 48½ × 39 in. (123.2 × 99.1 cm)
The Norton Simon Art Foundation, F.1972.05.P

Provenance

General Francesco Arese (1642–1721), Milan and Osnago, by 1711,[1] sold by his heirs in 1810 to; Prince Eugène de Beauharnais (1781–1824), Duke of Leuchtenberg, Stadtpalais, Munich,[2] by inheritance 1824 to his son; Maximilian de Beauharnais (1817–1852), 3rd Duke of Leuchtenberg, Prince Ramanowsky, Munich,[3] by inheritance to his son; Nicholas Maximilianovich de Beauharnais (1843–1890), 4th Duke of Leuchtenberg, who transferred the collection to the Marinepalais in St. Petersburg in 1863,[4] by inheritance to his son; Nicholas Nikolayevich de Beauharnais (1868–1928), sold 1917 to; [AB Nordiska Kompaniet, Stockholm, probably sold to];[5] Mrs. Hester Mullett, Buffalo, NY (estate sale, Parke-Bernet, New York, 15 November 1945, lot 45, sold to); Caledonio Vicente Pereda (1888–1970), Buenos Aires, sold 1972 to or through;[6] [Frederick Mont Inc., New York, sold 1972 to]; The Norton Simon Foundation.

Exhibited

On loan, Virginia Museum of Fine Arts, Richmond, 7 March–3 June 1972; on loan, Los Angeles County Museum of Art, 13 June 1972–26 November 1974; on loan, Chrysler Museum, Norfolk, VA, 3 November 1980–27 July 1981.

References

Muxel 1825/28, p. 38, no. 94; J. Smith 1829–42, vol. 9 (1842), p. 247, no. 17, ill.; Leuchtenberg 1843, p. 48, no. 129; Muxel 1845, p. 49, no. 129; Muxel 1851, p. 3, no. 94, line etching by Muxel; Passavant and Muxel 1851, p. 22, no. 110, ill. with Muxel's line etching; Passavant and Muxel 1852, p. 18, no. 110 (as 3 ft. 9 in. × 3 ft.), ill. with Muxel's etching; Waagen [1864] 1870, p. 383, no. 129, as Van Dyck; Rooses 1886–92, vol. 1 (1886), p. 146, vol. 5 (1892), p. 312; Wurzbach [1906–11] 1974, vol. 2 (1910), p. 511; Liphard-Rathshoff 1917, p. 48, no. 45 [110], ill.; Oldenbourg 1922, p. 101, fig. 58; Valentiner 1946, p. 159, no. 52, as Rubens and pupils, ca. 1615; Antwerp 1956, p. 50, no. 38; Held 1959, vol. 1, p. 104, no. 26, as Rubens, ca. 1615, "formerly in Leuchtenberg Collection and now in Mexico"; Burchard and D'Hulst 1963, vol. 1, pp. 116f., no. 70, as Rubens, early Antwerp period; Arese 1967, no. 21, p. 131; Held 1980, vol. 1, p. 43, no. 11, as Rubens, ca. 1615; Pasadena 1980, p. 46, ill.; D. W. S. 1981, n.pag., ill.; Silverman 1982, pp. 122ff.; Held 1986, p. 95, under no. 63, as Rubens, ca. 1615; Jaffé 1989, p. 221, no. 389, as Rubens, ca. 1616; D'Hulst and Vandenven 1989, pp. 125–28, no. 38, ill., as Rubens, ca. 1610–12 based on comparison with the drawings in Rotterdam and Montpellier; Møller and Vestergaard 1998, pp. 84, 86, fig. 18; Muchnic 1998, pp. 185, 276; Rotterdam 2001, p. 26, fig. 3; Pasadena 2003, p. 47, ill.; Jensen 2007, pp. 211, 217n15; Morandotti 2008, pp. 84ff.; S. Campbell 2010, pp. 135, fig. 1, 141, 336, no. 759, ill.; Sluijter 2015, pp. 191, 429n150, fig. III-83.

Technical Notes

The plain-weave canvas support has been lined, with the original edges removed. Over a warm white ground, Rubens applied a gray underpainting that is intermittently visible in the sky and below all flesh tones; it is especially obvious in the figure of David, around the contours of his hands and the hilt of the sword. A transparent golden-brown underpainting is in the lower part of the painting, left partially exposed as a mid-tone. The oil paint is generally of medium thickness, applied with vigorous brushwork. The flesh-colored paint is opaque and rich, blended wet-into-wet, with cool gray often used for modeling and dark red-brown for shadows. In darker passages Rubens used glossy transparent paint in a glaze-like consistency. X-radiography shows that prior damage at the edges caused paint losses of approximately ½ inch at each edge, but there is no damage within the main portion of the painting. Magnification reveals both solvent-related abrasion and pinpoint flake losses, both extensive, but especially noticeable in the blue sky and clouds. As a result, there is a great amount of retouching in the upper right quadrant. Numerous small repairs at the upper left may have been holes or small tears in the canvas. The painting was restored by Mario Modestini, New York, shortly before its acquisition by the Museum and was surface cleaned again in 1985. Ultraviolet light indicates the varnish to be an aged synthetic resin.

The Old Testament book of I Samuel recounts the story of the young shepherd David who slew Goliath, the Philistine giant whom no one had been able to conquer. When Goliath and the army of Philistines approached the Israelites, David confronted Goliath, who mocked him as being only a boy. David responded: "You come to me with a sword and with a spear and with a javelin, but I come to you in the name of the Lord of hosts, the God of the armies of Israel, whom you have defied. This day the Lord will deliver you into my hands, and I will strike you down and cut off your head." When the Philistine approached and "drew near to meet David, David ran quickly toward the battle line to meet him." Drawing a stone out of his bag, David hurled it with his sling and struck Goliath. "The stone sank into the giant's forehead; and he fell on his face to the ground." Rubens represented the final moment of the confrontation, when "David ran and stood over the Philistine, and took his sword and drew it out of its sheath and killed him and cut off his head with it." The painting's low horizon projects David against the sky,

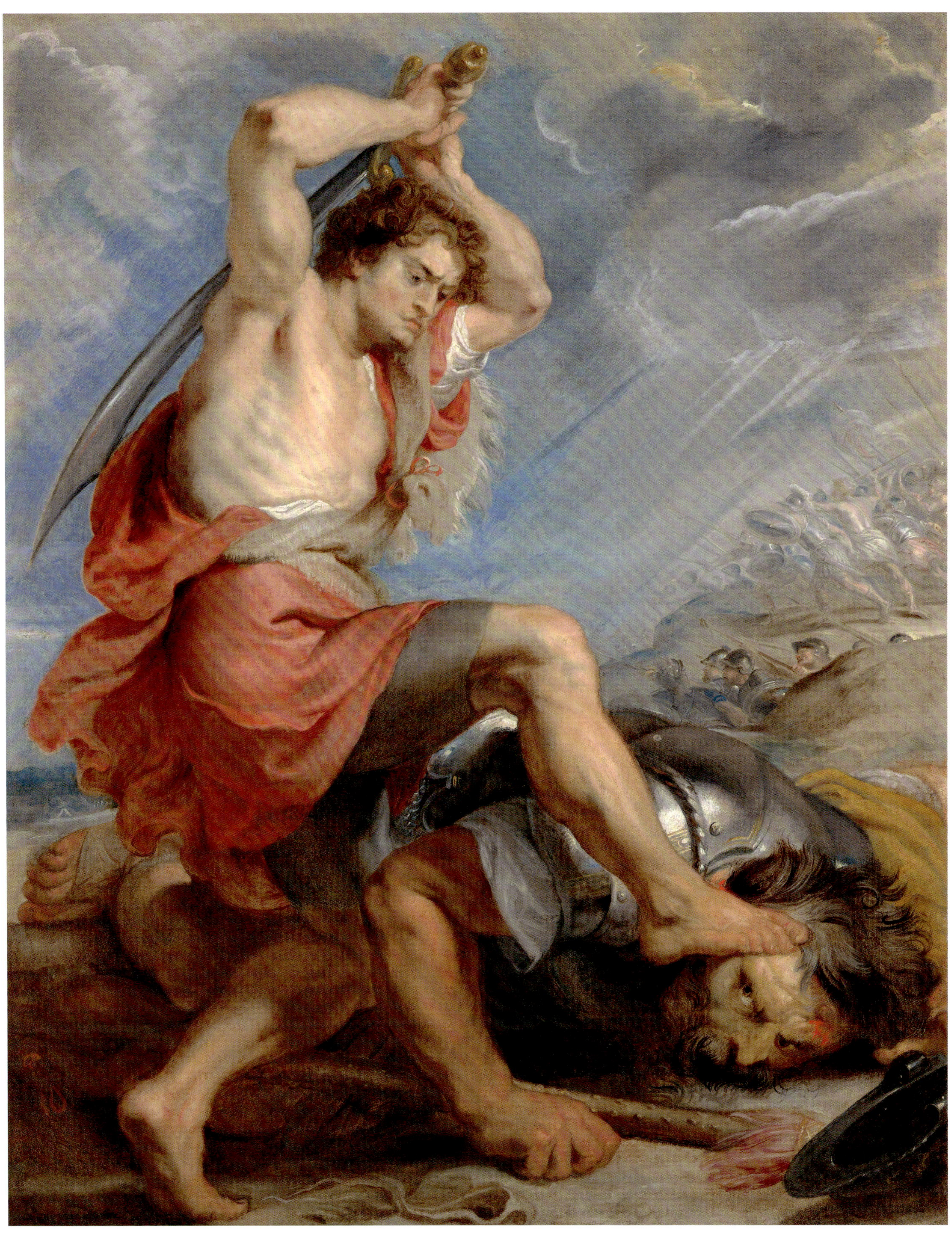

increasing the dramatic impact of the image. His face and muscles taut with tension, David raises the heavy sword with both hands over his head; in a moment the tension will break and the sword will crash down upon the massive neck of Goliath, who lies sprawled on the ground almost eye to eye with the spectator. Mortally wounded, Goliath glares up at his attacker. David's sling and Goliath's spear and helmet lie nearby.[7]

The victory of the "ruddy youth" David over the terrifying giant was regarded as the victory of good over evil and as a prefiguration of Christ's victory over the devil.[8] By representing David wearing only scant clothing, Rubens deviated from the biblical text, which recounts how "Saul armed David with his armor, and he put a helmet of bronze on his head and clothed him with a coat of mail."[9] By eliminating his armor, Rubens emphasized David's declaration that he depends solely on "the God of the armies of Israel" to overpower the larger man clothed in armor.

Rubens further emphasized the supremacy of the biblical hero by contrasting the powerful right arm of the giant struggling against the seemingly light restraint of David's right foot on his face. The extreme foreshortening of Goliath's torso contributes to the perception of his weighty bulk. By contrast, David's open posture creates the impression that his body is capable of spinning like a pinwheel around the axis of his hips but incapable of supporting his weight on his left leg bent beneath his body. Rubens increased the sense of David's mobility and power by using rapid, varied brushwork to describe the hero's knobby musculature, the sinews and veins of his arms and legs, and the fluttering red drapery of his tunic. Short strokes of hatching, characteristic of Rubens's technique, define and animate David's arms and legs as well as the fringe on the edges of the coarse wool cloth gathered over his shoulder and around his waist. Light, color, and diagonals create a sense of agitated movement that animates the composition. In the background, diagonal lines that suggest falling rain echo the line of David's sword, while other diagonals contribute to the impression of the forward movement of the armies pressing across the landscape.

Scholars have generally accepted *David Slaying Goliath* as a work by Rubens's own hand. Objections have been expressed only by Gustav Waagen, who attributed the painting to Anthony van Dyck (1599–1641), and Wilhelm Valentiner, who suggested that the painting was executed with the help of pupils.[10] R.-A. D'Hulst and M. Vandenven, who accept the painting as by Rubens himself, explain that previous doubts were the result of damage to the painting.[11] The diagonally applied imprimatura, the use of hatching, and the evenness of the rendering support the attribution to the master himself.

Rubens probably painted *David Slaying Goliath* ca. 1615–17. Although some scholars have dated it as late as the 1630s, the painting lacks the baroque unity of Rubens's works of the 1620s, in which light, color, and active brushstrokes create a unified composition based on a diagonal.[12] Rather, the Pasadena painting fits better into the transitional period of the mid-1610s. The figure of David is still relatively firmly painted—the light gray underpainting creates a hard, glimmering, almost mother-of-pearl effect of the skin. Yet there are few real lines; even in defining the eyes Rubens used a more painterly technique of hatchings, color, and light.[13]

This dating is supported by two drawings in Rotterdam (Museum Boijmans Van Beuningen) and Montpellier (fig. 70a), which are generally dated 1610–12 and show Rubens experimenting with the dramatic theme based on recollections of

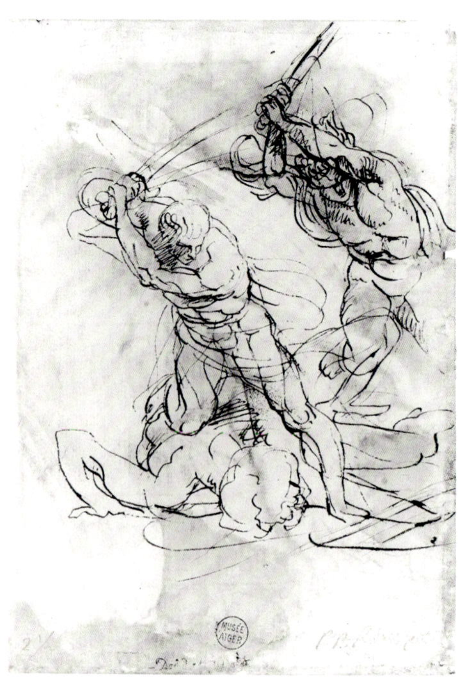

Fig. 70a. Peter Paul Rubens, *David and Goliath*, ca. 1610–12, ink on paper, 8 ½ × 6 ¼ in. (21.5 × 15.8 cm), Bibliothèque Universitaire, Collection Atger, Montpellier.

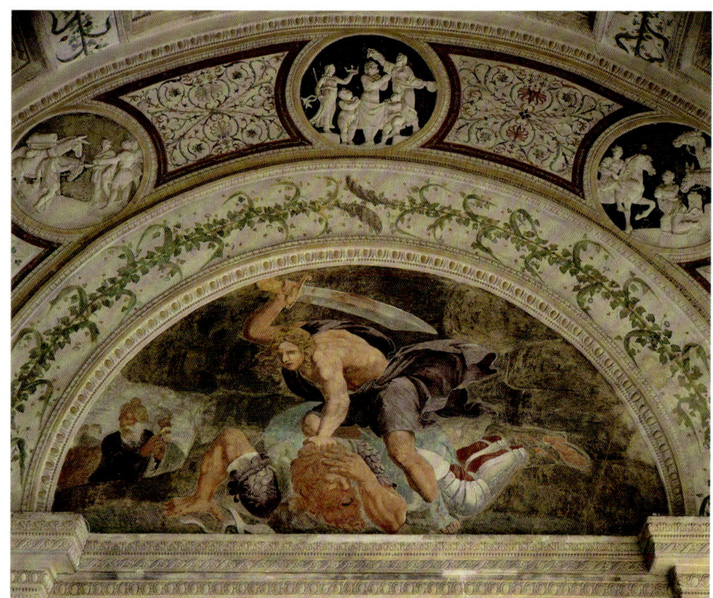

Fig. 70b. Giulio Romano, *David Slaying Goliath, Loggia of David*, 1526–28, fresco, Palazzo Te, Mantua.

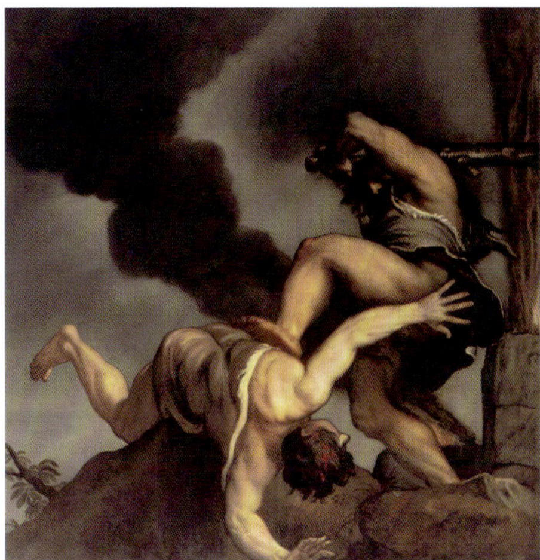

Fig. 70c. Titian, *Cain Slaying Abel*, 1543–44, oil on canvas, 115 × 110 ¼ in. (292 × 280 cm), Santa Maria Della Salute, Venice.

Italy.[14] The drawings reveal his knowledge of the semicircular fresco designed in 1532 by Giulio Romano (1499?–1546) and executed by an assistant for the loggia of the Palazzo Te, Mantua (fig. 70b). Rubens must have made sketches of it during his 1600–08 tenure as court painter to Vincenzo Gonzaga (1562–1612), Duke of Mantua. Rubens's figure of Goliath is particularly reminiscent of Romano's giant lying on the ground, his head turned toward the spectator and resting on his right hand.[15] The figure of David leaning over the fallen giant, his sword held high to strike the fatal blow, in the Pasadena painting relates both to that of the partial figure on the right in the Montpellier drawing and to *Cain Slaying Abel* by Titian (ca. 1488–1576), originally painted for Santo Spirito in Isola, Venice (fig. 70c).[16] Like Rubens's David, who raises the sword with two hands, Titian's figure of the murderous Cain stands with his legs apart, one foot restraining the struggling Abel, and two hands raising the club over his head.[17]

Rubens probably derived the idea of the distant phalanx of Philistine soldiers fleeing the Israelites from *David Slaying Goliath* in the Vatican Loggia, which was designed by Raphael (1483–1520) and executed by Perino del Vaga (1501–1547).[18] In contrast to his model, which portrays the soldiers surrounding the murder scene, however, Rubens moved the soldiers to the background, rendering them in loosely brushed, thinly applied, almost monochromatic blue and green paint. In this way, he retained the primary focus on the figures in the foreground while referencing the ultimate triumph of David's act: the Israelites' vanquishing of the Philistine army.

Rubens returned to the theme of David and Goliath in 1620 for one of the Old Testament scenes for the ceiling of the Jesuit church in Antwerp, which was destroyed by fire in 1718.[19] The extant oil sketch for the figure of David (fig. 70d) and the copies of the composition by Christian Benjamin Müller (1690–1758; drawing, Stedelijk Prentenkabinet, Antwerp) and Willem Panneels (ca. 1600–after 1632; engraving, 1630),[20] suggest that the composition was both closer to Romano's fresco and more "baroque" than the Pasadena painting, with which it shares important details, including the

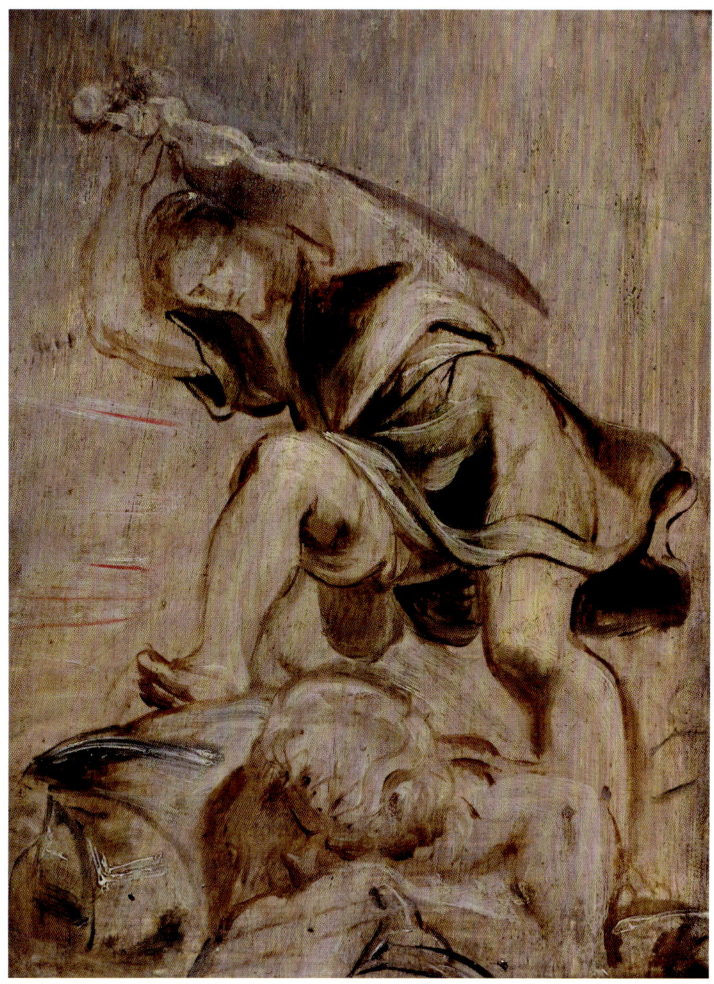

Fig. 70d. Peter Paul Rubens, *David Slaying Goliath*, 1620, oil on panel, 10 × 7 9⁄16 in. (25.5 × 19.2 cm), Courtauld Institute of Art Gallery, London.

general pose of David and the rush of soldiers in the background.[21] In contrast to the Pasadena composition, in which David's movement is essentially parallel to the picture plane, in the Antwerp version, seen from below, David steps from behind with his far leg pressing down on the shoulders of the giant sprawled prostrate beneath him. His heavy sword raised over his head poised to administer the fatal blow accentuates his diagonal movement forward and contributes to the perception of depth.

Nothing is known about the commission or intended placement of Rubens's *David Slaying Goliath*. As an example of how God grants power to the weak to overcome the mighty, the story of David and Goliath was often invoked for political purposes. The *Allegory of Frederik Hendrik as David*, painted by Jacob Gerritsz. Cuyp (1594–1652) for the City Hall of 's-Hertogenbosch to commemorate the capture of that city in 1629, for example, identifies the Dutch stadtholder as the victorious David and the Spanish as the defeated Goliath.[22] A closely related version of Rubens's painting signed and dated 1625 by the Dutch painter Isaac Isaacsz. (1598–1649; private collection) is one of a series of five compositions commissioned by Christian IV (1577–1648), Protestant king of Denmark and Norway, who in 1625 was engaged in the Thirty Years' War against Roman Catholic states of Germany.[23] The size and format of Rubens's *David Slaying Goliath* suggest that it, too, may have been intended as a similar political statement, but for whom is not known. The earliest documentation of the painting is 1711, when it was in the collection of General Francesco Arese (1642–1721) of Milan and Osnago.

1. Arese 1967, no. 21, p. 131; Morandotti 2008, pp. 84ff.

2. See Muxel 1825/28. Regarding the Arese sale, see Morandotti 2008, pp. 84ff.; and Miller 1990. The "adopted son" of Napoleon, Eugène de Beauharnais was Josephine's son by her first husband, General Viscount Alexandre de Beauharnais. Rising from service as Napoleon's aide de camp to that of brigadier general, Eugène de Beauharnais was named vice-regent of Italy in 1805, when Napoleon was proclaimed emperor and king of Italy. Beauharnais lived with his wife in the Villa Bonaparte (Villa Reale) in Milan, where he sought to establish a national picture gallery (Miller 1990). Milan was then the central collecting point for paintings confiscated by Napoleon's troops in northern Italy, a fact that contributed to the growth of the museum. Because of his position, Beauharnais was also the recipient of works of art confiscated by French troops throughout Europe and taken back to Paris as booty. Following the fall of Napoleon in 1814, Beauharnais installed his impressive personal collection in the Stadtpalais, Munich, where his father-in-law, Maximilian I (1756–1825), Elector and King of Bavaria, granted him the title Herzog von Leuchtenberg, Fürst von Eichstädt.

3. Maximilian de Beauharnais was married to the Grand Duchess Maria Nicolaevna (1819–1876), eldest daughter of the Russian Emperor Nicolas I (1796–1855).

4. See Waagen [1864] 1870, p. 383.

5. Miller 1990, p. 79, notes that the "exhibition sale" included "some ninety-three pictures from the Leuchtenberg collection. . . . These had been transported from . . . St. Petersburg during the turmoil of the Russian Revolution (a Dr. Nyblom was credited with this rescue)." Miller notes that thirty-nine of the paintings were subsequently shipped to Nordiska Kompaniet's branch store in Buenos Aires and exhibited together with a catalogue (*Nordiska Kompaniet S. A. Pintura Antigua*, Buenos Aires, n.d. [1920s]).

6. Apparently sold by his heirs. His son was also named Caledonio Vicente Pereda (1923–1983).

7. I Samuel 17:17–51.

8. I Samuel 17:42 describes Goliath's disdain for David, who "was but a youth, and ruddy, and of a fair countenance."

9. I Samuel 17:38.

10. Waagen [1864] 1870, p. 383, no. 129; Valentiner 1946, p. 159, no. 52.

11. D'Hulst and Vandenven 1989, p. 127.

12. Valentiner 1946, p. 159, followed by Held 1959, vol. 1, p. 104, date the painting ca. 1615. Held notes, "David's motion . . . closely resembles that of the tormentor of Christ near the right edge in the *Flagellation* sketch in Ghent [Museum voor Schone Kunsten] . . . of circa 1614. The [Pasadena] canvas seems to belong to the period of around 1615." D'Hulst and Vandenven 1989, p. 127, prefer a date slightly earlier, "around 1610–1612," noting that this is the generally accepted dating for the drawings of the same subject at Rotterdam and Montpellier. Other scholars have dated the painting somewhat later: In 1975, during a visit to the Norton Simon Museum, Justus Müller Hofstede suggested a date ca. 1625, and in 1994 Walter Liedtke suggested that the painting should be dated approximately the same time, "before Madrid." Michael Jaffé dated the painting to the 1630s (memorandum, 26 January 1984, NSM), but in his 1989 book he dates it 1616. A copy of the composition dated 1625 by Isaac Isaacsz. in the Staatens Museum for Kunst, Copenhagen, establishes the *terminus ante quem* for Rubens's painting. Regarding Isaacsz.'s painting, see Møller and Vestergaard 1998, passim, fig. 5.

13. Rubens's interest in representing dramatic, even violent movement is also found in a number of his other Old Testament paintings from the 1610s. See, for example, *Prometheus Bound*, ca. 1611–12, completed by 1618 (Philadelphia Museum of Art), and *Judith Beheading Holofernes* (D'Hulst and Vandenven 1989, no. 50; location unknown and presumed lost, known from a painted copy and an engraving).

14. Burchard and D'Hulst 1963, vol. 1, nos. 69–70, and D'Hulst and Vandenven 1989, nos. 36–37, figs. 83–84. Rubens was in Italy in 1600–03 and again in 1604–08. In 1603 he traveled to Spain on a diplomatic mission for the Duke of Gonzaga.

15. The relationship to the Palazzo Te fresco was first noted by Burchard and D'Hulst 1963, p. 115, and noted in D'Hulst and Vandenven 1989, p. 127.

16. J. R. Martin 1968, p. 71. D'Hulst and Vandenven 1989, p. 128n1, note that Rubens made a drawing after Titian's *Abraham's Sacrifice of Isaac* from the same *soffitto* in Venice (now in the Albertina, Vienna) and may also have made a drawing after *Cain Slaying Abel*.

17. In Titian's *David Slaying Goliath* from the same series, the artist represented David with his hands raised over his head in prayer to God. He does not hold the sword.

18. D'Hulst and Vandenven 1989, p. 127.

19. Regarding the ceiling, see J. R. Martin 1968. On p. 70, Martin notes that the etching by Panneels differs from the engravings by Jan Punt (1711–1779; see fig. 34), and Johann Justin Preissler (1698-1771; see fig. 32), which suggests that it was based on Rubens's lost *modello* rather than the final painting. Regarding the oil sketch, see Held 1980, vol. 1, pp. 42f., no. 11, pl. 12.

20. J. R. Martin 1968, p. 70, discusses Müller's drawing (fig. 31) and Panneel's engraving as important evidence of the destroyed painting of David and Goliath for the ceiling of the Jesuit Church Antwerp, although Müller's drawing is the most accurate. On pp. 72f., no. 5b, fig. 36, the author suggests that Panneels's engraving was based on the lost *modello* rather than on the actual ceiling painting.

21. See J. R. Martin 1968, figs. 31–36.

22. Bernstock 2000, pp. 155–69, notes that as early as the Middle Ages the French equated the biblical David and their own king as ancient and modern leaders of the chosen people. She argues that Nicolas Poussin's (1594–1665) painting *The Triumph of David*, ca. 1629–30 (Museo Nacional del Prado, Madrid; her fig. 18), celebrates three military victories of Louis XIII (David) over Philip IV of Spain (Goliath) between 1628 and 1629.

23. Significant differences between the two paintings indicate that Isaacsz., who was active in Antwerp and Copenhagen and traveled to Italy in 1622, did not copy Rubens's painting directly but probably relied on sketches and his memory. See Jensen 2007, esp. pp. 210f., pl. 112. The other paintings in the series are: *Melchisedek and Abraham* (1624), *Jacob's Dream* (1625), *Isaac's Sacrifice* (1625), and *Jews Gathering Manna* (date lost when the painting was cropped).

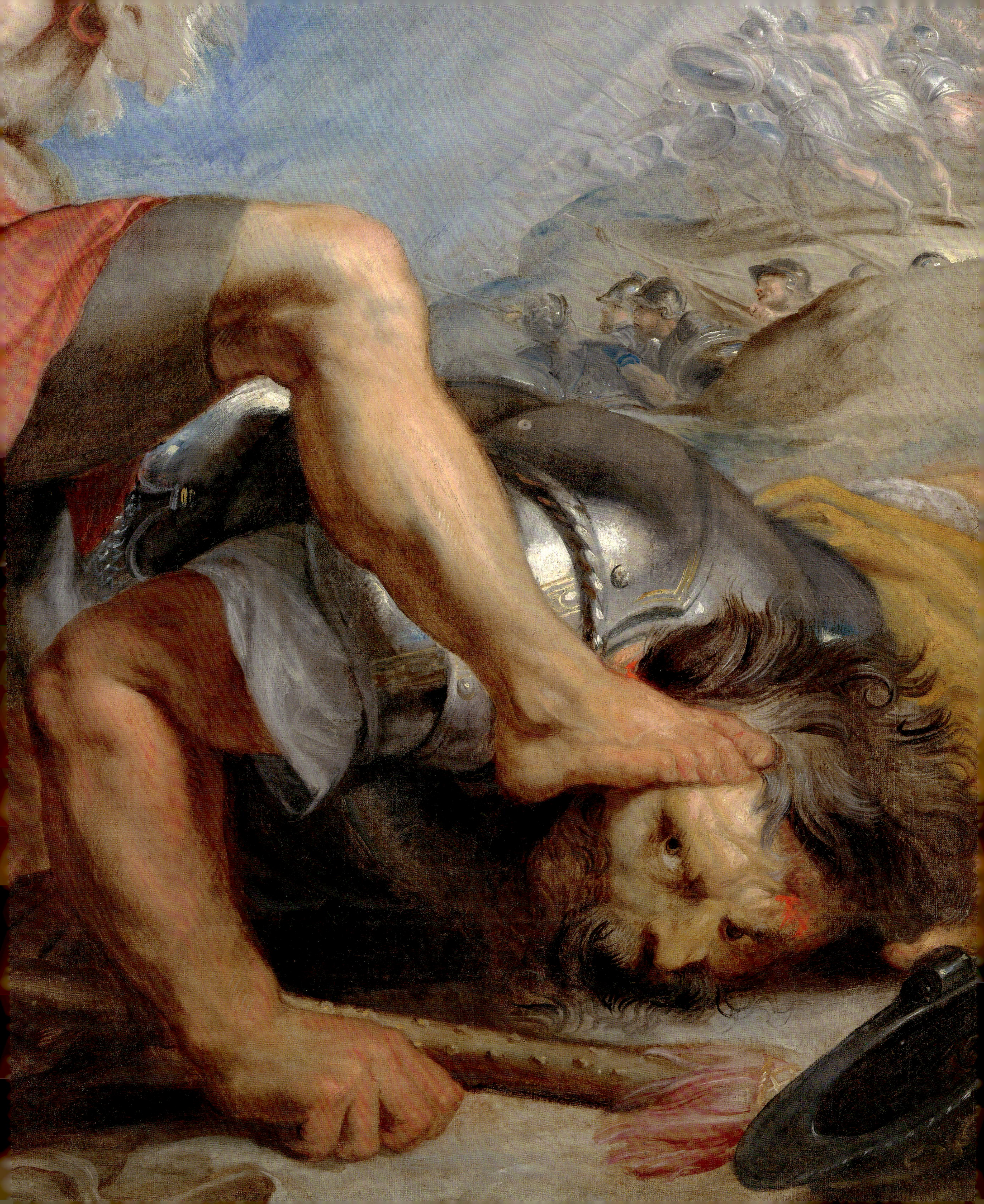

71

Peter Paul Rubens and workshop

Flemish
Siegen 1577–1640 Antwerp

The Holy Women at the Sepulchre

ca. 1612–14

Oil on panel, 34 5/8 × 42 in. (88 × 106.7 cm)
The Norton Simon Foundation, F.1972.51.P

Provenance

Friedrich Karl Ludwig (1723–1798), Freiherr von Moser, Ludwigsburg (private contract sale, Ludwigsburg, Württemberg, September 1794, lot 1, "Die Erscheinung der Engel denen zum Grabe Christi wallenden Weibern von Rubens, auf Holz, von unverletzter Schönheit, in einer ganz neuen modernen verguldten Rahme, breit 3 ½ Schuh, hoch 2 Schuh 10 Zoll, 4000 Rheinische Gulden," collection sold en bloc 1795 to);[1] Friedrich Karl Lang (1766–1822), Heilbronn (private contract sale, Heilbronn, 1796, lot 1, "Die Erscheinung der Engel den Weibern, die zum Grabe Christi gehen . . . Von anerkannten Originalität und unverletzter Schönheit auf Holz. P. P. Rubens, 2 Sch[uh]. 10 Z. hock, 3 ½ Sch[uh]. breit," bought in, probably sold ca. 1804 to);[2] [Dominik (a.k.a. Domenico) Artaria (1775–1842), Vienna and Mannheim, for];[3] Johann Rudolf (1757–1845), Count Czernin, Vienna, by descent to;[4] Czernin Collection, Vienna, until at least 1966. [Rudolf Heinemann/Pinakos, London and New York, sold 30 April 1971 to];[5] [Thomas Agnew & Sons, London, stock no. J7255, sold 12 June 1972 to]; The Norton Simon Foundation.

Exhibited

Brussels 1910, no. 322, as ca. 1620, 1 m 12 × 1 m 32; Vienna 1930, no. 80, as ca. 1612–14, 112 × 148 cm; Bern 1947–48, p. 16, no. 63; on deposit, Residenzgalerie, Salzburg, 1954–71;[6] on loan, Kunsthaus, Zurich;[7] on loan, Cleveland Museum of Art, 26 July 1972–10 September 1973; on loan, Los Angeles County Museum of Art, 14 September 1973–4 April 1974; on loan, De Young Museum, San Francisco, 10 April 1974–10 November 1974; on loan, Phoenix Art Museum, 21 November 1980–20 May 1981; on loan, Frick Collection, New York, 10 February–10 May 2009.

References

Bertuch 1808–10; J. Smith 1829–42, vol. 2 (1830), p. 281, no. 945, vol. 9 (1842), p. 328, no. 310; Perger 1853, pp. 236f.; Waagen 1866–67, vol. 1 (1866), p. 298, no. 24, as "3 F 7 Z h.; 4 F 8 Z br." and Rubens workshop; Mündler 1867; Lavice 1867, p. 449; Rooses 1886–92, vol. 2 (1888), pp. 151f., no. 340, as 112 × 146 cm, pl. 116 (Vorsterman print), vol. 5 (1892), p. 328;[8] Frimmel 1890, p. 542, as a sketch for the Melk painting of the same subject; Burckhardt 1898, p. 39; Rooses 1903, pp. 151f., pl. 116 (Vorsterman print); A. Rosenberg 1906, p. 204; Dillon 1909, pl. ccxv; Hymans 1910, p. 332; Rooses 1910, p. 295, no. 340;[9] *Trésor de l'art belge* 1912–13, vols. 1–2, no. 322; Oldenbourg [1921], p. 79; Baldass 1930, p. 136; Glück 1930, p. 168; Kieser 1933, p. 132; Wilczek 1936, pp. 76f., no. 168, fig. 24; Burckhardt 1950, p. 39; Buschbeck and Fuhrmann 1955, pp. 56f., no. 109, pl. 3; Jaffé 1961b, p. 13; Buschbeck and Fuhrmann 1962, pp. 72f., pl. 7; Stechow 1968b, pp. 55, 58, fig. 48; Gerson 1976, p. 163, fig. 3; Jaffé 1977, pp. 25, 81; Held 1980, vol. 1, pp. 52, 440f., 505, fig. 16; Pasadena 1980, p. 47, ill.; Agnew 1981, ill. p. 80; "Editorial: Art Treasures" 1981, pp. 145–46, pl. iii; De Grummond 1982, pp. 85f., fig. 10;[10] Freedberg 1984, pp. 21f., 39–42, no. 6, figs. 8–13;[11] Coffey 1984, pp. 9–14, pls. 3, 3a (detail), cover (detail); Held 1989; Steinberg 1989; Jaffé 1989, p. 198, no. 267; Bauman and Liedtke 1992, p. 363, fig. 422; White 1993, p. 152, fig. 6; Taft and Mayer 2000, p. 66, pl. 20; Müller Hofstede 2000, pp. 289f., fig. 4;[12] Rotterdam 2001, p. 316, fig. 2; S. Campbell 2010, pp. 141, 348, fig. 9, no. 890, ill.; Avery-Quash 2011, vol. 1, pp. 94, 521.

Related Works

Drawing after the painting[13]

- Lucas Vorsterman I (1595–1675), black and red chalk, with retouching and corrections, possibly by Rubens himself, 34.6 × 44.9 cm, Museum Boijmans Van Beuningen, Rotterdam (fig. 71a). Reference: Freedberg 1984, p. 42, no. 6a, ill. 10.

Engravings after the painting

- Lucas Vorsterman, with dedication: "Lectissimis Matronis, D. Mariae Nerot, D. Lodoici Clarisse, Senatoris Antverp. Conjugi: nec non D. Magdalenae De Schotte, D. Rogerii Clarisse, L. Fr. Vrbi Eleemosynis, Conjugi Cognomines Divas, observantiae testand. ergò offerebat Lucas Vorsterman"; inscription issuing from the mouth of the angel nearest to the women: "Nolite timere vos: scio enim quod Jesum qui crucifixus est quaeritis. Non est hic: surrexit enim sicut dixit et videte locum ubi positus erat Dominus. L. Vorsterman excudit cum priuilegijs."[14] References: Freedberg 1984, p. 42, no. 6a, copy, ill. 11; Voorhelm-Schneevoogt 1873, p. 56, no. 412.
- Anonymous; no inscriptions. Reference: Voorhelm-Schneevoogt 1873, p. 57, no. 413.

Painted copies[15]

- Oil on canvas, 161 × 224 cm, Melk Abbey, Austria.
- Oil on panel, 52.5 × 89 cm, Musée des beaux-arts, Dunkirk, inv. no. P.146. Provenance: Saint Winnoc's Abbey, Bergues, where it is attributed to van Hoeck.
- Oil on copper, 45 × 21 cm, Musée des beaux-arts, Besançon. Provenance: given to the museum by Canon Thiébaud.
- Oil on canvas, 92.5 × 115.5 cm, signed immediately below right foot of the second angel: "RvB" (?), location unknown. Provenance: Herbert Gilham, London, 1901.
- Oil on canvas, 83 × 110 cm, location unknown. Provenance: Hartveld, Antwerp; sale, Palais des beaux arts, Brussels, 21 May 1951, lot 123.
- Oil on canvas, 96.5 × 81.3 cm, location unknown. Provenance: Sir Ian Walker, Bart. (sale, Christie's, London, 17 May 1946, lot 77, as the "Foolish Virgins").
- [Oil on canvas?], 86 × 100 cm, collection C. de Jong, Soestdijk, Utrecht. Provenance: acquired from a castle in the Betuwe, Gelderland.[16]
- [Oil on canvas?], 81.3 × 114.3 cm, collection of M. Langlart, Lille.[17]

Technical Notes

The support is composed of four horizontally grained boards. The panel is strengthened by four horizontal battens that cover the three original joins as well as a long crack. The profiles of joins and cracks are visible in raking light. The entire panel has a convex warp with the grain. The white ground layer is thick enough to cover the texture of the wood completely. Very little underpainting was evident, as the upper paint layers cover a large percentage of the surface. Gray underpainting is occasionally visible within the flesh tones—

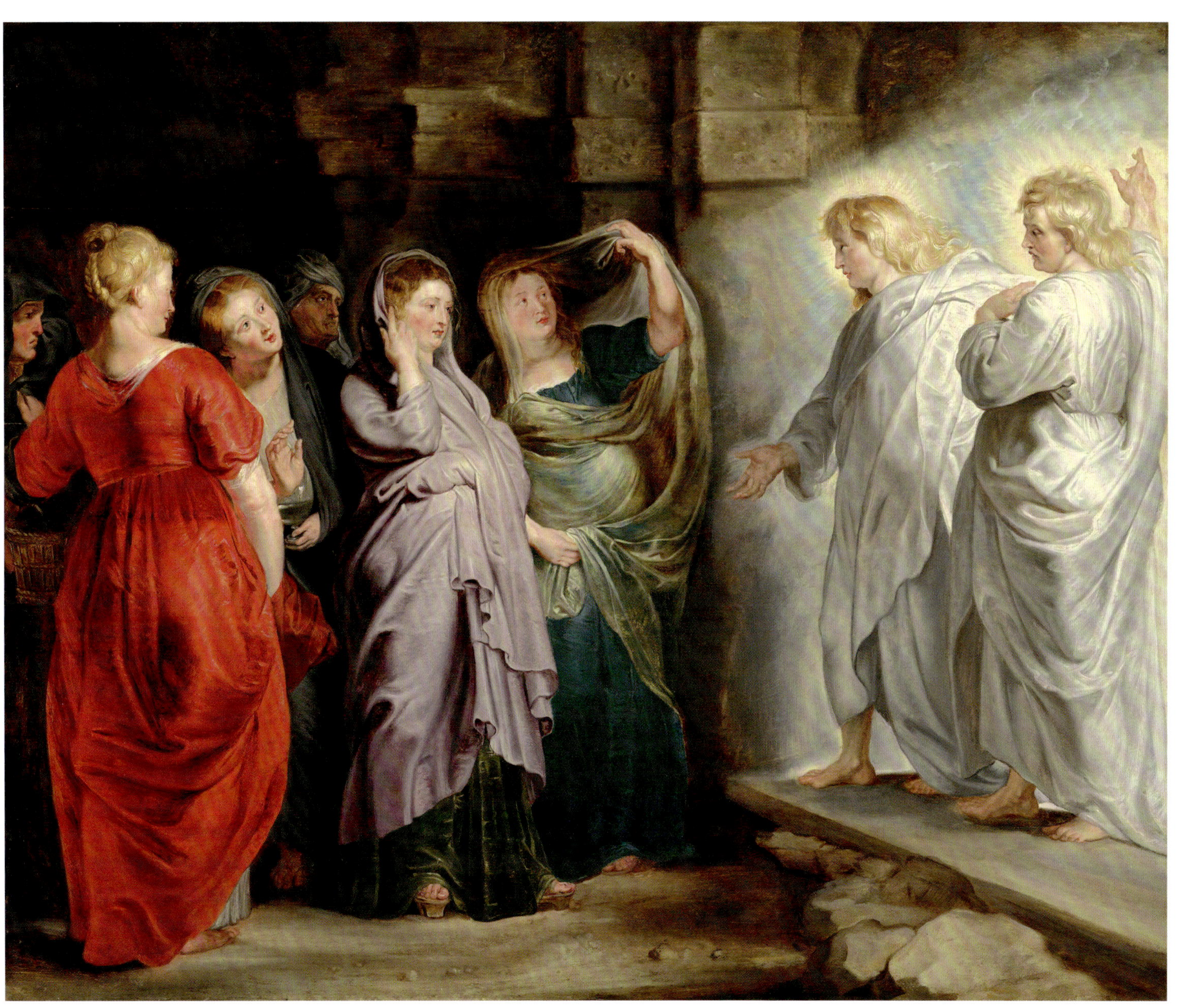

for example, in the faces of the women. Areas of sketchy drawing in darker paint, covered by the final paint layers, appear to be initial contours of feet, hands, and arms. The oil paint extends fully to all edges, suggesting the possibility of the panel having been trimmed, particularly at the left. The foreground was loosely brushed, lightly covering the ground. The upper background was painted with a simplified dark palette, accentuating the burst of light behind the two angels. The figures were painted with robust, opaque paint in a vibrant palette. There is energetic brushmarking throughout, including the thinly painted areas. The proper right hand of the woman in the red dress is covered with red paint yet remains clearly visible as a pentimento.[18] Contemporary engravings show her holding the basket against her left hip with her left hand around its outside. The black band at the edge of her left sleeve seems to have been a later change. The proper left side of her waist has been altered, where black paint now covers the red of the dress. The woman in the shadows at the extreme left was modified slightly, making it appear that she is holding the basket. Previous cleaning left the paint in a well-preserved state but with distracting residues of dirt left in the depressions of brushstrokes. Retouching is associated with the joins. A brand—showing two hands—associated with the Antwerp Joiner's Guild was identified on the verso of the panel by Jørgen Wadum. Another punched mark, mostly obscured by a fabric-reinforced adhesive mend to the panel, might be the castle symbol usually associated with the guild's brand.[19]

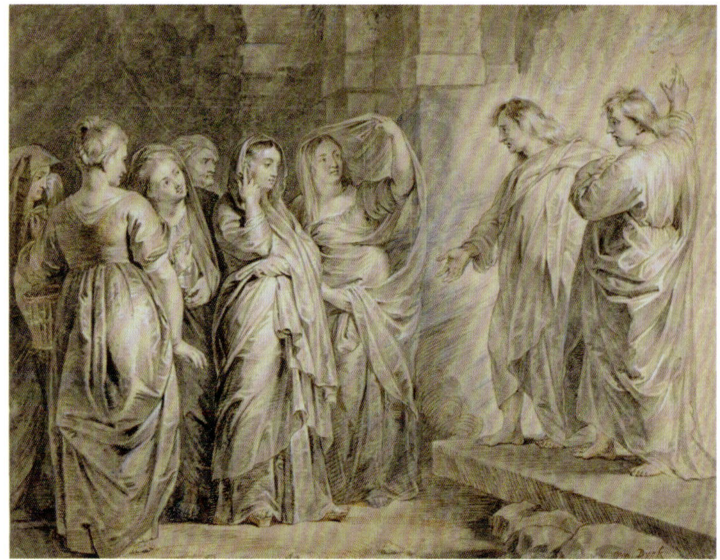

Fig. 71a. Lucas Vorsterman, *The Holy Women at the Sepulchre,* ca. 1619–20, black and red chalk, 13 ⅝ × 17 ¾ in. (34.6 × 44.9 cm), Museum Boijmans Van Beuningen, Rotterdam.

Early on Sunday morning following the Crucifixion, a group of women went to the tomb of Christ to anoint his body. Discovering that the huge stone that had covered the entrance to the tomb had been rolled aside, the women were told that Jesus was no longer there but had been resurrected. The story is told with slight variations in each of the Gospels.[20] Rubens's depiction comes closest to the description given in Luke 24:1–6: "On the first day of the week, at early dawn, they went to the tomb, taking the spices which they had prepared. And they found the stone rolled away from the tomb, but when they went in they did not find the body of the Lord Jesus. While they were perplexed about this, behold, two men stood by them in dazzling apparel. And as they were frightened and bowed their faces to the ground, the men said to them, 'Why do you seek the living among the dead? He is not here, but has risen!'"[21]

Luke's description of this encounter undoubtedly appealed to Rubens for its dramatic potential. Standing in the foreground before the heavy, rusticated stone walls of the tomb, a small group of women are illuminated by the supernatural light of two angels dressed like men in Roman togas who address them from the arched entrance of the tomb. The women respond to the apparition variously—one woman lifts her veil to shield her eyes from the intense glow, another casts her eyes to the ground, her right hand raised to her head in a chaste pose, while another woman peers around her, and a fourth stands on the left side of the composition, her back to the viewer.

Rubens's dramatic presentation of the scene—with its contrasts of light and dark, thick application of paint, and saturated colors—is characteristic of his work during the decade following his return from Italy in 1608. Typical, too, of this period is Rubens's reference to specific Italian models, both ancient and contemporary, for his composition and individual figures. David Freedberg suggests that Rubens derived the idea for the "isocephalic disposition" of the figures (meaning the consistent height of their heads), particularly the "*pleureur*-like" or mourning women, from Agostino Veneziano's (1490–1536) engraving *Three Women Going to the Sepulchre.*[22] Henri Hymans, writing in 1893 about Lucas Vorsterman's print after Rubens (fig. 71b), was the first to recognize that Rubens based his central female subject on the famous ancient Roman statue of Pudicitia (chastity; fig. 71c).[23] Rubens's careful recording of the details of the statue's costume, including the platform shoes, in the quick pen sketch of the marble original, then in Rome (now Pushkin Museum, Moscow), reflects his keen antiquarian interests.[24] Rubens repeated these details in the painting, where the Pudicitia figure wears a dark green Roman stola, a heavier, less clinging variation of the Greek chiton tunic; over this she wears a lilac palla, equivalent to the Greek himation, which serves as a mantle draped over her head and modestly covers her entire body. As in the statue, the central woman in Rubens's painting holds the palla modestly in place at her waist with her concealed left hand, while with her free right hand she holds it by her face. A. W. F. M. Meij

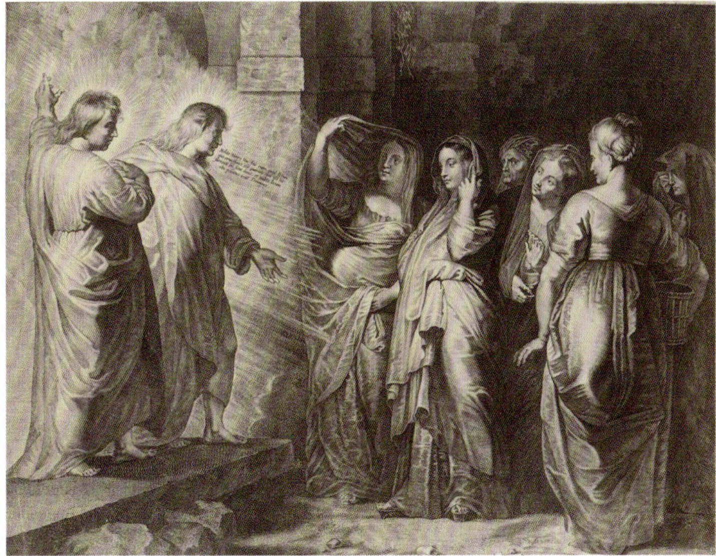

Fig. 71b. Lucas Vorsterman, after Peter Paul Rubens, *The Holy Women at the Sepulchre (1612–14)*, 1622–28, copperplate engraving, 14 × 17 ⅝ in. (35.5 × 44.9 cm), Albertina, Vienna.

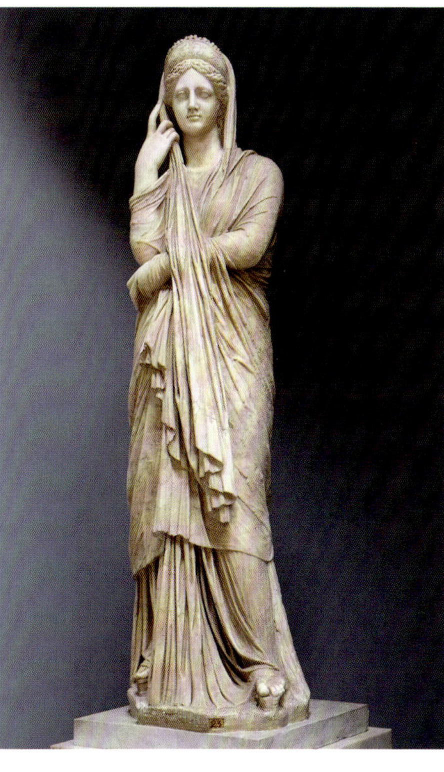

Fig. 71c. Rome, 1st century CE, *Personification of Pudicitia (Modesty, Demureness)*, copy of a Hellenistic original, marble, Braccio Nuovo, Museo Chiaramonti, Vatican Museums.

has suggested that Rubens referred to a second sculpture of Venus (fig. 71d) for the figure of the woman to the viewer's right who raises her veil as if shielding her eyes from the supernatural light.[25] In both figures Rubens succeeded in translating the cold, hard surfaces of the original marble into images of flesh and blood.

Like the Pudicitia figure, this woman closest to the male apparitions wears the costume of a noble Roman matron.[26] Raising the green palla to shield her eyes from the glare of the radiant vision, however, she reveals more of the dark blue stola beneath. In contrast to these women, the woman on the left with her back turned to the viewer does not cover her head, exposing her blond hair, which is braided and pinned to her head. Her red dress with a waist and open neck into which is tucked a white neckerchief more closely resembles contemporary European dress than that of antiquity.[27]

Comparison of the painting in its present state with Vorsterman's drawing (fig. 71a) and the print made after it (fig. 71b) reveals certain alterations that suggest the drawing was made before the painting reached final form.[28] In the drawing and the print, the woman with the basket at the left extends her right hand, bent at the wrist, toward the angels, whereas in the painting her hand appears only as a pentimento beneath the red fabric of her dress.[29] Careful examination of the red paint used in the overpainting reveals that it matches that of the fabric of her dress and thus probably represents Rubens's own rethinking of the painting, perhaps considering the unveiled hand too prominent. The panel also appears to have been cut by about two inches on the left, abbreviating the shadowy figure in the background and cutting the elbow of the woman in red. In the drawing and print, this figure wraps her arm over and around the basket, which in the painting is oddly separate. The covered left hand that the woman in the background on the far left raises to her face also appears to have been overpainted.[30] The weaker definition of these figures, as compared to the major figures on the right and the woman with her back to the viewer, suggests that they may have been painted by members of Rubens's workshop.

The story of the women going to the tomb of Christ is central to the liturgy of Easter, as they were the first witnesses to the Resurrection. As such, the story was often reenacted as part of the celebration of Easter and was depicted on liturgical objects in medieval art.[31] By the seventeenth century, however, the scene was represented only rarely. The four Gospels identify the women who visit the tomb on Easter morning as among the followers who accompanied Jesus to Jerusalem and witnessed the Crucifixion from a distance. The Gospels all agree that Mary Magdalene was present, but they vary regarding the identities of the other women. According to John 20:1, Mary Magdalene alone went to the tomb and discovered the rock rolled away from the entrance. Both Mark 15:40 and Luke 24:10 include Mary Cleophas (mother of James Minor) and other unnamed women. Whereas Mark identifies the third named woman as Mary Salome (the wife of Zebedee, the fisherman, and mother of James Major and John the Evangelist), Luke says it is Joanna. Matthew 28:1 mentions only two women, Mary Magdalene and "the other Mary," who, by reference to his identification of the two women who watched the burial of Jesus in the tomb, can be identified as Mary Cleophas. Mark and Luke are the only Gospels to mention the appearance

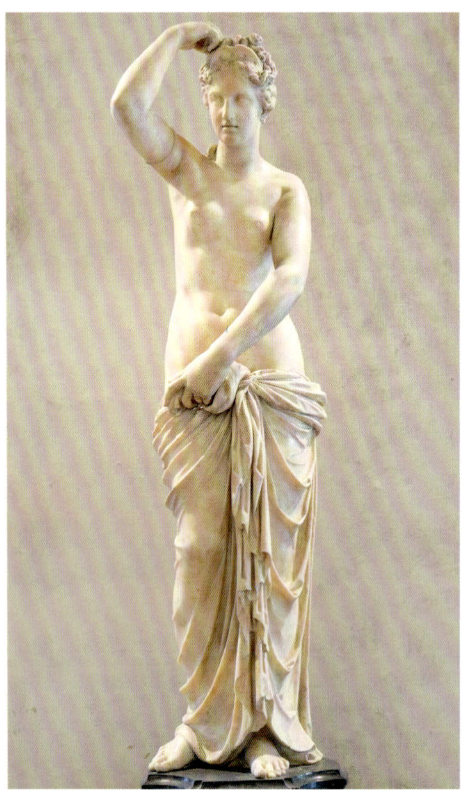

Fig. 71d. Rome, 1st century BCE, *Venus Urania*, marble, Gallerie degli Uffizi, Florence.

of angels: according to Luke there was only one, but Mark mentions two, whom he calls men.

Scholars have sought to identify the individual women represented by Rubens in *The Holy Women at the Sepulchre.* The woman who holds a container with oil and peers around the Pudicitia figure has been thought to represent Mary Magdalene; Wolfgang Stechow, however, suggested that Rubens actually intended the central figure to represent Mary Magdalene. According to Stechow, "Rubens saw the sinner Mary Magdalene transformed into a Pudicitia by her faith in the Resurrection announced to her by the angels."[32] By transforming this pagan figure into a Christian saint, Stechow contends, Rubens transformed the Magdalene into a figure of mourning and contrition, repentant for her former life of sin and thus a representation of the sufferings of the human soul and virtues of Christian piety.[33]

Stechow's identification of the Pudicitia figure as the Magdalene was generally accepted until 1989, when Julius Held reemphasized the theory he first proffered in 1980 that she represents not Mary Magdalene but the Virgin Mary.[34] In rejecting Stechow's identification, he points out that to justify Rubens's adoption of forms or actions, it is necessary to prove an underlying similarity or identity of meaning. But, as he notes, "the Pudicitia is chastity from head to toe," and not, therefore, a suitable model for Mary Magdalene.[35] Rather than the Magdalene, who Held believes is the woman who stands closest to the angels, the ancient image of chastity and virtue better suits the identity of the Virgin Mary, whom Rubens portrayed as the full-length Pudicitia figure in at least two other paintings of different subjects.[36]

The problem with this interpretation, as Held recognizes, is that none of the Gospels mention the presence of the Virgin Mary at the tomb of Christ. Held points, however, to the existence of a pictorial tradition cited by Johannes Molanus (1533–1585), professor of theology at Louvain, in 1570 when he criticized artists for erroneously representing the Virgin among the women at the tomb.[37] Noting that Rubens, who was keenly sensitive to Counter-Reformation theology, normally would have avoided such a breach of iconographic propriety, Held suggests the influence of a patron. The dedication on Vorsterman's print after Rubens's painting offers an important clue. In translation, the dedication reads, "To the most excellent matrons Lady Maria Nerot, wife of Lodovicus Clarisse, senator of Antwerp; and also to Magdalene de Schotte, wife of Master Rogier Clarisse, brother of Lodovicus, almoner of the city, Lucas Vorsterman dedicated the like-named divinities to attest his devotion."[38] Held, who dates the print to the first half of 1621, surmises that the dedication signed by Vorsterman also reflects Rubens's original intention and that the master may have painted the large panel for a member of the Clarisse family, who were his active patrons. Not only do the names of the two Clarisse women agree with those of the primary figures in the painting, but the two angels, he suggests, may also allude to the two Clarisse brothers.

Leo Steinberg, in an addendum to Held's 1989 article, supports Held's interpretation and strengthens the belief that the Clarisse family commissioned the painting. Steinberg recognizes the gesture of the woman shielding her eyes as a reenactment of an ancient ritual known to Rubens from Roman sarcophagi and other monuments as symbolizing the bridal or marital state. The hand appears as if either actively veiling or unveiling or as stilled at the veil's border, as in the Pudicitia figure. In either form, the gesture indicates consecration to the marital state and was thus an apt symbol of *pudicitia*, which should be understood as the virtuous fidelity of a wife rather than chastity. In *The Holy Women at the Sepulchre*, where Rubens represented both the active and the passive forms of the gesture, Steinberg suggests that Rubens may have "intended the still pudicitia *topos* to symbolize marriage as a *perpetuum*, and the veiling-unveiling to indicate entry into the married state." According to this reading, which supports Held's suggestion that the painting alludes to the marriages of the two Clarisse brothers, the painting was probably painted in late 1617, shortly after the marriage of Rogier Clarisse and his second wife, Magdalena de Schotte, on 28 May 1617.[39] The devotional painting, which Freedberg suggests may have been painted either as an altarpiece or as an epitaph, would thus not only celebrate their patron saints but also allude to the eternal fidelity of the two women, one of whom had been married since 1609, the other newly wed.[40]

The relationship of Vorsterman's print and Rubens's painting is critical to the dating and interpretation of *The Holy Women at the Sepulchre.* Between 1618 and 1623, when they had a falling out, Vorsterman was Rubens's exclusive printmaker. He thus played an important role in publicizing Rubens's paintings and establishing his international reputation. According to Andrew Hottle, in contrast to tradition, Rubens's dedications on prints published by Vorsterman "expunge all extraneous text in favor of bold proclamations to the worthiness of the dedicatees. . . . The inscriptions, which Rubens uniformly placed beneath the images, quite literally underscore his creations and imply an elevated status for both the artist and his work by associating his name and his inventions with persons of distinction."[41] Significantly, the subjects of Rubens's panegyrics were not, however, necessarily the patrons of the works reproduced in the prints, and in most cases they were not. In 1620 Rubens dedicated Vorsterman's print of his *Stigmatization of Saint Francis of Assisi* to Rogier Clarisse and his wife, praising the wealthy silk merchant's support of the Capuchins, a religious order of Franciscan friars.[42] Clarisse was not responsible, however, for commissioning the altarpiece Rubens painted for the high altar of the Capuchin church in Cologne that the print reproduces.

Recognition of Rubens's calculated use of dedications for political and professional benefit introduces new questions about the dating and biographical interpretation of *The Holy Women at the Sepulchre*. The dedication, notably, was not written by Rubens but by Vorsterman, who began to attach his own dedications to prints in 1621; indeed, the engraver does not even mention the painter. It appears that Vorsterman, like Rubens, was using the laudatory dedication to advance his own reputation by associating his craft and name to one of the wealthiest merchants in Antwerp with major international connections. The theory that the Clarisse brothers had commissioned the painting of *The Holy Women at the Sepulchre*, therefore, must be viewed with skepticism. On the basis of style, the painting probably dates before 1617. Ludwig Burchard suggested that the painting dates 1614/15, and David Freedberg dates the painting slightly before 1612–14—between the *Supper at Emmaus* "and at the latest, the Rockox epitaph."[43] If an earlier date is correct, then it dispels the association of the commission of the painting with the second marriage of Rogier Clarisse. Produced in about 1621, however, the reproductive print of Rubens's earlier composition with Vorsterman's dedication to the two Clarisse wives, Magdalena and Maria, was undoubtedly intended, by the printmaker if not the painter, to link the subject to the two women and their husbands.

1. Burton Fredericksen, letter dated 12 October 1999, reporting communications with Professor Jörg Jantzen, Munich (NSM). Fredericksen noted that Von Moser was a prominent official in the service of the court of Hessen-Darmstadt, functioning as a minister and chancellor 1770–80. Forced from office in 1781, he sold his collection of paintings and moved to Ludwigsburg. Fredericksen believes that Von Moser probably acquired the Pasadena painting between 1781 and 1794, closer to the end of that span, from either the Brussels or Antwerp art market. Fredericksen also notes that the asking price, printed in the catalogue, was the highest in the collection. The only known copy of the catalogue (unrecorded by Lugt 1938–87) is in a library in Weimar (it is transcribed in its entirety in GPI, Sales Catalog D-243). The results of the sale are not recorded in the unique copy, but sixty-three of the sixty-six paintings reappear in a subsequent sale held in Heilbronn in 1796 (GPI, Sales Catalog D-A255).

2. According to Professor Jörg Jantzen, Munich (letter, dated 16 May 1992, NSM), a letter written in 1796 by the German philosopher Friedrich Wilhelm Joseph Schelling (1775–1854) mentions that he had seen the original version of Rubens's painting of *The Holy Women at the Sepulchre* and the print by Vorsterman in the house of Friedrich Karl Lang (1766–1822) in Heilbronn. A lawyer by profession, Lang was an amateur draftsman and printmaker; he also wrote books on art as well as children's books. In 1798, following the failure of his publishing business, Lang was forced to flee Heilbronn, moving to Altona, Berlin, and Leipzig. He died in his home Wackerbartsruhe near Dresden. There are no recorded sales of Lang's collection. It seems very possible that Lang, or his creditors, sold the painting to Dominik Artaria in Mannheim. Heilbronn is situated between Stuttgart and Mannheim.

3. Artaria was primarily a publishing firm headquartered in Vienna with a branch in Mannheim. Dominik Artaria headed the family firm after 1802. In addition to being a publisher, he was an art dealer and, according to Frimmel 1913–14, vol. 1, p. 62, beginning in 1804 he bought paintings for Johann Rudolf, Count Czernin. See Tenner 1966, pp. 126ff.; and Natter 2003 for additional bibliography.

4. Avery-Quash 2011, vol. 1, p. 94. Charles Eastlake described seeing the Pasadena painting on an undated visit (but likely between 1830 and 1848) to the Czernin collection: "Rubens—angels appearing to women at Sepulchre—all draperies cold both that of angels & nearest females but a last, a woman to left, is [in] bright scarlet lake—the glory behind angels (& the flesh) the only warmth on other side." See also Juffinger and Brandhuber in Vienna 2010, pp. 67–75 (English trans. pp. 286–89), particularly the photograph on p. 73, where the Pasadena Rubens is shown installed in the Palais Czernin, Vienna. With thanks to Roswitha Juffinger for notifying us in 2009 of the existence of this photograph.

5. Pinakos, Agnew's, and Knoedler often owned paintings in shares, although Agnew's files do not indicate that in this case.

6. An unidentified label on the verso of the painting stating that it was sent from Salzburg to Prague on 18 June 1966 probably refers to the transfer of the painting from Salzburg to Czernin's residence in Prague and not to an exhibition.

7. This is based on a label on the verso, though the exhibition is unidentified.

8. In Rooses 1886–92, vol. 2 (1888) Rooses noted he had not seen the painting but accepted it on the basis of the print; in vol. 5 (1892), he cited Frimmel 1890 in saying that the Czernin painting was "une petite esquisse." Rooses considered the finished painting to be that at Melk Abbey, Austria.

9. Rooses 1910 rejected Frimmel's acceptance of the version at Melk Abbey as the original and says the painting with Czernin is authentic.

10. Incorrectly identified as in the Czernin Collection, Salzburg.

11. Freedberg gives incorrect dimensions (112 × 146 cm), which he apparently took from Rooses 1886–92, vol. 2 (1888).

12. Müller Hofstede 2000 dates the work 1615/17 and suggests (p. 304n60) that the fall of light from the right was influenced by *Calling of Saint Matthew*, 1599–1600, by Caravaggio (1571–1610; San Luigi del Francesi, Rome).

13. A drawing of a woman similar to the figure in red who is seen from behind and facing right in *The Holy Women at the Sepulchre* is depicted in Rubens's *Kostumstudie einer Frau in Rückenansicht* (black chalk with white highlights, 39.4 × 22.6 cm, Staatliche Museen Preußischer Kulturbesitz, KdZ 3236). Mielke and Winner 1977, pp. 93f., no. 33, date the drawing ca. 1630 and consider it an early study for Rubens's *Garden of Love*. Although the pose and costume resemble the woman dressed in red in *The Holy Women at the Sepulchre*, the more graceful and accomplished style suggests a date later than the Pasadena painting.

14. The inscription is from Matthew 28:5–6.

15. The first six copies are identified in Freedberg 1984, pp. 39f., no. 6.

16. Not mentioned by Freedberg 1984 but documented by a photograph at the RKD.

17. Not mentioned by Freedberg 1984. According to Avery-Quash 2011, vol. 1, p. 521, in November 1859 Charles Eastlake described a painting he saw at the dealer Langlart's at 10, rue de l'Entrepôt, Marché aux Charbons, Lille: "Rubens (School) 2 F. 8½ h, 3 F. 9 w. The Marys at the Sepulchre with attendants for there are six females (six heads) in all. The two angels are on the rt. & are finely painted—The heads of the women are rather dry & hard & thin draperies rather too full of small folds. The white drapery of the angels on the contrary is large and also fine in color, quite the taste of Rubens."

18. Andrea Rothe, paintings conservator at the J. Paul Getty Museum, memorandum, 25 January 1984 (NSM), noted that the red paint used to cover the hand was contemporary with that of the rest of the figure. He also noted that at some point in the past a restorer started to remove the red paint from the hand but stopped and repainted it.

19. Wadum 1998.

20. Matthew 28:1–8; Mark 16:1–8; Luke 24:1–10; and John 20:1–13.

21. Luke 24:1–6.

22. Freedberg 1984, p. 41. For Veneziano's *Three Women Going to the Sepulchre*, see Bartsch 1978–, vol. 14, no. 33.

23. Hymans 1893, no. 37. As Held 1989, p. 66, points out, Jacob Burckhardt actually may have preceded Hymans, since the connection appears in Burckhardt 1898, which was published posthumously.

24. In the seventeenth century the statue of Pudicitia was in the Mattei collection, Rome. Rubens later used the statue for the woman on the left of the center panel of the Ildefonso Altarpiece (Kunsthistorisches Museum, Vienna; Jaffé 1989, no. 998). Regarding Rubens's interest in the antique, see Stechow 1968b; White 1993; and especially Van der Meulen 1994–95. Regarding Rubens's interest in ancient costumes, see Belkin 1980; Rodee 1967; and De Grummond 1982.

25. Rotterdam 2001, p. 318.

26. The marble sculpture of Venus is nude except for a drape that wraps around her hips and falls to the ground; therefore, Rubens imagined the costume of her upper torso. The depiction of the fall of drapery for this figure and the others in the painting and drawing is awkward.

27. Freedberg 1984, p. 41, suggests that this woman "may simply have been intended as a servant carrying the basket of spices for the Holy Women."

28. Lucas Vorsterman (?), *The Holy Women at the Sepulchre*, pen and brown ink over black chalk in places, gray wash, heightened and corrected with white, indented for transfer, 34.6 × 44.9 cm, inscribed lower right in pen and brown ink: "Van Dyck." Freedberg 1984, p. 42, no. 6a, notes, "The drawing in chalk is almost certainly by Vorsterman, the reworking and corrections in pen and brown ink may be due to Rubens himself." He also suggests that the painting may have been cut down. See also Münster 1976, p. 220, nos. 164–65; and Rotterdam 2001, no. 98, pp. 316–18.

29. Because Vorsterman's print and the various other versions of the painting show the hand revealed, scholars have generally assumed that this alteration was made by a later hand rather than by Rubens. It has also been cited as a reason for dismissing Rubens's authorship. According to Freedberg 1984, p. 41, the concealed hand in the Pasadena painting led Ludwig Burchard to reject it in favor of the version in Melk Abbey. Freedberg disputes this opinion and judges the Melk painting a copy. The attribution of the Pasadena version to Rubens was previously questioned by Waagen 1866–67, p. 298, no. 24, "Obwohl ein ungemein ansprechendes Bild, dramatisch in den Motiven, fein im Gefühl, warm aber gemässigt in der Farbe, kann ich es doch nicht für ein Werk des Rubens halten. Die schlanken Gestalten, der antikisirende Geschmack in den Gewandfalten sprechen für einen Schüler." Rooses 1886–92, vol. 2 (1888), p. 152, defended the attribution of the painting, which, however, he apparently knew only from Vorsterman's print. Frimmel 1890, p. 542, considered the Czernin (now Pasadena) picture to be an authentic sketch ("Rubenssche echte Skizze") of the larger version at Melk Abbey, which is now considered to be a workshop piece. Freedberg 1984, p. 41, citing X-radiographs of the hand, convincingly argued for the authenticity of the Pasadena painting, although he considered that it "was evidently executed with a considerable amount of studio assistance."

30. See Technical Notes.

31. See, for example, the sixth-century Byzantine *Circular Box (pyxis) with the Women at Jesus's Tomb*, Metropolitan Museum of Art, New York, no. 17.190.57 a,b. Made from an elephant's tusk, the pyx was used to hold the wafer of the mass.

32. Stechow 1968b, p. 58.

33. Unpublished essay by Lucinda Reinold and Svetlana Alpers, written on the occasion of the 1974 loan of the painting to the De Young Museum, San Francisco (NSM).

34. Held 1989, passim.

35. Held 1989, p. 70. Margaret Iacono in New York 2009, pp. 37f., discusses the traditional associations of the Pudicitia with virtuous married women and associations with virginity and fidelity to a single spouse. Iacono suggests Rubens "knew that purple conferred honor to and indicated the status of the wearer."

36. Held 1989, p. 70.

37. Molanus 1570; Held 1989, p. 72.

38. Held 1989, p. 73.

39. Held 1989, p. 76n24, dates the painting 1617, noting that that Ludovicus Clarisse (bapt. 1588) was married to Maria Nerot (Noirot?) on 1 November 1609, and that Rogier Clarisse (bapt. 1593) married Magdalena de Schotte (Schot?) on 28 May 1617.

40. Steinberg 1989; Freedberg 1984, p. 22.

41. Hottle 2004, p. 60.

42. Rogier Clarisse and his first wife, Sara Breyell, founded a Capuchin house at Lier. Regarding Rubens's portraits of Rogier Clarisse (ca. 1611; Fine Arts Museums of San Francisco) and his first wife, Sara Breyell, with biographical information, see Jaffé 1953 and Jaffé 1961a. See also biographical information in Hottle 2004, pp. 77f.

43. Freedberg 1984, p. 41, who references without source Burchard's opinion, suggesting that it is noted in the file of the painting in the archive of Burchard's research at the Rubenianum in Antwerp.

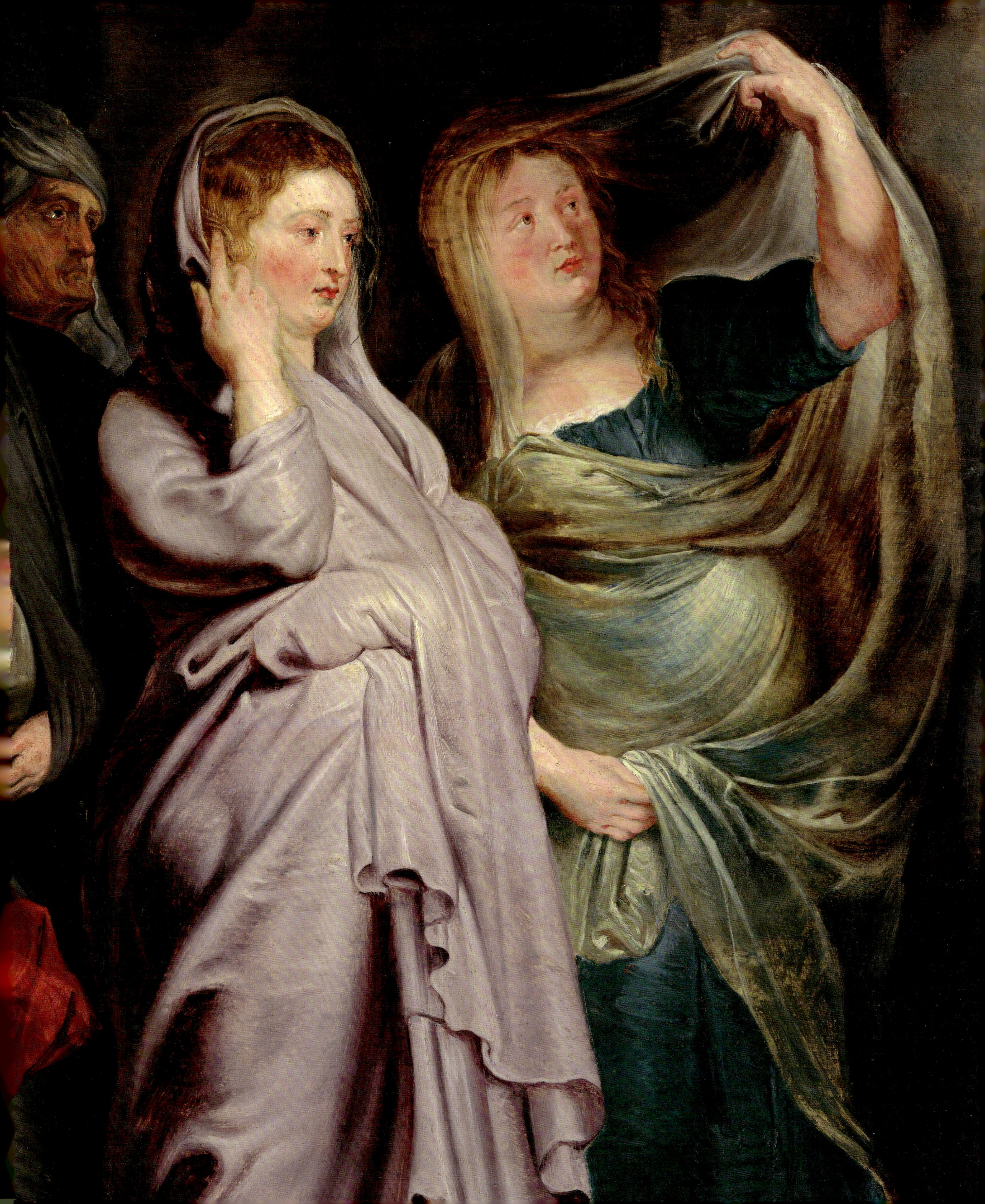

72

Peter Paul Rubens

Flemish
Siegen 1577–1640 Antwerp

The Hunt of the Calydonian Boar

ca. 1618–19

Oil on panel, 18 ¾ × 29 ⅛ in. (47.6 × 74 cm)
Norton Simon Art Foundation, M.1975.21.P

Provenance[1]
McMorrough Kavanagh Family, Borris House, County Carlow.[2] [Coutts & Co., London, sold 15 April 1959 to];[3] [Thomas Agnew & Sons, London, stock no. 2631, sold 28 October 1959 to]; [Rosenberg & Stiebel, New York, sold 1962 to]; Mr. and Mrs. Norton Simon, gift 1975 to; Norton Simon Art Foundation.

Exhibited
On loan, Los Angeles County Museum of Art, 18 January–16 April 1965; on loan, Los Angeles County Museum of Art, 1 August–14 December 1971; on loan, Los Angeles County Museum of Art, 25 April 1972–27 April 1973; on loan, Phoenix Museum of Art, 18 November 1980–20 May 1981.

References
Jaffé 1969, pp. 440, 443, fig. 28; Gerson 1976, p. 163, pl. 8; Vienna 1977, p. 93, fig. 19; Pasadena 1980, p. 46, ill.; Held 1980, vol. 1, pp. 337–39, no. 249, vol. 2, pl. 271; Adler 1980, p. 102, no. G38; Coffey 1984, p. 17, ill.; Balis 1986, pp. 158f., 161f., no. 10a, fig. 70; Jaffé 1989, p. 239, no. 483, ill.; Pasadena 1989, p. 55, ill.; Pasadena 2003, pp. 44–45, ill.; Kräftner, Seipel, and Trnek 2004, p. 228, fig. 1; S. Campbell 2010, pp. 44, 258, fig. 12, no. 112, ill.

Related Work
Peter Paul Rubens, *The Hunt of the Calydonian Boar*, oil on canvas, 101 ¼ × 163 ¾ in. (257 × 416 cm), Kunsthistorisches Museum, Vienna, inv. no. 523 (fig. 72a).

Technical Notes
The support is an uncradled oak panel composed of three vertically grained boards. Only the bottom edge is beveled; the top edge is somewhat uneven and may have been trimmed. The panel has a very slight cross-grain warp and was prepared with a smooth, moderately thick white ground. A light-brown imprimatura was then brushed quickly in all directions. This layer determines the tonality in much of the painting, remaining uncovered as a transitional tone or else covered very thinly, as in the body of the boar. Several figures were partially drawn with light brown paint to position them within the composition. Paint was applied in rapid, spontaneous brushstrokes. With thin liquid strokes of light gray, Rubens placed a backdrop for the standing figures and men on horseback. In some areas the light gray passes over the contour of a figure, as, for example, in the raised arm of the man on the white horse and his flowing robe. The paint is generally thin, sometimes brushed almost dry; the highlights are slightly thicker and more opaque. Contours of figures have a slight amount of brushmarking. There are numerous small losses at all the edges. A rather large loss at the lower left edge near the bottom has been partially filled but not retouched. The painting is very well preserved. A small amount of abrasion is located in the dark foliage and tree branches at the upper right and in the dark gray shadow of the central horse's rump. Retouching along the join at the left, as it passes through the dog and Meleager's proper right arm, is discolored and conspicuous. The varnish appears to be a thinly brushed natural resin.

The Hunt of the Calydonian Boar is one of Rubens's most exciting and beautiful oil sketches. Painted ca. 1618–19 with masterly bravura, the sketch captures the frenzy of the hunt with free and spontaneous brushstrokes that unify the composition but describe individual forms only generally. Rubens painted the Pasadena sketch in preparation for the larger painting of the same subject in Vienna (fig. 72a), which was chiefly executed by his workshop.

Oil sketches were a fundamental part of the working procedure Rubens adopted after his return to Antwerp from Italy in 1608, when he employed a large workshop to meet the growing demand for his paintings.[4] Rubens followed a procedure developed in Italy during the Renaissance: He began by working out his compositional ideas in pen, after which he developed them more fully in oil sketches on primed wood panels. Occasionally, as here, he drew directly on a panel with light brown paint and sketched over it in oil without known preliminary drawings on paper.[5] Following the initial oil sketch, or *bozzetto*, Rubens would refine the composition and forms by adding color and strengthening lines to produce a more elaborate *modello*, which was then presented to the patron, either for approval or simply as a valued gift of the artist's original invention.[6] *Modelli* were, however, essentially practical devices. Using the *modello* as a reference, Rubens would make chalk drawings of live models for the individual figures and then sketch in the design for the final painting, incorporating these drawings before turning the composition over to his assistants.[7]

The Hunt of the Calydonian Boar is typical of Rubens's *modelli* from the second decade of the seventeenth

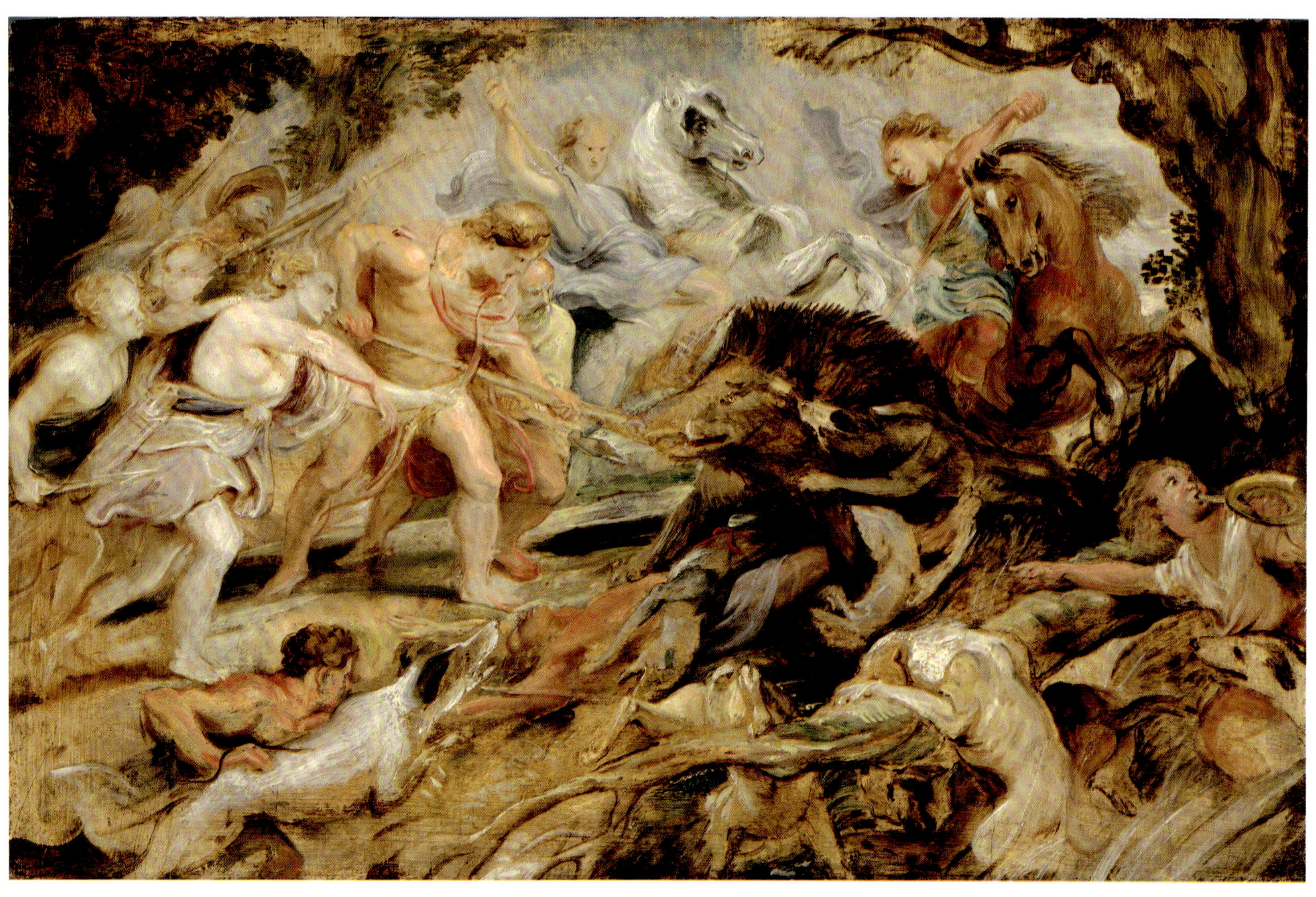

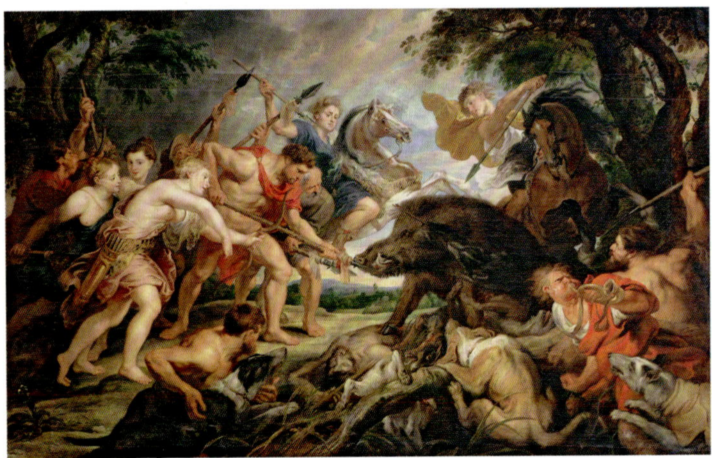

Fig. 72a. Peter Paul Rubens, *The Hunt of the Calydonian Boar*, ca. 1616–20, oil on canvas, 101¼ × 163¾ in. (257 × 416 cm), Kunsthistorisches Museum, Vienna.

century, when he painted on panels primed with white ground over which a film of medium brown was applied with the diagonal strokes of a coarse brush. This brown imprimatura serves as the middle tone, from which Rubens built up his forms. Here, the artist used thin layers of paint to "color" and define the forms of his initially freely rendered sketch, highlighting them with white and light colors and applying black to establish shadows, which visually push the three-dimensional forms forward.

Areas of light and dark also dramatically focus attention on the central event. Dark foliage frames the tense final moments of the fierce struggle of the powerful black boar. Nostrils flaring and eyes burning, the terrified animal reels around to defend itself against the frenzied assault of dogs and hunters who lunge forward with drawn bow and pike, as two men on rearing horses raise their spears to strike from behind. Rubens heightened the sense of tension by filling the scene with tightly coiled forms that anticipate an explosion of energy. Dogs scramble over and under fallen logs, driven by the scent of blood. One hound clings to the neck of the boar as it attacks its head; beneath the boar's front legs lie the body of a seminude man and dogs writhing in pain from wounds inflicted by the powerful beast.

Both the sketch and the larger painting in Vienna represent the classic story of Atalanta and Meleager killing the Calydonian boar, a subject Rubens treated throughout his career, including a slightly earlier version now at the J. Paul Getty Museum, Los Angeles.[8] The story is told in both the *Iliad* (9:430–605) and, more fully, in Ovid's *Metamorphoses* (8:260–546). According to Ovid, Diana, the goddess of the hunt, was offended by King Oeneus of Calydon and retaliated by sending a ferocious wild boar to ravage the countryside. Oeneus's son Meleager set out with a band of companions to kill the beast. Here, Rubens represents the dramatic moment of the story when the hunters corner the desperate boar. Atalanta, the virgin huntress whom Meleager loves, has wounded the boar with an arrow; now Meleager lunges forward to deal the fatal blow.[9]

Specific details and the relief-like quality of the Pasadena sketch suggest that Rubens referred to one of the ancient Greek or Roman sarcophagi on which the scene was often portrayed.[10] In common with the Pasadena painting, ancient Meleager sarcophagi typically include the lunging pose of Meleager who, wearing only the chlamys, thrusts his spear into the snout of the beast; the presence of Atalanta in the act of shooting an arrow (or, occasionally, taking an arrow from her quiver); a wounded or dead man; and two horsemen—almost certainly the Dioscuri, Castor and Pollux, whose presence was mentioned by Ovid.[11] Julius Held proposes that Rubens was influenced by a specific third-century sarcophagus (fig. 72b) he had seen over the door of a house next to Santa Maria sopra Minerva in Rome.[12]

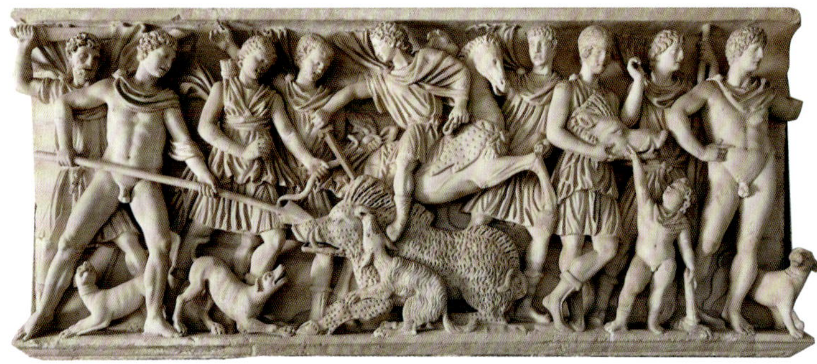

Fig. 72b. Rome, 280–90 CE, *Meleager Sarcophagus*, marble, Woburn Abbey, Bedfordshire.

Rubens, who possessed a voracious appetite for antiquities, recognized the challenge ancient sculpture presented to the painter.[13] In his Latin treatise *De imitatione statuarum*, the artist wrote: "I am convinced that in order to achieve the highest perfection [in art] one needs a full understanding of the [ancient] statues, nay a complete absorption in them; but one must make judicious use of them and before all avoid the effect of stone."[14] Rubens succeeded in avoiding the effect of stone in the Pasadena sketch, which not only appears in greater depth but also seems to pulsate with life. In addition to the sarcophagus, Rubens also apparently knew the famous marble sculpture of a wild boar rising to its feet (fig. 72c), which was displayed at the Gallerie degli Uffizi in Florence together with a statue of a youthful man in a short tunic and mantle standing in an attitude of attack.[15] It is, however, in the wonderful, animated forms of the eager dogs and the young man blowing the horn at the lower right that Rubens best demonstrated his skill and knowledge of anatomy.

Much of the dynamism and freedom of expression in the sketch is absent from the large Vienna canvas, which is now considered a product of the workshop, with little actual participation of Rubens.[16] In general, the tension of the sketch has been lost in the final painting, which stretches the

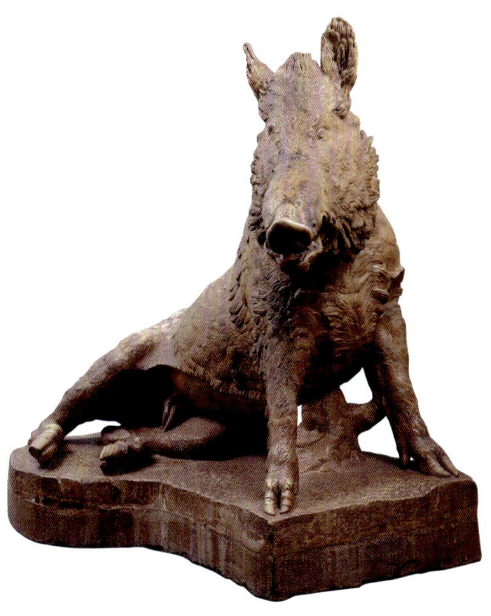

Fig. 72c. Anonymous, *Wild Boar*, 2nd–1st century BCE, copy of 4th-century BCE Lysippic bronze, marble, 37⅜ × 59½ in. (95 × 151 cm), Gallerie degli Uffizi, Florence.

compact composition of the sketch horizontally. The Vienna canvas generally follows the design of the Pasadena sketch, but with significant modifications: A figure launching a lance has been added in the lower right corner, where the youth blowing the horn is represented as a somewhat more substantial man; similarly, Meleager has been changed from a beardless youth to a stockier, bearded warrior. In the large canvas, the figures behind Atalanta are more clearly articulated than in the sketch and are moved back so that they appear more in line with the figures of Atalanta and Meleager; their rustic pitchforks have also been replaced with a lance and a horn. Finally, the Vienna painting differs in the positions of some of the hounds (especially the one clearing a fallen tree) and of the man killed by the boar.[17]

The commission for the large canvas in Vienna is unknown. The first reference to the painting is 1659, when it was included in the inventory of the collection of Archduke Leopold Wilhelm (1614–1662), who had served as governor of the Spanish Netherlands from 1647 to 1656, when he returned to Vienna. The archduke probably did not acquire the painting for his famous gallery until after Rubens's death in 1641. That the painting is now considered to have been painted by Rubens's assistants with little if any participation of the master may suggest that Rubens painted the sketch on speculation without a specific commission. The number of representations of the hunt (as individual paintings and as part of series of paintings) dating from the 1610s testifies to the renewed interest in the noble hunt and the related demand for images of hunting among the aristocracy of the Southern Netherlands. This predilection was apparently inspired by the archdukes' general policy of restoring the splendor of the court and legitimating an independent state and specifically by their issuance in 1613 of a hunting ordinance, which gave legal definition to the noble hunt. The ordinance stipulated that the "hunt of 'fur with fur and feather with feather,' a prerogative of the nobility, could only be carried out with hounds for the chase, a sword for administering the coup de grace and a hunting horn. Firearms, nets and other mechanical aids were forbidden."[18]

1. Balis 1986, p. 162, incorrectly associated the Pasadena painting with one sold from the collection of Edward Coxe (sale, Peter Coxe, London, 25 April 1807, lot 47). The description of that painting more closely agrees with one listed by Held 1980, vol. 1, no. 251, fig. 273, as in a Swiss private collection: "Rubens. The Boar Hunt, with the Death of Meleager. . . . The lifeless body of Meleager is finely contrasted by the animated Action of the surrounding Group, all eager to destroy the enraged Animal; while the Anxious Character of Atalante, bent on revenging the Death of her Lover, is told in impressive forcible Language. The Soul of Rubens is in this splendidly coloured Sketch . . . from the Calonne Collection." That work was sold to Sir Henry Rivers, 9th Bart., Kent (d. 1851). Balis's suggestion that the Pasadena painting was in the famous collection of Charles-Alexandre de Calonne (sale, Skinner and Dyke, London, 23–28 March 1795, lot 19: "Meleager and Atalanta Hunting the Wild Boar, a very fine finished sketch, full of magic genius") also seems wrong. Held 1980, vol. 1, no. 250, associates the painting in the Calonne sale with the later sketch of the same subject in the collection of Sir Francis Cook of Jersey.

2. According to the London dealer David Carritt and repeated in Held 1980, vol. 1, no. 2510, neither of whom, however, cite dates. Morgan Kavanagh, Borris House, confirms that the painting was sold by his grandmother in the 1950s (email, 9 October 2007). Although he notes that the family, which has occupied Borris House since the fifteenth century, has no documentary evidence of how the painting came to be there, they believe it was through Lady Harriet McMorrough Kavanagh (née Le Poer Trench, 1779–1885), an artist, traveler, and antiquarian who is believed to have been the first Irish woman to travel to Egypt. Her father, Richard, 2nd Earl of Clancarty (1767–1837), was ambassador to The Hague and a great collector, especially of porcelain. The Pasadena painting could have come through him or through Lady Harriet herself, who spent many years traveling through Europe.

3. Coutts & Co. is a bank and thus must have been representing the seller or seller's estate.

4. In a letter to the Flemish engraver, publisher, and numismatist Jacob de Bie (1581–ca. 1640), 11 May 1611, Rubens wrote: "I can tell you truly, without any exaggeration, that I have had to refuse over one hundred [young men who wanted to join the studio], even some of my own relatives or my wife's, and not without causing great displeasure among many of my best friends." Rooses and Ruelens 1887–1909, vol. 2 (1898), p. 35; Magurn 1971, p. 55.

5. Held 1986, pp. 26f., contradicting Van Puyvelde 1947, pp. 15 and 58, observes, "Although occasionally Rubens may have made no other drawings than those he traced directly on his panels or canvases, as a rule he prepared his pictures carefully in drawings on paper and in oil-sketches on panel." According to Held 1986, p. 25, the "primary function of drawings [for Rubens] is to serve as models for study, possibly also for the instruction of pupils, and as reference material." Rosand 1966, p. 236, notes that oil sketches "generally followed the artist's first pen sketches, the initial *pensieri* for a composition, and they represent a further elaboration

of the design giving it a firmer though not yet definitive statement."

6. Held 1980, vol. 1, p. 5, suggests that the relatively few examples of true *bozzetti* may be explained by Rubens's painting over them for the more refined *modelli*.

7. Regarding Rubens's working method, see introduction to Held 1986, esp. pp. 27–35. Held 1986, p. 26, refers to a report by the young Danish physician Otto Sperling, who had visited Rubens's house in 1621 and had observed in one room "many young painters who worked on different pieces on which Sr. Rubens had drawn with chalk and put a spot of colour here and there; the young men had to execute these paintings which then were finished off with lines and colours added by Rubens himself."

8. Regarding the Getty painting (acc. no. 2006.4), which until recently was known only from a copy, see Balis 1986, no. 1 (location unknown), and Woollett 2007. Regarding Rubens's other paintings of the subject, see Balis 1986, nos. 10 (Kunsthistorisches Museum, Vienna), 12 (location unknown), 12a (private collection, Switzerland), 18 (location unknown), and 20 (formerly Alcázar, Madrid, presumably lost).

9. Ovid relates how in triumph, the young prince presented the head and pelt of the dead animal to Atalanta, infuriating the others in the hunting party. Outraged, Meleager killed his two uncles, setting his own death into motion. Upon hearing that her son had murdered her brothers, Meleager's mother burned a log, which she had removed from the fire at the time of his birth when the Fates decreed that he would not die until the log was consumed by fire.

10. The literary source for the sarcophagi, according to Robert [1897–1919] 1969, vol. 3, p. 21 (cited by Held 1980, vol. 1, p. 338) was the lost play by Euripides.

11. Held 1980, vol. 1, p. 338. Robert [1897–1919] 1969, p. 22, identified the dead figure as Ancaeus, although Held 1980, vol. 1, p. 338, points out that Ovid mentions as the boar's victims Enaesimus, who died, and Hippasus, who was badly hurt. Held also mentions the fact that horses are white and roan, like the horses ridden by Castor and Pollux in Rubens's painting of the *Abduction by the Dioscuri of the Daughters of Leucippus* (Alte Pinakothek, Munich; Oldenbourg [1921], p. 131).

12. Held 1980, vol. 1, p. 338, notes that the Woburn Abbey sarcophagus (Robert [1897–1919] 1969, vol. 3 (1919), p. 224), which was placed over the doorway in the middle of the sixteenth century, includes the motif of a dog hanging onto one of the boar's ears, a detail Rubens employed in contemporary hunts of the wild boar, such as a picture in Marseilles (Jaffé 1989, no. 341). In accepting the Woburn Abbey sarcophagus as Rubens's source, Held corrects Jaffé 1969, p. 239, who associated the image with a sarcophagus now in the Palazzo dei Conservatori, Rome (Robert [1897–1919] 1969, vol. 3 [1919], p. 221, as that sarcophagus was not found until winter of 1872.

13. See Los Angeles 2021.

14. Quoted from the English translation in Stechow 1968b, p. 26.

15. The Roman marble figure of the man was destroyed by fire at the Uffizi in 1762. See Van der Meulen 1994–95, vol. 2, pp. 111f., vol. 3, pls. 179–80. See also Balis 1986, figs. 31–32, p. 92. Held 1980, vol. 1, p. 338n7, also mentions the possible influence of a bronze by Antico, now in the Victoria and Albert Museum, London (Kentner 1962, p. 172).

16. The painting originally measured approx. 207 × 360 cm and was apparently enlarged—by 40 cm at the top, 10 cm at the bottom, 30 cm at the left, and 25 cm at the right—to a final size of 257 × 416 cm. This alteration, however, does not affect the core of the painting. See Balis 1986, no. 10, pp. 156–61.

17. Held 1980, vol. 1, p. 338.

18. Koslow 1995, p. 224, with additional bibliography.

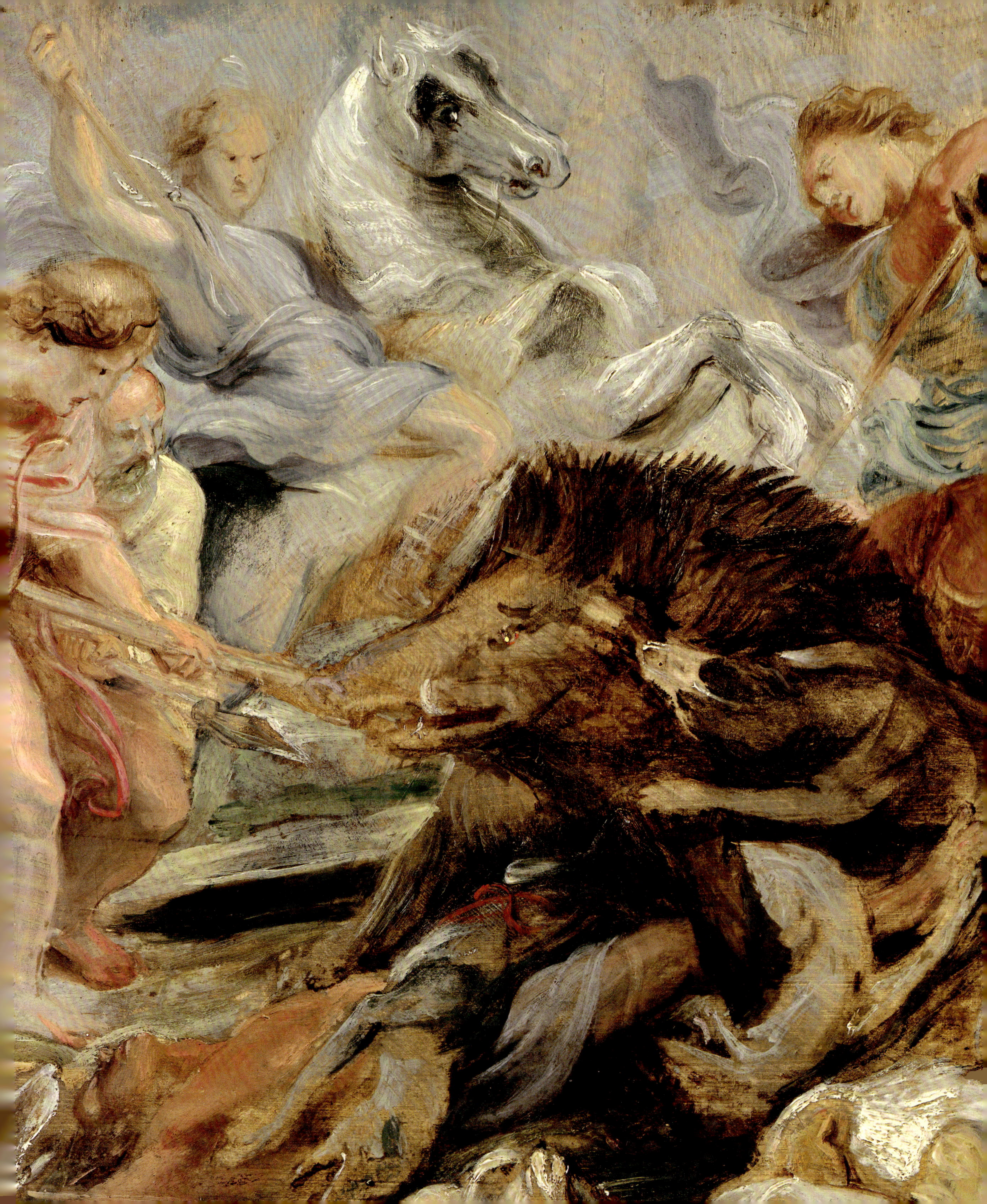

73

Peter Paul Rubens

Flemish
Siegen 1577–1640 Antwerp

Saint Ignatius of Loyola (1491–1556)

ca. 1616

Inscribed on page of open book: "AD / MAIOREM DEI / GLORIAM / QVICVNQVEHVIC / IESV CHRISI MII / TVE NOMEN D . . . / DERINT. DIE NO . . . / TEQVE SVCCIN . . . / TI LVMBOS ET . . . / TAM GRANDIS . . . / BITI SOLVTIONEM . . . / MPTI ESSE EBER. . . ."
Oil on canvas, 88¼ × 54¼ in. (224.2 × 137.8 cm)
Norton Simon Art Foundation, M.1975.03.P

Provenance

Jesuit Church, Brussels (sale, "Tableaux déposés au Collège de Bruxelles et provenant des ci-devant Jésuites de Bruxelles, de Louvain, de Namur, de Nivelles, de Malines, d'Alost et de Mons," Lannoy, Brussels, 12 May 1777, lot 2).[1] George Greville (1746–1816), 2nd Earl of Brooke and Warwick, by 1798,[2] by descent to; Charles Guy Fulke Greville (1911–1984), 7th Earl of Warwick, Warwick Castle (sale, Sotheby's, London, 11 December 1974, lot 36, sold to); Norton Simon Art Foundation.

Exhibited

Manchester 1857, no. 547;[3] Bruges 1956, no. 66; on loan, Virginia Museum of Fine Arts, Richmond, 13 August 1975–15 January 1976.

References

Mensaert 1763, vol. 1, p. 42; Descamps 1769, p. 64; J. F. M. Michel 1771, pp. 69f.; *Gentleman's Magazine* 1798;[4] Goede 1804–06, vol. 5 (1806), pp. 281f.;[5] Field 1815, pp. 186–88; J. Smith 1829–42, vol. 2 (1830), p. 51, vol. 9 (1842), p. 258, no. 66;[6] Passavant 1833, p. 219; Passavant 1836, p. 83; Waagen 1837–39, vol. 2 (1838), p. 367; Waagen 1854, vol. 3, pp. 214f.; Burger 1857, p. 195; Jerrold 1857, p. 17; Rooses 1886–92, vol. 2 (1888), pp. 285f., no. 449, pl. 151;[7] Dillon 1909, p. 237; Burchard 1930, vol. 1, pp. 127f.; Greville 1938, p. 50;[8] Evers 1942, p. 493n187; Van Puyvelde 1952, pp. 206f., as a copy; Grossmann 1957, p. 6; Van Puyvelde 1959, pp. 231f., as a copy; Van Puyvelde 1965, p. 188;[9] Lesuisse 1966; Vlieghe 1972–73, pp. 68–71, no. 113, fig. 36; Farington [1793–1821] 1978–84, vol. 5 (1979), p. 1588;[10] London 1979, p. 13; Pasadena 1980, p. 47, ill.; König-Nordhoff 1982, p. 82; Scheelen 1986, pp. 153–72; Buttery 1988, p. 42;[11] Jaffé 1989, p. 186, no. 203, as ca. 1613; Pasadena 1989, p. 40, ill.; Bauman and Liedtke 1992, p. 364, fig. 424; Roethlisberger and Bok 1993, vol. 1, pp. 434f., cat. C27, vol. 2, pp. 253, figs. 541f.; Vlieghe 1996, p. 291; Muchnic 1998, p. 276; Pasadena 2003, p. 46, ill.; S. Campbell 2010, pp. 171, 373, no. 1119, ill.; Sauerländer 2011, pp. 86–87, 287n7, ill.; Sauerländer 2014, pp. 84, 824, 283n7, fig. 29, ill.; Jonckheere 2016, p. 146n1 (re: no. R5); Bergvelt and Jonker 2021, DPG148 (*Miracles of the Blessed Ignatius of Loyola*, Dulwich Picture Gallery, London; related work 6b; https://dulwich-picture-gallery-ii.rkdstudies.nl/romeyn-rubens/peter-paul-rubens--dpg148/).

Related Works

- Copy, oil on canvas, 225 × 135 cm (88⅝ × 53⅛ in.), Muzeul Brukenthal, Sibiu, Romania, no. 995.
- Copy, oil on canvas, 224 × 140 cm (88⅛ × 55⅛ in.), Musée Communal, Nivelles.
- Copy, oil on canvas, 228 × 152 cm (89¾ × 59⅞ in.), Church of Notre Dame de la Chapelle, Brussels.
- Copy, oil on canvas, 216 × 121 cm (85 × 47⅝ in.), location unknown (formerly Museum voor Schone Kunsten, Ghent).
- Copy, oil on panel, 65 × 45 cm (25⅗ x 17¾ in.), Alte Pinakothek, Munich, inv. no. 4853.[12]
- Copy, attributed to Jan van Luyten (Jan of Utrecht), oil on canvas, 89½ × 53 in., Saint Louis University, acc. no. 1845:11, gift from the De Theux Collection, 1845.[13]
- Engraving by Schelte Adams à Bolswert (1586–1659); see Voorhelm-Schneevoogt 1873, p. 102, no. 70.
- Engraving by Schelte Adams à Bolswert; see Voorhelm-Schneevoogt 1873, p. 102, no. 71.
- Engraving by M. Sorrekens; see Voorhelm-Schneevoogt 1873, p. 102, no. 73.
- Engraving by Schelte Adams à Bolswert, half-length figure; see Voorhelm-Schneevoogt 1873, p. 215, no. 13.[14]
- Engraving by Schelte Adams à Bolswert, full-length figure of Saint Ignatius facing, within the same composition, the figure of Saint Francis Xavier from Rubens's lost painting; see Voorhelm-Schneevoogt 1873, p. 103, no. 79.

Technical Notes

The original support is a medium-weight plain-weave canvas that has been enlarged by a piece of canvas added to the bottom, 9 inches from the lower edge. The horizontal seam does not protrude, but the linear cracking associated with it is quite obvious. The original tacking edges of the canvas were unevenly trimmed before lining. There is evidence that the right edge was trimmed by as much as 1¾ inches. If so, the book held by the saint would have been entirely within the painting. Three rather large holes at the bottom center have been repaired. Two aged linings, both quite brittle and weak, are attached. The ground is cool white or pale gray. A medium-gray opaque underpainting beneath the figure of Saint Ignatius is visible around the outside contours of the proper right hand as well as between the thumb and the book held in the proper left hand. Beneath the brownish-black background, abraded and cracked paint reveals a lighter color, presumably the ground. Opaque, rich paint was applied in multiple layers of medium thickness. The red of the chasuble at the left side of the saint continues beneath the white habit across to the second fold of the fabric; the outer white fold (approximately from the waist to the ankle) appears to be a change by the artist. Brushmarking is obscured by the dense and conspicuous crackle pattern. There is only minimal impasto in the embroidery of the chasuble; there may have been a higher profile prior to lining. The edges of cracks in the dark background have been abraded, but abrasion within the figure is minimal. The painting was last cleaned in 1975 by Mario Modestini, New York. Several broad areas of retouching are located in

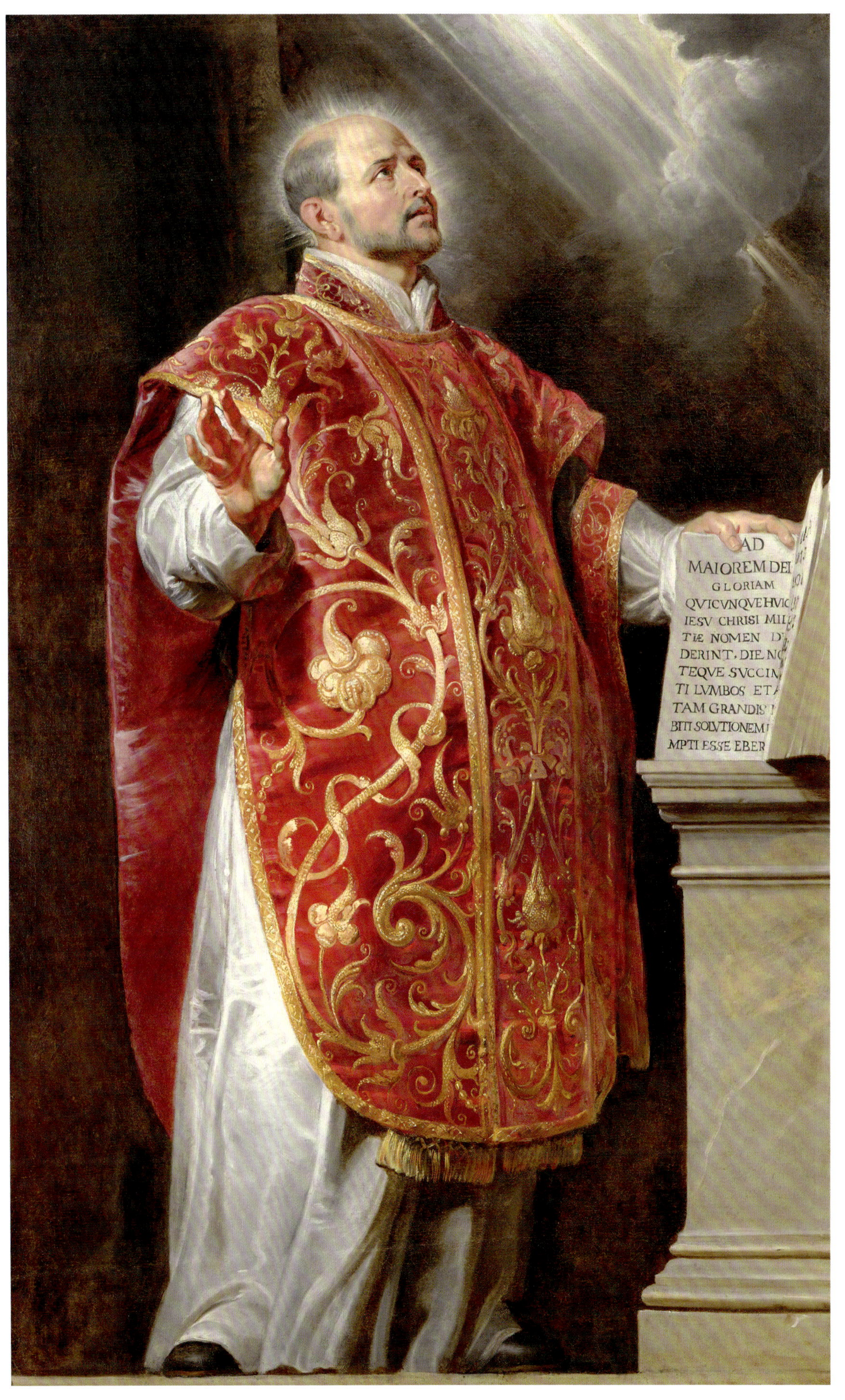
AD
MAIOREM DEI
GLORIAM
QVICVNQVE HVIC
IESV CHRISI MIL
TIÆ NOMEN D
DERINT. DIE NO
TEQVE SVCCIN
TI LVMBOS ET A
TAM GRANDIS
BITI SOLVTIONEM
MPTI ESSE EBER

the sky at upper right, at the lower right in the pedestal, at the bottom center, across the horizontal seam, and in the lower left background. A diagonal repair through the white collar of the habit has been overpainted. Ultraviolet light shows characteristic milky-blue fluorescence of an aged synthetic-resin varnish.

Rubens's commanding, monumental painting portrays Saint Ignatius of Loyola, one of the founders of the Society of Jesus, also known as the Jesuits.[15] Born into a noble Basque family in 1491, Ignatius was educated at the royal court of Castile and later entered the service of the Viceroy of Navarre. While recovering from a serious wound, he read books about the life of Christ and the saints and dedicated his life to the service of God. In his *Spiritual Exercises* (first published in 1548), Ignatius set out brief instructions to prepare one for active work as a soldier of the Church Militant: The individual was to employ all his faculties to achieve a realistic awareness of the subjects suggested for meditation—first, one was to contemplate sin, to see the flames of Hell, smell the stench, and hear the cries of the condemned. Later, the participant was instructed to imagine and relive Christ's life, death, and resurrection. Following a pilgrimage to Jerusalem and further study, Ignatius and six followers, including Saint Francis Xavier, took vows of poverty and chastity at Montmartre in 1534; they were ordained three years later. Unable to work as missionaries in the Holy Land because of the war with the Ottoman Turks, they offered their services to Pope Paul III. In 1539 they organized into a religious order, and in the following year a papal bull officially approved the Society of Jesus. As the first general of the society, Ignatius directed its aggressive missionary and educational activities from Rome until his death in 1556. Ignatius and Francis Xavier, the other leading member of the order, were canonized in 1622.

Wearing an elaborate red chasuble embroidered with gold over the white habit Jesuit priests wore to perform the mass, Ignatius, his head surrounded by an aureole of light, stands facing the viewer's right, his raised right hand pressing boldly forward into the viewer's space. With his left hand he supports a book resting on a rectangular plinth; the book is opened to a page on which is written his personal motto, "AD MAIOREM DEI GLORIAM" (To the greater glory of God). Tears flowing from his eyes, Ignatius looks toward the upper right corner of the canvas, where diagonal streaks of light break through clouds.

Rubens painted *Saint Ignatius of Loyola* to hang with a painting representing the full-length figure of Francis Xavier, his fellow cofounder of the Society of Jesus.[16] That painting, now destroyed, is known by a copy in the Brukenthal Museum, Sibiu, Romania (fig. 73a), where it hangs as a pendant to a copy of the Pasadena Saint Ignatius, presumably one of the copies of the original sold by the Jesuits in 1777.[17]

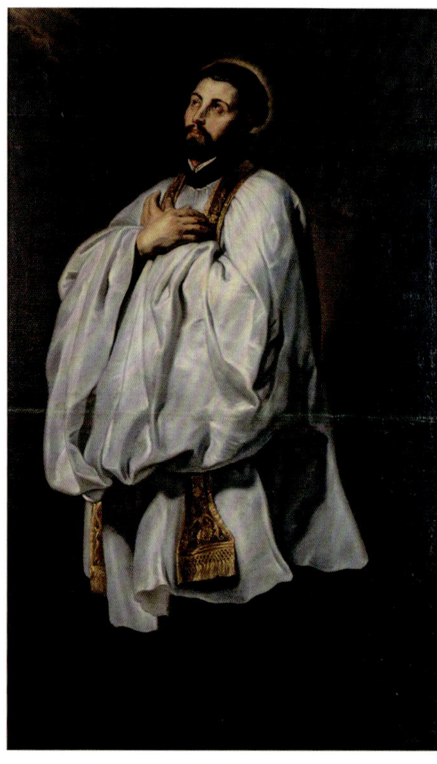

Fig. 73a. Workshop of Peter Paul Rubens, *Saint Francis Xavier*, 1618–33, oil on canvas, 88⅝ × 53⅜ in. (225.5 × 135.5 cm), Brukenthal National Museum, Sibiu.

Facing toward the viewer's left, Francis regards the diagonal streaks of light in the upper left corner, which appear to be a continuation of the apparition viewed by Ignatius. His eyes cast toward the beam of heavenly light, Francis crosses his arms over his chest, with the sleeves of his short white surplice billowing out over the regular black habit of the Jesuit order, an embroidered stole draped round his neck.

Rubens painted the two saints with minimal reference to the events of their lives. Francis Xavier, in particular, stands without attributes or even suggestions of time or place—the shadow of the saint's figure, cast by the strong light entering from the upper left, and the subtle suggestion of a corner are the only indications of his earthly presence. In this the paintings differ strikingly from the two enormous canvases dedicated to the miracles of the two founders of the Society of Jesus that Rubens painted in 1618 for the high altar of the new Jesuit church in Antwerp. The church, which was under construction between 1615 and 1622, was the first to be dedicated to Saint Ignatius (later rededicated to Saint Charles Borromeo). In each of the paintings for the high altar, both now in the Kunsthistorisches Museum, Vienna, the saint faces left and is elevated on a platform surrounded by references to his miraculous deeds (fig. 73b).[18] Unlike the enormous Vienna paintings, which were displayed alternately on the same altar, the smaller individual representations of Ignatius and Francis Xavier were apparently meant to hang as pendants, arranged so that they addressed each other and a common heavenly apparition.

Max Rooses was the first to associate the Pasadena painting and its pendant with the two works that the Flemish

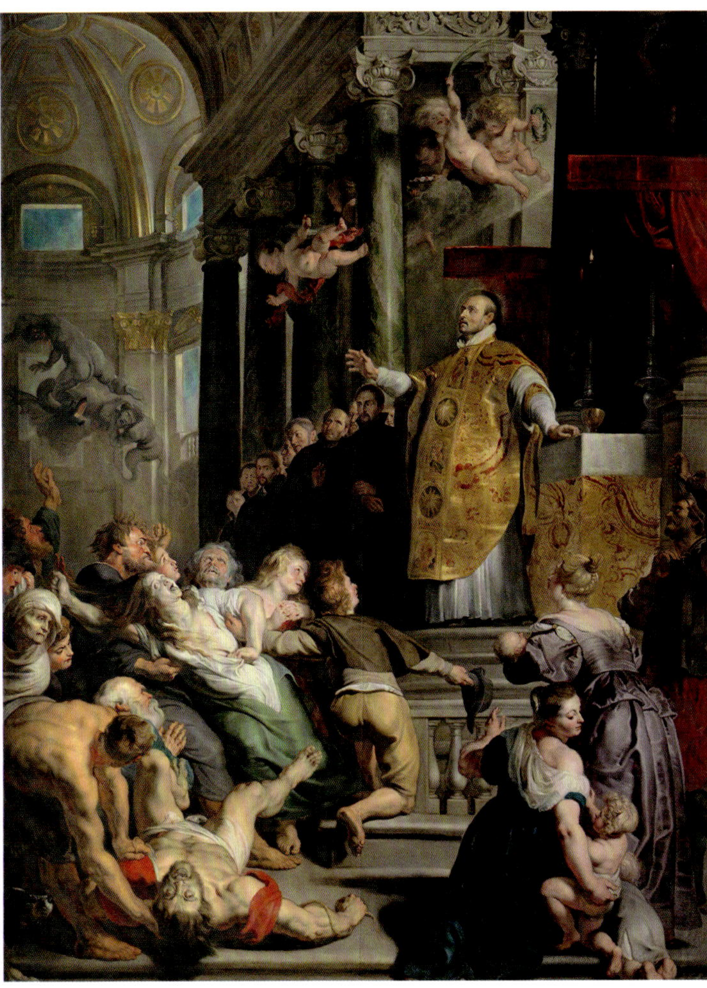

Fig. 73b. Peter Paul Rubens, *The Miracles of St. Ignatius of Loyola*, 1617/18, oil on canvas, 210½ × 155½ in. (535 × 395 cm), Kunsthistorisches Museum, Vienna.

painter and draftsman Guillaume Pierre Mensaert (1711–after 1777) and the French writer and artist Jean Baptiste Descamps (1714–1791) reported hanging on columns on either side of the high altar of the Jesuit Church in Brussels during the eighteenth century.[19] With the suppression of the Jesuits and the closure of the order's churches and convents, the paintings were sold in Brussels in 1777.[20] By 1798 the Pasadena painting was in the collection of George Greville, 2nd Earl of Brooke and Warwick, an avid collector who acquired a number of paintings by Rubens, Anthony van Dyck (1599–1641), and Rembrandt.[21] It remained in the Warwick Collection until 1974, when it was sold at auction to the Norton Simon Art Foundation. The painting of Saint Francis, which had been purchased separately, was destroyed by fire during the 1940 London blitz, when it was with the dealers Asscher and Welker.[22]

The documents related to the original commission for the paintings have never been found. Scholars have generally assumed that because eighteenth-century writers reported the paintings hanging against the pillars on either side of the high altar in Brussels, they must have been brought to the church from another location.[23] The paintings were considered to have been painted either for Il Gesù, the mother church of the Jesuit order in Rome, or for the Jesuits in Antwerp. Rubens, who was a member of the Jesuit Sodality in Antwerp, had already fulfilled numerous important commissions for the order both in the Netherlands and Italy.[24]

Two early sources suggest that Rubens painted the portraits for Il Gesù. In 1657 Francesco Scannelli (1616–1663) mentioned two paintings by Rubens there—one representing Saint Ignatius to the right of the high altar and one of Saint Francis Xavier to the left.[25] In the eighteenth century, François Mols (1722–1790) noted in his *Annotations manuscrites sur Rubens* that Rubens painted two works representing Saint Francis Xavier and Saint Ignatius for Il Gesù, displayed to the left and right of the main altar.[26] Both Ludwig Burchard and Hans Vlieghe suggest that Rubens executed the paintings for Il Gesù in 1620–22, possibly for the canonization of the saints on 12 March 1622.[27] In support of this dating Vlieghe cites the softer, less plastic painting of the figures, which is typical of Rubens's work ca. 1620. He also points to the appropriate inclusion of halos following the elevation of the founders to sainthood. Vlieghe theorized that the paintings were transported from Rome to Brussels during the late seventeenth or early eighteenth century, when Il Gesù was remodeled and new altars dedicated to the two saints were built—the altar to Saint Francis Xavier in 1673–78, and that to Saint Ignatius in 1696–1700.

An alternate theory that the paintings were originally intended for the Jesuits in Antwerp probably extends back at least to the late eighteenth century, when the Earl of Warwick acquired *Saint Ignatius of Loyola*. In 1815 the Reverend William Field noted that Rubens's *Saint Ignatius* "was painted originally for the Jesuits' College, at Antwerp; and brought thence to England, not many years ago."[28] Citing a contract dated 29 March 1620 between Rubens and Fr. Tirinus in Antwerp, Leo van Puyvelde suggested that Rubens painted two versions of the portraits of the Jesuit founders—one set for Rome in 1606–08, and another for Antwerp in celebration of the canonization of the saints in 1622.[29] This second version, Van Puyvelde contended, was transferred to Brussels by the eighteenth century. He believed that the paintings of Ignatius and Francis now in Sibiu, Romania, were the originals painted in Antwerp during the early 1620s; he dismissed the Pasadena painting (then with Warwick) and its pendant as inferior copies. Vlieghe and subsequent authors, however, accept the Pasadena painting and the destroyed painting of Francis as the original pair painted by Rubens. Vlieghe also dismisses Van Puyvelde's association of the Brussels paintings with the 1620 Antwerp contract; according to Vlieghe, Van Puyvelde misread the document, which actually concerns the two paintings of the miracles of the saints now in Vienna.[30]

Ursula König-Nordhoff, who accepts the Pasadena painting and its pendant as original, also proposes that Rubens painted the subject twice: once for Il Gesù between 1600 and 1608, and once in Antwerp ca. 1620, based on preparatory studies for the earlier commission. She believes that the Pasadena painting was part of the second set, explaining its more evolved style. The whereabouts of Rubens's hypothetical first treatment of the subject, which she believes was actually painted as a single composition, is no longer known. In her opinion, the Sibiu paintings are actually copies of the original Roman painting, divided into two separate compositions.[31]

Proponents of the two-set theory cite the inscriptions on Schelte Adams à Bolswert's engraving after the paintings, which refer specifically to the canonization of the two saints in 1622 (fig. 73c).[32] They also argue that the paintings must date from this year because the saints are shown with halos. This argument is not, however, supported by the evidence of other paintings and prints, which suggest that as early as 1600 images of the popular founders of the Society of Jesus were already circulated; at least some of these represent Ignatius without a hat and with his head surrounded by a circle of light. Walter Scheelen suggests that Rubens based the likeness of the saint in the Pasadena painting on a miniature copy of a portrait of Ignatius that had been commissioned by the Jesuits in Brussels in 1600 and sent to Rome, where it became his standard likeness. That copy (now in the Jesuit Residence, Brussels) was made in Rome in 1612 and brought to Brussels in 1614.[33] It is likely, however, that Rubens was already familiar with the image, which appeared as a full-page print in the *Vita Beati P. Ignatii Loiolae*, published by the Jesuit authorities in 1609 with contributions by Rubens.[34] Ignatius appears with a halo in both the 1612 painting and the *Vita Ignatii*, which was presumably published to coincide with the beatification of Ignatius by Pope Paul V on 27 July 1609 and to support his eventual canonization in 1622.

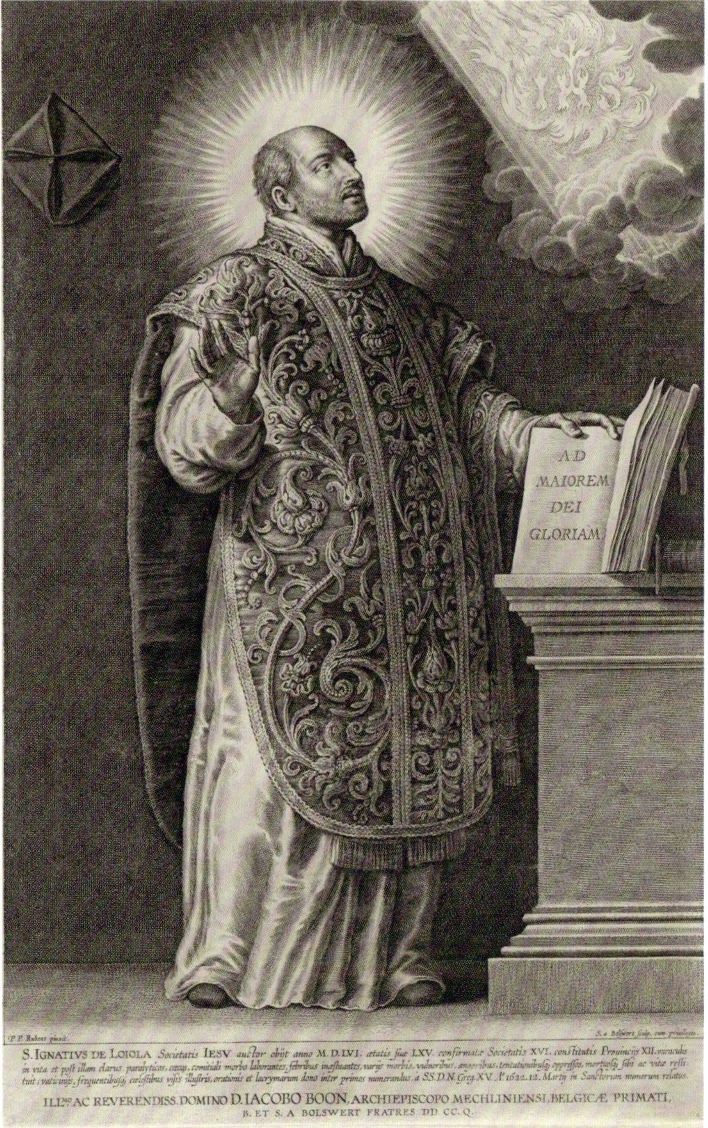

Fig. 73c. Schelte Adams à Bolswert, *Saint Ignatius Loyola, Standing and Holding an Open Book*, ca. 1623–33, after Peter Paul Rubens, *Saint Ignatius of Loyola (ca. 1616)*, engraving, 15⅝ × 10⅛ in. (39.7 × 25.7 cm), The Metropolitan Museum of Art, New York.

Introducing new documents concerning Rubens, Walter Scheelen proposes a fresh interpretation of the commissioning and completion of the paintings. According to Scheelen, Rubens painted only one original set of portraits—the Pasadena *Saint Ignatius* and its lost pendant. Scheelen also contends that Rubens actually painted these in Antwerp in 1616 for the Jesuit church in Brussels. Scheelen bases this hypothesis on two documents: a receipt written and signed by Rubens on 19 July 1616 in which he states that he had received "94 stucken van 8 schellinghen" from Fr. Jan van Dam;[35] and a brief history of the Jesuit residence in Brussels, ca. 1740, which identifies the two paintings as among the most important artworks in the residence.[36] Scheelen's theory that Rubens painted the two portraits of the saints in 1616 is supported by stylistic comparison of the Pasadena painting and Rubens's *Michiel Ophovius*, ca. 1615–18 (Mauritshuis, The Hague). Broadly painted to be comprehended from a distance, *Saint Ignatius* shows Rubens, under the influence of Italian painting, moving away from the hard, plastic manner of his early Antwerp paintings. This date also seems to be supported by the many copies of the pair that were produced by Rubens's workshop in Antwerp and appear to have been based on the actual paintings rather than on the prints made by Schelte Adams à Bolswert, which differ in significant ways from the paintings.[37] This, in itself, would seem to suggest that by about 1620 the original paintings were in the Southern Netherlands, not in Rome.

Scheelen offers that the paintings of the two Jesuit leaders, which were reported in Rome in 1657, were actually copies that had been sent to Rome to celebrate the elevation of the two saints. He notes that there is no documentary evidence that Rubens carried out work for Il Gesù and that no second version of the paintings is of high enough quality to be considered an original by the master. In addition, the first reference to any paintings of the two saints in Il Gesù appears in an inventory dated 1622/26, which notes that the paintings had been there for some time but gives no indication of how long. The inventory describes the paintings but does not attribute them to any artist. The only mention of Rubens appears in Scannelli's text of 1657. Later, however, two authors refer to the paintings in Il Gesù as by Van Dyck.[38] Scheelen believes these works were actually copies of the Brussels paintings and can be identified with those noted in 1936 by Redig de Campos in the Vatican Museum, where they were attributed to Van Dyck.[39]

Presuming that the Pasadena *Saint Ignatius* and its pendant were originally painted for Brussels, Scheelen proposes that they were never intended to serve as altarpieces but rather to hang on the first pillars of the choir, thus flanking the high altar on the level of the choir. *Saint Ignatius* was apparently placed in front of the chapel dedicated to the saint, and *Saint Francis Xavier* in front of the chapel of the Blessed Virgin.[40] Dressed in vestments appropriate for the performance of the Eucharist, Ignatius addresses the altar on which the sacrament was celebrated. The relationship of the saint in the Pasadena painting to the actual worshippers would thus have been similar to that of the saint and worshippers in the later altarpiece intended for the Jesuit church in Antwerp and now in Vienna (fig. 73b).

The paintings thus honor the two saints as defenders of the Eucharist, a major focus of the missionary work and teachings of the Jesuits. Their boldly displayed images were intended to serve as emotional stimuli to piety. His eyes turned toward the beams of heavenly light cast across the upper corner of the painting, Saint Ignatius appears to be experiencing a vision—and to be a vision himself. According to Ignatius, the faithful were to visualize the events of Christ's life and Passion as a means to their personal identification with and joyful acceptance of Christ's Passion. This direct involvement with religion was central to the teachings of the Post-Tridentine Roman Catholic Church after 1563. The low vantage point of the viewer relative to the figures of Ignatius and Francis Xavier and the one-sided orientation of the paintings support the idea that they hung on pillars at the entrance to the choir, where the light from the lantern would have illuminated the panels and suggested the heavenly light to which the two saints appear to be responding. The placement of the paintings of the two saints would, thus, have connected the worshipper to the events portrayed on the high altar as well as to the celebration of the mass, which honors the Passion of Christ.

Rather than paintings celebrating the canonization of the saints in 1622, Scheelen believes that the Pasadena *Saint Ignatius* and its pendant were part of the Jesuit's propaganda campaign for the two saints.[41] The numerous copies of the paintings confirm the demand for images of the two men, even before their canonization in 1622. In 1617, one year after receiving payment for the Brussels paintings, Rubens began work on the commission for the two monumental altarpieces for the high altar of the Jesuit church in Antwerp based on the earlier images but expanded to represent their miracles.

The Jesuit church in Brussels, like that in Antwerp, was still under construction in 1616 and not open to the public until 1621, suggesting that the Pasadena painting and its pendant were part of a comprehensive iconographic scheme for the altar of the church. It was not until 1624, however, that *Adoration of the Magi* by Abraham Bloemaert (1566–1651) was donated for the high altar in Brussels.[42] Marcel Roethlisberger suggests that Bloemaert, a Catholic artist from Utrecht in the Protestant Northern Netherlands, was chosen as part of an effort to extend the Jesuits' "foothold by calling on a leading painter from the north."[43] As he observes, however, the scale and style of Bloemaert's painting reflect his response to the paintings of the saints by Rubens and probably reflect the desires of the patron. One wonders, therefore, if the Jesuits in Brussels had originally also planned to have Rubens complete the painting for the high altar. Competing demands, and perhaps the lack of significant financial backing, may have delayed and eventually redirected an original commission given to Rubens.[44]

1. This was the second of three sales of the property of the Jesuits. Lot 2 was described as "Rubens, No. 2—Saint Ignace en contemplation, vêtu d'une Chasuble, ayant la main gauche posée sur un Livre ouvert reposant sur un Piedestal. Il est Peint plus grand que nature, d'un Coloris vrai et d'un Pinceau très-hardi. T(oile), 9 pieds 5 pouces sur 6 pieds 10 pouces [approx. 219 × 130 cm]." Lot 3 was "St. Francis-Xavier contemplant le Ciel . . ." with the same dimensions as the Pasadena painting. The sale also included as lots 208–15 "Copies d'après les fameux Originaux de P. P. Rubens," four sets of portraits of Ignatius and Francis Xavier. The Ignatius portraits measure: 6 pieds 10 pouces × 4 pieds 5 pouces (lot 208); 6 pieds 4½ pouces × 4 pieds (lot 210); 6 pieds 10 pouces × 4 pieds 6 pouces (lot 212); and 6 pieds 10 pouces × 4 pieds 3 pouces (lot 214). The first sale of Jesuit property took place in Ghent on 5 May 1777, and it included as lots 214 and 215 another set of copies of the two portraits of saints, noted as measuring 6 pieds 8 pouces × 4 pieds 6 pouces. The third sale was held in Antwerp on 20 May 1777. Van Puyvelde 1959, pp. 229–30.

2. The painting is included in the 1800 inventory of the Warwick collection (Warwick County Record Office: CR1886, Box 446). Francis, 1st Earl of Warwick, who died in 1773, was an important patron, but it was George Greville, 2nd Earl of Warwick, who was the great collector. The 1800 inventory includes more than 213 paintings.

3. As formerly from the College of the Jesuits at Antwerp, lent by the Earl of Warwick.

4. The list of paintings in Warwick Castle includes "Ignatius Loyola, standing, in a cope.

On a book, *ad majorem Dei gloriam.* Reubens." The painting hung next to Rubens's famous portrait of the Earl of Arundel (now in the Isabella Stewart Gardner Museum, Boston), which had entered the Warwick Collection by 1763. As early as 1788, William Gilpin [Gilpin 1788, vol. 1, p. 40], recording his observations from 1772, noted that in the collection of Warwick Castle, "its richest furniture is a choice collection of portraits by Rubens and Vandyke." Gilpin mentions no specific paintings.

5. Goede gives a full description of the painting and notes the Madrid Jesuits offered the Earl of Warwick 2,000 guineas for the painting. ("Als der Jesuiterorden noch in Spanien blühte, wurden einem Grafen Warwick von den Madrider Jesuiten zwei tausend Guineen für dieses Gemälde geboten, welches sie zur Ausschmückung einer ihrer Kirchen zu erlangen wünschten. Wie sehr muß es nicht jetz im Preise gestiegen seyn, wo die geistlichen und weitlichen Jünger des heiligen Ignas. stolzer, als je zuvor das haupt erheben!")

6. In 1830 Smith notes only the engraving by Bolswert, but twelve years later he identifies the original painting as belonging to the Earl of Warwick and as having formerly decorated the Jesuit church in Brussels.

7. Schelte Adams à Bolswert's engraving after the painting.

8. As hung in the Green Drawing Room at Warwick Castle and originally painted for the Jesuit College at Antwerp, where it remained until the French Revolution when it was acquired for the Castle by George, Earl of Warwick.

9. As a replica of the painting in Sibiu, Romania, which the author, Leo van Puyvelde, believes is the version formerly belonging to the college of the Jesuits in Antwerp.

10. Farington records a 15 August 1801 visit to Warwick Castle: "There are many excellent Portraits, particularly . . . Ignatius Loyola, whole length . . . [all by Rubens]." Among the other paintings mentioned by Farington are Rubens's portraits of the Marquis Spinola, the Earl of Arundel, and four portraits by Van Dyck.

11. Buttery notes that the painting was acquired toward the end of the eighteenth century by George, 2nd Earl of Warwick, who "was the great collector of the family acquiring works by Rembrandt, Rubens, and Van Dyck." Apparently aware of Scheelen 1986, he notes that the painting once hung in the Jesuit church in Brussels.

12. Jonckheere 2016, p. 146, no. R5.

13. We are grateful to Pam Ambrose, Saint Louis University, for her help in identifying this painting.

14. A painting of the same composition appeared in the sale of J. Schotel, Dordrecht, 24 April 1923, no. 19. Attributed to Rubens, the painting is probably an old copy of the print.

15. Regarding Saint Ignatius of Loyola, see Ignatius of Loyola 1991 and König-Nordhoff 1982.

16. The painting of Saint Francis Xavier was on canvas, 216 × 135 cm.

17. Baron Samuel von Brukenthal (1721–1803) purchased in Vienna the copies of the Pasadena Saint Ignatius and its pendant, Saint Francis Xavier. According to Van Puyvelde 1965, p. 188, who believed they were the originals, the copies (now in Sibiu, Romania) had been purchased from the Brussels sale of 1777 (see note 1 above) and brought to Vienna by by M. Donckers, an artistic adviser to the Austrian governor-general of the Netherlands in Brussels.

18. See G. Smith 1969, who observes how the paintings for the Antwerp church, which were part of the propaganda campaign for the canonization of the saints, incorporate references to the various miracles within each.

19. Rooses 1886–92, vol. 2 (1888), p. 286, no. 449; Mensaert 1763, vol. 1, p. 42; Descamps 1769, p. 64.

20. See note 1. The removal of all members of the Society of Jesus from most of Western Europe and their colonies began in 1759. In 1773 the order was abolished by the Holy See in Rome.

21. He assumed the titles of 2nd Earl of Brooke and of Warwick at the time of his father's death in 1773.

22. See the provenance in Vlieghe 1972–73, no. 114, p. 71.

23. Vlieghe 1972–73, p. 69.

24. Vlieghe 1972–73, p. 71, notes that Rubens received the following commissions for the Jesuits: the choir of Santissima Trinità, the Jesuit church at Mantua, 1604–05 (Jaffé 1989, no. 41a–i); *The Circumcision* for Sant'Ambrogio in Genoa, 1605–06 (Jaffé 1989, no. 54); and *The Miracles of Saint Ignatius of Loyola* for Sant'Ambrogio in Genoa, ca. 1620 (Jaffé 1989, no. 517; Vlieghe 1972–73, no. 116). In addition to these works, Rubens also painted an *Annunciation* for the chapel of the Jesuit Sodality in Antwerp (Jaffé 1989, no. 104; now Kunsthistorisches Museum, Vienna), and while in Italy he had provided illustrations for a biography of Ignatius of Loyola (Held 1972). See also Larsen and Hyde Minor 1977, p. 54, where the authors (citing Van Puyvelde 1965 without mention of Vlieghe 1972–73) incorrectly list "the two large 'Portraits' of *Saint Ignatius* and *Saint Francis Xavier* at the Brukenthal Museum, Sibiu, Rumania," as having been painted for the Jesuit church in Antwerp.

25. Scannelli [1657] 1966, p. 205.

26. Cited by Rooses 1886–92, vol. 2 (1888), p. 286, no. 449; and Scheelen 1986, p. 155. The manuscript for Mols's *Annotations manuscrites sur Rubens* is held in the Bibliothèque Royale de Belgique. We are grateful to Michiel Verweij there for his efforts to locate all of the Norton Simon paintings by Rubens mentioned in this large handwritten manuscript.

27. Burchard 1930, vol. 1, pp. 127f.; Vlieghe 1972–73, pp. 68–71, no. 113.

28. Field 1815, p. 186.

29. Van Puyvelde 1959, pp. 227f.

30. The 1620 contract refers to ƒ3,000 "for two large paintings of our holy Fathers Ignatius and Xavier, already painted by the said Sr. Rubbens for the aforesaid New Church." Rooses 1886–92, vol. 2 (1888), p. 266n1.

31. König-Nordhoff 1982, p. 82. In at least one of Schelte Adams à Bolswert's prints, the saints appear in a single composition as is if standing on opposite sides of an altar table and occupying the same physical space.

32. The British Museum dates its copy of the print 1623–33 and describes the inscription: "Lettered at bottom left 'P. P. Rubens pinxit,' right 'A. Bolswert sculp cum privilegio,' in lower margin five lines Latin with date 1622, and a dedication to Jacques Boon, Archbishop of Mechel[e]n, by B. and S. a Bolswert 'S. Ignatius de Loyola . . . fratres DD.CC.Q.'" The date of 1622 noted in the inscription refers to the canonization of the saint, not the date of the print. British Museum website, www.britishmuseum.org/collection/object/P_R-4-26, accessed August 29, 2023.

33. Scheelen 1986, pp. 165f. The miniature copy, now in the Jesuit Residence, Brussels, was sent in 1612 from Rome by Claudio Aquaviva, General of the Jesuits, to Fr. Manareus in Brussels. Scheelen believes that Rubens used this image as his model rather than a portrait of the saint painted by Alonso Sánchez Coello (ca. 1531–1588; destroyed in 1931; formerly in the Jesuit College, Madrid), which was modeled after a death mask of the saint. The elaborated death mask is now in the Professed House of the Society at Madrid. See Schamoni 1948, p. 134, fig. opp. p. 136.

34. Held 1972, attributes fourteen of the publication's illustrations of the life of Ignatius to Rubens. He does not, however, attribute the portrait of Saint Ignatius from the *Vita Ignatii* (fig. 50) to him.

35. Quoted in full as an appendix by Scheelen 1986, p. 171.

36. Scheelen 1986, pp. 159f. does not cite the location but identifies the MS. as ARAB, A.J.C.B., 3 bis: *Cartularium Templi Bruxellensis sacitis De Principi Collegii Bruxellensis* (ca. 1740), fol. 14.

37. Schelte Adams à Bolswert elaborated the settings and made various subtle changes in the composition that do not appear in the originals or in the painted copies.

38. Scheelen 1986, p. 156, cites Filippo Titi, *Ammaestramento utile e curioso di Pittura, Scultura et Architettura nelle Chiese di Roma* (Rome, 1686), p. 148; and Nicola Pio, *Le Vite de Pittori, Scultori e Architetti* (Rome, 1724).

39. Scheelen 1986, p. 156. He also questions why, if the paintings had been considered valuable original works by Rubens, they would have been removed from public view and displayed in the sacristy.

40. The Jesuits venerated the Virgin by establishing many new congregations of Our Lady.

41. The paintings were noted as having been among the many gifts to the Jesuits in Brussels, who were in straitened circumstances. Scheelen 1986, p. 160, suggests that the Jesuits may have commissioned the Pasadena painting and its pendant but turned to a donor to pay off the debt.

42. Scheelen 1989, p. 61, notes that there was no painting above the high altar before 1624. According to Roethlisberger and Bok 1993, vol. 1, pp. 253f., by 1660 the main altar of the Jesuit church in Brussels was fitted with pulleys, which permitted the alternation of three paintings depending on ecclesiastical needs. In addition to Bloemaert's *Adoration of the Magi* (Musée de Peinture et de Sculpture, Grenoble, inv. no. 87), the paintings included *Adoration of the Shepherds* by Jan Cossiers (1600–1671; anonymous donation for the main altar, 1655) and *Miracles of Saint Francis Xavier* of 1661 by Erasmus Quellinus II (1607–1678; now Gumpendorfer Pfarrkirche, Vienna).

43. Roethlisberger and Bok 1993, vol. 1, p. 253, point out that Bloemaert had close contacts with the Jesuits, including a painting he made of *The Vision of Saint Ignatius* for the Jesuits in 's-Hertogenbosch.

44. As noted above, the Jesuits in Brussels had financial difficulties and received many of their objects as donations.

74

Peter Paul Rubens and workshop

Flemish
Siegen 1577–1640 Antwerp

Portrait of Isabella Clara Eugenia, Governor of the Spanish Netherlands, as a Poor Clare

ca. 1625

Oil on canvas, 45 ⅝ × 35 ¼ in. (115.9 × 89.5 cm)
Norton Simon Art Foundation, M.1966.10.10.P

Provenance
Possibly Habsburg family, Vienna.[1] [Galerie Sanct-Lucas, Vienna, 1934, probably sold through]; [Rudolf J. Heinemann, Munich, to];[2] Heinrich Thyssen-Bornemisza (1875–1947), Schloss Rohoncz, Lugano, by 1935, by descent to his daughter; Baroness Gabrielle Bentinck Thyssen (1915–1999), sold 30 September 1957 through; [Rudolf J. Heinemann, Pinakos Inc., New York, to]; [Rosenberg & Stiebel, New York, sold 1959 to]; Mr. and Mrs. Norton Simon, gift 1966 to; Norton Simon Art Foundation.

Exhibited
Castagnola-Lugano 1949, no. 216; on loan, Hunt Branch Library, Fullerton, CA, 20 October 1967–27 April 1969; on loan, Los Angeles County Museum of Art, 30 April 1969–26 July 1972; Princeton 1972–74, no. 6, pp. 35–39, no. 6, p. 39 ill.; Paris 2017, pp. 108–10, 216, cat. 16.

References
Glück 1935, p. 142; Heinemann and Feulner 1937–41, vol. 1 (1937), p. 132, no. 360; Glück 1940, pp. 175, 178, ill.; J. R. Martin 1972, pp. 35–37; Steadman 1972, p. 35, fig. 4; London 1979, p. 13; Vlieghe 1987, pp. 121f., no. 111, fig. 130; Scribner 1989, pp. 16, 32, no. 5, fig. 1; Jaffé 1989, p. 296, no. 864 bis; P. Sutton 1989b, p. 6; P. Sutton 1993, p. 119, fig. 15; Jaffé 1997; Baciagalupe 1999, p. 41; S. Campbell 2010, pp. 32, 254, no. 80, ill.

Technical Notes
The tightly plain-woven canvas carries an old lining, and the original tacking edges have been removed. The smooth white ground is of medium thickness. A silvery gray underpainting is visible in the face, especially the eyes. The clear gray provides the basic color for the eyes, with a darker gray iris painted over it. Paint was applied in broad areas of smoothly blended color, using a limited palette of gray, black, white, and brown. The background, a liquid transparent brown, was loosely brushed directly over the white ground. The sitter's head is surrounded by horizontal striations of white paint. A black-and-white photograph of an undated X-radiograph shows paint losses throughout the painting, some of them fairly large. It is possible the canvas was removed from its stretcher and remained unsupported for a period of time. Extensive abrasion has further thinned paint, especially in the upper background, and has interrupted passages of subtle color. A 1957 conservation treatment by William Suhr included cleaning and retouching. In 1990 Bernie Rabin selectively cleaned the painting, removing varnish from the face, hands, and some parts of the habit. Filling and retouching are of uneven quality, which is probably a reflection of these two separate campaigns. Most of the retouching in the black habit is imprecise and covers the fine cracks. Toning in the background is much darker and denser than the warm translucent golden-brown of the original paint. The most recent retouching is around the perimeter, in the center right outside the edge of the veil in broad strokes, in long horizontal strokes above her head, and broadly applied at the bottom left corner. Layers of two different synthetic-resin varnishes impart uneven gloss, with some areas of yellowing noticeable in the lighter colors.

The Norton Simon Museum's *Portrait of Isabella Clara Eugenia, Governor of the Spanish Netherlands, as a Poor Clare* is considered the best version of Rubens's official portrait of his patroness, the Archduchess Isabella Clara Eugenia (1566–1633), which was destroyed in a fire at Coudenberg Palace, Brussels, in 1731.[3] The Pasadena portrait, like the lost original, portrays Isabella as governor of the Netherlands, a role she assumed following the death of her husband, Archduke Albert (1569–1621).[4] According to a contemporary, the day after Albert's death, Isabella discarded her elegant clothing and jewels, cut her hair, and put on the ash-colored tunic of the Poor Clares, the Second Order of Saint Francis founded by Saint Clare of Assisi (1194–1253).[5] On Saint Francis Day in October 1621, Isabella joined the Third Order of Saint Francis, known as the Tertiaries, an order of laymen and -women, making her vows before her confessor in a court chapel.[6] In adopting the habit of the Tertiaries—the light gray tunic tied with a knotted rope and the long black veil that covers the head and shoulders down to the floor—Isabella placed the traditional image of Franciscan piety at the center of her identity. Her likeness, which circulated in the form of prints and diplomatic gifts, declared her Roman Catholic faith and personal piety to substantiate her political authority. As a widow, she assumed the highly prestigious moral and ethical qualities that traditionally had been associated with widowhood since the early Church. According to Barbara Welzel, "When Isabella adopted the habit of the

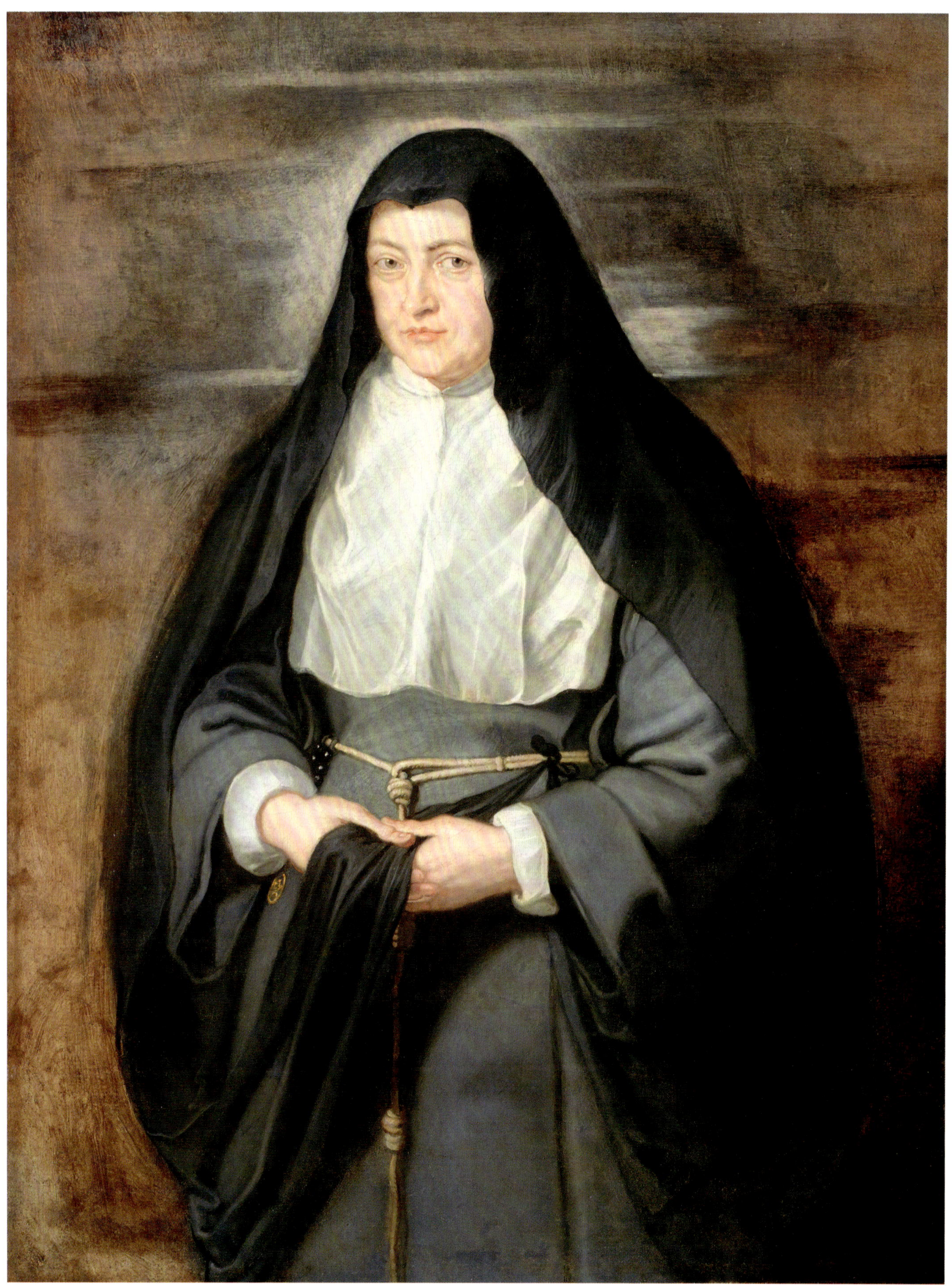

Tertiaries . . . the image of the pious widow underwent not only a religious intensification, but also an explicitly Catholic turn. In the Southern Netherlands, the confession of the Catholic faith likewise constituted a political confession of Habsburg rulership."[7]

Isabella, the favorite daughter of Philip II of Spain (r. 1556–98), married her cousin, Albert of Austria, the youngest son of the Habsburg emperor Maximilian II (r. 1564–76), in 1598, the same year Philip II died. In his will Philip named the couple joint sovereigns of the Spanish Netherlands as archdukes.[8] When Albert died without heir in 1621, Isabella as a woman was prohibited by law from ruling alone. Thus, direct rule reverted to Spain, and Isabella was reduced to governor of the Netherlands on behalf of the Spanish king. As a "princesse naturelle," however, she retained the social if not political status of a ruler and the admiration of her subjects as well as foreign statesmen. An English diplomat, Sir William Temple (1628–1699), wrote of her "generous and obliging disposition."[9] And in 1628, Rubens, who had become a confidante of Isabella following the death of her husband, observed: "She is a princess endowed with all the virtues of her sex; and long experience has taught her how to govern these people and remain uninfluenced by the false theories which all newcomers bring from Spain."[10]

Rubens's association with the Brussels court was formalized 23 September 1609, within a year of his return to Antwerp from Italy, when he accepted, at first reluctantly, an appointment as court painter.[11] Granted an annual pension of *f*500 with full privileges and honors, which included exemption from the regulations and dues of the local guild, Rubens was able to enroll a large workshop to carry out his many commissions. He also received special permission to live in Antwerp rather than at the court in Brussels. Increasingly, as his personal relationship with the rulers grew closer, Rubens functioned less as a court artist and more as a trusted courtier and diplomat, representing the political interests of the archdukes at the courts of Spain, England, and the Northern Netherlands. On many occasions, Isabella used Rubens's paintings and artistic services as diplomatic gifts to foreign courts.

Isabella probably sat for Rubens on her return to Brussels from Breda in 1625. On 6 June 1625, after a ten-month siege, Spanish troops led by Ambrogio Spinola (1569–1630) captured the town of Breda, a major stronghold of the Dutch on the northern border of Flanders. Within a month, Isabella visited Breda and returned victorious with Spinola to Brussels, stopping en route in Antwerp. According to a notation in the diary of Philippe Chifflet (1597–1663), Isabella's chaplain, she visited Rubens after lunch on 10 July 1625.[12] Like many of her contemporaries, Isabella was eager to see Rubens's famous collection of antiquities, rarities, and paintings.[13] Although Chifflet made no reference in his diary to Rubens's portrait of Isabella, later in his journal, he associated it with the year 1625: "1625, Rubens painted the Infante at Antwerp with a civic crown [a chaplet of oak leaves] about which M. Gevart made the verses that are in his letter."[14] In his *Obsidio Bredana armis Philippi IIII* (1626), Hermann Hugo (1588–1629) also refers to the now lost original portrait having been painted when Isabella was in Antwerp the previous year.[15]

Contemporary documents and prints indicate that the iconography established by Rubens's original portrait was closely associated with the conquest of the town of Breda. An allegorical print designed by Rubens and engraved by Paulus Pontius (1603–1658; fig. 74a) represents two angels

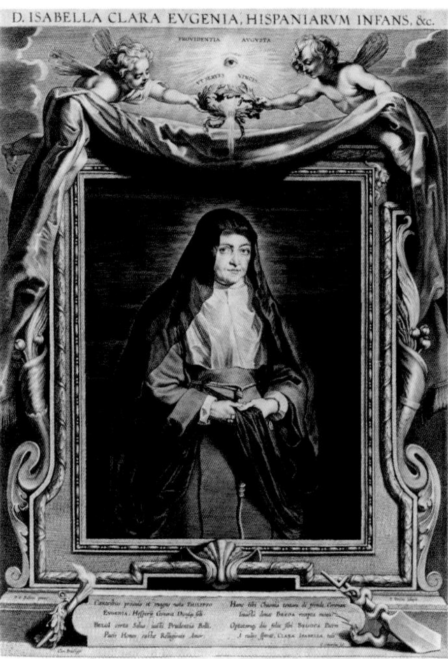

Fig. 74a. Paulus Pontius, after Peter Paul Rubens, *Portrait of Isabella Clara Eugenia, Infanta of Spain*, ca. 1630, copperplate engraving, 23½ × 17 in. (59.7 × 43.2 cm), Albertina, Vienna.

lifting a veil above the framed portrait of Isabella as they hold a crown of oak leaves above her. Rays of light from the all-seeing eye of Providence shine through the wreath, forming an aureole around her head. In a cartouche beneath the image, verses composed by Gevartius (Jan Gaspar Gevaerts; 1593–1666) refer to the glory of Isabella's victory at Breda and to the far-sightedness and glory of her government in general:[16] "Isabella, of the imperial dynasty and daughter of Philip II, is praised as the jewel of Spain and the salvation of Belgica. She is the prudence of just war, the honor of chaste peace, and the love of religion. She was crowned with the oak wreath after capturing Breda, bringing the longed-for peace to Belgica . . . the peace it [Belgica] had sought in the rays of Clara [shining] Isabella."[17]

Welzel notes, "The aureole around [Isabella's] head serves not only as a sign of majesty introduced as an attribute, but [also] constitutes the direct visualization of the person and her name."[18] In the context of Isabella's political ambitions and rivalry with her nephew, King Philip IV of Spain (r. 1621–65), the engraving, intended for wide distribution, was designed to assign credit for the conquest of

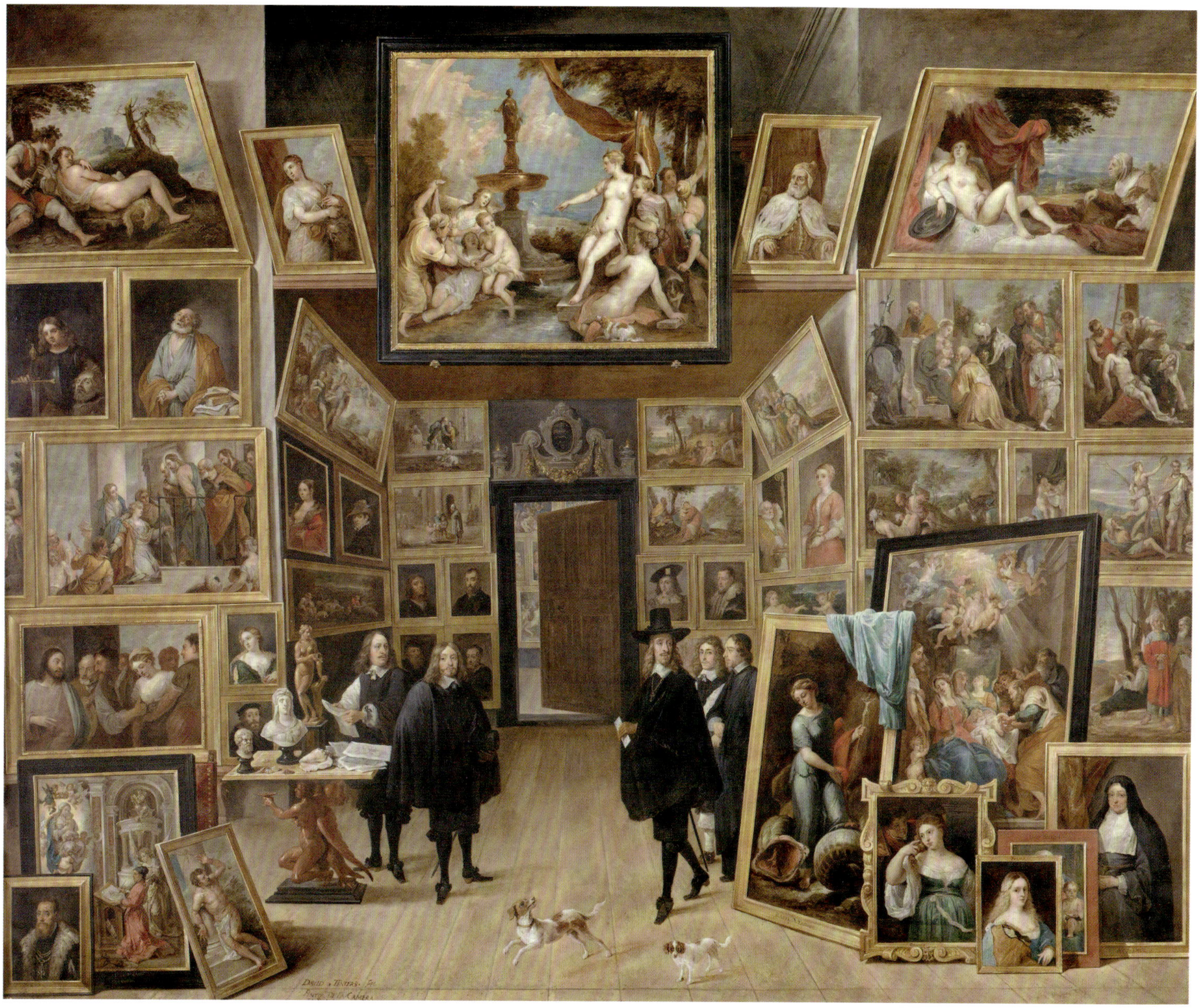

Fig. 74b. David Teniers II, *The Archduke Leopold Wilhelm in His Picture Gallery in Brussels*, 1647–51, oil on copperplate, 41¼ × 51⅜ in. (104.8 × 130.4 cm), (P001813), Museo Nacional del Prado, Madrid.

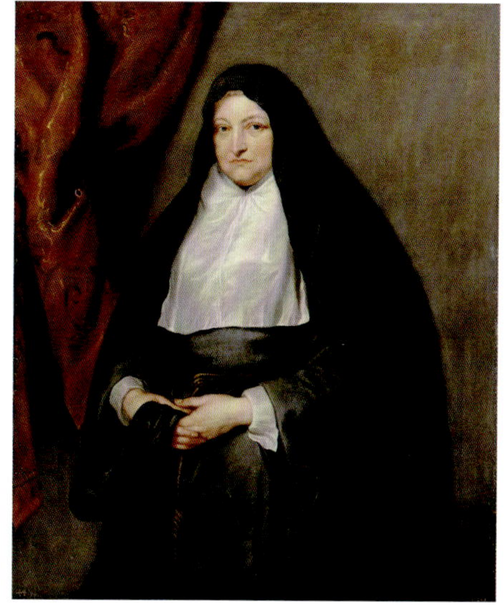

Fig. 74c. Anthony van Dyck, *Portrait of Isabella Clara Eugenia as a Poor Clare*, 1627, oil on canvas, 43 × 35 in. (109 × 89 cm), Kunsthistorisches Museum, Vienna.

Breda to Isabella alone. Like her patron, Saint Clare, who was venerated for having repulsed the infidels with the Holy Sacrament, Isabella was hailed for vanquishing the Protestant troops and reaffirming the Catholic faith and the Habsburg rule in the Spanish Netherlands (modern-day Belgium).[19] The archduchess further identified herself with Saint Clare in 1626 when she donated twenty tapestries designed by Rubens to the convent of the Descalzas Reales in Madrid. The Franciscan convent with Saint Clare as its patron had been founded by Isabella's aunt, the Infanta Juana, the youngest daughter of Charles V, King of Spain (r. 1516–56), later Charles V, Holy Roman Emperor (r. 1519–56). The tapestry series, which celebrates the Triumph of the Eucharist and includes two portraits of Isabella, was designated as decoration for the Feast of Corpus Christi.[20]

The Pasadena portrait represents Isabella with an aureole surrounding her head, extending in horizontal striations of light that suggest its reflection on the stone wall behind her. Welzel notes that only the original sketch (formerly in the Wertheimer Collection, Paris), the engraving, and the Pasadena painting include the aureole, which later versions of the portrait omit. Hans Vlieghe, who considers the Pasadena painting to be the closest extant version of the lost official portrait, notes: "The pictorial quality of the [facial] features [of the Pasadena painting] is . . . equal to that of the sketch-like Wertheimer version," and thus by Rubens.[21] The drapery, however, is probably the work of assistants.[22] Vlieghe contends that the high quality of the Pasadena painting indicates Rubens's actual participation in its execution, which implies that it was produced for a distinguished recipient.[23] His suggestion that it belonged to the Infanta herself and hung at Coudenberg Palace, Brussels—and through her successor as governor of the Spanish Netherlands, Archduke Leopold Wilhelm (r. 1647–56), passed to the Austrian branch of the Habsburg family prior to entering the Thyssen-Bornemisza collection—is, however, incorrect.[24] The only mention of a portrait of Isabella as a Poor Clare by Rubens in the archduchess's collection is the painting lost in the fire of 1731.[25] There is no documentation of a portrait of the Infanta by Rubens in either the 1649 or 1659 inventories of Leopold Wilhelm's collection.[26] The portrait of Isabella as a Poor Clare that appears in paintings by David Teniers II (1610–1690) of the gallery of Leopold Wilhelm in Madrid (fig. 74b) and possibly Munich (see fig. 75c) is the version by Anthony van Dyck (1599–1641).[27] That portrait, which is distinguished by a curtain on the side, was in Leopold Wilhelm's collection and is now in the collection of the Kunsthistorisches Museum, Vienna (fig. 74c).

1. Heinemann and Feulner 1937–41, vol. 1, no. 360, states that the painting had belonged to the Habsburg family, Vienna, but may have confused this painting with the version by Anthony van Dyck pictured in the gallery painting by David Teniers II and now in the Kunsthistorisches Museum, Vienna. See discussion below.

2. As stated in a letter from Gerald Stiebel to Barbara Roberts, 24 February 1970 (NSM). Rudolf Heinemann (1901–1975) was trained as an art historian and began his career as an apprentice to his father at E. A. Fleischmann's Hofkunsthandlung, later Galerie Fleischmann, Munich. Rudolf Heinemann assumed direction of the gallery in the late 1920s from his father, who died in 1931. In 1935 he moved to New York, continuing to work as an international dealer. During the 1940s and 1950s he also operated as Pinakos Inc. Heinemann worked closely with Heinrich Thyssen-Bornemisza to form the latter's collection in Lugano. For additional information, see "Heinemann, Rudolf J.," National Gallery of Art (Washington, DC) website, https://www.nga.gov/collection/provenance-info.8388.html, accessed August 29, 2023.

3. Rubens's original, destroyed painting is recorded in the collection formed by Isabella and Albert that remained, according to Isabella's will, in Brussels. De Maeyer 1955, doc. 263, "Inventory of the paintings of Her Highness in the wardrobe (garderobe), made between 1633 and 1650," no. 33 D: "De confeytselz van Huere Hoochde: Rubbens, hoch 4 3/11 d, breet 3 8/11 d."; doc. 271, "Inventory of paintings, furnishings and sculpture in the palace of Brussels, after 12 January 1659," no. 67: "Otra de dicho maestre [Rubens], representando la infanta doña Isabel vestida en religiosa"; doc. 275, "Inventory of the paintings from the palace at Brussels made between 1665–70 and 1698, probably before March 1692," no. 31: "Het contrefeijtsel, kniestuck, van d'infante Isabella op haer religeus gekleet, geschildert van Rubbens"; doc. 280, "Inventory, primarily of paintings from the palace of Brussels, which were not rediscovered after the fire of 3–4 February 1731; made by the controller J.-B. Aimé between 17 January and 1 April 1732," nos. 62 and 63: "Le pourtrait d'une reine de France; celluy d'une religieuse, où Isabelle habillée en Carmélite."

4. In 1615 Rubens had painted portraits of Isabella and Albert, which served as their official images until Albert's death. The prototype for those portraits was traditionally thought to have been the versions in Vienna, but dendrochronology has dated them to no earlier than 1620. Jaffé 1997 reconsiders the versions on canvas at the National Gallery, London, suggesting that they are autograph. Regarding the iconography of Isabella, see Welzel 1999.

5. Saint Clare of Assisi, a contemporary follower of Saint Francis of Assisi (1181–1226), founded the Order of Poor Ladies, a monastic religious order for women in the Franciscan tradition of strict poverty. Isabella was known for being extremely religious and particularly devoted to the Franciscans, who had served as her confessors.

6. Regarding Isabella, see Klingenstein 1910; De Villermont 1912; De Maeyer 1955; Brussels/Louvain 1998; and Thomas and Duerloo 1998.

7. Welzel 1999, p. 171.

8. By establishing this new political arrangement, Philip II hoped to extract Spain from the struggle in the Netherlands without losing prestige or the military foothold in the region.

9. Temple [1673] 1972.

10. Magurn 1971, p. 176. Rubens's nephew reported that Albert was particularly fond of Rubens, who named his first son after him (Lind 1946, p. 39).

11. Rubens, who had already worked at the court of Vincenzo I Gonzaga (r. 1587–1612), Duke of Mantua, and at the Spanish court, where Gonzaga had sent him on a diplomatic mission, stated in a letter to his doctor and friend in Rome, Jan Faber, 10 April 1609, "I have little desire to become a courtier again." Rooses and Ruelens 1887–1909, vol. 6 (1909), p. 324; Magurn 1971, p. 52.

12. "Après le diner S. A. fut voir le Panthéon de Rubens et toutes ses raretez." Philippe Chifflet, "Diare des choses arrivées à la Cour des Pais-Bas du temps de l'Infante Isabelle en l'an 1625," under 10 July, reprinted in De Maeyer 1955, p. 375, no. 197, and cited by Vlieghe 1987, p. 121n4, who notes that it is curious that Chifflet does not mention the portrait.

13. On Rubens as a collector, see J. M. Muller 1989.

14. "1625. Rubens peignit l'Infante à Anvers avec une coronne civique, sur laquelle M. Gevart fit les vers qui sont dans sa lettre." Philippe Chifflet, "Journal historique des choses mémorables arrivées en la cour des Pais-Bas depuis l'an 1559 jusques à l'an 1632 inclus," reprinted in De Maeyer 1955, p. 375, no. 199.

15. Hugo 1626, p. 125, quoted in Vlieghe 1987, p. 121n3. Bellori [1672] 1976, p. 265, quoted by Welzel 1999, p. 164, also refers to the event. According to Held 1980, vol. 1, p. 139, it may also have been during her visit to Antwerp in July 1625 that Isabella commissioned Rubens to design the cycle of tapestries known as *The Triumph of the Eucharist* for the convent of the Descalzas Reales in Madrid.

16. Voorhelm-Schneevoogt 1873, p. 178, no. 206. Vlieghe 1987, pp. 122f., no. 112 transcribes the full inscription. On p. 122 he notes: "The text refers to the oak wreath as a tribute from unconquered Breda, and to the expectation of a lasting peace. The hope of a return to prosperity is symbolized by the cornucopias with fruits of the earth, disposed decoratively around the frame."

17. Translation from Welzel 1999, p. 163, with my modification of the term *Belgica* for her use of Belgium, which is not an appropriate term until the nineteenth century. Both Chifflet and Hugo refer to the civic crown with which Isabella was represented in the original, now lost portrait by Rubens. Hugo specifically notes, "After this glorious triumph [the capture of Breda] she deserved to be depicted [with a civic crown], and by no other hand than that of the famed Apelles." Hugo 1626, p. 125, quoted in original Latin and in translation by Vlieghe 1987, p. 121. Bellori [1672] 1976, p. 265, quoted by Welzel 1999, p. 164, confirms the association.

18. Welzel 1999, p. 164.

19. Welzel 1999, passim, especially pp. 163ff.

20. As a young woman at the court of Spain, Isabella had been in frequent contact with the convent of the Descalzas Reales in Madrid, where she lived for a month in 1598. The oratory of the convent was the de facto chapel to the court in Madrid and the residence of many noble widows and unmarried women. Regarding Rubens's *Triumph of the Eucharist*, see Madrid/Los Angeles/Houston 2014–15, passim, and Scribner 2014, passim, with additional bibliography.

21. Regarding the Wertheimer sketch, see Vlieghe 1987, p. 119, no. 109, fig. 128 (oil on panel, 56.8 × 44 cm), and Paris 2017, pp. 108–09, cat. 15, ill., as private collection, formerly Wertheimer. Welzel 1999, p. 165, notes the many versions of the portrait represented by numerous artists as full-length, three-quarter, and bust portraits. She counts ten versions of the Van Dyck portrait of the Infanta. Vlieghe has suggested that the Wertheimer sketch of Isabella was one of many *editio princeps* of official portraits, which Rubens kept as prototypes to be used by his studio to meet the demand for portraits to be collected or given as statements of political and social alliances. Vlieghe notes the large number of portraits of royalty, nobles, and other dignitaries painted by Rubens that remained in his collection at the time of his death and later appear in the collection of his brother-in-law Arnold Lunden, where they are called "sketches." See Vlieghe 1987, p. 31; and Vlieghe 1977, pp. 195, 198; see also J. M. Muller 1989, pp. 60f.

22. Another version of the portrait, formerly in the Aldenham Collection, is in the Gallerie degli Uffizi–Galleria Palatina, Florence (inv. 1890 no. 4263). Vlieghe 1987, pp. 120f., notes that Burchard considered the Aldenham version (Vlieghe 1987, no. 110) to be wholly autograph and the best of the extant versions of the painting. Vlieghe, however, rejects the Aldenham painting as "not consonant with Rubens' style: above all the habit with its stiffly falling folds is clearly the work of an uninspired routine copyist." Jean-François Dubost (Paris 2017, pp. 108, 110, no. 17) published the Aldenham version as a work by Rubens, noting there are "two good versions [of the portrait]—Pasadena and, to a lesser degree, Florence."

23. López Navió 1962, p. 291 (cited by Vlieghe 1987, p. 121n6), mentions, for example, the 1655 inventory of Diego Felipez de Guzman (1580–1655), Marquis de Leganés, which lists: "498. Un retrato de medio cuerpo de la Ynfanta Doña Ysabel, bestida de terçiaria de mano de Rubens, en 400." Leganés fought for twenty years in the Spanish Netherlands in service of the archdukes until the death of Albert, when he returned to Madrid. Vlieghe 1987, p. 120, also notes that the Florence version, which he calls a copy, was first observed in the Grand-Ducal Collections of Tuscany, at Florence, ca. 1654–55.

24. Heinemann and Feulner 1937–41, no. 360.

25. See note 3 above.

26. See Berger 1883; Garas 1967; and Garas 1968.

27. Van Dyck, whose petition to paint the archduchess was refused, adapted Rubens's model in 1627, adding a curtain on the left side. Van Dyck's painting is also known in numerous versions, including one presented to the Dutch stadtholder Frederik Hendrik during Van Dyck's visit to The Hague in 1631. See A. Walsh 1994, pp. 228, 240n41. This may be the same painting noted as no. 73 in the 1632 inventory of the Palace at Noordeinde, "Een schilderie van de infante, hertoginne van Brabant." See Drossaers and Lunsingh Scheurleer 1974–76, vol. 147: 1632, Noordeinde, 210, no. 673. The 1632 inventory of the Palace at Noordeinde, one of the residences of Frederik Hendrik that served as the guest house for official visitors to the court, lists portraits of not only Isabella but also Charles V on horseback, Philip II, and Philip III. The paintings, which are unfortunately not attributed, appear in what are called the quarters of Amalia van Solms.

75

Workshop of Peter Paul Rubens

Flemish
Siegen 1577–1640 Antwerp

Portrait of Louis XIII, King of France

ca. 1622

Pendant to: *Portrait of Anne of Austria* (cat. 76)
Oil on canvas, 46½ × 38 in. (118.1 × 96.5 cm)
The Norton Simon Foundation, F.1965.1.060.P

Provenance[1]

Probably Isabella Clara Eugenia (1566–1633), Governor of the Spanish Netherlands, Coudenberg Palace, Brussels, by descent to; Cardinal Infante Ferdinand (1609–1641), Governor of the Spanish Netherlands, Coudenberg Palace, Brussels, by descent to; Archduke Leopold Wilhelm (1614–1662), Governor of the Spanish Netherlands, Coudenberg Palace, Brussels, where it remained until at least 1665, possibly 1698. Possibly Frederick I (1657–1713), Elector of Brandenberg, Duke of Prussia, after 1701, first King of Prussia, Schloss Charlottenburg, Berlin, by descent to his son; Frederick William I (1688–1740), Elector of Brandenburg and King of Prussia (r. 1713–40), Schloss Charlottenburg, Berlin, from at least 1725, by descent to his son;[2] Frederick II (1712–1786), Elector of Brandenburg and King of Prussia, Schloss Charlottenburg, Berlin, by descent to; Wilhelm II (1859–1941), King of Prussia, and 3rd Emperor of Germany (abdicated 1918), Schloss Charlottenburg, Berlin, sold by early 1928 to;[3] [Duveen Brothers, New York, stock no. 29280, sold 1965 to]; The Norton Simon Foundation.

Exhibited

Cincinnati 1933; Paris 1936, pp. 124f., no. 67; Detroit 1936, no. 25, ill.; New York 1943, no. 25; Los Angeles 1946, no. 26, ill.; Houston 1950, no. 13; on loan, Metropolitan Museum of Art, New York, 30 December 1965–23 March 1968; on loan, Minneapolis Institute of Art, 1 April–31 October 1968; on loan, Los Angeles County Museum of Art, 30 April 1969–13 September 1972; on loan, Museum of Fine Arts, Houston, 19 September–5 November 1973; Paris 2017, pp. 172n40, 174, 219, cover (detail), ill.

References

Mols n.d., no. 793; Winter 1768;[4] Oesterreich 1773, p. 97, no. 574;[5] Nicolai 1786, vol. 1, p. 1014; Rumpf 1823, vol. 2, p. 227;[6] Rooses 1886–92, vol. 4 (1890), p. 207, no. 980; Singleton 1929, pp. 176–80, ill.;[7] "Cincinnati Museum Notes" 1933, p. 127; Siple 1934, pp. 152, 184, 187, ill.; Valentiner 1936a, pp. 6–7, ill.; Richardson 1936, p. 63; "Detroit: Rubens" 1936, p. 181, ill.; Siple 1936, pp. 243–44; Carey 1936, p. 6; Decoen 1937, p. 46; Wescher 1937, p. 23; Glück 1940, pp. 178, 183, pl. IVa; Breuning 1946, p. 7; Frankfurter 1946, pp. 34–35, ill.; Millier 1946, p. 31; Valentiner 1946, p. 160, no. 80; Held and Goris 1947, p. 27, no. 8, pl. 22; De Hevesy 1948, pp. 97, 142; Valentiner 1948, p. 28; Larsen 1952, p. 217, no. 62; De Maeyer 1955, p. 126n5; Speth-Holterhoff 1957, p. 216n175; La Farge 1959b, p. 12; "Connoisseur's Diary" 1962, p. 261, ill., cover; Holmes 1964, pp. 67ff.; Huemer 1977, pp. 138–41, no. 21a, fig. 77; Moote 1989, p. 265, pl. 2, cover; Jaffé 1989, p. 270, no. 700; Pasadena 1989, p. 53; Hoff and Devapriam 1995, p. 258; Bernstock 2000, p. 161, fig. 25; Merle du Bourg 2004, pp. 26, 197f.; S. Campbell 2010, pp. 63, 445, no. D50a; Ducos 2011, p. 309.

Related Works

- Oil sketch, *Portrait of Louis XIII*, National Gallery of Victoria, Melbourne (fig. 75a).
- Engraving by Crispijn van de Passe II (ca. 1597–ca. 1670), in Antoine de Pluvinel (1552–1620), *Le Maneige Royal* (Paris, 1624).
- Engraving by J[acob]. Louys (1595 or 1600–1673) after P[ieter Claesz]. Soutman (ca. 1580–1657); see Voorhelm-Schneevoogt 1873, p. 172, no. 160.
- 17th-century French artist, *Portrait of a Man in Armor (possibly Louis XIII, King of France)*, oil on canvas mounted on fiberboard, 39½ × 33¼ in. (100.3 × 85.1 cm), Philadelphia Museum of Art, 1977-167-1084 (fig. 75b).
- David Teniers II (1610–1690), *Brussels Gallery No. 2*, ca. 1650, oil on canvas, 96 × 128 cm, Alte Pinakothek, Munich, inv. no. 1839.

Technical Notes

The support is a plain-weave canvas with the original tacking edges removed. There are slightly cusped threads along the top edge, stronger cusping at the right and bottom edges, and none at the left edge. James Roth, Kansas City, replaced a glue lining with a wax lining in 1969. The warm white ground appears rather thin. Microscopic examination revealed no underdrawing or underpainting. The opaque paint is generally smooth and of medium thickness, applied directly over the ground. Flesh tones are smoothly blended. Light colors were applied with thicker, opaque paint; cool shadows were thinly applied with nearly translucent paint. Some areas of the ground were left exposed, as in the right side of the lace collar where it overlaps the sky as well as in the fur trim of the cloak at lower left. Highlights, which were probably raised dots of white paint, have been flattened by lining. Brushmarking texture in general has been flattened in past interventions; chemical abrasion occurs throughout and is especially noticeable in the sky to the right of the head, in the blue cloak, and in the black armor. Fairly broad retouching might cause certain aspects of the artist's technique to be misunderstood (for example, the crisp contours might be the result of later strengthening). Retouching is found in all shadowed areas, such as the folds of the collar, all shadows throughout the cloak and armor, the plumes at right, the drapery at top right, under the chin, and in the hair. The 1969 treatment included varnishing with two different acrylic-resin solutions applied in thin layers.

Louis XIII (1601–1643) succeeded to the throne of France at the age of nine in 1610 following the murder of his father, Henry IV (1553–1610). He officially came of age in 1614, but his mother, Marie de' Medici (1575–1642), continued to rule as regent until 1617. In that year the young king personally ordered the murder of her chief minister, Concino Concini (1569–1617), Maréchal d'Ancre, and banished his mother to the

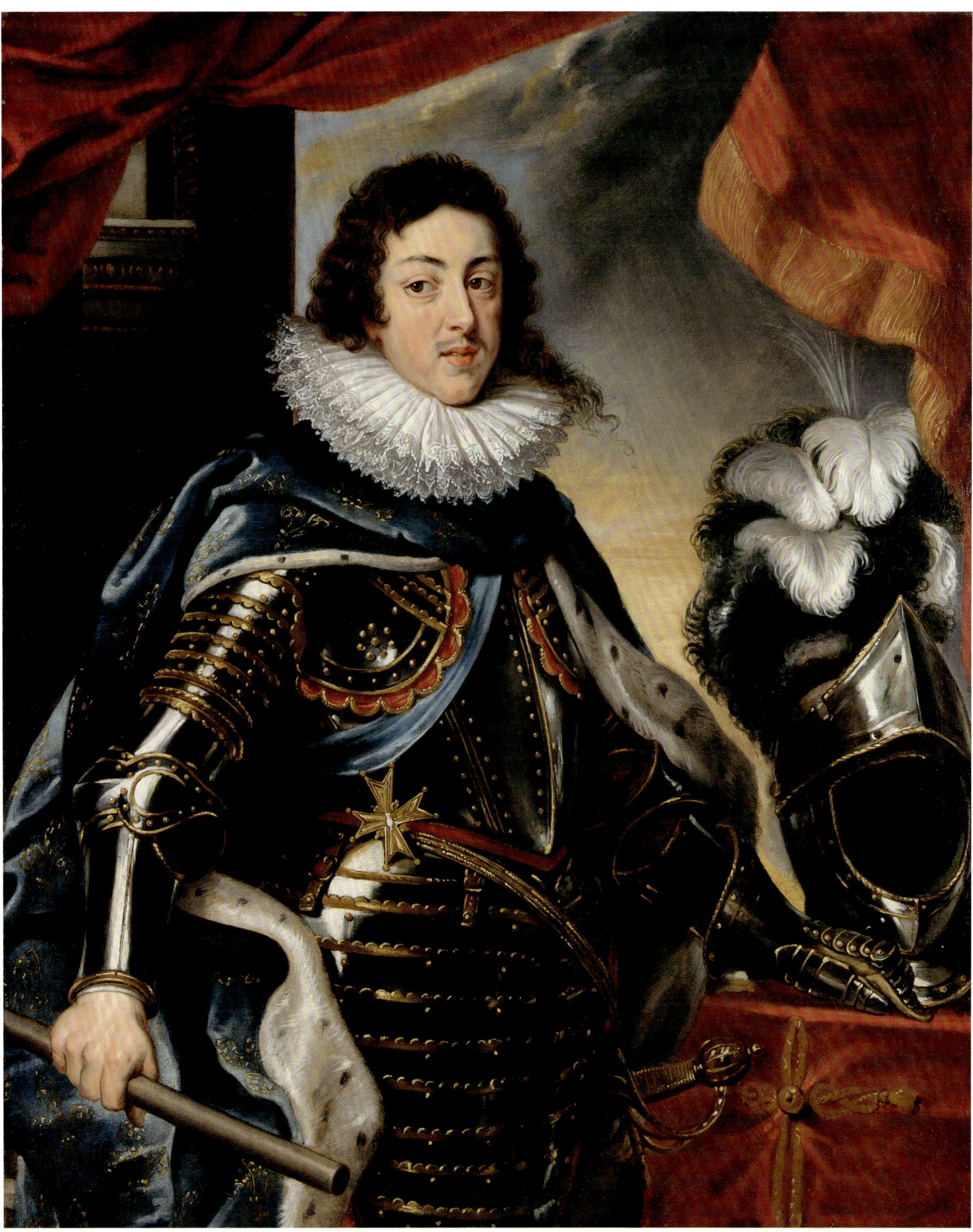

royal château at Blois. Less than two years later, in February 1619, Marie escaped from captivity and assembled an army supported by nobles against the authority of Louis's autocratic minister Charles d'Albert (1578–1621), Duke of Luynes. By August 1620 the king's army had suppressed the rebellion, and the queen mother, reconciled with her son, had returned to Paris. During the next two years, Louis followed an aggressive policy to restore former Catholic property to the church and to reestablish Catholic authority in nominally Protestant areas of France.[8] Louis's swift and successful response to the threats to his authority, as well as his belief in harsh justice, earned him the sobriquet "Le juste."[9]

Rubens arrived in Paris in early 1622 at the invitation of Marie de' Medici, who wanted the artist to decorate two galleries in her new residence, the Palais du Luxembourg, with two major painting cycles celebrating her life and that of her late husband, Henry IV.[10] Rubens brought with him a small dog wearing a collar decorated with twenty-four enameled plates, the gift of his patron Isabella (see cat. 74), Governor of the Spanish Netherlands, to the queen mother of France.[11] On 24 February Rubens and Marie de' Medici signed a contract to paint "twenty-four pictures in which will be represented the very illustrious life and heroic deeds of Madame the Queen."[12] Rubens was back in Antwerp in March. He returned to Paris during the spring of 1623, arriving in the city with the first nine paintings on 24 May 1623. He returned again to Paris in February 1625, when he brought the final fifteen paintings for the Marie de' Medici cycle. He was still in Paris at the time of the marriage by proxy of Marie's daughter Henrietta Maria (1609–1669) to Charles I (1600–1649) of England on 16 May 1625 and the official inauguration of the gallery of the Palais du Luxembourg on 27 May 1625.

It was probably during this first visit to Paris, from January to March 1622, that Rubens sketched the likenesses of the royal family, which he would need for the two large allegorical series commissioned by Marie de' Medici as well as for independent portraits.[13] Rubens's usual procedure was to make a drawing or oil sketch of the sitter from life, and then he or a member of his workshop would paint the formal portrait in his studio, without the sitter present. An unfinished portrait of Marie de' Medici and a portrait of the young queen, Anne of Austria (1601–1666), whom Louis XIII had married in 1615, appear as successive items in the inventory of Rubens's collection at the time of his death in 1640, suggesting that he had retained them as models.[14] A painting of the face of the young king, now in Melbourne (fig. 75a), is probably the sketch Rubens made of Louis XIII while in Paris and later used as the basis for portraits of the king, including the Pasadena portrait.[15] The stiff, unrefined quality of the costume and unexceptional treatment of the face in the Pasadena portrait of Louis XIII suggest that Rubens designed the composition but assigned its execution primarily to his workshop.

Louis wears ceremonial armor of polished steel ornamented with gold rivets and scallop trim and the white lace ruff and ermine-lined, bright blue silk cape of a courtier; the gold fleurs-de-lis embroidered on his cape are the emblem of the king of France. On his proper right side, at his waist, hangs the Cross of the Order of the Holy Spirit; on his left, a sword hangs from a gold belt. In the fist of his extended right arm the king clutches a baton, a symbol of leadership as well as strength and vigilance: He is a warrior-king. The antiquated helmet with its grand ostrich plumes was apparently a prop Rubens kept in his studio rather than an object belonging to the sitter.[16] Similar helmets appear in his other military portraits as well as in his later copy after Titian's (ca. 1488–1576) portrait of Holy Roman Emperor Charles V in armor. In conceiving the portrait of Louis XIII, Rubens probably referred to Titian's three-quarter portrait, which had established a powerful prototype for portraits of military heroes and rulers.[17] Rubens would have seen the famous portrait of the emperor when he was at the Spanish court in 1603, although it would not be until after his return to Madrid in the late 1620s that he would paint a copy of it.

No other versions of *Portrait of Louis XIII* by Rubens are known, but an unattributed portrait in the Philadelphia Museum of Art (fig. 75b) reflects the pose, lighting, and general appearance of the king in the Pasadena portrait.[18] In the Philadelphia portrait, however, the figure is pressing his right fist against his waist rather than grasping a baton. The Philadelphia painting also differs in execution, setting, and details such as the helmet and the absence of the royal cape and gauntlet, but the similarity of the armor in the two portraits, which differs from the actual armor of the king, suggests that the Philadelphia painting is based on the portrait of the king now in Pasadena.[19]

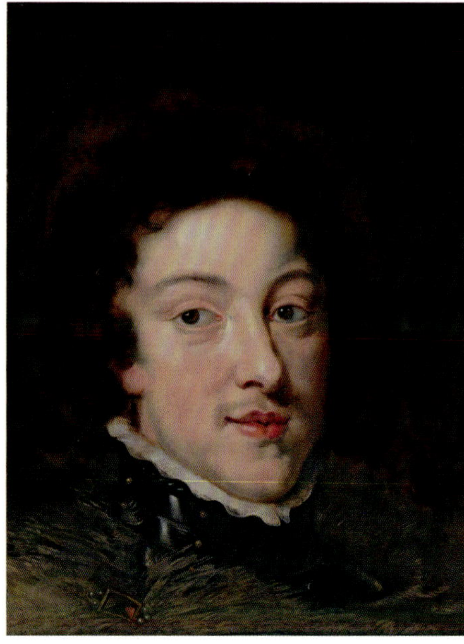

Fig. 75a. Peter Paul Rubens, *Louis XIII of France*, 1622, oil on paper on wood panel, 16 ¾ × 12 ⅞ in. (42.8 × 32.5 cm), National Gallery of Victoria, Melbourne, Everard Studley Miller Bequest, 1959.

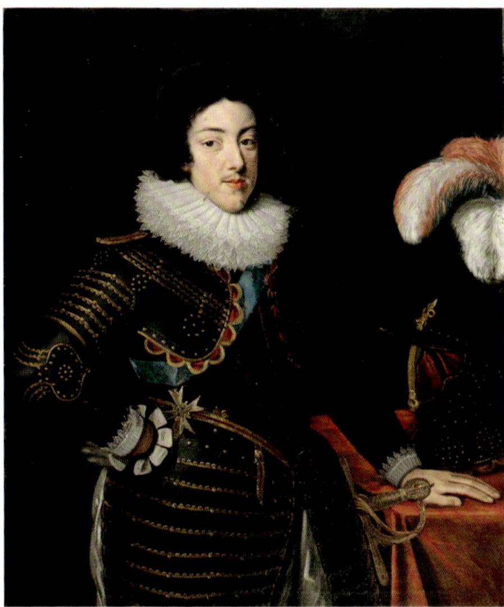

Fig. 75b. French, copy possibly after Frans Pourbus II, *Louis XIII*, 17th century, oil on canvas on fiberboard, 39½ × 33¼ in. (100.3 × 84.5 cm), Philadelphia Museum of Art, bequest of Carl Otto Kretzschmar von Kienbusch, 1977.

The *Portrait of Louis XIII* was painted to hang as a pendant to the *Portrait of Anne of Austria* (cat. 76), which was based on a portrait of Marie de' Medici by Frans Pourbus II (1569–1622), the queen mother's court painter who died while Rubens was in Paris.[20] In comparison with the portrait of her husband, that of Anne of Austria is compositionally self-contained and emotionally reserved. Hung together, the splendid blues and golds of the sitters' costumes unite the compositions, despite the differences in their backgrounds and stylistic renderings (see further discussion in the entry for cat. 76).

The commission for the portraits of Louis XIII and Anne of Austria is not known. There is no indication that the French court commissioned the paintings nor that they ever owned any versions of them. It is most likely that the portraits were painted for Rubens's patron, the Infanta Isabella, governor of the Spanish Netherlands.[21] Portraits of Louis XIII and Anne of Austria by Rubens—along with Anthony van Dyck's (1599–1641) three-quarter-length portraits of Charles I and Henrietta Maria of England and a portrait of *Isabella Clara Eugenia as a Poor Clare* by Van Dyck after Rubens—appear along the top row of the back wall in two paintings by David Teniers II (fig. 75c) of a gallery in Coudenberg Palace.[22] The palace was the official residence of the governors of the Spanish Netherlands in Brussels, where Teniers's patron, Archduke Leopold Wilhelm of Austria (1614–1662), lived from 1647 to 1656 before returning with his collection to Vienna. The portraits, which do not appear in either the 1649 or 1659 inventories of Leopold Wilhelm's famous collection, were among those that remained in the palace in Brussels, according to the instructions of Isabella's will.[23] They are recorded in three inventories of the palace made in 1659, 1665–70, and 1698 (possibly by March 1692).[24] By 1731, when the palace and much of its contents were

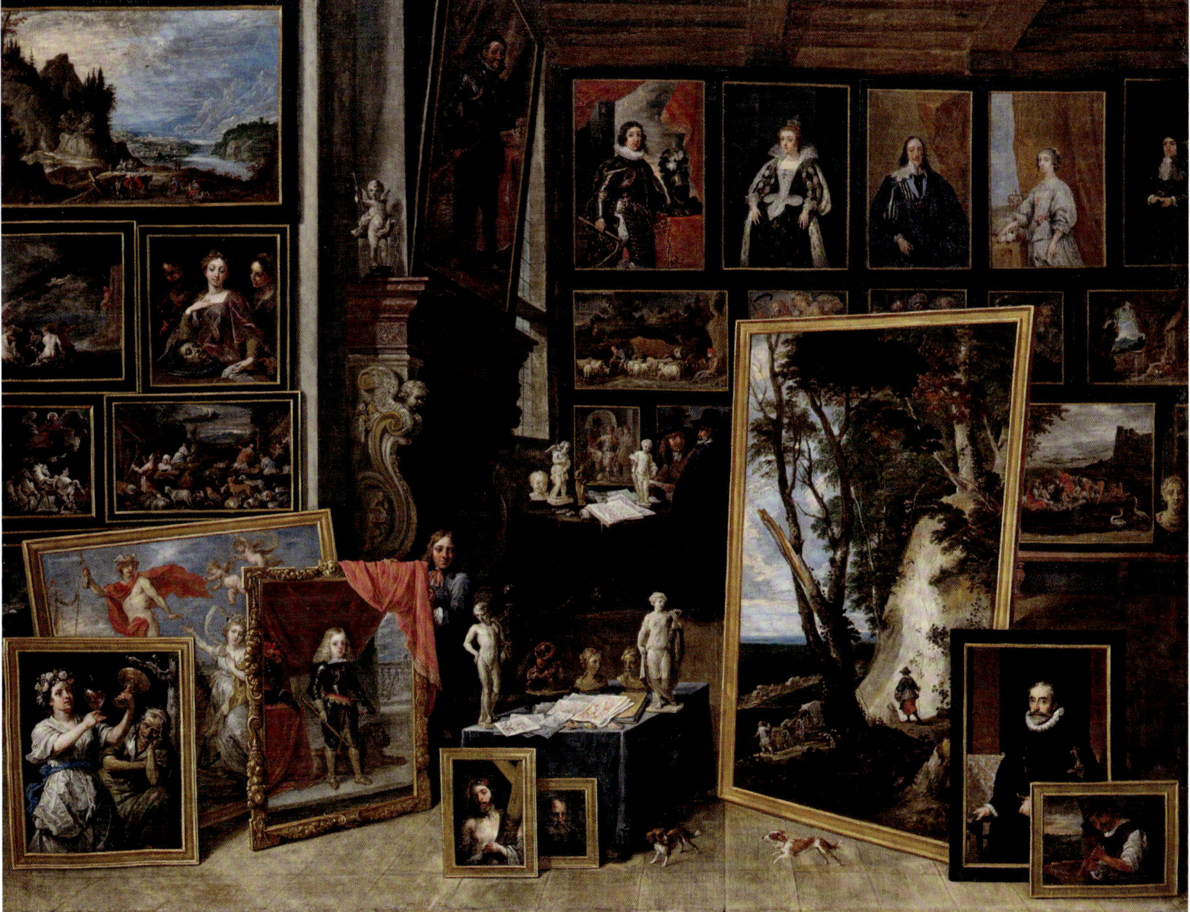

Fig. 75c. David Teniers II, *View of the Gallery of Archduke Leopold in Brussels (II)*, mid-17th century, oil on canvas, 37⅞ × 50⅜ in. (96 × 128 cm), Staatsgalerie Schleissheim, Bayerische Staatsgemäldesammlungen, Munich.

destroyed by fire, a large part of the collection had been dispersed piecemeal when funds were needed.[25] In 1708 the portraits of Charles I and Henrietta Maria by Van Dyck were among five paintings sold to the Duke of Marlborough.[26] The portraits of the French royal couple were thus probably sold or possibly given away during the early 1700s.

In 1725 the Pasadena paintings were recorded as in Schloss Charlottenburg, Berlin, one of the palaces of Frederick William I (1688–1740), King of Prussia. The king may have purchased them directly from the Brussels court, or he could have inherited them from his father, Frederick I (1657–1713), Elector of Brandenburg from 1688 to 1701. When he became the first king of Prussia, Frederick I sought to add prestige to his court through the decoration of his residences in Berlin. The possession of a gallery of royal portraits would have been a typical way of solidifying his public image.[27]

1. Rooses 1886–92, vol. 4 (1890), p. 207, no. 980, cites Mols n.d., no. 793, which mentions a 1725 document that locates the portraits of Louis and Anne at Charlottenburg. (With thanks to Michiel Verweij of the Bibliothèque Royale de Belgique for locating the exact citation in Mols's manuscript.) Rooses also mentions a portrait of Louis XIII by Rubens in the inventory of Quiryn van Biesum, Rotterdam, 18 October 1719; see Hoet 1752–70, vol. 1 (1752), p. 231. The portrait (lot 89), which was valued at ƒ44, was followed by lot 90, "De Reine Mère, door denzelven [Rubens]," valued at ƒ46. The "Reine Mère" may have been Marie de' Medici, but given the date of the inventory it may have been a reference to the mother of Louis XIV, Anne of Austria. The relatively low values of the paintings (in comparison with the ƒ500 for Van Dyck's full-length portrait of Abbot Veru in the same collection) suggests that the portraits of the French royal couple were workshop copies.

2. Frederick I was an important collector and Maecenas, who ca. 1706 owned about 2,500 paintings. His father had laid the foundation for the collection, and he added to it. As the grandson of Frederick William (1620–1688), Elector of Palatine and Brandenburg, known as the "Great Elector," and Louise Henriette (1627–1667), the daughter of the Dutch stadtholder Frederik Hendrik (1584–1647) and Amalia von Solms-Braunfels (1602–1675), he had inherited many of the paintings from his Dutch grandparents' collection, including works that had belonged to their grandson King William III (r. 1689–1702) of England and the Netherlands. Between 1720 and ca. 1754, his son and heir Frederick William I (r. 1713–40), King of Prussia, transferred the most valuable paintings from the stadtholder's residences to Berlin in four shipments. Frederick William's son and successor, Frederick II (r. 1740–86), shipped additional paintings to Berlin. It is possible that the Pasadena portraits of King Louis XIII and Anne of Austria were acquired by the Prussian royal collection directly from the sale of paintings from Coudenberg Palace or that they came through one of the collections of the heirs of Frederik Hendrik that were inherited by the Prussian kings. No portraits of Louis XIII or Anne of Austria by Rubens, however, appear in the collections of the stadtholder. See Vermeeren 1997–98, esp. pp. 73–75; and Winter 1768. Regarding Frederik Hendrik as a collector, see Hudig 1928; A. Walsh 1994; and The Hague 1997a and 1997b.

3. After the armistice of November 1918, Wilhelm II fled to the Netherlands, where he abdicated his throne and died in exile in 1941. The negotiations to sell the portrait of Louis XIII (incorrectly referred to in the documents as Louis III) were conducted in secrecy because of the suspected objections of the Germans. Wilhelm was a member of the Hohenzollern family.

4. According to Rooses 1886–92, vol. 4 (1890), p. 207.

5. "Rubens. 14 [reference to order within room]. Ludewig de Dreizehnte, König von Frankreich, halbe Figur in natüricher Größe." Hung in the concert room at Schloss Charlottenburg with twenty-six other paintings, including Rubens's *Portrait of Anne of Austria* (no. 578), which was not, however, hung immediately next to it, but presumably to its right.

6. As one of twenty-seven paintings in the Concert Room on the second floor of Charlottenburg.

7. As pendant to the portrait of Anne of Austria in the Museo Nacional del Prado, Madrid.

8. In 1624 Louis XIII entrusted Cardinal Richelieu (1585–1642) with total authority.

9. See Moote 1989.

10. Merle du Bourg 2004 publishes a document dated 9 September 1621 that indicates Armand-Jean du Plessis de Richelieu, then Bishop of Luçon and superintendent of Marie de' Medici's household, later Cardinal Richelieu, may have suggested and initiated contact with Rubens for the important commission. Merle du Bourg thus forces a revision of the reconstruction of the chronology of the commission by Held 1980, vol. 1, p. 89. Held knew of no mention of the commission before November 1621, when Nicolas-Claude Fabri de Peiresc (1580–1637), in a letter to Rubens, referred to the artist's planned visit to Paris, although he apparently did not know the purpose (Rooses and Ruelens 1887–1909, vol. 2 [1898], p. 294). The first actual mention of the commission known to Held was a letter from Peiresc to Rubens dated 23 December 1621 (Rooses and Ruelens 1887–1909, vol. 2 [1898], p. 319). By 11 January 1622, Peiresc had written in a letter to an Italian correspondent, Girolamo Aleandro, that Rubens had arrived in Paris because of the pictures for the queen's new palace (Rooses and Ruelens 1887–1909, vol. 2 [1898], p. 333).

11. De Maeyer 1955, p. 121.

12. Translation from Millen and Wolf 1989, p. 17. The contract, which was signed by the queen ("Marie"), her secretary Claude Bouthillier, Rubens ("Pietro Pauolo Rubens"), and two witnesses, Parque and Guerreau, is now in the Morgan Library and Museum, New York.

13. Huemer 1977, pp. 139f., notes the relationship of the Pasadena portrait and the engraving by Crispijn van de Passe II in Antoine de Pluvinel's book *Le Meneige Royal* (Paris, 1624) to the portrait of the king in *The Majority of Louis XIII* in the Medici series Rubens painted for the queen mother, now in the Louvre, Paris.

14. J. M. Muller 1989, p. 124, nos. 166–67. The paintings, which are now in the Museo Nacional del Prado, Madrid, were acquired from Rubens's estate by Philip IV of Spain after 1640. Two other paintings of Marie de' Medici by Rubens were acquired by Philip IV in 1659 from the former collection of Isabella (De Maeyer 1955, p. 435, doc. 270, [nos. 12–13]). One of those paintings may have been a finished version of the painting of Marie de' Medici that was left unfinished in Rubens's studio.

15. See Hoff and Devapriam 1995, p. 258; and Huemer 1977, no. 21, fig. 77. In addition to the Pasadena knee-length portrait, the sketch probably served as the model for a bust-length portrait of the king with a sash and cross known from the 1624 print by Crispijn van de Passe II (see Related Works above). The sketch may also have served as a model for an unattributed bust-length portrait of the king of France noted in inventories of Isabella's collection in Brussels: De Maeyer 1955, doc. 271, "Inventory of paintings, furnishings and sculpture in the palace of Brussels" [made after 12 January 1659], p. 436, [no. 12]: "Un retrato del rey de Francia Ludovico el Quarto [*sic*], hasta la cinta"; and doc. 275, "Inventory of paintings in Brussels, made between 1665–70 and 1698, probably before

March 1692," p. 460, [no. 123]: "Een borststuck, sonder leest, representerende den koninck van Vranckerijk."

16. Suggested in a letter dated 19 April 1979 to the Norton Simon Museum from Stuart W. Pyhrr of the Arms and Armor Department, Metropolitan Museum of Art, New York, citing the observation made by Holmes 1964 that the helmet does not belong to the armor worn by the king. Rather, the helmet is typical of those that sixteenth-century rulers wore for ceremonial events.

17. Titian's portrait of Charles V, which is now lost, is known by numerous copies, including full-length and three-quarter-length portraits by Juan Pantoja de la Cruz (1554–1608) from 1608 (Escorial, Madrid) and Rubens's version, painted ca. 1628–29, now in the Goepel collection, Detmold.

18. This is probably the painting noted by Huemer 1977, pp. 139f., as having been in the collection of the former Italian royal family and sold from the sale of "Furniture and Works of Art from the Castle formerly occupied by the Savoy Family in Venzuolo (Piedmont), Italy," American Art Association, New York, 16–18 February 1922, lot 396, ill., as A. Sánchez Coello. Huemer notes it was attributed to Pourbus by Ludwig Burchard and shows the same armor as is seen in the Pasadena portrait. In February 2010, in a conversation with the author, Blaise Ducos questioned the attribution to Pourbus of the original image upon which the Philadelphia painting is based.

19. See discussion by Holmes 1964, p. 69, who notes specific details such as the rivet heads of the Paris armor, which are all shaped like fleurs-de-lis—a detail included in later portraits of the king by Philippe de Champaigne (1602–1674; see, for example, Museo Nacional del Prado, Madrid, no. 2240). Holmes rightly suggests that Rubens typically would have been careful to render these details in his painting had he had the armor in front of him as he painted.

20. As painter to the French court, Pourbus had painted numerous portraits of the fifteen-year-old king at the time of his marriage. See, for example, the portrait of Louis painted in 1616 (Staatliche Kunsthalle Karlsruhe, inv. no. 2803). Ducos 2011 suggests that the presumed portrait of his bride, Anne of Austria (Staatliche Kunsthalle Karlsruhe, inv. no. 2804), is actually a portrait of Louis's sister, Elizabeth, the future queen of Spain.

21. As J. M. Muller 1989, p. 145, suggests, the portraits listed in the inventory of Rubens's collection at the time of his death probably represent sketches or finished paintings he kept on hand to satisfy such demands for additional portraits.

22. In addition to the painting now in the Staatsgalerie Schleissheim, Munich (fig. 75c), Rubens's portraits of Louis XIII and Anne of Austria also appear in Teniers's *Gallery of Archduke Leopold Wilhelm, Brussels*, 1641 (Staatsgalerie Stuttgart).

23. Leopold Wilhelm acquired most of his collection after becoming governor of the Spanish Netherlands in 1647; many of his paintings came from the sales of the great picture galleries of England, including the collections of the Dukes of Buckingham and Hamilton (1649) and that of Lord and Lady Arundel (beginning in 1654), but, surprisingly, not that of Charles I. Leopold Wilhelm's collection was the genesis of the Kunsthistorisches Museum in Vienna. Regarding the collection of Leopold Wilhelm, see Garas 1967 and Garas 1968. The 1659 inventory of Leopold Wilhelm's collection indicates that he owned 1,402 pictures, 517 of which were Italian and 885 of which were German and Netherlandish. In addition, the archduke acquired and sent to Prague approximately 100 paintings.

24. De Maeyer 1955, doc. 271, "Inventory of paintings, furnishings and sculpture in the palace of Brussels" [made after 12 January 1659], p. 436, [no. 2]: "Un retrato del rey de Ingalatera, hasta las rodillas, hecho por Van Dyck"; [no. 3]: "Otro del mismo tamaño, de la reynea su muyer, del dicho maestro"; [no. 5]: "Un retrato del rey de Francia Ludovico el Quarto [*sic*], hasta las rodillas, de Rubens"; [no. 6]: "Otro de la reyna, su muger, del mismo tamaño, hecho por el dicho Rubens"; p. 441, [no. 100]: "Otro de dicho maestre [Rubens], representando la infanta doña Isabel vestida en religiosa"; doc. 275, "Inventory of paintings, furnishings, and sculpture of the court at Brussels" [made between 1665–70 and 1698, probably before March 1692], p. 457, [no. 53]: "Het contrefeijtsel, kniestuck, van d'infante Isabella op haer religeus gekleet, geschildert van Rubbens"; [no. 64]: "Een kniestuck, het portrait van den koninck van Vranckerijck, Louis den Dertienden"; p. 458, [no. 65]: "Een kniestuck, wesende 't contrefeijtsel van sijne huysvrouwe"; p. 458, [no. 86]: "Een contrefeytsel, kniestuck, den koninck van Engelant Carolus Primus, geschildert van Van Deijck;" [no. 87]: "Item de koninginne , sijne huijsvrouwe, gheteeckent als in margine."

25. For a list of property destroyed in and saved from the fire, see De Maeyer 1955, docs. 279–81.

26. De Maeyer 1955, doc. 277.

27. See note 3 above.

76

Workshop of Peter Paul Rubens

Flemish
Siegen 1577–1640 Antwerp

Portrait of Anne of Austria, Queen of France

ca. 1622

Pendant to: *Portrait of Louis XIII* (cat. 75)
Oil on canvas, 47⅛ × 38⅛ in. (119.7 × 96.8 cm)
The Norton Simon Foundation, F.1965.1.059.P

Provenance

Probably Isabella Clara Eugenia (1566–1633), Governor of the Spanish Netherlands, Coudenberg Palace, Brussels, by descent to; Cardinal Infante Ferdinand (1609–1641), Governor of the Spanish Netherlands, Coudenberg Palace, Brussels, by descent to; Archduke Leopold Wilhelm (1614–1662), Governor of the Spanish Netherlands, Coudenberg Palace, Brussels, where it remained until at least 1665, possibly 1698. Possibly Frederick I (1657–1713), Elector of Brandenberg, Duke of Prussia, after 1701, King of Prussia, Schloss Charlottenburg, Berlin, by descent to his son;[1] Frederick William (1688–1740), Elector of Brandenburg and King of Prussia, Schloss Charlottenburg, Berlin, by 1725,[2] by descent to his son; Frederick II (1712–1786), Elector of Brandenburg and King of Prussia, Schloss Charlottenburg, Berlin, by descent to; Wilhelm II (1859–1941), King of Prussia and Emperor of Germany (abdicated 1918), Schloss Charlottenburg, Berlin, sold 1928 to; [Duveen Brothers, London and New York, stock no. 29761, sold 1965 to]; The Norton Simon Foundation.

Exhibited

New York 1943, no. 26, ill.; Los Angeles 1946, no. 27, ill.; Houston 1950, no. 13; on loan, Metropolitan Museum of Art, New York, 30 December 1965–23 March 1968; on loan, Minneapolis Institute of Art, 1 April–31 October 1968; on loan, Los Angeles County Museum of Art, 30 April 1969–13 September 1972; on loan, Museum of Fine Arts, Houston, 19 September–5 November 1973; Paris 2017, pp. 172–74, 219, no. 41, ill., back cover (detail).

References

Mols 1725, fol. 152v, no. 793; Winter 1768;[3] Oesterreich 1773, p. 98, no. 578; Rumpf 1823, vol. 2, p. 227;[4] Rooses 1886–92, vol. 4 (1890), pp. 124, noted under no. 887;[5] Paris 1936, p. 124, noted under no. 67; Glück 1940, pp. 178, 183, pl. IVb; Millier 1946, p. 31; Valentiner 1946, p. 163, no. 81, ill.; Valentiner 1948, p. 28; De Hevesy 1948, pp. 97, 142; Larsen 1952, p. 217, no. 63a;[6] La Farge 1959b, p. 12; Huemer 1977, pp. 138–41, no. 22, fig. 72; Moote 1989, p. 265, pl. 3; Jaffé 1989, p. 270, no. 701, ill.; Scarpa Sonino 1992, p. 100; Ost 2000, p. 66, fig. 9; Merle du Bourg 2004, pp. 26, 197f.; S. Campbell 2010, pp. 63, 445, no. D50b; Ducos 2011, p. 309, no. P. C. 48, rejects attribution to Frans Pourbus II.

Related Works

- Engraving, known with two different borders, by J[acob] Louys (1595 or 1600–1673) after P[ieter] C[laesz.] Soutman (ca. 1580–1657); see Voorhelm-Schneevoogt 1873, nos. 161–62.
- Copy with slight variations, including lighter hair, 52½ × 39⅞ in.; collection of Mrs. E. E., New York, 1952; see Larsen 1952, fig. 109, p. 170, where the author suggests it should be dated about 1650; Larsen does not mention the Pasadena painting, which was then with Duveen Brothers.

Technical Notes

The original support is a plain-weave canvas with portions of each tacking edge remaining. A large tear at the lower left and a smaller complex tear to the left of the head have been repaired. The canvas is lined, and the painting's surface texture has been altered. X-radiography indicates that the thin white ground was vigorously applied with large brushes or possibly a spatula. Especially along the left side of the painting and at the top edge, it was applied somewhat randomly or spontaneously. The opaque paint was applied directly over the ground; flesh tones were smoothly blended. The lace collar originally extended higher behind the head, as revealed in the X-radiograph. The decorative fleurs-de-lis in the brocade of the gown are not correctly adapted to the three-dimensional folds of the underlying fabric, as if they were added later. The paint in the figure is fairly well preserved, with few losses. Records from a 1969 conservation treatment by James Roth, Kansas City, state that the background had previously been completely repainted to cover losses and abrasion. The hair had also been repainted, considerably altering the original. The painting now has extensive retouching, and the background has been repainted again. Almost all the shadows in the folds of the dress have been broadly strengthened. There are scattered spots of retouching in the face and in both hands. The varnish consists of two different synthetic-resin layers of moderate thickness.

On 2 November 1615, after years of protracted diplomatic negotiations and maneuvers by Marie de' Medici (1575–1642), regent for her son Louis XIII of France (1601–1643), to arrange a double marriage between France and Spain, the Spanish Infanta Anne of Austria (1601–1666) was exchanged at the Franco-Spanish border for Elisabeth of France (1602–1644), who was to marry Philip IV of Spain (1605–1665). Rubens commemorated the event in the cycle of paintings for Marie de' Medici's Palais du Luxembourg (today in the Louvre, Paris). The daughter of Philip III of Spain (1578–1621) and Margaret of Austria (1584–1611), sister of Emperor Ferdinand II (1578–1637), Anne was destined to marry the young king of France, Louis XIII. Both were only fourteen at the time of their marriage by proxy in Burgos on 24 November 1615. From the beginning, Anne's attachments to the Roman Catholic Church and Spain made her loyalty to the French crown suspect. Largely ignored by her husband, Anne flirted with the Duke of Buckingham

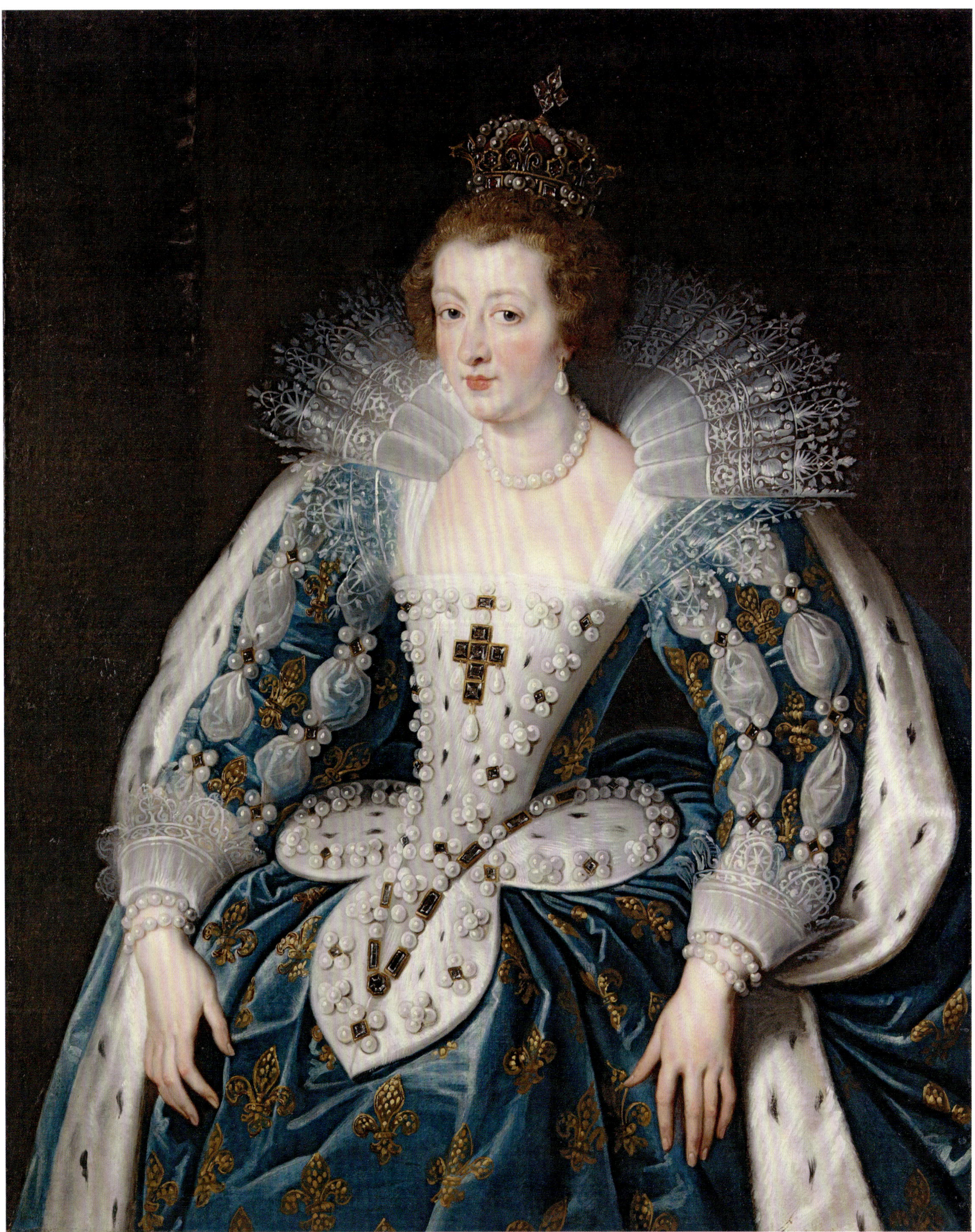

(1592–1628) and was implicated in court intrigues.[7] In 1638, after suffering a series of miscarriages, Anne gave birth to the future Louis XIV (1638–1715). Following the death of Louis XIII in 1643 (and against his wishes), Anne was named regent for the young Louis XIV, entrusting the government to Cardinal Mazarin (1602–1661). After Mazarin's death in 1661, Anne's role in governing France ended.

Praised for her exceptional beauty, Anne of Austria was twenty-one when she sat for Rubens in Paris in 1622. Rubens had arrived in the city in January to discuss the commission for the Marie de' Medici series for Palais du Luxembourg. The Infanta Isabella, Governor of the Spanish Netherlands, may have requested that Rubens bring her portraits of the French royal family. In addition to having diplomatic ties with the French court, Isabella was the aunt of the young queen.[8] By March 1622 Rubens was back in Antwerp, where he received a letter dated 14–15 April from his friend Nicolas-Claude Fabri de Pieresc (1580–1637), who said he was glad to hear that the Infanta Isabella, Rubens's patron, was pleased with the portraits of Marie de' Medici and Anne of Austria.[9] The portraits are presumed to be those of the two queens dressed in black in mourning for Anne's father, Isabella's brother, Philip III, who died in 1621. The portraits (figs. 76a–b) remained in Rubens's studio and were acquired from his estate by Philip IV of Spain.[10] The fresh immediacy of the unfinished portraits suggests that Rubens retained them as models from which he and his workshop could make other likenesses, including those for the Luxembourg series.[11]

Isabella probably requested that Rubens paint ceremonial portraits of Anne and Louis XIII (cat. 75) to hang in her gallery of heads of state. Two portraits of the king and queen by Rubens appear along the top row in a representation of the gallery of Leopold Wilhelm, Isabella's successor, painted by David Teniers II (1610–1690; fig. 75c)[12] and mentioned in inventories of the archducal collections at Coudenberg Palace, Brussels, from at least 1659 until possibly as late as 1698.[13] The portraits were probably painted shortly after Rubens's return to Antwerp from Paris in March 1622. The portrait of Anne was modeled on the state portrait of Marie de' Medici (fig. 76c) painted in 1611 by Frans Pourbus II (1569–1622) as a pendant to a portrait of Henry IV in armor. Rubens would have seen the portrait of the queen mother in Paris and possibly also in Brussels, where a portrait of the queen of France in her ceremonial robes is recorded in 1659.[14] Pourbus's portrait of Marie de' Medici was easily adapted as the model—formally and iconographically—for

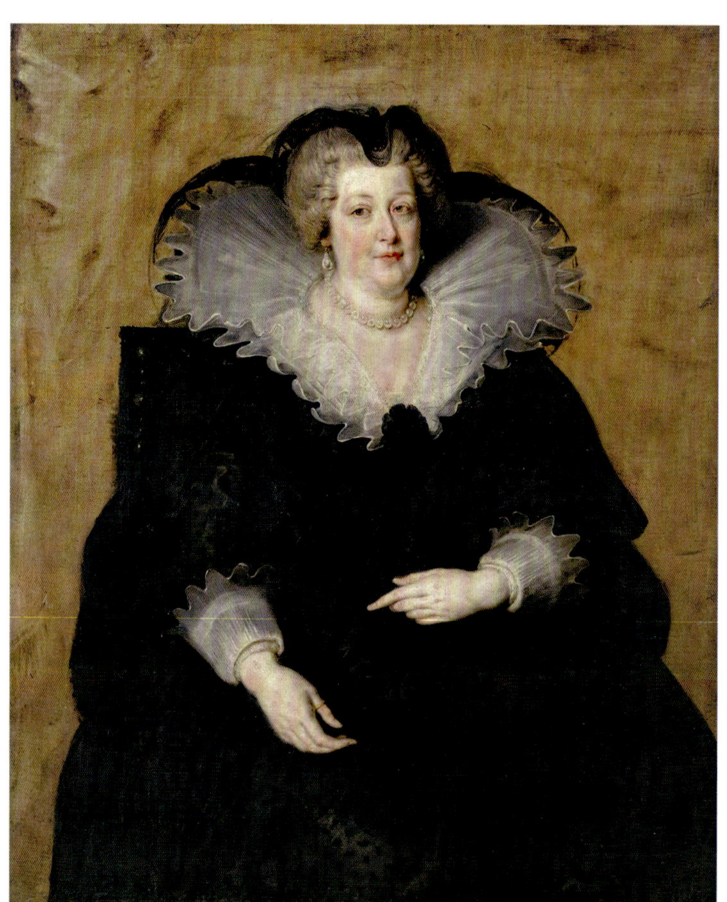

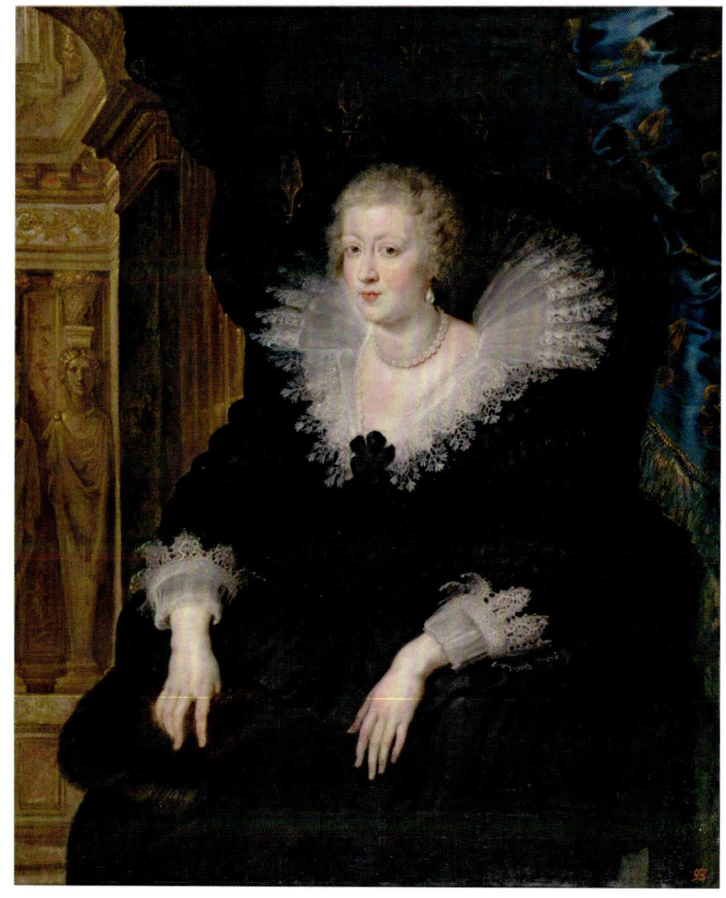

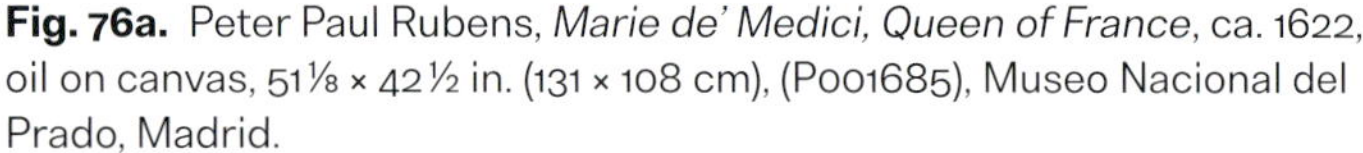

Fig. 76a. Peter Paul Rubens, *Marie de' Medici, Queen of France*, ca. 1622, oil on canvas, 51⅛ × 42½ in. (131 × 108 cm), (P001685), Museo Nacional del Prado, Madrid.

Fig. 76b. Peter Paul Rubens, *Anne of Austria, Queen of France*, ca. 1622, oil on canvas, 51⅛ × 42½ in. (130 × 108 cm), (P001689), Museo Nacional del Prado, Madrid.

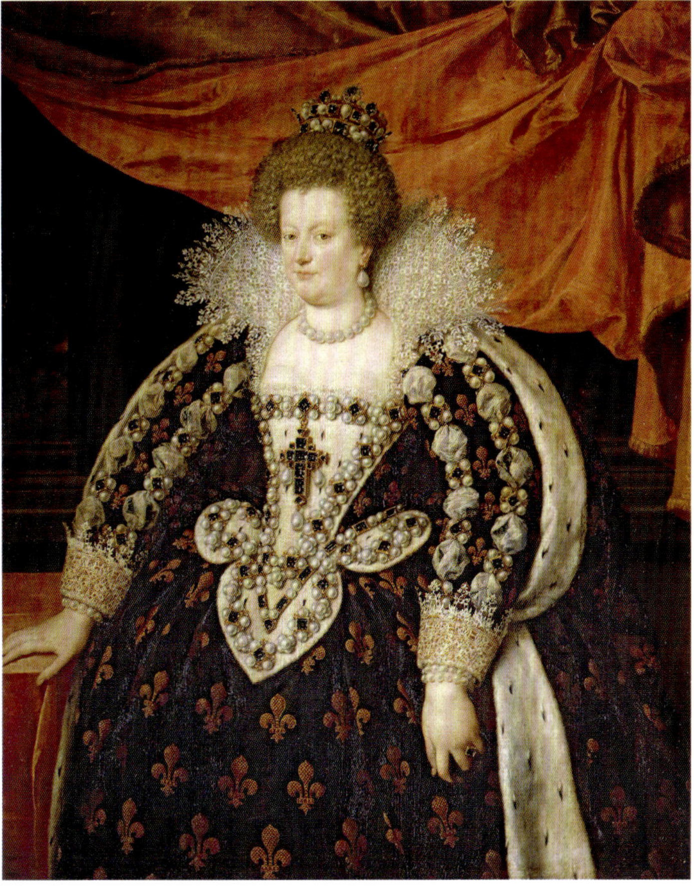

Fig. 76c. Frans Pourbus II, *Marie de' Medici, Queen of France*, 1611, oil on canvas, 56 × 50 in. (142 × 127 cm), Palazzo Pitti, Florence.

the portrait of Anne of Austria. Dressed in their coronation robes, the French queens appear in identical three-quarter-length poses. The portrait of Anne is, however, more focused, as the artist has omitted the architectural setting, the table, and the bunched hangings above Marie's head. Both women wear elegant blue silk gowns and stomachers of ermine embroidered with gold and ornamented with large pearls and jewels in the shape of fleurs-de-lis. A delicate standing linen "Medici collar" with fine Venetian lace gracefully frames the neck and head of each woman, and similar jeweled crowns balance on their heads.[15] Anne turns slightly to address the portrait of her husband, Louis XIII (cat. 75), which hung to her right, the viewer's left. The embroidered blue silk of her gown and ermine-lined cape match Louis's mantle and help to relate the portraits visually.

Ludwig Burchard recognized Rubens's hand in the rendering of the face and hands of the Pasadena portrait of Anne and also the influence of Pourbus's portrait of Marie de' Medici. Burchard suggested that Rubens may have completed a portrait begun by Pourbus, who died in February 1622 while Rubens was in Paris.[16] According to Blaise Ducos, however, it is doubtful that Marie de' Medici would ever have allowed Pourbus, her favorite court painter, to paint a portrait of Anne, of whom the queen mother was extremely jealous.[17] Citing weaknesses in the description of the figure of Anne and her costume that others have also noted, he dismisses the participation of either Pourbus or Rubens, two of the greatest portraitists of the seventeenth century.[18] The plastic quality of the forms, the costume, and the fussy details are uncharacteristic of Rubens and differ significantly from the freer handling of his contemporary portrait of the queen now in the Museo Nacional del Prado, Madrid.

Returning to Antwerp from Paris in 1622 with sketches of the royal couple he needed for the Luxembourg series, Rubens probably assigned his workshop to paint the Pasadena formal portraits of Anne of Austria and Louis XIII to hang as pendants in Isabella's portrait gallery in Brussels. Although likely based on Rubens's design, there is no evidence that he painted an "original" version of the portraits of the French royal couple that served as the model for the Pasadena paintings. Nor is there reason to believe that Isabella, as governor of the Spanish Netherlands, would have made copies of the portraits of the French king and queen to be distributed to other courts. Her interest was in diplomatically associating herself with the French monarchy through the images of Anne of Austria and Louis XIII.

Following the wishes of the Infanta Isabella, who stipulated in her will that the paintings in her three galleries at Brussels should remain in Coudenberg Palace, both portraits of Anne of Austria and Louis XIII remained in the archduchal collection in Brussels and did not go to Vienna with Leopold Wilhelm, governor of the Spanish Netherlands from 1647 to 1656. In addition to respecting the wishes of Isabella, it is likely that Leopold Wilhelm would have considered the portraits of the French monarchs out of date. Louis XIII and Anne are represented in his collection by later, more fashionably baroque portraits by Rubens's collaborator Justus van Egmont (1601–1674).[19] The Pasadena portraits, which were in the collection of the kings of Prussia by 1725, are probably those previously in the archduchal collection at Coudenberg Palace, Brussels until the late seventeenth century.

1. See cat. 75, note 2.

2. Mols n.d., no. 893.

3. Mentioned by Rooses 1886–92, vol. 4 (1890), p. 124, no. 887; on p. 207 Rooses cites Mols n.d., no. 89, which mentions a 1725 manuscript that documents the portraits of Louis and Anne were by then at Charlottenburg. With thanks to Michiel Verweij at the Bibliothèque Royale de Belgique for locating the exact citation for us.

4. Among twenty-seven paintings in the Concert Room on the second floor of Charlottenburg.

5. As in the collection of Charlottenburg in 1768.

6. "Another version of [Anne of Austria], cut down to be a companion piece to no. 62 [in Larsen 1952, referring to cat. 75 in this volume, Workshop of Peter Paul Rubens, *Portrait of Louis XIII, King of France*]. Probably the replica exacted by the Duchesse of Chevreuse from Rubens in payment of political information. Duveen Bros., Inc. New York, N.Y." Larsen calls a painting formerly in the collection of Mrs. E. E., New York (present location unknown; oil on canvas, approx. 130 × 100 cm) the "official court portrait, engraved by L. Louys and probably identical with the No. 167 listed in Rubens' estate. Dating from ca. 1625." The painting from Rubens's estate was, however, purchased by Philip IV and is now in the Museo Nacional del Prado, Madrid. The quality of the New York version is markedly weaker than that of the Pasadena version.

7. Moote 1989, p. 193, notes that Louis XIII believed Anne knew of plotting to remove him from the throne and replace him with his younger brother, Gaston. He apparently also thought that the queen planned to marry his successor. Alexandre Dumas père fictionalized a rumored affair between Anne of Austria and the Duke of Buckingham in *The Three Musketeers*.

8. When Rubens went to Madrid in 1628 to deliver eight paintings sent as a gift to the king from the infanta, Isabella commissioned the artist to paint for her portraits of all the Spanish royal family. See De Maeyer 1955, p. 125.

9. Nicolas-Claude Fabri de Pieresc to Rubens, 14–15 April 1622,: "M'è tutto carissimo d'intendere che con tanto gusto dell'Infanta si siano ricevuti i ritratti delle Regine; di che mene rallegro non poco con V. S." See Rooses and Ruelens 1887–1909, vol. 2, pp. 380f.

10. Jaffé 1989, nos. 697–98. See Huemer 1977, nos. 2 and 27. The paintings are nos. 166 and 167 in catalogue 1 of Rubens's collection (J. M. Muller 1989, p. 124). Rubens painted the portraits of the two women, who sit facing each other, to hang together as pendants. This pairing appears to have been rather unusual but perhaps reflects the powerful role Marie de' Medici maintained at court. After the death of Louis's autocratic minister Charles d'Albert (1578–1621), Duke of Luynes, and reconciliation with her son in 1621 (see cat. 75 in this volume), the queen mother dominated Anne of Austria. The two often appeared together in public, and Marie frequently took over the young queen's role as hostess, holding receptions at the Palais du Luxembourg rather than at the Louvre. A second portrait of Anne appears as no. 120 in the same catalogue of Rubens's collection (J. M. Muller 1989, p. 117). Huemer 1977, no. 3, identifies this as the portrait of the queen known by versions in the Rijksmuseum, Amsterdam, and in the Louvre, Paris.

11. See J. M. Muller 1989, p. 60.

12. In an unpublished entry on the painting from the early 1970s, Michael Jaffé notes, "Besides heightening the proportions of both portraits, Teniers took the further liberty of elaborating the backcloth behind the figure of the Queen" (NSM).

13. See cat. 74, note 24.

14. De Maeyer 1955, doc. 271, "1659, after 12 January, Inventory of the paintings, furnishings and sculpture in the palace at Brussels," no. 21: "Otro retrato a lo natural de la reyna de Francia, vestida conun bestido sembrado con flores de le y aforrado con pellagos blancos." The portraits of Louis XIII and Anne appear as nos. 5 and 6 in the same inventory of the grand gallery in Brussels, which was where the official portraits were displayed. According to Michael Jaffé, unpub. MS, pp. 1–2, (NSM), the prime version of Pourbus's three-quarter-length portrait of Marie de' Medici had been intended for Christina of Lorraine, Regent of Tuscany, but Marie kept the painting for herself. A replica of the portrait by Pourbus was ready to be sent to Florence on 15 February 1613 but was monogrammed and dated *F. P. F. Ao 1611*. That painting and its pendant hang together in the Appartamenti Imperiali e Reali of the Palazzo Pitti, Florence. Ducos 2011, p. 309, notes that numerous images of Anne of Austria, inspired by Pourbus's portrait of Marie de' Medici, were in circulation during the 1620s.

15. Jaffé, unpub. MS, p. 2 (NSM), notes that Rubens made "appropriate changes in the crown and in the pectoral cross in order to avoid competition with the setting envisaged for his *Louis XIII*."

16. Huemer 1977, p. 142, agrees with the suggestion made by Burchard "that Pourbus who was buried on 19 February 1622 had just time to begin the painting and that it was finished by Rubens, who, furthermore, tried to imitate the style of his predecessor especially in the face."

17. Blaise Ducos, personal communication to the author, February 2010. Ducos believes that the presumed portraits of Anne as a teenager (see, for example, the portraits of the young king and queen painted by Pourbus in 1616, now in the Staatliche Kunsthalle Karlsruhe) are actually portraits of Elizabeth of France, Louis's sister who married Philip IV of Spain.

18. Huemer 1977, p. 142, cites Burchard's notes. Details of Anne's costume in the Pasadena painting are awkward: the fleurs-de-lis are heavy and, rather than flowing with the fabric, appear almost "pasted" onto the costume. The artist also does not make effective use of the underpaint to define the ermine. The relationship of the dress to the body, especially the neck, is also awkward.

19. Berger 1883, p. cxxxv, listed as nos. 383 (Louis XIII) and 385 (Anne) in the 1659 inventory. The paintings remain in the collection of the Kunsthistorisches Museum, Vienna.

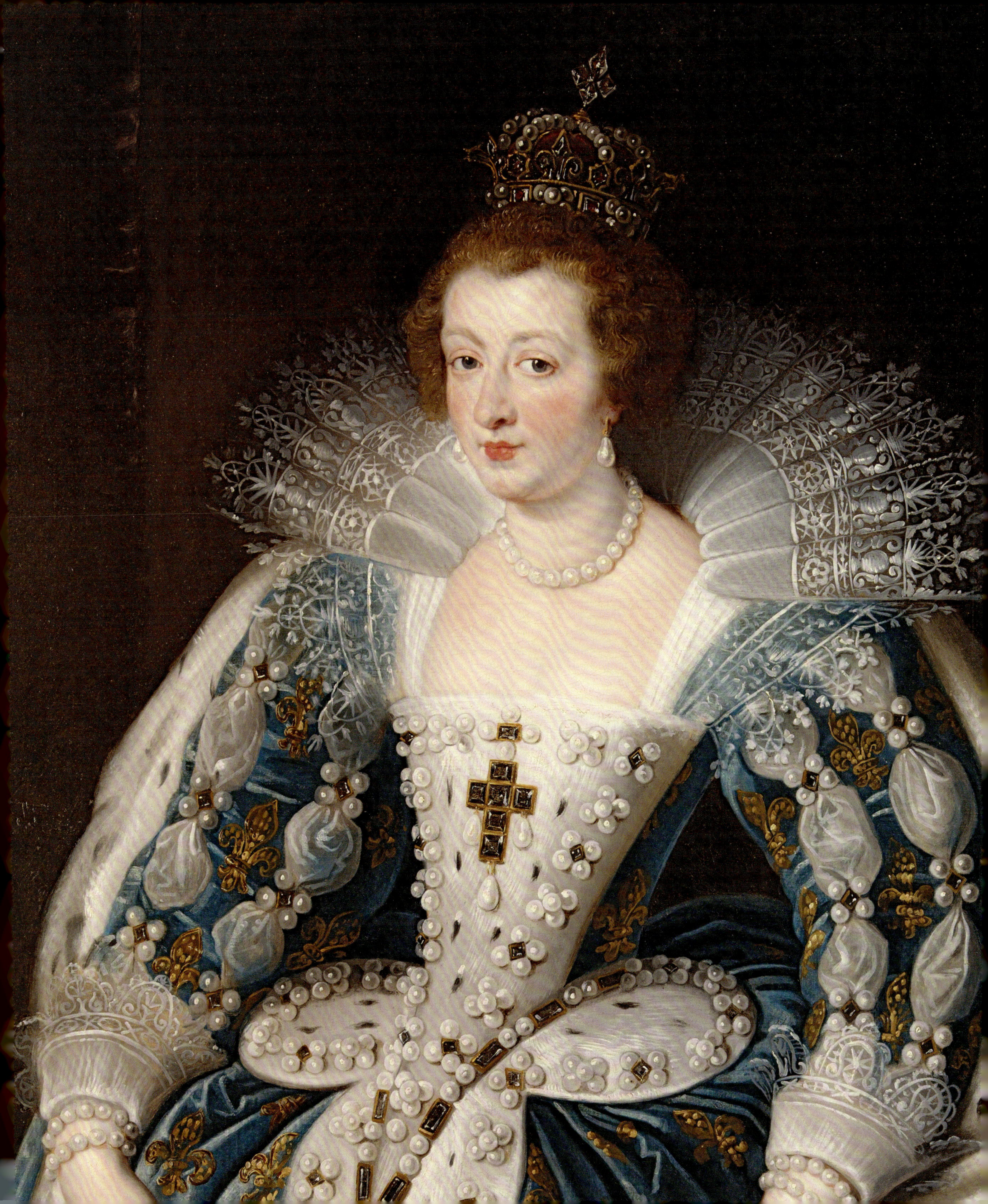

77

Jacob van Ruisdael

Dutch
Haarlem 1628/29–1682 Haarlem?

and

Nicolaes Berchem

Dutch
Haarlem 1621/22–1683 Amsterdam

Wooded Landscape with a Pool and Figures

ca. 1655

Signed, lower right: "JvRuisdael" (*JvR* in ligature)

Oil on panel, 27⅝ × 36¼ in. (70.2 × 92.1 cm)
Norton Simon Art Foundation, M.1969.33.P

Provenance
Reginald Hooper (1846–1898), Southbrook House, Starcross, Devon (sale, Christie's, London, 22 July 1893, lot 71, sold for £404 5s. to);[1] [Martin Colnaghi, London, sold 1894 to]; Sir Joseph B. Robinson, Bart. (1840–1929), London and South Africa[2] (sale, Christie's, London, 6 July 1923, lot 87, bought in at 900 guineas),[3] by descent to his daughter; Ida, Princess Labia (1880–1961), London and Cape Town.[4] [Thomas Agnew & Sons, London, sold 1968 to]; [P. & D. Colnaghi, London, sold 1969 to]; Norton Simon Art Foundation.

Exhibited
London 1894, no. 71; London 1958, p. 14, no. 12, ill.; Cape Town 1959, no. 57, ill.; Zurich 1962, no. 37; London 1968b, no. 18; on loan, Phoenix Art Museum, 6 December 1969–28 April 1970; on loan, Los Angeles County Museum of Art, 29 April 1970–7 July 1972; Princeton 1972–74, no. 9.

References
Hofstede de Groot 1908–27, vol. 4 (1912), p. 185, no. 586, figs. by Berchem, ca. 1650; J. Rosenberg 1928, p. 92, no. 335;[5] "Cape Town: Robinson" 1958, p. 96, no. 12; Schaar 1958, p. 36; J. R. Martin 1972, pp. 34, 44f., no. 9, ill.; Steadman 1973, p. 8; Gerson 1976, p. 171, fig. 10; Pasadena 1980, p. 64, ill.; P. Sutton 1986, p. 217; Pasadena 1989, p. 65, ill.; Slive 2001, pp. 250, 308, no. 408; Pasadena 2003, p. 60, ill.; Philadelphia/Los Angeles/London 2005–06, p. 8; S. Campbell 2010, pp. 95, 101n61, 326, no. 680, ill.; A. Walsh 2019b, p. 158.

Technical Notes
The uncradled wood support is composed of three horizontally grained oak boards with tightly closed joins that are flush on the front surface and slightly offset on the reverse to accommodate the variation in thickness of the three boards. The edges have shallow bevels. The thin smooth ground is a rose-beige color, and the texture of the wood remains faintly visible. Paint was applied directly over the ground with a variety of brushstrokes. The sky was strongly brushed with rich, opaque paint, where brushmarking is distinct. The artist's semidry brush left small gaps in the paint, allowing the rosy ground to show through. Tree leaves are short light dabs of fluid paint, applied with a variety of small brushstrokes. The foreground was painted with thinner, more liquid paint applied with a looser handling. Portions of the foreground are unclear and slightly difficult to interpret, owing to increasing transparency of the thin dark paint on the colored ground and to minor abrasion. Spots of exposed ground are numerous. The painting was cleaned by Joseph Fronek, Los Angeles, in 2005. Darkened varnish was preferentially thinned, discolored retouching in the sky was removed, and a synthetic-resin varnish applied.

A road deeply rutted by wagon wheels leads from the shadowy, uncultivated foreground into the composition of *Wooded Landscape with a Pool and Figures.* In the brilliant sunlit middle distance, a shepherd drives a herd of sheep forward on the road around a wooded dune. In the left foreground, two travelers rest beside a pool as one dips his foot into the cool water. On the opposite side, a couple accompanied by a boy and dog approach along a path on the edge of the woods without acknowledging the other travelers. Typical of Jacob van Ruisdael's landscapes, the staffage is compositionally significant but is not his subject; rather, as here, it is the rough, wooded dunes in which dramatic lighting and large, active skies create a brooding atmosphere. The foreground is shrouded in shadow, with trees set against a sky animated by a diagonally receding line of cumulous clouds and the sunlight cast on the herd of sheep.

Wooded Landscape with a Pool and Figures is characteristic of the baroque landscapes Ruisdael introduced during the second half of the 1640s, marking a major shift from the tonal landscapes of Jan van Goyen (1596–1656; see cat. 27) and Salomon van Ruysdael (1600/03–1670; see cats. 80 and 81). Typical of Ruisdael's paintings after 1653, *Wooded Landscape with a Pool and Figures* is signed but not dated. The panel support, theme, and composition of the painting relate to Ruisdael's earliest works, such as the 1646 *Dune Landscape* (Hermitage, St. Petersburg). As Seymour Slive suggests, however, a date in the first half of the 1650s is appropriate because of the close comparison of the Pasadena painting with *The Great Oak*, dated 1652 (fig. 77a). As in that work, the staffage of the Pasadena painting is attributed to Jacob van Ruisdael's

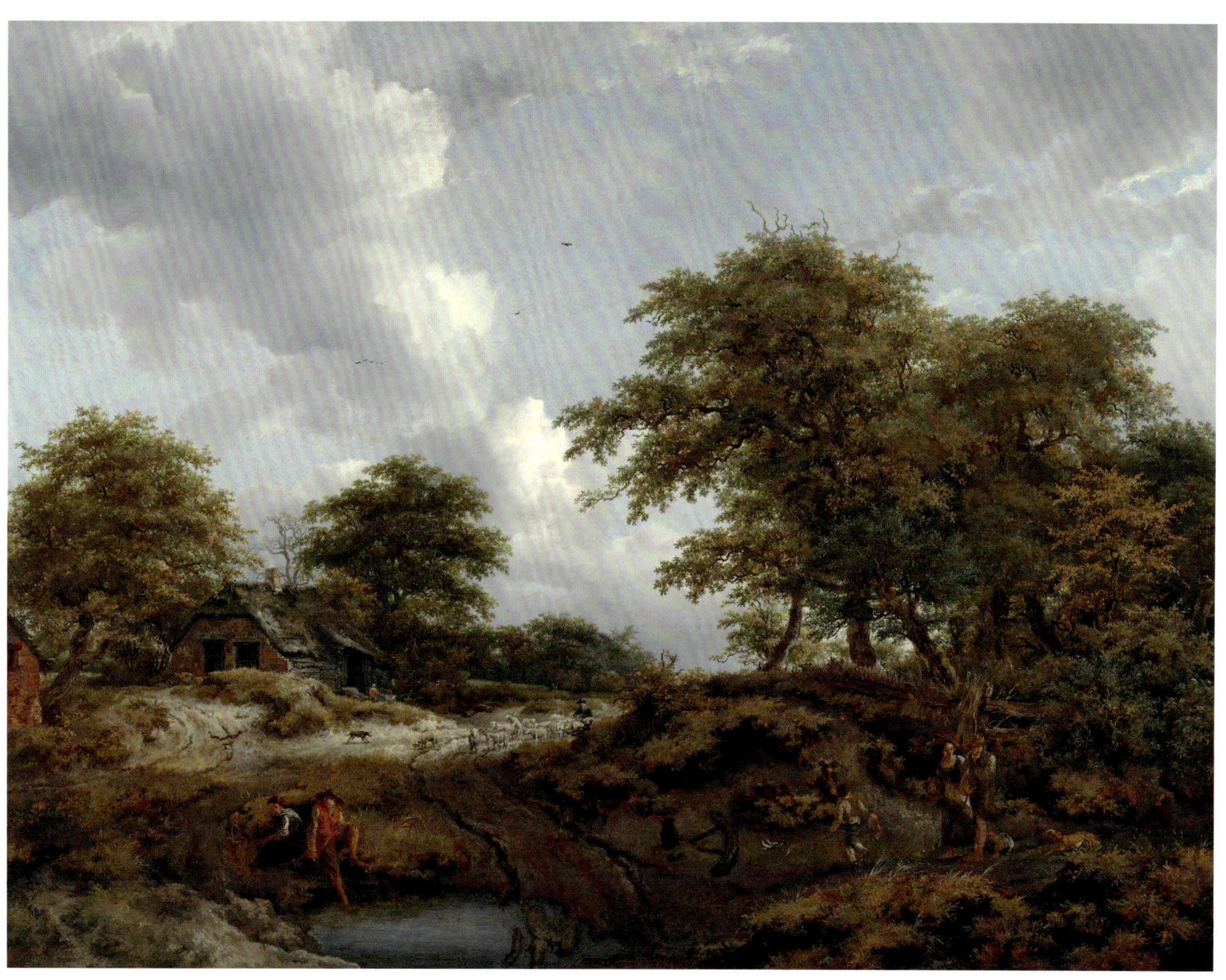

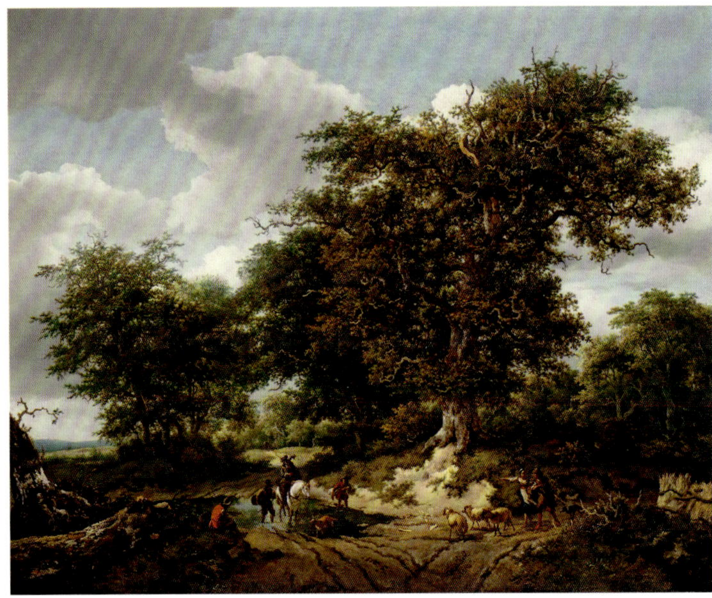

Fig. 77a. Jacob van Ruisdael, *The Great Oak*, 1652, oil on canvas, 34 × 42 in. (86.4 × 106.7 cm), Los Angeles County Museum of Art.

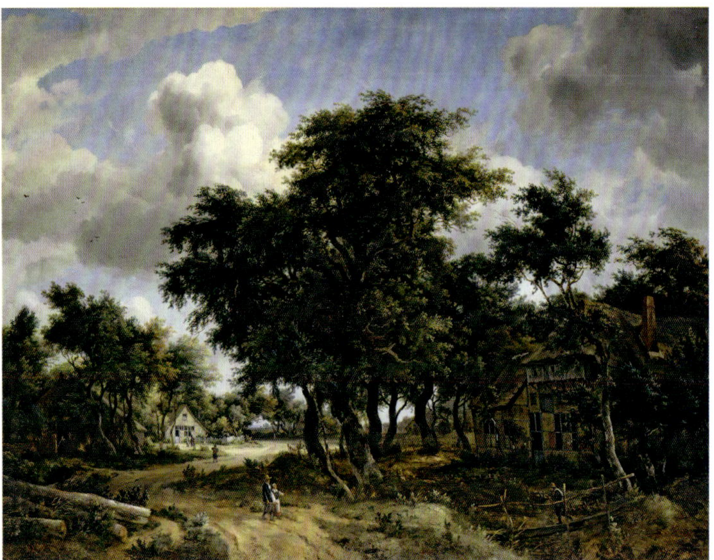

Fig. 77b. Meindert Hobbema, *Village Street under Trees*, ca. 1663, oil on canvas, 38¼ × 50¾ in. (97 × 129 cm), Gemäldegalerie, Staatliche Museen, Berlin.

friend Nicolaes Berchem—though, as was typical, Berchem's signature appears on neither painting.[6]

Differences in the compositions of *The Great Oak* and Pasadena paintings suggest that the latter dates to a few years later than the former. In *The Great Oak* a monumental tree dominates the composition; a traveler on horseback, accompanied by a man walking, moves forward and follows a road that winds around the great oak from the left, meeting in the foreground shepherds emerging from the woods on the right. In the Pasadena painting, Ruisdael presented a similar scene from a greater distance so that the major tree group diminishes in scale and the secondary group of trees and a house nestled in the dunes on the left is pushed further into the distance, creating an opening through which the deeply rutted road passes. An abandoned wagon wheel, all but submerged in the sand beside the road, echoes the circular movement of the road around the hill.[7]

By comparison with *The Great Oak*, the foliage of the trees in *Wooded Landscape with a Pool and Figures* is less dense and more feathery, allowing light to break through the branches and trunks, a device Ruisdael developed further in his later paintings. Tufts of grass, bushes, and sunlight slashing through the landscape help to organize the composition and suggest space. Sunlight appears to be arbitrary, picking out the thatched roof of the farmhouse and the hill in front of it and flickering across the shoulders of the figures in the foreground. The diminished scale and greater openness of the landscape in the Pasadena painting gives the sky more prominence than it has in *The Great Oak*, and bright clouds form a strong diagonal into the distance, echoing the direction of the road below. In his paintings of the 1660s and 1670s—such as *Mill at Wyck, near Duurstede* (Rijksmuseum, Amsterdam) and *Bleaching Fields Outside Haarlem* (Dr. L. Ruzicka Foundation, Kunsthaus Zürich), both from about 1670—Ruisdael increased the area of the sky and focused on the movement of the clouds, emphasizing the constant mutations of the weather and of nature as a whole.

Wooded Landscape with a Pool and Figures provides an important link between the baroque landscapes of Ruisdael and the loose, decorative paintings from the early 1660s of his student Meindert Hobbema (1638–1709). In *Village Street under Trees*, ca. 1663 (fig. 77b), for example, Hobbema adopted Ruisdael's organizational method of using masses of feathery trees and open spaces accented by light but moved the trees to the actual central axis of the painting and spaced them so that light penetrates the trees' foliage. Rather than employing Ruisdael's use of light and the sky to accentuate and complement the landscape, however, Hobbema dispersed light throughout the landscape, heralding the more decorative style of the following century.

1. With thanks to Marijke Booth, archives assistant, Christie's, London, for verifying the seller of this lot at the 1893 sale as Hooper. Wolfgang Stechow (per his notes after a visit to the Norton Simon Museum in November 1970, NSM) was the first to recognize that before 1893 the provenance of *Wooded Landscape with a Pool and Figures* was confused with that of two similar paintings. Slive 2001, no. 408, p. 308n1, concurs. A reference in the 1893 Christie's catalogue to the painting now in Pasadena having been in the David McIntosh collection ("A woody landscape, with a cottage on the right, a peasant driving a flock of sheep. . . . From the collection of David MacIntosh [*sic*], Esq.") is incorrect. The McIntosh sale (Christie's, London, 16 May 1857) included five wooded landscapes by Ruisdael. The closest description in the Christie's catalogue to the painting sold in 1893 is lot 47 (39 × 48½ in.); that work (see Hofstede de Groot 1908–27, vol. 4 [1912], p. 159, no. 507a) was, however, purchased by Lord Fitzwilliam for £210 and remains in the Fitzwilliam collection, Milton Hall, Peterborough, and therefore cannot be the Pasadena painting (letter from David Carritt, 1 August 1968, NSM). Neither the Pasadena nor the Fitzwilliam painting can be the same as that sold from the Perrin collection (Paris, 4–5 March 1816, lot 38), which the sale catalogue described as measuring 15 × 20 pouces and is therefore considerably smaller than *Wooded Landscape with a Pool*. The catalogue's description of the composition of the Perrin painting, although similar, also includes details not found in the Pasadena painting.

2. Joseph B. Robinson was born to British settlers in the Cape Colony. He made his fortune in the diamond and gold mines of South Africa and was an influential political figure at the turn of the century. Robinson was advised in building his collection by Sir George Donaldson and Charles Davis but was said to have made his own decisions. He was particularly fond of eighteenth-century French paintings and furniture as well as Dutch seventeenth-century paintings, many of which he bought from the Cornwall Legh collection in 1895. After Robinson's death, the collection passed to one of his daughters, Ida. See A. Scharf 1958; the biographical sketch by Ellis Waterhouse in London 1958; and that by Peter Cannon-Brookes in the sale catalogue of the Robinson collection, London, Sotheby's, 6 December 1989, n.pag.

3. According to Marijke Booth, Christie's, London, in an email to Carol Togneri 2 February 2011 (NSM).

4. According to an unidentified newspaper clipping dated 8 March 1961 (Collectors' File, GRI), the paintings were in storage in London at the time of Ida's death. They had been placed there in 1910, when Sir Joseph Robinson gave up his home in London and returned to South Africa. In 1925 Ida married Count Natale Labia (1877–1936). Following her death, the collection was divided between her two sons, Natale and Joseph.

5. J. Rosenberg 1928 assigned an asterisk to the number to indicate that he had not actually seen the painting and had relied on the entry in Hofstede de Groot 1908–27, vol. 4 (1912), p. 185, no. 586.

6. Hofstede de Groot 1908–27, vol. 4 (1912), p. 185, no. 586, attributed the figures to Berchem. Wolfgang Stechow rejected the attribution to Berchem (undated manuscript, ca. 1970, NSM), which has most recently been accepted again by Slive 2001, p. 308. For *The Great Oak*, see A. Walsh 2019b, pp. 156–61, cat. 25.

7. Seymour Slive in Philadelphia/Los Angeles/London 2005–06, p. 8, correctly rejects any attempt to read allegorical meaning into the broken wheel, animal bones, and crossroad in this painting and others.

78

Jacob van Ruisdael

Dutch
Haarlem 1628/29–1682 Haarlem?

Three Great Trees in a Mountainous Landscape with a River

Late 1660s

Signed, lower right: "J van Ruisdael"
Oil on canvas, 54⅜ × 68⅛ in. (138.1 × 173 cm)
The Norton Simon Foundation, F.1971.2.P

Provenance

Elizabeth, Lady Cooper (d. 1863),[1] London, in 1842, by descent to her son; Edward Henry Frederick Dawkins (1837–1912), Guilsborough Grange, Northampton, submitted January 1895 to Christie's, London, for auction but later withdrawn.[2] [C. Sedelmeyer, Paris, in 1895].[3] Maurice Kann (1839–1906), Paris (sale, Galerie Georges Petit, Paris, 9 June 1911, lot 59, ill., as *La Vallée* from the collection of Lady Cooper, sold for F41,000 to);[4] [Eugène Fischoff, New York and Paris, for];[5] [Galerie Sedelmeyer, Paris, 1925]. Baron Marczell von Nemes (1866–1930), Budapest and Munich (sale, Frederik Muller, Amsterdam, 13 November 1928, lot 62, bought in), (sale, Frederik Muller, Munich, 16 June 1931, lot 60, ill.). [Leo Collins (a.k.a. Cohen), Vienna, Paris, and New York, ca. 1932–34].[6] Gustav Oberlaender (1867–1936), Go-Al-Do Manor, Reading, PA,[7] by descent to his daughter; Dorothy (1899–after 1966), Mrs. Harold M. Leinbach, Reading (sale, Parke-Bernet Galleries, New York, 26 May 1939, lot 236, ill., as *The Valley [Landscape with Three Oaks]*, sold for $2,500).[8] John Bass, New York, by 1939 (sale, Parke-Bernet Galleries, New York, 25 January 1945, lot 22, ill., sold for $5,000).[9] [Galerie Nathan, Zurich, sold 1971 to]; The Norton Simon Foundation.

Exhibited

Paris 1895, p. 42, no. 36, ill.; San Francisco 1939–40, no. 199; on loan, Princeton University Art Museum, Princeton, NJ, 1971–72; The Hague/Cambridge 1981–82, p. 112, no. 38, ill.

References

J. Smith 1829–42, suppl. (1842), no. 8;[10] Hofstede de Groot 1908–27, vol. 4 (1912), nos. 673, 708, 725; Gillet 1909, p. 370; J. Rosenberg 1928, p. 98, no. 416; Simon 1930, p. 75; Simon 1935, p. 135; Nathan 1972, no. 13;[11] Gerson 1976, p. 171, fig. 11; Drucker 1979, p. 209; Pasadena 1980, p. 64, ill.; Brown 1982, p. 193; P. Sutton 1982, p. 150, fig. 4; Ashton, Davies, and Slive 1982, pp. 15–17, 28, pl. 10, cover; P. Sutton 1986, p. 217; Pasadena 1989, p. 65, ill.; Walford 1991, pp. 134, 138, fig. 147; Slive 2001, pp. 348f., no. 475, figs. 475, 475a; S. Campbell 2010, pp. 116, 161n21, 334, no. 743, ill.

Technical Notes

The original support is a plain-weave medium-weight canvas that has been glue-lined, with the original tacking edges removed. Two short horizontal tears, originating at the lower part of the right edge in the rocks, were repaired by the lining. A reddish-brown ground layer imparts a warm tonality throughout the painting, especially in the foreground, and also influences the appearance of the sky and the mountains. The sky and clouds are depicted with opaque paint directly applied with strong brushwork. The red-brown ground was left exposed in the trunks and branches of the three trees, providing the base color. Opaque white, black, and gray paint brushed in horizontal strokes depict the bark. Darker passages in the foreground were painted in nearly transparent washes, often allowing the ground to remain visible. Varieties of foliage are tiny individual brushstrokes and dabs of color applied more delicately with a smaller brush. X-radiography reveals a waterfall at the right side, in the middle of a rocky wall, falling into a pool of water and creating a frothy splash, but it is now almost invisible because of the increased transparency of the thin paint. The surrounding boulders and the water at the lower right corner have been abraded. Other areas in the foreground that are now quite thin, exposing a large amount of the ground, may also have been abraded, although microscopic examination does not establish this definitively. In a previous treatment, varnish was removed from the sky and the three tree trunks, but dark varnish was left in the foliage, significantly altering the chromatic balance of the painting. There are several scattered spots of retouching, primarily in the sky. An area of retouching directly above the tallest tree is conspicuous because of discoloration. Ultraviolet light indicates that a synthetic-resin varnish was applied overall, with natural-resin varnish remnants below.

Three monumental trees—two entwined oaks and a giant, battered birch—stand on the precipice of a hill overlooking a distant river valley. *Three Great Trees in a Mountainous Landscape with a River* represents the culmination of Jacob van Ruisdael's interest in prodigious trees, which had begun in the early 1650s with his etching *The Giant Beech; Two Peasants and Their Dog* (fig. 78a). As Seymour Slive observes, the painting's heroic mood and exaltation of creative power is unequaled.[12] Integrating light, color, perspective, and narrative, it is one of Ruisdael's most baroque landscapes. Light breaks through clouds that shroud the landscape, dramatically illuminating the three trees, which have just begun to adopt autumnal coloring. The white bark of the birch glimmers in the sunlight, but the exposed red wood of the broken trunk and branches reveals the violent history the tree has suffered. Red also appears mixed amid the leaves of the oak trees and in patches on the ground, where broken branches and roots exhibit the ravages of wind, water, and erosion.

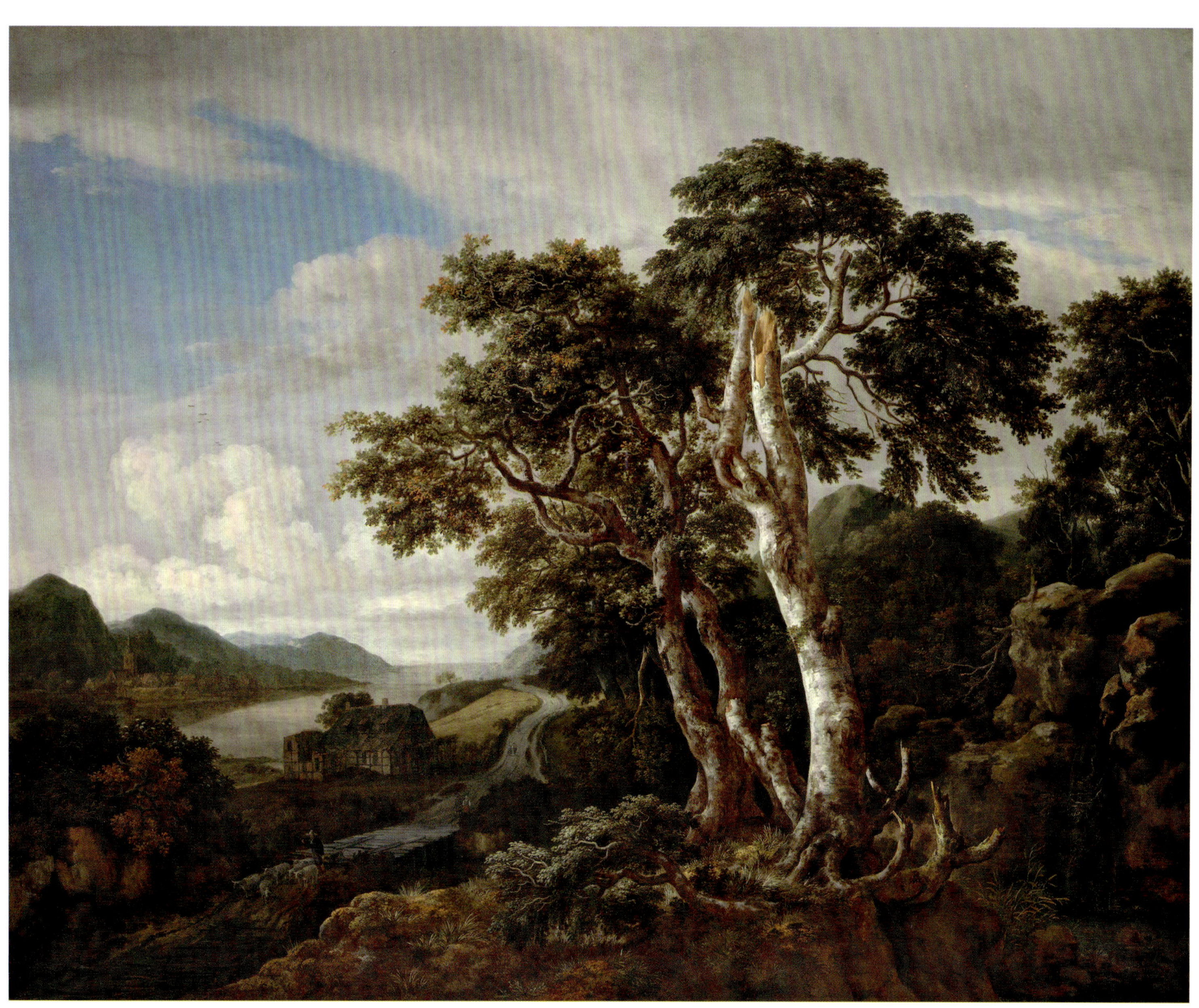

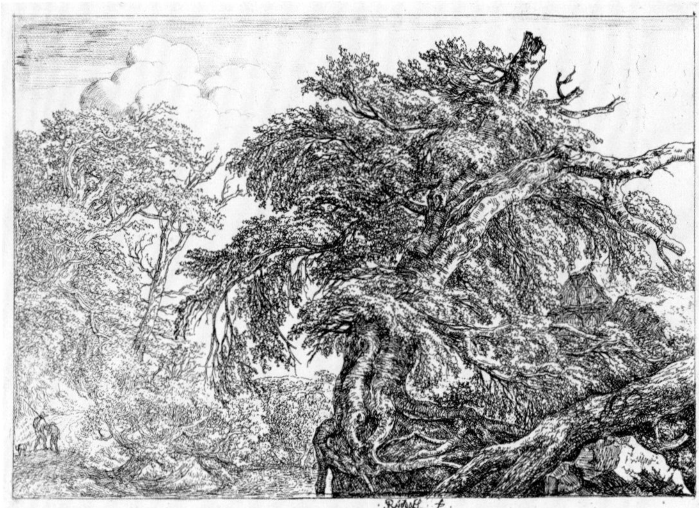

Fig. 78a. Jacob van Ruisdael, *The Giant Beech; Two Peasants and Their Dog*, 1650–82, etching, second state, image: 7¼ × 10 9⁄16 in. (18.4 × 26.8 cm), sheet: 7⅝ × 11 in. (19.4 × 27.9 cm), The Metropolitan Museum of Art, New York.

Painting over a reddish-brown ground, Ruisdael intensified the contrast between foreground and distance by varying not only the light but also the level of detail and application of paint. The thickly applied paint and clear details of the foreground stand out against the thinly painted, muted colors of the distance. The theme of transience and the mutability of nature is continued not only in the dilapidated farmhouse but also in the waterfall, the broad river, and the travelers. Yet the blasted tree, its roots dug deep into the soil, has survived the ravages of time, suggesting that Ruisdael may have been inspired by a more positive reference connected with the history of his native city of Haarlem. Following the devastating 1572–73 siege of Haarlem and destruction of the Haarlem woods, the blasted tree replaced the flourishing tree on the city's coat of arms. In the introductory poem to *Harlemias*, the history of the city of Haarlem published in 1647–48, Theodor Schrevelius (1572–1649) compared the strength of the citizens of Haarlem, who had grown steadfast through suffering, to the bare tree, which, through resisting the storms in the open field, had developed a stronger root system to survive.[13] Thus, the heroic tree, like the ruins of Bredero and Kleef, may have alluded to the history not only of Haarlem but also of the Netherlands, which triumphed over the Spanish through virtue and tenacity.[14]

The combination of powerful, closely seen forms with effects of great distance, typical of Ruisdael's paintings from the late 1660s, recalls but also significantly differs from the "world landscapes" of Pieter Bruegel I (ca. 1525–1569) and his contemporaries, whom Ruisdael would have known through prints and paintings. In those early landscapes there is typically a dramatic break between the foreground and distance. The latter appears to tilt upward toward a high horizon, and progression into the distance is marked by changes in color: earthy brown tones in the foreground, green in the middle ground, and light blue in the far distance. In Ruisdael's painting of the late 1660s, however, the elevated foreground is visually connected to the distance, and space is measurable, defined by natural variations in light and color as well as compositional devices such as the diagonal line of the river, which is bordered on one side by a low range of mountains and on the other by a broad road, where travelers draw the viewer's eye toward a distant patch of light.[15] A shepherd herding sheep over logs laid across the muddy road approaches the foreground, establishing a further connection between foreground and distance. The most important unifying devices, however, are the storm-driven clouds that sweep the sky, parting momentarily to allow the sun to scatter light across the landscape and illuminate the three heroic trees that cling tenaciously to the earth and dominate the monumental composition.

1. Elizabeth was the daughter of Rev. Sir Henry Cooper, Bart. She married Rev. Edward Henry Dawkins (1794–1859) in 1836.

2. Slive 2001 says Dawkins was from "Guisborough" Grange. A letter from N. Annesley, Christie's, London, dated 9 September 1971 (NSM), provides information regarding Christie's no. 944K, which is stenciled on a stretcher bar of the painting. According to the letter, the painting was submitted to Christie's for sale by Edward Dawkins of Guilsborough Grange on 21 January 1895. "Although [Christie's] sold a few other pictures that belonged to him, for some reason (not specified in [their] records) this particular picture was returned to him." Guilsborough Grange is now a wildlife park northwest of Northampton.

3. Visible on the left wall of the gallery in a photograph published as the frontispiece of Sedelmeyer 1906. The painting was not, however, included in the catalogue and had probably been sold within the previous ten years to Maurice Kann.

4. This was one of thirteen paintings by Ruisdael owned by Maurice Kann. In addition to the Dutch and Flemish seventeenth-century paintings and English eighteenth-century paintings offered at this sale, Kann had sold paintings to Duveen Gallery in 1909. Many of the paintings from Kann's collection now hang in the Metropolitan Museum of Art, New York, and in other public collections. Regarding Kann's collection, which was neither as rich nor as vast as that of his brother, Rodolphe Kann, see Gillet 1909 and the entry in this volume on Frans Hals's *Portrait of a Young Man* (cat. 29).

5. According to the catalogues—known in at least three versions—of the Kann sale (RKD). Eugène Fischoff was the son-in-law of Charles Sedelmeyer. Following his marriage to Emma Sedelmeyer in 1885, he became the New York representative of Sedelmeyer & Cie. In 1900 Emperor Franz Josef appointed him chief commissioner of fine arts in Austria.

6. Drucker 1979, p. 204, notes, "The three wonderful Ruysdael landscapes that to my eyes are the glories of the Norton Simon Museum

in Pasadena I saw first in Paarboom's . . . collection." In a telephone conversation on 10 July 1979 with David Steadman, then curator of paintings at the Norton Simon Museum, Peter Drucker acknowledged that Paarboom was a fictitious name and that this painting and the two by Salomon van Ruysdael (1600/03–1670; cats. 80 and 81) had belonged to Leo Cohen, who later anglicized his name to Collins. Leo C. Collins was originally from Vienna but lived in Paris until World War II, when he moved to New York; in 1953 he published a monograph on the seventeenth-century Dutch painter and printmaker Hercules Seghers (1589/90–ca. 1638). Elsewhere, Drucker 1979 states that Paarboom was an investment manager and had been a good customer of his firm, who moved from the Netherlands to England, where he was living in the 1930s. In a telephone conversation with Carol Togneri in April 2003, Drucker confirmed that Paarboom was a fictitious name for Cohen/Collins. In that conversation, he suggested that, because both names mean "pear tree," Paarboom may be an alias for David Birnbaum (a.k.a. David Bingham after 1946), a dealer connected to A. S. Drey in Munich who later settled in the United States. The only definite date associated with Collins's ownership of any of the three paintings is his acquisition of Ruysdael's *Landscape with Sandy Road* (cat. 80), which he purchased at auction in London in 1932. That painting was with Hoogendijk in Amsterdam by 1934. The third painting, Ruysdael's *Halt in Front of an Inn* (cat. 81), was in a private collection in Leipzig in 1929 and in Quebec by 1944. The identity of "Paarboom" remains a mystery. I am grateful to Bridget Lawler, archivist, Drucker Institute, Claremont, CA, for searching the Drucker archives for information about Paarboom and/or Collins, though she did not discover any mention of either name.

7. The painting is shown hanging in the "Museum Room" at Go-Al-Do Manor in a photograph on p. 36 of the 1939 Parke-Bernet sale catalogue.

8. The sale was identified as the collection of Gustav Oberlaender. The catalogue notes that the painting was accompanied by "a brochure with a MS. certificate by Comm. [*sic*] Hofstede de Groot, dated The Hague, July 1927." Harold Leinbach died in 1966.

9. The 1945 Parke-Bernet sale catalogue also states that the painting was sold with "a leather-bound brochure with a MS. certificate by Com. [*sic*] Hofstede de Groot, dated The Hague, July 1927."

10. Smith describes the painting in reverse according to the practice of describing the composition from the point of view of the painting.

11. Listed as in the collection of Fritz and Peter Nathan, although by the time of publication the painting had been sold to The Norton Simon Foundation.

12. Slive 2001, p. 340.

13. De Bièvre 1988, passim.

14. See A. Walsh 2019b, pp. 157f.

15. Ruisdael was apparently unhappy with the composition and extended the river, adding the third and fourth mountain in the distant left and effectively raising the horizon line.

79

Rachel Ruysch

Dutch
The Hague 1664–1750 Amsterdam

Nosegay on a Marble Plinth

ca. 1695

Signed, lower right: "Rachel Ruysch"
Oil on canvas,[1] 15 × 12 in. (38.1 × 30.5 cm)
The Norton Simon Foundation, F.1972.43.1.P

Provenance
Probably Molini (sale, Paris, 30 March 1778, lot 21, sold for 72 livres).[2] [Jean-Baptiste Pierre Lebrun (1748–1813), Paris, 1792]. Baron Hendrik Fagel III (1765–1838),[3] The Hague and London (sale, Hôtel Drouot, Paris, 4 May 1870, lot 17, bought in for F 800).[4] J. C. Bysterbos, Zwolle, or Mlle G. W. Dijk, Amsterdam (sale, Frederik Muller, Amsterdam, 7–8 March 1899, lot 40).[5] Dr. Cornelis Johannes Karel van Aalst (1866–1939), Huis te Hoevelaken, Holland, by descent in 1939 to his grandson;[6] Dr. N. J. van Aalst, sold 25 October 1972 through; [G. Cramer, The Hague, to]; The Norton Simon Foundation.

Exhibited
On loan, Virginia Museum of Fine Arts, Richmond, 27 September 1972–16 December 1974.

References
Lebrun 1792–96, vol. 2 (1792), n.pag., engraving by Vandermeer; J. Smith 1829–42, vol. 6, p. 502, no. 25, cites Lebrun catalogue; Hofstede de Groot 1907–28, vol. 10 (1928), p. 309, no. 4;[7] Grant 1956, p. 41, no. 179;[8] P. Sutton 1986, p. 215; S. Campbell 2010, p. 346, no. 861, ill.

Technical Notes
Although an 1899 sale catalogue refers to the painting as oil on panel" (see note 1 below), there is no physical evidence to suggest that this painting was once on panel and later transferred to canvas. The fine plain-weave canvas has been wax-lined with the original tacking edges removed. The paint layer continues over each tacking edge, indicating that the present stretched dimensions are smaller than the original measurements. X-radiography confirms that there are no cusped threads at the edges. The smoothly applied ground is a thin white layer. Opaque paint was directly applied to depict a tightly organized bouquet using meticulous brushwork in a finely finished technique. Some of the flowers and leaves were painted over the dried black background, notably the marigolds, where the edges of petals allow some of the black to be seen in reserve, while the brighter flowers may have been painted directly over the white ground. Although the paint is generally well preserved, some minor damages are present. The rather dense craquelure has a slightly dished profile, and the edges of the cracks are lightly abraded. The butterfly at center right has been damaged by abrasion and has not been retouched. The legs of the bumblebee and the small ants on the white rose have also been abraded. Two small spots of retouching are located at the upper right, and the four edges have been overpainted. The synthetic-resin varnish is slightly yellowed, with uneven surface gloss. There are also residues of lining adhesive, as well as old varnish left from a partial cleaning.

Painted about 1695, Rachel Ruysch's nosegay of wild and domesticated flowers casually laid on a mottled-pink marble ledge anticipates the relaxed, decorative compositions of the next century.[9] Originally influenced by the still lifes of Willem van Aelst (1627–1687), who had been her mentor in the early 1680s, Ruysch turned the nosegay—a small bouquet of flowers typically given as a gift—into a personal form, painting approximately twenty variations over the course of three separate decades: the 1680s, 1690s, and 1740s (fig. 79a).[10] In these paintings the flowers are at their peak of perfection. Reflecting the refined taste of collectors after the 1660s, the voluptuous forms of fully open roses, poppies, and marigolds and the complicated structure of the white snapdragons have replaced the crisply defined, tight blossoms of the early flower pieces painted by Jan Brueghel I (1568–1625) and Ambrosius Bosschaert (1573–1621; see cats. 8 and 9).

Nosegay on a Marble Plinth exhibits many of the ideals of the late seventeenth century that would be articulated approximately ten years later by the Dutch classicist Gerard de Lairesse (1640–1711) in *Het Groot Schilderboek* (The Great Painting Book; Amsterdam, 1707).[11] According to De Lairesse, the first author to offer a lengthy discussion of flower painting (to which he devoted a separate book), three things are required to make a good flower piece: "Firstly, beautiful and select flowers; secondly, a good arrangement and harmony; and thirdly, an exact, soft brush."[12] He decried the visual cliché of a bouquet in a vase, which he offered as an example of the lack of invention expressed by most still-life painters, and noted with disdain that flower painters have little knowledge of perspective, a failure he blamed on their reliance on drawings of individually observed flowers.[13]

Inherent in Ruysch's rendering of the Pasadena composition is her desire for variety and harmony of color, both of which were lauded as important characteristics of nature

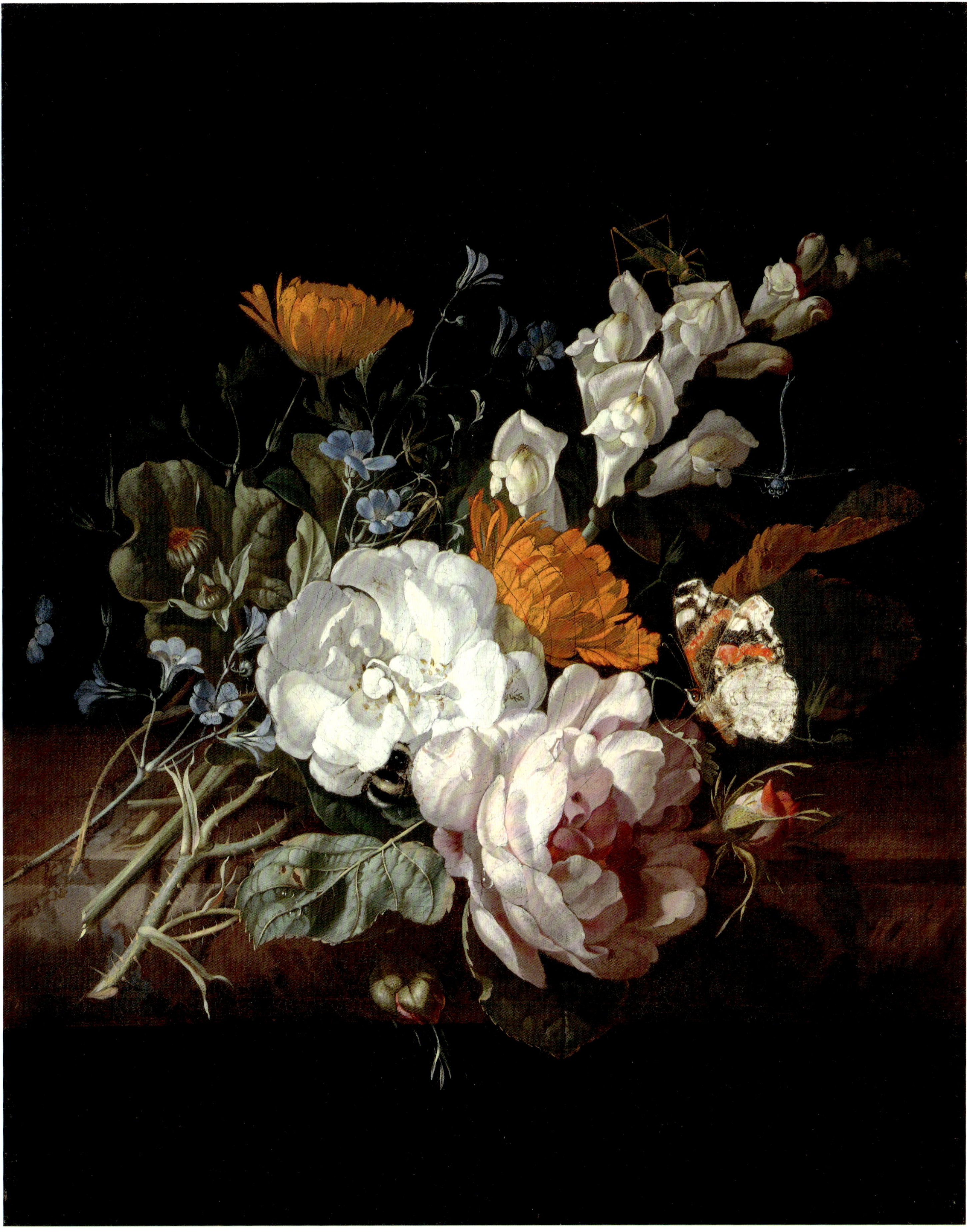

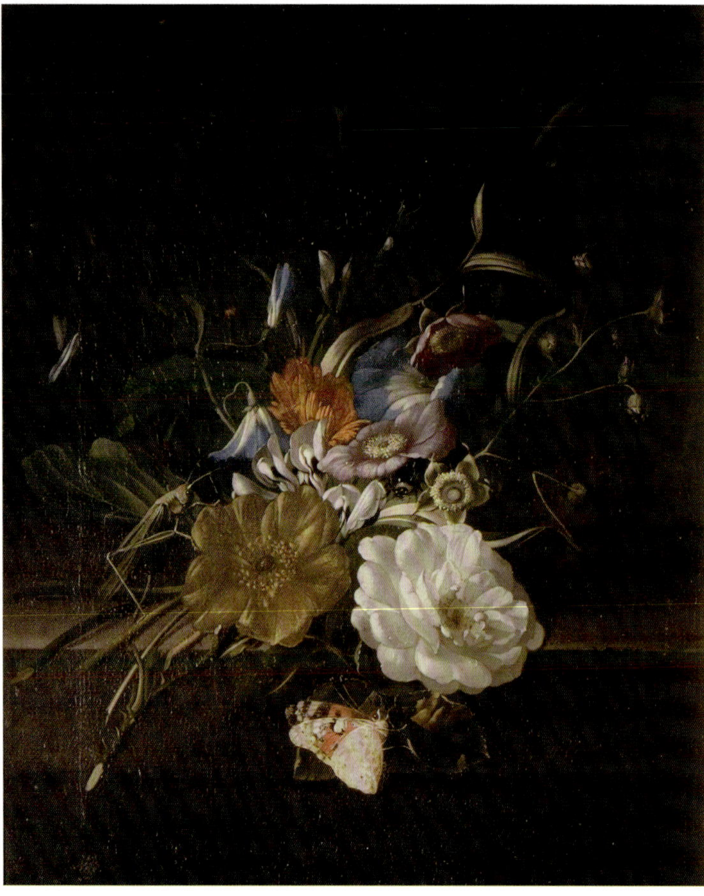

Fig. 79a. Rachel Ruysch, *A Still Life with a Spray of Flowers*, ca. 1685–1700, oil on canvas, 13½ × 10⅞ in. (34.2 × 27.6 cm), Victoria and Albert Museum, London.

worth copying.[14] Harmony of color was necessary for the creation of credible spatial relationships, "corresponding," according to De Lairesse, "to the concord and charming melody in Music."[15] Employing the meticulous painting technique of Van Aelst, carefully layering colored glazes to model the flowers in terms of light and color, Ruysch captured the illusion of fully rounded forms and depth within the nosegay.[16] Anticipating the advice of De Lairesse, Ruysch placed the brightest and largest flowers in the center of the composition, decreasing the size and intensity of light toward the outer edges.[17] De Lairesse advised artists to choose the background color of their paintings carefully so that the flowers appear to advance forward, creating an impression of three-dimensional volume. In Ruysch's painting, the black background, which provides little reflection, gives greater force to the pink and white roses, orange marigolds, and dramatic white snapdragons. The result is a bouquet that appears fully rounded. By placing her bouquet on a receding diagonal, Ruysch captured the illusion of a tangible volume existing in comprehensible space.

The daughter of Frederik Ruysch (1638–1731), a famous professor of anatomy and botany who was superintendent of the Amsterdam botanical gardens, Rachel Ruysch had easy access to the fresh flowers and insects she portrayed in her paintings. A portrait of the artist by Michiel van Musscher (1645–1705) with still-life details painted by Ruysch (fig. 79b) portrays her holding a palette in her left hand and fingering a blossom with her right; a large, loose bouquet of flowers just past their peak fills an unseen vase on the table at which she sits. Behind her is her easel with a large canvas. An open book of drawings of individual flowers and a large compositional sketch reveal that in addition to a live bouquet, she worked from drawings she had made from live flowers as well as, perhaps, from drawings by other artists.[18] A detail apparently painted by Ruysch in Musscher's portrait indicates that she also employed artificial flowers: the blossom she fingers with her right hand appears to be attached to a stick, the bottom of which she pinches with the forefinger and thumb of her left hand.[19] In *Het Groot Schilderboek*, De Lairesse described the technique of using artificial flowers: "Take a Parcel of Flowers of all Sorts, made of Paper or Silk, and with wired stalks, as they are sold by the Tire-women. Now, if you would make a Group, Festoon, or Basket of Flowers, or any such Thing, order and shift those Flowers by and upon one another, as they suit best; and thus you may exercise your self in Winter time, when you cannot have the Life; because those Flowers never wither."[20]

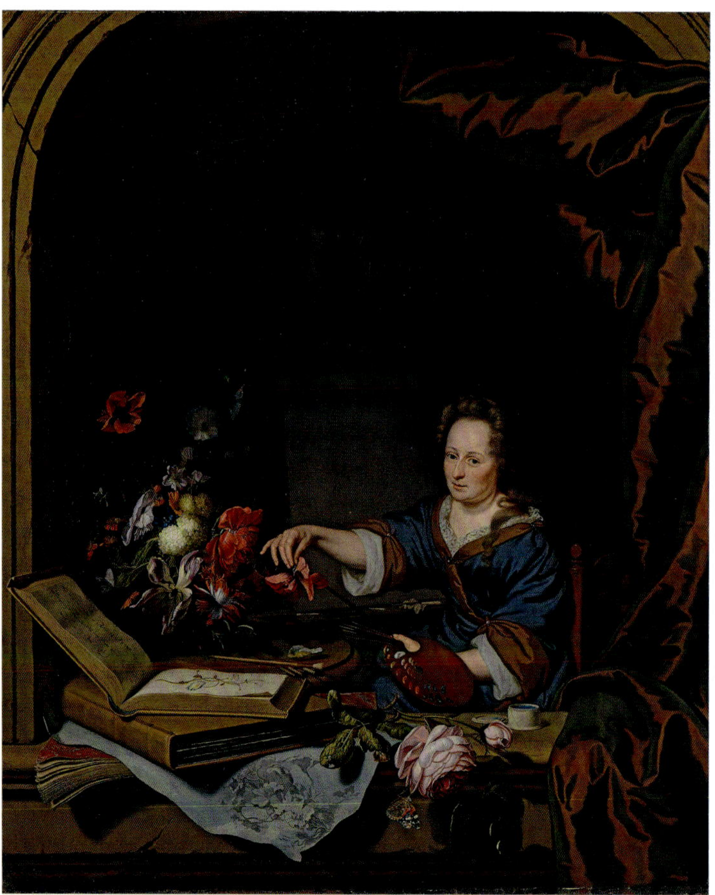

Fig. 79b. Rachel Ruysch and Michiel van Musscher, *Rachel Ruysch (1664–1750)*, 1692, oil on canvas, 30 × 25 in. (76.2 × 63.5 cm), The Metropolitan Museum of Art, New York.

Rather than exotic, rare breeds of imported flowers preferred by artists earlier in the century, the casual bouquet Ruysch depicted in *Nosegay on a Marble Plinth* is composed of domestic blossoms, seemingly picked by the artist and placed on the ledge awaiting a vessel in which to display them. The informal quality of the painting seems to deflect any overt symbolic significance, which might otherwise be suggested by the butterfly and dragonfly. Rather than a reference to transience, Ruysch and her contemporaries may have associated the painting with the simple personal pleasures of walking in the country, where one could enjoy the splendors of nature.[21] Executed during the last decade of the seventeenth century, the painting reflects the refined tastes and activities of those who built country houses in the vicinity of Amsterdam and The Hague. By 1701, the year De Lairesse published his popular lectures as *Grondlegginge der Teekenkonst* (Principles of Drawing) and Ruysch joined the confraternity of painters in The Hague, she was working for sophisticated members of the court circle who would have admired the illusion of an intimate nosegay picked from the garden and preserved throughout the long winter months.

1. In the catalogue of the sale of J. C. Bysterbos, Zwolle, or Mlle. G. W. Dijk, Amsterdam (sale, Amsterdam, Frederik Muller, 7–8 March 1899, no. 40), Frederik Muller stated that the painting was on panel, although J. Smith 1829–42, vol. 6, p. 502, no. 25, had previously noted it was on canvas. Early sales catalogues indicate that some paintings by Ruysch were painted on canvas mounted on panel. There is, however, no physical evidence that this canvas was ever mounted on panel (see Technical Notes). As Berardi 1998, p. 388, observes, "All of Ruysch's known works from 1680 to 1690 are on canvas rather than copper or wooden panel." She suggests, further, that Ruysch never worked on copper.

2. Described as "un bouquet de fleurs posé sur une table de marbre. Ce tableau sur toile porte de haut 1 pied 3 pouces, & de large 12 po."

3. Baron Henry (Hendrik III) Fagel, who was the sixth and last member of his family to hold the title of Clerk to the States General in The Hague, served as ambassador to England, where he lived in exile during the French occupation of the Netherlands. In 1790 he inherited the collection established during the eighteenth century by his grandfather Hendrik II (1706–1790; see Hoet 1752–70, vol. 2 [1752], pp. 409ff.). He may have purchased this painting from Lebrun in Paris in the early 1790s, when he was attempting to establish trade between England and France. Fagel married Agneta Margaretha Catherina Boreel (1770–1824) in 1790 but had no children, so it is unclear who owned the paintings between his death in 1838 and the sale in 1870. Regarding Fagel, see Molhuysen and Blok 1911–37, vol. 3 (1914), pp. 387ff; Bille 1961, vol. 1, pp. 65, 102, 115, 123, 140, 152; and Buchanan 1824, vol. 1, pp. 297–306, no. 45, which includes a catalogue of the Fagel collection.

4. "*Fleurs sur une table*. Deux roses aux tiges épineuses, des oeillets d'Inde, quelques fleurs des champs et des gueules de loup forment un charmant bouquet, autour duquel butinent un papillon et d'autres insectes. Au-dessous de la table, à droite, est la signature en toutes lettres. Toile: Haut., 38 cent.; larg., 30 cent."

5. "Fleurs. Quelques fleurs des champs, coupées et posées sur une plinthe. Des insectes, tels que papillon, abeille, libellule et sauterelle viennent y chercher leur nourriture. Très belle qualité et conservation parfaite. Signé: RACHEL RUIJS." Although the catalogue notes it is on panel measuring 40 × 30 cm, the illustrated painting appears identical to the Pasadena painting.

6. Not included in Moltke 1939.

7. Hofstede de Groot 1907–28, vol. 10 (1928), p. 309, no. 4, cites the Pasadena painting as either no. 9 or 25 in J. Smith 1829–42, vol. 6, and incorrectly places it in the Van Regteren Altena collection.

8. Grant 1956, who places it in the collection of Mrs. Carolus Ocavius van Regteren Altena, Bentveld (Zandvoort), confuses the Pasadena painting with his no. 132, which was sold at Christie's, London, 12 December 1986, lot 22.

9. A similar painting in the Gemäldegalerie Alte Meister, Dresden (canvas, 34.5 × 27.4 cm), is signed and dated "Rachel Ruysch MDCLXXXX." See also a painting dated 1695 (canvas, 31 × 24 cm) that was sold at Sotheby's, London, 3 April 1985, no. 70, now in a private collection, New York.

10. Berardi 1998, p. 258. Regarding the history of the nosegay motif and Ruysch's development of her distinctly personal style, see pp. 254–79, and 385–96.

11. For De Lairesse and his contemporaries, flower still lifes, although highly prized, were at the bottom of the theoretical hierarchy of painting. At the top of this hierarchy was history painting, which told a story through the dramatic actions and expressions of the figures. Still life was both honored and criticized for its verisimilitude and mimetic qualities. For Ruysch, one of the most successful independent female artists in the Netherlands, however, the genre was deemed ideally suited. Expressing what was apparently a common belief throughout the history of the genre, De Lairesse wrote, "There's nothing more feminine, or proper, for women than this [flower painting], and the reasons for this are so obvious," he observed, "that they need no explanation." Quoted in Taylor 1995, p. 100.

12. De Lairesse [1740] 1969, vol. 1, p. 113; quoted by Taylor 1995, p. 104.

13. Taylor 1995, pp. 106f.

14. Taylor 1995, p. 91, points out that there was considerable disagreement about which style of coloring actually agreed with nature.

15. Quoted in Taylor 1995, p. 90. Indeed, throughout the century, flower painting was considered to be an excellent way to study color relationships.

16. Berardi 1998, pp. 389f.

17. Taylor 1995, p. 110, discusses De Lairesse's advice.

18. The portrait, which was sold at auction in 2023, was apparently unknown to Berardi when she wrote her dissertation in 1998. Berardi 1998, p. 273, notes that there are no known drawings by Ruysch. On p. 388 she also notes, "I have not encountered credible references to compositional drawings by her mentioned in old sale catalogue and inventories. This seems to suggest that Ruysch designed her arrangements directly upon the canvas or panel she was painting, working both from life and from careful floral studies."

19. In her portrait, Ruysch may actually be attaching the flower to the stick with a wire. An indication that De Lairesse's advice reflected the practice of contemporary flower painters is also suggested by lots 125 and 126 of the joint estate sale of the artist Jan van Huysum (1682–1749) and the collector Johan Diederik Pomp van Meerdervoort (1697–1749) of Zwijndrecht (sale, Johannes Verkoije, Amsterdam, 14 October 1749), which record "Eenige Modellen van Bloemstukken" (several models of flower pieces; RKD). Found among other painting supplies, they may refer to drawings, or, possibly, artificial flowers. Although the joint sale does not identify the owner of individual lots, the painting supplies undoubtedly belonged to the artist rather than to the patron-collector.

20. "Of Flowers," in De Lairesse [1707] 1738, p. 628.

21. See Berardi 1998, pp. 274–79.

80

Salomon van Ruysdael

Dutch
Naarden 1600/03–1670 Haarlem

Landscape with Sandy Road

1628

Signed and dated, lower left: "S ·v ·RvyESDAEL / 1628"[1]
Oil on panel, 10⅝ × 14⅞ in. (27 × 37.8 cm)
The Norton Simon Foundation, F.1970.15.P

Provenance
Anonymous (sale, Sotheby's, London, 7 December 1932, lot 67, sold to); Leo Collins (a.k.a. Collings or Cohen), Vienna, Paris, and New York.[2] [D. A. Hoogendijk & Co., Amsterdam, by November 1934 until at least 1936].[3] [E. J. van Wisselingh & Co., Amsterdam, sold 1970 to]; The Norton Simon Foundation.

Exhibited
Amsterdam 1934, no. 5; Rotterdam 1934–35, no. 16; Amsterdam 1936a, no. 1;[4] Amsterdam 1936b, no. 141; on loan, Cleveland Museum of Art, March 1971–September 1973.

References
J. G. van Gelder 1933, p. 74; Bremmer 1934, p. 378; H. 1936, p. 57, ill.; Stechow 1938, pp. 17f., 94, no. 227, fig. 3; Stechow 1968a, p. 26; Stechow 1975, pp. 17f., no. 227, fig. 6; Gerson 1976, p. 167, fig. 8; Benesch 1979, p. 23, fig. 22; Pasadena 1980, p. 63, ill.; P. Sutton 1986, p. 217; Schama 1987a, p. 67, fig. 3; P. Sutton 1987, pp. 35f.; Amsterdam/Boston/Philadelphia 1987–88, p. 466; Pasadena 1989, p. 68, ill.; Madrid 1994, pp. 31–32, fig. 28; Liedtke 2003, p. 24; Pasadena 2003, pp. 58–59, ill.; S. Campbell 2010, p. 334, no. 741, ill.

Technical Notes
The uncradled wood panel—apparently oak—consists of a single board with a vertical grain. Rough tool marks on the reverse indicate that the original surface remains, including its shallow beveled edges. The white ground is a thin layer, leaving the texture of the wood grain apparent on the surface. A thin rose-beige layer, evident in the sky, appears to cover the entire ground. Although paint is generally thin, brushmarking is visible in the sky. The artist skillfully employed variations of opacity and transparency to depict textural differences among the earth, the sandy road, and grasses. Foliage and grasses are depicted by dabs of rich paint; the crisp, tiny strokes of delicate light green are vivid in raking light. A liquid transparent brown paint is overlaid with opaque, slightly thicker paint in lighter shades of brown to develop the broken dune in the foreground. The sandy road at the right was painted with the most opaque and thickly applied paint. The paint is very well preserved. Prior cleaning left some thin, scattered residues of darkened varnish on the large bush at the left center and the shrubs and grasses at the right, lending them a browner tone. Minor retouching in the sky is in thin vertical lines, covering small losses that follow the wood grain. Marco Grassi is recorded as applying "a spray/brush coat of gloss varnish (Rembrandt)" in 1978 because "the surface varnish had sunk-in in the dark foreground areas."[5]

Dated 1628, *Landscape with Sandy Road* is one of Salomon van Ruysdael's earliest and most effective paintings.[6] Nowhere else did he achieve such a stunning rendition of the dunes west of Haarlem. Here one feels the battle between the sun's warmth and the cool, damp winds off the sea that constantly shift the landscape, swallowing fences and huts, only to be uncovered by another shift in the wind. Viewed from a low vantage point, the dark form of a dune dominates the foreground and is balanced overhead by the dark clouds. At the left, a lanky man strides across the sunlit dune. Beyond him, half-hidden by the dune, a white horse draws a two-wheeled cart with two passengers toward the right.[7] Ruts in the brightly lit road that cuts through the dune anticipate the forward movement of the cart in a diagonal direction. In the distance, the roof of a humble house rises above the sand, while billowing gray clouds, punctuated by areas of white, animate the sky, echoing the diagonal movement of the figures as well as the pattern of the landscape. Like the trees and grasses bending in the wind and the dead tree trunks, the willowy man, hunched over, hands clasped behind his back, and face turned away from the viewer, appears to be part of the landscape.

Ruysdael's use of a dark wedge in the foreground and intense, raking light to define the composition of overlapping dunes marked a major shift in landscape painting that he shared with his contemporaries Jan van Goyen (1596–1656) and Pieter de Molijn (1595–1661). In Van Goyen's 1627 *Sandy Road with a Farmhouse* (fig. 80a) and Molijn's 1629 *Landscape with a Cottage* (Metropolitan Museum of Art, New York),[8] a house is all but swallowed by the waves of shifting dunes. Restricting their palettes to subtly varied tones of ochres, greens, and gray, the artists described the local landscape, capturing not only the images but also the feel of the cold wet wind off the North Sea. To differentiate the elements of the landscape, Ruysdael and his cohorts varied the application of paint. Thick, liquid yellow-white defines the areas in strongest light, while in areas of shadow, such as the broken face of the dune, oil with only a little brown pigment creates a translucent effect that suggests the reflected light

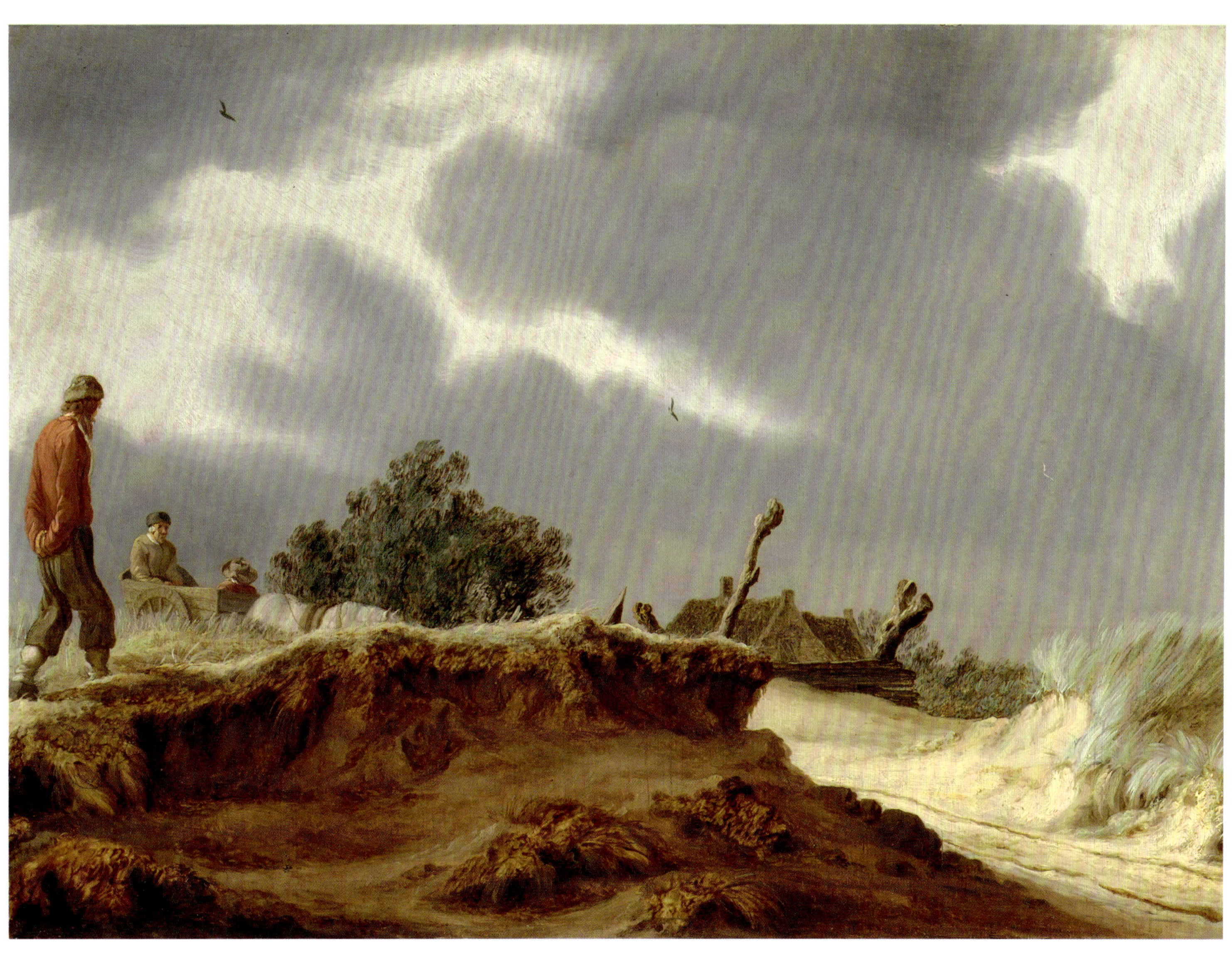

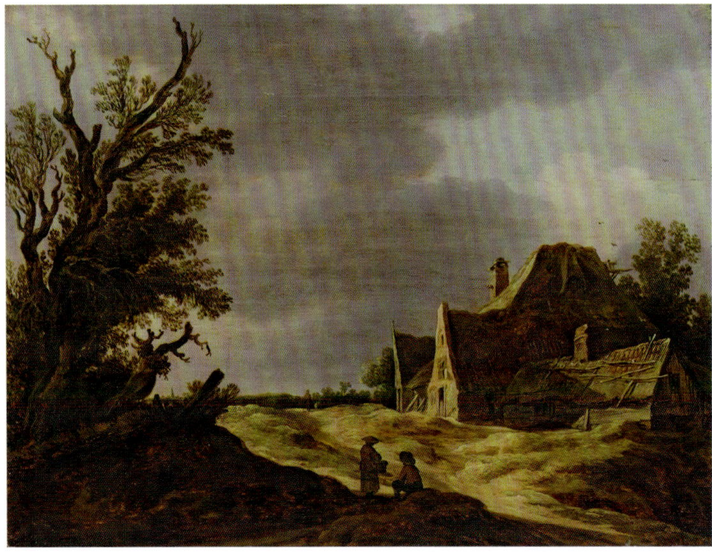

Fig. 80a. Jan van Goyen, *Sandy Road with a Farmhouse*, 1627, oil on wood, 12 ⅛ × 16 ¼ in. (30.8 × 41.3 cm), The Metropolitan Museum of Art, New York.

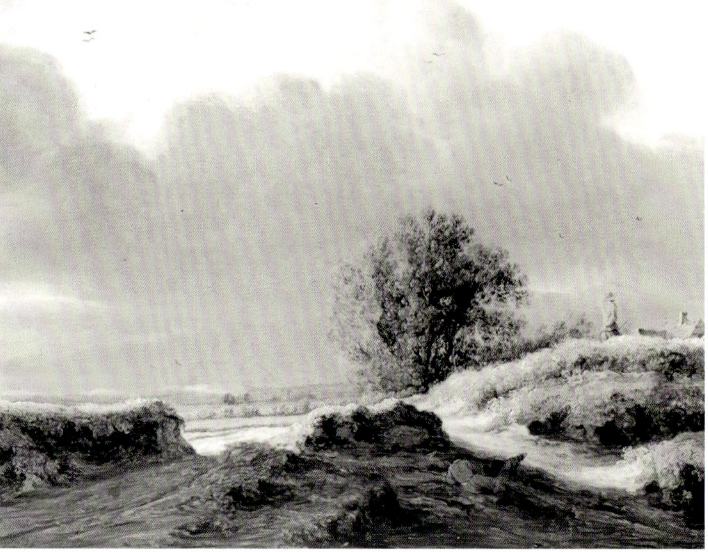

Fig. 80b. Salomon van Ruysdael, *River Landscape with Figures and a View of the Roof of a House*, 1628, oil on panel, 11 7⁄16 × 15 ½ in. (29 × 39.5 cm), sold, Sotheby's, London, 12 December 1979, lot 3, location unknown, image courtesy of Sotheby's.

of a daylight shadow. Thin, milky washes of opaque color moderate the shadows, giving distinction to the form of the dune. While not abandoning the definition of local colors, Ruysdael reduced the intensity of the man's red shirt and limits that of other details, contributing to a sense of atmospheric unity that he would develop further in the tonal landscapes of the next decade.

A comparison of the Pasadena painting and *River Landscape with Figures and a View of the Roof of a House* (fig. 80b), a closely related painting also dated 1628 by Ruysdael, reveals a dramatic development. Both paintings appear to represent the same location, but the Pasadena composition draws the viewer closer to the subject, positioning the man on the left edge of the panel so that he appears to stride into the composition from the undefined continuation of the landscape beyond the limits of the small panel. The surprisingly prominent figures and dunes in the Pasadena painting recall Molijn's series of four prints dated 1626, particularly the title page, which represents country folk in the immediate foreground resting in front of a house partially submerged in the sand (fig. 80c).[9] The relatively large scale and importance of the figures in the Pasadena work distinguish it and Ruysdael's other early paintings from the early work of Van Goyen and Molijn in which the figures are typically relatively small and unobtrusive. The careful placement of figures would remain an important compositional device used by Ruysdael throughout his career to suggest movement through his often vast landscapes.

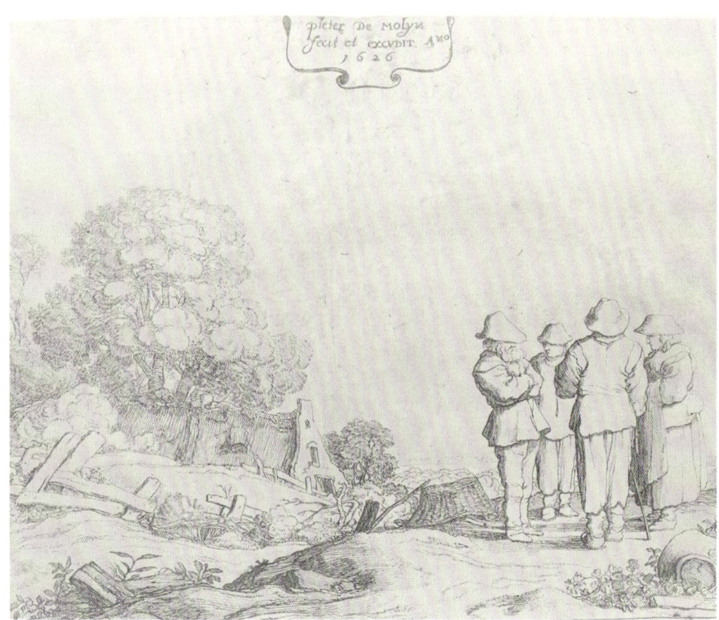

Fig. 80c. Pieter de Molijn, *Three Peasants and a Woman*, 1626, etching, 5 15⁄16 × 7 ¼ in. (15.1 × 18.4 cm), The Metropolitan Museum of Art, New York.

1. According to Stechow 1975, p. 11, in 1627 Ruysdael signed his first painting "S. V. Ruysdael," but between 1628 and 1631 he used the form "S. V. Ruyesdael."

2. Identified as "Collings" in an annotated copy of the 1932 sale catalogue. Possibly also known as Willem Paarboom, mentioned by Drucker 1979, p. 209. See cat. 78, note 6.

3. Label on the back of the panel: "D. A. Hoogendijk & Co." The invoice to The Norton Simon Foundation dated 5 January 1971 also states that the painting was once in the collection of the Hoogendijk dealership, Amsterdam.

4. Lent by a "private collection," most likely Hoogendijk, which exhibited the painting in 1934 and again in the summer of 1936.

5. NSM.

6. See Stechow 1968a, pp. 19–33; Amsterdam/Boston/Philadelphia 1987–88, pp. 34–39; and London 1986.

7. The horse-drawn two-wheel cart—which is very similar to that later depicted by Gerrit Claesz Bleker (active by 1625, d. 1656) in *Peasant Couple on Their Way to Market* (Hollstein 1949–2010, vol. 12, no. 11), dated 1643—was a typical conveyance for farmers of some means.

8. For more on Van Goyen and Molijn, see Liedtke 2007, vol. 1, pp. 225–27, no. 49, and pp. 490–92, no. 125.

9. Hollstein 1949–2010, vol. 14, p. 70, nos. 1–4; the title page is no. 1.

81

Salomon van Ruysdael

Dutch
Naarden 1600/03–1670 Haarlem

Halt in Front of an Inn

1643

Signed and dated, lower right: "S • vRuysdael • 1643" (*VR* in ligature)
Oil on panel, 24⅛ × 36½ in. (61.3 × 92.7 cm)
The Norton Simon Foundation, F.1970.09.P

Provenance
Leo Collins (a.k.a. Cohen), Vienna, Paris, and New York, ca. 1910s/20s.[1] [A. S. Drey, Munich, ca. 1925].[2] Walter Rieß (1884–1946), Leipzig, in 1929 and possibly still in 1938.[3] Jules Roos (1893–1968), Amsterdam and later Westmount, Quebec, by 1944, by bequest ca. 1968/69 to his son; Walter Roos (1923–1983), Palm Harbor, FL, sold October 1969 to; [Rosenberg & Stiebel, New York, sold 1970 to]; The Norton Simon Foundation.

Exhibited
Leipzig 1929, no. 94, ill.; Montreal 1944, no. 40; on loan, Allen Memorial Art Museum, Oberlin, 19 March–25 August 1970; on loan, Los Angeles County Museum of Art, 26 August 1970–26 November 1974.

References
Oertel 1929, p. 583; Stechow 1938, pp. 21, 84, no. 147, fig. 17; "Unbroken Tradition" 1944, p. 20, ill.; Stechow 1968a, p. 27, fig. 31; Stechow 1975, pp. 21f., 90, no. 147, ill.;[4] Gerson 1976, p. 167, fig. 9; Drucker 1979, p. 209; Pasadena 1980, p. 63, ill.; P. Sutton 1986, p. 217; Amsterdam/Boston/Philadelphia 1987–88, p. 470, fig. 1; Pasadena 1989, p. 67, ill.; Colnaghi 2003, no. 11; S. Campbell 2010, p. 332, no. 729, ill.

Technical Notes
The uncradled oak support is composed of two horizontally grained boards, with the tightly closed join located at the approximate center of the panel. Tool marks remain on the reverse of the panel, where the left and right sides have shallow bevels. The white ground is a thin layer, permitting the wood grain and vertical ridges from the saw marks to be part of the surface texture. A rose-beige imprimatura is apparent throughout the sky, but the warm earth colors of the lower portion of the painting make it difficult to identify in those areas. The deftly handled liquid paint is very thin. In many areas the monochromatic painting resembles a drawing. Colored areas are frequently thin washes applied with a minimum of brushstrokes. The central foreground was painted with a translucent brown paint, with plants rendered by small brushstrokes in richer brown paint. In the sky, the color applied last was blue, slightly overlapping the gray and white clouds, with perceptible brushmarking in those areas. The horse and travelers at the right are presented in slightly more vibrant colors. The texture of foliage in the large central tree and the lower shrubs at the right, rendered by dabs of rich paint, contrasts with the remainder of the smooth surface. The increasing transparency of thinly painted figures in the central portion, below the branches of the two trees, is probably beyond what the artist intended in his sketchy rendering of the buggy, three horses drinking from a trough, and other miscellaneous figures. The painting is in an excellent state of preservation. Small spots of minor retouching by Jeanne McKee from 1986 in Magna colors are primarily in the sky. Ultraviolet fluorescence is consistent with a thin natural-resin varnish.

Dated 1643, *Halt in Front of an Inn* is one of the earliest in a series of closely related paintings in which Salomon van Ruysdael depicted a country inn where a coach and an open cart filled with passengers bundled against the chill have halted to allow animals and passengers to refresh themselves.[5] Typically, the extremely low horizon emphasizes the dramatic, wind-swept clouds and flat landscape raked by the late afternoon sun that casts the facade of the inn in brilliant light.

The casual naturalism of *Halt in Front of an Inn* belies the complex organization of the composition, which successfully integrates the broad, flat landscape through the careful placement of figures and structures and especially the suggestion of movement. The massive tree placed at the center of the composition forms the apex of a dynamic triangle anchored and defined by the dark rise of earth in the foreground, a favorite device Ruysdael used during the 1640s to mark the visual progression into depth. The silhouetted figures of a man and woman resting on the hillock with their dog accent the primary lines of the composition. Echoing the line of the man's back, the major diagonal thrust runs along the dirt road from the lower right corner, along the facade of the inn, past the wagons and tree to the church tower at the distant left. In front of the enormous tree, a hunter, accompanied by his page and dog, approaches the inn along the same road, while on the left riders drive their cattle forward, following the secondary diagonal toward the lower left corner of the painting. The seated man leaning forward in the foreground marks the pivotal point, and the dog emphasizes the direction in which the cattle move.

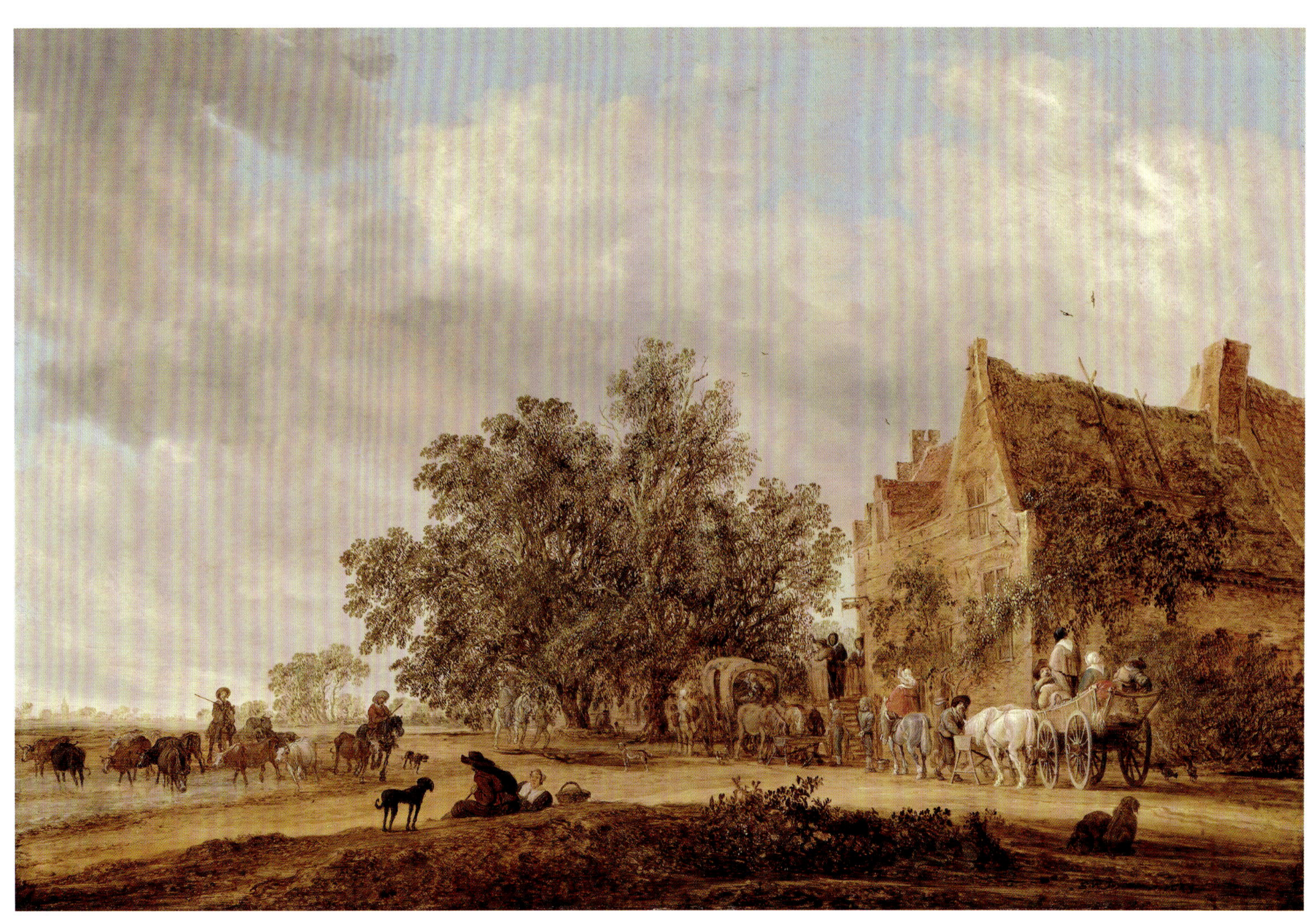

Halt in Front of an Inn is a masterpiece of subtle suggestion. Thinly applied paint deftly combined with fluid, calligraphic description imbues the figures and animals with a sense of natural movement and envelops the landscape in a unified atmosphere. In rendering the form of the two white horses eating from a trough in front of the inn, for example, Ruysdael used only a wash of white paint. In some places, such as the form of the man between the mounted rider and man feeding the white horses, the paint is so thin that the figures have faded away and taken on the appearance of ghosts. Very regular, short brushstrokes applied in a lively manner in parallel patterns define the leaves of the tree. Although the reactive effect of the linseed oil with copper oxide has caused the original green color of the giant tree to turn brown, Ruysdael also originally limited the color range of his painting to ochres with some light greens and grays, typical of the tonal landscapes of the 1640s.

In this and other landscapes by Ruysdael, the country inn primarily serves as an anecdotal compositional device and not as the focal point of a genre scene. In contrast to Isack van Ostade (1621–1649), a fellow member of the Haarlem painters' guild who, beginning in 1643, made a specialty of depicting the activity outside country inns, Ruysdael's primary concern was the description of a landscape. To animate and define his compositions, Ruysdael adopted elements from allegorical traditions, particularly allegories of the seasons. In the Pasadena painting, the cattle drive with horsemen and dogs, for example, suggests that it is autumn, when farmers transported the cattle to market for slaughter after grazing on the succulent Dutch meadows. Autumn was also a time when aristocratic hunters pursued their prey. By the 1640s these allusions to seasonal iconography had been absorbed into the general vocabulary of landscape and did not represent the primary significance of the painting, which had more to do with an appreciation of the country as a place for recreation and renewal. Reflecting the contemporary revival of Stoic philosophy, which extolled nature as a guide and remedy for those living in the city, the influential French philosopher, theologian, and humanist Pierre Charron (1541–1603) contended that the countryside offered "both spiritual and corporall, libertie, wisdom, innocencie, health, pleasure. In the fields the spirit is more free and more to itself. . . . This celestiall fire that is in us, will not be shut up, it loveth the aire, the fields; and therefore . . . the countrey life is the chosen of wisdom . . . which can not be without beautifull and free thoughts and meditations; which are hardly had and nourished among the troubles and molestations of the citie."[6]

The signing of the Twelve Years' Truce with Spain in 1609, although not the end of the war, had brought a new sense of peace and security to the seaward provinces of the Netherlands. The countryside became an inviting destination for those living in nearby cities, which had grown

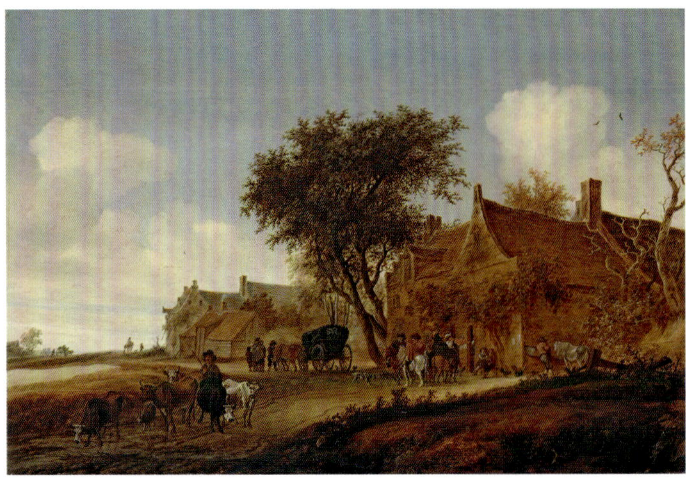

Fig. 81a. Salomon van Ruysdael, *Landscape with Travelers before an Inn*, 1665, oil on panel, 22 × 33¼ in. (56 × 84.5 cm), Rijksmuseum, Amsterdam.

crowded with immigrants from the countryside as well as those seeking religious freedom and economic opportunity. Successful burghers built country houses outside of the cities, and the less affluent made day trips to the country, seeking relief from the stress and competitiveness of the cities and the spiritual and physical health and refreshment offered by the country.[7] In 1678 a French visitor to the Netherlands remarked on the popular pleasure the urban Dutch from all strata of society took in excursions into the countryside: "Wherever one goes one finds as many people as would be seen elsewhere in a public procession. All these excursions end up at one of the inns which are to be found everywhere. . . . These inns are always packed with visitors, and the confused murmur of many voices is like the sound in a city square. These are the inexpensive pleasures which all, even the humblest labourer, can share."[8]

What seems to be the same large country inn, sometimes viewed from other angles, appears in several other paintings by Ruysdael. *Landscape with Travelers before an Inn* (fig. 81a), for example, is seen from the same viewpoint but with different surroundings.[9] Although the inn remains unidentified, these various images suggest that Ruysdael based its form on a specific place, which he could have sketched from different angles.[10] Contemporary prints, such as *Pleasant Places*, a series of twelve prints published in 1611 by Claes Jansz. Visscher (1587–1652), testify to the interest in local landmarks. Intended, as the title page says, for those who have no time to travel far, the prints guided the imaginations of the urban dweller out of the cities, across polders and dunes, past farms, and into villages.[11] It is likely that the person who purchased or commissioned this large painting would have recognized the inn as a local landmark or at least one typical of those in the vicinity and enjoyed the pleasant associations it evoked.

1. Regarding the identity of Leo Collins, see cat. 78, note 6.

2. According to the RKD photo mount.

3. Leipzig 1929 does not identify the lenders of specific paintings but does include Rieß in the list of lenders to the exhibition. Stechow 1938 lists Rieß as the owner of the painting.

4. Stechow 1975 incorrectly identifies the owner as "Jules Ross"—apparently an editorial mistake. A label on the back of the painting for the 1944 exhibition in Montreal identifies the lender as Jules Roos, as does the exhibition catalogue (Montreal 1944).

5. Among others, see *Travelers Halting outside an Inn*, panel, 54 × 85 cm, signed and dated 1643 (Stechow 1975, no. 146); *Travelers outside an Inn*, canvas, 62.5 × 94 cm, signed and dated 1644, (Stechow 1975, no. 149; formerly Julius Weitzner); *Landscape with Figures before an Inn*, 86.5 × 118.5 cm, signed and dated 1645 (Stechow 1975, no. 153A, with P. de Boer, 1967); *Landscape with a Carriage and Horsemen before an Inn, with Drovers and Cattle*, panel, 86 × 125.5 cm (Stechow 1975, no. 175, with Colnaghi, [Colnaghi 2003, no. 11]); *Village Inn with Wagons*, panel, 56 × 84.5 cm, signed and dated "SVR 1655", Rijksmuseum, Amsterdam); and *A Village Landscape with Carriages outside an Inn*, 55.3 × 74.6 cm, signed and dated 1660 (London, Christie's, 7 December 2006, lot 21).

6. Charron [ca. 1612] 1971, p. 207. Originally published in French in 1601, *De la sagesse* was widely read during the seventeenth century, translated into numerous languages, and published in eighty editions before the eighteenth century. An expression of neo-Stoic philosophy, it presents a carefully conceived didactic guide for the wise man in which Charron set down specific rules of behavior.

7. Echoing the sentiments of contemporary neo-Stoic writers and the *Georgics*, Virgil's first-century poem on agriculture, country-house poems published by many of the major Dutch poets of the seventeenth century celebrate the retreat to the local countryside. In contrast to pastoral literature inspired by Virgil's *Eclogues*, Georgic literature emphasized the practical, rustic aspects of the author's native landscape and introduced descriptions of realistic detail. *Den Binckhorst*, the first true country-house poem written in Dutch by Philibert van Borsselen (ca. 1575–1627) in 1613, typically describes the country as where virtue and happiness rule.

8. Quoted from Zumthor 1962, pp. 163f.

9. Ruysdael's *Travelers Halting before an Inn*, 1644 (formerly J. Paul Getty Museum, Los Angeles), and several other closely related paintings (including Stechow 1975, nos. 157 and 168) represent the inn from the opposite direction. Although somewhat altered, its basic construction appears to be based on the same prototype.

10. Ruysdael included topographical elements in a number of his paintings. See Niemeyer 1959 and Scholtens 1962.

11. Hollstein 1949–2010, vol. 39, nos. 149–60. The series, entitled "Plaisante Plaetsen," includes a title page and eleven prints, each showing a naturalistic view of an identified landscape in the vicinity of Haarlem. See also Levesque 1994, esp. pp. 35–54.

82

Roelandt Savery

Flemish
Kortrijk 1576–1639 Utrecht

Landscape with Ruins and Animals

1624

Signed and dated lower left on rock: "ROELAND FEO / SAVERY 1624"
Oil on wood, 20 ⅞ × 29 ⅞ in. (53 × 75.9 cm)
The Norton Simon Foundation, F.1972.36.1.P

Provenance
Prince of Wallenstein, since the beginning of the 18th century;[1] [Edward Speelman Ltd., London, sold 1972 to]; The Norton Simon Foundation.

Exhibited
On loan, Metropolitan Museum of Art, New York, 30 August 1972–28 March 1973; on loan, Princeton University Art Museum, Princeton, NJ, 29 March 1973–17 July 1974.

References
Gerson 1976, p. 164; Pasadena 1980, p. 61, ill.; Spicer 1983, p. 255; P. Sutton 1986, pp. 215, 310, ill.; Müllenmeister 1988, pp. 117f., no. 174; Pasadena 1989, p. 61, ill.; Pasadena 2003, p. 65, ill.; Poughkeepsie 2005, p. 33, fig. 21; S. Campbell 2010, pp. 141, 344, no. 846, ill.

Technical Notes
The uncradled oak support is a ¼-inch panel fabricated from three horizontally grained boards. A crack at the bottom right has been repaired, and the join of the lower board has been reinforced on the reverse with small pieces of wood. The smoothly applied white ground is moderately thick, leaving the texture of wood grain only slightly visible. A thin imprimatura appears to extend over the entire painting. A translucent brown provides the warm tonality in the foreground, where light green flora and fauna are delicately painted over it. It is also visible where it was left uncovered at the upper right corner of the white tower. Microscopic examination did not reveal underdrawing. The paint is in exceptionally good condition. Meticulously rendered details were painted with delicate brushstrokes of bright, opaque colors such as those depicting the foliage and animals. Dark areas of the composition (the foreground, the stone arches) were painted with a thin reddish-brown paint in a glaze-like consistency. The light-colored tower at the right was built up of thin pale layers. The thicker opaque paint of the sky extends up to reserves left for the trees, with tree branches and leaves painted last. Ultraviolet light reveals minor spots of retouching in the sky, foreground, and the bottom right corner, as well as traces of natural resin under a thin to moderate layer of synthetic-resin varnish.

Painted in 1624—ten years after Roelandt Savery left the court at Prague of Rudolf II (1552–1612), King of Hungary and Bohemia and Holy Roman Emperor, and returned to the Netherlands—*Landscape with Ruins and Animals* is the last of three known versions of the composition, including *Cattle and Deer near Ruins*, 1618 (Hermitage, St. Petersburg), and *Landscape with Cattle near Ruins*, 1622 (Herzog Anton Ulrich-Museum, Braunschweig).[2] The paintings combine two themes that dominated Savery's late career: scenes of animal combat and paradise. In the Pasadena painting, a ruined arch overgrown with foliage extends across the left half of the composition like a coulisse or stage flat, while on the right the composition opens to reveal a distant tower dramatically lit by the unseen sun. In the left foreground, amid the shadows of a lush forest, light illuminates two bulls locked in combat; twisting and turning, they are separated from a herd of peaceful cattle resting by a stream and three deer standing in a thicket before the arch. Flocks of birds and a hawk seemingly riding the sun's rays animate the sky and help to integrate the composition, while exotic birds and animals dispersed throughout the painting suggest the sounds and movement of the forest and draw the viewer into the painting in search of more details. The flickering light and fluid rhythms of the animals and grasses in the shadows of the foreground create an active surface design characteristic of Savery's later paintings.

Savery's composition recalls the romantic, overgrown forests painted by Gillis van Coninxloo (1544–1607) but replaces the sixteenth-century artist's preference for lush trees enclosing two views to the distance with a more naturalistic scene with views through a single open arch on the left and an opening to the distance framed on the right by only a narrow suggestion of foliage. Savery further integrated the composition by stressing the diagonal line of the hillside and limiting the use of local colors in the foreground, using a brown translucent glaze over a narrow range of opaque pigments and unpainted areas of preparatory ground to suggest an overall atmosphere. His brushstrokes are looser and more painterly

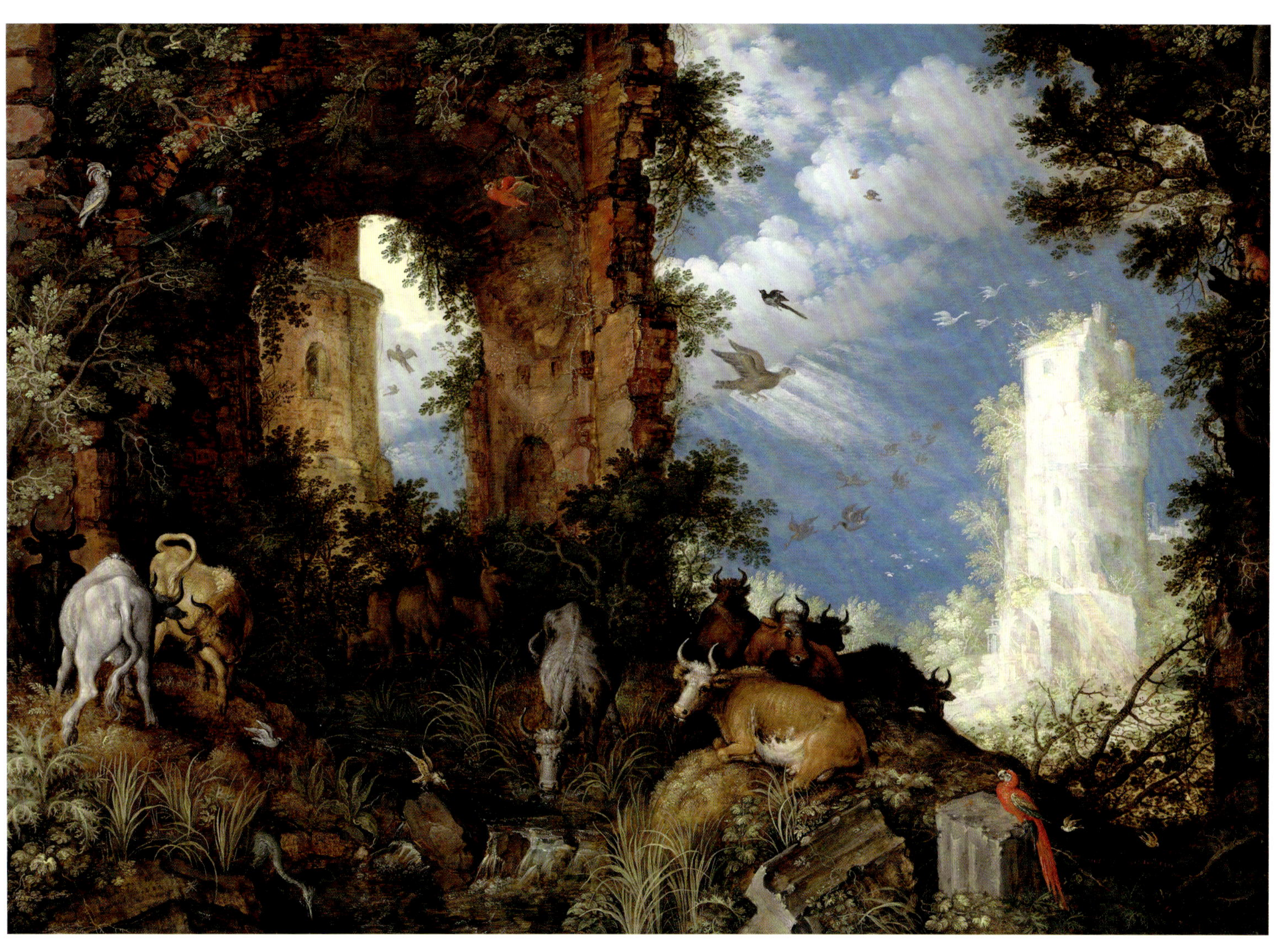

than the miniature-like refinement of his earlier paintings, such as the 1604 *Still Life* (Centraal Museum, Utrecht).[3]

As is typical for the artist, here Savery subordinated the details to the setting. Broken sections of a fluted column in the foreground recall the fascination with ruins introduced to the north by Paul Bril (1554–1626) and others who traveled to Rome. Overgrown with foliage, they are probably meant to oppose the vanity of human achievements and the permanence of nature and God.

The frequent repetition of both landscape elements and specific animal motifs in Savery's paintings suggests that he maintained a large collection of drawings and prints to use as reference material.[4] Among these were those he drew "naar het leven" (from life) from living specimens in the famous imperial menagerie in Prague as well as from mounted specimens, drawings, prints, and manuscripts in Rudolf II's fabulous Kunst- und Wunderkammer (collection of art and wonders of the world).[5] The convincing realism of the monkey perched in the tall tree on the right and the large colorful macaw in the lower right foreground of *Landscape with Ruins and Animals* is remarkable. Both are closely related to illustrations made from life by various artists and compiled together in a bestiary for Rudolf II, which Savery may have known (figs. 82a–b).[6] Savery's naturalistic rendering of the macaw in the Pasadena painting is striking in comparison with the stiff, two-dimensional character of the hawk flying in the center of the same work, which was probably modeled either from a print or drawn from his own imagination.

For the image of the fighting bulls on the left, Savery probably referred to a more complex motif from Antonio Tempesta's (1555–1630) popular series of stylized battles between pairs of animals (fig. 82c). Savery characteristically exploited the decorative potential of the prototype by exaggerating the curving lines of the horns, tails, and backs of the bulls and manipulating the positions of the animals to create a more dynamic and cohesive image. Savery used the motif in more than one painting: the same bulls appear in *Saint Elijah Being Fed by the Ravens* (Sint Eloyen Gasthuis, Utrecht), in which the biblical subject appears in the background framed by fighting bulls and a vignette of a lion attacking a horse in the foreground.[7]

Although compositionally similar to Savery's many depictions of paradise populated by domestic as well as exotic animals and figures of Adam and Eve, Noah, or Orpheus, the theme of the Pasadena painting appears to be more closely related to two paintings he signed and dated in 1616: one represents cattle resting (location unknown), the other, bulls attacked by a fox (fig. 82d). The two paintings were probably intended to be read as a pair and relate to an illustration in Jacob Cats's (1577–1660) *Spiegel van den Voorleden en Tegenwoordigen Tijt* (Mirror of the Past and Present Time; Amsterdam, 1632). The caption of Cats's illustration (in translation)—"Cattle fighting among themselves

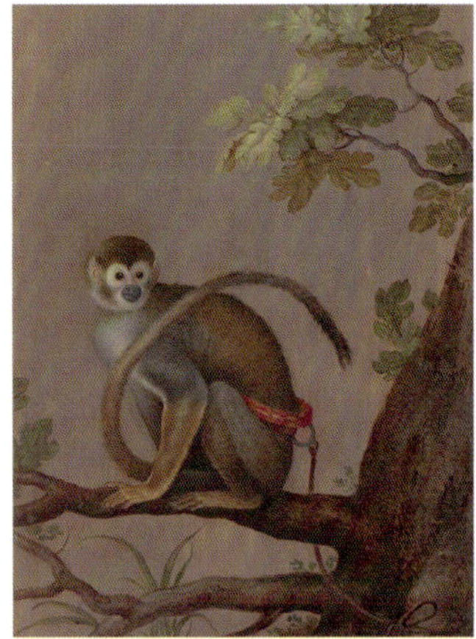

Fig. 82a. Unknown artist, *Monkey*, from *Bestiarium*, 1610, oil on paper, Cod. Min. 129, fol. 49, ÖNB/Vienna.

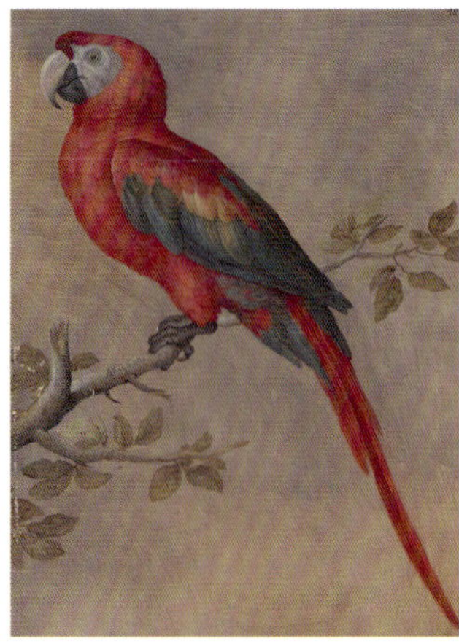

Fig. 82b. Daniel Fröschel, *Macaw*, from *Bestiarium*, 1610, oil on paper, Cod. Min. 130, fol. 17, ÖNB/Vienna.

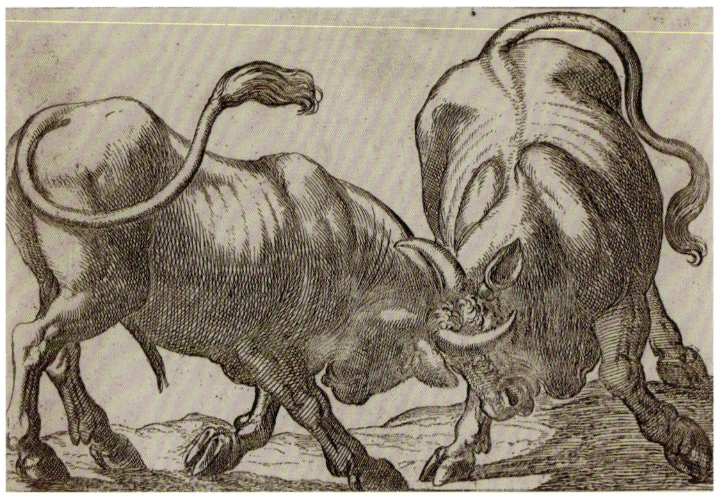

Fig. 82c. Antonio Tempesta, *Two Bulls Fighting*, from *Battling Animals*, 1600, engraving, 36⅝ × 51⅛ in. (93 × 130 cm), British Museum, Department of Prints and Drawings, London.

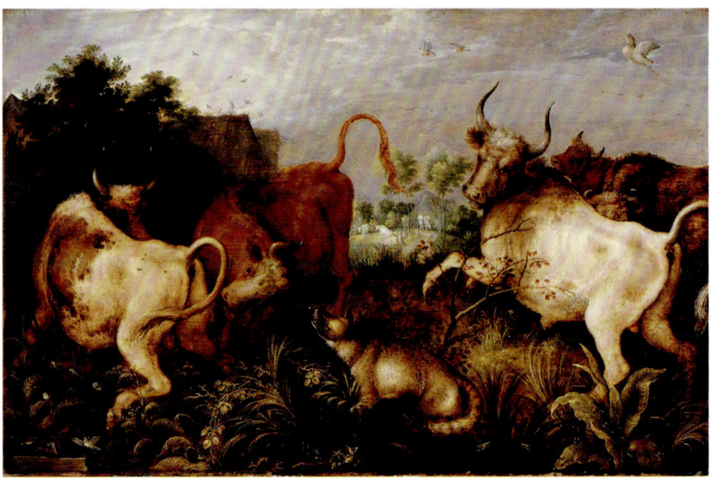

Fig. 82d. Roelandt Savery, *Landscape and Animals*, 1616, oil on wood, 20 1/16 × 32⅛ in. (51 × 81.5 cm), MAH Musée d'art et d'histoire, Ville de Genève. Legs Gustave Revilliod, Genève, 1890.

unite in defense when the wolf comes"—relates to the popular contemporary theme of vigilance, which may also be the theme of a related painting by Savery, *The Stag among the Oxen*, 1618 (Rijksmuseum, Amsterdam), representing a tale told and illustrated in the 1617 edition of Aesop's fables by Joost van den Vondel (1587–1679).[8] According to the fable, the stag asked the oxen for refuge from the hunters who were pursuing him. The cattle advise him to hide under the hay, but when the hunters leave, the farmer enters the barn and catches the stag. According to Van den Vondel, the moral of the fable is to beware of dangerous situations and avoid them.[9] In the Pasadena painting, the deer remain vigilant, their ears perked at attention, while the bulls spar among themselves.

Savery's numerous variations of *Landscape with Ruins and Animals*, as well as similar paintings of lush forests and exotic details that invite close inspection, attest to their popularity among his patrons. Visual pleasure was certainly a major part of their appeal. The combination of peaceful cattle with fighting bulls and alert deer, however, may also have been recognized in both general and specific terms as a reminder of the need for the country to remain vigilant, even in times of stability. The theme of vigilance appears in the literature and the visual arts of the Netherlands throughout the Eighty Years' War (1568–1648), but it was especially popular during and following the Twelve Years' Truce of 1609–21, a time when the desire for peace was equaled by the fear of the country's vulnerability to foreign attack.[10]

1. This information supplied by Edward Speelman in a letter to Norton Simon dated 12 June 1972 (NSM). Transcribed copies of four Wallenstein inventories were given by Lubor Machytka (Olomouc, Czech Republic) in the early 1990s to the GPI for its Collectors Files. All four documents record landscape paintings by Savery in the family collection between 1737 and 1900 but are not detailed enough to reliably connect to the Pasadena painting.

2. Müllenmeister 1988, nos. 172–73. On p. 118, Müllenmeister relates these paintings to two with similar but distinctly different settings and subjects: *Forest Landscape with Cattle* (Staatliche Galerie, Schloss Georgium, Dessau; Müllenmeister 1988, no. 171) and *Domestic Animals near Ruins*, 1617 (location unknown).

3. Savery's style was still in transition in the Pasadena painting. His use of a full brush to apply bright opaque colors for the background separates it atmospherically as well as coloristically from the foreground.

4. See Spicer 1979.

5. Regarding Savery's "naar het leven" drawings of figures, see Van Leeuwen 1970 and Spicer 1970. A number of important publications regarding Rudolf II's collection are sources for further bibliography. Among the most important are those by Eliška Fučíková, including Fučíková et al. 1991, Fučíková et al. 1997, Konečný et al. 1998, and Dijon 2002.

6. Rudolf II's bestiary in the Österreichische Nationalbibliothek, Vienna, Cod. Min. 129 and Cod. Min. 130, are reproduced in facsimile by Haupt et al. 1990. The manuscript, which consists of 180 gouaches on parchment, is attributed to various artists, including Daniel Fröschel (1563–1613), Joris (1542–1600) and Jacob Hoefnagel (1573–1632/33), and Dirk de Quade van Ravesteyn (1576–1612). The characteristic pose and physical appearance of the monkey in Savery's painting resemble those of a white-faced monkey with a leash around its waist sitting on the branch of a tree in a drawing included as fol. 49r (Haupt et al. 1990, pp. 194f., pl. 48). The large, red macaw is closely related to fol. 17r (Haupt et al. 1990, pp. 314f., pl. 106). The original image of the bird may have been derived from Savery's teacher Hans Bol (1534–1593), whose three-volume manuscript was copied by Jacopo Ligozzi (1547/49–1627) and others working in the imperial court. Bol's bestiaries, which are now housed in the Kongelige Bibliotek, Copenhagen, may have belonged to Joris Hoefnagel, who had also been a student of Bol and worked for the emperor. See Hendrix 1984, passim.

7. Müllenmeister 1988, no. 253.

8. Spicer 1983, pp. 255f.; Van den Vondel [1617], pp. 114f., fable 49.

9. Van den Vondel [1617], p. 114, equates the fable with the biblical story of the five Ammonite kings who take refuge from Joshua in a cave, only to be trapped there and later executed. The story is told in Joshua 10:16–27; Van den Vondel mistakenly cites Joshua 1:10.

10. Discussed in A. Walsh 1985, pp. 370ff.

83

Frans Snyders

Flemish
Antwerp 1579–1657 Antwerp

and

Cornelis de Vos

Flemish
Hulst ca. 1584/85–1651 Antwerp

Still Life with Fruit and Vegetables

ca. 1625–35

Signed on lower section of table leg: "F. Snyders fecit"
Oil on canvas, 68 ¼ × 101 in. (173.4 × 256.5 cm)
The Norton Simon Foundation, F.1973.16.P

Provenance

Field Marshal George Wade (1673–1748), sold before 1752 to;[1] Henry Pelham (1695–1754), by descent to his nephew;[2] Henry Fiennes Pelham-Clinton (1720–1794),[3] 9th Earl of Lincoln, after 1756, 2nd Duke of Newcastle-under-Lyne, Clumber Park, Worksop, Nottinghamshire, by descent to his son;[4] Thomas Pelham-Clinton (1752–1795), 3rd Duke of Newcastle-under-Lyne, 10th Earl of Lincoln, Clumber Park, Worksop, Nottinghamshire, by descent to his son; Henry Pelham Fiennes Pelham-Clinton (1785–1851), 4th Duke of Newcastle-under-Lyne, 11th Earl of Lincoln, Clumber Park, Worksop, Nottinghamshire, by descent to his son; Henry Pelham-Clinton (1811–1864), 5th Duke of Newcastle-under-Lyne, 12th Earl of Lincoln, Clumber Park, Worksop, Nottinghamshire, by descent to; Henry Pelham Alexander Pelham-Clinton (1834–1879), 6th Duke of Newcastle, 13th Earl of Lincoln, Clumber Park, Worksop, Nottinghamshire, by descent to his son; Henry Pelham Archibald Douglas Pelham-Clinton (1864–1928), 7th Duke of Newcastle, 14th Earl of Lincoln, Clumber Park, Worksop, Nottinghamshire, by descent to his brother; Henry Francis Pelham-Clinton-Pelham-Hope (1866–1941), 8th Duke of Newcastle, 15th Earl of Lincoln, Clumber Park, Worksop, Nottinghamshire, by descent to his son; Henry Edward Hugh Pelham-Clinton-Hope (1907–1988), 9th Duke of Newcastle, 16th Earl of Lincoln (sale, Christie's, London, 4 June 1937, lot 103, ill., sold to); [Polak]. Sir Harry Oakes (1874–1943),[5] London, by descent to his wife; Eunice, Lady Oakes (1898–1981), London (sale, Christie's, London, 29 June 1973, lot 100, sold to);[6] [Thomas Agnew & Sons, London, sold 1973 to]; The Norton Simon Foundation.

Exhibited

London 1851, no. 21;[7] Manchester 1857, either no. 545 or 572, both of which are titled *Market Scene* and lent by the Duke of Newcastle]; London 1879, no. 230, "Market Piece: Fruit, 67 × 99 in.," lent by the Duke of Newcastle.[8]

References

Walpole 1752, p. 80; Walpole 1767; Neale 1819–23, vol. 1 (1822), n.pag. [Clumber, Nottinghamshire]; Neale 1829–31, vol. 1 (1829), n.pag.; Waagen [1857] 1970, p. 508; *"Manchester Guardian"* 1857, p. 55, no. 545;[9] Thoré 1860, p. 227; Clumber 1872, no. 3; Graves [1913–15] 1970, vol. 3, pp. 1237–38; "Clumber House Treasures" 1937; "Clumber Old Masters" 1937; "Clumber Pictures" 1937; Greindl 1956, p. 181; Hairs 1955, p. 240; Hairs 1965, p. 412; Gerson 1976, p. 163; Los Angeles 1983, p. 20; Greindl 1983, pp. 75, 374, no. 48; Hairs 1985, p. 496; Robels 1989, pp. 27f., 66, 141, 205f., no. 41; Antwerp/Münster 1990, pp. 88f., fig. 57; Utrecht/Braunschweig 1991, pp. 25–26, 52, fig. 7; Bauman and Liedtke 1992, p. 369, fig. 456; Koslow 1995, pp. 134f., 137, figs. 109, 178; Pasadena 2003, p. 64, ill.; S. Campbell 2010, p. 357, no. 968, ill.

Technical Notes

The original plain-weave canvas support has been lined. Small fragments of the original tacking edges remain along the left, top, and bottom edges. Cusped threads are visible only at the top edge. Several minor tears in the canvas have been repaired. There is a moderately thick white ground. A light brown imprimatura painted over the ground influences the color of the thinly painted background. Paint in a variety of thicknesses has been applied with a loose and fluid handling. Thin paint in the background barely covers the imprimatura in some areas. At the top left, beside the red bowl of plums, a reserve may have been overlooked in the painting's final stages. Several artist's changes (pentimenti) have become evident as the paint has become more transparent: At the right corner of the table, a stem and upturned leaf were painted out, and the corner of the table appears to have been extended. At the left end of the table, an oval shape seems to be a pentimento from a plum that was never completed. The back of the woman's chair appears to have been painted at two different heights, with the first version lower. Increased transparency of the light-green grape leaf in the center allows the rim of the bowl behind it to show. The large dishes on the table were probably originally painted as blue-and-white Chinese export porcelain, possibly with indigo as the blue pigment, which has faded dramatically. The woman's apron, now noticeably damaged, may have been painted with smalt that lost its color over time. Subsequent cleaning may have caused the area further damage, which was compounded by overpainting. A condition report written by Herbert Lank, London, prior to acquisition in 1973 noted the severely damaged apron, as well as a significant amount of paint loss at the left, right, and bottom edges. Some abrasion had also occurred, and shadowed areas had been thinned. The loose and sketchy handling in several areas, as well as the transparency of the paint in other areas, may have given the impression that there was more abrasion than is actually the case. Despite multiple relinings, the paint is generally well preserved, with crisp contours and visible brushwork intact. The majority of restoration that followed is located at the edges of the painting. In 2009 Tiarna Doherty, of the paintings conservation department at the J. Paul Getty Museum, consolidated areas of loss and cracked paint principally along the bottom edge. Ultraviolet light indicates areas of both natural- and synthetic-resin varnish.

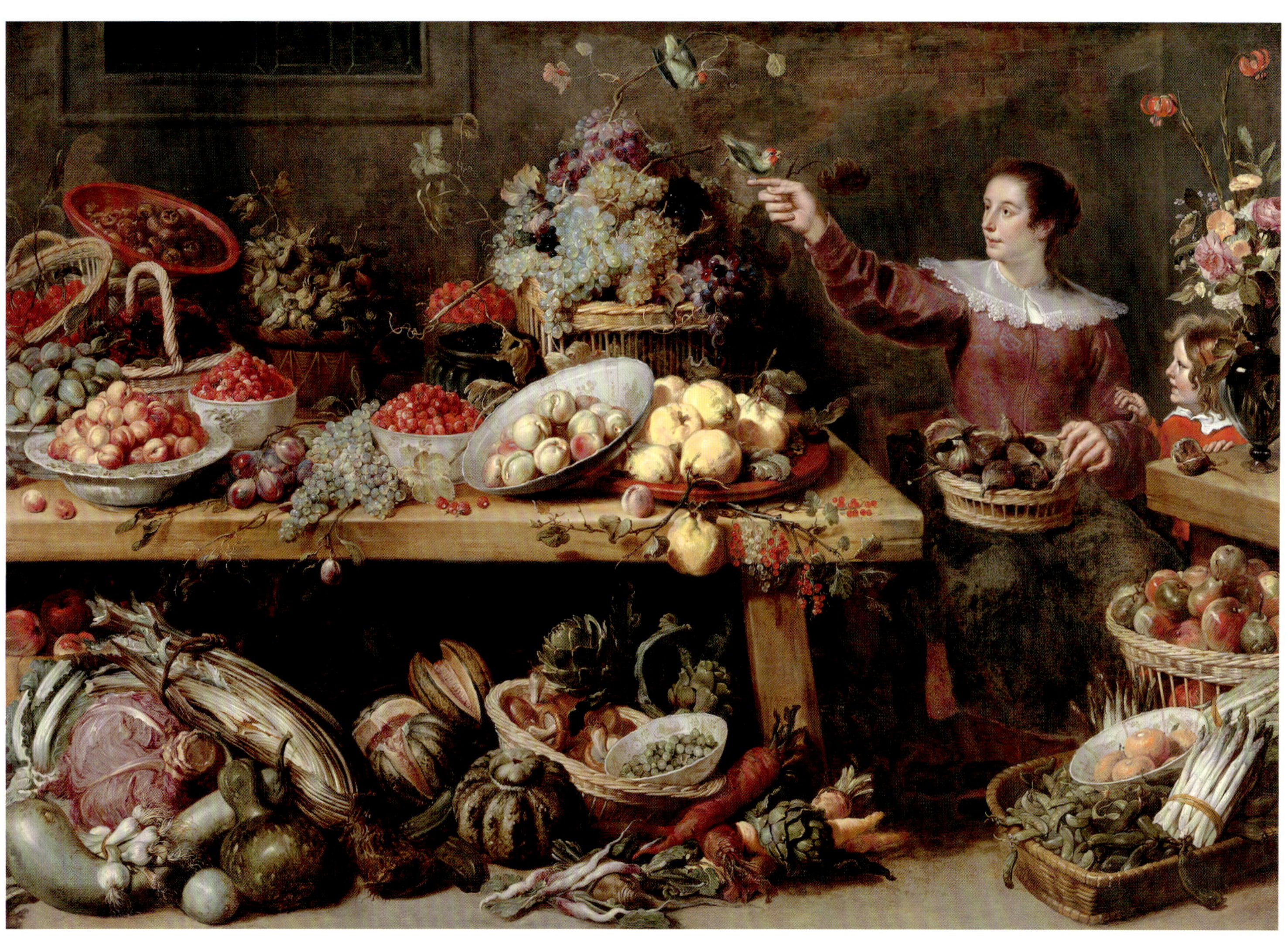

Still Life with Fruit and Vegetables is characteristic of Frans Snyders's paintings of markets and larders. Often of enormous proportions and hung in groups of two or four, these displays of abundance dominated even large rooms. From at least 1752 until 1937, the Pasadena painting hung as one of a group of four market scenes, including a game larder and two fish stalls.[10] Despite the similarity of dimensions and provenance, however, the inclusion of two works of the same subject suggests that these paintings may not originally have formed a set. The Pasadena painting and *A Game Stall* (fig. 83a) appear closest in terms of composition and size. Both are organized around a long rustic oak table set against a neutral wall; in the Pasadena painting, the wall is articulated only by the abstract geometric form of the lower portion of a leaded-glass window and a small area of rusticated bricks behind the woman. In *A Game Stall* the young man stands in front of an open door through which one can see the sky. In contrast to these two paintings, the two fish stalls (of which there are only written descriptions) included more figures and clearly set the scenes in the context of a market. Rather than a market, *A Game Stall* and the Pasadena painting probably represent the larder of a fine house.[11]

The large scale of *Still Life with Fruit and Vegetables* increases the impression of a voluptuous display of fresh produce piled freely on the floor and arranged on the table in wicker baskets and expensive blue-and-white Chinese export bowls.[12] Typically, Snyders depicted vegetables on the ground and the more precious fruit on the table. During the seventeenth century, fruit was a sign of wealth, grown only on estates, whereas vegetables were regarded as the mean basis of a peasant meal. The vegetables and fruits depicted by Snyders here are typical of those harvested locally: grapes, berries, cherries, quinces, red currants, and other fruits are represented in bowls and lying loosely on the plank table, while a red cabbage, onions, cardoons, chard, parsnips, carrots, beets, radishes, and artichokes are piled on the ground. Cantaloupes—overripe and split open—lie beneath the table.[13] A large basket on the right holds pears and apples. More precious vegetables, such as peas, mushrooms, and asparagus, are in bowls on the floor. The bouquet of flowers in a vase on the far right is reminiscent of those painted by Snyders's master, Jan Brueghel I (1568–1625).[14] Typical of contemporary flower arrangements, Snyders's display is fanciful as the fruits and vegetables ripen at different times.[15]

A young woman and a child who rests his hand on her arm animate the large still life. Seated at the end of the long table with a basket of figs in her lap, the woman and child direct their attention to a small colorful parrot perched on her finger. The identity of the pair is unclear. Wearing a red brocade dress with a dark apron, the original color of which has changed, and a white lace collar but no cap, the woman is better dressed than most of Snyders's market women and maids. In his closely related *Fruit and Vegetable Market* (Bayerische Staatsgemäldesammlungen, Munich), ca. 1620–30, for example, the maid wears a bright red jacket, dark skirt, black apron, and simple white collar and cap.[16] Like the similarly dressed young page in *A Game Stall*, the woman in the Pasadena composition is probably a member of the staff of an elegant household, perhaps a nurse with her charge.

Scholars generally agree that *Still Life with Fruit and Vegetables* is a collaborative work for which Snyders painted the produce and setting and another artist painted the figures. When first recorded in the collection of the Duke of Newcastle, the four paintings, including the Pasadena canvas, were identified as works by Snyders with figures by Lange Jan (Long John), the nickname for Jan Boeckhorst (ca. 1604–1668), a German painter originally from Münster, who worked with Rubens in Antwerp.[17] The figures in Boeckhorst's history paintings show the influence of Rubens but especially of Anthony van Dyck (1599–1641), Titian (ca. 1488–1576), and Paolo Veronese (1528–1588). The attribution of the figures to Boeckhorst is inadequate when one compares the relatively firmly modeled forms, especially the woman, in the Pasadena painting to his more painterly figures. Katelijne van der Stighelen was the first to propose the more likely attribution to the portraitist Cornelis de Vos, Snyders's brother-in-law, with whom he often collaborated.[18]

Snyders's combination of narrative figures with bountiful displays of produce recalls the sixteenth-century market scenes of Joachim Beuckelaer (1534–ca. 1574) and Pieter Aertsen (1507–1575) in which the foreground is occupied by fruits, vegetables, and game and related views of markets or religious vignettes are relegated to the background, which is physically detached by scale. In comparison with these earlier paintings, however, Snyders deemphasized the narrative, iconographic aspects of his market and larder scenes and focused more attention on the still life.

Snyders's monumental paintings draw on traditional allegorical associations to celebrate the productivity of the local countryside.[19] Working in the second quarter of the seventeenth century, Snyders naturalistically incorporated these concepts in scenes of everyday life. In addition to associations with the land, the Pasadena painting also discreetly refers to all the five senses: sight as well as taste by the succulent, ripe fruit; sound by the birds; smell by the flowers; and touch by the child's hand on the woman's arm.

More generally, Snyders's grandiose displays of abundance celebrate the productivity of the land, specifically of the Netherlands, a major theme of contemporary *hofdichten* (court poems) that were part of an international revival of Georgic literature. In these long poems celebrating the benefits of the country life, the author—the owner of the estate—mentions with great pride and satisfaction the table laid with food that has not been bought but has come entirely from his land. Snyders's still lifes celebrate precisely this point of pride in food produced locally. During

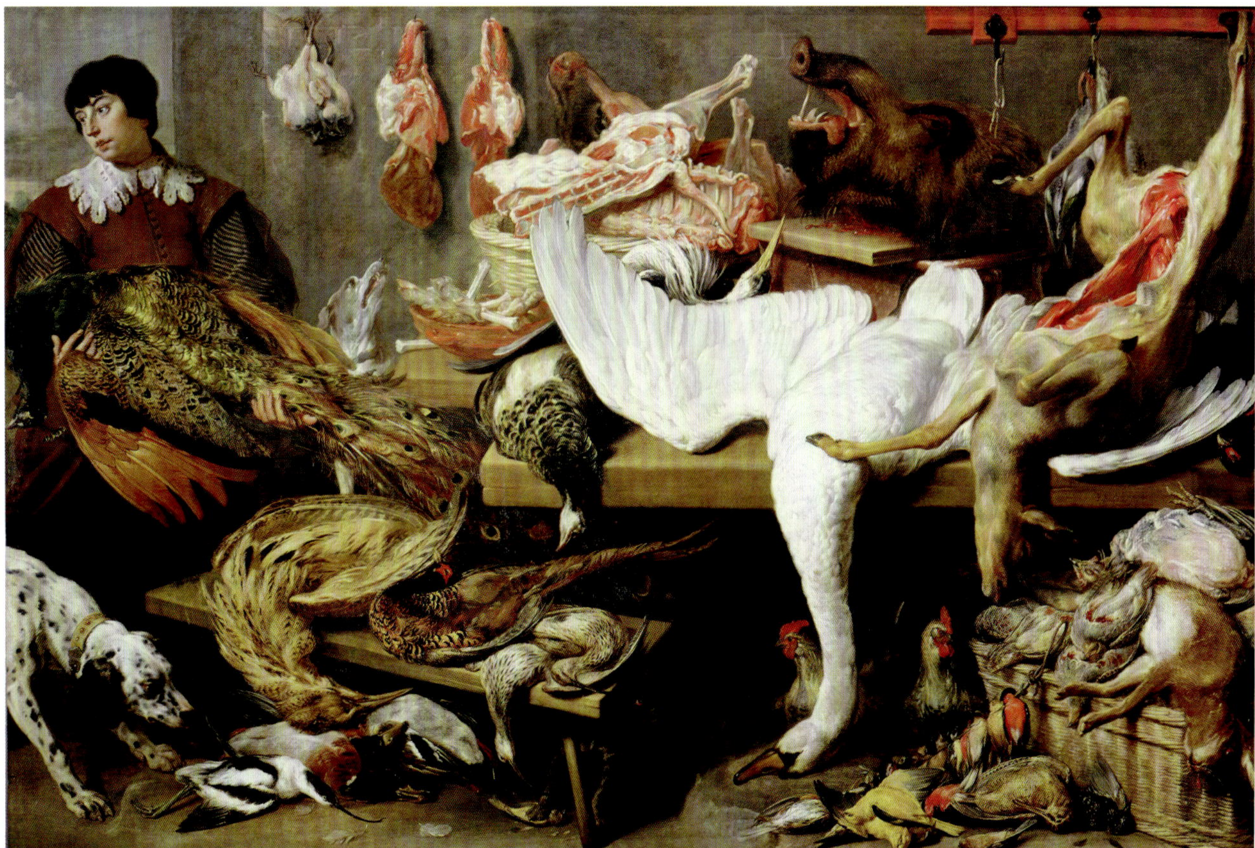

Fig. 83a. Frans Snyders, *A Game Stall*, 1625–35, oil on canvas, 67 × 100 in. (170 × 254 cm), City of York Art Gallery.

the sixteenth and seventeenth centuries, the Spanish Netherlands (present-day Belgium) was famous for the fruits and vegetables it exported to England. In 1581 Lodovico Guicciardini (1521–1589), a Florentine resident of Antwerp, published a description of the Netherlands in which he itemized the regional fruits and nuts, noting that pears and apples were especially plentiful and available throughout the year. Furthermore, Susan Koslow points out that the produce Snyders included in these paintings actually replicates that described in documents recording rent paid to the lord of an estate. The expensive Chinese bowls, the table overflowing with fruit, even the delicate figs in the woman's lap and the pet parrots, thus testify to the prosperity not only of a wealthy estate but also of the country in general. Writers since antiquity, including those of the *hofdichten*, have identified the prosperity of the land as one of the major benefits of political peace. It has also been considered a sign of God's providence. Significantly, Snyders began painting monumental still lifes such as the Pasadena painting during the Twelve Years' Truce established with the Dutch Republic in 1609.[20]

Some of Snyders's large larder and market scenes hung in public spaces; for example, a larder hung over the mantel in the banqueting room of Antwerp's city hall.[21] Snyders probably painted most of these paintings, however, for the wealthiest members of society, whose grand townhouses and country estates provided the necessary expanses of wall.[22] The commissioning of a series of large-scale paintings identified the patron as a man of taste and wealth, granting members of the new nobility and wealthy merchant class the social prestige they desired.

According to Horace Walpole (1717–1797), the Pasadena painting and its companions entered the collection of the Dukes of Newcastle before 1752, having been bought by "Mr. Pelham" from the sale of Field Marshal George Wade.[23] Walpole's information thus eliminates the possibility that the paintings were commissioned or bought directly from Snyders by William Cavendish (1593–1676), 1st Duke of Newcastle upon Tyne, who reportedly shared Charles I's love of painting and before 1649 had rented Rubens's house in Antwerp from the artist's widow.[24] They also cannot be identified with a set of paintings of the four elements that J. F. M. Michel in 1771 claimed Snyders had painted for Antoine Triest (1576–1657), Bishop of Bruges and later Ghent. Those paintings are noted in the archbishop's palace in Bruges in 1753 and 1763 and, according to Michel, were later transferred to the goldsmith's chamber in Brussels and sold to an English dealer before 1771.[25] Another suite of paintings that belonged to Jacques van Ophem (d. 1648)—a wealthy member of the lower nobility and Habsburg administrator responsible for collecting taxes who built a mansion on the rue Neuve, Brussels—was sold by his descendants ca. 1723 and acquired by the British statesman Robert Walpole (1676–1745), from whose estate they were later purchased by Empress Catherine II of Russia (r. 1762–96). Today they hang in the Hermitage, St. Petersburg.[26]

Henry Pelham, who was considered Robert Walpole's most capable disciple, was probably inspired by him to acquire Snyders's series, including the Pasadena painting, from Field Marshal Wade.[27] *Still Life with Fruit and Vegetables* later passed to Pelham's nephew, Henry Fiennes Pelham-Clinton, who married Pelham's oldest surviving daughter, Catherine (1727–1760) in 1744.[28] Henry Fiennes Pelham-Clinton was the son of Henry Pelham's sister Lucy. Neither Henry Pelham, whose sons had died young, nor his brother Thomas Pelham-Holles, 1st Duke of Newcastle-under-Lyne, who was childless but had served as guardian of Henry Fiennes Pelham-Clinton following the death of his father, had direct male heirs. At the time of the marriage of the two cousins, it was agreed that Henry Fiennes Pelham-Clinton would be the primary heir of both Henry Pelham and Thomas Pelham-Holles. In 1756, at the request of Pelham-Holles, the title Duke of Newcastle-under-Lyne was created for Henry Fiennes Pelham-Clinton, and he was given the properties in Nottinghamshire, where *Still Life with Fruit and Vegetables* remained until sold by the 9th Duke of Newcastle in 1937.

1. In Walpole 1752, p. 81, Horace Walpole discussed the four market scenes in his father's collection, noting that "Mr. Pelham has four Markets by Snyders like these, which he bought at Marshal Wade's Sale, the figures by Long John." The only known public sale of the Wade collection prior to 1752 was a sale of sculpture that took place in Wade's home in Burlington Gardens, London, by Cock and Langford, 18–20 May 1648 (GPI, Sales Catalog Br–A420). All other known sales from his collection postdate this notification: General Wade, Christie's, London, 19 April 1785 (Lugt 1938–87, vol. 1, no. 3865); and Edward Bearcroft and John Wade, both deceased, Christie's, London, 27–28 March 1797 (Lugt 1938–87, vol. 1, no. 5561). The second sale notes that John Wade's collection had been "originally collected by his father Field Marshal Wade, who was long distinguished for his correct Taste as a Connoisseur during his Command on the Continent." Field Marshal Wade led troops in Flanders for many years and may have acquired the paintings while there. One must presume that Pelham bought the painting at a private sale of part of Wade's collection, which probably took place at the time of his death in 1748.

2. According to Koslow 1995, p. 335n125, Mr. Pelham refers either to Thomas Pelham-Holles (1693–1768), 1st Duke of Newcastle-under-Lyne, or to his brother Henry Pelham. Both men were major political figures during the reign of King George II: Henry served as prime minister from 1742 until his death in 1754 and was succeeded in office by his older brother Thomas Pelham-Holles. Thomas was known as Newcastle after 1715, when he became duke, and Henry was referred to as Pelham; Horace Walpole, whose father was closely allied with both brothers, was also close to the family. In Walpole 1752, p. 81 (see note 1 above), he was probably referring to Henry Pelham, although the owner of the painting when it was lent to the British Institution in 1851 was noted as Newcastle.

3. Henry Fiennes Pelham-Clinton was the son of Henry Clinton, 7th Earl of Lincoln, and Lucy Pelham, the sister of Henry Pelham and the Duke of Newcastle. As heir to both Henry Pelham and Thomas, Duke of Newcastle, who had no children, Henry Fiennes Pelham-Clinton was made Duke of Newcastle-under-Lyne in 1756 to assure the continuation of the dukedom after the death of the 1st Duke of Newcastle upon Tyne.

4. Included in the inventory of Clumber House made at the time of the death of Henry Fiennes Pelham-Clinton. See the introduction to Clumber 1872, which identifies paintings marked with an asterisk in the catalogue as having been included in the 1794 catalogue. According to Neale 1819–23, vol. 1 (1822), n.pag., "In the state dining-room are four very large Market Pieces, beautifully painted by Snyders." The house at Clumber Park was built in 1767 from the designs of Stephen Wright and built of stone quarried on the estate. The house was destroyed in 1938, one year after the sale of the paintings.

5. Sir Harry Oakes was a Canadian-born gold-mining millionaire and collector who was murdered in the Bahamas in 1943. According to his grandson and namesake, Sir Harry Oakes (telephone conversation with Carol Togneri, 28 May 2002), the senior Sir Harry Oakes was buying paintings in the 1930s and early 1940s and probably acquired this painting shortly after the 1937 sale. Robels 1989, no. 41, confused the provenance of the Pasadena painting with that of her no. 40, which had been sold as lot 104 in the 1937 sale. Lot 104 was sold to Lycett Green, where it was noted by Bax 1952, pp. 104f. Both paintings were among the original four paintings by Snyders that hung at Clumber House.

6. The anonymous seller was Lady Oakes, Eunice Myrtle (née McIntyre), the widow of Sir Harry Oakes.

7. The Duke of Newcastle also lent three other paintings by Snyders, all said to have been painted with Jan Boeckhorst (a.k.a Lange Jan): *Poultry Market* (no. 14); *Fish Market* (no. 39); and *Fish Market* (no. 44).

8. The Duke of Newcastle also lent Snyders's *Market Piece, Fish*, 67 × 86 (no. 227); *Market Piece, Fish*, 67 × 97 (no. 244); and *Market Piece, Game*, 97 × 66 in. [dimensions reversed] (no. 252).

9. "This 'market scene,' which commands such universal admiration . . . is one of four which decorate the dining-room at Clumber. . . . The remaining three are less effective."

10. Walpole 1752, p. 80. Also included in the catalogue of the 1937 Christie's sale were: lot 104, ill., *A Game Stall*, "A youth on the right holding a dead peacock with a dog, swan, deer and other dead game on a table and on the ground," signed, 67 × 100 in., sold for £180 to Green [Lycett Green, South Africa; now York Art Gallery]; lot 105, *A Fish Stall*, "A lady buying fish from a young market woman; a cavalier and other figures in the background," 67 × 87 in., exhibited at Burlington House, 1879, no. 227, sold for £60 to W. Sabin [present location unknown]; lot 106, *A Fish Stall*, "A fisherman arranging a stall, with a quay scene and shipping in the background," 67½ × 56½ in., exhibited at Burlington House, 1879, no. 244, sold for £38 to Webster [present location unknown].

11. Koslow 1995, p. 38, refers to descriptions of larders in Roman treatises on husbandry. These accounts often mention that dining tables were placed in these cool rooms.

12. The blue pigment, probably indigo, Snyders used to describe the porcelain has deteriorated over time. See Technical Notes above.

13. Koslow 1995, p. 21, notes that Snyders apparently kept drawings of both local and foreign fruit. In his will, he left "all his paintings on paper of Italian fruit" to his studio assistant Hendrik de Rasiers, the second son of Snyders's eldest sister, Clara.

14. The Pasadena painting lacks the more precious leafy vegetables that appear in other paintings by Snyders such as *Fruit and Vegetable Market*, ca. 1620–30 (Bayerische Staatsgemäldesammlungen, Munich; Koslow 1995, fig. 173). Stone-Ferrier 1989, 442, notes the distinction between "grove" (coarse) and "fijn" (fine or leafy) vegetables, which were far more fragile and thus more precious.

15. We are grateful to Sean Lahmeyer of the Huntington Botanical Gardens for his help in identifying the produce displayed in this painting and pointing out that the display is fanciful because they do not ripen at the same time. See note 13 above re: Snyders's use of drawings to represent fruits and vegetables that were available at different times during the growing season.

16. The woman in the Pasadena painting is also distinguished from the fashionably dressed young woman who picks fruit from the display in a painting by Snyders and (attributed to) Theodor van Thulden (1606–1669), *Larder with Young Girl*, ca. 1640–50 (Gemäldegalerie Alte Meister, Dresden). See also *Kitchen Maid with Mortar and Pestle*, ca. 1610 (Wallraf-Richartz Museum, Cologne; Koslow 1995, fig. 44).

17. For Boeckhorst, see Galen 2012.

18. Van der Stighelen in Antwerp/Münster 1990, pp. 88f., fig. 57, contradicts the earlier opinion of Greindl 1944, pp. 107f., who asserted that there was no evidence that Cornelis de Vos worked with Snyders.

19. An engraving by Nicolaes de Bruyn (1571–1656) after Maarten de Vos (1532–1603), for example, represents the earth as a woman holding a cornucopia and surrounded by fruit, vegetables, and grazing animals.

20. Koslow 1995, pp. 38, 91–92.

21. Snyders was paid 300 guilders for the commission by the municipal government of Antwerp; see Koslow 1995, pp. 151, 338n211.

22. Koslow 1995, pp. 116, 120ff., fig. 142, discusses the arrangement of one series that Snyders painted for Jacques van Ophem's mansion in Brussels.

23. See note 1 above.

24. Regarding Cavendish, see Van Beneden and De Poorter 2006; and Trease 1979, pp. 160–64.

25. J. F. M. Michel 1771, pp. 364f. Regarding Triest, see Koslow 1995, pp. 111, 118–19, 334n121.

26. Regarding the provenance of the Hermitage paintings, see Koslow 1995, pp. 110–16, 120ff. The Hermitage suite of paintings was previously identified with the Antoine Triest group mentioned by Michel. According to Koslow, however, John Macky, acting on behalf of Robert Walpole, purchased the Van Ophem suite of paintings from Jacques-Ferdinand de Villegas (1658–1723), Baron of Hovorst and Seigneur of Bouchout, Viersel, and Werster. The sale probably took place in 1723. De Villegas was the eldest son of Marie-Isabelle van Ophem. Catherine I purchased the Hermitage paintings from the estate of Robert Walpole, whose famous picture gallery at Houghton House was sold by his heirs to pay off gambling debts.

27. The popularity of the group is indicated by the numerous copies made of the paintings now in Saint Petersburg. The two works identified as in the collection of the dukes of Newcastle, including that in Pasadena, however, represent a separate, distinct series.

28. See note 3 above.

84

Isaak Soreau

Dutch or German
Hanau 1604–after 1645 Frankfurt?

Still Life with Fruit and Flowers

ca. 1638

Possibly remnants of a signature, lower left on edge of table[1]
Oil on wood, 28 ⅝ × 40 ¼ in. (72.7 × 102.2 cm)
Norton Simon Art Foundation, M.1979.39.P

Provenance

Probably Ambrose Lanfear Norrie (1857–1910), New York, before 1900, by descent to;[2] "Dutch private collection" [heirs of Norrie Wells][3] (sale, Galerie Moos, Geneva, 23 May 1936, no. 114, ill., as Clara Peeters, bought in);[4] "Geneva private collection," 1962;[5] Mrs. Norrie Wells,[6] Geneva (sale, Christie's, London, 8 December 1972, lot 62, as Jan Soreau, sold for £27,300 to); Leadbeater. [Galeria Bernini, sold 1974 to]; [Paul Rosenberg & Co., New York, stock no. 6464–2754 (sale, Christie's, London, 2 July 1976, lot 6, as Jan Soreau, bought in)]; [Paul Rosenberg & Co., New York, sold 1979 to]; Norton Simon Art Foundation.

References

Bott 1962, pp. 46, 67, no. 21, ill.; Pasadena 1989, p. 73, ill.; Bott 2001, pp. 113, 184, no. WV.IS.39, pl. 97;[7] S. Campbell 2010, p. 429, no. 1636, ill.

Technical Notes

The horizontally grained oak panel underwent structural procedures before the museum's acquisition in 1979, presumably to repair several long cracks. These procedures included significant thinning before the attachment of a balsa-wood block and wax-resin backing. In 1984 the backing was removed and the cracks were stabilized. To support the thin panel, three vertical battens were installed to pass through small wooden brackets glued to the reverse at short intervals. A smooth white ground covers the wood texture. The artist blocked in the positions of various design elements with red-brown and ochre underpainting, now occasionally visible because of the increased transparency of the upper paint layers. Paint was applied in smooth layers, varying from opaque to quite thin in a glaze-like consistency. Details of every texture were meticulously rendered, such as veined leaves, soft flower petals, reflective glass, grapes, and the woven basket. The draftsman-like interpretation of the Chinese bowl, which is painted with hard, clean edges, contrasts with the more modulated skins of the fruits inside it. Pentimenti surrounding a pair of plums below the basket show that the artist originally planned for them to be larger in the underpainting. Much of the paint is well preserved, although loss along the long cracks was substantial. A relatively large loss is at the lower end of the left edge and a similarly large loss is at the center of the right edge. There have been minimal losses due to flaking in the lower portion of the painting. Extensive retouching appears to have been carried out in three campaigns and is related to losses surrounding the cracks as well as countless smaller losses in the lower part of the painting below the lowest crack. Conservation records indicate the varnishing consists of two spray-coatings of Acryloid B-72 followed by a brush-coating of Soluvar (Acryloid B-67).

Although only remnants remain of what we assume was once a signature, *Still Life with Fruit and Flowers* can be securely attributed to Isaak Soreau by comparing it with a painting closely related to *Fruits and Flowers* signed "I. Soreau 1638" (fig. 84a), the only painting Soreau is known to have signed and dated.[8] As in that painting, here the objects appear to rest, somewhat precariously, on the tilted surface of the wooden table that is viewed from a higher vantage point than the objects. The major motif of the still life is, typically, a tall wicker basket overflowing with grapes and peaches, which can be seen through the open weave of the basket. Within the visual triangle, the apex of which is the basket, are a blue-and-white export Chinese bowl known as Wan-li porcelain filled with fruit, and a prunt-glass rummer with a loosely arranged bouquet of flowers.[9] Loose grapes, cherries, plums, strawberries, and a single red-and-white carnation appear scattered on the table without apparent design. Decorative arabesques formed by vine tendrils and stems and the delicate, light outlines of the large grape leaf seemingly dancing against the dark, undefined background help to integrate the composition. Droplets of water and the stems of flowers and fruit extending over the forward edge of the table create a sense of immediacy and transience.

A dark gray tonality tempers the composition but does not diminish the local colors of the different fruits, which the artist defined with thinly applied washes of paint. The clear delineation of objects rendered in terms of their individual

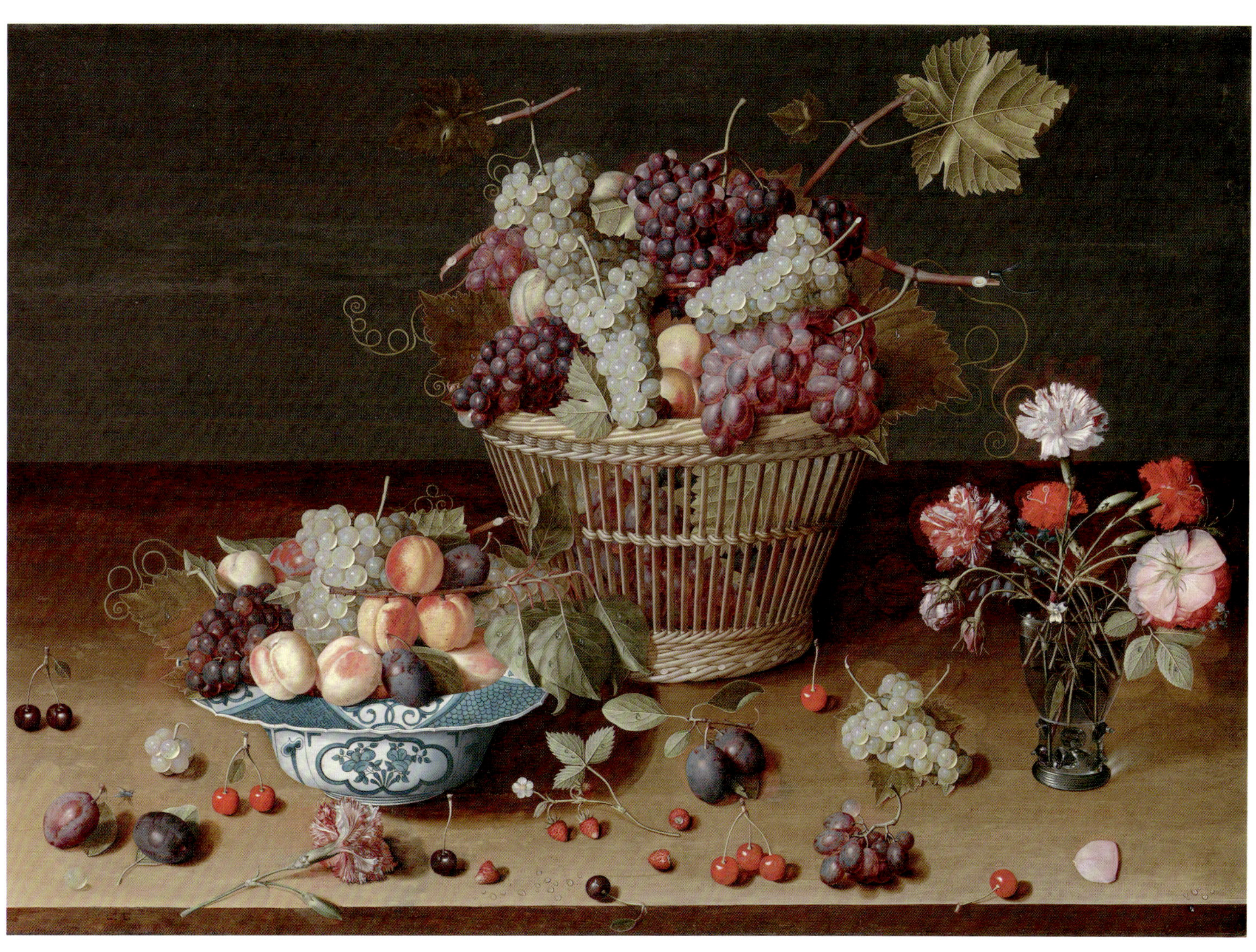

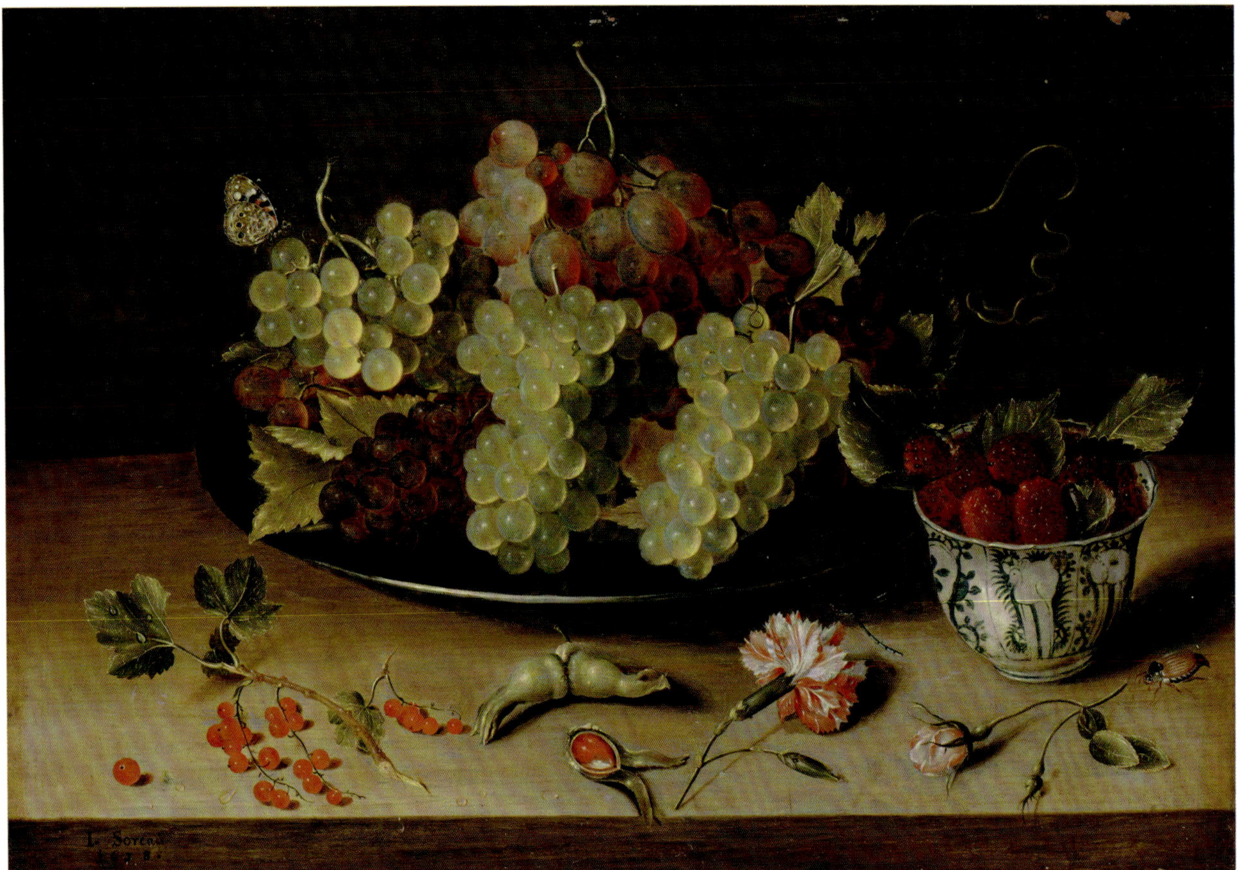

Fig. 84a. Isaak Soreau, *Fruits and Flowers*, 1638, oil on copper, 15⅜ × 22¼ in. (39 × 57 cm), Staatliches Museum, Schwerin.

light and color gives the painting an additive quality. Each of the grapes, for example, has a separate highlight and rim of light as if Soreau had followed a formula rather than his own direct observation of reality. Cast shadows likewise define the forms of separate objects rather than contribute to the unity of the composition, which relies on overlapping forms and the compositional structure of the implied pyramid. The limitations of this approach are evident in the fruit bowl, where each piece of fruit has independent volume but relates to the bowl as a two-dimensional form.

The cumulative effect of Soreau's composition is the result of his method of working from preparatory drawings of individual details. Pentimenti—of both overpainted motifs and areas originally left in reserve for objects, such as the double stem of plums in the center foreground, the fruit bowl, and the flowers—reveal that Soreau often reoriented his designs as he worked without changing their actual forms. His use of drawings as "stencils" explains not only the thinly overpainted areas of reserve but also the repetition of individual motifs from painting to painting. The carnation on the table and the double stem of cherries on the left, for example, reappear in a closely related painting in the Hamburger Kunsthalle, and the composition as a whole, with a reduced number of objects scattered on the table, is repeated in a work attributed to Isaak's older brother, Jan Soreau (1591–before 1626), on the Paris art market in 1964.[10]

The many versions of Isaak Soreau's still lifes of fruit and flowers and the similar still lifes of the Antwerp painter Jacob van Hulsdonck (1582–1647), with whom he may have studied, attest to their popularity among his patrons.[11] These medium and large cabinet paintings probably occupied prominent positions in the dining area of seventeenth-century homes, where they were admired for the beauty of their decorative compositions and the artist's skill in rendering reality. Viewers may have associated the theme of *vanitas* with the drops of water, the ripe fruit, and full-blown flowers, as well as the expensive Wan-li porcelain and the abundance of produce from the earth.

1. Bott 1962, p. 67, cites a letter of 3 March 1960 in which Edith Greindl says the painting is signed by Soreau.

2. Christie's 2 July 1976 sale catalogue cites the provenance as "Norrie Wells, England, before 1900." This is incorrect. "Mrs. Norrie Wells," the seller of the painting at Christie's on 8 December 1972, was Emily Margarita "Rita" Norrie Wells (1897–1981) of New York and Geneva, who married John Wells (1895–1951) of New York in 1917 and secondly Dr. Jacques de Morsier (1895–1962) of Geneva. She was the daughter of Ambrose Landfear Norrie and Ethel Lynde Barbey Norrie (1886–1959).

3. The anonymous seller was either Ambrose Norrie's widow, Ethel, or his daughter, Rita. In 1914, following Ambrose Norrie's death, Ethel Norrie married Count Armand de Jumilhac (1886–1966) and moved to Europe. She died in Paris. Regarding Rita, see note 2 above.

4. The sale catalogue does not specify from which collection the painting came. The collectors listed by the catalogue were Dr. C. T. van Valkenburg, Amsterdam; M. F. Uhlenbroek, Arnhem; and M. R. S. . . , Amsterdam.

5. Bott 1962, no. 21, cites the letter dated 3 March 1960 from Greindl for this provenance.

6. See note 2 above.

7. Bott 1962 and Bott 2001 erroneously cite the painting as on copper, 73 × 103 cm.

8. Because of the identical form of "I" and "J" during the seventeenth century, before Bott the painting was attributed to Isaak Soreau's older brother, Jan. As Bott 1962, p. 33, points out, however, the painting cannot have been by the elder sibling, who was baptized in Frankfurt in July 1591 and was buried in Hanau on 26 January 1626. Jan, Isaak, and Isaak's twin brother, Peter (1604–1672), were the sons and presumed students of the painter, architect, and wool merchant Daniel Soreau (1554–1619), who ran an important painting studio in Hanau. A Protestant family originally from Tornai, they had immigrated to Frankfurt in 1586 and in 1599 settled in Hanau, a newly established Walloon community near Frankfurt. Following the death of their father, the younger artists continued to work in the studio under the direction of Daniel Soreau's former student Sébastien Stoskopff (1597–1657), When Stoskopff left for Paris in 1621, the brothers took over the studio. In 1637 Peter Soreau married and established his own studio in Frankfurt, where Isaak may have joined him.

9. Rummers are large drinking glasses. Prunts, which resemble thorns, are formed by large glass drops broadly melted on the glass and pulled out to a point.

10. Sale, Paris, 8 December 1964, lot 89, panel, 76 × 96.5 cm. The Wan-li bowl and the flowers are closely related in the two paintings; indeed, many elements are repeated exactly in both works. The paintings also share several unusual details not found in Soreau's other works, most notably the wicker "stitching" midway up on the tall basket, which angles toward the left rather than the right, as it does in other paintings.

11. Although it is not documented, the close similarities of Isaak's still lifes and those of Jacob van Hulsdonck strongly suggest that the two artists were in contact, probably in Antwerp.

85

South German Master

Late 15th century

Christ Bearing the Cross

ca. 1490

Oil on panel, 20 × 14¾ in. (50.8 × 37.5 cm)
The Norton Simon Foundation, F.1965.1.036.P

Provenance
Private collection, Long Island, NY (sale, Parke-Bernet Galleries, New York, 13 March 1957, lot 4, as "Rhenish School, ca. 1490," sold for $900 to);[1] [Duveen Brothers, New York, as Master of the Karlsruhe Passion, stock no. 30275, sold 1965 to]; The Norton Simon Foundation.

Exhibited
Winston-Salem 1963, ill., as Follower of the Master of the Karlsruhe Passion, late 15th century; on loan, Museum of Fine Arts, Boston, 3 February 1965–4 December 1975.

Reference
S. Campbell 2010, p. 444, no. D36, ill.

Technical Notes
The support is a vertically grained hardwood panel made from a single board; now ¼-inch thick, it was probably thinned before its cradle was attached. Very little of the panel is exposed, making species identification difficult, although crack patterns in the paint at the sky and a sliver of wood exposed at the upper right edge suggest it is oak. The smooth white ground layer is moderately thick. The presence of a barbe at each side, where the wood was left without paint or ground, suggests that the panel was in a framework such as an altarpiece at the time it was prepared for painting. Microscopic examination of the surface did not reveal underdrawing. The paint appears to be an oil medium. The halos of Christ and the figures in the upper left were depicted with gold leaf and defined by incised outlines. Crisp, precise details of architecture and flora are highly finished. Generally the paint is not well preserved. Rather widespread abrasion is especially disfiguring in the face and robe of Christ. The halos have suffered extensive damage, with little remaining other than residues of gesso and traces of gold. The paint film is densely cracked in a fine web overall. Thin vertical cracks are often accompanied by lifting paint, with tiny losses at the edges. Magnification reveals a great number of small flake losses, some of which have been retouched without filling. Many flakes were previously dislodged and are now held in place by the thick varnish. In an undocumented prior treatment, cleaning of the painting left residues of dark varnish in all the recesses of the paint surface. Retouching is extensive, evident in numerous small spots throughout, including Christ's robe, Mary's robe, the raised arm and face of the soldier, and on the left shoulder of the foreground figure with a sword. Minor retouching is also located throughout the sky and foreground. The present natural-resin varnish is quite discolored, obscuring finely drawn details and distorting colors.

Christ Bearing the Cross represents one of the major scenes of the Passion of Christ as a contemporary event set outside a medieval German city. The robes and what remains of the flat, gold halos distinguish the holy personages from the laypeople dressed in late-fifteenth-century costumes. The iconography of the Pasadena panel expands the accounts of the Gospels with material derived from medieval narrative Passion texts.[2] Typical of late medieval Passion scenes, the painting includes details that emphasize the cruelties and suffering Christ endured at the hands of his tormentors as well as delicate emblematic flowers in the foreground.[3] The synoptic Gospels—Matthew, Mark, and Luke—refer to Simon of Cyrene as carrying the cross for Christ rather than Christ himself bearing the burden, as was normal for Roman prisoners. The Pasadena painting blends the two concepts, showing Christ stumbling beneath the burden of the large cross but assisted by the elderly figure of Simon dressed as a peasant. The image of the Virgin Mary—swooning at the gate of Jerusalem, supported on the left by John the Evangelist and on the right by Mary Magdalene—derives from Luke, who alone mentions the presence of the women. Veronica, who stands next to Mary Magdalene rather than near Christ, holds the cloth used to wipe the sweat from Christ's face, the likeness of which became permanently imprinted on it.

Christ Bearing the Cross may have served as the left wing of an altarpiece, the central image of which would have been a sculpture of the Crucifixion, and the right wing, the Resurrection.[4] It is also possible that it was one of two or more panels forming one of the wings of a large altarpiece. The composite of the individual panels is suggested by the inclusion of secondary events from the Passion of Christ in the background of the Pasadena panel: Judas, dressed in light-colored robes, leads a crowd of soldiers in the middle distance next to the city wall, and farther along the road,

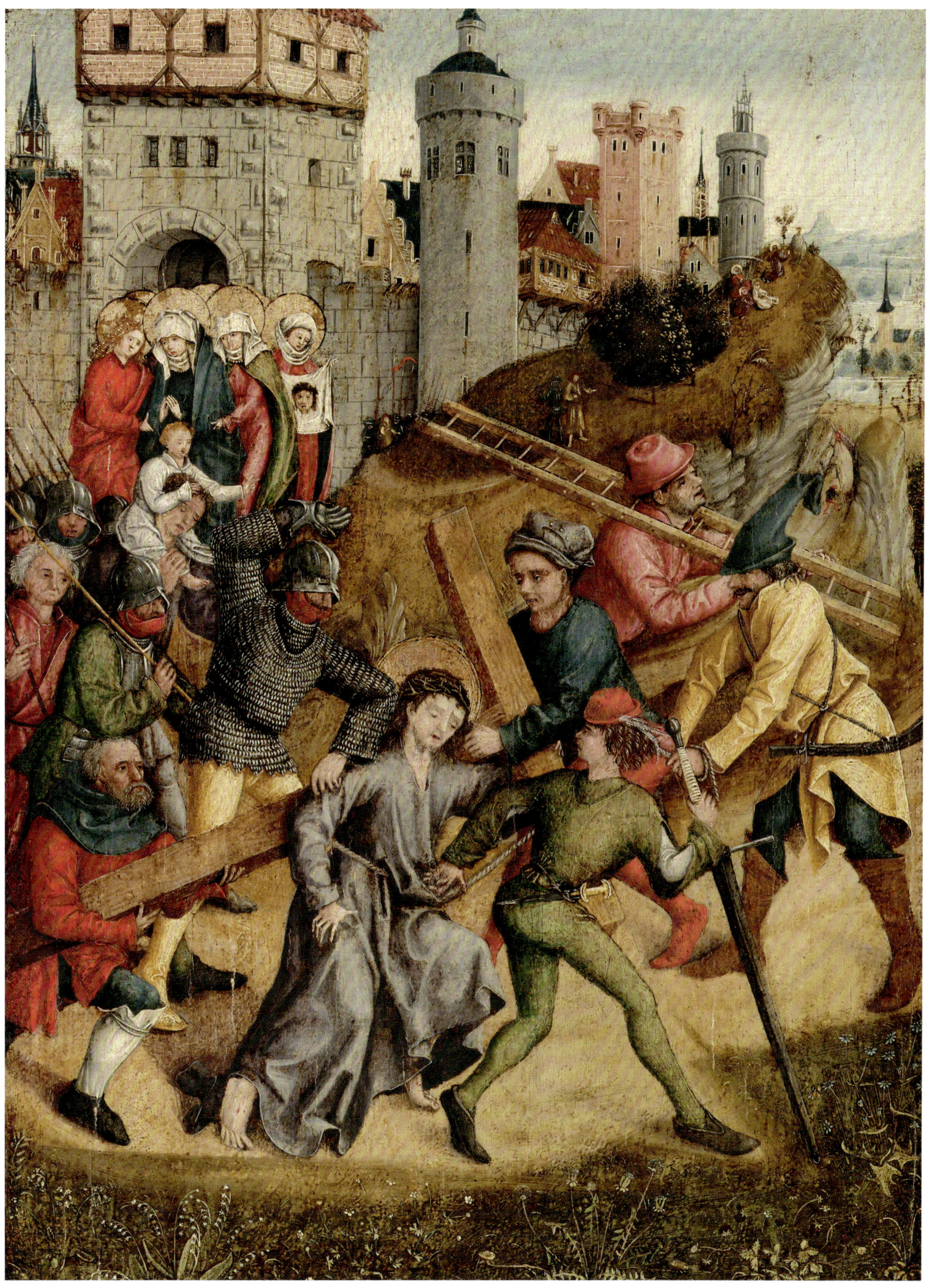

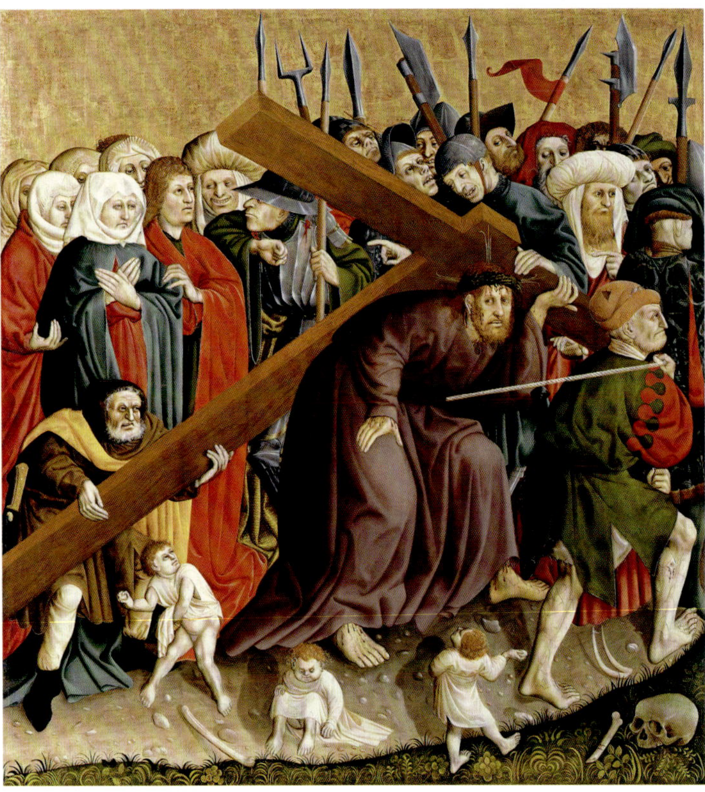

Fig. 85a. Hans Multscher, *Christ Carrying the Cross*, panel from the Wurzbach Altarpiece, 1437, oil on panel, 59 × 55⅛ in. (150 × 140 cm), Gemäldegalerie, Staatliche Museen, Berlin.

Judas directs a soldier to Christ, who prays on the Mount of Olives as his disciples Peter, James, and John sleep.

The attribution of this small panel remains unresolved. Max Friedländer attributed it to an anonymous painter active in southern Germany during the second half of the fifteenth century.[5] Duveen Brothers later attributed it to a follower of the Master of the Karlsruhe Passion, who was active in Strasbourg between 1420 and 1465.[6] Although the Pasadena painting shares with the works of this anonymous master a general similarity of iconography and interest in the costumes of the soldiers, this attribution is unconvincing. The slight figures and the landscape—integrated by winding roads, changes in scale, and aerial perspective—distinguish the Pasadena painting from these works. Distinctive details such as Christ supporting himself with his right hand on his leg and the brick and timber superstructure of the rusticated stone city gate may ultimately lead to the identification of the artist, who was probably active in the south of Germany during the late fifteenth century. The motif of Christ supporting himself with his hand on his thigh, for example, is found in *Christ Carrying the Cross* from the Wurzbach Altarpiece 1437 by Hans Multscher (1400–1467; fig. 85a), an influential painter and sculptor active in Ulm, as well as in the work of artists under his influence.[7]

1. In Sotheby's own marked catalogue of the 1957 Parke-Bernet sale, the seller for lots 4 and 21 is handwritten as either "Fontera" or "Santera." Neither of these names was recognized by Sotheby's staff. See emails from Lucian Simmons and Clarissa Post, 26 September and 1 October 2014 (NSM).

2. Matthew 27:32; Mark 15:1; Luke 23:26–32; John 19:17. Among the earliest and most influential narrative texts are the *Meditationes Vitae Christi* of Pseudo-Bonaventure of the late thirteenth century and the *Vita Christi* of Ludolph of Saxony (b. 1300) from the early fourteenth century. See Marrow 1977 and Marrow 1979. Marrow 1979, p. 145, notes that "by the late Middle Ages the Bearing of the Cross had become one of the most richly elaborated events of the passion, crowded with figures and replete with anecdotal incident."

3. The thistle to the right of center, for example, is an emblem of earthly sorrow and sin and thus a reference to the Passion of Christ. The flower on the far right appears to be a strawberry plant, which stood for perfect righteousness and was thus an emblem of the righteous man whose fruits are good works.

4. Such a sculpted scene of the Crucifixion would probably have been similarly packed with anecdotal detail. The Pasadena painting has been thinned and cradled, thus leaving no indication if it was originally painted on the reverse. No additional panels from the altarpiece have been identified.

5. Max Friedländer in an undated letter probably written to Duveen (NSM).

6. Although Senta Dietzel Bier was the first to publish this attribution in Winston-Salem 1963, pp. 102f., the records of Duveen Brothers (NSM) indicate that they were the first to associate this painting with the panels of the Karlsruhe Passion.

7. Ulm is located in the southern German state of Baden-Württemberg. The hand-on-thigh motif also appears in a painting attributed by Stange 1934–61, vol. 7 (1955), p. 107, no. 233, to the Master of the Saint Goar Altarpiece (active 15th century), an artist influenced by the Master of the Housebook (active ca. 1470–1500), who in turn was influenced by Multscher. A similar city gate appears in a painting attributed by Stange 1934–61, vol. 4 (1951), p. 31, no. 38, to a painter active in Konstanz (15th century).

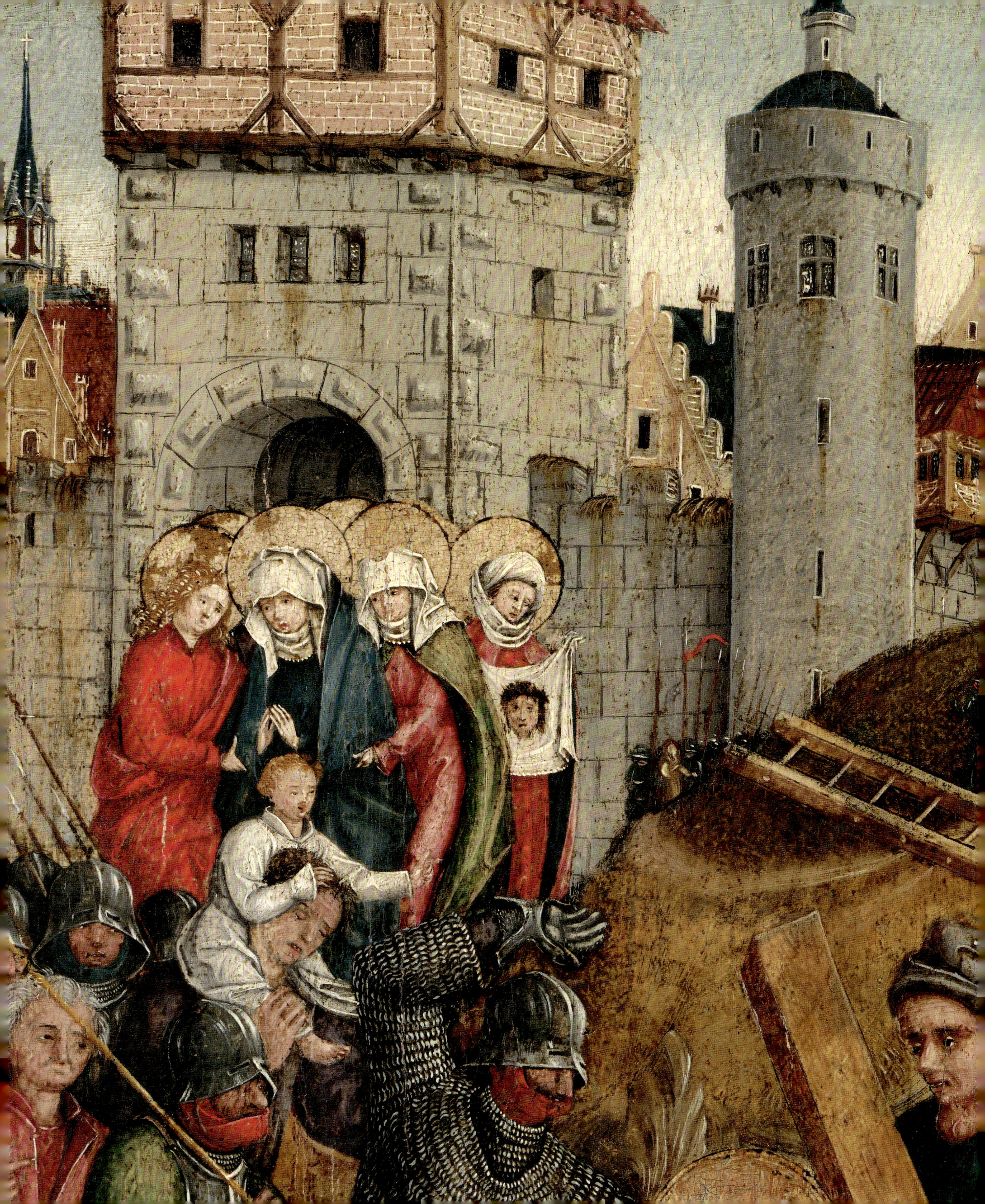

86

Jan Steen

Dutch
Leiden ca. 1626–1679 Leiden

Bathsheba

Late 1660s

Signed, bottom left corner: "JSteen" (*JS* in ligature)
Oil on panel, 15 × 12⅜ in. (38.1 × 31.4 cm)
The Norton Simon Foundation, F.1972.09.P

Provenance
Jacob van Zaanen (sale, Rietmulder, The Hague, 16 November 1767, lot 16).[1] John Stuart (1744–1814), 1st Marquess and 4th Earl of Bute, Luton Park, London, by January 1800; by descent to; John Crichton-Stuart (1881–1947), 4th Marquess of Bute, Luton Park, London, still in 1934.[2] [Galerie Internationale (H. Maas), The Hague, in 1938].[3] [D. Katz, Dieren, sold under duress 2 August 1940 to]; [Goudstikker/Miedl, Amsterdam, inv. no. 5238, sold 17 October 1940 to]; Reichs Chancellery, Berlin, recovered by Allied forces and transported to Munich Central Collecting Point, inv. no. 2349, returned in Dutch run no. 15 (Transport VI USFET) to; Dutch government, returned 13 November 1947 to; [Nathan Katz (1893–ca. 1950), The Hague (sale, Galerie Jean Charpentier, Paris, 7 December 1950, lot 58, sold for F 480,000)]. E. A. Klatte, Switzerland,[4] sold 1972 through; [G. Cramer Oude Kunst, The Hague, to]; The Norton Simon Foundation.

Exhibited
London 1882–83, p. 43, no. 147;[5] Glasgow 1884, no. 161; London 1909, no. 10; on loan, Allen Memorial Art Museum, Oberlin, 10 May 1972–8 May 1973; on loan, Los Angeles County Museum of Art, 9 May 1973–26 November 1974.

References
Hoet 1752–70, vol. 3 (1770), p. 652, no. 16; J. Smith 1829–42, vol. 4 (1833), p. 53, no. 158; Waagen 1854, vol. 3, p. 477, no. 4; Van Westrheene 1856, p. 122, no. 100;[6] "Marquis of Bute" 1882, p. 905; London 1882–83, no. 161; Hofstede de Groot 1908–27, vol. 1 (1908), no. 14; W. Martin 1909, p. 156; Schmidt-Degener and Van Gelder 1927, pp. 17f.; Gudlaugsson 1938, pp. 72f.; Gerson 1976, p. 171, fig. 12; Kirschenbaum 1977, pp. 49, 69, 91f., 115f., no. 14, fig. 70; K. Braun 1980, pp. 132f., no. 311, ill.; Pasadena 1989, p. 58, ill.; S. Campbell 2010, p. 337, no. 775, ill.; The Hague 2018, pp. 19–20, fig. 17.

Technical Notes
The vertically grained oak panel remains uncradled with no cracks or planar distortions. Narrow strips of wood have been attached to each side of the panel with finishing nails. The ground is a cream-colored smooth layer; moderately thick, it leaves the texture of the wood only slightly visible. Paint was directly applied over the ground. X-radiography reveals only a small change in the composition: The outline of Bathsheba's face and throat were altered slightly, and an area in the background directly behind her seems to have been changed to a darker, less distracting shape in the final painting. Steen used both thin paint, such as that in the architecture in the landscape at upper left and the foliage around the archway, and opaque, thicker paint in the figures and the interior scene. Faces were deftly handled and probably quickly painted. Fabrics, such as the proper right sleeve of Bathsheba's dress, employ thin paint and some use of glazes. Overall, the painting is quite well preserved, and abrasion is minimal. Retouching in an area above the old woman's head appears to compensate for drying cracks. The shadow below her proper right forearm has been strengthened slightly. A diagonally placed line of retouching was used, perhaps, to disguise the fact that the putto in the fountain was originally depicted urinating. The natural-resin varnish is slightly cloudy but not noticeably discolored.

One of the distinguishing characteristics of Jan Steen's paintings is his blending of history and genre. By integrating the two, he successfully implied the continuity of the historical subject's message for contemporary society.[7] This technique has, however, led to the frequent misidentification of his subjects. Such is the case with *Bathsheba*, formerly known as *The Love Letter*.[8]

In the Pasadena painting, Steen represented Bathsheba as a young woman on the porch of a well-appointed house. Dressed in elegant seventeenth-century clothing, she rests her left elbow on a stone table covered with a Persian rug; her chin supported by her left hand, she appears disinterested as she turns in response to an old woman who presents her with a letter on which is written, "LIEFE/MINNE" (sweet/love). Rather than look directly at the messenger, the young woman gazes knowingly toward the tiny figure of a man standing on the roof of the distant palace, directing the viewer to follow her gaze by the diagonal placement of the forefinger of her left hand. The animated dog suggests that the wizened woman has just arrived, an emissary from the palace. Fully clothed, Bathsheba is distinguished here from the images of the same subject by Rembrandt and others, who rendered her nude or seminude in the midst of her bath, tended to by maidservants who pare her toenails and comb her hair. The only indications of the bathing ritual in this painting are the fountain (in the middle distance between

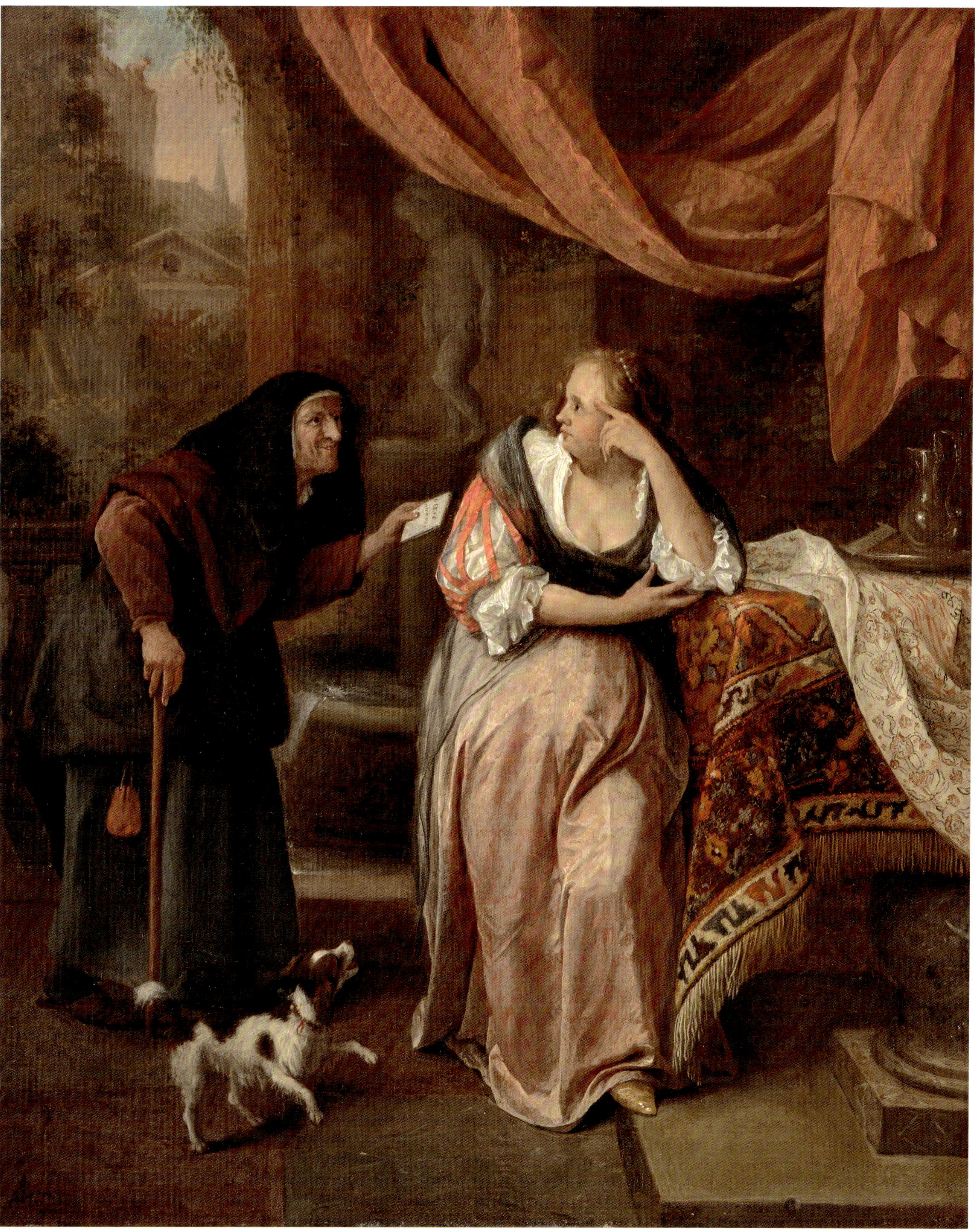

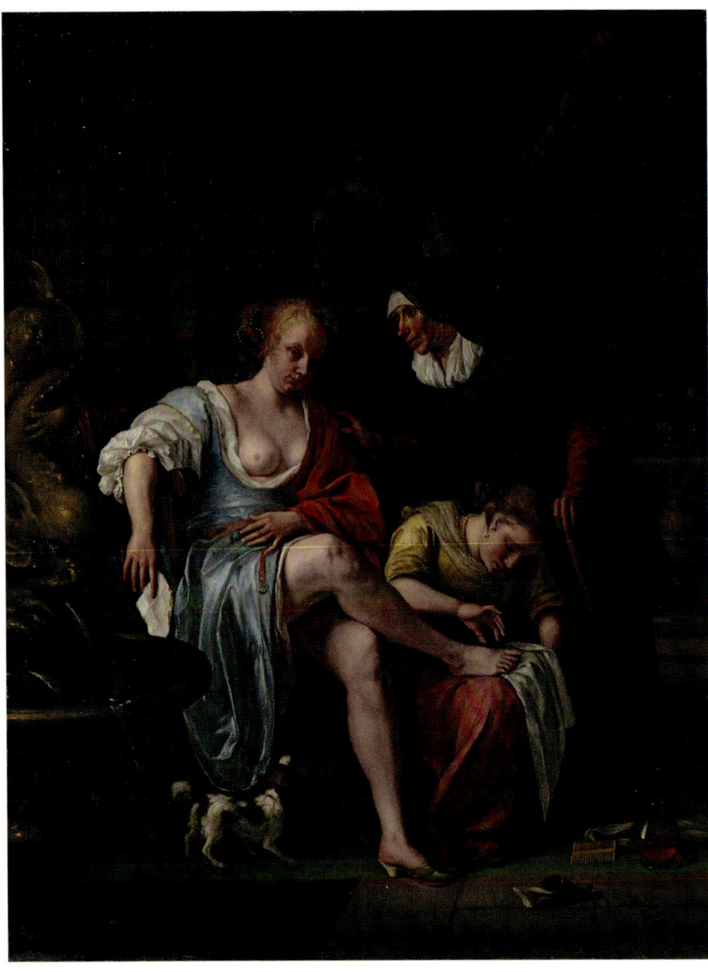

Fig. 86a. Jan Steen, *Bathsheba after the Bath*, ca. 1670–75, oil on panel, 22⅞ × 17 11⁄16 in. (57.5 × 44.5 cm), J. Paul Getty Museum, Los Angeles.

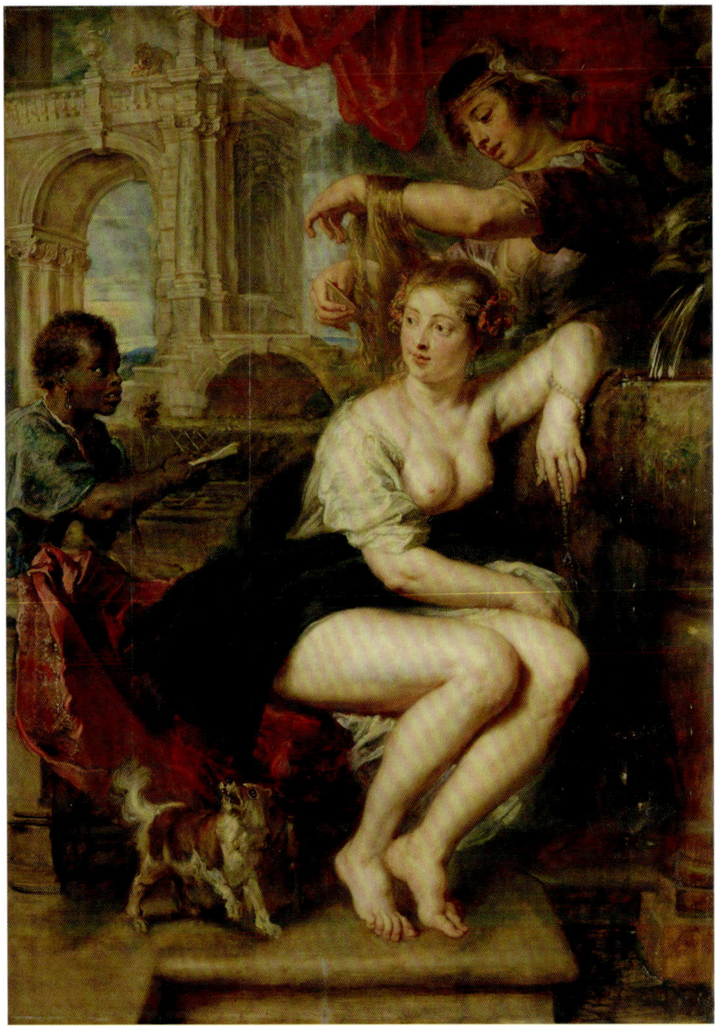

Fig. 86b. Peter Paul Rubens, *Bathsheba at the Fountain*, ca. 1635, oil on panel, 68⅞ × 49⅝ in. (175 × 126 cm), Gemäldegalerie Alte Meister, Staatliche Kunstsammlungen, Dresden.

the servant and Bathsheba) and the comb and oil ewer on a tray that lies on the carpeted stone table.

This painting is one of five versions of the story of Bathsheba that Steen painted beginning about 1659.[9] In each, Steen chose a slightly different aspect of the story, the biblical source of which is 2 Samuel 11:2–4. In the version in the J. Paul Getty Museum, Los Angeles (fig. 86a), Bathsheba sits next to a fountain fed by a stone dolphin; she crosses her right leg over her left so that a servant can give her a pedicure.[10] In her dropped right hand she holds a piece of paper; an old female servant with a cane leans forward as if speaking to her. Bathsheba's attention, however, is directed toward the viewer, whom she thus engages in the drama. Steen similarly incorporates the viewer in the other versions of the subject. In his last known treatment of the theme, that from the mid-1670s formerly in the Wetzlar Collection, Amsterdam, Bathsheba sits in the immediate foreground; her elbow resting on a table, she supports her head with her right hand and holds the letter from King David in her dropped left hand. Elegantly dressed, her hair falling loosely around her shoulders, she captivates the viewer with a seductive expression.[11]

The Pasadena painting, which Baruch Kirschenbaum dates to the late 1660s, in many ways integrates the characteristics of the Wetzlar painting and the earliest version of the story, now in a New York private collection.[12] In the New York painting, from about 1659/60, Steen portrayed Bathsheba as an elegant, refined young woman who closely resembles the women in paintings by his contemporary Gerard ter Borch (1617–1681). As in many scenes by these artists, Steen's early painting features a maid who has just presented the elegantly attired young woman with a letter, presumed to be a love letter.[13] Bathsheba in the Pasadena painting also resembles this type of woman. Dressed in a shimmering satin gown, she stands in the portico of an elegant home next to a table covered with a plush Persian carpet. Steen delighted in the play of the different textures against the muted background as well as the contrast of

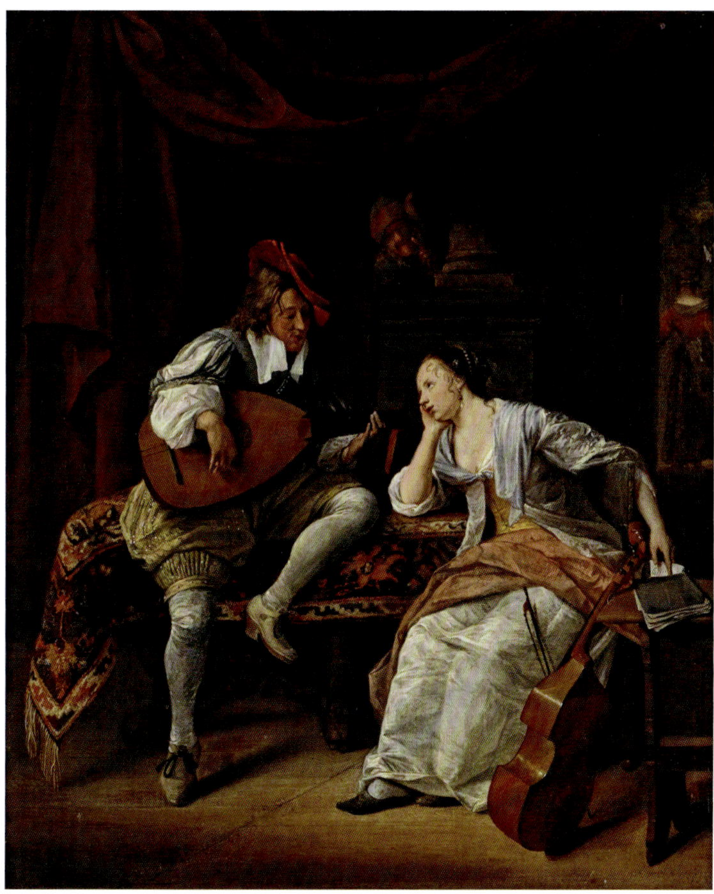

Fig. 86c. Jan Steen, *Ascanius and Lucilla*, ca. 1665–70, oil on panel, 15½ × 12½ in. (39.4 × 31.8 cm), The Bute Collection at Mount Stuart, Isle of Bute.

young and old women. In spite of her fine trappings, however, Bathsheba is disheveled, her hair loose and her décolletage too deep for a woman of refinement. Her ambiguous, perhaps bored, expression and casual pose further detach her from the contemporary ideal of a proper, moral woman. As she turns to the maid, she knowingly looks toward the distance where King David stands on the balcony.

It is this conflict between her refined setting and costume and her base behavior and appearance that creates a particularly strong image of debauchery. She is not the conflicted matron of Rembrandt's *Bathsheba Reading King David's Letter* (Musée du Louvre, Paris) who recognizes the gravity of her actions, reflected visually in the confining format of the painting.[14] Rather, in the Pasadena painting Steen's Bathsheba is already a fallen woman, the adulteress whom contemporary theologians and moralists used as an exemplum of *vanitas*. For it was Bathsheba's pride and love of wealth and pleasure that led her to King David and to the death of her husband, Uriah the Hittite. (See cat. 7, Cornelis Bisschop, *Bathsheba*, for the story.) The theme of *vanitas* is implied by the exotic details, such as the rug and the delicate white cloth with subtle black and red designs pulled back over it, as well as by the traditional contrast of an elegant young woman with an elderly one.[15] Here, too, one suspects that the statue of the urinating putto atop the fountain in the background refers both to Cupid and to love as well as to the bath that Bathsheba took in preparation for meeting the king.

In composing this *Bathsheba*, Steen may have referred to a painting of the subject by Rubens (fig. 86b), which he could have known from a print. In the vertical composition by the Flemish master, the seminude figure of Bathsheba sits next to a stone fountain as her maid combs her loose hair. Bathsheba turns to respond to a servant who offers her the letter from David, seen standing on the roof of the palace in the distant left. As in Steen's painting, a small spaniel yaps as Bathsheba responds with a bemused expression to the servant's entrance. A curtain is also used by both artists to distinguish the foreground space from the background.

The Pasadena *Bathsheba* was sold together with Steen's *Ascanius and Lucilla* (fig. 86c) in 1767 at the Van Zaanen auction, and the two paintings remained together in the Bute Collection through the early twentieth century, leading to the presumption that Steen painted them to hang as pendants. Although the paintings agree in dimensions, support, and internal structure (curtains and figural arrangements) and share, as Kirschenbaum observes, the common theme of love, there seems little reason to believe that Steen would have paired *Bathsheba*, a tale from the Old Testament, with *Ascanius and Lucilla*, a story from the ca. 1616 drama *Lucelle* by Gerbrand Adriaensz. Bredero (1585–1618).[16] The narratives respond neither as foils nor as parallels.[17] Rather than Steen, it may have been the eighteenth-century collector Jacob van Zaanen who created the pairing since there is no evidence that the two paintings were together before that time.

1. "Bathseba een Brief ontfangende, door Jan Steen; hoog 14, breet 11¾ duimen." Lot 16 was sold together with lot 17, "Ascagnes [Ascanius] en Lucella, door denzelven [Steen]; zijnde hoog en breet als 't vorige," for ƒ80. *Ascanius and Lucilla* was previously sold as lot 26 in the sale of the collection of Willem Fabricius, Haarlem, 19 August 1749. The Pasadena painting was not, however, included in that sale.

2. J. Smith 1829–42 (1833), vol. 4, no. 158, suggests that the Bute painting was "probably the picture which was sold in the collection of Greffier Fagel, 1801" as lot 45. That painting, described as "The Female Emissary delivering David's Letter to Bathsheba," cannot, however, be the Bute painting. The dimensions as recorded in a handwritten annotation are too large: "2 h. 1½ [w.] P. [panel]"; even more definitive, the painting was listed in an inventory of the Fagel collection published by Hoet 1752–70, vol. 1 (1752), p. 410. It cannot, thus, be identical with that in the Van Zaanen and Bute collections, which agree in terms of dimensions and the pairing with *Ascanius and Lucilla*. Regarding the twentieth-century provenance of the Pasadena painting, Andrew McLean, archivist, Bute Archives, Mount Stuart, Scotland, states that the painting is recorded in January 1800 at Luton Park in the North Red Dressing Room and that

there is no information about when and under what circumstances the painting left the Bute Collection (email to Carol Togneri, 14 November 2002, NSM). The painting was seen in the London residence of the Marquess of Bute by Ellis Waterhouse on 26 July 1934 (Ellis K. Waterhouse notebooks and research files, 1801–1987 [bulk 1924–1979], GRI).

3. According to the RKD photo mount.

4. G. Cramer Oude Kunst gallery records, series I. E. 1972, box 115, folder 8, Special Collections, GRI.

5. "Marquis of Bute" 1882 reviews the exhibition, mentioning that "no catalogue is yet available." The catalogue of the exhibition, London 1882–83, lists the Pasadena painting as no. 147, *The Love Letter*, a companion to no. 151, *A Cavalier Playing a Lute to a Lady [Ascanius and Lucilla]*. The latter work remains in the Bute Collection, Mount Stuart.

6. In his entry for the Pasadena painting, then with Bute, Van Westrheene 1856 cites the Van Zaanen sale of 1767 and notes that Descamps 1753–65, vol. 3 (1760), p. 29, mentioned the painting as being in the Van Slingeland collection, The Hague. Decamps, however, only notes the subject without description or dimensions—information too general to identify that work as the Pasadena painting. Van Westrheene also noted that Charles Blanc mentioned the painting but did not identify the source. Regarding Van Westrheene's suggestion that the painting was probably that which passed from Van Slingeland to the Greffier Fagel sale, see note 2 above.

7. In the present painting, for example, Steen's inclusion of exotic details suggests that the events take place in a distant place and time. By including the tower of a Dutch church in the distance, however, Steen draws the events back to the present.

8. The painting was known as *The Love Letter* by at least 1883, when it was exhibited in London 1882–83, p. 43, no. 147.

9. Regarding the theme of Bathsheba in the work of Steen, see Kirschenbaum 1977, pp. 59–70, nos. 14–15a. Kirschenbaum, however, discusses only four of the versions. Regarding the theme of Bathsheba in art, see Kunoth-Leifels 1962, passim, esp. "V. Rembrandt und die holländischen Bathseba Darstellungen des 17. Jahrhunderts," pp. 64–74.

10. Not included in Kirschenbaum 1977, it appears in Washington/Amsterdam 1996–97, no. 11, fig. 1, as about 1665–70.

11. Included in the posthumous sale of the collection of Dr. Hans Wetzlar, Sotheby Mak van Waay, Amsterdam, 9 June 1977, lot 68.

12. Washington/Amsterdam 1996–97, no. 11, pp. 132–34, color pl.

13. See A[rthur] K. W[heelock] in Washington/Amsterdam 1996–97, p. 132, for discussion of the nonbiblical tradition of David sending a letter.

14. Regarding Rembrandt's painting, see Adams 1998, passim.

15. Both the Persian rug and the dog, which appear often in Steen's paintings, were probably owned by the artist. According to Scheunemann 1954, the rug is typical of a group she terms the "Namenlose Gattung" (nameless genus), a group of small, simple rugs that appear only in Dutch seventeenth- and eighteenth-century paintings; no original rugs of this type are known to exist. For a discussion of these rugs in Dutch paintings, see Ydema 1991, pp. 99–107; on p. 187, no. 838, Ydema identifies the rug in Bathsheba as having the characteristics of the "Namenlose Gattung" group: a field pattern of a central star with rosettes and repeating corner stars and an irregular floral stem pattern.

16. Kirschenbaum 1977, p. 115, no. 14. Regarding *Ascanius and Lucilla*, see Kirschenbaum 1977, pp. 151f., add. 14, fig. 110, which he describes as panel, 15½ × 12½ in., signed in full on the paper held in the woman's hand. Regarding Bredero's play and representations of Ascanius and Lucilla, see Gudlaugsson 1947. Kirschenbaum, who knew the paintings only from photographs, was distraught over the apparent dissimilarity in the quality of the two paintings, considering *Ascanius and Lucilla* to be superior to *Bathsheba*, which he considered "weak in several areas, particularly in the painting of the old woman and the landscape." He noted further, "Perhaps it was this weakness that led Van den Marck to declare it a copy [Handex]." He was referring to the annotated copy of Hofstede de Groot 1908–27, vol. 1 (1908), no. 14, in the RKD. Examination of the painting, however, indicates that Steen intentionally painted these areas of the painting more broadly than the figure of Bathsheba to serve as a foil for her luxury, which he describes with delicate mastery of color, texture, and form. The background sky, painted with tones of pink to suggest the evening light, is thinly painted with a broad brush rather than severely damaged by abrasion.

17. In Bredero's play *Lucelle*, the daughter of a wealthy merchant of Lyon falls in love with her father's apprentice, spurns the love of a baron, is poisoned by her father's cook to save his reputation, and is spared death only when her father learns that her lover is actually the son of the Polish king (Gudlaugsson 1947, p. 178). Steen, like his contemporaries, represented the scene of the two lovers secretly meeting under the ruse of a music lesson, when they are spied on by the father's cook.

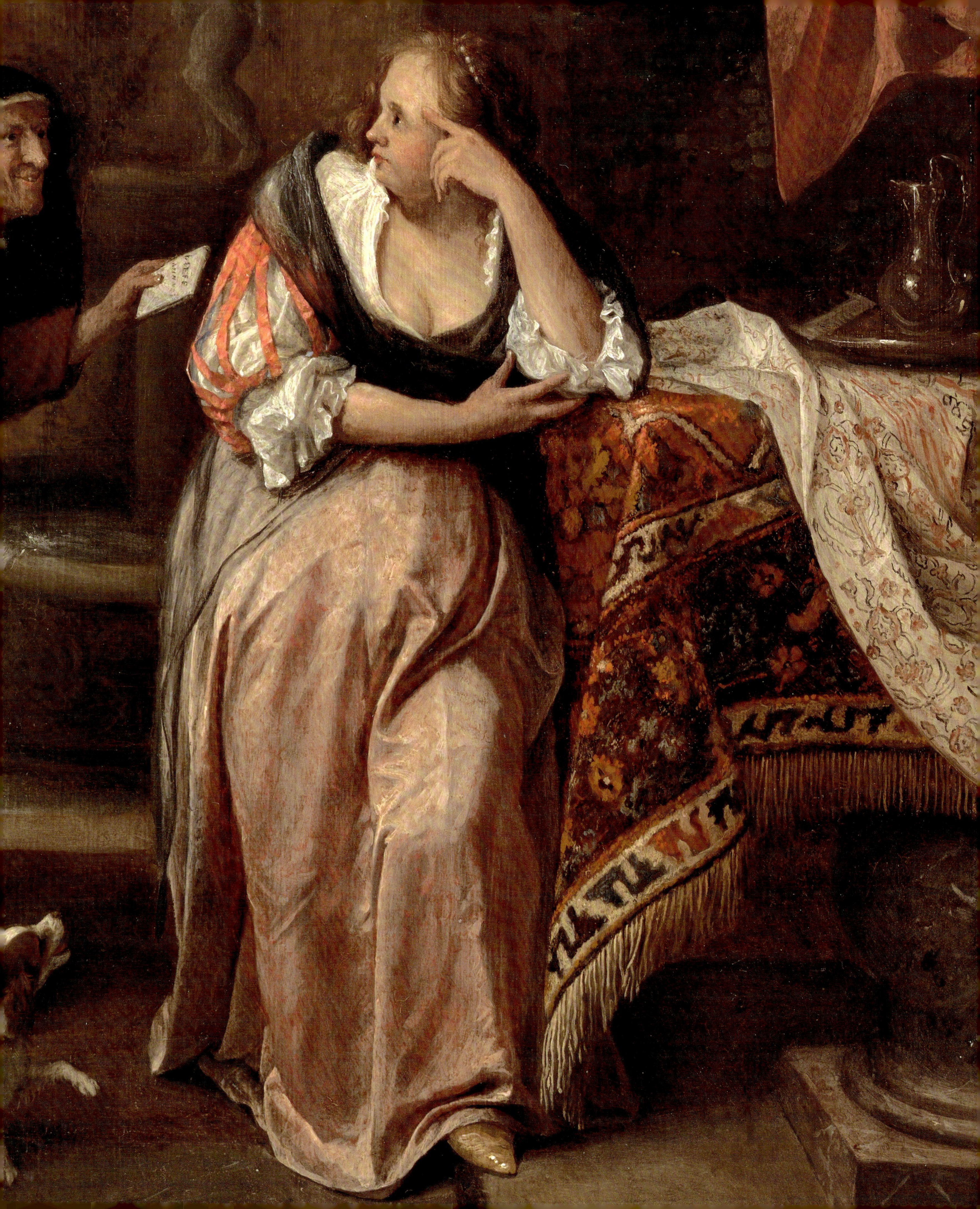

87

Jan Steen

Dutch
Leiden ca. 1626–1679 Leiden

Jacob Confronting Laban

1667/68

Signed, lower left: "JSteen" (*JS* in ligature)
Oil on panel, 18 ¾ × 23 ¼ in. (47.6 × 59.1 cm)
The Norton Simon Foundation, F.1969.10.1.P

Provenance

Anonymous (sale, Phillips, London, 7 June 1825, lot 124a). Hugh A. J. Munro (1797–1864), London and Novar, Scotland, by 1842–after 1865.[1] [Asscher-Welcker-Duits, London, 1925]. [Kunsthandel Gebr. Douwes, Amsterdam, stock no. 3560, 1926/27]. [Galerie Malmedé, Cologne and Bonn, 1949].[2] E. Meyer-Hohenberg, Hamburg, sold 1952 to; [Julius Böhler, Munich, stock no. 5280, sold 1958 to]; Hans A. Wetzlar (d. 1977), Amsterdam (sale, Charpentier, Paris, 3 December 1959, lot 25). [Alfred Brod, London, 1963, no. 12]. [Dr. William Katz, London, sold 1968 to]; [Schaeffer Galleries, New York, stock no. 2567, sold 1969 to]; The Norton Simon Foundation (sale, Christie's, New York, 16 April 1980, lot 72, unsold; sale, New York, Sotheby's, 12 December 1980, lot 86, unsold).

Exhibited

Leiden 1926, pp. 20f., no. 36; London 1963, no. 12; on loan, Allen Memorial Art Museum, Oberlin, 25 May–31 December 1969; on loan, Los Angeles County Museum of Art, 2 January 1970–26 November 1974.

References

J. Smith 1829–42, vol. 9 (1842), p. 509, no. 92; Van Westrheene 1856, p. 116, no. 76;[3] Frost 1865, p. 55; Hofstede de Groot 1908–27, vol. 1 (1908), p. 22, no. 54;[4] Trautscholdt 1937, p. 511, no. 54; Heppner 1939–40, pp. 37f., pl. 4b; Stechow 1945, vol. 27, pp. 229f., fig. 7; Kirschenbaum 1977, pp. 65f., 81, 144, fig. 81, no. 84b; K. Braun 1980, p. 130, no. 302, ill.; P. Sutton 1986, p. 219; Washington/Amsterdam 1996–97, p. 218, fig. 2; S. Campbell 2010, p. 322, no. 641, ill.; Kloek 2018, pp. 39, 52n24, fig. 11.

Technical Notes

Gertrude Blumel, New York, treated this panel prior to acquisition. At either this point or earlier, the support—a horizontally grained oak panel—was thinned considerably before being mounted onto a cross-grained board and a second thinner board. A partial cradle was attached to the reverse. The thin ground is white. Paint in differing thicknesses was directly applied. The background at upper left and the foreground at lower left are very thinly painted; the central figures are rendered in a somewhat more vivid palette. More robust paint was employed in the flesh tones and in the dark curtains. A pentimento is visible in the left side of the proper left leg of Jacob. The knee and calf were originally a bit wider or farther to the left. Abrasion is found throughout most of the painting, some of which can be seen with unassisted vision, primarily in dark or shadowed areas. The three figures at the lower right are the best preserved. At least two campaigns of extensive retouching have occurred; the figures at the left side have a significant amount of reinforcement. In an undocumented treatment, varnish was reduced from the white details of clothing, but the remaining natural-resin varnish is darkened, giving the painting a rather murky aspect overall.

Employing the devices of the theater and contemporary tableaux vivants, Jan Steen used rhetorical gesture and expression to create a highly charged dramatic scene in which a young man leaps from his bed, leaving behind a woman with her breast exposed lying beneath the covers, to confront an older man, behind whom stands an attentive young woman. The scene is framed by the theatrical device of a curtain seemingly draped across the upper edge of the painting.[5] Persian rugs covering the table and bed and exotic costumes—the older man's turban and the wrapped "togas"—set the scene in the biblical or historical past.[6]

Aspects of the narrative and iconography of this painting have inspired different interpretations of its theme. Now titled *Jacob Confronting Laban*, the subject of the painting was identified in the nineteenth century as *The Prodigal Son among Harlots*[7] and since at least 1926 as *Antiochus and Stratonice*.[8] Based on a historical king of Syria, the ancient story of Antiochus and Stratonice was revived during the Renaissance and remained popular in the seventeenth century.[9] According to the narrative, which was regarded as an example of a father's selfless love of his son, Antiochus falls hopelessly in love with Stratonice, the young wife of his father, King Seleucus. Alarmed by the deterioration of Antiochus's health, which had brought the lovesick prince close to death, the king asks a doctor to find the cause of his son's malady and to cure him. Seated by the bed of the young prince, the doctor realizes that Antiochus's spirits rise and fall as Stratonice enters and leaves the room. Informed of the source of his son's illness, Seleucus magnanimously cedes his wife to his son so that his life may be saved.[10]

Wolfgang Stechow interpreted Steen's painting as Antiochus leaping out of bed in response to the sight of Stratonice passing by his bedchamber: "The turbaned Seleucus already seems to be good-humoredly reconciled to the magnanimous deed expected of him, and Stratonice is delighted."[11] According to Stechow, Steen's unique omission of traditional elements within the story—especially the

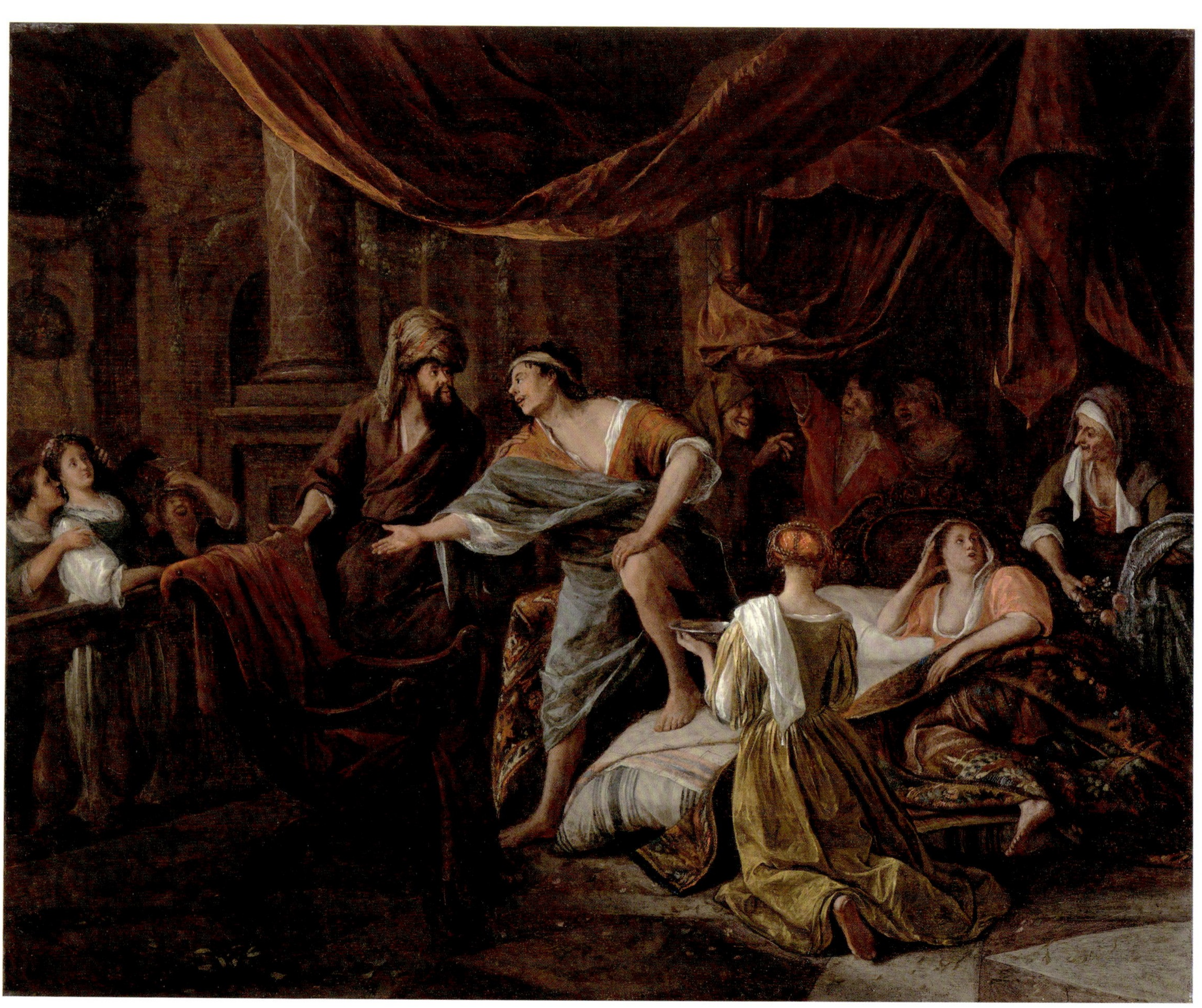

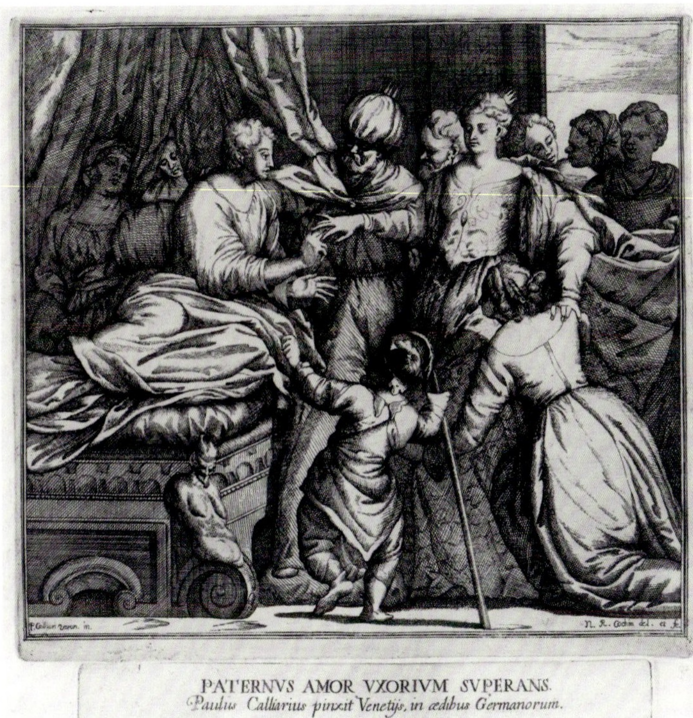

Fig. 87a. Noël-Robert Cochin II, after Paolo Veronese, *Antiochus and Stratonice*, from *Tabellae selectae ac explicatae* (Padua: Ex Typographia Seminarii, 1691), engraving, The Getty Research Institute, Los Angeles.

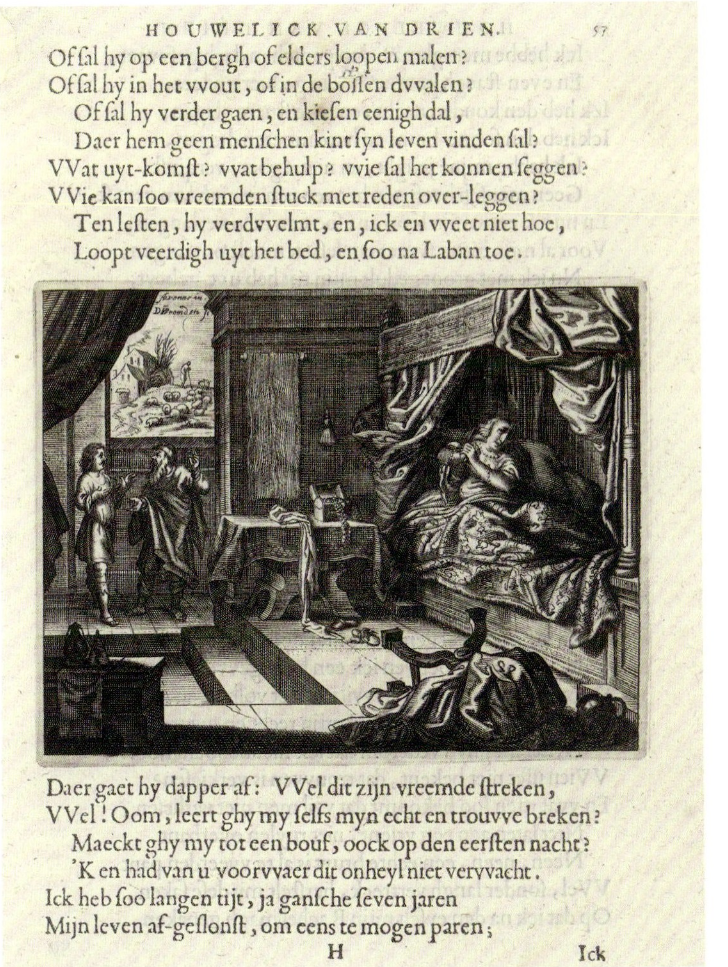

physician, whom other artists included—suggests a particularly close tie between his painting and Philippe Quinault's drama *Stratonice, tragi-comédie*, which also omits the physician.[12] Specifically, Stechow suggests that the painting represents the final scene in Quinault's play, where Antiochus falls at the feet of Stratonice. Here, however, the two lovers are separated rather than encouraged to unite. Other elements of the painting remain baffling or troubling when considered in terms of the play: There is no explanation for the woman in Steen's painting who lies on the bed, one breast exposed, as she turns questioningly toward an old woman who reveals a wedding crown from beneath a drape. Nor is there an explanation for the servant kneeling with a basin at the foot of the bed nor for other jocular figures who peer into the room from behind the curtains. Stechow suggested that the differences might be explained by an unrecorded *rederijker* (Dutch dramatic society) play but also remarked that the realistic-comic element of Steen's painting "is utterly at variance with the noble restraint characteristic of other renderings of the story."[13] Most notably, traditional representations of the tale of Antiochus and Stratonice typically show a lethargic, lovesick Antiochus reclining alone in bed.[14] In a print by Noël-Robert Cochin II (1622–1695) after a painting by Paolo Veronese (1528–1588; fig. 87a), Antiochus sits up in bed and reaches quietly toward the extended hand of the elegantly dressed Stratonice standing nearby; between them a turbaned man seems to encourage their contact. As in the

HOUWELICK VAN DRIEN. 57

Of ſal hy op een bergh of elders loopen malen?
Of ſal hy in het vvout, of in de boſſen dvvalen?
Of ſal hy verder gaen, en kieſen eenigh dal,
Daer hem geen menſchen kint ſyn leven vinden ſal?
VVat uyt-komſt? vvat behulp? vvie ſal het konnen ſeggen?
VVie kan ſoo vreemden ſtuck met reden over-leggen?
Ten leſten, hy verdvvelmt, en, ick en vveet niet hoe,
Loopt veerdigh uyt het bed, en ſoo na Laban toe.

Daer gaet hy dapper af: VVel dit zijn vreemde ſtreken,
VVel! Oom, leert ghy my ſelfs myn echt en trouvve breken?
Maeckt ghy my tot een bouf, oock op den eerſten nacht?
'K en had van u voorvvaer dit onheyl niet vervvacht.
Ick heb ſoo langen tijt, ja ganſche ſeven jaren
Mijn leven af-geſlonſt, om eens te mogen paren;
H Ick

Fig. 87b. Daniël van den Bremden, after Adriaen Pietersz. van de Venne, *Jacob Complains to Laban that He Has Given Him Leah instead of Rachel as His Wife*, ca. 1635–37, engraving, plate: 4 x 5¼ in. (10.2 x 13.3 cm), Rijksmuseum, Amsterdam.

Pasadena painting, the print, which Steen may have known, shows two women lurking in the shadows of the bed curtains behind the prince, while others surround the young woman.

J. Nieuwstraten has convincingly suggested that, rather than Antiochus and Stratonice, the Pasadena painting represents the biblical story of Jacob confronting Laban when he discovers that the older man had deceived him.[15] According to his agreement with Laban, Jacob had served seven years for the hand of Rachel, Laban's beautiful younger daughter, although tradition dictated that the older daughter should be the first to marry. On Jacob's wedding night, Laban arranged for his older daughter Leah to be brought to the young groom instead of her sister. Like the story of Antiochus and Stratonice, that of Jacob and Laban involved deceit and surprise, which presented the opportunity for Steen's comic interpretation.

The spontaneous reaction of the young man confronting the older turbaned man in the Pasadena painting agrees with story of Jacob confronting Laban the morning after his discovery of the deception. The narrative also explains many of the details in the painting that are unexplained by the literary source: The young woman in the bed from which the young man has suddenly sprung is Leah, the elder daughter, with whom Jacob had slept the previous night; at her feet is Zilpah, the handmaid Laban had given to the new bride. The old woman on the right, who draws a flower crown out from under a drapery, refers to the recent wedding and to the deceit. Rachel, Jacob's true love, is the demure woman at the left, coaxed by her maid, and the jocular observers are the celebrants from the previous night of feasting in celebration of the wedding. Ultimately, in response to Jacob's protests about the deception and his contracting to herd his father-in-law's sheep for seven additional years, Laban agrees to Rachel becoming Jacob's second wife.

The story of Jacob, Leah, and Rachel was known and discussed in the seventeenth century, most notably in "Houwelyck van Drien . . . " (Marriage of Three), a long poem first published in 1637 by the popular moralist and statesman Jacob Cats (1577–1660).[16] Following the narration of the biblical story, Cats debated, through the voices of two people, the moral implications of the story, questioning Jacob's choice of Rachel because of her beauty, Laban's deception, Jacob's ignorance of the identity of the woman he slept with, Rachel's complicity, and Leah's willingness to sleep with her sister's betrothed, as well as Jacob's taking a second wife. Although it is not known how Steen viewed the biblical story, he undoubtedly knew Cats's poem. In the print by Daniël van den Bremden (1586/87–1646/50), after Adriaen Pietersz. van de Venne (1589–1662; fig. 87b) that accompanies Cats's text, Leah sits in bed while Jacob confronts her father in the adjacent room. The animated conversation occurs in front of an open window with a view of a figure herding sheep on a hillside. The scene takes place in a Dutch interior, with only Laban's long beard and toga referencing the biblical source of the story. In the Pasadena painting, Steen transformed the event portrayed as a Dutch genre scene in the print into a dynamic, theatrical performance set in an exotic, imaginative past.

1. Hugh Munro (1797–1864) formed a famous collection of paintings known as the Novar Collection, among which were a large number of paintings by J. M. W. Turner (1775–1851), for whom he served as executor, and twenty-six paintings by Steen. The Pasadena painting, which is noted by J. Smith 1829–42 as in the Novar Collection in 1842, was not among the eleven works by Steen Waagen saw in London in 1835 (Waagen 1854, vol. 2, pp. 137f.). The painting is recorded by Frost 1865, p. 55, as in the Novar Collection, where it is called *The Prodigal Son*. (I am grateful to Charles Sebag-Montefiore for this reference.) This painting may have been either lot 159 or 171, identified only as "Steen, An Interior, with figures," in the first sale of Munro's collection (Christie's, London, 18 May 1867). The painting does not appear in Munro's posthumous sale at Christie's, London, 1 June 1878, nor does it appear in the sales of pictures from the estate of Henry Butler-Johnstone, which was formed by Munro (Christie's, London, 2 December 1876, 19–23 March 1880).

2. According to RKD photo mount.

3. As "*L'enfant prodigue chez des courtisanes*, canvas, 0.66 × 0.86 cm [dimensions erroneously repeated from no. 75], collection H. A. J. Munro, esq., London."

4. According to London 1963, the painting is "Hofstede de Groot, Supplement in manuscript at the Rijksbureau voor Kunsthistorische Documentatie, The Hague, with a certificate by Hofstede de Groot, no. 3003."

5. Regarding the function of these curtains for tableaux vivants as well as on the *rederijker* stage and Baroque theater, see Kalff 1895, pp. 26ff.

6. For a discussion of the particular rug, which was probably owned by Steen and appears in many of his paintings, see the discussion in cat. 89, *Marriage at Cana*. The major discussions of Steen and the theater are Heppner 1939–40, pp. 22–48; Van Gils 1942, pp. 57–62; Gudlaugsson 1975; and Kirschenbaum 1977, pp. 7–85. See also De Groot 1952; L. de Vries 1977; Washington/Amsterdam 1996–97, passim; Westermann 1997, pp. 276–312; and Cahill 2017.

7. J. Smith 1829–42, vol. 9 (1942), p. 509, no. 92.

8. Horst Schneider, cited in Leiden 1926, no. 36, was the first to suggest the story of Antiochus and Stratonice. This attribution was later discussed by Heppner 1939–40, pp. 22ff., and Stechow 1945, pp. 221–31.

9. Among others, Rubens portrayed the subject in a now lost painting that was enthusiastically described in 1781 by Sir Joshua Reynolds (1723–1792). See McGrath 1997, vol. 1, figs. 66, 68, and vol. 2, pp. 95ff. See also Stechow 1945, p. 229.

10. According to Stechow 1945, p. 222, the tale of the lovesick Antiochus was revived during the Renaissance by Plutarch, Appian, and Pseudo-Lucien, who introduced a new element: a ruse. The clever physician tells the king that Antiochus has fallen in love with his own (the doctor's) wife. For the sake of his son, the king entreats the physician to cede his wife to the lovesick prince, whereupon the doctor informs him of the true situation and pleads with him to follow his own advice.

11. Stechow 1945, p. 230.

12. Quinault's play was originally performed in Paris in 1657, and published in French in 1660. Abraham Bogaert published a Dutch translation in 1694.

13. Stechow 1945, p. 229. Westermann 1997, p. 311n64, in agreement with Gudlaugsson 1975, pp. 5ff., observes, however, that the relationship between seventeenth-century plays and history paintings, including those by Steen, should be considered more general than specific; as she points out, Steen typically inserted anecdotal, comic elements into his historical subjects.

14. See Stechow 1945.

15. Genesis 29:25. Wouter Kloek in Washington/Amsterdam 1996–97, p. 218n8, credits the original attribution of the subject to Horst Schneider and the suggestion that it represents Jacob to J. Nieuwstraten. Kirschenbaum 1977, no. 84B/54, noted and dismissed a previous attribution of the subject as Jacob and Laban but gives no reference.

16. Originally published in *'s Werelts begin, midden, eynde, besloten in den trov-ringh, met den proef-steen van den selven* (Dordrecht, 1637), the poem is included in Jacob Cats, *Alle de Werken*, Amsterdam, 1658. See Cats 1880, part 2, pp. 17–26. In addition to Genesis, Cats also cites the first-century Roman-Jewish historian Flavius Josephus, *Romeinsche oudheden*, 1.17–18, as a source for the story. Josephus's work is known in English as *The Antiquities of the Jews*; the story of Jacob, Laban, and his daughters is told in 1.19.1–11 in the English translation.

88

Jan Steen

Dutch
Leiden ca. 1626–1679 Leiden

Wine Is a Mocker

ca. 1668/70[1]

Signed at left, on well: "JSteen" (*JS* in ligature)
Inscribed over doorway: "De Wÿn is een Spoter. Proverbyn . . . 20.1"
Oil on canvas, 34⅜ × 41¼ in. (87.3 × 104.8 cm)
Norton Simon Art Foundation, M.1969.05.P

Provenance
Possibly anonymous (sale, Amsterdam, 17 September 1727, lot 12, for ƒ265).[2] Edward Solly (1776–1844),[3] London and Berlin (sale, Foster and Son, London, 31 May 1837, lot 68, as 41 × 34½ in. [reversed], sold for £86 2s. to); Norbury [?].[4] M. C. Hoogendijk, The Hague, by 1899 (sale, Frederick Muller & Cie., Amsterdam, 14 May 1912, lot 80, as 81 × 100 cm, "Jan Steen [d'après]"). Ten Bos, Almelo, Twenthe, Netherlands, in 1938.[5] [D(aniël) Katz, Dieren, inv. no. 513, sold 25 June 1941 to];[6] Hans Posse (1879–1942) for; Führermuseum Linz, inv. no. 1906, sent to storage at; Altaussee, inv. no. 2827, recovered by the Allies and sent to; Munich Central Collecting Point, inv. no. 4090, returned via Transport VIII USFET, inv. no. 1780 to; Dutch government by July 1946, restituted 13 November 1947 to];[7] [Benjamin (b. 1891) and Nathan Katz (1893–1949)]. Madame K. L. (sale, Galerie Jean Charpentier, Paris, 30 November 1954, lot 32, pl. xiii, as 87.5 × 105 cm).[8] K. L. Sander, Bloemendaal, 1957.[9] K. Gratma, Heemstede, in 1961 (sale, Sotheby's, London, 30 June 1965, lot 100, unsold), sold through [G. Cramer Oudekunst, The Hague, 1969 to]; Norton Simon Art Foundation.

Exhibited
The Hague 1899–1900, no. 17; Rotterdam 1938, no. 147; Haarlem 1946, no. 125; on loan, Phoenix Art Museum, 20 February–8 July 1969; Princeton 1972–74, no. 11; Washington/Amsterdam 1996–97, no. 38, ill.

References
Hoet 1752–70, vol. 1 (1752), p. 319, no. 12; J. Smith 1829–42, vol. 9 (1842), p. 487, no. 37. Van Westrheene 1856, p. 163, no. 390; Hofstede de Groot 1908–27, vol. 1 (1908), p. 39, no. 103;[10] W. Martin 1954, p. 73; "Notable Works of Art" 1968; Cramer 1968b, no. 59; Steadman 1972, p. 36, fig. 7; K. Braun 1980, p. 112, no. 191, ill.; Pasadena 1980, p. 59, ill.; Rumsey 1985, pp. 324f.; Pasadena 1989, p. 59, ill.; Westermann 1997, pp. 122f., 279, 281, 292, fig. 60; Rousová 2004, pp. 36–37, fig. 10; S. Campbell 2010, pp. 93, 313, no. 569, ill.; Suchtelen and Buvelot 2016, pp. 270–71, fig. 48d; Westermann 2018, p. 62, fig. 11.

Technical Notes
The fine plain-weave canvas has been lined. The original tacking edges no longer remain, but cusped threads visible at all sides indicate that the original dimensions have not changed. Two vertical tears in the lower right quadrant have been repaired. The ground layer is not easily accessible. Abraded dark paint in the foreground partially reveals what appears to be a ground layer of medium value, possibly tan or light gray. Salmon-colored underpainting is below the central figure of the recumbent woman but does not extend further. Paint was applied throughout in thin multiple layers, often leaving lower layers partially exposed. An example is at the lower left, where the dog was painted over a greenish-brown layer, with a reddish-brown paint applied last. At the center right, the young boy clutching a flask was painted on a light area (the wall of the house); Steen then toned the wall a bit darker while leaving the lighter color around the curly hair. Faces were painted with quick brushstrokes of flesh color using a small brush. Although paint was originally fairly thin and liquid, it has been further thinned by cleaning. Lining pressure has exaggerated the canvas texture on the surface, while also flattening the brushmarking. X-radiographs reveal a considerable number of small losses along the bottom edge and along the right side. Extensive retouching includes some strengthening of contours as well as compensation for losses. The retouching in several faces subtly alters expressions—for example, a dab of blue-black in the drunken woman's proper right eye, added to an area of damaged paint, gives a distinct and presumably unintended direction to her gaze. The natural-resin varnish is moderately yellowed.

The many versions and copies of *Wine Is a Mocker* attest to the seventeenth-century popularity of Jan Steen's darkly humorous interpretation of a verse from Proverbs.[11] As a crowd watches, two youths struggle to lift a woman into a wooden wheelbarrow. Totally disheveled, her fur-lined jacket open and exposing a breast, her skirt raised up above her red stockings to reveal her bare legs, and her slippers and kerchief carelessly discarded on the ground, the woman has collapsed before a doorway, having fallen into a drunken stupor.

For Steen and his viewers, the woman's physical collapse was understood as a metaphor for her moral downfall. An inscription on the facade of the wooden awning over the door in the Pasadena painting—"De Wÿn is een Spoter. [Wine is a mocker]. Proverbyn . . . 20.1"—clearly states Steen's meaning here. The full passage from Proverbs 20:1 is "Wine is a mocker, strong drink a brawler, and whoever is led astray by it is not wise." Steen cites the same verse in *Gamblers Quarreling* (fig. 88a), where drink has resulted in a fight in an inn, overturning chairs, knocking over a backgammon game, and sending cards, a wine pitcher, crockery braziers, and

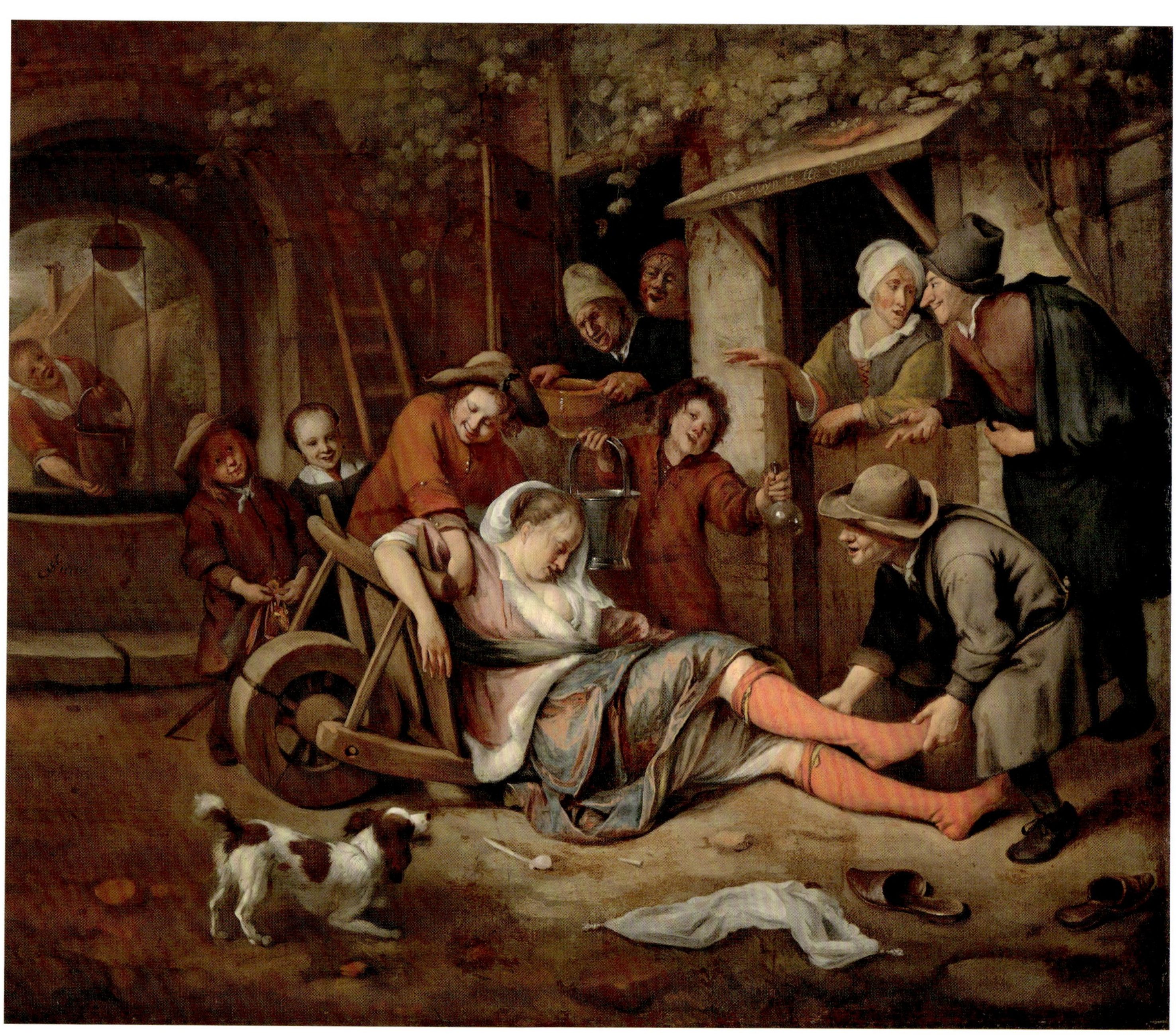

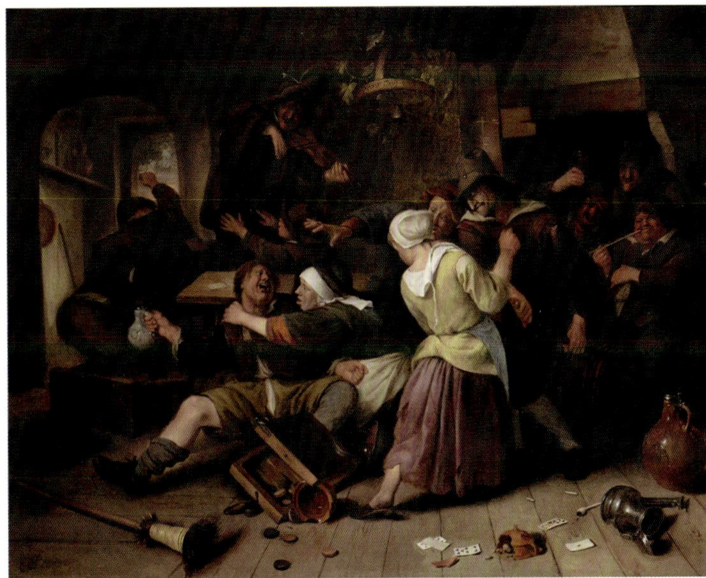

Fig. 88a. Jan Steen, *Gamblers Quarreling*, ca. 1665, oil on canvas, 27 ¾ × 35 in. (70.5 × 88.9 cm), Detroit Institute of Arts, Gift of James E. Scripps, 89.46.

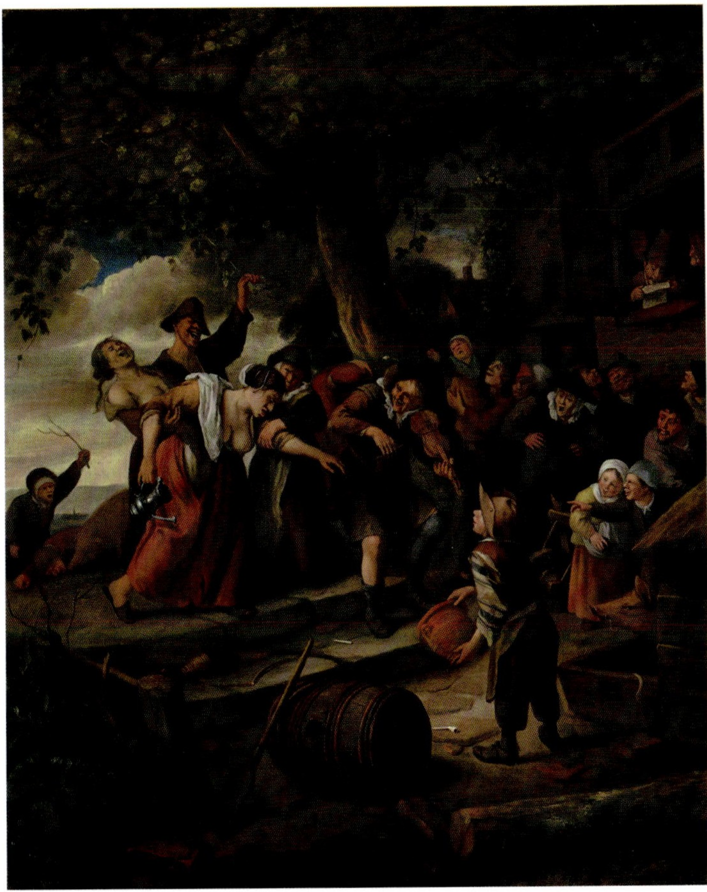

Fig. 88b. Jan Steen, *A Pig Belongs in the Sty*, ca. 1673–75, oil on canvas, 33 ⅞ × 28 ⅜ in. (86 × 72 cm), Mauritshuis, The Hague.

pipes to the ground.[12] A woman abandons her work, dropping her broom on the floor, to try to wrestle the men apart.

Overindulgence in drink was a matter of serious public concern in the seventeenth century. The Dutch of all social levels were renowned for their addiction to both smoking and alcohol.[13] Preachers railed against intemperance from pulpits, and publishers turned out numerous tracts on the subject: Jacobus Sceperus's (1607–1677) tract *Bacchus, Den ouden en huyden-daegschen Dronckeman* (Bacchus, The Drunkard of Past and Present Times) of 1665 typically warned that drink "leads men to whoring, adultery, lewdness, and dishonor."[14] The title of a book of emblems published in Leeuwarden in 1645 by Petrus Baardt (ca. 1595–1677/78), *Deugden-spoor in de on-deughden des werelts aff-gebeeldt* (Exhortations to Virtue through the Portrayal of the World's Vices) helps to understand the illustration of moral shortcomings in many of Steen's paintings. Rather than the harsh words of preachers, Steen expressed the same messages through entertaining scenes of contemporary life.[15]

A number of Steen's paintings address the particular consequences for women who drink too much. While inebriated men may fight or engage in lewd behavior, drunken women collapse on the steps, as in *The Marriage at Cana* (see fig. 89b), or lie provocatively across the lap of a male companion, as in *Drunken Pair* (Rijksmuseum, Amsterdam). Popular opinion of the period held that women were by nature weaker and more susceptible to sloth and drunkenness than men.[16] Because of a woman's key role in the Dutch household, her overindulgence had disastrous consequences, which Steen was quick to exploit comically. In *Luxury Beware* (Kunsthistorisches Museum, Vienna), for example, he depicted a household turned upside down when a housewife falls into a drunken sleep: a boy smokes a pipe and a girl steals from a cabinet, while her husband cavorts with a sex worker.

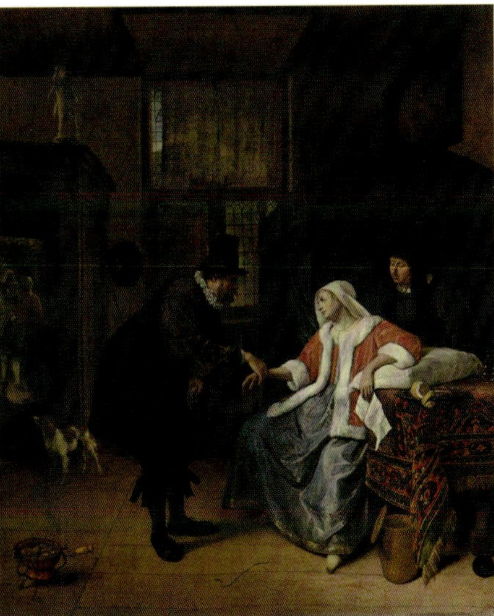

Fig. 88c. Jan Steen, *The Doctor's Visit*, 1661/63, oil on canvas, 24 × 20 ½ in. (61 × 52.1 cm), Alte Pinakothek, Bayerische Staatsgemäldesammlungen, Munich.

In the Pasadena painting, the state of disarray and exposed flesh of the woman dressed in a luxurious fur-trimmed pink jacket and skirt of pink-and-blue *changeant*

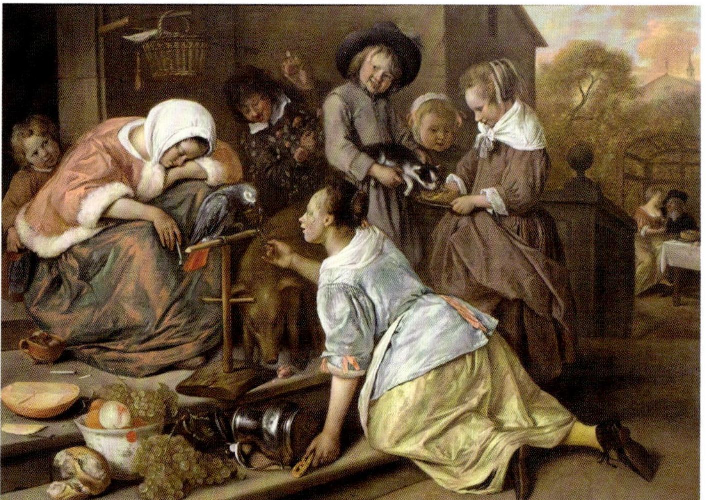

Fig. 88d. Jan Steen, *The Effects of Intemperance*, 1663–65, oil on wood, 30 × 42 in. (76 × 106.5 cm), The National Gallery, London.

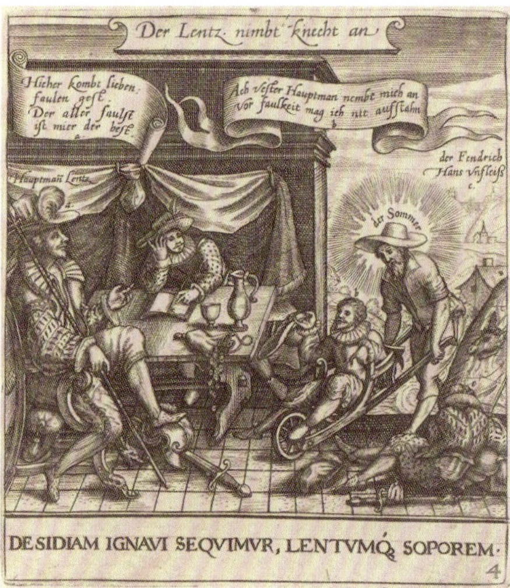

Fig. 88e. Johann Theodor de Bry, *Emblem of a Foppish Man in a Wheelbarrow*, from *Emblemata Saecularia, Mira et iucunda* (Frankfurt, 1596), National Gallery of Art, Washington, DC.

satin, who has collapsed onto the ground, suggest that she is a fallen woman is all senses of the term. Her red stockings and discarded slippers reinforce the impression that she may be a sex worker.[17] In *A Pig Belongs in the Sty* (fig. 88b) Steen represented two obviously inebriated women, their clothes askew, one of them dangling a wine pitcher in her right hand, stumbling toward a crowd of laughing townsfolk.[18] Led by a fiddler, the festive group is probably returning from a fair or yearly market on the outskirts of town, where sex workers plied their trade.[19] A pig trough in the foreground and a woman chasing pigs with a switch behind the drunken women emphasize their excesses. A moment later one of these women could end up sprawled on the ground and need to be lifted up like the subject of the Pasadena painting—a wooden wheelbarrow is visible amid the crowd.

It is unclear whether the scene in the Pasadena painting takes place in a village outside a house, an inn, or perhaps a *musico*. Run by a procuress-hostess, *musicos* were known for providing drink, entertainment, and dancing as well as being sites for obtaining sexual services.[20] In the Pasadena painting, a woman at the door carries on a lively conversation with a sharp-featured man dressed in a tall hat and cape, the type of character Steen often cast as a visitor to a brothel or as a "quack," a pseudo-medical doctor who attends "lovesick" women—that is, women generally recognized as having become pregnant through sex work (fig. 88c).

As they do here, children often underscore the moralizing purpose in Steen's paintings.[21] In *The Effects of Intemperance* (fig. 88d), for example, a woman dressed in clothes like those of the woman in the Pasadena painting has fallen asleep with a pipe in her hand in the presence of children. The parrot alludes to the negative effect of her behavior on the children, one of whom picks her pockets as another feeds pie to a cat and wine to the parrot.[22] In *Wine Is a Mocker*, the only person to connect with the viewer is the boy standing next to the intoxicated woman. In his right hand he holds a shopping bucket and in his left he holds a bulbous glass bottle.[23] Two younger children behind the wheelbarrow watch the scene with amusement. Steen's painting suggests, however, that they, too, may succumb to the same deception if not properly taught. The little boy rides a hobbyhorse, which an emblem in Jacob Cats's (1577–1660) widely read book *Houwelyck* (Marriage) associates with the folly of self-delusion, for the child "thinks he rides a brave horse . . . but he who considers well finds there only wood and nothing else."[24]

Steen emphasized that the sorry state of the woman is due to her overindulgence by repeating the theme of vessels: the pail and glass bottle held by the boy, the bucket at the well, and the bowl at the window. The woman herself is also a vessel for drink. Rather than a bowl of water to throw on the inebriated woman, the man in the window probably holds a chamber pot, like "Sleazy Bess" in a print by Hendrik Brary (1640–1707) after Frans van Mieris I (1635–1681).[25] Both the chamber pot here and the earthenware bucket held by the boy in *A Pig Belongs in the Sty* appear to refer to the degraded state of the women.[26] By contrast, the woman drawing water from the well may allude to purity and virtuous behavior.

Steen thus illustrated the maxim "Wine is a mocker" by emphasizing the humiliation and self-deception brought about by drink and luxury in general, which leads to sexual laxity and neglect of duty. The prominent inscription confirms Steen's didactic purpose, permitting an interpretive approach to the details in the painting, including the wheelbarrow, which was itself probably a reference to the moral of Proverb 20:1 that excess leads to dissipation.[27] The caption and verses of an emblem illustrated with a foppish man pushed in a wheelbarrow published by Johann Theodor de Bry (1561–1623; fig. 88e) refer to the dangers of drink, which brings about sloth and dull sleep, leading men, too, to neglect their duties.

1. According to Washington/Amsterdam 1996–97, no. 38. Westermann 1997 dates it ca. 1660.

2. "Een Dronk Wyf op een Kruywagen, met Omstanders. geestig en Potzig, verbeelt, door Jan Steen. 265 - 0": Hoet 1752–70, vol. 1 (1752), p. 320.

3. Regarding Solly, see Herrmann 1967–68; and Haskell 1976, pp. 41f.

4. This name comes from a copy of the 1837 Solly sale catalogue annotated by Frank Simpson (GRI). In an email of 28 January 2011 from Burton Fredericksen (NSM), he cites another copy of the 1837 catalogue held in the National Art Library, London, which has the following annotation for lot 68: "well executed. 'tumbled out of' instead of 'on' – red stocking – complete brutal drunkenness – capital – see Emmerson's Cat. of this year No.[blank] described as representing his own family satirically." That reference is to the dealer Thomas Emmerson's sale at Phillips auction house in London, 19 and 20 May 1837, lot 163: "An Interior, with his Wife and Children satirically represented, a first rate specimen of the master." The price was £389, but the buyer's name is not given. The Pasadena painting is not an "Interior," and it seems unlikely that Solly would have purchased the painting at this sale and then sold it two weeks later on 31 May. Perhaps the National Art Library annotation refers to the subject of drunkenness and folly in another painting sold just prior to the Solly sale.

5. A copy of Rotterdam 1938 annotated by J. G. van Gelder (GRI) identifies the lender listed as "Part. verz., Twenthe" (private collector, Twenthe) as "ten Bos, Almelo." Probably Johan Lucas ten Bos (1866–1949) or his son and successor, Frederik Henri ten Bos (b. 1910), textile manufacturers in Almelo.

6. Documentation of the Stichting Nederlands Kunstbezit (SNK), The Hague, lists this painting as having been taken from the firm D. Katz, Dieren, by the German occupation authorities in 1941.

7. The documentation card for Munich Central Collecting Point, inv. no. 4090, at the SNK incorrectly notes the dimensions as 70 × 80 cm. However, the verso of the Pasadena painting bears the number 4090 in blue chalk, and it also has the letters "DK III," presumably for the firm D. Katz. The card identifies the owner as Katz, Dieren, but also notes as "Origin," Coll. Clarenbeek, Rotterdam, apparently based on a photograph at the RKD inscribed "bij Notaris van Clarenbeek, Noordblank, Rotterdam."

8. The entry for lot 32 appears in part 1, paintings belonging to Madame K. L., of the sale of "Collection Madame K. L. et diverse Amateurs," but notes, "Collection privée, Twente, Hollande"—probably a reference to the former collection of Ten Bos. Frits Lugt annotated the mount of the photograph at the RKD: "echt, maar grof" (genuine but coarse).

9. RKD photograph from Sander.

10. Hofstede de Groot confuses the provenance of his no. 103 (then in the Strauss collection, Vienna, sold Glückselig, Vienna, 22–23 March 1926) with that of the painting now in Pasadena. According to Hofstede de Groot, the provenance of the Strauss painting was: anonymous (sale, Amsterdam, 17 September 1727, lot 12, sold for ƒ265); Huybert Ketelaar (sale, Amsterdam, 19 June 1776, lot 223, sold for ƒ11 to); Wubbels. Edward Solly (sale, Foster and Son, London, 1837, lot 68, sold for 82 guineas). The sharp drop in value of the painting between 1727 and 1776, however, suggests that these are different paintings. The paintings associated by Hofstede de Groot with no. 103 also have different dimensions: the Ketelaar version is noted as 43½ × 67 *duim* (1 *duim* = about 1 inch); the catalogue of the 1837 Solly sale gives the dimensions as 41 × 34½ in. (apparently reversed). The Pasadena painting closely matches the dimensions of the Solly painting, while the Strauss painting (Bredius 1927, no. 67, 108.7 × 167.5 cm; 42⅝ × 66 in.) matches that sold from the Ketelaar collection. Hofstede de Groot himself notes, "It is uncertain whether the picture of the Edward Solly sale, 1837 (mentioned by Sm[ith] and W[aagen]) was the original or a copy, but Sm[ith]. gives its dimensions as 34½ inches by 41 inches." Hofstede de Groot 1908–27, vol. 1 (1908), p. 39, mentions as copies works in the Cologne Museum; the Hoogendijk collection, The Hague; and the Arthur Campbell sale, London, April 23, 1904, no. 90. In addition to those versions noted by Hofstede de Groot, photographs at the RKD record the following versions: Wilhelm Itzinger, Berlin (sale, Lepke, Vienna, 21 April 1903, lot 113, panel, 54 × 74 cm); Swiss collection (sale, Helbing, Munich, 24 November 1911, no. 60, pl. 17, canvas, 92 × 108 cm, gold frame [as "Atelierkopie nach Jan Steen"]); Gal. H. Abels, Cologne, 1935; Collection Ferdinand Bek, Ulm, ("Corr. M.H. 1939," nos. B48 and 49); Collection Chr. de Marinitch (photo Giraudon no. 16432).

11. See note 10.

12. In that work, "Prov. Cap. xx. Vers. I." is inscribed on a crown hanging over the scene.

13. Schama 1987b, p. 189.

14. Quoted in Washington/Amsterdam 1996–97, no. 38.

15. See Baardt 1645.

16. Washington/Amsterdam 1996–97, no. 38, cites Slive 1968, pp. 452–59, which includes a bibliography on drunkenness and sleep.

17. Regarding stockings and shoes or slippers as sexual metaphors, see De Jongh 1968–69, pp. 36f. During the seventeenth century, the Dutch word for stocking, *kouse*, was also used to refer to the female genitals. Westermann 2018, p. 62, refers to the woman in the Pasadena painting only as "an urban woman who has collapsed in a village."

18. Westermann 1996, p. 54, discusses *A Pig Belongs in the Sty* as an illustration of a famous comic song by Gerbrand Adriaensz. Bredero (1585–1618) in which a middle-class urban narrator visits a country fair. Initially, he enjoys the peasant festivities and dialect spoken by the peasants, but rushes for cover when the fighting begins.

19. These special occasions were generally regarded with greater tolerance. See Van Deursen 1978, vol. 2, pp. 34–38.

20. Schama 1987b, p. 472, notes that the Amsterdam slang for *musicos* was "Meniste Bruiloft," a Mennonite wedding.

21. Washington/Amsterdam 1996–97, no. 38, suggests that the children may have been modeled after Steen's own family. Children are often placed in the role of observers of both positive and negative behavior. In a print published in 1610, which is thematically related to *Wine Is a Mocker*, for example, Salomon Savery (1594–1678) represents a child observing three women beating a drunken man with his pants down (Hollstein 1949–2010, vol. 24, no. 45). A yapping dog responds to the commotion.

22. Regarding smoking, which was referred to as "drinking smoke" by people in the seventeenth century, see cat. 13 in this volume, Quiringh Gerritsz. van Brekelenkam, *The Shoemaker's Shop*.

23. The combination of the woman at the door and the theatrically dressed man with the hat and cape recall both procuress scenes and so-called scenes of lovesick maidens, in which a similarly dressed man holds up a bottle, like that held by the boy. In those scenes, the bottle filled with urine signaled a test for pregnancy.

24. See Washington/Amsterdam 1996–97, no. 38, who quotes from Durantini 1983, p. 236.

25. Washington/Amsterdam 1996–97, no. 38, suggests that the man was preparing to douse her with water. Regarding the print by Brary, see Schama 1987b, p. 431.

26. Regarding chamber pots, see De Jongh 1968–69, pp. 45–47.

27. Washington/Amsterdam 1996–97, no. 38.

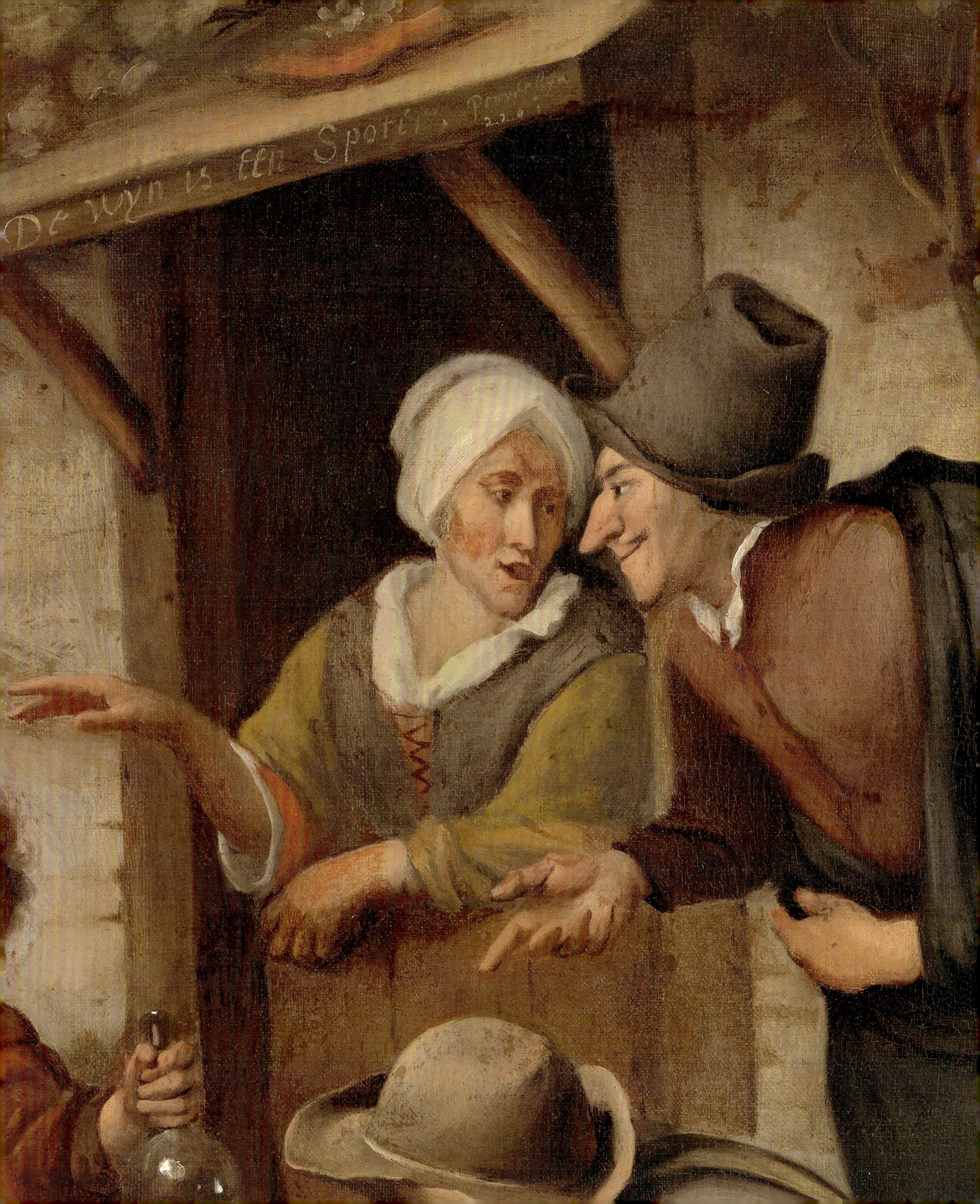
De wyn is een Spoter

89

Jan Steen

Dutch
Leiden ca. 1626–1679 Leiden

Marriage at Cana

1676

Signed and dated lower right: "JSteen 1676" (*JS* in ligature)
Oil on canvas, 31⅜ × 43 in. (79.7 × 109.2 cm)
The Norton Simon Foundation, F.1969.21.P

Provenance
Johanna Ghijs, widow of Pieter Anthony Bonenfandt, Zoeterwoude (sale, 19 April 1775, lot 6). [John Blackwood (d. by 1778), London (sale, Christie's, London, 20–21 February 1778, lot 62)].[1] John Lecomte (sale, Hôtel Drouot, Paris, 18 January 1877, lot 27, bought in by John Lecomte).[2] Prince Paul Anatolii Demidoff (1839–1885), Palais de San Donato, Florence[3] (sale, Pillet, Palais de San Donato, Florence, 15 March 1880, lot 1126, sold for F 10,000). Anonymous[4] (sale, 27 January 1882, Hôtel Drouot, Paris, lot. 84).[5] Alexis-Joseph Febvre (1810–1881), Paris[6] (sale, Hôtel Drouot, Paris, 17–20 April 1882, lot 84, bought in or sold for F 4,355 to); [(Hector) Brame (1831–1899), Paris (sale, Hôtel Drouot, Paris, 20 March 1883, lot 49, sold for F 4,400)].[7] Vincent Claude Laurent-Richard (1811–1886), Paris[8] (sale, Galerie Georges Petit, Paris, 28–29 May 1886, lot 45, sold or bought in for F 7,200; to Laurent-Richard's daughter); Madame Jean Martin Charcot (née Victoire Augustine Laurent-Richard [1834–1899]), Paris (sale, Chevallier, Paris, 6–9 July 1900, lot 12, ill.). [Galerie Charles Sedelmeyer, Paris, from at least 1906 (sale, Paris, 25–28 May 1907, lot 176, sold for F 27,000 to)];[9] S. Oppenheimer for; Otto Gerstenberg (1848–1935), Berlin, still in 1929.[10] [D. Katz, Dieren]. [Duits, London, no. 6073, from August 1930; half share from 1935 with Goudstikker, Amsterdam (no. 2643), forced sale July 1940 to]; Hermann Goering (1893–1946), sold 31 March 1942 to; [Goudstikker/Miedl, Amsterdam]; sent 1942 by Alois Miedl to Switzerland, where recovered in 1945.[11] [Duits, London (?)]. [P. de Boer, Switzerland, on consignment to P. de Boer, Amsterdam, July 1956; sold August, 1956 to]; Prof. Adriaan Hendrik Kleiweg de Zwaan (1879–1962), Nederlangbroek, by descent to; heirs of A. H. Kleiweg de Zwaan, on consignment to; [P. de Boer, Amsterdam, sold 1968 to]; [Frederick Mont Inc., New York, sold 1969 to]; The Norton Simon Foundation.

Exhibited
Amsterdam 1906, no. 115; Amsterdam 1938, no. 102; Amsterdam 1939, p. 103, no. 121b, ill.; on deposit, Kunstmuseum Bern, ca. 1951;[12] Amsterdam 1955–56, ill.; Amsterdam 1956, ill.; Dordrecht 1957, no. 75, ill.; Bordeaux 1959, p. 67, no. 127; Utrecht 1962, p. 88, no. 94; on loan, Allen Memorial Art Museum, Oberlin, 23 May–31 December 1969; on loan, Los Angeles County Museum of Art, 2 January 1970–6 August 1974; on loan, Henry Art Gallery, University of Washington, Seattle, 2 August–9 December 1974.

References
Sedelmeyer 1906, no. 38, p. 46, ill.; Hofstede de Groot 1908–27, vol. 1 (1908), p. 14, no. 50; Saint-Groux 1907, pp. 17, 20, ill.; Errera 1920–21, vol. 1 (1920), p. 343; J. G. van Gelder 1926, pp. 209f.; Bredius 1927, p. 34; W. Martin 1927–28, p. 328; Fischel 1935, pp. 60, 65; Heppner 1939–40, p. 43, as 1671; De Jonge 1940, p. 58, ill.; De Groot 1952, p. 178; Bax 1952, pp. 115, 122n6; W. Martin 1954, pp. 71, 80; Stechow 1972a, pp. 80f., 83n22; Weston 1974b; Gerson 1976, p. 171, pl. C; Kirschenbaum 1977, pp. 52, 54, 73, 82, 95, 133, no. 50, fig. 95; K. Braun 1980, p. 142, no. 369, ill.; Pasadena 1980, p. 59, ill.; P. Sutton 1982–83, p. 20, fig. 15; Haak 1984, pp. 430f.; P. Sutton 1986, p. 219; Venema 1986, pp. 170, 584, 598; Pasadena 1989, p. 59, ill.; Ydema 1991, p. 188, no. 854; L. de Vries 1996, p. 238, fig. 1; Washington/Amsterdam 1996–97, p. 238, fig. 1; Buomberger 1998, pp. 88f., 466, no. 70; Heuss 1998, pp. 108, 144, no. 70; Hollander 1998, pp. 119–21; Cornew 1999, pp. 114ff.; Francini, Heuss, and Kreis 2001, pp. 287, 377, 387ff.; Kloek 2005, pp. 74f.; Prescott 2005, pp. 53f.; Yeide 2009, p. 57, no. A245; S. Campbell 2010, pp. 95, 324, no. 660, ill.; J. Scharf et al. 2012, vol. 1, pp. 316–22, fig. 320, vol. 2, pp. 213–14, no. 1327; The Hague 2018, pp. 138f., fig. 14b.

Technical Notes
The plain-weave canvas has been lined. The surface texture of the canvas weave, which is rather pronounced, was probably exaggerated by the lining pressure. Irregularities in the canvas such as slubs and knots protrude slightly below the paint and ground. The moderately thick ground is off-white or pale gray. X-radiography suggests that the ground was applied with a trowel or spatula in rather large strokes. Visual examination seems to confirm this supposition, as the ground layer is not entirely smooth. Steen's preparatory drawing consists of dark-brown painted lines that position the figures and other elements of the composition. Many of these lines, which were left uncovered as Steen developed the painting, function as shadows in the finished work. It appears that Steen made some changes as he painted: Specular and raking light reveal anomalies in the surface texture where brushstrokes are discernible below the visible image yet are unrelated to the final picture. Figures in the background, under the portico and surrounding Christ, were painted in a quickly executed shorthand, as were the face and hands of Christ. The figures on the balcony were painted in a subdued palette in flat tones, making them seem remote from the central activity. In the central frieze of figures, from the wine casks across to the bride at the right, Steen used a brighter palette, with more details of facial features and costume. Microscopic examination reveals rather widespread thinning of the paint layer, especially the portions that were thinly painted originally. Retouching is found along the bottom edge and the upper third of the right edge. Scattered small lines of retouching strengthen shadows or reinforce contours. The varnish, likely a thin synthetic resin based on ultraviolet fluorescence, does not saturate well, but it is clear.

The story of the Marriage at Cana is found only in the Gospel of John (2:1–11). Following his baptism and the selection of his first disciples, Christ attended a wedding in

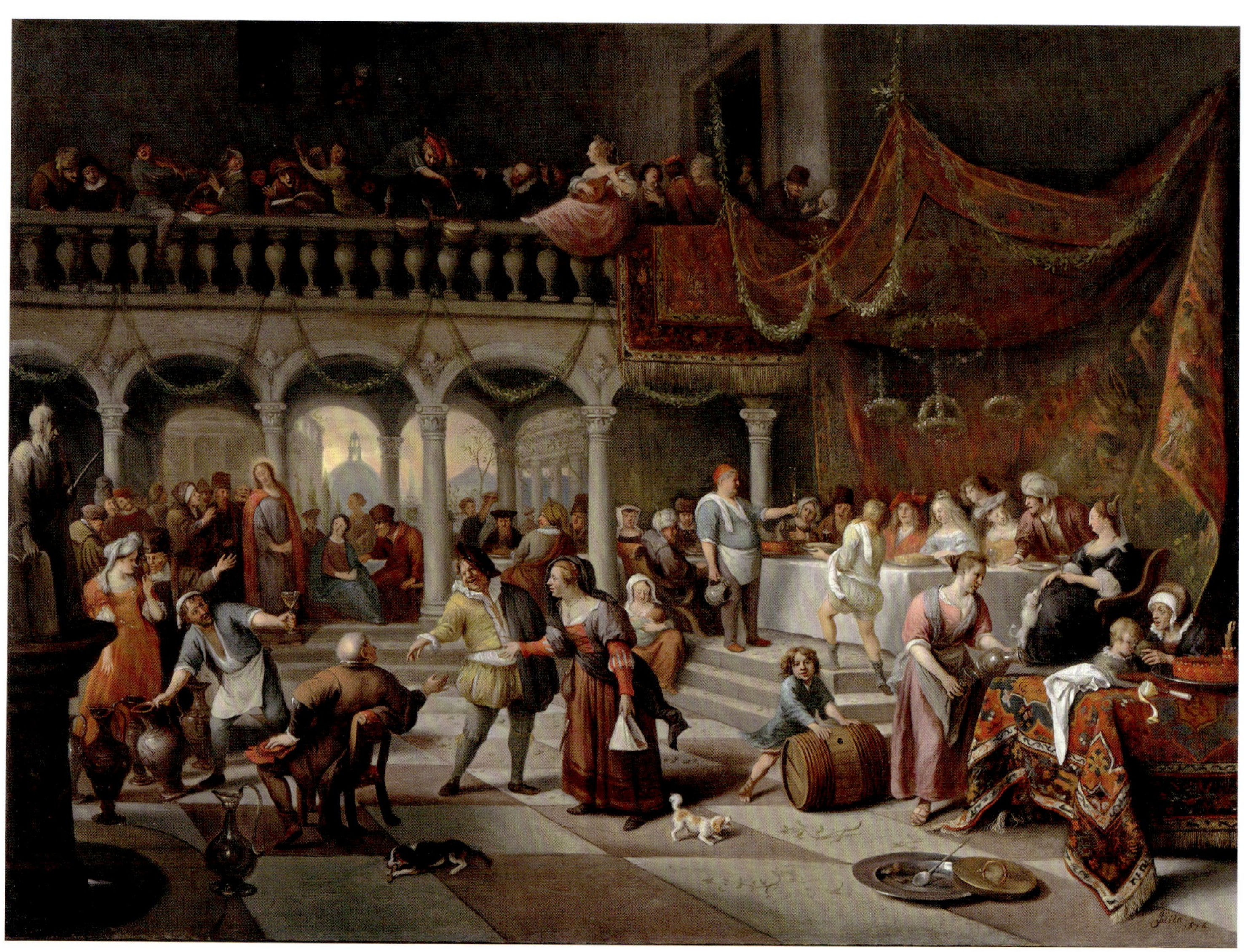

Cana. When he arrived, his mother, Mary, told him that the guests had drunk all the wine. Christ performed his first miracle by transforming six vessels of water into wine. Jan Steen painted the scene at least six times over a period of twenty years; the Pasadena painting, dated 1676, is the last of these.[13] Each version is unique, although all share Steen's conception of the biblical story of the first miracle as a pseudomodern event visited by figures from the biblical past and defined by exotic Middle Eastern costumes and carpets.

In the Pasadena painting, as in the other versions, Steen places Christ in the background and gives prominence to anecdotal detail that creates an atmosphere of celebration and expands the theme of Christ's first miracle.[14] The spaciousness of the Pasadena composition is typical of Steen's paintings from the late 1670s. Rather than focusing on a single dramatic moment, as in *Amnon and Tamar* (Wallraf-Richartz Museum, Cologne) and *Jacob Confronting Laban* (cat. 87), Steen integrated multiple dramatic incidents into a dynamic compositional pattern emphasized by light and dashes of color. Steen subtly directed the viewer's attention to Christ, who has a discreet halo of light and stands quietly before a column of the arcade, his hands folded in front of him directly above a glass of transformed wine offered to guests by a servant in the foreground.[15] Surrounded by men with the long beards and tall hats of Old Testament rabbis, Christ initiates the viewer's suggested journey with the tilt of his head, directing attention to the turbaned woman who listens to one of the rabbis as she sips wine from a glass she politely holds by the stem. On the far left, a statue of Moses with his staff and the tablets of the Ten Commandments stands above a fountain, in front of which are the six pitchers of wine that Christ transformed from water. The compositional line swings through the steward and seated man, on to the central couple, and then to a mother nursing her infant on the steps of the dais. It continues to the waiter who gestures toward the bride, through the wedding table, down to the woman giving a child a drink from a cup behind the richly carpeted table, and finally to the boy rolling a barrel; he is the only person to make eye contact with the viewer.

Steen includes in the painting some of his stock types, such as the portly man in outdated clothing and a woman in the center of the composition who holds a napkin containing leftovers from the meal. One of Steen's often-repeated motifs, they may represent the guests who were departing because of the lack of wine.[16] The boy rolling an empty barrel also appears in the version in the National Gallery of Ireland, Dublin (fig. 89a) and that formerly in the collection of the Duke of Arenberg.[17] Typically, however, Steen repeated only the type and not the exact form.

Rather than give direct testimony to the miracle, which has already taken place, Steen defines the event by including numerous details related to drinking: the boy swallowing from a cup held by a woman, the woman nursing her infant, the turbaned woman who sips wine, and the steward who offers the departing couple a glass of wine as if to draw them back to the party.[18] The respectability of the guests in the Pasadena painting contrasts with a version from about 1674/78 (fig. 89b), in which Steen alludes to the excesses of the wedding guests who had consumed all the wine before Christ arrived by prominently portraying a woman sprawled out on a step across the foreground; obviously inebriated, she dangles a jug from her right hand and offers a young boy a drink from a glass she holds in her left hand.

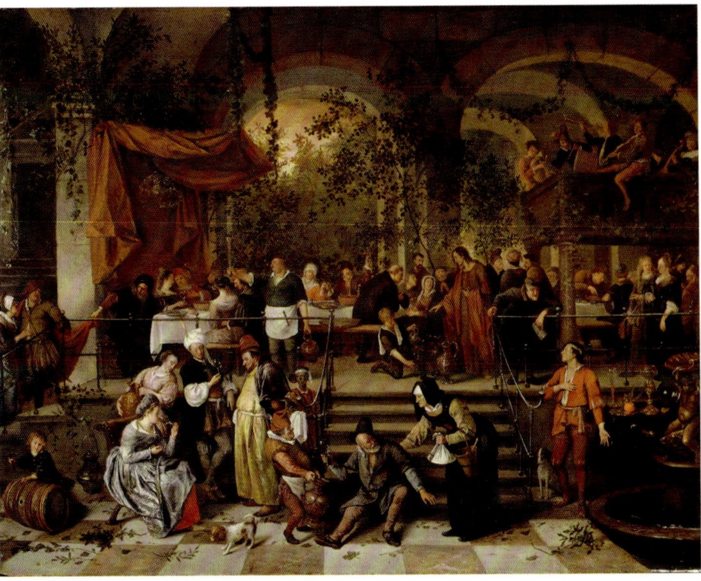

Fig. 89a. Jan Steen, *The Marriage Feast at Cana*, ca. 1670–72, oil on wood panel, 25 × 32½ in. (63.5 × 82.5 cm), National Gallery of Ireland, Dublin.

The Pasadena version is unique in its inclusion of the statue of Moses on the fountain from which was drawn the water that Christ changed into wine. This detail holds the key to the interpretation of the painting. In his left hand Moses holds the staff with which he struck the rock in the desert to provide water for the people of Israel.[19] For the Catholic Church, the story of Moses striking the rock is a prefiguration of Christ's miraculous transformation of water into wine at the Marriage at Cana, and both are typologically linked to the Eucharist, which represents the transformation of the communion wine into the blood of Christ.

Subsidiary details, such as the musicians performing in the balcony, allude to love and marriage, providing the context for Christ's miracle. Light and the waiter's gesture, as well as the three floral crowns and the enormous Persian rug, signal the importance of the bride seated in the center of a long table at the right. The nursing mother and sprigs of myrtle scattered on the floor allude to fertility; sacred to Aphrodite, one sprig of myrtle flowers into many.

Steen's ties to the theater, especially to the informal productions of the *rederijkers* (Dutch dramatic societies), have often been noted.[20] His vocabulary of gestures and

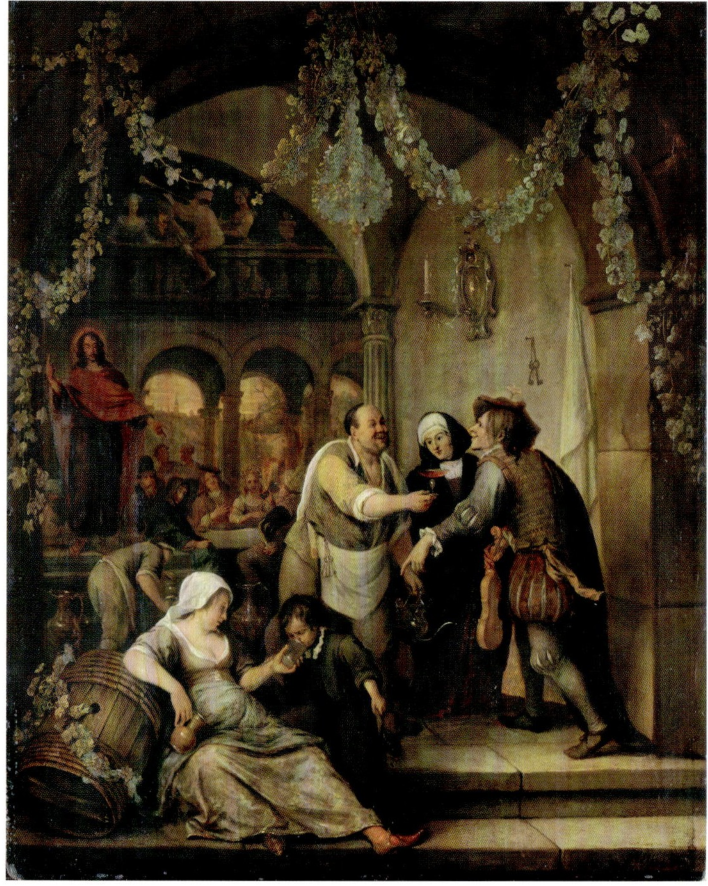

Fig. 89b. Jan Steen, *The Wedding at Cana*, around 1674/78, oil on oak panel, 23 ⅛ x 18 ⅞ in. (58.7 x 48 cm), Gemäldegalerie Alte Meister, Staatliche Kunstsammlungen, Dresden.

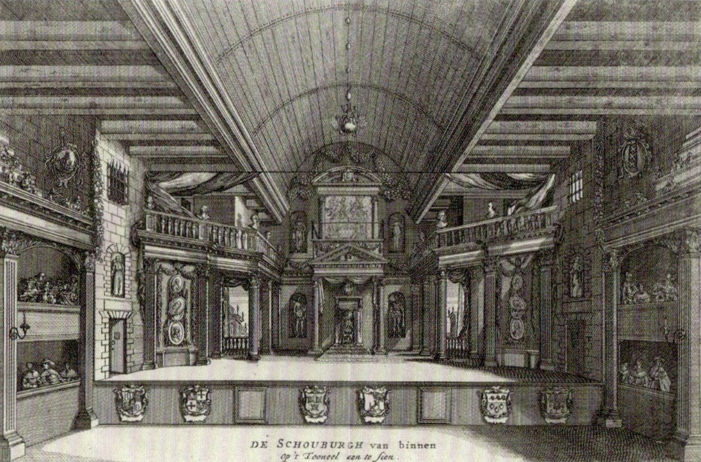

Fig. 89c. Salomon Savery, *Stage of the Amsterdam Schouwburg*, 1658, engraving, 7 ⅜ × 11 ½ in. (18.7 × 29.2 cm), by permission of the Folger Shakespeare Library, Washington, DC.

expressions is clearly informed by dramatic performances, as is his practice of repeating stock characters in different poses and combinations as if working with a repertory of actors.[21] In his seminal articles about art and the theater, Oskar Fischel observed that the Pasadena painting is similar to the view of the stage that a person sitting in a box in the Amsterdam Schouwburg would have had: "Past the canopy to the pillars and the row of pilasters with the balcony and the door in the short wall."[22] Albert Heppner, who considered the painting "pure Baroque theater," saw the entire scene as similar to a permanent architectural stage setup, with grandiose extensions to the stage in the form of colonnades with a musical gallery above.[23] Steen's combination of the colonnade and balcony has, in fact, strong similarities to the stage of the Amsterdam Schouwburg as represented in an engraving of 1658 by Salomon Savery (1594–1678; fig. 89c). The draping of the huge carpet over the dais in the Pasadena painting, furthermore, suggests an effect similar to that created by the curtains pulled back above the balcony in the print.[24]

Steen's numerous versions of the Marriage at Cana attest to the popularity of the subject among his contemporaries. Heppner suggested that the paintings were commemorations of actual wedding celebrations at which *rederijkers* performed the story of the Marriage at Cana.[25] Stechow, however, dismissed this hypothesis, noting the absence of documentation that these performances actually took place at weddings, and Gudlaugsson objected that the 1617 Synod of Dordrecht forbade the performance of events from the life of Christ.[26] Kirschenbaum nevertheless considers the possibility that the paintings do reflect actual performances, citing Bax, who suggests that the figures grouped around Christ, who are dressed in turbans and wrapped robes to identify them as biblical characters, represent players in *tafelspelen* (skits), which were common at seventeenth-century weddings.[27] One such performance appears on the left in Steen's *Village Wedding* (Boijmans Van Beuningen Museum, Rotterdam), but the subject is not recognizable.[28] Bax also explains the boisterousness of Steen's versions of the story by noting that in the Catholic calendar the Miracle at Cana is commemorated on 6 January, the same day as Twelfth Night, the usually raucous celebration of the arrival of the Magi in Bethlehem.[29] There seems to be, however, no need to extend the associations to this celebration; the celebration of the wedding is enough reason for the excitement, and Steen included no specific reference to the events of Twelfth Night.

As an artist, Steen was also influenced by visual sources. In his late history paintings Steen often looked to sixteenth-century prototypes for their "vocabulary of form."[30] He appears to have known, for example, a print after Raphael's (1483–1520) *School of Athens* (1509–11), which influenced his rendering of *The Marriage at Cana* in Dublin.[31] The open space defined by grand architecture and the small scale of groups of animated figures, concentrated around the perimeter, especially within the open colonnade in the distance of the Pasadena painting, are reminiscent of *Feast in the House of Levi* by the Venetian painter Paolo Veronese (1528–1588; fig. 89d), which Steen could have known through a print by

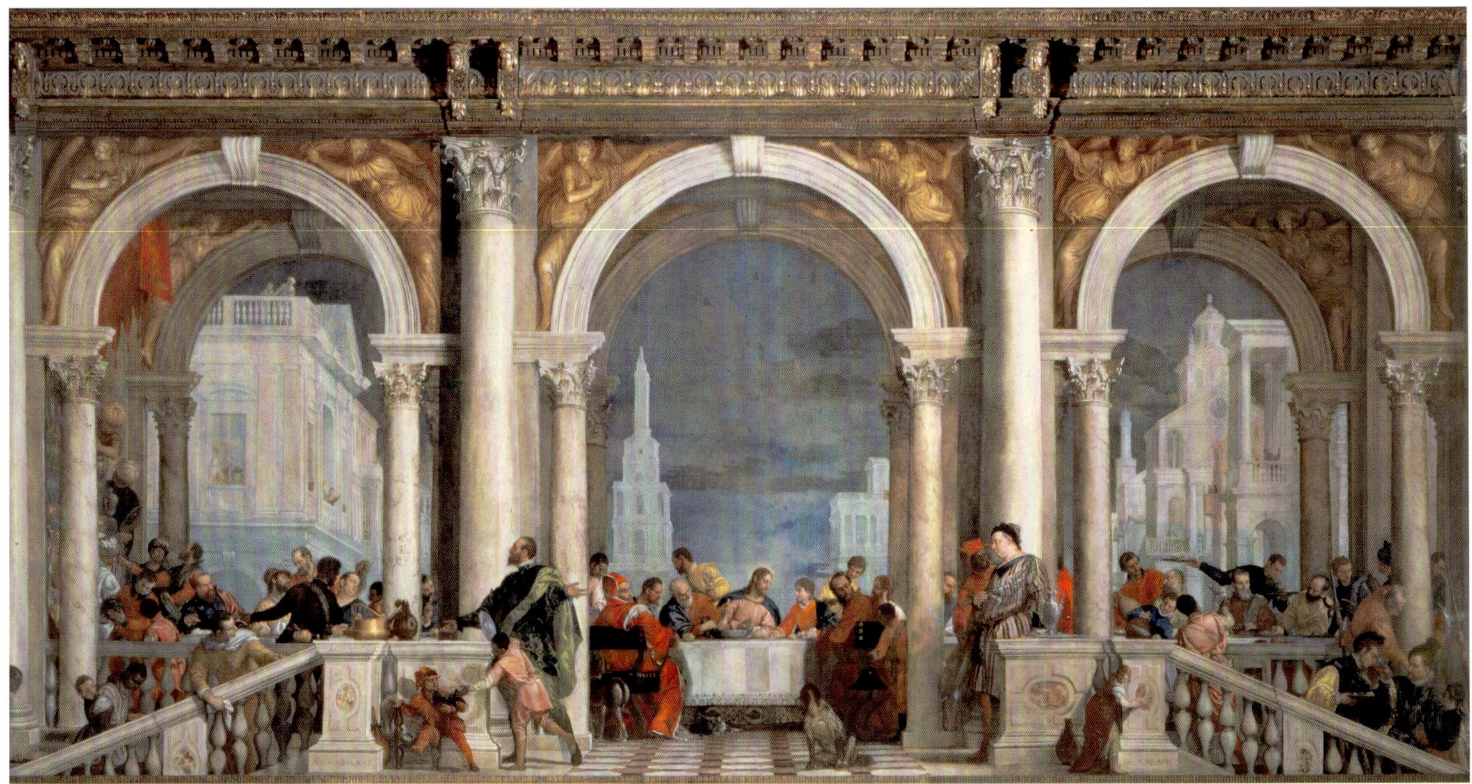

Fig. 89d. Paolo Veronese, *Feast in the House of Levi*, 1573, oil on canvas, 218 ½ × 504 in. (555 × 1280 cm), Gallerie dell'Accademia, Venice.

Giovanni Temini (active ca. 1622). Typically, however, Steen has absorbed and redefined his sources, adding the balcony from the Amsterdam theater and musicians and celebrants to create an image reminiscent of Gerrit van Honthorst's (1592–1656) illusionistic paintings, such as his 1622 *Musical Group* (J. Paul Getty Museum, Los Angeles). Steen's renewed interest in the work of Pieter Bruegel I (ca. 1525–1569) is evident in his placement of the bridal table on a diagonal in the middle distance on the right. Bruegel's *Peasant Wedding* (Kunsthistorisches Museum, Vienna) is similar in its theme and focus on the bride who sits under a wedding crown as well as its diagonal placement of the table. In 1604 Karel van Mander mentioned that Bruegel's painting was in an Amsterdam collection; thus, Steen could have seen it.[32]

Kirschenbaum suggested that these paintings were made to be placed in drinking halls and taverns because of Steen's emphasis on consumption.[33] While this assertion bears some consideration in terms of Steen's familiar mixture of history with genre, which demystifies the events and brings messages of his paintings into the context of the viewer, Kirschenbaum's hypothesis seems unlikely given Steen's references to the doctrine of the Catholic Church.

The scale of *Marriage at Cana* and the care Steen took to paint it indicate that he probably executed it as a commission rather than for the open market. The patron was, like Steen himself, most likely a Catholic who would have appreciated the painting's reference to transubstantiation, the belief that communion wine is transformed into the blood of Christ. Of fundamental significance for the Catholic faith, transubstantiation was a major focus of debate between Catholics and Protestants.[34]

In 1926 Jan van Gelder referred to Steen's *Expulsion from the Temple* as the pendant of the Pasadena *Marriage at Cana* based on the appearance of both paintings in a 1778 sale.[35] This has been rejected by subsequent scholars.[36] Kirschenbaum noted that although the paintings are related in terms of size and general format, and their subjects (both from the life of Christ) are possible as pendants, there is no cogent iconographical relationship between them.[37] Rather than Steen, who seems to have used standard-sized canvases, it is therefore more likely that John Blackwood, a merchant and picture dealer, was responsible for pairing the two history paintings during the eighteenth century.

1. John Blackwood, described as a merchant who dealt in pictures, was a major buyer in London salerooms between the 1740s and mid-1770s and held auctions on his own. Most of his collection was sold posthumously.

2. The painting was included in what was identified as the Edouard O(utran) sale.

3. Paul P. Demidoff was the nephew and sole heir of Anatole Demidoff (1812–1870), Prince of San Donato. Like his uncle, Paul was an avid collector. His sale of most of the pictures and furnishings from San Donato in 1880 was even more sensational than Anatole's sale of 1868. By 1880, Paul and his family were living in the Medici property of Pratolino, where he died in 1885. Regarding Paul Demidoff, see Haskell et al. 1994, p. 28; and Tonini 1996.

4. A handwritten annotation on the title page notes the seller as "Baron Beurnonville [*sic*] or Brame," a reference to Étienne-Edmond Martin, Baron de Beurnonville (1825–1906), who had recently died, or Hector Brame (see note 7).

5. Because Hector Brame's name appears in several sales within a short time, it is possible he was acting as an agent, possibly originally for Beurnonville, in the 1882 sale.

6. The catalogue describes Febvre as having been a former expert.

7. The title page of the sale lists the sellers as Patureau, Double, De Beurnonville, et al. A handwritten inscription on the title page of the copy of the sale catalogue at GRI reads "Vente Brame," undoubtedly a reference to Hector Brame, a dealer in Paris who is also listed as the buyer of the painting at the 17–20 April 1882 sale. Brame was also the seller in another sale, Hôtel Drouot, Paris, 24 April 1883. In 1864 Brame merged his gallery with that of Jean Lorenceau to form Galerie Brame & Lorenceau. The family-owned gallery continues to operate under the management of the descendants of the original owners, specializing in nineteenth- and early twentieth-century paintings.

8. Regarding the Laurent-Richard collection of eighteenth- and nineteenth-century paintings, see Ménard 1873 and De Lostalot 1878.

9. Annotated sale catalogue, GRI.

10. Information regarding Gerstenberg's ownership kindly supplied by Julietta Scharf, Stiftung Sammlung Dieter Scharf zur Erinnerung an Otto Gerstenberg, in a letter received 17 August 2009 (NSM). See J. Scharf et al. 2012, vol. 2, pp. 213–14, no. 1327; see also Donath 1909 and Donath 1929.

11. Regarding the extended legal dispute over this painting between Goudstikker, Duits, Miedl, and Arthur Wiederkehr, see Francini, Heuss, and Kreis 2001, pp. 388–92. In 1951 Duits and Goudstikker withdrew their claim to the painting.

12. Francini, Heuss, and Kreis 2001, p. 390.

13. See Stechow 1972a, pp. 73–83.

14. Only in the version from the late 1660s formerly in the Moss Collection, Berlin (Stechow 1945, fig. 3), does Steen give Christ a prominent position in the foreground.

15. Stechow 1972a, p. 80, notes that Christ's attitude in the Pasadena painting is very close to that in Steen's *The Wedding at Cana*, ca. 1667/68, Gemäldegalerie Alte Meister, Dresden (fig. 89b).

16. As in Jan Steen, *Marriage at Cana* (Beit Collection, National Gallery of Ireland).

17. Although the motifs are the same, they are not identical. The boy in the Arenberg painting approaches from the right rather than the left and rolls his barrel parallel with the picture plane rather than toward it, as in the Pasadena painting.

18. In the Dublin version, for example, Christ is actually in the act of transforming the wine.

19. Regarding the motif of the horned Moses, see Mellinkoff 1970.

20. The major discussions of Steen and the theater are Heppner 1939–40, pp. 22–48; Giltaij and Lammertse 2001, pp. 57–62; Gudlaugsson 1975; and Kirschenbaum 1977, pp. 7–85. See also De Groot 1952; L. de Vries 1977; Washington/Amsterdam 1996–97, passim; Westermann 1997, pp. 276–312; and Cahill 2017.

21. For example, the boy with the barrel, the woman with the leftovers, the singers, and the waiter in the red cap with a white apron tied around his bulging middle. Regarding Steen's use of rhetorical gestures from the theater, see Cahill 2017, especially pp. 23–26.

22. Fischel 1935, no. 383, part 2, p. 65, refers to the paintings as "formerly in the Sedelmeyer collection in Paris."

23. Heppner 1939–40, p. 43, mistakenly says that the painting, which he notes was formerly in the Sedelmeyer Collection, is dated 1671.

24. Ydema 1991, p. 188, no. 854, identifies the rug in the Marriage at Cana as typical of the "Namenlose Gattung" group identified by Scheunemann 1954. See cat. 86, note 15.

25. Heppner, 1939–40, p. 44.

26. Gudlaugsson 1975, pp. 5f.; Stechow 1972a, pp. 73f.

27. The costumes, which were considered biblical, reflect the presence of numerous merchants from the Middle East whom Steen would have often seen in Amsterdam. See, for example, Gerrit Adriaensz. Berckheyde (1638–1698), *The Town Hall on Dam Square*, 1672 (Rijksmuseum, Amsterdam, inv. SK-A-34).

28. Kirschenbaum 1977, p. 82; Bax 1952, pp. 115, 122n6.

29. Bax 1952, p. 115.

30. L. de Vries 1996, p. 218.

31. Washington/Amsterdam 1996–97, no. 43.

32. Van Mander/Miedema 1994–99, vol. 1 (1994) pp. 192–93 (fol. 233v), "In Amsterdam with the art lover Mr Herman Pilgrims, there is a *Peasant Wedding* in oils which is most subtle."

33. Kirschenbaum 1977, p. 96.

34. According to Protestant belief, the wine only symbolizes Christ's blood; it is not actually transformed into it, as in Catholic and Eastern Orthodox belief. Washington/Amsterdam 1996–97, p. 238, no. 43.

35. Kirschenbaum 1977, p. 224, fig. 94. J. G. van Gelder 1926, p. 210n3, calls them pendants but does not explain.

36. Notably Stechow 1972a, p. 83n22; and Kirschenbaum 1977, p. 133.

37. Kirschenbaum 1977, p. 133, citing Stechow 1972a, p. 83n22.

90

Hendrick van Steenwijck II

Flemish
Antwerp ca. 1580/82–1649 The Hague?

The Liberation of Saint Peter

1618

Signed and dated, lower right: "HENRI. V. / STEINWICK / 1618"

Oil on panel, 19⅞ × 25½ in. (50.5 × 64.8 cm)
Norton Simon Art Foundation, M.1979.58.P

Provenance
"English private collection." [Brian Koetser Gallery, London, in 1971].[1] M. J. Green (sale, Sotheby's, London, 10 July 1974, lot 112, sold to); Norton Simon, gift 1979 to; Norton Simon Art Foundation.

Exhibited
London 1971; on loan, Henry Art Gallery, University of Washington, Seattle, 12 August–9 December 1974.

References
Goldner 1988, vol. 1, p. 222, ill.; Díaz Padrón 1995, vol. 2, p. 1310, cited in no. 2139; Howarth 2009, pp. 77, 299n64, 303n8, 486, fig. II.C.12; S. Campbell 2010, p. 369, no. 1071, ill.

Technical Notes
The original oak panel may have been fabricated from two boards, but an X-radiograph suggests that it was probably a single horizontally oriented, wavy-grained board that later split. The right end of the split has irregular edges, which would be an unlikely condition if done by a cabinetmaker. The repaired join is located 9 inches from the top edge. In 1976 the panel underwent a major structural intervention at the Los Angeles County Museum of Art by Ben Johnson and George Wight, at which time vertical battens, which had restricted movement of the panel and had led to some deformation and separation at the join, were removed. The overall curvature of the readhered panel was reestablished, and the back was sealed with wax resin. The panel was then adhered with wax-resin adhesive to an auxiliary support composed of small balsa blocks put together with the same adhesive. The blocks were, in turn, covered with wax-resin-saturated fabric. In 1983 Andrea Rothe of the J. Paul Getty Museum paintings conservation department noted the join was not stable and recommended consolidation with a low-viscosity adhesive. No documentation exists, but it is assumed this was carried out at this time. The white ground is a thin layer, leaving parallel lines of the wood grain visible on the front surface. Examination with infrared reflectography showed the painting to be completely underdrawn. A tiny hole 9 inches from the bottom and 12¾ inches from the right edge is at the exact center of the horizontal axis and slightly below center on the vertical axis; it determines the vanishing point. Lines of perspective, many of which are visible with normal vision in the lighter-colored areas of the floor, fully establish the interior architecture and all the figures. The interior space was first established with translucent thin paint, subtly modulated to indicate different surfaces and light levels. Darker lines depicting the details of the architecture were painted with a fine brush. Denser paint in slightly more vibrant colors was used in the figures. The paint was thinly applied throughout, and time has increased its transparency, revealing many of the underdrawn lines. There are many tiny drying cracks in every area, which create a distraction in the dark areas. A diagonal scratch in the upper left quadrant, almost 9 inches long, has penetrated the varnish and paint layers. The dull varnish saturates poorly. Some light-colored accretions at the bottom left could be residues of wax, now covered with discolored varnish, including a thin synthetic resin layer.

The Liberation of Saint Peter is one of approximately twenty-five versions of the subject Hendrick van Steenwijck II painted beginning by or before 1604. Steenwijck was living in London in 1618, the date he inscribed on the Pasadena painting, but he may actually have begun the painting in Antwerp, the probable origin of the oak panel.[2] The subject of Peter's release from prison by an angel, which could be interpreted as symbolic of the Church's coming deliverance from persecution, may have appealed to the Protestant artist and his clientele for religious and political reasons.[3] It is, however, more likely that Steenwijck selected the story of Saint Peter's rescue because the interior setting in a dark crypt gave him the opportunity to render space in terms of the rules of perspective and dramatic light effects.

Light draws the viewer's attention through a series of vaults, past guards who have apparently fallen asleep during a card game, to the tiny shapes of Saint Peter and his liberating angel barely visible in the shadows of the distant dark hallway. The figures animate the scene but submit to the architecture. The painting is typical of Steenwijck's mature works, which are set at night or in a dark crypt, allowing the artist to depict readable architectural space using light and shadows cast by various sources. Here, light from a primitive chandelier fills the foreground vault, reflected by the surfaces and edges of the surrounding architecture.

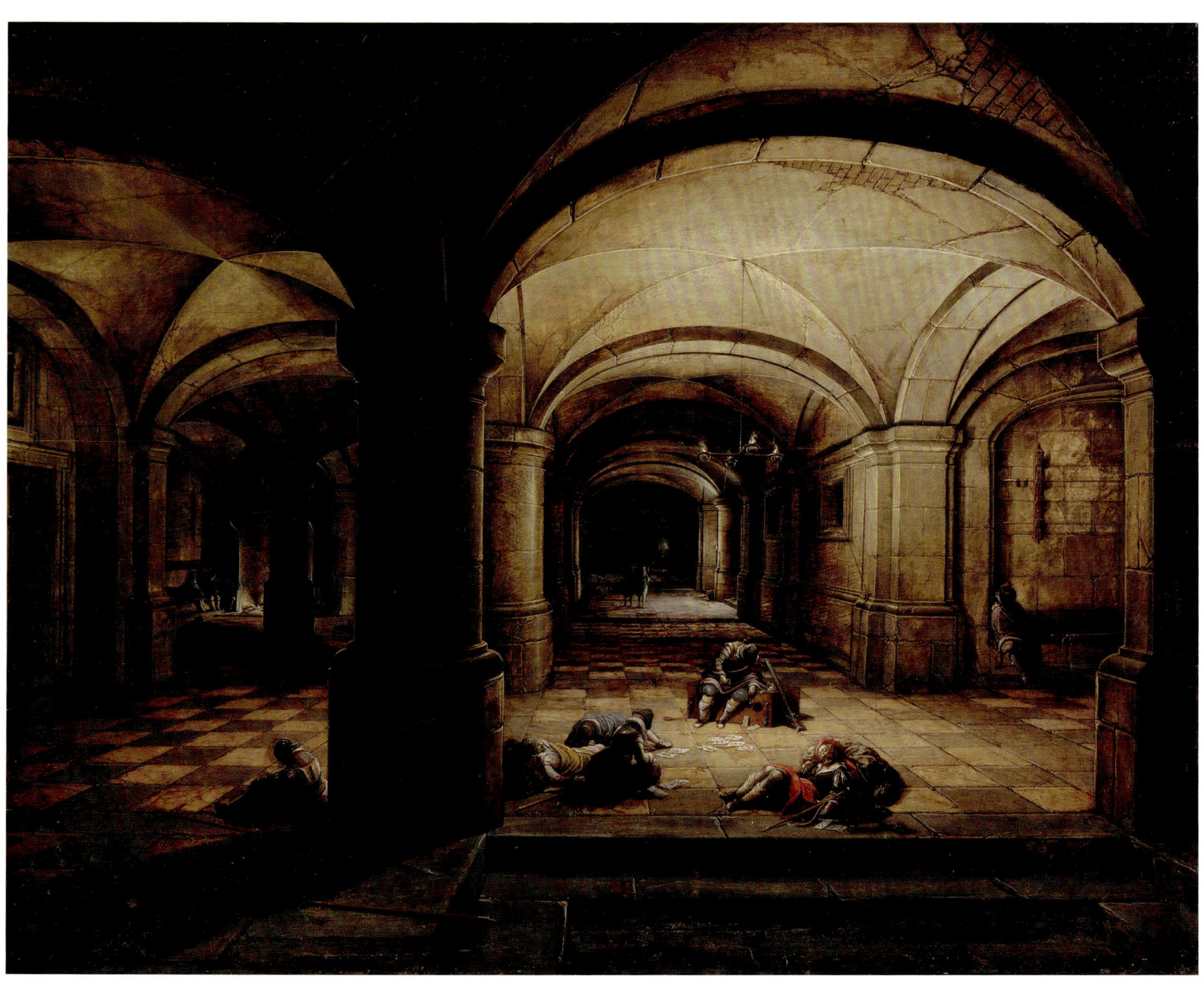

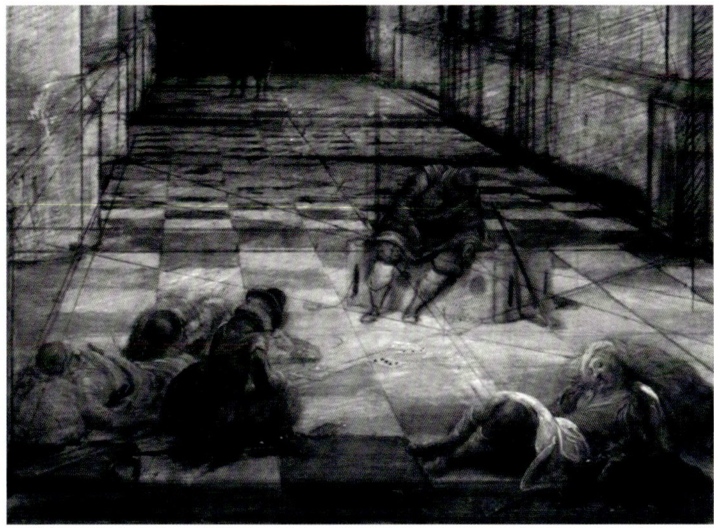

Fig. 90a. Detail of infrared photograph of *The Liberation of Saint Peter*, image courtesy of J. Paul Getty Museum, Los Angeles.

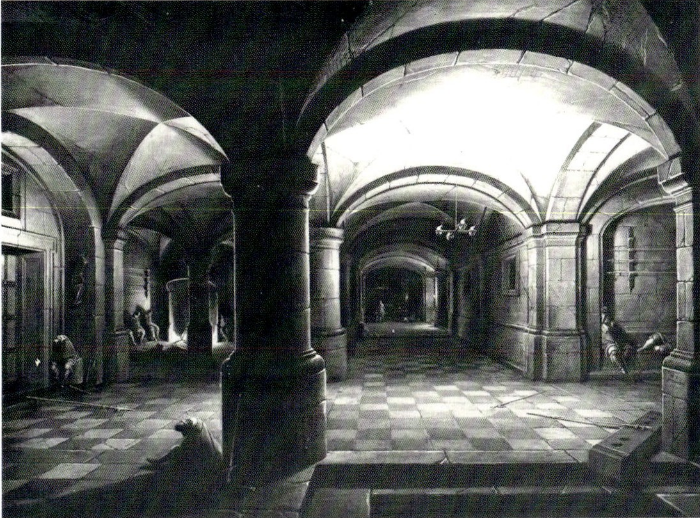

Fig. 90b. Hendrick van Steenwijck II, *The Liberation of Saint Peter*, 1617, oil on panel, 19 × 25¾ in. (48.3 × 65.4 cm), location unknown, image courtesy of Christie's.

Infrared reflectography (fig. 90a) confirms what is partly visible through the thinly painted surface: Steenwijck composed the architecture of the painting on the basis of a geometric scheme. Rather than describing what he saw, the artist used geometry and rules of perspective to construct this imaginary space. Drawn onto the hard, white ground of the panel, the major orthogonals meet at a focal point marked by a small hole in the panel to the left of the eyes of the angel and Saint Peter. Steenwijck based his architectural rendering on the principles of perspective described in albums published in Antwerp by Hans Vredeman de Vries (1527–ca. 1606) between 1560 and 1604.[4] Vredeman de Vries's consistent and didactic application of the principles of perspective made these publications highly influential as models for artists, architects, garden designers, and furniture makers. Steenwijck was undoubtedly first introduced to these theories by his father, Hendrick van Steenwijck I (ca. 1550–1603), who had studied with Vredemen de Vries and had himself painted according to his teachings.

By applying a mathematical formula, Steenwijck could repeat his architectural composition exactly without the need of preparatory drawings or other aids.[5] Indeed, Steenwijck appears to have applied the same formula to produce two other versions of the Pasadena painting dated 1617 (one of which was sold in 1974; fig. 90b).[6] Although the individual figures vary, the size of the three panels and the description of the architecture are identical in each painting. This working method would explain why, in spite of the complicated architectural spaces of his interiors, no compositional drawings by Steenwijck are known.[7] Although it seems likely that he relied on drawings for his figures, only one such work, *The Crypt of a Church with Two Men Sleeping* (fig. 90c), has been attributed to him. The polished quality of that drawing depicting slumbering soldiers in a vaulted space suggests, however, that it was a presentation drawing rather than a preparatory work.

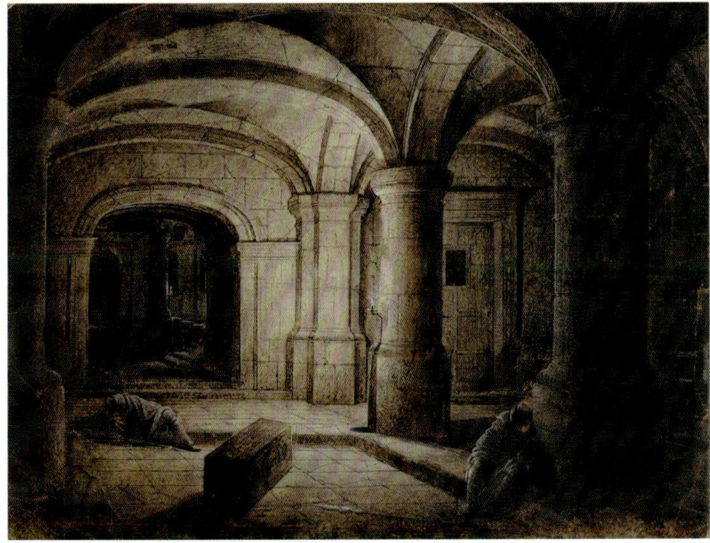

Fig. 90c. Hendrick van Steenwijck II, *The Crypt of a Church with Two Men Sleeping*, ca. 1625, pen and brown ink, brown wash, graphite, and white gouache on tan paper, 4 13⁄16 × 6½ in. (12.3 × 16.5 cm), J. Paul Getty Museum, Los Angeles.

Steenwijck's primary orientation to architecture rather than to narrative is further indicated by Dutch seventeenth-century inventories that refer to his paintings as "perspectives." Karel van Mander (1548–1606), writing in 1604, used the expression to mean a painting that displayed an artist's mastery of the rules of perspective. The term apparently referred not only to cabinet paintings but also to illusionistic murals. This employment of science in the service of art appealed to the late Mannerist taste for fantasy and deception by which courtiers delighted in surprising their guests with the unexpected. Indeed, Van Mander notes that the Prince of Orange and many others were deceived by Vredeman de Vries's life-sized "perspectives."[8] The inventories of the Dutch stadtholder Frederik Hendrik (1584–1647) and Amalia von Solms, as well as of the English king Charles I (1600–1649), for whom Steenwijck worked, confirm that the smaller perspectives, which often depict palatial settings populated by courtiers, were popular among members of the Dutch and English courts as well as wealthy and socially prominent collectors.[9] These were the people who were most interested in the advances of science and who would have known, if not owned, copies of books on architecture published by Vredeman de Vries as well as those by Sebastiano Serlio (1475–1554) and the ancient Roman architect Vitruvius, whose *Ten Books on Architecture* was published in the sixteenth century by Pieter Coecke van Aelst (1502–1550). The collector who acquired the Pasadena panel would have been impressed by Steenwijck's ability to suggest interior volume and depth accurately by the application of mathematical formulas and artistic control of dramatic lighting effects.

1. Advertisement, *Art Quarterly* 34, no. 3 (Autumn 1971): p. 384.

2. Jørgen Wadum, former keeper of conservation, Statens Museum for Kunst, Copenhagen, and currently director of Wadum Art Technological Studies, as well as an associate researcher at the RKD, and a specialty adviser on Dutch and Flemish art at the Nivaagaard Collection, Nivå, Denmark, has connected the unique wavelike wood grain of the panel to a group of paintings dated 1618 by Steenwijck and works by other Antwerp painters, suggesting that the panels had been made by the same Antwerp panel maker. In conversation with the author (Aachen, March 2009).

3. Acts 12:1–19 tells the story of the imprisonment of Saint Peter by King Herod and his liberation by the angel of God.

4. For more on Vredeman de Vries's principles of perspective, see Heuer 2009.

5. Koopstra 2019 discusses Steenwijck's use of prints by Albrecht Dürer (1471–1528) in the creation of his paintings of Saint Jerome in his study. There is no evidence of his reference to prints for the paintings of the liberation of Saint Peter.

6. Howarth 2009, p. 211, fig. II.C.10 (sale, Christie's, London, 28 June 1974, lot 23, sold to Duncan). The other version is Howarth 2009, p. 211, fig. II.C.11 (sale, Sotheby's, London, 11 December 1985, lot 118, oil on panel, 19¼ × 25½ in., signed and dated 1617).

7. This working method streamlined the artist's work and allowed him to produce compositions in multiples, and thus on speculation, while maintaining the impression of a highly skilled work. Like a print, which was produced in multiple and often engraved by one artist after the design of another, the value in these paintings, all of which appear to have been painted by Steenwijck, is not in the unique status of the image but in the artist's original conception, which is indeed unique.

8. Van Mander 1604, fol. 266r: "For Gillis Hofman, on a site opposite a gateway, he made a large perspective looking like a vista in a garden. Later some German noblemen as well as the Prince of Orange were deceived by this, thinking it to be a real building with a view." Translation from Van Mander/Miedema 1994–99, vol. 1 (1994), p. 322.

9. According to the painter Adriaen van Nieulandt I (1587–1658), Steenwijck, who was in London by at least 1617, often worked for the court of Charles I (r. 1625–49) painting perspectives for the backgrounds of portraits by Anthony van Dyck (1599–1641) and others. Steenwijck's signature appears on the portrait of Charles I by Daniël Mijtens I (ca. 1590–ca. 1647) in Turin, Italy. Steenwijck also painted the architectural backgrounds of two small full-length portraits of Charles I and his wife, Henrietta Maria, dated 1637. The figure of Charles I is a copy after the Turin painting. See Jantzen [1910] 1979, p. 38. Two of the six paintings now in the English royal collection were owned by Charles I. Number CA 74-C138-R in the 1866 catalogue of the collection of the Earl of Craven is identified as Steenwijck, *Liberation of Saint Peter*, dated 1617, from the collection of Frederick of the Palatine (1596–1632) and Elizabeth Stuart of England (1596–1662), the king and queen of Bohemia. Also known as the Winter King and Queen, the couple took refuge in The Hague following their defeat by the emperor's forces in Prague; see Hoogsteder 1986; and Montias 1991, pp. 25–28.

91

Matthias Stom

Dutch
Amersfoort ca. 1600–after 1652 Sicily or northern Italy

The Mocking of Christ

ca. 1632–35

Oil on canvas, 43½ × 63¼ in. (110.5 × 160.7 cm)
Norton Simon Art Foundation, M.1977.25.P

Provenance
Possibly Alexandre-Louis Roëttiers de Montaleau (1748–1808), et al. (sale, Paillet, Paris, 19–29 July 1802, lot 54, as Honthorst, "Un tableaux offrant Jésus-Christ flagella et couronné d'épines, à qui des bourreaux présentent le roseau; composition de cinq figures éclairés à la lueur d'un flambeau dans une prison. Sur toile, haut de 115, large de 160 c.," sold to); Commarieux. Possibly Nicolai Nikitich Demidoff (1773–1828), Conte de San Donato (sale, Claude-Joseph Rouget, Paris, 2 April 1812, lot 4, as Honthorst, "Le Christ flagellé," sold to);[1] [Constantin]. Anonymous (sale, Hôtel Drouot, Paris, 20 March 1950, lot 64, as Honthorst).[2] Private collection, France, 1953.[3] Possibly Carl dal Lago (1869–1949), in 1964.[4] [Chicago art market, 1970].[5] [Richard L. Feigen & Co., New York, sold 1977 to]; Norton Simon Art Foundation.

Exhibited
On loan, Princeton University Art Museum, Princeton, NJ, 22 February 1978–8 January 1979, and 11 December 1980–23 July 1981.

References
Pauwels 1953, pp. 151f., 187; Nicolson 1977, fig. 3, App. no. 46, p. 243; Nicolson 1979, p. 94; Pasadena 1980, p. 58, ill.; P. Sutton 1986, p. 219; Pasadena 1989, p. 51, ill.; Raleigh/Milwaukee/Dayton 1998–99, p. 235, no. 7, ill.; Judson and Ekkart 1999, p. 352; Pasadena 2003, p. 57, ill.; S. Campbell 2010, p. 409, no. 1460, ill.; A. Walsh 2019a, p. 42; Osnabrugge 2019, pp. 188n44, 211, 290, fig. 60.

Technical Notes
The medium-weight plain-weave canvas was lined by Gertrude Blumel, New York, in 1977. The original tacking edges are cut off. X-radiography reveals cusped threads at the left and right edges of the painting; the top and bottom edges are less distinct. Comparison of measurements on the X-radiograph and the painting indicate that the bottom edge has been trimmed approximately ⅝ inch. Several tears in the original canvas were repaired by the lining. The white ground layer underlies several shades of dark brown used for underpainting. A dark brown is visible beneath the flesh tones and clothing of the figures. A slightly darker brown predominates as the background color, although it is not monochromatic. Executed with a warm palette in limited colors, the painting features dramatic lighting that required clear, crisp contours. The body of Christ was painted with short firm strokes of light-colored paint that permits the dark layer beneath to be seen, accentuating the direction of the brush. Shadows on the flesh tones were rendered with full-bodied hues of darker paint mixed on the palette. The brushmarking of the moderately thick paint may have been smoothed somewhat by lining pressure. X-radiography also shows past damages or losses of paint, which appear to be primarily flake losses. There is no evidence of chemical abrasion. Retouching is extensive, located in the repaired damages and scattered areas throughout. More broadly toned areas are behind Christ's proper left arm, and along the lower and the left edges. Ultraviolet-light examination indicates a synthetic-resin varnish.

Following the arrest of Christ in the Garden of Gethsemane, soldiers led him to the house of the high priest Caiaphas, where lawyers and elders considered what charges to bring against him. Jesus remained silent until the high priest asked him directly if he were the Christ, the Son of God. When Christ replied, "From now on, you will see the Son of Man seated at the right hand of Power and coming on the clouds of heaven," Caiaphas tore his robes and cried, "Blasphemy!" The others joined in, hurling abuse, spitting in Christ's face, and striking him with their fists. The following morning, Jesus was turned over to Pilate, the Roman governor, who ordered him flogged and crucified. The Roman soldiers stripped him and dressed him in a scarlet mantle, placing a crown of thorns on his head and a cane in his right hand, mocking those who claimed that he was king of the Jews. Kneeling before him, they jeered and beat him with the cane. Finally, they stripped him and dressed him in his own clothes.[6]

The Pasadena painting is one of four versions of the mocking of Christ that Matthias Stom is known to have painted. Although not a popular subject during the seventeenth century, it was treated by major sixteenth- and seventeenth-century painters, including Rubens, Titian (ca. 1488–1576), Ludovico Carracci (1555–1619), Anthony van Dyck (1599–1641), and Caravaggio (1571–1610), all of whom adopted the late medieval scheme of the tormented Christ seated frontally as he is crowned with thorns, beaten with sticks, and spat on.[7] By comparison, Stom's composition is benign and contemplative. Rather than the violent

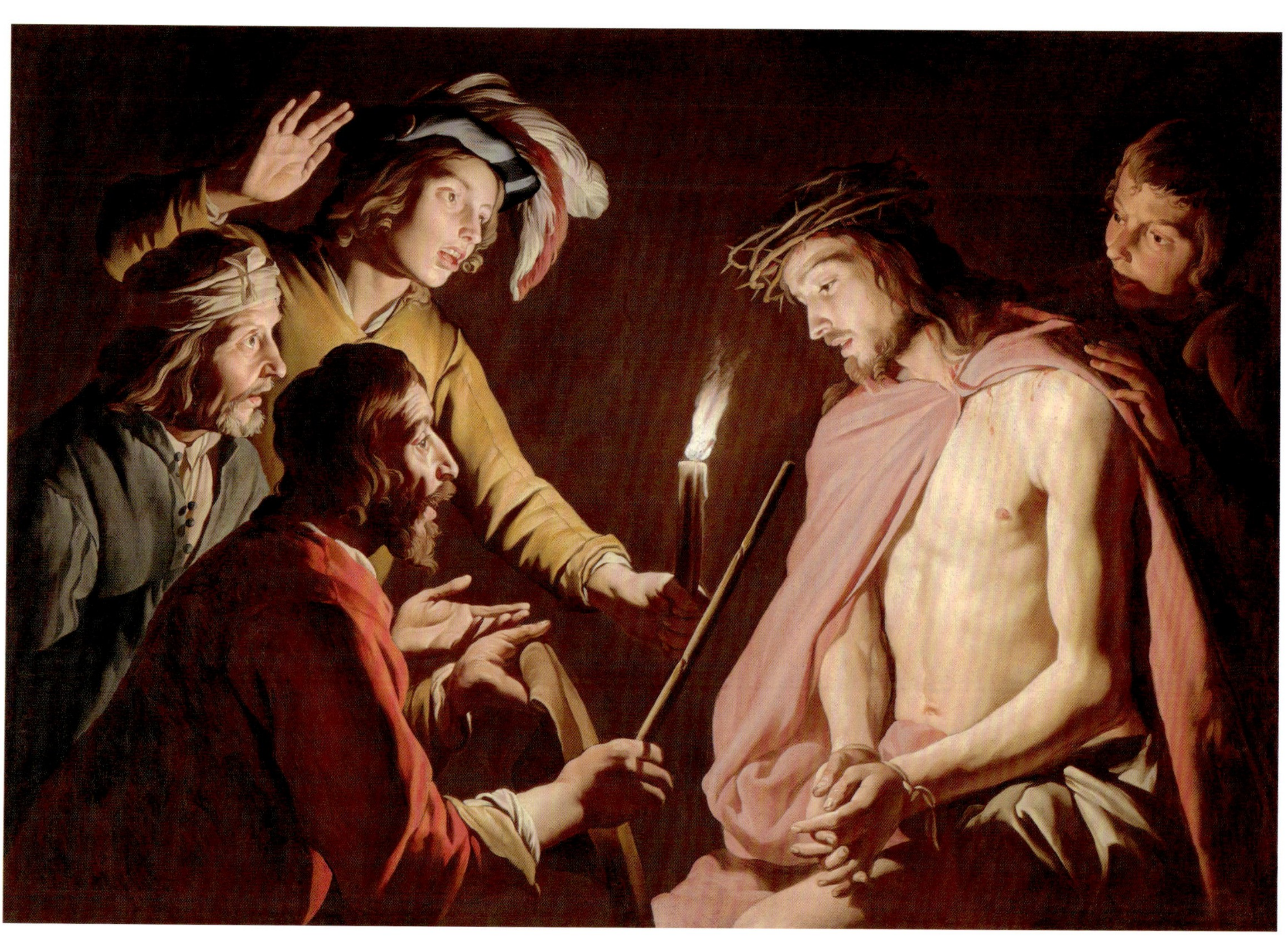

episode of physical torture, Stom represents the subsequent moments of the story. Seated in profile at the right, Christ wears a scarlet mantle and crown of thorns. Two men kneel before him, offering a cane in place of a scepter and a cloth in mock homage to him as king of the Jews. Light from a candle thrust forward by a young man breaks through the enveloping darkness, illuminating only the naked body and downcast face of Christ and the dramatically charged faces and hands of the others. The taunting has turned from harsh brutality to animated questioning, and the mood and composition have moved closer to Stom's depictions of *The Supper at Emmaus* (University of Göttingen) and *The Incredulity of Thomas* (formerly Collection Barone Scotti, Bergamo).[8]

The emotional intensity of *The Mocking of Christ*, and especially Stom's use of the open candle as a focal point to emphasize the quiet suffering of Christ and the faces of his tormentors in an otherwise oppressive darkness, are similar to the effects achieved in the early works of his compatriot Gerrit van Honthorst (1592–1656), who was in Rome from abut 1610/12 to 1620, when he returned to Utrecht. Honthorst depicted the subject of Christ crowned with thorns in at least three paintings[9] and the mocking of Christ in at least three others.[10] Stom's specific source for the Pasadena painting was probably Honthorst's *The Mocking of Christ* from about 1617 (fig. 91a), which combines general compositional ideas from Caravaggio and his followers with works by Francesco da Ponte, called Francesco Bassano (1549–1592), in which light from torches heightens the drama of his subjects.[11] A similar composition, Bassano's *Mockery of Christ*, ca. 1577 (fig. 91b), portrays Christ seated in profile on the right surrounded by seven men, one of whom reaches forward with a torch that illuminates him. Similarities with Honthorst's example, particularly the group of four men opposite Christ on the left,

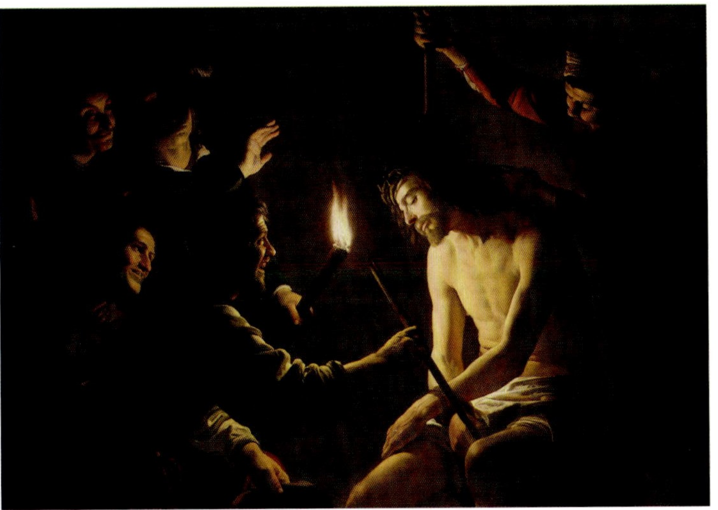

Fig. 91a. Gerrit van Honthorst, *The Mocking of Christ*, ca. 1617, oil on canvas, 57½ × 81½ in. (146 × 207 cm), Los Angeles County Museum of Art.

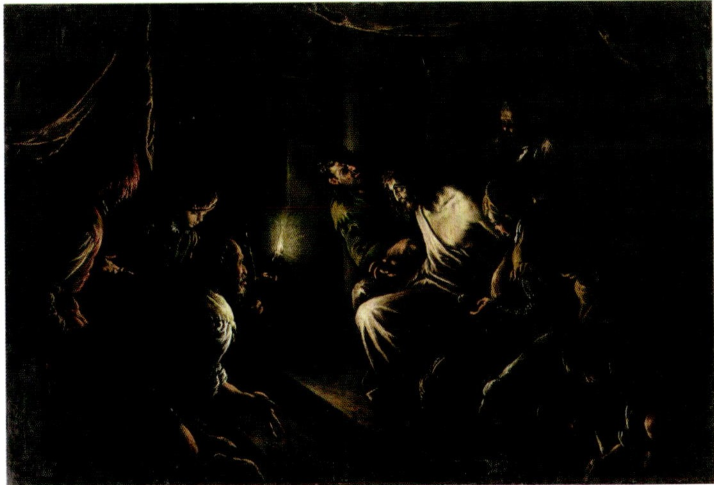

Fig. 91b. Francesco Bassano, *Mockery of Christ*, ca. 1577, canvas, 24¾ × 36¾ in. (62.8 × 93.2 cm), Kunsthistorisches Museum, Vienna.

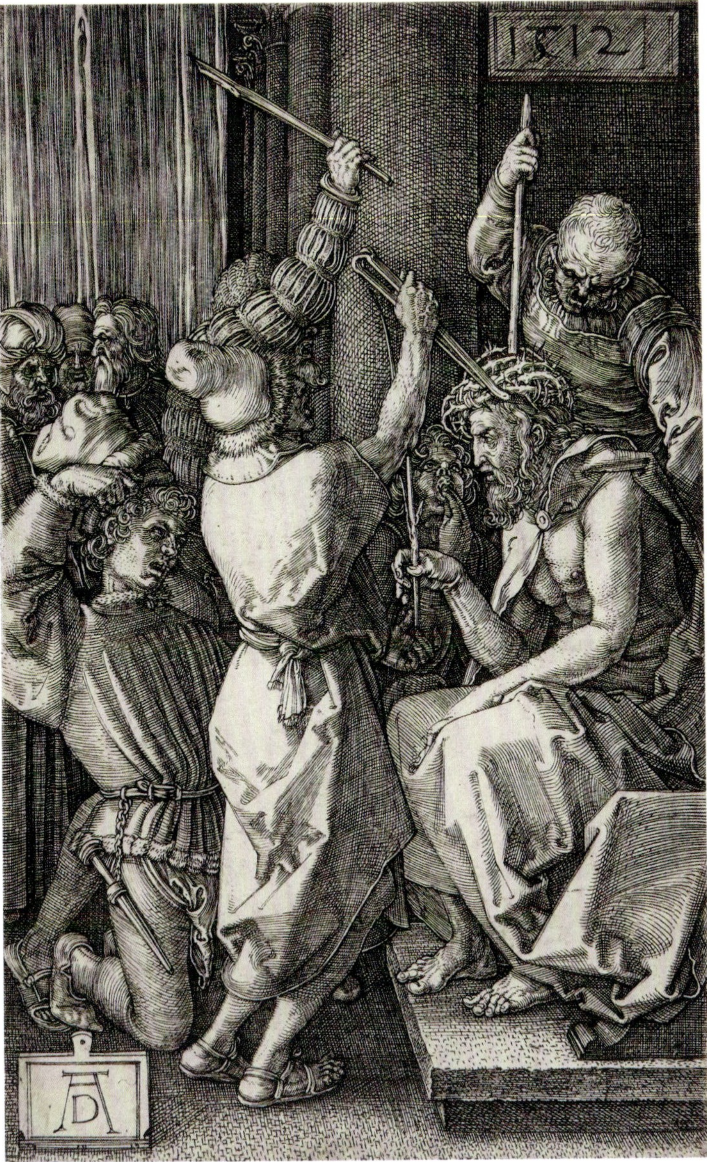

Fig. 91c. Albrecht Dürer, *Christ Crowned with Thorns*, from *The Engraved Passion*, 1512, woodcut, 4⅞ × 3 in. (12.4 × 7.6 cm), Norton Simon Museum, Pasadena, Gift of Mrs. Edward C. Crossett, 1968.

suggest that he must have known Bassano's treatment of the subject. Stom, following Honthorst's example, increased the drama and the emotional intensity of the scene by eliminating Bassano's indications of setting and decreasing the number of figures. Reflecting the influence of Caravaggio, the two northern artists draw the viewer closer to the event by replacing Bassano's full-length figures with larger, three-quarter-length figures and by exaggerating their expressions and hand gestures. The general composition and details indicate that both Honthorst and Bassano knew Albrecht Dürer's (1471–1528) woodcut *Christ Crowned with Thorns* (fig. 91c).[12]

Even more than Honthorst's painting, Stom's interpretation and presentation of the subject conform to the demands of the Council of Trent (1563) to employ art in the service of faith by making it more accessible to believers through greater clarity of form and content. Contrasting light and shadow and employing unbroken colors and simplified garments and postures, Stom rendered the clear impression of solid, three-dimensional forms within a shallow space. Like Bassano and the Dutch Caravaggesque painters, including Honthorst, he portrayed historical figures as his contemporaries and without idealization.[13] This naturalism demystifies the religious event and makes it more accessible to the viewer, who in Stom's painting is invited to enter the incomplete circle formed by Christ and the three men around the central axis of the candle.

The lack of dated works makes Stom's chronology difficult to establish.[14] Marije Osnabrugge, concurring with Benedict Nicolson, dates *The Mocking of Christ* to Stom's Neapolitan period. The circular organization of the three-quarter-length figures around a central exposed candle, which emphasizes their dramatic expressions, and the specific figure types relate *The Mocking of Christ* to a group of paintings Stom is believed to have painted while in Naples. The figures in the Pasadena painting are particularly close in both physiognomy and costume to the men seated with Christ in three versions by Stom of *The Supper at Emmaus* (Museo e Real Bosco Capodimonte, Naples; Kunstsammlung der Universität Göttingen; and Museo Nacional Thyssen-Bornemisza, Madrid).[15] New documentation places Stom in Naples between 1632, when he was last recorded in Rome, and by at least early spring 1639, possibly by July 1638, when he arrived in Sicily. He is first documented in Palermo in January 1640.[16]

The original commission and intended destination for the Pasadena painting are not known. Engaging the viewer through identification with the dramatic responses of the protagonists, it may have been painted as an independent, devotional image for a private patron in Naples. More probably it was painted as part of a passion cycle for a church or private patron.[17]

1. This information is taken from a "Notice" found in the Bibliothèque Nationale de France, Paris, and published online in GPI, Sales Catalog F-377. It is not a sale catalogue in the traditional sense, but an advertisement for a sale that would take place on site at 49, rue du Mont-Blanc, Paris.

2. We are grateful to Burton Fredericksen for supplying information about the 1802, 1812, and 1950 sales. While the connection of the Pasadena painting to the 1812 sale and owner remains tenuous, it is interesting to consider that the buyer of the "Honthorst" at the 1802 sale was listed as Commarieux, most likely the engraver J. A. Commarieux (ca. 1757–1809). Commarieux's stepson was the architect Auguste Montferrand (1786–1858), who worked in Russia for the Demidoff family. Commarieux purchased at least eight lots at the 1802 sale, three of which have been traced by Fredericksen to the 1812 Demidoff sale and three of which went to the Troubetzkoy collection.

3. Pauwels 1953, p. 152n36, credits R.-A. d'Hulst, adjunct curator of the Koninklijk Museum voor Schone Kunsten, Brussels, for informing them of the painting and sending them a photograph of it.

4. According to the RKD photo mount. The origin of this information is unknown and is questionable. If correct, the collection must have belonged to an heir in 1964, because the Austrian writer Carl dal Lago died in 1949.

5. Nicolson 1977, fig. 3. The 1970 reference may be to Richard Feigen, who was active as a dealer in Chicago as well as New York.

6. The most complete account of the story can be found in Matthew 26:57–68 and 27:11–31.

7. In Titian's influential image in the Alte Pinakothek, Munich, Christ is seated in the center of the composition facing the viewer, tormented by angry soldiers and men who jab him from behind with sticks and twist staves into his crown of thorns like the spokes of a wheel. Caravaggio's lost painting of the crowning with thorns, known only from copies and variants, eliminates the secondary elements of the scene but retains the central placement of Christ and the violent action of the traditional images. Regarding Caravaggio's lost version of the subject, see the painting attributed to a follower in the Kunsthistorisches Museum, Vienna (Utrecht/Braunschweig 1986–87, p. 21, ill. 7).

8. Pauwels 1953, ills. 4, 6.

9. Judson and Ekkart 1999, no. 59, J. Paul Getty Museum, Los Angeles; no. 60, Rijksmuseum, Amsterdam; no. 61, a lost composition known from a copy belonging to the Parish of Saints Mary and Ursula, Delft, on loan to the City of Delft and exhibited at Museum Prinsenhof Delft.

10. Judson and Ekkart 1999, no. 62, Santa Maria della Concezione, Rome; and two paintings included in the Addendum, pp. 349–52, one in the Spier Collection, London, and the other in the Los Angeles County Museum of Art. Regarding the Los Angeles version, see A. Walsh 2019a.

11. Judson and Ekkart 1999, p. 351. The representation of the actual light source by both Stom and Honthorst is typical of northern artists under the influence of Caravaggio but not actually of Caravaggio himself.

12. *Christ being crowned with thorns*, Hollstein 1954–2019, vol. 7, p. 123, no. 142. Honthorst apparently knew the print himself since he included the motif of the stick and the cloth held by the man directly confronting Christ, details that are present but less accentuated in the Bassano painting but reappear in the painting by Hendrick ter Brugghen (1588–1629) also tempered the Caravaggist prototype with northern elements derived from sixteenth-

century prints. In *Christ Crowned with Thorns*, signed and dated 1620 (Statens Museum for Kunst, Copenhagen), Ter Brugghen turned to a print by Lucas van Leyden (ca. 1494–1533; see Utrecht/Braunschweig 1986–87, pp. 83–87).

13. Caravaggio's *Calling of Saint Matthew* (Contarelli Chapel, San Luigi dei Francesi, Rome) was especially influential and served as the inspiration for Bartolomeo Manfredi's (1582–1622) popular genre scenes of figures gathered around a table. The type of foppish young man with a feathered hat in the background of the Pasadena painting is often found in these paintings.

14. Osnabrugge 2019, p. 176, notes that only four paintings by Stom are dated.

15. Osnabrugge 2019, p. 188, believes that Stom also painted two of the other four known versions while in Naples.

16. Osnabrugge 2014. Regarding Stom's stylistic development, see Nicolson 1977, and Osnabrugge 2019, pp. 181ff. According to Nicolson 1977, p. 234, "All Stomer's famous and biblical scenes done in north Sicily differ from their Neapolitan predecessors by their vast dimensions and the ease with which monumentality is grasped." Nicolson points out that paintings from Stom's Neapolitan period tend to be quieter and less dramatic (p. 238).

17. According to Osnabrugge 2019, pp. 182–86, in 1692 Carlo Celano reported paintings by Stom in the church of Sant'Eframo Nuovo in Naples, but did not mention their subjects. In 1789, however, De Dominici Sigismondo noted, "Behind the main altar there are some paintings of Christ at the column, crowned with thorns and a crucifixion surrounded by several crying angels, which were painted by Giovani Stomer [the] German" (also noted by Nicolson 1977, p. 232). Borean and Cecchini 2002, pp. 159ff., observe that a series of thirteen paintings depicting the Passion of Christ by Stom are recorded in the 7 January 1677 inventory of the widow of the Venetian merchant Giovanni Andrea di Ottavio Lumaga (1607–1672), who had business in Naples and Milan, as well as in Germany and France: "Tredeci con tutta la Passione del Signore pieni di figure quanto al naturale fino al ginocchio tutti di notte al lume del Matteo fiamengo." (GPI, Archival Inventory I-3641, item 0016). Osnabrugge 2019, p. 198, believes that Lumaga purchased the paintings from the collection of Gaspar de Roomer (ca. 1596/1608–1674), a wealthy Antwerp-born merchant and ship owner in Naples. In that collection the paintings—identified as by "Stopper"—were seen by Giulio Cesare Cappachio, as reported in *Il Forastier dialogi di Giulio Cesare Cappachio, Academica Otioso* (Naples, 1634; see Penta 1990, p. 254n2). Finally, see Labrot 1992, p. 130, no. 7, where a painting entitled "l'Incoronatione di spine di Monsù Matteo Stroma" appears in the 1676 inventory of the Neapolitan merchant Pompeo d'Anna (GPI, Archival Inventory I-8, p. 2, item 0007 [Anna]). According to Osnabrugge 2019, p. 188, because the inventories do not cite dimensions, it is not possible to identify the paintings mentioned in the Neapolitan collections of Pompeo d'Anna or Pietro Giacomo d'Amore (1656) with any of the known versions, including the Pasadena painting.

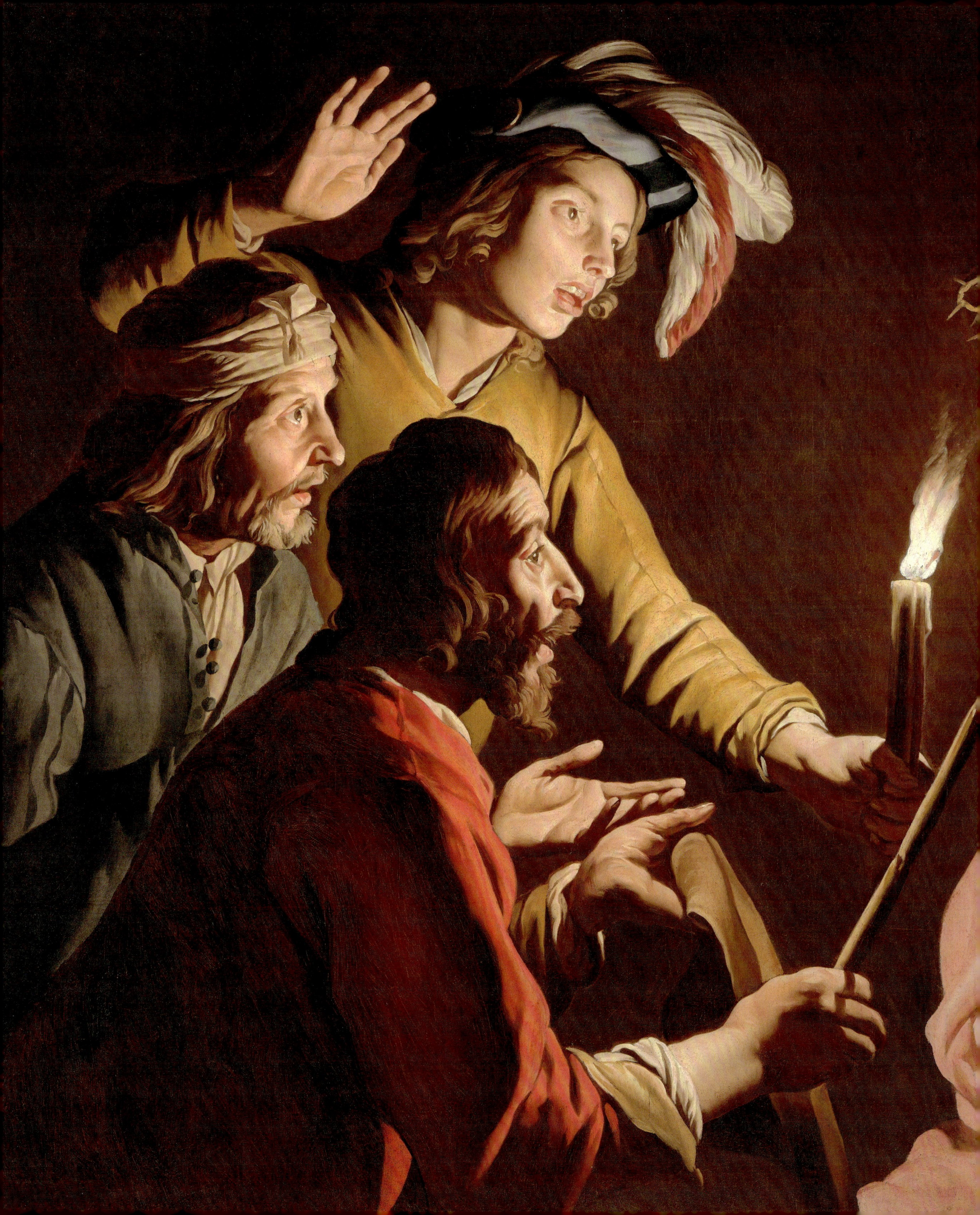

92

Sébastien Stoskopff

Alsatian or German
Strasbourg 1597–1657 Idstein

Still Life with Empty Glasses

ca. 1640

Oil on canvas, 34 × 43¼ in. (86.4 × 109.9 cm)
The Norton Simon Foundation, F.1972.18.2.P

Provenance
Private collection, Vienna. [Galerie Sanct Lucas, Vienna, 1969].[1] [Galerie Nathan, Zurich, sold 25 November 1971 to]; [Paul Rosenberg and Co., New York, stock no. 6416-2693, sold 1972 to]; The Norton Simon Foundation.

Exhibited
On loan, Phoenix Art Museum, 5 June 1972–6 July 1973; on loan, Los Angeles County Museum of Art, 9 July 1973–26 August 1974; San Francisco 1974–76, pp. 16f., no. 1, ill., as 1644; Paris/New York/Chicago 1982, pp. 202–03, 322f., 373, no. 103, ill.

References
Faré 1974, p. 129, ill.; Pasadena 1980, p. 66, ill.; *La Chronique des arts* 1982, p. 3; Lesné 1982, p. [3], ill.; Chicago 1982, p. 11; Gruber 1983, pp. 212–15, fig. 1; Bergamo 1983, p. 218, ill.; Wright 1985, p. 262;[2] Idstein 1987, p. 27, no. 18, p. 82, ill.; Pasadena 1989, p. 74, ill.; London 1993, p. 36, no. 11, fig. 2; Hahn-Woernle 1996, no. 44, pp. 204–06; S. Campbell 2010, p. 340, no. 802, ill.

Technical Notes
The support is a medium-weight double-weave canvas. It has been lined, with the original tacking edges removed; cusped threads at all edges indicate that the painting's dimensions are probably unchanged. The smoothly applied ground is white. Microscopic examination suggests that the composition was completely underdrawn. Such lines, possibly drawn in graphite, define the table edge as well as the edges of the stacked tumblers, for example. Paint in the darker areas is moderately thin but not transparent, directly applied over the light-colored ground. Larger elements of the composition were smoothly brushed and blended as rather flat, dark colors. Opaque white paint was used to capture reflections. Tiny, precisely placed dots of thick white paint describe the decorative details of varied objects and textures. Although the painting's appearance is not seriously compromised, there have been past damages. X-radiography reveals damage around the perimeter and a large loss at the bottom right corner. Lining pressure has altered the original surface characteristics of the paint, softening the impasto and suppressing the raised painted dots. Abrasion is scattered throughout, although it is not always evident with normal vision. A vertical line of damage near the left side seems to have been caused by creasing or folding of the canvas. Retouching includes repairs at the outer edges, the upper left side, an area at top center, and the filled loss at the bottom right. All retouching underlies the natural-resin varnish.

Using a limited palette of subdued, smoothly applied tones of brown and gray, Sébastien Stoskopff depicted the poorly lit corner of a kitchen where fine glasses are washed and stored after a meal. On a simple wooden table a wicker-covered glass flask lies on its side next to an overturned green rummer with raspberry prunts. A tall brass bucket, decoratively incised both inside and outside the rim, stands behind. Inside a similarly decorated oblong copper tub used for washing is a hexagonal pewter flask with a screw top. On the top of a wooden cupboard on the right, a wicker basket is filled with delicate Venetian wineglasses and a lobed, gilded goblet. Fragments of a similar broken Venetian wineglass lie on the table in the center foreground next to the handle of a turned wood stick used in washing glasses. To the right, a stack of six silver- and gold-colored beakers stands close to the table's edge. To the far right, precariously close to the corner, is a tall, clear Venetian glass goblet, distinguished from the others by its slimmer proportions and simple, delicate silhouette.[3] Barely visible in the center of the shadowy background is a niche with a glass tazza filled with what is probably red wine.

Stylistically and compositionally, *Still Life with Empty Glasses* resembles works Stoskopff painted following his return to Strasbourg from Paris in 1641. Wicker baskets of delicate Venetian glasses appear in several of his paintings, including *Still Life with Glasses in a Basket* (1644; Musée de l'Œuvre Notre-Dame, Strasbourg) and *Still Life with Glasses and Goblets* (fig. 92a). The latter also includes the washing tub and broken glass. During the approximately twenty years he lived in Paris, Stoskopff moved away from the style of his mentor, the Flemish painter and architect Daniel Soreau (1554–1619), and had developed a style similar to that of the contemporary Flemish still-life artists Jacques Linard (ca. 1600–1645), Pierre Boucle (ca. 1610–1673), and Lubin Baugin (ca. 1612–1663), all active in Paris. In addition to a repertoire of objects, Stoskopff shared with these artists a

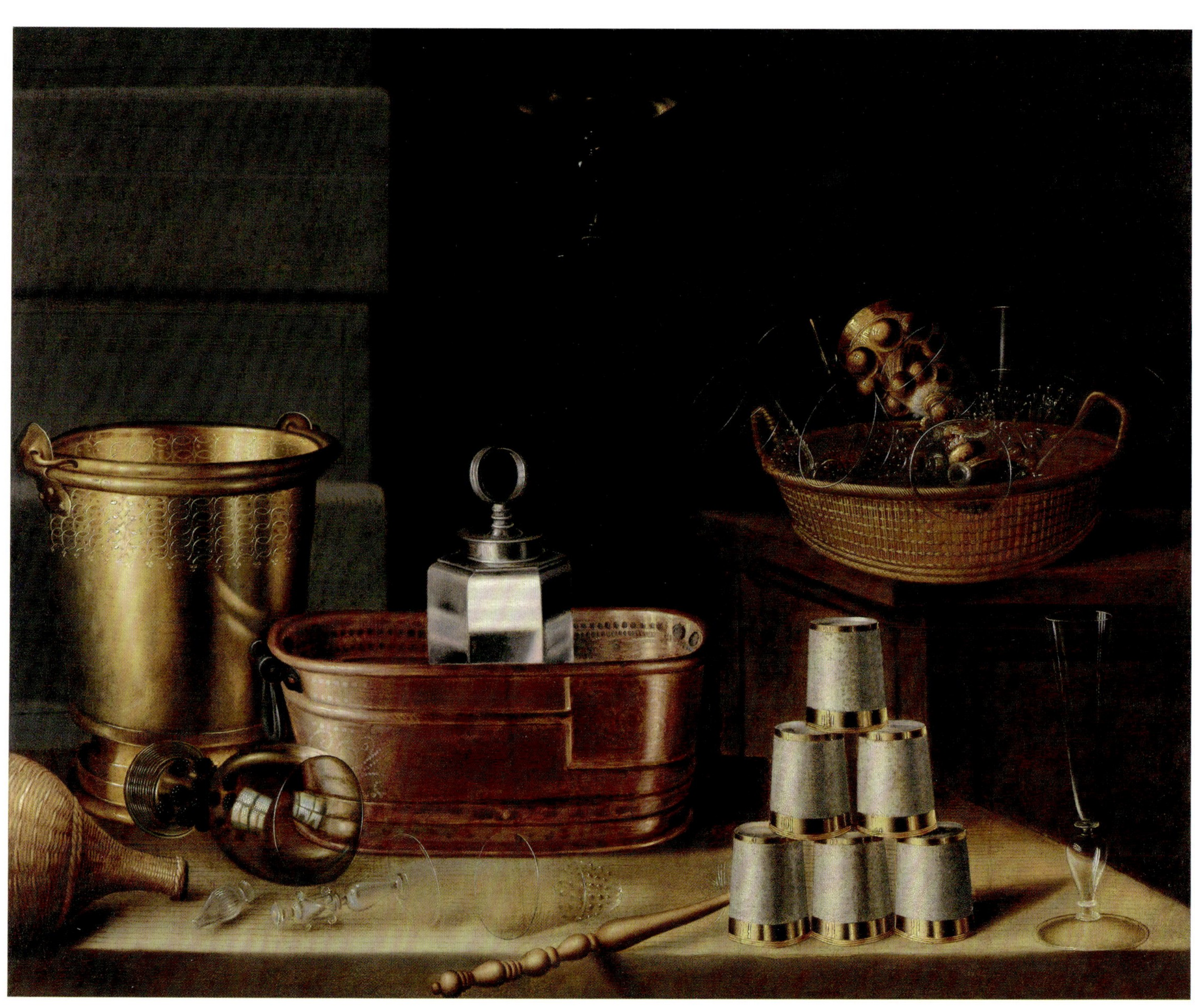

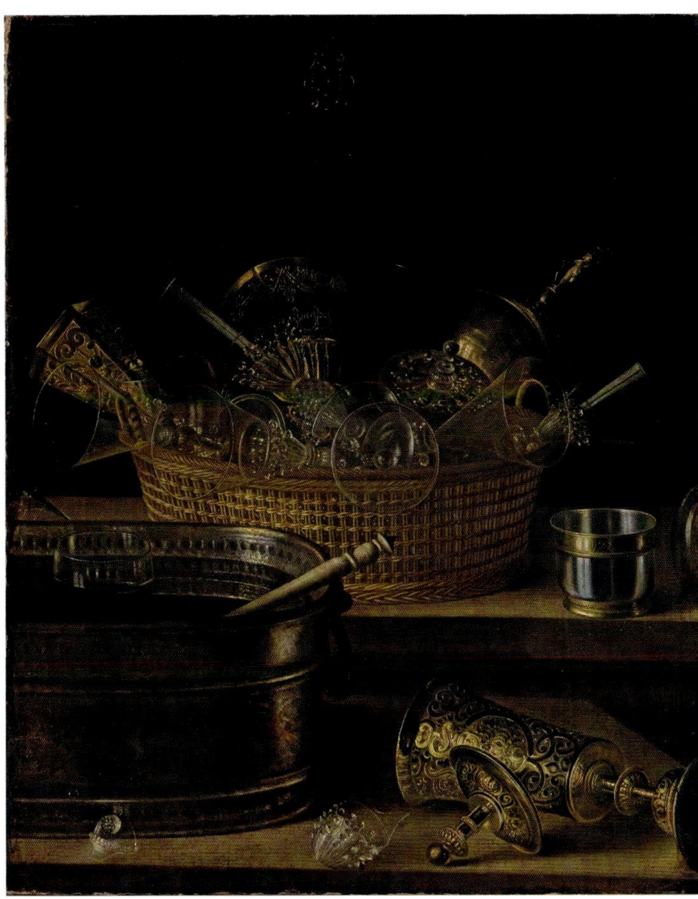

Fig. 92a. Sébastien Stoskopff, *Still Life with Glasses and Goblets*, ca. 1645, oil on canvas, 25 5/8 × 21 1/4 in. (65 × 54 cm), Staatliche Kunsthalle, Karlsruhe.

preference for austere compositions that emphasize individual items through precise draftsmanship and controlled light.

Stoskopff's primary compositional concern was the description of light as it strikes and defines different surfaces, emphasizing the geometric forms and establishing the degree of translucency of each object. Relieved from the dark surroundings by light, the objects cast reflections and shadows on surrounding surfaces. Stoskopff consciously played the smooth, glistening surface of the six-sided pewter container against the rough surface of the rusticated stone wall and captures the reflection of the copper tub in the brass pail. The reflective quality of these smooth surfaces also plays off against the incised detail of the same metal vessels, as well as against the flat surface of the table, defined only by the wood grain. White paint applied in a regular pattern of raised dots renders the effect of light reflected on the rough texture of the beakers, while white paint applied more smoothly suggests the reflection of the window on the beaker at the left.

The informality of *Still Life with Basket of Glasses* belies the artist's careful preparation of the composition, as evidenced by the precision of the drawing beneath. There is great subtlety in the crisp lines of the underdrawing—probably rendered in graphite or metal point rather than chalk—to define the fragility of the delicate Venetian glasses. Stoskopff described the distant rims of the glasses by using only the lines of the underdrawing: thin glazes of white paint washed over the dark background suggest the transparent glass, while delicate lines of white paint define the light following the rims of the glasses in the foreground.

By the mid-seventeenth century, Venetian glass was used by the well-to-do throughout Europe.[4] The expensive metalwork Stoskopff included in this and many of his other paintings was probably produced in Strasbourg, where members of his mother's family, the Riedingers, were silversmiths.[5] All of these objects would have been found in the kitchens of wealthy households or inns. The silver beakers on the right, however, were called *Ratsherrenbechers* in Strasbourg and thus may refer to the *Ratskeller*, a restaurant in the cellar of the townhall.[6]

Like many of the *pronk* (ostentatious) still lifes of his contemporaries, Stoskopff's painting of sumptuous objects celebrates wealth while subtly warning of the fragility of life and the vanity of earthly possessions and activities that can distract one from spiritual responsibilities. The beakers, for example, may refer to measure and moderation, while the broken glass is a familiar reference to the fragility of life frequently cited by contemporary emblematic literature, in which life is compared to a beautiful glass that is easily broken.[7] The inclusion of the glass tazza with red wine may, furthermore, be a reference to the Eucharist, a specific reminder of spiritual life.

1. Hahn-Woernle 1996, p. 204.

2. Wright 1985 incorrectly notes the painting is signed and dated 1644.

3. Hahn-Woernle 1996, p. 204, identifies this as a *Kelchglas*.

4. Stoskopff himself may have first come into contact with Venetian glass when he visited Venice while living in Paris, although the beautiful, delicate glasses were admired throughout Europe.

5. Hahn-Woernle 1996, p. 204.

6. Hahn-Woernle 1996, p. 204, with reference in note 2 to Haug 1978, figs. 32, 45, 46. Hahn-Woernle 1996 (p. 206) reproduces a painting attributed to either Pieter Gerritsz. van Roestraten (1629/30–1700) or Theodor Roos (1638–1687), *Drinking Vessels*, from the second half of the seventeenth century (oil on canvas, 44.7 × 50.3 cm; private collection, Hungary). It represents virtually the same stack of beakers, which she considers to have been based on Stoskopff's example but which may also imply a specific iconographic significance.

7. Hahn-Woernle 1996, p. 205n4, refers to a poem by Josua Stegmann (1588–1632), cited in Van Ingen 1966, p. 63.

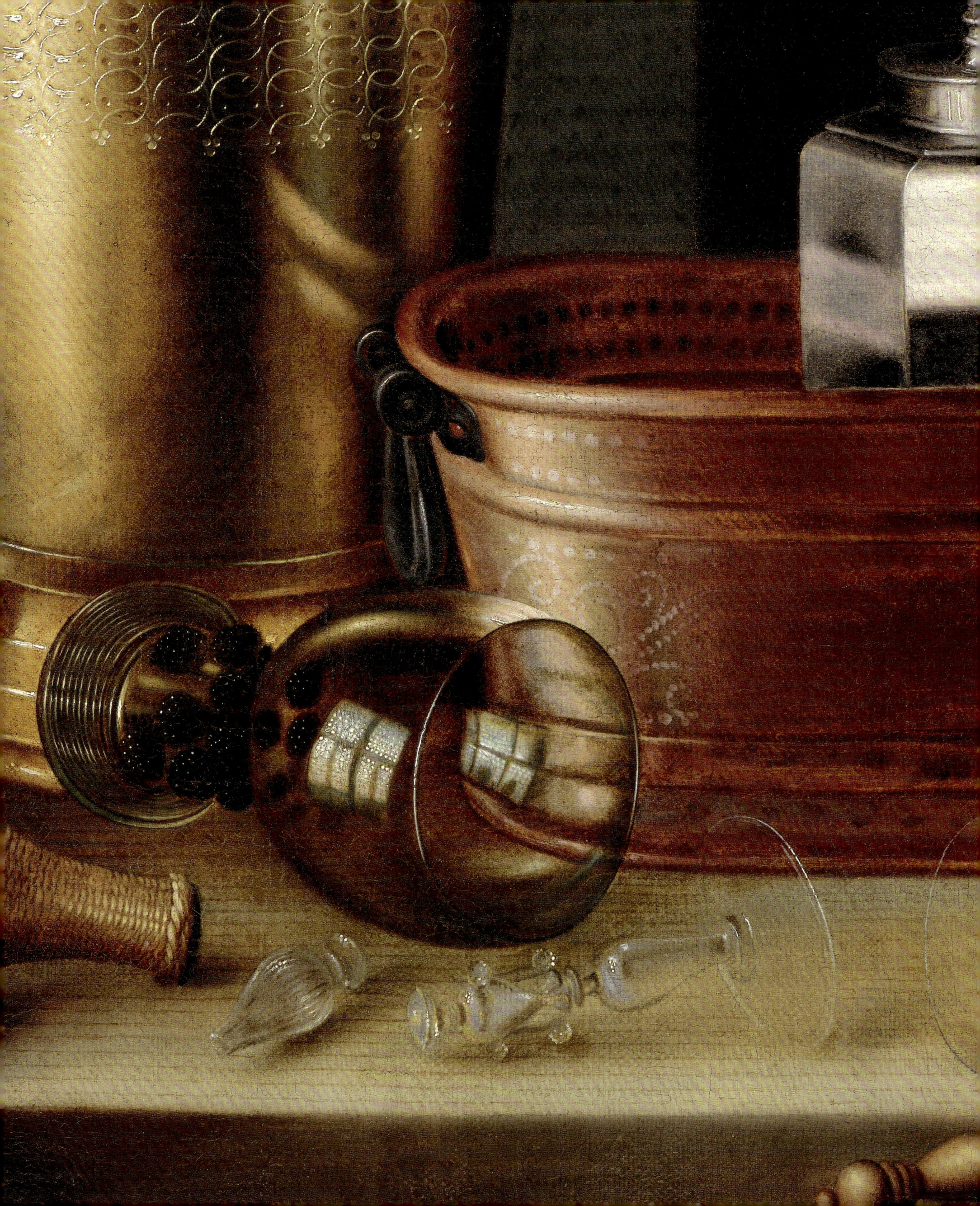

93

Justus Sustermans, also known as Giusto Suttermans

Flemish
Antwerp 1597–1681 Florence

Portrait of a Woman

ca. 1635–45

Oil on canvas, 21 × 17¼ in. (53.3 × 43.8 cm)
Norton Simon Art Foundation, M.2010.1.200.P

Provenance

Dr. Ernst Heldring (1871–1954), Amsterdam (sale, Frederik Muller, 15 Amsterdam, May 1934, lot 10, ill., sold for ƒ11,000 to); [Nicolas Beets (1878–1963), Amsterdam]. Hans Ludwig Larsen (1892–1937), Wassenaar, in 1937, by descent to his widow; Suzanne Larsen-Menzel (1911–2001), later Mrs. Frank E. Brower, Wassenaar (sale, Parke-Bernet Galleries, New York, 6 November 1947, lot 37, ill., sold for $2,400 to); M. Shapiro. Anonymous (sale, Sotheby Parke-Bernet, New York, 30 May 1979, lot 86, sold to); Norton Simon, gift to; Jennifer Jones Simon Art Trust, bequest 27 September 2010 to; Norton Simon Art Foundation.

Exhibited

Rotterdam 1938, p. 45, no. 183, fig. 171.

References

Florence 1983, p. 14, fig. 2; S. Campbell 2010, p. 426, no. 1605, ill.

Technical Notes

The medium-weight plain-weave canvas is lined, with the original edges cut off. X-radiography reveals that only the top edge has cusped threads. A vertical tear through the proper left eyebrow of the sitter and a short diagonal tear at the bottom left have been repaired by the lining. The smooth white ground is moderately thick, not covering the canvas weave entirely. A warm gray-brown paint, visible in the unfinished lower portion of the painting, appears to extend over the entire surface; below the face, it is visible at the corners of both eyes and in cool shadows such as those surrounding the lips. Opaque, rich paint was smoothly blended in the luminous face, with light flesh tones over thin, cool shadows. Only the face was fully finished; the bodice was left in reserve with the outlines of the white collar loosely painted over it. The paint is generally well preserved, although there are numerous small flake losses in the lower portion. Ultraviolet light indicates that the varnish in the face, neck, and pearls was reduced in prior selective cleaning. Retouching is in two generations: The older retouching is found at the top of the hair, in some small losses on the proper right shoulder, and along the bottom edge of the painting; more recent retouching is in the proper left eyebrow and proper left cheek, in the red rose above the left ear, and along the top edge of the painting. A thin layer of synthetic-resin varnish, likely Acryloid B-72, overlies the natural-resin varnish.

Left unfinished, this bust-length portrait of an unidentified young woman has the freshness and directness of a sketch made directly from life. Seen in three-quarter view, the sitter looks at the viewer out of the corners of her eyes, the slight hint of a smile further animating her expression. Light floods her face; falling strongly on her forehead, it dances over her eyelids and the bridge of her nose, striking the individual pearls of her choker and reflecting up under her chin. Rose-red paint blushes her cheeks and defines her mouth. A red flower ornaments her hair.[1]

After blocking out the sitter's general form, Sustermans fully rendered only her face, leaving the bodice in reserve, defined only by quick strokes of black paint. The artist apparently originally planned to represent the sitter wearing a soft "petal" collar, but then painted over the area with the dark background color, using white to roughly sketch in the outlines of a stiff, flat collar visible on the viewer's right.[2] The thinly applied gray-brown paint of the bodice appears to underlie the entire composition. In some areas, including the neck and the dark shadows of the face as well as the background, Sustermans toned this lighter color with one or more layers of dark paint, giving the painting a warm brown tonality. The woman's wavy hair, tied back with loose strands falling on the side, is a warm brown color brushed with lighter shades around her face; brown, rather than black, is also used to suggest the deepest, sharpest shadows and to define her eyes.[3]

Only the linear description of the sitter's eyes recalls Sustermans's early training with the Flemish painter Frans Pourbus II (1569–1622), a style to which he returned briefly in the 1640s. His use of brown and red to soften the transitions of forms is, however, characteristic of the more painterly style of his later work. Introduced to the work of Titian (ca. 1488–1576) in Rome and further stimulated by the arrival in Florence during the 1630s of numerous Venetian paintings in the dowry of Vittoria della Rovere (1622–1694), wife of Ferdinando II de' Medici (1610–1670), Grand Duke of Tuscany, Sustermans loosened his brushwork and lightened his palette. In 1649, attracted to Anthony van Dyck's (1599–1641) Genoese portraits as well to the work of Guercino (1591–1666), Rubens

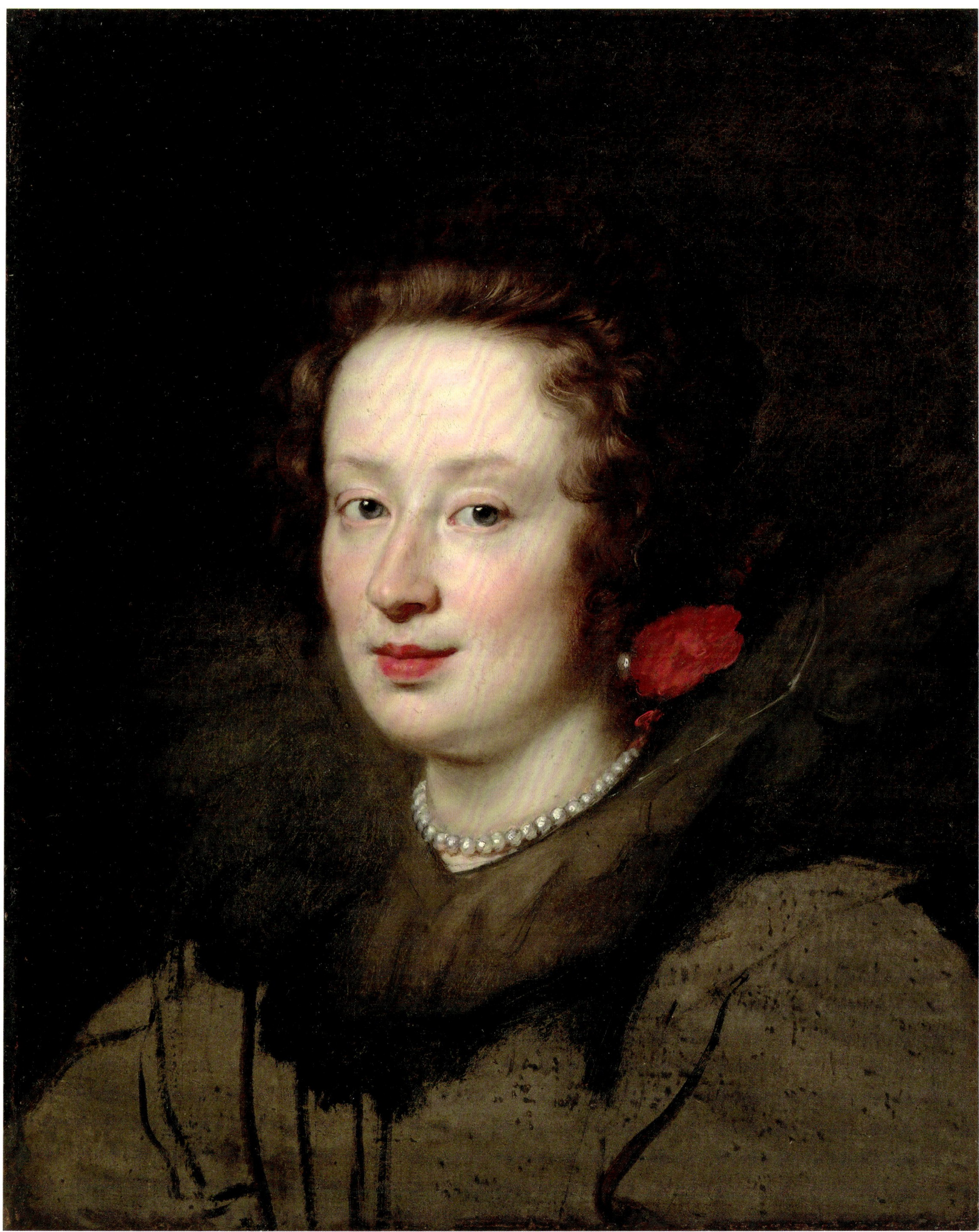

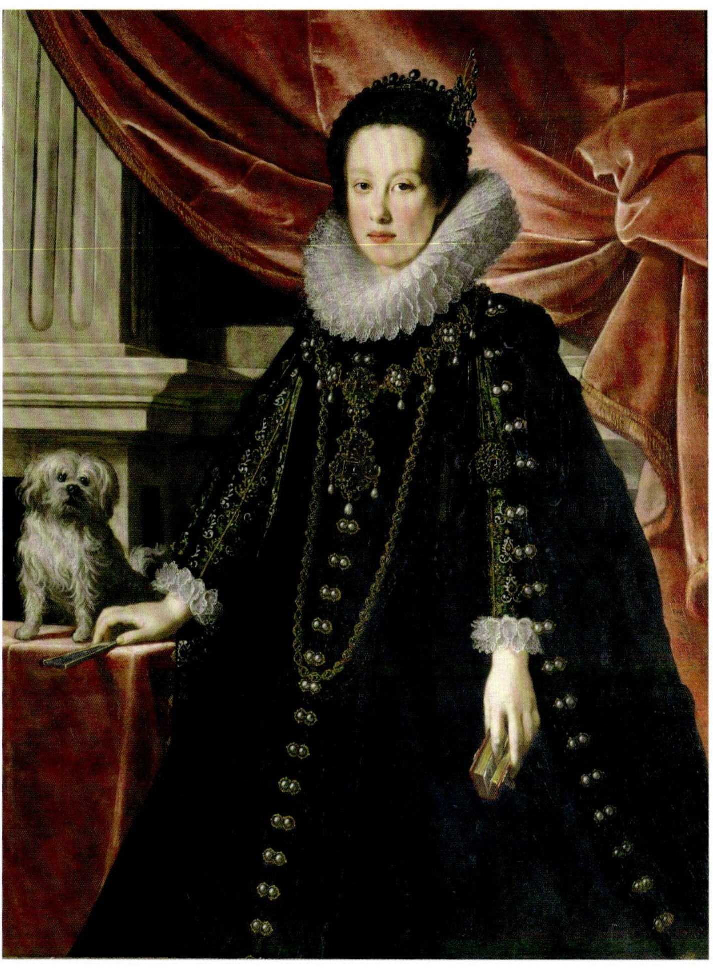

Fig. 93a. Justus Sustermans, *Anna di Cosimo II de' Medici*, ca. 1630, oil on canvas, 78⅜ × 50⅞ in. (199 × 129 cm), Kunsthistorisches Museum, Vienna.

(1577–1640), and Velázquez (1599–1660), Sustermans's palette and style changed.

The most significant influence evident in the Pasadena portrait is probably that of Velázquez, whose *Portrait of Francesco I d'Este*, 1638 (Pinacoteca Estense, Modena), Sustermans admired in Modena.[4] The soft modeling of forms, the warm brown tones, and the gray-brown underpainting of the unfinished portrait in Pasadena resemble Velázquez's technique. A similar greenish ochre painted over a preliminary sketch in brown characterizes a number of portraits left unfinished by Velázquez, such as *Portrait of a Little Girl*, ca. 1638–44 (Hispanic Society, New York).

The Pasadena painting—which earlier had been identified as a "Medici Princess"[5]—may never have been intended as a formal portrait; rather, like Rubens and many court painters, Sustermans may have painted it as a sketch to keep in his studio as a prototype for repetition in formal portraits of the sitter. The position of her head and torso agree with the traditional pose of the many full-length portraits Sustermans painted of the Medicis in Florence. While the sitter resembles in both general type and physical attributes various female members of the Medici family, such as *Anna di Cosimo II de' Medici* (fig. 93a), she cannot be identified with any of these Medici women with certainty.[6] Part of the problem in identifying the sitter rests with the difference between the relatively free, spontaneous nature of the sketch and the more labored character of formal state portraits, which emphasize the sitter's official identity rather than her individual personality.

1. Freely rendered diagonal "squiggles" of red paint above and below the blossom suggest that Sustermans may have planned to create a line of flowers in her hair, as in his portrait of Isabella d'Este (Cassa di Risparmio, Prato; Paolucci and Lapi Ballerini 2004, pp. 93–96, cat. 30).

2. The black paint surrounding the collar appears to have been painted to define the reserved sections of the collar and dress. The stiff collar would have been similar, for example, to that worn by the sitter in Sustermans's portrait of *Maria Maddalena of Austria* (1622; Musée des Beaux Arts, Brussels). Lisa Goldenberg Stoppato stated, "I would date the [Pasadena] painting no later than the mid-1630s, since the sitter's collar is cut in a form that went out of fashion shortly afterwards" (e-mail to Carol Togneri, 30 September 2009, NSM). Florence 1983, pp. 13f., dates the Simon picture closer to 1649.

3. Her hair appears to extend farther into the shadows of the background. This undefined area, which reflects differently under ultraviolet light, may represent an area originally left in reserve and later toned without definition rather than an area of later retouching or change.

4. Florence 1983, p. 14.

5. See 1934 Heldring sale, lot 10.

6. For Sustermans's Medici portraits, see Goldenberg Stoppato 2003 and Goldenberg Stoppato 2006.

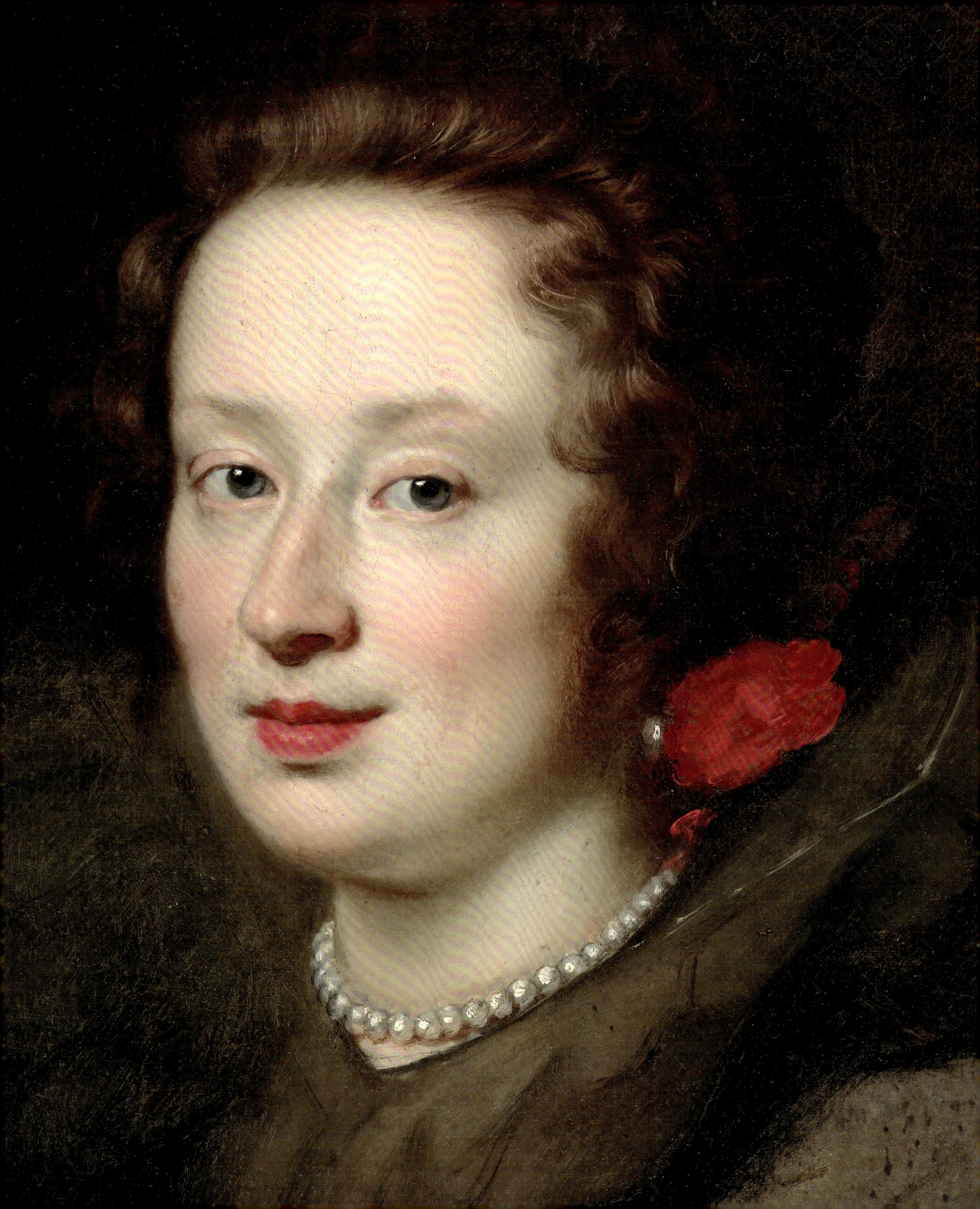

94

Follower of Willem van de Velde II

Dutch
Leiden 1633–1707 Greenwich

Vessels Offshore in a Calm

ca. 1670

Inscribed, lower right in water: "A Stork"
Oil on canvas, 16 3/8 × 20 3/4 in. (41.6 × 52.7 cm)
Norton Simon Art Foundation, M.1969.24.5.P

Provenance
Hubert George de Burgh-Canning (1832–1916), 2nd Marquess of Clanricarde, acquired in the nineteenth century,[1] by descent to his nephew; Henry George Lascelles (1882–1947), 6th Earl of Harewood, Harewood House, York (estate sale, Christie's, London, 29 June 1951, lot 96, sold to); [Edward Speelman Ltd., London]. [John Mitchell Gallery, London, 1959].[2] Anonymous (sale, Sotheby's, London, 26 March 1969, lot 98, sold through); [R. M. Light and Co., Boston, to]; Norton Simon Art Foundation.

Exhibited
On loan, Phoenix Art Museum, 15 July–19 October 1969; on loan, Los Angeles County Museum of Art, 20 October 1969–26 July 1972; Princeton 1972–74, pp. 46–47, no. 10, ill.

References
Borenius 1936, p. 93, no. 189, as Seascape (signed, 15 ½ × 20 ¼ in.); Pasadena 1980, p. 65, ill.; S. Campbell 2010, p. 316, no. 594, ill.

Technical Notes
The original support, a lightweight plain-weave canvas, has an aged lining. After the painting was lined and restretched, narrow wood strips were nailed to the left and right sides of the stretcher, increasing the total width of the painting by ½ inch. The canvas has a smoothly applied, warm beige ground of moderate thickness. Some canvas texture is evident, but this may be a result of lining pressure. For the most part the paint is opaque. Ships and figures are crisply drawn, and details are often hard-edged and linear. The top sides of the two added strips were prepared with a white ground before applying paint that continues the colors and design of the original painting. Minor abrasion is noticeable in most of the thin dark lines of the rigging and in the hull of the larger ship in the left foreground. The blue paint of the flag of the larger boat, second from the left, is particularly abraded. In September 1978 the painting was treated by Marco Grassi, New York, to lay down minor blistering and remove darkened varnish; some blistering was again addressed, along with some filling and retouching, by Rosamund Westmoreland in 2008. There are small scattered retouchings in the sky, and wide overpainted edges at the left and right sides where the added strips join the original painting. The present varnish, a synthetic resin, is slightly yellowed. Microscopic observations suggest that the "A Stork" signature was applied very early on, before the craquelure was established, and that it seems consistent with the application of similar finishing touches in the painting, namely the rigging. Some reinforcements to the lettering, possibly executed with a quill and ink, may be relatively old, perhaps made by a restorer before any revarnishing. Further examination with ultraviolet light may better show the extent of the reinforcements.

In the calm, shallow waters of an inlet at low tide, Dutch coastal craft used for fishing and local transport prepare to sail with the rising tide. On the right, five men launch a small fishing boat known as a *weyschuit*,[3] while on the left, crews ready three larger boats, their anchors already raised.[4] The cluster of boats set back from the foreground and arranged to enhance the three-dimensional perception of depth counterbalances the deep, open space on the right, where the diminishing size and clarity of the ships mark the recession into the distance. Their details obscured by the suggestion of morning mist, a fleet of seagoing frigates lies at anchor; a two-decker, viewed from the port side in the right middle distance, fires guns from both sides. The fleet may have recently arrived, for the partially lowered positions of the sails and the limited activity on the ship suggest that the crew is drying the sails rather than preparing for departure. A launch carrying men from ship to ship or from ship to shore appears in the center of the painting in the middle distance.

Vessels Offshore in a Calm, which is inscribed "A Stork" in the water on the lower right, has traditionally been attributed to Abraham Storck (ca. 1635–1710), the best known member of a family of marine painters active in Amsterdam in the last third of the seventeenth century. His paintings, which enjoyed popular success during his lifetime, represent river and coastal scenes, sea battles, and naval parades, as well as topographical views made from the perspective of boats in the harbors of Amsterdam and other Dutch and foreign cities.[5] The traditional attribution of the Pasadena painting to Storck is drawn into question on the basis of the weak quality of the painting. The superficial, sketchy white highlights on the stern of the large merchant ship on the right, the imprecise description of the rigging of the sails,

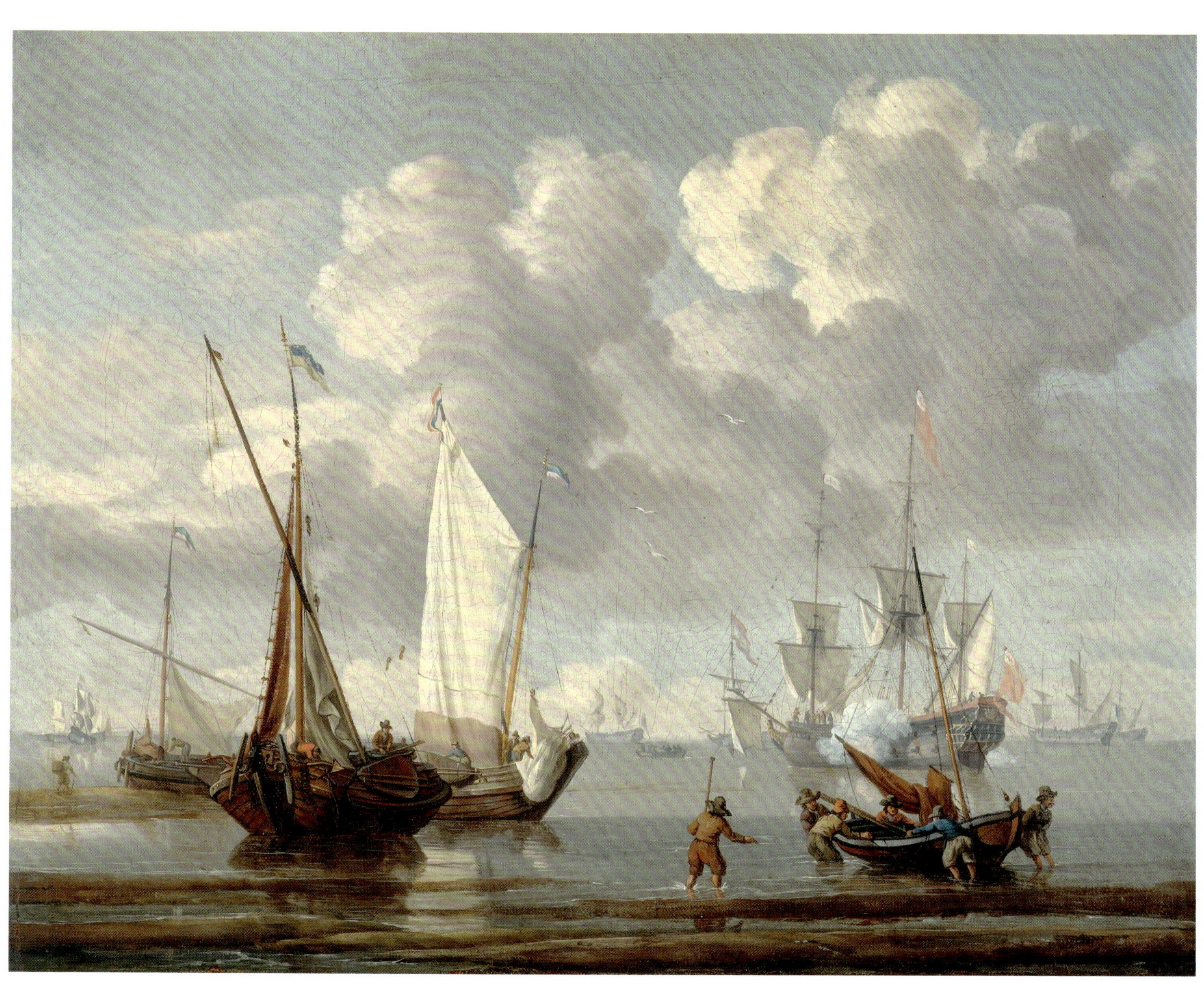

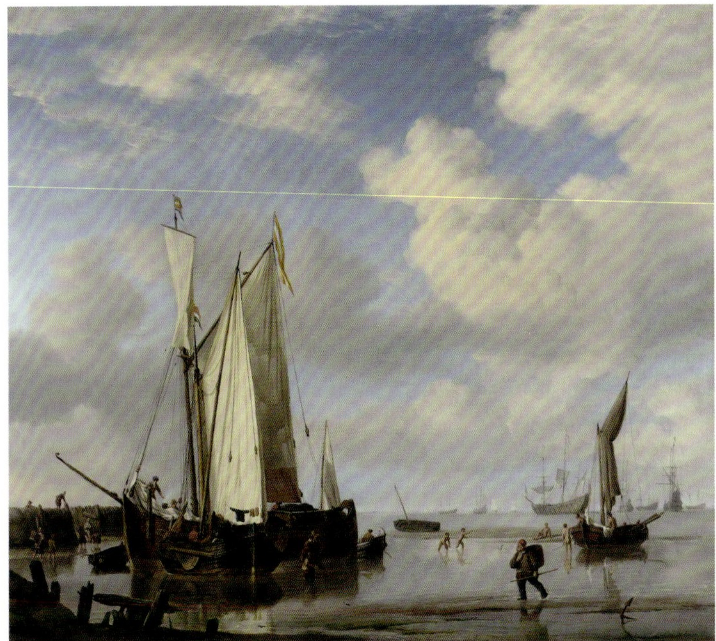

Fig. 94a. Willem van de Velde II, *Dutch Vessels Inshore and Men Bathing*, 1661, oil on canvas, 24 ⅞ × 28 ⅜ in. (63.2 × 72.2 cm), The National Gallery, London.

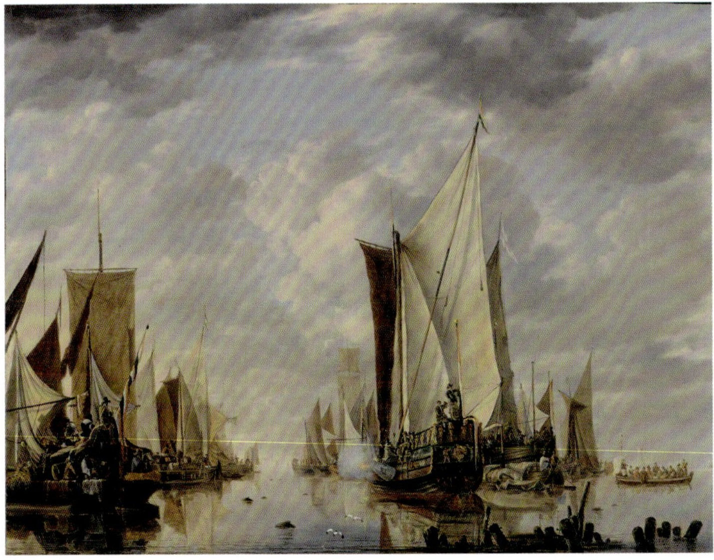

Fig. 94b. Jan van de Cappelle, *Shipping in a Calm at Flushing with a States General Yacht Firing a Salute*, 1649, oil on oak panel, 27 ½ × 36 ¼ in. (69.9 × 92.1 cm), J. Paul Getty Museum, Los Angeles.

and other faulty details of the vessels suggest that it was not painted by Abraham Storck, who was particularly attentive to the technical details and riggings of ships.[6] The rejection of the traditional attribution is supported by the false signature. Although the inscription appears to be contemporary with the painting, it differs from the artist's authentic signature: "A: Storck." Similar inscriptions have been noted on other paintings, and especially on drawings, falsely attributed to Abraham Storck.[7]

The composition and details of *Vessels Offshore in a Calm* reflect the dominant influence that Willem van de Velde II exerted over Dutch marine painting during the second half of the seventeenth century. As in Van de Velde's *Dutch Vessels Inshore and Men Bathing*, dated 1661 (fig. 94a),[8] and *A Smalschip at Anchor with a Kaag and Other Vessels Close Inshore*, ca. 1661 (Wallace Collection, London), here the low horizon projects the ships against the broad sky animated by billowing clouds. Other compositional devices were also derived from Van de Velde's paintings. The movement of two figures—a man on the left using a walking stick and bearing a package on his back and another in the center carrying a pole and walking through the shallow water toward the boat—helps to integrate the composition. Vertical reflections of the figures and boats in the still water enliven the alternating horizontal bands of light and dark, which help to pace the progression into depth without the use of repoussoir elements such as pilings or a sand barge.

The number of small-scale paintings of seemingly everyday scenes of the Dutch coastline suggests their broad appeal for a country whose economy depended on the sea and was frequently the source of friction with England throughout the second half of the seventeenth century. In *Vessels Offshore in a Calm*, which represents a generic rather than specific event, the local fishing and transport vessels fly the "common Dutch flag" with horizontal stripes of red, white, and blue, while the large frigate on the right flies the English flag—a red field with a white canton (the rectangular corner at the top of the flag) bearing a red cross—at the mainsail and as an ensign at the stern.[9] Two white flags (fore and aft of the mainsail) suggest it is the flagship of the rear admiral of the squadron.[10] The activity of the crewmen on the boats and ships as well as the quiet of the water clearly suggests a peaceful encounter between the vessels of the two countries rather than the tension of war. The English ship fires its cannons in salute, not in hostility. This was typically done to announce the ship's arrival or departure or in celebration, as in *Shipping in a Calm at Flushing with a States General Yacht Firing a Salute*, by Jan van de Capelle (1626–1679; fig. 94b).

1. Borenius 1936, p. 93, no. 189.

2. Advertisement, *Burlington Magazine* 101, no. 670 (January 1959): p. v.

3. See M. S. Robinson 1990, vol. 2, for a glossary of sea terms and diagrams of different types of seventeenth-century vessels and their dating.

4. Closest to the foreground is a Dutch *kaag*, its bow pointed toward the viewer; at its stern is a *smalschip*, its spritsail set and its foresail apparently being raised from the foredeck. Further back on the left is another *kaag*, its sprit nearing a horizontal position in preparation for raising the sail.

5. M. Russell 1996, p. 721, observes that in addition to the compositional influence of Willem van de Velde II, the pictorial treatment of the sky and water in Storck's river and coastal scenes recall the paintings of the Amsterdam marine painter Ludolf Backhuysen I (1630–1708), and his naval battles reveal the influence of Jan Abrahamsz. Beerstraten (1622–1666). Middendorf 1989, p. 47, also notes the similar use of blue-green and rose-red colors with accents of white in a number of Storck's early paintings from the second half of the 1660s, such as *Ships at Anchor on the Coast of Den Helder* (National Maritime Museum, Greenwich), and paintings by Hendrik Jacobsz. Dubbels (1621–1707).

6. M. Russell 1996, p. 721, notes that Storck, like the Van de Veldes, was particularly attentive to the accuracy of his details. Walter Liedtke, in conversation with the author February 2011, noted that the overlapping, rounded, cauliflower clouds and the detached areas of highlights on the water and ships recall the characteristic style of Dubbels, who he suggested might have painted the Pasadena picture. However, the quality of the painting, which Liedtke knows only from a digital image, is not high enough to warrant the attribution to Dubbels.

7. Pieter Roelofs, who is studying Storck, rejects the attribution to the artist, noting, "I have seen it [the signature] a few times, and in the same hand, especially on drawings. It seems to be a false signature on a painting by someone who was working in his slipstream. The only name I can come up with at this moment is the young Adam Silo (Amsterdam 1674–1760), but this is probably a little too far-fetched." Email to the author, 29 June 2011 (NSM).

8. A second version is in the Akademie der bildenden Künste, Vienna.

9. An ensign is a national flag most often flown at the stern (rear) of a naval or merchant vessel to indicate nationality while in port. Regarding technical information about ships and shipping, see the glossary of M. S. Robinson 1990, vol. 2, pp. 1127ff.

10. During the seventeenth century, English fleets were normally organized into three squadrons, each of three divisions. The "van," or front squadron, was commanded by the vice admiral, the central division by the admiral, and the rear division by the rear admiral. See Corbett 1917, p. 580.

95

Johannes Cornelisz. Verspronck

Dutch
Haarlem 1601/03–1662 Haarlem

Portrait of a Woman

1641

Signed and dated, lower left: "[Spr]onck an° 1641"[1]
Oil on canvas, 31 × 26 in. (78.7 × 66 cm)
The Norton Simon Foundation, F.1973.34.2.P

Provenance
David P. Sellar (1833–1901), London, by 1888 (sale, Galerie Georges Petit, Paris, 6 June 1889, lot 90, as "Portrait de la femme du peintre Th. Wyck [lot 89]," sold for £3,400 to); [Colnaghi, London].[2] Probably Stephenson Clarke (1824–1891), Haywards Heath, Sussex, by descent to his wife; Agnes Mara Bridger Clarke (1838–1921), Brook House,[3] Haywards Heath, Sussex, by 1903, by descent to her son; Col. Stephenson Robert Clarke (1862–1948), Haywards Heath, Sussex, by descent to his son;[4] Col. Ralph Stephenson Clarke (1892–1970), Borde Hill House, Cuckfield, Hayward Heath, Sussex (sale, Christie's, London, 29 June 1973, lot 17, sold to); [Edward Speelman Ltd., London, sold 1973 to]; The Norton Simon Foundation.

Exhibited
London 1888, p. 18, no. 65;[5] London 1903, no. 191;[6] London 1904, no. 363; London 1925, p. 7, no. 11;[7] London 1929b, no. 368, pl. LXXXI; London 1952–53, vol. 1, p. 49, no. 326, ill.; on loan, Virginia Museum of Fine Arts, Richmond, 25 June–16 December 1974.

References
Bryan 1889, p. 662; Moes 1892–1905, vol. 1 (1892), p. 3, no. 24; Mireur 1901–12, vol. 7 (1912), p. 352; N. N. 1903, pp. 53, 55, ill.;[8] Wurzbach [1906–11] 1974, vol. 2 (1910), p. 783; Clarke 1910, MS, p. 20, no. 197;[9] Graves [1913–15] 1970, vol. 4 (1914), p. 1578; Balet 1921, p. 338; Witt 1929b, p. 91, fig. 109; London 1929a, no. 109; Kelly and Charmet 1953, n.pag., ill.;[10] Plietzsch 1960, p. 169; Slive 1970–74, vol. 3 (1974), p. 123; Gerson 1976, pp. 166f., 171n6, fig. 7; Ekkart 1979, pp. 45, 87f., 162, no. 35; Roach, Musa, and Hollander 1980, p. 89, no. 76, ill.; P. Sutton 1986, p. 216; Pasadena 1989, p. 79, ill.; S. Campbell 2010, p. 360, no. 996, ill.; Hindlip 2016, p. 90, ill.; Speelman 2022, pp. 129–30, fig. 48.

Technical Notes
The primary support is a plain-weave medium-weight canvas that was originally in a rectangular format. At some point the canvas was cut down to create an oval, losing the first three letters of the signature at the lower left as well as part of the fan and the back side of the ruff. Slight differences in surface texture indicate the stretched dimensions of the oval probably were 29 × 24 ½ inches. The support was altered a second time to return the painting to a rectangular shape and its present dimensions by adding canvas of similar weight and weave around the oval. It is lined to the canvas. The smoothly applied ground is cream or pale beige. Verspronck typically worked from a complete underdrawing, portions of which are visible in areas where light-colored paint is becoming increasingly transparent, such as the fingers and the bracelet. Paint was smoothly applied in a very refined handling and controlled brushwork. The modeling of the face is delicately blended, with nearly translucent cool shadows. Cuffs were smoothly painted in white and gray with delicate brushwork; a very small brush was used for the patterned lace. The gold bracelet was rendered with tiny round drops of paint. The paint is very well preserved. Retouching disguises tiny losses and stains in the face and ruff. Infrared viewing reveals minor changes in the contours of two fingers on the proper right hand and in the outline of the bracelet. The varnish is clear within the oval and slightly discolored outside the join; ultraviolet light indicates that the two areas are coated with different resins.

The conservative black dress with starched lace cuffs and large millstone ruff of elaborately pleated and starched linen identify the young woman in Johannes Cornelisz. Verspronck's portrait as a member of the prosperous Dutch burgher class.[11] Placed off center and posed so that her body appears in profile to the left, she turns her head and addresses the viewer with a pleasant, relaxed smile.[12] Although the pose and spontaneous expressions were inspired by Verspronck's presumed teacher Frans Hals (1582/83–1666), this portrait is distinguished by its more restrained brushwork and greater attention to detail.

Independent portraits of women were rare during the seventeenth century. A painting such as this one, depicting a woman alone turned toward the left, was typically designed to hang as a pendant to a portrait of her husband, often painted on the occasion of the couple's marriage. Details of costume thus refer not only to the sitter's position in society but also to the event and institution of marriage. The ample folds of black fabric here suggest that the dress was made of wool that had been pressed with a hot, patterned iron to give it the shiny appearance of the more costly silk brocade.[13] The black silk stomacher, decorated with gold buttons and flowers embroidered with gold and terminating in a small,

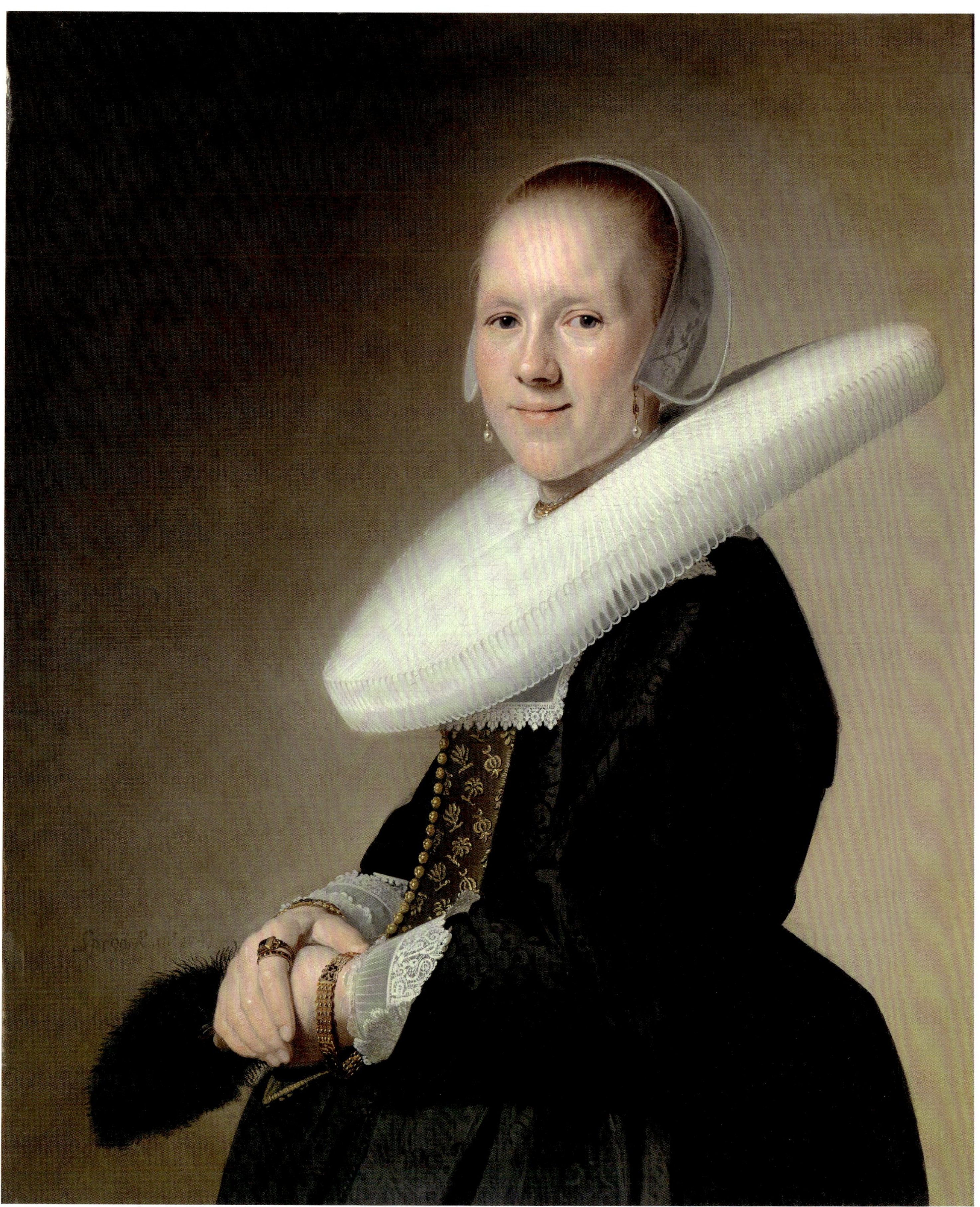

pointed peplum, was probably a wedding present from her husband, as were the lace cuffs, gold necklace, bracelets, rings, drop-pearl earrings, and black feather fan that she clutches in her left hand.[14] A simple embroidered linen cap covers her hair, which she probably wears in a chignon, a popular hair style at the time.

In the seventeenth century, a couple went with their families and friends to the notary to sign the marriage contract, after which they exchanged gifts—ring, marriage token (*huwelijkspenning*), gloves, handkerchief, knife, needle, and scissors—and the betrothal was announced.[15] The bride placed her gifts from the groom in a basket decorated with flowers and ribbons, which was displayed in the bride's family home until the actual wedding day, when the gifts were moved to the couple's new home. In Verspronck's portrait the sitter wears a stone-studded version of the traditional plain gold wedding band and another with a beveled gemstone, probably a square-cut diamond.[16] In *Houwelyck* (1625), his popular handbook on marriage, Jacob Cats (1577–1660) praised the gift of such a ring as a symbol of the bond of marriage, patience, and the dominant role of the husband.[17]

Until 1889 the Pasadena portrait hung in the collection of David Sellar as a pendant to *Portrait of a Man* (fig. 95a). Both canvases had been cut to oval formats and later restored to rectangles with similar dimensions.[18] The man, who is dressed in a black doublet with white lace collar and cuffs, has traditionally been identified as the Haarlem painter Thomas Wijck (ca. 1616–1677). On the basis of this attribution, the Pasadena portrait has been supposed to be his wife, Trijntje Adamsdr. The origin of the identification of the man as Wijck is unknown and is now generally rejected as the sitter does not appear to be the person who is depicted in accepted portraits of the artist.[19] Perhaps more significantly, scholars have noted that the 1641 date on *Portrait of a Woman* precedes the couple's 1644 marriage by three years. Both sitters, therefore, remain anonymous, but they were presumably members of the Catholic society of Haarlem, to which many if not most of Verspronck's patrons belonged.

Compositionally, psychologically, and socially, *Portrait of a Woman* interacts with her pendant portrait and the viewer. By 1640 Verspronck had established the standard poses for his portraits of married couples, which adopt the traditional position of the woman on her husband's left, the viewer's right.[20] Their poses complement one another: In the male portrait, the sitter's elbow protrudes forward into the viewer's space, and the sharp silhouette of his torso curves outward in the direction of his wife. The more demure figure of the woman responds to the figure of her husband with the gentle concave slope of her stomacher, which is extended by the dramatic forty-five-degree pitch of the ruff that gracefully balances on her shoulders and frames her face and is matched by the convex curve of the silhouette of her back against the light ochre background. The soft, rounded silhouette of her costume was preferred by women after about 1625.

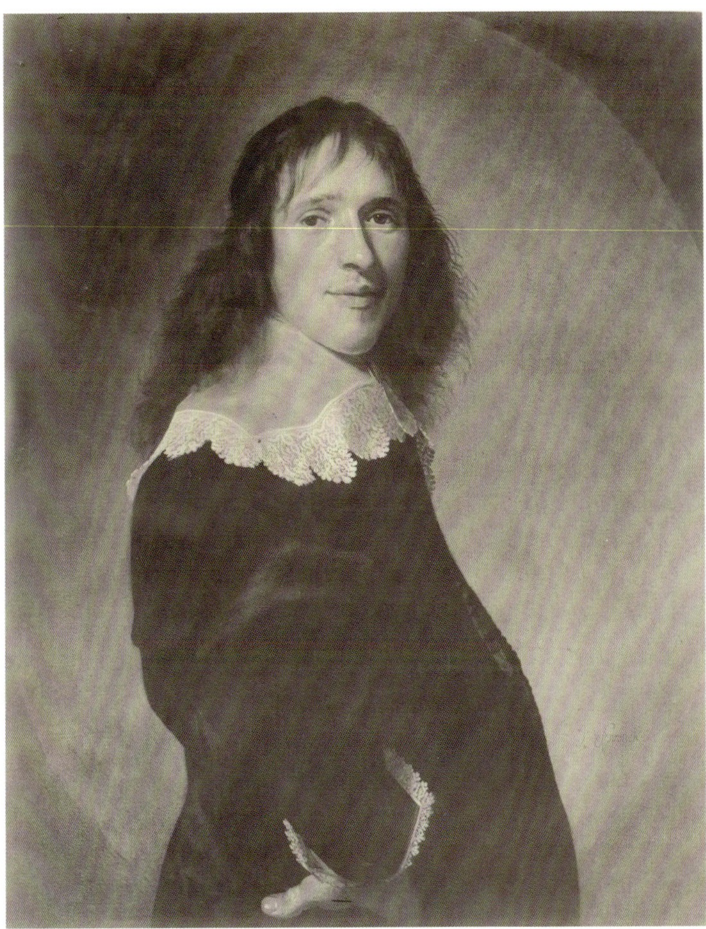

Fig. 95a. Johannes Cornelisz. Verspronck, *Portrait of a Man*, 1641?, oil on canvas, 31¼ × 26¼ in. (79.4 × 66.7 cm), location unknown (last known in Nathan Katz collection, sold in Paris, 1950).

In complementing the form of her husband, the sitter in the Pasadena portrait nevertheless maintains her own independent character, perhaps reflecting the improved status women had achieved in the Netherlands by the mid-seventeenth century, when they were in many ways considered equal to men. The husband remained the head of household, but the wife was also well respected for her domestic virtues and industriousness.[21] The importance of domesticity for seventeenth-century Dutch men and women is witnessed by the number of books, such as Cats's *Houwelyck*, that gave advice on the practical and psychological problems associated with marriage. The Dutch considered marriages a partnership and companionship a priority, which perhaps explains the casual openness of the sitter in Verspronck's *Portrait of a Woman*.

1. The beginning of the signature appears to have been cut when the painting was reduced to an oval. See Technical Notes.

2. A stamp on an early mount of a photograph of the painting from the archive of Duits Ltd., London, consulted at the GRI Photo Archive, reads: "Louis Morant, 9, Cork Street, London." Morant was active during the interwar years as international dealer associated with Lenygon & Morant, London decorators and antique dealers. If the painting were with Morant, then it was probably following Colnaghi and before it entered the collection of the Stephenson Clark family, where it is documented in 1910. See note 10 below.

3. The 1910 inventory of the collection indicates that the painting hung in the dining room of Brook House. See note 10 below.

4. In 1952 the painting was lent to an exhibition at the Royal Academy of Arts, London, by "Mrs. C. G. Stephenson Clark[e]." She has not been identified. Stephenson Robert Clark was married in 1890 to the former Edith Gertrude Godman (d. 1941). His heir, Ralph Stephenson Clarke, was married in 1921 to the former Rebekah Mary Buxton (1900–1985).

5. As "Portrait of Catherine Adams . . . A native of Haarlem; m. 1644, Thomas Wyck [no. 61]."

6. As "wife of T. Wyck."

7. Although the catalogue does not mention the lender, a stamp on the back of the canvas with "2/5/25" (2 May 1925) probably refers to this exhibition.

8. Illustrated as a rectangle; dated as "1643."

9. As "*Portrait of a Lady. Wife of Thomas Wyck*, dated 1614 [*sic*], from the collection of Mr. David Seller. Guildhall 1903, R.A., *Old Masters* 1888." A copy of the original manuscript is in the GRI, Collectors Files.

10. As owned by Mrs. C. G. Stephenson Clarke; see note 4 above.

11. Ruffs came into fashion in the late sixteenth century, inspired by the wide starched collars worn in India and Ceylon to protect clothes from long, oiled hair.

12. According to Hendriks 1998, pp. 242ff., without exception the portraits she examined revealed that Verspronck had made a preliminary sketch of the heads and collars directly on the primed support.

13. Pieter Biesboer, curator of the Frans Hals Museum, Haarlem, made this observation in the Norton Simon Museum galleries in November 1995.

14. According to Du Mortier 1989, p. 51, pendant earrings first came into fashion in the Netherlands during the 1630s. Those portrayed in Verspronck's *Portrait of a Woman* are actually attached to the headband that forms the frame of her cap rather than to her ears. First introduced in the second quarter of the sixteenth century, fans gained popularity in the Netherlands with the introduction of the French style in the early seventeenth century. Regarding fans, see Du Mortier 1992.

15. Du Mortier 1989, p. 48.

16. The specific bracelet and square ring, as well as the embroidered stomacher, appear in other portraits by Verspronck. While they may indicate contemporary fashion, they may also have been studio props owned by the painter rather than the sitter. In 1620 Willem Baudertius noted that in Holland "we invest more in pearls and diamonds than gold" (quoted by Adams 1985, vol. 1, p. 306).

17. Du Mortier 1989, p. 46, citing Cats [1625] 1712, pp. 17f.

18. The last known location of the man's portrait was in the Nathan Katz sale, Charpentier, Paris, 7 December 1950, lot 69. It measures 31 ¼ × 26 ¼ in. (76.8 × 66.7 cm). The reshaping of the man's portrait probably explains the absence of a date, which typically would have appeared to the right of the artist's signature, which abuts the cut edge on the right. According to Hendriks 1998, p. 229, "considering Verspronck's oeuvre as a whole, the majority of paintings fall within a range of 70–90 cm tall and 60–70 cm wide, with some a little bigger or smaller and only very few of quite different format. This shows a much greater consistency compared to the portraits of Frans Hals for example."

19. The identification of the sitters was first noted in London 1888, p. 18, no. 65, and questioned in London 1929b, no. 368. See Slive 1970–74, vol. 3 (1974), pp. 122, cat. L.14.

20. See, for example, Verspronck's *Portrait of a Woman*, 1640 (Galleria Corsini, Rome).

21. See Franits 1993; and Schama 1987b, pp. 375–480 and passim.

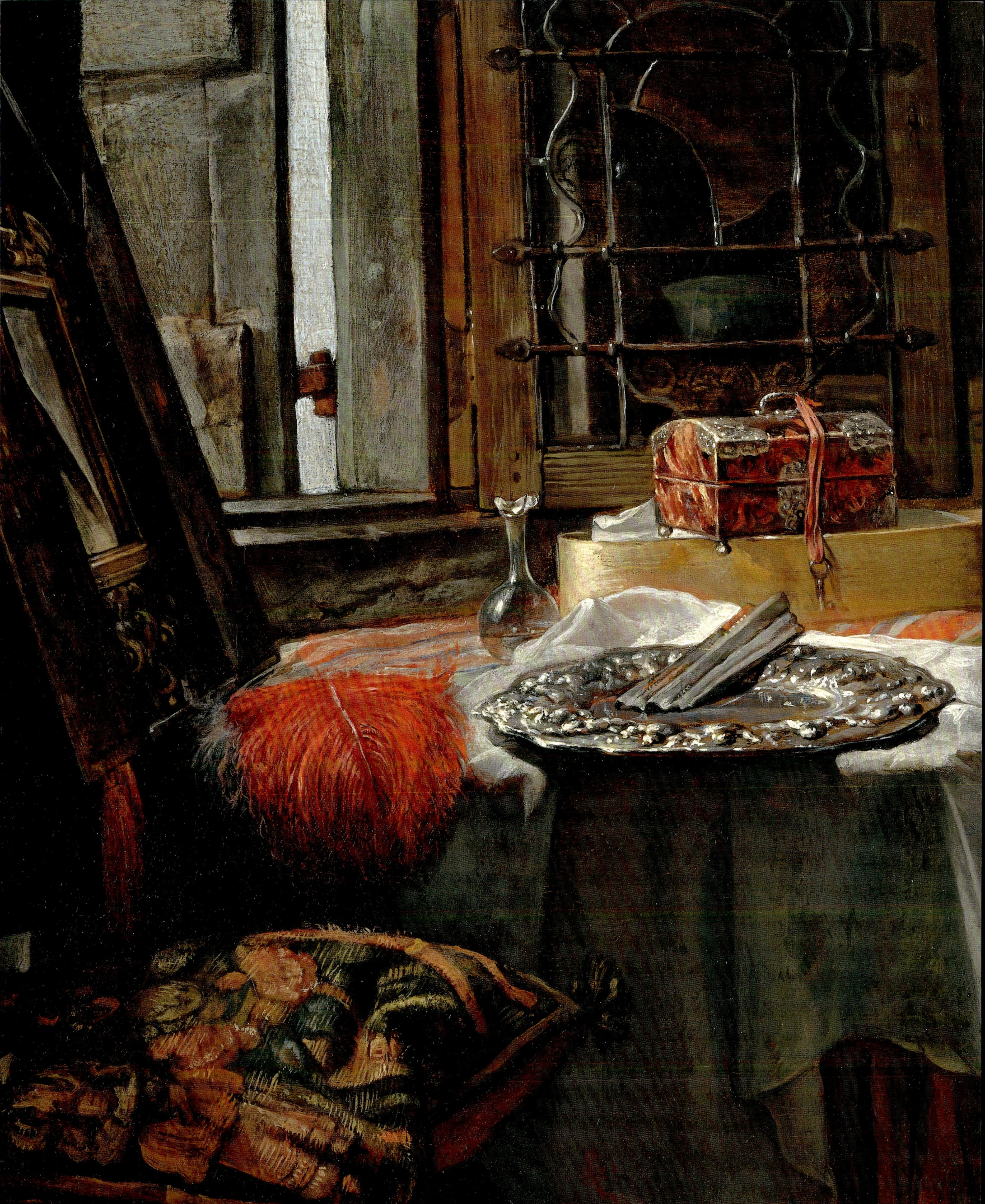

Sources and Exhibitions Cited

Frequently cited sources have been identified with the following abbreviations:
GPI: Getty Provenance Index: http://www.getty.edu/research/conducting_research/provenance_index/
GRI: Getty Research Institute
NSM: Norton Simon Museum curatorial files
RKD: Netherlands Institute for Art History

Unless otherwise noted, all biblical citations come from the *ESV Study Bible* (Wheaton: Crossway, 2008), https://www.biblegateway.com/.

Van der Aa 1852–78
Aa, Abraham Jacob van der. *Biographisch woordenboek der Nederlanden*. 21 vols. in 17. Haarlem, 1852–78.

Aachen/Gotha 2016
Ayooghi, Sarvenaz, Sylvia Böhmer, and Timo Trümper, eds. *Die Stillleben des Balthasar van der Ast (1593/94–1657)*. (Exh. cat. Suermondt-Ludwig-Museum, Aachen, 10 March–5 June 2016; Herzogliches Museum, Stiftung Schloss Friedenstein, Gotha, 2 July–2 October 2016.) Text by Sarvenaz Ayooghi et al. Translated by Heinrich Becker and Marlene Müller-Haas. Petersberg, 2016.

"Acquisitions" 1978
"Acquisitions." *Art Journal* 37/4 (summer 1978): p. 351.

Adams 1985
Adams, Ann Jensen. "The Paintings of Thomas de Keyser (1596/7–1667): A Study of Portraiture in Seventeenth-Century Amsterdam." 4 vols in 2. PhD diss., Harvard University, 1985.

Adams 1998
Adams, Ann Jensen, ed. *Rembrandt's "Bathsheba Reading King David's Letter."* New York and Cambridge, 1998.

Adams 2020
Adams, Ann Jensen. "Connoisseurship and the Archive: A Version of Thomas de Keyser's Portrait of Dirck van Wissel and His Son Jacob." *Connoisseurship: Essays in Honour of Fred G. Meijer*. Leiden, 2020.

Adler 1980
Adler, Wolfgang. *Jan Wildens, der Landschaftsmitarbeiter des Rubens*. Fridingen, 1980.

Agnew 1981
Agnew, Geoffrey. *A Dealer's Record: Agnew's 1967–1981*. London, 1981.

Aikema 1996
Aikema, Bernard. *Jacopo Bassano and His Public*. Translated by Andrew P. McCormick. Princeton, 1996.

Aikema 1999
Aikema, Bernard. "The Lure of the North: Netherlandish Art in Venetian Collections." In Venice 1999–2000, pp. 82–91.

Aikema and Brown 1999
Aikema, Bernard, and Beverly Louise Brown. "Painting in Fifteenth-Century Venice and the Ars Nova of the Netherlands." In Venice 1999–2000, pp. 176–83.

Ainsworth 1988
Ainsworth, Maryan W. "Gerard David's Drawings for the 'Justice of Cambyses' Once Again." *Burlington Magazine* 130/1024 (1988): pp. 528–30.

Ainsworth 1989
Ainsworth, Maryan W. "Northern Renaissance Drawings and Underdrawings." *Master Drawings* 27/1 (1989): pp. 5–38.

Ainsworth 1990a
Ainsworth, Maryan W. "'Paternes for Phiosioneamyes': Holbein's Portraiture Reconsidered." *Burlington Magazine* 132/1044 (March 1990): pp. 173–86.

Ainsworth 1990b
Ainsworth, Maryan W. "Review of H. J. van Miegroet, 'Gerard David.'" *Art Bulletin* 72 (1990): pp. 649–54.

Ainsworth 1991
Ainsworth, Maryan W. "Methods of Copying in the Portraiture of Hans Holbein the Younger." In *Colloque 8* 1991, pp. 11–13, pls. 1–3.

Ainsworth 1993
Ainsworth, Maryan W. "Gerard David's Workshop Practices: An Overview." In *Colloque 9* 1993, pp. 11–33, pls. 1–10.

Ainsworth 1994
Ainsworth, Maryan W. "Hans Memling as a Draughtsman." In *Hans Memling: Essays*. Bruges, 1994, pp. 78–100.

Ainsworth 1998
Ainsworth, Maryan W. *Gerard David: Purity of Vision in an Age of Transition*. New York, 1998.

Alexandre 1927
Alexandre, Arsène. "Memling chez Reynolds." *La Renaissance de l'art français et des industries de luxe* 10/2 (February 1927): pp. 61–67.

Allen et al. 2003
Allen, Denise, et al. *Masterpieces of Paintings in the J. Paul Getty Museum*. Los Angeles, 2003.

Alpers 1975–76
Alpers, Svetlana. "Realism as a Comic Mode: The Peasant." *Simiolus* 8/3 (1975–76): pp. 115–44.

Altes et al. 2003
Altes, Everhard Korthalls. *De verovering van de internationale kunstmarkt door de zeventiende-eeuwse schilderkunst: Enkele studies over de verspreiding van Hollandse schilderijen in de eerste helft van de achttiende eeuw*. Leiden, 2003.

Althorp House 1851
Catalogue of Pictures at Althorp House. London, 1851.

Amsterdam 1898
Hofstede de Groot, C[ornelis]. *Rembrandt, schilderijen bijeengebracht ter gelegenheid van de inhuldiging van Hare Majesteit Konigin Wilhelmina*. (Exh. cat. Stedelijk Museum, Amsterdam, 8 September–31 October 1898.) Amsterdam, 1898.

Amsterdam 1906
Maîtres Hollandais du XVIIe siècle . . . en l'honneur du Tercentenaire de Rembrandt. (Exh. cat. Frederik Muller & Cie., Amsterdam, 1906.) Introduction by Frits Lugt. Accompanied by *Album de planches de l'exposition de maîtres hollandais du XVIIe siècle. . . .* Amsterdam, 1906.

Amsterdam 1933
Catalogus der tentoonstelling "Het Stilleven" ten bate van de Vereeniging "Rembrandt." (Exh. cat. Kunsthandel J. Goudstikker, Amsterdam, 1933.) Amsterdam, 1933.

Amsterdam 1934
Oude schilderijen. (Exh. cat. D. A. Hoogendijk & Co., Amsterdam, November 1934.) Amsterdam, 1934.

Amsterdam 1936a
Catalogus der tentoonstelling van werken door Salomon van Ruysdael. (Exh. cat. Kunsthandel J. Goudstikker, Amsterdam, 1936.) Amsterdam, 1936.

Amsterdam 1936b
Catalogus van de tentoonstelling van oude kunst uit het bezit van den internationalen handel. (Exh. cat. Rijksmuseum, Amsterdam, 1936.) Amsterdam, 1936.

Amsterdam 1937
Jan van der Heyden. (Exh. cat. Amsterdamsch Historisch Museum de Sint Anthonies Waag, Amsterdam, 1937.) Amsterdam, 1937.

Amsterdam 1938
Gedenck-Clanck: Muziecktentoonstelling ter gelegenheid van het 50-jarig bestaan van het Concertgebouw. Introduction by H. E. Enthoven (Exh. cat. Stedelijk Museum, Amsterdam, May 1938.) Amsterdam, 1938.

Amsterdam 1939
Schmidt-Degener, Frederik, et al. *Tentoonstelling bijbelsche kunst.* (Exh. cat. Rijksmuseum, Amsterdam, 1939.) Amsterdam, 1939.

Amsterdam 1952
Drie eeuwen portret in Nederland. (Exh. cat. Rijksmuseum, Amsterdam, 1952.) Amsterdam, 1952.

Amsterdam 1955–56
Kersttentoonstelling, 1955. (Exh. cat. Kunsthandel P. de Boer, Amsterdam, [December] 1955–31 January 1956.) Amsterdam, 1955.

Amsterdam 1956
Catalogue of Old Pictures. . . . (Exh. cat. Kunsthandel P. de Boer, Amsterdam, Summer–30 September 1956.) Amsterdam, 1956.

Amsterdam 1958–59
Catalogue of Old Pictures. . . . (Exh. cat. Kunsthandel P. de Boer, Amsterdam, Winter 1958–59.) Amsterdam, 1958.

Amsterdam 1959
Catalogue of Old Pictures. . . . (Exh. cat. Kunsthandel P. de Boer, Amsterdam, Summer 1959.) Amsterdam, 1959.

Amsterdam 1962
Tentoonstelling van oude meesters. (Exh. cat. Kunsthandel Gebr. Douwes, Amsterdam, 1962.) Amsterdam, 1962.

Amsterdam 1963
Catalogue of Old Pictures. . . . (Exh. cat. Kunsthandel P. de Boer, Amsterdam, 1963.) Amsterdam, 1963.

Amsterdam 1966–67
Winter Exhibition 1966/67. (Exh. cat. Kunsthandel P. de Boer at Museum Amstelkring, Amsterdam, 1966–67.) Amsterdam, 1966.

Amsterdam 1968
Old Masters. (Exh. cat. Kunsthandel Gebr. Douwes, Amsterdam, 1968.) Amsterdam, 1968.

Amsterdam 1969
Rembrandt 1669/1969. (Exh. cat. Rijksmuseum, Amsterdam, 1969.) Amsterdam, 1969.

Amsterdam 1971
Oude Meesters, Tentoonstelling van Hollandse en Vlaamse schilderijen uit de 16e en 17e eeuw. (Exh. cat. Kunsthandel Gebr. Douwes, Amsterdam, 15 November–23 December 1971.) Amsterdam, 1971.

Amsterdam 1977
Kloek, Wouter Th. *Alleen kijken naar meisjes of jongetjes.* (Exh. cat. Rijksmuseum, Amsterdam, 1977.) Amsterdam, 1977.

Amsterdam 1983
Blankert, Albert, et al. *The Impact of a Genius: Rembrandt, His Pupils and Followers in the Seventeenth Century.* (Exh. cat. K. & V. Waterman Gallery, Amsterdam, in collaboration with the Groninger Museum, 1983.) Amsterdam, 1983.

Amsterdam 1992
Bergvelt, Elinoor, and Renée Kistemaker, eds. *De Wereld binnen handbereik: Nederlandse kunst- en rariteitenverzamelingen, 1585–1735.* (Exh. cat. Amsterdams Historisch Museum, Amsterdam, 1992.) Zwolle and Amsterdam, 1992.

Amsterdam 2007
Kilian, Jennifer M. *Karel du Jardin, 1626–1678.* (Exh. cat. Rijksmuseum, Amsterdam, 2007.) Amsterdam, 2007.

Amsterdam/Aachen 2008
Brink, Pieter van den, and Jaap van der Veen. *Jacob Backer (1608–1651).* (Exh. cat. Rembrandthuis, Amsterdam; Suermondt-Ludwig-Museum, Aachen, 2008.) Zwolle, 2008.

Amsterdam/Boston/Philadelphia 1987–88
Sutton, Peter C., with Albert Blankert et al. *Masters of 17th-Century Dutch Landscape Painting.* (Exh. cat. Rijksmuseum, Amsterdam; Museum of Fine Arts, Boston; Philadelphia Museum of Art, 1987–88.) Boston, 1987.

Amsterdam/Salem 2015–16
Corrigan, Karina, et al. *Asia in Amsterdam: The Culture of Luxury in the Golden Age.* (Exh. cat. Rijksmuseum, Amsterdam, 15 October 2015–17 January 2016; Peabody Essex Museum, Salem, 27 February–5 June 2016.) Salem and Amsterdam, 2015.

Anderson 1980
Anderson, Jaynie. "Giorgione, Titian, and the Sleeping Venus." In *Tiziano e Venezia: Convegno internazionale di studi, Venezia, 1976.* Venice, 1980, pp. 337–42.

Andersson 1985
Andersson, Christiane D. "'Livelier than Life,' in Amsterdam and Frankfurt." *Print Collector's Newsletter* 16/4 (1985): pp. 132–35.

Antwerp 1956
Burchard, Ludwig, and R.-A. d'Hulst. *Catalogus Tekeningen van P. P. Rubens.* (Exh. cat. Rubenshuis, Antwerp, 1956.) Antwerp, 1956.

Antwerp/Münster 1990
Luchardt, Jochen, et al. *Jan Boeckhorst, 1604–1668: Maler der Rubens.* (Exh. cat. Rubenshuis, Antwerp; Westfälisches Landesmuseum für Kunst und Kulturgeschichte, Münster, 1990.) Freren, 1990.

Arese 1967
Arese, Franco. "Una quadreria Milanese della fine del Seicento." *Arte Lombarda* 12/1 (1967): pp. 127–42.

Arnhem 1953
17e eeuwse meesters uit Gelders bezit. (Exh. cat. Gemeentemuseum, Arnhem, 1953.) Arnhem, 1953.

Arnold 1985
Arnold, Janet. *Patterns of Fashion: The Cut and Construction of Clothes for Men and Women, ca. 1560–1620.* London and New York, 1985.

Arpino and Lecaldano 1969
Arpino, Giovanni, and Paolo Lecaldano. *L'opera pittorica completa di Rembrandt.* Milan, 1969.

Arundel 1909
Arundel Club Portfolio. London, 1909.

Ashton, Davies, and Slive 1982
Ashton, Peter Shaw, Alice I. Davies, and Seymour Slive. "Jacob van Ruisdael's Trees." *Arnoldia* 42/1 (1982): pp. 2–31.

Van Asperen de Boer 1975
Asperen de Boer, J. R. J. van. "A Technical Examination of the Frame of Engebrechtsz.'s 'Crucifixion' and Some Other 16th-Century Frames." *Nederlands kunsthistorisch jaarboek* 26 (1975): pp. 73–87.

Van Asperen de Boer and Wheelock 1973
Asperen de Boer, J. R. J. van, and Arthur K. Wheelock Jr. "Underdrawings in Some Paintings by Cornelis Engebrechtsz." *Oud Holland* 87 (1973): pp. 61–94.

Avery-Quash 2011
Avery-Quash, Susanna. "The Travel Notebooks of Sir Charles Eastlake." 2 vols. *The Volume of the Walpole Society* 73 (2011).

Baardt 1645
Baardt, Petrus. *Deugden-spoor in de on-deughden des werelts aff-gebeeldt.* Leeuwarden, 1645.

Bachmann 1975
Bachmann, Fredo. "Die Herkunft der Frühwerke des Aert van der Neer." *Oud Holland* 89 (1975): pp. 213–22.

Bachmann 1982
Bachmann, Fredo. *Aert van der Neer, 1603/4–1677*. Bremen, 1982.

Baciagalupe 1999
Baciagalupe, Miguel Ángel Echevarria. "Los Archiduques y su tiempo (1599–1633)." In *El Arte en la Corte de los Archiduques Alberto de Austria e Isabel Clara Eugenia (1598–1633), Un Reino Imaginado*, pp. 32–45. Edited by Alejandro Vergara. (Exh. cat. Salas de Exposiciones Temporales del Palacio Real, Madrid, 1999.) Madrid, 1999.

Badstübner 2011
Badstübner, E. "Der Hochalter der Stendaler Marienkirche als Spiegel mitteleuropäischer Kunstströmungen in der zweiten Hälfte des 15. Jahrhunderts." In *Die Altmark von 1300 bis 1600: Eine Kulturregion im Spannungsfeld von Magdeburg, Lübeck, und Berlin*, pp. 362–72. Edited by J. Fajt, W. Franzen, and P. Knüvener. Berlin, 2011.

Baer 1990
Baer, Ronni. "The Paintings of Gerrit Dou (1613–1675)." PhD diss., New York University, 1990.

Baer 2015
Baer, Ronni. *Class Distinctions: Dutch Painting in the Age of Rembrandt and Vermeer*. Boston, 2015.

Bagot 1824
Bagot, William, 2nd Baron. *Memorials of the Bagot Family*. Blithfield, 1824.

Bailey et al. 2011
Bailey, Colin B., et al. *Rembrandt and His School: Masterworks from the Frick and Lugt Collections*. New York, 2011.

Baldass 1930
Baldass, Ludwig von. "Drei Jahrhunderte Flämische Malerei." *Pantheon* 5 (1930): pp. 130–36.

Baldass 1940
Baldass, Ludwig von. "Zur Bildniskunst der Dürerschule; II. Die Bildniskunst des Jörg Pencz und Bartel Beham." *Pantheon* 26 (November 1940): pp. 253–59.

Balen 1677
Balen, Matthys Jansz. *Beschryvinge der stad Dordrecht, vervatende haar begin, opkomst, toeneming, en verdere stant. . . .* 3 vols. in 2. Dordrecht, 1677.

Balet 1921
Balet, Leo. "Die Sammlung Bachstitz." *Cicerone* 13 (1921): pp. 331–38.

Balis 1986
Balis, Arnout. *Hunting Scenes*. Corpus Rubenianum Ludwig Burchard 18/2. London, 1986.

Bangs 1999
Bangs, Jeremy Dupertuis. "The Masters of Alkmaar and Hand X: The Haarlem Painters of the Van Waterlant Family." *Wallraf-Richartz-Jahrbuch* 60 (1999): pp. 65–152.

Barker 1994
Barker, Nicolas. *Hortus Eystettensis: The Bishop's Garden and Besler's Magnificent Book*. New York, 1994.

Barnes and Rose 2002
Barnes, Donna R., and Peter G. Rose. *Matters of Taste: Food and Drink in Seventeenth-Century Dutch Art and Life*. Albany and Syracuse, 2002.

Bartsch 1797
Bartsch, Adam von. *Catalogue raisonné de toutes les estampes qui forment l'œuvre de Rembrandt, et ceux de ses principaux imitateurs*. 2 vols. Vienna, 1797.

Bartsch 1803–21
Bartsch, Adam von. *Le peintre graveur*. 21 vols. Vienna, 1803–21.

Bartsch [1854–70] 1970
Bartsch, Adam von. *Le peintre graveur*. 4 vols. Hildesheim, 1970. [Repr. of 21 vol. 1854–70 Leipzig ed.; 1st ed. 1803–21.]

Bartsch 1978–
Bartsch, Adam von. *The Illustrated Bartsch*. Founding ed. Walter L. Strauss; general eds. Anthony Kaufman and John T. Spike. 166 vols. New York, 1978–.

Bauch 1926
Bauch, Kurt. *Jakob Adriaensz. Backer, ein Rembrandtschüler aus Friesland*. Berlin, 1926.

Bauch 1929
Bauch, Kurt. "Ausstellung holländischer Kunst von 1450–1900 in London." *Zeitschrift für bildende Kunst* 63 (1929): pp. 9–23.

Bauch 1966
Bauch, Kurt. *Rembrandt Gemälde*. Berlin, 1966.

Bauch 1973
Bauch, Kurt. "Diskussion" [responding to Gerson 1973b]. In Simson and Kelch 1973, pp. 217f.

Bauman and Liedtke 1992
Bauman, Guy C., and Walter A. Liedtke, eds. *Flemish Paintings in America: A Survey of Early Netherlandish and Flemish Paintings in the Public Collections of North America*. Antwerp, 1992.

Baumstark 1974
Baumstark, Reinhold. "Iconographische Studien zu Rubens Krieges und Friedensallegorien." *Aachener Kunstblätter* 45 (1974): pp. 125–234.

Bax 1952
Bax, Dirk. *Hollandse en Vlaamse schilderkunst in Zuid-Afrika*. Amsterdam, 1952.

"A Bearded Man" 1977
"Special Exhibition. Rembrandt Portrait: 'A Bearded Man in a Wide-Brimmed Hat.'" *Bulletin* (St. Louis Art Museum) 13/4 (July–August 1977): p. 135 (ill.).

"Bearwood" n.d.
"Catalogue of Pictures at Bearwood for Insurance with the Fine Art and General Insurance Company Limited," n.d. County Archive, Berkshire Record Office, Shire Hall, Reading, no. D/EWL F12[2]. Photocopy, GRI.

"Bearwood" 1884
"Catalogue of Pictures at Bearwood, Insured in the Sun Office by Policy No. 3236176, Policy dated Feby 14, 1884." County Archive, Berkshire Record Office, Shire Hall, Reading, no. D/EWL F12[1]. Photocopy, GRI.

Beck 1972–87
Beck, Hans-Ulrich. *Jan van Goyen, 1596–1656: Ein Oeuvre Verzeichnis*. Introduction by Wolfgang Stechow. 3 vols. Amsterdam, 1972–87.

Bedaux 1987
Bedaux, Jan Baptist. "Fruit and Fertility: Fruit Symbolism in Netherlandish Portraiture of the Sixteenth and Seventeenth Centuries." *Simiolus: Netherlands Quarterly for the History of Art* 17, nos. 2–3 (1987): pp. 150–68.

Bedaux 1990
Bedaux, Jan Baptist. *The Reality of Symbols: Studies in the Iconology of Netherlandish Art, 1400–1800*. 's-Gravenhage, 1990.

Belkin 1980
Belkin, Kristin Lohse. *The Costume Book*. Corpus Rubenianum Ludwig Burchard 24. Brussels, 1980.

Belkin 2009
Belkin, Kristin Lohse. *Copies and Adaptations from Renaissance and Later Artists: German and Netherlandish Artists*. 2 vols. Edited by Carl Van de Velde, Ria De Boodt, and Prisca Valkeneers. Corpus Rubenianum Ludwig Burchard 26/1. London, 2009.

Bellori [1672] 1976
Bellori, Giovan Pietro. *Le vite de' pittori, scultori e architetti moderni*. Edited by Evelina Borea. Turin, 1976. [Repr. of 1672 ed.]

Belting and Kruse 1994
Belting, H., and C. Kruse. *Die Erfindung des Gemäldes: Das erste Jahrhundert der niederländischen Malerei*. Munich, 1994.

Bendall 2017
Bendall, Sarah. "Rebato Collar, c. 1600–1625. Part One: Brief History and Materials." Sarah A. Bendall, Material Culture and Dress Historian (website). December 18, 2017. https://sarahabendall.com/2017/12/18/rebato-collar-c-1600-1625-part-one-materials/.

Van Beneden and De Poorter 2006
Beneden, Ben van, and Nora de Poorter. *Royalist Refugees: William Cavendish in the Rubens House, 1648–1660*. Antwerp, 2006.

Benesch 1928
Benesch, Otto. *Die Zeichnungen der niederländischen Schulen des XV. und XVI. Jahrhunderts*. Beschreibender Katalog der Handzeichnungen in der Graphische Sammlung Albertina, vol. 2. Vienna, 1928.

Benesch 1935
Benesch, Otto. *Rembrandt, Werk und Forschung*. Vienna, 1935.

Benesch 1979
Benesch, Otto. *From an Art Historian's Workshop*. Edited by Eva Benesch. Lucerne, 1979.

Benesch/Benesch 1970
Benesch, Otto. *Rembrandt, Werk und Forschung*. Lucerne, 1970. [Repr. of 1935 ed., with corrections and additions by Eva Benesch.]

Benesch/Benesch 1973
Benesch, Otto. *The Drawings of Rembrandt: Complete Edition*. 6 vols. [Repr. of 1954–57 ed., enlarged and edited by Eva Benesch.] London, 1973.

Bénézit 1976
Bénézit, Emmanuel. *Dictionnaire critique et documentaire des peintres, sculpteurs, dessinateurs et graveurs de tous les temps et de tous les pays. . . .* 10 vols. Rev. ed. Paris, 1976.

Berardi 1998
Berardi, Marianne. "Science into Art: Rachel Ruysch's Early Development as a Still-life Painter." PhD diss., University of Pittsburgh, 1998.

Bergamo 1983
Veca, Alberto. *Simposio: Cerimonie e apparati*. Galleria Lorenzelli, Bergamo. Catalogue by Alberto Veca with Pietro Lorenzelli. Bergamo, 1983.

Berger 1883
Berger, Adolf. "Inventar der Kunstsammlung des Erzherzogs Leopold Wilhelm von Österreich." *Jahrbuch der kunsthistorischen Sammlungen des allerhöchsten Kaiserhauses* 1 (1883): LXXIXff.

Bergström 1970
Bergström, Ingvar. "Notes on the Boundaries of Vanitas Significance." In *Ijdelheid der Ijdelheden: Hollandse vanitas-voorstellingen uit de zeventiende eeuw*. Edited by Ingvar Bergström and M. I. Wurfbain. (Exh. cat. Stedelijk Museum de Lakenhal, Leiden, 1970). Leiden, 1970.

Bergvelt and Jonker 2021
Bergvelt, Ellinoor, and Michiel Jonker. *Dulwich Picture Gallery II: Catalogue of the Dutch, Flemish, and German Schools, with Addenda to the British School*. The Hague, 2021. https://dulwich-picture-gallery-ii.rkdstudies.nl. [Enlarged digital version of *Dutch and Flemish Paintings: Dulwich Picture Gallery* (London, 2016).]

Berlin 1931
Die Sammlung Dr. Hans Wendland, Lugano. (Auction cat. Hermann Ball and Paul Graupe, Berlin, 24–25 April 1931.) Introduction by C. F. Foerster. Berlin, 1931.

Bermingham 1986
Bermingham, Ann. *Landscape and Ideology: The English Rustic Tradition, 1740–1860*. Berkeley, 1986.

Bern 1947–48
Europäische Barockmalerei aus Wiener Privatgalerien: Czernin, Harrach, Schwarzenberg. Introduction by Max Huggler. (Exh. cat. Kunstmuseum Bern, 21 December 1947–31 March 1948.) Bern, [1947].

Bernstock 2000
Bernstock, Judith. *Poussin and French Dynastic Ideology*. New York, 2000.

Bernt 1957–58
Bernt, Walther. *Die niederländischen Zeichner des 17. Jahrhunderts*. 2 vols. Foreword by J. Q. van Regteren Altena. Munich, 1957–58.

Bertram 1983
Bertram, Helmut. *Stillebenbilder der Kunsthalle*. Hamburg, 1983.

Bertuch 1808–10
Bertuch, Carl. *Bemerkungen auf einer Reise aus Thüringen nach Wien in Winter 1805 bis 1806*. Weimar, 1808–10.

Van Beuningen 1954
"Entretien avec M. D. C. van Beuningen." *Connaissance des arts* 34 (December 1954): pp. 57–61.

Białostocki 1976
Białostocki, Jan. "Fifteenth-Century Pictures of the Blessing of Christ Based on Rogier van der Weyden." *Gesta* 15 (1976): pp. 313–20.

Białostocki and Walicki 1955
Białostocki, Jan, and Michał Walicki. *Malarstwo europejskie w zbiorach polskich, 1300–1800*. Kraków, 1955.

Bieneck 1992
Bieneck, Dorothea. *Gerard Seghers, 1591–1651; Leben und Werk des Antwerpener Historienmallers*. Lingen, 1992.

Biesboer 2001
Biesboer, Pieter. *Netherlandish Inventories I: Collections of Paintings in Haarlem 1572–1745*. Documents for the History of Collecting, Getty Provenance Index. Edited by Carol Togneri. Los Angeles, 2001.

Biesboer 2006
Biesboer, Pieter. "Nicolaes Pietersz. Berchem, Master Painter of Haarlem." In Haarlem/Zurich/Schwerin 2006, pp. 11–35.

De Bièvre 1988
Bièvre, Elisabeth de. "Violence and Virtue: History and the Art in the City of Haarlem." *Art History* 11/3 (1988): pp. 303–34.

Bijlsma 1911
Bijlsma, R. "De Brouwerij 'Twee Witte Klimmende Leeuwen.'" *Rotterdamsche Jaarboek* 9 (1911): pp. 127–38.

Bille 1961
Bille, Clara. *De Tempel der Kunst of het Kabinet van den Heer Braamcamp*. 2 vols. Amsterdam, 1961.

Blaeu 1649
Blaeu, Joan. *Toonneel der steden van de vereenighde Nederlanden, met hare beschrijvingen; Toonneel der steden van's konings Nederlanden, met hare beschrijvingen*. Amsterdam, 1649.

Blaker and Urquhart 1963
Blaker, Hugh, and Murray Urquhart. "The Blaker Diary: Some Extracts with a Memoir by Murray Urquhart." *Apollo* 78 (October 1963): pp. 293–98.

Blanc 1857–58
Blanc, Charles. *La trésor de la curiosité. . . .* 2 vols. Paris, 1857–58.

Blanc 1861
Blanc, Charles. *Histoire des Peintres de toutes les écoles. École hollandaise*. 2 vols. Paris, 1861.

Blankert et al. 1975–79
Blankert, Albert, with contributions by Rob Ruurs and N. Köhler. *Amsterdams Historisch Museum: Schilderijen daterend van voor 1800*. Amsterdam, 1975–79.

Blankert 1995
Blankert, Albert. "Vermeer's Modern Themes and Their Tradition." In *Johannes Vermeer*, pp. 31–45. By B. P. J. Broos et al. (Exh. cat. National Gallery of Art, Washington, DC; Royal Cabinet of Paintings, Mauritshuis, The Hague, 1995.) The Hague, 1995.

Blussé and Falkenburg 1987
Blussé, Léonard, and Reindert L. Falkenburg. *Johan Nieuhofs beelden van een Chinareis, 1655–1657*. Middelburg, 1987.

Bock and Gaehtgens 1987
Bock, Henning, and Thomas Gaehtgens, eds. *Holländische Genremalerei im 17. Jahrhundert: Symposium, Berlin 1984*. Jahrbuch Preußischer Kulturbesitz 4. Berlin, 1987.

Bode 1883
Bode, Wilhelm von. *Studien zur Geschichte der holländischen Malerei*. Braunschweig, 1883.

Bode 1900
Bode, Wilhelm von. *Gemäldesammlungen des Herrn Rudolf Kann*. 2 vols. Vienna, 1900.

Bode 1907
Bode, Wilhelm von. *Catalogue de la collection Rodolphe Kann*. 2 vols. Paris, 1907.

Bode 1914
Bode, Wilhelm von, ed. *Frans Hals: Sein Leben und seine Werke*. 2 vols. Text by M. J. Binder. Berlin, 1914.

Bode 1915
Bode, Wilhelm von. "Jan van der Heyden." *Zeitschrift für bildende Kunst* N.F. 26 (1915): pp. 181–87.

Bode 1919
Bode, Wilhelm von. *Die Meister der holländischen und vlämischen Malerschulen*. Leipzig, 1919. [2nd enlarged ed.]

Bode 1923
Bode, Wilhelm von. *Rembrandt und seine Zeitgenossen: Charakterbilder der grossen Meister der holländischen und vlämischen Malerschule im siebzehnten Jahrhundert*. Leipzig, 1923.

Bode and Hofstede de Groot 1897–1906
Bode, Wilhelm von, with Cornelis Hofstede de Groot. *The Complete Work of Rembrandt*. 8 vols. Translated from the German by Florence Simmonds. Paris, 1897–1906.

Bode/Plietzsch 1958
Bode, Wilhelm von. *Die Meister der holländischen und flämischen Malerschulen*. Previously published as *Rembrandt und seine Zeitgenossen*. Edited and expanded by Eduard Plietzsch. Leipzig, 1958.

Bogendorf Rupprath: See also **Kortenhorst-von Bogendorf Rupprath 1993**

Bogendorf Rupprath 2003
Bogendorf Rupprath, Cynthia von. "De Muzen van het vroeg-17de-eeuwse Haarlem: Bronnen van genremotieven." In *Satire en vermaak: Schilderkunst in de 17de eeuw—Het genrestuk van Frans Hals en zijn tijdgenoten 1610–1670*, pp. 8–31. Edited by Pieter Biesboer and Martina Sitt. (Exh. cat. Frans Hals Museum, Haarlem, 2003.) Zwolle and Haarlem, 2003.

Böhm 1980
Böhm, Elga. "Matthias Joseph De Noël (1782–1849): Erster Konservator des Kölner Museums 'Wallrafianum.'" *Wallraf-Richartz-Jahrbuch* 41 (January 1980): pp. 159–221.

Bol 1960
Bol, Laurens J. *The Bosschaert Dynasty: Painters of Flowers and Fruit*. Leigh-on-Sea, 1960.

Bomford 1986
Bomford, David. "Techniques of the Early Dutch Landscape Painters." In London 1986, pp. 45–56.

Bomford, Roy, and Smith 1986
Bomford, David, Ashok Roy, and Alistair Smith. "The Techniques of Dieric Bouts: Two Paintings Contrasted." *National Gallery Technical Bulletin* (London) 10 (1986): pp. 39–57.

Bonafoux 1990
Bonafoux, Pascal. *Rembrandt: Le clair, l'obscur*. Paris, 1990.

Bonnet 1994
Bonnet, Anne-Marie. "Der Akt im Werk Lucas Cranachs." In Kronach 1994, pp. 139–49.

Borchert 1995
Borchert, Till-Holger. "Memling's Antwerp 'God the Father' with Music-Making Angels." In *Colloque 10* 1995, pp. 153–67, pls. 75–77.

Bordeaux 1954
Martin-Méry, Gilberte. *Flandres, Espagne, Portugal du XVe au XVIIe siècle*. (Exh. cat. Musée des Beaux-Arts de Bordeaux, 1954.) Bordeaux, 1954.

Bordeaux 1959
Martin-Méry, Gilberte. *Exposition internationale [9th : 1959 : Bordeaux] La découverte de la lumière des primitifs aux impressionists*. (Exh. cat. Galerie des Beaux-Arts, Bordeaux, 20 May–31 July 1959.) Bordeaux, 1959.

J.-L. Bordeaux 1986
Bordeaux, Jean-Luc. "Authentique sans réserves." *Connaissance des arts* 413–14 (July–August 1986): pp. 36–41.

Borean and Cecchini 2002
Borean, Linda, and Isabella Cecchini. "Microstorie d'affari e di quadric. I Lumaga tra Venezia e Napoli." In *Figure di collezionisti a Venezia tra Cinque e Seicento*, pp. 159–231. Udine, 2002.

Borenius 1932
Borenius, Tancred. "Shorter Notices: The Stephan von Auspitz Collection." *Burlington Magazine* 61/357 (December 1932): pp. 283, 286–88.

Borenius 1936
Borenius, Tancred. *Catalogue of the Pictures and Drawings at Harewood House and Elsewhere in the Collection of the Earl of Harewood*. Oxford, 1936.

Boston/Toledo 1993
Sutton, Peter C., with Marjorie E. Wieseman et al. *The Age of Rubens*. (Exh. cat. Museum of Fine Arts, Boston; Toledo Museum of Art, 1993.) Boston, 1993.

Bott 1962
Bott, Gerhard. "Stillebenmaler des 17. Jahrhunderts: Isaak Soreau—Peter Binoit." *Kunst in Hessen und am Mittelrhein* 2 (1962): pp. 27–93.

Bott 2001
Bott, Gerhard. *Ein Stück von allerlei Blumenwerk, ein Stück von Früchten, zwei Stück auf Tuch mit Hecht: Die Stillebenmaler Soreau, Binoit, Codino und Marrell in Hanau und Frankfurt 1600–1650*. Hanau, 2001.

Brandt [1720–23] 1979
Brandt, Geeraert. *The History of the Reformation and Other Ecclesiastical Transactions in and about the Low Countries. . . .* 4 vols. Translated by John Chamberlayne. New York, 1979. [Repr. of 1720–23 London ed.]

Braun and Hogenberg [1618–23] 1966
Braun, Georg, and Frans Hogenberg. *Civitates orbis terrarum*. Introduction by R. A. Skelton. 6 vols. in 3. Cleveland, 1966. [Facsimile of ca. 1618–23 Antwerp ed.; 1st ed. 1581.]

J. Braun 1928
Braun, J. "Die Ikonographie des Dreikönigenschreins." *Kunstwissenschaftliches Jahrbuch der Görresgesellschaft* 1 (1928): pp. 29–39.

K. Braun 1980
Braun, Karel. *Alle tot nu toe bekende schilderijen van Jan Steen*. Rotterdam, 1980.

Braun-Ronsdorf 1967
Braun-Ronsdorf, Margarete. *History of the Handkerchief*. Leigh-on-Sea, 1967.

Braunschweig 2006
Gatenbröcker, Silke. *Familienglück: Rembrandt und sein Braunschweiger Meisterwerk*. (Exh. cat. Herzog Anton Ulrich-Museum, Braunschweig, 2006.) Braunschweig, 2006.

Bredius 1892
Bredius, Abraham. "De schilder Johannes van de Cappelle." *Oud Holland* 10 (1892): pp. 26–40.

Bredius 1906
Bredius, Abraham. "De nalatenschap van Carel Du Jardin." *Oud Holland* 24 (1906): pp. 223–32.

Bredius 1912
Bredius, Abraham. "De nalatenschap van Jan van der Heyden's weduwe." *Oud Holland* 30 (1912): pp. 129–51.

Bredius 1915
Bredius, Abraham. "De nachlass-inventar von Jan Miense Molenaer." In Bredius 1915–22, vol. 1 (1915), pp. 1–26.

Bredius 1915–22
Bredius, Abraham. *Künstler-Inventare, Urkunden zur Geschichte der holländischen Kunst. . . .* 8 vols. The Hague, 1915–22.

Bredius 1927
Bredius, Abraham. *Jan Steen*. Amsterdam, 1927.

Bredius 1935
Bredius, Abraham. *Rembrandt, Gemälde. 630 Abbildungen*. Vienna, 1935.

Bredius/Gerson 1969
Bredius, Abraham. *Rembrandt: The Complete Edition of the Paintings*. 3rd ed. Revised by Horst Gerson. London, 1969.

Bredius and Hirschmann 1921
Bredius, Abraham, and Otto Hirschmann. "Der Künstlerische Nachlas van Cornelis Cornelisz. van Haarlem." In Bredius 1915–22, vol. 7 (1921): pp. 77–99.

Brejon de Lavergnée 1994
Brejon de Lavergnée, Arnauld. "La collection de tableaux d'Henri Heugel (1844–1916.)" *Bulletin de la Société de l'histoire de l'art français* (1994): pp. 215–38.

Bremmer 1934
Bremmer, H. P. "Tentoonstelling: Amsterdam. . . . Oude schilderijen bij D. L. [*sic*] Hoogendijk & Co." *Maandblad voor beeldende kunsten* 11 (1934): pp. 374–79.

Brenninkmeijer-De Rooij 1996
Brenninkmeijer-De Rooij, Beatrijs. *Roots of Seventeenth-Century Flower Painting: Miniatures, Plant Books, Paintings*. Leiden, 1996.

Breuning 1939
Breuning, Margaret. "Classic Nudes." *Magazine of Art* (Washington, DC) 32/5 (May 1939): pp. 298–99.

Breuning 1946
Breuning, Margaret. "Masters of Yesteryear." *Art Digest* 20 (15 February 1946): pp. 7, 30.

Brière-Misme 1950
Brière-Misme, Clotilde. "Un petit maître hollandais Cornelis Bisschop (1630–1674.)" *Oud Holland* 65 (1950): pp. 24–40, 104–16, 139–51, 178–92, 227–40.

Briganti 1983
Briganti, Giuliano. "The Myth of the Window Opened on to Life." In *The Bamboccianti*, pp. 13ff. By Giuliano Briganti, Ludovica Trezzani, and Laura Laureati; translation by Robert Erich Wolf. Rome, 1983.

Briganti, Trezzani, and Laureati 1983
Briganti, Giuliano, Ludovica Trezzani, and Laura Laureati. *I Bamboccianti, pittori della vita quotidiana a Roma nel Seicento*. Rome, 1983.

Van den Brink 2001
Brink, Peter van den. "The Art of Copying and the Serial Production of Paintings in the Low Countries in the Sixteenth and Seventeenth Centuries." In *Brueghel Enterprises,* pp. 12–43. Edited by Peter van den Brink, with Dominique Allart et al. (Exh. cat. Bonnefantenmuseum, Maastricht; Musées Royaux des Beaux-Arts de Belgique, Brussels, 2001.) Maastricht, 2001.

Brochhagen 1957
Brochhagen, E. "Dujardins spate Landschaften." *Bulletin—Musées Royaux des Beaux-Arts de Belgique* 6 (1957): pp. 236–55.

Brochhagen 1958
Brochhagen, E. "Karel Dujardin; ein Beitrag zum Italianismus in Holland im 17 Jahrhundert." PhD diss., University of Cologne, 1958.

Brockwell 1917
Brockwell, Maurice W. "Notable Collections: The Cook Collection, pt. II.—The Flemish and Dutch Schools." *Connoisseur* 48 (May–August 1917): pp. 20–29.

Brockwell 1932
Brockwell, Maurice W. *Abridged Catalogue of the Pictures at Doughty House, Richmond, Surrey, in the Collection of Sir Herbert Cook, bart*. London, 1932.

Brook 2008
Brook, Timothy. *Vermeer's Hat: The Seventeenth Century and the Dawn of the Global World*. New York and London, 2008.

Brooks 1985
Brooks, Valerie F. "The 'Thrill of a Lifetime.'" *ARTnews* 84/5 (1985): pp. 19–20.

Broos 1997
Broos, Ben. "Karel du Jardin, 'Paul Healing the Crippled Man at Lystra,' 1663." *Biuletyn Historii Sztuki* (Warsaw) 59/3–4 (1997): pp. 218–25.

Brown 1976
Brown, Christopher. "Rembrandt's 'Portrait of a Boy.'" *Connoisseur* 193/777 (November 1976): pp. 216–19.

Brown 1977
Brown, Christopher. *Dutch and Flemish Painting*. Oxford and New York, 1977.

Brown 1979
Brown, Christopher. *Rembrandt*. London, 1979.

Brown 1982
Brown, Christopher. "Boston, Jacob van Ruisdael at the Fogg." *Burlington Magazine* 124/948 (March 1982): pp. 190–94.

Brown 1989
Brown, Christopher. "Review of D. Wolfthal, *The Beginnings of Netherlandish Canvas Painting 1400–1530*." *Times Literary Supplement*, November 10–16, 1989, p. 1247.

Brown 1992
Brown, Christopher. "Utrecht and Cologne, I Bamboccianti." *Burlington Magazine* 134/1066 (1992): pp. 54–56.

Brown et al. 1991
Brown, Christopher, et al. *Rembrandt: The Master and His Workshop (Paintings)*. London, 1991.

Bruges 1949
Friedländer, Max J. *Gerard David*. (Exh. cat. Stedelijk Museum voor Schone Kunsten [Groeningemuseum], Bruges, 18 June–21 August 1949.) Brussels, 1949.

Bruges 1956
L'art flamand dans les collections Britanniques et la Galerie Nationale de Victoria. (Exh. cat. Stedelijk Museum voor Schone Kunsten [Groeningemuseum], Bruges, August–September 1956.) Brussels, 1956.

Bruges 1960
Pauwels, H., et al. *Le siècle des primitifs flamands*. (Exh. cat. Stedelijk Museum voor Schone Kunsten [Groeningemuseum], Bruges, 26 June–11 September 1960.) Bruges 1960.

Bruges 1994
De Vos, Dirck, with Dominique Marachal and Willy Le Loup. *Hans Memling: Five Centuries of Fact and Fiction*. (Exh. cat. Stedelijk Museum voor Schone Kunsten [Groeningemuseum], Bruges, 1994.) Translated by Ten Atkins and Marcus Cumberledge. Brussels, 1994.

Bruges 1998
Martens, Maximiliaan P. J., ed. *Bruges and the Renaissance: Memling to Pourbus*. (Exh. cat. Memlingmuseum, Oud Sint-Janshospitaal, Bruges, 1998.) Bruges, 1998.

De Brune 1970
Brune, Johan de. *Emblemata of Zinne-werck*. Introduction by P. J. Meertens. Soest, 1970.

Brunner-Bulst 2004
Brunner-Bulst, Martina. *Pieter Claesz.: Der Hauptmeister des Haarlemer Stillebens im 17. Jahrhundert: Kritischer Oeuvrekatalog*. Lingen, 2004.

Brussels 1873
Exposition de tableaux et dessins d'anciens maîtres organisée par la Société Néerlandaise de Bienfaisance à Bruxelles. (Exh. cat. Brussels, 1873.) Brussels, 1873.

Brussels 1910
Exposition d'art ancien. L'art belge au XVIIe siècle. (Exh. cat. Musée du cinquantenaire, Brussels, June–November 1910.) Brussels, 1910.

Brussels 1963
De eeuw van Bruegel: De schilderkunst in België in de 16e eeuw. (Exh. cat. Musées Royaux des Beaux-Arts de Belgique, Brussels, 1963.) Brussels, 1963.

Brussels 1977
Anzelewsky, Fedja, Matthias Mende, and Paul Eeckhout. *Albert Dürer aux Pays-Bas: Son voyage (1520–1521), son influence*. (Exh. cat. Palais des beaux-arts, Brussels, 1 October–27 November 1977.) Brussels, 1977.

Brussels/Delft 1957–58
Vries, A. B. de. *Dieric Bouts*. (Exh. cat. Palais des Beaux-Arts, Brussels; Museum Prinsenhof, Delft, 1957–58.) Brussels, 1957.

Brussels/Louvain 1998
Thomas, Werner, and Luc Duerloo, eds. *Albert & Isabelle, 1598–1621*. (Exh. cat. Musées Royaux d'Art et d'Histoire, Brussels; Université catholique de Louvain, 1998.) 2 vols. Turnhout, 1998.

De Bruyn Kops 1965
Bruyn Kops, C. J. de. "De Amsterdamse verzamelaar Jan Gildemeester Jansz." *Bulletin van het Rijksmuseum* 13 (1965): pp. 70–141.

De Bruyn Kops 1976
Bruyn Kops, C. J. de. "De Zeven Werken van Barmhartigheid van de Meester van Alkmaar gerestaureerd." *Bulletin van het Rijksmuseum* 23/14 (February 1976): pp. 203–26; English summary 249–51.

Bryan 1889
Bryan, Michael. *Bryan's Dictionary of Painters and Engravers*. London, 1889.

Buchanan 1824
Buchanan, William. *Memoirs of Painting*. 2 vols. London, 1824.

Buendia 1993
Buendia, J. Rogelio. *A Basic Guide to the Prado: A View of the Museum According to Styles*. Madrid, 1993.

Buijnsters-Smets 1995
Buijnsters-Smets, Leontine. *Jan Massys: Een Antwerps schilder uit de zestiende eeuw*. Zwolle, 1995.

Buijsen 1996
Buijsen, Edwin. "A Rediscovered Wing of a Diptych by Hans Memling (c. 1440–1494.)" *Oud Holland* 110 (1996): pp. 57–69.

Buijsen 2001
Buijsen, Edwin. *Onder de Huid van Oude Meesters, zeventiende-eeuwse schilderijen onderzocht met infraroodreflectografie*. The Hague, 2001.

Buomberger 1998
Buomberger, Thomas. *Raubkunst-Kunstraub: Die Schweiz und der Kandel mit gestohlenen Kulturgütern zu Zeit des Zweiten Welt-kriegs*. Zurich, 1998.

Burchard 1930
Burchard, Ludwig. "Die Seitenaltäre van Rubens für il Gesù in Rome." In *Actes du XIIe Congrès International d'histoire de l'art*, vol. 1 of 2, pp. 127f. Brussels, 1930.

Burchard and D'Hulst 1963
Burchard, Ludwig, and R.-A. d'Hulst. *Rubens Drawings*. 2 vols. Brussels, 1963.

Burckhardt 1898
Burckhardt, Jacob. *Erinnerungen aus Rubens*. Basel, 1898.

Burckhardt 1950
Burckhardt, Jacob. *Recollections of Rubens*. Edited with an introduction by Horst Gerson. Burchkhardt's essay translated by Mary Hottinger. Selected letters translated by R. H. Boothroyd and I. Grafe. London, 1950.

Burger 1857
Burger, W. *Trésors d'art exposés a Manchester en 1857*. Paris, 1857.

Burrows 1929
Burrows, Carlyle. "Exhibition of Flemish Primitive Painting." *Parnassus* 1/7 (November 1929): pp. 6–9.

Buschbeck and Fuhrmann 1955
Buschbeck, Ernst H., and Franz Fuhrmann. *Katalog der Residenzgalerie Salzburg mit Sammlung Czernin*. Salzburg, 1955.

Buschbeck and Fuhrmann 1962
Buschbeck, Ernst H., and Franz Fuhrmann. *Katalog der Residenzgalerie Salzburg mit Sammlung Czernin und Sammlung Schönborn-Bruchheim*. Salzburg, 1962.

Buttery 1988
Buttery, David. "The Glory that Was Warwick." *Antique Collector* 12 (1988): pp. 41–46.

Cahill 2017
Cahill, Nina. "Staging the Old Testament: Jan Steen and the Theatre." In *Pride and Persecution: Jan Steen's Old Testament Scenes*, pp. 20–33. By Robert Wenley, Nina Cahill, and Rosalie van Gulick. (Exh. cat. Barber Institute of Fine Arts, Birmingham, 2017.) Birmingham, 2017.

L. Campbell 1995a
Campbell, Lorne. "Bruges: Hans Memling." *Burlington Magazine* 137 (April 1995): pp. 264f.

L. Campbell 1995b
Campbell, Lorne. "Memling's Creative Processes as Seen in His Paintings in the National Gallery, London." In *Colloque 10* 1995, pp. 149–52, pls. 72–75.

L. Campbell 1998
Campbell, Lorne. *The Fifteenth-Century Netherlandish Schools*. London, 1998.

S. Campbell 2010
Campbell, Sara. *Collector Without Walls: Norton Simon and His Hunt for the Best*. New Haven, 2010.

Canepa 2019
Canepa, Teresa. *Jingdezhen to the World: The Lurie Collection of Chinese Export Porcelain from the Late Ming Dynasty*. London, 2019.

"Cape Town: Robinson" 1958
"Cape Town's Gain: London's Loss—The Robinson Pictures." *Connoisseur* 142/572 (November 1958): pp. 95–97.

Cape Town 1959
The Sir Joseph Robinson Collection, Lent by the Princess Labia. Introduction by John Paris; biography by L. S. le Roux. (Exh. cat. National Gallery of South Africa, Cape Town, 1959.) 2nd rev. ed. Cape Town, 1959.

Carey 1936
Carey, C. B. C. "Sixty Paintings Show the Art of Rubens, Master of Many Talents." *Art Digest* 10/10 (15 February 1936): pp. 5–6.

Carter 1905
Carter, Joseph H. *Catalogue of the Collection of Paintings at High Legh Hall. . . .* Birmingham, 1905.

Castagnola-Lugano 1949
Aus dem Besitz der Stiftung Sammlung Schloss Rohoncz. Edited by Rudolf Heinemann and Adolf Feulner. (Exh. cat. Villa Favorita, Castagnola-Lugano, 1949.) 2 vols. Castagnola-Lugano, 1949.

Castelfranchi Vegas 1984
Castelfranchi Vegas, Liana. *Italie et Flandres dans la peinture du XVe siècle*. Milan, 1984.

Castiglione 1561
Castiglione, Baldassare. *The Courtyer of Count Baldessar Castilio*. Translated by Thomas Hoby. London, 1561.

Cats [1625] 1712
Cats, Jacob. *Houwelyck, dat is, de gansche gelegenheyt des echten-staets*. Amsterdam, 1712. [1st ed. 1625.]

Cats [1632] 1658
Cats, Jacob. *Spiegel van den ouden ende nieuwen tijdt. . . .* Amsterdam, 1658 [1st ed. 1632.]

Cats 1880
Cats, Jacob. *Alle de Werken van Jacob Cats*. Dordrecht, 1880.

Cennini 1971
Cennini, Cennino. *Il libro dell'arte*. Vicenza, 1971.

Chaban-Delmas 1954
Chaban-Delmas, Jacques. "Flandres, Espagne, Portugal: Des Primitifs à Rubens." *Visages du monde* 107 (1954): pp. 3–21.

Chamot 1929a
Chamot, Mary. "Dutch Art." *Country Life* 65 (5 January 1929): pp. 16–23.

Chamot 1929b
Chamot, Mary. "Rembrandt at Burlington House." *Country Life* 65 (26 January 1929): pp. 133–36.

Chamot 1932
Chamot, Mary. "The von Auspitz Collection." *Country Life* 72 (1932): pp. 561–63.

Chapman 1989
Chapman, H. Perry. "Rembrandt's 'Burgerlijk' Self-Portraits." *Leids Kunsthistorisch Jaarboek* 8 (1989): pp. 203–15.

Charron [ca. 1612] 1971
Charron, Pierre. *Of Wisdome*. New York, 1971. [Repr. of ca. 1612 ed.]

Chicago 1961
Treasures of Chicago Collectors. (Exh. cat. Art Institute of Chicago, 15 April–7 May 1961.) Chicago, 1961.

Chicago 1982
Wise, Susan, et al. *France in the Golden Age: Seventeenth-Century French Paintings in American Collections*. (Exh. cat. Art Institute of Chicago, 1982.) Chicago, 1982. [Abr. ed. of Paris/New York/Chicago 1982.]

Chicago/Minneapolis/Detroit 1969
Rembrandt after Three Hundred Years: An Exhibition of Rembrandt and His Followers. (Exh. cat. Art Institute of Chicago; Minneapolis Institute of Art; Detroit Institute of Arts, 1969.) Foreword by C. C. Cunningham; introduction by E. Haverkamp-Begemann; catalogue by J. R. Judson. Chicago, 1969.

Chong 1992
Chong, Alan. "Aelbert Cuyp and the Meanings of Landscape." PhD diss., New York University, 1992.

Chong 2001
Chong, Alan. "Aristocratic Imaginings: Aelbert Cuyp's Patrons and Collectors." In Washington/London/Amsterdam 2001, pp. 34–51.

Christiansen 2004
Christiansen, Keith. "Giovanni Bellini and the Practice of Devotional Painting." In *Giovanni Bellini and the Art of Devotion*, pp. 3–57. Edited by R. Kasl. Indianapolis, 2004.

Christlieb 1969
Christlieb, Wolfgang. "Rembrandt: Der grosse Verschwender." *Epoca* 12 (December 1969): pp. 50–60, fig. 53.

***La Chronique des arts* 1980**
La Chronique des arts. Supplement to *Gazette des beaux-arts* (December 1980).

***La Chronique des arts* 1982**
La Chronique des arts. Supplement to *Gazette des beaux-arts* (July–August 1982).

Cincinnati 1933
Exhibition of Old Masterpieces. (Exh. cat. Cincinnati Art Museum, 1–14 November 1933.) Cincinnati, 1933.

"Cincinnati Museum Notes" 1933
"Museum Notes." *Cincinnati Art Museum Bulletin* 4/4 (1933): pp. 125–28.

Claremont 1974
The Fine Art of Food. (Exh. cat. Lang Art Gallery, Scripps College, Claremont, CA, 5 November–3 December 1974.) Claremont, 1974.

Clarke 1910
Collection of Pictures and Water Colour Drawings Belonging to Mrs. Stephenson Clarke 1910. Manuscript copy, GRI.

Clemen 1905
Clemen, Paul. *Die Kunstdenkmäler der Rheinprovinz, im auftrage des Provinzialverbandes, fünfter band, III: Die Kunstdenkmäler der Stadt und des Kreises Bonn*. Düsseldorf, 1905.

Clement de Ris 1877
Clement de Ris, L. *Les amateurs d'autrefois*. Paris, 1877.

Cleveland 1936
Twentieth Anniversary Exhibition of the Cleveland Museum of Art, the Official Art Exhibit of the Great Lakes Exposition. (Exh. cat. Cleveland Museum of Art, 1936.) Cleveland, 1936.

Cleveland 1944
The Elisabeth Severance Prentiss Collection: Bequest of Elisabeth Severance Prentiss, 1944. (Exh. cat. Cleveland Museum of Art, 1944.) Cleveland, 1944.

De Clippel and Van der Linden 2015–16
De Clippel, Karolien, and David van der Linden. "The Genesis of the Netherlandish Flower Piece: Jan Brueghel, Ambrosius Bosschaert and Middelburg." *Simiolus* 38/1–2 (2015–16): pp. 73–83.

Clumber 1872
Catalogue of Pictures: Being Part of the Clumber Collection, The Property of His Grace the Duke of Newcastle. London, 1872.

"Clumber House Treasures" 1937
"More Treasures from Clumber House to Be Sold at Christie's." *Morning Post* (London), 14 April 1937.

"Clumber Old Masters" 1937
"In the Sale Room, Old Masters from Clumber." *Morning Post* (London), 31 May 1937.

"Clumber Pictures" 1937
"Pictures from Clumber." *Morning Post* (London), 5 June 1937.

Coffey 1984
Coffey, Susan C. *Peter Paul Rubens: Norton Simon Museum*. Maedaenas Monographs on the Arts. Pasadena, 1984.

Collins and Keene 2022
Collins, Kristen M., and Bryan Keene, eds. *Balthazar: A Black African King in Medieval and Renaissance Art*. Los Angeles, 2022.

***Colloque 8* 1991**
Verougstraete-Marcq, Hélène, and Roger van Schoute, eds. *Dessin sous-jacent dans la peinture. Colloque 8, 8–10 September 1989: Dessin sous-jacent et copies*. Université Catholique de Louvain, Institut Supérieur d'Archéologie et d'Histoire de l'Art. Document de travail 26. Louvain-la-Neuve, 1991.

***Colloque 9* 1993**
Verougstraete-Marcq, Hélène, and Roger van Schoute, eds. *Dessin sous-jacent dans la peinture. Colloque 9, 12–14 September 1991. Louvain: Dessin sous-jacent et pratiques d'atelier*. Université Catholique de Louvain, Institut Supérieur d'Archéologie et d'Histoire de l'Art. Document de travail 27. Louvain-la-Neuve, 1993.

***Colloque 10* 1995**
Verougstraete-Marcq, Hélène, and Roger van Schoute, eds. *Dessin sous-jacent dans la peinture. Colloque 10, 5–7 September 1993, Louvain-la-Neuve: Le dessin sous-jacent dans le processus de création*. Université Catholique de Louvain, Institut Supérieur d'Archéologie et d'Histoire de l'Art. Document de travail 28. Louvain-la-Neuve, 1995.

Colnaghi 2003
P. & D. Colnaghi Co. *Old Master Paintings and Drawings*. Preface by Konrad O. Bernheimer. London, 2003.

Cologne 1995
Kier, Hiltrud, and Frank Günter Zehnder. *Lust und Verlust, Kölner Sammler zwischen Trikolore und Preußenadler*. (Exh. cat. Wallraf-Richartz-Museum, Josef-Haubrich-Kunsthalle, Cologne, 1995.) Cologne, 1995.

Cologne/Antwerp/Vienna 1992
Mai, Ekkard, and Hans Vlieghe, eds. *Van Brueghel bis Rubens: Das Goldene Jahrhundert der flämischen Malerei*. (Exh. cat. Wallraf-Richartz-Museum, Cologne; Museum voor Schoone Kunst, Antwerp; Kunsthistorische Museum, Vienna, 1992.) Cologne, 1992.

Cologne/Utrecht 1987
Mai, Ekkehard, and Christiane Stukenbrock, eds. *Nederlandse 17de eeuwse schilderijen uit Boedapest*. (Exh. cat. Wallraf-Richartz-Museum, Cologne; Centraal Museum, Utrecht, 1987.) Cologne, 1987.

Cologne/Utrecht 1991
Levine, David A., and Ekkehard Mai. *I Bamboccianti: Niederländische Malerrebellen im Rom des Barock*. (Exh. cat. Wallraf-Richartz-Museum, Cologne; Centraal Museum, Utrecht, 1991.) Milan, 1991.

"Connoisseur's Diary" 1962
"The Connoisseur's Diary . . . Rubens and Louis XIII." *Connoisseur* 150/606 (August 1962): pp. 260f.

Cook 1914
Cook, Herbert, ed. *A Catalogue of Paintings at Doughty House, Richmond, and Elsewhere in the Collection of Sir Frederick Cook*. Vol. 2, *Dutch and Flemish Schools*. By J. O. Kronig. London, 1914.

Cook 1915
Cook, Herbert, ed. *A Catalogue of Paintings at Doughty House, Richmond, and Elsewhere in the Collection of Sir Frederick Cook*. Vol. 3, *English, French, Early Flemish, German, and Spanish Schools, and Addenda*. By M. W. Brockwell. London, 1915.

Cooper 1954
Cooper, Douglas. *The Courtauld Collection*. London, 1954.

Coornhert [1586] 1942
Coornhert, Dirck Volkertsz. *Zedekunst, dat is Wellevenskunste*. Edited and annotated by B. Becker. Leiden, 1942. [Based on 1586 ed.]

Corbett 1917
Corbett, Julian Stafford. *England in the Mediterranean; A Study of the Rise and Influence of British Power within the Straits, 1603–1713*. London, 1917.

Cornette and Mérot 1999
Cornette, Joël, and Alain Mérot. *Histoire artistique de l'Europe: Le XVIIe Siècle*. Paris, 1999.

Cornew 1999
Cornew, Clive. "The Battle of Changing Times: Picaresque Parodies from Bruegel to Grosz." PhD diss., University of South Africa, 1999.

***Corpus* 1982**
Rembrandt Research Project Foundation. *A Corpus of Rembrandt Paintings I: 1625–1631*. By J. Bruyn et al. Translated by D. Cook-Radmore. The Hague, 1982.

***Corpus* 1986**
Rembrandt Research Project Foundation. *A Corpus of Rembrandt Paintings II: 1631–1634*. By J. Bruyn et al. Translated by D. Cook-Radmore. The Hague, 1986.

***Corpus* 1989**
Rembrandt Research Project Foundation. *A Corpus of Rembrandt Paintings III: 1635–1642*. By J. Bruyn et al. Translated by D. Cook-Radmore. The Hague, 1989.

***Corpus* 2005**
Rembrandt Research Project Foundation. *A Corpus of Rembrandt Paintings IV: The Self-Portraits*. By Ernst van de Wetering et al. Translated by Jennifer Kilian, Katy Kist, and Murray Pearson. Dordrecht, 2005.

Corti and Faggin 1969
Corti, Maria, with Giorgio T. Faggin. *L'opera completa di Memling*. Classici dell'arte 27. Milan, 1969.

Cramer 1966–67
Cramer Oude Kunst. *Important Paintings by Old Masters, no. 13*. The Hague, 1966–67.

Cramer 1968a
Cramer Oude Kunst. *Important Paintings by Old Masters, no. 14*. The Hague, 1968.

Cramer 1968b
Cramer Oude Kunst. *Important Paintings by Old Masters, no. 15*. The Hague, 1968.

Cramer 1975
Cramer Oude Kunst. *Paintings by Old Masters*. The Hague, 1975.

"Cramer" 1975
"Cramer—Gemälde alter Meister." *Weltkunst* 45/23 (December 1975): p. 2292.

Cranach Digital Archive n.d.
Cranach Digital Archive. Stiftung Museum Kunstpalast, Düsseldorf, Cologne Institute of Conservation Sciences, and Cologne University of Applied Sciences. Accessed August 1, 2023. https://lucascranach.org/home.

Crombie 1978
Crombie, T. "Round the Galleries: Vernal Variety." *Apollo* 107/195 (May 1978): p. 432.

"Current and Forthcoming Exhibitions" 1975
"Current and Forthcoming Exhibitions." *Burlington Magazine* 117/873 (1975): p. 820.

Czobor 1963
Czobor, Ágnes. "Zu Vinckboons' Darstellungen von Soldatenszene." *Oud Holland* 78 (1963): pp. 150–53, 157–59.

Dacier 1913
Dacier, Émile. "Galleries et collections: La collection Marczell de Nemes." *Revue de l'art* 33/195 (June 1913): pp. 453–62.

Dangers 1928
Dangers, Robert. *Die Rembrandt-Fälschungen*. Hanover, 1928.

Danziger 2004
Danziger, Elon. "The Cook Collection, Its Founder and Its Inheritors." *Burlington Magazine* 146 (July 2004): pp. 444–58.

Davenport 1948
Davenport, Millia. *The Book of Costume*. 2 vols. New York, 1948.

Davies 1953
Davies, Martin. *The National Gallery, London*. Primitifs flamands 3. 2 vols. Antwerp, 1953.

Davies 1968
Davies, Martin. *Early Netherlandish School*. 1945. 3rd rev. ed. London, 1968.

Dayot 1911
Dayot, Armand. "Grands et petits maîtres hollandaise." *L'art et les artistes* 13 (April 1911): pp. 50–64.

Dayot 1912a
Dayot, Armand. *Grands et petits maîtres hollandaise du XVIIe siècle*. Paris, 1912.

Dayot 1912b
Dayot, Armand. "La peinture hollandaise." *L'art et les artistes* 15 (April–September 1912): pp. 193–97.

Dechamps 1977a
Dechamps, Christine. "Albert Bouts, alias le Maître de l'Assomption de la Vierge." PhD diss., University of Louvain, 1977.

Dechamps 1977b
Dechamps, Christine. "Albert Bouts, alias le Maître de l'Assomption de la Vierge." PhD diss., University of Louvain, 1977. Abstract. *Revue des archéologues et historiens d'art de Louvain* 10 (1977): pp. 304–06.

Decoen 1937
Decoen, Jean. "Rubens in Paris." *Burlington Magazine* 70/406 (January 1937): p. 46.

Delft 1963
XVe Oude Kunst- en Antiekbeurs der vereniging van handelaren in oude kunst in Nederland. (Exh. cat. Stedelijk Museum Het Prinsenhof, Delft, 1963.) Delft, 1963.

Delft 1967
XIX Oude Kunst- en Antiekbeurs, Delft. (Exh. cat. Stedelijk Museum Het Prinsenhof, Delft, 1967.) Delft, 1967.

Delft 1972
XXIVe Oude Kunst- en Antiekbeurs. (Exh. cat. Stedelijk Museum Het Prinsenhof, Delft, 1972.) Delft, 1972.

Delft 1975
XXVIIe Oude kunst en antiekbeurs. (Exh. cat. Stedelijk Museum Het Prinsenhof, Delft, 1975.) Delft, 1975.

Delft/Cambridge/Fort Worth 1988
Segal, Sam, and William B. Jordan, eds. *A Prosperous Past: The Sumptuous Still Life in the Netherlands, 1600–1700*. (Exh. cat. Stedelijk Museum Het Prinsenhof, Delft; Fogg Museum, Cambridge; Kimbell Art Museum, Fort Worth, 1988.) The Hague, 1988.

Denucé 1931–49
Denucé, Jean. *Bronnen voor de geschiedenis van de Vlaamsche kunst*. 5 vols. Antwerp, 1931–49.

Denucé 1932
Denucé, Jean. *De Antwerpsche "konstkamers": Inventarissen van kunstverzamelingen te Antwerpen in de 16e en 17e eeuwen* (1932). Vol. 2 of *Bronnen voor de geschiedenis van de Vlaamsche kunst*. 5 vols. Antwerp, 1931–49.

Descamps 1753–65
Descamps, Jean-Baptiste. *La vie des peintres flamands, allemands et Hollandais*. 4 vols. Paris, 1753–65.

Descamps 1769
Descamps, Jean-Baptiste. *Voyage pittoresque de la Flandre et du Brabant*. Paris, 1769.

Descargues 1969
Descargues, Pierre. "Le Dernier sourire de Rembrandt." *Plaisir de France* 371 (October 1969): pp. 2–9.

Destrée 1923
Destrée, Joseph. "Jérôme Busleyden, mécène, possesseur d'un triptyque de Hugo van der Goes." In *Compte rendu du Ve Congrès International des sciences historiques, 5th Congrès*. pp. 359f. Brussels, 1923.

Destrée 1926
Destrée, Joseph. "Un triptyque de Hugo van der Goes." *Bulletins de la classe des beaux-arts* (Acadèmie Royale de Belgique) 8 (1926): pp. 25–37.

Detroit 1935
An Exhibition of Fifty Paintings by Frans Hals. Introduction by Wilhelm R. Valentiner. (Exh. cat. Detroit Institute of Arts, 1935.) Detroit, 1935.

Detroit 1936
An Exhibition of Sixty Paintings and Some Drawings by Peter Paul Rubens. (Exh. cat. Detroit Institute of Arts, 1936.) Detroit, 1936.

Detroit 1941
Masterpieces of Art from European and American Collections. (Exh. cat. Detroit Institute of Arts, 1941.) Introduction by E. P. Richardson. Detroit, 1941.

Detroit 1960
Pauwels, H., et al. *Flanders in the Fifteenth Century: Art and Civilization.* (Exh. cat. *Masterpieces of Flemish Art: Van Eyck to Bosch*, Detroit Institute of Arts, October–December 1960.) Detroit, 1960.

"Detroit: Rubens" 1936
"Detroit. Une exposition Rubens." *Revue de l'art* 69/369 (April 1936): p. 181.

Van Deursen 1978
Deursen, A. Th. van. *Het kopergeld van de Gouden Eeuw*. Assen, 1978.

Díaz Padrón 1995
Díaz Padrón, Matías, with Aída Padrón Mérida. *El Siglo de Rubens en el Museo del Prado: Catálogo Razonado de Pintura Flemenca del Siglo XVII*. 2 vols. Madrid, 1995.

Dibbits 2006
Dibbits, Taco. "Ooit Rembrandts 'vermaarde schilderij': De receptiegeschiedenis van *Heilige Familie bij avond*." *Bulletin van het Rijksmuseum* 54/2 (2006): pp. 100–21.

Dibdin 1822
Dibdin, Thomas Frognall. *Aedes Althorpianae*. London, 1822.

Dictys 1966
Dictys. *The Trojan War: The Chronicles of Dictys of Crete and Dares the Phrygian*. Translated, notes, and introduction by R. M. Frazer Jr. Indiana University Greek and Latin Classics. Bloomington, 1966.

DiFuria 2017
DiFuria, Arthur J. "The Timeless Space of Maerten van Heemskerck's Panoramas: Viewing 'Ruth and Boaz.'" In *The Primacy of the Image in Northern European Art, 1400–1700; Essays in Honor of Larry Silver*, pp. 405–18. Edited by Debra Taylor Cashion, Henry Luttikhuizen, and Ashley D. West. Leiden and Boston, 2017.

DiFuria 2019
DiFuria, Arthur J. *Maarten van Heemskerck's Rome: Antiquity, Memory, and the Cult of Ruins*. Leiden and Boston, 2019.

Dijkstra 1990
Dijkstra, Jeltje. *Origineel en kopie: Een onderzoek naar de navolging van de Meester van Flémalle en Rogier van der Weyden*. Amsterdam, 1990.

Dijon 2002
Fučíková, Eliška, Emmanuel Starcky, and Rémi Cariel. *Praga magica 1600: L'art à Prague au temps de Rodolfe II*. (Exh. cat. Musée National Magnin, Dijon, 2002.) Dijon, 2002.

Dillon 1909
Dillon, Edward. *Rubens*. London, 1909.

***DNB* [1921–22] 1973**
Dictionary of National Biography. 22 vols. London, 1973. [Repr. of 1921–22 ed.]

***DNB* 1992**
Concise Dictionary of National Biography, from the Earliest Times to 1985. 3 vols. Oxford and New York, 1992.

Donahue 1969
Donahue, Susan S. "Two Paintings by Ochtervelt in the Wadsworth Atheneum." *Wadsworth Atheneum Bulletin* 5/2 (1969): pp. 46–59.

Donath 1909
Donath, Adolf. "Galerie Gerstenberg in Berlin." *Internationale Sammler-Zeitung* 1/22 (1909): p. 360.

Donath 1929
Donath, Adolf. "Der Berliner Kaufmann als Kunstfreund." In *Berlins Aufstieg zur Weltstadt. Ein Gedenkbuch*. Berlin, 1929, pp. 241–310.

Dordrecht 1957
Mens en Muziek, Neerlandse meesters uit vijf eeuwen. (Exh. cat. Dordrechts Museum, 1957.) Dordrecht, 1957.

Dordrecht 1977
Groot, J. M. de. *Aelbert Cuyp en zijn familie, schilders te Dordrecht: Gerrit Gerritsz. Cuyp, Jacob Gerritsz. Cuyp, Benjamin Gerritsz. Cuyp, Aelbert Cuyp Schilderijen/tekeningen*. (Exh. cat. Dordrechts Museum, 1977.) Dordrecht, 1977.

Douglas 1946
Douglas, R. Langton. "Gerard David: Blessed Virgin as Queen of Heaven." *Art in America* 34/3 (July 1946): pp. 161–63.

Douglas 1951
Douglas, R. Langton. "Some Portraits of Ceremony of the Jacobean School." *Connoisseur* 126 (January 1951): pp. 162–66, 220.

Drossaers and Lunsingh Scheurleer 1974–76
Drossaers, S. W. A., and T. H. Lunsingh Scheurleer, eds. *Inventarissen van de inboedels in de verblijven van de Oranjes en daarmede gelijk te stellen stukken, 1567–1795*. Rijks Geschiedkundige Publicatiën, Grote ser., 147–49. 's-Gravenhage, 1974–76.

Drost 1943
Drost, W. *Die Danziger Gemälde-Galerie: Neuerwerbungen*. Danzig, 1943.

Drucker 1979
Drucker, Peter F. *Adventures of a Bystander*. New York, 1979.

Dublin 1815
Catalogue of Pictures, By the Old Masters with which the Proprietors Have Favoured the Royal Irish Institution. (Exh. cat. Royal Irish Institution, Dublin, 1815.) Dublin, 1815.

Dublin 1853–54
Sproule, John, ed. *The Irish Industrial Exhibition of 1853*. (Exh. cat. Irish Industrial Exhibition, Dublin, 1853–54.) Dublin, 1854.

Dublin 1865
Dublin International Exhibition of Arts and Manufactures. (Exh. cat. Exhibition Palace, Dublin, 1865.) Dublin, 1865.

Dublin 1872
Dublin Exhibition of Arts, Industries, and Manufactures, and Loan Museum of Works of Art. (Exh. cat. Fine Arts Department, Exhibition Palace, Dublin, 1872.) 3rd ed. Dublin [1872].

Dublin/Amsterdam/Washington 2010–11
Waiboer, Adriaan, E. et al. *Gabriel Metsu*. (Exh. cat. National Gallery of Ireland, Dublin; Rijksmuseum, Amsterdam; National Gallery of Art, Washington, DC, 2010–11.) New Haven and London, 2010.

Dubois et al. 1997
Dubois, H., et al. "A Late Fifteenth Century Italian *Tüchlein*." *Zeitschrift für Kunsttechnologie und Konserviering* 11/2 (1997): pp. 228–37.

Ducos 2006
Ducos, Blaise. *Rembrandt: Bethsabée tenant la lettre du roi David*. Paris, 2006.

Ducos 2011
Ducos, Blaise. *Frans Pourbus le jeune (1569–1622): Le portrait d'apparat à l'aube du Grand Siècle entré Habsbourg, Médicis et Bourbons*. Paris, 2011.

Dudok van Heel 1992
Dudok van Heel, S. A. C. "Enkele observaties bij het portret van een 83-jarige dame uit 1634 door Rembrandt." *Maandblad Amsteldamum* 79 (1992): pp. 6–15.

Dudok van Heel 1994
Dudok van Heel, S. A. C. "De remonstrantse wereld van Rembrandts opdrachtgever Abraham Anthoniszn Recht." *Bulletin van het Rijksmuseum* 42/4 (1994): pp. 34–46.

Dudok van Heel 2006
Dudok van Heel, S. A. C. "De jonge Rembrandt onder tijdgenoten: Godsdienst en schilderkunst en Leiden." PhD diss., University of Nijmegen, 2006.

Dudok van Heel 2008
Dudok van Heel, S. A. C. *Van Amsterdamse burgers tot Europese aristocraten hun geschiedenis en hun portretten: De Heijnen-maagschap 1400–1800*. 2 vols. The Hague, 2008.

Dudok van Heel 2011
Dudok van Heel, S. A. C. "De schilders Jacob Cornelisz alias Jacob War en Cornelis Buys uit Oostzaan." *De Nederlandsche Leeuw* 128 (2011): pp. 49–79.

Dudok van Heel 2020a
Dudok van Heel, S. A. C. "Rembrandt als portretschilder bij Hendrick Uylenburgh, 1631–1635, met opdrachten in Den Haag, Leiden en Rotterdam." *Amstelodamum* 107/2 (April–June 2020): pp. 54–91.

Dudok van Heel 2020b
Dudok van Heel, S. A. C. "Rembrandt's Surprising Start as a Portrait Painter: Hendrick Uylenburgh's Role in the Production of Portraits in Amsterdam." In *Rembrandt and Amsterdam Portraiture, 1590–1670*, pp. 129–51. Edited by Norbert Middelkoop. (Exh. cat. Museo Nacional Thyssen-Bornemisza, Madrid, 2020.) Madrid, 2020.

Dülberg 1930
Dülberg, Franz. *Frans Hals: Sein Leben und sein Werk*. Stuttgart, 1930.

Dunkerton 1999
Dunkerton, Jill. "North and South: Painting Techniques in Renaissance Venice." In Venice 1999–2000, pp. 92–103.

Dunkerton et al. 1991
Dunkerton, Jill, et al. *Giotto to Dürer: Early Renaissance Painting in the National Gallery*. New Haven and London, 1991.

Durantini 1983
Durantini, Mary Frances. *The Child in Seventeenth-Century Dutch Painting*. Studies in the Fine Arts. Iconography 7. Ann Arbor, 1983.

Duret-Robert 1986
Duret-Robert, François. "Le faux du siècle?" *Connaissance des arts* 412 (January 1986): pp. 86–91.

Düsseldorf 1904
Firmenich-Richartz, Eduard, and Paul Hartmann. *Kunsthistorische Ausstellung*. (Exh. cat., Düsseldorf, 1904.) Introduction by Paul Clemen. Düsseldorf, 1904.

Dutuit 1885
Dutuit, Eugène. *Tableaux et dessins de Rembrandt; catalogue historique et descriptif. . . .* Paris, 1885. [Supplement to *L'oeuvre complet de Rembrandt*. 2 vols. Paris, 1883–84].

Duverger 1984–2009
Duverger, Erik. *Antwerpse kunstinventarissen uit de zeventiende eeuw*. Fontes historiae artis Neerlandicae. 14 vols. Brussels, 1984–2009.

D. W. S. 1981
D. W. S. [David Steadman]. "Hals, Manet, Rubens on Loan." *Chrysler Museum* 11/1 (January 1981): n.pag.

Dyballa 2015
Dyballa, Katrin. *Georg Pencz*. Berlin, 2015.

Eastlake 1858–60
Eastlake, Charles. Manuscript Notebooks. National Gallery of Art Library, London, 1858–60. Published in Avery-Quash 2011.

Ebert 2011
Ebert, Anja. "Adriaen van Ostade und die komische Malerei der 17. Jahrhunderts." PhD diss., Universität Dortmond, 2011.

Edinburgh 1950
An Exhibition of Paintings by Rembrandt: Arranged by the Arts Council of Great Britain for the Edinburgh Festival Society. (Exh. cat. National Gallery of Scotland, Edinburgh, 1950.) Introduction by Ellis Waterhouse. Edinburgh, 1950.

"Editorial: Art Treasures" 1981
"Editorial: Art Treasures on the Move." *Apollo* 114/235 (September 1981): pp. 144–47.

Edwards 1982
Edwards, JoLynn. "Alexandre Joseph Paillet (1743–1814): Study of a Parisian Art Dealer." PhD diss., University of Washington, 1982.

Edwards 1996
Edwards, JoLynn. *Alexandre Joseph Paillet, expert et marchand de tableaux à la fin du XVIIIe siècle*. Paris, 1996.

Eeckhout 1992–93
Eeckhout, P. "De Justus de Gand à Hugo van der Goes ou le mythe de Joos van Wassenhove." *Bulletin des Musées Royaux de Beaux-Arts de Belgique* 41–42/1–4 (1992–93): pp. 9–33.

Chr. P. van Eeghen 1946
Eeghen, Chr. P. van. "Dirk Valkenburg–boekhouder–schrijver–kunstschilder voor Jonas Witsen." *Oud Holland* 61 (1946): pp. 58–69.

I. H. van Eeghen 1952
Eeghen, Isabella H. van. "Aantekeningen uit het Archief van het Burgerweeshuis te Amsterdam II." *Oud Holland* 67 (1952): p. 124.

I. H. van Eeghen 1966
Eeghen, Isabella H. van. "De vier huizen van Cromhout." *Maandblad Amstelodamum* 53 (1966): pp. 53–59.

I. H. van Eeghen 1973
Eeghen, Isabella H. van. "Archivallia betreffende Jan van der Heyden." *Maandblad Amstelodamum* 60 (1973): pp. 29–36, 54–61, 73–79, 99–106, 128–34.

I. H. van Eeghen et al. 1976
Eeghen, Isabella H. van, et al. *Vier eeuwen Herengracht: Geveltekeningen van alle huizen aan de gracht*. Amsterdam, 1976.

Egerton 1978
Egerton, Judy. *British Sporting and Animal Paintings, 1655–1867*. Sport in Art and Books. The Paul Mellon Collection. London, 1978.

Eisler 1988
Eisler, Colin. "What Takes Place in the Getty Annunciation?" *Gazette des beaux-arts* 130/3 (1988): pp. 193–202.

Ekkart 1979
Ekkart, Rudolf E. O. *Johannes Cornelisz. Verspronck: Leven en werken van een Haarlems Portretschilder uit de 17de eeuw*. Haarlem, 1979.

Ekkart 2011
Ekkart, Rudolf E. O. *Old Masters' Gallery Catalogues, Szépmüvészeti Múzeum Budapest*. Vol. 1, *Dutch and Flemish Portraits, 1600–1800*. Leiden and Budapest, 2011.

Ekkart and Van den Donk 2021
Ekkart, Rudolf E. O., and Claire van den Donk. "Rembrandt's Portrait Commissions outside Amsterdam." In *Rembrandt in Amsterdam: Creativity and Competition*, pp. 148f. (Exh. cat. National Gallery of Canada, Ottawa; Städel Museum, Frankfurt, 2021.) Edited by Stephanie S, Dickey and Jochen Sander. Ottawa and New Haven, 2021.

Ekkart et al. 1999–2004
Ekkart, Rudolf E. O., et al. *Herkomst Gezocht*. . . . 6 vols. The Hague, 1999–2004.

Ekserdjian 2007
Ekserdjian, David. *Alle origini della natura morta*. Milan, 2007.

Elias [1903–05] 1963
Elias, Johan E. *De vroedschap van Amsterdam, 1578–1795*. 2 vols. Amsterdam, 1963. [Repr. of 1903–05 ed.]

Erasmus 1992
Erasmus of Rotterdam. *Patristic Scholarship: The Edition of St. Jerome*. Collected Works of Erasmus 61. Edited, translated, and annotated by James F. Brady and John C. Olin. Toronto, 1992.

Errera 1920–21
Errera, Isabella. *Répertoire des peintures dates*. 2 vols. Brussels, 1920–21.

Ertz 1979
Ertz, Klaus. *Jan Brueghel der Ältere (1568–1625): Die Gemälde mit kritischem Oeuvrekatalog*. Cologne, 1979.

Ertz 1984
Ertz, Klaus. *Jan Brueghel der Jüngere (1601–1678): Die Gemälde mit kritischem Oeuvrekatalog. Flämische Maler im Umkreis der grossen Meister 1*. Freren, 1984.

Ertz 1997
Ertz, Klaus, and Christa Nitze-Ertz. *Pieter Brueghel, der Jüngere—Jan Brueghel der Ältere. Flämische Malerei um 1600. Tradition und Fortschritt*. Vienna, 1997.

Ertz and Nitze-Ertz 2012
Ertz, Klaus, and Christa Nitze-Ertz. *Die Maler Jan Van Kessel, Kritische Kataloge der Gemälde*. Lingen, 2012.

Evelyn 1906
Evelyn, John. *The Diary of John Evelyn*. 3 vols. Introduction and notes by Austin Dobson. London, 1906.

Evers 1942
Evers, Hans Gerhard. *Peter Paul Rubens*. Munich, 1942.

Fahy 1969
Fahy, Everett. "A Madonna by Gerard David." *Apollo* 90 (September 1969): pp. 190–95.

Fahy 1998–99
Fahy, Everett. "How the Pictures Got Here." In New York 1998–99, pp. 63–75.

Failing 1983
Failing, Patricia. *Best-loved Art from American Museums*. New York, 1983.

Fajt, Franzen, and Knüvener 2011
Fajt, J., W. Franzen, and P. Knüvener. *Die Altmark von 1300 bis 1600. Eine Kulturregion im Spannungsfeld von Magdeburg, Lübeck und Berlin*. Berlin, 2011.

Faré 1974
Faré, Michel. *Le grand siècle de la nature morte en France*. Fribourg and Paris, 1974.

Faries 1993
Faries, Molly. "Master and Pupil: A North Netherlandish Example." In *Colloque 9* 1993, pp. 102f.

Farington [1793–1821] 1978–84
Farington, Joseph. *The Diary of Joseph Farington*. 16 vols. Studies in British Art. Edited by Kenneth Garlick and Angus Macintyre. New Haven, 1978–84. [Repr. of 1793–1821 ed.]

Feßel 2016
Feßel, Sonja. "Fotografie zwischen Kunstmarkt und Wissenschaft. Zum Glasplattenbestand der Kunsthandlung Fritz Gurlitt, Berlin, im Deutschen Dokumentationszentrum für Kunstgeschichte—Bildarchiv Foto Marburg." *Rundbrief Fotografie* 23/3 (2016): pp. 8–22.

Fiebig 2020
Fiebig, Nils. *Alois Miedl: Der Bankier Und Die Raubkunst: Geschäfte Im Schatten Der Macht*. Würzburg, 2020.

Field 1815
Field, William. *An Historical and Descriptive Account of the Town and Castle of Warwick; and of the Neighbouring Spa of Leamington. . . .* Warwick, 1815.

Filedt Kok 1999
Filedt Kok, Jan Piet. "The Workshop Practice of Cornelis Engebrechtsz. Some Preliminary Remarks." In *La peinture dans les pays-bas au 16e siècle: Pratiques d'atelier: infrarouges et autres methods d'investigation. Colloque 12, 1997, Bruges: Dessin sous-jacent et de la technologie dans la peinture*, pp. 19–28. Edited by Hélène Verougstraete-Marcq and Roger van Schoute. Leuven, 1999.

Filedt Kok 2008
Filedt Kok, Jan Piet. "Master of Alkmaar." In *Vroege Hollanders. Schilderkunst van de late Middeleeuwen*, pp. 150–56. Friso Lammertse and Jeroen Giltaij, eds. (Exh. cat. Museum Boijmans Van Beuningen, Rotterdam, 2008.) Rotterdam, 2008.

Filedt Kok et al. 2014
Filedt Kok, Jan Piet, et al. *Cornelis Engelbrechtsz., A Sixteenth-Century Leiden Artist and His Workshop*. Edited by Yvette Bruijnen. Turnhout, 2014.

Filipczak 1995
Filipczak, Zirka Zaremba. "A New Studio Practice of Claesz. and Heda: Composing with Real Objects." In *Shop Talk: Studies in Honor of Seymour Slive, Presented on His Seventy-Fifth Birthday*, pp. 71–73. Edited by Cynthia P. Schneider, William W. Robinson, and Alice I. Davies. Cambridge, 1995.

Fischel 1935
Fischel, Oskar. "Art and Theater." *Burlington Magazine* 66 (1935): pp. 4–14, 54–67.

Fishman 1982
Fishman, Jane Susannah. *Boerenverdriet—Violence between Peasants and Soldiers in Early Modern Netherlands Art*. Ann Arbor, 1982.

Florence 1983
Chiarini, Marco, and Claudio Pizzorusso. *Sustermans: Sessant'anni alla corte dei Medici*. (Exh. cat. Palazzo Pitti, Florence, July–October 1983.) Florence, 1983.

Foister 1983
Foister, Susan. *Drawings by Holbein from the Royal Library, Windsor Castle*. London, 1983.

Foister 1993
Foister, Susan. "Workshop or Followers? Underdrawing in Some Portraits Associated with Hans Holbein the Younger." In *Colloque 9* 1993: pp. 113–24, pls. 43–46.

Foister 2015
Foister, Susan. "Lucas Cranach the Elder, Portrait of a Woman." National Gallery (London) website. 2015. www.nationalgallery.org.uk/paintings/research/lucas-cranach-the-elder-portrait-of-a-woman.

Förster 1931
Förster, Otto H. *Kölner Kunstsammler vom Mittelalter bis zum Ende des Bürgerlichen Zeitalters*. Berlin, 1931.

Fowkes 1978
Fowkes, Charles. *The Life of Rembrandt*. London, 1978.

Fowles 1976
Fowles, Edward. *Memories of Duveen Brothers*. London, 1976.

Francini, Heuss, and Kreis 2001
Francini, Esther Tisa, Anja Heuss, and Georg Kreis. *Fluchtgut-Raubgut: Der Transfer von Kulturgütern in und über die Schweiz 1933–1945 und die Frage der Restitution*. Veröffentlichungen der UEK/Publications de la CIE 1. Zurich, 2001.

Franits 1993
Franits, Wayne E. *Paragons of Virtue: Women and Domesticity in Seventeenth-Century Dutch Art*. New York, 1993.

Franits 1995
Franits, Wayne. "Young Women Prefered White to Brown: Some Remarks on Nicolaes Maes and the Cultural Context of Late Seventeenth-Century Dutch Portraiture." *Nederlands kunsthistorisch jaarboek* 46 (1995): pp. 395–415.

Franits 2010
Franits, Wayne. "Gabriel Metsu and the Art of Luxury." In Dublin/Amsterdam/Washington 2010–11, pp. 53–71.

Frankau 1904
Frankau, Julia. *William Ward A.R.A., James Ward R.A.: Their Lives and Works*. Eighteenth Century Artists and Engravers. London, 1904.

Franken 2005
Franken, Michiel. "'Pour mon honneur et pour vostre contentement': Nicolas Poussin, Paul Fréart de Chantelou and the Making and Collecting of Copies." In *The Learned Eye, Regarding Art, Theory, and the Artist's Reputation: Essays for Ernst van de Wetering*, pp. 180–89. Edited by Marieke van den Doel et al. Amsterdam, 2005.

Franken and Van der Kellen 1883
Franken, D., and J. Ph. van der Kellen. *L'oeuvre de Jan van de Velde*. Amsterdam, 1883.

Frankfurter 1932
Frankfurter, Alfred M. "Paintings by Hans Memling in American Collections." *Fine Arts* (March 1932): p. 22.

Frankfurter 1939
Frankfurter, Alfred M. "The Classic Nude: 1460–1905, from Pollaiuolo to Picasso in a Magnificent Anthology." *Art News* 37/29 (15 April 1939): pp. 9–11, 21.

Frankfurter 1946
Frankfurter, Alfred M. "International Portraits of Baroque Royalty." *Art News* 45 (March 1946): pp. 32–35, 64.

Fredericksen 1988
Fredericksen, Burton. *Masterpieces of Painting in the J. Paul Getty Museum*. Malibu, 1988.

Fredericksen and Jaffé 1997
Fredericksen, Burton, and David Jaffé. *Masterpieces of the J. Paul Getty Museum: Paintings*. Malibu, 1997.

Freedberg 1984
Freedberg, David. *The Life of Christ after the Passion*. Corpus Rubenianum Ludwig Burchard 7. London, 1984.

Fried 2010
Fried, Michael. *The Moment of Caravaggio*. Princeton, 2010.

M. Friedländer 1915
Friedländer, Max J. "Der Meister der Mansi-Magdalena." *Jahrbuch der königlich preussischen Kunstsammlungen* 36 (1915): pp. 6–12.

M. Friedländer 1924–37
Friedländer, Max J. *Die altniederländische Malerei*. 14 vols. Berlin, 1924–37; vols. 12–14 published in Leiden.

M. Friedländer 1927
Friedländer, Max J. "Zur Londoner Leihausstellung Belgischer Kunst." *Der Cicerone* 19 (April 1927): pp. 207–16.

M. Friedländer 1928
Friedländer, Max J. "Adriaen Ysenbrant als Porträtmaler." *Pantheon* 1 (January 1928): pp. 2–7.

M. Friedländer 1967–76
Friedländer, Max J. *Early Netherlandish Painting*. Leiden, 1967–76. [English ed. of M. Friedländer 1924–37; vol. 14 includes supplement bound separately.]

M. Friedländer and Rosenberg 1932
Friedländer, Max. J., and Jakob Rosenberg. *Die Gemälde von Lucas Cranach*. Berlin, 1932.

M. Friedländer and Rosenberg 1978
Friedländer, Max. J., and Jakob Rosenberg. *The Paintings of Lucas Cranach*. Translated by Heinz Norden. Introduction translated by Ronald Taylor. Ithaca, 1978.

W. Friedländer 1955
Friedländer, Walter. *Caravaggio Studies*. New York, 1955.

Friedmann 1980
Friedmann, Herbert. *A Bestiary for Saint Jerome*. Washington, DC, 1980.

Frimmel 1890
Frimmel, Theodor von. "Kunstgeschichtliches." *Kunstchronik* 1/32 (August 1890): p. 542.

Frimmel 1913–14
Frimmel, Theodor von. *Lexikon der Wiener Gemäldesammlungen*. 2 vols. Munich, 1913–14.

Fritz 1967
Fritz, Rolf, ed. *Sammlung Becker: 1: Gemälde alter Meister*. Dortmund, 1967.

Frost 1865
Frost, William. *Catalogue of the Paintings in the Collection of Hugh Andrew Johnstone Munro, Esq., of Novar*. London, 1865.

Fučíková et al. 1991
Fučíková, Eliška, et al. *Die Kunst am Hofe Rudolfs II*. 2nd ed. Prague, 1991.

Fučíková et al. 1997
Fučíková, Eliška, et al., eds. *Rudolf II and Prague: The Court and the City*. Prague, London, and New York, 1997.

Gaillard 1863
Gaillard, J. *Maison de Zuylen, histoire et généolographie*. Bruges, 1863.

Galen 2012
Galen, Maria. *Johann Boeckhorst: Gemälde und Zeichnungen*. Hamburg, 2012.

Gamber 1958
Gamber, Ortwin. "Der Italienische Harniesch im 16. Jahrhundert." *Jahrbuch der kunsthistorischen Sammlungen in Wien* 54/N.F. 18 (1958): pp. 104–20.

Gans and Duyvené de Wit-Klinkhamer 1961
Gans, M. H., and Th. M. Duyvené de Wit-Klinkhamer. *Dutch Silver*. Translated by Oliver van Oss. London, 1961.

Ganz 1950
Ganz, Paul. *Hans Holbein der Jüngere: Die Gemälde, eine Gesamtausgabe*. Basel, 1950.

Ganz 1956
Ganz, Paul. *The Paintings of Hans Holbein, First Complete Edition*. Translated by Marguerite Kay. Introduction translated by R. H. Boothroyd. London, 1956.

Garas 1967
Garas, Klara. "Die Entstehung der Galerie des Erzherzogs Leopold Wihelm." *Jahrbuch der kunsthistorischen Sammlungen in Wien* 63 (1967): pp. 39–80.

Garas 1968
Garas, Klara. "Das Schicksal der Sammlung des Erzherzogs Leopold Wilhelm." *Jahrbuch der kunsthistorischen Sammlungen in Wien* 64 (1968): pp. 181–285.

Garff 1971
Garff, Jan. *Den Kongelige Kobberstiksamling: Tegninger af Maerten van Heemskerck*. Copenhagen, 1971.

Gaskell 1987
Gaskell, Ivan. "Tobacco, Social Deviance, and Dutch Art in the Seventeenth Century." In Bock and Gaehtgens 1987, pp. 117–37.

Gaskell 1990
Gaskell, Ivan. *Seventeenth-Century Dutch and Flemish Painting: The Thyssen-Bornemisza Collection*. London, 1990.

Gee 2007
Gee, Malcolm. "Noailles, de." *Grove Art Online*. Accessed 12 September, 2007. http://www.groveart.com.

H. E. van Gelder 1942
Gelder, H. E. van. *Rembrandt en zijn tijd*. Amsterdam, 1942.

H. E. van Gelder [1948]
Gelder, H. E. van. *Rembrandt en zijn portret*. Palet serie. Amsterdam, [1948].

J. G. van Gelder 1926
Gelder, J. G. van. "Een vroeg werk van Jan Steen." *Oud Holland* 43 (1926): pp. 202–10.

J. G. van Gelder 1933
Gelder, J. G. van. *Jan van de Velde, 1593–1641, Teekenaar-Schilder*. The Hague, 1933.

J. G. van Gelder 1949
Gelder, J. G. van. "The Gerard David Exhibition at Bruges." *Burlington Magazine* 91 (September 1949): pp. 253f.

J. G. van Gelder 1950
Gelder, J. G. van. "The Rembrandt Exhibition at Edinburgh." *Burlington Magazine* 92 (November 1950): pp. 327–29.

J. G. van Gelder 1977
Gelder, J. G. van. "Tekeningen van Aelbert Cuyp." In Dordrecht 1977, pp. 112–77.

Génard [1865–66]
Génard, P. "De nalatenschap van P. P. Rubens." *Antwerpsch Archievenblad* 2, n.d. [1865–66], pp. 69ff.

Geneva 1974
Loche, Renée. *De Genève à l'Ermitage: Les collections de François Tronchin*. (Exh. cat. Musée Rath, Geneva, with collaboration of the Hermitage Museum, Geneva, 1974.) Geneva, 1974.

Van Gent 2012
Gent, Judith van. *Bartholomeus van der Helst (ca. 1613–1670): Een studie naar zijn leven en werk*. Zwolle, 2012.

***Gentleman's Magazine* 1798**
Gentleman's Magazine: and Historical Chronicle 48 (October 1798): 836.

Gerson 1968
Gerson, Horst. *Rembrandt Paintings*. Amsterdam, London, New York, 1968.

Gerson 1973a
Gerson, Horst. "Symposium: Rembrandt's Workshop and Assistants." In *Rembrandt after Three Hundred Years: A Symposium; Rembrandt and His Followers*, pp. 19–31. Edited by Deirdre C. Stam. Chicago, 1973.

Gerson 1973b
Gerson, Horst. "Zur Nachwirkung von Rembrandts Kunst." In Simson and Kelch 1973, pp. 207–17.

Gerson 1976
Gerson, Horst. "Dutch and Flemish Painting [in the Norton Simon Museum of Art at Pasadena]." *Connoisseur* 193/777 (November 1976): pp. 163–71.

Gerszi et al. 2019
Gerszi, Teréz, et al. *Jan Brueghel: A Magnificent Draughtsman*. Translated by Steve Kane. Antwerp, 2019.

Getty 1985
J. Paul Getty Museum. "Recent Acquisitions: Paintings." *Calendar/The J. Paul Getty Museum* (April 1985): n.pag.

De Gheyn I [1607] 1971
Gheyn, Jacob de, I. *Wapenhandelinghe van roers, musquetten, en spiessen achtervolgende de' ordre van syn excellente Maurits Prince van Orangie, Graue van Nassou, etc. . . .* Lochem, 1971. [Repr. of 1607 ed.]

De Gheyn II 1619
Gheyn, Jacob de, II. *Wapenhandelinghe van roers, musquetten ende spiessen. Polyglot Maniement d'armes, d'arqvebvses, mousqvets, & picques: selon l'ordre de monseig. Le Prince Maurice.* . . . Zutphen, 1619.

Ghilarov 1929
Ghilarov, Sergei Alekseyevich. *A Recently Discovered Work by Cranach in Museum of Art.* Kiev, 1929. Written in Ukrainian with a French summary; English translation by Dr. Tatiana Mikheeva; NSM.

Gibson 1972–73
Gibson, Walter S. "Imitatio Christi: The Passion Scenes of Hieronymus Bosch." *Simiolus* 6/2 (1972–73): pp. 83–93.

Gibson 1977
Gibson, Walter S. *The Paintings of Cornelis Engebrechtsz.* Outstanding Dissertations in the Fine Arts. New York, 1977. [Originally PhD diss., Harvard University, 1969.]

Gibson 2000
Gibson, Walter S. *Pleasant Places: The Rustic Landscape from Brueghel to Ruisdael.* Berkeley, Los Angeles, and London, 2000.

Gifford 1983
Gifford, E. Melanie. "A Technical Investigation of Some Dutch Seventeenth-Century Tonal Landscapes." *AIC Preprints* 11 (1983): pp. 39–49.

Gifford 1995
Gifford, E. Melanie. "Style and Technique in Dutch Landscape Painting in the 1620s." In *Historical Painting Techniques, Materials, and Studio Practice*, pp. 140–47. Edited by Arie Wallert, Erma Hermens, and Marja Peek. Preprints of a Symposium, University of Leiden, 26–29 June 1995. Marina del Rey, 1995.

Gifford 1996
Gifford, E. Melanie. "Jan van Goyen en de techniek van het naturalistische landschap." In *Jan van Goyen*, pp. 70–79, 81. By Christiaan Vogelaar et al. (Exh. cat. Stedelijk Museum "De Lakenhal," Leiden, 1996.) Zwolle and Leiden, 1996.

Gifford 2010
Gifford, E. Melanie. "Fine Painting and Eloquent Impression: Gabriel Metsu's Painting Technique" In Dublin/Amsterdam/Washington 2010–11, pp. 155–79.

Gillet 1909
Gillet, Louis. "La Collection Maurice Kann." *Revue de l'art ancien et moderne* 26 (1909): pp. 361–74, 421–34.

Gilpin 1788
Gilpin, William. *Observations, Relative Chiefly to Picturesque Beauty Made in the Year 1772, on Several Parts of England; Particularly the Mountains and Lakes of Cumberland, and Westmoreland.* 2 vols. 2nd ed. London, 1788.

Van Gils 1942
Gils, J. B. F. van. "Jan Steen in de Schouwburg." *Oud Holland* 59 (1942): pp. 57–62.

Giltaij and Lammertse 2001
Giltaij, Jeroen, and Friso Lammertse. "Maintaining a Studio Archive. Drawn Copies by the De Braij Family." *Master Drawings* 39/4 (2001): pp. 367–94.

Ginzburg 2001
Ginzburg, Carlo. "'Your Country Needs You.' A Case Study in Political Iconography." In *History Workshop Journal* 52 (2001): pp. 1–22.

Ginzburg 2015
Ginzburg, Carlo. *Paura reverenza terrore.* Milan, 2015.

Glasgow 1884
Richter, Jean Paul. *Catalogue of the Collection of Paintings Lent for Exhibition by the Marquess of Bute.* (Exh. cat. Corporation Galleries, Glasgow, 1884.) Glasgow, 1884.

Glück 1900
Glück, Gustav. "Die Gemäldesammlung des Herrn Rudolf Kann in Paris." *Die Graphischen Künste* 23 (1900): pp. 85–94.

Glück 1930
Glück, Gustav. "Drei Jahrhunderte Vlämischer Kunst: Ausstellung in der Wiener 'Secession.'" *Belvedere* 9/5 (1930): pp. 167–74.

Glück 1935
Glück, Gustav. "Peter Paul Rubens." In Thieme-Becker 1907–50, vol. 29 (1935): pp. 137–46.

Glück 1940
Glück, Gustav. "Rubens as Portrait Painter." *Burlington Magazine* 76/447 (June 1940): pp. 173–83.

Gmelin 1961
Gmelin, Hans Georg. "Georg Pencz Als Maler." PhD diss., Freiburg im Breisgau, 1961.

Gmelin 1966
Gmelin, Hans Georg. "Georg Pencz als Maler." *Münchner Jahrbuch der bildenden Kunst*, 3rd ser., 17 (1966): pp. 49–126.

Gmelin 1968
Gmelin, Hans Georg. "Georg Pencz." In *Fränkische Lebensbilder. Veröffentlichungen Der Gesellschaft für Fränkische Geschichte Reihe VII A. Fränkische Lebensbilder. Neue Folge der Lebensläufe aus Franken, 2. Band.* Würzburg, 1968.

Goede 1804–06
Goede, Christian August Gottlieb. *England, Wales, Irland und Schottland: Erinnerungen an Natur und Kunst aus einer Reise in den Jahren 1802 und 1803.* 5 vols. Dresden, 1804–06.

Goffen 1997
Goffen, Rona. *Titian's "Venus of Urbino."* Cambridge and New York, 1997.

Goldenberg Stoppato 2003
Goldenberg Stoppato, Lisa. "Suttermans, Painter and Courtier of the Medici." In *Italian History and Culture* (Villa Le Balze, Florence, Georgetown University) 9 (2003): pp. 31–42.

Goldenberg Stoppato 2006
Goldenberg Stoppato, Lisa. *The Grand Duke's Portraitist: Cosimo III de' Medici and His "Chamber of Paintings" by Giusto Suttermans.* Livorno, 2006.

Goldgar 2007
Goldgar, Anne. *Tulipmania: Money, Honor, and Knowledge in the Dutch Golden Age.* Chicago, 2007.

Goldner 1988
Goldner, George. *European Drawings 1: Catalogue of the Collections, J. Paul Getty Museum.* Malibu, 1988.

Van Gouthoeven 1636
Gouthoeven, Wouter van. *D'oude chronijcke ende historien van Holland (met West-Vriesland), van Zeeland ende van Utrecht.* The Hague, 1636.

Gozzano 2015
Gozzano, Natalia. *Lo "specchio della corte," Il maestro di casa.* Rome, 2015.

Graevenitz 1972
Graevenitz, Antje von. "Was wird die Delfter Antiekbeurs bringen?" *Die Weltkunst* 42/17 (September 1972): pp. 1184–87.

Grant 1956
Grant, M. H. *Rachel Ruysch 1664–1750.* Leigh-on-Sea, 1956.

Graves [1913–15] 1970
Graves, Algernon. *A Century of Loan Exhibitions, 1813–1912.* 5 vols. in 3. Bath, 1970. [1st ed. London, 1913–15.]

Greenwich/Amsterdam 2006–07
Sutton, Peter C., et al. *Jan van der Heyden.* (Exh. cat. Bruce Museum, Greenwich; Rijksmuseum, Amsterdam, 2006–07.) Greenwich, 2006.

Greenwich/New York 2008–09
Sutton, Peter C., et al. *Reclaimed: Paintings from the Collection of Jacques Goudstikker.* (Exh. cat. Bruce Museum, Greenwich; The Jewish Museum, New York, 2008–09.) New Haven and London, 2008.

Greindl 1944
Greindl, Edith. *Corneille de Vos, portraitiste flamand (1584–1651).* Brussels, 1944.

Greindl 1956
Greindl, Edith. *Les peintres flamands de nature morte au XVIIe siècle.* Brussels, 1956.

Greindl 1983
Greindl, Edith. *Les peintres flamands de nature morte au XVIIe siècle.* 2nd rev. ed. Sterrebeek, 1983.

Greville 1938
Greville, Elfrida Marjorie. *Warwick Castle: A Brief Account of the Earls of Warwick, Together with a Description of the Castle and Some of the More Notable Works of Art Therein (1930–1931)*. Sevenoaks, 1938.

Grimm 1972
Grimm, Claus. *Frans Hals: Entwicklung, Werkanalyse, Gesamtkatalog*. Berlin, 1972.

Grimm 1991
Grimm, Claus. *Rembrandt Selbst: Eine Neubewertung seiner Porträtkunst*. Stuttgart and Zurich, 1991.

Grimm 2023–24
Grimm, Claus. *Frans Hals and His Workshop*, A4.3.40. The Hague, 2023–24. Accessed July 29, 2024. https://frans-hals-and-his-workshop.rkdstudies.nl/a4-paintings-created-frans-halss-workshop/a43-portraits/a4325-a4340/.

Grimm and Montagni 1974
Grimm, Claus, with E. C. Montagni. *L'opera completa di Frans Hals*. Classici dell'arte 76. Milan, 1974.

Groen and Murray 1991
Groen, Karin, and Sarah Murray. "Underdrawing in Four Early Seventeenth Century Flower Paintings." In *Colloque 8* 1991: pp. 151–54, pls. 82–84.

Groeneweg 1995
Groeneweg, Irene. "Regenten in het swart: vroom en deftig?" *Nederlands kunsthistorisch jaarboek* 46 (1995): pp. 199–251.

De Groot 1952
Groot, C. W. de. *Jan Steen: Beeld en woord*. Utrecht and Nijmegen, 1952.

Grosshans 1980
Grosshans, Rainald. *Maerten van Heemskerck, die Gemälde*. Berlin, 1980.

Grossmann 1957
Grossmann, F. "Flemish Paintings at Bruges." *Burlington Magazine* 99 (1957): pp. 3–9.

Gruber 1983
Gruber, Alain. "Un autoportrait caché dans la peinture du XVIIe siècle." In *Von Angesicht zu Angesicht: Porträtstudien: Michael Stettler zum 70. Geburtstag*, pp. 212–15. Edited by Florens Deuchler, Mechthild Flury-Lemberg, and Karel Otavsky. Bern, 1983.

De Grummond 1982
Grummond, Nancy de. "The Study of Classical Costume by Philip, Albert, and Peter Paul Rubens." *Ringling Museum of Art Journal* (1982): pp. 78–90.

Gudlaugsson 1938
Gudlaugsson, Sturla J. *Ikonographische Studien über die holländische Malerei und das Theater des 17 Jahrhunderts*. Würzburg, 1938.

Gudlaugsson 1947
Gudlaugsson, Sturla J. "Bredero's Lucelle door eenige zeventiende eeuwshe meesters uitgebeeld." *Nederlands kunsthistorisch jaarboek* 1 (1947): pp. 177–94.

Gudlaugsson 1959–60
Gudlaugsson, Sturla J. *Geraert Ter Borch*. 2 vols. The Hague, 1959–60.

Gudlaugsson 1968
Gudlaugsson, Sturla J. "Kanttekeningen bij de ontwikkeling van Metsu." *Oud Holland* 83 (1968): pp. 13–43.

Gudlaugsson 1975
Gudlaugsson, Sturla J. *The Comedians in the Work of Jan Steen and His Contemporaries*. Translated by James Brockway. Introduction translated by Patricia Wardle. Soest, 1975. [Originally published as *Komedianten bij Jan Steen en zijn tijdgenooten* (The Hague, 1945).]

Guicciardini [1567] 1612
Guicciardini, Lodovico. *Beschrijvinghe van alle de Nederlanden*. Translated by Cornelis Kiel and Petrus Montanus. Amsterdam, 1612. [Originally published as *Descrittione di tutti I Paesi Bassi* (Antwerp, 1567).]

Guillaud and Guillaud 1986
Guillaud, Jacqueline, and Maurice Guillaud. *Rembrandt: The Human Form and Spirit*. Paris, 1986.

Gutmann 1980
Gutmann, Myron P. *War and Rural Life in the Early Modern Low Countries*. Princeton, 1980.

H. 1936
H. "Tentoonstellingen: Amsterdam . . . Saloman van Ruysdael bij Goudstikker." *Maandblad voor beeldende kunsten* 13/2 (1936): pp. 55–59.

Haak 1984
Haak, Bob. *The Golden Age: Dutch Painters of the Seventeenth Century*. Translated and edited by Elizabeth Willems-Treeman. New York, 1984.

Haarlem 1934
Tentoonstelling van schilderijen van oudhollandsche meesters uit de collectie Katz te Dieren. (Exh. cat. Frans Hals Museum, Haarlem, 1934.) Haarlem, 1934.

Haarlem 1946
Haarlemsche meesters uit de eeuw van Frans Hals. Tentoonstelling ter gelegenheid van de viering van het 700-jarig bestaan van Haarlem als stad. (Exh. cat. Frans Hals Museum, Haarlem, 1946.) Haarlem, 1946.

Haarlem 1974
Tulpomania: Tentoonstelling Rondom Het Tulpenboek Van Judith Leyster. (Exh. cat. Frans Hals Museum, Haarlem, 1974.) Haarlem, 1974.

Haarlem 1986a
Jongh, Eddy de. *Portretten van echt en trouw: Huwelijk en gezin in de Nederlandse kunst van de zeventiende eeuw*. (Exh. cat. Frans Hals Museum, Haarlem, 1986.) Zwolle and Haarlem, 1986.

Haarlem 1986b
Veldman, Ilja M. *Leerrijke reeksen van Maarten van Heemskerck*. (Exh. cat. Frans Hals Museum, Haarlem, 1986.) Haarlem, 1986.

Haarlem/Worcester 1993
Welu, James A., and Pieter Biesboer, eds. *Judith Leyster: A Dutch Master and Her World*. (Exh. cat. Frans Hals Museum, Haarlem; Worcester Art Museum, 1993.) Zwolle and Worcester, 1993.

Haarlem/Zurich/Schwerin 2006
Biesboer, Pieter, et al. *Nicolaes Berchem: In the Light of Italy*. (Exh. cat. Frans Hals Museum, Haarlem; Kunsthaus Zürich; Staatliches Museum, Schwerin, 2006.) Haarlem and Ghent, 2006.

Hadeln 1923
Hadeln, Detlev von. "La nuda von Bernardino Licinio." *Belvedere* 3 (1923): p. 6.

Van Haeften 2003
Van Haeften, Johnny. *Dutch and Flemish Old Master Paintings*. London, 2003.

The Hague 1899–1900
Catalogus van schilderijen van Oud Hollandsche meesters: Collectie C. Hoogendijk. (Exh. cat. Pulchri Studio, The Hague, 1899–1900.) The Hague 1899–1900.

The Hague 1922a
Tentoonstelling collectie Goudstikker in "Pulchri Studio," 's Gravenhage. (Exh. cat. Pulchri Studio, The Hague, 1922.) The Hague, 1922.

The Hague 1922b
Hermsen, Theodorus. *Huys van Johan de Witt, collectie Dorus Hermsen: Voortdurende tentoonstelling van schilderijen der oude Hollandsche school*. (Exh. cat. Huys van Johan de Witt, The Hague, 1922.) The Hague, [1922].

The Hague 1926
Nederlandsche stillevens uit vijf eeuwen. (Exh. cat. Gemeentemuseum voor Moderne Kunst, The Hague, 27 February–31 March 1926.) The Hague, 1926.

The Hague 1928–29
Tentoonstelling van schilderijen door oud-Hollandsche en Vlaamsche meesters. (Exh. cat. Koninklijke Kunstzaal Kleykamp, The Hague, 1928–29.) The Hague, 1928.

The Hague 1997a
Keblusek, Marika, and Jori Zijlmans. *Princely Display: The Court of Frederik Hendrik of Orange and Amalia van Solms*. (Exh. cat. Haags Historisch Museum, The Hague, 1997.) Zwolle and The Hague, 1997.

The Hague 1997b
Ploeg, Pieter van der, and Carola Vermeeren, with Ben Broos et al. *Princely Patrons: The Collection of Frederick Henry of Orange and Amalia of Solms in The Hague*. (Exh. cat. Mauritshuis, The Hague, 1997.) The Hague and Zwolle, 1997.

The Hague 2001–02
Suchtelen, Ariane van, et al. *Holland Frozen in Time, The Dutch Winter Landscape in the Golden Age*. (Exh. cat. Mauritshuis, The Hague, 2001–02.) The Hague and Zwolle, 2001.

The Hague 2018
Suchtelen, Ariane van, et al. *Jan Steen's Histories*. (Exh. cat. Mauritshuis, The Hague, 2018.) The Hague and Zwolle, 2018.

The Hague/Cambridge 1981–82
Slive, Seymour, and Hans R. Hoetink. *Jacob van Ruisdael*. (Exh. cat. Mauritshuis, The Hague; Fogg Art Museum, Harvard University, Cambridge, 1981–82.) New York, 1981.

The Hague/London 1999
White, Christopher, and Quentin Buvelot, eds. *Rembrandt by Himself*. (Exh. cat. Mauritshuis, The Hague; National Gallery, London, 1999.) The Hague and London, 1999.

The Hague/London 2007–08
Ekkart, Rudi, et al. *Dutch Portraits: The Age of Rembrandt and Frans Hals*. Edited by Quentin Buvelot. Translated by Beverly Jackson. (Exh. cat. Mauritshuis, The Hague; National Gallery, London, 2007–08.) Zwolle, 2007.

The Hague/London 2019–20
Suchtelen, Ariane van, Bart Cornelis, Marijn Schapelhouman, and Nina Cahill. *Nicolaes Maes: Dutch Master of the Golden Age*. (Exh. cat. Mauritshuis, The Hague, 17 October 2019–19 January 2020; National Gallery, London, 22 February–31 May 2020.) Zwolle and London, 2019.

The Hague/San Francisco 1990
Broos, Ben, et al. *Great Dutch Paintings from America*. (Exh. cat. Mauritshuis, The Hague; Fine Arts Museums of San Francisco, 1990.) The Hague and Zwolle, 1990.

Hahn-Woernle 1996
Hahn-Woernle, Birgit. *Sebastian Stoskopff: Mit einem kritischen Werkverzeichnis der Gemälde*. Stuttgart, 1996.

Hairs 1955
Hairs, Marie-Louise. *Les peintres flamands de fleurs au XVIIe siècle*. Paris and Brussels, 1955.

Hairs 1965
Hairs, Marie-Louise. *Les peintres flamands de fleurs au XVIIe siècle*. 2nd rev. ed. Brussels, 1965.

Hairs 1985
Hairs, Marie-Louise, with Dominique Finet. *The Flemish Flower Painters in the XVIIth Century*. Translated by Eva Grzelak. Brussels, 1985.

Ardelia Hall Collection 1946–51
Ardelia Hall Collection. Records of U.S. Occupation Headquarters, World War II. Record Group 260. National Archives, Washington, DC. Microfilm copies at the National Gallery of Art, Washington, DC, and the GRI.

Van Hall 1963
Hall, H. van. *Portretten van Nederlandse beeldende kunstenaars*. Amsterdam, 1963.

Hamann 1936
Hamann, Richard. "Hagars Abschied bei Rembrandt und im Rembrandtkreis." *Marburger Jahrbuch für Kunstwissenschaft* 8/9 (1936): pp. 471–578a.

Hand 1980
Hand, John Oliver. "The Portrait of Sir Bryan Tuke by Hans Holbein the Younger." *Studies in the History of Art* 9 (1980): pp. 33–49.

Hand 1992
Hand, John Oliver. "*Salve sancta facies*: Some Thoughts on the Iconography of the *Head of Christ* by Petrus Christus." *Metropolitan Museum Journal* 27 (1992): pp. 7–18.

Hand 2004
Hand, John Oliver. *Joos van Cleve: The Complete Paintings*. New Haven, 2004.

Hanover/Raleigh/Atlanta 1991
Kenseth, Joy, ed. *The Age of the Marvelous*. (Exh. cat. Hood Museum of Art, Dartmouth College, Hanover; North Carolina Museum of Art, Raleigh; High Museum of Art, Atlanta, 1991.) Hanover, 1991.

Harbison 1995
Harbison, Craig. *The Mirror of the Artist: Northern Renaissance Art in Its Historical Context*. New York, 1995.

Harding and Harding 1891
Harding, George R., and H. W. Harding, eds. *Catalogue of the Furniture, Porcelain, Pictures, &c. at Camelford House, Park Lane, The Town Residence of Lord Hillingdon*. London, 1891.

Harrison 1987
Harrison, Jefferson C. "The Paintings of Maerten van Heemskerck: A Catalogue Raisonné." 4 vols. PhD diss., University of Virginia, Charlottesville, 1987.

Hart 1952
Hart, G.'t. "Nicolaas Witsen en ZijnVoorouders." *Oud Holland* 67 (1952): pp. 74–95.

Haskell 1976
Haskell, Francis. *Rediscoveries in Art: Some Aspects of Taste, Fashion, and Collecting in England and France*. London, 1976.

Haskell et al. 1994
Haskell, Francis, et al. *Anatole Demidoff, Prince of San Donato (1812–70)*. Collectors of the Wallace Collection 1. London, 1994.

Haug 1978
Haug, Hans. *L'orfèvrerie de Strasbourg dans les collections publique françaises*. Paris, 1978.

Haupt et al. 1990
Haupt, Herbert, et al. *Le bestiaire de Rodolphe II*. Translated by Léa Marcou. Paris, 1990.

Haverkamp-Begemann 1959
Haverkamp-Begemann, Egbert. *Willem Buytewech*. Amsterdam, 1959.

Haverkamp-Begemann 1969
Haverkamp-Begemann, Egbert. "Rembrandt und seine Schule." *Kunstchronik* 22/10 (October 1969): pp. 281–89, figs. 1–7.

Hazlitt 1900
Hazlitt, W. Carew. *The Venetian Republic: Its Rise, Its Growth, and Its Fall, 421–1797*. 2 vols. London, 1900.

Hearn 2002
Hearn, Karen. *Marcus Gheeraerts II: Elizabethan Artist in Focus*. London, 2002.

Hedinger 1986
Hedinger, Bärbel. *Karten in Bildern: Zur Ikonographie der Wandkarte in holländischen Interieurgemälden des siebzehnten Jahrhunderts*. Hildesheim and New York, 1986.

Hedinger 1987
Hedinger, Bärbel. "Karten in Bildern. Zur politischen Ikonographie der Wandkarte bei Willem Buytewech und Jan Vermeer." In Bock and Gaehtgens 1987, pp. 139–68.

Van Heemstra 2000
Heemstra, G. van. "Space, Light, and Stillness: A Description of Saenredam's Painting Technique." In *Pieter Saenredam, the Utrecht Work. Paintings and Drawings by the 17th-Century Master of Perspective*, pp. 73–90. Edited by L. M. Helmus. (Exh. cat. Centraal Museum, Utrecht, 2000.) Utrecht, 2000.

Heinemann 1958–64
Heinemann, Rudolf. *Sammlung Schloss Rohoncz*. Castagnola-Lugano, 1958; addendum 1964. [Nachtrag, 1959]

Heinemann 1969
Heinemann, Rudolf, ed. *The Thyssen-Bornemisza Collection*. 2 vols. Text by J. C. Ebbinge Wubben et al. Castagnola-Lugano, 1969.

Heinemann 1971
Heinemann, Rudolf, ed. *The Thyssen-Bornemisza Collection*. 2 vols. Text by J. C. Ebbinge Wubben et al. Castagnola-Lugano, 1971.

Heinemann and Feulner 1937–41
Heinemann, Rudolf, and Adolf Feulner, eds. *Stiftung Sammlung Schloss Rohoncz*. 3 vols. Castagnola-Lugano, 1937–41.

Held 1931
Held, Julius S. *Dürers Wirkung auf die Niederländische Kunst Seiner Zeit*. The Hague, 1931.

Held 1959
Held, Julius S. *Rubens, Selected Drawings*. 2 vols. London, 1959.

Held 1969
Held, Julius S. *Rembrandt's Aristotle and Other Rembrandt Studies*. Princeton, 1969.

Held 1972
Held, Julius S. "Rubens and the *Vita Beati P. Ignatii Loiolae* of 1609." In *Rubens Before 1620*, pp. 93–133. Edited by John Rupert Martin. Princeton, 1972.

Held 1980
Held, Julius S. *The Oil Sketches of Peter Paul Rubens*. 2 vols. Princeton, 1980.

Held 1986
Held, Julius S. *Rubens, Selected Drawings*. 2nd rev. ed. Mt. Kisco, 1986.

Held 1989
Held, Julius S. "*The Holy Women at Christ's Sepulchre* by Rubens." *Source: Notes in the History of Art* 8–9 (1989): pp. 66–76.

Held and Goris 1947
Held, Julius S., and Jan-Albert Goris. *Rubens in America*. New York, 1947.

Henderiks 2006
Henderiks, Valentine. "Le *Triptyque de l'Assomption de la Vierge* d'Albrecht Bouts: analyse critique." *Annales d'Histoire de l'Art et d'Archéologie de l'Université Libre de Bruxelles* 28 (2006): pp. 1–24.

Henderiks 2011
Henderiks, Valentine. *Albrecht Bouts (1451/55–1549)*. Contribution à l'étude des Primitifs flamands 10. Brussels, 2011.

Hendriks 1998
Hendriks, Ella. "Johannes Cornelisz. Verspronck. The Technique of a Seventeenth-Century Haarlem Portraitist." In *Looking Through Paintings: The Study of Painting Techniques and Materials in Support of Art Historical Research*. Edited by Erma Hermens. Baarn, 1998.

Hendrix 1984
Hendrix, Marjorie Lee. "Joris Hoefnagel and the *Four Elements*: A Study in Sixteenth-Century Nature Painting." PhD diss., Princeton University, 1984.

Hendrix 1992
Hendrix, [Marjorie] Lee. "Conquering Illusion: Bartholomeus Spranger's Influence in *Venus and Mars Surprised by Vulcan* by Hendrick Goltzius." In *Hendrick Goltzius and the Classical Tradition*, pp. 66–72. Edited and with an introduction by Glenn Harcourt. (Exh. cat. Fisher Gallery, University of Southern California, 1992.) Los Angeles, 1992.

Van Hengel 1990
Hengel, J. H. van. *Early Golf*. 3rd ed. Naarden, 1990.

Hengeveld 1865–70
Hengeveld, G. J. *Het Rundvee, zijne verschillende soorten, rassen en veredeling. . . .* 2 vols. Haarlem, 1865–70.

Henkel 1934
Henkel, M. D. "'The Denial of St. Peter' by Rembrandt." *Burlington Magazine* 64 (April 1934): pp. 153–56, 159.

Heppner 1939–40
Heppner, Albert. "The Popular Theatre of the Rederijkers in the Work of Jan Steen and His Contemporaries." *Journal of the Warburg and Courtauld Institutes* 3/1–2 (1939–40): pp. 22–48.

Herbert 1990
Herbert, John. "How Rembrandt's *Titus* Was Sold." In *Inside Christie's*, pp. 100–19. London, 1990.

Herrmann 1967–68
Herrmann, Frank. "Who Was Solly?" *Connoisseur* 164 (1967): pp. 229–34; 165 (1967): pp. 12–18, 153–61; 166 (1967): pp. 10–18; 169 (1968): pp. 12–17.

Herrmann [1972] 1999
Herrmann, Frank, ed. *The English as Collectors: A Documentary Sourcebook*. 1972. 2nd ed., revised and expanded. New Castle and London, 1999.

Heuer 2009
Heuer, Christopher P. *The City Rehearsed: Object, Architecture, and Print in the Worlds of Hans Vredeman de Vries*. London, 2009.

Heuss 1998
Heuss, Anje. "The Goudstikker Case: The Netherlands and Looted Art." In *Das Geschäft mit der Raubkunst: Fakten, Thesen, Hintergründe*, pp. 105–10. Edited by Matthias Frehner. Zurich, 1998.

De Hevesy 1948
Hevesy, André de. "Rubens à Paris." *Gazette des beaux-arts* 34 (August 1948): pp. 89–106.

Heydenreich 2007a
Heydenreich, Gunnar. "Adam and Eve in the Making." In *Temptation in Eden: Lucas Cranach's Adam and Eve*, pp. 18–33. Edited by Caroline Campbell. (Exh. cat. Courtauld Institute of Art Gallery, London, 2007.) London, 2007.

Heydenreich 2007b
Heydenreich, Gunnar. *Lucas Cranach, the Elder: Painting Materials, Techniques and Workshop Practice*. Amsterdam, 2007.

Heydenreich 2008
Heydenreich, Gunnar. "The Color of Canvas: Historical Practices for Bleaching Artist's Linen." In *Preparation for Painting, Artist's Choice and Its Consequences*, pp. 30–41. Edited by Joyce Townsend et al. London, 2008.

Higginson 1842
A Descriptive Catalogue of the Gallery of Pictures Collected by Edmund Higginson, Esq. of Saltmarshe. London, 1842.

Hind 1915–32
Hind, Arthur, ed. *Catalogue of Drawings by Dutch and Flemish Artists Preserved in the Department of Prints and Drawings in the British Museum*. 5 vols. London, 1915–32.

Hindlip 2016
Hindlip, Charles. *An Auctioneer's Lot: Triumphs and Disasters at Christie's*. London, 2016.

Hochstrasser 2007
Hochstrasser, Julie Berger. *Still Life and Trade in the Dutch Golden Age*. New Haven, 2007.

Hoet 1713
Hoet, Gerard. *Ontslote deure der tekenkunst waarin, door natuurlyke voorbeelden veelerlei stant en gebaar van hoofden en tronien als mede de beweegingen van handen en voeten, midsgaders veele volkomene beelden zoo mannen als vrouwen, in hunne verscheide gestalten als leggende, staan de . . . vertoont woorden: alles ooirspronkelyk getekent door Gerard Hoet en met etznaalde in 't koper gebragt door Pieter Bodart*. Leeuwarden, 1713.

Hoet 1752–70
Hoet, Gerard. *Catalogus of naamlyst van schilderyen met derzelver pryzen. . . .* 3 vols. Vols. 1–2, The Hague, 1752; vol. 3, edited by Pieter Terwesten, The Hague, 1770.

Hoff and Devapriam 1995
Hoff, Ursula, with Emma Devapriam. *European Paintings before 1800 in the National Gallery of Victoria*. 4th ed. Melbourne, 1995.

Hofstede de Groot 1906
Hofstede de Groot, Cornelis. *Die Urkunden über Rembrandt (1575–1721)*. The Hague, 1906.

Hofstede de Groot 1907–28
Hofstede de Groot, Cornelis. *Beschreibendes und kritisches Verzeichnis der Werke der hervorragendsten Holländischen Maler des XVII Jahrhunderts nach dem Muster von John Smith's Catalogue Raisonné*. 10 vols. Esslingen, 1907–28.

Hofstede de Groot 1908–27
A Catalogue Raisonné of the Works of the Most Eminent Dutch Painters of the Seventeenth Century; Based on the Work of John Smith. Translated and edited by Edward G. Hawke. 8 vols. London, 1908–27.

Hohenzollern-Hechingen [1859]
Verzeichnis der Gemäldesammlung seiner Hoheit des Fürste Hohenzollern-Hechingen. Löwenberg, [1859].

Hollander 1998
Hollander, Pieter den. *De Zaak Goudstikker*. Amsterdam, 1998.

Hollander 2009
Hollander, Pieter den. *Roofkunst: Goudstikker.* Amsterdam, 2009.

Hollstein 1949–2010
Hollstein, F. W. H., et al. *Dutch and Flemish Etchings, Engravings, and Woodcuts, ca. 1450–1700.* 72 vols. Amsterdam, 1949–2010.

Hollstein 1954–2019
Hollstein, F. W. H. *German Engravings and Woodcuts, ca. 1400–1700.* 104 vols. Amsterdam, 1954–2019.

Hollstein 1993–
Hollstein, F. W. H. *The New Hollstein: Dutch and Flemish Etchings, Engravings, and Woodcuts, 1450–1700.* 33 vols. Rosendaal, 1993–.

Holmes 1964
Holmes, Martin. "Two Helmets Painted by Rubens." *Connoisseur Year Book* (1964): pp. 67–69.

Holst 1938
Holst, Niels von. "Baltische Kunstsammlungen der Neuzeit. I. vom Barocken Raritätenkabinett zur Galerie Herzog Peters von Kurland." *Baltische Monatshefte* 10 (October 1938): pp. 561–77.

Hooft 1912
Hooft, C. G. 't. *Amsterdamsche stadsgezichten van Jan van der Heyden.* Amsterdam, 1912.

Hoogewerff 1936–47
Hoogewerff, G. J. *De Noord-Nederlandsche Schilderkunst.* 5 vols. 's-Gravenhage, 1936–47.

Hoogsteder 1986
Hoogsteder, Willem-Jan. "De schilderijen van Frederik en Elizabeth, koning en koningin van Bohemen." Proefschrift, Universiteit te Utrecht, 1986.

Hottle 2004
Hottle, Andrew D. "Commerce and Connections: Peter Paul Rubens and the Dedicated Print." *Netherlands Kunsthistorisch Jaarboek (NKJ) / Netherlands Yearbook for the History of Art* 55 (2004): pp. 54–85.

Houbraken 1718–21
Houbraken, Arnold. *De groote schouburgh der Nederlantsche konstschilders en schilderessen.* 3 vols. Amsterdam, 1718–21.

Houbraken [1753] 1976
Houbraken, Arnold. *De groote schouburgh der Nederlantsche konstschilders en schilderessen.* 3 vols. Amsterdam, 1976. [Repr. of 1753 's-Gravenhage ed.; 1st ed. Amsterdam, 1718–21.]

Houston 1950
Seventeen Masters of Painting. (Exh. cat. Museum of Fine Arts, Houston, 1950.) Houston, 1950.

Houston 1972–74
Masterpieces of Five Centuries: Forty-eight Paintings and Sculptures from the Norton Simon Foundation and the Norton Simon Inc. Museum. Museum of Fine Arts, Houston, 4 October 1972–8 September 1974.

Hout 1998
Hout, Nico van. "Meaning and Development of the Ground Layer in Seventeenth Century Painting." In *Looking through Paintings: The Study of Painting Techniques and Materials in Support of Art Historical Research,* pp. 199–225. Edited by Erma Hermens, Annemiek Ouwerkerk, and Nicola Costaras. Leids Kunsthistorisch Jaarboek 11. Baarn, 1998.

Howarth 2009
Howarth, Jeremy. *The Steenwyck Family as Masters of Perspective.* Turnhout, 2009.

Hudig 1928
Hudig, Ferrand W. *Frederik Hendrik en de kunst van zijn tijd.* Amsterdam, 1928. Inaugural speech delivered at Universiteit van Amsterdam, 1 October 1928.

Huemer 1977
Huemer, Frances. *Portraits Painted in Foreign Countries.* Corpus Rubenianum Ludwig Burchard 19/1. Brussels, 1977.

Hugo 1626
Hugo, Hermann. *Obsidio Bredana armis Philippi IIII.* Antwerp, 1626.

D'Hulst and Vandenven 1989
D'Hulst, R.-A., and M. Vandenven. *The Old Testament.* Corpus Rubenianum Ludwig Burchard 3. London, 1989.

Humfrey 1993
Humfrey, Peter. *The Altarpiece in Renaissance Venice.* New Haven, 1993.

Hussey 1947
Hussey, Christopher. "Malahide Castle, Co. Dublin, II." *Country Life* 101 (25 April 1947): pp. 760–63.

Huygens 1629–31
Huygens, Constantijn. "Autobiographical Fragment (in Latin), 1629–1631, Koninklijk Bibliotheck, The Hague." In *Mijn Jeugd,* pp. 84–90. Translated by Chris L. Heesakkers. Amsterdam, 1987.

Huygens 1892–99
Huygens, Constantijn. *De gedichten van Constantijn Huygens, naar zijn handschrift uitg.* 9 vols. Edited by Jacob Adolf Worp. Groningen, 1892–99.

Huys Janssen 1994
Huys Janssen, Paul. "Jan van Bijlert (1597/98–1671), Schilder in Utrecht." PhD diss., Universiteit te Utrecht, 1994.

Huys Janssen 1998
Huys Janssen, Paul. *Jan van Bijlert 1597/98–1671: Catalogue Raisonné.* Amsterdam and Philadelphia, 1998.

Hymans 1886
Hymans, Henri. "Correspondance de Belgique, l'exposition rétrospective de Bruxelles." *Gazette des beaux-arts,* 2nd ser. 34 (1886): pp. 331–38, 424–35.

Hymans 1893
Hymans, Henri. *Lucas Vorsterman: Catalogue raisonné de son oeuvre. . . .* Brussels, 1893.

Hymans 1910
Hymans, Henri. "Correspondance de Bruxelles, l'exposition de l'art Belge au XVIIième siècle." *Gazette des beaux-arts* 4/4, pt. 2 (1910): pp. 326–44.

Idstein 1987
Müller, Wolfgang J., and Silvia Berger. *Sebastian Stoskopff: sein Leben, sein Werk, seine Zeit.* (Exh. cat. Stadthalle Idstein, 1987.) Idstein, 1987.

Ignatius of Loyola 1991
Ignatius of Loyola: Spiritual Exercises and Selected Works. Edited by George E. Ganss. New York, 1991.

Indianapolis 1950
Holbein and His Contemporaries. (Exh. cat. John Herron Art Museum, Indianapolis, 22 October–24 December 1950.) Indianapolis, 1950.

Indianapolis 2006
Dickey, Stephanie S. *Rembrandt Face to Face.* (Exh. cat. Indianapolis Museum of Art, 2006.) Indianapolis, 2006.

Ingelheim am Rhein 1988
Ingelheim am Rhein. *Sebastian Münster: Katalog zur Ausstellung aus Anlass des 500. Geburtstages am 20. Januar 1988 im Museum-Altes Rathaus Ingelheim am Rhein.* (Exh. cat. Museum-Altes Rathaus, Ingelheim am Rhein, 1988.) Ingelheim am Rhein, 1988.

Van Ingen 1966
Ingen, Ferdinand van. *Vanitas und Memento Mori in der deutschen Barocklyrik.* Groningen, 1966.

"In the Galleries" 1909
"In the Galleries." *International Studio* 39 (November 1909): xvii.

Israel 1995
Israel, Jonathan. *The Dutch Republic: Its Rise, Greatness, and Fall, 1477–1806.* Oxford History of Early Modern Europe. Oxford, 1995.

Jacob 1979
Jacob, Sabine. "Zur Entwicklung der Landschaftmalerei von Jan Lievens." In *Jan Lievens, ein Maler im Schatten Rembrandts,* pp. 21–25. By Rudolf E. O. Ekkart, Sabine Jacob, and Rüdiger Klessmann. Translated by Wolfgang Müller and Hans Seyffert. (Exh. cat. Herzog Anton Ulrich-Museum, Braunschweig, 1979.) Braunschweig, 1979.

Jager 2001
Jager, Janine. "Reger Handel mit den Niederlanden." In *Verkaufte Kultur: Die Sowjetischen Kunst- und Antiquitäten Exporte 1919–1938*, pp. 151–70. Edited by Waltraud Bayer. Frankfurt, 2001.

Jaffé 1953
Jaffé, Michael. "Portrait of Rogier Clarisse." *Burlington Magazine* 95/609 (December 1953): pp. 387–90.

Jaffé 1961a
Jaffé, Michael. "The Companion to Rubens' 'Portrait of Rogier Clarisse.'" *Burlington Magazine* 103/694 (January 1961): pp. 2, 4–6.

Jaffé 1961b
Jaffé, Michael. "*The Return from the Flight into Egypt* by Peter Paul Rubens." *Wadsworth Atheneum Bulletin* 5/8 (1961): pp. 10–26.

Jaffé 1969
Jaffé, Michael. "Rediscovered Oil Sketches by Rubens, I." *Burlington Magazine* 108 (1969): pp. 435–44.

Jaffé 1977
Jaffé, Michael. *Rubens and Italy*. Ithaca, 1977.

Jaffé 1989
Jaffé, Michael. *Catalogo Completo Rubens*. Translated by Germano Mulazzani. Milan, 1989.

Jaffé 1997
Jaffé, Michael. "Rubens's Portraits of the Archduke Albert and the Infanta Isabella." *Burlington Magazine* 139 (1997): pp. 194–95.

Janson 1982
Janson, Carol Louise. "The Birth of Dutch Liberty: Origins of the Pictorial Imagery." PhD diss., University of Minnesota, 1982.

Jantzen [1910] 1979
Jantzen, Hans. *Das Niederländische architekturbild*. 2nd rev. ed. Braunschweig, 1979. [1st ed. Leipzig, 1910.]

Jensen 2007
Jensen, H. Ragn. "Isaac Isaacsz." In *Pieter Isaacsz (1569–1625): Court Painter, Art Dealer and Spy*, pp. 205–17. Edited by B. Noldus and J. Roding. Turnhout, 2007.

Jerrold 1857
Jerrold, W. Blanchard, ed. *Jerrold's Guide to the Exhibition: How to See the Art Treasures Exhibition*. Manchester, 1857.

Jestaz 2007
Jestaz, Bertrand. *L'art de la renaissance*. Paris, 2007.

Johnson and Cairns 1972
Johnson, Ben, and Thomas Cairns. "Art Conservation: Culture under Analysis." Pts. 1 and 2. *Analytical Chemistry* 44/1 (January 1972): pp. 24–36; 44/2 (February 1972): pp. 30–38.

Johnson, Metzger, and Wolfthal 2017
Johnson, D., C. Metzger, and D. Wolfthal. "Weave Match and Its Implications: The Case of Dirk Bout." In *The Workshop Practice in Early Netherlandish Painting: Case Studies from Van Eyck through Gossart*, pp. 37–47. Edited by Maryan W. Ainsworth. Turnhout, 2017.

Jonckheere 2016
Jonckheere, Koenraad. *Portraits after Existing Protypes*. Corpus Rubenianum Ludwig Burchard 19/4. London, 2016.

Jones 1996
Jones, Alison, ed. *Chambers Dictionary of Quotations*. London, 1996.

De Jonge 1940
Jonge, Caroline Henriette de. *Jan Steen*. Palet serie. Amsterdam, 1940.

De Jongh 1968–69
Jongh, Eddy de. "Erotica in vogelperspectief: De dubbelzinnigheid van een reeks 17de-eeuwse genre-voorstellingen." *Simiolus* 3 (1968–69): pp. 22–74.

De Jongh 1982
Jongh, Eddy de. "The Interpretation of Still-Life Paintings: Possibilities and Limits." In 1982 *Still-Life In the Age of Rembrandt*, pp. 27–37. (Exh. cat. Auckland City Art Gallery, Auckland; National Art Gallery, Canberra; McDougall Art Gallery, Christchurch, 1982.) By Eddy de Jongh et al. Auckland, 1982.

De Jongh 2001
Jongh, Eddy de. "De mate van ikheid in Rembrandt's zelfportretten." *Kunstschrijft* 4 (2001): pp. 13–23.

Judson 1964
Judson, J. Richard. "Pictorial Sources for Rembrandt's *Denial of St. Peter*." *Oud Holland* 79 (1964): pp. 141–51.

Judson 1969
Judson, J. Richard. "Rembrandt in Canada." *Burlington Magazine* 111 (November 1969): pp. 703–04.

Judson and Ekkart 1999
Judson, J. Richard, and Rudolf E. O. Ekkart. *Gerrit van Honthorst 1592–1656*. Doornspijk, 1999.

Jullian 1964
Jullian, Philippe. "Une des maisons—clés pour l'histoire du gout au XXe siécle, l'hôtel du vicomte et de la vicomtesse de Noailles, à Paris." *Connaissance des arts* 130 (October 1964): pp. 68–91.

Kahr 1966
Kahr, Madlyn Millner. "Rembrandt's *Esther*: A Painting and an Etching Newly Interpreted and Dated." *Oud Holland* 81 (1966): pp. 228–44.

Kahr 1982
Kahr, Madlyn Millner. *Dutch Painting in the Seventeenth Century*. 1978. New York, 1982.

Kalff 1895
Kalff, Gerrit. "Bijdrage tot de geschiedenis van het Amsterdamsch tooneel in the 17de eeuw." *Oud Holland* 13 (1895): pp. 1–33.

Kauffmann 1923
Kauffmann, Hans. "Die Farbenkunst des Aert van der Neer." In *Festschrift für Adolph Goldschmidt zum 60. Geburtstag am 15. Januar 1923*, pp. 106–10. Leipzig, 1923.

Kauffmann 1926
Kauffmann, Hans. "Overzicht der literatuur betreffende Nederlandsche kunst." *Oud Holland* 43 (1926): pp. 235–48.

Kaufman 1995
Kaufman, Lea Eckerling. "The Paintings of Isack van Ostade." 2 vols. PhD diss., University of California, Los Angeles, 1995.

Kaufmann 1985
Kaufmann, Thomas Da Costa. "Éros et poesia: La peinture à la cour de Rodolphe II." *Revue de l'art* 69 (1985): pp. 29–46.

Kaufmann 1988
Kaufmann, Thomas Da Costa. *The School of Prague: Painting at the Court of Rudolf II*. Chicago, 1988.

Kelly and Charmet 1953
Kelly, Gerald, and Raymond Charmet. *Rembrandt, Franz Hals et les maîtres hollandais à la Royal Academy*. Art et style 28. Paris, 1953.

Kennedy and Nolan 2011
Kennedy, Trinita, and John Nolan. *Northern Renaissance Paintings from the Bob Jones University Museum and Gallery*. Nashville, 2011.

Kentner 1962
Kentner, H. "Italianische Kleinbronzen." *Kunstchronik* 15 (1962): pp. 169–77.

Kettering 1974
Kettering, Alison McNeil. "The Batavian Arcadia: Pastoral Themes in 17th-Century Dutch Art." PhD diss., University of California, Berkeley, 1974.

Kettering 1982
Kettering, Alison McNeil. *The Dutch Arcadia: Pastoral Art and Its Audience in the Golden Age*. Montclair and Woodbridge, 1982.

Kettering 2007
Kettering, Alison McNeil. "Men at Work in Dutch Art, or Keeping One's Nose to the Grindstone." *Art Bulletin* 89/4 (2007): pp. 694–714.

Kier and Zehnder 1998
Kier, Hiltrud, and Frank Günter Zehnder. *Lust und Verlust, Corpus-Band zu Kölner Gemäldesammlungen 1800–1860*. Cologne, 1998.

Kieser 1933
Kieser, Emile. "Antikes im Werke des Rubens." *Münchner Jahrbuch der bildenden Kunst*, n.F. 10 (1933): pp. 110–37.

Kilian 1993
Kilian, Jennifer M. "The Paintings of Karel du Jardin." PhD diss., New York University, 1993.

Kilian 2005
Kilian, Jennifer M. *The Paintings of Karel Du Jardin, 1626–1678: Catalogue Raisonné*. Amsterdam, 2005.

Kinderen-Besier 1950
Kinderen-Besier, J. H. der. *Spelevaart der Mode. De kledij onzer voorouders in de zeventiende eeuw*. Foreword by I. Q. van Regteren Altena. Amsterdam, 1950.

King's Lynn 1958
Exhibition of 17th-Century Dutch Pictures. (Exh. cat. Fermoy Art Gallery, King's Lynn, 26 July–9 August 1958. Organized by Thos. Agnew & Sons, London.) By Geoffrey Agnew. London, 1958.

King's Lynn 1965
The Heathcoat Amory Collection. (Exh. cat. Fermoy Art Gallery, King's Lynn, July 1965; organized by Thos. Agnew & Sons, London.) London, 1965.

Kirsch and Levenson 2000
Kirsch, A., and R. S. Levenson. *Seeing Through Paintings: Physical Examination in Art Historical Studies*. New Haven, 2000.

Kirschenbaum 1977
Kirschenbaum, Baruch D. *The Religious and Historical Paintings of Jan Steen*. New York, 1977.

"Kleinberger/Flemish Primitives" 1929
"Partial List of Flemish Primitives in Kleinberger Show." *Art News* 28/2 (12 October 1929): p. 5.

"Kleinberger/Flemish Show" 1929
"Flemish Show Opens Today at Kleinberger's." *Art News* 28/4 (26 October 1929): pp. 3–9, 12.

Klingenstein 1910
Klingenstein, L. *The Great Infanta Isabel, Sovereign of the Netherlands*. London, 1910.

Kloek 1992
Kloek, Wouter Th. "Over Rembrandts Portret van Uyttenbogaert, nu in het Rijksmuseum." *Bulletin van het Rijksmuseum* 40 (1992): pp. 346–52.

Kloek 2005
Kloek, Wouter Th. *Jan Steen (1626–1679)*. Amsterdam, 2005.

Kloek 2017/2020–
Kloek, Wouter Th. "Peasants Merrymaking Outside an Inn (Previously "Fair at Warmond")" (2017.) In *The Leiden Collection Catalogue*. Edited by Arthur K. Wheelock Jr. and Lara Yeager-Crasselt. 3rd ed. New York, 2020–. Accessed April 04, 2023. https://theleidencollection.com/artwork/peasants-merrymaking-outside-an-inn.

Kloek 2018
Kloek, Wouter Th. "Jan Steen, His Repertoire of Motifs and History Painting." In The Hague 2018, pp. 32–53.

Knight, Frank & Rutley 1915
A Catalogue of the Sydney Collection at Frognal, Chislehurst, Kent. (Sale cat., Knight, Frank & Rutley, London, 7 June 1915). London, 1915.

Knuttel 1956
Knuttel, G. *Rembrandt, de meesteren zijn werk*. Amsterdam, 1956.

Koch 1988
Koch, Robert A. "The Getty 'Annunciation' by Dieric Bouts." *Burlington Magazine* 130/1024 (July 1988): pp. 509–16.

Koeman [1663] 1970
Koeman, Cornelis. *Joan Blaeu and His Grand Atlas*. Amsterdam, 1970. [Facsimile ed. of *Le grand atlas*, 1663.]

Koerner 1985
Koerner, Joseph Leo. "The Mortification of the Image: Death as a Hermeneutic in Hans Baldung Grien." *Representations* 10 (Spring 1985): pp. 52–101.

Konečný et al. 1998
Konečný, Lubomír, with Beket Bukovinská and Ivan Muchka, eds. *Rudolf II, Prague, and the World: Papers from the International Conference, Prague, 2–4 September 1997*. Prague, 1998.

König-Nordhoff 1982
König-Nordhoff, Ursula. *Ignatius von Loyola. Studien zur Entwicklung einer neuen Heiligen-Ikonographie im Rahmen einer Kanonisationskampagne um 1600*. Berlin, 1982.

Koning 1986
Koning, Hans. "The Real Rembrandt." *Connoisseur* (April 1986): pp. 106–12.

Koopstra 2019
Koopstra, Anna. "New Insights into Hendrik van Steenwijck the Younger's Working Methods and Milieu." Appendix by Thomas Fusenig. *Journal of Historians of Netherlandish Art* 11/1 (Winter 2019). https//:doi.org/10.5092/jhna.2019.11.1.3.

Kortenhorst-von Bogendorf Rupprath 1993
Kortenhorst-von Bogendorf Rupprath, Cynthia. "Catalogue." In Haarlem/Worcester 1993.

Koslow 1975
Koslow, Susan. "Frans Hals's Fisherboys: Exemplars of Idleness." *Art Bulletin* 57 (1975): pp. 418–32.

Koslow 1995
Koslow, Susan. *Frans Snyders. The Noble Estate: Seventeenth-Century Still-Life and Animal Painting in the Southern Netherlands*. Antwerp, 1995.

Kräftner, Seipel, and Trnek 2004
Kräftner, Johann, Wilfried Seipel, and Renate Trnek, eds. *Rubens in Vienna: The Masterpieces*. Vienna, 2004.

Krelage 1942
Krelage, E. H. *Bloemenspeculatie in Nederland: De tulpomanie van 1636–1637 en de Hyacintenhandel 1720–1736*. Amsterdam, 1942.

Krempel 2000
Krempel, León. *Studien zu den datierten Gemälden des Nicolaes Maes (1634–1693)*. Studien zur internationalen Architektur- und Kuntgeschichte 9. Petersberg, 2000.

Kren 1978
Kren, Thomas. "Jan Miel: A Flemish Painter in Rome." PhD diss., Yale University, 1978.

Kronach 1994
Grimm, Claus, Johannes Erichsen, and Evamaria Brockhoff. *Lucas Cranach: Ein Maler-Unternehmer aus Franken*. (Exh. cat. Festung Rosenberg, Kronach, 1994.) Veröffentlichungen zur Bayerischen Geschichte und Kultur 26/94. Augsburg, 1994.

Kronig 1910
Kronig, J. O. "Deux tableaux de maîtres primitifs néerlandais dans les collections de S. M., le Roi de Portugal." *Les arts: Revue mensuelle des musées, collections, expositions* 9/99 (March 1910): p. 28.

Kuhn 1936
Kuhn, Charles L. *A Catalogue of German Paintings of the Middle Ages and Renaissance in American Collections*. Cambridge, 1936.

Kühnen and Herm 2016
Kühnen, Renate, and Christoph Herm. "Protein Fibres as Intermediate Layer on Medieval Shields, Panel Paintings and Altarpieces." *Zeitschrift für Kunsttechnologie und Konservierung* 30 (2016): pp. 36–46.

Ter Kuile 1985
Kuile, Onno ter. *Seventeenth-Century North Netherlandish Still Lifes*. The Hague and Amsterdam, 1985.

Kunoth-Leifels 1962
Kunoth-Leifels, Elisabeth. *Über die Darstellungen der "Bathseba im Bade," Studien zur Geschichte des Bildthemas 4. bis 1. Jahrhundert*. Essen, 1962.

Kuretsky 1971
Kuretsky, Susan Donahue. "Jacob Ochtervelt." 2 vols. PhD diss., Harvard University, 1971.

Kuretsky 1979
Kuretsky, Susan Donahue. *The Paintings of Jacob Ochtervelt (1634–1682)*. Montclair, 1979.

Kuretsky 2000
Kuretsky, Susan Donahue. "Ochtervelt, Jacob." In *From Rembrandt to Vermeer: 17th-Century Dutch Artists*, pp. 235f. Edited by Jane Turner. Grove Dictionary of Art. New York, 2000.

Kurz 1953
Kurz, Otto. "Huius Nympha Loci: A Pseudo-Classical Inscription and a Drawing by Dürer." *Journal of the Warburg and Courtauld Institutes* 16/3–4 (1953): pp. 171–77.

Kurz and Kurz 1972
Kurz, Hilde, and Otto Kurz. "The Turkish Dresses in the Costume-book of Rubens." *Nederlands Kunsthistorisches Jaarboek* 23 (1972): pp. 275–90.

Kuus 1994
Kuus, Saskia. "Rokkenkinderen in de Nederlanden 1560–1660. Een onderzoek naar het verschil in kleding tussen meijses en jongens in rokken." In *Kostuum: Jaaruitgave van de Nederlandse Kostuum Vereninging voor mode en streekdracht*, pp. 6–13, 57–58. Amersfoort, 1994.

Kuus 2000
Kuus, Saskia. "Children's Costume in the Sixteenth and Seventeenth Centuries." In *Pride and Joy: Children's Portraits in the Netherlands, 1500–1700*, pp. 73–83. Edited by Jan Baptist Bedaux and Rudolf E. O. Ekkart. Amsterdam, 2000.

Labrot 1992
Labrot, Gérard, with Antonio Delfino. *Italian Inventories 1: Collections of Paintings in Naples 1600–1780*. Edited by A. Cera Sones and C. Togneri. Munich and New York, 1992.

La Farge 1959a
La Farge, Henry A. "Jacobean Portraits." *Art News* 58 (March 1959): p. 12.

La Farge 1959b
La Farge, Henry A. "Reviews and Previews." *Art News* 58/6 (October 1959): pp. 10–16.

De Lairesse [1707] 1738
Lairesse, Gerard de. *The Art of Painting, in All Its Branches, Methodically Demonstrated by Discourses and Plates. . . .* Translated by John Frederick Fritsch. London, 1738. [Originally published as *Het Groot Schilderboek*, 2 vols., Amsterdam, 1707.]

De Lairesse [1740] 1969
Lairesse, Gerard de. *Het Groot Schilderboek. . . .* 2 vols. in 1. [Doornspijk], 1969. [Repr. of 1740 Haarlem ed.; 1st ed. 1707.]

Lammertse 1998
Lammertse, Friso, with contributions by Jeroen Giltaij and Anouk Janssen. *Dutch Genre Paintings of the 17th Century: Collection of the Museum Boijmans van Beuningen*. Rotterdam, 1998.

Lammertse 2008
Lammertse, Friso. "Salomon de Bray, Painter, Architect, and Theorist." In *Painting Family: The De Brays, Master Painters of 17th Century Holland*, pp. 10–16. By Pieter Biesboer et al. (Exh. cat. Frans Hals Museum, Haarlem; Dulwich Picture Gallery, London, 2008.) Zwolle, 2008.

Lammertse and Van der Veen 2006
Lammertse, Friso, and Jaap van der Veen. *Uylenburgh & Son: Art and Commerce from Rembrandt to De Lairesse, 1625–1675*. Zwolle and Amsterdam, 2006.

B. G. Lane 1980
Lane, Barbara G. *Hans Memling, Werkverzeichnis*. Die grossen Meister der Malerei. Frankfurt, 1980.

B. G. Lane 2009
Lane, Barbara G. *Hans Memling, Master Painter in Fifteenth-Century Bruges*. Turnhout, 2009.

J. W. Lane 1939
Lane, James W. "Notes from New York." *Apollo* 29/174 (June 1939): pp. 296–99.

Langedijk 1976
Langedijk, Karla. "Baccio Bandinelli's Orpheus: A Political Message." *Mitteilungen des Kunsthistorischen Instituts in Florenz* 20 (1976): pp. 33–52.

Laren 1963
Modernen van Toen, 1570–1630, Vlaamse schilderkunst en haar invloed. (Exh. cat. Singer Museum, Laren, 1963.) Laren, 1963.

Larsen 1952
Larsen, Erik. *P. P. Rubens: With a Complete Catalogue of His Works in America*. Antwerp, 1952.

Larsen and Hyde Minor 1977
Larsen, Erik, and Vernon Hyde Minor. "Peter Paul Rubens and the Soceity of Jesus." *Kunsthistorisk tidskift* 46 (1977): pp. 48–54.

Lasius 1989
Lasius, Angelika. "Die Schuhmacher- und Schneiderdarstellungen des niederländischen Malers Quiringh Gerritsz. van Brekelenkam." *Wallraf-Richartz-Jahrbuch* 50 (1989): pp. 141–61.

Lasius 1992
Lasius, Angelika. *Quiringh van Brekelenkam*. Doornspijk, 1992.

Lasius 1996
Lasius, Angelika. "Brekelenkam, Quiringh (Quirijn) Gerritsz. van." In *Saur Algemeines Kunstler-Lexikon*, vol. 14 (1996), pp. 95f. Edited by Günter Meisser. 119 vols. Munich, Leipzig, 1992–.

Laurentius, Niemeijer, and Ploos van Amstel 1980
Laurentius, Th., J. W. Niemeijer, and G. Ploos van Amstel. *Cornelis Ploos van Amstel, 1726–1798: Kunstverzammlaar en prentuitgever*. Assen, 1980.

Lauritzen 1978
Lauritzen, Peter. *Venice: A Thousand Years of Culture and Civilization*. New York, 1978.

Lauts 1940
Lauts, Jan. *Antonello da Messina*. Vienna, 1940.

Lavice 1867
Lavice, André. *Revue des musées d'Allemagne*. Paris, 1867.

Lawner 1987
Lawner, Lynne. *Lives of the Courtesans: Portraits of the Renaissance*. New York, 1987.

Lawrence 1988
Goddard, Stephen H., ed., with Patricia A. Emison et al. *The World in Miniature: Engravings by the German Little Masters, 1500–1550*. (Exh. cat. Spencer Museum of Art, University of Kansas, Lawrence, 1988.) Lawrence, 1988.

Lebrun 1792–96
Lebrun, [Jean-Baptiste-Pierre]. *Galerie des peintres flamands, hollandais et allemands. . . .* 3 vols. Paris, 1792–96.

Leeds 1868
National Exhibition of Works of Art at Leeds. (Exh. cat. Leeds, 1868.) Leeds, 1868.

Van Leeuwen 1970
Leeuwen, Frans van. "Iets over het handschrift van de 'naar het leven' tekenaar." *Oud Holland* 85 (1970): pp. 25–32.

Lefèvre 1676
Lefèvre, Raoul. *The Destruction of Troy: In Three Books. . . .* 9th ed. Translated by William Caxton. London, 1676.

Leiden 1926
Martin, W. *Jan Steen, over zijn leven en zijn Kunst*. (Exh. cat. Stedelijk Museum "De Lakenhal," Leiden, 1926.) Leiden, 1926.

Leiden 1966
Thyssen, Lucia. *Gabriel Metsu*. Introduction by J. N. van Wessem. (Exh. cat. Stedelijk Museum "De Lakenhal," Leiden, 1966.) Leiden, 1966.

Leipzig 1929
Alte Meister aus Privatbesitz. (Exh. cat. Museum der Bildenden Kunst, Leipzig, 1929.) Leipzig, 1929.

Leonard et al. 1988
Leonard, Mark, et al. "Dieric Bouts's 'Annunciation': Materials and Techniques, A Summary." *Burlington Magazine* 130/1024 (1988): pp. 517–22.

Lesné 1982
Lesné, Claude. "La peinture française du XVIIe siècle dans les collections américaines." *Le petit journal des grandes expositions* 116 (1982): n.pag.

Lesuisse 1966
Lesuisse, René. "Les St. Ignace et St. François Xavier de Rubens: Warwick, Sibiu, Nivelles." *Annales de la Société archéologique et folklorique de Nivelles et du Brabant Wallon* 19 (1966): pp. 281–317.

Leuchtenberg 1843
Verzeichniss der Bildergallerie seiner königlichen Hoheit des Prinzen Eugen, Herzogs von Leuchtenberg in München. Munich, 1843.

Levesque 1994
Levesque, Catherine. *Journey through Landscape in Seventeenth-Century Holland: The Haarlem Print Series and Dutch Identity*. University Park, 1994.

Levy 1988
Levy, Janey L. "The Erotic Engravings of Sebald and Barthel Beham." In Lawrence 1988, pp. 40–53.

Liedtke 1988
Liedtke, Walter. "Toward a History of Dutch Genre Painting II: The South Holland Tradition." In *The Age of Rembrandt: Studies in Seventeenth-Century Dutch Painting*, pp. 94–131. Edited by Roland E. Fleischer and Susan Scott Munshower. Papers in Art History from the Pennsylvania State University 3. University Park, 1988.

Liedtke 1995
Liedtke, Walter. "Rembrandt's 'Man in a Gorget and Plumed Cap' in the J. Paul Getty Museum." *Burlington Magazine* 137 (July 1995): pp. 458–62.

Liedtke 1997
Liedtke, Walter. "Reconstructing Rembrandt and His Circle: More on the Workshop Hypothesis." In *Rembrandt, Rubens, and the Art of their Time: Recent Perspectives*, pp. 37–59. Edited by Susan Scott. Papers in Art History from the Pennsylvania State University 11. University Park, 1997.

Liedtke 2003
Liedtke, Walter. "Cottage Industry, Some Haarlem Landscapes of the Early Seventeenth Century." *Apollo* 158/498 (August 2003): pp. 21–31.

Liedtke 2004
Liedtke, Walter. "Rembrandt's 'Workshop' Revisited." *Oud Holland* 117/1–2 (2004): pp. 48–73.

Liedtke 2007
Liedtke, Walter. *Dutch Paintings in the Metropolitan Museum of Art*. 2 vols. New York, New Haven, and London, 2007.

Liedtke et al. 1995
Liedtke, Walter, et al. *Rembrandt/Not Rembrandt in the Metropolitan Museum of Art: Aspects of Connoisseurship*. Vol. 2, *Paintings, Drawings, and Prints: Art-Historical Perspectives*. New York, 1995.

Liège 1910
Exposition d'oeuvres d'art anciennes & modernes. (Exh. cat. Palais des Fêtes, Liège, 1910.) Liège, 1910.

Lieure [1924–27] 1969
Lieure, Jules. *Jacques Callot*. 8 vols. New York, 1969. [Repr. of 1924–27 Paris ed.].

Lilian 2007
Solomon Lilian Gallery. *Old Masters*. Geneva and Amsterdam, 2007.

Lilian 2014
Salomon Lilian Gallery, *Old Masters 2014*. Geneva and Amsterdam, 2014.

Lillie 2003
Lillie, Sophie. *Was Einmal War: Handbuch der enteigneten Kusntsammlungen Wiens*. Vienna, 2003.

Lind 1946
Lind, L. R. "The Latin Life of Peter Paul Rubens by His Nephew Philip." *Art Quarterly* 9 (1946): pp. 37–44.

Liphard-Rathshoff 1917
Liphard-Rathshoff, Renaud de. *Leuchtenbergska Tavelsamlingen*. Stockholm, 1917.

Liverpool 1959
The Heywood-Lonsdale Loan. (Exh. cat. Walker Art Gallery, Liverpool, 1959.) Liverpool, 1959.

Lokin 2016
Lokin, Daniëlle. "Schöne als die Wirklichkeit. Der Maler und Inventor Balthasar van der Ast," In Aachen/Gotha 2016, pp. 54–67.

London 1829
Pictures by Italian, Spanish, Flemish, Dutch and English Masters. (Exh. cat. British Institution, London, 1829.) London, 1829.

London 1847
Pictures by Italian, Flemish, Dutch, French and English Masters. (Exh. cat. British Institution, London, June 1847.) London, 1847.

London 1851
Pictures by Italian, Flemish, Dutch, French and English Masters. (Exh. cat. British Institution, London, June 1851.) London, 1851.

London 1854
Pictures by Italian, Flemish, Dutch, French and English Masters. (Exh. cat. British Institution, London, 1854.) London, 1854.

London 1860
Pictures by Italian, Flemish, Dutch, French and English Masters. (Exh. cat. British Institution, London, 1860.) London, 1860.

London 1863
Pictures by Italian, Spanish, Flemish, Dutch, French and English Masters. (Exh. cat. British Institution, London, 1863.) London, 1863.

London 1867
The National Portrait Exhibition. (Exh. cat. South Kensington Museum, London, 1867.) London, 1867.

London 1878
Works by the Old Masters. (Exh. cat. Royal Academy of Arts, London, 1878.) London, 1878.

London 1879
Works by the Old Masters and by Deceased Masters of the British School. (Exh. cat. Royal Academy of Arts, London, Winter 1879.) London, 1879.

London 1882–83
Richter, Jean Paul. *Catalogue of the Collection of Paintings Lent for Exhibition by the Marquis of Bute, K. T.* (Exh. cat. Science and Art Department of the Committee of the Council on Education, South Kensington, at Bethnal Green Branch Museum, London, 1882–83.) London, 1883.

London 1888
Exhibition of Works by the Old Masters. (Exh. cat. Royal Academy of Arts, London, Winter 1888.) London, 1888.

London 1890
Exhibition of Works by the Old Masters. (Exh. cat. Royal Academy of Arts, London, 1890.) London, 1890.

London 1891
Exhibition of Works by the Old Masters. (Exh. cat. Royal Academy of Arts, London, 1891.) London, 1891.

London 1894
Exhibition of Works by the Old Masters. (Exh. cat. Royal Academy of Arts, London, Winter 1894.) London, 1894.

London 1895
Fair Children. (Exh. cat. Grafton Galleries, London, 1895.) London, 1895.

London 1899
Exhibition of Works by Rembrandt. (Exh. cat. Royal Academy of Arts, London, Winter 1899.) London, 1899.

London 1903
Temple, Alfred George. *Exhibition of a Selection of Works by Early and Modern Painters of the Dutch School*. (Exh. cat. Guildhall Art Gallery, London, 1903.) London, 1903.

London 1904
Dutch Exhibition. (Exh. cat. Whitehall Art Gallery, London, 1904.) London, 1904.

London 1907
38th Winter Exhibition. (Exh. cat. Royal Academy of Arts, London, 1907.) London, 1907.

London 1909
Loan Exhibition of Pictures by Jan Steen. (Exh. cat. Dowdeswell and Dowdeswell, London, May–June 1909.) London, 1909.

London 1922
Pictures by Old Masters on Behalf of Lord Haig's Appeal for Ex-Servicemen. . . . (Exh. cat. Thomas Agnew & Sons, London, November–December 1922.) London, 1922.

London 1925
Loan Exhibition of Pictures by Old Masters: On Behalf of the Royal Northern Hospital, Holloway. (Exh. cat. Thos. Agnew & Sons, London, May–June 1925.) London, 1925.

London 1927a
Lambotte, Paul, et al. *Exhibition of Flemish and Belgian Art, 1300–1900. Organized by the Anglo-Belgian Union*. (Exh. cat. Royal Academy of Arts, London, 1927.) London, 1927.

London 1927b
Loan Exhibition of Flemish & Belgian Art. . . . (Exh. cat. Royal Academy of Arts, London, 1927.) London, 1927.

London 1929a
Dutch Art: An Illustrated Souvenir of the Exhibition of Dutch Art at Burlington House. (Exh. cat. Royal Academy of Arts, Burlington House, London, 1929.) London, 1929.

London 1929b
Exhibition of Dutch Art 1450–1900. (Exh. cat. Royal Academy of Arts, Burlington House, London, 1929.) London, 1930.

London 1932
An Exhibition of the von Auspitz Collection of Old Masters, by Courtesy of Herr Walter Bachstitz. (Exh. cat. Thos. Agnew & Sons, London, November–December 1932.) London, 1932.

London 1936–37
Exhibition of Pictures, Drawings, Furniture, and Other Objects of Art. (Exh. cat. Burlington Fine Arts Club, London, 1936–37.) London, 1936.

London 1938
Exhibition of 17th Century Art in Europe. (Exh. cat. Royal Academy of Arts, London, Winter 1938.) London, 1938.

London 1946
Thirty-five Masterpieces of European Painting in Aid of the Soldiers', Sailors' and Airmen's Families Association. (Exh. cat. Thos. Agnew & Sons, London, November–December 1946.) London, 1946.

London 1948
1948 Exhibition of Dutch and Flemish Masters. (Exh. cat. Eugene Slatter, London, 5 May–10 July 1948.) London, 1948.

London 1949
Masterpieces of Dutch and Flemish Painting: Loan Exhibition in Memory of Ralph Warner. (Exh. cat. Eugene Slatter, London, 16 February–16 March 1949.) London, 1949.

London 1952–53
Dutch Pictures, 1450–1750. . . . (Exh. cat. Royal Academy of Arts, London, Winter 1952–53.) London, 1952.

London 1953a
An Exhibition of Paintings and Drawings by European Masters. (Exh. cat. Marlborough Gallery, London, November–December 1953.) London, 1953.

London 1953b
Rembrandt's Influence in the 17th Century. (Exh. cat. Matthiesen Gallery, London, 20 February–2 April 1953.) Introduction by Horst Gerson. London, 1953.

London 1953–54
Flemish Art, 1300–1700. . . . (Exh. cat. Royal Academy of Arts, London, Winter 1953–54.) London, 1953.

London 1958
Waterhouse, Ellis K. *The Robinson Collection: Paintings from the Collection of the Late Sir J. B. Robinson, Bt., Lent by the Princess Labia*. (Exh. cat. Royal Academy of Arts, London, 1958.) London, 1958.

London 1962
Exhibition of Fine Paintings of the Seventeenth-Century Dutch, Flemish and French Schools. (Exh. cat. H. Terry-Engell Gallery, London, 1962.) London, 1962.

London 1963
Annual Autumn Exhibition of Paintings by Old Dutch and Flemish Masters. (Exh. cat. Brod Gallery, London, 17 October–16 November 1963.) London, 1963.

London 1968a
Paintings by Old Masters. (Exh. cat. P. & D. Colnaghi, London, 7–24 May 1968.) London, 1968.

London 1968b
Recent Acquisitions. (Exh. cat. T. Agnew & Sons, London, 12 March–10 April 1968.) London, 1968.

London 1971a
Dutch and Flemish Paintings. (Exh. cat. Brian Koetser Gallery, London, October–December 1971.) London, 1971.

London 1971b
Herner-Wengraf Quarterly Catalogue 9. (Exh. cat. Old Masters Gallery, London, Winter 1971.) London, 1971.

London 1979
Cohen, Alfred R., E. Young, and E. Cohen. *Trafalgar Galleries at the Royal Academy II*. (Exh. cat. Royal Academy of Arts, London, 1979.) London, 1979.

London 1986
Brown, Christopher. *Dutch Landscape: The Early Years, Haarlem and Amsterdam, 1590–1650*. (Exh. cat. National Gallery, London, 1986.) London, 1986.

London 1993
Cohen, Alfred R., Ronald Cohen, and W. J. van de Watering. *Trafalgar Galleries XII*. (Exh. cat. Royal Academy of Arts, London, 1993.) London, 1993.

London/The Hague 1999
White, Christoper, and Quentin Buvelot, eds. *Rembrandt by Himself*. (Exh. cat. National Gallery, London; Mauritshuis, The Hague, 1999.) Essays by Ernst van de Wetering, Volker Manuth, and Marieke de Winkel, catalogue by Edwin Buijsen et al. London, 1999.

London/The Hague 2007
Ekkart, Rudolf E. O., et al. *Dutch Portraits: The Age of Rembrandt and Frans Hals / Hollanders in beeld. Portretten uit de Gouden Eeuw*. (Exh. cat. National Gallery, London; Mauritshuis, The Hague, 2007.) Translated by Beverly Jackson. The Hague, London, and Zwolle, 2007.

London, ON, 1957
Loan Exhibition, 15th-, 16th-, 17th- Century Flemish Masters. (Exh. cat. McIntosh Memorial Gallery, University of Western Ontario, London, 1957.) Foreword by Julius Held. London, ON, 1957.

Longhi 1914
Longhi, Roberto. "Piero della Francesca e lo sviluppo della pittura veneziana." *L'arte* (Milan) 17 (1914): pp. 198–221, 241–56.

Longhi 1961
Longhi, Roberto. "Piero della Francesca e lo sviluppo della pittura Veneziana, 1914." In *Scritti giovanili, 1912–1922*. Vol. 1, bk. 1 of *Edizione delle Opere complete di Roberto Longhi*, pp. 61–109. Florence, 1961.

A. van Loon 2008
Loon, Annelies van. *Color Changes and Chemical Reactivity in Seventeenth-Century Oil Paintings*. London, 2008.

G. van Loon 1723
Loon, Gerard van. *Beschryving der Nederlandsche historipenningen. . . .* 10 pts. The Hague, 1723.

López Navió 1962
López Navió, J. "La gran collección de pinturas del Marqués de Leganés." *Analecta Calasanctiana* 8 (1962): pp. 259–330.

Los Angeles 1946
Valentiner, Wilhelm R. *Loan Exhibition of Forty-Three Paintings by Rubens and Twenty-Five Paintings by Van Dyck*. (Exh. cat. Los Angeles Museum of History, Science, and Art, 19 November–22 December 1946.) Los Angeles, 1946.

Los Angeles 1965
Special Exhibition of the Collection of Mr. and Mrs. Norton Simon for the College Art Association. Los Angeles County Museum of Art, 18 January–16 April 1965.

Los Angeles 1983
Albuquerque, Lita, Robert Kramer, and Harold Budd. *ABHASA Image Bearing Light* (Exh. cat. Fisher Gallery, University of Southern California; part of "Collaboration," L.A. Institute of Contemporary Art, 1983.) Los Angeles, 1983.

Los Angeles 2001
The J. Paul Getty Museum: Handbook of the Collection. Los Angeles, 2001.

Los Angeles 2017
Gasparotto, Davide, ed. *Giovanni Bellini: Landscapes of Faith in Renaissance Venice*. (Exh. cat. J. Paul Getty Museum, Los Angeles, 2017.) Los Angeles, 2017.

Los Angeles 2018
Kren, Thomas, et al. *The Renaissance Nude.* (Exh. cat. J. Paul Getty Museum, Los Angeles, 2018.) Los Angeles, 2018.

Los Angeles 2021
Woollett, Anne T., Davide Gasparotto, and Jeffrey Spier, eds. *Rubens: Picturing Antiquity.* (Exh. cat. J. Paul Getty Museum, Los Angeles, 2021.) Los Angeles, 2021.

Los Angeles 2023–24
The World Made Wondrous: The Dutch Collector's Cabinet and the Politics of Possession. (Exh. cat. Los Angeles County Museum of Art, 17 September 2023–3 March 2024.) By Diva Zumaya. Los Angeles, 2023.

Los Angeles *Annual Report* 1968
Annual Report, Bulletin of the Los Angeles County Museum of Art 18/1–2 (1968).

Los Angeles/Boston/New York 1981–82
Walsh, John, Jr., and Cynthia P. Schneider. *A Mirror of Nature: Dutch Paintings from the Collection of Mr. and Mrs. Edward William Carter.* (Exh. cat. Los Angeles County Museum of Art; Museum of Fine Arts, Boston; Metropolitan Museum of Art, New York, 1981–82.) Los Angeles, 1981.

De Lostalot 1878
Lostalot, Alfred de. "La Collection Laurent Richard." *Gazette des beaux-arts*, per. 2, 17 (1878): pp. 459–72.

Lowenthal 1995
Lowenthal, Anne W. *Joachim Wtewael: Mars and Venus Surprised by Vulcan*. Getty Museum Studies on Art. Malibu, 1995.

Lubberhuizen-van Gelder 1947–49
Lubberhuizen-van Gelder, A. M. "Japonsche Rocken." Pts. 1 and 2. *Oud Holland* 62 (1947): pp. 137–52; 64 (1949): pp. 25–38.

Lucco 1997
Lucco, Mauro. "Un'eco fiamminga di Giovanni Bellini." In *Scritti per l'Istituto Germanico di Storia dell'Arte di Firenze*, pp. 199–204. Edited by C. A. Luchinat et al. Florence, 1997.

Lucco 2004
Lucco, Mauro. "Bellini and Flemish Painting." In *The Cambridge Companion to Giovanni Bellini*, pp. 75–94. Edited by P. Humfrey. Cambridge, 2004.

Lugt 1938–87
Lugt, Frits. *Répertoire des catalogues de ventes publiques. . . .* 4 vols. The Hague, 1938–87.

Lugt 1956
Lugt, Frits. *Les marques de collections de dessins et d'estampes. . . .* La Haye, 1956.

D. F. Lunsingh Scheurleer 1974
Lunsingh Scheurleer, D. F. *Chinese Export Porcelain, Chine de Commande*. New York, 1974.

Th. H. Lunsingh Scheurleer 1973
Lunsingh Scheurleer, Th. H. "Jacob de Wit beschildert kunstkasten." In *Album Amicorum J. G. van Gelder*, pp. 226–33. Edited by Josua Bruyn et al. The Hague, 1973.

Luton MS catalogue 1799
1799 manuscript inventory of Luton Hoo, Bute Archives at Mount Stuart, Isle of Bute.

Van Maarseveen 1998
Maarseveen, Michel P. van. "Dorpsplunderingen in de schilderkunst van de eerste helft van de zeventiende eeuw." In *Beelden van een strijd, oorlog en kunst vóór de Vrede van Munster 1621–1648*, pp. 148–63. Edited by Michel P. van Maarseveen, J. W. L. Hilkhuijsen, and Jacques Dane. (Exh. cat. Stedelijk Museum Het Prinsenhof, Delft, 1998.) Delft, 1998.

MacLaren 1960
MacLaren, Neil. *The Dutch School*. National Gallery Catalogues. London, 1960.

Madou 1998
Madou, Mirelle. "Vestmenaire aspectem." In *Dirk Bouts, Leuven in de late Middeleeuwen, het laatse Avondmaal*, pp. 196–203. Edited by Anna Bergmans. Tielt and Brussels, 1998.

Madresfield [1889]
Catalogue of the Pictures, Chiefly Historical Portraits at Madresfield Court, to which is Added a List of Miniatures and Enamels. London, [1889].

Madrid 1994
Sutton, Peter C., with John Loughman. *El Siglo de oro del paisaje Holandés.* (Exh. cat. Fundación Colección Thyssen-Bornemisza, Madrid, 1994.) Madrid, 1994.

Madrid/Los Angeles/Houston 2014–15
Vergara, Alejandro, and Anne T. Woollett, eds. *Spectacular Rubens: The Triumph of the Eucharist.* (Exh. cat. Museo Nacional del Prado, Madrid, 25 March–29 June 2014; J. Paul Getty Museum, Los Angeles, 14 October 2014–11 January 2015; Museum of Fine Arts, Houston, 15 February–10 May 2015.) Los Angeles, 2014.

De Maeyer 1955
Maeyer, Marcel de. *Albrecht en Isabella en de Schilderkunst*. Verhandelingen van de Koninklijke Vlaamse Academie voor Wetenschappen, Letteren en Schone Kunsten van België, Klasse der Schone Kunsten 9. Brussels, 1955.

Magurn 1971
Magurn, Ruth Saunders, transl. and ed. *The Letters of Peter Paul Rubens*. Cambridge, 1971.

Malraux 1974
Malraux, André. *La metamorphose des dieux, l'irréel*, vol. 2. Paris, 1974.

Manchester 1857
Art Treasures of the United Kingdom. (Exh. cat. Manchester, 1857.) With essays by Owen Jones, Digby Wyatt, et al. London, 1857.

***"Manchester Guardian"* 1857**
Handbook to the Paintings by Ancient Masters in the Art Treasures Exhibition, Being a Reprint of Critical Notices Originally Published in "The Manchester Guardian." London, 1857.

Van Mander 1604
Mander, Karel van. *Het schilder-boeck*. Including pt. 4, *Wtlegghingh op den Metamorphosis. . . ,* and pt. 5, *Uytbeeldinge der figueren. . . .* Haarlem, 1604.

Van Mander/Miedema 1994–99
Mander, Karel van. *The Lives of the Illustrious Netherlandish and German Painters, from the First Edition of the Schilder-boeck (1603–1604).* 6 vols. Edited by Hessel Miedema. Doornspijk, 1994–99.

Mantz 1873
Mantz, Paul. "La galerie de M. Rothan." Pts. 1 and 2. *Gazette des beaux-arts,* 2nd période, t. 7 (1873): pp. 273–94, 428–49.

Manuth 1998
Manuth, Volker. "Zum Nachleben der Werke Hans Holbeins d. J. in der holländischen Malerei und Graphik des 17. Jahrhunderts." *Zeitschrift* für *Schweizerische Archäologie und Kunstgeschichte (ZAK)* 55/2–4 (1998): pp. 323–35.

Manuth 1999
Manuth, Volker. "Rembrandt and the Artist's Self-portrait: Tradition and Reception." In London/The Hague 1999, pp. 46ff.

Manuth and De Winkel 2019
Manuth, Volker, and Marieke de Winkel. *Rembrandt: The Self-Portraits*. Cologne, 2019.

Manuth, De Winkel, and Van Leeuwen 2019
Manuth, Volker, Marieke de Winkel, and R. van Leeuwen. *Rembrandt: The Complete Paintings*. Cologne, 2019.

Marette 1961
Marette, Jacqueline. *Connaissance des primitifs par l'étude du bois, du XIIe au XVIe siècle*. Paris, 1961.

Marguillier 1903
Marguillier, Auguste. "La collection de M. Rodolphe Kann." Pt. 2. *Les arts: Revue mensuelle des musées, collections, expositions* 2/14 (February 1903): pp. 30–31.

Marijnissen 1988
Marijnissen, R.-H. "Notes on Technique." *Academiae Analecta: Mededelingen van de Koninklijke Academie voor Wetenschappen, Letteren en Schone Kunsten van België* 49/1 (1988): pp. 107–14.

Marlier 1957
Marlier, Georges. *Ambrosius Benson et la peinture à Bruges au temps de Charles-Quint*. Damme, 1957.

"Marquis of Bute" 1882
"The Marquis of Bute's Pictures at Bethnal Green (first notice)." *Athenaeum* 2879 (30 December 1882): p. 905.

"Marquis of Bute" 1883
"The Marquis of Bute's Pictures at Bethnal Green." *Athenaeum* 2880 (6 January 1883): pp. 23–24.

Marrow 1977
Marrow, James H. "*Circumdederunt me canes multi*: Christ's Tormentors in Northern European Art of the Late Middle Ages and Early Renaissance." *Art Bulletin* 59 (1977): pp. 167–81.

Marrow 1979
Marrow, James H. *Passion Iconography in Northern European Art of the Late Middle Ages and Early Renaissance: A Study in the Transformation of Sacred Metaphor into Descriptive Narrative*. Kortrijk, 1979.

Marshall 1993
Marshall, David Ryley. *Viviano and Niccolò Codazzi and the Baroque Architectural Fantasy*. Milan, 1993.

J. R. Martin 1968
Martin, John Rupert. *The Ceiling Paintings for the Jesuit Church in Antwerp*. New York, 1968.

J. R. Martin 1972
Martin, John Rupert. "Northern 17th-Century Painting." In Princeton 1972–74, pp. 34–49.

W. Martin 1909
Martin, Wilhelm. "L'exposition Jan Steen à Londres." *L'art flamand et hollandais* 12 (1909): pp. 129–58.

W. Martin 1911
Martin, Wilhelm. "De tentoonstelling van oudhollandsche schilderijen te Parijs." *Elseviers maandblad* 21/42 (1911): pp. 240–54.

W. Martin 1913
Martin, Wilhelm. *Gérard Dou: Des Meisters Gemälde in 247 Abbildungen*. Klassiker der Kunst in Gesamtausgaben 24. Stuttgart and Berlin, 1913.

W. Martin 1927–28
Martin, Wilhelm. "Neues über Jan Steen." *Zeitschrift für bildende Kunst* 61 (1927–28): pp. 325–41.

W. Martin 1954
Martin, Wilhelm. *Jan Steen*. Bibliotheek der nederlandse kunst. Amsterdam, 1954.

W. Martin and Moes 1912
Martin, Wilhelm, and Ernst Wilhelm Moes. *Oude schilderkunst in Nederland: Schilderijen van Hollandsche en Vlaamsche meesters in raadhuizen...*, vol. 1. 's-Gravenhage, 1912.

Martínez Leiva and Rodríguez Rebollo 2015
Martínez Leiva, Gloria, and Ángel Rodríguez Rebollo. *El Inventario del Alcázar de Madrid de 1666, Felipe IV y su colección artística*. Madrid, 2015.

Masschelein-Kleiner et al. 1978–79
Masschelein-Kleiner, Liliane, et al. "Examen et traitement d'une de tempe sur toil attribuée à Thierry Bouts." *Bulletin* (Institut royal du Patrimoine artistique) 17 (1978–79): pp. 5–20.

Massing 1991
Massing, J. M. "Three Panels by the Master of the View of Ste-Gudule in the Chapel of Queens' College, Cambridge." *Burlington Magazine* 133 (1991): pp. 690–93.

Matsche 1994
Matsche, Franz. "Lucas Cranachs mythologische Darstellungen." In Kronach 1994, pp. 81ff.

McCleery 1974
McCleery, W. "A Businessman and Art Collector Talks of Art and Business." *University* (Princeton University) 60 (spring 1974): p. 10.

McGrath 1997
McGrath, Elizabeth. *Subjects from History*. 2 vols. Corpus Rubenianum Ludwig Burchard 13/1. London, 1997.

McNamee 1972
McNamee, Maurice B. "The Origin of the Vested Angel as a Eucharistic Symbol." *Art Bulletin* 54 (1972): pp. 263–78.

McNamee 1998
McNamee, Maurice B. *Vested Angels: Eucharistic Allusions in Early Netherlandish Paintings*. Louvain, 1998.

Meaume 1860
Meaume, Eduoard. *Recherches sur la vie et les ouvrages de Jacques Callot*. 3rd ed., 2 vols. Paris, 1860.

Van der Meer 1969
Catalogue of Our Collection of 16th- and 17th-Century Paintings: A. van der Meer, Amsterdam. Amsterdam, 1969.

D. C. Meijer 1886
Meijer, D. C., Jr. "De familieportretten der Alewijns." *De Gids* (1886): pp. 326–39.

F. G. Meijer 2012
Meijer, F. G. *Jan Davidsz. de Heem, Utrecht 1606–1683/4 Antwerp. A Still Life of a Vase of Flowers, a Silver Tazza and Two Pewter Dishes of Fruit on a Table Draped with an Oriental Carpet and a Red Cloth*. London, 2012.

F. G. Meijer 2016
Meijer, F. G. "Jan Davidsz. de Heem 1606–1684." PhD diss., Amsterdam School of Historical Studies, University of Amsterdam, 2016. https://dare.uva.nl/search?identifier=b57017f0-4361-423c-a85e-46dc01608fd7.

Meiss 1966
Meiss, Millard. "Sleep in Venice. Ancient Myths and Renaissance Proclivities." *Proceedings of the American Philosophical Society* 110/5 (1966): pp. 348–82.

Meiss 1974
Meiss, Millard. "Scholarship and Penitence in the Early Renaissance: The Image of St. Jerome." *Pantheon* 32 (April–June 1974): pp. 134–40.

Meldrum 1923
Meldrum, D. S. *Rembrandt's Paintings*. London, 1923.

Mellinkoff 1970
Mellinkoff, Ruth. *The Horned Moses in Medieval Art and Thought*. California Studies in the History of Art 14. Berkeley, 1970.

Ménard 1873
Ménard, René. "Collection Laurent Richard." *Gazette des beaux-arts*, per. 2, 7 (1873): pp. 177–96.

Mensaert 1763
Mensaert, Guillaume Pierre. *Le peintre amateur et curieux, ou description générale des tableaux des plus habiles maîtres. . . .* 2 vols. Brussels, 1763.

Merle du Bourg 2004
Merle du Bourg, Alexis. *Peter Paul Rubens et la France, 1600–1640*. Histoire de l'art. Temps, espace et société, 873. Villeneauve d'Ascq, 2004.

Van der Meulen 1994–95
Meulen, Marjon van der. *Copies after the Antique*. 3 vols. Edited by Arnout Balis. Corpus Rubenianum Ludwig Burchard 23. London, 1994–95.

De Meyere 1986–87
Meyere, Jos A. L. de. "Hendrik ter Brugghen en tijdgenoten (I): Nieuw licht op de Gouden Eeuw." *Antiek* 21 (1986–87): pp. 341–53.

E. Michel 1893
Michel, Emile. *Rembrandt*. Paris, 1893.

E. Michel 1901
Michel, Emile. "La Galerie de M. Rodolphe Kann (premier article)." *Gazette des beaux-arts*, ser. 3, 25 (1901): pp. 385–400, 493–506.

J. F. M. Michel 1771
Michel, Jean François Marie. *Histoire de la vie de P. P. Rubens, Chevalier, & Seigneur de Steen*. Brussels, 1771.

Middendorf 1989
Middendorf, Ulrike. *Hendrik Jacobsz. Dubbels (1621–1707): Gemälde und Zeichnungen mit kritischem Oeuvrekatalog*. Freren, 1989.

Miedema 1977
Miedema, Hessel. "Realism and Comic Mode: The Peasant." *Simiolus* 9/1 (1977): pp. 205–19.

Miedema 1981
Miedema, Hessel. "Feestende boeren—lachende dorpers. Bij twee recente aanwinsten van het Rijksprentenkabinet." *Bulletin van het Rijksmuseum* 29/4 (1981): pp. 191–213.

Van Miegroet 1988
Miegroet, Hans J. van. "The Getty Annunciation and Early Netherlandish Canvases: Bouts in Perspective." *Academiae Analecta: Mededelingen van de Koninklijke Academie voor Wetenschappen, Letteren en Schone Kunsten van België, Klasse der Schone Kunsten* 49/1 (1988): pp. 91–106.

Van Miegroet 1989
Miegroet, Hans J. van. *Gérard David*. Antwerp, 1989.

Van Miegroet 1992a
Miegroet, Hans J. van. "Dieric Bouts, *The Annunciation*." In Bauman and Liedtke 1992, pp. 63f.

Van Miegroet 1992b
Miegroet, Hans J. van. "Gérard David, *The Coronation of the Virgin*." In Bauman and Liedtke 1992, pp. 94f.

Mielke 1979
Mielke, Hans. *Manierismus in Holland um 1600: Kupferstiche, Holzschnitte und Zeichnungen aus dem Berliner Kupferstichkabinett*. Berlin, 1979.

Mielke and Winner 1977
Mielke, Hans, and Matthew Winner. *Peter Paul Rubens Kritischer Katalog der Zeichnungen, Originale-Umkreis Kopien. Staatliche Museen Preussischer Kulturbesitz*. Berlin, 1977.

Milan 1872a
Catalogo delle opere d'arte antica: Esposte nel Palazzo di Brera. (Exh. cat. Palazzo Brera, Milan, 26 August–7 October 1872.) 2nd ed. Milan, 1872.

Milan 1872b
Guida all'Esposizione d'arte nel Palazzo di Brera. (Exh. cat. Palazzo Brera, Milan, 1872.) Milan, 1872.

Millar 1953
Millar, Oliver. "Catalogue of the Works at Malahide Castle." Unpub. MS, 1953.

Millen and Wolf 1989
Millen, Ronald Forsyth, and Robert Erich Wolf. *Heroic Deeds and Mystic Figures: A New Reading of Rubens' Life of Maria de' Medici*. Princeton, 1989.

Miller 1990
Miller, Dwight C. "A Note on the Collection of the Duke of Leuchtenberg." *Paragone*, n.s. 24/489 (November 1990): pp. 76–83.

Millier 1946
Millier, A. "Los Angeles Stages Important Review of Rubens and Van Dyck." *Art Digest* 21/5 (1 December 1946): pp. 5, 31.

Minneapolis/Houston/San Diego 1985
Keyes, George S., et al. *Dutch and Flemish Masters: Paintings from the Vienna Academy of Fine Arts*. (Exh. cat. Minneapolis Institute of Arts; Museum of Fine Arts, Houston; San Diego Museum of Art, 1985.) Minneapolis, 1985.

Mireur 1901–12
Mireur, H. *Dictionnaire des ventes d'art faites en France et à l'étranger pendant les XVIIIme & XIX siècles*. 7 vols. Paris, 1901–12.

De Mirimonde 1962
Mirimonde, A. P. de. "Jan Massys dans les musées de Province Français." *Gazette des beaux-arts* per. 6, 60 (1962): pp. 543–68.

De Mirimonde 1966
Mirimonde, A. P. de. "La musique dans les allégories de l'amour." *Gazette des beaux-arts* 68 (1966): pp. 265–90.

Moes 1892–1905
Moes, Ernst Wilhelm. *Iconographia Batava*. 2 vols. Amsterdam, 1892–1905.

Moes 1909
Moes, Ernst Wilhelm. *Frans Hals: sa vie et son oeuvre*. Translated by J. de Bosschere. Brussels, 1909.

Moes 1910
Moes, Ernst Wilhelm. "Brekelenkam, Quiringh Gerritsz. van." In Thieme-Becker 1907–50, vol. 4 (1910): pp. 574f.

Moes 1911
Moes, Ernst Wilhelm. "De inventaris van den inboedel nagelaten door Dirck Alewijn in 1637." *Jaarboek der Vereeniging Amstelodamum* 9 (1911), pp. 31–54.

Molanus 1570
Molanus, Johannes. *De picturis et imaginibus sacris, liber unus. . . .* Louvain, 1570.

Molhuysen and Blok 1911–37
Molhuysen, P. C., and P. J. Blok, eds. *Nieuw Nederlandsch biografisch woordenboek*. 10 vols. Leiden, 1911–37.

Møller and Vestergaard 1998
Møller, Vibeke Andersson, and Karin Vestergaard. "Maleren Isaac Isaacsz. opdaget på Ledreborg." *Nationalmuseets Arbejdsmark* (1998): pp. 72–86.

Mols n.d.
François Mols. *Rubeniana*. vol. 1 of 3. KBR MS 5725, fol. 152v. Handwritten manuscript. Rubenshuis Bibliotheek, Antwerp.

Moltke 1938–39
Moltke, Joachim Wolfgang von. "Salomon de Bray." *Marburger Jahrbuch für Kunstwissenschaft* 11–12 (1938–39): pp. 309–414.

Moltke 1939
Moltke, Joachim Wolfgang von, ed. *Dutch and Flemish Old Masters in the Collection of Dr. C. J. K. van Aalst, Huis-te-Hoevelaken, Holland*. Foreword by Wilhelm R. Valentiner. Verona, 1939.

De Montfaucon 1719
Montfaucon, Bernard de. *L'Antiquité expliquée et représentée en figures. . . .* 5 vols. Paris, 1719.

Montias 1991
Montias, John Michael. "'Perspectives' in 17th-Century Inventories." In *Perspectives: Saenredam and the Architectural Painters of the 17th Century*, pp. 19–38. (Exh. cat. Museum Boijmans Van Beuningen, Rotterdam, 1991.) By Jeroen Giltaij and Guido Jansen. Rotterdam, 1991.

Montreal 1944
Loan Exhibition of Great Paintings: Five Centuries of Dutch Art. (Exh. cat. Art Association of Montreal, 1944.) Montreal, 1944.

Montreal/Toronto 1969
Rembrandt and His Pupils: A Loan Exhibition of Paintings Commemorating the 300th Anniversary of Rembrandt. (Exh. cat. Montreal Museum of Fine Arts; Art Gallery of Ontario, Toronto, 1969.) London, 1969.

Moore-Gwyn 2007
Moore-Gwyn, David. "Ashford, William." *Grove Art Online*. Accessed July 24, 2007. http://www.groveart.com.

Moote 1989
Moote, A. Lloyd. *Louis XIII, the Just*. Berkeley, 1989.

Morandotti 2008
Morandotti, Alessandro. *Il Collezionismo in Lombardia: Studi e Ricerche tra '600 e '800*. Milan, 2008.

Morse 1979
Morse, J. D. *Old Master Paintings in North America*. New York, 1979.

Du Mortier 1989
Mortier, Bianca M. du. "Costume in Frans Hals." In *Frans Hals*, pp. 45–60. Edited by Seymour Slive. (Exh. cat. National Gallery of Art, Washington, DC; Royal Academy of Arts, London; Frans Hals Museum, Haarlem, 1989.) London, 1989.

Du Mortier 1992
Mortier, Bianca M. du. *Waaiers en waaierbladen 1650–1800 / Fans and Fan Leaves 1650–1800*. Amsterdam and Zwolle, 1992.

Du Mortier 2010
Mortier, Bianca M. du. "Costumes in Gabriel Metsu's Paintings: Mode and Manners in the Mid-Seventeenth Century." In Dublin/Amsterdam/Washington 2010–11, pp. 126–53.

Du Mortier et al. 2016
Mortier, Bianca M. du, et al. *Costume and Fashion*. Amsterdam, 2016.

Moxey 1981–82
Moxey, Keith P. F. "Sebald Beham's 'Church Anniversary Holidays': Festive Peasants as Instruments of Repressive Humor." *Simiolus* 12/2–3 (1981–82): pp. 107–30.

Muchnic 1998
Muchnic, Suzanne. *Odd Man In: Norton Simon and the Pursuit of Culture*. Berkeley, 1998.

Muchnic 2019
Muchnic, Suzanne. *Odd Man in: Norton Simon and the Pursuit of Culture*. Second ed. Pasadena, 2019.

Müllenmeister 1978–81
Müllenmeister, Kurt J. *Meer und Land im Licht des 17. Jahrhunderts*. Bk. 2, *Tierdarstellungen in Werken niederländischer Künstler A–M*. 2 vols. Bremen, 1978–81.

Müllenmeister 1988
Müllenmeister, Kurt J. *Roelant Savery . . . die Gemälde mit kritischem Œuvrekatalog*. Freren, 1988.

J. M. Muller 1989
Muller, Jeffrey M. *Rubens: The Artist as Collector*. Princeton, 1989.

Müller Hofstede 2000
Müller Hofstede, Justus. "Rubens in Italien 1600–1608. Rangstufen der Skulptur in der Imitatio von Antike und Florentiner Cinquecento." In *L'Europa e l'arte Italiana*, pp. 283–305. Edited by Max Seidel. Venice, 2000.

Mündler 1867
Mündler, O[tto]. Review of G. F. Waagen 1866. *Zeitschrift für bildende Kunst* 2 (1867): p. 48.

Mundy 1980
Mundy, E. James. "Gerard David Studies." PhD diss., Princeton University, 1980.

Munich 1962
Hiepe, Richard. *Meister des Manierismus: Gemälde, Handzeichnungen, Druckgraphik*. (Exh. cat. Galerie Wolfgang Gurlitt, Munich, 1962.) Munich, 1962.

Munich 1973
Krempel, Ulla. *Jan van Kessel d. Ä, 1626–1679: die vier Erdteile*. (Exh. cat. Alte Pinakothek, Munich, 1973.) Munich, 1973.

Münster 1976
Langemeyer, Gerhard, and Reinhart Schleier. *Bilder nach Bildern, Druckgrafik und die Vermittlung von Kunst*. (Exh. cat. Westfälisches Landesmuseum für Kunst und Kulturgeschichte, Münster, 1976.) Münster, 1976.

Muxel 1825/28
Muxel, J. N. *Catalogue des tableaux de la galerie de feu son altesse royale, monseigneur le prince Eugène, duc de Leuchtenberg à Munich*. Munich, 1825; repr. 1828.

Muxel 1845
Muxel, J. N. *Catalogue des tableaux de la galerie de feu son altesse royale, monseigneur le prince Eugène, duc de Leuchtenberg à Munich*. Munich, 1845.

Muxel 1851
Muxel, J. N. *Gemälde Sammlung in München . . . des Dom Augusto, Herzogs von Leuchtenberg und Santa Cruz . . . Fürsten von Eichstädt. . . .* Munich, 1851.

Nagler, Andresen and Clauss 1858–79
Nagler, Georg Kaspar, Andreas Andresen, and Carl Clauss. *Die Monogrammisten und diejenigen bekannten und unbekannten Künstler aller Schulen*. 5 vols. Munich, 1858–79.

J. Nash 1972
Nash, J. M. *The Age of Rembrandt and Vermeer*. New York, 1972.

S. Nash 2008
Nash, S. *Northern Renaissance Art*. New York, 2008.

Nathan 1972
Nathan, Peter. *Dr. Fritz Nathan und Dr. Peter Nathan, 1922–1972*. Zurich, 1972.

Natter 2003
Natter, G. Tobias. "Artaria." *Grove Art Online*. 2003. http://www.groveart.com.

Neale 1819–23
Neale, J[ohn] P[reston]. *Views of the Seats of Noblemen and Gentlemen, in England, Wales, Scotland, and Ireland*. 6 vols. London, 1819–23.

Neale 1824–29
Neale, J[ohn] P[reston]. *Views of the Seats of Noblemen and Gentlemen, in England, Wales, Scotland, and Ireland*. 2nd ser. 5 vols. London, 1824–29.

Neale 1829–31
Neale, J[ohn] P[reston]. *Jones' Views of the Seats, Mansions, Castles, etc. of Noblemen and Gentlemen in England*. 3 vols. London, 1829–31.

Neale 1847
Neale, J[ohn] P[reston]. *The Mansions of England or Picturesque Delineations of the Seats of Noblemen and Gentlemen, from drawings by J. P. Neale, Esq.re Arranged in Counties*. 2 vols. London, 1847.

Nehlsen-Marten 2003
Nehlsen-Marten, Britta. *Dirck Hals 1591–1656. Oeuvre und Entwicklung eines Haarlemer Genremalers*. Weimar, 2003.

Newton 1999
Newton, Stella Mary. *Fashion in the Age of the Black Prince: A Study of the Years 1340–1365*. Woodbridge, Suffolk, and Rochester, 1999.

New York 1913
Bode, Wilhelm von. *The Collection of Pictures of the Late Herr A. de Ridder, Formerly in His Villa at Schönberg near Cronberg in the Taunus*. Translated by Harry Virgin. (Exh. cat. F. Kleinberger Galleries, New York, 1913.) New York, 1913.

New York 1915
Loan Exhibition of Masterpieces by Old and Modern Painters. (Exh. cat. M. Knoedler & Co., New York, 6–14 April 1915.) New York, 1915.

New York 1929
Loan Exhibition of Flemish Primitives in Aid of the Free Milk Fund for Babies Inc. By Harry G. Sperling; preface by Max J. Friedländer. (Exh. cat. F. Kleinberger Galleries, New York, 28 October–16 November 1929.) New York, 1929.

New York 1939a
Masterpieces of Art. Catalogue of European Paintings and Sculpture from 1300–1800. Compiled by George Henry McCall; edited by William R. Valentiner. (Exh. cat. New York World's Fair, May–October 1939.) New York, 1939.

New York 1939b
Masterpieces of Art: Official Souvenir Guide and Picture Book. (Exh. cat. New York World's Fair, 1939.) New York, 1939.

New York 1939c
Pollaiuolo to Picasso: Classics of the Nude. (Exh. cat. M. Knoedler & Co., New York, 10–29 April 1939.) New York, 1939.

New York 1940
Masterpieces of Art. Catalogue of European and American Paintings, 1500–1900. (Exh. cat. New York World's Fair, May–October 1940.) New York, 1940.

New York 1942a
Flemish Primitives. (Exh. cat. M. Knoedler & Co., New York, 13 April–9 May 1942.) New York, 1942.

New York 1942b
Paintings by the Great Dutch Masters of the Seventeenth Century: Loan Exhibition in Aid of the Queen Wilhelmina Fund and the American Women's Voluntary Services. (Exh. cat. Duveen Brothers, New York, 8 October–7 November 1942.) New York, 1942.

New York 1943
A Loan Exhibition of Fashion in Headdress, 1450–1943. (Exh. cat. Wildenstein & Co., New York, 27 April–27 May, 1943.) New York, 1943.

New York 1946a
An Exhibition of Flemish Paintings of the Fifteenth and Early Sixteenth Centuries. (Exh. cat. Duveen Brothers, New York, 1946.) New York, 1946.

New York 1946b
Paintings from the 16th to the 18th Centuries. (Exh. cat. Duveen Brothers, New York, 1946.) New York, 1946.

New York 1964
Masterworks of Flemish and Related Art: Exhibition of Painting and Sculpture. (Exh. cat. Duveen Brothers, New York, February–April 1964.) New York, 1964.

New York 1967
Dutch Seventeenth-Century Paintings. (Exh. cat. H. Shickman Gallery, New York, October 1967.) New York, 1967.

New York 1974–75
The Grand Gallery at the Metropolitan Museum of Art. Sixth International Exhibition Presented by C.I.N.O.A., la Confédération internationale des négociants en œuvres d'art. (Exh. cat. Metropolitan Museum of Art, New York, 19 October 1974–5 January 1975.) New York, 1974.

New York 1992–93
Masterworks from the Musée des Beaux-Arts, Lille. (Exh. cat. Metropolitan Museum of Art, New York, 27 October 1992–17 January 1993.) New York, 1992.

New York 1998–99
Ainsworth, Maryan, and Keith Christiansen, eds. *From Van Eyck to Bruegel: Early Netherlandish Painting in the Metropolitan Museum of Art.* (Exh. cat. Metropolitan Museum of Art, New York, 22 September 1998–3 January 1999.) New York, 1998.

New York 2004
Evans, Helen C., ed. *Byzantium: Faith and Power 1261–1557.* (Exh. cat. Metropolitan Museum of Art, New York, 23 March–4 July 2004.) New York, 2004.

New York 2009
Margaret Iacono, with essay by Sara Campbell. *Masterpieces of European Painting from the Norton Simon Museum.* (Exh. cat. Frick Collection, New York, 2009.) New York, 2009.

Nicholas 1994
Nicholas, Lynn. *The Rape of Europa: The Fate of Europe's Treasure in the Third Reich and the Second World War.* New York, 1994.

Nicolai 1786
Nicolai, Friedrich. *Beschreibung der königlichen Residenzstädte Berlin und Potsdam.* 3 vols. Berlin, 1786.

Nicolle 1908
Nicolle, Marcel. "La Collection Rodolphe Kann." *Revue de l'art ancien et modern* 23 (1908): pp. 187–204.

Nicolson 1958
Nicolson, Benedict. *Hendrick Terbrugghen.* London, 1958.

Nicolson 1971
Nicolson, Benedict. "Gerard Seghers and the 'Denial of St. Peter.'" *Burlington Magazine* 113 (1971): pp. 304–09.

Nicolson 1977
Nicolson, Benedict. "Stomer Brought Up-to-date." *Burlington Magazine* 119/889 (April 1977): pp. 230–45.

Nicolson 1979
Nicolson, Benedict. *The International Caravaggesque Movement.* Oxford, 1979.

Nicolson/Vertova 1990
Nicolson, Benedict. *Caravaggism in Europe.* Revised and expanded by Luisa Vertova. 3 vols. Turin, 1990. Rev. ed. of Nicolson 1979.

Niemeyer 1959
Niemeyer, J. W. "Mededelingen van het Rijksbureau voor Kunsthistorische Documentatie. Het topografisch element in enkele riviergezichten van Salomon van Ruysdael nader beschouwd." *Oud Holland* 74 (1959): pp. 51–56.

Niessen 2010
Niessen, Judith. "De Meester van Alkmaar en zijn werkplaats, een heroverweging." *Oud Holland* 123 (2010): pp. 260–304.

N. N. 1903
N. N. "The Dutch Exhibition at the Guildhall. Article 1: The Old Masters." *Burlington Magazine* 2/4 (June 1903): pp. 50–63.

Noble et al. 2012
Noble, Petra, et al. "Rembrandt and/or Studio, *Saul and David,* c. 1655: Visualising the Curtain Using Cross-section Analyses and X-ray Fluorescence Imaging." *Technè: La science au service de l'histoire de l'art et des civilisations* 35 (2012): 36–45.

Noe 1930
Noe, Sidney P. "Flemish Primitives in New York." *American Magazine of Art* 21/1 (January 1930): pp. 30–39.

Noël 1837
Noël, Matthias Joseph de. *Catalogue of the Collection of the Paintings of the Late J. Lyversberg Esq. at Cologn.* Cologne, 1837.

"Notable Works of Art" 1966
"Notable Works of Art." *Burlington Magazine* 108 (1966): advertising supplement following p. 650.

"Notable Works of Art" 1968
"Notable Works of Art Now on the Market." *Burlington Magazine* 110 (December 1968): p. xlii.

Nuremburg 1952
Aufgang der Neuzeit: Deutsche Kunst und Kultur von Dürers Tod bis zum Dreißigjährigen Kriege, 1530–1650. (Exh. cat. Germanisches Nationalmuseum, Nuremburg, 15 July–15 October 1952.) Nuremburg, 1952.

Nuttall 2012
Nuttall, Paula. "Reconsidering the Nude: Northern Tradition and Venetian Innovation." In *The Meanings of Nudity in Medieval Art,* pp. 299–318. Edited by Sherry C. M. Lindquist. Farnham, 2012.

Nuttall 2004
Nuttall, Paula. *From Flanders to Florence: The Impact of Netherlandish Painting, 1400–1500.* New Haven and London, 2004.

Nuttall 2013
Nuttall, Paula. *Face to Face: Flanders and Renaissance Painting.* San Marino, 2013.

Oakland 1969
Art Treasures in California. (Exh. cat. Oakland Museum, 1969.) Oakland, 1969.

Odom and Salmond 2009
Odom, Anne, and Wendy R. Salmond, eds. *Treasures into Tractors: The Selling of Russia's Cultural Heritage, 1918–1938.* Seattle, 2009.

Oertel 1929
Oertel, R. "Alte Meister aus Leipziger Privatbesitz." *Pantheon* (December 1929): pp. 582–83.

Oesterreich 1773
Oesterreich, Matthias. *Beschreibung aller Gemählde, Antiquitäten, und anderer kostbarer und merkwürdiger Sachen, so in denen beyden Schlössern von Sans-Souci, wie auch in dem Schlosse zu Potsdam und Charlottenburg enthalten sind.* Berlin, 1773.

Olbricht 1972
Olbricht, Klaus-Hartmut. "Eine Qualitätsmesse mit Rekordverkäufen." *Die Kunst und das schöne Heim* 84/12 (December 1972): pp. 755f.

Oldenbourg 1911
Oldenbourg, Rudolf. *Thomas de Keysers Tätigkeit als Maler, ein Beitrag zur Geschichte des holländischen Porträts.* Leipzig, 1911.

Oldenbourg [1921]
Oldenbourg, Rudolf, ed. *P. P. Rubens, Des Meisters Gemälde in 538 Abbildungen.* Klassiker der Kunst in Gesamtausgaben 5. 4th rev. ed. Stuttgart, [1921].

Oldenbourg 1922
Oldenbourg, Rudolf. *Peter Paul Rubens, Sammlung der von Rudolf Oldenbourg veröffentlichten oder zur Veröffentlichung vorbereiteten Abhandlungen über den Meister.* Edited by W. von Bode. Munich and Berlin, 1922.

Olivar 2010
Olivar, John. "The First Woman Architect." *Architects' Journal,* 11 November 2010. https://www.architectsjournal.co.uk/practice/culture/the-first-woman-architect.

Orlers 1641
Orlers, J[an] J[ansz]. *Beschryvinge der Stadt Leyden. . . .* 2nd ed. Leyden [Leiden], 1641.

Osnabrugge 2014
Osnabrugge, Marije. "New Documents for Matthias Stom in Naples." *Burlington Magazine* 156/1331 (February 2014): pp. 107f.

Osnabrugge 2019
Osnabrugge, Marije. *The Neapolitan Lives and Careers of Netherlandish Painters, 1575–1655.* Amsterdam, 2019.

Ost 2000
Ost, Hans. "Anna von Österreich und Elisabeth von Frankreich: Zu einigen Porträts von Frans Pourbus d.J., Peter Paul Rubens und Cornelis de Vos." *Jahrbuch der Staatlichen Kunstsammlungen in Baden-Württemberg* 37 (2000): pp. 57–80.

Osten 1973
Osten, Gert von der. *Deutsche und niederländische Kunst der Reformationzeit*. Cologne, 1973.

Osten and Vey 1969
Osten, Gert von der, and Horst Vey. *Painting and Sculpture in Germany and the Netherlands, 1500 to 1600*. Baltimore, 1969.

Paderborn 2015
Wandschneider, Andrea, et al. *Die Brueghel Familie = The Brueghel Family*. (Exh. cat. Städische Galerie in der Reithalle, Paderborn, 2015.) Paderborn, 2015.

Padovanni et al. 1996
Padovanni, S., et al. *L'Età di Savonarola: Fra Bartolomeo e la scuola di San Marco*. Venice, 1996.

Panofsky 1958
Panofsky, Erwin. *Early Netherlandish Paintings: Its Origins and Character*. Charles Eliot Norton Lectures, 1947–48. 2 vols. Cambridge, 1958.

Panofsky 2005
Panofsky, Erwin. *The Life and Art of Albrecht Dürer*. Princeton, 2005.

Paolucci and Lapi Ballerini 2004
Paolucci, Antonio, and Isabella Lapi Ballerini, eds. *Palazzo degli Alberti. Le collezioni d'arte della Cariprato*. Milan, 2004.

Paris 1895
The Second Hundred Paintings by Old Masters. (Ill. cat. Galerie Sedelmeyer, Paris.) Paris, 1895.

Paris 1911
Exposition des grands et petits maîtres hollandais du XVIIe siècle. (Exh. cat. Salle du Jeu de Paume, Paris, 1911.) Paris, 1911.

Paris 1936
Sterling, Charles. *Rubens et son temps*. (Exh. cat. Musée de l'Orangerie, Paris, 1936.) Paris, 1936.

Paris 1969
Maîtres anciens. (Exh. cat. M. Knoedler & Co., Paris, 4 June–31 July 1969.) Paris, 1969.

Paris 1970
Le siècle de Rembrandt: Tableaux hollandaise des collections publiques françaises. (Exh. cat. Musée du Petit Palais, Paris, 1970.) Paris, 1970.

Paris 2017
Jacquot, Dominique, et al. *Rubens, Portraits princiers*. (Exh. cat. Musée Luxembourg, Paris, 2017.) Paris, 2017.

Paris/New York/Chicago 1982
Rosenberg, Pierre. *France in the Golden Age: Seventeenth-Century French Paintings in American Collections / La peinture Française au XVIIe siècle dans les collections américaines*. (Exh. cat. Galeries Nationales du Grand Palais, Paris; Metropolitan Museum of Art, New York; Art Institute of Chicago, 1982.) Paris and New York, 1982.

Parker 2004
Parker, Geoffrey. *The Army of Flanders and the Spanish Road, 1567–1659: The Logistics of Spanish Victory and Defeat in the Low Countries' War*. Cambridge and New York, 2004.

Parthey 1863–64
Parthey, G[ustav]. *Deutscher Bildersaal. Verzeichniss der in Deutschland vorhandenen Oelbilder verstorbener Maler aller Schulen*. 2 vols. Berlin, 1863–64.

Pasadena 1980
Selected Paintings at the Norton Simon Museum, Pasadena, California. Introduction by Frank Herrmann. London and New York, 1980.

Pasadena 1989
Campbell, Sara, ed. *Masterpieces from the Norton Simon Museum*. Pasadena, 1989.

Pasadena 2003
Campbell, Sara, Christine Knoke, and Gloria Williams, eds. *Handbook of the Norton Simon Museum*. Pasadena, 2003.

Passavant 1833
Passavant, Johann David. *Kunstreise durch England und Belgien*. . . . Frankfurt, 1833.

Passavant 1836
Passavant, Johann David. *Tour of a German Artist in England*. London, 1836.

Passavant and Muxel 1851
Passavant, Johann David. *Galerie Leuchtenberg: Gemälde-Sammlung . . . des Herzogs von Leuchtenberg in München*. Engravings by J. N. Muxel. 2nd rev. ed. Frankfurt, 1851; rev. ed. of Muxel 1851.

Passavant and Muxel 1852
Passavant, Johann David. *The Leuchtenberg Gallery: A Collection of Pictures Forming the Celebrated Gallery of His Imperial Highness the Duke of Leuchtenberg, at Munich*. Engravings by J. N. Muxel. Frankfurt and London, 1852. [English ed. of Passavant and Muxel 1851.]

Van de Passe 1643–44
Passe, Crispijn van de. *La prima-[quinta] parte della luce del dipingere et disegnare*. . . . Amsterdam, 1643–44.

Pauli 1911
Pauli, Gustave. *Hans Sebald Beham: Nachtraege zu dem kritischen Verzeichnis seiner Kupferstiche, Radierungen und Holzschnitte*. Strassburg, 1911.

Pauwels 1953
Pauwels, C. H. "De schilder Matthias Stomer." *Gentse bijdragen tot de kunstgeschiedenis* 14 (1953): pp. 139–92.

Pavord 1999
Pavord, Anna. *The Tulip*. London, 1999.

Van Peer 1971
Peer, H. F. van. *Beeld van een oude stad, Gezicht op Gorcum*. Alphen aan den Rijn, 1971.

Péladan 1912
Péladan, Joséphin. *Frans Hals, 1580(?)–1666*. Paris, 1912.

Pennisi 2007
Pennisi, Meghan S. W. *The Flower Still-life Painting of Ambrosius Bosschaert the Elder in Middelburg*. PhD diss., Northwestern University, 2007.

Penta 1990
Penta, Maria Teresa. "Un'opera di Matthias Stom a Napoli." *Storia dell'Arte* 69 (1990): pp. 245–55.

Perger 1853
Perger, A[nton], Ritter von. "Die Kunstchatze Wiens, V: Die Gallerie des Grafen von Czernin." *Österreichische Blätter für Literatur und Kunst* 41 (10 October 1853): pp. 236–37.

Pérez Sánchez 1985
Pérez Sánchez, Alfonso E. *Juan Carreño de Miranda (1614–1685)*. Avilés, 1985.

Pérez Sánchez 1986
Pérez Sánchez, Alfonso E. *Carreño, Rizi, Herrera y la pintura madrileña de su tiempo*. Madrid, 1986.

Peri 1992
Peri, Paolo. *The Handkerchief*. Modena, 1992.

Périer-d'Ieteren 1994
Périer-d'Ieteren, Catherine. "La technique de Memling et sa place dans l'évolution de la peinture flamande du XVe siècle." In Bruges 1994, pp. 67–77.

Périer-d'Ieteren 2006
Périer-d'Ieteren, Catherine, with Valentine Henderiks, foreword by Paul Philippot. *Dieric Bouts, The Complete Works*. Brussels, 2006.

Phenix and Lee 2013
Phenix, Alan, and Lynn Lee. *Collections Research Laboratory Analytical Report*. Getty Conservation Institute, 2013.

Philadelphia 1922
Philadelphia Museum of Art. *Catalogue of the W. P. Wilstach Collection: Memorial Hall*. Philadelphia, 1922.

Philadelphia/Berlin/London 1984
Sutton, Peter, et al. *Masters of Seventeenth-Century Dutch Genre Painting*. (Exh. cat. Philadelphia Museum of Art; Gemäldegalerie, Staatliche Museen Preußischer Kulturbesitz, Berlin; Royal Academy of Arts, London, 1984.) Philadelphia, 1984.

Philadelphia/Los Angeles/London 2005–06
Slive, Seymour. *Jacob van Ruisdael: Master of Landscape*. (Exh. cat. Philadelphia Museum of Art; Los Angeles County Museum of Art; Royal Academy of Arts, London, 2005–06.) London, 2005.

Philipp 2020
Philipp, Michael. "Turbans and Silk Robes: Bringing the Orient Home." In *Rembrandt's Orient: West Meets East in Dutch Art of the Seventeenth Century*, pp. 102–03. Edited by Gary Schwartz et al. Munich, 2020.

Phoenix 1999
Komanecky, Michael K., ed. *Copper As Canvas: Two Centuries of Masterpiece Paintings on Copper, 1575–1775*. (Exh. cat. Phoenix Art Museum, 1999.) Oxford, 1999.

Pinder [1943] 1950
Pinder, Wilhelm. *Rembrandts Selbstbildnisse*. Königstein im Taunus, 1950. [1st ed. 1943.]

Plietzsch 1937
Plietzsch, Eduard. "Jacob Ochtervelt." *Pantheon* 20 (December 1937): pp. 364–72.

Plietzsch 1956
Plietzsch, Eduard. "Randbemerkungen zur holländischen Interieurmalerei am Beginn des 17. Jahrhunderts." *Wallraf-Richartz-Jahrbuch* 18 (1956): pp. 174–96.

Plietzsch 1960
Plietzsch, Eduard. *Holländische und flämische Maler des XVII. Jahrh*. Leipzig, 1960.

Pliny 1967
Pliny the Elder. *Natural History*. Translated by H. Rackham et al. Loeb Classical Library, 10 vols. Cambridge and London, 1967.

Ploos van Amstel 1980
Ploos van Amstel, G. *Portret van een koopman en uitvinder, Cornelis Ploos van Amstel: Maatschappelijk, cultureel en familieleven van een achttiende eeuwer*. Assen, 1980.

Poortenaar [1940]
Poortenaar, Jan. *Rembrandt: Zijn kunst en zijn leven*. Antwerp, [1940].

Poughkeepsie 2005
Kuretsky, Susan Donahue, et al. *Time and Transformation in Seventeenth-Century Dutch Art*. (Exh. cat. Frances Lehman Loeb Art Center, Vassar College, Poughkeepsie, 2005.) Poughkeepsie, 2005.

Preibisz 1911
Preibisz, Leon. *Martin van Heemskerck: Ein Beitrag zur Geschichte des Romanismus in der niederländischen Malerei des XVI. Jahrhunderts*. Leipzig, 1911.

Prescott 2005
Prescott, Theodore L., ed. *A Broken Beauty*. Grand Rapids, 2005.

Prévost-Marcilhacy 2022
Prévost-Marcilhacy, Pauline. "Rodolphe (1845–1905) and Maurice Kann (1839–1906)," *Journal of the History of Collections* 34/3 (2022): pp. 481–94.

Priem 1997
Priem, Ruud. "The 'Most Excellent Collection' of Lucretia Johanna van Winter: The Years 1809–22." *Simiolus* 25/2–3 (1997): pp. 103–235.

Princeton 1972–74
Steadman, David W., ed. *Selections from the Norton Simon Inc. Museum of Art*. (Exh. cat. Princeton University Art Museum, 3 December 1972–17 July 1974.) Princeton, 1972.

Van Puyvelde 1947
Puyvelde, Leo van. *The Sketches of Rubens / Les esquisses de Rubens*. Translated by Eveline Winkworth. London, 1947.

Van Puyvelde 1952
Puyvelde, Leo van. *Rubens: Peintres flamands du XVIIe siècle*. Paris and New York, 1952.

Van Puyvelde 1959
Puyvelde, Leo van. "Les 'Saint Ignace' et 'Saint François Xavier' de Rubens." *Gazette des beaux-arts*, per. 6, vol. 53 (1959): pp. 225–36.

Van Puyvelde 1965
Puyvelde, Leo van. "Saint Ignace." In *Le siècle de Rubens*, pp. 187–88, no. 197. (Exh. cat. Musées Royaux des Beaux-Arts de Belgique, Brussels, 15 October–12 December 1965.) Brussels, 1965.

Rademaker 1725
Rademaker, Abraham. *Kabinet van Nederlandsche outheden en gezichten. . . .* Amsterdam, 1725.

Raleigh/Indianapolis/Manchester 2002–03
Weller, Dennis P., with Cynthia von Bogendorf Rupprath and Mariët Westermann. *Jan Miense Molenaer, Painter of the Dutch Golden Age*. (Exh. cat. North Carolina Museum of Art, Raleigh; Indianapolis Museum of Art, Columbus Gallery; Currier Museum of Art, Manchester, 2002–03.) Raleigh, 2002.

Raleigh/Milwaukee/Dayton 1998–99
Weller, Dennis P., with Leonard Slatkes and Roger Ward. *Sinners and Saints: Darkness and Light. Caravaggio and His Dutch and Flemish Followers*. (Exh. cat. North Carolina Museum of Art, Raleigh; Milwaukee Art Museum; Dayton Art Institute, 1998–99.) Raleigh, 1998.

Ratouis de Limay 1913
Ratouis de Limay, Paul. "Un Collectionneur Rouennais au XVIII-siècle: Le président Robert de Saint-Victor." *Archives de l'art français* 7 (1913): pp. 422–39.

Rearick 1978
Rearick, W. R. "Jacopo Bassano and Changing Religious Imagery in the Mid-Cinquecento." In *Essays Presented to Myron P. Gilmore*. Vol. 2, *History of Art, History of Music*, pp. 331–43. Edited by Sergio Bertelli and Gloria Ramakus. Florence, 1978.

Van Regteren Altena 1929
Regteren Altena, I. Q. van. "De tentoonstelling in London, een nabeschouwing." *Maandblad voor beeldende kunsten* 6 (April 1929): pp. 113–24.

Reiss 1975
Reiss, Stephen. *Aelbert Cuyp*. Boston, 1975.

Reithmeier 2010
Reithmeier, Irene. *Johann Konrad von Gemmingen: Fürstbischof von Eichstätt (1593/95–1612); Landesherr und Diözesanvorstand im Späthumanismus*. Regensburg, 2010.

Rem 2003
Rem, Paul H. "Vinckboons, (2) Philips Vingboons." *Grove Art Online*. 2003. http://www.groveart.com.

Reynolds 1980
Reynolds, Catherine. "Dieric Bouts—A Resurrection." In *Art at Auction: The Year at Sotheby Parke Bernet, 1979–1980*, pp. 12–21. London, 1980.

Rice 1985
Rice, Eugene, Jr. *Saint Jerome in the Renaissance*. Johns Hopkins Symposia in Comparative History 13. Baltimore, 1985.

Richardson 1936
Richardson, E. P. "The Rubens Exhibit." *Bulletin of the Detroit Institute of Arts* 15/5 (February 1936): pp. 61–63.

Richardson 1941
Richardson, E. P. "Augmented Return Engagement and Positive Farewell Appearance of the Masterpieces of Art from Two World's Fairs." *Art News* 40/6 (1941): pp. 17–18, 39.

Richmond 1957
England's World of 1607. (Exh. cat. Virginia Museum of Fine Arts, Richmond, 1957.) Richmond, 1957.

Richmond 1970–72
Recent Acquisitions of the Norton Simon Foundation Inc. (Exh. cat. Virginia Museum of Fine Arts, Richmond, 1970–72.) Richmond, 1972.

De Ridder 1989
Ridder, Juliaan H. A. de. *Gerechtigheidstaferelen voor schepenhuizen in de zuidelijke Nederlanden in de 14de, 15de en 16de eeuw*. Verhandelingen van de Koninklijke Vlaamse Academie voor Wetenschappen, Letteren en Schone Kunsten van België, Klasse der Schone Kunsten 51/45. Brussels, 1989.

Rietbergen 1986
Rietbergen, P. J. A. N. "Witsen's World: Nicolaas Witsen (1641–1717) between the Dutch East India Company and the Republic of Letters." In *All of One Company: The VOC in Biographical Perspective*, pp. 121–34. Utrecht, 1986.

Rinaldi 1989
Rinaldi, Maura. *Kraak Porcelain: A Moment in the History of Trade*. London, 1989.

Ringbom 1962
Ringbom, Sixten. "Maria in Sole and the Virgin of the Rosary." *Journal of the Warburg and Courtauld Institute*. 25/3–4 (1962): pp. 326–30.

Ringbom 1965
Ringbom, Sixten. *Icon to Narrative: The Rise of the Dramatic Close-up in Fifteenth-Century Devotional Painting*. Åbo, 1965.

Roach, Musa, and Hollander 1980
Roach, Mary Ellen, Kathleen Ehle Musa, and Anne Hollander. *New Perspectives on the History of Western Dress: A Handbook*. New York, 1980.

Robels 1989
Robels, Hella. *Frans Snyders, Stilleben- und Tiermaler 1579–1657*. Munich, 1989.

Robert [1897–1919] 1969
Robert, Carl. *Einzelmythen. Die Antiken Sarkophar-Reliefs 3*. 3 vols. Rome, 1969. [Repr. of 1897–1919 Berlin ed.]

B. Roberts 2012
Roberts, Benjamin B. "Appearance and Clothing in the 1620s and 1630s." In *Sex and Drugs before Rock 'n' Roll: Youth Culture and Masculinity during Holland's Golden Age*, pp. 45–72. Amsterdam, 2012.

W. Roberts 1935
Roberts, W. "The Voorhelms of Haarlem." *Journal of the Royal Horticultural Society* 60 (1935), pp. 199–208.

F. W. Robinson 1974
Robinson, Franklin W. *Gabriel Metsu (1629–1667): A Study of His Place in Dutch Genre Painting of the Golden Age*. New York, 1974.

M. S. Robinson 1990
Robinson, Michael S. *Van de Velde: A Catalogue of the Paintings of the Elder and the Younger Willem van de Velde*. 2 vols. Greenwich, 1990.

W. W. Robinson 1993
Robinson, William W. "Nicolaes Maes: Some Observations on His Early Portraits." In *Rembrandt and His Pupils: Papers Given at a Symposium in Nationalmuseum, Stockholm, 2–3 October 1992*, pp. 98–118. Edited by Görel Cavalli-Björkman. Stockholm, 1993.

W. W. Robinson 1996
Robinson, William W. "The Early Works of Nicolaes Maes, 1653–1661." 3 vols. PhD diss., Harvard University, 1996.

Robson 1819–
Robson, William. *Robson's London Directory, Street Guide and Carriers' List*. London, 1819–.

Rodee 1967
Rodee, Howard D. "Rubens' Treatment of Antique Armor." *Art Bulletin* 49 (1967): pp. 223–30.

Roelofs 2010
Roelofs, Pieter. "Early Owners of Paintings by Metsu in Leiden and Amsterdam." In Dublin/Amsterdam/Washington 2010–11, pp. 96–125.

Roethlisberger and Bok 1993
Roethlisberger, Marcel G., and Marten Jan Bok. *Abraham Bloemaert and His Sons: Paintings and Prints*. 2 vols. Doornspijk, 1993.

Rohlmann 1999
Rohlmann, M. "Flanders and Italy. Flanders and Florence. Early Netherlandish Painting in Italy and Its Particular Influences on Florentine Art. An Overview." In *Italy and the Low Countries—Artistic Relations. The Fifteenth Century, Proceedings from Symposium, Museum Catharijneconvent, Utrecht, 14 March 1994*, pp. 39–67. Edited by V. M. Schmidt. Florence, 1999.

Rolf 1967
Rolf, Fritz. *Sammlung Becker. I: Gemälde alter Meister*. Dortmund, 1967.

Rolland 1967
Rolland, Victor. *V. & H. V. Rolland's Illustrations to the Armorial Général by J.-B. Rietstap*. 6 vols. in 3. Baltimore, 1967. Originally published as *Armoiries des familles contenues dans l'Armorial général de J. B. Rietstap* (Paris, 1903–26).

Rooses 1886–92
Rooses, Max. *L'oeuvre de P. P. Rubens*. 5 vols. Antwerp, 1886–92.

Rooses 1903
Rooses, Max. *Rubens' leven en werken*. Antwerp, 1903.

Rooses 1908
Rooses, Max. *Jacob Jordaens: His Life and Work*. London, 1908. Originally published as *Jordaens: Sa vie et ses oeuvres* (Antwerp, 1906).

Rooses 1910
Rooses, Max. "L'oeuvre de Rubens: Addenda et corrigenda." *Rubens-bulletijn, Jaarboeken. . . .* 5/4 (1910): pp. 279–330.

Rooses and Ruelens 1887–1909
Rooses, Max, and Ch. Ruelens, eds. *Correspondance de Rubens et documents épistolaires concernant sa vie et ses oeuvres, publiés, traduits, annotés par Ch. Ruelens*. Codex diplomaticus Rubenianus 1–6. 6 vols. Antwerp, 1887–1909.

Rosand 1966
Rosand, David. "State of Research in Rubens Drawings." *Art Bulletin* 48 (1966): pp. 235–47.

Rosand 1969
Rosand, David. "Rubens's Munich *Lion Hunt*: Its Sources and Significance." *Art Bulletin* 51 (1969): pp. 29–40.

Rosenauer 2016
Rosenauer, Artur. *Titian: The Grimani Risen Christ; An Early Masterpiece*. Munich, 2016.

Rosenbaum 1982
Rosenbaum, Lee. *The Complete Guide to Collecting Art*. New York, 1982.

A. Rosenberg 1906
Rosenberg, Adolf, ed. *P. P. Rubens, des Meisters Gemälde*. Klassiker der Kunst 5. 1905. 2nd ed. Stuttgart and Leipzig, 1906.

J. Rosenberg 1928
Rosenberg, Jakob. *Jacob van Ruisdael*. Berlin, 1928.

J. Rosenberg 1948
Rosenberg, Jakob. *Rembrandt*. 2 vols. Cambridge, 1948.

J. Rosenberg 1964
Rosenberg, Jakob. *Rembrandt, Life and Work*. London, 1964.

Rotterdam 1922–23
Tentoonstelling Collectie Goudstikker. (Exh. cat. Rotterdamsche Kunstkring, Rotterdam, 22 December 1922–4 January 1923; organized by Kunsthandel J. Goudstikker.) Catalogue no. 23. Amsterdam, 1922.

Rotterdam 1926
Catalogue de la collection Goudstikker d'Amsterdam. (Exh. cat. Rotterdamsche Kunstkring, Rotterdam, 10–25 April 1926; organized by Kunsthandel J. Goudstikker.) Catalogue no. 31. Amsterdam, 1926.

Rotterdam 1934–35
Tentoonstelling van oude en modernen schilderijen. (Exh. cat. Museum Boijmans, Rotterdam, 1934–35.) Rotterdam, 1934.

Rotterdam 1936–37
Tentoonstelling van schilderijen en antiquiteiten: geexposeerd door den Kunsthandel J. Goudstikker N. V. (Exh. cat. Rotterdamsche Kunstkring, Rotterdam, 17 December 1936–10 January 1937; organized by Kunsthandel J. Goudstikker.) Amsterdam, 1936.

Rotterdam 1938
Meesterwerken uit vier eeuwen, 1400–1800. (Exh. cat. Museum Boijmans Van Beuningen, Rotterdam, 1938.) Rotterdam, 1938.

Rotterdam 1977
Van wambuis tot frac: Het kostuum in de prentkunst circa 1450–circa 1800. (Exh. cat. Prentenkabinet, Museum Boijmans Van Beuningen, Rotterdam, 1977.) Catalogue no. 6. Rotterdam, 1977.

Rotterdam 1990
Poorter, Nora de, Guido Jansen, and Jeroen Giltaij. *Rubens en zijn tijd / Rubens and His Time*. (Exh. cat. Museum Boijmans Van Beuningen, Rotterdam, 1990.) Rotterdam, 1990.

Rotterdam 2001
Meij, A. W. F. M., and Maartje de Haan, eds. *Rubens, Jordaens, Van Dyck and Their Circle: Flemish Master Drawings from the Boijmans van Beuningen Museum*. (Exh. cat. Museum Boijmans Van Beuningen, Rotterdam, 2001; organized by the Museum Boijmans Van Beuningen and the American Federation of the Arts.) Rotterdam, 2001.

Rousová 2004
Rousová, Andrea. *Petr Brandl, A Painter of Worldy Vices*. Prague, 2004.

Rowlands 1985
Rowlands, John. *Holbein: The Paintings of Hans Holbein the Younger*. Oxford, 1985.

Roy 1992
Roy, Alain. *Gérard de Lairesse (1640–1711)*. Paris, 1992.

Rózsaffy 1931–34
Rózsaffy, Dezsö. "Jegyzetek a Szépmüvészeti Múzeum van der Heyden-csendéletéhez." *Az Országos Magyar Szépmüvészeti Múzeum Évkönyvei* 7 (1931–34) [published 1935]: pp. 165–71; summary in German: pp. 216–17, pl. 2.

Rumpf 1823
Rumpf, J. D. F. *Berlin und Potsdam: Eine Beschreibung aller Merkwürdigkeiten dieser Städte und ihrer Umgebungen*. 2 vols. Berlin, 1823.

Rumsey 1985
Rumsey, Thomas R. *Men and Women in Revolution and War, 1600–1815*. Wellesley Hills, 1985.

F. Russell 2004
Russell, Francis. *John; 3rd Earl of Bute, Patron and Collector*. London, 2004.

M. Russell 1996
Russell, Margarita. "Storck [Sturck; Sturckenburch]." In Turner 1996, vol. 29, pp. 720f.

Rutherglen 2017
Rutherglen, Susannah. "'Resplendent Brushes': Giovanni Bellini's 'Resurrection' Altarpiece for San Michele di Murano, Venice." "Studies in Renaissance Art and Culture in Honor of Debra Pincus." Special issue, *Artibus et Historiae* 38/76 (2017): pp. 9–32.

Saarinen 1968
Saarinen, Aline. "Portrait of the Artist's Son, Titus." *McCall's* 95 (January 1968): pp. 40f.

Sadie 1980
Sadie, Stanley. *The New Grove Dictionary of Music and Musicians*. London, 1980.

Saint-Groux 1907
Saint-Groux, A. "La collection de Charles Sedelmeyer." *Les arts: Revue mensuelle des musées, collections, expositions* 6 (May 1907): pp. 17–27.

Salerno 1977–80
Salerno, Luigi. *Pittori di paesaggio del Seicento a Roma / Landscape Painters of the Seventeenth Century in Rome*. 3 vols. Rome, 1977–80.

Sander 1992
Sander, Jochen. *Hugo van der Goes. Stilentwicklung und Chronologie*. Berliner Schriften zur Kunst 3. Mainz, 1992.

Sander 1997
Sander, Jochen. "Ein unbekanntes Werk Gerard Davids. Die Beweinung Chrisi in Halbfigur." *Städel-Jahrbuch* 16 (1997): pp. 159–70.

Sanfuentes Echeverría 2023
Sanfuentes Echeverría, Olaya. "Adoración de los Magos de Cornelis Engebretsz. Propuesta de interpretación a la luz de la idea de Imperio Universal." *Tiempos Modernos* 46 (June 2023): pp. 287–306.

Sandrart [1675] 1925
Joachim von Sandrarts Academie der Bau-, Bild- und Mahlerey-Künst von 1675. Edited with commentary by A. R. Penzer. Munich 1925.

San Francisco 1939–40
Masterpieces of Five Centuries, Golden Gate International Exposition. (Exh. cat. Palace of Fine Arts, San Francisco, 1939–40.) San Francisco, 1939.

San Francisco 1974–76
Three Centuries of French Art, Vol. II: Selections from the Norton Simon Inc. Museum of Art and the Norton Simon Foundation. (Exh. cat. California Palace of the Legion of Honor, San Francisco, 19 October 1974–15 June 1976.) Edited by Jacques de Caso. San Francisco, 1975.

San Francisco/Toledo/Boston 1966–67
The Age of Rembrandt: An Exhibition of Dutch Paintings of the Seventeenth Century. (Exh. cat. California Palace of the Legion of Honor, San Francisco, 10 October–13 November 1966; Toledo Museum of Art, 26 November 1966–8 January 1967; Museum of Fine Arts, Boston, 21 January–5 March 1967.) New York, 1966.

Sauerländer 2011
Sauerländer, Willibald. *Der Katholische Rubens, Heilige und Märtyrer*. Munich, 2011.

Sauerländer 2014
Sauerländer, Willibald. *The Catholic Rubens: Saints and Martyrs*. Los Angeles, 2014.

Saxl 1957
Saxl, Fritz. *A Heritage of Images: A Selection of Lectures by Fritz Saxl*. Edited by Hugh Honour and John Fleming. London, 1957.

Scaff 1970
Scaff, Villy. "Ioannes Qvintini Massiis Pingebat." In *Mélanges d'archéologie et d'histoire de l'art offerts au professeur Jacques Lavalleye*, pp. 259–80. Louvain, 1970.

Scailliérez 2007
Scailliérez, Cécile. *Quentin Metsys, Sainte Madeleine*. Collection Solo 34. Paris, 2007.

Scannelli [1657] 1966
Scannelli, Francesco. *Il Microcosmo della pittura*. Milan, 1966. [Repr. of 1657 Cesena ed.]

Scarpa Sonino 1992
Scarpa Sonino, Annalisa. *Cabinet d'amateur, Le grandi collezioni d'arte nei dipinti dal XVII al XIX secolo*. Milan, 1992.

Schaar 1958
Schaar, Eckhard. "Studien zu Nicolaes Berchem." PhD diss., University of Cologne, 1958.

Schabaelje 1654
Schabaelje, Jan Philipsz. *Den grooten emblemata sacra, bestaande in meer dan drie hondert bybelsche figueren, soo des Ouden als des Nieuwen Testaments*. Amsterdam, 1654.

Schama 1987a
Schama, Simon. "Dutch Landscapes: Culture as Foreground." In Amsterdam/Boston/Philadelphia 1987–88, pp. 64–83.

Schama 1987b
Schama, Simon. *The Embarrassment of Riches: An Interpretation of Dutch Culture in the Golden Age*. New York, 1987.

Schamoni 1948
Schamoni, Wilhelm. *The Face of the Saints*. London, 1948.

A. Scharf 1958
Scharf, Alfred. "The Robinson Collection." *Burlington Magazine* 100 (September 1958): pp. 298–304.

J. Scharf et al. 2012
Scharf, Julietta, with Hanna Strzoda and Janina Dahlmanns. *Die Historische Sammlung Otto Gerstenberg*. 2 vols. Ostfildern, 2012.

Schatborn 1973
Schatborn, Peter. "Olieverfschetsen van Dirck Hals." *Bulletin van het Rijksmuseum* 21 (1973): pp. 107–16.

Schatborn 1974
Schatborn, Peter. "Figuurstudies van Nicolaes Berchem." *Bulletin van het Rijksmuseum* 22 (1974): pp. 3–16; English summary: 56–57.

Scheelen 1986
Scheelen, Walter. "De herkomst en de datering van Rubens' voorstellingen van de H. Ignatius van Loyola en de H. Franciscus Xaverius." *Koninklijk Museum voor Schone Kunsten Jaarboek* (1986): pp. 153–72.

Scheelen 1989
Scheelen, Walter. "De bemiddelende rol van de Jezuïetenbij het tot stand komen van hun kunstpatrimonium." *De zeventiende eeuw* 5/1 (1989): pp. 60–66.

Scheunemann 1954
Scheunemann, Brigitte. "Anatolische Teppiche auf abendländischen Gemälden." PhD diss., Berlin, 1954.

Schilder and Welu 1980
Schilder, Günter, and James Welu. *The World Map of 1611 by Pieter van den Keere*. Wall-maps of the 16th and 17th Centuries 3. Amsterdam, 1980.

Schlégl and Berkes 1971
Schlégl, István, and Sàndor Berkes. *Praktischer Führer durch die Sammlung Thyssen-Bornemisza*. Castagnola-Lugano, 1971.

Schmid 1948
Schmid, Heinrich Alfred. *Hans Holbein der Jüngere*. 2 vols. Basel, 1948.

Schmidt 1931
Schmidt, James A. "Adam and Eve von Cranach." *Pantheon* (May 1931): pp. 35–36; English summary: 194–95.

Schmidt-Degener 1917
Schmidt-Degener, F. "Het genetische probleem van de Nachtwacht: IV. De compositie." *Onze Kunst* 31 (April 1917): pp. 97–102.

Schmidt-Degener and Van Gelder 1927
Schmidt-Degener, Frederik, and H. E. van Gelder. *Jan Steen: Forty Reproductions in Photogravure of the Artist's Principal Works*. London, 1927.

Schnackenburg 1970
Schnackenburg, Bernhard. "Die Anfänge des Bauerinterieurs bei Adriaen van Ostade." *Oud Holland* 85 (1970): pp. 158–69.

Schnackenburg 2016
Schnackenburg, Bernhard. *Jan Lievens: Friend and Rival of the Young Rembrandt*. Petersburg, 2016.

Schneede 1968
Schneede, Uwe M. "Gabriel Metsu und der holländische Realismus." *Oud Holland* 83 (1968): pp. 45–61.

C. Schneider 1984
Schneider, Cynthia. "A New Look at the Landscape with an Obelisk." *Fenway Court* (Isabella Stewart Gardner Museum), 1984, pp. 7–19.

C. Schneider 1990
Schneider, Cynthia. *Rembrandt's Landscapes*. New Haven, 1990.

H. Schneider 1921
Schneider, Hans. "Der Maler Jan Tengnagel." *Oud Holland* 39 (1921): pp. 10–27.

H. Schneider/Ekkart 1973
Schneider, Hans. *Jan Lievens, sein Leben und seine Werke*. Amsterdam, 1973; rev. ed. of 1932 Haarlem ed., edited with supplement by Rudolf E. O. Ekkart.

Schoen 2001
Schoen, Christian. *Albert Dürer: Adam und Eva; die Gemälde, ihre Geschichte und Rezeption bei Lucas Cranach d.Ä. und Hans Baldung Grien*. Berlin, 2001.

Scholtens 1962
Scholtens, H. J. J. "Salomon van Ruysdael in de contreien van Holland's landengte." *Oud Holland* 77 (1962): pp. 1–10.

Schulz 2002
Schulz, Wolfgang. *Aert van der Neer*. Zwolle, 2002

Schütz 2002
Schütz, Karl. "Naturstudien und Kunstkammerstücke." In *Das Flämische Stilleben, 1550–1680*, pp. 60–109. Edited by Christa Nitze-Ertz et al. (Exh. cat. Kunsthistorisches Museum, Vienna; Kulturstiftung Ruhr, Essen, 1 Sepetmber–8 December 2002.) Lingen, 2002.

Schwartz 1985
Schwartz, Gary. *Rembrandt, His Life, His Paintings*. New York, 1985. [English ed. of *Rembrandt, zijn leven, zijn schilderijen* (Maarssen, 1984).]

Schwarz 2004
Schwarz, Birgit. *Hitler's Museum, die Fotoalben Gemäldegalerie Linz: Dokumente zum "Führer museum."* Vienna, 2004.

Scott 1986
Scott, Margaret. *The Fourteenth and Fifteenth Centuries, A Visual History of Costume*. London, 1986.

Scribner 1989
Scribner, Charles, III. *Peter Paul Rubens*. New York, 1989.

Scribner 2014
Scribner, Charles, III. *The Triumph of the Eucharist: Tapestries Designed by Rubens*. New York, 2014.

Sebag-Montefiore 1988
Sebag-Montefiore, Charles. "Three Lost Collections of London." *NACF Magazine* (National Art-Collections Fund) 38 (Christmas 1988): pp. 50–56.

Sedelmeyer 1906
Sedelmeyer Gallery. *Illustrated Catalogue of the Tenth Series of 100 Paintings by Old Masters*. Paris, 1906.

Seelig 2006
Seelig, Gero. "The Reception of Berchem's Painting in Eighteenth-Century France." In Haarlem/Zurich/Schwerin 2006, pp. 59–69.

Seelig 2010
Seelig, Gero, with Kerstin Binzer and Ellis Dullaart. *Die holländische Genremalerei in Schwerin. Bestandskatalog Staatliches Museum Schwerin*, Schwerin and Petersberg, 2010.

Segal 1984
Segal, Sam. "Still-life Painting in Middelburg." In *Masters of Middelburg: Exhibition in the Honour of Laurens J. Bol*, pp. 25–95. By Noortje Bakker et al. (Exh. cat. Kunsthandel K. & V. Waterman B. V., Amsterdam, 1984.) Amsterdam, 1984.

Segal 1987a
Segal, Sam. "A Flower Piece by Cornelis de Heem." *Tableau* 9 (Summer 1987): pp. 32–33.

Segal 1987b
Segal, Sam. "Rectificatie, Cornelis de Heem." *Tableau* 10 (November 1987): p. 48.

Segal 1987c
Segal, Sam. *Tulips by Anthony Claesz: 56 seventeenth century watercolour drawings by Anthony Claesz (ca. 1607/08–1649)*. London, 1987.

Segal 1992
Segal, Sam. *De Tulp verbeeld: Hollandse tulpenhandel in de 17de eeuw*. Amsterdam, 1992.

Segal 2007
Segal, Sam, with Mariël Ellens and Joris Dik. *The Temptations of Flora / De verleiding van Flora: Jan van Huysum, 1682–1749*. Zwolle, 2007.

Seldis 1972
Seldis, Henry J. "Simon Says." *ARTnews* 71 (December 1972): pp. 24–28.

"Selected Old Masters" 1946
"Selected Old Masters; Duveen Presents Some Rarely Seen Paintings." *Pictures on Exhibit* 7 (February 1946): p. 8.

Selleck 1977
Selleck, Jack. *Faces*. Insights to Art. Worcester, 1977.

Sellin 2006
Sellin, Christine Petra. *Fractured Families and Rebel Maidservants: The Biblical Hagar in Seventeenth-Century Dutch Art and Literature*. New York and London, 2006.

Senenko 2009
Senenko, Marina. *The Pushkin State Museum of Fine Arts, Collection of Dutch Paintings XVII–XIX Centuries*. Moscow, 2009.

Serlio [1611] 1980
Serlio, Sebastiano. *Tutte l'opere d'architettura*. New York, 1980. [Repr. with facsimile of 1611 ed.]

Silver 2011
Silver, Larry. *Pieter Bruegel*. New York and London, 2011.

Silverman 1982
Silverman, R. *Learning about Art: A Practical Approach*. Newport Beach, 1982.

Simon 1930
Simon, Kurt Erich. *Jacob van Ruisdael: Eine Darstellung seiner Entwicklung*. Berlin, 1930.

Simon 1935
Simon, Kurt Erich. "'Doctor' Jacob van Ruisdael." *Burlington Magazine* 67/390 (September 1935): pp. 132–35.

Simons 1956
Simons, Menno. *The Complete Writings of Menno Simons*. Translated by Leonard Verduin. Edited by John C. Wenger. Scottdale, 1956.

Simson and Kelch 1973
Simson, Otto Georg von, and Jan Kelch, eds. *Neue Beiträge zur Rembrandt-Forschung*. Berlin, 1973.

Singleton 1929
Singleton, Esther. *Old World Masters in New World Collections*. New York, 1929.

Siple 1934
Siple, Ella S. "A Rubens Portrait and Other Old Masters." *Burlington Magazine* 64/373 (April 1934): pp. 152 (frontispiece), 184, 187.

Siple 1936
Siple, Ella S. "Art in America—The Rubens Exhibition at Detroit." *Burlington Magazine* 68/398 (May 1936): pp. 243–44.

Skinner 1781
Skinner, J. R. *Voyage historique et litteraire la Suisse Occidentale*. 2 vols. Neufchatel, 1781.

Slatkes 1983
Slatkes, Leonard J. *Rembrandt and Persia*. New York, 1983.

Slatkes 1991
Slatkes, Leonard J. "E Pluribus Unum: Rembrandt Research Project." *Journal of Art* 4 (May 1991): p. 73.

Slatkes 1992
Slatkes, Leonard J. *Rembrandt: Catalogo completo dei dipinti*. Florence, 1992.

Slim 1993
Slim, H. Colin. "Images of Music in Three Prints after Maarten van Heemskerck." In *Iconography at the Crossroads*, pp. 229–39. Edited by Brenden Cassidy. Princeton, 1993.

Slim 1997
Slim, H. Colin, "On Parnassus with Maarten van Heemskerck: Instrumentaria and Musical Repertoires in Three Paintings in the U.S.A., pt. I." *Musica Disciplina: A Yearbook of the History of Music* (American Institute of Musicology) 51 (1997): pp. 1–70.

Slim 1998–2002
Slim, H. Colin, "On Parnassus with Maarten van Heemskerck: Instrumentaria and Musical Repertoires in Three Paintings in the U.S.A., pt. II." *Musica Disciplina: A Yearbook of the History of Music* (American Institute of Musicology) 52 (1998–2002): pp. 181–232.

Slive 1953
Slive, Seymour. *Rembrandt and His Critics, 1630–1730*. The Hague, 1953.

Slive 1968
Slive, Seymour. "Een dronkende slapende meyd aan een tafel by Jan Vermeer." In *Festschrift Ulrich Middeldorf*, pp. 453–59. Edited by Antje Kosegarten and Peter Tigler. 2 vols. Berlin, 1968.

Slive 1970–74
Slive, Seymour. *Frans Hals*. 3 vols. London, 1970–74.

Slive 1979
Slive, Seymour. "Rembrandt's *Portrait of a Woman* in the Speed Art Museum." *J. B. Speed Art Museum Bulletin* 32/2 (September 1979): pp. 3–10.

Slive 2001
Slive, Seymour. *Jacob van Ruisdael: A Complete Catalogue of His Paintings, Drawings, and Etchings*. New Haven and London, 2001.

Slive 2014
Slive, Seymour. *Frans Hals*. 3 vols. Rev. 2nd ed., London, 2014.

Van der Sloot 1959
Sloot, R. B. F. van der. "Harnassen uit einde 16e en begin 17e eeuw in de noordelijke Nederlanden." *Nederlands kunsthistorisch jaarboek* 10 (1959): pp. 99–124.

Sluijter 1973
Sluijter, Eric Jan. "Boekbespreking: Helga Wagner, *Jan van der Heyden 1637–1712*." *Oud Holland* 87 (1973): pp. 244–52.

Sluijter 1986
Sluijter, Eric Jan. "De 'heydensche fabulen' in de Noordnederlandse schilderkunst, circa 1590–1670." PhD diss., Rijksuniversiteit, Leiden, 1986.

Sluijter 1991–92
Sluijter, Eric Jan. "Venus, Visus en Pictura." *Nederlands kunsthistorisch jaarboek* 42–43 (1991–92): pp. 337–96.

Sluijter 1998
Sluijter, Eric Jan. "Rembrandt's Bathsheba and the Conventions of a Seductive Theme." In *Rembrandt's Bathsheba Reading King David's Letter*, pp. 48–99. Edited by Ann Jensen Adams. Masterpieces of Western Painting. Cambridge and New York, 1998.

Sluijter 2006
Sluijter, Eric Jan. *Rembrandt and the Female Nude*. Amsterdam, 2006.

Sluijter 2015
Sluijter, Eric Jan. *Rembrandt's Rivals: History Painting in Amsterdam, 1630–1650*. Amsterdam and Philadelphia, 2015.

Smeyers 1998
Smeyers, M. *Dirk Bouts. Peintre du silence*. Tournai, 1998.

D. R. Smith 1982
Smith, David R. *Masks of Wedlock: Seventeenth-Century Dutch Marriage Portraiture*. Ann Arbor, 1982.

G. Smith 1969
Smith, Graham. "Rubens' Altargemälde des Hl. Ignatius von Loyola und des Hl. Franz Xaver für die Jesuitenkirche in Antwerpen." *Jahrbuch der Kunsthistorischen Sammlungen in Wien* 65 (1969): pp. 39–60.

H. C. Smith 1944
Smith, H. Clifford. "Mr. Churchill's Globe." *Country Life* 95/2451 (18 February 1944): pp. 284f.

J. Smith 1829–42
Smith, John. *A Catalogue Raisonné of the Works of the Most Eminent Dutch, Flemish, and French Painters*. 9 vols. London, 1829–42.

Snoep 1975
Snoep, D. P. *Praal en propaganda: Triumfalia in de Noordelijke Nederlanden in de 16de en 17de eeuw*. Alphen aan den Rijn, 1975.

Snow-Smith 1982
Snow-Smith, Joanne. *The Salvator Mundi of Leonardo da Vinci*. Seattle, 1982.

Snyder, Silver, and Luttikhuizen 2005
Snyder, J., L. Silver, and H. Luttikhuizen. *Northern Renaissance Art: Painting, Sculpture, the Graphic Arts from 1350 to 1575*. Upper Saddle River, 2005.

Sonnenburg 1995
Sonnenburg, Hubert von. *Rembrandt/Not Rembrandt in the Metropolitan Museum of Art: Aspects of Connoisseurship*. Vol. 1, *Paintings: Problems and Issues*. New York, 1995.

Sotheby's 1968
Art at Auction: The Year at Sotheby's and Parke-Bernet, 1967–68. London, 1968.

Speelman 2022
Speelman, Anthony. *A Tale of Two Monkeys: Adventures in the Art World*. London, 2022.

"Lord Spencer" 1911
"In Lord Spencer's Collection." *Connoisseur* 29 (January 1911): p. 17.

Speth-Holterhoff 1957
Speth-Holterhoff, S. *Les peintres flamands de cabinets d'amateurs au XVIIe siècle*. Paris and Brussels, 1957.

Spicer 1970
Spicer, Joaneath. "The 'Naer het Leven' Drawings: By Pieter Breugel or Roelandt Savery?" *Master Drawings* 8 (1970): pp. 3–30.

Spicer 1979
Spicer, Joaneath. "The Drawings of Roelandt Savery." PhD diss., Yale University, 1979.

Spicer 1983
Spicer, Joaneath. "'De Koe voor d'aerde statt': The Origins of the Dutch Cattle Piece." In *Essays in Northern European Art Presented to Egbert Haverkamp Begemann on His Sixtieth Birthday*, pp. 251–56. Edited by Anne-Marie Logan. Doornspijk, 1983.

Spieth 2018
Spieth, Darius A. *Revolutionary Paris and the Art Market for Netherlandish Art*. Studies in the History of Collecting and Art Markets 3. Leiden and Boston, 2018.

Spring 2017
Spring, Marika. "New Insights into the Materials of Fifteenth- and Sixteenth-Century Netherlandish Paintings in the National Gallery, London." *Heritage Science* 5/40 (2017): n.pag. https://doi.org/10.1186/s40494-017-0152-3.

Stange 1934–61
Stange, Alfred. *Deutsche Malerei der Gotik*. 11 vols. Berlin, 1934–61; vols. 4–11 published in Munich.

A. Staring 1965
Staring, A. "Vier familiegroepen van Nicolaas Maes." *Oud Holland* 80/3 (1965): pp. 169–80.

W. M. Staring 1947
Staring, W. M. "De Maria-Hemelvaart van Albert Bouts." *Oud Holland* 62 (1947): pp. 182–88.

Steadman: See also **D. W. S. 1981**

Steadman 1972
Steadman, David. "The Norton Simon Exhibition at Princeton." *Art Journal* 32/1 (fall 1972): pp. 34–40.

Steadman 1973
Steadman, David. "The Landscape in Art." *University: A Princeton Quarterly* 57 (summer 1973): p. 8.

Stechow 1935
Stechow, Wolfgang. "Cornelis van Haarlem en de hollandsche laat-mannieristische schilderkunst." *Elsevier's geillustreerd maandschrift* 45/90 (1935): pp. 73–91.

Stechow 1938
Stechow, Wolfgang. *Salomon van Ruysdael, eine Einführung in seine Kunst*. Berlin, 1938.

Stechow 1945
Stechow, Wolfgang. "'The Love of Antiochus with Faire Stratonica' in Art." *Art Bulletin* 27 (December 1945): pp. 221–31.

Stechow 1968a
Stechow, Wolfgang. *Dutch Landscape Painting of the Seventeenth Century*. National Gallery of Art Kress Foundation Studies in the History of European Art 1. 1966. 2nd ed. New York, 1968.

Stechow 1968b
Stechow, Wolfgang. *Rubens and the Classical Tradition*. Martin Classical Lectures 22. Cambridge, 1968.

Stechow 1972a
Stechow, Wolfgang. "Jan Steen's Representations of the Marriage in Cana." *Nederlands kunsthistorisch jaarboek* 23 (1972): pp. 73–83.

Stechow 1972b
Stechow, Wolfgang. "Some Thoughts on Rubens as a Copyist of Portraits, 1610–1620." In *Rubens before 1620*, pp. 23–44. Edited by John Rupert Martin. Princeton, 1972.

Stechow 1975
Stechow, Wolfgang. *Salomon van Ruysdael, eine Einführung in seine Kunst*. 1938. 2nd rev. ed. Berlin, 1975.

Stefes 2006
Stefes, Annemarie. "Nicolaes Berchem as a Draughtsman." in Haarlem/Zurich/Schwerin 2006, pp. 97–115.

Steinberg 1989
Steinberg, Leo. "Addendum to Julius Held's Paper." *Source: Notes in the History of Art* 8/9 (1989): pp. 77–79.

Stewart 1990–95
Stewart, Ann M. *Irish Art Loan Exhibitions 1765–1927, Index of Artists*. Introduction by S. B. Kennedy. 3 vols. Dublin, 1990–95.

Stichting Geschiedschrijving Holland 2002
Stichting Geschiedschrijving Holland. *Geschiedenis van Holland (History of Holland)*. Utrecht, 2002.

Stockholm 1956
Dahlbäck, Bengt, and Per Bjurström. *Rembrandt*. (Exh. cat. Nationalmuseum, Stockholm, 1956.) Stockholm, 1956.

Stone-Ferrier 1989
Stone-Ferrier, Linda. "Gabriel Metsu's *Vegetable Market at Amsterdam*." *Art Bulletin* 71 (1989): pp. 428–52.

Stourton 2007
Stourton, J. *Great Collectors of Our Time: Art Collecting since 1945*. London, 2007.

Stratton 1994
Stratton, Suzanne L. *The Immaculate Conception in Spanish Art*. Cambridge and New York, 1994.

Strauss and Van der Meulen 1979
Strauss, Walter L., and Marjon van der Meulen. *The Rembrandt Documents*. With the assistance of S. A. C. Dudok van Heel and P. J. M. de Baar. New York, 1979.

Van Strein 1993
Strien, C. D. van. *British Travellers in Holland during the Stuart Period: Edward Browne and John Locke as Tourists in the United Provinces*. Leiden: 1993.

Stroganoff 1800
Catalogue raisonné des tableaux, qui composent la collection du Comte A. de Stroganoff. St. Petersburg, 1800.

Strong 1969a
Strong, Roy C. *The English Icon: Elizabethan and Jacobean Portraiture*. Studies in British Art. London and New York, 1969.

Strong 1969b
Strong, Roy C. *Tudor and Jacobean Portraits*. London, 1969.

Stroo et al. 1996–2013
Stroo, Cyriel, et al. *The Flemish Primitives: Catalogue of Early Netherlandish Painting in the Royal Museums of Fine Arts of Belgium*. 6 vols. Brussels, 1996–2013.

Suchtelen and Buvelot 2016
Suchtelen, Ariane van, and Quentin Buvelot. *Genre Paintings in the Mauritshuis*. The Hague and Zwolle, 2016.

Sumowski 1956–57
Sumowski, Werner. "Bemerkungen zu Otto Beneschs Corpus der Rembrandt-Zeichnungen I." *Wissenschaftliche Zeitschrift der Humboldt-Universität zu Berlin, Gesellschafts- und Sprachwissenschaftliche Reihe* 6/4 (1956–57): pp. 255–81.

Sumowski 1983–93
Sumowski, Werner, ed. *Gemälde der Rembrandt-Schüler*. 6 vols. Landau, 1983–93.

Surh and Rahusen 2017/2020
Surh, Dominique, and Henriette Rahusen. "Portrait of a Gentleman with a Walking Stick" (2017). In *The Leiden Collection Catalogue*. 3rd ed. Edited by Arthur K. Wheelock Jr. and Lara Yeager-Crasselt. New York, 2020–. Accessed 8 October 2020. https://theleidencollection.com/artwork/portrait-of-a-gentleman-with-a-walking-stick/

D. Sutton 1979
Sutton, Denys. "Robert Langton Douglas, Part 4." *Apollo*, n.s. 109/209 (July 1979): pp. 2–56.

P. Sutton 1978
Sutton, Peter C. "Jacob Ochtervelt, *Family Portrait (The Elsevier Family?)*." In *Wadsworth Atheneum Paintings: The Netherlands and the German-Speaking Countries, Fifteenth-Nineteenth Centuries*, pp. 168f. Edited by Egbert Haverkamp-Begmann. Hartford, 1978.

P. Sutton 1982
Sutton, Peter C. Review of *Jacob van Ruisdael*, Mauritshuis and Fogg Art Museum, 1981–82. *Art Journal* 42/2 (summer 1982): pp. 147–51.

P. Sutton 1982–83
Sutton, Peter C. "The Life and Art of Jan Steen." "Jan Steen, Comedy and Admonition." Special double issue, *Philadelphia Museum of Art Bulletin* 337–38 (Winter 1982–Spring 1983): pp. 3–64.

P. Sutton 1986
Sutton, Peter C. *A Guide to Dutch Art in America*. Washington, DC, 1986.

P. Sutton 1987
Sutton, Peter C. Introduction to Amsterdam/Boston/Philadelphia 1987–88, pp. 1–63.

P. Sutton 1989a
Sutton, Peter C. "A Pair by Van Bijlert." *Mercury* 8 (1989): pp. 4–16.

P. Sutton 1989b
Sutton, Peter C. "Rubens's *Sacrifice of the Old Covenant* from the Coolidge Collection." *Journal of the Museum of Fine Arts, Boston* 1 (1989): pp. 5–21.

P. Sutton 1990
Sutton, Peter C. "Recent Patterns of Public and Private Collecting of Dutch Art." In The Hague/San Francisco 1990, pp. 104–19.

P. Sutton 1992
Sutton, Peter C. *Dutch and Flemish Seventeenth-Century Paintings in the Harold Samuel Collection*. Cambridge and New York, 1992.

P. Sutton 1993
Sutton, Peter C. "The Spanish Netherlands in the Age of Rubens." In Boston/Toledo 1993, pp. 106–30.

P. Sutton 1995
Sutton, Peter C. *The William Appleton Coolidge Collection*. Boston, 1995.

P. Sutton 2006–07
Sutton, Peter C. "Jan van der Heyden." In Greenwich/Amsterdam 2006–07, pp. 17–81.

P. Sutton et al. 2008
Sutton, Peter C., et al. *Reclaimed: Paintings from the Collection of Jacques Goudstikker*. New Haven, 2008.

Szafran 2014
Szafran, Yvonne. Conservation Report (L.2012.33), 2014. Paintings conservation department archives, J. Paul Getty Museum; also NSM.

Taft and Mayer 2000
Taft, W. Stanley, and James W. Mayer. *The Science of Paintings*. New York, 2000.

Talbot 1987
Talbot, Charles. "Lucas Cranach the Younger. 10. Nymph of Spring." In *The Robert Lehman Collection*. Vol. 2, *Fifteenth- to Eighteenth-Century European Paintings*, pp. 48–54. Edited by Charles Sterling et al. New York and Princeton, 1987.

Tatlock 1923
Tatlock, R. "Sir Bryan Tuke, by Holbein." *Burlington Magazine* 42/242 (May 1923): pp. 246–51, ill.

Taylor 1995
Taylor, Paul. *Dutch Flower Painting, 1600–1720*. New Haven and London, 1995.

Temple [1673] 1972
Temple, William. *Observations upon the United Provinces of the Netherlands*. Edited by George Clark. Oxford, 1972. [Repr. of 1673 London ed.]

Tenner 1966
Tenner, Helmut. *Mannheimer Kunstsammler und Kunsthändler bis zur Mitte des neunzehnten Jahrhunderts*. Heidelberg, 1966.

Van Thiel 1992
Thiel, Pieter J. J. van. "De Rembrandt-tentoonstelling van 1898." *Bulletin van het Rijksmuseum, Amsterdam* 40/1 (1992): pp. 11–92.

Van Thiel 1999
Thiel, Pieter J. J. van. *Cornelis Cornelisz van Haarlem, 1562–1638: A Monograph and Catalogue Raisonné*. Translated by Diane L. Webb. Doornspijk, 1999.

Thieme-Becker 1907–50
Thieme, Ulrich, and Felix Becker. *Allgemeines Lexikon der bildenden Künstler von der Antike bis zur Gegenwart*. 37 vols. Leipzig, 1907–50.

Thiery 1986
Thiery, Yvonne. *Les peintres flamands de paysage au XVIIe siècle, des pécurseurs à Rubens*. Brussels, 1986.

Thomas and Duerloo 1998
Thomas, Werner, and Luc Duerloo, eds. *Albert & Isabella, 1598–1621: Essays*. Turnhout, 1998.

Thompson 1997
Thompson, John L. "Hagar, Victim or Villain? Three Sixteenth-Century Views." *Catholic Biblical Quarterly* 59/2 (1997): 213–33.

Thoré 1860
Thoré, Théophile E. J. [William Bürger]. *Trésors d'art en Angleterre*. Brussels, 1860.

Thoré 1864
Thoré, Théophile E. J. [William Bürger]. "Galerie de Mm. Pereire." *Gazette des beaux-arts* 16 (1864): pp. 193–213, 297–317.

Thornton 1978
Thornton, Peter. *Seventeenth-Century Interior Decoration in England, France, and Holland*. New Haven and London, 1978.

Van Tielhof and Van Dam 2006
Tielhof, Milja van, and Petra J. E. M. van Dam. *Waterstaat in Stedenland: Het hoogheemraadschap van Rijnland voor 1857*. Utrecht, 2006.

Tietze-Conrat 1955
Tietze-Conrat, E. *Mantegna*. London, 1955.

Tipping 1918
Tipping, H. Avray, "Shavington–II. Shropshire, the Seat of Lt.-Col. Heywood-Lonsdale." *Country Life* 44 (10 August 1918): pp. 112–17.

Tissink and De Wit 1987
Tissink, Fieke, and H. F. de Wit. *Gorcumse schilders in de ouden eeuw*. Gorinchem, 1987.

Tokyo/Kyoto 1968–69
Karnebeek, D. A.- née van Roijen. *The Age of Rembrandt: Dutch Paintings and Drawings of the 17th Century*. (Exh. cat. National Museum of Western Art, Tokyo; Kyoto Municipal Museum, 1968–69.) Tokyo, 1968.

Toledo/Toronto 1944–45
Masterpieces from the Cook Collection. (Exh. cat. Toledo Museum of Art; Art Gallery of Toronto, 1944–45.) Toledo, [1944].

Tomasi 1997
Tomasi, Lucia Tongiorgi. *An Oak Spring Flora: Flower Illustrations from the Fifteenth Century to the Present Time*. London and New Haven, 1997.

Tomkiewicz 1950
Tomkiewicz, W. *Catalogue of Paintings Removed from Poland by the German Occupation Authorities during the Years 1939–1945. I: Foreign Paintings*. Ministry of Culture and Art, Publications of the Reparations Section 9. Warsaw, 1950.

Tonini 1996
Tonini, Maria Lucia. *I Demidoff a Firenze e in Toscana*. Cultura e memoria 2. Florence, 1996.

Trautscholdt 1937
Trautscholdt, Eduard. "Jan Steen." In Thieme-Becker 1907–50, vol. 31 (1937): pp. 509–15.

Trease 1979
Trease, Geoffrey. *Portrait of a Cavalier: William Cavendish, First Duke of Newcastle*. London, 1979.

***Trésor de l'art belge* 1912–13**
Trésor de l'art belge au XVIIe siècle: mémorial de l'exposition d'art ancien à Bruxelles en 1910. 2 vols. Brussels and Paris, 1912–13.

Trezzani 1983
Trezzani, Ludovica. "Willem Reuter." In Briganti, Trezzani, and Laureati 1983, pp. 327–35.

Trivas 1941
Trivas, Numa S. *The Paintings of Frans Hals*. London, 1941.

Trnek 1992
Trnek, Renate. *Die Holländischen Gemälde des 17. Jahrhunderts in der Gemäldegalerie der Akademie der bildenden Künste in Wien*. Vienna, 1992.

Tronchin 1780
Tronchin, François. *Catalogue des tableaux de mon cabinet*. Geneva, 1780.

Tümpel 1986
Tümpel, Christian, with Astrid Tümpel. *Rembrandt*. Amsterdam and Antwerp, 1986.

Tümpel 1993
Tümpel, Christiaan, with Astrid Tümpel. *Rembrandt: All Paintings in Colour*. Antwerp and New York, 1993.

Turner 1996
Turner, Jane, ed. *The Dictionary of Art*. 34 vols. New York, 1996. See also https://www.oxfordartonline.com.

"Unbroken Tradition" 1944
"Holland's Unbroken Tradition: 5-Century Review at Montreal." *Art News* 43/4 (1944): p. 20.

Upjohn 1939
Upjohn, E. M. "Exhibitions: Classics of the Nude." *Art in America* 27/3 (July 1939): pp. 133f.

Upton 1990
Upton, Joel M. *Petrus Christus: His Place in Fifteenth-Century Flemish Painting*. University Park, 1990.

Urquhart 1948
Urquhart, Murray. "Hugh Blaker, Collector." In *Catalogue of an Exhibition of Selected Paintings, Drawings and Sculpture from the Collection of the Late Hugh Blaker*. (Exh. cat. Leicester Galleries, London, 1948.) London, 1948, pp. 2–4.

Utrecht 1962
Het Wonder: Miracula Christi. (Exh. cat. Aartsbisschoppelijk Museum, Utrecht, 29 June–26 August 1962.) Recklinghausen, 1962.

Utrecht 1980
Jong, Erik de. *De Slapende Mars van Hendrick ter Brugghen*. (Exh. cat. Centraal Museum, Utrecht, 1980.) Utrecht, 1980.

Utrecht/Braunschweig 1986–87
Blankert, Albert, et al. *Nieuw licht op de Gouden Eeuw: Hendrick ter Brugghen en zijn tijdgenoten*. (Exh. cat. Centraal Museum, Utrecht; Herzog Anton Ulrich-Museum, Braunschweig, 1986–87.) Utrecht, 1986.

Utrecht/Braunschweig 1991
Segal, Sam, with Liesbeth Helmus. *Jan Davidsz. de Heem en zijn kring*. (Exh. cat. Centraal Museum, Utrecht; Herzog Anton Ulrich-Museum, Braunschweig, 1991.) The Hague, 1991.

Utrecht/Frankfurt/Luxembourg 1993
Brink, Peter van den, et al. *Het gedroomde land: Pastorale schilderkunst in de Gouden Eeuw*. (Exh. cat. Centraal Museum, Utrecht; Schirn Kunsthalle, Frankfurt; Musée National d'Histoire et d'Art, Luxembourg, 1993.) Zwolle and Utrecht, 1993.

Valentiner 1908
Valentiner, Wilhelm R., ed. *Rembrandt: Des Meisters Gemälde*. . . . Klassiker der Kunst in Gesamtausgaben 2. 3rd ed. Stuttgart, 1908.

Valentiner 1921a
Valentiner, Wilhelm R., ed. *Frans Hals, des Meisters Gemälde*. Klassiker der Kunst in Gesamtausgaben 28. Stuttgart, 1921.

Valentiner 1921b
Valentiner, Wilhelm R., ed. *Rembrandt: Wiedergefundene Gemälde (1910–1920)*. Klassiker der Kunst in Gesamtausgaben 27. Stuttgart and Berlin, 1921.

Valentiner 1921c
Valentiner, Wilhelm R. *The Work of Rembrandt*. 3rd ed. New York, 1921.

Valentiner 1923a
Valentiner, Wilhelm R., ed. *Frans Hals, des Meisters Gemälde*. Klassiker der Kunst in Gesamtausgaben 28. Stuttgart and Berlin, 1921; also 2nd ed., Stuttgart, Berlin, and Leipzig, 1923.

Valentiner 1923b
Valentiner, Wilhelm R., ed. *Rembrandt: Wiedergefundene Gemälde (1910–1922)*. Klassiker der Kunst in Gesamtausgaben 27. 2nd rev. ed. Stuttgart, 1923.

Valentiner 1924
Valentiner, Wilhelm R. "Jacob Ochtervelt." *Art in America* 12 (1924): pp. 269–84.

Valentiner 1936a
Valentiner, Wilhelm R. "The Art and Personality of Rubens in a Great Loan Exhibition of Sixty Paintings at Detroit." *Art News* 34/20 (15 February 1936): pp. 5–7.

Valentiner 1936b
Valentiner, Wilhelm R. *Frans Hals Paintings in America*. Westport, 1936.

Valentiner 1939
Valentiner, Wilhelm R. Foreword to Moltke 1939, p. xiv.

Valentiner 1941
Valentiner, Wilhelm R. "Jan van de Cappelle." *Art Quarterly* 4/4 (1941): pp. 272–95.

Valentiner 1946
Valentiner, Wilhelm R. "Rubens' Paintings in America." *Art Quarterly* 9/2 (1946): pp. 153–68.

Valentiner 1948
Valentiner, Wilhelm R. "A Portrait of Louis III [*sic*] by Pourbus." *Los Angeles County Museum Bulletin* 1/3–4 (Spring 1948): pp. 27–28.

Valls 2005
"2005 Recent Acquisitions." Rafael Valls Ltd. (Dealer catalogue.) London, 2005.

Vandenbroeck 1982
Vandenbroeck, Paul. "Laatmiddeleeuwse doekschilderkunst in de Zuidelijke Nederlanden." *Jaarboek van het Koninklijk Museum voor Schone Kunsten Antwerpen* 21 (1982): pp. 29–59.

Vaughan 1927
Vaughan, Malcolm. "Holbein Portraits in America." Pts. 1 and 2. *International Studio* 88/366 (November 1927): pp. 21–27; 88/367 (December 1927): pp. 63–68, 94.

Vaughan 1929
Vaughan, Malcolm. "A Loan Exhibition of Flemish Primitives." *International Studio* 94/390 (November 1929): pp. 38–41.

Vaughan 1961
Vaughan, Malcolm. "The Connoisseur in America." *Connoisseur* 146 (January 1961): pp. 293–98.

Van der Veen 2000
Van der Veen, Jaap. "Eenvouding en stil: Studeerkamers in zenventiende-eeuwse woningen, voornamelijk te Amsterdam, Deventer en Leiden." Special issue, *Wooncultuur in de Nederlanden / The Art of Home in the Netherlands, 1500–1800*. Edited by Jan de Jong et al. *Nederlands kunsthistorisch jaarboek* 51 (2000): pp. 137–72. https://doi.org/10.1163/22145966-90000662.

Van der Veen 2003
Van der Veen, Jaap. "*Onbekende opdrachtgevers van Rembrandt* (3) Portretten van leden van de familie Sijen door Rembrandt." *Kroniek van het Rembrandthuis* 1–2 (2003): pp. 46–60.

Veldman 1980
Veldman, Ilja M. "Seasons, Planets, and Temperaments in the Work of Maarten van Heemskerck: Cosmo-astrological Allegory in Sixteenth-Century Netherlandish Prints." *Simiolus* 11/3–4 (1980): pp. 149–76.

Veldman 1985
Veldman, Ilja M. "The 'Concert of the Muses' in the Work of Maarten van Heemskerck." *Mercury* 1 (1985): pp. 35–41.

Veldman 1986
Veldman, Ilja M. "Leerzame dwaasheid: De invloed van het 'Sotten schip' (1548) op zottenvoorstellingen van Maarten van Heemskeerck en Willem Thibaut." *Nederlands kunsthistorisch jaarboek* 37 (1986): pp. 195–224.

Veldman 1992
Veldman, Ilja M. "Images of Labor and Diligence in Sixteenth-Century Netherlandish Prints: The Work Ethic Rooted in Civic Morality or Protestantism?" *Simiolus* 21/4 (1992): pp. 227–64.

Veldman 1996
Veldman, Ilja M. "The Two Sides of Nature: An Allegory by Maarten van Heemskerck." *Simiolus* 24/2–3 (1996): pp. 128–39.

Veldman 2019
Veldman, Ilja M. "A Rediscovered Painting by Maarten van Heemskerck: A Moral Allegory in the Form of a Prodigal Son." *Simiolus* 41/1–2 (2019): pp. 39–51.

Venema 1986
Venema, A. *Kunsthandel in Nederland, 1940–1945*. Amsterdam, 1986.

Venice 1999–2000
Aikema, Bernard, and Beverly Louise Brown, eds. *Renaissance Venice and the North: Crosscurrents in the Time of Bellini, Dürer, and Titian*. (Exh. cat. Palazzo Grassi, Venice, 5 September 1999–9 January 2000.) New York, 1999.

Vermeeren 1997–98
Vermeeren, Carola. "'For the Preservation of Her Legacy' The Vicissitudes of Frederick Henry and Amalia of Solms' Collection of Paintings." In The Hague 1997b, pp. 61–75.

Verougstraete-Marcq and Van Schoute 1989
Verougstraete-Marcq, Hélène, and Roger van Schoute. *Cadres et supports dans la peinture flamande aux 15e et 16e siècles*. Heure-le-Romain, 1989.

G. H. Veth 1884
Veth, G. H. "Aelbert Cuyp, Jacob Gerritsz. Cuyp en Benjamin Cuyp." *Oud Holland* 2 (1884): pp. 233–90.

J. Veth 1941
Veth, Jan. *Rembrandt's leven en kunst*. 2nd ed. Amsterdam, 1941.

Vienna 1930
Drei Jahrhunderte Vlämischer Kunst, 1400–1700. (Exh. cat. Wiener Secession, Vienna, 11 January–23 February 1930.) Vienna, 1930.

Vienna 1977
Peter Paul Rubens, 1577–1640. (Exh. cat. Kunsthistorisches Museum, Vienna, 1977.) Introduction by Günther Heinz. Vienna, 1977.

Vienna 1984–85
Herzig, Robert. *Gemälde alter Meister: Winter 1984/85*. (Cat. Galerie Sanct Lucas, Vienna, 1984–85.) Vienna, 1984.

Vienna 2010
Haag, Sabine, et al. *Vermeer, Die Malkunst: Spurensicherung an einem Meisterwerk*. (Exh. cat. Kunsthistorisches Museum, Vienna, 2010.) Vienna, 2010.

De Villermont 1912
Villermont, M. de. *L'Infanta Isabelle gouvernante des Pays-Bas*. 2 vols. Paris, 1912.

Villers 1991
Villers, Caroline. Review of *The Beginnings of Netherlandish Canvas Painting, 1400–1530* by Diane Wolfthal. *Burlington Magazine* 133/1057 (April 1991): pp. 258f.

Visscher 1614
Visscher, Roemer. *Sinnepoppen*. Amsterdam, 1614.

Vlieghe 1972–73
Vlieghe, Hans. *Saints*. 2 vols. Corpus Rubenianum Ludwig Burchard 8. London, 1972–73.

Vlieghe 1977
Vlieghe, Hans. "Une Grande Collection Anversoise du dix-septième siècle: Le cabinet d'Arnold Lunden, beau-frère de Rubens." *Jahrbuch der Berliner Museen* 19 (1977): pp. 172–204.

Vlieghe 1987
Vlieghe, Hans. *Portraits of Identified Sitters Painted in Antwerp*. Corpus Rubenianum Ludwig Burchard 19/2. London, 1987.

Vlieghe 1996
Vlieghe, Hans. "Peter Paul Rubens." In Turner 1996, vol. 27, pp. 287–303.

Vollmer 1930
Vollmer, Hans. "Memling, Hans." In Thieme-Becker 1907–50, vol. 24 (1930): pp. 374–77.

Van den Vondel [1617]
Vondel, Joost van den. *Vorstelycke warande der dieren*. Leiden, [1617].

Van den Vondel 1927–40
Vondel, Joost van den. *De Werken van Vondel*. 10 vols. Netherlands, 1927–40.

Voorhelm-Schneevoogt 1873
Voorhelm-Schneevoogt, C[arl] G[ottfried]. *Catalogue des estampes gravées d'après P. P. Rubens: Avec l'indication des collections où se trouvent les tableaux et les gravures*. Haarlem, 1873.

Vorenkamp 1933
Vorenkamp, Alphonsus P. A. "Bijdrage tot de geschiedenis van het hollandsch stilleven in de zeventiende eeuw." Proefschrift, Rijksuniversiteit, Leiden, 1933.

Vos 1726
Vos, Jan. *Alle de Gedichten van Jan Vos*. 2 vols. Amsterdam, 1726.

De Vos 1987
Vos, Dirk de. "Memling, Hans." In *Naational biografisch woordenboek*, vol. 12 (1987): pp. 519–34.

De Vos 1994
Vos, Dirk de. *Hans Memling: The Complete Works*. London, 1994.

A. de Vries 1981
Vries, Anik de. "Sébastien Erard: Un amateur d'art du début du XIXè siècle et ses conseillers." *Gazette des beaux-arts* 97 (1981): pp. 78–86.

J. de Vries 1974
Vries, Jan de. *The Dutch Rural Economy in the Golden Age, 1500–1700*. New Haven, 1974.

L. de Vries 1977
Vries, Lyckle de. "Jan Steen, 'de kluchtschilder.'" PhD diss., Rijksuniversiteit, Groningen, 1977.

L. de Vries 1989
Vries, Lyckle de. "Tronies and Other Single Figured Netherlandish Paintings." In *Nederlandse Portretten*, pp. 185–202. Edited by H. Blasse-Hegeman et al. Lieds Kunsthistorisch Jaarboek 8. The Hague, 1989.

L. de Vries 1996–97
Vries, Lyckle de. "Steen's Artistic Evolution in the Context of Dutch Painting." In Washington/Amsterdam 1996–97, pp. 238–40.

Vroom 1980–99
Vroom, N. R. A. *A Modest Message as Intimated by the Painters of the "Monochrome Banketje*." English translation by Peter Gidman. 3 vols. Schiedam, 1980–99.

Waagen 1837–39
Waagen, Gustav F. *Kunstwerke und Künstler in England und Paris*. 3 vols. Berlin, 1837–39.

Waagen 1854
Waagen, Gustav F. *Treasures of Art in Great Britain*. 3 vols. London, 1854.

Waagen [1857] 1970
Waagen, Gustav F. *Galleries and Cabinets of Arts in Great Britain. . . .* Translated by Lady Eastlake. London, 1970. [Facsimile of 1857 London ed.; supplement to Waagen 1854.]

Waagen [1864] 1870
Waagen, Gustav F. *Die Gemäldesammlung in der kaiserlichen Ermitage zu St. Petersburg: Nebst Bemerkungen über andere dortige Kunstsammlungen*. St. Petersburg, 1870. [Repr. of 1864 Munich ed.]

Waagen 1866–67
Waagen, Gustav F. *Die vornehmsten Kunstdenkmäler in Wien*. 2 vols. Vienna, 1866–67.

Van de Waal 1952
Van de Waal, H. *Drie eeuwen vaderlandsche geschiedenis uitbeelding 1500–1800, een iconologische studie*. 2 vols. The Hague, 1952.

Wadum 1998
Wadum, Jørgen. "The Antwerp Brand on Paintings on Panel." In *Looking through Paintings: The Study of Painting Techniques and Materials in Support of Art Historical Research*, pp 179–95. Edited by Erma Hermens. London, 1998.

Wagenaar [1760–67] 1971–72
Wagenaar, Jan. *Amsterdam, in zyne opkomst, aanwas, geschiedenissen, voorregten, koophandel, gebouwen, kerkstaat, schoolen, schutterye, gilden en regeeringe*. 4 vols. Amsterdam, 1971–72. [Facsimile of 1760–67 ed.]

Wagner 1971
Wagner, Helga. *Jan van der Heyden, 1637–1712*. Amsterdam, 1971.

Waiboer 2012
Waiboer, Adriaan E. *Gabriel Metsu, Life and Work, a Catalogue Raisonné*. New Haven and London, 2012.

Walford 1991
Walford, E. John. *Jacob van Ruisdael and the Perception of Landscape*. New Haven and London, 1991.

Wallace 1968
Wallace, Robert. *The World of Rembrandt*. New York, 1968.

Wallen 1971
Wallen, Burr. "The Portraits of Jan Sanders van Hemessen." *Oud Holland* 86 (1971): pp. 70–87.

Wallert 2006–07
Wallert, Ari. "Refined Technique or Special Tricks? Painting Methods of Jan van der Heyden." In Greenwich/Amsterdam 2006–07, pp. 91–103.

Walpole 1752
Walpole, Horace. *Aedes Walpolianaei: or, A Description of the Collection of Pictures at Houghton-Hall in Norfolk, the Seat of the Right Honourable Sir Robert Walpole, Earl of Orford*. 2nd ed., with additions. London, 1752.

Walpole 1767
Walpole, Horace. *Aedes Walpolianaei: or, A Description of the Collection of Pictures at Houghton-Hall in Norfolk, the Seat of the Right Honourable Sir Robert Walpole, Earl of Orford*. 3rd ed. London, 1767.

A. Walsh 1985
Walsh, Amy L. "Paulus Potter: His Works and Their Meaning." PhD diss., Columbia University, 1985.

A. Walsh 1994
Walsh, Amy L. "Van Dyck and the Court of Frederik Hendrik." In *Van Dyck 350*, pp. 223–44. Edited by Susan J. Barnes and Arthur K. Wheelock Jr. Washington, DC, 1994.

A. Walsh 1996
[Walsh, Amy L.] "Randon de Boisset, (Pierre-Louis-) Paul." In Turner 1996, vol. 25, p. 888.

A. Walsh 1997
Walsh, Amy L. "Rural Life and Views." In *Dutch Art: An Encyclopedia*, pp. 338–40. Edited by Sheila D. Muller. New York, 1997.

A. Walsh 2019a
Walsh, Amy L. "Gerrit van Honthorst." In *Gifts of European Art from the Ahmanson Foundation*. Vol. 3, *Dutch Painting, Flemish Painting, Spanish Painting and Sculpture*, pp. 40–43. Edited by Leah Lehmbeck. Los Angeles, 2019.

A. Walsh 2019b
Walsh, Amy L. *The Mr. and Mrs. Edward Carter Collection of Dutch Paintings, Los Angeles County Museum of Art*. Edited by Leah Lehmbeck. Los Angeles, 2019.

J. Walsh 1986
Walsh, John. "Acquisitions/1985." *The J. Paul Getty Museum Journal* 14 (1986): pp. 173–286.

Warsaw 1939
Walicki, Michal. *Malarze Martwej Natury*. (Exh. cat. National Gallery, Warsaw, 1939.) Warsaw, 1939.

Washington 1975
Russell, H. Diane. *Jacques Callot, Prints and Related Drawings*. (Exh. cat. National Gallery of Art, Washington, DC, 1975.) Washington, DC, 1975.

Washington 1988
Cafritz, Robert, Lawrence Gowing, and David Rosand. *Places of Delight: The Pastoral Landscape*. (Exh. cat. National Gallery of Art, Washington, DC, 1988.) Washington, DC, and New York, 1988.

Washington 1993
Hand, John Oliver, with Sally E. Mansfield. *German Paintings of the Fifteenth Through Seventeenth Centuries*. Washington, DC, 1993.

Washington/Amsterdam 1996–97
Chapman, H. Perry, et al. *Jan Steen: Painter and Storyteller*. (Exh. cat. National Gallery of Art, Washington, DC; Rijksmuseum, Amsterdam, 1996–97.) Washington, DC, 1996.

Washington/London/Amsterdam 2001
Wheelock, Arthur K., Jr., ed. *Aelbert Cuyp*. (Exh. cat. National Gallery of Art, Washington, DC; National Gallery, London; Rijksmuseum, Amsterdam, 2001.) Washington, DC, 2001.

Washington/Milwaukee/Amsterdam 2008
Wheelock, Arthur K., Jr., et al. *Jan Lievens, A Dutch Master Rediscovered*. (Exh. cat. National Gallery of Art, Washington, DC; Milwaukee Art Museum; Rembrandthuis, Amsterdam, 2008.) Washington DC, 2008.

Weddigen 1984
Weddigen, Erasmus. "Jacopo Tintoretto und die Musik." *Artibus et historiae* 10 (1984): pp. 67–119.

Weisbach 1926
Weisbach, W. *Rembrandt*. Berlin, 1926.

Weitzner 1936
A Selection of Paintings. (Sale cat., Julius H. Weitzner Inc., New York.) New York, 1936.

Weller 2009
Weller, Dennis P. *Seventeenth-Century Dutch and Flemish Paintings*. Raleigh, 2009.

Welu 1975
Welu, James A. "Vermeer: His Cartographic Sources." *Art Bulletin* 57 (1975): pp. 529–47.

Welu 1991
Welu, James A. "Strange New Worlds: Mapping the Heavens and Earth's Great Extent." In Hanover/Raleigh/Atlanta 1991, pp. 101–12.

Welzel 1999
Welzel, Barbara. "Princeps Vidua, Mater Castrorum, The Iconography of Archduchess Isabella as Governor of the Netherlands." In *Jaarboek Koninklijk Museum voor Schone Kunsten Antwerpen 1999 / Antwerp Royal Museum Annual* (1999): pp. 159–75.

Wéra 1951
Wéra, Marguerite. "Contribution à l'étude d'Albert Bouts." *Revue belge d'archéologie et d'histoire de l'art* 20 (1951): pp. 139–44.

Wescher 1930
Wescher, Paul. "Massys (Metsys), Jan." In Thieme-Becker 1907–50, vol. 24 (1930): pp. 226–27.

Wescher 1936
Wescher, Paul. "Zum Werk des Jörg Pencz." *Pantheon* 18/9 (September 1936): pp. 280–84; English summary: 34ff.

Wescher 1937
Wescher, Paul. "Die Pariser Ausstellung 'Rubens und seine Zeit.'" *Pantheon* 19 (1937): pp. 21–24.

Westermann 1996
Westermann, Mariët. "Steen's Comic Fictions." In Washington/Amsterdam 1996–97, pp. 53–68.

Westermann 1997
Westermann, Mariët. *The Amusements of Jan Steen*. Zwolle, 1997.

Westermann 2002–03
Westermann, Mariët. "Jan Miense Molenaer in the Comic Mode." In Raleigh/Indianapolis/Manchester 2002–03, pp. 55ff.

Westermann 2018
Westermann, Mariët. "Steen's Great History Pageant." In The Hague 2018, pp. 54–72.

Weststeijn 2022
Weststeijn, Thijs. "Unease with the Exotic: Ambiguous Responses to Chinese Material Culture in the Dutch Republic." In *Making Worlds: Global Invention in the Early Modern Period*, pp. 436–76. Edited by Angela Vanhaelen and Bronwen Wilson. Toronto, 2022.

Weston 1974a
Weston, Wallace. "An Allegory of Nature by Maerten van Heemskerck." *Quarto* (Henry Art Gallery, University of Washington, Seattle) 1 (January 1974): n.pag.

Weston 1974b
Weston, Wallace. "A Marriage at Cana by Jan Steen." *Quarto* (Henry Art Gallery, University of Washington, Seattle) 3 (July 1974): n.pag.

Weston 1978
Weston, Wallace. "On the Road with Nicolaes Berchem." *Quarto* (Henry Art Gallery, University of Washington, Seattle) 5 (July 1978): n.pag.

Van Westrheene 1856
Westrheene, Tobias van. *Jan Steen: Étude sur l'art en Hollande*. The Hague, 1856.

Van de Wetering 1983
Wetering, Ernst van de. "Isaac Jouderville, a Pupil of Rembrandt." In Amsterdam 1983, pp. 59–77.

Van de Wetering 1991
Wetering, Ernst van de. "Verdwenen tekeningen en het gebruik van afwisbare tekenplankjes en 'tafeletten.'" *Oud Holland* 105/4 (1991): pp. 210–27.

Van de Wetering 1997
Wetering, Ernst van de. *Rembrandt: The Painter at Work*. Amsterdam, 1997.

Van de Wetering 2000
Wetering, Ernst van de. *Rembrandt: The Painter at Work*. Berkeley, Los Angeles, and London, 2000. Paperback ed. of Van de Wetering 1997.

Van de Wetering 2003
Wetering, Ernst van de. *Rembrandt's Hidden Self-Portraits / Rembrandts verborgen zelfportretten*. Amsterdam, 2003.

Van de Wetering 2016
Wetering, Ernst van de. *Rembrandt: The Painter Thinking*. Edited by Wardy Poelstra. Amsterdam, 2016.

Van de Wetering 2017
Wetering, Ernst van de, with Carin van Nes. *Rembrandt's Paintings Revisited, A Complete Survey*. Dordrecht, 2017. [Repr. of *A Corpus of Rembrandt Paintings VI: Rembrandt's Paintings Revisited, A Complete Survey*. (The Hague and Boston, 2015.]

Wheelock 1995
Wheelock, Arthur K., Jr. *Dutch Paintings of the Seventeenth Century*. Washington, DC, 1995.

White 1982
White, Christopher. *The Dutch Pictures in the Collection of Her Majesty the Queen*. Cambridge, London, and New York, 1982.

White 1992
White, Christopher. "Exhibition Review: Rembrandt, Amsterdam and London." *Burlington Magazine* 134 (April 1992): pp. 264–68.

White 1993
White, Christopher. "Rubens and Antiquity." In Boston/Toledo 1993, pp. 146–57.

Wieseman 2010
Wieseman, Marjorie E. "Rembrandt's Portrait(s) of Frederik Rihel." *National Gallery* (UK) *Technical Bulletin* 31 (2010): pp. 96–111.

Wiesner 1986
Wiesner, Merry E. *Working Women in Renaissance Germany*. New Brunswick, 1986.

Wilczek 1936
Wilczek, Karl. *Katalog der Graf Czernin'schen Gemäldegalerie in Wien*. Vienna, 1936.

Wilenski 1929
Wilenski, R. H. *An Introduction to Dutch Art*. London, 1929.

Wilenski 1945
Wilenski, R. H. *Dutch Painting*. 1929; rev. ed. London, 1945.

Willemse 2005
Willemse, Frans. *The Mystery of the Tulip Painter*. Translated by Marja Smolenaars. Lisse, 2005.

Wilson 1995
Wilson, Jean C. "Adriaen Isenbrant and the Problem of His Oeuvre." *Oud Holland* 109 (1995): pp. 1–17.

Wind 1967
Wind, Edgar. *Pagan Mysteries in the Renaissance*. Harmondsworth, 1967.

De Winkel 1999
Winkel, Marieke de. "Costume in Rembrandt's Self-portraits." In London/The Hague 1999, pp. 68f.

De Winkel 2005
Winkel, Marieke de. "Rembrandt's Clothes—Dress and Meaning in His Self-Portraits." In *Corpus* 2005, pp. 45–87.

De Winkel 2006
Winkel, Marieke de. *Fashion and Fancy: Dress and Meaning in Rembrandt's Paintings*. Amsterdam, 2006.

Winkler 1960
Winkler, Friedrich. "Ausstellung altniederländischer Bilder aus Amerika in Brügge. . . ." *Kunstchronik* 13 (1960): pp. 312–18.

Winner 1961
Winner, Matthias. "Zeichnungen des älteren Jan Brueghel." *Jahrbuch der Berliner Museen* 3 (1961): pp. 190–241.

Winston-Salem 1963
Dietzel Bier, Senta. *Collectors' Opportunity*. (Exh. cat. Gallery of the Public Library of Winston-Salem and Forsyth County, 22 April–3 May 1963.) Winston-Salem, 1963.

Winter 1768
Winter, Georg Ludwig. *Beschreibung aller Seltenheiten der Kunst und übrigend Alterthüme . . . in dem königlichen Lust-Schlosse Charlottenburg*. Berlin, 1768.

Winternitz 1967
Winternitz, Emanuel. *Gaudenzio Ferrari, His School, and the Early History of the Violin*. New York, 1967.

De Witt 2007
De Witt, David A. *Jan van Noordt: Painter of History and Portraits in Amsterdam*. Montreal, Kingston, London, and Ithaca, 2007.

Witt 1929
Witt, Robert. "The Dutch Exhibition at the Royal Academy." *Burlington Magazine* 54/310 (January 1929): pp. 3–17.

Wolfthal 1989
Wolfthal, Diane. *The Beginnings of Netherlandish Canvas Painting, 1400–1530*. Cambridge and New York, 1989.

Wolfthal and Metzger 2014
Wolfthal, Diane, and Cathy Metzger. *Los Angeles Museums*. Corpus of Early Netherlandish Painting 22. Brussels, 2014.

Wolleswinkel 2005
Wolleswinkel, E. J. "Collectie: Wapenboekjes Joris Sijen Pietersz. Uit de collecties van de Hoge Raad van Adel." *De Nederlandsche Leeuw* 122/3 (2005): pp. 173–83.

Woodall 1990
Woodall, Joanna. "Status Symbols: Role and Rank in Seventeenth-Century Netherlandish Portraiture." *Dutch Crossing* 42 (Autumn 1990): pp. 34–68.

Woods 2007
Woods, K. M. "Netherlandish Networks." In *Locating Renaissance Art*, pp. 65–99. Edited by C. M. Richardson. New Haven, 2007.

Woollett 2007
Woollett, Anne T. "The 'Calydonian Boar Hunt': A Rubens for the J. Paul Getty Museum." *Burlington Magazine* 149 (February 2007): pp. 82–84.

Woollett 2009
Woollett, Anne T. *Rembrandt in Southern California*. Los Angeles, 2009.

Wright 1982
Wright, Christopher. *Rembrandt: Self-Portraits*. London, 1982.

Wright 1985
Wright, Christopher. *The French Painters of the Seventeenth Century*. London, 1985.

Wright 2001
Wright, Christopher. *Rembrandt*. Paris, 2001.

Wurzbach 1886
Wurzbach, Alfred von. *Rembrandt Galerie*. Stuttgart, 1886.

Wurzbach [1906–11] 1974
Wurzbach, Alfred von. *Niederländisches Künstler-Lexikon*. 3 vols. Amsterdam, 1974. [Repr. of 1906–11 Vienna and Leipzig ed.]

De Wyzewa and Perreau 1890
Wyzewa, T. de, and X. Perreau. *Les Grands Peintres des Flandres, de la Hollande, de l'Italie et de la France*. Paris, 1890.

Ydema 1991
Ydema, Onna. *Carpets and Their Datings in Netherlandish Paintings, 1540–1700*. Leiden, 1991.

Yeide 2009
Yeide, Nancy H. *Beyond the Dreams of Avarice: The Hermann Goering Collection*. Dallas, 2009.

Yeide, Akinsha, and Walsh 2001
Yeide, Nancy, Konstantin Akinsha, and Amy L. Walsh. *The AAM Guide to Provenance Research*. Washington, DC, 2001.

Zandvliet 2006
Zandvliet, Kees. *De 250 rijksten van de Gouden Eeuw. Kapitaal, macht, familie en levensstijl*. Amsterdam, 2006.

Zanotti and Iacoviello 2015
Zanotti, Anna Letizia, and Antonella Iacoviello. "Con l'occhio del naturalista, Per un riconoscimento delle specie botaniche nei dipinti di natura morta." In *La natura morta di Federico Zeri*, pp. 287–320. By Andrea Bacchi, Francesca Mambelli, and Elisabetta Sambo. Bologna, 2015.

Zeldenrust 1983
Zeldenrust, Manja. "Aert van der Neers 'Rivierlandschap bij maanlicht' opgehelderd." *Bulletin van het Rijksmuseum* 31/1 (1983): pp. 99–104; English summary: p. 140.

Zeri 1954
Zeri, Federico. *La Galleria Spada in Roma, Catalogo dei dipinti*. Florence, 1954.

Zeri 1987
Zeri, Federico. *La pittura in Italia. Il Quattrocento*. 2 vols. Milan, 1987.

Zirpolo 2008
Zirpolo, L. *Historical Dictionary of Renaissance Art*. Lanham, 2008.

Zumthor 1962
Zumthor, Paul. *Daily Life in Rembrandt's Holland*. London, 1962.

Zurich 1962
Sammlung Sir Joseph Robinson, 1840–1929. (Exh. cat. Kunsthaus, Zurich, 1962.) Zurich, 1962.

Photographic Credits

Unless otherwise noted, all figure illustrations are courtesy of the Norton Simon Art Foundation, Pasadena. All images of artworks in the Norton Simon Art Foundation, The Norton Simon Foundation, and the Norton Simon Museum collections are copyrighted to their respective owning entities. All other image credits are listed below, including material supplied by other institutions, agencies, and individual photographers. A good-faith effort has been made to secure permission from copyright holders. In instances where no copyright holder has been located, any information is appreciated and will be included in future editions.

The Albertina, Vienna: figs. 25e, 71b, 74a.
© Alinari / Art Resource, NY: figs. 72c, 89d.
© Veneranda Biblioteca Ambrosiana / Mondadori Portfolio: fig. 9c.
© Amgueddfa Cymru–National Museum Wales: fig. 66b.
Art Gallery of Ontario: fig. 29b.
© Auktionshaus im Kinsky GmbH, Vienna: fig. 63c.
Image courtesy of Jean-Luc Baroni Ltd.: fig. 48d.
Bayerische Staatsgemäldesammlungen–Alte Pinakothek München: figs. 42a, 58c, 62a, 75c, 88c.
Bibliothèque universitaire, Collection Atger, Montpellier: fig. 70a.
Sarah Campbell Blaffer Foundation, Houston: fig. 62b.
bpk Bildagentur / Gemäldegalerie Alte Meister, Museumslandschaft Hessen Kassel / Art Resource, NY: fig. 36b.
bpk Bildagentur / Gemäldegalerie Alte Meister, Staatliche Kunstsammlungen / Photo: Elke Estel, Hans-Peter Klut / Art Resource, NY: fig. 86b.
bpk Bildagentur / Staatliches Museum Schwerin / Art Resource, NY: fig. 84a.
bpk, Berlin / Alte Pinakothek, Bayerische Staatsgemäldesammlungen, Munich / Art Resource, NY: fig. 37a.
bpk, Berlin / Gemäldegalerie Alte Meister, Staatliche Kunstsammlungen / Photo: Elke Estel, Hans-Peter Klut / Art Resource, NY: fig. 89b.
bpk, Berlin / Kupferstichkabinett / Photo: Joerg P. Anders: fig. 54c.
© The Trustees of the British Museum. All rights reserved: fig. 32a, 34c, 41b, 68c, 82c.
© The Trustees of the British Museum / Art Resource, NY: figs. 14b, 20c.
Brukenthal National Museum: fig. 73a.
The Bute Collection at Mount Stuart: fig. 86c.
The Bute Collection at Mount Stuart / Photo: Keith Hunter: fig. 5b.
Cameraphoto Arte, Venice / Art Resource, NY: fig. 70c.
© Centraal Museum Utrecht: fig. 6b.
© Christie's Images / The Bridgeman Art Library: fig. 53a.
Image courtesy of Christie's: fig. 90b.
© The Samuel Courtauld Trust, The Courtauld Gallery, London: fig. 70d.
© DeA Picture Library / Photo: G. Dagli Orti / Art Resource, NY: fig. 70b.
Detroit Institute of Arts: fig. 88a.
Image courtesy of Douwes Fine Art (since 1770), Amsterdam, The Netherlands: fig. 8c.
Agnes Etherington Art Centre, Queen's University, Kingston, Canada: Introduction, fig. 5.
Photo by Evening Standard / Hulton Archive / Getty Images: Introduction, fig. 3.
Fine Arts Museums of San Francisco, Gift of Dr. Ludwig A. Emge: fig. 68b.
© The Fitzwilliam Museum, Cambridge: fig. 28b.
Folger Shakespeare Library, Folger Imaging Department: fig. 89c.
Frans Hals Museum, Haarlem: fig. 28c.
Image courtesy of Frick Art Reference Library: fig. 95a.
Gemäldegalerie der Akademie der bildenden Künste Wien: figs. 28d, 68a.
Getty Research Institute, Los Angeles; digital images courtesy of the Getty's Open Content Program: figs. 3b, 6a, 13a, 13b, 64a, 64b, 87a.
Photo: Tom Haartsen / © Foto Marburg / Art Resource, NY: fig. 29a.
Collection of the Haggerty Museum of Art, Marquette University: Introduction, fig. 6.
Photo: Erik and Petra Hesmerg: fig. 33c.
Image courtesy Hoogsteder & Hoogsteder: fig. 56d.
IRR: © RKD, The Hague: fig. 58b.
J. Paul Getty Museum, Los Angeles; digital images courtesy of the Getty's Open Content Program: figs. 11a, 16a, 86a, 90c, 94b.
© KHM-Museumsverband: figs. 25f, 26a, 48c, 72a, 73b, 74c, 91b.
Leonard Koetser Gallery Ltd., London: fig. 42b.
Koninklijk Museum voor Schone Kunsten, Antwerp / © Lukas-Art in Flanders VZW: fig. 21a.
Kunstmuseum Basel / Photo: Martin P. Bühler: fig. 33b.
Kupferstich-Kabinett, Staatliche Kunstsammlungen Dresden: fig. 27a.
Latvian National Museum of Art: fig. 35a.
The Leiden Collection, New York: fig. 22b.
Erich Lessing / Art Resource, NY: fig. 93a.
Los Angeles County Museum of Art (www.lacma.org): figs. 9b, 9d, 60a, 65c, 77a, 91a.
Mauritshuis, The Hague: figs. 22a, 30a, 88b.
The Metropolitan Museum of Art, New York: figs. 17b, 23a, 31e, 51a, 51b, 54b, 56a, 73c, 78a, 79b, 80a, 80c.
Minneapolis Institute of Arts: fig. 23b.
The Morgan Library & Museum, New York. Gift; Purchased by J. Pierpont Morgan (1837–1913), 1910. MS M.399, fol. 13v: fig. 63d.
The Morgan Library & Museum, New York. Purchased by J. Pierpont Morgan (1837–1913), 1910. MS M.399., fol. 13v: fig. 20b.
Musea Brugge / Photo: Hugo Maertens: fig. 55c.
© Musée d'art et d'histoire, Ville de Genève, inv. no. CR0143 / Photo: Bettina Jacot-Descombes: fig. 82d.
© Museo Nacional Thyssen-Bornemisza, Madrid: figs. 8a, 8b, 34a.
Collection Museum Boijmans Van Beuningen / Bruikleen / Loan: Rijksdienst voor het Cultureel Erfgoed 1990 (NK-collectie): fig. 40c.
Collection Museum Boijmans Van Beuningen, from the estate of F. J. O. Boijmans, 1847: fig. 71a.
Collection Museum Boijmans Van Beuningen, from the estate of F. J. O. Boijmans, 1847 / Photo: Studio Tromp: fig. 35b.
Collection Museum Boijmans Van Beuningen, gift of Henry Deterding, 1936 / Photo: Studio Tromp: fig. 56b.

Collection Museum Boijmans Van Beuningen, Loan from the Museum Boijmans Van Beuningen Foundation, purchased with the support of Rembrandt Association and 120 friends of the museum, 1940: fig. 67d.
Museum Bredius: fig. 58a.
Museum De Lakenhal, Leiden / Photo: Rik Klein Gotink: fig. 25d.
© 2024 Museum of Fine Arts, Boston: fig. 55a.
© The National Gallery, London: figs. 11b, 88d, 94a.
National Gallery of Art, Washington, D.C.: figs. 37b, 67b, 88e.
National Gallery of Art, Washington, D.C., Gallery Archives; RG26B, National Gallery of Art Events Images–Exhibitions and Installations, 26B7_163_007: Introduction, fig. 4.
National Gallery of Art, Washington, D.C., Painting Conservation Department: fig. 67a.
© The National Gallery of Ireland: fig. 89a.
National Gallery of Victoria, Melbourne: fig. 75a.
© National Trust Images / Photo: John Hammond: fig. 19a.
Image courtesy of Otto Naumann Ltd., New York: fig. 45a.
The New York Public Library: fig. 50b.
Image courtesy of Noortman Master Paintings, Maastricht: fig. 14a.
North Carolina Museum of Art: figs. 23c, 49a.
Odessa Museum of Western and Eastern Art: fig. 66d.
ÖNB/Vienna: figs. 82a, 82b.
Philadelphia Museum of Art: figs. 16b, 26b, 75b.
© Photographic Archive Museo Nacional del Prado: figs. 17c, 17d, 69a, 74b, 76a, 76b.
Regional Picture Gallery, Tver, Russia: fig. 12a.
© Réunion des Musées Nationaux (PBA, Lille) / Photo: Philipp Bernard / Art Resource, NY: fig. 40b.
Collection Rijksbureau voor Kunsthistorische Documentatie (RKD), The Hague: fig. 28a.
Rijksmuseum, Amsterdam: figs. 1a, 4a, 5a, 6c, 16c, 20a, 33d, 46a, 46b, 48a, 48b, 50a, 66c, 81a, 87b.
Image courtesy of Rijksmuseum, Amsterdam, when the object was housed there: fig. 12c.
© RMN-Grand Palais / Art Resource, NY: fig. 36a.
© RMN-Grand Palais / Photo: Bulloz / Art Resource, NY: fig. 51c.
© RMN-Grand Palais / Photo: Michel Urtado / Art Resource, NY: fig. 4b.
© RMN-Grand Palais / Photo: Thierry Le Mage / Art Resource, NY: fig. 38a.
© RMN-Grand Palais / Photo: Tony Querrec / Art Resource, NY: figs. 40a, 55d.
Royal Collection Trust / © His Majesty King Charles III, 2024: fig. 57a.
© Royal Museums of Fine Arts of Belgium, Brussels / Photo: J. Geleyns: figs. 10a, 10b, 11c, 53b.
© Scala / Ministero per i Beni e le Attivà culturali / Art Resource, NY: figs. 55b, 64c.
Scala / White Images / Art Resource, NY: figs. 40d, 76c.
Image courtesy of Sotheby's: figs. 49b, 80b.
Spencer Museum of Art, Lawrence, Kansas, gift of the Mark L. Morris Jr. Family. 1992.0037: fig. 2a.
Staatliche Kunsthalle Karlsruhe: fig. 92a.
Staatliche Museen zu Berlin, Gemäldegalerie: fig. 65b.
Staatliche Museen zu Berlin, Gemäldegalerie / Photo: Jörg P. Anders: figs. 77b, 85a.
Staatliche Museen zu Berlin, Gemäldegalerie / Property of Kaiser Friedrich Museumsverein / Photo: Christoph Schmidt: fig. 54a.
Statens Museum for Kunst, Copenhagen: fig. 59a.
Statens Museum for Kunst, Copenhagen / Photo: Hans Petersen: fig. 3a.
St. John's Hospital / www.artinflanders.be: fig. 39a.
© Szépmüvészeti Múzeum / Museum of Fine Arts, Budapest, 2024: figs. 34b, 61a.
The Speed Art Museum: fig. 65a.
Toledo Art Museum: fig. 56c.
Urheberrecht Foto: Horst Kolberg, Neuss / Nutzungsrecht Foto: Kunst-palast, Düsseldorf / Kunstpalast–Horst Kolberg–ARTOTHEK: fig. 7a.
Image courtesy of Rafael Valls Ltd.: fig. 15b.
Image courtesy of Johnny Van Haeften Gallery, London: fig. 12b.
© Vanni / Art Resource, NY: fig. 71c.
© Victoria and Albert Museum, London: figs. 41a, 79a.
© Wallace Collection, London, UK / Bridgeman Images: fig. 67c.
Image courtesy of The Weiss Gallery, London: Introduction, fig. 7.
From the Woburn Abbey Collection, Bedfordshire, UK: fig. 72b.
Yale Center for British Art: fig. 20d.
© York Museums Trust (York Art Gallery), UK / The Bridgeman Art Library: fig. 83a.
Zoonar GmbH / Alamy Stock Photo: fig. 71d.

Index

Note: Page numbers in italic type indicate illustrations.

Abbas I, Shah, 321
Adams, Ann Jensen, 226, 231
Adamsdr., Trijntje, 470
Aelst, Willem van, 394, 396
Aertsen, Pieter, 412
Aesop, 409
Agostino Veneziano, *Three Women Going to the Sepulchre*, 348
Ainsworth, Maryan, 118–19, 197
Albert, Archduke, 95, 370
Alewijn, Dirck (grandfather), 250
Alewijn, Dirck Fredericksz., 248, 250–52
Alewijn, Frederick Dircksz., 250–51
Alfonso V, King of Portugal, 266
Alkmaar, Master of. *See* Master of Alkmaar
Altdorfer, Albrecht, 260
Alva, Duke of, 167, 168
Amberger, Christoph, 336
Amman, Joost
  Eygentliche Beschreibung aller Stände (Exact Description of All Ranks), 80
  The Shoemaker, 80, *80*
Andrea, Giovanni, 62
Anne, Queen of England, 216
Anne of Austria, Queen of France, 376–77, 380, 382–83
Anslo, Cornelis Claesz., 313
Antonello da Messina, 264
Apollo Belvedere, *102*
Arenberg, Duke of, 442
Arese, Francesco, 344
Arkel, Roelof van, 285
Artois, Jacques d', 200
Arundel, Thomas Howard, 14th Earl of, 329
Ascensius, Jodocus Badius, 167
Asperen de Boer, J. R. J. van, 141
Asscher and Welker (art dealers), 363
Ast, Balthasar van der, 26, 28, 51
  Flowers in a Chinese Vase, *50*, 51
  Fruit Still Life with Two Parrots, 28, *28*
  Still Life with Fruits and Flowers (cat. 3), 26, *27*, 28–29, 51
Avercamp, Hendrick, *Winter Scene on a Frozen Canal*, 286, *288*

Baardt, Petrus, *Deugden-spoor in de on-deughden des werelts aff-gebeeldt* (Exhortations to Virtue through the Portrayal of the World's Vices), 436
Bachmann, Fredo, 284
Backer, Jacob Adriensz., 235
Bader, Alfred, 240
Baldung Grien, Hans, 102
Bamboccianti, 32, 332, 334–35
Bangs, Jeremy, 23–24
Bartoli, Daniello, *Povertà Contenta* (Contented Poverty), 335
Bassano, Francesco, *Mockery of Christ*, *452*, 452–53
Bassano, Jacopo, 32
  Proclamation to the Shepherds (engraving by Aegidius Sadeler after Bassano), 30, *32*
Bauch, Kurt, 235, 329
Baudouin, Comte de, 322
Baugin, Lubin, 456
Bax, Dirk, 443
Beck, Hans-Ulrich, 150
Beert, Osias, *Still Life with Cherries and Strawberries in Porcelain Bowls*, 28
Beham, Barthel, 307
Beham, Sebald, 307
  Death and the Maiden, 307
  Death and the Sleeping Woman, 307
Belkin, Kristin, 336, 338
Bellini, Giovanni
  Agony in the Garden, 69
  Resurrection Altarpiece, 69
  The Transfiguration, 69
Bellori, Pietro, 128
Bening, Simon
  April, from the *Da Costa Hours*, 112, *112*
  Pig Slaughter, The Month of November, from the *Da Costa Hours*, 302, *302*
Benson, Ambrosius, 206
  Deipara Virgo, 118, *118*
Berchem, Nicolaes, 30, 32, 34, 36, 202, 388
  An Extensive Wooded Landscape with Peasants on a Path, 34, *36*
  Pastoral Scene (cat. 4), 30, *31*, 32–33
  Shepherds and a Young Woman on a Donkey (etching by Johannes Visscher after Berchem), 34, *36*
  Shepherds and Their Flocks, 30
  Shepherds with a Woman Washing, 30
  Study of a Young Farm Woman, *32*
  Study of Six Sheep, 32, *32*
  Wooded Landscape with a Pool and Figures (cat. 77) (with Jacob van Ruisdael), 386, *387*, 388–89
Berchem, Nicolaes (after), *Evening Landscape with Tower and Figures and a Distant View of Mount Soratte, Rome* (cat. 5), 34, *35*, 36–37
Berckheyde, Gerrit Adriaensz., 176
Beuckelaer, Joachim, 412
Beyeren, Abraham van, 91
Bible, 66, 122, 124, 183, 230, 244, 256
Bicker, Agatha, 248, 250–52
Bicker, Andries, 251
Bicker, Eva Jacobsdr., 250–51
Bicker, Hendrik Jacobsz., 251
Bicker, Jan, 251
Bicker, Wendela, 251
Biesboer, Pieter, 158
Bijlert, Jan van, 38, 40–41
  Mars in Armor, 40
  Mars Overpowered by Cupid, 40
  Mars Vigilant (Man in Armor Holding a Pike) (cat. 6), 38, *39*, 40–41
Bilhamer, Joost Jansz., 177
Binoit, Peter, 57, 394
Bisschop, Cornelis, 44
  Bathsheba (cat. 7), 42, *43*, 44–46, *47* (detail), 427
  The Concert, 45
  Contest between Marsyas and Apollo, 44
  Joseph and Potiphar's Wife, 44, *44*
  Mercury and Argus, 44
  Pilate Washing His Hands, 44
Bisschop, Jan de, *Beckeneelhuisje aan de Nieuwe Kerk te Amsterdam*, 177, *177*
Blackwood, John, 444
Blaeu, Joan, *Atlas Maior*, 183
Blaeu, Willem Jansz., *Theatrum Orbis Terrarum*, 180
Blaker, Hugh, 197
Bloemaert, Abraham, 302
  Adoration of the Magi, 365
  Terra [Earth] (engraving by Cornelis Bloemaert II after Abraham Bloemaert), 112, *112*
Bloemaert, Cornelis, II, *Terra [Earth]* (engraving after Abraham Bloemaert), 112, *112*
Bode, Wilhelm, 329
Boeckhorst, Jan (Lange Jan [Long John]), 412
Bol, Laurens, 56, 57
Bolswert, Boetius Adams, 302

Bolswert, Schelte Adams à, 129, 211
Saint Ignatius Loyola, Standing and Holding an Open Book (engraving after Rubens), 364, *364*
Borch, Gerard ter, 270, 426
Curiosity, 292
Lady at Her Toilet, 292
A Woman Having Her Hair Combed by a Maid, 270
Borromeo, Charles, 362
Borromeo, Federico, 56, 86, 162
Bosch, Marretje Arents, 313
Bosschaert, Ambrosius, I, 28, 50, 51, 54, 56–57, 394. *See also* Circle of Ambrosius Bosschaert I
Bouquet in an Arched Window, 56
Bouquet of Flowers on a Ledge, 56, *56*, *57* (detail)
Chinese Vase with Flowers, Shells, and Insects, *50*, 51
Flowers in a Glass Beaker, 56
Still Life with Flowers in a Vase, 51
Bosschaert, Ambrosius, II, *A Bouquet of Flowers in a Wan-Li Vase Surrounded by Some Shells, Grapes, and a Butterfly* (with Johannes Bosschaert), 51, *51*
Both, Jan, 34, 112, 202
Boucle, Pierre, 456
Bouts, Albrecht, 62–63.
The Penitence of Saint Jerome, *60*, 62
Triptych of the Assumption of the Virgin, *62*, 63
Bouts, Albrecht, Workshop of, *The Penitence of Saint Jerome* (cat. 10), 60, *61*, 62–63
Bouts, Dieric, 66
The Adoration, 67–68
The Annunciation, 16, 64, 66, *67*, 67–68
The Crucifixion, 68–69, *69*
The Entombment, 16, 64, 66, 67–68, *68*
Passion Altarpiece, 69
The Resurrection (cat. 11), 16, 64, *65*, 66–71
Braamcamp, Gerrit, 36
Bradford, Mary, Countess of, 323
Bradford, Richard Newport, 2nd Earl of, 323
Brary, Hendrik, 437
Braun, Georg, and Franz Hogenberg, *View of Dordrecht*, from *Civitates Orbis Terrarum (Towns of the World)*, *244*, 245
Bray, Salomon de, 75
The Expulsion of Hagar and Ishmael (cat. 12), 72, *73*, 74–76, *75* (infrared photograph), *77* (detail)
Expulsion of Hagar and Ishmael (drawing), 75, *75*
The Expulsion of Hagar and Ishmael (London), 74, *74*
The Expulsion of Hagar and Ishmael (Tver, Russia), 74, *74*
Bredero, Gerbrand Adriaensz.
Boeren Geselschap, 298
Lucelle, 427
Brekelenkam, Quiringh Gerritsz. van, 78, 80–81
The Shoemaker's Shop (cat. 13), 16, 78, *79*, 80–82, *83* (detail)
Bremden, Daniël van den, *Jacob Complains to Laban that He Has Given Him Leah instead of Rachel as His Wife* (engraving after Adriaen Pietersz. van de Venne), *432*, 433
Brink, Peter van den, 235
British, glass color print depicting the interior of a tavern with three men drinking, 214, *214*
Brouwer, Adriaen, 234, 238, 298
Brown, Christopher, 329–30
Bruegel, Pieter, I, 335, 392, 444
Haystacks, 303
Kermis at Hoboken, 298
Peasant Wedding, 444
Brueghel, Abraham, 56
Brueghel, Ambrosius, 51
Brueghel, Jan, I, 28, 54, 56–57, 84, 86, 162, 394, 412
Flowers in a Golden Tazza, 84, 86, *86*
Flowers in a Tazza (formerly attributed to Brueghel I), 84, 86, *86*
Flower Still Life, 56, *57*
Brueghel, Jan, II, 28, 56, 222
Flowers in a Gilt Tazza (cat. 14), 84, *85*, 86–87
Flowers in a Glass Beaker (cat. 9), 26, 54, *54* (detail), *55*, 56–58, *59* (detail), 84
Brugghen, Hendrick ter
Mars Asleep, 40, *40*
Trik-trak Players, 40
Brune, Johan de, *Emblemata of Zinne-werck*, *80*, 81
Bry, Johann Theodor de, *Emblem of a Foppish Man in a Wheelbarrow*, 437, *437*
Buckingham, Duke of, 380
Burchard, Ludwig, 351, 363, 383
Busleyden, Hieronymus, 118
Butler, Richard, 36
Buys, Cornelis, I, 23, 24
Buytewech, Willem Pietersz.
Allegory of the Deceitfulness of Spain and the Liberty and Prosperity of the Dutch Republic, *40*, 41

cabinets of curiosities (*Kunstkammern*, *Wunderkammern*), 28, 50, 132, 408
Cagnacci, Guido, 16
Callot, Jacques, 334–35
The Fair at Impruneta, 334, *334*
frontispiece for *Il Solimano*, 335
The Palace Gardens at Nancy, 334
Calvin, John, 72
Calvinism, 313
Campbell, Lorne, 69
Campbell Abdo, Sara, 13
Campos, Redig de, 365
Cappelle, Jan van de, 158
Shipping in a Calm at Flushing with a States General Yacht Firing a Salute, 466, *466*
Capuchin order, 351
Caravaggio, 128–29, 450, 452, 453
The Denial of Saint Peter, 128, *128*
Caravaggisti, 38, 40, 128–29, 332
Carlos II, King of Spain, 334
Carracci, Ludovico, 450
Carreño de Miranda, Juan, 274
Casanova, Giuseppe, 67
Castiglione, Baldassare, *The Courtier*, 155
Catherine II, Empress of Russia, 322, 414
Catholic Church, 81, 167, 284–85, 344, 362–65, 368, 370–71, 376, 380, 444, 446
Cats, Jacob, 42, 72, 95, 244
Houwelyck (Marriage), 437, 470
"Houwelyck van Drien . . ." (Marriage of Three), 433
Spiegel van den Voorleden en Tegenwoordigen Tijt (Mirror of the Past and Present Time), 408
Cavendish, William, 413

Cennini, Cennino, 66
Cerquozzi, Michelangelo, 332
Chance, Peter, 13
Charles I, King of England, 41, 224, 376–78, 413, 449
Charles V, Holy Roman Emperor, 119, 371, 376
Charron, Pierre, 404
chiaroscuro, 214, 244, 332. *See also* sfumato
Chifflet, Philippe, 370
Christian IV, King of Denmark and Norway, 344
Christie's, 13–14, 331
Christus, Petrus, *Head of Christ*, 265
Circle of Ambrosius Bosschaert I
Flowers in a Glass Beaker (cat. 9), 26, 54, *54* (detail), *55*, 56–58, *59* (detail), 84
Large Bouquet in a Wan-Li Vase with a Gilt Mount (cat. 8), 48, *49*, 50–52, *53* (detail)
Claesz., Anthony, 135
Claesz., Pieter, 88, 90
A Still Life of a Crab on a Pewter Plate, a Salt Cellar, a Roemer, a Knife, a Lemon, and Two Oysters on a Pewter Plate, All Resting on a Draped Table, 90, *90*
Still Life with Rummer (cat. 15), 88, *89*, *90* (detail), 90–91
Clare of Assisi, Saint, 368, 371
Clarisse, Lodovicus, 350–51
Clarisse, Rogier, 350–51
Clarke, Simon H., 114
Claudius, 307
Cleve, Joos van, 336
Portrait of an Old Man, 336, 338, *338*
Cleyburgh, Haesje Jacobsdr. van, 314
Clodion, 16
Clusius, Carolus (Charles de l'Écluse), 50, 132
Cochin, Noël-Robert, II, *Antiochus and Stratonice* (engraving after Paolo Veronese), 432, *432*
Cock, Hieronymus, 170
Codde, Pieter, 228, 230–31, 278, 280
Portrait of Hendrick Meurs (engraving by Paulus Pontius after Codde), 228, *230*, 230–31
Portrait of Judith Kotermans (engraving by Paulus Pontius after Codde), 228, 230, *230*
Coecke van Aelst, Pieter, 449
Comes, Natale, 167
Concini, Concino, 374
Coninxloo, Gillis van, 406
Cook Collection, 13
Coornhert, Dirck Volkertsz., 94, 167, 168, 170, 172
Boaz and Ruth (engraving and etching after Maarten van Heemskerck), 170, *172*, 172–73
Council of Trent, 453
Council of Troubles, 168
Couwenhoven, Jacob Allertsz. van, 313

Couwenhoven, Jacob Jacobsz. van, 16, 313–14
Cranach, Lucas, I, 101
Adam (cat. 17), 15, 98, *99*, *101* (detail), 101–4
Adam (Dresden), 101
Adam (Florence), 101
Adam (Vienna), 102
Eve (cat. 18), 15, 98, *99*, 101–4, *105* (detail)
Eve (Dresden), 101
Eve (Florence), 101
Eve (Vienna), 102
Nymph of the Spring, 304
Portrait of a Woman, 100
Portrait of Johannes Feige, 100
Craven, Earl of, 220
Critz, John de, I, 106
Portrait of a Woman (possibly by de Critz) (cat. 19), 106, *107*, 108–9
Croos, Anthonie van der, *Views of The Hague, with Twenty Scenes in the Neighborhood*, 150
Cuyp, Aelbert, 112
Boats at a Pier on a River, 112, *112*
Evening in the Meadows (cat. 20), 32, 110, *111*, 112–14, *115* (detail)
Herdsmen and Their Cattle at a Bridge, 112
View of Dordrecht, 112
Cuyp, Jacob Gerritsz., 250
Allegory of Frederik Hendrik as David, 343

Daret, P., 129
David, Gerard
Christ Carrying the Cross, with the Crucifixion, from *Lamentation* Triptych, 23
The Coronation of the Virgin, Maria in Sole (cat. 21), 16, 116, *117*, 118–20, *121* (detail)
David, Jessica, 106
Davis, John Scarlett, *The Interior of the British Institution Gallery*, *113*, 114
De Lairesse, Gerard. *See* Lairesse, Gerard de
Descalzas Reales, 371
Descamps, Jean Baptiste, 363
De Twee Klimmende Leeuwen (The Two Climbing Lions) brewery, 313, 314
Dictys, *Diary of the Trojan War*, 192
DiFuria, Arthur J., 173
Dominican order, 118
Dou, Gerrit, 125, 268, 270
Portrait of a Gentleman with a Walking Stick, 124–25, *124*
Portrait of a Woman (cat. 22), 15, 122, *123*, 124–25, 230, 252
The Young Mother, 122, *124*
A Young Woman at Her Toilet, 270, *271*
Douglas, Robert Langton, 106, 108
Duck, Jacob, *Woman Playing a Theorbo*, 270
Ducos, Blaise, 383
Dudok van Heel, S. A. C., 314
Dughet, Gaspard, 200
Dujardin, Karel, 128–29
The Denial of Peter (cat. 23), 126, *127*, 128–30, *131* (detail)
Dürer, Albrecht, 101, 260, 304, 338
Adam, 101–2, *102*
Adam and Eve, 101, *102*
Christ Crowned with Thorns, *452*, 453
Eve, 101–2, *102*
Dutch East India Company, 183, 292–93
Dutch Reformed Church, 72, 122
Dutch Republic, 41, 132, 211, 240, 285, 413. *See also* Netherlands
Dutuit, Eugène, 329
Duveen Brothers, 16, 422
Dyck, Anthony van, 210, 234, 236, 251, 323, 342, 363, 365, 377–78, 412, 450, 460
Portrait of Isabella Clara Eugenia as a Poor Clare, *371*, 372, 377
An Unknown Genoese Noblewoman (formerly *Marchesa Lomellini Durazzo*), 14–15, *16*

East India Company, 232. *See also* Dutch East India Company
Eastlake, Charles Lock, 67–69
Edward VI, King of England, 329
Egmont, Justus van, 383
Eighty Years' War (1568–1648), 38, 183, 284, 409
Ekkart, Rudi, 293
Elisabeth of France, Queen of Spain, 380
Elizabeth, Princess (of England, exiled queen of Bohemia), 41
Elizabeth I, Queen of England, 108
Elizabeth Stuart, Queen of Bohemia, 276
Engebrechtsz., Cornelis, 141–42
Christ Taking Leave of His Mother, 141, 142
Esther before Ahasuerus, *141*, 142
Lamentation with Donors and Saints, 142
Naamen Bathing in the Jordan, from the *Triptych with the Healing of Naamen*, *141*, 142
Triptych with the Crucifixion of Christ, *140*, 141, 142
The Triumph of Mordecai, 142
Engebrechtsz. (?), Cornelis, Workshop of
The Adoration of the Magi (cat. 25), 138, *138* (closed triptych), *139* (open triptych), *140* (infrared photographs), 140–43
The Adoration of the Magi (Chicago), 141
England, wars and politics of, 41, 216
Erasmus, Desiderius, 167
Ertz, Klaus, 84, 86, 220, 222
Evelyn, John, 197
Eyck, Jan van, 234
Christ as Salvator Mundi (early 17th-century copy after), 264–65, *265*
Holy Face, 264–65

Fabri de Pieresc, Nicolas-Claude, 382
Fabritius, Carel, 320
Falda, Giovanni Battista, *Piazza di Santa Maria in Trastevere ampliata di N.S. Papa Alessandro VII*, *334*
Ferdinand, Holy Roman Emperor, 380
Ferdinand II, King of Aragon, 119
Fernando II de' Medici, Grand Duke of Tuscany, 460
Field, William, 363
Filedt Kok, Jan Piet, 142
Filipczak, Zirka, 90
Fine Arts Museums of San Francisco, 15
Fischel, Oskar, 443
Flémalle, Master of. *See* Master of Flémalle
Fletcher, John, 196
Flinck, Govaert, 322–23
Foister, Susan, 197
Follower of Willem van de Velde II, *Vessels Offshore in a Calm* (cat. 94), 464, *465*, 466–67
Followers of Jan van Kessel I
Still Life with Fruit (cat. 44), 222, *223*
Still Life with Fruit and a Bird (cat. 43), 218, *219*, 220–22
Still Life with Fruit and Vase of Flowers (cat. 42), 218, *219*, 220–22
Foscari, Federico, 69
Foscari, Francesco (1373–1457), 69–70
Foscari, Francesco (1704–1790), 69
Franciscan order, 67, 70, 118, 351, 368
Francis Xavier, Saint, 362, 364–65
Frederick, King of Bohemia, 276
Frederick I, Elector of Brandenburg, 378
Fredericksen, Burton, 44
Frederick the Wise, Elector of Saxony, 102
Frederick William I, King of Prussia, 378
Frederik Hendrik, Prince of Orange, 40, 41, 276, 285, 314, 329, 449
Freedberg, David, 348, 350, 351
Frick, Henry Clay, 16
Friedländer, Max, 141, 206, 260, 336, 422
Fröschel, Daniel, *Macaw*, from *Bestiarium*, 408, *408*
Fyt, Jan (Johannes), 144
Still Life with a Red Curtain (cat. 26), 144, *145*, 146, *147* (detail)

Galle, Philips, 170
Geelvinck, Eva, 251
Geelvinck, Jan Cornelisz., 251
Geeraerts, Marcus, II, 106
Gelder, J. G. van, 278, 444
Gemmingen, Johann Konrad von, 50, 135
Gent, Judith van, 314
George I, King of England, 216
George II, King of England, 216
Gerson, Horst, 235, 329
J. Paul Getty Museum, Los Angeles, 15, 16
Gevartius (Jan Gaspar Gevaerts), 370
Gheyn, Jacob de, II
A Pike Bearer, 38, 40, *40*
Wapenhandelinghe, 38, 40
Gibson, Walter, 142
Giorgio, Francesco di, 16
Giorgione, 16, 32
Sleeping Venus, 306
Giulio Romano, 173, 306
David Slaying Goliath, Loggia of David, *342*, 343
Goes, Hugo van der, *Deipara Virgo Foretold by the Prophets and the Sibyls*, 118
Goltzius, Hendrick, 94, 95
Mars and Venus, 94, *94*
Gossaert, Jan, 321
Goyen, Jan van, 132, 148, 150, 398, 400
Ferry with Three Cattle and Six Passengers, 150
River Landscape with a Village Church (cat. 27), 90, 148, *149*, 150–51, 386
Sandy Road with a Farmhouse, 398, *400*
Village Behind Trees by the Water, Ferry with People, 150, *150*

Graeff, Cornelis de, 251
Graeff family, 251
Greville, George, 15, 363
Gro[o]tewal, Marretje Cornelisdr. van, 312–13
Groot, Catharina de, 32
Gudlaugsson, Sturla, 443
Guercino, 16, 460
Guicciardi, Diego, 67, 69–70
Guicciardi, Paolo, 67
Guicciardi family, 16, 68
Guicciardini, Lodovico, 78, 81, 413

Haarlem, Cornelis Cornelisz. van, 94–95
Mars and Venus (cat. 16), 15, 92, *93*, 94–97
Haarlem Classicists, 128
Habsburg dynasty, 167, 370–72
The Hague, 41
Hals, Dirck, 152, 154–55, 278, 280
Elegant Company Playing Music in an Interior, 152, *154*
A Fiddler (cat. 28), 152, *153*, 154–55
The Lute Player, 154
A Seated Man Playing the Violin, 152, *154*
The Soloist, 154, *154*
Woman Playing a Flute, 154, *154*
Hals, Frans, 152, 156, 468
De Heer Bodolphe, 158
Officers and Subalterns of the St. George Civic Guard, 158, *158* (detail)
Portrait of a Young Man, formerly called *Jan van de Cappelle* (cat. 29), 14, 156, *157*, 158–59
Vincent Laurensz. van der Vinne, 158, *158*
Willem van Heythuysen, 278
Hamann, Richard, 75
Hand, John, 196
Hanneman, Adriaen, *Portrait of Prince William III*, 293
Harrison, Jefferson C., 166
Heda, Pieter Claesz., 88
Heem, Jan Davidsz. de, 91, 162
Memento Mori, 162
Still Life with Crucifix and Skull, 162
Vase of Flowers (cat. 30), 160, *161*, 162–63
Vase with Flowers (The Hague), 162, *162*
Vivat Oraenge, 162
Heemskerck, Maarten van, 164, 166–68, 170, 172–73
Allegory of Nature (cat. 31), 15, 164, *164* (detail), *165*, *166* (details), 166–69, *167* (detail)
Boaz, His Kinsman, and the Elders at the Gate (cat. 32), 15, 170, *171*, 172–73
Boaz and Ruth (engraving and etching by Dirck Volkertsz. Coornhert after Van Heemskerck), 170, *172*, 172–73
Held, Julius, 336, 338, 350, 356
Helst, Bartholomeus van der, 314
Hemessen, Jan Sanders van, 338
Henderiks, Valentine, 63
Henrietta Maria, Queen of England, 376–78
Henry IV, King of France, 374, 376
Henry VIII, King of England, 194
Heppner, Albert, 443
Heusch, Willem de, 36
Heyden, Jan van der, 168, 174, 176
Corner of a Library, 180, *182*, 182–83
Dam Square in Amsterdam, 176
Dam Square in Amsterdam against City Hall and Nieuwe Kerk, 176, *177*
The Herengracht, Amsterdam, from the Leliegracht, 177, 251
Library Interior with Still Life (cat. 34), 14, 180, *181*, 182–84, *185* (detail)
Room Corner with Rarities, 180, *182*, 182–83
Townscape with Gothic Church (cat. 33), 174, *175*, *176* (detail), 176–78, *179* (detail)
Hieronymites, 62, 63
Hobbema, Meindert, 388
Village Street under Trees, 388, *388*
Hoet, Gerard, I, 188–90
The Finding of Moses, 188, *188*
Mercury and Herse, formerly known as *Festival in Honor of Mercury* (cat. 35), 186, *187*, 188–89
Paris Presenting Helen at the Court of Priam, formerly known as *Achilles Taking Brisais Back to Her Parents* (cat. 36), 190, *191*, 192–93
Pyrrhus Snatching Astyanax from the Arms of His Mother, *192*, 193
Hofstede de Groot, Cornelis, 235
Hogenberg, Franz. *See* Braun, Georg
Holbein, Hans, II, 196–97, 329, 336
Portrait of Edward VI as a Child, 329, *329*, 330
Portrait of Sir Bryan Tuke (attributed), 196, *196*
Sir Bryan Tuke, 196, *196*, 197
Holbein, Hans, II (after), *Sir Bryan Tuke* (cat. 37), 194, *195*, 196–98, *199* (detail)
Holland. *See* Netherlands
Hollar, Wenceslaus, 329, 330
Holsteyn, Pieter, II, 135
Homer
Iliad, 192, 356
Odyssey, 92, 186, 192
Honthorst, Gerrit van, 128, 444, 452–53
The Denial of Saint Peter, 128, *128*
The Mocking of Christ, *452*, 452–53
Musical Group, 444
Hortus Eystettensis, 50, 135
Hottle, Andrew, 351
Houbraken, Arnold, 176, 285, 330
Houckgeest, Gerard, 176
House of Orange, 38, 162
Hulsdonck, Jacob van, 218, 222, 418
Hulst, R.-A. D', 342
hunting, 146, 167, 216, 329, 356–57
Huygens, Constantijn, 231, 234
Hofwijk, 302
Huysmans, Cornelis, 200, 202
Forest Edge with Lumberjacks, 200, *202*
Huysmans, Jan Baptist, 200
A Wooded Italianate Landscape (cat. 38), 200, *201*, 202, *203* (detail)
Hymans, Henri, 348
Hypnerotomachia Poliphili, 304, *306*

Ignatius of Loyola, Saint, 362, 364–65
imitatio Christi, 22
Isaacsz., Isaac, 343
Isabella, Queen of Castile, 119
Isabella Clara Eugenia, Archduchess (earlier, Infanta of Spain and Portugal), 95, 368, 370, 376–77, 382–83
Isenbrant, Adriaen, 206
Young Man with a Rosary (cat. 39), 204, *205*, *206* (detail), 206–7

Jacobite uprising (1745–46), 216
Jacobus de Voragine, *The Golden Legend*, 140
Jacot, Balthasar, 250
Jaffé, Michael, 336, 338
James I, King of England, 108, 276
James II, King of England, 216
Janssen, Paul Huys, 40
Jerome, Saint, 60, 62
Jesuits, 362–65
Jordaens, Jacob, 208, 210–11
Mercury and Argus (cat. 40) (with Jan Wildens), 16, 208, *209*, 210–12, *213* (detail)
Mercury and Argus (Lyon), 211, *211*
Mercury and Battus, 210–11, *211*
Study of Five Cattle, 210, *210*
Jouderville, Isaac de, 235, 236
Bust of a Young Man, 235
Juana, Infanta, 371–72
Judson, Richard, 44
Juncker, Justus, 214
Interior with a Man Seated before a Table Smoking a Pipe, 214
Sportsmen in a Tavern (cat. 41) (attributed), 214, *215*, 216, *217* (detail)

Kahr, Madlyn, 271
Kalf, Willem, 91
Karlsruhe Passion, Master of the. *See* Master of the Karlsruhe Passion
Keijser, Dorothea Adriaensdr., 314
Kessel, Ferdinand van, 220
Allegory of Europe, 220
Kessel, Jan van, I, 220, 222. *See also* Followers of Jan van Kessel I
The Four Continents: Europe, 220, *220*
Reconstruction of the Craven Panels' Arrangement with Paintings Attributed to Jan van Kessel I, 220, *220*
Kessel, Jan van, II, 220, 222
Keyser, Hendrik de, 224, 250
Keyser, Thomas de, 125, 224, 226, 228, 231, 250, 278
Dirck van Wissel and His Son Jacob (cat. 45), 224, *225*, 226–27
Portrait of a Gentleman and His Son, 226–27, *226*
Portrait of a Man (cat. 46) (or painted by a follower), 228, *229*, 230–31
Portrait of a Woman (cat. 47) (or painted by a follower), 228, *229*, 230–31
Kierincx, Alexander, 282
Kirschenbaum, Baruch, 426, 443–44
Kneller, Godfrey, 216
Knoedler and Co., 14
König-Nordhoff, Ursula, 364
Koslow, Susan, 413
Kotermans, Judith, 230
Krelage, Ernst Heinrich, 135

Kren, Thomas, 332, 334
Kretschmar, F. G. L. O., 226
Kunstkammern. See cabinets of curiosities

Laer, Pieter van, 32
Lairesse, Gerard de, 36, 183, 190
Grondlegginge der Teekenkonst (Principles of Drawing), 397
Het Groot Schilderboek (The Great Painting Book), 190, 192, 202, 394, 396
The Landing of Helen Led by Paris at the Palace of Priam, In Troy, 190, 192–93, *192*
Mercury and Herse, *186*, 188
Lampsonius, Dominicus, *Pictorum aliquot celebrium Germaniae inferioris effigies*, 321
landscape painting, 32, 36, 148, 200, 202, 386, 392, 398, 400
Lasius, Angelika, 78
Leeuw, Willem van der, *Portrait of an Unknown Young Man with Beret*, 234, *234*, 235, 236
Lefèvre, Raoul, *Recueil des histories de Troie*, 193
Lely, Peter, 323
Lentulus, Publius, and the Lentulus Letter, 264
Leopold Wilhelm, Archduke, 357, 372, 377, 382, 383
Lesueur, J. B., 322
Leveck, Jacobus, *Portrait of a Woman, probably Hendrickje Stoeffels* (formerly attributed to Rembrandt), 14, *15*
Lievens, Jan, 235–36, 238
Bust of an Old Woman (Rembrandt's Mother?), 235
Fantastic Landscape, 240, *240*
Head of a Young Man with a Cap, 235–36, *236*, 238
Landscape with a Church, 240
A Man Fishing in a River, 240, *240*
Old Man, 235, *236*
Panoramic Landscape (cat. 49), 15, 238, *239*, 240–41
Portrait of Constantijn Huygens, 235
Prince Charles Louis of the Palatinate with His Tutor Wolrad von Plessen in Historical Dress, 235, 236, 238
Young Man with Red Beret (cat. 48) (attributed), 16, 232, *233*, 234–37
Linard, Jacques, 456
Lindsay, Patrick, 13
notes by, *13*
Lipsius, Justus, 167
Lisle, Robert Sidney, Lord (later 4th Earl of Leicester), 197
Lockey, Rowland (possibly; after British School), *Lady Arabella Stuart, Later Duchess of Somerset (1575–1615), aged 13 1/2*, 108, *108*
Loose, E. de, *The Scholar* (engraving after Nicolaes Maes), 182, *183*
Los Angeles County Museum of Art (LACMA), 15
Louis XIII, French, copy possibly after Frans Pourbus II, 376, *377*
Louis XIII, King of France, 374, 376–77, 380, 382
Louis XIV, King of France, 382
Lowenthal, Anne, 94, 95
Luca d'Olanda, 67
Luther, Martin, 102
Lutma, Johannes, 272
Luynes, Charles d'Albert, Duke of, 376
Lyversberg, Jakob Johann Nepomuk, and the Lyversberg collection, 258, 260

Maes, Nicolaes, 44, 242, 244, 250–52
Abraham Dismissing Hagar and Ishmael, 44
Admiral Jacob Binkes, *250*, 251
Dordrecht Family in an Interior (cat. 50), 242, *243*, 244–46, *247* (detail)
Ingena Rotterdam (died 1704), Betrothed of Admiral Jacob Binkes, *250*, 251
The Lacemaker, 44, 244
Portrait of Agatha Bicker (cat. 52), 248, *249*, 250–53
Portrait of Dirck Fredericksz. Alewijn (cat. 51), 248, *249*, 250–53
The Scholar (lithograph by E. de Loose after Maes), 182, *183*
Mander, Karel van, 32, 95, 112, 141, 170, 211, 312, 444, 448
Mansi, Giovanni Battista, 260
Mansi Magdalen, Master of the. *See* Master of the Mansi Magdalen
Mantegna, Andrea
Agony in the Garden, 69
The Resurrection, 69
San Zeno Altarpiece, 69
Mantua, Vincent Gonzaga, Duke of, 343
Manuel II, King of Portugal, 266
Manuth, Volker, 329
Margaret of Austria, 380
Margaret of Parma, 168
Marie de' Medici, Queen of France, 374, 376–77, 380, 382–83
Marlborough, Duke of, 378
Marrel, Jacob, 135
Mary Stuart, Queen of England, 252, 329
Massys, Jan, 256, 260
Susanna and the Elders (Brussels), 254, 256, *256*
Susanna and the Elders (cat. 53), 254, *255*, 256–57
Susanna and the Elders (private collection), 254, *256*
Master of Alkmaar, 23–24
The Arrest of Christ, *23*, 24
Christ before Pilate, 23
Christ Carrying the Cross (cat. 2), 20, *21*, 22–25
The Flagellation of Christ (cat. 1), 20, *21*, 22–25
The High Priest Refusing Joachim's Sacrifice, 23
The Meeting of Joachim and Anna under the Golden Gate, 23
Pilate Washing His Hands, 23, 24
The Resurrection of Christ, 23, 24
St. Adrian, 23
St. Antony Abbot, 23
Triptych with Adoration of the Magi, 23
Visiting the Sick, from *The Seven Works of Mercy*, *22*, 23
Master of Flémalle, *Christ and the Virgin*, 264
Master of the Karlsruhe Passion, 422
Master of the Mansi Magdalen, 260–61
Heads of Two Old Bearded Men, *260*, 261
The Lamentation (cat. 54), 258, *259*, 260–61
Mary Magdalene, 260, *260*
Virgin and Child, 260, *260*
Matham, Jacob, 95
Mars and Venus, 95, *95*
Maurits, Prince of Orange and Nassau, 38, 40, 285, 313
Maximilian II, Emperor, 370
Mazarin, Cardinal, 382
McNamee, Maurice, 66–67
Meckenem, Israhel van, II, 24
Meij, A. W. F. M., 348–49
Meijer, D. C., Jr., 250
Meijer, Fred, 51, 162
Meleager Sarcophagus (Roman), 356
Mellon, Paul, 214
Melzi, Vittorio, 67
Memling, Hans, 266
Christ as the Man of Sorrows, 265
Christ Blessing, 14, 262, 265
Christ Giving His Blessing (cat. 55), 14, 262, *263*, 264–66, *267* (detail)
Christ with the Musical Angels, 264
Diptych of Maarten van Nieuwenhove, 204, *204*
Portrait of a Man, 262
The Virgin in Prayer, 265
Mennonites, 312–13
Mensaert, Guillaume Pierre, 363
Metsu, Gabriel, 268, 270–71
A Musical Party, 268, *270*
Woman at Her Toilette (cat. 56), 15, 268, *269*, 270–73
Metsys, Quentin, 256, 260–61
Metzger, Cathy, 69, 266
Meurs, Hendrick, 230–31
Michelangelo, 173
Michiel, J. F. M., 413
Miegroet, Hans van, 118–19
Miel, Jan, 332
Mierevelt, Michiel Jansz. van, *Amalia, Countess von Solms*, 276
Mieris, Frans van, I, 270, 437
Mitjens, Daniël, I, 274
Elizabeth, Queen of Bohemia (1596–1662), 274, *276*
Portrait of a Young Noblewoman (cat. 57) (in the style of), 16, 274, *275*, *276* (detail), 276–77
Molanus, Johannes, 350
Molenaer, Jan Miense, 154–55, 278
Allegory of Fidelity, 280
Allegory of Vanity, 270, *271*
The Departure of the Prodigal Son, 280
Landscape with a Cottage, 398
A Painter in His Workshop, 90, 280, *280*, *280* (infrared photograph)
Portrait of a Gentleman (cat. 58) (attributed), 278, *279*, 280–81
Self-Portrait with Skull, *280*, 281
The Wedding Portrait of Willem van Loon and Margaretha Bas, 278, 280
Molijn, Pieter de, 148, 398, 400
Three Peasants and a Woman, 400, *400*
Molinet, R. P. Claude du, 183

Mols, François, 363
Moltke, Joachim Wolfgang von, 75
Monkey (unknown artist), from *Bestiarium*, 408, *408*
Montfaucon, Bernard de, *Fountain Nymph*, 304, *306*
moralizing in painting. See also *vanitas* theme
peasant behavior, 302
religiosity, 72
sexuality, 44, 94
thought and behavior, 166, 409, 433, 436, 437
women's behavior, 256, 307, 368, 427, 433, 434, 437
More, Thomas, 196
Moreelse, Paulus, 95, 250
Morland, George, *Sportsman's Hall* (mezzotint by William Ward after), 214, 216, *216*
Muchnic, Suzanne, 13
Müller, Christian Benjamin, 343
Muller, Jeffrey, 338
Multscher, Hans, *Christ Carrying the Cross*, 422, *422*
Münster, Sebastian, 336, 338
Musscher, Michiel van, *Rachel Ruysch* (with Rachel Ruysch), 396, *396*
Mytton, Elizabeth, 323

Naiad-Venus Observed by Satyrs, from *Hypnerotomachia Poliphili*, 304, *306*
Nanteuil, Robert, *Portrait de Madame de Sévigné*, *251*, 252
National Gallery, London, 16
National Gallery of Art, Washington, DC, 14, 15
Neer, Aert van der, 282, 284–86
Soldiers and Villagers Leaving a Burning Village (cat. 59), 282, *283*, 284–85
Winter Scene with Figures Playing Kolf (cat. 60), 286, *287*, 288–89
neo-Stoicism, 302
Nerot, Mary, 350–51
Netherlands
cattle raising and dairy production in, 112–13
drinking and smoking in, 298, 436–37
fruits and vegetables in, 413
landscape painting in, 36
literary genres in, 32
religion in, 285
tulip industry in, 132
wars and politics of, 38, 41, 95, 167–68, 211, 251, 284, 370–71, 404, 409
Niarchos, Stavros, 14
Nicolson, Benedict, 453
Nieuwe Kerk, Amsterdam, 176–77, *177*
Nieuwstraten, J., 432
Nitze-Ertz, Christa, 220, 222
Noordt, Jan van, *A Boy with a Hawk and Leash*, 329, 330, *330*
Noordt, Johannes van, *The Toilette of Esther*, 271, *272*
Norton Simon Museum, Pasadena, 15, *16*, 17

Ochtervelt, Jacob, 293
Family Portrait (cat. 61), 290, *291*, 292–94, *295* (detail)
Family Portrait (Hartford, Connecticut), 293
Portrait of a Family, 290, *292*
Tric-trac Players, 290
Oldenbourg, Rudolf, 231
Oosten de Jonge, Gerrit van, 251
Ophem, Jacques van, 413
Orlers, Jan Jansz., 81
Osnabrugge, Marije, 453
Ostade, Adriaen van, 296, 298, 302
Carousing Peasants (cat. 62), 296, *297*, 298–99
Drinking Figures and Crying Children, 298, *298*
Men and Women in a Barn Interior, *296*, 298
Peasants Playing Cards, 298
Ostade, Isack van, 296, 302, 404
Peasants Outside a Farmhouse Butchering a Pig (cat. 63), 300, *300* (detail), *301*, *302* (detail), 302–3
Rural Scenery in front of a Farm House, 302, *302*
Ovid, *Metamorphoses*, 92, 94, 186, 188, 208, 211, 356

Paffenrode, Jacob van, 285
Panneels, Willem, 343
Passe, Crispijn van de, I, 54
Paul, Saint, 126, 128, 140
Paul III, Pope, 362
Paul V, Pope, 364
Peace of Münster (1648), 211
Peace of Utrecht (1713), 216
Pelham, Catherine, 414
Pelham, Henry, 414
Pelham, Lucy, 414
Pelham-Clinton, Henry Fiennes, 414
Pelham-Holles, Thomas, 414
Pencz, Georg, 306–7
Sleeping Female Nude, Vanitas (cat. 64), 304, *305*, 306–8, *309* (detail)
Perino del Vaga, *David Slaying Goliath* (with Raphael), 343
Personification of Pudicitia (Modesty, Demureness), Roman copy of Hellenistic original, 348, *349*, 350
perspective
aerial, 422
linear, 28, 176, 220, 231, 256, 334, 394, 446, 448–49
Pesser, Dammas Jansz., 313–14
Pesser, Dirck Jansz., 313–14
Pesser, Marritge Jansdr., 313–14
Peter, Saint, 140
Philip II, King of Spain, 370
Philip III, King of Spain, 380
Philip IV, King of Spain, 338, 370, 380, 382
Plantijn, Christoffel, 170
Pliny, 50
Pontius, Paulus
Portrait of Hendrick Meurs (engraving after Pieter Codde), 228, 230–31, *230*
Portrait of Isabella Clara Eugenia, Infanta of Spain (engraving after Rubens), 370, *370*
Portrait of Judith Kotermans (engraving after Pieter Codde), 228, 230, *230*
Poor Clares, 368
Post, Pieter, 323
Potter, Paulus, 202
Peasant on the Dung Heap, 303
Pourbus, Frans, II, 377, 460
Louis XIII (copy possibly after), 376, *377*
Marie de' Medici, Queen of France, 377, 382–83, *383*
Pre-Rembrandtists, 188
Primaticcio, 256
Protestantism, 72, 81, 284, 344, 446. *See also* Calvinism; Dutch Reformed Church; Mennonites; Reformed Calvinist Church
Puyvelde, Leo van, 363

Quast, Pieter Jansz., 278
Queen Anne's War (1702–13), 216
Quinault, Philippe, *Stratonice, tragi-comédie*, 432

Rademaker, Abraham, *Kabinet van nederlandsche outheden en gezichten*, 150
Raimondi, Marcantonio, 260, 306
Raphael, 173, 234
David Slaying Goliath (with Perino del Vaga), 343
School of Athens, 443
Reformed Calvinist Church, 284
Rembrandt and His Pupils (exhibition), 44
Rembrandt Harmensz. van Rijn, 14, 74, 158, 232, 234–36, 238, 240, 242, 298, 312–14, 322–23, 363, 424
Bathsheba Reading King David's Letter, 427
Christ at Emmaus, 298
An Elderly Man as Saint Paul, 328
Esther Preparing to Intercede with Ahasuerus, 270–71
Moses Breaking the Tables of the Law, 330
The Philosopher (formerly attributed to Rembrandt), 14, *15*
The Polish Rider, 330
Portrait of a Bearded Man in a Wide-Brimmed Hat, Probably Jacob Jacobsz. van Couwenhoven (ca. 1594–1661), Heer van de Oude en Nieuwe Sruyten (cat. 65), 16, 310, *311*, 312–16, *317* (detail)
Portrait of a Boy in Fancy Costume (cat. 67), *12* (detail), 13–14, *14*, 16, 326, *327*, *328* (X-radiograph), 328–31
Portrait of a Forty-Year-Old Woman, Possibly Marretje Cornelisdr. van Grotewel, 312, *312*
Portrait of Amalia von Solms, 234
Portrait of Dirck Jansz. Pesser, 313, 314, *314*
Portrait of Jacob Trip, 328
sales of works by, 13
Self-Portrait (cat. 66), 15, 318, *319*, 320–25, *320* (infrared photograph)
Self-Portrait in a Soft Hat and Embroidered Cloak, 321
Self-Portrait in Velvet Cap and Plume, 321, *321*
Stormy Landscape, 240
Titus at His Desk, 329, *330*
Young Girl Leaning on a Window-sill, 330
Young Man in a Beret, 329
Rembrandt Research Project, 235, 320
Rembrandt School, copy of *Self-Portrait*, 322, *322*

Remonstrant Brotherhood, 313–14
Reuter, Willem
Festival in the Piazza di Spagna, Rome, 332, *332*, 334
Market Scene, 332, 334
A Roman Market (cat. 68), 16, 332, *333*, 334–35
Ribera, Luini, 16
Rijckere, Bernaert de, 338
Rijn, Titus van, 329–30
Roethlisberger, Marcel, 365
Rombouts, Catharina, 226–27
Rombouts, Jacob, 226
Rooses, Max, 211, 362
Rosa, Salvator, 200
Rovere, Vittoria della, 460
Royal Academy of Arts, London, 36
Rubens, Peter Paul, 210–11, 234, 238, 338, 350–51, 354, 356, 362–65, 370, 376–77, 380, 382–83, 412–13, 450, 460, 462. *See also* Rubens, Peter Paul, Workshop of
Anne of Austria, Queen of France, 382, *382*
Autograph Letter (Written in Secretary's Hand in Dutch, Signed by Rubens on Verso), 16, *17*
Bathsheba at the Fountain, *426*, 427
David and Goliath (drawing), *342*, 342–43
David and Goliath (painting), 343, *343*
David Slaying Goliath (cat. 70), 15, 340, *341*, 342–44, *345* (detail)
The Holy Women at the Sepulchre (cat. 71) (and workshop), 15, 346, *347*, 348–52, *353* (detail)
The Hunt of the Calydonian Boar (cat. 72), 14–15, 354, *355*, 356–58, *359* (detail)
The Hunt of the Calydonian Boar (painting), 354, *356*, 356–57
Louis XIII of France, 376, *376*
Marie de' Medici, Queen of France, 382, *382*
Michiel Ophovius, 364
The Miracles of St. Ignatius of Loyola, 362, *363*, 365
Portrait of an Elderly Man, formerly known as *Sebastian Münster*; copy after a 16th-century Flemish portrait attributed to Joos van Cleve (cat. 69), 15, 336, *337*, 338–39
Portrait of Isabella Clara Eugenia, Governor of the Spanish Netherlands, as a Poor Clare (cat. 74) (and workshop), 15, 368, *369*, 370–73
Saint Ignatius of Loyola (cat. 73), 15, 360, *361*, 362–67
Stigmatization of Saint Francis of Assisi, 351
Supper at Emmaus, 351
Rubens, Peter Paul, Workshop of
The Holy Women at the Sepulchre (cat. 71) (Rubens and), 15, 346, *347*, 348–52, *353* (detail)
Portrait of Anne of Austria, Queen of France (cat. 76), 15, 377, 380, *381*, 382–84, *385* (detail)
Portrait of Isabella Clara Eugenia, Governor of the Spanish Netherlands, as a Poor Clare (cat. 74) (Rubens and), 15, 368, *369*, 370–73
Portrait of Louis XIII, King of France (cat. 75), 15, 374, *375*, 376–79, 382, 383
Saint Francis Xavier, *362*, 362–65
Ruckers, Hans, I, *Double Virginal*, 168, *168*
Rudolf II, Holy Roman Emperor, 406, 408
Ruisdael, Jacob van, 200, 386, 388, 392
Bleaching Fields Outside Haarlem, 388
Dune Landscape, 386
The Giant Beech; Two Peasants and Their Dog, 390, *392*
The Great Oak, 386, 388, *388*
Mill at Wyck, near Duurstede, 388
Three Great Trees in a Mountainous Landscape with a River (cat. 78), 15, 390, *391*, 392–93
Wooded Landscape with a Pool and Figures (cat. 77) (with Nicolaes Berchem), 386, *387*, 388–89
Russell, Margaretta, 158
Ruysch, Frederik, 396
Ruysch, Rachel, 394, 396–97
Nosegay on a Marble Plinth (cat. 79), 394, *395*, 396–97
Rachel Ruysch (with Michiel van Musscher), 396, *396*
A Still Life with a Spray of Flowers, 394, *396*
Ruysdael, Salomon van, 148, 398, 400, 402, 404
Halt in Front of an Inn (cat. 81), 90, 298, 386, 402, *403*, 404–5
Landscape with Sandy Road (cat. 80), 90, 386, 398, *399*, 400–401
Landscape with Travelers before an Inn, 404, *404*
River Landscape with Figures and a View of the Roof of a House, 400, *400*

Sachs, Hans, 80
Sadeler, Aegidius, *Proclamation to the Shepherds* (engraving after Jacopo Bassano), 30, *32*
Saftleven, Herman, 303
Santvoort, Dirck, 250
Savery, Roelandt, 406, 408–9
Cattle and Deer near Ruins, 406
Landscape and Animals, 408, *408*
Landscape with Cattle near Ruins, 406
Landscape with Ruins and Animals (cat. 82), 406, *407*, 408–9
Saint Elijah Being Fed by the Ravens, 408
The Stag among the Oxen, 409
Still Life, 408
Savery, Salomon, 278
Portrait of a Young Man with a Beret with a Feather on His Head after *Young Man with Red Beret*, 234, *234*, 236
Stage of the Amsterdam Schouwburg, 443, *443*
Scannelli, Francesco, 363, 365
Sceperus, Jacobus, *Bacchus, Den ouden en huyden-daegschen Dronckeman* (Bacchus, the Drunkard of Past and Present Times), 436
Schaar, Eckard, 34
Schabaelje, Jan Philipsz., 236
Schaffers-Bodenhausen, Karen, 226
Schatborn, Peter, 152
Scheelen, Walter, 364–65
Schmidt-Degener, F. 329
Schnackenburg, Bernhard, 235
Schneevoogt, George Voorhelm, 135
Schneider, Cynthia, 240
Schotte, Magdalene de, 350–51
Schouten, Aeltje Gerritsdr., 313
Schrevelius, Theodor, *Harlemias*, 392
Scorel, Jan van, 173, 260
Seghers, Daniel, 220
Seghers, Gerard, *The Denial of St. Peter*, 129, *129*
Seghers, Hercules, 240
Sellar, David, 470
Serlio, Sebastiano, 176, 449
Serwouters, Johannes, 272
Seymour, William, 108
sfumato, 118, 119. *See also* chiaroscuro
Siberechts, Jan, 202
Sijen, Joris Pietersz., 313
Sijen, Pieter, 312–13
Sijen, Pieter Pietersz., 313
Simon, Jennifer Jones, 16
Simon, Lucille Ellis, 14, *14*
Simon, Norton, 13–17, 331
notes on bidding strategy of, *13*
photograph of, *14*
Simons, Menno, 42, 44. *See also* Mennonites
Sixtus IV, Pope, 118
Slatkes, Leonard, 321
Slive, Seymour, 156, 158, 278, 386, 390
Smids, Ludolf, *Polyxena*, 183
Snyders, Frans, 144, 218, 222, 412–14
Fruit and Vegetable Market, 412
A Game Stall, 412, *413*
Small Game and a Cat, 144, 146, *146*
Still Life with Fruit and Vegetables (cat. 83) (with Cornelis de Vos), 410, *411*, 412–15
Society of Jesus. *See* Jesuits
Solms, Amalia von, 449
Soreau, Daniel, 456
Soreau, Isaak, 416, 418
Fruits and Flowers, 416, *418*
Still Life with Fruit and Flowers (cat. 84), 416, *417*, 418–19
Soreau, Jan, 418
Sotheby's, 16
South German Master, *Christ Bearing the Cross* (cat. 85), 420, *421*, 422, *423* (detail)
Spain, wars and politics of, 38, 40–41, 95, 113, 167–68, 176, 211, 284, 370–71, 404
Spencer, Earl of, 13, 329
Spinola, Ambrogio, 370
Staring, W. M., 245
States General, 41, 122, 285
Stechow, Wolfgang, 150, 350, 430, 432, 443
Steen, Jan, 424, 426, 432, 434, 436–37, 442–44
Amnon and Tamar, 442
Ascanius and Lucilla, 427, *427*
Bathsheba (cat. 86), 424, *425*, 426–28, *429* (detail)
Bathsheba after the Bath, 426, *426*
The Doctor's Visit, *436*, 437
Drunken Pair, 436
The Effects of Intemperance, 437, *437*
Expulsion from the Temple, 444
Gamblers Quarreling, 434, 436, *436*

Steen, Jan *(continued)*
Jacob Confronting Laban (cat. 87), 430, *431*, 432–33, 442
Luxury Beware, 436
The Marriage at Cana, 436
Marriage at Cana (cat. 89), 15, 440, *441*, 442–45
The Marriage at Cana (Dresden), 442, *443*
The Marriage Feast at Cana, 442, *442*
A Pig Belongs in the Sty, *436*, 437
Village Wedding, 443
Wine Is a Mocker (De wijn is een Spoter) (cat. 88), 15, 434, *435*, 436–38, *439* (detail)
Steenwijck, Hendrick van, I, 448
Steenwijck, Hendrick van, II, 446, 448–49
The Crypt of a Church with Two Men Sleeping, 448, *448*
The Liberation of Saint Peter (cat. 90), 446, *447*, *448* (infrared photography), 448–49
The Liberation of St. Peter, 448, *448*
Steinberg, Leo, 350
Stighelen, Katelijne van der, 412
still lifes, 26, 28–29
Stoicism, 167, 404. *See also* neo-Stoicism
Stom, Matthias, 450, 453
The Incredulity of Thomas, 452
The Mocking of Christ (cat. 91), 450, *451*, 452–54, *455* (detail)
The Supper at Emmaus, 452, 453
Stone, Henry, 226
Storck, Abraham, 464, 466
Stoskopff, Sébastien, 456, 458
Still Life with Empty Glasses (cat. 92), 456, *457*, 458, *459* (detail)
Still Life with Glasses and Goblets, 456, *458*
Still Life with Glasses in a Basket, 456
Strong, Roy, 106, 108
Stroo, Cyriel, 68
Stuart, Arabella, 108
Sumowski, Werner, 44, 235, 238
Sustermans, Justus (also known as Giusto Sustermans), 460, 462
Anna di Cosimo II de' Medici, 462, *462*
Portrait of a Woman (cat. 93), 460, *461*, 462, *463* (detail)
Sweerts, Emanuel, 54
Sweerts, Michiel, 334

Talbot, Althea, 330
Temini, Giovanni, 444
Tempesta, Antonio, *Two Bulls Fighting*, from *Battling Animals*, 408, *408*
Temple, William, 370
Tengnagel, Jan, *Allegory of the Blossoming of the Republic of the United Netherlands during the Stadhoudership of Prince Maurits*, 113
Teniers, David, II, 368
The Archduke Leopold Wilhelm in His Picture Gallery in Brussels, *371*, 372
View of the Gallery of Archduke Leopold in Brussels (II), 372, 377, *377*, 382
Tertiaries, 368, 370
Thirty Years' War (1618–48), 344
Thomas Agnew & Sons, 23
Thyssen-Bornemisza, Baron, 16
Titian, 32, 306, 376, 412, 450, 460
Cain Slaying Abel, 343, *343*
Venus of Urbino, 306, *306*
Toonneel des Aerdrijkx, ofte Nieuw Atlas (Theatre of the World, or the New Atlas), 180
Townshend, John Robert, 197
Townshend, Robert Marsham, 197
Triest, Antoine, 413
tronies (studies of human expression or character), 234, 235, 328, 330
Tuke, Bryan, 194, 196–97
Tuke, Charles, 197
A Tulip Book (cat. 24), 14, 50, 132, *133*, *134*, 134–36, *137* (detail)
tulips, 132, 134–35
Twelve Years' Truce (1609–21), 40, 95, 113, 211, 284, 404, 409, 413

Uden, Lucas van, 208
United Provinces of the Netherlands. *See* Netherlands
Ursula, Saint, 140
Uylenburgh, Hendrick, 312–14

Vaillant, Wallerant, 250
Valentiner, Wilhelm, 158, 329, 342
Vandenven, M., 342
vanitas theme, 28–29, 81, 90, 162, 180, 183, 196, 270, 304, 307, 418, 427
Vasari, Giorgio, 170
Vecellio, Cesare, 274
Veen, Jaap van der, 312–13
Velázquez, Diego, 462
Portrait of a Little Girl, 462
Portrait of Francesco I d'Este, 462
Velde, Adriaen van de, 176
Velde, Esaias van de, 282, 284–85
A Village Looted at Night, 282, *284*
Velde, Willem van de, II, 466. *See also* Follower of Willem van de Velde II
Dutch Vessels Inshore and Men Bathing, 466, *466*
A Smalschip at Anchor with a Kaag and Other Vessels Close Inshore, 466
Veldman, Ilja, 166–67
Venne, Adriaen Pietersz. van de, *Jacob Complains to Laban that He Has Given Him Leah instead of Rachel as His Wife* (engraving by Daniël van den Bremden after), *432*, 433
Venus Urania (Roman), 349, *350*
Vermeer, Johannes, 16
Veronese, Paolo, 412
Antiochus and Stratonice (engraving by Noël-Robert Cochin II after), 432, *432*
Feast in the House of Levi, 443, *444*
Verspronck, Johannes Cornelisz., 468
Portrait of a Man, 470, *470*
Portrait of a Woman (cat. 95), 252, 468, *469*, 470–71
Villeers, Jacob de, 238
Vinne, Vincent Laurensz. van der, 158
Virgil
Aeneid, 186
Eclogues, 32
Georgics, 32, 302
Visscher, Claes Jansz., *Pleasant Places*, 404
Visscher, Johannes, *Shepherds and a Young Woman on a Donkey* (etching after Nicolaes Berchem), 34, *36*
Visscher, Nicolaes, II, 183
Visscher, Roemer, *Tis misselijck waer een geck zijn gelt aen leijt*, 28, *28*
Vita Beati P. Ignatii Loiolae, 370–71
Vitruvius, 449
Vlieghe, Hans, 363, 372
Vondel, Joost van den, 230, 409
Voorhelm, Dirck, 135
Voorhelm, Simon, 135
Vorsterman, Lucas, 350–51
The Holy Women at the Sepulchre (drawing), *348*, 349
The Holy Women at the Sepulchre (engraving after Rubens), 348, 349, *349*, 350
Stigmatization of Saint Francis of Assisi (print after Rubens), 351
Vos, Cornelis de, 412
Still Life with Fruit and Vegetables (cat. 83) (with Frans Snyders), 410, *411*, 412–15
Vredeman de Vries, Hans, 448–49
Vries, Lyckle de, 44

Waagen, Gustav, 342
Wade, George, 413, 414
Wagenaar, Jan, 177
Walker, John, *14*
Walpole, Horace, 413
Walpole, Robert, 413–14
Ward, William, *Sportsman's Hall* (mezzotint after George Morland), 214, 216, *216*
War of the Austrian Succession (1742), 216
War of the Spanish Succession (1701–14), 216
Waterlant, Claas van, 23
Waterlant, Mourijn van, 23
Weenix, Jan, *Still Life with a Hare and Birds*, 146, *146*
Weller, Dennis, 278, 280
Welzel, Barbara, 368, 370, 372
Weston, Wallace, 166, 168
Wetering, Ernst van de, 320–22, 330
Weyden, Rogier van der, 67, 69, 264
Braque Triptych, 264–65, *265*
The Descent from the Cross, 69
Miraflores Altarpiece, 69
Wheelock, Arthur, 330
Wierix, Johannes, *Portrait of Jan Gossart*, 321, *322*
Wijck, Thomas, 470
Wilbraham, Thomas, 323
Wildens, Jan, 208, 210
Landscape, 208, 210, *210*
Mercury and Argus (cat. 40) (with Jacob Jordaens), 208, *209*, 210–12, *213* (detail)
Wildens, Jeremias, 210–11
Willaerts, Adam, 245
Willem II, Prince of Orange, 329
William of Orange (later William III, King of England), 162, 168, 197, 216, 252, 285, 329
Winkel, Marieke de, 232, 313, 321–22
Winner, Matthias, 84
Wissel, Dirck van (father), 226–27
Wissel, Dirck van (son), 226–27
Wissel, Jacob van, 226–27

Witsen, Cornelis Jan, 271–72
Witsen, Jonas, 271–72
Witsen, Jonas Cornelis, 271
Witsen, Jonas (grandson of Jonas Witsen), 272
Witsen, Lambert, 271
Witsen, Nicolaas, 271
Witt, Johann de, 251
Witte Leeuw (White Lion) brewery, 313
Wolfthal, Diane, 68–70, 266
Wolleswinkel, E. J., 313
Wolsey, Thomas, 194
women, attitudes toward/representations of, 256, 307, 427, 434, 436–37
Workshop of Albrecht Bouts. *See* Bouts, Albrecht, Workshop of
Workshop of Cornelis Engebrechtsz. (?). *See* Engebrechtsz. (?), Cornelis, Workshop of
Workshop of Peter Paul Rubens. See Rubens, Peter Paul, Workshop of
Wtenbogaert, Johannes, 313–14
Wtewael, Joachim, *Mars and Venus Surprised by Vulcan*, *94*, 94–95
Wunderkammern. *See* cabinets of curiosities

Zaanen, Jacob van, 427
Zeeuw, Cornelis de, *Pierre de Moucheron* (formerly attributed to), 244, *244*
Zeuxis, 50
Zuccaro, Federico, 106
Zuylen, Paul van, 168
Zuylen van Nyevelt, Willem van, 168

Library of Congress Cataloging-in-Publication Data: 2025
Names: Norton Simon Museum (Pasadena, Calif.), author. | Walsh, Amy, author. | Togneri, Carol, writer of introduction. | Westmoreland, Rosamond, contributor. | Birkmaier, Ulrich, contributor. | Forman, Lisa, contributor. | Ormond, Devi, contributor. | Robinson, William W., contributor. | Sander, Gloria Williams, contributor. | Watters, Mark, contributor. | Yocco, Nancy E., contributor.
Title: Northern European Art in the Norton Simon Museum / Amy Walsh; technical notes by Rosamond Westmoreland; introduction by Carol Togneri; with contributions by Ulrich Birkmaier, Lisa Forman, Devi Ormond, William W. Robinson, Gloria Williams Sander, Mark Watters, Nancy E. Yocco.
Description: Pasadena, California: Norton Simon Art Foundation, [2025] | Includes bibliographical references and index. | Summary: "Northern European Art in the Norton Simon Museum celebrates the strengths of the Norton Simon Museum's holdings and features Dutch, Flemish, Early Netherlandish, and German paintings from the fifteenth through the eighteenth centuries. Northern European Art in the Norton Simon Museum illuminates ninety-five extraordinary paintings and works on paper across a rich range of genres, from portraiture and landscape to still life and religious themes. An introductory essay by Carol Togneri, former Chief Curator at the Norton Simon Museum, addresses Simon's ambition and foresight as a collector and recounts some of his most public and dramatic acquisitions. The catalogue's entries—authored by curator and provenance researcher Amy Walsh, with technical reports by conservator Rosamond Westmoreland and contributions from a number of specialists in the field—offer insights into the historical context, ownership trajectories, and conservation assessment of these objects." —Provided by publisher.
Identifiers: LCCN 2024014985 | ISBN 9780300272338 (hardcover)
Subjects: LCSH: Art, Northern European—Catalogs. | Art—California—Pasadena—Catalogs. | Norton Simon Museum (Pasadena, Calif.)—Catalogs. | BISAC: ART / European | ART / Collections, Catalogs, Exhibitions / Permanent Collections
Classification: LCC N6754 .N67 2024 | DDC 709.4074/79493—dc23/eng/20240527
LC record available at https://lccn.loc.gov/2024014985

ISBN: 978-0-300-27233-8

Published by the Norton Simon Art Foundation
411 West Colorado Boulevard
Pasadena, California 91105
nortonsimon.org

Distributed by Yale University Press
302 Temple Street
P.O. Box 209040
New Haven, CT 06520-9040
yalebooks.com/art

Produced by Marquand Books, Seattle
marquandbooks.com

Edited by Tom Fredrickson
Designed by Thomas Eykemans
Typeset in Bw Nista International by Katrina Noble
Proofread by Tanya Heinrich
Indexed by Dave Luljak
Color management by I/O Color, Seattle
Printed and bound in China by C&C Offset Printing Co.

Authorized Representative in the EU Details: Easy Access System Europe, Mustamäe tee 50, 10621 Tallinn, Estonia, gpsr.requests@easproject.com

Front cover: Johannes Cornelisz. Verspronck, *Portrait of a Woman*, 1641 (cat. 95).
Back cover: Jan Davidsz. de Heem, *Vase of Flowers*, mid-1670s (cat. 30).